The Law of Performance Bonds

Second Edition

LAWRENCE R. MOELMANN
MATTHEW M. HOROWITZ
KEVIN L. LYBECK
EDITORS

TORT TRIAL & INSURANCE PRACTICE SECTION

AMERICAN BAR ASSOCIATION
Defending Liberty
Pursuing Justice

Cover design by ABA Publishing

The materials contained herein represent the opinions and views of the authors and/or the editors, and should not be construed to be the views or opinions of the law firms or companies with whom such persons are in partnership with, associated with, or employed by, nor of the American Bar Association or the Tort Trial and Insurance Practice Section unless adopted pursuant to the bylaws of the Association.

Nothing contained in this book is to be considered as the rendering of legal advice, either generally or in connection with any specific issue or case. Nor do these materials purport to explain or interpret any specific bond or policy, or any provisions thereof, issued by any particular insurance company, or to render insurance or other professional advice. Readers are responsible for obtaining advice from their own lawyer or other professional. This book and any forms and agreements herein are intended for educational and informational purposes only.

© 2009 American Bar Association. All rights reserved. No part of this publication may be reproduced, stored in a retrieval system, or transmitted in any form or by any means, electronic, mechanical, photocopying, recording, or otherwise, without the prior written permission of the publisher. For permission contact the ABA Copyrights & Contracts Department, copyright@abanet.org or via fax at 312-988-6030

Printed in the United States of America

Library of Congress Cataloging-in-Publication Data on File

Discounts are available for books ordered in bulk. Special consideration is given to state bars, CLE programs, and other bar-related organizations. Inquire at Book Publishing, ABA Publishing, American Bar Association, 321 North Clark Street, Chicago, Illinois 60654.

www.ababooks.org

Preface

This publication has been prepared for use in conjunction with the spring surety program of the Fidelity & Surety Law Committee of the Tort and Insurance Practice Section of the American Bar Association, held in La Jolla, California on May 21-22, 2009. The first edition of *The Law of Performance Bonds* was published in 1999, and was the basis for the mid-winter meeting for the Fidelity & Surety Law Committee held in San Francisco on January 28, 2000. Lawrence R. Moelmann and John T. Harris were the editors of the first edition.

In 1997, Kevin L. Lybeck and H. Bruce Shreves envisioned a series of books to be published by the Fidelity & Surety Law Committee that would not only cover the most significant legal issues pertaining to surety bonds, but would also serve as a research and reference source for all surety practitioners. As editors, they published *The Law of Payment Bonds* in 1998, which was presented at the mid-winter program held in San Francisco in January, 2000. That publication served as the predecessor to the first edition of *The Law of Performance Bonds*.

Following that format, the Fidelity & Surety Law Committee published *The Law of Miscellaneous and Commercial Surety Bonds* which was presented at the mid-winter meeting held in New York City on January 26, 2001. Todd C. Kazlow and Bruce C. King were the Co-Chairs and Publication Editors for that program. That successful program was followed by *The Law of Probate Bonds* presented at the annual meeting held in Chicago, Illinois on August 6, 2001. William A. Downing and Jeffrey M. Frank were the Co-Chairs and Publication Editors for that program. Because of significant judicial decisions rendered in recent years, the Fidelity & Surety Law Committee now is updating these publications so that current practitioners may continue to have the benefit of these valuable resource materials.

We have organized this publication, following the format of these prior publications, in a manner that surety practitioners will find informative and useful. It is intended that these publications will be used as a primary source of reference for experienced practitioners. For those lawyers who only occasionally have surety issues, these publications can be extremely useful in presenting a comprehensive overview of the relevant issues. Entry-level practitioners in the field of suretyship can use these publications as their initial source material from which to learn this complex area of law. It should be noted that the ideas and opinions expressed in this book are solely those of the authors and may not coincide with those of their employers or of the other authors and editors of this publication.

In order to facilitate the use of this publication as a reference source, a detailed table of contents has been included at the beginning of this book which sets forth the various topics that are addressed in each chapter. The most current cases addressing these and other performance bond issues are discussed in a comprehensive and informative manner.

The editors wish to thank all authors and other contributors to this project for their hard work and dedicated efforts. Special appreciation is extended to all of the secretaries, legal assistants, and law clerks who have had to set aside other responsibilities in order to meet the seemingly endless demands that such a project requires. Without those efforts, this publication would not have been possible. We especially want to thank Susan Evans Jones, Gintare Grenier, and Michelle Himes-Wiederschall, of Wolf, Horowitz & Etlinger, LLC and Clifford E. Yuknis, Albert L. Chollet, III and Daniel R. Degen of Hinshaw & Culbertson LLP for their editing and input for this publication and Robin Bangham for her assistance with formatting. We want to extend special appreciation to Deborah McKenna for having the final responsibility in compiling and formatting this publication, which is the same responsibility she undertook for the first edition of *The Law of Performance Bonds*.

Last, but certainly not least, special recognition must be extended to E. A. "Seth" Mills, Jr. who is serving as the current Chair of the ABA/TIPS Fidelity & Surety Law Committee. He has truly been the driving force behind this publication. Our goal was to attain the same standard of excellence that the contributors achieved in the prior publications. Under his watchful eye and guidance, we believe that this publication has met that goal.

> Lawrence R. Moelmann
> Matthew M. Horowitz
> Kevin L. Lybeck
> Program Co-Chairs and Publication Editors
> May, 2009

Contributing Authors and Editors

Phillip G. Alber • Founding Shareholder in the regional law firm Alber Crafton, P.S.C., with offices in Michigan, Ohio, and Kentucky. He is a *cum laude* graduate of the University of Michigan with a degree in economics and received his J.D. degree from Wayne State University in Detroit, Michigan. He is a past Vice Chair of the Fidelity & Surety Law Committee, a member of the Surety Claim Institute and Program Chair for the National Bond Claims Association.

George J. Bachrach • Partner with the law firm of Whiteford, Taylor & Preston, L.L.P. He is a graduate of Harvard University, B.A., *cum laude*, 1971, and Georgetown University Law Center, J.D. 1974. He is a past Chair of the ABA/TIPS Fidelity & Surety Law Committee (2001-2002).

Lee McGraw Brewer • Partner in the Columbus, Ohio office of Alber Crafton, P.S.C. She received her B.S. degree from the University of Tennessee, her M.B.A. degree from Capital University and her J.D. degree from Capital University, *cum laude*.

Bogda M.B. Clarke • A *summa cum laude* and *phi peta kappa* graduate of Rutgers University, she received her J.D. degree from New York University School of Law. She is a Vice Chair of the Fidelity & Surety Law Committee of the Tort and Insurance Practice Section and the Forum on the Construction Industry of the American Bar Association and the Fidelity and Surety Law Section of the New Jersey Bar Association. She presently serves as a Director of the National Bond Claims Association.

R. Scott Cochrane • Vice President of Bond Claims for Hartford Fire Insurance Company in Hartford, Connecticut. He was formerly the Director of Surety Claims, Western Division, St. Paul Fire and Marine Insurance Company and was with Reliance Surety before that. Mr. Cochrane graduated from Boston University in 1976 with a B.A. degree in American History and received a J.D. degree from the University of Puget Sound Law School (now Seattle University) in 1982. He is a member of the ABA/TIPS Fidelity & Surety Law Committee and a member of the Washington State Bar Association.

Brett D. Divers • Founding Shareholder with Mills Paskert Divers, P.A. in Tampa, Florida. He graduated from Dartmouth College with a B.A. degree in English, and received his J.D. degree from the University of Florida College of Law.

James D. Ferrucci • Partner in the West Orange, New Jersey and New York firm of Wolff & Samson PC. He received a B.A. degree, *cum laude* and with highest honors in Political Science, from Williams College in 1969 and a J.D. degree from Harvard Law School in 1972. Mr. Ferrucci is a past Vice Chair of the ABA/TIPS Fidelity & Surety Law Committee and a member of the Editorial Board of its *Fidelity & Surety Digest* and is a past Chair of the Fidelity and Surety Law Committee of the New Jersey State Bar Association.

Julia Blackwell Gelinas • Member of the Indianapolis, Indiana office of Frost Brown Todd LLC. She graduated from St. Mary's College at Notre Dame, Indiana and received her J.D. degree from Indiana University Law School at Indianapolis. She has served as a Vice Chair of the ABA/TIPS Fidelity & Surety Law Committee.

Kenneth M. Givens, Jr. • Executive Bond Counsel with Arch Insurance Company in Philadelphia, Pennsylvania. He graduated from Hamilton College with a B.A. degree, and received his J.D. degree from Villanova University School of Law.

Matthew Horowitz • Partner in the law firm of Wolf, Horowitz & Etlinger, LLC based in Hartford, Connecticut. He received a B.A. degree from Tufts University and a J.D. degree from New York University School of Law. He is a member of the Connecticut and Massachusetts Bars. He has been a Vice Chair of the ABA/TIPS Fidelity & Surety Law Committee and a co-editor and contributing author of numerous ABA publications.

Marchelle ("Marci") M. Houston • Senior Vice President of Claims for Travelers Bond and Financial Products. Ms. Houston received her undergraduate degree from Michigan State University and her J.D. from DePaul University's College of Law. She is also a Vice Chair of the ABA/TIPS Fidelity & Surety Law Committee.

Nicholas Hyslop • Vice President and Regional Claims Manager with Liberty Mutual Surety in Seattle, Washington. He is a graduate of the United States Military Academy and the University of Illinois Law School. He has been with the surety industry for 14 years (12 years with Safeco) and is a member of the Washington Bar. He has the CPCU, AFSB, and AIM insurance designations.

Peter E. Karney • Bond Claims Supervisor for Nationwide Insurance in Des Moines, Iowa. He graduated from Grinnell College with a B.A. in 1978. Mr. Karney then received his J.D. with honors from the Illinois Institute of Technology/Chicago-Kent College of Law in 1981. He is a former Vice Chair of the Fidelity and Surety Law Committee.

Charles W. Langfitt • Vice President with The Travelers and leads the company's Western Regional Surety Claim Office located in Federal Way, Washington. Mr. Langfitt graduated from the University of Oregon in 1977 with a B.S. in History, and received his J.D. from Gonzaga University School of Law in 1980, with honors. He is a member of the Washington State Bar Association.

Keith A. Langley • Partner in the Dallas, Texas law firm of Langley Weinstein Hamel LLP. He received his J.D. from the University of Virginia in 1985 and a B.S. in Criminal Justice, *summa cum laude*, from Old Dominion University.

Bennett J. Lee • Partner in the law firm of Watt, Tieder, Hoffar & Fitzgerald, LLP, San Francisco, California. Mr. Lee obtained his B.S. in Accounting from Georgetown University, and his J.D. from Georgetown University Law Center.

Benjamin D. Lentz • Partner in the law firm of Torre, Lentz, Gamell, Gary & Rittmaster, LLP. He is a graduate of Haverford College, Honors in Philosophy and Sociology & Anthropology, 1973, and New York University School of Law, J.D. 1976. He is a past Vice Chair of the ABA/TIPS Fidelity & Surety Law Committee.

Jacqueline Lewis • A past Vice Chair of the ABA/TIPS Fidelity & Surety Law Committee, she studied philosophy and economics at Albertus Magnus College and received her J.D. degree from the University of Connecticut School of Law.

P. Keith Lichtman • Shareholder with Mills Paskert Divers, P.C. in Atlanta, Georgia. He received a B.A. in History and Political Science, as well as a J.D., from the University of Alabama.

Kevin L. Lybeck • Vice President of Surety Claims for Travelers Bond and Financial Products where he is responsible for leading the surety claim organization for The Travelers. He received his B.A. degree, with honors, from Montana State University in 1982, and received his law degree, *cum laude*, from Gonzaga University School of Law in 1985. Mr. Lybeck has served as a Vice Chair of the Fidelity & Surety Law Committee, and is a former Chair of the Law Division of that committee.

Kim McNaughton • Vice President of Bond Claims Eastern Region for Liberty Mutual Surety in Plymouth Meeting, Pennsylvania. He was formerly the Vice President of Travelers Bond, East Division, and was with Reliance Surety before that. Mr. McNaughton graduated from Brigham Young University with a B.S. degree in Finance and received a J.D. degree from the University of Puget Sound Law School (now Seattle University) in 1985. He is a member of the Washington State Bar Association.

Lawrence R. Moelmann • Partner in the Chicago law firm of Hinshaw & Culbertson LLP. He received his A.B. degree, *magna cum laude*, from Princeton University and his J.D. degree, *cum laude*, from the University of Michigan Law School. He is currently a Vice Chair of the ABA/TIPS Fidelity & Surety Law Committee. He is former Chair of the Fidelity and Surety Committee of the International Association of Defense Counsel and former Chair of the Fidelity and Surety Committee of the Defense Research Institute. Mr. Moelmann was an editor of the first edition of *The Law of Performance Bonds*.

Steven D. Nelson • Executive Vice President and General Counsel of SureTec Insurance Company and President of its construction risk management and consulting firm, SureTec Information Systems, Inc. He is past Chair of the Construction Law Sections of the Dallas Bar Association, Austin Bar Association, and the Construction Law Section of the State Bar of Texas. He is a Fellow of the American College of Construction Lawyers, a Fellow of the Center for Public Policy Dispute Resolution, and an Adjunct Professor at the University of Texas at Austin School of Engineering. Mr. Nelson has a B.A. in Economics and a J.D. degree from Southern Methodist University.

Robert C. Niesley • Senior Partner in the Irvine, California office of Watt, Tieder, Hoffar & Fitzgerald, LLP. He specializes in construction and surety litigation. He is a graduate of the University of San Diego, B.A., 1984, and J.D., 1987.

David C. Olson • Member of Frost Brown Todd LLC practicing in the firm's Cincinnati, Ohio office. He graduated from Williams College with a B.A. degree, *cum laude*, and obtained his J.D. from The Ohio State University. He is a Vice Chair of the Fidelity & Surety Law Committee and a member of the Surety Claims Institute and the National Bond Claims Association.

Sam H. Poteet, Jr. • Partner in the Nashville, Tennessee law firm of Manier & Herod, P.C. He received his undergraduate degree from Tennessee Technological University and his J.D. degree from the University of Tennessee. He is a past Vice Chair of the ABA Fidelity & Surety Law Committee.

Jeffrey S. Price • Partner in the Nashville, Tennessee law firm of Manier & Herod, P.C. He received his undergraduate degree from Gardner Webb University and his J.D. degree from the University of Tennessee.

Denise C. Puente • Partner in the New Orleans, Louisiana law firm of Simon, Peragine, Smith & Redfearn, LLP. She received her undergraduate and law degrees from Louisiana State University.

Cynthia E. Rodgers-Waire • Partner with the law firm of Whiteford, Taylor & Preston, L.L.P. She received her B.A. from the University of Virginia in 1989 and her J.D., with honors, from the University of Maryland School of Law in 1992. She is a former Vice Chair of the ABA/TIPS Fidelity & Surety Law Committee.

Chad L. Schexnayder • Partner in the Phoenix, Arizona law firm of Jennings, Haug & Cunningham, LLP. He graduated with a B.A. degree, *cum laude*, from Washington University in St. Louis, Missouri, and received his J.D. degree, *cum laude*, from Arizona State University.

Genise W. Teich • Senior Managing Claims Counsel for International Fidelity Insurance Company in Newark, New Jersey. She received her A.B. degree in Biology from Brandeis University in 1977 and her J.D. degree from Boston University in 1980.

Richard E. Towle • Vice President of Chubb & Son and the worldwide manager of Surety Claims. He has a B.A. from the University of Notre Dame, an M.B.A. from Baldwin-Wallace College, and a J.D. from Cleveland-Marshall College of Law, Cleveland State University. He is a past Vice Chair of the ABA Fidelity & Surety Law Committee.

Thomas J. Vollbrecht • Partner in the Minneapolis, Minnesota office of Faegre & Benson LLP. He graduated with a B.A. degree, *cum laude*, from St. John's University and received his J.D. degree from Harvard Law School. He currently serves as a Case Law Spotlight Editor for the Fidelity & Surety Law Committee Newsletter.

Christopher R. Ward • Partner in the Dallas, Texas law firm of Strasburger & Price, LLP. Mr. Ward is a graduate of the University of Colorado at Boulder, B.A., *summa cum laude*, and the University of Texas School of Law, J.D., with honors. He is a Vice Chair of the ABA/TIPS Fidelity & Surety Law Committee and Co-Chair of the Law Division of the ABA/TIPS Fidelity & Surety Law Committee.

J. Blake Wilcox • Vice President, Liberty Mutual Surety. He is a graduate of Louisiana Tech University, B.S. in Finance, 1989 and Louisiana State University–Paul M. Hebert School of Law, J.D. 1992. Mr. Wilcox is a past Vice Chair of the Bonding and Insurance Committee of the ABA's Public Contract Law Section and a current Vice Chair of the ABA/TIPS Fidelity & Surety Law Committee.

The Law of Performance Bonds, 2d Ed.

Table of Contents

Chapter 1 - Creation Of The Relationship
Thomas J. Vollbrecht, Jacqueline Lewis

Introduction 1

I. History and Purpose 2
    A. Bonds Through the Ages 2
    B. What A Bond Is 4
    C. The Relationships Created by a Performance Bond 5

II. Underwriting Considerations 6
    A. Reinsurance 8
    B. Co-Suretyship 8

III. Types of Bonds 9
    A. Defeasance Bond 9
    B. The A312 Performance Bond 9
    C. The A311 Performance Bond 11
    D. Indemnity Bonds 12
    E. Miller Act/Federal Standard Form 25 13
    F. Little Miller Acts 13
    G. Subcontractor Bonds 14
    H. Bid Bonds 14

IV. Execution, Delivery and Acceptance 15

V. Consideration 16
    A. Indemnity Agreement Executed After Bond Issues 16
    B. Subsequent Indemnity Agreements Omit
        Certain Indemnitors 17

VI. Fraud by the Principal 17

VII. Fraud by the Obligee 18

VIII. Unauthorized Acts by Agent 19

Table of Contents

IX.	Mistake	19
X.	Illegality	19

Conclusion 20

Chapter 2 - Conditions Precedent To Asserting A Performance Bond Claim
Benjamin D. Lentz, Kim McNaughton

Introduction 21

I. What Constitutes a Contractor's Default 22
    A. The Distinction Between Breach and Default;
        Default Defined 22
    B. What Is Material? 24
    C. Contract Provisions Defining Default: Are
        the Contract Provisions Exclusive? 25
    D. Summary 27

II. The AIA 311 Bond—Conditions Precedent or Not? 28
    A. Introduction 28
    B. Decisions Supporting the Conclusion That Default
        and Notice to the Surety of Such Default Are
        Conditions Under the A311 Bond Form 29
    C. Decisions Which Require That the Surety
        Demonstrate Prejudice Where No Notice Is
        Given Under the AIA 311 Bond 33
    D. Decisions Holding That Notice to the Surety
        Is Not a "Condition Precedent" Under
        the AIA 311 Bond 35
    E. Summary 40

III. The AIA 312 Bond: Compliance With the Express
     Conditions Precedent 41
    A. The Section 3.1 Condition: Notice of the
        Pre-Default Conference 42

Table of Contents

    B. The Section 3.2 Condition: Declare a Contractor Default and Formally Terminate the Contractor's Right to Complete..43
    C. The Section 3.3 Condition: Obligee's Agreement to Pay the Balance of the Contract Price 50
    D. Do the AIA 312 Conditions Apply Where There Is Not a Completion Claim But Solely a Claim for Damages (e.g. Delay Damages)? 52

IV.   Defeasance Bonds 54

Conclusion...56

Chapter 3 - Performance Options Available To The Surety
Charles W. Langfitt, Bennett J. Lee, Robert C. Niesley

Introduction 59

I.   The Surety's Investigation 60
    A. Need for Default and Declaration Thereof 61
    B. Nature of Investigation 62
        1. The Surety's File 63
        2. The Obligee...63
        3. The Principal 65
    C. Obligee's Rights and Duties During the Investigation 66
    D. Assembling the Team 66
    E. The Focus of the Investigation...67
        1. Delays..67
        2. Defective Work 67

II.   The Surety's Performance Obligations 68

III. Right of Surety to Takeover and Complete Performance of the Bonded Project..69
    A. Domination/Alter Ego..74
    B. Abuse of Rights 75
    C. Wrongful Interference With Contractual Relationship..........76

Table of Contents

```
     D.  Loss of Prospective Economic Advantage ........................ 76
     E.  Other Issues to be Considered in Takeover
         and Completion Agreements ....................................... 77
     F.  General Provisions for Takeover and
         Completion Agreements ........................................... 79
         1.  The Takeover Agreement ..................................... 79
         2.  Completion Agreement ....................................... 81
     G.  Matters to be Considered in Drafting the
         Agreement Between the Surety and the Obligee ................... 82
         1.  Limitation of the Surety's Liability to the
             Bond Penalty ............................................... 82
         2.  Preservation of Claims ..................................... 82
         3.  Contract Balances .......................................... 83
         4.  Latent Defects and Warranties .............................. 83
         5.  Subcontract Hold or Ratification Agreements ................ 84
         6.  Liquidated Damages/Extension of Time ....................... 84

IV.  Tendering of a New Contractor ......................................... 85
     A.  Is Tendering Possible? ............................................ 86
     B.  Possible Complications in Implementing a Tender ................... 86
     C.  Advantages of Tendering ........................................... 87
     D.  Special Considerations ............................................ 87
         1.  Liquidated Damages ............................................ 88
         2.  Patent and Latent Defects ..................................... 88
         3.  Warranties .................................................... 89
         4.  Principal's Claims Against the Obligee ........................ 89
     E.  Drafting of the Agreement ......................................... 89

V.   Financing the Principal ............................................... 90
     A.  The Benefits of Financing the Principal ........................... 90
         1.  Reduction of the New Contractor Premium ....................... 90
         2.  Time Savings .................................................. 91
         3.  Preservation of Claims ........................................ 91
         4.  Salvage Considerations ........................................ 92
     B.  The Detriments to Financing the Principal ......................... 92
         1.  The Bond Penalty .............................................. 92
         2.  Expense of Monitoring Performance of the Job .................. 93
         3.  Elimination of Fixed Cost ..................................... 93
         4.  Contractor's/Principal's Overhead ............................. 93
         5.  Tax Considerations ............................................ 94
```

Table of Contents

        6. Liability Under a Theory of Alter Ego
           or Domination 94
        7. Potential Claim for Failure to Finance 95
    C. Elements to Consider When Deciding Whether
       to Finance...95
       1. Progress of the Job 95
       2. Contractor Ability/Integrity..96
       3. Subcontractor Relations 96
       4. Competition..96
       5. Amount of Unbonded Work..97
       6. Availability of Collateral...98
    D. Effect of Financing on Subrogation Rights 99
    E. Financing Through Advancing Funds for Obligations
       Owed Under the Payment Bond 101
    F. Guaranteeing of Bank Loan Versus Surety
       Providing Financing...101
    G. The Agreements..102
    H. Joint Control Accounts 105
    I. Control of Overhead Expenses 106

VI. Completion By the Bond Obligee 107
    A. Limitations on the Surety's Right to Require
       Completion by the Obligee...107
    B. Factors to be Considered by Surety 108

VII. Comparing The Various Performance Bond Forms....................110

VIII. Options Prior to Obligee's Declaration of Default 154
    A. Financing 155
    B. Assignment of Bonded Contracts 158

Conclusion..160

Table of Contents

Chapter 4 - The Performance Bond Surety's Rights To The Contract Funds
George J. Bachrach, Cynthia E. Rodgers-Waire

Introduction 161

I. The Starting Point–The Obligee's Rights to
   the Contract Funds 162
   A. The Obligee's Contractual Right to Complete
      the Performance of the Work 165
   B. The Obligee's Contractual Right to Pay
      the Principal's Subcontractors/Suppliers 166
   C. The Obligee's Other Contractual, Statutory and
      Common-Law Rights 168
      1. Contract Rights 168
      2. Statutory Rights (The Right to Withhold
         Contract Funds Under Mechanics' Lien and
         Stop Notice Statutes) 169
      3. Common-Law Setoff Rights 170
   D. The Obligee's Default and/or Termination of
      the Principal 170

II. The Theoretical Bases for the Performance Bond
    Surety's Rights to the Contract Funds 171
    A. The Performance Bond Surety's Rights to the
       Contract Funds 173
    B. The Performance Bond Surety's Indemnity
       Agreement Rights to the Contract Funds 175
       1. The Surety's Indemnity Agreement Perfected
          Security Interest in the Contract Funds Under
          the Uniform Commercial Code 175
       2. The Surety's Trust Fund Rights Under the
          Indemnity Agreement 177

Table of Contents

  C. The Performance Bond Surety's Subrogation
    Rights to the Contract Funds 178
    1. Subrogation Rights–Definition and Elements 179
    2. Subrogation Rights–Type of Contract Funds 182
    3. Subrogation Rights–Conditions Precedent 183
    4. The Surety's Notice 188
    5. The Parties' Rights to Which the Surety
     is Subrogated 189

III. The Performance Bond Surety's Competitors for
  the Contract Funds 195
  A. Contractual Competitors 198
    1. The Obligee (Contractual and Setoff Claims) 198
    2. The Principal 203
    3. The Principal's Assignees/Lenders (The "Bank") 204
  B. Statutory Competitors 207
    1. The Obligee as a Taxing Authority 207
    2. The Principal's Subcontractors and Suppliers
     (The "Claimants") 208
    3. The Trustee in Bankruptcy/The Principal as
     Debtor-In-Possession (The "Debtor") 209
    4. Taxing Authorities Other Than the Obligee 213
  C. Legal Competitors, Including the Principal's
    General Creditors and Judgment Creditors
    (Hereinafter the "General Creditors") 215
  D. Setoff Issues: The Surety's Subrogation Rights to the
    Obligee's Setoff Rights to Defeat the Claims of
    Other Claimants ("Common Obligee Theory") 217

IV. Unique Issues Involving The Federal Government
  As Obligee 219
  A. Surety Bonding with the Federal Government 220
    1. The Miller Act 220
    2. The Federal Acquisition Regulations 220
  B. The Surety's Performance Bond Options When the
    Federal Government Defaults the Principal 221
  C. The Surety's Disputes with the Federal Government–
    Jurisdictional Issues 223
    1. The Tucker Act–Generally 224
    2. Contracts Under the Tucker Act 225

Table of Contents

    3. The Contract Disputes Act 230
    4. Comparing and Contrasting the Surety's Claims in the Claims Court Under the Tucker Act and the Contract Disputes Act 234
D. The Use of a Surety's Subrogation Rights to Establish Tucker Act Jurisdiction 239
E. The Surety's Claim to the Contract Funds Under a Takeover Agreement 242
    1. Contract Funds 242
    2. Claims and Extras for Delay, Acceleration, Wrongful Termination, Etc. 243
    3. Liquidated Damages 245
    4. Improper Payments 245
F. The Traditional Surety Claims for the Contract Funds Under the Tucker Act That Are Not Recoverable Under the Contract Disputes Act 248
    1. Overpayment/Impairment of Suretyship 249
    2. Wrongful Termination and Pre-termination Claims–Takeover Agreement Required 252
    3. Contesting the Assessment of Liquidated Damages 254
G. The Performance Bond's Surety's Competitors for the Contract Funds Held by the Federal Government 255
    1. Surety v. Government Exercising its Setoff Rights 256
    2. Surety v. Assignee/Lenders 257
    3. Surety v. Trustees in Bankruptcy/Debtors in Possession 258
    4. Surety v. Subcontractors and Suppliers on the Bonded Projects 258
    5. Common Obligee Theory 259
H. The Impact of the Blue Fox Case on the Surety's Use of the Tucker Act in Pursuit of its Claims Against the Federal Government 259
    1. What is the Blue Fox Case? 259
    2. Why Does the Blue Fox Case Matter to Sureties? 260
    3. Tucker Act Decisions Involving Sureties Since Blue Fox 261

Table of Contents

V. The Surety's Rights to the Contract Funds in
the Principal's Bankruptcy Case 265

Conclusion 266

Chapter 5 - Surety's Rights of Recovery Rights Against Principals And Indemnitors Under The General Indemnity Agreement And The Common Law
Brett D. Divers, Kenneth M. Givens, Jr., P. Keith Lichtman

Introduction 267

I. General Indemnity Agreement 267
   A. Surety's Rights Prior to Payment 269
      1. The Right to Indemnity Against Liability 269
      2. The Collateral Deposit Clause 271
      3. Right to Have Indemnitors Obtain Release of Surety 281
      4. Right to Review Books and Records of the
Principal and Indemnitors and to Obtain
Other Financial Information 282
      5. Right to Financial Information From Third-Parties 283
   B. Surety's Rights After Payment 284
      1. Indemnity After Loss 284
      2. Prima Facie/Conclusive Evidence Clauses 285
      3. Indemnity Against Expenses, Including
Attorney's Fees 286

II. Quia Timet and Exoneration 289
   A. Quia Timet 290
   B. Exoneration 290
   C. Distinction Between Quia Timet And Exoneration 291
   D. Enforcement 292

III. Reimbursement and Contribution 293
   A. Reimbursement 293
   B. Contribution 295

Conclusion 296

Table of Contents

Chapter 6 – Surety's Rights Under The General Indemnity Agreement To Minimize Loss
Richard E. Towle, Sam H. Poteet, Jr., Jeffrey S. Price

Introduction 297

I. Provisions to Minimize Surety's Loss...................................299
    A. Collateral Deposit Demand (without Regard to Settlement of Claims) 299
    B. The UCC Provision...302
    C. Power-of-Attorney or Attorney-in-Fact..............................304
    D. Assignment of Contract Rights and Subcontracts, Including Receivables on Bonded and Unbonded Contracts 305
        1. Contract Proceeds..308
        2. Claims 310
    E. Assignment of Material and Equipment on Bonded Projects 310
    F. Right of Surety to Takeover or Complete Performance of Bonded Contracts...................................314
    G. Surety's Right to Finance Principal and Recover Financing Under Indemnity Agreement 317
    H. Designation of Contract Funds as Trust Funds..................319
        1. Observe Local Law 320
        2. Courts Finding That a Trust was Formed....................320
        3. Courts Finding that a Trust was not Formed..............323
    I. Right to Compromise or Settle Claims 326
        1. Absence of Right-to-Settle Clause 327
        2. Exercise of Discretion 328
        3. Burden of Proving Reasonableness of Settlement of Claim..329
        4. Prima Facie or Conclusive Evidence Provision 332
        5. Failure to Mitigate Damages 333
        6. The Bond v. the Indemnity Agreement 333
        7. Notice to Indemnitors..335
        8. Deposit of Collateral 336
        9. Affirmative Claims of Principal..................................339

Table of Contents

    J. Principal's Obligation to Cooperate in
Defense of Claims 342
    K. Right to Have Indemnitors Obtain Release of Surety........... 343

II. Other Provisions of The Indemnity Agreement 345
    A. Rights of Co-Sureties and Reinsurers.................................. 345
    B. Severability.. 346
    C. Surety's Right to Bring Separate Suit.................................. 346
    D. Waiver of Notice.. 347
    E. Waiver of Homestead and Other Exemptions 347
    F. Right to Financial Information from Third-Parties.............. 348

Conclusion... 349

Chapter 7 - Right Of The Surety To Pursue Claims Against Third Parties
Christopher R. Ward, Nicholas Hyslop

Introduction 351

I. Source of a Surety's Rights Against Third Parties 352
    A. Subrogation.. 352
    B. Assignment 355
    C. Exoneration and Indemnification.. 357

II. Claims Against Subcontractors and Material Suppliers.............. 358

III. Claims Against Design Professionals... 361
    A. Potential Causes of Action Against Design
Professionals 361
        1. Breach of Contract Claims Asserted by
Subrogation or Assignment.. 361
        2. Negligence.. 363
        3. Impact of Economic Loss Rule on
Negligence Claims 372

Table of Contents

IV. Claims Against the Principal's Accountant 374
    A. The Type of Financial Statement's Effect on the Accountant's Liability 375
    B. Potential Causes of Action Against the Principal's Accountant 378
        1. Negligent Misrepresentation 379
        2. Breach of Contract–The Surety as a Third-Party Beneficiary 392
        3. Fraud/Intentional Misrepresentation 393
    C. Potential Defenses that May be Asserted by the Accountant 394
        1. Limitations by Statute 394
        2. Lack of Causation 394
        3. Contributory/Comparative Negligence 395
        4. Failure to Mitigate 396
        5. Statute of Limitations 396

V. Claims Against Lenders 397
    A. Misrepresentation 398
    B. Negligent Disbursement of Project Funds 400
    C. Improper Set-Off of Construction Funds 401

VI. Claims Against Third Parties for Violations of Trust Fund Statutes and Fraudulent Transfers 402
    A. Claims Based on Violations of Trust Fund Statutes 403
    B. Claims Based on Fraudulent Transfer Laws 406

VII. Insurance Claims 410
    A. Commercial General Liability Coverage 410
        1. Coverage 411
        2. Exclusions 416
    B. Builder's Risk Coverage 426
        1. Risks Covered 426
        2. Insureds 428

Conclusion 429

Table of Contents

Chapter 8 - Liability Of The Performance Bond Surety For Damages (Under Contract Of Suretyship)
Keith A. Langley, Marchelle M. Houston

Introduction 431

I. General Principles of Construction and Interpretation 431
    A. Contract Principles of Interpretation 431
    B. Suretyship Distinguished From Insurance 433
        1. Liability of the Surety is Secondary 433
        2. No Actuarial Based Expected Loss 433

II. Performance Bond Forms 434
    A. Statutory Bonds 435
    B. Common Law Bonds 435

III. Design-Build 438
    A. Nature of the Design-Build Delivery Method 438
    B. Managing and Allocating the Risk of the
        Design-Build Contract 440

IV. Claims by the Obligee 443
    A. Costs to Complete 443
    B. Consequential Damages 444
        1. Liquidated Damages 445
        2. Actual Damages From Delay 448
    C. Attorneys' Fees and Interest 452
    D. Warranty Claims and Latent Defects 454
    E. Dual Obligees 455

V. Claims by a Non-Obligee 455
    A. Subcontractors and Suppliers 456
    B. Assignees, Successors and Purchasers 456
    C. Miscellaneous Claims 457

VI. Limitations to Liability 458
    A. The Penal Limit 458
    B. The Surety's Performance Options 462

Table of Contents

VII.	Defenses	464
	A. Substantial Completion	464
	B. Material Alteration	466
	C. Overpayment or Improper Payment	468
	D. Termination for Convenience and Release of the Principal	469

Conclusion 470

Chapter 9 - Extra-Contractual Liability Of Performance Bond Sureties
David C. Olsen, Peter E. Karney

Introduction		471
I.	Bad Faith	472
	A. Recovery From Surety by Obligee For Surety's Alleged Bad Faith	474
	1. Recovery Against Surety Allowed	474
	2. Recovery Against Surety Not Allowed	481
	B. Recovery From Surety by Principal for Surety's Alleged Bad Faith	483
	C. Statutory Causes of Action - Model Unfair Claims Settlement Practices Act	486
II.	Fraudulent or Illegal Activities of the Principal	488
	A. Fraud Committed on the Surety	488
	B. Penalties/Punitive Damages	490
III.	Tort Claims Against the Principal	493
IV.	Tax Obligations of the Principal	495
	A. Miller Act Bonds	495
	B. Little Miller Act Bonds	497
V.	Interest and Attorney Fees	499
	A. Interest	499
	B. Attorney Fees	501

Table of Contents

VI. Liability for Environmental Claims 505
    A. Federal Statutes Governing Hazardous Materials and Environmental Degradation 505
        1. Liability Under CERCLA 507
        2. Liability Under RCRA 507
        3. Liability Under SMCRA 508
    B. Practical Application of Federal Statutes to Sureties 508
    C. Mold–The Performance Bond Surety's New Generation of Environmental Claims 510
        1. Basis For The Mold-Related Bond Claim 510
        2. The Surety's Response To Mold-Related Bond Claims 511

Conclusion 512

Chapter 10 - Claims And Defenses Asserted By Principals Or Indemnitors Against The Surety
Lee McGraw Brewer, Bogda M.B. Clarke, Phillip G. Alber

Introduction 513

I. The Surety's Duty to Act in Good Faith Stems Either From the Indemnity Agreement or Common Law. 514

II. Affirmative Claims Asserted by Indemnitors Against the Surety 516
    A. Claims That Surety Breached Duty of Good Faith 516
        1. Lambert (Surety Asserts Rights to Contract Balances and Refuses Further Financial Assistance) 516
        2. Standards for the Surety's Good Faith 520
        3. Cases Finding No Tort Claim For Surety's Alleged Failure to Act in Good Faith 528
    B. Claims Based Upon Breach of Fiduciary Duties 533
    C. Claims Based Upon Abuse of Rights 535

III.	Defenses Raised By Indemnitors to Surety's Indemnity Claims 536	
	A. Breach of Covenant of Good Faith and Fair Dealing 536	
	B. Wrongful Settlement and Release of the Principal's Affirmative Claims 541	
	C. Obligee's Breach of Its Duties to the Principal 544	
	D. Demand for Collateral by Surety is Excessive 546	
	E. Failure to Litigate Claims Asserted by Obligee...................551	
	F. Settlement Motivated by Bad Faith Claims Asserted By Obligee 555	
	G. Attorney's Fees Incurred by the Surety Are Excessive or Incurred in Bad Faith..558	
	1. Burden of Proof Issues 558	
	2. Surety Not Limited to "Reasonable and Necessary" Expenses..566	
	3. Case Law or Statute Might Override the Express Language of the Indemnity Agreement..........................568	
	H. Surety Failed to Mitigate its Damages..................................569	
	I. Burden of Proof 570	

Conclusion...574

Chapter 11 - Defenses Available To The Surety
Julia Blackwell Gelinas, Genise W. Teich

Introduction..575

I.	The Surety Succeeds to All of the Defenses of Its Principal........576	
	A. The Obligee's Failure to Provide Plans and Specifications Which are Free From Defects 577	
	B. Obligee's Failure to Act 579	
	C. Impossibility of Performance...580	
	D. Obligee's Wrongful Termination of the Principal's Contract 583	
	E. Failure to Provide Notice and An Opportunity to Cure........585	
	F. Setoffs or Counterclaims 587	
	G. Prior Material Breach by Obligee...589	

Table of Contents

II.	Acts of the Obligee Prejudicial to the Surety	590
	A. Surety Must Be Given Notice of Default and Opportunity to Perform	590
	1. Declaration of Default Must be Clear	590
	2. Surety Must Be Given An Opportunity To Perform	594
	B. Material Alteration in the Underlying Contract	595
	1. Prejudice to the Surety	597
	2. Cardinal Change	599
	3. Changes in the Parties to the Contract	602
	C. Prepayments and Overpayments by the Obligee	603
	D. Extensions of Time	607
	E. Failure to Mitigate	607
	F. Other Actions of the Obligee	608
III.	Impairment to Security or Collateral	610
	A. Impairment of Collateral	610
	B. Release of Collateral	612
IV.	Release or Discharge of Principal	613
V.	Obligee's Lack of Good Faith	616
	A. Concealment	616
	B. Non-Disclosure	617
	C. Misrepresentation	618
VI.	Matters Affecting the Bonded Obligation	619
Conclusion		621

Chapter 12 - Litigation Issues
Denise C. Puente, Steven D. Nelson

Introduction		623
I.	Federal Court Jurisdiction	623
	A. Diversity Jurisdiction	624
	B. Federal Question Jurisdiction	625
	C. Counterclaims and Cross-Claims	628

Table of Contents

  D. Ancillary Jurisdiction 629
  E. Abstention 631

II. Venue 636
  A. Forum Non Conveniens 639
  B. Forum Selection Clauses 645
  C. Bankruptcy Venue 651

III. Change of Venue in Bankruptcy Cases 654

IV. Removal of State Proceedings to Federal Court 655
  A. Actions Removable Generally Under
    28 U.S.C. § 1441 655
  B. Removal to Bankruptcy Court Under
    § 28 U.S.C. § 1452 658
    1. Jurisdictional Requirements of 28 U.S.C. § 1452 659
    2. Exceptions of Removal Under 28 U.S.C. § 1452 660
    3. Procedure for Removal Under 28 U.S.C. § 1452 660
    4. Remand 661

V. Issues Relating to Limitations 661
  A. Contractual Limitations 662
    1. Limitation Periods Stated in the Bond 662
    2. Limitation Periods Stated in the
      Underlying Contract 667
  B. Statutory Limitations 670
    1. Statutes 670
    2. Miller Act Claims 672
    3. Tax Claims 673
  C. Impact of Bankruptcy 673

Conclusion 675

Table of Contents

Chapter 13 - Effect Of An Arbitration Provision In The Principal's Contract With The Obligee
James D. Ferrucci, R. Scott Cochrane

Introduction 677

I. Arbitration in General–A Brief Overview 679
   A. Statutory Framework 679
   B. Limited Judicial Review of Arbitration Awards 683
   C. The Consensual Nature of Arbitration 688

II. The Surety's Obligation to Arbitrate 690
   A. Direct Compulsion–Incorporation by Reference 692
      1. Incorporation–The Basic Principle 692
      2. Super Incorporation 702
      3. Limited Incorporation 710
      4. Rediscovery of Limited Incorporation 716
   B. Direct Compulsion–As Performing Surety 726
   C. Indirect Compulsion–Preclusion 731
   D. Statutory Compulsion 733

III. The Obligee's Obligation to Arbitrate 736

IV. Consolidation of Related Arbitrations 740
   A. Under the Federal Arbitration Act 741
      1. Before Green Tree 741
      2. After Green Tree 746
   B. Under State Statutes 751
      1. Statutes Which Do Not Address Consolidation 752
      2. The Revised Uniform Arbitration Act 754

V. Preclusion 757
   A. Basic Principles of Preclusion 757
      1. Res Judicata, Collateral Estoppel and Privity 759
      2. Due Process Limitations on Nonparty Preclusion ... 762
   B. Preclusion in the Suretyship Context 773
      1. Extent of Preclusive Effects 774
      2. Conditions Affecting the Imposition of
         Preclusive Effects 780

Table of Contents

    C. Preclusive Effect of an Arbitration Award Against the Principal 797
    D. Suretyship Defenses 807
        1. Under General Preclusion Principles 807
        2. Under the Incorporation Doctrine 812

Conclusion 814

Chapter 14 – Bankruptcy
Chad L. Schexnayder, J. Blake Wilcox

Introduction 815

I. Fundamental Purposes and Principles of Bankruptcy Law 816
    A. Forgiveness of Indebtedness 817
    B. Sharing 817
    C. Breathing Space 818
    D. An Important Definition–"Property of the Estate" 820

II. The Impact of Bankruptcy on the Completing Surety 821
    A. The Need for Information–Bankruptcy Rule 2004 Examination 822
    B. Notice of Default/Termination of Bonded Contracts 824
    C. Assumption or Rejection of Executory Contracts. 826
        1. Standards for Assumption 827
        2. Opposing the Assumption 828
    D. Right to Use Debtor's Subcontractors 831
    E. Right to Use Debtor's Equipment and Tools in Completion of Bonded Projects 832
        1. The Surety as a Creditor With an Interest in the Equipment. 833
        2. Surety's Right to Use Debtor's Equipment Obtained by Subrogation to Obligee's Position. 834
    F. Taking Control Over or Compromising Debtor's Affirmative Claims 834
    G. Non-Dischargeability of the Indemnity Obligation 835

Table of Contents

- III. The Surety's Rights in Bonded Contract Proceeds 839
  - A. Are Bonded Contract Proceeds Property of the Estate? 840
    1. Contract Funds Are Not Property of the Estate............. 842
    2. Bonded Contract Proceeds Held to be Property of the Estate... 848

- IV. Actions to Protect Surety's Rights in Bonded Contract Proceeds 850
  - A. Giving Notice to the Obligee 850
  - B. Motion For Relief From The Automatic Stay Regarding Bonded Contract Proceeds. 854
  - C. Motion to Sequester Cash Collateral and, Alternatively, for Adequate Protection 857
  - D. Common Obligee–The Surety's Right to Contract Proceeds From Other Projects. 860

- V. Impact of Bankruptcy Upon the Surety's Ability to Finance the Principal's Completion of Bonded Work 863
  - A. Pre-Petition Financing of the Principal................................. 863
    1. Introduction.. 863
    2. The Law of Preference Liability 864
    3. Other Financing Clauses That May Assist the Surety in Bankruptcy.. 871
  - B. Post-Petition Financing of the Principal 873
    1. Introduction.. 873
    2. The Four Types of Post-Petition Credit 874
    3. Cross-Collateralization... 878
    4. The Safe-Harbor for the Post-Petition Financier............ 878
    5. Implementing the Post-Petition Financing Agreement and Order... 880

- VI. Opposing the Principal's Control of the Reorganization 882
  - A. Motion to Convert Chapter 11 Reorganization to Chapter 7 Liquidation 885
  - B. Motion to Appoint Trustee or Examiner............................... 885
    1. Trustee.. 885
    2. Examiner 888
  - C. The Creditor Plan... 889

Table of Contents

VII. Surety's Use of Involuntary Bankruptcy Remedy 891
    A. The Involuntary Petition 891
    B. Principal Advantages of an Involuntary Bankruptcy 895
    C. Principal Disadvantages of Filing an
        Involuntary Petition 896

Conclusion 898

1

CREATION OF THE RELATIONSHIP

Thomas J. Vollbrecht
Jacqueline Lewis

Introduction

The construction industry is historically and endemically exposed to enormous risks, with each business cycle placing strains on its financial capacity.[1] Performance bonds serve to provide the industry with a measure of financial stability.

Performance bonds are express, bilateral contracts with trilateral rights and obligations. In addition, they can, and often do, incorporate equitable and statutory precepts and provisions. This chapter provides a grounding in the history and development of performance bonds and also discusses issues surrounding creation of the bonding relationship.[2]

---

[1] See Arnold, *The Compensated Surety*, 26 COL. L. REV. 171, 172 (1926) ("Prior to 1894 . . . at nearly every session of Congress, bills were introduced for the relief of debtors who had guaranteed the [construction] obligations of another to the United States."); Crenner, *Maintaining Favorable Credit Ratings*, in CONSTRUCTION BUSINESS HANDBOOK, 12-2 (1978) ("Construction failures climbed in 1975 to 2,262, an eight-year high . . . Casualties of construction contractors comprised 19.8% of total failures in 1975, up from 15.2% in 1974, and the highest portion in two decades."); Schmalz, *Analyzing and Assessing Risk: The Role of Surety Bonds*, in CFMA BUILDING PROFITS, 79 (March/April 1999) ("In 1997, more than 11,000 contractors failed, leaving a trail of liabilities totaling more than $1.8 billion; 37% of these firms had been in business a decade or more.").

[2] The author is indebted to the excellent scholarship on this topic contained in Chapter 1 of the first edition of THE LAW OF PERFORMANCE BONDS (Lawrence R. Moelmann & John T. Harris eds., 1999) authored by Roger P. Sauer. It is simply not practicable to footnote all references in this edition to Mr. Sauer's earlier work. For similar reasons, a general (and appreciative) reference is provided at the outset to 4 PHILIP L. BRUNER & PATRICK J. O'CONNOR, JR., BRUNER & O'CONNOR ON CONSTRUCTION

I. History and Purpose

A. *Bonds Through the Ages*

Suretyship has existed for millennia. A tablet dated to 2750 B.C. from the library of Sargon I, King of Accad, documents a merchant's promise to guarantee a farmer's agreement to cultivate another's land and return half the produce.[3] Ancient suretyship involved a simple pledge by an individual assuring the performance of another's obligation, frequently secured by becoming or providing a hostage.[4]

Just as ancient are the warnings against accepting the obligations of suretyship. A tablet in the Delphian Temple and attributed to Thales, a Greek sage and philosopher, was inscribed with following warning: "suretyship is the precursor of ruin."[5] The Book of Proverbs, authored by another noted sage, King Solomon, is replete with similar advice:

> He who gives surety for a stranger will smart for it but he who hates suretyship is secure. (Proverbs 11:15).
>
> A man without sense gives a pledge, and becomes surety in the presence of his neighbor. (Proverbs 17:18).
>
> My son, if you have become surety for your neighbor, you have given your pledge for a stranger; if you are snared in the utterance of your lips, caught in the words of your mouth, then do this, my son, and save yourself, for you have come into your neighbor's power; Go, hasten, and importune your neighbor. Give your eyes no sleep and your eyelids

---

LAW, ch. 12, *Suretyship Assuring Contract Performance* (2002 & Supps.).

[3] See generally Willis D. Morgan, *The History and Economics of Suretyship*, 12 CORNELL L.Q. 153 (1926) and 13 CORNELL L.Q. 487 (1927).

[4] See OLIVER W. HOLMES, JR., THE COMMON LAW, 248 (1881) ("the surety of ancient law was the hostage and the giving of hostages was by no means confined to international dealings.").

[5] GEORGE W. CRIST, JR., CORPORATE SURETYSHIP, 1 (2d ed. 1950).

no slumber; save yourself like a gazelle from the hunter, like a bird from the hand of the fowler. (Proverbs 6:1-5).[6]

Rome in 106 B.C. provides the earliest recorded reference to the use of suretyship to guarantee completion of a construction project.[7] The Magna Carta, 1215 A.D., specifically recognized the surety's right of indemnity out of the principal's collateral.[8] By the time of Blackstone's Commentaries on the English common law, the practice of suretyship was well established.[9]

Performance bonds arose in the American construction industry in the late nineteenth century in an attempt to protect public treasuries against the risk of default on public projects.[10] Prior to the 1890s, most sureties were individuals and uncompensated, although a few corporate sureties had been organized.[11] In response to the financial panic of 1893, the Heard Act was enacted.[12] It required that the performance and payment obligations of federal contractors be guaranteed by a surety bond issued by "good and sufficient" sureties, including compensated corporate sureties approved by the Treasury Department.[13] In 1935, the Miller Act[14] replaced the Heard Act.

---

[6] Those admonitions have rung down through the ages echoed, for example, by Sir Walter Raleigh:
> If any desire thee to be his surety, give him a part of what thou hast to spare; if he press thee further, he is not thy friend at all, for friendship rather chooses harm to itself than offer it.

Morgan, *The History and Economics of Suretyship*, 12 CORNELL L.Q. 153, 162 (1926).

[7] *See* Harry Cross, *Suretyship Is Not Insurance*, 30 INS. COUNS. J. 235 (1963).

[8] *See* STEPHENSON AND MARCHAU, SOURCES OF ENGLISH CONSTITUTIONAL LAW, 117 (1937).

[9] *See* Loyd, *The Surety*, 66 U. PA. L. REV. 40 (1916); *see also* THOMAS M. COOLEY, BLACKSTONE'S COMMENTARIES ON THE LAWS OF ENGLAND 1872 (2d ed.).

[10] *See generally* Lynn M. Schubert, *Modern Contract Bonds–An Overview*, in THE LAW OF SURETYSHIP, 3-1 (Edward G. Gallagher ed., 1993).

[11] *See* Morgan, *The History and Economics of Suretyship*, 13 CORNELL L.Q. 487-492 (1927).

[12] Heard Act (Aug. 13, 1894) Ch. 280, 28 Stat. 278.

[13] 28 Stat. at L.279, 5 Ch. 282.

[14] 40 U.S.C.S. §§ 3131, *et seq.* (2009).

B. What a Bond Is

The performance bond is, first and foremost, a contract. Apart from statutory bonds that, by definition, can incorporate legislatively mandated requirements and proscriptions,[15] all others are ultimately nothing more than a function of what the parties agree to.[16] And that agreement should be in writing. Almost all states (except Louisiana) require a writing signed by the party to be charged as a condition precedent to enforcement of a promise of suretyship.[17]

At early common law, the rule of *strictissimi juris* was utilized by courts to restrict the surety's liability to the narrowest reasonable scope. Although some jurisdictions still apply that rule,[18] it is now usually limited to the truly gratuitous surety and not to compensated sureties, including the corporate entities typically issuing performance bonds.[19] At the same time, the obligee remains obligated to satisfy express conditions precedent to trigger surety responsibility and liability under the bond.[20]

Governmental regulation of the surety industry has historically paralleled regulation of the insurance industry, and the National Association of Insurance Commissioners (NAIC) model legislation defined "insurance" to include any "contract of suretyship" despite the fact that suretyship has fundamental differences from traditional insurance. A benefit of including suretyship within insurance was that doing so provided the surety industry with the same antitrust, price fixing and reserve setting exemptions, practices and federal tax treatment as the insurance industry. However, including suretyship within the NAIC definition of the

---

15 *See, e.g.*, United States *ex rel.* Sherman v. Carter, 353 U.S. 210, 215-216 (1957) ("The surety's liability on a Miller Act bond must be at least coextensive with the obligations imposed by the Act if the bond is to have its intended effect.").

16 Which has led contemporary sages to proclaim that anyone who wants to understand what a bond does and does not provide should start by doing the following: "RTFB," i.e. "Read The . . . Bond."

17 *See* RESTATEMENT (THIRD) OF SURETYSHIP AND GUARANTY § 11 cmt. a (1996).

18 *See* Graham Arch'l Prods. Corp. v. St. Paul Mercury Ins. Co., 303 F. Supp. 2d 274, 281 (E.D.N.Y. 2004).

19 *See, e.g., In re* Fischel, 103 B.R. 44, 47 (N.D.N.Y. 1989).

20 *See* Enter. Capital, Inc. v. San-Gra Corp., 284 F. Supp. 2d 166, 176-177 (D. Mass. 2003).

"business of insurance" has also led to significant controversy regarding the applicability to sureties of state laws governing insurers' claims practices duties.[21]

C. The Relationships Created by a Performance Bond

Performance bonds always create a tripartite relationship. There is the "principal" (typically the general contractor) who has assumed a contractual undertaking. There is the "obligee" (typically the project owner) who is due the benefits of the principal's performance. And there is the "surety" who provides the performance bond that secondarily guarantees to the obligee performance of the principal's contractual undertaking.[22] While the language of a bond may tend toward the archaic, its purpose is straight-forward: A performance bond provides available funds to complete the principal's contract should the latter be in default of the performance it owes the obligee.

Typically, the surety's obligation tracks that of the principal under the bonded contract[23] up to the stated penal sum, subject to the specific terms and limitations in the bond, and is conditioned upon the principal's material default of its performance obligations under the bonded contract. Determining the surety's preferred and/or required course of action after a claim is made, however, can be complicated because of the cumulative effect of:

1. The surety's multiple independent obligations to the obligee, the principal and the principal's indemnitors;

2. Murky and heavily contested factual and technical issues involving design adequacy, construction conformance, and competing claims by the principal, the obligee and others of contract breach and default that often require expert analysis;

---

21   *See infra*, Chapter 9 "Extra-Contractual Liability of Performance Bond Sureties."
22   *See* RESTATEMENT (THIRD) OF SURETYSHIP AND GUARANTY § 1 (1996).
23   *See* Cates Constr., Inc. v. Talbot Partners, 980 P.2d 407, 413 (Cal. 1999) (as a general rule, "the obligation of a surety must be neither larger in amount nor in other respects more burdensome than that of the principal.").

3. The surety's interest in mitigating loss to itself and its principal by controlling the cost of completion, efficiently utilizing remaining contract funds and holding third-parties accountable for loss they caused or contributed to; time and resource limitations; and the multitude of response options provided in the bond.[24]

Many of these complexities are addressed at length in subsequent chapters of this book.

II. Underwriting Considerations

A primer on surety underwriting is beyond the scope of this chapter. Still, a review of basic surety underwriting considerations can enhance understanding of the role of performance bonds and also highlights clear differences between performance bonds and "typical" insurance.

"Typical" insurance underwriters start with large groups of individuals who they place into risk pools based upon characteristics that lead the underwriter to conclude that the individuals in one pool present a materially different risk that a valid claim will some day be presented than the individuals making up the other risk pools. The underwriter then builds models of anticipated loss and structures premiums to (hopefully) provide: (1) sufficient funds to draw upon when the expected losses occur; and (2) sufficient funds to cover overhead and profit. This actuarial approach to underwriting works not because any *individual* insured acts exactly according to expectations, but because the risk pool *as a generalized whole* conforms to its profile. It is also important to understand that the insured absolutely anticipates that it will have to pay claims under the policies it issues.

Performance bond underwriting is much different. It looks at the *unique* characteristics of a given principal and only issues a bond if claims are *not* expected. As a general rule, performance bond premiums are not adjusted to account for the perceived risk of loss, meaning that bond premiums are not calculated to cover anticipated claims. If there is a sufficient perceived risk of claims, the bond should not be issued at all.

---

24 *See* Philip L. Bruner & Tracey L. Haley, *Strategic "Generalship" of the Complex Construction Surety Case*, in MANAGING AND LITIGATING THE COMPLEX SURETY CASE, 2-9 (Bruner & Haley eds., 2d ed. 2007).

The bond premium is effectively an administrative fee based upon the surety's assessment that its underwriting is sufficiently rigorous that there will be few or no defaults under its bonded contracts. As such, a performance bond is really an extension of standby credit to the bond principal, meaning that individual risk assessments are critical.[25] To make underwriting assessments, performance bond sureties look to the "three Cs": the character, capacity and capital of the principal. "Character" analyzes the experience, caliber and history of the company's management and major support personnel. "Capacity" involves the fit (or lack thereof) between the principal and the work to be done under the proposed contract, including the type, size and location of the work. Finally, "capital" involves numbers crunching: analysis of whether the company has adequate financing, cash flow, financial reporting, etc., such that it is likely to remain viable throughout the term of the surety's proposed secondary responsibility. Unless the underwriter is satisfied with all three Cs, the bond should not to be written. As discussed above, performance bond premiums do not allow the surety to simply charge a higher rate to compensate for a higher risk. It is a "yes or no" calculation.

An additional surety underwriting consideration is indemnification which, again, differentiates surety bonds from standard insurance policies. A typical insurance policyholder is not expected or obligated to reimburse his or her insurer after making a claim under the insurance policy. A performance bond principal, on the other hand, *is* expected to indemnify its surety against all costs, expenses, damages, losses, etc. incurred by the surety when a claim is made on its performance bond. In the ordinary course, the principal, its owners and possibly others,[26] will be required to execute a general indemnity agreement for any bond that is issued. This places the ultimate responsibility for any performance default with the party who is primarily responsible for that performance, i.e., the principal, together with the individuals who control the principal, rather

---

25 *See generally* Stewart R. Duke, *How Contract Bonds Are Underwritten*, in THE LAW OF SURETYSHIP, 4-1 (Edward G. Gallagher ed., 1993).

26 *See id.*, in LAW OF SURETYSHIP, 4-1, 4-13 (1993) ("We feel that [providing personal indemnity to the surety] is a manifestation by the stockholders and/or partners of a construction firm, that they are fully behind their company and have faith enough in their company to, as we say, 'get on the line'."

than with the surety who is only secondarily responsible for that performance.

A. Reinsurance

Under the standards followed by the United States Treasury in maintaining its Treasury List of approved sureties for federal projects, the amount of any single bond that a surety can write is limited to no more than 10 percent of its surplus.[27] Sureties routinely reinsure to pass off some of their performance bond risk and to allow them to write larger books of contract bond business.

Two types of reinsurance are typically utilized: "treaty reinsurance" in which the reinsurer agrees to automatically accept a share of any risk that the surety chooses to place with it; and "facultative reinsurance" in which each bond submitted by the surety is individually underwritten by the reinsurer. Sureties customarily have treaty reinsurance with one or more reinsurers to whom they cede their surety bond risk over a specified retained amount. Facultative reinsurance usually comes into play only when a particular bond is larger than what the surety can write within the limits of its retained capacity under its existing reinsurance treaties.[28]

B. Co-Suretyship

Sureties may enter into co-surety agreements when issuing bonds for joint ventures whose principals are bonded by different companies, or when the bond required by a single contractor exceeds the underwriting limits (or appetite) of its regular surety. Co-surety agreements define the relationship between the co-sureties, including each surety's exposure to risk. Absent agreement to the contrary, each co-surety on the same bond must pay its "contributive share"[29] as a principal obligor.[30] Unless the agreement makes clear that the relationship is one of "sub-suretyship"—

---

[27] See 31 C.F.R. § 223.10 (2009).
[28] Duke, *How Contract Bonds Are Underwritten, in* LAW OF SURETYSHIP, 4-1, 4-16 to 4-17 (1993). *See also* William Hoffman, *Facultative Reinsurance Contract Formation, Documentation and Integration*, 38 TORT TRIAL & INS. PRAC. L. J. 763 (Spring 2003).
[29] *See* RESTATEMENT (THIRD) OF SURETYSHIP AND GUARANTY § 57 (1996).
[30] *See id.* § 55.

where one surety is expressly primary and the other expressly secondary—there is a presumption in favor of co-suretyship.[31]

III. Types Of Bonds

The performance bond obligation is traditionally expressed in conditional defeasance language declaring that the obligation is "null and void" upon performance of the bonded contract, thereby assuring that the bond obligation is terminated without need for express cancellation and confirming that the bond obligation is at most co-extensive with the principal's obligation under the bonded contract. With respect to the surety's obligations upon notice of default by its principal, the choice of bond form and bond language is, of course, crucial, as that language will define the nature and extent of those obligations.

A. *Defeasance Bond*

Traditionally, performance bonds are defeasance bonds, meaning that the surety's performance obligation is expressed in conditional "defeasance" language. That language declares that the bond obligation is null and void upon performance of the underlying bonded contract in conformance with its terms and conditions such that the bond remains in full force and effect until that performance is completed. Although archaic in form and ancient in history, this defeasance language continues to serve an important function: it assures that the bond obligation will become void automatically upon completion of the bonded contract without need for express cancellation.

Definition and explication of the rights and obligations of the surety and obligee pursuant to that standard defeasance language upon alleged nonperformance by the principal depends upon all of the other provisions contained in the particular bond form being utilized. A brief description of several of those forms follows.

B. *The A312 Performance Bond*

The AIA A312 Performance Bond is perhaps the most widely used performance bond form. Important provisions of the A312 bond include:

---

31 *See id.* § 53(3) cmt. f.

1. *Scope of the bond obligation*: Paragraphs 1 and 2 make clear that the surety and principal are jointly and severally liable for "the performance of a construction contract" which is "incorporated herein by reference" and that no obligation arises under the bond so long as "the contractor performs the construction contract." The construction contract is expressly defined to include: "The agreement between the Owner and the Contractor identified on the signature page, including all Contract Documents and changes thereto."[32]

2. *Trigger*: Paragraph 3 provides that the surety's obligation arises only if: (a) the owner is not in default; (b) the owner notifies the contractor and surety that it is considering default; (c) the owner requests a conference with the contractor and surety; (d) following that conference, the owner declares a default and formally terminates the contractor's right to perform; and (e) the owner agrees to pay the contract balance to the surety or a contractor selected to take over performance.

3. *Surety options*: Paragraphs 4 and 5 provide the surety with numerous options after the bond is appropriately triggered: the surety may: (a) with the obligee's consent, arrange for completion by the principal; (b) take over and complete itself; (c) tender a substitute contractor to the owner; (d) buy back the bond; or (e) deny liability.

4. *Liability limitations*: The bond extends coverage to post-completion correction of defective work and delay damages, plus completion of the contract, additional legal and design professional costs, liquidated or actual damages, and costs resulting from actions or inactions of the surety under paragraph 4. The owner cannot reduce or set off the Contract Balance against unrelated obligations owed to it by the principal.

---

32 Paragraph 8 provides that: "The Surety hereby waives notice of any change, including changes of time, to the Construction Contract, or to related subcontracts, purchase orders and other obligations."

5. *Suit limitation period*: Paragraph 9 provides the obligee with two years in which to commence suit after the date of contractor default, after the contractor stops work or after the surety refuses or fails to perform its obligations, whichever occurs first.

6. *Statutory requirements*: Paragraph 11 provides that, when the bond has been provided to comply with a statutory or other legal requirement in the location where the construction is to be performed, the bond will be construed in conformation with the statutory requirements. In such circumstances, "[t]he intent is that this Bond shall be construed as a statutory bond and not as a common law bond." Despite that provision, many jurisdictions hold that, where the scope of the bond obligations or time for suit commencement is stated in broader terms than what is required by the statute, those broader terms will still be enforced as a voluntary grant of protection beyond that required by the statute.[33]

C. *The A311 Performance Bond*

The AIA A311 Performance Bond is the predecessor to the A312 bond form.[34] It remains in use but is much less detailed in its terms. Akin to the A312 bond, it makes clear that the surety and principal are jointly and severally liable for performance of the construction contract which is incorporated by reference, and the surety again waives notice of alterations and extensions of time. However, the bond "trigger" and surety options are much less detailed. The trigger description is limited to: "Whenever Contractor shall be, and declared by Owner to be in default under the Contract, the Owner having performed Owner's obligations thereunder." The surety options consist of: (a) remedying the default; (b) completing the contract; or (c) rebidding the remaining work, arranging a contract between the lowest responsible bidder and the owner, and making available sufficient funds (up to the penal sum of the bond), less the contract balance, to pay the cost of completion. The A311

---

33 *See* Nelson Roofing & Contr'g, Inc. v. C. W. Moore Co., 245 N.W.2d 866 (Minn. 1976); Reliance Ins. Co. v. Trane Co., 184 S.E.2d 817 (Va. 1971).
34 The A311 dates to 1970; the A312 dates to 1984.

performance bond also provides that suit must be instituted before the expiration of two years from the date on which final payment under the construction contract falls due.[35]

D. Indemnity Bonds

Under an indemnity bond, the surety's performance obligation is limited to reimbursing the obligee up to the penal sum for any cost of completion in excess of the unpaid contract balance at contract termination. There is no true performance obligation or option, meaning that the surety has no control over completion by the obligee and the costs incurred therein. Although completion costs must be reasonable, the surety's burden of proving unreasonableness is not easily satisfied.[36] Moreover, indemnity bonds have been construed to cover a variety of consequential damages, including delay and lost profits.[37] One advantage to the surety is the absence of obligation to any third-party so long as the indemnification is clearly stated to run only to the obligee.[38]

---

35 Cases discussing differences between the A312 and A311 bond forms include Walter Concrete Constr. Corp. v. Lederle Labs., 788 N.E.2d 609 (N.Y. 2003), *and* 120 Greenwich Dev. Assocs. v. Reliance Ins. Co., No., 01 Civ. 8219 (PKL), 2004 WL 1277998, 2004 U.S. Dist. LEXIS 10514 (S.D.N.Y. June 8, 2004).

36 *See* Prudence Co. v. Fid. & Deposit Co. of Md., 297 U.S. 198 (1936); Schmidt Bros. Constr. v. Raymond Y.M.C.A., 163 N.W. 458, 462 (Iowa 1917) (owner "not required to submit the cost of completing the structure to competitive bidders, nor to complete the same at the lowest possible cost, but had the right to expend such sum for labor and material as was fairly and reasonably necessary").

37 *See* Capua v. W. E. O'Neil Constr. Co., 367 N.E.2d 669 (Ill. 1977); Bossier Med. Props. v. Abbott & Williams Constr. Co. of La., 557 So. 2d 1131 (La. Ct. App. 1990).

38 *See* Am. Rad. & Stand. San. Corp. v. Forbes, 259 F.2d 147 (9th Cir. 1958); Camelot Excav'g Co. v. St. Paul Fire & Marine Ins. Co., 301 N.W.2d 275 (Mich. 1981), *overruled in part on other grounds by* Rory v. Continental Cas. Co., 703 N.W.2d 23 (Mich. 2005).

E. Miller Act/Federal Standard Form 25

The Miller Act[39] provides, in part, that contractors awarded contracts of more than $100,000 for the construction, alteration or repair of any public building or public work of the United States must provide a performance bond with a surety or sureties satisfactory to the officer awarding such contract in such amount as the officer considers adequate for the protection of the government, including coverage for taxes.[40]

The Miller Act does not prescribe the form of the required performance bond, but the Code of Federal Regulations does provide a standard form, the Federal Standard Form 25 Performance Bond,[41] that is commonly used. Federal Standard Form 25 is, on its face, a pure indemnity bond that provides for payment up to the penal sum as the only performance option. This bond form has left to the Miller Act, itself, federal regulations, court and boards of contract appeals decisions the task of defining the true scope of the surety's obligations and options under the Miller Act.[42] Among other things, the Miller Act will be liberally construed to protect the United States,[43] and the surety's options upon default are not necessarily limited to payment but can include whatever the government agrees to accept.[44]

F. Little Miller Acts

All states have adopted some form of a "Little Miller Act." A review of each state statute and the related case law is well beyond the scope of this chapter. Consequently, although it is safe to state as a general proposition that each Little Miller Act seeks in some fashion to mirror the Miller Act in terms of purpose and scope, it is also prudent and necessary to specifically state that individual research and review is required when a "Little Miller Act" inquiry moves from the abstract to a concrete application in a particular state. For

---

39 40 U.S.C.S. § 3131-3134 (2009).
40 *Id.* at § 3131(b)(1) and (c)(1).
41 48 C.F.R. § 53.228.
42 *See* Gavin et al., *Public Works Projects, in* BOND DEFAULT MANUAL (Duncan L. Clore ed., 2d ed. 1995).
43 Clifford F. MacEvoy Co. v. United States *ex rel.* Calvin Tomkins Co., 322 U.S. 102, 107 (1944).
44 *See* Aetna Cas. & Surety Co. v. United States, 845 F.2d 971, 975 (Fed. Cir. 1988).

example, Connecticut's Little Miller Act (Conn. Gen. Stat. §§ 49-41a and 49-42) does not require a performance bond at all.

G. Subcontractor Bonds

Subcontractor performance bonds (i.e., bonds where the general contractor is the obligee and the subcontractor is the principal) are routinely required, particularly on large construction projects. The form of the bond often mirrors industry forms, such as the A311 performance bond, and the rules of construction and enforcement likewise mirror the rules applicable to those forms. Typically, there is no concern that legislative requirements of the Miller Act or Little Miller Acts will override or rewrite the terms of the bond, since subcontractor performance bonds are seldom required by those statutes. The project owner is typically unable to seek direct enforcement against the subcontract surety in the absence of express language naming it as a dual obligee or providing conditional assignment consents by the subcontractor and the surety. This is so despite standard subcontract language that invariably incorporates by reference the prime contract terms and conditions.[45]

H. Bid Bonds

Almost all public bid invitations, and many private invitations, require each bidder to provide bid security to insure that the bidder will enter into the contract if it is determined to be the lowest responsible bidder. That bid security has traditionally been between 5 and 10 percent of the bid. The form of the bid security is usually a bid bond, letter of credit or cashier's check. Because most sureties do not charge a premium for the bid bonds of their client contractors, bid bonds are often the security of choice.

A typical bid bond provides that, if the principal is awarded the contract but fails to enter into the contract and provide required payment and performance bonds, the obligee can make claim against the bid bond for its actual resultant damages—usually the additional cost of

---

[45] *See* S. Patrician Assocs. v. Int'l Fid. Ins. Co., 381 S.E.2d 98 (Ga. Ct. App. 1989); *see also* Young v. Gen. Ins Co. of Am., 337 N.E.2d 739 (Ill. App. Ct. 1975).

contracting with the next lowest bidder—up to the penal sum of the bond. However, some statutes, and some advertisements for bids, may mandate that the bid security constitutes liquidated damages. In that circumstance, so long as the obligee can meet the general requirements for establishing an enforceable liquidated damages provision, the entire penal sum may be forfeited without regard to any actual damages suffered by the obligee.[46]

The bid bond surety is ordinarily under no obligation to issue performance or payment bonds after furnishing the bid bond,[47] despite the fact that the surety's failure to provide that bonding may well lead to termination of the contractor for breach of contract if it cannot secure bonding from another surety. Ordinarily, that consequence does not provide grounds for recovery by the contractor from the surety for at least two reasons: (1) the standard general indemnity agreement between the contractor and surety specifically negates any such duty; and (2) the bid bond makes clear that the obligation to furnish performance and payment bonds rests primarily with the contractor, and the surety's secondary obligation and exposure to damages is limited to the penal sum of the bid bond.[48]

IV. Execution, Delivery and Acceptance

Case law supports the proposition that the bond does not become effective against the surety until it is delivered to and accepted by the obligee.[49] Similarly, at least in the case of a subcontractor bond, case law supports a surety's right to withdraw its bond before delivery and acceptance by the obligee, even though the latter had relied upon advice from the principal's attorney that valid bonds had been issued.[50]

---

46 *See* City of Lake Geneva v. States Improv. Co., 172 N.W.2d 176 (Wis. 1969).
47 Some state statutes do require that the bid bond be accompanied by, or serve as consent of the surety to issue, performance and payment bonds. *E.g.*, N.J. Stat. 40A:11-22 (2009).
48 *See* Chas. H. Tompkins Co. v Lumbermens Mut. Cas. Co., 732 F. Supp. 1368 (E.D. Va. 1990).
49 Rachman Bag Co. v. Liberty Mut. Ins. Co., 46 F.3d 230, 238 (2d Cir. 1995).
50 S.S. Silberblatt Inc. v. Seaboard Surety Co., 417 F.2d 1043, 1051-52 (8th Cir. 1969).

V. Consideration

Like any other contract, the performance bond must be supported by consideration, and whatever constitutes sufficient consideration for other contracts will ordinarily suffice to support a contract of suretyship.[51] In at least one reported case, *United States v. Simpkins*,[52] that required consideration was held to be absent. The court reasoned that a common law bond is an obligation knowingly incurred in order to obtain "some right or benefit to which the principal would not otherwise be entitled." In that case, the principal had secured a bond for excise taxes upon the basis of a perceived statutory duty that, in fact, no longer existed. The court therefore found that the principal did not obtain any benefit or achieve any purpose in keeping the bond in effect and so denied recovery.[53] On the other hand, there is authority for the proposition that a contract of suretyship "under seal" need not be shown as supported by consideration.[54]

A. Indemnity Agreement Executed After Bond Issues

On occasion, the press of business may result in a surety issuing the performance bond before the principal and other indemnitors have executed the general indemnity agreement. At least one reported decision has held that the delay in execution does not negate the surety's rights under that agreement. In *American Druggists' Insurance Co. v. Shoppe*,[55] the surety issued performance and payment bonds in April 1979 but the indemnity agreement was not executed until February 1980. Still, the court held the indemnitors liable, reasoning that the bonds were consideration for the indemnity agreement, and issuance of the bonds and execution of the indemnity agreement were a unitary act. Moreover, it was a common

---

51   72 C.J.S. *Principal and Surety*, § 64, at 550 (2008).
52   313 F. Supp. 1045 (E. D. Tex. 1970).
53   *Id*. at 1048.
54   Johnston v. Missouri Pac. R.R. Co., 160 S.W.2d 39 (Ark. 1942); Smalley v. Bassford, 13 S.E.2d 662 (Ga. 1941); Central-Penn Nat'l Bank of Phila. v. Tinkler, 40 A.2d 389 (Pa. 1945); Billings v. Roth, 40 A.2d 910 (Pa. Super. Ct. 1945).
55   448 N.W.2d 103 (Minn. Ct. App. 1989).

industry practice to issue the bonds before fully executing the indemnity agreement.[56]

B. Subsequent Indemnity Agreements Omit Certain Indemnitors

The execution of one or more renewals of the indemnity agreement generally does not operate as a novation[57] of the earlier agreement.[58] Most indemnity agreements provide that the surety's release of one indemnitor does not operate to release any of the other indemnitors. Those agreements also often include an express waiver of notice of any act, fact or information concerning or affecting the rights or liabilities of the indemnitors. Consequently, an indemnitor will have great difficulty supporting an argument that its indemnity obligations are extinguished by the surety's subsequent omission or release of other indemnitors.

VI. Fraud by the Principal

As a general rule, fraud by the principal will not discharge the surety's obligations to the obligee under the performance bond, so long as the obligee is not itself involved in the fraud[59] and so long as the obligee does not become aware, before entering into its contract with the principal, that the principal has defrauded the surety.[60]

---

56   *Id. See also* Elk River Concrete Prods. Co. v. Am. Cas. Co., 129 N.W.2d 309 (Minn. 1964).
57   Novation "is the substitution of a new obligation for an existing one, which is thereby extinguished." Cincinnati Ins. Co. v. Leighton, 403 F.3d 879, 887 (7th Cir. 2005).
58   *See* Nat'l Surety Corp. v. Prairieland Constr., Inc., 354 F. Supp. 2d 1032 (E.D. Mo. 2004); Olympic Dev. Group, Inc. v. Am. Druggists' Ins. Co., 333 S.E.2d 622 (Ga. Ct. App. 1985); Travelers Indem. Co. v. Ducote, 380 So. 2d 10 (La. 1979). *But see* Cincinnati Ins. Co. v. Leighton, 403 F.3d 879 (7th Cir. 2005).
59   *E.g.*, Rachman Bag Co. v. Liberty Mut. Ins. Co., 46 F.3d 230, 237 (2d Cir. 1995); G. & S. Foods, Inc. v. Vavaroutsos, 438 F. Supp. 122, 125 (N.D. Ill. 1977); Nat'l Union Fire Ins. Co. of Pittsburgh v. Robuck, 203 So. 2d 204, 206 (Fla. Dist. Ct. App. 1967), *cert. denied*, 212 So. 2d 869 (Fla. 1968); Casoni v. Jerome, 58 N.Y. 315, 321 (1874).
60   RESTATEMENT (THIRD) OF SURETYSHIP AND GUARANTY § 12(2) (1996).

The rationale is straightforward: the performance bond is issued to protect the obligee; therefore, so long as the obligee acts in good faith, it should not be denied that protection. Moreover, the surety is ordinarily in the best position to detect the fraud of its own principal and, in any event, retains a remedy against the principal for any losses it incurs through the indemnity agreement (and equitable principles), even in the absence of fraud.

VII. Fraud by the Obligee

Fraud or misrepresentation by the obligee that induces the surety to issue a bond can make the surety's obligations under that bond voidable.[61] Actionable circumstances can include intentional misstatement, nondisclosure or concealment.[62] However, the obligee must be shown to have a duty to disclose the information[63] and that the information is not something that the surety should have independently known.[64] For example, if the obligee knew that the surety would not bond the full cost of the contemplated contract and work out an agreement under which only a portion of the project is submitted for bonding—without disclosing to the surety the true scope of the overall undertaking—the surety may be entitled to discharge.[65]

---

61 *Id.* § 12(1) ("If the secondary obligor's assent to the secondary obligation is induced by a fraudulent or material misrepresentation by the obligee upon which the secondary obligor is justified in relying, the secondary obligation is voidable by the secondary obligor."); *see also* Marine Bank, N.A. v. Meat Counter, Inc., 826 F.2d 1577 (7th Cir. 1987); Falco v. Alpha Affiliates, Inc., No. 97-494 (MMS), 2000 WL 727116, 2000 U.S. Dist. LEXIS 7480, at *14-15 (D. Del. Feb. 9, 2000) (surety contracts voidable due to material misrepresentations).

62 *See* Ground Improv't Techniques, Inc. v. Merchants Bonding Co., 63 F. Supp. 2d 1272, 1276 (D. Colo. 1999) (denying plaintiff's motion for summary judgment on surety's counterclaim for rescission because issues of fact surrounding whether issuance of bond was induced by concealment of material information).

63 Rachman Bag Co. v. Liberty Mut. Ins. Co., 46 F.3d 230 (2d Cir. 1995).

64 Iowa Concrete Breaking Corp. v. Jewat Trucking, Inc., 444 N.W.2d 865, 868 (Minn. Ct. App. 1989).

65 *See* Employers Ins. of Wausau v. Constr. Mgmt. Engineers of Fla., Inc., 377 S.E.2d 119 (S.C. Ct. App. 1989).

VIII. Unauthorized Acts by Agent

It is difficult for a surety to contest the authority of a purported agent to bind it to the terms of a performance bond. "The authority of persons who signed a bond for a surety company may not ordinarily be questioned by the company where, with knowledge of the bond, it received the premium owing to it without repudiating the authority of such persons."[66] Moreover, statutes in many states establish an irrebuttable presumption of the apparent authority of an agent to bind the surety company, where that agent has been generally employed to receive bond applications and/or deliver bonds, and that agent in fact delivers a bond apparently executed by the surety to a person who accepts that delivery in good faith.[67]

IX. Mistake

General principles of contract law, including the concept of mistake, are applicable to surety bonds.[68] Moreover, as a secondary guarantor of its principal's performance, the surety may generally assert any defenses it has in its own right,[69] together with such defenses as may be available to its principal on the underlying contract.[70] At the same time, courts are not predisposed to accept a surety's claim of mistake or misunderstanding regarding the terms of the suretyship agreement.[71]

X. Illegality

Similarly, in appropriate circumstances, the surety can assert the defense of illegality of the underlying contract[72] or of the performance bond itself.[73] However, a claim that the bond is illegal because it fails to conform to statutory requirements is unlikely to prevail. If the bond

---

66 74 AM. JUR. 2D SURETYSHIP § 254 (2008).
67 *Id.*
68 RESTATEMENT (THIRD) OF SURETYSHIP AND GUARANTY § 5 (1996).
69 *Id.* § 12 cmt. k.
70 *Id.* §§ 19(b), 34.
71 *E.g.*, United States v. Country Kettle, Inc., 738 F. Supp. 1358, 1360-61 (D. Kan. 1990); *see* 72 C.J.S. *Principal and Surety* § 78 (2008).
72 72 C.J.S. *Principal and Surety* § 20 (2008).
73 *Id.* § 79.

terms conflict with statutory requirements, however, the judicial response is not to declare the bond illegal but rather to hold that the statutory provisions control.[74] Furthermore, the illegality of the underlying contract may be insufficient to discharge the surety if the obligee retains causes of action against the principal other than in contract.[75]

Conclusion

Despite their ancient pedigree, occasionally arcane language and other unique characteristics, performance bonds are contracts first and foremost. The language of the bond will, in the main, create and govern the relationships between the surety, obligee and principal. Consequently, the importance of careful drafting, careful selection and careful review of bond forms cannot be overstated. The following chapters will further discuss and explore the rights and obligations of the parties pursuant to those relationships.

---

[74] *See* Wichita Sheet Metal Supply, Inc. v. Dahlstrom & Ferrell Constr. Co., 792 P.2d 1043, 1046 (Kan. 1990); Sheldon Pollack Corp. v. Pioneer Concrete of Tex., Inc., 765 S.W.2d 843, 846 (Tex. App. 1989); 17 AM. JUR. 2d *Contractors' Bonds* § 8 (2008).

[75] 17 AM. JUR. *Contractors' Bonds* § 9 (2008).

2

CONDITIONS PRECEDENT TO ASSERTING A PERFORMANCE BOND CLAIM

Benjamin D. Lentz
Kim McNaughton*

Introduction

The law on conditions precedent has been defined as follows:

> A condition precedent is an act or event, other than a lapse of time, which, unless the condition is excused, must occur before a duty to perform a promise in the agreement arises . . . Conditions can be express or implied. Express conditions are those agreed to and imposed by the parties themselves. Implied or constructive conditions are those imposed by law to do justice. Express conditions must be literally performed, whereas constructive conditions, which ordinarily arise from language or promise, are subject to the precept that substantial compliance is sufficient . . . [1]

There is a substantial body of case law addressing whether an obligee has no rights under a performance bond due to the obligee's failure to comply with conditions precedent to the surety's obligations or performance. Possible conditions precedent under performance bond forms that are commonly in use include the following:

- Whether the obligee is required to comply with its obligations to the contractor under the bonded contract;
- Whether the obligee is required to hold a pre-default meeting;

---

*   Jason A. Lange of Torre, Lentz, Gamell, Gary & Rittmaster, LLP rendered substantial assistance with respect to the research and preparation of this chapter.

[1] Int'l Fid. Ins. Co. v. County of Rockland, 98 F. Supp. 2d 400, 434 (S.D.N.Y. 2000) (quoting Oppenheimer & Co. v. Oppenheim, Appel, Dixon & Co., 660 N.E.2d 415 (N.Y. 1995)).

- Whether the obligee is required to formally default the principal and terminate its right to complete the contract;
- Whether the obligee is required to give notice to the surety of the default and termination of its principal so that the surety has an opportunity to select its preferred performance or completion option; and
- Whether the obligee is required to dedicate the undisbursed contract balance to the completion of the bonded contract.

The case law is sharply split as to whether the AIA 311 bond form requires that the obligee provide notice to the surety that it has defaulted the principal as a condition precedent that must be performed by the obligee. By contrast, the AIA A312 bond form sets out explicit language regarding an obligee's conditions precedent (obligee compliance with its obligations, predefault meetings, formal default/termination and dedication of contract balance), though there are some conflicting decisions regarding the extent of their application. Typical defeasance bonds are even less precise in terms of setting out explicit conditions precedent.

Issues regarding possible conditions precedent in connection with each of these bond forms are discussed in this chapter. Because many bond forms have language suggesting that the principal's default is a precondition to a bond claim, the consideration of each common bond form in this chapter is preceded by a discussion of what constitutes a "default" as referenced in the bond forms—including consideration of the differences between a contractor's breach of contract and a contractor's default in performance of the contract, what constitutes a material breach, and whether contract provisions defining default are exclusive.

I. What Constitutes a Contractor's Default

A. *The Distinction Between Breach and Default; Default Defined*

The first step in dealing with the issue of when a breach of contract justifies termination of the contractor's right to perform the contract for default is to understand the distinction between the terms "breach" and "default." This issue cuts across all bond forms for the surety's obligation is always triggered by the contractor's default. Stated alternatively, if there is no contractor default, then there is no need for the obligee to make demand upon the surety.

While the terms "breach" and "default" are sometimes mistakenly used interchangeably, there is a clear difference between the two terms, for not every breach of a construction contract justifies a termination of the contractor's right to complete the contract for default. This distinction between breach and default was articulated by the Fifth Circuit in *L&A Contracting Company v. Southern Concrete Services, Inc.*,[2] as follows:

> Although the terms breach and default are sometimes used interchangeably, their meanings are distinct in construction suretyship law. Not every breach of a construction contract constitutes a default sufficient to require the surety to step in and remedy it. To constitute a legal default, there must be (1) material breach or series of material breaches (2) of such magnitude that the obligee is justified in terminating the contract. Usually the principal is unable to complete the project, leaving termination of the contract the obligee's only option.[3]

While *L&A Contracting* stands for the proposition that there is a distinction between "breach" and "default," it is important to notice that the word breach is used in the definition of default, namely a material breach or breaches of such magnitude that the obligee is justified in terminating the contract. The distinction between breach and default found in *L&A Contracting* has been applied in *John A. Russell Corp. v. Fine Line Drywall, Inc.*,[4] where the district court found that "[t]he *L&A* approach offers a clear benchmark for determining whether a default has occurred by requiring a material breach."[5] Furthermore, the distinction has been applied in *Colorado Structures, Inc. v. Insurance Co. of the West*,[6] where the Supreme Court of Washington followed *L&A*

---

[2] 17 F.3d 106 (5th Cir. 1994). As discussed in Section II A, *supra*, the Fifth Circuit rejected the obligee's argument that job correspondence complaining about the principal's (subcontractor's) performance constitutes an unequivocal declaration of default.

[3] *Id.* at 110.

[4] No. 2:05-CV-321, 2008 WL 501273 (D. Vt. Feb. 21, 2008).

[5] *Id.* at *3.

[6] 167 P.3d 1125 (Wash. 2007). We have cited the *L&A Contracting* and *Colorado Structures* decisions since they are in accord regarding the distinction between "breach" and "default." However, as discussed

Contracting for the limited purpose of distinguishing between breach and default. *Colorado Structures* found "that a principal is 'in default under the subcontract' if he or she materially breaches the subcontract, thereby permitting (but not requiring) the obligee to terminate or cancel the subcontract."[7]

Thus, since default is defined as material breach (or breaches) which justify terminating the contract, the next task is to focus on the definition of materiality.

B. What Is Material?

As was set forth in *L&A Contracting* and adopted by *John A. Russell* and *Colorado Structures*, in order for a breach (or breaches) to justify a default termination, the breach (or breaches) must be material. In interpreting materiality, courts in various jurisdictions will often look to the Restatement (Second) of Contracts §241, which provides as follows:

> In determining whether a failure to render or to offer performance is material, the following circumstances are significant:
>
> (a) the extent to which the injured party will be deprived of the benefit which he reasonably expected;
>
> (b) the extent to which the injured party can be adequately compensated for the part of that benefit of which he will be deprived;
>
> (c) the extent to which the party failing to perform or to offer to perform will suffer forfeiture;
>
> (d) the likelihood that the party failing to perform or to offer to perform will cure his failure, taking account of all the circumstances including any reasonable assurances;
>
> (e) the extent to which the behavior of the party failing to perform or to offer to perform comports with standards of good faith and fair dealing.

---

below, they are not in accord regarding whether "declaration of default" and "notice" to the surety are "conditions" to the surety's obligations under the non-AIA 312 form; in fact, *Colorado Structures* expressly rejects the reasoning of *L&A Contracting* regarding the "conditions" issue.

7   *Id.* at 1132.

For example, in *In re Decker Oaks Development II, Ltd.*,[8] a bankruptcy court sitting in Texas found that when determining whether a breach was material "the Court must apply a list of considerations set forth in the Restatement of Contracts."[9] In *Gallagher v. Southern Source Packaging, LLC*,[10] a district court sitting in North Carolina and applying Indiana law found that "courts look to the Restatement (Second) of Contracts to determine whether a breach is material."[11]

In *Decker Oaks*, the court noted that "[w]hether a breach of contract is material is a question of fact."[12] Thus, materiality is determined by the facts and circumstances on a case-by-case basis. For example, the first element set forth in the RESTATEMENT, the extent of harm, is fact specific. Therefore, while this chapter started with *L&A Contracting* for the proposition that there is a distinction between breach and default, the key factor marking that distinction, materiality, is defined by the facts and circumstances of each case. Materiality is not dependent upon the bond form that is used; rather it is dependent upon the facts and circumstances of each case.

Given the factual nature of materiality, the surety must carefully examine the contract to see if the parties have defined default or set forth events of default, as discussed in the next section.

C. Contract Provisions Defining Default: Are the Contract Provisions Exclusive?

The underlying contract is generally incorporated by reference into the performance bond. The initial recital clause in the performance bond customarily refers to the contract between the contractor and owner, and often expressly states that the contract is "made a part hereof" or employs similar language. Thus, the contract is the first place for the surety to look to see if the parties have defined the term "default," or have defined "events of default" which would justify the owner's (1) termination of the contractor's right to complete performance of the contract, and (2) invoking the surety's performance bond obligations.

---

8   No. 07-35557 and Adversary No. 07-03421, 2008 WL 2356098 (Bankr. S.D. Tex. June 5, 2008).
9   *Id.* at *25.
10   564 F. Supp. 2d 503 (E.D.N.C. 2008).
11   *Id.* at 509.
12   2008 WL 2356098 at *25 (citations omitted).

This is another issue that cuts across all bond forms, namely whether the underlying contract defines default.

An example of a typical clause for a large public construction contract (the New York City Transit Authority) is as follows:

> An event of Default shall mean a material breach of the Contract by the Contractor which, without limiting the generality of the foregoing and in addition to those instances specifically referred to in the Contract as a material breach or an Event of Default, shall include a determination by the Engineer that: (i) performance of this Contract is unnecessarily or unreasonably delayed; (ii) the Contractor is willfully violating any of the provisions of the Contract Documents or is not executing the same in good faith and in accordance with this Contract; (iii) the Contractor has abandoned the Work; (iv) Contractor has become insolvent (other than as a bankrupt), or has assigned the proceeds of this Contract for the benefit of creditors, or taken advantage of any insolvency statute or debtor or creditor law or if his property or affairs have been put in the hands of a receiver; (v) Contractor has failed to obtain an approval required by the Contract; or (vi) the Contractor has failed to provide 'adequate assurance' as required under paragraph (b) hereof.[13]

This public owner has expressly set forth a broad definition of contractor "default" (essentially the common law definition of "a material breach of the Contract by the Contractor"). Further, while this owner has set forth six "events of default," these six events are not exclusive, and this owner may simply rely upon the common law definition to establish a default.

This leads to the next question which is what happens where the default provision, by its terms, does not provide that it is "exclusive" or "not exclusive." More specifically, if the contract default provision is silent as to whether it is exclusive, can the owner assert a basis or ground for default that is not contained in the contract? In *Olin Corporation v. Central Industries, Inc.*,[14] the court noted the split in authority between what the court referred to as (1) the "Corbin view," namely that "where such a termination provision is included in a contract, it constitutes the exclusive means of terminating the contract,"[15] and (2) the "Williston

---

[13] New York City Transit Authority Contract (on file with the authors of this chapter).
[14] 576 F.2d 642 (5th Cir. 1978).
[15] 6 Arthur Corbin, CORBIN ON CONTRACTS § 1266 at 64 (1962).

view," namely that "[u]nless a contract provision for termination for breach is in terms exclusive (citation omitted), it is a cumulative remedy and does not bar the ordinary remedy of termination for a 'breach which is material, or which goes to the root of the matter or essence of the contract.'"[16] Given the split in authority, where the contract does not expressly state whether or not the default or termination provisions are exclusive, the law of the applicable jurisdiction will determine whether the owner can resort to a non-specified basis for defaulting the contractor and making demand upon the surety.

By analogy, *Granite Computer Leasing Corp. v. Travelers Indemnity Co.*,[17] involves a subcontractor abandoning the project based upon a ground not contained in the subcontract. The subcontract provided that the subcontractor "may stop work if any progress payment is not made . . . within ten (10) days after the due date." The court held that this language did not preclude the subcontractor from asserting other reasons to justify abandonment of performance (government delays in design approval), stating as follows:

> Although this provision listed no further ground of which National could cease performance it did not thereby establish nonpayment as the sole contractual ground for termination. Had it been contemplated that no other contractual ground could justify termination by National, the contract could easily have provided that National may stop work only if any progress payment is not made. Interpleaded as one express justification which could warrant National terminating the subcontract, this provision did not preclude National from terminating for other reasons, such as government delays in claim resolution.[18]

D. Summary

In summary, the principal must be in material breach of contract for the obligee to successfully make a demand upon the performance bond.

---

16 Samuel Williston, 15 WILLISTON ON CONTRACTS § 44:55 (4th ed. 2008).
17 894 F.2d 547 (2d Cir. 1990).
18 *Id.* at 553.

II. The AIA 311 Bond–Conditions Precedent or Not?

A. *Introduction*

The operative terms of the AIA 311 bond form arguably create conditions precedent to the surety's liability:

> Whenever Principal shall be, and declared by Obligee to be in default under the subcontract, the Obligee having performed Obligee's obligations thereunder:
>
> (1) Surety may promptly remedy the default, subject to the provisions of paragraph 3 herein, or;
>
> (2) Obligee after reasonable notice to Surety may, or Surety upon demand of Obligee may arrange for the performance of Principal's obligation under the subcontract subject to the provisions of paragraph 3 herein;
>
> (3) The balance of the subcontract price, as defined below, shall be credited against the reasonable cost of completing performance of the subcontract....[19]

Based on this language, it can be argued that the conditions precedent to an owner successfully asserting a claim under the bond include the owner's compliance with its obligations under the bonded contract, its commitment to dedicate the undisbursed contract balance to completion of the project, the termination of the principal, and timely notice of the termination to the surety.[20] Of these possible conditions precedent, there is extensive and conflicting precedent regarding whether the surety is entitled to receive timely notice of the contractor's default and, if so, what are the consequences (if any) to the owner if such notice is not given. These issues are addressed herein.

---

[19] There are many manuscripted bond forms that incorporate some or all of this language and therefore the analysis herein may be applicable in whole or part to bond forms that incorporate some or all of the A311 text.

[20] *See* Roel Partnership v. Amwest Sur. Ins. Co., 258 A.D. 2d 780, 781-82 (N.Y. App. Div. 3d Dept. 1999) (surety properly denied performance bond claim where obligee breached condition precedent by failing to properly pay principal).

This section will start with the Fifth Circuit's *L&A Contracting* decision, which sets forth several important principles that have been applied by later courts, including that (1) the obligee's obligation to inform the surety of the principal's default is a "condition" to the surety's performance bond liability, and (2) the obligee's failure to give such notice (or satisfy such condition) results in the discharge (no liability) of the performance bond surety, without a showing of prejudice.[21]

B. Decisions Supporting the Conclusion That Default and Notice to the Surety of Such Default Are Conditions Under the A311 Bond Form

In *L&A Contracting*, the general contractor L&A recovered a judgment for delay damages against both the concrete subcontractor Southern and its surety F&D. The court stated that the form of the subcontract performance bond provided that F&D would become liable to take certain actions to remedy Southern's breach "[w]henever the Principal shall be, and shall be declared by Obligee to be in default under the subcontract, the Obligee having performed Obligee's obligations thereunder."

Both F&D and Southern appealed. The Fifth Circuit, applying Florida law, reversed as to F&D, stating that:

> The Bond in this case imposes liability on F&D for Southern's breach only if two conditions exist. First, Southern must have been *in default* of its performance obligations under the subcontract. Second, L&A must have *declared* Southern to be in default.

Since the court found that the general contractor L&A had failed to declare the subcontractor Southern in default, the court found that F&D did not breach the terms of its bond, and accordingly had no liability under the bond. (See the separate discussion below regarding whether job correspondence is insufficient to constitute a declaration of default.) It is important to note that while the judgment against the surety was reversed, the judgment against the subcontractor for delay damages was sustained, pointing out the difference between the liability of the principal and surety under this bond form.

---

21   17 F.3d 106 (5th Cir. 1994).

The obligee/general contractor argued on appeal that the performance bond phrase "declared . . . to be in default" was ambiguous, and urged that this phrase should be defined as any communication that the principal failed to fulfill a contractual duty. The court disagreed, finding this phrase to be unambiguous, citing three factors. First, the court stated that the obligee's definition "impermissibly blurs the distinct concept of breach and default."[22] Second, the obligee's definition was "impractical" because "[g]iven the consequences that follow a declaration of default, it is vital that the declaration be made in terms sufficiently clear, direct, and unequivocal to inform the surety that the principal has defaulted on its obligations and the surety must immediately commence performing under the terms of the bond."[23] Third, the obligee's proposed definition does not promote the purpose behind the notice of default provision, namely, "to avoid the common-law rule that a secondary obligor such as F&D is not entitled to notice when the time for its performance is due."[24]

Accordingly, the court found as a matter of law that the proposed evidence of default, namely the job correspondence, was insufficient to establish the required declaration of default. None of these letters sent by the obligee/contractor to the subcontractor and surety even mentioned the term "default," nor was there "an unequivocal declaration of default." The court stated that correspondence from the general contractor attempting to prod subcontractors into improved performance are inevitably abundant on large construction projects, but such correspondence does not constitute the required declaration of default. As for this required declaration, the court stated as follows:

> The declaration must inform the surety that the principal has committed a material breach or series of material breaches of the subcontract, that the obligee regards the subcontract as terminated, and that the surety must immediately commence performing under the terms of its bond.[25]

---

22 *Id.* at 110.
23 *Id.* at 111.
24 *Id.*
25 *Id.*

In *Bank of Brewton, Inc. v. International Fidelity Insurance Co.*,[26] the court stated that job correspondence does not constitute a declaration of default, stating:

> Although the correspondence details many threats to declare a contractor default, perhaps intended to inspire greater diligence on the part of the contractor, a mere threat is not sufficient to trigger the obligations of a surety.[27]

The decision in *Balfour Beatty Construction, Inc. v. Colonial Ornamental Iron Works, Inc.*,[28] is strikingly similar to *L&A Contracting*. The relevant bond language was the same, "whenever principal shall be, and declared by Obligee to be in default under the subcontract." Again the obligee's failure to give notice resulted in a total discharge or release of liability of the performance bond surety. The court stated that "[a]s a result, the plaintiff [obligee] fails to meet a necessary condition for NSC's [the surety's] liability under the bond and the defendant's motion for summary judgment is granted."[29] The court rejected the obligee's contention that two letters sent by the obligee, both complaining of delays by the supplier, constituted a sufficient notice of default.

In addition to the "condition" rationale that was employed in *L&A Contracting*, the *Balfour* court employed another rationale supporting the total discharge or release of the surety, namely that the failure of the obligee to give notice to the surety of the contractor's default deprived the surety of its performance bond options. The court observed that, under a performance bond, the surety generally has two options upon its principal's default. "First, the surety may undertake to complete the principal's work itself; this obligation may be satisfied by the surety funding the principal to complete its work. Second, the surety has the option of paying the obligee under the bond its damages, essentially, the

---

26   827 So. 2d 747 (Ala. 2002).
27   *Id.* at 754. *Cf.* Siegfried Constr., Inc. v. Gulf Ins. Co., No. 98-2808, 2000 U.S. App. LEXIS 1304 (4th Cir. Feb. 2, 2000) (multiple notices found sufficient to constitute "notice of default" where the notices were headed "Termination for Failure to Perform," stated specific grounds justifying termination, and indicated an intent to either terminate the principal or supplement its work force.
28   986 F. Supp. 82 (D. Conn. 1997).
29   *Id.* at 86.

obligee's cost of completion."[30] The court then stated that the obligee improperly "allowed Colonial [the principal] to complete the project, thereby denying the defendant [surety] the opportunity to exercise any of its options under the performance bond."[31]

The court in *Insurance Company of North America v. Metropolitan Dade County*[32] also construed a bond with language similar to that of an AIA 311. The court adopted the reasoning that "Dade's [the owner's] failure to comply with INA's bond notice provisions stripped the surety of its liability for the instant claim."[33] In *INA*, the latent defects were discovered in 1992, when certain portions of the roofs of the project blew off during Hurricane Andrew. Dade County obtained a default judgment against the contractor, commenced a separate action against INA, and obtained summary judgment. INA argued that it was relieved of liability because it was not notified when the defects were discovered, but was only notified after the repairs had been made and when the action was commenced against the contractor. Under its performance bond, INA, upon notification, was required to either complete the contract, or at the county's option, obtain bids and arrange for completion. Since Dade County failed to notify INA, the court reversed the judgment in favor of the county. Again, the surety was not required to demonstrate prejudice, namely that it would have completed at a lower cost.

In *Hunt Construction Group, Inc. v. National Wrecking Corp.*[34] the general contractor/obligee terminated the subcontract months after the subcontractor had completed its work, and sought to hold the subcontractor's surety liable for delay damages. The court held in favor of the surety, stating:

> Where the obligee fails to notify a surety of an obligor's default in a timely fashion, so that the surety can exercise its options under the

---

30   *Id.* (quoting Granite Computer Leasing Corp. v. Travelers Indem. Co., 894 F.2d 547 (2d Cir. 1990)).

31   *Id. See* Sch. Bd. of Escambia County v. TIG Premier Ins. Co., 110 F. Supp. 2d 1351 (N.D. Fla. 2000) (following *Balfour Beatty*, the court affirmed the surety's denial of a performance bond claim due to a lack of timely notice irrespective of whether the lack of notice caused prejudice).

32   705 So. 2d 33 (Fla. Dist. Ct. App. 1997).

33   *Id.* at 35.

34   542 F. Supp. 2d 87 (D. D.C. 2008).

controlling performance bond, the obligee renders the bond null and void.[35]

In *CC-Aventura, Inc. v. Weitz Co., LLC*,[36] the court held that the "reasonable notice" provision of the performance bond was not inconsistent with the contract provisions regarding subcontractor default and the general contractor's right to perform the defaulted subcontractor's work. The court, in granting summary judgment to the surety, stated that the general contractor was required to give the surety "reasonable notice" before making its own arrangements to complete the subcontractor's work.

C. Decisions Which Require That the Surety Demonstrate Prejudice Where No Notice Is Given Under the AIA 311 Bond

In contrast to the "condition" and "loss of rights" rationales discussed above, certain courts have held that the surety is not relieved of liability where it did not receive notice under the AIA 311 bond unless the surety can demonstrate prejudice.

In *Blackhawk Heating & Plumbing Co. v. Seaboard Surety Co.*,[37] the court permitted the surety to establish a defense to the extent that the surety's damages would have been reduced had notice to the surety been given. Seaboard testified that it was its practice, when notified of problems on a bonded project, to respond and take whatever steps are necessary to resolve them. In *Blackhawk*, Seaboard denied performance bond liability claiming,

> that an implied condition of the performance bond for recovery of additional costs due to the subcontractor's delays was that the general contractor would notify Seaboard of any delays and give Seaboard the opportunity to remedy those delays, and that failure to give notice bars *any* recovery by Blackhawk.[38]

---

35   *Id.* at 96.
36   No. 06-21598-CIV, 2008 WL 2937856 (S.D. Fla. July 14, 2008).
37   534 F. Supp. 309 (N.D. Ill. 1982).
38   *Id.* at 315.

The court agreed in part with Seaboard, stating that to the extent that Seaboard could have remedied the delays, and thereby avoided the additional costs, Seaboard was not liable. However, to the extent that the additional costs could not have been avoided, then the failure to give notice was immaterial.

Plowden & Roberts, Inc. v. Conway,[39] also applies a prejudice or injury standard, stating "[t]he compensated surety's liability is merely reduced by any harm which it has suffered by the fact that it was not accorded its rights to remedy the default."[40] In *Plowden*, the performance bond provided that the surety's obligations were triggered when the principal shall be and declared by the general contractor to be in default. In contrast to the total release cases, the court stated:

> These provisions permitting U.S.F.&G. to remedy the default by completing the contract or arranging for a contract for completion are not made conditions precedent to suit. The fact that Plowden does not allege a demand upon U.S.F.&G. to remedy the default, complete the contract or obtain a contract for completion, does not totally relieve the compensated surety from all obligations under the performance bond. The bond does not specifically so provide and under the circumstances U.S.F.&G. must plead and prove the damages, if any, resulting from Plowden's failure to permit it to promptly remedy the alleged default in accordance with the terms of the bond.[41]

These decisions requiring that the surety demonstrate prejudice are clearly wrong if one assumes that notice is a "condition precedent," for as set forth at the outset of this chapter a "condition precedent" is an act that must be performed by the obligee before the surety's performance bond duty arises. However, as demonstrated by the case law discussed in the next section, it is hotly disputed whether the AIA 311 bond language is recognized as "condition precedent" language.

---

39   192 So. 2d 528 (Fla. Dist. Ct. App. 1966).
40   *Id.* at 533.
41   *Id.*

D. Decisions Holding That Notice to the Surety Is Not a "Condition Precedent" Under the AIA 311 Bond

In *Walter Concrete Construction Corp. v. Lederle Laboratories*[42] the plaintiff Fred Holt, Inc., entered into a subcontract with the defendant subcontractor, Walter Concrete to construct a building project. The surety issued an AIA A311 subcontract performance bond, which contains an identical paragraph to the one cited in *L&A Contracting*, namely "[w]henever contractor shall be, and declared by the owner to be in default under the contract, ..."

Walter Concrete eventually abandoned the project, but the general contractor did not request the surety to complete the construction project. Rather, the general contractor and owner hired other contractors to complete the subcontractor's work. The obligee made demand upon the surety for the excess completion costs. The surety refused, "claiming that it had not received a declaration of default which, it asserted, was a necessary precursor to its liability under the bond."[43] The court of appeals (New York's highest court) disagreed, stating that "the AIA-311 performance bond contains no explicit provision requiring notice of default as to condition precedent to any legal action on the bond." The court went on further to distinguish the A312 and the AIA-311 performance bonds by stating.

> Surety bonds–like all contracts–are to be construed in accordance with their terms. Unlike the AIA-312 bond, another industry standardized bond, an action on the AIA-311 bond is not tied to a declaration of default, the principal's cessation of work or the surety's refusal to perform under the bond. Rather, an action on the AIA-311 need only be commenced within two years from the date on which final payment under the contract is due. Had the parties to the contract desired notice of the default as a precursor to liability under the bond, they could have elected to issue the more specific AIA-312, which by its terms requires pre default notification be given to the contractor and surety by the owner.[44]

---

42   788 N.E.2d 609 (N.Y. 2003).
43   *Id.* at 610.
44   *Id.*

The New York Court of Appeals in *Walter* cited with approval two appellate division decisions, *Babylon Associates v. County of Suffolk* and *Menorah Nursing Home, Inc. v. Zukov*. In *Babylon Associates*,[45] the court stated

> While the bond does require that the county declare the bond in default, this provision was satisfied by the county's allegation in its counterclaim stating, 'the Performance Bond is in default.'[46]

By reversing this dismissal, the appellate court is clearly holding that the bond requirement of declaration of default is not a "condition" because this requirement can be satisfied by the owner's litigation pleadings.

In *Menorah Nursing Home, Inc.*,[47] the owner of the construction project and others sued the surety (Travelers) of the general contractor (Blitman) for "economic damages" (the nature of which was not indicated in the opinion). Travelers impleaded several of the subcontractors of the general contractor, including the surety (National) one of the subcontractors, Mopal. The court rejected National's argument that Traveler's third-party action should be dismissed because its principal, Mopal, was never declared in default, and Blitman (the general contractor) had actually certified that Mopal's work had been satisfactorily completed. The court stated:

> National also argues that Travelers' third-party action should be dismissed because the obligee named in its bond (Blitman), far from ever declaring a default by Mopal in the performance of its subcontract, actually certified that Mopal's work had been satisfactorily completed. This argument must fail for the basic reason that National's bond contains no provision which expressly requires a notice of default as a condition precedent to any legal action on the bond.[48]

RLI Insurance Co. v. St. Patrick's Home For The Infirm And Aged[49] is a recent decision applying New York law that rejects the surety's

---

45 475 N.Y.S.2d 869 (N.Y. App. Div. 1984).
46 *Id.* at 875.
47 548 N.Y.S.2d 702 (N.Y. App. Div. 1989).
48 *Id.* at 708.
49 452 F. Supp. 2d 484 (S.D.N.Y. 2006).

argument that the performance bond language ("wherever principal shall be, and declared by obligee to be in default . . .") constitutes "a condition precedent to the surety's obligation to pay under the bond." The surety had cited to *Elm Haven Construction Ltd. Partnership v. Neri Construction LLC*[50] and *Seaboard Surety Co. v. Town of Greenfield ex rel. Greenfield Middle School Building Committee*,[51] cases construing the A312 bond, and the court distinguished these cases on the grounds that "the performance bond in this case does not include an explicit notice requirement."[52]

In *Colorado Structures* the court expressly stated that *L&A Contracting* was "wrongly decided" with respect to the default and notice of default as "conditions" of the surety's liability. The Washington Supreme Court found that "by the plain terms of the bond, the obligee was not required to formally declare the principal in default. . . ."[53]

In that case, the subcontractor was "seriously behind schedule." The general contractor, Action, chose not to terminate the subcontract, but rather decided to supplement the subcontractor's terms and took other steps to minimize expense and delay. In November 1998, after the subcontractor's work was substantially complete, the general contractor declared the subcontractor in default and demanded that the surety pay the excess costs of completion. The surety refused to pay "because CSI has not formally declared Action to be in default before Action had substantially completed the work."

The court's reasoning in rejecting *L&A Contracting* is based upon the "condition clause" of the performance bond and the use of the word "otherwise" within that clause. To understand the reasoning of *Colorado Structures*, it is necessary to set forth terms of the performance bond, and the brackets "[A]" "[B]," and "[C]" employed by the court. The form of performance bond at issue reads as follows:

> [A] Action Excavating & Paving, Inc. . . ., hereinafter called Principal, and Insurance Company of the West. . ., hereinafter called Surety, are held and firmly bound unto CSI Construction Co. . . ., hereinafter called Obligee, in the amount of . . . $472,290. . . .

---

50 376 F.3d 96 (2d Cir. 2004).
51 370 F.3d 215 (1st Cir. 2004).
52 452 F. Supp. 2d at 488.
53 167 P.3d at 1130.

[B] WHEREAS, Principal has ... entered into a subcontract with Obligee ..., which subcontract is by reference made a part hereof, and is hereinafter referred to as the subcontract, NOW

THEREFORE, THE CONDITION OF THIS OBLIGATION IS SUCH THAT, if Principal shall promptly and faithfully perform said subcontract, then this obligation shall be null and void; otherwise it shall remain in full force and effect.

[C] Whenever Principal shall be, and declared by Obligee to be in default under the subcontract, the Obligee having performed Obligee's obligations thereunder:

(1) Surety may promptly remedy the default, subject to the provisions of paragraph 3 herein, or;

(2) Obligee after reasonable notice to Surety may, or Surety upon demand of Obligee may arrange for the performance of Principal's obligation under the subcontract subject to the provisions of paragraph 3 herein;

(3) The balance of the subcontract price, as defined below, shall be credited against the reasonable cost of completing performance of the subcontract. If completed by the Obligee, and the reasonable cost exceeds the balance of the subcontract price, the Surety shall pay to the Obligee such excess, but in no event shall the aggregate liability of the Surety exceed the amount of this bond. If the Surety arranges completion or remedies the default, that portion of the balance of the subcontract price as may be required to complete the subcontract or remedy the default and to reimburse the Surety for its outlays shall be paid to the Surety at the times and in the manner as said sums would have been payable to Principal had there been no default under the subcontract. The term "balance of the subcontract price," as used in this paragraph, shall mean the total amount payable by Obligee to Principal under the subcontract and any amendments thereto, less the amounts heretofore properly paid by Obligee under the subcontract.[54]

In determining that the surety was liable under the performance bond, the court analyzed the "condition" set forth in Paragraph B of the bond. In relevant part the court found that Paragraph B of the bond:

by its plain terms ... conditions the liability created by Paragraph A on one–and only one–express condition subsequent. Paragraph B states

---

54 *Id.* (the relevant provisions are quoted here to better illustrate the court's analysis of the performance bond).

that "the condition of this obligation is such that, if [the] Principal shall promptly and faithfully perform said subcontract, then this obligation shall be null and void; *otherwise* it shall remain in full force and effect." By using the word "condition" in its singular form, Paragraph B manifests that the liability created by Paragraph A is subject to only one condition–that the principal "promptly and faithfully perform" the offsite subcontract. By using the word "otherwise," which we have italicized, Paragraph B expressly eliminates all other conditions. Read together, Paragraphs A and B state that the surety's obligation commences when it executes the bond and continues until the principal promptly and faithfully performs.[55]

The court continued its analysis by reading Paragraph C to "provide for certain remedies and measures of damage," but only when (1) the principal is in default, (2) the owner has declared a default, and (3) the owner has performed under the contract.[56] Employing this analysis, the court ultimately determined that "*L&A* was wrongly decided,"[57] because the *L&A Contracting* court concluded that "the events described in the preamble to Paragraph C condition not just the use of remedies described in Paragraph C, but also the *liability* in Paragraph A."[58] The court rejects *L&A* by stating that:

> To so hold, however, plainly violates the language of the bond. As already discussed, Paragraphs A and B of the bond create liability, subject to a single express condition subsequent (the principal's prompt and faithful performance). By using the word "otherwise," Paragraph B explicitly eliminates any other conditions on liability. Paragraph C imposes express conditions precedent (including that the principal be "in default" and that the obligee have declared the principal to be in default) on the use of the remedies described therein, *but not* on the liability described in Paragraphs A and B.[59]

Also, in *DCC Constructors, Inc. v. Randall Mechanical, Inc.*,[60] the court held that the AIA 311 bond "does not require termination of the

---

55   *Id.* at 1131-32 (footnotes omitted).
56   *Id.* at 1132.
57   *Id.* at 1134.
58   *Id.* (emphasis in original).
59   *Id.* (emphasis in original).
60   791 So. 2d 575 (Fla. Dist. Ct. App. 2001).

subcontract with Randall as a condition precedent to any action on the performance bond."[61] DCC Contractors distinguished *L&A Contracting* on the ground that *L&A Contracting* "does not hold that liability under a performance bond only occurs when the general contractor actually terminates the subcontract."[62]

Finally, in *Dooley & Mack Constructors, Inc. v. Developers Surety & Indemnity Co.*[63] the court held that the general contractor could make claim against the surety where the general contractor had not formally notified the surety that it was making its own completion arrangements. The court stated that under a "standard surety bond," such a failure would result in a discharge of the surety. However, that rule did not apply since the bond incorporated the subcontract, and the subcontract permitted the general contractor to complete the subcontractor's work and thereafter look to the surety for damages. The "logic" of *Dooley & Mack Constructors, Inc.* was expressly rejected in *CC-Aventura, Inc.* where the court stated "to the extent the logic in *Dooley* would lead to a different result here, the court rejects it."[64]

E. Summary

There is no definitive statement that can be made regarding the issue of whether notice to the surety of the contractor's default under an AIA 311 or like bond form is a "condition" to the surety's obligation. Some cases adopt a "condition" rationale (*L&A Contracting*); by contrast, other cases reject such a rationale (*Walter Concrete* and *Colorado Structures*). Some cases adopt a "loss of surety's rights" rationale without any required demonstration of prejudice (*Balfour*); by contrast, other cases require that the surety demonstrate prejudice (*Blackhawk* and *Plowden*). All of these issues should become moot when the AIA 312 bond form is used, since that form expressly provides for three "conditions precedent" for the surety's obligation, as discussed below.

---

61 *Id.* at 577.
62 *Id.*
63 972 So. 2d 893 (Fla. Dist. Ct. App. 2007).
64 No. 06-21598-CIV 2008 WL 2937856 at *7 (S.D. Fla. July 14, 2008).

III. The AIA 312 Bond: Compliance With the Express Conditions Precedent

Paragraph 3 of the AIA 312 performance bond expressly provides that "[i]f there is no Owner default," the surety's obligation shall arise after the Owner meets the following additional conditions precedent:

> If there is no Owner Default, the Surety's obligation under this Bond shall arise after:[65]
>
> 3.1 The Owner has notified the Contractor and the Surety at its address described in Paragraph 10 below that the Owner is considering declaring a Contractor Default and has requested and attempted to arrange a conference with the Contractor and the Surety to be held not later than fifteen days after receipt of such notice to discuss methods of performing the Construction Contract. If the Owner, the Contractor and the Surety agree, the Contractor shall be allowed a reasonable time to perform the Construction Contract, but such an agreement shall not waive the Owner's right, if any, subsequently to declare a Contractor Default; and
>
> 3.2 The Owner has declared a Contractor Default and formally terminated the Contractor's right to complete the Contract. Such Contractor Default shall not be declared earlier than twenty days after the Contractor and the Surety have received notice as provided in Sub-paragraph 3.1; and
>
> 3.3 The Owner has agreed to pay the Balance of the Contract Price to the Surety in accordance with the terms of the Construction Contract or to a contractor selected to perform the Construction Contract in accordance with the terms of the contract with the Owner.

Under Paragraph 3, the owner must be in compliance with its obligations under the bonded contract as a precondition to the surety's liability. In addition, the bond sets out three enumerated conditions precedent.

---

65 The case law regarding what constitutes an "Owner Default" is addressed at Chapter 11.

A. The Section 3.1 Condition: Notice of the Pre-Default Conference

The AIA 312 Performance Bond expressly provides that the surety's obligation "shall arise after" the owner satisfies or meets three "conditions." The first "condition" is that the owner has notified the contractor and surety that the owner is considering declaring a contractor default, and has requested a conference to discuss methods of performing the construction contract.

In *153 Hudson Development, LLC v. DiNunno,*[66] the New York Appellate Division sustained the granting of summary judgment in favor of the surety where the owner failed to give notice regarding a pre-default conference, stating that "this bond mandates that pre-default notification be given to the contractor and surety by the owner."[67]

In *United States ex rel. Platinum Mechanical, LLC v. United States Surety Co.*,[68] the court also granted summary judgment in favor of the surety where the owner had failed to comply with the paragraph 3.1 requirement of notice of a pre-default conference.

By contrast, in *RLI Insurance Company v. Indian River School District*,[69] the court refused to apply the paragraph 3.1 condition of a pre-default meeting because the Delaware Procurement Act does not require such meeting. Paragraph 11 of the A312 bond provides in relevant part that "[w]hen this Bond has been furnished to comply with a statutory or other legal requirement . . . any provision in this Bond conflicting with said statutory or legal requirement shall be deemed deleted . . ."[70] The court found that because the bond was issued to comply with Delaware statutory requirements, the surety cannot rely on any defense/bond that is inconsistent with the statute. In *Indian River*, the court found that Delaware's "Procurement Act does not require a pre-default conference,

---

66 778 N.Y.S.2d 482 (N.Y. App. Div. 2004). While the published decision did not indicate whether the performance bond in question was an A312 bond, the surety's opposition papers do in fact identify the performance bond as an A312 bond.
67 *Id.* at 483.
68 No. 07 CV 3318 (CLB), 2007 WL 4547849 (S.D.N.Y. Dec. 21, 2007).
69 556 F. Supp. 2d 356 (D. Del. 2008).
70 *Id.* at 365.

and any defense asserted by RLI Insurance on this basis is inconsistent with the purpose of Delaware's statutory requirements. . . ."[71]

Finally, in *Mid-State Surety Corp. v. Thrasher Engineering, Inc.*,[72] the court stated that all that paragraph 3.1 required was that the obligee "attempt" to arrange for a pre-default conference. The court rejected the surety's argument that paragraph 3.1 required the obligee to actually hold such a conference.

B. The Section 3.2 Condition: Declare a Contractor Default and Formally Terminate the Contractor's Right to Complete

The second "condition" to the surety's obligation is that the owner has "declared a contractor default and formally terminated the contractor's right to complete the contract." The owner must wait at least twenty days after the contractor and surety have received notice of the pre-default conference before declaring such contractor default.

In *Elm Haven*,[73] the Court of Appeals for the Second Circuit in construing the A312 bond found that the obligee's "declaration of default had to be made to [the surety] in precise terms."[74] In *Elm Haven*, the obligee sent several letters to the bond principal, with copy to the surety, setting forth that the principal was not performing under its subcontract, as well as establishing its continued failure to respond to inquiries. Additionally, the obligee sent several letters to the surety directly informing the surety that certain work for which the principal was responsible would be performed by others because the principal failed to perform its contractual obligations. Specifically, the obligee drafted a letter dated April 30, 2001 to the surety that stated that the obligee, "Elm Haven 'hereby provides notice to [principal] that this work will be performed by others in accordance with' the default provision of the subcontract agreement."[75] The obligee further indicated in a subsequent letter that it was forced to find others to do the work and that it sustained losses. The surety simply responded that it was not liable because there

---

71 *Id.*
72 575 F. Supp. 2d 731 (S.D. W. Va. 2008).
73 376 F. 3d 96 (2d Cir. 2004).
74 *Id.* at 100.
75 *Id.* at 99.

was no formal declaration of default, precluding the surety from properly investigating the obligee's claims.

The court granted the surety's motion for summary judgment, stating:

> At best, the earlier letters notified [principal] and [surety] that Elm Haven was exercising its rights under the default provisions of the subcontract agreement. However, the letters clearly evidenced Elm Haven's desire to continue its arrangements with [principal] and to keep the subcontract agreement in place. If Elm Haven wanted to trigger the Performance Bond at that point, it would have had to terminate its relationship with [principal] and give [surety] an opportunity to complete the project itself . . . [t]o the contrary, these letters provided notice that part of [principal's] work would be performed by others, indicating only that [principal] would continue to perform some work under the agreement . . .[76]

In *LBL Skysystems (USA), Inc. v. APG-America, Inc.*,[77] the surety argued that the general contractor did not comply with the paragraph 3.2 condition because the general contractor did not comply with the twenty day waiting period between notice of the pre-default conference and the declaration of default. The paragraph 3.1 pre-default notice was sent on April 23, 2002, and the declaration of default occurred eighteen days later on May 10, 2002. The court rejected the surety's argument, stating that:

> LBL did not fail to comply with the twenty-day requirement because it sent the notice on the last business day, May 10, 2002, before the twenty-day period expired.[78]

In addition, the surety argued that the May 10 letter did not comply with paragraph 3.2 because it merely declared the subcontractor in default, and stopped short of formally terminating the subcontractor's right to complete the contract. The court disagreed, stating that the bond

---

76   *Id.* at 100-01.
77   No. 02-5379, 2006 WL 2590497 (E.D. Pa. Sept. 8, 2006).
78   *Id.* at *24.

"did not require LBL to declare APG in default and terminate APG in the same letter."[79]

In *Enterprise Capital, Inc. v. San-Gra Corp.*,[80] the court found that the surety was not obligated because the obligee's "letter was not clear, direct, and unequivocal notice of termination to San-Gra [contractor], and therefore, failed to meet the requirements of paragraph 3.2 of the Performance Bond. . ."[81] In that case, subsequent to the paragraph 3.1 meeting, the obligee sent two letters which it contends provided notice to the surety and contractor of the contractor's default.[82] The first such letter, sent on June 21, 2001, stated that the obligee would "proceed to procure the completion of the project." The court found that the letter did not clearly provide clear notice of termination, and in fact, "[t]o the contrary, it requested participation by San-Gra in furtherance of that end and referred to San-Gra as the 'General Contractor on the job' in the present tense."[83] On August 3, 2001, the obligee sent another letter that clearly declared the contractor in default and terminated San-Gra's right to complete performance of the contract. However, the court determined that the obligee failed to meet the condition precedent because the August 3 letter was addressed only to the surety, and not to both the surety and contractor, stating that the August 3 letter "was not, however, a clear, direct and unequivocal formal declaration of termination to the contractor, that is San-Gra."[84] The surety was released from its obligations under the performance bond.

In *Mid-State Surety*, the court held that the obligee's letter complied with paragraph 3.2 where it stated that it was "a notification under Article 3.2 of the captioned Performance Bond of a contractor default."[85] The court rejected the surety's argument that this letter was inadequate

---

79   *Id.* at n. 86.
80   284 F. Supp. 2d 166 (D. Mass. 2003).
81   *Id.* at 180.
82   Additionally, the obligee argued that under Massachusetts law, a compensated surety may not be discharged of liability absent a showing of loss, injury or prejudice. In a footnote, the court determined that the principal did not receive notice, thereby defeating the obligee's argument.
83   *Id.*
84   *Id.* at 181.
85   575 F. Supp. 2d at 742.

because it did not also expressly state that the contractor's rights were "terminated."[86]

In *United States Fidelity & Guaranty Co. v. Braspetro Oil Services Co.*,[87] the Second Circuit stated that a "condition precedent to the Sureties' obligations under the Bonds was a clear notice of default terminating the Consortium's [principal] rights under the Contracts."[88] The Second Circuit affirmed the trial court's finding that the obligees complied with this condition "since the termination notices sent by Petrobas [obligee] plainly declared the Consortium in default on the Contracts and terminated the Consortium's right to complete the Contracts."[89] On appeal, the sureties argued that the termination notices were insufficient because (1) the "obligations of Consortium remained intact" and (2) the Consortium continued to perform under the contract.[90]

The Second Circuit disagreed, stating:

> Nor does the fact that the Consortium remained on the Projects for some time post-default alter the fact that the Consortium's rights under the Contracts had been terminated. All of the Consortium's work on the Projects subsequent to the Obligees' declarations of default was subject to "new financial arrangements" between Brasoil and the Consortium, arrangements that were entered into subsequent to the declarations of default and independent of the Contracts.[91]

Furthermore, the Second Circuit affirmed the district court's "fact finding and reasoning regarding the Obligee's efforts to mitigate their damages," stating:

> Moreover, the District Court found that the Obligees had a duty to mitigate their damages and that keeping the Consortium on the Projects post-default was, given the exorbitant expense that moving the platforms would have represented, a form of mitigation. *See* [District Court decision] *at 451, 482-83*. Thus, this case is plainly distinguishable from those in which a court released a surety on the

---

86 *Id.*
87 369 F.3d 34 (2d Cir. 2004).
88 *Id.* at 57.
89 *Id.*
90 *Id.*
91 *Id.* at 58.

grounds that the obligee-owner simply "allowed" the defaulting contractor to remain on the job to finish the contract. *See, e.g., Balfour Beatty Constr.*, 986 F.Supp. at 86 (finding that the surety was discharged where the obligee-general contractor "allowed [the defaulting subcontractor] to complete the project," failed to notify the surety of the default, and thereby "den[ied] the [surety] the opportunity to exercise any of its options under the performance bond").[92]

Regarding mitigation and damages, the district court[93] stated as follows:

> Brasoil completed the projects in a reasonable manner and mitigated its damages by continuing to use the P-19 Consortium. Furthermore, Brasoil did nothing to diminish the Sureties' ability to arrange for completion, their ability to take any other measures under ¶ 4 of the Bonds once the defaults were declared, or their status as sureties and/or subrogees under the Bonds and other instruments.[94]

It is important to observe that in both the Second Circuit and district court opinions in *Braspetro*, the courts determined that there was no incompatibility between the obligees' mitigation efforts and the obligees' rights to make claim under the AIA 312 performance bond. Stated alternatively, the obligee exercised its common law duty to mitigate damages and still complied with the conditions precedent and preserved its rights under the AIA 312 performance bond. The AIA 312 bond, by its terms, does not attempt to negate the obligee's common law duty to mitigate its damages. *Braspetro* appears to stand for the proposition that as long as the obligee satisfies the three conditions precedent, the obligee may make completion (mitigation) arrangements that do not "diminish the sureties' ability to arrange for completion."[95]

The court in *Braspetro* stated that its situation was different from that in *Balfour Beatty* where the surety was discharged where the defaulted contractor was allowed to complete the contract and no notice was given to the surety. In *Braspetro*, the defaulted contractor was allowed to complete (albeit under different contractual arrangements), but notice

---

92   *Id.*
93   219 F. Supp. 2d 403 (S.D.N.Y. 2002), *vacated in part on other grounds*, 369 F.3d 34 (2d Cir. 2004).
94   *Id.* at 482-83.
95   *Id.* at 483.

was given to the surety (the obligee complied with the conditions precedent). The Second Circuit affirmed the district court's finding that the obligee ". . . did nothing to diminish the Sureties' ability to arrange for completion." Clearly, this finding is not meant to be interpreted literally, for any completion work performed by the obligee is completion work that will not be performed by the surety. Rather, taken in context, what this finding may mean is that the obligee can take certain steps to mitigate damages while preserving the surety's ability to arrange for completion. For example, we can envision that *Braspetro* would approve of the situation where the obligee mitigates damages by completing critical path work on a time and material basis while simultaneously complying with the conditions precedent to afford the surety the opportunity to exercise its completion options.

Another mitigation of damages case is *Commercial Casualty Insurance Company of Georgia v. Maritime Trade Center Builders*.[96] In *Commercial Casualty*, the court rejected the surety's "condition precedent" defense of late notice under the AIA 312 bond because the subcontract provided for a 48-hour notice requirement to the subcontractor (and not the surety) after which subcontract afforded the general contractor the right to supplement the subcontractor's labor and materials. The court stated that "[b]ecause the bond incorporated the subcontract by reference, we must construe them together" and "[t]he plain language of the executed documents leads to only one reasonable interpretation, that the contractor was not required to give the surety notice before supplementing the subcontractor's labor or materials to collect under the performance bond." The reasoning of *Commercial Casualty* is similar to that of *Dooley and Mack Constructors*[97] where the court essentially ruled that the contract (no notice to surety) provisions take precedent over the bond notice provisions. This stands on its head the proposition that a performance bond incorporates the terms of the bonded contract subject to the express conditions and limitations of the bond.[98] As noted above, the "logic" of *Dooley and Mack Constructors*

---

96   572 S.E.2d 319 (Ga. Ct. App. 2002).
97   972 So. 2d 893 (Fla. Dist. Ct. App. 2007).
98   See Samuel Grossi & Sons, Inc. v. United States Fid. & Guar. Co., No. 3590, 2007 Phila. Ct. Com. Pl. LEXIS 198 (June 29, 2007); Downingtown Area Sch. Dist. v. Int'l Fid. Ins. Co., 769 A.2d 560, 566 n. 13 (Pa. Commw. Ct. 2001).

was expressly rejected in *CC-Aventura, Inc.*,[99] where the court essentially held that the bond notice provisions took precedence over the contract (no notice to surety) provisions. In summary, the cases are in at least some conflict as to whether contract provisions "trump" or take precedence over bond provisions or vice versa.[100]

Developers Surety & Indemnity Co. v. Dismal River Club, LLC,[101] is a recent decision where the surety obtained summary judgment that it had no liability under the AIA 312 performance bond because the owner had failed to comply with both the paragraph 3.1 and 3.2 conditions precedent since the owner had failed (1) to formally terminate the contractor's right to complete the project and (2) to agree to pay the contract balance. There are two interesting aspects to *Developers Surety*. First, the court rejected the owner's argument that the surety must prove prejudice, stating:

> . . . . it is immaterial whether Developers could have completed the project for less than the amount spent by Dismal River—or, more to the point, for less than the amount of the bond—if Developers' obligation to perform was never triggered by Dismal River meeting the conditions of paragraph 3.

Second, the court addressed whether the owner may still satisfy the conditions precedent of paragraph 3 even after the construction was completed.[102] The court noted that the only time limit stated in

---

99   2008 WL 2937856 (S.D. Fla.).
100 *See* Solai & Cameron, Inc. v. Plainfield Cmty. Consol. Sch. Dist. No. 202, 871 N.E.2d 944 (Ill. App. Ct. 2007), in which the obligee argued that the contract provisions take precedence over the surety bond and permit the obligee to hire a replacement contractor. The court rejected the obligee's incorporation by reference argument because (1) the electrical subcontract contained no requirement that the subcontractor obtain a performance bond, and (2) the performance bond was executed before the subcontract was executed, and thus incorporation by reference was not possible since the subcontract did not exist when the performance bond was executed.
101 No. 4:07CV3148, 2008 WL 2223872 (D. Neb. May 22, 2008).
102 In *Developers Surety*, the court cited to Seaboard Surety Co. v. Town of Greenfield *ex rel.* Greenfield Middle School Building Committee, 370 F.3d 215 (1st Cir. 2004) and its discussion that the owner's failure to give the surety notice under paragraph 5 defeated its claim as a matter of law

paragraph 3 was the twenty day waiting period in paragraph 3.12 after the notice of pre-default meeting in paragraph 3.1. The court found that since the owner had already completed the project, the surety's "ability to discharge its obligations under paragraph 4 would be prejudicial, [and] it is no longer possible for those conditions precedent to be satisfied by [the owner]."[103]

C. The Section 3.3 Condition: Obligee's Agreement to Pay the Balance of the Contract Price

The third "condition" to the surety's obligation is that the owner agreed to pay the "Balance of the Contract Price" to either the owner or its completion contractor.

The phrase "Balance of the Contract Price" is defined at paragraph 12.1, as follows:

> 12.1 Balance of the Contract Price: The total amount payable by the Owner to the Contractor under the Construction Contract after all proper adjustments have been made, including allowance to the Contractor of any amounts received or to be received by the Owner in settlement of Insurance or other claims for damages to which the Contractor is entitled, reduced by all valid and proper payments made to on behalf of the Contractor under the Construction Contract.

In *Braspetro*, the Second Circuit stated that:

> First, in determining whether the Obligee's complied with this condition precedent, the relevant inquiry is whether the Obligees actually agreed to pay the Balance of the Contract Price, not as Sureties urge, whether the Obligees agreed with the Sureties' assessment of what the respective Balances were at the time of the declaration of default.[104]

The district court found that the obligees, in their notice of default, informed the sureties that they agreed to pay the balance of the contract,

---

(the owner had complied with the paragraph 3 conditions precedent, and the court assumed that the surety had failed to promptly perform its obligations under paragraph 4).

103 2008 WL 2223872 at *13.
104 369 F. 3d at 58.

but that there was no balance remaining. The Second Circuit, in affirming this part of the district court decision (by finding no clear error), found that the obligees were in compliance with paragraph 3.3 because:

> In light of the foregoing facts, the sureties–although they may have disagreed with the Obligees' position that the Balances remaining due under the Contracts were zero–cannot reasonably maintain that the Obligees did not agree to pay the Balance of the Contract Price; nor can we gainsay the court's ultimate finding that the Obligees agreed to pay the sureties the Balances as required under the Bonds.[105]

As an additional point, the sureties had contended that the district court was incorrect in subtracting certain "contractual loans" and payments "outside the contract" to determine the balance. The Second Circuit disagreed, stating that the sureties' "interpretation of the Bonds [was] inconsistent with their plain meaning and with the underlying purpose of the Sureties' undertaking (i.e., to secure the obligee's right to performance under the Contracts), and we therefore reject it." [106]

In *Brewton,* the court, applying Alabama law, determined that even if the owner adequately declared a contractor default, the owner's failure to agree to pay the balance of the contract price to the surety (or to a proposed completion contractor) and therefore, "did not substantially comply with the performance bond."[107]

Finally, in *Mid-State Surety,*[108] where the arbitrator had found that there was no contract balance to be paid, and in fact damages were due from the contractor, the court stated that it was not possible for the obligee to comply with paragraph 3.3 and excused the obligee from this requirement.[109]

---

105 *Id.*
106 *Id.* at 60.
107 827 So. 2d at 754.
108 575 F. Supp.2d 731 (S.D. W. Va. 2008).
109 *Id.* at 743.

D. Do the AIA 312 Conditions Apply Where There Is Not a Completion Claim But Solely a Claim for Damages (e.g. Delay Damages)?

In *L&A Contracting*,[110] the court reversed a decision awarding delay damages against a surety because the owner had failed to provide the surety with notice of the principal's termination, which the court held was a condition precedent under a bond incorporating A311 language. In contrast, the decisions in *International Fidelity Insurance Co. v. County of Rockland*[111] and *Mid-State Surety Corp. v. Thrasher Engineering, Inc.*[112] have raised the question of whether there are circumstances under which the conditions precedent under the A312 bonds may not be found applicable to performance bond claims solely for damages.

International Fidelity and *Mid-State* involve similar facts. In both cases, the original contractor defaulted, the surety for the original contractor ("Surety No. 1") retained a completion contractor, and the completion contractor's obligations were bonded by its own surety ("Surety No. 2") pursuant to an AIA 312 bond.

In *International Fidelity*, the court discussed, in the context of summary judgment motions, the claims of Surety No. 1 against Surety No. 2 for indemnity against the owner's claims against Surety No. 1 for delay arising from the late performance by the completion contractor bonded by Surety No. 2. Surety No. 2 argued that the indemnification claims (for the owner's delay damages) must be dismissed since Surety No. 1 did not comply with the paragraph 3 conditions precedent.[113] Surety No. 1 argued that these conditions only applied to claims regarding the completion of the project claims, where the surety must take one of the actions specified in paragraph 4 of the bond.[114] The court stated that it need not decide this argument of Surety No. 1 because the obligations of Surety No. 2 arose not only from the bond, but also from the completion contract that was incorporated by reference into the bond.[115]

---

110   17 F.3d 106 (5th Cir. 1994).
111   98 F. Supp. 2d 400 (S.D.N.Y. 2000).
112   575 F. Supp. 2d 731 (S.D. W. Va. 2008).
113   98 F. Supp. 2d at 429, 430.
114   *Id.* at 433.
115   *Id.*

The court also stated that the paragraph 3 steps were "promises" as opposed to "conditions precedent." This part of the decision has been overruled by *Braspetro*, where the Second Circuit expressly held that the language contained in paragraph 3 constituted conditions precedent. However, in *Braspetro* the Second Circuit did not overrule the part of *International Fidelity* regarding the liability of the surety under the indemnification provision of the completion contract, stating "paragraph 3 of the AIA 312 form did not establish conditions precedent to surety's liability for indemnification where construction contract contained separate indemnification provision."[116]

In *Mid-State*, the court held that Surety No. 1 (as obligee or owner) had complied with the paragraph 3 conditions. As an alternative theory of recovery, the court held that aside from the paragraph 3 conditions, Surety No. 1 was entitled to recover under the indemnification provision in the completion contract, which is incorporated by reference into the performance bond.[117]

These two decisions are favorable to the obligee where the obligee has a post-project completion claim against the contractor and its surety. One example of such a claim is an indemnification claim for owner delay damages. This situation can arise from the fact pattern of the two cases discussed above, *International Fidelity* and *Mid-State Surety*, where Surety No. 1 is seeking indemnity from Surety No. 2. Another fact pattern for such an indemnification claim is where the general contractor (or its surety) makes claim against the subcontractor (or its surety). Another example of a post-project completion claim is a warranty claim against the contractor (and its surety).

In these examples, the obligee could "comply" with the conditions precedent (pre-default meeting, formal default/termination, dedication of contract balance). However, based on the foregoing case law, some courts may decide that these conditions logically serve as predicates to the surety's "actions" under paragraph 4 of the AIA 312 bond only, which actions contemplate situations where the project is still not complete. Where a project is complete but the contractor still has contractual obligations to the owner (e.g., indemnification and warranty), it is possible that some courts will deem the A312 conditions precedent inapplicable.

---

116   219 F. Supp. 2d at 477.
117   575 F. Supp. 2d at 745.

IV. Defeasance Bonds

A typical defeasance bond provides that if the contractor shall faithfully perform the contract, then the surety's obligations under the bond shall be null and void, otherwise to remain in full force and effect. These bonds must be carefully reviewed for any language suggesting conditions precedent to the surety's obligations, such as formal default, notice to the surety of such default, and dedication of the remaining contract balance to the completion of the project. Likewise, as the first case below demonstrates, the underlying construction contract, which is incorporated by reference into the performance bond, must be carefully reviewed to see if it contains any conditions precedent.

In *Dragon Construction, Inc. v. Parkway Bank & Trust*,[118] the court held that the owner's "failure to provide adequate notice of Dragon's (the contractor's) termination and their hiring of a successor contractor before NAIC [the surety] received the late notice stripped NAIC of its right to limit its liability and constituted a material breach of contract which rendered the surety bonds null and void."[119] In *Dragon*, the performance bond did not contain a notice provision; however the default clause of the contract required (amongst other things) that the owner provide seven days written notice to the contractor and surety prior to termination. The performance bond provided that upon the contractor's termination, the surety may either complete the contract or obtain bids and select the lowest responsible bidder. It is important to note that there was no notice requirement in the performance bond itself; the notice requirements of the contract were incorporated into the bond.

The owner failed to give timely notice, and had actually engaged a completing contractor prior to giving any notice to the surety. The court found that such conduct constituted a material breach of the performance bond by the owner, because the surety was "stripped of its contractual right [the seven day notice provision] to minimize its liability under the performance bond by ensuring that the lowest responsible bidder was selected to complete the job."[120] Moreover, the *Dragon* court did not require that the surety demonstrate that it was prejudiced by the owner's making completion arrangements before notifying the surety. The court

---

118   678 N.E. 2d 55 (Ill. App. Ct. 1997).
119   *Id.* at 58.
120   *Id.*

did not (1) require that the surety prove that it could have arranged to complete the project at a lesser cost, nor (2) reduce the owner's claim to the extent that the surety's arrangements would have yielded a lower cost.

Contrary to *Dragon*, some courts have held that the owner's breach of contractual notice requirements does not discharge the surety in the absence of prejudice. In *Winston Corp. v. Continental Casualty Co.*,[121] the court held (applying Georgia law) that the "appellant's [owner's] failure to give seven days notice was an insubstantial breach in light of the circumstances of this case, and that it caused no prejudice or injury to the surety."[122] In *Winston*, the performance bond contained no notice provision; however, Article 22 of the contract required that the surety receive seven days written notice before the contractor could be terminated. After numerous problems arose during the course of construction, the owner and contractor had reached an agreement dated April 7, 1999, whereby the owner took possession of the premises, assumed construction of the project, and took an assignment of the contractor's subcontracts and other rights. In defense of the owner's claim under the performance bond, the surety took the position that this April 7 agreement constituted a termination of the contractor, and since the required seven day notice was not given, the surety was released. The court disagreed, stating that whether the April 7 agreement is viewed as an assignment or termination of the contract, it did not discharge the surety. The court found that the surety was aware of the contractor's financial problems, the delays on this project, and the surety had declined to attend several meetings to discuss construction problems, including the one that led to the April 7 agreement. As set forth above, the court held that the owner's failure to give the surety seven days notice was an "insubstantial breach," stating:

> Had the April 7 agreement provided that it would not become effective until seven days after receipt by Continental, there is no doubt that Continental would not have been discharged. We do not believe that this insignificant distinction, in light of Continental's knowledge of the

---

121   508 F. 2d 1298 (6th Cir. 1975).
122   *Id.* at 1304.

construction problems and its rejection of Winston's repeated invitations to discuss them, should require a different result.[123]

Finally, with regard to the prejudice or harm rationale, mention should be made of *Continental Bank & Trust Co., v. American Bonding Co.*,[124] where the Eighth Circuit stated that the lower court had improperly determined damages against the surety (completion costs as of the date of trial), and stated that damage must be determined as of the date of the principal's default. While the circuit court noted that a surety need not receive notice of its principal's default in the absence of a bond provision requiring notice, citing the Restatement of Security §136 (1941), the circuit court made the important point that

> ... the obligee may not delay before notifying the surety and then insist that the measure of the surety's liability includes escalated costs arising in the interim between default and demand.[125]

Thus, even where there is no requirement that (either in the bond itself or the contract provisions incorporated into the bond) that the owner notify the surety of the contractor's default, the owner should not be able to recover higher damages that arise in the period between the contractor's default and the owner's demand upon the surety.

Conclusion

Our conclusions regarding the related and intertwined issues of contractor's material breach, contractor's default, and conditions precedent to the surety's performance bond liability, incorporation by reference of the underlying contract and any prejudice requirement, are as follows:

(1) While there is an important distinction between a contractor's breach of contract and a contractor's default, this distinction may be easier to articulate as an abstract matter rather than to apply since default is defined as a material breach that justifies terminating the contractor's right to complete the contract, and what is material

---

123 *Id.*
124 605 F.2d 1049 (8th Cir. 1979).
125 *Id.* at 1054 n. 17.

requires an inquiry into the relevant facts and contract provisions.

(2) While the surety may receive copies of job correspondence complaining about the contractor's performance, such correspondence does not constitute a default of the contractor and the termination of its right to complete performance of the contract.

(3) While the surety's performance bond obligation is triggered by whether the contractor is in default, the case law involving the AIA 311 bond form is split as to whether notice to the surety of such default is a "condition" to the surety's obligation, with (a) some jurisdictions holding that such notice is a "condition," while others hold that interpretation is not justified based upon the bond language and that noting that the AIA 312 bond form (with its explicit "condition precedent" language) could have been used, and (b) some jurisdictions hold that failure to give the surety such notice deprives the surety of the opportunity to exercise its performance bond options, while others require that the surety demonstrate that it suffered prejudice as a result of such lack of notice.

(4) The case law regarding the "defeasance bond" (non-AIA 311 and 312 bond forms) is likewise split regarding whether notice is a condition and whether the surety must demonstrate prejudice.

(5) The AIA 312 bond should resolve the dispute about "conditions" since this bond form contains three express "conditions precedent" (pre-default meeting; default and formal termination of contractor's right to complete the contract; and agreement to pay contract balance), and the express condition precedent language should render moot the prejudice issue (because under basic contract law the condition precedent should be enforced regardless of prejudice). However, the obligee, while complying with the "conditions precedent," may take steps to mitigate damages and continue the defaulted contractor's work under the theory that the obligee had the common law duty to mitigate damages or had the contractual right to mitigate damages.

(6) The incorporation by reference of the underlying construction contract into the performance bond is a "two-edged sword," for (1) the surety will want to incorporate notice provisions of the contractor's default, and (2) the obligee will want to incorporate the indemnity provisions regarding damages as constituting a separate promise from the surety's completion obligations, and incorporate provisions permitting the obligee to take steps to mitigate damages without notice to the surety.

3

PERFORMANCE OPTIONS AVAILABLE TO THE SURETY

Charles W. Langfitt
Bennett J. Lee
Robert C. Niesley*

Introduction

It is often said that when handling a performance bond claim the surety is "driving an ambulance and not a hearse." This saying should have special meaning to every surety claim professional trying to investigate and resolve a performance bond claim quickly and fairly. Every case has varying levels of urgency, obligee and principal cooperation, agreement or disagreement among the project players, document and personnel availability, complications associated with ongoing litigation or a bankruptcy, completion options, among many other challenges too numerous to identify in this short chapter. Whatever the adversity, the surety claim professional should try to get through the challenge quickly and as thoroughly as possible within the legal and contractual limitations of the bond and the practicalities of the real world.

This chapter attempts to provide a framework within which the surety claim professional can evaluate his or her options in response to a performance bond claim. Regardless of the varying facts and adversities, the options available to the surety remain basic and few. This chapter begins with a discussion of the first step of the claim process–the surety's investigation. Next, the surety's options–takeover, tender, financing, obligee completion, buy-out and denial of the claim–are discussed. Then, this chapter addresses the effect of particular bond forms upon the

---

* Katy Ross and Yanna J. Li of Watt, Tieder, Hoffar & Fitzgerald, LLP rendered substantial assistance with respect to the research and preparation of this chapter.

decision-making process, and continues with a brief discussion of the surety's pre-default options.[1]

Finally, this chapter generally explains the surety's options, but does not thoroughly cover every law and statute in every state or federal jurisdiction. If the reader is using this chapter to assist with a bond claim in a particular jurisdiction, attention should be paid to the particular cases, statutes or administrative laws in that jurisdiction, which may define the surety's rights and duties with more particularity.

I. The Surety's Investigation

The surety's first obligation upon receiving a performance bond claim is to commence an investigation of the claim in order to determine the most appropriate response. The manner and timing of the surety's investigation is a function of the context and facts and may be subject to state laws and regulations.[2] The surety's investigation is a fact-finding mission intended

---

[1] Although all of the surety options discussed herein are usually, but not always, available when a principal or obligee has filed bankruptcy, this chapter does not address any bankruptcy law or strategies. These issues are addressed in Chapter 14.

[2] See, for example, ALASKA STAT. § 21.36.125 (Michie 2008); ARIZ. REV. STAT. § 20-461 (2008); ARK. CODE ANN. § 23-66-206 (Michie 2008); Cal. Ins. Code § 790.03(h) (Deering 2008); COLO. REV. STAT. § 10-3-1104(1)(h) (2008); DEL. CODE ANN. tit. 18, § 2304(16) (2008); FLA. STAT. ch. 626.9541(1)(i) (2008); GA. CODE ANN. § 33-6-33, *et seq.* (2008); HAW. REV. STAT. ANN. § 431:13-103(a)(11) (Michie 2008); IDAHO CODE § 41-1329 (Michie 2008); 215 Ill. Comp. Stat. 5/154.6 (2008); IND. CODE ANN. § 27-4-1-4.5 (Michie 2008); IOWA CODE § 507B.4(9) (2008); KAN. STAT. ANN. § 40-2404(9) (2007); KY. REV. STAT. ANN. § 304.12-230 (Michie 2008); ME. REV. STAT. ANN. tit. 24-A, § 2164-D (West 2008); MASS. GEN. LAWS ch. 176D, § 3(9) (2008); MICH. COMP. LAWS § 500.2026 (2008); MINN. STAT. §§ 72A.20(12), 72A.201(4) (2008); MONT. CODE ANN. § 33-18-201 (2007); NEB. REV. STAT. § 44-1540 (2008); NEV. REV. STAT. § 686A.310 (2008); N.H. REV. STAT. ANN. § 417:4(XV) (2009); N.J. REV. STAT. ANN. § 17:29B-4(9) (West 2008); N.M. STAT. ANN. § 59A-16-20 (Michie 2008); N.Y. INS. LAW § 2601 (Consol. 2008); N.C. GEN. STAT. § 58-63-15(11) (2008); N.D. CENT. CODE § 26.1-04-03(9) (2008); OR. REV. STAT. § 746.230 (2007); 40 PA. CONS. STAT. § 1171.5(a)(10) (2008); S.C. CODE ANN. § 38-59-20 (2007); S.D. CODIFIED LAWS § 58-33-67 (Michie 2008); TENN.

to promptly discern whether (i) its bond principal is, in fact, in default of its contractual obligations, and (ii) if so, whether the surety has liability under the performance bond. Because the surety's investigation will determine its response to the claim, thereby playing a significant role in the surety's ability to control its bond loss, it is imperative that the surety conduct its investigation in an expeditious and comprehensive manner, gathering as much information as is reasonably available.

It is important to note that the surety is *not* required to completely resolve all factual disputes between the obligee and the principal, nor is it expected to make a final determination regarding the apportionment of liability. The surety's investigation is aimed toward finding the most efficient means of fulfilling the surety's bond obligations, if any, based on the information available at the time the surety receives a demand for performance under its bond.

A. *Need For Default and Declaration Thereof*

Under many performance bonds, before a surety is required to do anything, the obligee must formally declare the principal in default of its contractual obligations. A default is generally defined as a "(1) material breach or series of material breaches (2) of such magnitude that the obligee is justified in terminating the contract."[3] Some construction contracts will expressly define what constitutes a material breach or default, so the surety must be sure to consult the contract documents for any such applicable definitions. In all cases, however, the materiality of a breach is defined by the facts and circumstances of the particular project.[4]

Depending on the particular bond form and its interpretation by the applicable courts, an obligee's failure to comply with the bond provisions or the underlying contract terms for declaring a principal in default may discharge or exonerate the surety's liability.[5] Close attention

---

CODE ANN. § 56-8-104(8) (2008); UTAH CODE ANN. § 31A-26-303 (2008); VA. CODE ANN. § 38.2-510 (Michie 2008); W. VA. CODE § 33-11-4(9) (2008); WYO. STAT. ANN. § 26-13-124 (Michie 2008).

[3] L&A Contracting Co. v. S. Concrete Servs., Inc., 17 F.3d 106, 110 (5th Cir. 1994).

[4] This issue is addressed in greater detail in Chapter 2.

[5] *L&A Contracting Co.*, 17 F.3d at 109; Seaboard Sur. Co. v. Town of Greenfield, 266 F. Supp.2d 189, 196 (D. Mass. 2003), aff'd, 370 F.3d

should be paid to the details of the bond form and the underlying bonded contract to confirm that the principal has been properly held in default.[6]

Determining the appropriate time to act can be problematic where no termination or declaration of default is necessary under the contractual language in order to trigger the surety's investigation obligation.[7] For example, when the bond does not require the obligee to declare a default and the obligee has not terminated the principal, but the surety has been advised that the principal is in default of its bonded obligations, it may be prudent for the surety to begin an investigation. In many cases, it is in the surety's best interest to have a clear and unambiguous declaration of default from the obligee. Under some circumstances, the surety may insist that the obligee issue such a declaration against the principal in order to avoid any later misunderstandings with the obligee or principal.

B. Nature of Investigation

It is important for the surety's investigation to be as thorough as circumstances reasonably allow. Therefore, the surety must gather as much information as possible from as many sources as possible, the most important of which are: (1) the surety's own files; (2) the obligee; and (3) the bond principal.

  215, 219 (1st Cir. 2004); Ins. Co. of N. Am. v. Metro. Dade County, 705 So.2d 33, 35 (Fla. Dist. Ct. App. 1997); Dragon Constr., Inc. v. Parkway Bank & Trust, 678 N.E.2d 55, 58 (Ill. App. Ct. 1997).
6 This issue is addressed in greater detail in Chapter 2.
7 *See, e.g.*, Siegfried Constr., Inc. v. Gulf Ins. Co., 203 F.3d 822 (4th Cir. 2000), reported in full at 2000 U.S. App. LEXIS 1304 (Feb. 2, 2000), *cert. denied*, 530 U.S. 1275 (2000) (holding Virginia law does not require the obligee to terminate the bond principal before the surety's obligations are triggered); DCC Constructors, Inc. v. Randall Mech., Inc., 791 So.2d 575 (Fla. Dist. Ct. App. 2001) (holding that after the obligee gave the principal multiple notices that it was in default and the principal made no attempt to cure the defaults, the contract was considered abandoned by the principal and thus the obligee did not need to declare a default).

1. The Surety's File

The surety's in-house claim professional may be aware of problems before there is a formal declaration of default. It is not uncommon for the obligee to copy the surety on correspondence in which the obligee is alleging a material breach of the contract or threatening to terminate the principal, giving a preview of a future performance bond claim. This pre-claim correspondence is generally not a claim per se and does not trigger any duties by the surety to investigate. Nevertheless, the surety claim professional should have an understanding of the contents of the surety's claim file at the commencement of any investigation.

The underwriting file provides a copy of the bond and documents leading to the issuance of the bond, a general overview of the principal's operations and financial condition, its other bonded projects and the resources and assets it has available for use in the completion of bonded work. This information will help the surety determine coverage limitations, timing requirements, whether its principal has encountered a single difficult project, or whether it has more extensive operational problems. These are important factors in the surety's consideration of its performance options.

2. The Obligee

The surety should attempt to understand the obligee's perspective regarding the status of the bonded project and the reasons the obligee defaulted or terminated the bond principal. In many contexts, the surety will attempt to speak or meet with the obligee or its representatives as soon as practicable after the declaration of default, for a detailed discussion of the obligee's alleged problems with the principal and the work that remains incomplete.

The parties may attempt to meet at the project site so that they can simultaneously review and document the remaining and/or allegedly defective work at issue. The surety should request that the obligee provide copies of all relevant project documents, including, but not necessarily limited to, complete contract documents, payment applications received and checks issued, meeting minutes, significant correspondence and project work schedules. The types of documents requested can be limited or expanded, depending upon the issues raised by the obligee and the principal. The types of documents that the obligee can provide include:

- the construction contract, including all addenda, alternates, attachments, etc.
- contract drawings
- contract specifications
- contract general and special conditions
- copies of all executed change orders, including time extensions
- applications for payment, including schedules of values
- material procurement/delivery status report
- on-site and off-site materials inventory
- project schedule–baseline schedule plus all updates in electronic format
- all reports from the obligee, the obligee's engineer, architect, and/or any other person pertaining to any alleged defaults by the bond principal
- contract by and between the obligee and all of its engineers, architects, consultants, inspectors, etc.

In addition, depending upon the size and scope of incomplete work, the surety may want to ask that the following documents be made available for inspection:

- any and all correspondence related to project(s)
- project daily reports
- shop drawing and submittal log
- request for information (RFI) log
- all RFIs
- change order log
- all change order requests or proposals submitted by the principal
- all evaluations and assessments by the obligee of change order requests or proposals
- all submitted requests for time extensions
- all notices of non-conforming work or deficiencies–also known as deficiency and omission reports
- all punch lists and punch list inspection reports
- progress meeting minutes
- photographs of progress or case-specific issues
- contract bid tabulation

- listing of all outstanding/unresolved backcharges
- listing of any outstanding disputed issues, including all applicable correspondence
- all engineer, architect and consultant project files

Of course, the facts of each case will dictate the most relevant documents and the level of detail required to complete the surety's investigation. The listing above, however, covers the typical documents the surety will want to request during its investigation.

3. The Principal

In order to develop a balanced understanding of the facts, the surety should investigate the bond principal's side of the story.[8] Even where a defaulted bond principal is defensive and uncooperative as a result of its termination, most general indemnity agreements require the principal to cooperate with the surety, and many specifically require the principal to provide any documents or information requested by the surety. An uncooperative principal should be reminded of its duties under the applicable indemnity agreement, and that the failure to honor its obligations to the surety may operate to the harm of the principal and its indemnitors. At a minimum, the uncooperative principal will complicate the surety's handling of bond claims.[9]

Once the principal agrees to cooperate, the surety may be advised to request a meeting with the principal's project management personnel, among others, to hear the principal's responses to the obligee's specific allegations, as well as any documents which support the principal's position.

In cases where the principal is alleged to be behind schedule, the surety should try to understand the project schedule, obligee-caused delays and disruptions, and any changes to the principal's original scope of work. In cases involving defective work, the surety should gather from

---

[8] For purposes of this section, it is assumed that the obligee has declared a default and has demanded performance by the surety, rather than the principal voluntarily defaulting and asking the surety to perform or requesting the surety's assistance in order to prevent a default.

[9] *See* Mountbatten Sur. Co. v. Szabo Contracting, Inc., 812 N.E.2d 90 (Ill. App. Ct. 2004).

the principal the contract's technical plans and specifications, contractor submittals, and relevant inspection and defect reports.

The surety should inquire as to any problems that the principal has had with the obligee over payment, problems in an obligee-supplied design, approval of change orders, granting of time extensions, and obligee interference. The surety should also gather information regarding the principal's other projects, both bonded and unbonded, in order to evaluate the principal's overall status and the possibility of completing the bonded work by retaining the defaulted principal.

C. Obligee's Rights and Duties During the Investigation

While the surety generally has a duty to conduct an investigation, the obligee has a corresponding duty to act in good faith toward the surety by cooperating with the surety and allowing completion of the investigation. Before the surety is obligated to respond, the obligee must provide the surety with all available documentation and information supporting its performance bond claim.[10] The obligee also must afford the surety the opportunity to investigate the performance bond claim and determine its preferred course of action. By undertaking completion of the work before the surety has had a chance to fulfill its bond obligations, the obligee risks a discharge of all or part of the surety's liability.[11]

D. Assembling the Team

At the outset of the investigative stage the surety needs to determine if the investigation can be handled in-house or requires the formation of an investigative team. Of course, many claims can be handled in-house from beginning to end. Some claims are more factually complex or may involve legal issues in a particular jurisdiction. In those cases, a team should be put together, as needed, including legal counsel, accountants, general construction consultants, and/or specialists in discrete fields of

---

10 *See* Farmer's Union Cent. Exch., Inc. v. Reliance Ins. Co., 675 F. Supp. 1534, 1542 (D.N.D. 1987).

11 *See* Elm Haven Constr. Ltd. P'ship v. Neri Constr., L.L.C., 376 F.3d 96 (2d Cir. 2004) (holding where obligee hires replacement principal before giving notice of the default to the terminated principal's surety, the surety's obligations are discharged).

construction. The addition of legal counsel to the team adds the protection of the work product and attorney-client privileges, which is sometimes needed in claims involving litigation.

E. The Focus of the Investigation

Allegations of breach of contract arising out of alleged delays and/or defective work are at the center of many principal defaults. While it is beyond the scope of this chapter to explore all of the potential causes of delay and defective work, the following are general guidelines for the surety in investigating alleged delays and defective work.

1. Delays

In any construction delay case, the central issue concerns the principal's progress relative to a project schedule properly adjusted for all excusable delays. To properly investigate such delays, the surety must first understand the actual status of physical work on the project. This can be done through an inspection of the project site, review of the principal's project schedule, periodic status reports, project videos, and obligee inspection reports.

With an understanding of the physical status of work, the surety can then compare project status to the contract schedule. To the extent that the work is deemed to be behind where the principal should be pursuant to the contract schedule, the surety must come to understand the extent and causes of the delay. Depending on the complexity of the project, the surety may want to retain a capable scheduling consultant to assist in its investigation. Although this is not required, the consultant can help identify the project's critical path and the extent of work delays up to the time of the alleged default. More importantly, the consultant can identify the magnitude and causes of delay. If it is ultimately determined that the principal was maintaining adequate progress against a contract schedule properly adjusted for excusable delays, then the principal should not be found to be in default of the contract for alleged lack of progress.

2. Defective Work

The principal typically has a contractual duty to construct the project in accordance with the approved project design. In cases where the obligee has supplied the design, the obligee warrants that the plans and specifications are proper and that if the principal constructs the project in accordance therewith, it has satisfied its contractual obligations to the obligee. So when an obligee alleges that the principal's work is incomplete or defective in some material way, the surety must compare (i) the principal's installed work with (ii) the project's design.

Again, depending on the complexity of the project and the alleged deficiency, the surety may want to retain a technical consultant to assist in the investigation. Often the assessment of construction quality involves scrutinizing the contract's plans, specifications, modifications, contractor submittals, deficiency reports, and RFIs. With any confirmed deficiency, the surety must then determine where the deficiency stands in significance relative to the overall project and what it should do in response.

II. The Surety's Performance Obligations

Once it completes the investigation, the surety must decide the most appropriate means of responding to the obligee's performance bond claim. While many bond obligees typically view a performance bond as a promise that the surety itself will automatically complete the project upon default by the principal, the general rule is that the surety's only obligation is to pay monetary damages resulting from the principal's default, up to the penal limit of the bond. As a result, the surety actually has several options as to how it may fulfill its bond obligations, assuming that the surety does not decide to deny the bond claim altogether.

In some cases, the surety's performance options are limited by the terms of the bond and the underlying contract. Thus, it is always important to review the bond and the contract at the time the surety begins its investigation to see what, if any, limitations there are on the surety's options. Assuming there are no such written limitations, the surety generally has six options:

1. takeover and complete the bonded project;
2. tender a new contractor;
3. finance the bond principal's completion of the work;
4. indemnify the obligee;
5. buy-out the bond obligation; or
6. deny the claim.

Each of these performance options is discussed in detail in this chapter. The selection of a particular completion method does not require absolute mastery of every fact and figure on the project. Nor does selection of a completion method require the surety to resolve ongoing disputes between the principal and obligee. Sometimes the project can be completed with a reservation of rights for the sole purpose of capping the loss, completing the work, and saving the fight with the obligee over coverage until another day in the future.

III. Right of Surety to Takeover and Complete Performance of the Bonded Project

In many cases, the surety will decide to "step into the shoes" of its defaulted principal and complete the bonded project. When the project is near completion at the time the default is declared, the surety may find that taking over completion allows maximum control for the surety over the cost to complete, thereby allowing the surety to minimize its potential losses under the bond. Conversely, takeover may not be the best option when the project is far from finished, and the surety risks seeing its cost to complete skyrocket because of previously unknown design issues, unforeseen site conditions or other unexpected events. The more work there is to be done, the greater the chance that some unforeseeable event or condition will cause an unexpected and dramatic rise in the cost to complete.[12]

---

12 There are a number of books, articles and papers that discuss the surety's takeover and completion option, including Gregory L. Daily & Todd C. Kazlow, *Takeover and Completion*, in BOND DEFAULT MANUAL 223, 223-41 (Duncan L. Clore, Richard E. Towle & Michael J. Sugar, Jr. eds., 3d ed. 2005); Bruce C. King, *Takeover and Completion of Bonded Contracts by the Surety*, BRIEF Fall 1997, Vol. 27, No. 1, at 22; Luther P. Cochrane, *Obligations of the Principal's Subcontractors and Suppliers on Default or Takeover by the Surety*, 14 FORUM 896 (1979); Gregory S. Arnold, Christopher Morkan & Matthew M. Horowitz, *Issues and Practical Considerations for the Surety in Using Subcontractor Ratification Agreements* 7-4 (unpublished paper submitted at the Seventeenth Annual Northeast Surety & Fidelity Claims Conference on Sept. 21, 2006); Michael J. Sugar, Jr., Elizabeth E. Spiker & Richard D. Davis, *Challenges of a Unit Price Contract Re-Let* 4 (unpublished paper submitted at the Fifteenth Annual Northeast Surety & Fidelity Claims Conference on Sept. 30, 2004).

Importantly, if the surety opts to take over and then encounters unforeseen events that significantly raise the costs of completion, the surety risks losing far more than the penal sum of its bond. The surety's liability is generally limited to the penal sum of the bond.[13] However, if the surety elects to take over and complete the bonded project, then it may no longer be able to limit its liability to the penal sum because the surety is bound under a new, separate contract to complete the work.[14] This result should be avoided by requiring the obligee to agree to a provision in the takeover agreement which acknowledges that the surety's obligation to complete is limited by the unexpended amount of the penal sum of the bond. Some obligees will be reluctant to agree to any such provision, as it subjects them to the possibility that the surety will expend the entire amount of the bond before the work is finished. If the obligee refuses to acknowledge the penal sum cap, the surety should examine other completion options and/or be very confident that the law in the subject jurisdiction will enforce the penal cap and/or obtain assurances that its cost-to-complete will not exceed the penal sum of the bond.

Once the surety decides that it will take over, it must decide how it wants to complete the work. The surety can opt to hire a new contractor to perform the completion work, or forego the hiring of a general contractor and simply hire a construction manager to supervise the completion of the work by the original subcontractors.[15] The surety also has the option of "rehiring" the defaulted bond principal, but should only do so after it determines that the principal is actually capable of

---

13 *See, e.g.*, Turner Constr. Co. v. First Indem. of Am. Ins. Co., 829 F. Supp. 752, 759 (E.D. Pa. 1993), *aff'd*, 22 F.3d 303 (3d Cir. 1994); Long v. City of Midway, 311 S.E.2d 508 (Ga. Ct. App. 1983); Peerless Ins. Co. v. S. Boston Storage & Warehouse, Inc., 491 N.E.2d 253 (Mass. 1986); Great Am. Ins. Co v. N. Austin Mun. Util. Dist. No. 1, 908 S.W.2d 415 (Tex. 1995).

14 *See, e.g.*, McWaters & Bartlett v. U.S., 272 F.2d 291 (10th Cir. 1959); Caron v. Andrews, 284 P.2d 544 (Cal. Ct. App. 1955); Employer's Mut. Cas. Co. v. United Fire & Cas. Co., 682 N.W.2d 452 (Iowa Ct. App. 2004); Klein v. J.D. & J.M. Collins, 106 So. 120 (La. 1925).

15 No contractor's license is required for work on federal property. Everywhere else, some type of license may be required and the surety should make sure that its completion principal or construction manager has the license(s) required to finish the project.

completing the work. Retaining the defaulted principal is often an attractive option where there is minimal work left, as there is minimal profit to be made and the surety might have trouble finding a new contractor willing to undertake a relatively small project.

However, some obligees may be hesitant to allow the defaulted principal to return to the project. While it is questionable as to whether the obligee has a legal right to dictate the means of completion by the surety, some bond forms specifically require that the obligee consent to the surety's proposed completion plan. Regardless of the specific bond language, it is always preferable to have the obligee's consent and cooperation when trying to get the work finished as quickly and efficiently as possible. Thus, the surety who wants to complete the work using the defaulted principal may consider hiring a consultant who can act as the construction manager or otherwise manage the completion effort, providing a buffer between a wary obligee and a principal who has already been terminated once.

Even if resistant, the obligee may have no choice but to accept the surety's preferred method of completion, as long as the surety acts within the terms of the bond. In at least one case, the surety's bond obligations were wholly exonerated due to the obligee's refusal to accept a completion proposal which conformed to the terms of the bond.[16] In *St. Paul Fire & Marine Insurance Co. v. City of Green River*, the obligee terminated its contractor following significant delays and made a claim against the performance bond. Under the terms of the performance bond, the surety could, among other options: (1) arrange for the terminated contractor to complete the project, with the obligee's consent; or (2) undertake completion itself, "through its agents or through independent contractors[.]"[17] The surety began its investigation immediately, and simultaneously entered into negotiations with both the obligee and the terminated contractor. As a result of those negotiations, the surety proposed a compromise wherein, among other things, the surety would complete the project itself utilizing the personnel of the terminated contractor. Under the surety's proposed completion compromise, the

---

16   St. Paul Fire & Marine Ins. Co. v. City of Green River, 93 F. Supp.2d 1170, 1179 (D. Wyo. 2000), *aff'd*, 6 Fed. Appx. 828 (10th Cir. 2001).
17   *Id.* at 1172.

project would be completed approximately five months after the completion date called for in the original contract.[18]

The obligee informed the surety that it considered the proposal to be an anticipatory breach of the bond on the grounds that: (1) the surety was bound by the original completion date in the contract; and (2) the surety was not entitled to use the personnel of the terminated contractor without the obligee's consent.[19] On those grounds, the obligee refused to allow the surety to complete the project. The surety immediately filed suit seeking a declaratory judgment that the obligee's refusal to allow the surety to complete the project was a material breach that exonerated the surety from any further bond liability. The obligee immediately counterclaimed for breach of contract, breach of the covenant of good faith and fair dealing, tortious bad faith and violation of certain insurance statutes.[20]

The *Green River* court came down squarely on the side of the surety. First, the court held that the surety's proposed completion date was not an anticipatory breach of the bond terms. The surety would still be liable for liquidated damages in the event of late completion, but the bond called for the surety to proceed "with reasonable promptness" and did not expressly bind the surety to the original completion date. The court found that the performance bond expressly contemplated late completion due to contractor delays, and that the obligee's attempt to bind the surety to the original completion date was "unreasonable in light of the fact that a performance bond surety's duty of performance is typically triggered only when the construction project is already in trouble and behind schedule."[21] Concluding that the obligee's interpretation led to "impractical and commercially absurd results," the court went on to find that the surety had a good faith basis to believe that its interpretation of the bond (i.e. that it was not bound by the original completion date) was correct such that the surety's offer to complete in accordance with its interpretation of the bond could not be an anticipatory breach.[22]

The *Green River* court then turned its attention to the issue of whether the surety was permitted to undertake completion itself, utilizing

---

18   *Id.*
19   *Id.* at 1173.
20   *Id.*
21   *Id.* at 1175-76.
22   *Id.* at 1176-77.

the personnel of the terminated contractor. The obligee argued that, if the surety opted to arrange for completion by the original contractor, then the obligee's consent was required. However, the surety had expressly stated that it intended to undertake completion under a different performance option, wherein the surety itself assumed contractual responsibility for completion. Under the performance option chosen by the surety, no consent was required.[23] The obligee argued that if the surety opted to complete the project itself, then it was barred from using the terminated contractor's personnel.

On this issue, the court again sided with the surety, finding that the performance option selected by the surety places no restrictions on who the surety could utilize in completing the project. The *Green River* court rejected the obligee's attempt to "graft" the consent requirement from one performance option onto another performance option.[24] Based on its rejection of the obligee's claims of anticipatory breach by the surety, the court found that the obligee's refusal to allow the surety to complete the project was wrongful, and exonerated the surety from any further performance obligations.[25]

Thus, an obligee takes a significant risk by refusing to allow a surety to perform if the surety's performance plan conforms to the terms of the bond. However, before the surety decides to take over and complete the project work, the surety needs to consider the legal risks and repercussions associated with its decision, several of which are discussed below. While this chapter does not provide an exhaustive analysis of every element that the surety might consider when making its decision, it does look at some of the primary risks and benefits associated with taking over and completing a bonded project, and offers practical advice for minimizing the surety's potential liability.[26]

---

23   *Id.* at 1177.
24   *Id.* at 1177-78.
25   *Id.* at 1179.
26   The following text addresses a surety's exposures to claims from principals sounding in "Domination/Alter Ego," "Abuse of Rights," and "Wrongful Interference with Contractual Relationship" which can arise as a result of a surety's decision to take over and complete a bonded project. These issues are also addressed in Chapter 8.

A. Domination/Alter Ego

One of the risks for a surety who opts to take over and complete the project with its defaulted principal is that the surety may be subject to various claims based on domination and alter ego, two similar and sometimes interchangeable doctrines. The essence of each doctrine is that the surety–by taking over the principal's obligations, becoming involved in the business and financial dealings of the principal and essentially acting as the principal's decision maker–has become so intertwined with the principal as to dominate it or become its alter ego. Based on either of these theories, other parties might seek damages from the surety which they would not otherwise be entitled to.

For example, the bond obligee may attempt to recover extra contractual damages from the surety that would not be available under the terms of the bond. The principal itself, along with its indemnitors, may seek damages from the surety for its allegedly wrongful domination of the principal's business and, in some instances, for destroying the principal's business.[27] Further, third-party creditors of the principal have, on occasion, argued domination or alter ego as a basis for trying to hold a surety liable for the principal's unrelated, unbonded debts.[28] However, courts have generally rejected such arguments.[29] Nonetheless, these claims are a nuisance and can be costly to defend against.

As a result, the surety will want to take certain precautions aimed at preventing such claims from ever arising. For instance, if the surety enters into a completion agreement with the defaulted principal, the

---

27   This claim most often arises when the surety agrees to provide financing to its principal, then later decides to discontinue the funding. In such instances, principals and their indemnitors have raised claims that the surety's decision to discontinue financing caused the principal's business to fail, because the surety had taken control of the business by providing financing in the first place. These claims against a financing surety, and the appropriate way to avoid them, are discussed in Section V below.

28   *See, e.g.*, James E. McFadden, Inc. v. Baltimore Contractors, Inc., 609 F. Supp. 1102 (E.D. Pa. 1985).

29   *Id. See also* U.S. *ex rel.* Maris Equip. Co. v. Morganti, Inc., 163 F. Supp.2d 174 (E.D.N.Y. 2001); John G. Lambros Co. v. Aetna Cas. & Sur. Co., 468 F. Supp. 624 (S.D.N.Y. 1979); Irwin & Leighton, Inc. v. W.M. Anderson Co., 532 A.2d 983 (Del. Ch. 1987); Lambert v. Md. Cas. Co., 403 So.2d 739 (La. Ct. App. 1981), *aff'd*, 418 So.2d 553 (La. 1982).

completion agreement must specifically delineate the relationship between the surety and its principal, as well as the obligations being undertaken by the surety and its reasons for undertaking them. In other words, the completion agreement must specifically state that the surety is involved in the project because of its own obligations under the bond and clearly establish that the surety is not acting as an agent, representative, partner, parent company or other controlling entity of the principal. By reaffirming that the surety is acting in order to fulfill its bond obligations and as a result of its own potential liability, the surety can at least avoid claims by the principal or its indemnitors that the surety overtook the principal's business, thereby avoiding claims based on domination and/or alter ego.

B. Abuse of Rights

Another potential issue related to the takeover of a bonded project is that the surety may face claims that it has abused its rights. A claim of abuse of rights arises when a party has acted within its rights, but with the intent to cause harm.[30] Such claims are most commonly seen as an affirmative defense to indemnity claims, when the principal or its indemnitors claim that the surety technically acted within its rights by taking over the bonded work, but did so improperly because it acted with the intent to harm the principal.

As long as the surety has a reasonable justification for its actions, a claim based on abuse of rights should be rejected, unless there is affirmative evidence of a malicious or harmful intent.[31] However, the surety should still memorialize its reasons for taking over the work, reciting them in both the takeover agreement executed with the obligee and the completion agreement signed with the contractor (regardless of whether its bond principal is the completion contractor or not). By including such recitals in its agreements, the surety can usually insulate itself from these types of abuse of rights claims.

---

30 See *Lambert*, 403 So.2d 739.
31 *Id.* at 757. *See also* Wilcon, Inc. v. Travelers Indem. Co., 654 F.2d 976 (5th Cir. 1981) (holding plaintiff must show an ulterior motive that is improper or malicious to sustain an abuse of process claim, which is the procedural equivalent of an abuse of rights claim).

C. Wrongful Interference With Contractual Relationship

A principal or its indemnitors may claim that the surety, by taking over the work, has interfered with the principal's contract with the obligee. Such claims have generally been rejected on the grounds that the surety is within its *own* contractual rights to take over a bonded project.[32] While there is no uniform standard, the general rule is that, in order to prevail, a party claiming wrongful interference must show malice in inducing a breach of contract, and that the wrongful acts were done intentionally.[33] In other words, in order to prevail on a claim of wrongful interference, the bond principal would need to demonstrate that the surety maliciously and intentionally induced the obligee to breach its contract with the principal.

Again, the surety should prevail against these types of claims as long as there is a reasonable basis for the surety's actions. However, it is still important for the surety to thoroughly document its investigation and memorialize its reasons for taking over the bonded project. It is also beneficial to obtain a detailed written statement from the obligee regarding its reasons for defaulting the principal if one is not voluntarily provided by either the principal or the obligee. As long as the surety's records are thorough and provide a sound justification for the surety's actions, the surety should not be liable for wrongful interference.

D. Loss of Prospective Economic Advantage

A bond principal who has seen its surety take over a project will sometimes complain that the surety is responsible for depriving the principal of its expected benefits under the contract in question, namely the profit it expected to earn from the project. A failed principal might also argue that a surety who decided to stop issuing bonds on its behalf made it impossible for the principal to obtain future contracts, depriving the principal of its ability to continue turning a profit or even stay in business. These claims of "loss of prospective economic advantage" can

---

32 *See* Travelers Cas. & Sur. Co. of Am. v. Amoroso, No. C03-5746 PJH, 2004 WL 1918890 (N.D. Cal. Aug. 24, 2004).

33 *See* Gerstner Elec., Inc. v. Am. Insur. Co., 520 F.2d 790 (8th Cir. 1975); Zoby v. Am. Fidelity Co., 242 F.2d 76 (4th Cir. 1957).

be costly if successful.[34] As with claims of contractual interference, the surety can protect itself from such allegations by thoroughly documenting its investigation and the reasonable basis for its decisions. The general indemnity agreement gives the surety broad discretion to resolve claims in a reasonable manner to protect the surety. The surety has no legal or contractual obligation to protect the principal or to issue new surety credit. Great care should be taken by the surety to work through its bond claims within the permissive language of the general indemnity agreement.

E. Other Issues to be Considered in Takeover and Completion Agreements

In addition to concerns over certain types of legal claims arising from its decision to takeover a bonded project, the surety must take a number of other factors into consideration before making its decision to complete. In order to get a clear idea of the remaining scope of work, and the time and money necessary to complete that work, the surety will want to pay particular attention to other facts that can dramatically impact the progress of the work. For example, liquidated damages, or the threat of liquidated damages, is often an issue. The surety should generally seek a waiver of liquidated damages (sometimes in the form of a time extension) in exchange for its promise to complete. At minimum, the surety should request that no liquidated damages be taken out of the contract balance so that the entire amount can be dedicated to completion. If the obligee is unwilling to make any such agreement, the surety may have to reach into its own pocket to fund completion.

Furthermore, evidence of previous design issues on the project in the form of a high volume of change orders, can be a red flag to the surety that the completion of the project might be more costly than is represented by the obligee. Consequently, the surety should anticipate that its completion effort might also involve a significant number of change orders and/or design issues, even if it appears there is a minimal amount of work left to be performed.

---

34 Arntz Contracting Co. v. St. Paul Fire & Marine Ins. Co., 54 Cal. Rptr. 2d 888 (Cal. Ct. App. 1996) (affirming award to principal of $16.5 million in breach of contract damages for profits allegedly lost as a result of the refusal to provide further bonding).

The quality of the work performed by the defaulted principal is also a critical consideration. If the obligee asserts numerous defective work items by the principal and the surety finds that the work is indeed defective, the surety should be more concerned about latent defect liability than it otherwise might be. A completion contractor will charge a higher price if it is expected to assume liability for latent defects, even more so if it is already known that the original contractor performed shoddy work.

The surety should also be sure to pay attention to the obligee's behavior while the surety is conducting its investigation. The manner in which the obligee conducts itself with respect to the surety and its investigation can be an excellent barometer of how the obligee has conducted itself, and will continue to conduct itself, during the course of the project work. If the obligee proves to be contentious and uncooperative during the surety's investigation or the defaulted principal shows that it has had prior difficulty dealing with the obligee, then the surety must realize that its own relationship with the obligee could be problematic and increase the cost to complete.

A surety considering takeover also needs to assess the resources necessary for completion, and whether those resources are readily available. This includes both the surety's own resources, and the resources of the potential completion contractors who might be hired to finish the work. For example, if the project in question requires a contractor with highly specialized equipment and there are few potential contractors who have that equipment available to dedicate to the project, then the surety may want to consider other options, such as financing its defaulted principal, instead of taking over completion itself.

The surety will also want to assess the principal's relationships with its subcontractors in order to determine the extent to which the same subcontractors might be kept on the job following the principal's default. There are a number of benefits to utilizing the original subcontractors, not the least of which is that the obligee has already agreed to accept the use of those subcontractors. Retaining the original subcontractors will also reduce the cost of completion by avoiding the time and expense associated with mobilizing an entirely new workforce, as well as avoiding the escalation costs that would no doubt accompany a reletting of all the subcontracts. However, if the defaulted principal has failed to pay its subcontractors or has been responsible for poor management of the project and caused schedule delays, the surety will have to work a little harder to convince the original subcontractors to remain on the project.

In some instances, subcontractors may feel a certain amount of loyalty to the terminated principal, making them reluctant to remain on the job if the principal is removed. Moreover, if the principal has alleged delays caused by the obligee or that the obligee owes additional funds, the subcontractors may agree with the principal's allegations and demand that the surety pay additional monies (e.g. for outstanding change orders) that are purportedly owed by the obligee before they are willing to continue. Depending upon the amount of money being demanded, it may be preferable to allow new subcontractors onto the job. However, if the obligee has withheld funds from the principal due to stop notices or mechanics' liens, then the surety can often negotiate the release of those funds, use them to pay the disgruntled subcontractors and get the project back on track.

Depending upon the facts and circumstances of the particular project at issue, there may be other considerations which will help the surety make its decision as to whether it will takeover and complete the project. The most important thing is that the surety gather as much information and consider as many elements of the completion effort as possible before executing any takeover agreement.

F. General Provisions for Takeover and Completion Agreements

Once the surety decides to take over the bonded project, it will typically need to execute: (1) a takeover agreement with the bond obligee; and (2) a completion agreement with its selected contractor.

1. The Takeover Agreement

If the surety is taking over completion of the work, the first step is to ask the obligee to enter into a takeover agreement which clearly sets forth the surety's obligations for completing the project. Some obligees will be reluctant to execute a takeover agreement, operating under the belief that it is not necessary to do so because the surety is already obligated under the bond to complete the project. However, many bonds provide options for the surety, meaning that a takeover agreement is important for establishing the surety's election to complete and defining its completion obligations. Moreover, most bonds simply provide indemnity and nothing else. Most obligees are willing to execute a takeover agreement in order to keep the project moving, and in order to specifically reserve any rights and claims the obligee may have against the principal. If, notwithstanding the above, an obligee is still reluctant to sign a takeover agreement, the surety should reconsider whether this is the best completion option for the surety.

In addition to the standard contract provisions (i.e. an incorporation clause, attorneys' fee provision, etc.), the essential elements of a takeover agreement include:

a. the identification of the parties, the bonded project and the bond, and a recitation of the circumstances of the principal's termination;
b. a description of the remaining work that is as thorough and detailed as possible, including corrective work;
c. a recitation of the original contract amount, any approved change orders, amounts paid to the principal, the status of any other change orders (not approved, disputed, pending), and the remaining contract balance;
d. a promise by the obligee to apply the remaining contract balance to the completion of the project;
e. the method for paying out funds and administering the work, typically achieved by referencing the procedures set out in the original contract;
f. a new completion date;
g. reaffirmation by the obligee that the surety's liability is limited to the penal sum of the bond, and that any amounts advanced by the surety for completion of the project will reduce the penal sum of the bond accordingly;
h. a specific reservation of rights, by one or both parties, with respect to issues that cannot be resolved in the takeover agreement, including a specific reservation of all the principal's rights under the original contract;
i. where appropriate, a provision dealing with the issue of liquidated damages and whether the obligee will waive them, in whole or in part;
j. an acknowledgement of the obligee's acceptance of the selected completion contractor, or of the surety's assumption of the role as completion contractor; and

k. a description of the role of the completion contractor on the project and exactly which contractual duties the completion contractor is authorized to perform.

Negotiating a takeover agreement can be tricky, particularly where there are disputes over the quality of the work performed and the amount of work remaining, and must be drafted carefully. For example, if the surety cannot determine to a reasonable degree of certainty whether the default was warranted, the reservations of rights in the takeover agreement are critical. Obligees will often fight for language in the takeover agreement that concedes the principal's liability. In other words, the obligee will try to include a statement that unconditionally admits that the alleged default was warranted or that the principal performed defective work. The surety needs to guard against prematurely making any such statements, or it may face problems if it later determines that the termination was wrongful or that the work was not defective.

2. Completion Agreement

In conjunction with the takeover agreement, the surety will also need to execute an agreement with the contractor it selects to complete the project, whether it employs the bond principal or brings another contractor onto the job. Necessary terms include:

a. identification of the project and the identification of the parties;

b. a precise definition of the scope of work, which can be taken directly from the corresponding takeover agreement, or which can be as broad as "completion of the principal's contract and correction of the defective work;"

c. a provision addressing whether the completion contractor must provide new payment and performance bonds, and the insurance requirements for the new contractor;

d. the contract price and terms of payment, the latter of which is often taken from the original contract and adapted to include the surety's review or submission of the new contractor's payment applications;

e. the new completion date and liability for liquidated damages that might accrue thereafter;

f. the warranty responsibility and latent defect liability of the completion contractor;
g. an assignment in favor of the completion contractor of all materials and supplies on the project site and, where possible, an assignment of the original subcontracts to the completion contractor;
h. terms for administering the completion contract, tailored to fit the level of supervision that the surety determines is necessary or appropriate; and
i. the method for providing any notices.

Just as it does with the takeover agreement, the surety needs to draft the completion agreement with a critical eye toward each and every provision. The completion effort will slow down, and be more expensive, if there are disputes over the contractor's responsibilities because of a poorly drafted contract.

G. Matters to be Considered in Drafting the Agreement Between the Surety and the Obligee

1. Limitation of the Surety's Liability to the Bond Penalty

The surety should make every effort to obtain an agreement from the obligee in its takeover agreement that the surety's completion costs are limited to the penal sum of the bond. As mentioned earlier, obligees may be wary of including a limitation on the surety's completion costs because it leaves open the possibility that the surety will expend the full amount of the bond before the project is finished. However, if the obligee does not agree to the penal sum cap, the surety should consider other options.

2. Preservation of Claims

More often than not, the surety will encounter disputes between the principal and the obligee that cannot be resolved before the execution of the takeover agreement. In those instances, the preservation of all parties' rights becomes an important issue. A reservation of the principal's rights and claims can reassure the principal that the surety has not totally dismissed its allegations regarding the obligee, as well as protecting the surety from future claims that the surety impaired or interfered with whatever rights the principal may believe that it has. Similarly, the obligee will be assured that its project will get completed and it will still be allowed to later seek damages from the defaulted principal, while the surety is allowed to proceed with completion and minimize its potential liability.

3. Contract Balances

The determination of the contract balance remaining at the time of termination can be a complicated issue. There may be conflicting claims about the amount due under change orders, or what is considered additional work for which the contractor should be compensated. If there have been delays, then the obligee will often claim it is withholding payment due to an assessment of liquidated damages. The surety and obligee will need to come to an agreement regarding the amount of contract funds left, and the manner in which those funds will be paid to the surety or the completion contractor. If such an agreement is not possible within the time constraints of a particular transaction, the surety can agree to disagree, accept the obligee's accounting, and reserve rights to claim additional funds later.

4. Latent Defects and Warranties

Latent defect and warranty liability can also be a tricky issue, especially when the project work is performed by two different contractors. Contractors are seldom, if ever, willing to assume liability for latent defects in work they did not perform themselves, or to warrant work done by another contractor. The surety should attempt to include in the takeover agreement an acknowledgement by the obligee that all work performed by the defaulted principal was in accordance with the plans and specifications, except for specifically identified defective work, if any. Then, the surety can have its completion contractor assume warranty and latent defect liability only for the corrective and completion work, while warranty and latent defect liability for the pre-default work remains with the defaulted principal and/or the surety.

Alternatively, in some circumstances the surety may want or need to attempt to negotiate a price for the completion contractor to assume the principal's warranty/latent defect liability on a unit price, change order basis. Using this method gives the obligee a single warranty from the completion contractor, but does not transfer the risk associated with warranty obligations and latent defects arising from the principal's work. In effect, the surety backs the portion of the warranty that relates to the principal's work.

5. Subcontract Hold or Ratification Agreements

Provided they are competent, it is typically more efficient for the surety to complete the bonded work with the subcontractors and materialmen who already contracted with the defaulted principal to work on the project. Pursuant to the express terms of most indemnity agreements, the surety is assigned all subcontracts of its principal on a bonded project. Moreover, when a surety steps into the shoes of its principal, it is subrogated to the rights of the principal. As the assignee and subrogee of the principal, the surety may be entitled to compel a subcontractor to continue performing its subcontract.

Typically, a surety will approach all necessary subcontractors and suppliers in an attempt to negotiate a "Hold Agreement" or "Ratification Agreement," which is the same thing with two different titles. These short agreements provide as follows: (1) that the surety will pay the past due amounts owed by the principal to the subcontractor or supplier on the bonded project; and (2) that the subcontractor or supplier will, if needed by the completion contractor, complete its original scope of work for the original price. Depending upon the circumstances, the surety will sometimes need to negotiate a new price or resolve claims as part of the ratification process.

6. Liquidated Damages/Extension of Time

Depending upon the jurisdiction, default situations may involve the assessment of liquidated damages or the threat of assessing liquidated damages by the obligee. It can be difficult for the surety to quickly determine whether the assessment of liquidated damages is appropriate, and thus the parties will often postpone the resolution of the liquidated damages issue until after completion of the bonded work. A simple reservation of rights can preserve this issue, giving the parties time to analyze the schedule, the cause(s) of delay, and the law of the relevant jurisdiction.

In some cases, the surety can negotiate a resolution much earlier. For example, the surety may convince the obligee to waive its assessment of liquidated damages up through the date the takeover agreement is executed if the surety makes a corresponding concession, such as using the obligee's preferred contractor as its completion contractor. The surety may also negotiate a reasonable new completion date with the obligee and have the completion contractor assume liability for any liquidated damages assessed as a result of failing to meet the new completion date. Another option is to have the completing contractor bid two alternates: making the existing date or bidding a new date. This way the surety can determine how much an acceleration will cost, or how much it may have to pay in liquidated damages, then can make decisions and negotiate with the obligee over a reasonable completion date.

IV. Tendering of a New Contractor

Under some circumstances, it may be preferable for a performance bond surety to offer up a new contractor, along with a new performance bond surety when possible, rather than completing the bonded project itself.[35] The tendering of a new contractor requires the surety to solicit bids from potential completion contractors. The surety selects the lowest responsible bidder and offers, or "tenders," the designated contractor to the bond obligee. The bond obligee then contracts directly with the designated contractor, with the surety either paying the difference between the remaining balance on the original contract and the new contract price, or paying out the penal sum of its bond, whichever is less.

Tendering a new contractor is more likely to be a viable option if the work on the bonded contract has either not commenced or is in its early stages. It can be difficult to generate interest on the part of potential bidders if there is minimal work to be performed, and thus minimal profit to be earned. Further, there is a significant amount of time and expense involved in soliciting bids from potential completion contractors. Undertaking the time and expense of re-letting the project is justifiable only when the time and expense involved in completing the project is significantly greater. However, the benefits of the tender option, discussed in detail in this section, can make it an attractive option.

---

35 There are a number of books, articles and papers that discuss the surety's tender option, including E.A. "Seth" Mills, Jr. & Susan M. Moore, *Tender, in* BOND DEFAULT MANUAL 243, 243-67 (Duncan L. Clore, Richard E. Towle & Michael J. Sugar, Jr. eds., 3d ed. 2005) and the citations contained therein.

A. Is Tendering Possible?

If the surety is considering tendering a new contractor, it must first confirm that it is allowed to do so. Bonds do not typically explicitly provide that tender is an option for the surety. However, the standard AIA performance bond does expressly permit tender,[36] and tender is allowed by law in most jurisdictions.[37] Frequently, the obligee prefers the tender option because it provides a new bonded contractor a chance to complete without the surety's involvement in day-to-day activities, and a chance to resolve all issues up front without further administrative or legal expense.

If the bonded project at issue is a public works project, the bond obligee will frequently have concerns that accepting a tender violates competitive bidding statutes. If tender is expressly provided for in the bond, this may satisfy the public entity obligee. In addition, several jurisdictions have statutory provisions which make tender a viable option. For example, under federal law, a contracting officer has the discretion to decide the appropriate means of completing a project under a performance bond. The surety should investigate the applicable law prior to presenting its tender offer so that it can address any concerns over competitive bidding at the outset of its negotiation with the public owner obligee.

B. Possible Complications in Implementing a Tender

There are possible complications that may arise in arranging a tender. For example, the obligee may be seeking swift action by the surety and an immediate start to the work. However, the process of investigating the status of the project, soliciting bids, evaluating bids and negotiating with both the completion contractor and the obligee can be time consuming.

From the surety's perspective, tender of a new contractor typically involves the use of a lump sum or fixed price contract so that the surety can quantify the amount that it must pay the obligee. Thus, if it appears

---

36 AIA Document A312-1984, *Performance Bond* (Am. Inst. of Architects 1984) [hereinafter "AIA 312"].

37 *See* Granite Computer Leasing Corp. v. Travelers Indem. Co., 894 F.2d 547, 551 (2d Cir. 1990); United States v. Seaboard Sur. Co., 817 F.2d 956, 959 (2d Cir. 1987); Aetna Cas. & Sur. Co. v. United States, 845 F.2d 971 (Fed. Cir. 1988).

from the surety's investigation that a cost-plus contract is more appropriate, tender is usually not the best option unless the surety can convince the obligee to accept some risk or the surety agrees to indemnify the obligee for costs over the tendered sum. If the surety is planning to assert its principal's claims after having tendered a new contractor, the surety needs to consider as part of a tender making arrangements with the new contractor so that evidence needed for the claim is developed and preserved.

C. Advantages of Tendering

In spite of these disadvantages, there are distinct benefits to tendering that can make it an attractive option for sureties. In most default situations, the surety is thrust into the middle of an acrimonious and tense relationship between the obligee and the defaulted contractor. By tendering a new contractor, the surety extricates itself from this difficult position between two adversarial parties, and avoids dealing with the concerns and complaints of the obligee, who is uncomfortable with allowing the defaulted contractor to complete the work even with the surety's supervision.

Further, the surety has greater control over its losses. The use of a fixed price contract, as is necessary in the tender situation, allows the surety to cap its losses at a much earlier stage than if it decides to complete the project itself. The surety also avoids the extended investment of time and money that typically accompanies the supervision of a takeover situation. In addition, if the surety can negotiate the appropriate terms, it can avoid unforeseen claims and potential future costs, such as the costs associated with delay (including liquidated damages), warranty obligations, latent defects and unforeseen project conditions.

D. Special Considerations

There are several issues that must be considered, and addressed, in order for the surety to take full advantage of the benefits of tendering. These include: (1) liquidated damages; (2) patent and latent defects; (3) warranties; and (4) the principal's claims against the obligee.

1. Liquidated Damages

Most default situations involve claims that the project completion has been, or certainly will be, delayed. First and foremost, the surety must negotiate with the obligee for a new, reasonable completion date for the completion contractor. To the extent possible, the surety can endeavor to have the completion contractor attempt to make up some delays and reduce the obligee's claim for liquidated damages.

Frequently, obligees will claim that they have already assessed liquidated damages against the defaulted contractor. The surety can negotiate with the obligee and attempt to eliminate or reduce the obligee's claim by offering other concessions. If the surety's investigation makes it clear that the defaulted contractor would indeed be liable for liquidated damages, then the surety can factor the liquidated damages claim into its payment to the obligee by reducing the balance of the original contract by the amount of the liquidated damages claim. However, it is rare that such a determination can be made quickly, and often the surety will need to reserve the liquidated damages issue for later resolution in order to proceed with the tender.

2. Patent and Latent Defects

Obligees will often identify patent defects as part of their justification for declaring a default of the original contractor. Any patent defects should be identified in the surety's investigation and included as part of the completion contractor's scope of work. The issue of repairing latent defects, however, poses a more difficult problem for the surety. Bidders will typically add contingencies to their bids for the possibility that they will encounter major latent defects, raising the cost of completion. Depending upon the size of the project, these allowances can be substantial. As a result, the surety may prefer to exclude liability for latent defects from the completion contract and retain liability for potential latent defects. Sureties can also test the market, and solicit bids with a specific line item value assigned for repairing latent defects. This allows the surety to decide whether it should retain the risk of paying for latent defects after the bidders have put a price on doing so or negotiate a side agreement with a new contractor and offer to provide direct reimbursement for correcting latent defects based on some objective measure—i.e., time and materials plus mark-up.

3. Warranties

Warranties are partly related to latent defects, and are an equally significant issue for a surety considering tender as an option. Completion contractors rarely are willing to assume warranty liability for the principal's work. If the completion contractor can be convinced to assume all warranty liability, it will mean an additional cost being added to the completion contract. Often times a provision will be included in the tender agreement providing for the surety to pay the completion contractor or reimburse the obligee, on a time and materials basis or other agreed price, for warranty work below a certain dollar threshold. For larger dollar warranty issues, the tender agreement sometimes provides for notice to the surety and an opportunity to investigate and resolve its potential warranty liability.

4. Principal's Claims Against the Obligee

When presented with the tender of a new contractor, obligees will almost always seek a waiver of all claims or potential claims that the principal has alleged, or could allege, against the obligee. The principal's claims should be thoroughly investigated. Where the principal's claims appear to have merit, they can be used as a bargaining chip by the surety, as the subrogee or assignee of those claims, to reduce the amount of its overall exposure (i.e. to lessen the amount that the surety will pay to the obligee as part of the tender transaction, or as a coverage defense). If the obligee is not willing to recognize any value in the principal's claims or refuses to allocate a sufficient value, then the surety should reserve its rights and resolve the claims at a later date.

E. Drafting of the Agreement

Unlike the takeover method of completion where there are two agreements (the takeover agreement and the completion agreement), with a tender there is usually only one agreement between the obligee, completion contractor and surety. The tender agreement provisions affecting the obligee and completion contractor include the circumstances of contracting, the cost, a new completion date, and the scope and all agreed upon terms and conditions for completion of the work. The tender agreement provisions affecting the obligee and surety include the price the surety will pay, the timing of payment, a release of the surety and any exceptions to the surety's release (e.g. warranties, latent defects or other project specific issues) subject, as always, to the penal sum of the performance bond.

V. Financing the Principal

The surety has no legal or nonlegal obligation, arising out of the issuance of its bonds, to finance a principal. If the surety determines that, provided with an infusion of cash, the principal can finish the bonded project in a timely and workmanlike manner, then it may decide to finance the principal's completion of the work. However, given the distinct possibility that the contractor is having severe and systemic financial problems, the surety should proceed with financing cautiously and only after completing a thorough investigation.[38]

A. The Benefits of Financing the Principal

1. Reduction of the New Contractor Premium

As noted several times in this chapter, there are additional costs associated with the hiring of a new contractor. A new contractor will build contingencies into its bid (and thus into the contract price) to account for the possibility that there are unknown defects in the defaulted contractor's work, and will expect to be paid for assuming warranty liability. There are also costs associated with the mobilization of a new contractor, and allowances must be made for the time it will take a new contractor to familiarize itself with the project.

---

[38] There are a number of books, articles and papers that discuss the surety's financing of its principal option, including George J. Bachrach & Matthew L. Silverstein, *Financing the Principal, in* BOND DEFAULT MANUAL 155, 155-221 (Duncan L. Clore, Richard E. Towle & Michael J. Sugar, Jr. eds., 3d ed. 2005); T. Scott Leo, *The Financing Surety and the Chapter 11 Principal*, 26 TORT & INS. L.J. 45 (1990); Gilbert J. Schroeder, *Providing Financial Support to the Contractor*, 17 FORUM 1190 (1982); Gilbert J. Schroeder, *Procedures and Instruments Utilized to Protect the Surety Who Finances a Contractor*, 14 FORUM 830 (1979); Francis J. McGrath, George J. Bachrach & Adam Cizek, *The Financing Surety as a Performing Surety–Law and Practice* 1 (unpublished paper submitted at the Fourteenth Annual Northeast Surety & Fidelity Claims Conference on Sept. 18, 2003).

By financing the bond principal through completion, the surety can avoid this "new contractor premium." Financing the principal provides an element of continuity and helps minimize the delay and other damages stemming from the principal's default. In addition, financing the principal allows the surety to avoid some of the administrative burdens associated with the surety taking over the project.

2. Time Savings

Finding and hiring a completion contractor takes weeks or months to accomplish. Some obligees will not wait that long. Some projects have high liquidated damages or other reasons motivating the surety to minimize delays. Financing the principal is typically the fastest way to keep a project moving forward, provided that the principal has the capacity to effectively prosecute the work, which may not be the case.

3. Preservation of Claims

In many default situations, the contractor will assert its own claims against the obligee. However, when the surety takes over the project, the defaulted principal may see itself as having little vested interest in the successful completion of the project and prosecution of claims notwithstanding its indemnity obligation. Moreover, the principal may be hostile toward its surety if it perceives that the surety turned its back on the principal by taking over the work. In other words, the principal loses sight of the fact that, even after default, it is still in the principal's best interest to help the surety complete the work as quickly and efficiently as possible.

When the surety chooses to finance the principal, rather than taking over the principal's contract rights, the principal retains a direct and substantial interest in the project and may see the surety as supportive rather than adversarial. As a result, the contractor is far more likely to mitigate construction costs and take pains to preserve (and provide to the surety) the evidence supporting its claims. Financing the principal helps keep the project team(s) together long enough to develop the claims while the project is being completed. Otherwise, the project team will be assigned to different projects, or they will leave the employment of the principal, either of which could result in little or no cooperation from the percipient witnesses in the claim development process and heavier reliance upon expensive outside consultants.

4. Salvage Considerations

A surety has no obligation to finance its principal, and the principal has no right to demand financing. Most contractors, however, are eager for the opportunity to complete the project on their own. Thus, the principal and its indemnitors are often willing to pledge assets to the surety as security for funds provided by the surety. This volunteer process could yield new assets not recoverable through litigation, and/or new indemnitors, and/or save time and dollars spent pursuing indemnification, and/or avoid a personal bankruptcy, and/or all or some of the above.

B. The Detriments to Financing the Principal

There are also serious concerns involved with financing a defaulted principal. Before entering into any financing agreement, the surety should make every effort to address these concerns and thus protect its investment.

1. The Bond Penalty

Unless the obligee agrees in writing to a contrary arrangement, financing provided to the principal may not result in a corresponding reduction of the surety's bond penalty. In order to avoid this situation, as part of the process of executing its financing agreement with the principal, the surety can solicit an agreement from, or give notice to the obligee that funds advanced to the principal for completion of the bonded project will reduce the surety's penal sum accordingly.

With most principals, there is no law requiring disclosure of loan and other confidential financial information. Sometimes the principal and surety may decide that public disclosure of the financing arrangement could cause harm to the project, such as reduced negotiating leverage of the principal, harsher credit terms with subcontractors and vendors, slower payment from the obligee, violations of lender loan covenants, among other adverse consequences. In those cases, obtaining pre-financing consent from the owner would not be possible and the surety will need to evaluate the risk of the job cost exceeding the penal sum and whether financing is a viable option for a particular project.

2. Expense of Monitoring Performance of the Job

As noted above, one of the advantages of financing the principal is that it allows the surety to avoid the time and expense of completing the bonded project with a completion contractor. However, a surety that finances its principal will still need to closely monitor the principal's completion of the work. Thus, some of the surety's savings will be offset by the time and expense involved with monitoring the principal's progress, which monitoring is frequently performed by outside consultants.

3. Elimination of Fixed Cost

If the surety opts to take over the bonded project or to tender a new contractor, it usually receives the benefit of a fixed price contract, or has remedies available if the agreed-upon price is exceeded. In most circumstances, this means that the surety avoids the possibility of an increased loss. The same cannot be said of a surety who agrees to finance its principal. There is a risk, usually unquantifiable, that the principal's cost to complete will grow over time, leaving the surety with a difficult decision as to whether it should continue financing or take over the project after having already spent a significant amount. This is particularly risky if the obligee refuses to agree that money advanced to the contractor counts against the penal sum of the bond.

4. Contractor's/Principal's Overhead

Overhead can be a significant and complicated issue. The surety will need to first identify the number of projects, both bonded and unbonded, that the contractor is working on at the time, and determine the amount of overhead attributable to the particular bonded project accordingly. For example, if the number of projects underway is minimal or decreasing, then a large portion of the contractor's overhead will be attributable to the bonded project at issue. If the contractor is working on a large number of unbonded projects, then the proportion will be smaller. In any case, the financing agreement should specifically set forth the amount, or method for calculating the amount, of overhead expenses being paid from the funds provided by the surety.

The importance of the surety's investigation of the issue of overhead cannot be overemphasized. The surety must fully familiarize itself with the overall financial status and outlook of its principal, and come to an accurate conclusion as to what the principal's overall overhead expenses are. If the contractor has little or no additional work coming in, or few projects underway, then it is relatively certain that the amount of overhead being paid by the surety will continue to increase.

5. Tax Considerations

When a surety decides to finance its principal, it may also become liable for some of the principal's tax liabilities. For example, because the financing surety has control over the principal's payment of wages, federal law makes the financing surety liable for withholding taxes.[39] Federal law dictates that a surety paying a contractor's employees' wages is liable for all withholding taxes *and interest* owed by the contractor.[40] Further, if a surety finances the principal's payroll and has notice that the principal does not intend to make any deposits toward its withholding taxes, then the surety can be liable for all such taxes *and interest of up to 25 percent*.[41] There are also potentially significant penalties to which the surety may be exposed.[42] When financing, the surety should pay all taxes directly to the state and federal authorities. Handling the payments itself can eliminate all risks.

6. Liability Under a Theory of Alter Ego or Domination

As noted earlier in this chapter, depending on the jurisdiction, a surety that exercised an improper amount of influence or control over the principal's affairs may be liable under a theory of alter ego or domination.[43] At a minimum, the principal, and more likely its indemnitors, may assert an alter ego or domination claim as a defense to indemnity. These claims are mostly futile attempts to avoid indemnity obligations.[44] As such, they usually fail, but cost a great deal to defeat.

---

39   26 U.S.C. § 3505 (2008).
40   *Id.* (emphasis added).
41   *Id.* (emphasis added).
42   26 U.S.C. § 6672 holds that a party who is required to pay and account for taxes can be penalized in an amount equal to the amount of the tax evaded. In other words, the surety can be liable for two times the amount of taxes that the principal fails to pay.
43   *See* Lambert v. Md. Cas. Co., 403 So.2d 739 (La. Ct. App. 1981), *aff'd*, 418 So.2d 553 (La. 1982).
44   See Chapter 8 for further analysis of these issues.

The drafting of the financing documents can assist in avoiding or defeating any such claim. The surety should clearly have the right to advance or not advance funds in its sole and unilateral discretion. Any attempt by the principal to create a mandatory funding obligation should be rejected and treated as non-negotiable. Additionally, the financing documents should include a release by the principal and indemnitors of the surety for events past, present, and future, arising out of or related to the financing transaction. Many jurisdictions will not allow an advance waiver of fraudulent conduct, but most other claims, whether in contract or tort, can be waived in advance, thereby avoiding future alter ego or domination allegations and attempts to reduce the surety's entitlement to repayment. Any attempt by the principal to reject a waiver and preserve its remedies should be reviewed closely by the surety before entering into a financing relationship.

7. *Potential Claim for Failure to Finance*

Although a surety has no obligation to finance its principal, the principal may feel entitled to receive continued funding after the surety agrees to provide some funds. Thus a termination of financing may lead to a principal asserting a claim that the surety terminated funding in bad faith. As such, it is imperative that any financing agreement expressly sets forth the surety's right to terminate financing at any time and for any reason.

C. Elements to Consider When Deciding Whether to Finance

There are specific factors, detailed below, that must be analyzed when the surety is considering financing its principal. These are all factors which should be looked at as part of the surety's initial investigation, but which deserve special emphasis if the surety is seriously considering providing funding to the defaulted principal.

1. *Progress of the Job*

Obviously, the closer the project is to completion, the more realistic it is that financing is a viable option. The further the project is from completion, the more likely it is that problems will arise and the cost to complete will continue to increase, requiring the surety to provide more funding than originally anticipated. Conversely, as the project approaches completion, it may be more efficient to have the defaulted contractor, who is familiar with the job and remaining work, stay on the job. Additionally, finding a replacement contractor who is willing to complete the job when there is minimal work remaining can be difficult.

2. Contractor Ability/Integrity

The defaulted principal will most likely represent to the surety that it is ready, willing and able to complete the project, regardless of whether this is true. However, the surety must conduct its own analysis of the resources, including materials, equipment and personnel, that the principal has available for the completion effort. Further, the surety should assess the contractor's management personnel and their level of knowledge to the greatest extent possible, in order to gauge the likelihood that the contractor can complete the work as promised. Another issue is whether the contractor can stay in business over an extended period and/or whether its key employees can be locked in at least until the bonded projects are completed. The surety should pay special attention to the contractor's overall integrity, including its willingness to act reasonably and ability to follow through on its promises. To this end, the contractor's conduct and level of cooperation during the surety's initial investigation is a significant indicator.

3. Subcontractor Relations

The principal's relationships with its subcontractors and suppliers, as well as its creditors and other project obligees, are also an important consideration. If the principal has maintained good relations with these third-parties, there is a greater likelihood that the financing effort will result in successful completion of the bonded project. On the other hand, if these relationships have turned acrimonious or entered litigation, the surety should view the financing option less favorably. On occasion, adding a third-party construction consultant to the project team, one who works for the surety, can help to solve communication issues or other sources of tension on the project.

4. Competition

When deciding between financing the defaulted principal and possibly employing a different contractor, the surety needs to know what its options are with respect to potential replacements. If there are several other qualified contractors available to perform the work, then financing is not necessarily the better option. Conversely, if the surety fails to find a satisfactory selection of potential replacement contractors available to work on the project, then financing the defaulted principal becomes more attractive.

5. Amount of Unbonded Work

Unbonded projects are a potential source of income for the defaulted principal, and thus increase the possibility that the surety will be able to recover the funds that it lends to the principal. Accordingly, the surety will want to evaluate the number of unbonded projects being performed by the principal, as well as the profits that those projects are expected to generate. The surety will also need to determine whether the principal requires financial assistance to complete the unbonded projects, and whether it is beneficial for the surety to fund the unbonded work in addition to the bonded project (or projects) being financed.[45]

If the principal has both bonded and unbonded work, the surety will also want to evaluate exactly how its financing of the principal's overhead is to be allocated. Frequently, the principal's desire to have financial assistance to pay for overhead leads to additional collateral that perhaps the surety would not otherwise be entitled to. In other circumstances, the surety only finances a portion of the overhead and looks to the principal to pay the balance from revenues on unbonded projects.

Absent an assignment of rights from the principal, the surety does not have an automatic right to the proceeds from unbonded work. A

---

45 Absent a common obligee, the surety will typically not have the same subrogation rights with respect to unbonded projects, as the surety is not legally obligated to act with respect to work which it has not guaranteed. The surety could argue that its funding for the unbonded work was necessary as part of its effort to sustain the principal's business and prevent any defaults on the bonded projects. However, there appears to be minimal precedent for asserting subrogation rights with respect to unbonded work. The surety would have to rely on the assignment in order to assert any right to recover unbonded contract funds. This means that the surety's rights will not necessarily take priority over other creditors as they would with a subrogation claim. These issues are addressed in Chapter 4.

financing surety will want to obtain an assignment from the principal of those proceeds as part of the financing arrangement, in order to assure that any profits being brought in by the contractor for unbonded work is applied to the debt created by the financing of bonded work.

6. Availability of Collateral

It is very rare for the surety to finance the principal's obligations without new collateral. Typically, very early in the financing discussion with the principal and its indemnitors, updated financial statements are obtained for the surety to analyze: (a) the current financial condition of the principal and indemnitors; (b) the status of assets that the principal and indemnitors had when the bond(s) were issued; (c) the ability of the principal and indemnitors to repay the surety; and (d) to identify specific assets that may be pledged to the surety as collateral.

When taking collateral for any loan by the surety, attention should be paid to documenting the consideration for the loan. Typically, the indemnity agreement expressly provides for the surety taking collateral if it sets a reserve or otherwise believes a loss is possible, in which case the consideration for the new collateral is already established in the original transaction. In other situations, the surety can offer a forbearance for a defined period of the surety's immediate rights and remedies under the indemnity agreement. For example, the surety could forbear from filing an indemnity suit for a defined period of time. In other situations, a new indemnitor (e.g. a new trust or a relative) pledges collateral for the loan, in which case the consideration needs to be specifically thought through. It is not difficult to find consideration for any aspect of the loan, provided the issue is identified and thoroughly contemplated early in the transaction.

When considering what collateral to take, independently verify that the person or entity pledging the asset has unencumbered legal title to do so. Check the Secretary of State records for UCC-1 Financing Statements that may affect title. Also, obtain a title report for any real property being pledged. In some transactions, the surety may want to obtain title insurance guaranteeing its position on the title of a particular real property asset. Finally, pay attention to state laws affecting sureties' remedies in case the principal or indemnitors default.

D. Effect of Financing on Subrogation Rights

The right of equitable subrogation is a powerful tool for the surety. The surety's subrogation rights have been recognized and affirmed by the Supreme Court on numerous occasions, for more than a century.[46] In essence, the doctrine of subrogation holds that, when a surety satisfies an obligation owed by the principal to a third-party creditor, the surety assumes the rights previously held by the creditor whose debt was satisfied. Therefore, if a performance bond surety satisfies the principal's obligation to complete a bonded project, then the surety has an equitable right to the remaining contract balance.[47]

Subrogation is an equitable remedy, arising independently of any contractual agreement. In order to establish the surety's subrogation rights, there are generally four elements which must be shown: (1) an obligation of the principal to the obligee; (2) the principal's default with respect to that obligation; (3) rights vested in the obligee as a result of the principal's default; and (4) the surety's performance of the defaulted obligation, pursuant to the bond issued on behalf of the principal.

The surety's subrogation rights to contract funds will be considered superior to the rights of any lender who has loaned funds to the principal or anyone whose rights to contract funds are derived solely from an assignment of rights executed by the principal. As explained by the Supreme Court in the seminal *Prairie State* case:

> [The principal] could not transfer to the bank any greater rights in the fund than they themselves possessed. Their rights were subordinate to...the sureties. Depending, therefore, solely upon rights claimed to have been derived...by express contract with [the principal], it necessarily results that the equity, if any, acquired by the Prairie Bank in the...fund then in existence...was subordinate to the equity which had arisen in favor of the surety Hitchcock.

---

46   *See* Pearlman v. Reliance Ins. Co., 371 U.S. 132 (1962); United States v. Munsey Trust Co., 332 U.S. 234 (1947); Henningsen v. U.S. Fid. & Guar. Co., 208 U.S. 404 (1908); Prairie State Bank v. United States, 164 U.S. 227 (1896).

47   *Prairie State Bank*, 164 U.S. 212. This issue is addressed in greater detail in Chapter 4.

The financing surety's subrogation rights should be no different than the subrogation rights which vest in a surety that completes the project itself.[48] When its principal has been declared to be in default of its obligations and the surety opts to finance the principal's completion of the project rather than undertaking completion, it does so as a result of its bond obligations. It does not do so as a volunteer. In order to affirm that the surety is providing funding to the principal as a result of its bond obligations, the written financing agreement between the surety and the principal must include a recitation that the surety is financing the principal as a result of the principal's default on its bonded obligations. The necessary terms of the financing agreement are discussed in further detail below.

The surety's subrogation right may come under greater attack from lenders if the surety decides to finance the principal prior to any declaration of default by the obligee, but after the principal advises the surety that it does not have the financial capacity to complete its bonded work. The argument, in essence, is that the surety has acted as a voluntary lender, and therefore should not be able to assert that its rights are superior to those of other lenders. However, there is a substantial amount of case law affirming the financing surety's ability to assert subrogation rights regardless of whether there has been a formal declaration of default by a bond obligee.[49] Courts have found that, even where the surety is acting to prevent a default rather than acting as the result of a default, the surety is acting as a result of its bond obligations.

---

48   *See* Lacy v. Md. Cas. Co., 32 F.2d 48 (4th Cir. 1929).
49   Mass. Bonding & Ins. Co. v. New York, 259 F.2d 33, 37-38 (2d Cir. 1958); Morgenthau v. Fid. & Deposit Co. of Md., 94 F.2d 632, 635 (D.C. Cir. 1937); Aetna Cas. & Sur. Co. v. United States, 845 F.2d 971, 975 (Fed. Cir. 1988); First Ala. Bank of Birmingham v. Hartford Accident & Indem. Co., 430 F. Supp. 907, 911 (N.D. Ala. 1977); Travelers Indem. Co. v. W. Ga. Nat'l Bank, 387 F. Supp. 1090, 1094 (N.D. Ga. 1974); Indem. Ins. Co. of N. Am. v. Lane Contracting Corp., 227 F. Supp. 143, 148 (D. Neb. 1964); Mass. Bonding and Ins. Co. v. Fago Constr. Corp., 82 F. Supp. 619, 622 (D. Md. 1948); Equibank v. Ram Constr., Inc. (In re Ram Constr., Inc.), 32 B.R. 758, 759 (Bankr. W.D. Pa. 1983); Morrison Assurance Co. v. United States, 3 Cl. Ct. 626, 634 (Cl. Ct. 1983); Great Am. Ins. Co. v. United States, 481 F.2d 1298, 1308 (Ct. Cl. 1973); Fid. & Deposit Co. of Md. v. United States, 393 F.2d 834, 837 (Ct. Cl. 1968); Royal Indem. Co. v. United States, 371 F.2d 462, 464 (Ct. Cl. 1967).

The surety's financing of a principal prior to a declaration of default is discussed later in this chapter.

E. Financing Through Advancing Funds for Obligations Owed Under the Payment Bond

Sometimes the principal only needs financial help with payment of laborers, material suppliers and subcontractors on a particular bonded project or projects. If the surety pays these debts, cash can be freed up for the principal to pay its other bonded performance obligations or necessary overhead. The resolution of a few payment bond obligations can usually be accomplished quickly and with minimal paperwork.

As a general practice, the above approach should not be used if the surety anticipates a loss nearing its performance bond penal sum. By intentionally allocating financing dollars to the payment bond, the surety does not get the credit against the performance bond penal sum that it may want or need in the future. If a penal sum loss is possible, it is usually better to structure the transaction so that all surety payments are counted against the performance bond.

Even when the surety is simply advancing funds for obligations owed under the payment bond, care should be taken to document the financing transaction up front with the principal and indemnitors so that there is a clear understanding of how and when the surety will be repaid.

F. Guaranteeing of Bank Loan Versus Surety Providing Financing

In most financing situations, the surety will opt to lend the principal money from the surety's own funds. However, if the principal has no cash but there are substantial assets available for repayment of any loan made, then the surety may decide it is preferable to guarantee a bank loan for the principal, who will then bear the risk of non-payment, rather than using its own money. There are additional costs associated with bank loans, namely interest and financing charges. However, as long as those additional costs can be covered by the principal's pledged assets, the surety does not need to be concerned that it will have to pay those additional costs. Moreover, pledging assets to a bank rather than the surety should protect the principal from a later finding that the transaction was a voidable preference under bankruptcy laws.[50]

Guaranteeing a loan is also preferable where the project or projects at issue involve federal construction contracts. Federal law does not recognize an assignment to a surety, but will recognize an assignment to a financial institution.[51] Thus, if a bank takes an assignment of contract funds instead of the surety, the federal government can be prevented from taking offsets against the assigned contract funds.

G. *The Agreements*

The financing agreement between the surety and the principal (referred to herein as the "Financing Agreement"[52]) must be carefully drafted in order to assure that the surety is well protected.[53] Among other things, the Financing Agreement needs to set forth in detail the structure of the arrangement between the parties, and the specific means by which the loaned funds will be controlled, and the timetable for repayment.

To start, the Financing Agreement must recite and reaffirm the indemnity obligations of the principal and the indemnitors in favor of the surety. The Financing Agreement also *must* include a statement regarding the principal's default on its bonded obligations (or inevitable default in the absence of the surety's agreement to finance), the request by the principal and indemnitors that the surety provide financing and the surety's decision to provide financing in order to satisfy its obligations under the performance bond (or decision to provide financing in order to prevent a default which will result in a demand on the surety's performance bond). The Financing Agreement should also include an acknowledgement that the surety's loan is a financial accommodation to the principal and indemnitors, who are direct beneficiaries of the loan.

---

50   *See* 11 U.S.C. § 547 (2008).
51   *See* 41 U.S.C. § 15(b) (2008).
52   The financing agreement can have a number of different titles–"Loan and Security Agreement," "Joint Control Trust Agreement" or "Financing and Collateral Agreement," to name a few. The particular title given to the document is not of high importance, so long as the necessary terms are included.
53   Cross-reference forms in BOND DEFAULT MANUAL (Duncan L. Clore, Richard E. Towle & Michael J. Sugar, Jr. eds., 3d ed. 2005).

It is imperative that the Financing Agreement contain a statement that the surety is not obligated to provide funding, and that the funding can be stopped at any time and for any reason, at the sole discretion of the surety. Also, the Financing Agreement should provide that the principal will execute voluntary letters of default and termination for each bonded project and give them to the surety. It should then be within the surety's sole discretion as to when, if ever, the surety should take over the bonded projects and send the letters of default to the corresponding bond obligees.

With respect to funding, the Financing Agreement must set forth a specific and comprehensive definition of the surety's loss (in other words, each and every expense, loss and/or expenditure by the surety which must be repaid by the principal and indemnitors) and the collateral security being provided by the principal and indemnitors in exchange for the surety's financing. The value of the collateral provided should be commensurate with the amount of financing being provided, but may go so far as to grant the surety lien rights in all personal and real property of the principal and indemnitors. Regardless of its value, the surety will also need to assure that its lien rights are perfected after the Financing Agreement is executed, including the execution and filing of trust deeds against real property and the filing of UCC-1 financing statements. Laws can vary from state to state with respect to the perfecting of a security interest, and the surety should consult the applicable law to assure that it has properly perfected its security interests for that jurisdiction.

Frequently, the Financing Agreement provides for the establishment of a special bank account ("Special Account") into which bonded contract funds and the money loaned by the surety will be deposited. Regardless of the type of account established, the surety will also want to include a statement in the Financing Agreement that the Special Account funds are trust funds solely for the uses and purposes set forth in the Financing Agreement.[54] Further, if the principal is already a customer of the bank where the Special Account is established, the surety must include a provision stating that the Special Account is not affected by any previous relationship or transactions between the bond principal and

---

54 The surety must consult the applicable state law regarding the formation of trusts for any other terms which must be included in order to properly establish the Special Account as a trust.

the selected bank, and that the funds cannot be used to offset any other debt owed by the principal to the bank.

The surety will also want to include a provision requiring the bank to notify the surety if any other creditor of the principal attempts to garnish or lien the Special Account funds. This will allow the surety to go to court to have any such garnishment or lien removed. Finally, the Financing Agreement should require the principal to provide a letter of direction for each bonded project, instructing the bond obligees to make all future payments to the principal and surety jointly and transmit all payment to the surety for deposit into the Special Account. This allows the surety to monitor the payments being received and afford the surety greater control over the situation. In some cases when the existence of the Financing Agreement is confidential, the payment instructions to the obligee can simply be to pay into a designated numbered account rather than disclosing the surety's financing role.

In addition to establishing the Special Account, the Financing Agreement should specifically set out the uses for the funds deposited in the Special Account, including a specification of which overhead expenses, if any, are to be paid from the Special Account. If the surety opts to only finance the principal's completion of bonded work, then the Financing Agreement should set forth that the Special Account is solely for labor and material costs which are necessary to complete the work on bonded projects for which the surety would be liable under its bonds.

Finally, the Financing Agreement should set out the timetable for the principal and its indemnitors to repay the surety. This includes setting out the specific circumstances under which the surety is permitted to sell the assets that were pledged as collateral security. The sale of the collateral security is usually conditioned upon a default of the repayment obligations, but the particular facts and circumstances of the situation may call for the sale of collateral as a means of making periodic payments. The surety may also want to include in the Financing Agreement a waiver by the principal and its indemnitors of any claims that they might have alleged against the surety prior to and up to the execution of the Financing Agreement, thereby depriving the principal and indemnitors of the ability to assert any such claims as justification for failure to repay the surety.

With a carefully drafted Financing Agreement, the surety can avoid many of the hazards that might accompany the surety's decision to finance its bond principal. Because there may be facts and circumstances unique to the bond principal and jurisdiction in question, which require modifications to or alterations of the standard provisions used in such agreements, the surety may want to consider utilizing outside counsel to review its Financing Agreement before execution.

H. Joint Control Accounts

When establishing a Special Account under the Financing Agreement, the surety can opt for one of several types of accounts that will allow the surety to exercise control over the principal's expenditure of the funds. Prior to the execution of the Financing Agreement, the surety will need to find a bank that is willing to accommodate the terms and conditions agreed to by the parties and set forth in the Financing Agreement.

The most common type of Special Account is the joint control account. With this type of account, all bonded contract funds and funds provided by the surety are deposited into a single account. Thereafter, both the principal and the surety must sign any check drawn on the account. As such, the principal cannot make any payment unless the surety agrees that the payment is necessary and allowed under the terms of the Financing Agreement. However, this type of account can prove time consuming for the surety and lead to logistical problems under certain circumstances. For instance, if the principal is required to make an immediate payment, it will be unable to do so unless the surety has a local representative who is authorized to sign the joint control account checks.

There are other types of account structures available. For instance, the surety can elect to establish two different special accounts, meaning one for the surety and one for the principal, and establish a corresponding special operating account. No money is held in the special operating account at any time. Instead, the principal presents the surety with any number of bills which must be paid, and writes checks drawn on the special operating account. Once the surety agrees to pay some or all of the bills presented, the surety transfers funds from its special account to the principal's special account. After the checks are sent out to the payees and received back by the bank, the bank transfers the funds from the principal's special account into the special operating account. Under this arrangement, the principal is only able to pay those bills that the surety agrees should be paid. If the special operating account is ever overdrawn, then the surety immediately knows that the principal has made payments which were not approved by the surety.

There may be other types of joint control accounts available, but irrespective of the type of account established, the surety will want to maintain as much control over the disbursement of funds as is reasonably possible. The surety must take into consideration the cost and time associated with monitoring the type of Special Account agreed to by the parties, and it is incumbent upon the surety to find a bank that is willing to honor the terms of the Financing Agreement. Once the Special Account is established, the surety must continue to conscientiously monitor the use of its funds by the principal.

I. *Control of Overhead Expenses*

Because it can be difficult to apportion overhead costs, and because the amount of overhead being paid by the surety may change over time, it is necessary for the surety to include special terms in the Financing Agreement regarding the payment of overhead. Although overhead costs are not directly attributable to the performance of the bonded work, they obviously must be paid in order for a financially troubled principal to stay in business and fulfill its obligations. There are several means of addressing the surety's concerns regarding the payment of overhead expenses.

The surety may decide not to include a provision in the Financing Agreement that obligates the surety to pay a specific amount of overhead, and instead require that the principal seek the surety's approval of any overhead payments to be made from the Special Account. This allows the surety to determine on a case-by-case basis whether it will pay particular overhead expenses. Alternatively, the surety can agree to pay a predetermined percentage of the principal's overhead. The surety could agree to pay additional overhead expenses as it sees fit, but would not be required to do so under the Financing Agreement.

Regardless of how the surety determines what overhead expenses it will pay, the surety must be sure to address the issue prior to the execution of the Financing Agreement. The principal will almost certainly want the surety to pay for all overhead expenses, and the failure to address the issue in detail can lead to disputes between the parties.

VI. Completion by the Bond Obligee

The surety generally has the option of allowing the obligee to complete the bonded project on its own, then indemnifying the obligee for covered expenses up to the penal sum of the bond. This method is frequently chosen when the contract balance in the obligee's possession exceeds the anticipated cost-to-complete plus unpaid payables. In determining whether this is the best course of action, the surety must carefully weigh a host of considerations. The exposure to the surety can be expected to increase when it relinquishes control over completion to a third-party obligee.[55]

A. *Limitations on the Surety's Right to Require Completion by the Obligee*

As always, the surety must first review the terms of its bond to determine its available options for fulfilling its bond obligations. Unless the bond or applicable law expressly requires otherwise, the surety has the option of allowing the obligee to complete any remaining work itself. For instance, the AIA performance bond form specifically allows the surety to waive its performance and tender options, and instead simply conduct an investigation, determine the amount for which it may be liable and make a payment.

The Miller Act performance bond form required for federal contracts does not explicitly set forth the options available to the surety, but case law indicates that the surety's only obligation is to pay monetary damages arising from the bond principal's default.[56] Thus, the surety also has the option of having the obligee complete bonded federal projects. It is clear that, in most situations, the surety has the option of simply paying the obligee for completion costs beyond the remaining contract balance.

---

[55] There are a number of books, articles and papers that discuss the completion by the obligee option, including Deborah S. Griffin & Stephen J. Beatty, *Completion by the Bond Obligee*, in BOND DEFAULT MANUAL 269, 269-86 (Duncan L. Clore, Richard E. Towle & Michael J. Sugar, Jr. eds., 3d ed. 2005) and the citations contained therein.

[56] *See, e.g.*, United States v. Seaboard Sur. Co., 817 F.2d 956, 959 (2d Cir. 1987); Trinity Universal Ins. Co. v. United States, 382 F.2d 317, 321 (5th Cir. 1967).

However, the court's decision in one case, *Continental Realty Corp. v. Andrew J. Crevolin Co.*,[57] indicates that this is not always the case, and that the surety's decision to "do nothing" may leave the surety vulnerable. In *Continental*, the surety issued a performance bond wherein the surety had the right either to take over completion of the project or to pay the obligee the reasonable cost of completion minus any contract balance at the time of the default.[58] Rather than elect either of those two options, the surety chose to deny the obligee's bond claim. The court later held that the surety had breached its obligation to the obligee by failing to exercise either of the performance options specified in the bond. Thus, the surety's liability was theoretically expanded to the full amount of damages sustained by the obligee as a result of the breach of the bond without regard to the penal sum limit of the bond.[59] Thus, before electing to do nothing and allow the obligee to perform, the surety must be certain that this is a viable action under the bond and applicable law.

B. Factors to be Considered by Surety

A surety is never permitted, in fact, to do nothing in response to a performance bond claim. As stated previously, a surety must first conduct a reasonable investigation of any alleged default and associated demand on the bond. Only then can the surety determine the appropriate course of action. In making its decision to allow obligee completion, there are certain factors that the surety must consider.

First, experience tells us that the surety is better at mitigating completion costs than an obligee or project owner. Where a surety is motivated to complete remaining work for the least cost possible, obligees often view performance bonds as a blank check to be written when the project is completed. Believing that it will ultimately collect its excess completion costs from either the defaulted contractor or its surety, an obligee-owner will often finish the project in the manner it had envisioned all along, with never a shortage of manpower, supervision, materials and equipment. In addition, in cases where the obligee is

---

57 Cont'l Realty Corp. v. Andrew J. Crevolin Co., 380 F. Supp. 246 (S.D. W. Va. 1974).
58 *Id.* at 248.
59 *Id.* at 252.

completing, there are the inevitable disputes over betterments and the obligee's attempt to make the surety liable for post-default changes. By remanding control to the obligee, the surety's loss exposure is normally increased pending a final resolution of liability.

Second, an obligee will often limit the surety's access to the project post-default once the surety has elected not to perform. The disadvantage here is that the obligee will often continue to build its case against the defaulted contractor and surety by documenting problems in the principal's work as it is uncovered by a third-party completion contractor. This is a risk that, for instance, would not exist where the surety takes over using the principal as the completion contractor.

Third, when a surety elects to take over a project itself, it is usually afforded the benefit of a takeover agreement that expressly preserves its rights and defenses under the bond. Conversely, as mentioned previously, a surety that elects to allow the obligee to assume control over the completion process is sometimes precluded from objecting to the actions the obligee undertook to complete the bonded work.

There are several other considerations that may factor into the surety's decision-making process, depending on the particular facts and circumstances of the situation. These include: (1) the financial viability of the principal (and other indemnitors); (2) the ability to avoid disputes with other creditors over the contract balance; and (3) the surety's appetite for litigation.

The aforementioned risks are balanced against the main benefit of not performing. The surety, by electing to do nothing, avoids the immediate cash outlay attendant with funding the completion of a construction project. There is no need to pay contractors (often on a time-and-materials basis), suppliers, consultants, lawyers, construction managers, etc., on what is undoubtedly a troubled project with an upset obligee. If the surety believes that any declaration of default by the obligee was improper (and is ultimately proven correct in that position), then the surety has saved significant expense in completing a project for which it had no underlying liability.

But any short-term "savings" may be simply deferred until the obligee completes the project[60] and elects to pursue any excess

---

60 The federal performance bond form does not require the surety to make a payment until after the work is completed and the final completion cost has been determined. *See* 48 C.F.R. 49.406 (2008). However, the AIA

completion costs against the principal and surety, often in litigation. In such a case, the surety often faces an increased exposure from an obligee that has "gold plated" its completion effort along with the attorneys' fees associated with repelling such a claim. On the other hand, it is often understood among the parties that the underlying project, while undoubtedly troubled, will be the subject of litigation regardless of the completion costs. In such cases, the specter of litigation and its associated costs will exist regardless of whether the surety performs or not.

In the end, a surety's decision to do nothing hinges on (1) whether the surety believes that the default is improper, (2) the likely excess completion costs, if any, and (3) the surety's ability to later cover for any damages assessed against the performance bond.

VII. Comparing the Various Performance Bond Forms

Any analysis concerning a surety's completion options under a bond must logically start at the source document. Although there are "industry" standard bond forms, such as the AIA 312[61] and AIA 311,[62] which do set out a surety's options, many bonds do not have that same specificity. This last category of bond form merely recites defeasance

---

performance bond form requires the surety to tender payment "as soon as practicable" following a determination of what the reasonable completion cost will be. AIA 312, *supra* note 36, at para. 4.

Further, the bond obligee may insist on waiting until its actual completion costs have been incurred before accepting payment from the surety. In those cases, the surety is faced with having committed itself to pay for the completion costs, while simultaneously having surrendered control over completion costs to the obligee. If the bond obligee has been hostile or contentious with the principal, then the surety can expect that its own relationship with the obligee will be difficult and the completion costs will be driven higher. This can lead to later disputes with the obligee regarding what are legitimate completion costs, and it may be difficult for the surety to determine whether the obligee's costs are rightfully recoverable under the bond. The surety can opt to monitor the obligee's completion effort, but this reduces the amount of effort and money saved by opting to have the obligee complete the work itself.

61   AIA 312, *supra* note 36.
62   AIA Document A 311-1970, *Performance Bond* (Am. Ins. of Architects 1970) [hereinafter "AIA 311"].

language and not much more. A typical defeasance bond innocuously recites that if the "contractor shall promptly and faithfully perform [the] contract . . . then this obligation shall be void; otherwise it shall remain in full force and effect."[63] Nothing is mentioned concerning the surety's options such as financing the contractor, taking over the work, or tendering a new contractor.

Such a defeasance bond may leave the uninitiated scratching their heads in puzzlement as to a surety's completion options. For the surety industry, the answer is a bit like discussing the unwritten English Constitution: tradition provides the answer. Taking this approach results in the conclusion that the surety's traditional options of financing the contractor, taking over the work and tendering[64] are implied terms which

---

[63] Standard Accident Ins. Co. v. Rose, 234 S.W.2d 728, 730 (Ky. 1950). *See also* 4 PHILIP L. BRUNER & PATRICK J. O'CONNOR, BRUNER & O'CONNOR ON CONSTRUCTION LAW § 12:14 (West 2008) [hereinafter "BRUNER & O'CONNOR ON CONSTRUCTION LAW"].

[64] The applicable state common law supplies the "tradition" along with surety industry practices. In the tradition permeating these defeasance bonds, the surety's options "were perceived as the specific 'means and methods' to be implemented by the surety in satisfying its bond obligations. . . ." This conclusion is similar to the tradition in the construction world, where the party shouldering the obligation to achieve a certain outcome is also granted the right to choose the means and methods to reach that outcome. *See, e.g.*, Stephen M. Rae et al., *A Surety's Inherent Right to Perform* 11 (unpublished paper submitted at the Eighteenth Annual Northeast Surety & Fidelity Claims Conference on Sept. 27, 2007); BRUNER & O'CONNOR ON CONSTRUCTION LAW, *supra* note 63, at § 12:77. Of course, in the surety/construction world, as in the real world, some people's traditions are different than those of "mainstream" society. *See, e.g.*, Sch. Bd. of Broward County v. Great Am. Ins. Co., 807 So.2d 750 (Fla. Dist. Ct. App. 2002) (ruling that the surety's tender of a new principal with a new bond did not "correct" the defunct principal's default). The *Broward* defeasance bond did not expressly prohibit a tender. In fact, no surety options were mentioned other than the surety "correcting" the default. In breathing life into this dead phraseology, the court held that the surety's obligation to "correct" the default meant that the surety had to take over the project. *Id.* at 751-52. *See also* Millgard Corp. v. E.E. Cruz/Nab/Frontier-Kemper, No. 99 Civ. 2952 (LBS), 2002 WL 31812710, at *12 (S.D.N.Y. Dec. 12, 2002) (commenting that "[t]he type of obligation imposed on the surety and

are read into a defeasance bond, supported by the significant legal defense of "mitigation."

Yet, tradition is not everything when it comes to a defeasance bond. There is a sub-class of defeasance bonds that provide for "payment" as the bond's only performance option, written in the form of an indemnity obligation. Despite the "payment" only language, certain of these bonds are equipped with options other than payment and ones which are not based on tradition. This important sub-class is the Miller Act bond for federal projects.[65] Unlike most defeasance bonds, a Miller Act bond comes with federal regulations which supplant or supplement a surety's traditional options.[66]

---

thus the surety's 'menu' of remedial options upon a principal's default is determined by the language of the bond itself rather than simply the label 'performance' bond"). Unfortunately, the *Millgard* court's rationale does not address dilemmas such as the one confronting the surety in *Broward*. If a bond's menu of options is vague, such as providing an option to "correct" the default, as in *Broward*, then a court's refusal to accept the surety's traditional options as implied terms may lead to counterintuitive results such as the outcome in *Broward*. Logically, a surety tendering a new contractor should "correct" a default notwithstanding the *Broward* court's contrary conclusion. Eradicating bond forms such as the *Broward* bond is not easy. Unlike the insurance industry with insurance policies, in many settings a surety does not control bond terms. Instead, the obligee mandates the bond's terms. This marketplace reality impedes a surety's ability to eliminate problematic bond forms.

[65] 40 U.S.C. § 3131 is commonly called the Miller Act. 40 U.S.C.A. § 3131 (West 2006). 48 C.F.R. § 53.301-25 (2008) specifies the Miller Act bond form, a Standard Form SF-25. "[T]he Federal Standard . . .Performance Bond is a type of statutory indemnity bond that simply provides for "payment" as the only performance option." BRUNER & O'CONNOR ON CONSTRUCTION LAW, *supra* note 63, at § 12:18.

[66] *See* Rae, *supra* note 64, at 1. "This bond form has left to the Miller Act, federal regulations, and courts and boards of contract appeal the task of defining the scope of the surety's obligations." BRUNER & O'CONNOR ON CONSTRUCTION LAW, *supra* note 63, at §12:18. *See also* Appeal of Milner Constr. Co., DOTBCA No. 2043, 91-3 B.C.A. ¶ 24,195 (D.O.T.B.C.A. July 17, 1991), where the administrative judge determined the scope of the Miller Act surety's obligation by referring to the default clause proscribed by 48 C.F.R. 52.249-10, ruling that by issuing the bond guaranteeing that the principal would perform all of the principal's

Performance Options Available to the Surety

Many subcontract bonds in the marketplace contain terms adopted from two of the bond forms already mentioned: the AIA 311 and the AIA 312. In the past, many subcontract bonds borrowed heavily from the AIA 311, and now, increasingly, from the AIA 312. Subcontract bonds, however, do defy any broad generalizations as to completion options because so many subcontract bonds are customized. Despite this impediment, the widespread usage of these AIA-based subcontract bonds dictates their inclusion in this chapter.

To start this section, we will compare a surety's options under an AIA 312 with the options available under an AIA 311. Next, we will discuss a surety's options under a defeasance bond, including a Miller Act bond. Finally, we will conclude with a brief discussion of a surety's options under two AIA-based subcontract bonds. With each bond type, as discussed previously in this chapter, there are six surety options to consider: financing the principal; takeover; tender; obligee completion; cash payment, also known as buying back the bond; and denying the claim.

A quick glance at the AIA 312 reveals that the provisions concerning a surety's options reside in paragraphs 4, 5 and 6. In particular, a surety's options are laid out in paragraph 4 in a series of subparagraphs. The phrase "financing the Contractor" or other similar nomenclature does not appear in these paragraphs. Nevertheless, paragraph 4.1 does contain language which permits the surety to select a financing completion option. The language in paragraph 4.1 provides the surety with the option to promptly "arrange for the Contractor, with the consent of the Owner, to perform and complete the Construction Contract. . . ."[67]

The bond's language permits a surety to select the principal to complete the bonded contract, with or without the surety funding that

---

contractual obligations, the surety bound itself to satisfy any liability which might arise under the default clause.

[67] The complete text of paragraph 4.1 and its preamble in paragraph 4 read as follows: "When the Owner has satisfied the conditions of Paragraph 3, the Surety shall promptly and at the Surety's expense take one of the following actions: 4.1 Arrange for the Contractor, with the consent of the Owner, to perform and complete the Construction Contract; . . ." The term "promptly" as used in paragraph 4 is really a "reasonable promptness" standard because of the interplay between the AIA 312's paragraph 4 and paragraph 5. The "reasonable promptness" standard resides in paragraph 5.

undertaking, depending, of course, on the principal's financial condition. The catch, of course, is that the obligee must consent to the principal returning to the project. Many times, the principal-obligee relationship is irretrievably broken by this time, with finger pointing and mudslinging having preceded the principal's termination. If this is the surety's situation, then the obligee may prevent the surety from selecting this financing option by withholding consent.

The AIA 311 does not have a series of numbered subparagraphs similar to the AIA 312's paragraph 4.[68] Looking at the AIA 311's second page, however, there is some pertinent language above the two Arabic numbered subparagraphs. In this preamble resides a surety option phrased such that "the surety *may* promptly remedy the default."[69] (emphasis added).

---

[68] Some commentators have noted that while the AIA 312 generally codifies the surety's common law performance options, the AIA 311 has been held to restrict those common law options, citing National Fire Ins. Co. of Hartford v. Fortune Constr. Co., 320 F.3d 1260 (11th Cir. 2003), where the court ruled that the surety did not have the option to decline to perform and later tender the completion costs to the obligee instead of initially performing the work. *See* Rae, *supra* note 64, at 4. However, in Balfour Beatty Constr., Inc. v. Colonial Ornamental Iron Works, Inc., 986 F. Supp. 82, 85-6 (D.Conn. 1997), the court noted in dicta that a surety has the right to pay an obligee's completion costs in lieu of performance under a bond with A311 language. Compare *School Board of Broward County*, 807 So.2d at 750, where the court ruled that the surety who issued a defeasance bond could not tender a principal to "correct" the principal's default. The bond merely provided that the surety was to "correct" the principal's default within a reasonable time. Nothing was said about any surety options. The *Broward County* court ruled that "correct" meant the surety either had to serve as the general contractor or supervise the new completion contactor's work. *Id.* at 751. Given the counterintuitive outcome in *Broward*, that court's interpretation of the term "correct" should not receive general acceptance.

[69] The pertinent text for this part of the AIA 311 reads as follows: "Whenever Contractor shall be, and declared by the Owner to be in default under the Contract, the Owner having performed the Owner's obligations thereunder, the Surety *may* promptly remedy the default. . . ." *See* AIA 311, *supra* note 62 (emphasis added). In *Cooper Industries, Inc. v. Tarmac Roofing Systems, Inc.*, 276 F.3d 704 (5th Cir. 2002), the court construed this language in conjunction with the surety's other options

Taken at face value, this phrase grants the surety the option to promptly remedy the principal's default.[70] How the surety does so is left to the surety's discretion, but the surety must use the principal to do so.[71] Some jurisdictions follow the *L&A Contracting Co. v. Southern Concrete Services, Inc.* line of cases[72] where the obligee must first terminate the principal as a condition precedent to making a claim. Under this case authority, the surety inherently has the option to offer its principal as the surety's prompt remedy to the obligee's completion

---

under an AIA 311-based subcontract bond as follows: "IFIC reads the performance bond as affording IFIC three options upon Castro's default: (1) IFIC *may* remedy the default; or IFIC *shall* (2) take over and complete the contract; or (3) obtain a new contract for Cooper [tender a new principal]. IFIC does not contend that it obtained a new contract for Cooper, but asserts that it remedied Castro's default. For this to be correct, the default must have been one that, once remedied, allowed Castro to continue to perform under the contract. Any other interpretation of the first option would render superfluous IFIC's other two options, *i.e.*, completing the contract or obtaining a new contract for Cooper. [citations omitted] ('Courts must construe contracts so they give effect to all provisions.'). Therefore, if Castro was unable to complete the contract, even with IFIC's assistance, then IFIC was required to complete the contract or obtain a new contract for Cooper." *Id.* at 712 (emphasis in original).

70   See AIA 311, *supra* note 62. A surety has the right to exercise this option in its discretion, but if the surety does so, then the surety must use the principal as its remedy. *Cooper Industries*, 276 F.3d at 712. Please note the *Cooper Industries* court's interpretation of this bond's options. If a surety does not select the remedy option, then the surety faces a mandatory choice between the last two options: completing the contract, that is, a takeover, or obtaining a new contract for the obligee, that is, a tender. For an opinion which may be used to supplement the *Cooper Industries* court's interpretation of the AIA 311, *see* George J. Bachrach & Matthew L. Silverstein, *Financing The Principal*, in BOND DEFAULT MANUAL 155, 174 (Duncan L. Clore, Richard E. Towle & Michael J. Sugar, Jr. eds., 3d ed. 2005), where the author opines that the "Complete the Contract" option under paragraph 1 includes both the option to finance by using the principal as the takeover contractor and the option to take over using another contractor.
71   *Cooper Industries*, 276 F.3d at 712.
72   L&A Contracting Co. v. S. Concrete Servs., Inc., 17 F.3d 106 (5th Cir. 1994).

demand, even post-default termination. Because the obligee does not have a valid performance bond claim without a default termination, and the surety is granted the option to promptly remedy this default termination, it follows logically that a principal's previous default termination does not bar the surety from selecting the principal as the surety's remedy.[73] Of course, the surety and principal must take steps to remedy the alleged defaults which formed the basis of the earlier default termination or the surety is not satisfying the remedy requirement of this option.

Unlike the AIA 312's paragraph 4.1, however, the AIA 311's "Surety may promptly remedy" option does not require the obligee's consent. This language's flexibility makes the AIA 311 facially more appealing to the surety than the AIA 312's paragraph 4.1.

There is an important distinction between the AIA 311 and AIA 312 which does reduce the apparent superior appeal of the AIA 311's financing option. Although both bonds use the word "promptly" to describe the alacrity with which a surety is to exercise its options, the AIA 312 further qualifies this standard in paragraph 5.[74] There, the AIA

---

73   For example, in Hunt Constr. Group, Inc. v. National Wrecking Corp., 542 F. Supp.2d 87, 95 (D.D.C. 2008), the court suggested that the sureties' "remedy the default" option included doing something to aid the principal in speeding up the work, such as hiring more trucks, more workers, more oversight, or whatever, in their judgment, would assist the principal. These remedial activities may occur after the principal's default termination given the *L&A Contracting* line of cases which the *Hunt* court followed in rejecting the obligee's claim and rendering a summary judgment of dismissal in favor of the sureties. *Id.* at 92, 95. The *Hunt* court's suggestion about the surety's "remedy the default" option presumes, correctly, that the AIA 311 surety can return its principal to the project post-default. A different conclusion would contradict the *L&A Contracting* rationale the *Hunt* court used to dismiss the obligee's claim and also read the "remedy the default" option out of the bond. Further support for this proposition is furnished by the *Cooper Industries* decision. There, the court interpreted the AIA 311 surety's "remedy the default" option as a solution which allowed the principal to continue to perform under the contract once the default is remedied. *Cooper Industries*, 276 F.3d at 712.

74   In pertinent part, paragraph 5 provides that: "If the Surety does not proceed as provided in Paragraph 4 with *reasonable promptness*, the Surety shall be deemed to be in default on this Bond fifteen days after

312 requires a surety to proceed with "*reasonable* promptness" in exercising its options under paragraph 4.[75] Note that the AIA 312's usage

---

75   receipt of an additional written notice from the Owner...". *See* AIA 312, *supra* note 36 (emphasis added).

75   *Id.* The court in *International Fidelity Insurance Co. v. County of Rockland*, 98 F. Supp.2d 400 (S.D.N.Y. 2000), interpreted the surety's reasonable promptness obligation under an AIA 312 bond as the surety promptly either: (1) taking one of the steps specified in the bond necessary to initiate the steps necessary to resume construction; or (2) notifying the obligee it will not do so and that the obligee should step in. *Id.* at 420-421. In coming to this conclusion, the *Rockland* court distinguished *International Fidelity Insurance Co. v. County of Chautauqua*, 245 A.D.2d 1056 (N.Y. App. Div. 1997). Unlike in *Rockland*, the *Chautauqua* court defined the surety's reasonable promptness obligation as an obligation to complete the contract promptly. *Chautauqua*, 245 A.D.2d at 1057. Obviously, there is a substantial difference between initiating an activity within a certain timeframe and having to complete an activity within that same timeframe. Moreover, the *Rockland* court appropriately rejected the *Chautauqua* court's improper interpretation of what appears to have been the AIA 312's paragraph 6. Not appreciating some important legal distinctions, the *Chautauqua* court levied both actual and liquidated damages against the surety. In rejecting the *Chautauqua* decision, the *Rockland* court politely noted that there was a well recognized distinction in standard trade usage between "'actual damages caused by delayed performance' on the one hand, [AIA 312 subparagraph 6.3 which provides for the exclusivity of liquidated damages unless they are not specified by the contract] and 'additional legal, design professional and delay costs' on the other [the AIA 312's subparagraph 6.2]." *Rockland*, 98 F. Supp.2d at 420 (emphasis added). Noting that the *Chautauqua* court had made a simple conclusion, without analysis or citation, that the term "delay costs" included "delay damages," the *Rockland* court rejected the *Chautauqua* court's decision as contrary to extensive literature and case law. Applying this extensive authority, the *Rockland* court decided that delay damages were not recoverable under the AIA 312's subparagraph 6.2 because that subparagraph only included costs, and not damages. Importantly, the *Rockland* court also recognized that damages (costs) resulting from a surety's delay under subparagraph 6.2 are merely for the surety's delay in arranging for the completion or taking over of the contract, and not for the surety's delay in completing the underlying contract. The practical outcome was the *Rockland* court refused to permit a double recovery, as was granted in the *Chautauqua*

of the qualifier "reasonable" provides the surety with a more flexible performance standard than the AIA 311.[76] Even though there is a poorly

---

decision. In that decision, the *Chautauqua* court erroneously allowed the recovery of both liquidated damages and lost income damages by declaring the loss income damages recoverable "delay costs" despite the extensive authority holding that these damages should have been categorized as actual damages subsumed by the liquidated damages clause.

76 A very good discussion of the flexible nature of AIA 312's reasonable promptness standard is contained in *Seaboard Surety Co. v. Town of Greenfield*, 266 F. Supp.2d 189 (D. Mass. 2003). Relying on some commentators and cases, the *Greenfield* court formulated this standard as to whether the surety's response was reasonable, given the default of the principal and considering the status and complexity of the remaining work, with the surety provided a reasonable amount of time for investigating and selecting from the bond's performance options. *Id.* at 194. Likewise, the surety is allowed a reasonable time to perform a due diligence of the work completed and to analyze the tasks remaining for completion. *Id.* As such, the surety's time spent investigating a claim and formulating the proper response is part of the surety's reasonably prompt performance. *Id. See also* Solai & Cameron, Inc. v. Plainfield Cmty. Consol. Sch. Dist. No. 202, 871 N.E.2d 944, 957 (Ill. App. Ct. 2007) (ruling that the obligee's demand for the surety to perform was improper because that demand did not afford the surety any time to act with reasonable promptness to investigate its options under paragraph 4 and then decide a course of conduct to either complete the project or pay damages). In *Solai & Cameron*, the obligee's demand was made nearly contemporaneously with the notice of the subprincipal's termination. *Id.* The bond at issue was a subcontract bond based on the AIA 312. *Cf.* Developers Sur. & Indem. Co. v. Dismal River Club, L.L.C., No. 4:07CV3148, 2008 WL 2223872 (D. Neb. May 3, 2008) (ruling that paragraph 5 imposed an implied obligation on an obligee to exercise that paragraph's 15-day surety cure notice option within a reasonable time and that failure to do so discharged the surety from any duty to perform). *But see* Dadeland Depot, Inc. v. St. Paul Fire & Marine Ins. Co., 483 F.3d 1265, 1277-78 (2007) (reversing a summary judgment in the surety's favor, determining that there was a triable issue of material fact as to the surety's reasonable promptness under paragraph 5 when the surety's response to the obligee's 15-day cure notice in the form of a denial was 12 days late, the court noting that it disagreed with the district court's finding that the surety acted "with reasonable promptness"). On the other

reasoned AIA 312 decision which effectively rejects this standard, the AIA 312 still has an advantage over the AIA 311 because this aberrant case runs counter to the overwhelming weight of authority that is in favor of enforcing these AIA 312 provisions, and this trend allows a surety to substantially discount this decision's potentially adverse impact.[77]

---

hand, the AIA 311 does not specify a standard for the surety's response beyond "promptly." Nevertheless, the court in Hunt Constr. Group, Inc. v. National Wrecking Corp., 542 F. Supp.2d 87, 94-96 (D.D.C. 2008), endorsed an AIA 311 surety's right to investigate, and the obligee's need to cooperate with that investigation, by noting that on top of its other sins, the obligee in that case "even then [after failing to timely declare a default] sat on its hands and failed to assist the Sureties in their legitimate investigation." *See also* Howard Constr. Co. v. Teddy Woods Constr. Co., 817 S.W.2d 556 (Mo. App. 1991) (ruling that the surety failed to promptly complete or obtain completion of the bonded subcontracts when the surety could not secure replacement contractors before the obligee did so two and then five weeks after the default). In *Howard*, the surety had a potential replacement contractor candidate meet the obligee within the five weeks, but this candidate declined the opportunity. The obligee completed some work within the five weeks to keep the projects moving. The court allowed the obligee to recover its damages rejecting the surety's exoneration argument that the obligee had unilaterally taken over the projects thereby precluding the surety from completing the work. *Id.* In all material respects, the bond was an unadulterated AIA 311 form even though it was a subcontract bond.

[77] In a poorly reasoned, unpublished decision, the court ignored most of the AIA 312's provisions along with any case law which stood in the court's path towards a pre-determined result. See Kilpatrick Bros. Painting v. Chippewa Hills Sch. Dist., No. 262396, 2006 WL 664210 (Mich. Ct. App. Mar. 16, 2006). The *Kilpatrick* court chose to rip up the AIA 312 bond thereby sticking the surety with the completion bill, reasoning that "[a]s the school district argues, the bond does not guarantee that, at the time of default termination, all of the options listed in ¶4 will be available." *Id.* at *6. In *Kilpatrick*, the obligee had hired contractors to correct and complete the principal's work before default termination. *Id.* at *7. After default termination, the obligee called on the surety, which indicated it was investigating under a complete reservation of rights, with the surety, evidently, making no specific objection to the obligee's hiring of completing contractors pre-default termination. *Id.* at *6. In the ensuing litigation, the surety argued that the obligee had improperly affected the surety's right to select from paragraph 4's options by hiring

Nevertheless, in comparing the two bond forms, one should partially discount the advantages of the AIA 312's reasonable promptness standard because paragraph 4.1 lacks flexibility. The reason for this comparative lack of flexibility lies in paragraph 4.1's requirement that a surety secure the obligee's consent to return the contractor to the project. In contrast, the AIA 311 does not require a surety to secure the obligee's consent before returning the contractor to the project. With the AIA 312, however, if the obligee objects to the contractor returning to the project, then the surety may have to forego paragraph 4.1's financing option, and explore other completion alternatives available under the bond.[78]

---

contractors pre-default termination, which action exonerated the surety. *Id.* at *3. Unfortunately, the *Kilpatrick* court concluded that "by electing to investigate without objection, Merchants (the surety) effectively made a choice to proceed under ¶4.4 of the bond." *Id.* at *6. This reasoning left the surety with one option: pay or deny the claim. To reach this outcome, the *Kilpatrick* court eviscerated paragraph 5 by permitting letters issued 16 months after the default termination to "satisfy" paragraph 5's 15-day cure notice provision. *Id.* at *7. Although not specifically stated, it appears that the principal's work had been completed by the obligee's new contractors before these letters were sent. Supporting this conclusion is the nature of the obligee's "cure" letters. These letters demanded not performance with reasonable promptness, but payment. *Id.* By taking this approach, the *Kilpatrick* court ignored the clear purpose of the 15-day notice provision which is to provide a surety with an opportunity to cure. Further, the 15-day cure notice allows the obligee to prod and then remove the surety from the completion effort if the obligee does not believe the surety is proceeding with reasonable promptness. *Id.* The *Kilpatrick* decision is contrary to the overwhelming weight of authority on the AIA 312 bond. *See* BRUNER & O'CONNOR ON CONSTRUCTION LAW, *supra* note 63, at § 12.41 nn. 1-3, for the proposition that the AIA 312's notice provisions continue to be enforced strictly.

78 St. Paul Fire & Marine Insurance Co. v. City of Green River, 93 F. Supp.2d 1170 (D. Wyo. 2000), *aff'd*, 6 Fed. Appx. 828 (10th Cir. 2001), is an example of one such alternative. There, the surety retained a consultant who in turn hired some of the principal's employees to finish the project. The surety then elected to complete under the AIA 312's paragraph 4.2 which does not require obligee consent. If the surety is deemed to have added inappropriate conditions to its paragraph 4.2 election, however, a court may rule that the obligee's rejection of the surety's election does not exonerate the surety. *See generally* N.V. Heathorn, Inc. v. U.S. Fid. & Guar. Co., Nos. A112107, A112345, 2007

The surety is always concerned about limiting its potential maximum exposure to the bond amount, and, further, whether this exposure varies from project to project given that the AIA 312 and AIA 311 have different terms. With the AIA 312's paragraph 4.1 financing option, the surety's exposure is limited to the bond's penal sum amount.[79] Selecting

---

WL 141174 (Cal. Ct. App. Jan. 22, 2007) (referencing an unappealed ruling from a motion judge in a different lawsuit concerning the same surety and contractor in which the motion judge declined to exonerate the surety for this reason). Given this procedural history, the conditional paragraph 4.4 election issue was not before the *N.V. Heathorn* court. For this reason, and its unpublished/noncitable status, *N.V. Heathorn* does not have precedential value for the proposition that the surety may not condition its paragraph 4.2 election. Alternatively, if the obligee unreasonably refuses to consent to the principal returning to the project, then the surety may appropriately take the position that the obligee is unfairly depriving the surety of the benefit of its bargain which is the right to use the principal as a completion option. This argument is available in those jurisdictions in which there is a covenant of good faith and fair dealing implied in a contract. If an obligee unreasonably refuses to consent to the principal's return, then the obligee may have breached the implied covenant thereby relieving the surety of any liability. *See* RESTATEMENT (SECOND) OF CONTRACTS § 205 (2008). *See, e.g.*, Speedway SuperAmerica, L.L.C. v. Tropic Enters., Inc., 966 So.2d 1 (Fla. Dist. Ct. App. 2007) (applying the implied covenant to protect the parties' reasonable commercial expectations and reversing the trial court's ruling that the landlord had the unfettered right to deny consent where the lease did not contain any standard to measure the landlord's conduct in consenting or refusing to consent to an assignment, providing only that prior written consent was required). *Accord* Castle v. McKnight, 866 P.2d 323 (N.M. 1993).

79 BRUNER & O'CONNOR ON CONSTRUCTION LAW, *supra* note 63, at § 12:16 ("If the surety exercises option[] (1) [the AIA 312's paragraph 4.1's financing option] ... the surety's liability is limited to the amount of the bond."). A related consideration is what might happen if the surety finances the principal without a declared default termination under either the AIA 312 or the AIA 311. At least one court has determined that by financing a principal without first securing the obligee's consent, a surety does not waive either the AIA 312's conditions precedent under paragraph 3 or the 15-day cure provision granted by paragraph 5. Tishman Westside Constr. L.L.C. v. ASF Glass, Inc., 33 A.D. 3d 539, 540 (N.Y. App. Div. 2006). On the other hand, in an AIA 311 setting, an

this option grants the surety penal sum protection with the obligee's consent, but the surety must first leap the initial hurdle, which is securing the obligee's consent. However, this may not be possible.[80] So even after partially discounting the value of the AIA 312's financing option because that option requires the obligee's consent, this option "caps" the surety's exposure at the bond's penal sum amount.

---

aberrant decision resulted in the financing surety losing its subrogation rights. Liberty Mut. Ins. Co. v. Constr. Mgmt. Servs., Inc., No. 99 C 6906, 2004 WL 2271811 (N.D. Ill. Oct. 6, 2004). There, the surety did not secure the obligee's consent before financing the principal. If the surety had secured a declaration from the obligee that the principal was in default, then the surety would have avoided being blindsided by the subsequent adverse outcome. Citing the *L&A Contracting* line of cases and other authority, the *Liberty* court rejected the principal's voluntary letter of default and letter of direction because the obligee had not declared a default and termination. Reasoning that only the obligee had the right to declare a default under the bond, the *Liberty* court ruled this requisite condition precedent to the surety's liability was never triggered. Without any bond liability, the financing surety did not have any subrogation rights. *Id.* at *5. Under existing case law, the poor surety could not have reasonably anticipated this outcome. This case does demonstrate, however, that a surety should seriously consider securing the obligee's consent before financing, even though that consent is not required by the AIA 311 as a precursor to such financing.

80   See BRUNER & O'CONNOR ON CONSTRUCTION LAW, *supra* note 63, at § 12:16 for the rule that the surety liability is limited to its bond amount, if the surety selects the AIA 312's paragraph 4.1 financing option. The potential difficulty a surety may encounter in securing the obligee's consent to return a principal to the project is illustrated by St. Paul Fire & Marine Insurance Co. v. City of Green River, 93 F. Supp.2d 1170 (D. Wyo. 2000), *aff'd*, 6 Fed. Appx. 828 (10th Cir. 2001). The obligee in *Green River* refused to let the surety use the defaulted principal's personnel to finish the project even though the surety was proceeding pursuant to paragraph 4.2, which did not require the obligee's consent, instead of paragraph 4.1, which did require the obligee's consent. The *Green River* court rejected the obligee's argument that the surety was merely attempting to circumvent the AIA 312's consent requirement, as stipulated by paragraph 4.1. Green River, 93 F. Supp.2d at 1178. *See* BRUNER & O'CONNOR ON CONSTRUCTION LAW, *supra* note 63, at § 12:78 and n. 10.50.

Unfortunately, on the other hand, the AIA 311's financing option is less advantageous than the AIA 312's financing option with reference to bond penal sum protection. The surety runs the risk that these financing expenditures will not reduce the surety's exposure, as measured by the bond limits.[81] The solution is a separate written agreement with the obligee whereby the obligee agrees that funds supplied by the surety to the principal or completion contractor are credited against the bond's penal sum. If a surety does not secure such an agreement, then the surety's bond amount remains in its undiminished original sum, as does the surety's possible exposure. So even though the surety may select the AIA 311's financing option without first securing the obligee's consent, if the AIA 311 surety does so then that surety's exposure is not limited to the bond's penal sum.

The AIA 312 bond form also provides the surety the option of takeover. Paragraph 4.2 provides that the surety may undertake to perform and complete the construction contract itself, through its agents or through independent contractors.[82] This is an option even though three alternatives are presented, and the word "takeover" is not used. To carry out one of these alternatives, the surety can use the principal's employees and resources to complete without first securing the obligee's consent.[83]

---

[81] "Unless the obligee is notified of and consents to the surety's financing as made pursuant to the surety's performance bond obligation, sums advanced by the surety may not be credited against the limit of the bond amount." BRUNER & O'CONNOR ON CONSTRUCTION LAW, *supra* note 63, at § 12:78. *See also* George J. Bachrach & Matthew L. Silverstein, *Financing the Principal*, in BOND DEFAULT MANUAL 155, 174-75, 178 (Duncan L. Clore, Richard E. Towle & Michael J. Sugar, Jr. eds., 3d ed. 2005).

[82] The complete text of paragraph 4.2 and its preamble are as follows: "When the Owner has satisfied the conditions of Paragraph 3, the Surety shall promptly and at the Surety's expense take one of the following actions: . . . 4.2 Undertake to perform and complete the Construction Contract itself, through its agents or through independent principals; . . ." *See* AIA 312, *supra* note 36.

[83] *See Green River*, 93 F. Supp.2d at 1178 (reasoning that: "While the Board accuses St. Paul of trying to 'create a hybrid action from the two paragraphs' it is actually the Board that is attempting to graft the owner consent provision contained in Paragraph 4.1 onto the performance option actually selected by St. Paul, Paragraph 4.2. Because St. Paul had the right to utilize Westates personnel as part of its project team, St. Paul's

One way a surety may carry out this option is to contract with a consultant, although the use of a construction manager may suffice.[84] The consultant, or construction manager, in turn, hires or contracts with key employees or subcontractors of the principal.[85]

---

[84] plan to use such personnel could not constitute an anticipatory breach."). *But see* N.V. Heathorn, Inc. v. U.S. Fid. & Guar. Co., Nos. A112107, A112345, 2007 WL 141174 (Cal. Ct. App. Jan. 22, 2007).

[84] *Green River*, 93 F. Supp.2d at 1178 (noting that "it is common practice for a surety that elects to perform the project itself to hire the principal's employees under the direction of a consultant, just as St. Paul did here.").

[85] *Id. But see N.V. Heathorn*, 2007 WL 141174. Beyond its status as an unpublished, non-citable decision, this case does not set any precedent concerning a paragraph 4.2 election because the issues discussed by the court were not directly before that tribunal. Instead, the *N.V. Heathorn* court recited events from other related litigation. In *N.V. Heathorn*, the surety conditioned its paragraph 4.2 *Green River*-styled election to return its principal to the project with a reservation of rights. This reservation concerned the propriety of the principal's termination, limited the surety's exposure to the bond amount, and requested that the obligee not withhold any liquidated damages. The obligee rejected the surety's paragraph 4.2 election as inappropriately conditioned with terms contrary to the AIA 312. The surety's subsequent effort to secure a summary determination that the surety was exonerated failed after a motion judge sided with the obligee. This exoneration issue, however, was not before the *N.V. Heathorn* court, as the dispute under review was between the surety and its indemnitors, and not the surety and the obligee. Moreover, the *N.V. Heathorn* court noted that whether the bond actually did compel the obligee to accept an unconditional election under paragraph 4.2 was a legal issue that the court need not, and did not, resolve. Because the *Green River* exoneration issue was not fully before the *N.V. Heathorn* court, a surety still has a *Green River* exoneration defense available in California post-*N.V. Heathorn*. The obligee in the litigation related to this *N.V. Heathorn* case asserted that the surety waived all of its defenses if the surety proceeded under paragraph 4.2, including the surety's right to challenge the propriety of the principal's default. The issue now is what conditions, if any, the surety should consider attaching to its election understanding that there is no binding authority preventing the surety from conditioning its election. Please note that the surety's election under paragraph 4.2 in *Green River* was conditioned on a number of issues, including a reservation of rights and yet the court still exonerated the surety. *Green River*, 93 F. Supp.2d at 1172-1173. *See also* BRUNER &

Alternatively, the surety may undertake a formal re-bidding process complete with a solicitation for offers. With this process, the successful bidder enters into a completion contract directly with the surety. Although the obligee may complain that the surety is taking too much time, the surety's response is found in paragraph 4.2. This provision only requires the surety to promptly "undertake" this completion option, and not to complete that option within any set time.[86] So when paragraph 4.2

O'CONNOR ON CONSTRUCTION LAW, *supra* note 63, at § 12:79 n 15 (citing *N.V. Heathorn* for the following proposition: "Although the takeover surety has the discretion to award the completion contract to its defaulted principal, the surety is under no obligation to do so.").

[86] There is a difference between the reasonable promptness standard which applies to paragraph 4.1 versus the standard for paragraph 4.2. The distinction is based on paragraph 4.2's use of the word "undertake." Turning to the Webster's New World Dictionary definition of "undertake," the court in International Fidelity Insurance Co. v. County of Rockland, 98 F. Supp.2d 400, 420-22 (S.D.N.Y. 2000), noted that the response standard under option 4.2 was quite different than that under option 4.1 because: "The obligation that the drafters imposed on a surety ... was a very specific and limited one: to 'agree' or 'guarantee' to perform and complete; to *enter into* a commitment—that is, to 'contract'; and to 'take over' the completion obligation 'as a charge.' Once the surety has promptly *contracted* for and *entered into* its completion task— and certainly once it has actually 'taken over' that completion under a formal takeover agreement and commenced the work-it has fulfilled its obligation under 4.2." *Rockland*, 98 F. Supp.2d at 420-22 (emphasis added). In contrast, under the other sections of paragraph 4, including paragraph 4.1, the surety must either: (1) promptly undertake one of the specified alternatives necessary to initiate the steps required to resume construction, or (2) notify the owner that the surety will not do so and the owner should step in. *Id.* Under these options, the goal is to ensure that the resumption of construction will not be unduly delayed. *Id.* The practical distinction is one with a real world difference. Applying the *Rockland* court's reasoning, under paragraph 4.2, the takeover option, the surety may satisfy its completion obligation by executing a takeover agreement with the obligee, without the resumption of construction. *Id.* If the surety does not timely complete the project, the *Rockland* court noted, then that is a breach of the takeover agreement, and not the bond, because the surety's bond obligation under paragraph 4.2 was satisfied by the execution of the takeover agreement, and any subsequent performance, or lack thereof, is controlled by the takeover agreement, and not the bond.

is read in conjunction with paragraph 5's reasonable promptness standard, the obligee does not have a legitimate complaint provided that the surety has undertaken, that is, the surety has promptly *contracted* for and *entered into* its completion task, which certainly includes a takeover agreement.[87]

Further, so long as the surety is proceeding with reasonable promptness with the completion of the contract, the obligee may not be able to terminate the surety for finishing the contract later than the original completion day.[88] Instead, the obligee's remedy is liquidated damages which are the surety's obligation under the AIA 312 if the late

---

[87] *Id.* On the other hand, under paragraph 4.1, the financing option, the surety's initial completion obligation is satisfied by taking the steps necessary to resume construction, and not merely by the execution of an agreement with the obligee, if such an agreement is sought. *Id.* As for paragraph 4.3, the tender option, the necessary steps the surety must take are specified in great detail, such as obtaining bids, and the surety must promptly take these steps and complete them in order to satisfy the surety's completion obligation of resuming construction. *Id.* Although the term "promptly" is used here, that term, in practice, is modified by paragraph 5 into a reasonable promptness standard given the interplay of paragraphs 4 and 5. *See supra* note 67. Also, the *Green River* court approached the surety's obligations under paragraph 4.2 differently than the *Rockland* court, looking to the bond's language as controlling, post takeover, although that may be attributable to the lack of a takeover agreement in the *Green River* case. *See infra* notes 93, 94, 102.

[87] *Rockland*, 98 F. Supp.2d 400. *See also supra* note 67. *Accord* Seaboard Sur. Co. v. Town of Greenfield, 266 F. Supp.2d 189, 194-95 (D. Mass. 2003), *aff'd*, 370 F.3d 215, 219 (1st Cir. 2004).

[88] The *Green River* court ruled that St. Paul's performance pace was unambiguously defined by paragraph 5's reasonable promptness standard. *Green River*, 93 F. Supp.2d at 1175. Moreover, the bond's express contemplation of a tardy completion by the surety due to principal delays was manifested by the bond's provision for liquidated damages, which intent ran contrary to the notion that the obligee could terminate the surety if the surety exceeded the original completion date. *Id.*

completion is not otherwise excused under the contract.[89] Importantly, the obligee may not have the right to terminate a surety for failure to accelerate construction to make up for the principal's delays.[90]

---

[89] The *Green River* court recited the well known rule that the surety's liability is co-extensive with its principal's liability and that if the principal is liable for liquidated damages under the contract then the surety is likewise liable for those damages. The court then noted that the bond's paragraph 6.3 explicitly provided that the surety was liable for liquidated damages caused by the principal. *Green River*, 93 F. Supp.2d at 1175. In firmly rejecting the obligee's argument that the obligee could terminate St. Paul for not completing the project within the original schedule, the court noted that the surety's performance duty is typically triggered only when the project is already in trouble and behind schedule, e.g., it is not unusual for a principal on a two year project that is one year behind to be terminated shortly before the completion deadline. *Id.* The bond contemplated this typical event and provided the obligee with recourse for the surety's tardy completion by covering liquidated damages. If the court accepted the obligee's unreasonable position, however, then the obligee could insist that the surety deliver the project by the original completion date leading to an impractical and commercially absurd result. The imposition of such an absolute duty of timely delivery would permit an obligee to terminate a surety if the surety did not complete a one year project in a day. The court declined to interpret the bond in such a manner which would have impermissibly required St. Paul to be "superhuman." *Id.*

[90] *Id.* at 1176. Also, on appeal, the 10th Circuit commented that "it was not unreasonable for the surety to seek compensation from the Board for the cost of accelerating performance beyond the 'reasonable promptness' standard the bond specified." St. Paul Fire & Marine Ins. Co. v. City of Green River, 6 Fed. Appx. 828, 830 (10th Cir. 2001).

Commentators have stated that the surety's liability is not limited to the amount of the bond, if the surety selects paragraph 4.2 as its completion option.[91] To support this proposition, however, the commentators relied on a non-AIA 312 case.[92] This is a distinction

---

91 BRUNER & O'CONNOR ON CONSTRUCTION LAW, *supra* note 63, at §12:16.
92 In *Rockland*, 98 F. Supp.2d 400, the court did not fully appreciate paragraph 6's "to the limit of the amount of this Bond" language, but instead went straight to commentators and case law which support the proposition that the surety surrenders its bond penal sum limits if the surety takes over a project. After making this swift movement, the court glossed over the proposition that the AIA 312's completion option selection process in combination with paragraph 6's to the "limit of the amount of this Bond" language required a different outcome. In short, if a surety selects an authorized completion option such as paragraph 4.2's takeover option, then a fair reading of the bond is that the surety's maximum liability is the bond's amount, as specified by paragraph 6. Unfortunately, the court reasoned that the bond did not contain any limit on the amount of surety-caused delay damages, as those damages fell under the takeover agreement, and that paragraph 6's provision limiting the surety's obligation "to the limit of the amount of this Bond" only addressed completion costs and principal-caused delay damages. *Id.* at 428. The court figuratively sawed the surety in half with its analysis that the surety's pre-takeover activities and liability for the contractor's breaches were governed by the bond, the limits of which were waived by the takeover, but that the surety's post-takeover activities were governed by the takeover agreement, a whole new agreement, which did not, in the court's mind, contain a properly drafted provision that successfully limited the surety's liability to the penal sum. As such, the court claimed that under either the bond or the takeover agreement the surety was not protected by the bond's penal sum. *Id.* at 428-430. Taking this tack, the *Rockland* court ignored the most logical end result of its bond interpretation which is that the absence of the surety damage category the court was endeavoring to find in paragraph 6 meant that these damages were not a surety liability. An example of such an outcome is provided by North American Specialty Insurance Co. v. Chichester School District, 158 F. Supp.2d 468, 471-73 (E.D. Pa. 2001). There, the court correctly determined that the bond is the proper place to start analyzing whether a surety is liable for certain types of damages, not the underlying contract. *Id.* Finding paragraph 6 controlling, the court ruled that the surety's liability was strictly limited to the identified damages. *Id.* As such, although the surety's performance obligations are measured by the

which makes a difference because the AIA 312's paragraph 6 states: "To the limit of the amount of this Bond, but subject to the commitment by the Owner of the Contract Price to mitigation of costs and damages on the Construction Contract, the Surety is obligated without duplication for: . . . ." Despite this comforting language, new obligations are oftentimes created when a surety takes over for its defaulted principal

---

underlying contract as imposed upon the surety by the bond's paragraph 1, the remedies to which the obligee is entitled for the breach of those obligations are restricted by paragraph 6. *Id.* Given this conclusion, the court ruled that the underlying contract language was irrelevant for damage determination purposes. *Id.* It is interesting to note that the surety in *Chichester* completed under paragraph 4.2 without a takeover agreement. *Id.* Moreover, even though this iteration of the *Chichester* case concerned only attorneys fees, the *Chichester* court relied on Downingtown Area School District v. International Fidelity Insurance Co., 769 A. 2d 560 (Pa. Commw. Ct. 2001), which addressed a surety's responsibility for delay damages under an AIA 311 bond. There, the *Downingtown* court ruled that whether or not a surety is liable for delay damages depends upon the language of the bond, and not the underlying contract. Such an analytical approach has even more merit when applied to an AIA 312 bond given that bond's greater specificity, particularly paragraph 6's recitation of recoverable damage items. *See infra* note 94. Under this more fairly reasoned interpretation of the AIA 312 bond, the surety's bond penal sum limit remains intact. *See also Green River*, 93 F. Supp.2d 1170, where the court indicated that the obligee's remedy for the surety's late completion under paragraph 4.2 was governed by paragraph 6, which, of course, includes the protective "To the limit of the amount of this Bond" language. As such, the *Green River* court appears to have determined that the obligee's liquidated damage claim for the surety's late completion is covered by paragraph 6, a conclusion contrary to the *Rockland* court's AIA 312 interpretation. Accepting this analysis for the purposes of our bond penal sum discussion provides an alternative argument that the surety's selection of paragraph 4.2's completion option limits the surety's liability accordingly because of the "To the limit of the amount of this Bond" language; a feature not available with other bond forms because of the lack of such limiting language. As a general proposition, however, takeover sureties face a developed body of case law to the contrary. *See Daily & Kazlow, supra* note 12, at 227-228 & nn. 1 & 3.

and a court may determine that these obligations are not subject to the bond penal sum amount.[93]

---

[93] BRUNER & O'CONNOR ON CONSTRUCTION LAW, *supra* note 63 at § 12:16 n.5.50 (citing Employers Mut. Cas. Co. v. United Fire & Cas. Co., 682 N.W.2d 452 (Iowa Ct. App. 2004). Admittedly, there is a well developed body of authority standing for the proposition that a completing surety surrenders its bond penal sum limits in non-AIA 312 settings. With the exception of the outlier *Rockland* case, however, case law explicitly gutting the AIA 312's bond limit language does not exist. Even though the AIA 312's penal sum limits were pierced by one court in U.S. Fid. & Guar. Co. v. Braspetro Oil Servs. Co., 369 F.3d 34 (2d Cir. 2004), that outcome, reached without any explanation or penal sum discussion, does not change the outlier status of *Rockland*. This state of affairs makes relevant today the 13 year-old question posed in the Second Edition of the Bond Default Manual by Chapter 5's author, whereby he suggests that the AIA 312 bond's different terms required a different outcome: "Query, however, if the situation is different where either the bond itself, on its face, gives the surety the option to complete the work, such as the. . . [AIA 312] form, or where the bond requires the surety to complete. To argue in such a situation that by completing the surety waives the protection of its bond penalty would make the bond penalty surplusage and the bond contradictory on its face." Richard A. Kowalczyk & Todd C. Kazlow, *Takeover and Completion*, in BOND DEFAULT MANUAL 175, 180 (Duncan L. Clore ed., 2d ed. 1995). That this author's interpretation is the correct reading of the AIA 312, is supported further by the following passage: "The surety's liability under the AIA 312 Bond includes correction of defective work, completion of the contract, additional legal, design professional, and delay costs resulting from the contractor's default, liquidated or actual damages caused by delayed performance or non-performance, and any costs resulting from the 'actions or failure to act' of the surety under paragraph 4. The bond therefore reasserts the primacy of the limitation of the bond amount as a cap on the surety's liability for any breach of the bond, and in exchange, grants to the obligee the right to be protected for specified consequential delay and other damages." BRUNER & O'CONNOR ON CONSTRUCTION LAW, *supra* note 63, at § 12:16. Further, the AIA 312's paragraph 6 grants penal sum limit protection no matter what option the surety selects by using the phrase "To the limit of the amount of this Bond . .the Surety is obligated for. . ." As noted in BRUNER & O'CONNOR ON CONSTRUCTION LAW, *supra* note 63, at § 12:21, this language is intended to minimize the risk of liability for damage awards in excess of the bond

The more simplistic AIA 311 provides for a surety takeover option with paragraph 1.[94] Although this sparse language does not restrict the surety by listing the steps by which a surety may "complete" the contract, the lack of some guiding terms like the AIA 312's paragraph 4.2 may lead to a dispute about how—and how quickly—the surety must take over and complete. Nevertheless, a reasonable reading of this language provides the surety with the latitude to solicit bids or take other steps to complete that are similar to the AIA 312. The AIA 312, however, provides greater clarity as to timing and how the obligee may "terminate" the surety, if the surety is not proceeding with reasonable promptness.[95] With the AIA 311's takeover option comes some risk concerning the surety's limit of liability based on the penal sum. Although countervailing and persuasive arguments exist that the surety does not waive its bond limits by performing under the AIA 311's

---

amount arising out of judicial "bond busting." An unpublished, non-citable California decision discusses the surety's bond penal sum protection in the context of a paragraph 4.2 election which was rejected by the obligee. N.V. Heathorn, Inc. v. U.S. Fid. & Guar. Co., Nos. A112107, A112345, 2007 WL 141174 (Cal. Ct. App. Jan. 22, 2007). The court, however, never fully addressed the bond limits issue given a motion judge's issuance of an earlier order refusing to summarily dismiss the surety on a *Green River* exoneration argument. The motion judge ruled that the conditions the surety attached to its paragraph 4.2 election were contrary to, or inconsistent with, the terms of the bond, so the election was not a valid offer of performance. The surety's conditions included a reservation of rights concerning the surety's penal sum as the limit of the surety's liability.

94 In pertinent part paragraph 1 and its preamble read as follows: "[T]he Surety . . . shall promptly 1) Complete the Contract in accordance with its terms and conditions . . . ." See AIA 311, *supra* note 62.

95 AIA 312 paragraph 5 provides: "If the Surety does not proceed as provided in Paragraph 4 with reasonable promptness, the Surety shall be deemed to be in default on this Bond fifteen days after receipt of an additional written notice from the Owner to the Surety demanding that the Surety perform its obligations under this Bond, and the Owner shall be entitled to enforce any remedy available to the Owner. If the surety proceeds as provided in Subparagraph 4.4, and the Owner refuses the payment tendered or the Surety has denied liability, in whole or in part, without further notice the Owner shall be entitled to enforce any remedy available to the Owner." See AIA 312, *supra* note 36.

paragraph 1, there is an established body of authority to the contrary, primarily addressing defeasance bonds.[96] This authority is primarily driven by the determination that the surety has independently "picked up" new liabilities either through performing the underlying contract or via the takeover agreement.[97]

Although the tender option is discussed in treatises as a surety option, neither the AIA 312 nor the AIA 311 use this term.[98] Nevertheless, this option is provided for by both bond forms.

AIA 312, paragraph 4.3 provides for a tender process as a surety option. The selection process starts from a pool of qualified contractors, acceptable to the obligee, with the new contractor entering into a direct contract with the obligee, but only after this contractor is first selected with the obligee's concurrence.[99] The specified selection process is either soliciting bids or negotiating proposals. Bonds for the new contractor are required. Please note that the financial terms of this provision provide for a lump sum payment by the surety to the obligee. This payment is based

---

96   *See* Bruce C. King, *Takeover and Completion of Bonded Contracts by the Surety*, BRIEF Fall 1997, Vol. 27, No. 1, at 25-28; ROBERT F. CUSHMAN ET AL., HANDLING FIDELITY, SURETY AND FINANCIAL RISK CLAIMS 127 (2d ed. 1990). *See also supra* notes 63 and 64. One example of a persuasive argument in favor of capping a completing surety's liability at its bond amount is the citation of California Code of Civil Procedure Section 996.470 which provides that: "Notwithstanding any other statute . . ., the aggregate liability of a Surety to all persons for all breaches of the condition of a bond is *limited to the amount of the bond*." Cal. Civ. Proc. Code § 996.470 (2008) (emphasis added).

97   *See* Int'l Fid. Ins. Co. v. County of Rockland, 98 F. Supp.2d 400, 423 (S.D.N.Y. 2000).

98   *See* AIA 312, *supra* note 36, at subpara. 4.3; AIA 311, *supra* note 62, at para. 1. *See also Mills & Moore, supra* note 35, at 251-52.

99   Paragraph 4.3 provides that the surety shall promptly: "Obtain bids or negotiated proposals from qualified principals acceptable to the Owner for a contract for performance and completion of the Construction Contract, arrange for a contract to be prepared for execution by the Owner and the contractor selected with the Owner's concurrence, to be secured with performance and payment bonds executed by a qualified surety equivalent to the bonds issued on the Construction Contract, and pay to the Owner the amount of damages as described in Paragraph 6 in excess of the Balance of the Contract Price incurred by the Owner resulting from the Contractor's default." *See* AIA 312, *supra* note 36.

on the damages described in paragraph 6, but only to the extent they are in excess of the contract price.[100] In particular, paragraph 6's language limits the surety's liability to the amount of the bond.[101] Moreover, with paragraph 4.3's lump sum payment, followed by the surety's graceful exit, the AIA 312's tender option provides a "clean break" for both the obligee and the surety.[102]

---

[100] Paragraph 4.3 requires "pay[ing] to the Owner the amount of damages as described in paragraph 6 in excess of the Balance of the Contract Price incurred by the Owner resulting from the Contractor's default." *See* AIA 312, *supra* note 36. In pertinent part, paragraph 6 and its subparts provide "[T]he Surety is obligated without duplication for: 6.1 The responsibilities of the Contractor for correction of defective work and completion of the Construction Contract; 6.2 Additional legal, design professional and delay costs resulting from the Contractor's Default, and resulting from the actions or failure to act of the Surety under paragraph 4; and 6.3 Liquidated damages, or if no liquidated damages are specified in the Construction Contract, actual damages caused by delayed performance or non-performance of the Contractor." *Id.* If an obligee does not negotiate the amount of these damages in a fair manner, then that obligee may face a *Green River*-styled exoneration argument, that is, the obligee is attempting to prevent the surety from using this option by unreasonably refusing to accept a lump sum payment which properly includes paragraph 6's damage items.

[101] *See supra* notes 92-94 and accompanying text. *See also* BRUNER & O'CONNOR ON CONSTRUCTION LAW, *supra* note 63, at § 12:16 ("If the surety exercises options ... [subparagraph 4.3] the surety's liability is limited to the amount of the bond..."). By tendering, the surety is not performing under a takeover agreement but under the bond. With the tender option, a surety avoids the takeover process. The takeover process creates potential entanglements that may lead a court to assume the surety has elected to shoulder a burden greater than its bond obligations.

[102] "Too often, by the time a surety is called in on a potential default, an acrimonious relationship has existed between the obligee and the principal for months, and the well intended surety is immediately immersed in those hostilities which can and often do continue throughout the performance and completion of the bonded obligation. Tender allows the surety and the obligee to extricate themselves from an otherwise acrimonious relationship, establish a clean break, and from the obligee's point of view start anew." James H. Baumgartner, Jr., *Tender*, in BOND DEFAULT MANUAL 193, 200 (Duncan L. Clore ed., 2d ed. 1995).

The tender option is also addressed in paragraph 2 of the AIA 311. Unlike the AIA 312, this provision does not provide for the obligee to pre-qualify the bidders. Note that the surety is authorized to select the lowest responsible bidder unless the obligee affirmatively elects to jointly select the winning bidder with the surety.[103] The reprocurement process specified by the AIA 311 also does not expressly include negotiating proposals that are authorized by the AIA 312.

Moreover, the AIA 311 does not require the new contractor's performance to be secured by bonds. The lack of bonds may explain the AIA 311's different financial terms. Instead of a lump sum payment, an AIA 311 surety must make sufficient funds available "as Work progresses" to pay the cost of completion less the balance of the contract price.[104] This latter stipulation leaves the surety in for the duration as the permanent funding mechanism for the project, with that funding not

---

103   In pertinent part, paragraph 2 and its preamble provide: "[T]he Surety . . . shall promptly . . .[o]btain a bid or bids for completing the Contract . . . and upon determination by Surety of the lowest responsible bidder, or, if the Owner elects, upon determination by the Owner and the Surety jointly of the lowest responsible bidder, arrange for a contract between such bidder and Owner, and make available as Work progresses (even though there should be a default or a succession of defaults under the contract or contracts of completion arranged under this paragraph) sufficient funds to pay the cost of completion less the balance of the contract price; but not exceeding, including other costs and damages for which the Surety may be liable hereunder, the amount set forth in the first paragraph hereof." See AIA 311, *supra* note 62.

104   *Id.*

exceeding, however, the bond's limit.[105] With the AIA 312, however, the surety makes one lump sum payment to satisfy its obligation.[106]

As stated previously, obligee completion of the project is another option available to the surety. Obligee completion may take one of two forms. The first form is whether or not the obligee has the option to complete. This iteration includes whether the obligee may "supplement" the principal's work at the surety's expense without the surety's consent or participation. The second form is whether or not a surety has the option to compel the obligee to complete.

Neither the AIA 312 nor the AIA 311 expressly authorize an obligee to complete the project at the surety's expense. In certain settings,

---

105   The surety shall ". . . make available as Work progresses (even though there should be a default or a succession of defaults under the contract or contracts of completion arranged under this paragraph) sufficient funds to pay the cost of completion less the balance of the contract price; but not exceeding, including other costs and damages for which the Surety may be liable hereunder, the amount set forth in the first paragraph hereof." *See* AIA 311, *supra* note 62. In Downingtown Area School District v. International Fidelity Insurance Co., 769 A.2d 560 (Pa. Commw. Ct. 2001) and American Home Assurance Co. v. Larkin General Hospital, Ltd., 593 So. 2d 195 (Fla. 1992), the courts interpreted this language from the AIA 311's tender option as limiting a surety's liability to the amount of its bond. *Downingtown*, 769 A.2d at 564; *Larkin*, 593 So. 2d at 197 (citing Ken Sobel, *Owner Delay Damages Chargeable to Performance Bond Surety*, 21 CAL. W.L. REV. 128, 137 (1984) ("it is obvious that the provision was intended to limit the surety's liability, not expand it")). In practice, this "for the duration" funding provision is less desirable from both a surety and obligee perspective. The surety is deprived of its "clean break." The obligee, on the other hand, is left with a depleted AIA 311 bond from the original surety, as opposed to receiving a new bond from the completing principal's surety, as contemplated by the AIA 312's subparagraph 4.3. In all probability, the new bond posted pursuant to the AIA 312's tender option has a higher bond amount, that is, more available funds, than the soon to be depleted original bond. In the AIA 311 setting, this depleted original bond has to stay in place under the tender option. In the AIA 312 setting, however, this old depleted bond is replaced with a new and undiminished bond.

106   AIA 312, *supra* note 36, at para. 4.3.

however,[107] the surety may discover that an obligee may attempt to eliminate the surety's options under an AIA 312 or AIA 311 by completing the work or "supplementing" the principal.

Contrary to the overwhelming trend in AIA 312 cases, there is at least one published decision which permitted a general contractor obligee to avoid the AIA 312's default termination requirements by supplementing the principal's work.[108] Yet, this case is an isolated decision that is directly contrary to the better reasoned weight of authority which strictly enforces the AIA 312's default termination and notice provisions.[109] At the top of the citation list in support of this proposition is *Solai & Cameron, Inc. v. Plainfield Community Consolidated School District No. 202*, where the court strictly enforced the AIA 312's condition precedent requirements.[110]

---

107 The supplementation cases have typically arisen in subcontractor bond settings.

108 In Commercial Casualty Insurance Co. of Georgia v. Maritime Trade Center Builders, 572 S.E.2d 319, 322 (Ga. App. 2002) the court acknowledged that the bond contained detailed notice provisions in the event of default. Nevertheless, the court determined that the bond did not address the contingency of the principal-obligee supplementing the subprincipal-principal's work before default. *Id.* To support its decision in favor of the supplementing obligee, the court turned to the bonded subcontract's terms which only required a 48-hour notice to the subprincipal and did not specify that the surety was to receive any notice. *Id.* These same terms provided that the surety agreed to pay the principal for losses incurred because of the subprincipal's breach or failure to perform. *Id.* Construing these documents, the court came to the conclusion that the general contractor obligee was not required to give the surety notice as a pre-condition to collecting under the bond before supplementing the subprincipal's work. *Id.*

109 *See* BRUNER & O'CONNOR ON CONSTRUCTION LAW, *supra* note 63, at § 12:41 nn. 1-3, for the proposition that the AIA 312's notice provisions continue to be enforced strictly.

110 871 N.E.2d 944 (Ill. App. Ct. 2007). Although not cited in the decision, the *Solai & Cameron* court applied the same AIA 312 analysis as the authors of a well respected construction law treatise who conclude that an obligee must satisfy all of these conditions, that is, paragraph 3's pre-default meeting, followed by a declaration of default and formal termination, amongst other conditions precedent, to have a valid bond claim. BRUNER & O'CONNOR ON CONSTRUCTION LAW, *supra* note 63, at

In the AIA 311 setting there are cases that have misconstrued the bond's language and have declined to accept or fully accept the rationale of the *L&A Contracting* case and its progeny.[111] A number of these decisions concern AIA 311-based subcontract bonds. The end result is that the general contractor is permitted to either complete or supplement the subcontractor's work and then just send the surety a bill.[112] Shorn of its options, the surety is never given the opportunity to control its own financial destiny.[113] These subcontract bond obligees argue that the *L&A*

---

§ 12:16. This same treatise collects the cases which reflect the trend to strictly enforce the AIA 312's conditions precedent. *Id.* at § 12:16 nn. 1, 3, 3.50, 4, 4.50, § 12:41 nn. 1, 2, 3. The result should not be any different when the AIA 312 is used as a subcontract bond. *See, e.g.*, Current Builders of Fla., Inc. v. First Sealord Sur., Inc., 984 So. 2d 526 Fla. Dist. Ct. App. 2008).

[111] This issue is addressed in greater detail in Chapter 2.

[112] *See, e.g.*, Siegfried Constr., Inc. v. Gulf Ins. Co., No. 98-2808, 2000 U.S. App. LEXIS 1304 (4th Cir. Feb. 2, 2000) (published without opinion at 203 F.3d 822) (holding that the obligee had properly declared a default, but rejected *L&A Contracting* by ruling that the bond's language did not require termination); Dooley & Mack Constructors, Inc. v. Developers Sur. & Indem. Co., 972 So. 2d 893 (Fla. Dist. Ct. App. 2008) (holding bond's declaration of default provision "trumped" by subcontract provision which permitted the general contractor obligee to cure the principal's default itself without notice to the surety and at the surety's expense); DCC Constructors, Inc. v. Randall Mech., Inc., 791 So. 2d 575 (Fla. Dist. Ct. App. 2001) (declaration of default, without a termination, sufficient to trigger surety's liability given subcontract's extensive reference to what constituted a default, and that termination was just one option provided to the obligee by the subcontract).

[113] *Siegfried Constr.*, 2000 U.S. App. LEXIS 1304; *Dooley & Mack Constructors*, 972 So. 2d 893; *DCC Constructors*, 791 So. 2d 575. *See, however*, Hunt Constr. Group, Inc. v. National Wrecking Corp., 542 F. Supp. 2d 87, 94-96 (D. D.C. 2008), where the court endorsed an AIA 311 surety's right to investigate, and the obligee's need to cooperate with that investigation, by noting that on top of its other sins, the obligee in that case "even then [after failing to timely declare a default] sat on its hands and failed to assist the Sureties in their legitimate investigation." The *Hunt* court followed the *L&A Contracting* line of authority, including Elm Haven Constr. L.P. v. Neri Constr. L.L.C., 281 F. Supp. 2d 406 (D. Conn. 2003), and Balfour Beatty Constr., Inc. v. Colonial Ornamental Iron Works, 986 F. Supp. 82 (D. Conn. 1997), in ruling that the obligee's

Contracting line of authority is satisfied by a declaration of default without a termination.[114] Some obligees have argued that a surety has no

---

[114] failure to give the sureties reasonable notice of the principal's default rendered the bonds null and void.

In *Siegfried Constr.*, the court determined that a declaration of default without a termination was sufficient to trigger an AIA 311-based subcontract bond. 2000 U.S. App. LEXIS 1304. The *Siegfried* court reasoned that although other courts such as *L&A Contracting* have required obligees to terminate, Virginia law did not counsel this result. Ruminating about the bond's terms, the court opined that had the parties actually intended *Siegfried* to terminate the subprincipal before making a claim on the bond, then such a provision would surely have been inserted in the bond by some clear language; but such was not the case. *Id.* Similar reasoning was used by the court in *DCC Constructors*, but applied in such a manner as to require only a declaration of default, with the court distinguishing *L&A Contracting* on its facts and reconfiguring the holding of that case so a declaration of default, without a termination, triggers a surety's liability. 791 So. 2d at 577. *See also Dooley & Mack Constructors*, 972 So. 2d 893. There, the court reversed a summary judgment in favor of the surety and allowed the general contractor obligee to complete the subprincipal's work at the surety's expense without a termination. The *Dooley* court determined that the subcontract's provisions "trumped" the bond's declaration of default terms by granting the general contractor the right to cure the subprincipal's default itself by completing the work and then holding the surety liable. *Id.* The vigorous dissent in *Dooley* presents a more cogent analysis that: "The majority . . . seizes upon an obscure provision of the subcontract . ., not signed by the surety, to afford *Dooley & Mack* a remedy not contemplated either in the default provisions of the subcontract or the bond." *Id.* at 895-96. Subsequently, the dissent's reasoning was adopted by a later decision but in a slightly different context. *See* CC-Aventura, Inc. v. Weitz Co., LLC, No. 06-21598-CIV, 2008 WL 2937856 (S.D. Fla. July 14, 2008). There, the court embraced the *Dooley* dissenting opinion's reasoning that an obscure subcontract provision could not override a bond term which required notice to the surety. Having found that the obligee properly declared a default, the court proceeded to rule that the obligee had not complied with this bond form's additional notice requirement. The obligee advising the surety, in a declaration of default letter, that the obligee was also completing the work and would seek reimbursement from the surety did not comply with the bond's additional notice requirement. The bond provision at issue required the obligee to provide completion options under an AIA 311-based subcontract bond, except for the ones the obligee is willing to grant the surety.[115] In these jurisdictions an obligee may very well advance this supplementation argument in

---

reasonable notice to the surety if the obligee chose the bond's option which allowed the obligee to complete the principal's work. Because the obligee had already hired a replacement subcontractor and commenced incurring expenses by the time the obligee sent the surety the declaration of default/notice letter, the court ruled that this letter was not reasonable notice under the bond. In exonerating the surety, the court rejected the obligee's argument that the subcontract's default provisions, which did not require this surety notice, overrode the bond's explicit reasonable notice requirement.

115   In Colorado Structures, Inc. v. Insurance Co. of the West, the Washington State Supreme Court butchered the plain language of an AIA 311-based subcontract bond. 167 P. 3d 1125 (Wash. 2007). There, the court ruled that because the law and subcontract gave the obligee the option, but not the obligation, to declare a default, that the obligee could decline to declare a default, and supplement the principal subprincipal's work at the surety's expense. *Id.* at 1133. This case's practical effect is to provide the obligee with complete control over the surety's options. If the obligee does not declare a default, then the obligee may complete at the surety's expense. On the other hand, the obligee may declare a default thereby activating the surety's options under the bond. A better reasoned interpretation of the AIA 311's language is found elsewhere. In particular, the *Hunt* court's rationale offers a more cogent and complete example of proper contract construction, unlike the approach taken by the court in *Colorado Structures*: "This Court respectfully declines to adopt the reasoning of *Colorado Structures*, as it would turn a performance bond surety into a commercial guarantor—an undertaking well beyond the limits of the surety bond. Rendering a 'surety' absolutely liable for all costs and expenses, without notice, under Paragraphs A and B would also read Paragraph C [which contains all the surety's performance options] out of the performance bond, and allow the obligee to wait for indefinite periods before demanding 'performance'." *Hunt Constr. Group*, 542 F. Supp. 2d at 94-95. Other courts that have recently followed the *L&A Contracting* line of authority post-*Colorado Structures* are CC-Aventura, Inc. v. Weitz Co., LLC, No. 06-21598-CIV, 2007 WL 2986371, at *2 (S.D. Fla. Oct. 10, 2007) and Memphis-Shelby County Airport Authority v. Illinois Valley Paving Co., No. 01-3041 B, 2007 WL 2904539, at *4-6 (W.D. Tenn. Oct. 3, 2007).

support of obligee completion in the obligee-general contractor AIA 311 setting.

Neither the AIA 312 surety nor the AIA 311 surety have the express right to compel the owner-obligee to complete. As a practical matter, however, the AIA 312's subparagraph 4.4's tender payment or deny liability provisions have the effect of compelling obligee completion. In this scenario, obligee completion occurs either voluntarily after a settlement between the surety and the obligee, with the obligee completing, assisted by surety money, or involuntarily, and without surety money, following the surety's denial. Obviously, if a surety denies the obligee's claim, then the obligee is entitled to enforce any available remedy and, if successful, recoup its damages from the surety, subject to paragraph 6's limitations.

On the other hand, it is not clear that an AIA 311 surety can compel an obligee to complete, as at least one court has held that this option is not available to the surety while another court has indicated in dicta that a surety has the right to allow an obligee to complete and reimburse the obligee for its completion costs to the extent recoverable under the bond.[116] As with the AIA 312, however, this does not mean that an AIA 311 surety cannot deny a claim, even though an AIA 311 bond does not

---

116 "National Fire [the Surety] could not, as the district ruled, simply 'do nothing' and pay for any excess construction costs. As noted in one treatise: 'The seductive enticement of the 'do nothing' option to the surety is avoiding the immediate cost of completion, but this course of action remains advantageous only if the surety is correct in its analysis that it has no liability to the obligee... Some bond forms remove the surety's 'do nothing' option. These instruments require the surety to act. If the surety believes it has a defense, it may reserve its rights and litigate–but it must perform." Nat'l Fire Ins. Co. of Hartford v. Fortune Constr. Co., 320 F.3d 1260, 1272 n.16 (11th Cir. 2003) (citing BRUNER & O'CONNOR ON CONSTRUCTION LAW, *supra* note 63, at § 12:82 n. 5, where the court had an AIA 311-based subcontract bond under consideration). Bruner & O'Connor note that certain bond forms require the surety to perform, but they do not address whether the AIA 311 is that kind of bond. In contrast, the court in Balfour Beatty Constr., Inc. v. Colonial Ornamental Iron Works, Inc. noted in dicta that a surety has the right to pay an obligee's completion costs in lieu of performance under a bond with A311 language. 986 F. Supp. 82, 85-86 (D. Conn. 1997).

have an explicit "pay or deny" provision like the AIA 312's paragraph 4.4.[117]

In its last option paragraph, the AIA 312 authorizes the surety to either make a cash offer to the obligee, following an investigation, or deny liability, in whole or in part.[118] In doing so, the surety waives its right to perform and complete, arrange for completion, or obtain a new contractor.[119] The same reasonable promptness standard applies to this option, as it does to all the previous ones.[120] Of course, the obligee does not have to accept either the amount tendered by the surety to buy back its bond or surety's denial decision. If the surety does not proceed with reasonable promptness under paragraphs 4.1, 4.2, 4.3 or the obligee

---

[117] See Roel Partnership v. Amwest Surety Insurance Co., 658 N.Y.S.2d 832, 833 (N.Y. App. Div. 1999), where the court upheld an AIA 311 surety's denial based on an obligee's failure to pay under the construction contract. The AIA 311 conditioned the obligee's rights on the "Owner having performed Owner's obligations thereunder [the contract] ... ," which is standard AIA 311 language contained in the AIA 311's "Whenever" clause. *Id.* Because the obligee breached the contract by failing to pay the principal, the obligee had not performed its obligations under the contract. As such, a precondition for the surety's liability had not been satisfied and the AIA 311 surety was entitled to a summary dismissal in its favor. The outcome in *Roel* survives the later New York cases declining to follow *L&A Contracting*. The long-standing proposition that a surety's liability is co-extensive with the principal's liability, and therefore, if the principal is not liable, then neither is the surety, should carry the day. In short, the obligee's breach of contract relieves both the principal and the surety of any liability. The holdings of two related New York cases which declined to follow *L&A Contracting*, the 2001 decision in Walter Concrete Constr. Corp. v. Lederle Laboratories and the 2003 decision in Walter Concrete Constr. Corp. v. Lederle Laboratories, should not impede the surety from denying an obligee's claim based on a breach of contract defense. 734 N.Y.S.2d 80 (N.Y. App. Div. 2001); 788 N.E.2d 609 (N.Y. 2003). *See also* BRUNER & O'CONNOR ON CONSTRUCTION LAW, *supra* note 63, at § 12:37 ("Absent express bond language to the contrary, the surety's conditional liability does not arise if the owner is in default of its obligations under the bonded contract.").

[118] AIA 312, *supra* note 36, at subpara. 4.4.
[119] *Id.*
[120] *Id.*

refuses the surety's cash offer or claim denial under paragraph 4.4, then the obligee may enforce any remedy available.[121]

Although not expressly authorized in the bond, there is nothing to suggest that an AIA 311 surety cannot offer to buy its bond back or deny the claim.[122] Doing nothing, however, is probably not desirable.[123]

An important further consideration is whether or not a bond's specified options have been overridden by a statutorily required bond form. If the statute pursuant to which the surety furnished the AIA bond dictates a particular bond form, then there is a distinct possibility that the surety may have fewer or different options than those listed in either the AIA 311 or AIA 312 bond.[124]

---

121 *Id.* at para. 5.
122 *See supra* note 68. *See also* BRUNER & O'CONNOR ON CONSTRUCTION LAW, *supra* note 63, at §12:15 n. 5 and §12:77 for a description of the "buy back" option and its general availability.
123 *See supra* notes 69, 123.
124 *See* Gloucester City Bd. of Educ. v. Am. Arbitration Ass'n, 755 A.2d 1256, 1262-67 (N.J. Super. Ct. App. Div. 2000) (ruling that the surety could not raise the AIA 312's condition precedent defenses, including the requirement that the obligee first default and terminate the principal). There, the court noted that the state bond statute provided for a performance bond in "substantially" the same form as that set forth in the statute. *Id.* This statutory form was a bare bones defeasance bond without any of the AIA 312's default termination notice requirements, or, for the sake of our discussion, any of the AIA 312's completion options. *Id.* Given the difference in terms, the court ruled that the AIA 312 did not substantially conform to the statutory bond form, making the AIA 312's extraneous provisions unenforceable surplusage. *Id.* Moreover, the *Gloucester* court pointed to the AIA 312's "read in-read out" provision in paragraph 11 as an alternative means to defeat the surety's argument. In short, this paragraph "reads out" of the bond those provisions which conflicted with a statute and then "reads in" the applicable statutory provisions. Paragraph 11 applies when the AIA 312 bond is posted to comply with a statutory requirement or other legal requirement. The *Gloucester* court's rationale may apply to eliminate an AIA 312's completion options in other jurisdictions which require substantial compliance with a stipulated statutory bond form. *See, e.g.*, RLI Ins. Co. v. Indian River Sch. Dist., 556 F. Supp. 2d 356 (D. Del. 2008) (outcome similar to that in *Gloucester*). Although *Gloucester* is an AIA 312 decision, there is nothing to suggest that the *Gloucester* court's reasoning will not apply to an AIA 311 bond.

The defeasance bond has the standard absence of terms.[125] At first blush, the absence of specific bond terms describing a surety's options seems to grant the surety great latitude. Under this defeasance bond, a surety may clearly exercise three options: takeover; financing the principal pre-default; or paying the obligee, that is, buying the bond back.[126] However, in practice, a defeasance bond surety may have fewer options than an AIA 312 or AIA 311 surety, including not having a tender option.[127] If such an interpretation is accepted in that jurisdiction,

---

125 See supra notes 63 and 64.
126 "Under a performance and completion bond, a surety generally has two options upon its principal's default. First, the surety may undertake to complete the principal's work itself; this obligation may be satisfied by the surety funding the principal to complete its work. Second, the surety has the option of paying the obligee under the bond its damages, essentially the obligee's cost of completion." Granite Computer Leasing Corp. v. Travelers Indem. Co., 894 F.2d 547, 551 (2d Cir. 1990) (citations omitted). A closer reading of this decision reveals that the *Granite* court dropped the surety's takeover and financing options into one category called "the surety undertaking to complete the principal's work." Taking this view of the *Granite* decision means that the defeasance bond surety really has three options and not just two. The surety's three options are: (1) undertaking to complete the work itself, that is, the takeover option; (2) financing the principal pre-declared default; and (3) paying the obligee under the bond its damages, that is, the obligee's cost of completion. That the foregoing is the correct interpretation of the *Granite* decision is supported by reviewing one of the cases cited by the *Granite* court, Aetna Casualty & Surety Co. v. United States, 845 F.2d 971, 975 (Fed. Cir. 1988), where the *Aetna* court lists three surety options, and not just two. Although not recited in *Granite* as such, the *Aetna* court recognized the Miller Act surety's option to allow the project to be defaulted, thereby permitting obligee completion, with the government completing and the surety responsible for the costs in excess of the contract price. *Id.*
127 "The type of obligation imposed on the surety, and thus the surety's 'menu' of remedial options upon a principal's default, is determined by the language of the bond itself rather than simply the label 'performance bond'." Millgard Corp. v. E.E. Cruz/Nab/Frontier-Kemper, No. 99 CIV. 2952 (LBS), 2002 WL 31812710, at *12 (S.D.N.Y. Dec. 12, 2002). The *Millgard* court's bold statement makes a point, but begs a major question: if the bond is either silent or innocuously describes the surety's sole option as an opportunity to "correct" a default, what are the surety's

then the surety is left with the three previously referenced options of takeover, financing, or buying the bond back by a cash payment.

Unfortunately, some obligees may argue that the surety cannot return the principal to the project post-declared default, leaving the surety with just two options: takeover or buy the bond back. Eventually, reality may boil these two options down to one–taking over the project–if the obligee's cost to buy back the bond is too unrealistic. Nevertheless, the surety may still provide pre-default financing to the principal and head-off the reinstatement issue entirely.

Obligee completion, if compelled by a defeasance bond surety, may not be prudent if the surety is declining to perform without first conducting an investigation and presenting an appropriate claim denial.[128] Still, some courts have determined that a surety is protected by

---

options? Faced with such a situation, another court in School Board of Broward County v. Great American Insurance Co., 807 So.2d 750, 751 (Fla. Dist. Ct. App. 2002), took a narrow view of the term "correct" by ruling that the surety's tender of a new principal with a new surety did not correct the defunct principal's default. 807 So. 2d 750, 751. The fact that the obligee rejected the tender in the first place is astonishing given the circumstances of the principal's default. The principal defaulted before even starting the project. The tendered principal was an original bidder on the project. The new tendered contract was for the same price and was supported by bonds issued by another surety company. In exchange, the previous surety asked for a release. Evidently, this was too much for the obligee and the *Broward* court which ruled that the obligee was entitled to insist on performance by the original surety. What was that performance given the paucity of terms? The surety was bound to serve either as the general contractor, handling disbursements of the obligee's money, or supervising the new completing contractor's work. Tender was not an option. A potential alternative to avoid this outcome is "stacking" the original bond and the tender principal's bond. The original surety is not released. Instead, the tender principal's bond is made "primary" and the original surety's bond is made "excess." Under this proposal, the obligee may not "access" the original surety's bond unless and until the tender principal's bond is first exhausted. Whether the *Broward* obligee would have accepted such a proposal is unknown, but a "stacking" offer does remove what was the main objection to the surety's tender proposal: the surety's release.

128   See *Griffin & Beatty, supra* note 55, at 276–80.

its bond amount if the surety does not perform.[129] A major, and quite important qualification, however, is that the defeasance bond must not contain terms susceptible to the interpretation that the surety has only one choice: completion.[130] Therefore, compelling obligee completion or doing nothing may not be available surety options under a defeasance bond.[131] Improperly invoking one of these alternatives may expose the surety to additional liability.[132] Nevertheless, the proper cure is the traditional tonic of an investigation followed by an appropriate decision to either complete or deny the claim.[133]

None of these options limits the surety's exposure to the bond amount, other than the obligee accepting a cash offer in exchange for a release or, if appropriate, a claim denial, following an investigation which is subsequently determined to have been reasonable.[134] Defeasance bonds were at the heart of the original adverse decisions that did not limit the surety's liability to the bond amount.[135] Understanding this important point should make the surety cautious as it analyzes its options under a defeasance bond. Arguing traditional surety options is an

---

[129] Bill Curphy Co. v. Elliot, 207 F.2d 103 (5th Cir. 1953) (considering a bond with the same surety options as the AIA 311). *See also* Miracle Mile Shopping Ctr. v. Nat'l Union Indem. Co., 299 F.2d 780 (7th Cir. 1962); *Griffin & Beatty, supra* note 55, at 276-80. *But see* Nat'l Fire Ins. Co. of Hartford v. Fortune Constr. Co., 320 F.3d 1260 (11th Cir. 2003) (ruling that the surety did not have the option under an AIA 311-based subcontract bond to decline to perform and instead tender the completion costs to the obligee).

[130] *See, e.g.*, Cont'l Realty Corp. v. Andrew J. Crevolin Co., 380 F. Supp. 246 (S.D. W. Va. 1974); *Griffin & Beatty, supra* note 55, at 276-80.

[131] *See supra* notes 64-66.

[132] *Id.*

[133] *See generally* James J. Mercier & John T. Harris, *Rights of Surety in Event of Default*, in THE LAW OF PERFORMANCE BONDS, 37, 38 (Lawrence R. Moelmann & John T. Harris eds., 1999); William S. Piper & Carl C. Coe, Jr., *The Surety's Investigation*, in BOND DEFAULT MANUAL 43, 49-54 (Duncan L. Clore, Richard E. Towle & Michael J. Sugar, Jr. eds., 3d ed. 2005).

[134] *See supra* note 134. *See also supra* note 116 and, specifically, *supra* note 57, concerning one court's perspective on the surety's alleged "do nothing" option which may not have been even exercised as the surety claimed it had tendered a completing contractor.

[135] *See Daily & Kazlow, supra* note 12, at 228.

important avenue to provide what are, in effect, "gap filler" terms for sparse defeasance bonds, but one may run the risk that what one thinks is traditional, others may consider to be radical.[136]

Miller Act bonds do not present the same uncertainty as to the surety's options. Even though the Federal Standard Form 25 Miller Act performance bond does not provide a list of surety options, case law and regulations supply "gap filler" terms which establish a surety's options and make up the federal "tradition" which breathes life into this otherwise dead bond form.[137] Federal regulations, such as 48 C.F.R. 49.404 (e), actually establish a process for a surety takeover of a government project, including terms. Using this process, a Miller Act

---

[136] *See, e.g.,* Sch. Bd. of Broward County v. Great Am. Ins. Co., 807 So.2d 750, 751-52 (Fla. Dist. Ct. App. 2002). There, the surety tendered a new principal, a traditional surety remedy, which the obligee rejected. In ruling for the obligee, the court construed the pertinent bond language very narrowly. This language merely required the surety to "correct" its principal's default. Surprisingly, the court ruled that the surety did not "correct" its principal's default by tendering only a new deal. In *Broward*, the obligee was entirely protected given that the principal defaulted before the project began, the tender contract was in the same amount as the original contract, and the tendered contract was supported by bonds from a new surety. The surety did request a release. Nevertheless, the court did not think that a tender, under these facts, served as a correction of the principal's default.

[137] *See* 48 C.F.R. 53.301-25 (2009) for the Miller Act Bond Form 25 which merely provides: "The above obligation is void if the Principal – (a) 1) Performs and fulfills all the undertakings, covenants, terms, conditions, and agreements of the contract during the original term of the contract and any extensions thereof that are granted by the Government, with or without notice to the Surety(ies), and during the life of any guaranty required under the contract, and 2) performs and fulfills all the undertakings, covenants, terms, conditions, and agreements of any and all duly authorized modifications of the contract that hereafter are made. Notice of those modifications to the Surety(ies) are waived. (b) Pays to the Government the full amount of the taxes imposed by the Government, if the said contract is subject to the Miller Act, . . . , which are collected, deducted, or withheld from wages paid by the Contractor in carrying out the construction contract with respect to which this bond is furnished." *See also Griffin & Beatty, supra* note 55, at 270-72 and *Daily & Kazlow, supra* note 12, at 238-40, for the gap filling nature of the Federal Acquisition Regulations.

performing surety may formally take over the project and contract for its completion. Alternatively, the surety may allow the project to be defaulted and let the government complete or contract for the completion of the project, in which case the surety is responsible for the costs in excess of the contract price, subject to the bond's penal sum limit. A performing surety may also satisfy its obligation by providing funds to an insolvent contractor to complete performance.[138] A Miller Act surety may also challenge the propriety of a default termination, thereby, in effect, denying liability on the bond.[139]

Unlike the options described previously, there is an open question concerning a Miller Act surety's tender option. What is open to question is the extent to which this option exists for a Miller Act surety, although the better-reasoned approach is that this option is available.[140] This same open question exists concerning a surety's option to buy its bond back with a cash payment. The better-reasoned interpretation is that a surety's

---

[138] Aetna Cas. & Sur. Co. v. United States, 845 F.2d 971, 975 (Fed. Cir. 1988). *See also* Ins. Co. of the West v. United States, 243 F.3d 1367, 1370 (Fed. Cir. 2001).

[139] United States v. Seaboard Sur. Co., 817 F.2d 956, 959-60 (2d Cir. 1987). *See also* BRUNNER & O'CONNOR ON CONSTRUCTION LAW, *supra* note 63, at § 12:37 ("Absent express bond language to the contrary, the surety's conditional liability does not arise if the owner is in default of its obligations under the bonded contract").

[140] *See Mills & Moore, supra* note 35, at 262-63, where the author notes that tender is not disallowed in the federal context which implies the contrary: it is permissible. The author also suggests that the surety should cite 48 C.F.R. § 49.405 to satisfy any government objection that it is necessary to go through the entire public bidding process again for the tender. If a surety declines to complete, this regulation grants the contracting officer the discretion to select a range of methods to complete the defaulted work including not conducting a public bid. Even though this regulation is designed to address what happens if the surety does not complete, the natural, logical segue is that if the contracting officer has such discretion when the government completes, does not this mean that the contracting officer has similar discretion to accept a tender without a public bid process when the surety completes? The answer should be "yes," particularly when the other applicable Federal Acquisition Regulations are examined. *See infra.* note 149.

right to "cash out" clearly exists, so the surety does not have to wait to receive a completion bill from the government.[141]

A Miller Act surety may finance, take over, allow obligee completion, deny the claim, and, impliedly, tender or buy back the bond. The "rub," however, is how those options are implemented in a Miller Act setting.

Put plainly, the surety's options under a Miller Act bond have been described as whatever performance the government agrees to accept.[142] Unlike most other bonds, a Miller Act surety does not have an inherent right to complete a project.[143] Instead, the government's contracting officer is directed to consider the surety's request to take over the project, but the officer is not bound to accept the surety's proposal.[144] Taking this approach to its logical conclusion means that the Miller Act sanctions obligee completion which either the surety or the government may initiate.[145] The government is thus authorized to send the surety a

---

141 See Griffin & Beatty, supra note 55, at 271-72, where the author cites 48 C.F.R. §49.402-3(i) and other regulations for the proposition that this is an acceptable option, by implication.

142 BRUNER & O'CONNOR ON CONSTRUCTION LAW, supra note 63, at § 12:77.

143 48 C.F.R. § 49.404(b), (c) (2009). See Appeal of Milner Constr. Co., DOTBCA No. 2043, 91-3 B.C.A. ¶ 24,195 (D.O.T.B.C.A. July 17, 1991), where the administrative law judge ruled that there is no absolute requirement in law or regulation that a surety must be given a right of first refusal to complete a contract. Instead, the guiding principle is that the contracting officer is to take action based upon what is in the government's best interest. The administrative law judge ruled that 48 C.F.R. § 49.404(c) vested in the contracting officer the discretion to decide how to complete the work with that discretion being measured by what was in the government's best interest. See also 48 C.F.R. § 49.402-3(i) (2009).

144 48 C.F.R. § 49.404(b), (c) (2009). See also 48 C.F.R. § 402-3(h) (2008), which advises the contracting officer to ask the surety if the surety desires to arrange for the completion of the work.

145 Morrison Assur. Co., Inc. v. United States, 3 Cl. Ct. 626, 632 (Cl. Ct. 1983). See also Ins. Co. of the West v. United States, 243 F.3d 1367, 1370 (Fed. Cir. 2001); Trinity Universal Ins. Co. v. United States, 382 F.2d 317, 321 (5th Cir. 1967). Support for these cases is found in the applicable regulations such as 48 C.F.R. § 52.249-10(a) (2008), the default clause for fixed price construction, and 48 C.F.R. § 49.405 (2008)

claim for the government's cost of completion in excess of the remaining contract price.[146] On the other hand, the surety's right to finance the principal's completion pre-default without government consent is recognized, but reinstating the principal post-default termination may present difficulties, if the government objects.[147]

---

which provides that the contracting officer normally will arrange for completion, if the surety does not do so. *See also Griffin & Beatty, supra* note 55, at 271-72 n.9, where the author comments that a Miller Act bond does not provide explicit guidance to the surety as to the circumstances under which the surety may respond to the government's demand by requesting the government to complete, and later present the surety with a claim for damages. Nevertheless, the author concludes, correctly, that based on existing case law, the surety may do so. *Id.* at 271-272.

[146] *Morrison Assurance Co.*, 3 Cl. Ct. at 632. See 48 C.F.R. § 52.249-10(a), which is the default clause for fixed price construction which may be summarized, in pertinent part, as permitting the government to take over the work and complete it by contract or otherwise, with the principal and its sureties liable for any damage to the government. *See also* 48 C.F.R. § 49.406 (2009), which authorizes the contracting officer to collect the government's damages in excess of the contract balance from the principal and surety. *See* BRUNER & O'CONNOR ON CONSTRUCTION LAW, *supra* note 63, at 12:82 n. 3 ("[T]he Federal Acquisition Regulation, 48 C.F.R. 49.402-3 and 49.404 confirms that the government has the right to elect whether it will complete the contract and send the bill for excess costs to the surety or whether it will accept a completion proposal submitted by the surety."). *See generally Griffin & Beatty, supra* note 55, at 271-72.

[147] *Aetna Cas. & Sur. Co v. United States*, 845 F.2d 971 (Fed. Cir. 1988). *See* 48 C.F.R. § 49.404(c) (2009) ("The contracting officer should permit surety offers to complete the contract, unless the contracting officer believes that the persons or firms proposed by the surety to complete the work are not competent and qualified or the proposal is not in the best interest of the Government."). This regulation appears broad enough to grant the contracting officer sufficient discretion to decline a surety offer to return the principal to the project post-default termination. As support for this proposition, *see Appeal of Milner Constr. Co. Inc.*, DOTBCA No. 2043, 91-3 B.C.A. ¶ 24,195 (D.O.T.B.C.A. July 17, 1991), where the administrative law judge rejected a financing surety's argument that it should have been given the first opportunity to complete the work after the principal's termination. Made through its principal, the surety's argument was based on 48 C.F.R. 49.404(c), but did not include returning

A proposal to tender a contractor may encounter some resistance, typically with the government maintaining that it does not have the authority to do so. This objection, however, ignores the power vested in the contracting officer by the Federal Acquisition Regulations.[148] The same is true concerning the Miller Act surety making a cash offer to buy its bond back.[149]

With each option, other than financing and takeover, a Miller Act surety's exposure is limited to the bond amount. Moreover, if the surety has any bond limit concerns, the surety may decline to perform and let the government complete.[150] In this scenario, the government's

---

the principal to the project given the principal's manifest inability to perform. Nevertheless, if the surety had made such an argument, there is no doubt that the administrative law judge would have given that position "short shrift" followed by a quick burial. *See also* 48 C.F.R. § 49.402-4(a) which provides authority for the contracting officer in his or her discretion to take the opposite position by granting the contracting officer the discretion to allow the principal, surety, or a guarantor, to continue performance of the contract in lieu of a termination for default, when that decision is in the government's best interest.

148 48 C.F.R. §49.404 (b) and (c) (2008). These regulations charge the contracting officer with the obligation to consider carefully the surety's proposals for completing the contract and that the officer should permit surety offers to complete the contract, unless the officer believes the persons or firms proposed by the surety to complete are not competent or qualified. A fair reading of these regulations leads to the conclusion that the contracting officer has the discretion to accept a tender. If the government objects, claiming a tender requires a new formal public bidding process because the end result is a contract between the government and the completing contractor, then the government's attention should be directed to 48 C.F.R. §49.405. This regulation authorizes a contracting officer to secure a new contract to complete the defaulted work by the "result of a sealed bid or any other appropriate contracting method or procedure." Although this regulation is designed to provide for the situation when a surety does not arrange for completion, the principle for which this regulation stands is nevertheless the same: the government does not have to conduct a public bid process before securing a new contractor to finish the work. *See also Mills & Moore, supra* note 35, at 262-63.

149 *See supra* note 149. *See also Griffin & Beatty, supra* note 55, at 272.

150 *Morrison Assurance Co.*, 3 Cl. Ct. at 632. *See also* Aetna Cas. & Sur. Co. v. United States, 845 F.2d 971 (Fed. Cir. 1988); United States v.

recoverable damages, are those incurred in excess of the contract price, but subject to the limiting "cap" of the bond's amount.[151]

Having summed up the surety's Miller Act options, we come to the last two bonds. These subcontract bonds are based on the AIA 312 and AIA 311, respectively. The AIA 312-based subcontract bond is an unadulterated rendition of the original AIA 312. Therefore, the same analysis used for the obligee-general contractor version of the AIA 312 applies to the subcontract version of this form. The risk of obligee completion, against the surety's will, is a higher probability with a subcontract bond. A general contractor, unlike a typical obligee, has greater flexibility to call on its own resources, or its subcontractors, to supplement the principal's work. Such an approach, however, is subject to attack as a violation of the AIA 312's terms. Given the weight of authority in favor of strictly enforcing the AIA 312's conditions precedent and notice terms, the surety should prevail if faced with such a dilemma.

When reviewing the AIA 311-based subcontract bond, a number of different terms stand out. Unlike the standard AIA 311, this subcontract bond iteration provides for obligee completion in paragraph 2. There, the obligee, after reasonable notice to the surety may, or the surety upon the demand of the obligee may, arrange for the performance of the principal's obligations under the subcontract.[152] Under these alternative options, which are completion by the surety or completion by the obligee, it is the obligee, and not the surety, who selects the completion option.[153] Further, this revision of the original AIA 311's "complete the contract" takeover option inserts new and additional notice and demand provisions. These new notice and demand requirements are the "triggers" used by the obligee to activate one of these two completion options. In

---

Seaboard Sur. Co., 817 F.2d 956 (2d Cir. 1987); Trinity Universal Ins. Co. v. United States, 382 F.2d 317, 321 (5th Cir. 1967).

151 *Morrison Assurance Co.*, 3 Cl. Ct. at 632.

152 Paragraph (2) provides: "Obligee after reasonable notice to Surety may, or Surety upon demand of Obligee may arrange for the performance of the Principal's obligation under the subcontract subject to the provisions of paragraph 3 herein."

153 Nat'l Fire Ins. Co. of Hartford v. Fortune Constr. Co., 320 F.3d 1260, 1273 (11th Cir.).

short, the obligee may provide reasonable notice to the surety, and then arrange for completion, or, alternatively, demand that the surety do so.[154]

The subcontract bond does not directly address the tender option, although the AIA 311 does provide such an option. This does not mean, however, that the tender option is not available. The subcontract bond does not use the "complete the contract" language of the AIA 311's paragraph 1, but, instead, uses the following phraseology: "may arrange for the performance of the principal's obligations under the subcontract."[155] This language is flexible enough to include a tender as an "arrangement" and clearly encompasses a takeover.[156] Despite this reasonable interpretation, however, a surety tendering a contractor under this provision probably needs to secure the obligee's approval, unlike the AIA 311. Although such approval is not directly required by the subcontract bond's terms, the way these provisions operate together

---

154   *Id. See also* CC-Aventura, Inc. v. Weitz Co., LLC., No. 06-21598-CIV, 2008 WL 2937856 (S.D. Fla. July 14, 2008) (obligee's failure to provide reasonable notice to the surety under this notice provision discharged the surety from all liability).

155   *See supra* text accompanying note 95.

156   In National Fire Insurance Co. of Hartford, 320 F.3d at 1278-79 (citing St. Paul Fire & Marine Ins. Co. v. City of Green River, 93 F. Supp. 2d 1170 (D. Wyo. 2000)), the court mentioned, *in dicta*, that if the general contractor obligee did prevent the surety from completing by refusing to accept the surety's tender, then the surety could assert this fact as an affirmative defense with the court. The court's comment suggests two things. First, that the subcontract bond's usage of the phrase "may arrange for the performance" in describing the surety's completion option is broad enough to include a tender. Second, that a surety in a non-AIA 312 setting may assert a *Green River* exoneration defense if the obligee rejects a tendered principal. It is important to note, however, that the bonds in *National Fire Ins. Co.* were two subcontract bonds, one an exact replica of the standard AIA 311 and the other a substantially modified version of an AIA 311. These bonds' different terms distinguish the *National Fire Ins. Co.* decision from another court's ruling rejecting a tender in School Board of Broward County v. Great American Insurance Co., 807 So. 2d 750 (Fla. Dist. Ct. App. 2002). In *Broward County*, the court ruled that the surety did not have a tender option under a defeasance bond, which provided that the surety was to "correct" the defunct principal's default, and, as such, the surety was not exonerated by the obligee's rejection of the surety's tender. *Id.*

dictate that the surety needs the obligee to "trigger" the surety's tender or takeover options in the first place. Using the subcontract bond's paragraph 2, the obligee controls whether the surety is completing because the bond cedes to the obligee in the first instance the right to demand that the surety arrange performance. If the surety proposes a tender, without first receiving a demand, the obligee may elect, instead, to provide the surety with reasonable notice, and arrange the completion on its own.[157] This outcome is only possible because pursuant to this bond form the obligee, not the surety, controls whether the surety completes. 320 F.3d at 1273. Nevertheless, the surety has a possible mitigation defense because this bond form only requires the surety to pay the "reasonable costs" of completing performance. One way of presenting this defense is using the tendered contract amount as a "measuring stick," presuming the surety had a tender contractor ready to proceed. This approach allows the surety to argue that any obligee expenditures in excess of the tender contract amount are per se unreasonable.

Alternatively, this analysis does not mean that a surety needs the obligee to "trigger" the surety's "promptly remedy option" which is contained in the subcontract bond's paragraph 1. Instead, this surety option is not subject to any conditions precedent other than the requisite default termination requirement, provided one is in a jurisdiction which follows *L&A Contracting*, or similar authority.[158] If the jurisdiction follows the rationale of the *Cooper Industries* court, then this "promptly remedy" language provides a surety with a financing option.[159] As such, a surety may elect to finance post-default using this provision without

---

157 For example, *see* National Fire Insurance Co. of Hartford, 320 F.3d 1260, where the court held that the general contractor obligee, and not the surety, could choose whether the general contractor obligee would voluntarily complete, or, for that matter, whether the surety would complete. The court noted that there were material issues of fact about whether the surety's failure to perform constituted a breach of the performance bond. The surety claimed it appropriately tendered a completion principal to the general contractor obligee, but that the general contractor obligee refused the tender. On the other hand, the general contractor obligee claimed that a completion contractor was never tendered despite its demands.
158 *See supra* text accompanying notes 72 and 73.
159 *Id.*

first receiving the obligee's prior demand or notice concerning who is to complete pursuant to paragraph 2.[160]

Under this subcontract bond, the surety has the right to deny the claim, but may not be able to compel involuntary obligee completion, if the project is located in a jurisdiction which does not permit this approach.[161] Other than the obligee completion option available with this bond, but not the AIA 311, the surety faces the same bond penalty issues with this bond as it does with the AIA 311.[162]

VIII. Options Prior to Obligee's Declaration of Default

Sometimes, the surety is confronted with a bond principal who has not been formally declared in default by a bond obligee, but who nonetheless

---

160 *Id.*
161 See *Nat'l Fire Ins. Co. of Hartford*, 320 F.3d at 1272-73. The *National Fire Insurance Co. of Hartford* court's analysis that the surety was not entitled to ignore the obligee's demands to perform and thereby force the obligee to complete, with the surety paying the completion bill later, did not address the issue of a denial. Such an option was available to the surety in *National Fire Insurance Co. of Hartford* because the two AIA 311-based bonds retained the standard AIA 311 condition precedent term which requires the obligee to have performed its obligations under the bonded contract. Accordingly, the surety in *National Fire Insurance Co. of Hartford* could have denied the claim on that basis, or any other appropriate basis, if the facts warranted such a decision. *See* discussion *supra* note 117.
162 In pertinent part, this subcontract bond provides as follows in paragraph (3): "The balance of the subcontract price ... shall be credited against the reasonable cost of completing performance of the subcontract. If completed by the Obligee, and the reasonable cost exceeds the balance of the subcontract price, the Surety shall pay to the Obligee such excess, but in no event shall the aggregate liability of the Surety exceed the amount of this bond." This is the only provision in the subcontract bond's option terms which references that the surety's liability is limited to the bond amount. By its express terms, this protective provision only applies to obligee completion. Accordingly, other than obligee completion, the surety faces the same questions concerning whether or not this subcontract bond "caps" the surety's exposure at the bond's limits that it faces with the standard AIA 311. *See supra* notes 112, 115, 116, 117 and 127.

informs the surety that it is no longer able to meet its contractual obligations. It is in the best interests of the surety to try and prevent any formal termination of the bonded contract in order to minimize the delays and associated costs that almost always accompany a termination for default. Because the same financial woes that make a troubled bond principal a poor indemnitor, the surety will want to make every effort to minimize the amount of indemnity it will have to seek from the principal. The most common pre-default solutions employed by sureties are (1) financing the principal or (2) accepting an assignment of the bonded contract(s) from the principal or facilitating the assignment of a bonded contract from the principal to a third-party contractor.

A. *Financing*

For one reason or another, a bond principal may be faced with temporary or permanent insolvency. The surety may deem it in the surety's best interest to finance the principal in order to prevent a default rather than doing so after the principal has already failed to meet its contractual obligations. The surety will need to thoroughly review the principal's financial situation to see if the financial difficulties are temporary and can be overcome, or whether recovery is impossible. If the principal has numerous unbonded projects under contract, but which will not provide cash flow in time for the principal to meet its bonded obligations, then providing funds might be appropriate. Conversely, if the principal is faced with diminishing margins, has failed to make a profit for a number of years, and has no new work on the horizon, then it may be more cost effective for the surety to simply take over the bonded obligations rather than loaning money to the principal to do so.

The surety also needs to perform an overall assessment of the principal's business operations to determine whether the principal's financial difficulties are the result of systematic inefficiencies and poor management, or whether there was an unusual event that led to temporary insolvency on either a company-wide or project-specific basis. For instance, a surety is unlikely to provide financing to a principal that has failed to turn a profit for several years and has consistently failed to complete its work on time, but may decide to fund a principal that has been in business for a number of years but simply encountered a particularly problematic project that caused a severe, but temporary, cash shortage.

If the surety does decide to finance its principal prior to a declaration of default by an obligee, it will want to execute the same type of financing and control agreements that it would if a default had been declared. However, in those situations, the recitals regarding the principal's inability to complete its bonded obligations become particularly important for protecting the surety's subrogation rights. There is a substantial body of case law that holds that a formal declaration of default is not required in order for subrogation rights to vest in the surety. All that is required is a *de facto* default, meaning that the principal was unable to fulfill its obligations under the bonded contract. Thus, as long as the agreements include confirmation that the principal is unable to complete the work in the absence of the surety's financing, the surety's subrogation rights are preserved. As one court pointed out:

> Both the State and the United States vehemently argue that the default contemplated in the contract between the bankrupt and the surety never occurred, and hence the assignment never matured; nor did the surety acquire a lien by way of subrogation. To some extent, the arrangement created by the bankrupt and the surety whereby construction costs were paid out of the joint account into which they deposited progress payments supports this argument, for nominally the bankrupt continued its operations subject only to financial supervision by the surety. In this way, construction activity never ceased and bills were paid without material delay. But to analyze these facts so as to deprive the surety of its claim based on subrogation when it actually provided over $136,000 of its own money to pay laborers and materialmen is too technical to warrant serious consideration. The nub of the bankrupt's default was its inability to continue paying its bills. Whether the surety stepped in prior to or after the bankrupt failed to pay these bills is of little moment. The important fact is that the surety expended large sums of its own money to complete the contracts for which it has not been recompensed.[163]

---

[163] Mass. Bonding & Ins. Co. v. New York, 259 F.2d 33, 37-38 (2d Cir. 1958) (citation omitted). In this case, the surety had provided financing to a bond principal that later went bankrupt. Both the federal government and the State of New York asserted tax liens. The financing surety argued that it was entitled to the remainder of the bankrupt principal's estate based on its subrogation rights, but the governmental entities argued that

Performance Options Available to the Surety

The general rule, therefore, is that a surety that finances its principal prior to a declaration of default is still acting because of its legal obligation, not acting as a volunteer, and its subrogation rights remain intact.

Another alternative is to simply have the principal execute a voluntary letter of default and termination addressed to the bond obligee. This should eliminate any later potential dispute with the bond principal and indemnitors over whether there was a valid default or not. The surety should always have the principal execute voluntary letters of default, which can be sent at the appropriate time as determined by the surety, even if they are not sent right away. Generally speaking, however, most contractors will want to avoid taking a voluntary termination, as it may impair a contractor's ability to bid on other projects in the future. In such cases, the surety, principal and indemnitors can execute joint agreements wherein the parties expressly agree that there is a default on a bonded project thereby necessitating financing from the surety.

One problem for the surety who opts to fund its principal prior to any default is the penal sum of the bonds and the handling of the obligee. When a default has already been declared, the surety can seek an agreement from the obligee that funds provided to the principal for the completion of the bonded project will correspondingly reduce the penal sum of the bond. However, in deciding to fund a bond principal prior to default, the surety is often trying to keep the principal in business and prevent the multitude of issues which accompany the declaration of default (other obligees demanding financial assurances, subcontractors who learn about the default and stop work, etc.). Such efforts, the obligee will argue, do not serve to reduce the penal sum of the bond. Therefore, before financing the principal pre-default, the surety should feel confident that, but for the financial issues, the principal is capable of completing the bonded work. At a minimum, the surety must have personnel overseeing the principal's project and company performance, in order to protect its investment. Otherwise, the surety can be left in the unenviable position of having to fund completion of the project twice.

---

the surety had no subrogation rights because there had been no technical default under the terms of the contract. The court rejected the argument that a formal default was required and the surety prevailed.

B. Assignment of Bonded Contracts

If a bond principal encounters a particularly problematic project and approaches its surety for assistance, the surety can try to negotiate with the obligee and principal for an assignment of the bonded contract to the surety.[164] This approach is sometimes preferred when the obligee has a time-consuming default termination process that would delay the transition to the surety and ultimately cost the surety more money in delay or other damages. Under this scenario, the surety typically takes over completion of the work without a formal termination for default and without having to complete an investigation. The surety can then arrange for the project to be completed by a licensed completion contractor.

If the bonded contract is assigned, the surety also assumes the right to receive payments from the obligee, reducing the amount of indemnity it will have to seek from the principal and indemnitors. In theory, assuming that the obligee has not overpaid the principal, there should be sufficient funds remaining in the contract balance to complete the remaining work. By the time a project has reached this point, however, the contractor (and thus the assignee surety) are usually in a cash negative position due to unresolved change orders, bid deficiencies, subcontractor claims, deficiencies, liquidated damages, etc. It would be prudent for the surety to attempt to reduce, if not eliminate, the obligee's contractual setoffs at the time of the assignment in order to improve cash flow on the project. Obligees, in the interest of getting the project back on track, often will at least agree to forbear from withholding money from the surety for problems caused by the contractor.

In addition, the surety will want to have its own consultants overseeing and managing the project, in addition to personnel from the bond principal, which represents additional costs, as well. For these reasons, among others, the surety will likely incur a loss by the end of the project, and will want to ensure that any assignment package includes an agreement wherein the principal and indemnitors reaffirm their joint obligations for any surety loss.

---

164   Sometimes the surety can arrange for the assignment to go from the principal directly to a new completion contractor, with obligee ratification. This is essentially the "tender" option without a default termination. The same considerations apply here as to the tender option discussed earlier in this chapter.

By accepting an assignment of the bonded contract from its principal, the surety steps into the identical shoes of its principal and thereby may not be able to claim any protections afforded under the bond or any limitations on its liability created under the bond.

In the alternative, the surety can attempt to arrange an assignment of the bonded contract from its principal to a third-party contractor, with the third-party contractor either providing its own bonds or the surety agreeing to permit its bonds to remain operative. This option is most feasible either where the construction work has not commenced or is in its initial phases or where the work is substantially complete or approaching substantial completion. This pre-default option is analogous in certain respects to a tender following a default. One principal advantage over a post-default tender may be that a "pre-default" assignment can include an assignment of the principal's subcontracts and thereby bind the subcontractors to complete at their original pricing.

Assignments may be subject to anti-assignment clauses in the operative contracts. Although some courts will invalidate an attempted assignment altogether when the contract contains an anti-assignment provision, the modern trend is to hold that such provisions only limit a parties' right to assign a contract, not its power to do so, unless the clause specifically declares any assignment to be void.[165] Under this reasoning, unless an anti-assignment clause specifically voids an assignment, the assignment is valid and the party contesting the assignment is relegated to a remedy in damages due to a breach of the clause. Typically,

---

[165] *See, e.g.,* Bank of Am., N.A. v. Moglia, 330 F.3d 942, 947-48 (7th Cir. 2003); Bel-Ray Co. v. Chemrite Ltd., 181 F.3d 435, 441-43 (3d Cir. 1999); Pravin Banker Assocs. Ltd. v. Banco Popular Del Peru, 109 F.3d 850, 856 (2d Cir. 1997); Cedar Point Apartments, Ltd. v. Cedar Point Inv. Corp., 693 F.2d 748, 753-54 (8th Cir. 1982); Wonsey v. Life Ins. Co. of N. Am., 32 F. Supp. 2d 939, 943-44 (E.D. Mich. 1998); Int'l Telecomms. Exch. Corp. v. MCI Telecomms. Corp., 892 F. Supp. 1520, 1533-34 (N.D. Ga. 1995); Pro Cardiaco Pronto Socorro Cardiologica S.A. v. Trussell, 863 F. Supp. 135, 137-38 (S.D.N.Y. 1994); Lomas Mortgage U.S.A., Inc. v. W.E. O'Neil Constr. Co., 812 F. Supp. 841, 843-44 (N.D. Ill. 1993); In re Freeman, 232 B.R. 497, 501-02 (Bankr. M.D. Fla. 1999); Rumbin v. Utica Mut. Ins. Co., 757 A.2d 526, 532-34 (Conn. 2000); Travertine Corp. v. Lexington-Silverwood, 683 N.W.2d 267, 272-74 (Minn. 2004); In re Kaufman, 37 P.3d 845, 851-52 (Okla. 2001).

monetary damages do not flow from an assignment in derogation of an anti-assignment clause.

Notably, as mentioned earlier, federal law does not recognize an assignment in favor of a surety by a contractor.[166] Therefore, when dealing with a federal government contract, assigning the bonded contract to the surety may not be a viable option. Under those circumstances, the surety can prepare its completion proposal, and have the principal execute a voluntary letter of default. Then, the surety can present the bond obligee with the letter of default and its proposal simultaneously. If the principal and obligee have had a positive working relationship, the surety may even approach the obligee prior to presenting the letter of default in order to negotiate the terms of its takeover before taking any formal action. This can drastically reduce the delays that might otherwise be encountered if the surety waited for a declaration of default.

Conclusion

By issuing a performance bond, the surety has committed itself to facilitating the completion of the principal's work in some manner in the event of a principal's default, whether it completes the work itself or simply pays for someone else to do so. As this chapter makes clear, there are numerous potential scenarios for the surety who is faced with a bond claim. Above all else, the surety must act swiftly and judiciously, focusing on conducting a reasonable investigation, determining its potential liability, and, if necessary, completing the work. Each of these decisions carry significant legal consequences, so they must be weighed carefully. The surety cannot afford to be shortsighted nor can it afford to ignore the fact that its actions will directly affect a number of other parties.

---

166   41 U.S.C. § 15(b) (2008).

4

THE PERFORMANCE BOND SURETY'S RIGHTS TO THE CONTRACT FUNDS

George J. Bachrach
Cynthia E. Rodgers-Waire*

Introduction

During its fact-gathering investigation of a performance bond claim and based upon its analysis of the information obtained, the performance bond surety will determine its rights and obligations and choose its performance option or options. A critical element in the performance bond surety's investigation and analysis is the status of the contract funds that the obligee is contractually obligated to pay, first to the principal to perform the work under the construction contract and then, upon the principal's default and/or termination, to complete the performance of the work, whether the obligee or the surety completes the performance of the work.

A performance bond surety has rights to the contract funds to complete the performance of the work and/or to mitigate its loss. This chapter will review the rights of the various parties to the contract funds, including the obligee, the principal, the principal's subcontractors and suppliers, and the surety, and those other parties who may compete with and contest the performance bond surety's rights to the contract funds. In addition, this chapter will address the unique issues involving the federal government, as obligee, and the performance bond surety.

---

* Adam Cizek of Whiteford, Taylor & Preston, LLC rendered assistance with respect to the research and preparation of this chapter.

I. The Starting Point–The Obligee's Rights to the Contract Funds

When an obligee and a principal enter into a construction contract,[1] the principal has a reasonable expectation that the obligee will pay the contract funds to the principal for its performance of the work. There are many different forms of construction contracts between obligees and principals, but the two most frequently used form construction contracts are the AIA Standard Form of Agreement[2] in conjunction with the AIA General Conditions,[3] and the new ConsensusDOCS Standard Agreement and General Conditions.[4]

Whether the contract funds are defined as the "Contract Sum" under the AIA Standard Form of Agreement[5] and the AIA General

---

[1] This chapter will always address the owner (or general contractor, when applicable) as the "obligee" under the performance bond and the general contractor (or subcontractor, when applicable) as the "principal" under the performance bond.

[2] AIA Document A101-2007, *Standard Form of Agreement Between Owner and Contractor Where the Basis of Payment is a Stipulated Sum* (Am. Inst. of Architects 2007) (hereinafter the "AIA Standard Form of Agreement"). As between a general contractor and a subcontractor, see AIA Document A401-2007, *Standard Form of Agreement Between Contractor and Subcontractor* (Am. Inst. of Architects 2007).

[3] AIA Document A101-2007, *General Conditions of the Contract for Construction* (Am. Inst. of Architects 2007) (hereinafter the "AIA General Conditions").

[4] ConsensusDOCS 200, *Standard Agreement and General Conditions Between Owner and Contractor (Where the Contract Price is a Lump Sum)* (ConsensusDOCS 2007) (hereinafter the "CD Agreement"). As between a general contractor and a subcontractor, see ConsensusDOCS 750, *Standard Form of Agreement Between Contractor and Subcontractor* (ConsensusDOCS 2007).

[5] AIA Standard Form of Agreement, *supra* note 2, § 4.1. The Contract Sum may be changed by certain alternates (§ 4.3) and allowances (§ 4.4), and by the terms of the AIA General Conditions, including additions and deductions for Changes in the Work (Article 7), delays and extensions of time (§ 8.3 and Article 15), liquidated damages, corrective work and others.

Conditions,[6] or as the "Contract Price" under the CD Agreement,[7] the obligee agrees to pay the principal for its performance of the work under the contract. The critical importance of the obligee's obligation and ability to pay the contract funds to the principal is highlighted in both the AIA General Conditions and the CD Agreement. The AIA General Conditions provide not only that the principal is entitled to information concerning the obligee's ability to pay the contract funds for the principal's performance of the work,[8] but also that the obligee must furnish the principal with information concerning the principal's ability to perfect and enforce its mechanics' lien rights.[9] The CD Agreement requires not only that the obligee provide the principal with the information concerning the obligee's financial ability to pay the contract funds for the principal's performance of the work,[10] but also that the obligee must furnish the principal with information concerning the principal's ability to perfect and enforce its mechanics' lien rights.[11]

Normally the principal is entitled to the payment of the contract funds based upon its performance and eventual completion of the work required under the contract. Most form construction contracts provide for the payment of progress payments to the principal during the time of the principal's performance of the work, and for final payment when the work is complete. The AIA Standard Form of Agreement,[12] the AIA

---

[6] AIA General Conditions, *supra* note 3, § 9.1. The AIA General Conditions then provide for the Contractor's submission of a Schedule of Values (§ 9.2), the Contractor's submission of an Application for Payment (§ 9.3), and the Architect's issuance of a Certificate for Payment (§ 9.4).
[7] CD Agreement, *supra* note 4, § 7.1. Article 8 concerns Changes in the Work that may lead to an increase or decrease in the Contract Price.
[8] AIA General Conditions, *supra* note 3, § 2.2.1.
[9] *Id.* § 2.1.2.
[10] CD Agreement, *supra* note 4, § 4.2.
[11] *Id.* § 4.5.
[12] AIA Standard Form of Agreement, *supra* note 2, § 5.1.1. The Standard Form of Agreement provides for the Architect certification of the amount due to the Contractor within a specified period of time (§ 5.1.3), that each Application for Payment be based upon the most recent schedule of values (§ 5.1.4), and the manner and methods for the computation of the progress payment. Final payment under the AIA Standard Form of Agreement is found in § 5.2.

General Conditions[13] and the CD Agreement[14] each provide detailed provisions with respect to the obligee's payment of the contract funds to the principal.

Notwithstanding the principal's performance of the work and its submission of its application for payment of the contract funds, the obligee has contractual rights to withhold the payment of the contract funds. Under the AIA General Conditions, the architect may withhold approval of the principal's application for payment of the contract funds.[15] The CD Agreement provides the obligee with a similar right to adjust or reject a principal's application for payment of the contract funds.[16]

The provisions of the AIA Standard Form of Agreement and the AIA General Conditions and those of the CD Agreement (or the provisions of whatever construction contract exists between the obligee and the principal) constitute one of the starting points in determining the surety's rights to the contract funds in the event that the obligee makes a claim against the surety's performance bond. As discussed later in this chapter, many performance bonds require an obligee to "pay the balance of the contract price" to the surety upon the surety's performance of its performance bond obligations. Furthermore, those performance bonds may incorporate by reference the underlying construction contract.

Long before the principal may be determined to be in default and subsequently terminated from the performance of the work under the contract, there may be tension between the obligee and the principal concerning the payment of the contract funds. The principal submits its application for the payment of the contract funds to the obligee because it wants to be paid for the performance of the work. The principal's performance or lack of performance of the work may or may not lead to

---

13   *See generally* the AIA General Conditions, *supra* note 3, Article 9, and specifically § 9.6, which provide more details concerning the Owner's payment of the progress payments. Final completion and final payment under the AIA General Conditions is found in § 9.10.

14   CD Agreement, *supra* note 4, § 9.2 requires the Contractor to prepare and submit to the Owner a schedule of values and progress payment Applications in accordance with the procedures set forth in § 9.1 and § 9.2. Final completion and final payment under the CD Agreement is found in § 9.8.

15   AIA General Conditions, *supra* note 3, § 9.5.1.

16   CD Agreement, *supra* note 4, § 9.3.

the obligee's decision either to withhold certification for the payment of the contract funds or to adjust the principal's payment application. From the obligee's standpoint, the obligee must have both the ability to pay the principal and also the obligation to pay the principal, if, in fact, the principal is entitled to the payment of the contract funds.

When an obligee refuses to pay the principal and asserts the obligee's rights under the contract against the contract funds, the obligee may be justified due to the principal's failure to perform the work and/or to comply with its contractual obligations, or the obligee may be in default under the contract due to its failure or refusal to pay the principal. In either instance, the result may lead to the obligee's default and subsequent termination of the principal's right to perform the work under the contract and a claim against the surety's performance bond. The obligee has various rights under the construction contract that may significantly affect the surety's rights to the contract funds in the event that the obligee makes a claim against the surety's performance bond.

A. *The Obligee's Contractual Right to Complete the Performance of the Work*

Many form construction contracts provide the obligee with the right to withhold payment of the contract funds from the principal when the principal repeatedly fails to carry out the performance of the work in accordance with the contract,[17] when there is reasonable evidence that the principal's performance of the work cannot be completed for the unpaid balance of the contract funds,[18] and/or when there is reasonable evidence that the principal's performance of the work cannot be completed within the contract time and schedule.[19] As a result, the obligee may assert its contractual rights to complete the principal's performance of the work under the contract.

The AIA General Conditions provide the obligee with the right to perform the work even if the principal is not in default and/or has not

---

17   *See* the AIA General Conditions, *supra* note 3, § 9.5.1.7, and the CD Agreement, *supra* note 4, § 9.3.1.
18   *See* the AIA General Conditions, *supra* note 3, § 9.5.1.4, and the CD Agreement, *supra* note 4, § 9.3.6.
19   *See* the AIA General Conditions, *supra* note 3, § 9.5.1.6, and the CD Agreement, *supra* note 4, § 9.3.5.

been terminated.[20] The CD Agreement requires the obligee to provide a notice to cure a default to the principal, but also authorizes the obligee to perform the work under the contract.[21]

The obligee's election to enforce its contractual right to complete the principal's performance of the work, whether or not the principal is in default and/or has been terminated from the contract, will inevitably lead to a reduction in the balance of the contract funds. This reduction of the contract funds may or may not prejudice the surety ultimately investigating the obligee's performance bond claim. The language of the surety's performance bond may allow the obligee to complete the performance of the work, it may allow the surety to use the principal to perform the work, and/or it may authorize the surety to either take over and complete the performance of the work or tender a completion contractor to the obligee conditioned upon the obligee's "payment of the contract balance" to the surety.[22] Because the obligee's cost to perform the principal's work may be different (most likely higher than the principal's cost to perform the work, and possibly the surety's cost to perform the work), the surety may deny the obligee's claim against the surety's performance bond.

B. The Obligee's Contractual Right to Pay the Principal's Subcontractors/Suppliers

There are other grounds for the obligee's refusal to pay the contract funds to the principal. The obligee may withhold the payment of the contract funds to the principal if the principal fails to properly pay its subcontractors and suppliers[23] or there is reasonable evidence that third-party mechanics' lien claims and other claims may be asserted against the obligee or the obligee's property.[24]

---

20 AIA General Conditions, *supra* note 3, § 2.4.
21 CD Agreement, *supra* note 4, § 11.2.
22 *See* Chapter 3, *supra* (describing the performance bond surety's options, including takeover and completion, tender, financing the principal and completion by the obligee).
23 *See* the AIA General Conditions, *supra* note 3, § 9.5.1.3, and the CD Agreement, *supra* note 4, § 9.3.3.
24 *See* the AIA General Conditions, *supra* note 3, § 9.5.1.2, and the CD Agreement, *supra* note 4, § 9.3.7.

Obligees want their principals to pay their subcontractors and suppliers the amounts due for their respective performance of the work and supplying of materials on the project as soon as possible after the principal receives payment from the obligee. The AIA General Conditions and the CD Agreement are no different in the results that they want to achieve, but they come from different angles.

The AIA General Conditions provide two protections to the principal's subcontractors and suppliers. First, unless there is a surety payment bond, the principal must hold the contract funds for payment to its subcontractors and suppliers.[25] Second, the AIA General Conditions provide the obligee with the ability to issue joint checks in the event that the principal fails to make proper payments to its subcontractors and suppliers under section 9.5.1.3 of the AIA General Conditions,[26] thereby reducing the balance of the contract funds.

The CD Agreement also authorizes the obligee to make an adjustment to a principal's payment application if the principal fails to properly pay its subcontractors and suppliers following receipt of the progress payment from the obligee.[27]

From the surety's standpoint, the principal's failure to pay its subcontractors and suppliers is just as much a failure of the principal to perform as the principal's failure to perform the work under the contract.[28] However, while the obligee's use of the contract funds to pay

---

25 AIA General Conditions, *supra* note 3, § 9.6.7.
26 *Id.* § 9.5.3.
27 CD Agreement, *supra* note 4, § 9.3.3.
28 Many cases have found no distinction between the principal's default in its failure to perform the work under the contract and the principal's default in its failure to pay the claims of its subcontractors and suppliers. *In re* Larbar Corp., 177 F.3d 439, 443 (6th Cir. 1999); *In re* Modular Structures, Inc., 27 F.3d 72, 77-78 (3d Cir. 1994); United States v. Pa. Dep't of Highways, 349 F. Supp. 1370, 1379-80 (E.D. Pa. 1972); Fid. & Cas. Co. of N.Y. v. Dykstra, 208 F. Supp. 717, 721-22 (D. Minn. 1962); Atl. Ref. Co. v. Cont'l Gas Co., 183 F. Supp. 478, 483-84 (W.D. Pa. 1960); Transam. Premier Ins. Co. v. United States, 32 Fed. Cl. 308, 312 (1994); U.S. Fid. & Guar. Co. v. Triborough Bridge Auth., 74 N.E.2d 226, 227-28 (N.Y. 1947). Furthermore, the obligee may compel the surety to keep the bonded project free and clear of all mechanics' liens. Third Nat'l Bank in Nashville v. Highlands Ins. Co., 603 S.W.2d 730 (Tenn. 1980).

the principal's subcontractors and suppliers on the project may ultimately increase the surety's performance bond loss because of the obligee's use of the contract funds, it should reduce the surety's payment bond loss to the extent that the principal's subcontractors and suppliers on the project are paid from the contract funds otherwise due to the principal on that project.[29]

C. The Obligee's Other Contractual, Statutory and Common-Law Rights

The obligee may have other contract, statutory and common-law rights that allow the obligee to withhold payments to the principal under the construction contract. Generally, these other rights include the following:

1. Contract Rights

In addition to its contractual rights to complete the performance of the principal's work and to pay the principal's subcontractors and suppliers, the obligee may have other contractual rights to withhold the payment of the contract funds to the principal.

 a. *Claims (defective work, warranty work, etc.)*. The obligee may withhold payment of the contract funds to the principal resulting from the principal's performing work that is rejected, non-conforming or defective, and not corrected in a timely fashion.[30]

 b. *Delay (liquidated damages and/or actual damages)*. The obligee may withhold payment of the contract funds to the principal when there is reasonable evidence that the principal's performance of the work cannot be completed within the contract time and schedule and/or the unpaid balance of the contract funds would not be adequate to cover the

---

29 This statement assumes that the subcontractors and suppliers will apply the obligee's payments from the project contract funds to the principal's obligations to the subcontractors and suppliers on that project. If the obligee's payments are applied by the subcontractors and suppliers to other obligations that the principal may have to those subcontractors and suppliers, the surety may lose the benefit of the contract funds for either the performance of the principal's work or the payment of the principal's obligations to its subcontractors and suppliers on the project.

30 *See* the AIA General Conditions, *supra* note 3, § 9.5.1.1, and the CD Agreement, *supra* note 4, § 9.3.4.

actual or liquidated damages that the obligee may incur as a result of the anticipated delay.[31]

c. *Contractual setoff rights.* Neither the AIA General Conditions nor the CD Agreement provides the obligee with a contractual right to setoff obligations under the contract with the principal against any other obligations that the principal may have to the obligee not related to the contract or the project (i.e., under other contracts and projects that the obligee may have with the principal). However, there are a number of non-standard form, manuscript contracts that allow the obligee to setoff amounts owed to a principal on one contract (bonded by the surety) against amounts that the principal may owe to the obligee on an entirely different contract for an entirely different project (whether or not it is bonded by the surety).[32] When such contractual setoff rights exist, the surety that anticipates that it will have access to the "balance of the contract price" for its performance of the work under its subcontract performance bond (the subcontractor principal is in default and has been terminated from its performance of the work) may face the situation where the general contractor obligee attempts to reduce the "balance of the contract price" under the bonded subcontract as a result of the obligations of the subcontractor principal to the general contractor obligee that have nothing to do with the subcontract for which the surety executed its subcontract performance and payment bonds.

2. Statutory Rights (The Right to Withhold Contract Funds Under Mechanics' Lien and Stop Notice Statutes)

The obligee may have statutory rights to withhold payment of the contract funds to the principal as a result of mechanics' liens filed by the principal's subcontractors and suppliers and/or due to the obligee's

---

31   *See* the AIA General Conditions, *supra* note 3, § 9.5.1.6, and the CD Agreement, *supra* note 4, § 9.3.5.
32   Neither the AIA General Conditions, *supra* note 3, nor the CD Agreement, *supra* note 4, and neither the AIA Document A401-2007 Standard Form of Agreement Between Contractor and Subcontractor, *supra* note 2, nor the ConsensusDOCS 750 Standard Form of Agreement Between Contractor and Subcontractor, *supra* note 4, contain such an express contractual setoff provision and right for the obligee against the principal.

receipt of a "stop notice" authorized under various state statutes.[33] While mechanics' liens typically attach to real property, "stop notice" statutes address the contract funds in the hands of the obligees or lenders.[34] "Stop notice" statutes allow a party that is owed money on a construction project to provide the obligee or lender with notice of the party's claim to prevent the obligee's disbursement of the contract funds to the principal until the party's debt is satisfied.[35]

3. Common-Law Setoff Rights

In addition to its contractual and statutory rights, an obligee may also have its common-law setoff rights to withhold the payment to the principal of the contract funds from one contract with the principal as a result of the principal's obligations to the obligee under a different and separate contract or for any other reason (including tax obligations).[36]

D. The Obligee's Default and/or Termination of the Principal

The obligee's final contractual rights to the contract funds arise when the obligee terminates the principal for default under the contract. While the grounds for default and termination and the procedures for default and

---

[33] See, e.g., MD. CODE ANN., REAL PROP. § 9-104(f)(1) (2009). Each state has enacted a mechanics' lien law. See Philip L. Bruner & Patrick J. O'Connor, Jr., 3 BRUNER & O'CONNOR ON CONSTRUCTION LAW § 8:124 (2002). For a detailed discussion of each state's mechanics' lien law, see FIFTY STATE CONSTRUCTION LIEN & BOND LAW, 2d ed. (2000).

[34] Mechanics' liens are typically not available on public projects. At least one state has enacted a statute that allows parties to claim a lien on contract funds held by the obligee on public construction projects. See S.D. CODIFIED LAWS § 5-22-1 (2009).

[35] For examples of state "stop notice" statutes, see ALASKA STAT. § 34.35.062 (2009); ARIZ. REV. STAT. §§ 33-1051, et seq. (2009); CAL. CIV. CODE §§ 3156, et seq. (2008). See also Curtis R. Reitz, Construction Lender's Liability to Contractors, Subcontractors, and Materialmen, 130 U. PA. L. REV. 416 (1981).

[36] See, e.g., Transamerica Ins. Co. v. United States, 989 F.2d 1188 (Fed. Cir. 1993); District of Columbia v. Aetna Ins. Co., 462 A.2d 428 (D.C. 1983); Morash v. New York, 703 N.Y.S.2d 55 (N.Y. App. Div. 2000).

termination may differ, the ultimate result is the obligee's withholding of the payment of the contract funds to the principal.

Pursuant to the AIA General Conditions, the obligee has several grounds for terminating the principal's contract and right to perform the work under the contract.[37] The AIA General Conditions then set forth the procedures, including written notice, for the termination of the principal[38] and the effect on the payment of the contract funds after the obligee terminates the principal.[39] The CD Agreement also provides for the obligee's notice to the principal to cure the defaults prior to termination,[40] and then defines the obligee's rights to terminate the principal for default.[41]

When an obligee terminates the principal for default under the contract, the obligee is no longer obligated to pay the contract funds to the principal unless the actual cost of the obligee's completing the work that was to be performed by the principal results in contract funds remaining after the obligee has deducted all of its costs and expenses for performing the work. Furthermore, the principal's default and termination may lead to the obligee's demand and/or claim against the surety's performance bond. The surety's rights to the contract funds upon the default and termination of its principal are many and varied, but they start with the rights of either the obligee or the principal to the contract funds from the inception of the contractual relationship until the principal's default and termination, and continue forward to encompass the surety's own contractual and other rights to the contract funds.

II. The Theoretical Bases for the Performance Bond Surety's Rights to the Contract Funds

In the event that the principal is unable to perform or complete the performance of its work under the contract, whether because of a declared default, termination, or for any other reason, the obligee has the right (contractual, statutory and/or common-law) to withhold the balance

---

37   AIA General Conditions, *supra* note 3, § 14.2.
38   *Id.* § 14.2.2. Section 14.2.2 sets forth the actions that the Owner may take to "terminate employment of the Contractor," but "subject to any prior rights of the surety."
39   *Id.* § 14.2.3.
40   CD Agreement, *supra* note 4, § 11.2.
41   *Id.* § 11.3.1.

of the contract funds and to use the balance of the contract funds to pay for the performance of the remaining work and the other obligations under the contract. To the extent that the costs to perform the remaining work exceed the balance of the contract funds, the obligee has the right to bring an action against the principal for reimbursement of its excess costs to complete the performance of the work under the contract and to pay the claims of the principal's subcontractors and suppliers on the project.

When the principal and its surety provide a performance bond to the obligee, the obligee has additional protection in the event of the principal's default, termination and/or other failure to perform the work under the contract because the obligee may make a claim against the surety's performance bond. However, notwithstanding the existence and obligations of the surety's performance bond, the obligee is contractually bound to pay someone the balance of the contract funds for the further performance and completion of the work under the contract. The obligee's payment may be to the surety that performs under its performance bond.

Performance bonds are not insurance. Rather, suretyship is a credit transaction.[42] By providing its credit to the principal in order for the principal to enter into a construction contract with the obligee, the surety guarantees that the principal will perform the work under the contract in accordance with the terms of the contract, including the obligee's payment of the contract funds. When the surety is called upon to perform and elects its options, if any, under its performance bond, the surety has a right and expectation that the contract funds will be used by the obligee to complete the performance of the work under the contract.

---

42 *See* George J. Bachrach, Ch. 1, *The Surety's Rights to Obtain Salvage–Exoneration, Reimbursement, Subrogation and Contribution*, in SALVAGE BY THE SURETY 1, 1 (George J. Bachrach ed., 1998).

A. The Performance Bond Surety's Rights to the Contract Funds

Practically every performance bond is different from every other performance bond.[43] The surety's rights to the contract funds depend upon the performance bond language as well as the underlying construction contract that may be incorporated into the performance bond, and the surety's statutory and common-law rights. When the obligee defaults and terminates a principal on a contract and makes a demand against the surety's performance bond, the surety begins its investigation by reviewing its rights and obligations contained in the performance bond.

In order to obtain the contract funds, the performance bond surety must perform.[44] While some performance bonds do not set forth any

---

[43] See Chapters 1 through 3, *supra*, for discussions of the many basic types of performance bonds, including but not limited to standard form private performance bonds, statutorily required performance bonds, indemnity bonds, manuscript bonds, completion bonds, and others that an obligee may request or require and a principal and a surety may execute. The standard form performance bonds that relate to the AIA Documents are the AIA Document A311 Performance Bond (Am. Inst. of Architects 1970) and the AIA Document A312 Performance Bond (Am. Inst. of Architects 1984). The standard form performance bond that relates to the ConsensusDOCS is the ConsensusDOCS 260 Performance Bond (ConsensusDOCS 2007). Occasionally, the "standard" performance bond may become a "manuscript" performance bond that shifts the "normal construction risks and liabilities" in some fashion such that it may become "onerous" to one party (usually the surety) or another. Steven D. Nelson, "Onerous" Bond Forms–A Look at Departures from Standard Performance and Payment Bond Provisions (2004) (unpublished paper submitted at the ABA Forum on the Constr. Indus./TIPS Fid. & Surety Law Comm. program on Jan. 29, 2004 at the 2004 ABA Mid-Winter Meeting).

[44] In order for a performance bond surety to be deemed a performing surety, there is no requirement that its principal be declared in default by the obligee, the principal's contract be terminated by the obligee, or the surety assume primary responsibility for the completion of the contract. Aetna Cas. & Sur. Co. v. United States, 845 F.2d 971, 975 (Fed. Cir. 1988); Great Am. Ins. Co. v. United States, 481 F.2d 1298, 1307-08 (Ct. Cl. 1973). Generally, a surety may perform under its performance bond in

options for the performance bond surety to perform its obligations, others spell out in some detail those options that the surety may exercise to perform its obligations under the performance bond.[45]

The AIA Document A311 Performance Bond, the AIA Document A312 Performance Bond, and the ConsensusDOCS 260 Performance Bond all provide that the surety may exercise certain performance options. The performance bond surety's theoretical rights to the contract funds start with the performance bond option that the surety may elect.

Chapter 3 describes in detail the frequent options that a performance bond surety may have under the applicable performance bond, which may include the takeover and completion option, the tender option, the financing of the principal option, the completion by the obligee option, and the surety's denial of liability under the performance bond option.[46] Regardless of which option the performance bond surety chooses, the surety will have direct rights to the contract funds if it enters into some agreement with the obligee (the takeover and completion option) or

---

a number of ways. The surety may make payments to the obligee as a result of its principal's default, it may undertake the completion of the contract in some fashion, or it may finance its principal in order to complete the contract. Aetna Cas. & Sur. Co. v. United States, 845 F.2d 971, 975 (Fed. Cir. 1988); Transamerica Ins. Co. v. United States, 31 Fed. Cl. 532 (1994) (the surety facilitated the completion of the contract by tendering a completion contractor to the federal government and paying the completion contractor to complete the work). There is no distinction between a performing surety that discharges its obligations by taking over and completing a project and one that finances its principal in order to allow its principal to complete the project. Morgenthau v. Fid. & Dep. Co. of Md., 94 F.2d 632, 635-36 (D.C. Cir. 1937). By providing a principal with financial assistance prior to a formal default, a surety minimizes the delay in completion of the project and protects the interests of the principal, obligee and the surety. *See* Morrison Assurance Co. v. United States, 3 Cl. Ct. 626 (1983).

45 *See* Chapter 3, *supra*.
46 *See also* George J. Bachrach, "The Surety Performance Bond Lifeboat: Bailing Out and/or Salvaging Someone Else's Wreck" (2007) (unpublished paper submitted at the ABA Forum on the Construction Industry Fall program on Oct. 26, 2007), *republished* as "A Primer for the Surety's Handling of Performance Bond Claims" (2008) (unpublished paper submitted at the Nineteenth Annual Northeast Sur. & Fid. Claims Conference on Sept. 18, 2008).

indirect rights to the contract funds if the obligee is compelled to use the contract funds for the completion of the performance of the work (the tender option, the completion by the obligee option, and the surety's denial of liability under the performance bond option). If the surety exercises its option to finance the principal, then the contract funds will be paid either to the principal or the surety depending upon the controls and procedures established pursuant to the financing arrangement. Therefore, theoretically, all of the contract funds will be used to complete the performance of the work required under the underlying contract.

B. The Performance Bond Surety's Indemnity Agreement Rights to the Contract Funds

In addition to the performance bond surety's direct contractual rights to the contract funds held by the obligee pursuant to the terms of the performance bond and the underlying construction contract that is incorporated into the performance bond, the surety may also have contractual rights to the principal's claims to the contract funds pursuant to the surety's indemnity agreement. These rights under the indemnity agreement include the surety's assignment rights and perfected security interest in the contract funds and the surety's rights to the contract funds under the indemnity agreement's trust fund provision.[47]

1. The Surety's Indemnity Agreement Perfected Security Interest in the Contract Funds Under the Uniform Commercial Code

Most sureties require their principals, and other third-party indemnitors, to execute an indemnity agreement that provides for the assignment of certain of the principal's property rights to the surety, including the contract funds on any bonded project, and allows the surety to perfect its assignment rights and security interest.[48] If the surety has filed a notice

---

47   See Chapter 6, *infra*, for a more detailed discussion of these surety rights.
48   See Chapter 6, *infra*; *see also* THE SURETY'S INDEMNITY AGREEMENT: LAW AND PRACTICE 307-22 (Marilyn Klinger et al. eds., 2d ed. 2008). The surety may also take collateral at the time that it underwrites the bonds for its principal, including a perfected security interest in the

of its indemnity agreement as a financing statement under the Uniform Commercial Code,[49] or has otherwise filed or recorded some other financing statement executed by the principal as a result of a financial arrangement or pursuant to some other security agreement, the surety obtains a perfected security interest in the contract funds. The surety's rights and priorities to the contract funds based upon its perfected security interest are treated like any other perfected security interest under the Uniform Commercial Code.[50] However, the surety's assignment and perfected security interest in the contract funds may not be effective when the contract funds are held by a federal government obligee under a federal government contract.[51]

---

contract funds and other real and personal property owned by the principal and the indemnitors. *Id.* at 130-56.

49 The surety's filing of its indemnity agreement as a financing statement under the Uniform Commercial Code is not an election of remedies nor is it a waiver of the surety's subrogation rights. Am. Oil Co. v. L. A. Davidson, Inc., 290 N.W.2d 144 (Mich. Ct. App. 1980). Sureties have obtained priority to the contract funds by filing their indemnity agreements as a financing statement under the Uniform Commercial Code. Travelers Cas. & Sur. Co. of Am. v. Target Mech. Sys., Inc., 800 N.Y.S.2d 358 (N.Y. Sup. Ct. 2004).

50 If the surety's assignment rights are not perfected as a security interest against the contract funds, the surety may lose its assignment rights to a later assignment which has been recorded and perfected as a security interest. Travelers Indem. Co. v. Clark, 254 So. 2d 741 (Miss. 1971); Third Nat'l Bank in Nashville v. Highlands Ins. Co., 603 S.W.2d 730 (Tenn. 1980).

51 The Federal Assignment of Claims Act, 31 U.S.C. § 3727, and Anti-Assignment Act, 41 U.S.C. § 15, forbid an assignment of contract funds due under a contract with the United States other than to a financing institution. The courts have held that a surety is not a financing institution. Gen. Cas. Co. v. Second Nat'l Bank of Houston, 178 F.2d 679 (5th Cir. 1949); Royal Indem. Co. v. United States, 93 F. Supp. 891 (Ct. Cl. 1950). The act, however, is solely for the benefit of the federal government and does not affect the assignment as between other parties. Martin v. Nat'l Sur. Co., 300 U.S. 588 (1937); United Pac. Ins. Co. v. United States, 358 F.2d 966 (Ct. Cl. 1966); United Pac. Ins. Co. v. First Nat'l Bank of Oregon, 222 F. Supp. 243 (D. Ore. 1963). An assignment, therefore, can be valid as between the principal and the surety, but the federal government remains free to pay the principal.

2. The Surety's Trust Fund Rights Under the Indemnity Agreement

Frequently, an indemnity agreement contains a trust fund provision.[52] If the indemnity agreement has a trust fund provision that provides that the principal holds all contract funds in trust in order to pay its subcontractors and suppliers, or to pay the surety in the event that the surety is obligated to pay the subcontractors and suppliers under the performance or the payment bond, the principal has a fiduciary duty to the surety to hold the contract funds in accordance with the terms of the trust fund provision of the indemnity agreement.[53] If a valid express trust is created by the trust fund provision in the indemnity agreement, the surety's trust fund rights will be protected.[54]

---

52 See Chapter 6, *infra*; *see also* THE SURETY'S INDEMNITY AGREEMENT: LAW AND PRACTICE 291-307 (Marilyn Klinger et al. eds., 2d ed. 2008); *see generally* Robert L. Lawrence et al., *Ch. 2, The Agreement of Indemnity–The Surety's Handling of Contract Bond Problems: Enforcement of the Surety's Rights Against the Principal and the Indemnitors Under the Agreement of Indemnity*, in THE AGREEMENT OF INDEMNITY–PRACTICAL APPLICATIONS BY THE SURETY (George J. Bachrach ed., 1990).

53 See THE SURETY'S INDEMNITY AGREEMENT: LAW AND PRACTICE 489-92 (Marilyn Klinger et al. eds., 2d ed. 2008).

54 Whether the trust fund provision of the indemnity agreement constitutes an express trust and provides a surety with an interest in the contract funds must be determined under state law. *See* George J. Bachrach & Cynthia E. Rodgers-Waire, *The Surety's Rights to the Contract Funds in the Principal's Chapter 11 Bankruptcy Case*, 35 TORT & INS. L. J. 1, 15-20 (1999). In *In re* Alcon Demolition, Inc., 204 B.R. 440 (Bankr. D.N.J. 1997), the court found that the four elements for the establishment of an express trust under New Jersey law were met by the trust fund provision in the indemnity agreement, thus establishing a valid and enforceable express trust under New Jersey law. 204 B.R. at 448-49. The debtor had no beneficial interest in the contract funds to the express extent of the payments made by the surety, and the debtor was bound by its fiduciary duty to pay the contract funds to the surety as the beneficiary of the express trust under the trust fund provision of the indemnity agreement. *Id.* at 449; *In re* Maxon Eng'g Servs., Inc., 332 B.R. 495 (Bankr. D. P.R. 2005) (the trust fund provision of the indemnity agreement made the debtor a trustee of the contract funds for the benefit of persons furnishing labor or material and for the benefit of the surety). *Cf., In re* Eastern

C. The Performance Bond Surety's Subrogation Rights to the Contract Funds

Much has been written about the surety's subrogation rights generally[55] and specifically about the performance bond surety's subrogation rights to the contract funds.[56]

Concrete Paving Co., 293 B.R. 704 (Bankr. E.D. Mich. 2003) (the trust fund provision in an indemnity agreement was insufficient to prevent the contract funds from becoming property of the debtor's estate because it did not establish the intent of the project obligee, who transferred the funds, to hold the funds in trust).

55 George J. Bachrach & John V. Burch, Ch. 23, *The Surety's Subrogation Rights*, in THE LAW OF SURETYSHIP 419-53 (Edward G. Gallagher ed., 2d ed. 2000); Daniel Mungall, Jr., *Ch. 1, The Subrogation Rights of the Contract Bond Surety: Some Basics*, in SUBROGATION RIGHTS OF THE CONTRACT BOND SURETY 1 (George J. Bachrach ed., 1991).

56 *See* Edward G. Gallagher, *Ch. 4, Entitlement to Contract Proceeds*, in THE LAW OF PERFORMANCE BONDS 61-75 (Lawrence R. Moelmann & John T. Harris eds., 1999); G. Steven Ruprecht, *Ch. 5, Surety's Rights and Remedies Against Principals and Against Indemnitors Under the General Indemnity Agreement*, in THE LAW OF PERFORMANCE BONDS 77-121 (Lawrence R. Moelmann & John T. Harris eds., 1999); George J. Bachrach & Cynthia E. Rodgers-Waire, *The Surety's Rights to the Contract Funds in the Principal's Chapter 11 Bankruptcy Case*, 35 TORT & INS. L.J. 1 (1999); Francis J. McGrath et al., *The Financing Surety as a Performing Surety–Law and Practice* (2003) (unpublished paper submitted at the Fourteenth Annual Northeast Surety & Fidelity Claims Conference on Sept. 18, 2003). THE SUBROGATION DATABASE: CASES CONCERNING THE SUBROGATION RIGHTS OF THE CONTRACT BOND SURETY (George J. Bachrach ed., 1995) contains all of the cases concerning the subrogation rights of the surety organized in an outline (matrix) form. The outline (matrix) lists the significant issues concerning the subrogation rights of the surety and provides a framework or structure to identify, organize and categorize all cases concerning the surety's subrogation rights. *See also* George J. Bachrach, *Ch. 1, The Surety's Rights to Obtain Salvage-Exoneration, Reimbursement, Subrogation and Contribution*, in SALVAGE BY THE SURETY 1 (George J. Bachrach ed., 1998).

1. Subrogation Rights—Definition and Elements

The surety that performs its obligations under a performance bond and completes its principal's contractual performance obligations is subrogated to the rights of the obligee and the principal,[57] including the obligee's rights to the contract funds,[58] because by performing its obligations under a performance bond, the surety confers a benefit upon the obligee.[59]

---

57 Pearlman v. Reliance Ins. Co., 371 U.S. 132 (1962); Cont'l Cas. Co. v. Am. Sec. Corp., 443 F.2d 649, 652 (D.C. Cir. 1970); Trinity Universal Ins. Co. v. United States, 382 F.2d 317, 320 (5th Cir. 1967), *cert. denied*, 390 U.S. 906 (1968).

58 *See, e.g.*, Transamerica Ins. Co. v. United States, 989 F.2d 1188, 1190 (Fed. Cir. 1993); Aetna Cas. & Sur. Co. v. United States, 845 F.2d 971, 975 (Fed. Cir. 1988); Framingham Trust Co. v. Gould-National Batteries, Inc., 427 F.2d 856 (1st Cir. 1970); Am. Fire & Cas. Co. v. First Nat'l City Bank of N.Y., 411 F.2d 755, 758 (1st Cir. 1969); Trinity Universal Ins. Co. v. United States, 382 F.2d 317, 320 (5th Cir. 1967), *cert. denied*, 390 U.S. 906 (1968); Morgenthau v. Fid. & Dep. Co. of Md., 94 F.2d 632 (D.C. Cir. 1937); Fed. Ins. Co. v. Constructora Maza, Inc., 500 F. Supp. 246, 250 (D. P.R. 1979); Morrison Assurance Co. v. United States, 3 Cl. Ct. 626 (1983); Great Am. Ins. Co. v. United States, 481 F.2d 1298, 1308 (Ct. Cl. 1973); Sec. Ins. Co. of Hartford v. United States, 428 F.2d 838, 842 (Ct. Cl. 1970); Castro v. Malcolm, 226 P. 976 (Cal. 1924); Dist. of Columbia v. Aetna Ins. Co., 462 A.2d 428, 430 (D.C. 1983); Miller-Stauch Constr. Co. v. Williams-Bungart Elec., Inc., 959 S.W.2d 490, 495 (Mo. Ct. App. 1998); Fin. Co. of Am. v. United States Fid. & Guar. Co., 353 A.2d 249, 252 (Md. 1976); Globe Indem. Co. v. Peterson McCaslin, 303 P.2d 414 (Nev. 1956); Bd. of Educ. of Linden v. Vail, 154 A. 531 (N.J. Ch. 1931); Scarsdale Nat'l Bank & Trust Co. v. United States Fid. & Guar. Co., 190 N.E. 330 (N.Y. 1934); Sundheim v. Sch. Dist. of Phila., 166 A. 365, 369 (Pa. 1933). *See also*, OKLA. STAT. ANN. tit. 15, § 382 (2008); S.D. CODIFIED LAWS § 56-2-17(1) (2009).

59 *See* Am. Fire & Cas. Co. v. First Nat'l City Bank of N.Y., 411 F.2d 755, 758 (1st Cir. 1969) ("But for the surety's completion of the work, the obligee on the bond, be he owner or prime contractor, would have been entitled to apply the funds against the cost of completion. It is the surety's performance which frees the funds, and, in our view, the surety is entitled to them."); *see also* Fed. Ins. Co. v. Constructora Maza, Inc., 500 F. Supp. 246, 250 (D. P.R. 1979) (completing "surety may be seen as filling the shoes of the owner, whose benefits from the completion of the

The Restatement (Third) Of Suretyship And Guaranty (1996), Section 28, provides that a surety who satisfies its principal's obligations to a creditor (in the Restatement, the creditor is referred to as the "obligee") is subrogated, to the extent it contributed to that satisfaction, in the following way:

a. To the rights of the obligee against the principal (in the Restatement, the principal is referred to as the "principal obligor") pursuant to the underlying obligation;
b. To the rights of the obligee against other sureties;
c. To the interests of the obligee in property in which the obligee has no continuing interest; and
d. To the rights of the obligee against other persons whose conduct has made them liable to the obligee.[60]

Comment *a.* to the Restatement (Third) of Suretyship and Guaranty (1996), section 27, states that, when the property of one person is used to discharge the debt of another, the person whose debt is discharged is unjustly enriched by the retention of the benefit conferred. Consequently, the person who satisfied the debt is placed in the position of the obligee. Comment *a.* to section 27 goes on to say that, although subrogation does not spring from contract, "it may be confirmed or qualified by contract [such as where the indemnity agreement confirms the surety's rights]," and that subrogation "is a rule that the law adopts to compel the eventual satisfaction

---

project, may be unjustly enriched if the surety who assumed completion of a project were precluded from seeking reimbursement" from the contract funds); Sec. Ins. Co. of Hartford v. United States, 428 F.2d 838, 842 (Ct. Cl. 1970) ("The surety who undertakes to complete the project is entitled to the funds in the hands of the government not as a creditor and subject to setoff, but as a subrogee having the same rights to the funds as the government.").

60 RESTATEMENT (THIRD) OF SURETYSHIP AND GUARANTY § 28 (1996). *See also* Pearlman v. Reliance Ins. Co., 371 U.S. 132, 138 (1962); Prairie State Nat'l Bank v. United States, 164 U.S. 227 (1896); Aetna Life Ins. Co. v. Middleport, 124 U.S. 534, 548 (1888); Patrick J. O'Connor, Jr., *Ch. III, The Surety's Rights of Restitution and Subrogation–Setoff Principles Under the Restatement of the Law, Suretyship and Guaranty, in* THE RESTATEMENT OF SURETYSHIP & GUARANTY: A TRANSLATION FOR THE PRACTITIONER 23 (T. Scott Leo & Daniel Mungall, Jr. eds., 2005).

of an obligation by the one who ought to pay it." Furthermore, in the suretyship context, subrogation provides a surety with all of the obligee's rights "with respect to the underlying obligation as though that obligation had not been satisfied."[61]

In the performance bond context, comment *a.* to section 27 means that the surety that performs the principal's obligations under the construction contract is subrogated to all of the rights of the obligee, including those rights which would arise if the principal's construction contract had not been completed. Obviously, if the obligee were an owner of a construction project, it would use the contract funds to pay for the completion of the project. Thus, the surety that completes the project is entitled to use the contract funds to reimburse itself for all of its costs in completing the project.

Subrogation is dependent upon the equities and the particular facts and circumstances of each situation.[62] Yet, no matter how one defines subrogation, there are certain essential elements present in every context in which subrogation is asserted. These are:[63]

1. The existence of an obligation of the principal to the obligee;
2. The failure of the principal to perform that obligation;
3. Rights in the obligee arising from the principal's failure to perform; and
4. The performance by the surety, pursuant to the suretyship, of the obligation that the principal failed to perform.[64]

---

61   RESTATEMENT (THIRD) OF SURETYSHIP AND GUARANTY § 27 cmt. a (1996).
62   73 AM. JUR. 2D, SUBROGATION § 11 (1974).
63   Dist. of Columbia v. Aetna Ins. Co., 462 A.2d 428, 430 (D.C. 1983); Daniel Mungall, Jr., *Ch. 1, The Subrogation Rights of the Contract Bond Surety: Some Basics,* in SUBROGATION RIGHTS OF THE CONTRACT BOND SURETY 1 (George J. Bachrach ed., 1991); Daniel Mungall, Jr., *The Subrogation Rights of the Contract Bond Surety–A Primer* (1986) (unpublished paper submitted at the ABA/TIPS Fid. & Sur. Law Comm. program on Jan. 31, 1986 at the 1986 Mid-Winter Meeting).
64   For an application of one or more of these elements, *see* Prairie State Nat'l Bank v. United States, 164 U.S. 227 (1896); *In re* L. H. Duncan & Sons, 127 F.2d 640 (3d Cir. 1942); Travelers Indemnity Co. v. West Georgia Nat'l Bank, 387 F. Supp. 1090 (N.D. Ga. 1974); Nat'l Union

The first three elements are issues of contract law. The principal's obligations to the obligee arise from the contract between the parties. The principal's failure to perform, or default, is determined by the acts of the principal, the contract between the parties and the rules of contract interpretation. The rights of an obligee arising from the principal's failure to perform are governed by the contract and the law of contract damages. Finally, in order for the right of subrogation to exist, the surety, pursuant to the suretyship, must perform an obligation that the principal failed to perform.

2. Subrogation Rights–Type of Contract Funds

The courts have attempted to define the various types of contract funds that may be in dispute and subject to the surety's subrogation rights. Frequently used terms are the following:

- "Progress payments," which are those contract funds that the obligee periodically pays to the principal based upon satisfactory performance of the work.[65]
- "Earned but unpaid contract funds," which are those contract funds for work that has been performed by the principal that have not yet been paid by the obligee to the principal. Earned but unpaid contract funds include progress payments.
- "Retainage," which is that portion of each progress payment that is withheld by the obligee under the provisions of the construction contract to ensure the completion of the contract and the payment of outstanding obligations owed to the obligee.

Fire Ins. Co. of Pittsburgh v. United States, 304 F.2d 465 (Ct. Cl. 1962); Continental Cas. Co. v. United States, 169 F. Supp. 945 (Ct. Cl. 1959). California recognizes the following prerequisites to the assertion of subrogation: (1) payment must have been made by the subrogee to protect his own interest; (2) the subrogee must not have acted as a volunteer; (3) the debt paid must be one for which the subrogee was not primarily liable; (4) the entire debt must have been paid; and (5) subrogation must not work any injustice to the rights of others. Golden Eagle Ins. Co. v. First Nationwide Fin. Corp., 31 Cal. Rptr. 2d 815, 822 (Cal. Ct. App. 1994).

65   *In re* Glover Constr. Co., 30 B.R. 873, 875 (Bankr. W.D. Ky. 1983).

- "Extras," "claims," and "bonuses," which are payments for amounts due for work performed by the principal that are beyond the scope of the original construction contract.

Generally, the surety's subrogation rights to the contract funds held by the obligee do not depend upon the type of contract funds involved.[66] For example, the surety has subrogation rights to current earned and unpaid estimates,[67] retainages,[68] claims,[69] amounts due under a changed conditions clause in the contract,[70] bonuses for early substantial completion of the contract,[71] rebates of liquidated damages assessed by the obligee,[72] and the proceeds of an arbitration award resulting from the obligee's wrongful termination of the principal's right to perform the contract.[73] As discussed below, there are instances when the courts have drawn distinctions between the various types of contract funds. For the purposes of this chapter, all contract funds held by the obligee at the time the surety asserts its subrogation rights are referred to collectively as the "contract funds."

3. Subrogation Rights—Conditions Precedent

a. *Condition Precedent No. 1—The Necessity of the Principal's Default.* In most construction contracts, the principal's failure to perform

---

[66] Balboa Ins. Co. v. United States, 775 F.2d 1158, 1163 (Fed. Cir. 1985) ("[T]here is no valid distinction between money held by the [obligee] which is a 'retainage' and a 'progress payment.'"). "In either case, the 'total fund' remaining in the [obligee]'s possession, to the extent the surety has obligations arising under the contract, is available to the surety." *Id.*
[67] Lacy v. Md. Cas. Co., 32 F.2d 48 (4th Cir. 1929).
[68] Pearlman v. Reliance Ins. Co., 371 U.S. 132 (1962).
[69] *In re* Alliance Properties, Inc., 104 B.R. 306 (Bankr. S.D. Cal. 1989).
[70] *In re* Dutcher Constr. Corp., 378 F.2d 866 (2d Cir. 1967).
[71] Aetna Cas. & Sur. Co. v. Port of N.Y. Auth., 182 F. Supp. 671 (S.D.N.Y. 1960).
[72] Transamerica Ins. Co. v. United States, 31 Fed. Cl. 532 (1994) (surety can assert claim to contract balance as of the time the surety notified the federal government of the principal's default and challenge the federal government's subsequent assessment of liquidated damages); *In re* Cummins Constr. Corp., 81 F. Supp. 193 (D. Md. 1948).
[73] *In re* Alcon Demolition, Inc., 204 B.R. 440 (Bankr. D.N.J. 1997).

is called a default. The principal's default is at the heart of the surety's subrogation rights because a default triggers the surety's performance of its bonded obligations.[74] Without the principal's default, the surety may be deemed to perform as a "volunteer," and the surety's performance as a "volunteer" does not provide the foundation necessary for the surety's assertion of its subrogation rights.[75]

Before the surety may be compelled to perform, the principal must be in default.[76] In general terms, default is the principal's failure to do that which it is obligated to do. Default typically is a fact issue that often defies a bright line analysis and depends upon the particular circumstances of each case.

Default may take many forms. There may be a formal default declaration, but this may not be necessary.[77] All that may be required is that the principal be in default as a matter of fact. The construction contract may define the events of default. When the contract fails to define default, or there has been no formal declaration of default or termination, the material breach concept is often used to determine the existence of the principal's default.[78] A material breach is the failure to

---

74 RESTATEMENT (THIRD) OF SURETYSHIP AND GUARANTY § 27 cmt. c (1996); William M. Dolan, III, *Ch. 2, The Contractor's Default as a Condition Precedent to the Contract Bond Surety's Right of Subrogation (Out of the Darkness and Into the Light)*, in SUBROGATION RIGHTS OF THE CONTRACT BOND SURETY 41 (George J. Bachrach ed., 1991).

75 Nat'l Shawmut Bank of Boston v. New Amsterdam Cas. Co., 411 F.2d 843 (1st Cir. 1969); Anderson v. United States, 97 Ct. Cl. 545 (1942).

76 Fid. & Dep. Co. of Md. v. United States, 393 F.2d 834, 837 (Ct. Cl. 1968); First Ala. Bank of Birmingham v. Hartford Acc. & Indem. Co., 430 F. Supp. 907, 911-12 (N.D. Ala. 1977); *In re* Ram Constr. Co., 32 B.R. 758, 760 (Bankr. W.D. Pa. 1983).

77 "It is not necessary that there be a formal declaration of the contractor's default. All that is necessary for the surety to prevail is that the contractor be in default as a matter of fact; and that as a result of such default, the surety has become obligated to pay under its payment or performance bond." Fid. & Dep. Co. of Md. v. United States, 393 F.2d 834, 837 (Ct. Cl. 1968). *Accord* First Ala. Bank of Birmingham v. Hartford Acc. & Indem. Co., 430 F. Supp. 907, 911-12 (N.D. Ala. 1977); Travelers Indem. Co. v. West Ga. Nat'l Bank, 387 F. Supp. 1090, 1093 (N.D. Ga. 1974); Royal Indem. Co. v. United States, 371 F.2d 462 (Ct. Cl. 1967).

78 Fid. & Dep. Co. of Md. v. Scott Bros. Constr. Co., 461 F.2d 640, 643 (5th Cir. 1972); Fid. & Cas. Co. of N.Y. v. Dykstra, 208 F. Supp. 717, 722 (D.

perform by one party to the contract that discharges the other party's duty to perform.[79] The material breach concept is important because it fleshes out varying degrees of non-performance and pinpoints when a failure to perform constitutes a default. Without a default, the surety's subrogation rights cannot arise.[80]

In order to find default, one must look to the principal's obligations. The principal's default may arise out of the underlying construction contract,[81] such as the principal's abandonment or repudiation of the construction contract with the obligee or the principal's failure to pay subcontractors and suppliers.[82] Default may arise out of the performance bond,[83] which may also take the form of the principal's abandonment or repudiation.

The effect of default is two-fold. First, it triggers the surety's performance of its obligations under the bonds. Second, it acts as the foundational support for the surety's assertion of its subrogation rights. Until default, the surety has no obligation to begin performance under its bonds and, therefore, cannot avail itself of any of the rights that subrogation provides.[84]

b. *Condition Precedent No. 2–The Necessity of the Surety's Performance*. Once the principal defaults, the surety's performance to

---

Minn. 1962); Atl. Ref. Co. v. Cont'l Cas. Co., 183 F. Supp. 478, 482 (W.D. Pa. 1960). *Cf.*, Liberty Mut. Ins. Co. v. Constr. Mgmt. Servs., Inc., No. 99 C 6906, 2004 WL 2271811. 2004 U.S. Dist. LEXIS 23635 (N.D. Ill. Oct. 6, 2004).

79 Fid. & Cas. Co. v. Dykstra, 208 F. Supp. 717 (D. Minn. 1962) (citing RESTATEMENT OF CONTRACTS §§ 274, 275).

80 Lacy v. Md. Cas. Co., 32 F.2d 48, 53 (4th Cir. 1929); First Ala. Bank of Birmingham v. Hartford Acc. & Indem. Co., 430 F. Supp. 907, 911-12 (N.D. Ala. 1977); *In re* Ram Constr. Co., 32 B.R. 758, 760 (Bankr. W.D. Pa. 1983); Fid. & Dep. Co. of Md. v. United States, 393 F.2d 834, 837 (Ct. Cl. 1968).

81 *In re* Modular Structures, Inc., 27 F.3d 72 (3d Cir. 1994); *In re* L. H. Duncan & Sons, 127 F.2d 640 (3d Cir. 1942); Atl. Ref. Co. v. Cont'l Cas. Co., 183 F. Supp. 478 (W.D. Pa. 1960); Cont'l Cas. Co. v. United States, 169 F. Supp. 945 (Ct. Cl. 1959).

82 Fireman's Fund Ins. Co. v. United States, 421 F.2d 706 (Ct. Cl. 1970); City of Detroit v. Fid. & Dep. Co. of Md., 215 N.W. 394 (Mich. 1927).

83 Lambert v. Md. Cas. Co., 403 So. 2d 739 (La. Ct. App. 1981).

84 Cotton States Mut. Ins. Co. v. Citizens & S. Bank, 308 S.E.2d 199 (Ga. Ct. App. 1983).

remedy the principal's default is also necessary to the surety's assertion of its subrogation rights.[85] The necessary surety performance varies according to the circumstances. The surety's performance, however, is always dictated by the performance bond that it provided to the obligee on behalf of the principal. Typically, the performance bond will incorporate the construction contract. Therefore, the surety's performance is a question of the interpretation of the performance bond in relation to the construction contract.

Generally, the surety must fully satisfy the principal's failure to perform before the surety may assert its subrogation rights.[86] This still begs the question of what the surety must perform or pay in order to assert these rights. Some cases hold that the surety's subrogation rights are not enforceable until the creditor's claim is paid in full.[87] This means that, even if the surety pays the penal sum of its bond that is inadequate to cover all claims, the surety may not assert its subrogation rights.[88] The rationale is that it is inequitable to allow subrogation in a way that would reduce the protection of the beneficiaries of the bonds. This provides some harsh results for the surety.

However, exceptions do exist. Some cases hold that the requirement of full performance and/or payment may only be asserted by the obligee.[89] Because subrogation is equitable in nature, some cases hold

---

85 RESTATEMENT (THIRD) OF SURETYSHIP AND GUARANTY § 27 cmt. b (1996); David W. Slaughter, *Ch. 3, The Contract Bond Surety's Performance as a Condition Precedent to its Rights of Subrogation (Beyond a Twiddling of Thumbs),* in SUBROGATION RIGHTS OF THE CONTRACT BOND SURETY 73 (George J. Bachrach ed., 1991).

86 Equilease Corp. v. United States Fid. & Guar. Co., 565 S.W.2d 125, 126 (Ark. 1978); Gen. Ins. Co. of Am. v. State Highway Comm'n., 414 P.2d 526, 530 (Mont. 1966).

87 Fid. & Dep. Co. of Md. v. Hay, 9 F.2d 749, 750 (3d Cir. 1926), *cert. denied,* 271 U.S. 663 (1926); Martin v. Nat'l Sur. Corp., 262 A.2d 672, 675 (Pa. 1970). *See generally* Annotation, *Payment of Entire Claim of Third Person as Condition of Subrogation,* 9 A.L.R. 1596 (1920), *supplemented by,* 32 A.L.R. 568 (1924), 46 A.L.R. 857 (1927), 53 A.L.R. 304 (1928), and 91 A.L.R. 855 (1934).

88 Am. Sur. Co. v. Westinghouse Elec. Mfg. Co., 296 U.S. 133, 137 (1935); Covenant Mut. Ins. Co. v. Able Concrete Pump, 609 F. Supp. 27, 31 (N.D. Cal. 1984).

89 R.C. Mahon Co. v. R.S. Knapp Co., 255 N.W. 453 (Mich. 1934).

that the partially performing or paying surety may assert subrogation rights.[90] As an example, one court allowed a surety to recover unpaid contract amounts, but only in excess of the amounts that the obligee had the right to pay for unpaid material and labor.[91] Another court allowed a surety to assert its subrogation rights to the contract retainage by distinguishing between the surety as the subrogee of the obligee and the surety as the subrogee of the principal.[92] Under similar equities, some courts have been willing to grant subrogation rights to the surety when the surety fully performs with respect to the performance bond, but only partially performs with respect to the payment bond.[93]

It is absolutely essential that the surety's performance be in discharge of a legal obligation that the surety owes to the obligee or some other third-party.[94] Put another way, the surety must perform "under compulsion of the surety bond."[95] The surety that performs

---

90 *See generally* Corn Constr. Co. v. Aetna Cas. & Sur. Co., 295 F.2d 685 (10th Cir. 1961); United States Fid. & Guar. Co. v. Sweeney, 80 F.2d 235 (8th Cir. 1935); United Pac. Ins. Co. v. United States, 319 F.2d 893 (Ct. Cl. 1963); Martin v. Nat'l Sur. Corp., 262 A.2d 672 (Pa. 1970).

91 Fid. & Dep. Co. of Md. v. Hay, 9 F.2d 749 (3d Cir. 1926), *cert. denied*, 271 U.S. 663 (1926).

92 Covenant Mut. Ins. Co. v. Able Concrete Pump, 609 F. Supp. 27 (N.D. Cal. 1984). (As subrogee of the obligee, the surety's rights to the contract funds prevail over those rights of unpaid suppliers. The obligee has a right of set off that the surety can assert against the contract funds held by the obligee. As subrogee of the principal, however, the surety is obligated to pay the claims of laborers and materialmen. The court ultimately reasoned that the surety's completion of the contract and full tender of its payment bond penalty satisfied all of the surety's obligations and entitled it to the retainage as the obligee's subrogee.).

93 Fid. & Dep. Co. of Md. v. Hay, 9 F.2d 749 (3d Cir. 1926); Am. Fid. Fire Ins. Co. v. United States, 513 F.2d 1375 (Ct. Cl. 1975). *See also* Int'l Fid. Ins. Co. v. United States, 25 Cl. Ct. 469 (1992); Fireman's Fund Ins. Co. v. United States, 421 F.2d 706 (Ct. Cl. 1970).

94 Nat'l Shawmut Bank of Boston v. New Amsterdam Cas. Co., 411 F.2d 843, 848 (1st Cir. 1969); Lacy v. Md. Cas. Co., 32 F.2d 48, 53 (4th Cir. 1929); Md. Cas. Co. v. City of Pittsburgh, 51 F. Supp. 459 (W.D. Pa. 1943); United States Fid. & Guar. Co. v. N.J.B. Prime Investors, 377 N.E.2d 440, 443 (Mass. App. Ct. 1978); Martin v. Nat'l Sur. Corp., 262 A.2d 672, 675 (Pa. 1970).

95 4 Corbin, CONTRACTS § 51.8 (2007).

outside of its bond obligations is a volunteer for which no rights of subrogation are available.[96] Conversely, the surety that performs pursuant to its bond obligations is not a volunteer and is entitled to assert its subrogation rights.[97]

4. The Surety's Notice

In the performance bond context, the surety does not have to provide notice to the obligee of its subrogation rights with respect to the particular bonded contract.[98] The obligee is the entity holding the contract funds, and when it makes a claim against the surety under the performance bond, the obligee should realize or know that it has rights to the contract funds it is holding (and may understand that the surety also has rights to the contract funds). This is unlike the situation when the surety receives notice of claims against its principal's payment bond from the principal's subcontractors and suppliers who have not been paid. Under that situation, the surety may have to provide notice to the obligee of the existence of the payment bond claims and payments in order to assert its subrogation rights to the contract funds held by the obligee.[99]

---

96   Mass. Bonding & Ins. Co. v. Fago Constr. Corp., 82 F. Supp. 619, 622 (D. Md. 1949); United States Fid. & Guar. Co. v. N.J.B. Prime Investors, 377 N.E.2d 440, 443 (Mass. App. Ct. 1978); Cagle, Inc. v. Sammons, 254 N.W.2d 398, 403 (Neb. 1977).

97   Henningsen v. United States Fid. & Guar. Co., 208 U.S. 404 (1908); Prairie State Nat'l Bank v. United States, 164 U.S. 227 (1896); Nat'l Shawmut Bank of Boston v. New Amsterdam Cas. Co., 411 F.2d 843, 844 (1st Cir. 1969); Morgenthau v. Fid. & Dep. Co. of Md., 94 F.2d 632, 635 (D.C. Cir. 1937); Mass. Bonding & Ins. Co. v. Fago Constr. Corp., 82 F. Supp. 619, 621-22 (D. Md. 1949).

98   The performance bond surety asserting its subrogation rights to the obligee's setoff rights under the "common obligee theory" must provide notice to the obligee when it asserts those subrogation rights. *See* this chapter, *infra*, Section IV.D.

99   *See* Marilyn Klinger, *Ch. 4, The Surety's Notice: What Does it Say and Does it Work?*, in SUBROGATION RIGHTS OF THE CONTRACT BOND SURETY 111 (George J. Bachrach ed., 1990); George J. Bachrach & Robert F. Carney, *The Surety and the United States Court of Federal Claims - Revisited* (1999) (unpublished paper submitted at the Tenth Annual Northeast Sur. & Fid. Claims Conf. on Oct. 21, 1999); George J.

5. The Parties' Rights to Which the Surety Is Subrogated

The surety that pays under its performance bond is subrogated to the obligee's rights,[100] the rights of third-party beneficiaries under the surety's payment bond (hereinafter the "claimants"),[101] and the principal's rights.[102] Obligees, claimants and principals have many rights arising under contract, at law and in equity. Upon the failure of the principal to perform its obligations to the obligee, and the surety's performance of those obligations, the surety may step into the shoes of the obligee, the claimant and/or the principal[103] to enforce whatever rights they may have against the contract funds. The following are the kinds of rights to which the surety may be subrogated.

a. *The Obligee's Rights.* The obligee has rights against the principal and the contract funds to which the surety may be subrogated. Those rights include the obligee's rights to the contract funds under the construction contract[104] as well as common-law setoff rights.[105]

(1) *The obligee's contractual rights to the contract funds under the underlying contract with the principal.* The principal's rights to receive the contract funds are governed by its underlying contract with the obligee. To the extent that the provisions in the underlying contract authorize the obligee to restrict the principal's rights to the contract

---

Bachrach & Robert F. Carney, *The Surety and the United States Court of Federal Claims* 40-44 (1995) (unpublished paper submitted at the Sur. Claims Inst. program on June 22, 1995 at the 1995 Annual Meeting).

100 Framingham Trust Co. v. Gould-National Batteries, Inc., 427 F.2d 856 (1st Cir. 1970).
101 Pearlman v. Reliance Ins. Co., 371 U.S. 132 (1962).
102 Henningsen v. United States Fid. & Guar. Co., 208 U.S. 404 (1908).
103 Nat'l Shawmut Bank of Boston v. New Amsterdam Cas. Co., 411 F.2d 843 (1st Cir. 1969); *In re* QC Piping Installations, Inc., 225 B.R. 553 (Bankr. E.D.N.Y. 1998); *In re* John's Insulation, Inc., 221 B.R. 683 (Bankr. E.D.N.Y. 1998); *In re* Alcon Demolition, Inc., 204 B.R. 440 (Bankr. D. N.J. 1997); Transamerica Premier Ins. Co. v. United States, 32 Fed. Cl. 308 (1994).
104 *In re* Modular Structures, Inc., 27 F.3d 72 (3d Cir. 1994); Am. Fire & Cas. Co. v. First Nat'l City Bank, 411 F.2d 755 (1st Cir. 1969); Home Ins. Co. v. United States, 46 Fed. Cl. 160 (2000); Cont'l Cas. Co. v. United States, 169 F. Supp. 945 (Ct. Cl. 1959).
105 Merritt Comm'l Sav. & Loan, Inc. v. Guinee, 766 F.2d 850 (4th Cir. 1985).

funds, the principal has not "earned" the contract funds, and is not entitled to payment of the contract funds until the principal complies with the provisions of the underlying contract.[106]

As described in Section II of this chapter in the discussion of the AIA Standard Form of Agreement, the AIA General Conditions and the CD Agreement, the obligee has a number of rights to the contract funds under its construction contract with the principal, including but not limited to its rights to withhold payments to the principal for various reasons (in order to complete the performance of the work, to pay the principal's subcontractors and suppliers, as a result of the principal's defective work and delay in performance, and in the event of the principal's default and/or termination under the construction contract). Because of these kinds of contract provisions, the surety, pursuant to its subrogation rights, may have an interest in the contract funds to the extent that they are necessary for the performance of the work under the contract and for the payment of the bills of subcontractors and suppliers on the contract for which the surety may become liable under its bonds.

The surety's rights to the contract funds, when such contract provisions exist, are fully discussed in the bankruptcy case of *In re Modular Structures, Inc.*,[107] but the court's analysis of the surety's rights in *Modular Structures* may also be used in non-bankruptcy cases. *Modular Structures* involved a dispute over the contract funds between the surety and a secured creditor (bank) claiming through the debtor (the principal). The court reviewed the terms of the contract between the debtor and the obligee to determine whether the debtor was entitled to final payment under the terms of the contract. The court specifically cited the following provision of the contract:

> Neither final payment nor any remaining retained percentage shall become due until the Contractor submits to the Architect (1) an affidavit that payrolls, bills for materials and equipment, and other indebtedness connected with the Work for which the Owner or the Owner's property might be responsible or encumbered (less amounts withheld by Owner) have been paid or otherwise satisfied, . . . (4) consent of surety, if any, to final payment and (5) if required by the Owner, other data establishing payment or satisfactions of obligations, such as receipts, releases and waivers of liens, claims, security interests

---

106 *In re* Modular Structures, Inc., 27 F.3d 72 (3d Cir. 1994).
107 27 F.3d 72 (3d Cir. 1994).

or encumbrances arising out of the Contract to the extent and in such form as may be designated by the Owner.[108]

The court found that the debtor was obligated to pay its subcontractors and submit proof thereof before it could receive final payment from the obligee. Because the debtor could not satisfy these conditions precedent, the court held that none of the contract funds in the hands of the obligee were due or owing to the debtor, and thus could not be properly considered to be part of the debtor's bankruptcy estate.[109] Other bankruptcy courts have come to similar conclusions.[110]

(2) *The obligee's statutory rights to the contract funds.* If the principal fails to comply with its statutory obligations to promptly pay all subcontractors and suppliers from the contract funds the principal receives from the obligee, the principal has not earned the contract funds and is not entitled to the obligee's payment of the contract funds until the principal complies with its statutory obligations.[111] To the extent that an obligee has any rights to the contract funds under a federal or state statute or regulation, the surety that performs and/or pays the principal's obligations is subrogated to the obligee's statutory rights to the contract

---

108   *Id.* at 75.
109   *Id.* at 76-77.
110   *In re* Pacific Marine Dredging & Constr., 79 B.R. 924 (Bankr. D. Or. 1987) (holding that the contract between the debtor and the obligee required the debtor to promptly pay its subcontractors for the work that they provided under the contract, that the debtor's failure to pay its subcontractors and suppliers is just as much a failure to perform the contract as the abandonment of the work (citing United States v. Commonwealth of Pa., Dep't of Highways, 349 F. Supp. 1370 (E.D. Pa. 1972) and Atl. Ref. Co. v. Cont'l Gas Co., 183 F. Supp. 478 (W.D. Pa. 1960)), and that the surety that pays the subcontractors and suppliers is subrogated to the obligee's rights in the contract funds). *See also In re* Comcraft, Inc., 206 B.R. 551 (Bankr. D. Or. 1997) (holding that the contract provision not only obligated the debtor to make payments to its subcontractors and suppliers, but also required the debtor to make those payments to the subcontractors and suppliers out of the payments of the contract funds the debtor received from the obligee).
111   *In re* Comcraft, Inc., 206 B.R. 551 (Bankr. D. Or. 1997).

funds. Such statutes include, but are not limited to, mechanics' lien statutes, stop notice statutes and prompt payment statutes.[112]

b. *The Principal's Rights.* The surety is subrogated to its principal's rights against the obligee under the construction contract,[113] mechanics' lien rights,[114] other statutory rights,[115] including prompt payment rights, and common-law rights.[116] The surety may assert its subrogation rights to the principal's rights in order to seek reimbursement from the contract funds for losses incurred as a result of payments under the surety's performance bond.

c. *The Subcontractors/Suppliers' Rights.* Claimants, the principal's subcontractors and suppliers on the bonded project, may have direct claims against the obligee to which the surety may be subrogated. With respect to private and public contracts, there may be express provisions in the construction contract and the payment bond.[117] Claimants may also have mechanics' lien rights against the obligee[118] and statutory trust

---

112 For a general discussion of such statutes, *see* this chapter, Section II.C.2., *supra*, and notes 126 and 127, *infra*.

113 Pearlman v. Reliance Ins. Co., 371 U.S. 132 (1962); Nat'l Sur. Corp. v. United States, 118 F.3d 1542 (Fed. Cir. 1997); Cont'l Cas. Co. v. Am. Sec. Corp., 433 F.2d 649 (D.C. Cir. 1970); *In re* Alcon Demolition, Inc., 204 B.R. 440 (Bankr. D.N.J. 1997) (The court found that the surety's subrogation rights put the surety in the position to exercise the debtor's rights to identifiable contract funds, thereby removing the contract funds as property of the debtor's estate. The court found that the surety stands in the shoes of the obligee, subcontractors and suppliers, and the debtor with respect to the contract funds.). *See also In re* Johns Insulation, Inc., 221 B.R. 683 (Bankr. E.D.N.Y. 1998) (holding that the performing surety's claims to the contract funds prevailed over the debtor's claims to the contract funds).

114 Third Nat'l Bank in Nashville v. Highlands Ins. Co., 603 S.W.2d 730 (Tenn. 1980).

115 Dole Co. v. Aetna Cas. & Sur. Co., 269 F. Supp. 72 (D. Me. 1967).

116 Fed. Ins. Co. v. Constructora Maza, Inc., 500 F. Supp. 246 (D. P.R. 1979).

117 Active Fire Sprinkler Corp. v. United States Postal Serv., 811 F.2d 747 (2d Cir. 1987); *In re* L.H. Duncan & Sons, 127 F.2d 640 (3d Cir. 1942); *In re* Comcraft, Inc., 206 B.R. 551 (Bankr. D. Or. 1997).

118 Golden Eagle Ins. Co. v. First Nationwide Fin. Corp., 31 Cal. Rptr. 2d 815 (Cal. Ct. App. 1994); William Aupperle & Sons, Inc. v. Am. Indem. Co., 394 N.E.2d 725 (Ill. App. Ct. 1979).

fund rights[119] or stop notice/withhold/direct payment rights under state law[120] to which the surety may be subrogated in order to obtain the contract funds. A surety may be subrogated to the rights of the principal's subcontractors and suppliers that have state law mechanics' lien rights against the obligee or the property of the obligee.[121]

Claimants may have state law statutory trust fund rights against the contract funds to which the surety may be subrogated. Many states have trust fund statutes that give subcontractors and suppliers a trust interest in any contract funds paid by an obligee to a contractor or by a contractor to a subcontractor.[122]

In *Universal Bonding Insurance Co. v. Gittens & Sprinkle Enterprises, Inc.*,[123] the Third Circuit Court of Appeals addressed the surety's interest in the contract funds claimed by a New Jersey debtor from the contracts bonded by the surety. The court found that the

---

119 Universal Bonding Ins. Co. v. Gittens & Sprinkle Enters., Inc., 960 F.2d 366 (3d Cir. 1992).
120 Butler v. Pac. Nat'l Ins. Co., 375 F.2d 518 (9th Cir. 1967); *In re Comcraft, Inc.*, 206 B.R. 551 (Bankr. D. Or. 1997).
121 A problem that arises for the surety is that no mechanics' lien claim may exist if the subcontractor or the supplier fails to perfect its mechanics' lien rights properly under state law. *See In re* Wm. Cargile Contractor, Inc., 151 B.R. 854 (Bankr. S.D. Ohio 1993). Under Ohio law, mechanics' liens are only effective once filed and do not relate back to the date that the subcontractor commenced work. The surety in *Wm. Cargile* was not subrogated to any lien rights of the subcontractors because their mechanics' liens filed post-petition were unenforceable and violated the automatic stay. *Id.* at 858. *See also* Ohio ex rel. Star Supply v. City of Greenfield, 528 F. Supp. 955 (S.D. Ohio 1981) (the surety had no right to the retainage as subrogee of subcontractors and/or suppliers because they had not complied with the requirements of the mechanics' lien statute and all claims under the statute were time-barred).
122 Robert F. Carney & Adam Cizek, *Payment Provisions in Construction Contracts and Construction Trust Fund Statutes: A Fifty State Survey* (2004) (unpublished paper submitted at the Fifteenth Annual Northeast Sur. & Fid. Claims Conference on Sept. 30, 2004); Kim McNaughton et al., *The Surety's Rights to Contract Funds Under Trust Fund Provisions in Indemnity Agreements and Trust Fund Statutes* (1999) (unpublished paper submitted at the Surety Claims Institute program on June 25, 1999 at the 1999 Annual Meeting).
123 960 F.2d 366 (3d Cir. 1992).

contract funds were subject to the New Jersey Trust Fund Act and must be paid over to the debtor ("Gittens") as debtor-in-possession. But the court stated as follows:

> [We do] not agree with the bankruptcy court and the district court that monies that Gittens has received or will receive from the state and municipal agencies after the filing of its petition may be allocated to, and be distributed to, general creditors or used by Gittens in its effort to reorganize. Rather, we hold that Gittens, once it has received the monies from the various agencies, must hold those monies subject to the statutory trust imposed by the New Jersey Trust Fund Act.[124]

Whether Gittens received the contract funds either before or after the filing of its bankruptcy case, the court determined that there was no difference in the trust fund nature of the contract funds from the New Jersey state and municipal agencies under the New Jersey Trust Fund Act. The court found that Gittens' right to the contract funds did not change the moment that Gittens filed its bankruptcy case, and held:

> [M]onies received by Gittens from the state and municipal agencies constitute trust funds for the benefit of laborers and materialmen. Moreover, when and if [the surety] pays Gittens' indebtedness to laborers or materialmen, it may pursue the statutory remedies of the laborers or materialmen by proceeding against such funds.[125]

When state law provides for a statutory trust over the contract funds, the principal must hold all contract funds in trust for the benefit of its subcontractors, suppliers, laborers and materialmen. By virtue of its subrogation rights, the surety has an interest in the contract funds. The principal's only right to the contract funds is to hold the contract funds in trust to protect the interests of the beneficiaries, whether they are the subcontractors, suppliers, laborers and materialmen, or the surety, which may be liable to the subcontractors, suppliers, laborers and materialmen pursuant to its obligations under the bonds.

Claimants may have other federal and/or state law statutory rights against the obligee, the principal, or the contract funds, including stop

---

124   *Id.* at 371.
125   *Id.* at 373-74.

notice/withhold/direct payment rights[126] and prompt payment rights,[127] to which the surety may be subrogated. It is beyond the scope of this chapter to list all of the potential statutory rights that claimants may have against the obligee, the principal, or the contract funds that would entitle the claimants to receive direct payments of the contract funds from the obligee or others, thereby bypassing the principal's rights, if any. To the extent that such federal and/or state statutes exist, and assuming that the claimants have perfected their rights under the statutes, the surety would be entitled to be subrogated to the rights of the claimants against the obligee, the principal, and the contract funds under federal and/or state law.

III. The Performance Bond Surety's Competitors For the Contract Funds

In the competition for the contract funds, the question arises as to when the surety's subrogation rights accrue and become enforceable against the claims of other parties. Many cases hold that the surety's subrogation rights arise at the time of the execution of the bonds.[128] Although the

---

126 For examples of such statutes, *see* ALASKA STAT. § 34.35.062 (2009); ARIZ. REV. STAT. §§ 33-1051, *et seq.*, (2008); CAL. CIV. CODE §§ 3156, *et seq.* (2008); S.D. CODIFIED LAWS § 5-22-1 (2009); MD. CODE ANN., REAL PROP. § 9-104(f)(1) (2008).

127 The federal government has a Prompt Payment Act, 31 U.S.C. § 3903(b)(1)(B). Pursuant to the Federal Prompt Payment Act, a contractor's payment request may not be approved by the federal government unless it includes a certification by the contractor, to the best of the contractor's knowledge and belief, that payments to subcontractors and suppliers have been made from previous payments received by the contractor under the contract, and that timely payments will be made from the proceeds of the payment covered by the certification in accordance with the subcontract and purchase order agreements between the contractor and its subcontractors and suppliers. The Federal Prompt Payment Act is implemented through the Federal Acquisition Regulations, 48 C.F.R. 52.232-5(c).

128 Henningsen v. United States Fid. & Guar. Co., 208 U.S. 404 (1908); Prairie State Nat'l Bank v. United States, 164 U.S. 227 (1896); *In re Larbar Corp.*, 177 F.3d 439 (6th Cir. 1999); Ins. Co. of the West v. United States, 55 Fed. Cl. 529 (2003); Aetna Cas. & Sur. Co. v. Harvard Trust Co., 181 N.E.2d 673, 678 (Mass. 1962); United States Fid. & Guar.

surety's subrogation rights may not be available and enforceable until all of the essential elements and conditions precedent are met, the right relates back to the time of the execution of the bonds. The "relation back concept" allows the surety to assert all the rights that were available to the obligee, the principal and/or the claimants at the time of the execution of the bonds. The "relation back concept" applies to both performance bond sureties[129] and payment bond sureties.[130]

However, the surety's reliance upon the "relation back concept" to defeat the claims of competing parties to the contract funds has been criticized as being "wide of the mark."[131] As stated by one commentator:

> When the contractor defaults in the performance of its contract obligations, the owner, as a matter of contract law, has rights and remedies, the most obvious of which is the right to withhold his further performance until the contractor's default is cured. Thus, upon the occurrence of a major default, there is nothing due to the contractor and it follows inexorably that no one claiming through the contractor has any right to contract funds. This applies to a lending bank, an assignee, an attaching creditor and even tax claims.
>
> When the controversy over contract funds is with an adversary claiming rights derived through the contractor, the surety's first position should be that there is nothing due the contractor because of his default and thus there is nothing which the adversary's claim can

---

Co. v. Triborough Bridge Auth., 74 N.E.2d 226, 227 (N.Y. 1947); Int'l Fid. Ins. Co. v. Ashland Lumber Co., 463 S.E.2d 664 (Va. 1995).

129 Prairie State Nat'l Bank v. United States, 164 U.S. 227 (1896); First Ala. Bank of Birmingham v. Hartford Acc. & Indem. Co., 430 F. Supp. 907 (N.D. Ala. 1977); District of Columbia v. Aetna Ins. Co., 462 A.2d 428 (D.C. 1983); Aetna Cas. & Sur. Co. v. Harvard Trust Co., 181 N.E.2d 673 (Mass. 1962); First State Bank v. Reorganized Sch. Dist. R-3, 495 S.W.2d 471 (Mo. Ct. App. 1973).

130 Henningsen v. United States Fid. & Guar. Co., 208 U.S. 404 (1908); First Ala. Bank of Birmingham v. Hartford Acc. & Indem. Co., 430 F. Supp. 907 (N.D. Ala. 1977); Fid. & Dep. Co. of Md. v. United States, 393 F.2d 834 (Ct. Cl. 1968); Royal Indem. Co. v. United States, 371 F.2d 462 (Ct. Cl. 1967); United States Fid. & Guar. Co. v. Triborough Bridge Auth., 74 N.E.2d 226 (N.Y. 1947).

131 Daniel Mungall, Jr., *Ch. 1, The Subrogation Rights of the Contract Bond Surety: Some Basics, in* SUBROGATION RIGHTS OF THE CONTRACT BOND SURETY 1, 5 (George J. Bachrach ed., 1991).

reach. Courts indicate that the contractor has no property rights and no title in the contract balances; that there is no property and no debt due him; that he has no rights to or interest in the balances; and that he cannot assign what he does not have. If the contractor is not entitled to the unpaid contract funds, there is nothing which assignees and attaching creditors including United States tax liens may reach.[132]

In those jurisdictions that subscribe to the "relation back concept," and hold that the surety's subrogation rights arise as of the time of the principal's default and relate back to the date of the execution of the bonds, sureties may use the "relation back concept" to the extent that it provides "priority" over the claims of competing parties to the contract funds. However, the real essence of the surety's subrogation rights lies in the simple concept that the surety has performed its obligations under its bonds when the principal has failed to perform, thus leaving "no debt" due from the obligee to the principal and nothing that any party taking through the principal, whether it is an assignee, attaching creditor or tax lienor, can reach. The surety obtains the contract funds through its subrogation rights to those entities that have rights to the contract funds to the exclusion of the competing parties. A surety asserting its subrogation rights should recover the contract funds notwithstanding the claims of competing parties alleging that their rights were perfected prior to the surety's having issued the bonds.[133]

---

132   *Id.* (citations omitted).
133   Framingham Trust Co. v. Gould-National Batteries, Inc., 427 F.2d 856 (1st Cir. 1970); Am. Fire & Cas. Co. v. First Nat'l City Bank of N.Y., 411 F.2d 755 (1st Cir. 1969); Centex-Simpson Constr. Co. v. Fid. & Dep. Co. of Md., 795 F. Supp. 35, 39-41 (D. Me. 1992); In re Pac. Marine Dredging & Constr., 79 B.R. 924, 928-9 (Bankr. D. Or. 1987); First Ala. Bank of Birmingham v. Hartford Acc. & Indem. Co., 430 F. Supp. 907, 910-11 (N.D. Ala. 1977).

A. Contractual Competitors

1. The Obligee (Contractual and Setoff Claims)[134]

Assuming there are no other competing claimants to the contract funds, a surety may pursue the obligee for the contract funds necessary for reimbursement of its performance bond losses. A surety is subrogated to the principal's rights to the contract funds under the underlying construction contract.[135] The obligee, however, may have contractual defenses to the payment of the contract funds.[136] For example, the obligee may contend that it has backcharges against the principal, there are liquidated damages or other delay claims as a result of the principal's late performance (or the surety's late performance as the completing contractor), or there are damages as a result of other breaches of the construction contract.[137] When the surety is pursuing the contract funds

---

134 *See generally* Patrick J. O'Connor, Jr., *Ch. III, The Surety's Rights of Restitution and Subrogation–Set-off Principles Under the Restatement of the Law, Suretyship & Guaranty, in* THE RESTATEMENT OF SURETYSHIP & GUARANTY: A TRANSLATION FOR THE PRACTITIONER 23 (T. Scott Leo & Daniel Mungall, Jr. eds., 2005) (Section 31 of the RESTATEMENT (THIRD) OF SURETYSHIP AND GUARANTY (1996) and its comments reject the doctrine articulated in United States v. Munsey Trust Co., 332 U.S. 234 (1947)); Daniel Mungall, Jr., *The Buffeting of the Subrogation Rights of the Construction Contract Bond Surety by U.S. v. Munsey Trust Co.*, 46 INS. COUNS. J. 607 (1979); George J. Bachrach & Robert F. Carney, *The Surety and the United States Court of Federal Claims–Revisited* (1999) (unpublished paper submitted at the Tenth Annual Northeast Sur. & Fid. Claims Conference on Oct. 21, 1999), updating George J. Bachrach & Robert F. Carney, *The Surety and the United States Court of Federal Claims* (1995) (unpublished paper submitted at the Sur. Claims Inst. program on June 22, 1995 at the 1995 Annual Meeting).

135 Transamerica Ins. Co. v. Barnett Bank of Marion County, N.A., 540 So. 2d 113 (Fla. 1989).

136 *See* this chapter, Section II, *supra*.

137 *See* United States Fid. & Guar. Co. v. West Rock Dev. Corp., 50 F. Supp. 2d 127 (D. Conn. 1999) (an obligee cannot defeat a completing surety's entitlement to payment of the contract funds by arguing that the original contractor never completed the project or that the project was uncompleted due to punchlist items not affecting substantial completion); *see also* Int'l Fid. Ins. Co. v. County of Rockland, 51 F. Supp. 2d 285

held by the obligee pursuant to its subrogation rights to the principal's rights, the resolution of the disputes with the obligee are straight contract law issues and not suretyship issues. The surety is standing in the shoes of its principal to enforce the terms of the construction contract for the payment of the contract funds, and the obligee may or may not have good defenses to the payment of those contract funds to the surety.

The surety's subrogation rights do come into play when the obligee admits owing the contract funds, but attempts to reduce the contract funds to be paid to the surety as a result of setoffs claimed by the obligee against the principal. Two examples frequently arise. The obligee may attempt to setoff against the contract funds amounts owed to the obligee by the principal on other contracts or obligations between the obligee and the principal. When the surety is a performance bond surety, the obligee may not exercise those setoff rights against the contract funds.[138]

A second example is the obligee that is also a government taxing authority attempting to setoff against the contract funds certain taxes due and owing by the principal to the government obligee. When the surety has acted to perform the contract and incurred losses under its performance bond, the government obligee has not been successful in setting off against the contract funds the amounts of those taxes due from the principal.[139]

(S.D.N.Y. 1999) (surety brought suit against obligee to obtain contract funds which obligee claimed were not due because of project delays); Pac. Employers Ins. Co. v. City of Berkeley, 204 Cal. Rptr. 387 (Cal. Ct. App. 1984).

[138] Sec. Ins. Co. of Hartford v. United States, 428 F.2d 838 (Ct. Cl. 1970); United States Fid. & Guar. Co. v. Mo. Highway & Transp. Comm'n, 783 S.W.2d 516 (Mo. Ct. App. 1990) (principal's obligation in an unrelated condemnation proceeding). A performing surety's right to the contract funds is superior to the obligee's right to offset from such contract funds monies owed to the obligee by the principal for a debt not related to the bonded contract. Miller-Stauch Constr. Co. v. Williams-Bungart Elec., Inc., 959 S.W.2d 490 (Mo. Ct. App. 1998).

[139] Trinity Universal Ins. Co. v. United States, 382 F.2d 317 (5th Cir. 1967), cert. denied, 390 U.S. 906 (1968); Teamsters Health & Welfare Fund v. Net Constr., Inc., 334 F. Supp. 2d 751 (E.D. Pa. 2004); Sec. Ins. Co. of Hartford v. United States, 428 F.2d 838 (Ct. Cl. 1970); United States Fid. & Guar. Co. v. Mo. Highway & Transp. Comm'n., 783 S.W.2d 516 (Mo. Ct. App. 1990) (surety financing principal). However, the surety has not been as successful against the federal government claims under the

The most frequent situation is when the obligee holds contract funds that it admits are due and owing to the principal, but refuses to pay them to the surety because the obligee has received notice of the claims of others to the same contract funds. In this instance, the obligee is a mere stakeholder, having no independent interest in the contract funds. For its own protection, the obligee may hold onto the contract funds pending a resolution of the disputes between the surety and the competing claimants, or the obligee may interplead the contract funds into court, name all of the competing parties to the contract funds as parties to the litigation, and receive a release and discharge from any further obligation with respect to the interpled contract funds.[140] Whether the surety or one or more of the competing claimants are ultimately entitled to the contract funds depends upon the same arguments with respect to the competition between the surety and one or more of the other competing claimants as described below in this chapter.

At times, the obligee *should* have been a stakeholder with respect to the contract funds because it had no interest in the contract funds. Yet, despite receiving conflicting claims to the contract funds from the surety and other claimants, the obligee has paid the contract funds to the principal, assignees/lenders, and others. The surety has pursued the

---

Davis-Bacon Act and with the state government claims under their labor statutes by asserting its subrogation rights to the contract funds. See Michael A. Stover & Susan Getz Kerbel, *"Look Who's Bringing Home the Bacon"–How Recent Decisions Interpreting the Davis-Bacon Act Can Negatively Affect the Surety* (2003) (unpublished paper submitted at the Fourteenth Annual Northeast Sur. & Fid. Claims Conference on Sept. 18, 2003); Darryl Weissman & Scott D. Baron, *The Surety's Priority Battle With State Labor Departments Over Unpaid Contract Funds–Whatever Happened to Subrogation?* (1998) (unpublished paper submitted at the Ninth Annual Northeast Sur. & Fid. Claims Conference on Oct. 22, 1998).

140 Newark Ins. Co. v. United States, 169 F. Supp. 955, 957 (Ct. Cl. 1959) ("Surely a stakeholder, caught in the middle between two competing claimants, cannot, in effect, decide the merits of their claims by the mere physical act of delivering the stake to one of them. If his position as stakeholder becomes uncomfortable, and the claimants do not take steps to get a judicial solution of the question, the law has provided him with an interpleader proceeding by which he can deposit the stake in court and walk out free of annoyance of being in the middle.").

obligee as a result of the alleged wrongful payment, and has succeeded in having the obligee pay a second time, this time to the surety, as a result of its prior payment to the principal,[141] the assignee/lender[142] and taxing authorities other than the obligee.[143]

There is one final issue between the obligee and the surety seeking to enforce its subrogation rights. During the principal's performance of the construction contract, the surety may be placed on notice of various claims of laborers and materialmen who have provided work or materials on the bonded project. Whether or not the surety has paid the claims, the surety may place the obligee on notice of the claims and make demand for sufficient contract funds to pay the claims.[144] The obligee, however,

---

141 Pa. Nat'l Mut. Cas. Ins. Co. v. City of Pine Bluff, 354 F.3d 945 (8th Cir. 2004); Nat'l Sur. Corp. v. United States, 118 F.3d 1542 (Fed. Cir. 1997); Nat'l Sur. Corp. v. United States, 319 F. Supp. 45 (N.D. Ala. 1970); Home Indem. Co. v. United States, 313 F. Supp. 212 (W.D. Mo. 1970); Hanover Ins. Co. v. United States, 279 F. Supp. 851, 853 (S.D.N.Y. 1967); Home Ins. Co. v. United States, 46 Fed. Cl. 160 (2000); Int'l Fid. Ins. Co. v. United States, 41 Fed. Cl. 706 (1998); Transamerica Premier Ins. Co. v. United States, 32 Fed. Cl. 308 (1994); Int'l Fid. Ins. Co. v. United States, 25 Cl. Ct. 469 (1992); Am. Fid. Fire Ins. Co. v. United States, 513 F.2d 1375 (Ct. Cl. 1975); Fireman's Fund Ins. Co. v. United States, 421 F.2d 706 (Ct. Cl. 1970); Home Indem. Co. v. United States, 376 F.2d 890, 893-94 (Ct. Cl. 1967); Dist. of Columbia v. Aetna Ins. Co., 462 A.2d 428 (D.C. 1983). *But cf.* United States Fid. & Guar. Co. v. United States, 475 F.2d 1377 (Ct. Cl. 1973).
142 Reliance Ins. Co. v. Alaska State Hous. Auth., 323 F. Supp. 1370 (D. Alaska 1971); Great Am. Ins. Co. v. United States, 492 F.2d 821, 824-25 (Ct. Cl. 1974); Argonaut Ins. Co. v. United States, 434 F.2d 1362 (Ct. Cl. 1970); Newark Ins. Co. v. United States, 169 F. Supp. 955, 957 (Ct. Cl. 1959).
143 Home Indem. Co. v. United States, 313 F. Supp. 212 (W.D. Mo. 1970).
144 The issue of the surety's notice to the obligee is complex. *See* Marilyn Klinger, *Ch. 4, The Surety's Notice: What Does it Say and Does it Work?*, *in* SUBROGATION RIGHTS OF THE CONTRACT BOND SURETY (George J. Bachrach ed., 1991); George J. Bachrach & Robert F. Carney, *The Surety and the United States Court of Federal Claims–Revisited* (1999) (unpublished paper submitted at the Tenth Annual Northeast Sur. & Fid. Claims Conference on Oct. 21, 1999), *updating* George J. Bachrach & Robert F. Carney, *The Surety and the United States Court of Federal Claims* (1995) (unpublished paper submitted at the Surety Claims Institute program on June 22, 1995 at the 1995 Annual Meeting). In many instances, notice must be provided by the surety directly to the obligee, and notice from the principal's unpaid subcontractors and suppliers is

may want the principal to receive the progress payments in order to continue the performance of the contract. The courts have found that the obligee has a vital interest in the principal's timely and efficient completion of the work, which allows the obligee broad discretion and flexibility in determining whether to withhold the progress payments for the benefit of the surety or to pay the progress payments to the principal to continue the performance of the contract.[145] However, despite this discretion, when the surety has provided notice to the obligee that the principal is in default, the obligee has an obligation to take reasonable steps to determine for itself that the principal has the capacity and intention to perform the work and complete the project.[146] If the obligee pays the progress payments to the principal after notice to the obligee, the surety may hold the obligee liable again if the obligee has engaged in arbitrary or capricious action or abuse of discretion, or deliberate and fraudulent conduct (bad faith).[147]

---

insufficient. Fireman's Fund Ins. Co. v. United States, 909 F.2d 495 (Fed. Cir. 1990). When notice is given by the surety to the obligee, and the obligee's role is as a stakeholder of the contract funds, and the obligee pays an entity other than the surety, the obligee may have to pay a second time, this time to the surety. However, the surety does not need to give notice to the obligee when the obligee is in breach of its contract with the principal. Nat'l Sur. Corp. v. United States, 118 F.3d 1542 (Fed. Cir. 1997) (obligee paid the retainage to the principal in breach of the terms of the contract).

145 United Bonding Ins. Co. v. Catalytic Constr. Co., 533 F.2d 469 (9th Cir. 1976); Fireman's Fund Ins. Co. v. United States, 362 F. Supp. 842 (D. Kan. 1973); United States Fid. & Guar. Co. v. United States, 676 F.2d 622 (Ct. Cl. 1982); United States Fid. & Guar. Co. v. United States, 475 F.2d 1377, 1384 (Ct. Cl. 1973); Argonaut Ins. Co. v. United States, 434 F.2d 1362 (Ct. Cl. 1970).

146 Fireman's Fund Ins. Co. v. United States, 362 F. Supp. 842 (D. Kan. 1973); United States v. Cont'l Cas. Co., 346 F. Supp. 1239 (N.D. Ill. 1972); Royal Indem. Co. v. United States, 529 F.2d 1312 (Ct. Cl. 1976).

147 Balboa Ins. Co. v. United States, 775 F.2d 1158, 1163 (Fed. Cir. 1985) (listing eight factors considered by the court to be important in determining whether the obligee has exercised reasonable discretion in disbursing the contract funds to the principal); United Pac. Ins. Co. v. United States, 16 Cl. Ct. 555 (1989) (surety entitled to judgment against government obligee as a result of abuse of discretion in releasing progress

2. The Principal

On the rare occasion, the surety may compete for the contract funds in the hands of the obligee against its own principal. The surety, which may have completed the principal's performance of the work and/or paid the principal's subcontractors and suppliers on the bonded project, claims the contract funds pursuant to its subrogation rights to the rights of the subcontractors and suppliers against the principal and to the rights of the obligee holding the contract funds.[148]

When the surety has paid subcontractor and supplier claimants in excess of the contract funds, it is entitled to the contract funds ahead of the principal.[149] When the surety makes advances to the principal to pay for labor and materials which the principal is unable to pay for, the surety does not become a "volunteer" as a result of the advances because it has a legal obligation to perform the contract and pay claims for labor and material on the bonded contract. As a result, the surety is entitled to the contract funds.[150] However, if the bonded contract is completed at a profit, the principal may be entitled to that profit and not the surety.[151]

---

payment to principal); Royal Indem. Co. v. United States, 529 F.2d 1312 (Ct. Cl. 1976).

[148] *In re* Johns Insulation, Inc., 221 B.R. 683 (Bankr. E.D.N.Y. 1998) (holding that the performing surety's claims to the contract funds prevailed over the principal debtor's claims to the contract funds); *In re* Alcon Demolition, Inc., 204 B.R. 440 (Bankr. D. N.J. 1997); *In re* Four Star Constr. Co., 151 B.R. 817 (Bankr. N.D. Ohio 1993).

[149] Cont'l Cas. Co. v. Am. Sec. Corp., 443 F.2d 649, 652 (D.C. Cir. 1970); *In re* Alcon Demolition, Inc., 204 B.R. 440 (Bankr. D. N.J. 1997); *In re* Four Star Constr. Co., 151 B.R. 817 (Bankr. N.D. Ohio 1993); Home Indem. Co. v. United States, 313 F. Supp. 212 (W.D. Mo. 1970); Hanover Ins. Co. v. United States, 279 F. Supp. 851 (S.D.N.Y. 1967).

[150] Mass. Bonding & Ins. Co. v. Fago Constr. Corp., 82 F. Supp. 619 (D. Md. 1949).

[151] United States Fid. & Guar. Co. v. Worthington & Co., 6 F.2d 502 (5th Cir. 1925); Howell Constr., Inc. v. United Pac. Ins. Co., 824 F. Supp. 105 (W.D. Ky. 1993); Home Ins. Co. v. United States, 46 Fed. Cl. 160 (2000).

3. The Principal's Assignees/Lenders (The "Bank")[152]

Conflicting claims to the contract funds between the surety and the bank squarely pit the surety's subrogation rights to the principal's rights,[153] the labor and material claimants' rights,[154] and the obligee's rights[155] to the contract funds against the bank's perfected security interest under the Uniform Commercial Code in all of the principal's accounts receivable. The courts have uniformly held that the surety's subrogation right to the contract funds is not a security interest requiring perfection under the Uniform Commercial Code.[156] As a result, the courts have held that the surety completing the contract under its performance bond has priority to the contract funds over the claims of the bank under its perfected security

---

152 Sam H. Poteet, Jr. & J. Michael Franks, *Entitlement to Contract Funds Among Competing Surety, Lender, Contractor and the Internal Revenue Service*, 9 CONSTR. LAW. 11 (1989).

153 Transamerica Ins. Co. v. Barnett Bank of Marion County, N.A., 540 So. 2d 113, 115 (Fla. 1989).

154 United States Fid. & Guar. Co. v. First State Bank of Salina, 494 P.2d 1149, 1154 (Kan. 1972).

155 Pearlman v. Reliance Ins. Co., 371 U.S. 132, 137 (1962); Fin. Co. of Am. v. United States Fid. & Guar. Co., 353 A.2d 249, 252 (Md. 1976).

156 Nat'l Shawmut Bank of Boston v. New Amsterdam Cas. Co., 411 F.2d 843, 845 (1st Cir. 1969); United States Fid. & Guar. Co. v. APAC-Kansas, Inc., 151 F. Supp. 2d 1297 (D. Kan. 2001); *In re* Alcon Demolition, Inc., 204 B.R. 440 (Bankr. D. N.J. 1997); *In re* Comcraft, Inc., 206 B.R. 551 (Bankr. D. Or. 1997); Home Indem. Co. v. United States, 433 F.2d 764, 765 (Ct. Cl. 1970); Transamerica Ins. Co. v. Barnett Bank of Marion Co., N.A., 540 So. 2d 113, 117 (Fla. 1989); Argonaut Ins. Co. v. C&S Bank of Tifton, 232 S.E.2d 135, 140 (Ga. Ct. App. 1976); Fin. Co. of Am. v. United States Fid. & Guar. Co., 353 A.2d 249, 253 (Md. 1976); Jacobs v. Northeastern Corp., 206 A.2d 49, 54-55 (Pa. 1965). A different rule may apply if the surety attempts to use its subrogation rights to acquire priority in the principal's personal property other than the contract funds (inventory, equipment, etc.) over a bank which has a perfected security interest under the Uniform Commercial Code in that personal property. State Bank & Trust Co. v. Ins. Co. of the West, 132 F.3d 203, 206 (5th Cir. 1997); Aetna Cas. & Sur. Co. v. J.F. Brunken & Son, Inc., 357 F. Supp. 290 (D. S.D. 1973).

interest.[157] The surety's performance bond subrogation rights in the contract funds are superior to those of the bank even though the proceeds of the bank's loan to the principal were used to pay suppliers of labor and materials to whom the surety would otherwise have been liable.[158] A surety does not waive its subrogation rights to the contract funds even if it perfects a security interest in the contract funds because assignment rights are independent from subrogation rights.[159]

A surety is subrogated to the obligee's rights and can exercise those rights to apply the contract funds to completing the construction contract and paying the principal's subcontractors and suppliers.[160] The obligee does not owe any contract funds to the principal until the obligations owed to the obligee and to the principal's subcontractors and suppliers are satisfied.[161] The principal's bank, who takes the contract funds with the same rights as the principal, is therefore subject to the surety's superior rights.[162] Furthermore, the surety's subrogation rights relate back to the date that the bonds are executed to defeat the bank's claims, whose rights to the contract funds only arise through the principal and upon the completion of the work.[163]

---

157 Prairie State Nat'l Bank v. United States, 164 U.S. 227 (1896); Indus. Bank of Wash. v. United States, 424 F.2d 932, 934 (D.C. Cir. 1970); Alaska State Bank v. Gen. Ins. Co. of Am., 579 P.2d 1362, 1368 (Alaska 1978).

158 Nat'l Shawmut Bank of Boston v. New Amsterdam Cas. Co., 411 F.2d 843, 847 (1st Cir. 1969); Union Indem. Co. v. New Smyrna, 130 So. 453 (Fla. 1930); State ex rel. S. Sur. Co. v. Schlesinger, 151 N.E. 177 (Ohio 1926).

159 Old Kent Bank-Southeast v. City of Detroit, 444 N.W.2d 162, 165 (Mich. Ct. App. 1989).

160 Fin. Co. of Am. v. United States Fid. & Guar. Co., 353 A.2d 249, 252 (Md. 1976).

161 *In re* Modular Structures, Inc., 27 F.3d 72 (3d Cir. 1994); Centex-Simpson Constr. Co. v. Fidelity & Dep. Co. of Md., 795 F. Supp. 35, 39 (D. Me. 1992).

162 Nat'l Shawmut Bank of Boston v. New Amsterdam Cas. Co., 411 F.2d 843, 848 (1st Cir. 1969).

163 Prairie State Nat'l Bank v. United States, 164 U.S. 227 (1896); Pembroke State Bank v. Balboa Ins. Co., 241 S.E.2d 483, 484-85 (Ga. Ct. App. 1978); Third Nat'l Bank in Nashville v. Highlands Ins. Co., 603 S.W.2d 730, 734 (Tenn. 1980); Interfirst Bank Dallas, N.A. v. United States Fid. & Guar. Co., 774 S.W.2d 391, 397-99 (Tex. App. 1989).

The priority of the surety's subrogation rights over the contract funds does not depend upon the type of the contract funds in the hands of the obligee.[164] Therefore, the courts have held that the surety's subrogation rights have priority over the bank with regard to earned but unpaid funds, including unpaid progress payments,[165] retainage held by the obligee during the principal's performance of the contract,[166] as well as all other funds held by the obligee, whether they are for extras, bonuses, claims or lease payments.[167]

The surety's rights to progress payments that have either been paid to its principal and then sent to the principal's bank or paid directly to the principal's bank depend on a number of factors. When the progress payments are earned and paid to the bank prior to the principal's default,[168] or if the bank receives payment from the principal without notice or knowledge that the principal has failed to pay its subcontractors and suppliers,[169] the surety has been unable to recover from the bank the

---

164 Am. Fire & Cas. Co. v. First Nat'l City Bank of N.Y., 411 F.2d 755, 758 (1st Cir. 1969), *cert. denied*, 396 U.S. 1007 (1970); Trinity Universal Ins. Co. v. United States, 382 F.2d 317, 320 (5th Cir. 1967), *cert. denied*, 390 U.S. 906 (1968).

165 Nat'l Shawmut Bank of Boston v. New Amsterdam Cas. Co., 411 F.2d 843, 848 (1st Cir. 1969); Alaska State Bank v. Gen. Ins. Co. of Am., 579 P.2d 1362, 1368 (Alaska 1978); First Fed. State Bank v. Town of Malvern, 270 N.W.2d 818 (Iowa 1978); First Hutchings-Sealy Nat'l Bank of Galveston v. Aetna Cas. & Sur. Co., 532 S.W.2d 114 (Tex. Civ. App. 1976).

166 Prairie State Nat'l Bank v. United States, 164 U.S. 227, 233 (1896); Trinity Universal Ins. Co. v. United States, 382 F.2d 317, 320-21 (5th Cir. 1967), *cert. denied*, 390 U.S. 906 (1968); Centex-Simpson Constr. Co. v. Fid. & Dep. Co. of Md., 795 F. Supp. 35, 39-40 (D. Me. 1992); Fid. & Cas. Co. of N.Y. v. Ind. Nat'l Bank, 216 N.E.2d 857, 860 (Ind. Ct. App. 1966); Fid. Nat'l Bank of Okla. City v. United States Cas. Co., 131 P.2d 75, 77-78 (Okla. 1942).

167 London & Lancashire Indem. Co. of Am. v. Endres, 290 F. 98 (8th Cir. 1923); In re Alliance Props., Inc., 104 B.R. 306, 311-12 (Bankr. S.D. Cal. 1989); Equilease Corp. v. United States Fid. & Guar. Co., 565 S.W.2d 125, 126-27 (Ark. 1978).

168 Reliance Ins. Co. v. U.S. Bank of Wash., N.A., 143 F.3d 502 (9th Cir. 1998); Am. Fire & Cas. Co. v. First Nat'l City Bank, 411 F.2d 755, 758 (1st Cir. 1969), *cert. denied*, 396 U.S. 1007 (1970).

169 Reliance Ins. Co. v. U.S. Bank of Wash., N.A., 143 F.3d 502 (9th Cir. 1998); Bank of Ariz. v. Nat'l Sur. Corp., 237 F.2d 90, 93-94 (9th Cir. 1956).

payments received from the bonded contracts despite losses incurred by the surety. The bank prevails over the surety even if the check from the principal was not collected from the drawee bank until after a declaration of default.[170] Generally, in the absence of knowledge or fraud on the part of the bank, progress payments paid to the bank may not be collected by the surety from the bank pursuant to its subrogation rights.[171]

Banks have been held to be on notice of the surety's subrogation rights.[172] When the principal is in default under the construction contract prior to the payment of the progress payment, and the bank is aware of the default, the surety may be entitled to obtain the progress payment received by the bank.[173] Furthermore, when the bank received the contract funds with notice of the principal's default, the bank is not entitled to offset debts owed to it by the principal that are unrelated to the construction contract.[174]

B. *Statutory Competitors*

1. The Obligee as a Taxing Authority

An obligee may also be a government taxing authority attempting to setoff against the contract funds certain taxes due and owing by the principal to the government obligee. When the surety has acted to perform the contract and incurred losses under its performance bond, the

---

170 Fid. & Dep. Co. of Md. v. Scott Bros. Constr. Co., 461 F.2d 640, 643 (5th Cir. 1972).
171 Am. Fid. Co. v. Nat'l City Bank of Evansville, 266 F.2d 910, 915-17 (D.C. Cir. 1959).
172 Standard Acc. Ins. Co. of Detroit v. Fed. Nat'l Bank of Shawnee, 112 F.2d 692, 695 (10th Cir. 1940); Nat'l Sur. Corp. v. United States, 133 F. Supp. 381, 384-85 (Ct. Cl. 1955); Royal Indem. Co. v. United States, 93 F. Supp. 891, 894 (Ct. Cl. 1950).
173 Ins. Co. of N. Am. v. Northampton Nat'l Bank, 708 F.2d 13, 15 (1st Cir. 1983); Travelers Indem. Co. v. W. Ga. Nat'l Bank, 387 F. Supp. 1090, 1094 (N.D. Ga. 1974).
174 Fed. Ins. Co. v. Fifth Third Bank, 867 F.2d 330, 334-36 (6th Cir. 1989); Pac. Indem. Co. v. Grand Ave. State Bank of Dallas, 223 F.2d 513, 518-19 (5th Cir. 1955); Cent. Nat'l Ins. Co. of Omaha v. Tri-County State Bank, 823 F. Supp. 652 (D. Minn. 1993).

government obligee has not been successful in setting off against the contract funds the amounts of those taxes due from the principal.[175]

2. The Principal's Subcontractors and Suppliers (The "Claimants")

In the normal course of business, claimants with valid claims against a surety's payment bond will be paid by the surety. Therefore, there will be no competing claims between the surety and the claimants for the contract funds.[176] There are circumstances when potential claimants under a payment bond are not paid by the surety for various reasons, and the claimants compete with the surety for the contract funds. In these instances, the claimants assert an equitable interest in the contract funds in order to defeat the surety's claim under its subrogation rights.[177]

When the surety both completed the performance of the contract at a cost greater than the contract funds, and had deposited the full amount of the payment bond with the court, the surety was subrogated to the rights of the government obligee to the contract funds even though the payment bond did not fully compensate all of the claimants.[178] However, if the surety is not required to make any payments on the performance bond, and pays the full penal sum of the payment bond, if the payment bond

---

175 Trinity Universal Ins. Co. v. United States, 382 F.2d 317 (5th Cir. 1967), *cert. denied*, 390 U.S. 906 (1968); Sec. Ins. Co. of Hartford v. United States, 428 F.2d 838 (Ct. Cl. 1970); United States Fid. & Guar. Co. v. Mo. Highway & Transp. Comm'n, 783 S.W.2d 516 (Mo. Ct. App. 1990) (surety financing principal).

176 United States v. TAC Constr. Co., 760 F. Supp. 590, 594 (S.D. Miss. 1991).

177 Edward Graham Gallagher, *Unpaid Subcontractor's or Supplier's Right to Payment Out of Contract Funds*, 10 CONSTR. LAW. 9 (1990); Gordon S. Elkins, *Rights of Subcontractors, Laborers and Materialmen to Contract Balances*, 18 FORUM 695 (1983); Francisco Castro-Amy, *The Contest for Contract Retainage Between the Surety and Suppliers Without Recourse Under the Bond*, 16 FORUM 1073 (1981); Kenneth M. Cushman, *Who Gets the Funds? Surety's Costs Exceed Retained Funds—But Claimant Fails to Notify or Sue on Time*, 11 FORUM 1160 (1976); Annotation, *Relative Rights, As Between Surety on Public Work Contractor's Bond and Unpaid Laborers or Materialmen, In Percentage Retained By Obligee*, 61 A.L.R.2d 899 (1958).

178 Covenant Mut. Ins. Co. v. Able Concrete Pump, 609 F. Supp. 27, 31 (N.D. Cal. 1984).

was insufficient to cover all of the claims of the claimants, the claimants' rights to the contract funds may be superior to the surety.[179]

3. The Trustee in Bankruptcy/The Principal as Debtor-In-Possession (The "Debtor")[180]

The conflicting claims for the contract funds between the surety and the debtor or trustee in bankruptcy has begun anew since the enactment of the United States Bankruptcy Code[181] (hereinafter the "Code") in 1978 and the repeal of the old Bankruptcy Act. The seminal case under the Bankruptcy Act is *Pearlman v. Reliance Insurance Co.*,[182] which was decided prior to the enactment of the Code. In finding that the surety that paid the claims of the bankrupt principal's laborers and materialmen has priority to the contract funds retained by the government obligee as against the claims of the bankrupt principal's trustee, the Supreme Court held that:

> the [obligee] had a right to use the retained fund to pay laborers and materialmen; that the laborers and materialmen had a right to be paid out of the fund; that the contractor, had he completed his job and paid his laborers and materialmen, would have become entitled to the fund; and that the surety, having paid the laborers and materialmen, is entitled to the benefit of all these rights to the extent necessary to reimburse it.[183]

Since the enactment of the Code, bankruptcy courts have had to address the issue of whether *Pearlman* is still good law under the Code.[184] In *Pearlman*, the Supreme Court held that the contract funds were subject to the surety's equitable lien and not property of the estate

---

179 United States Fid. & Guar. Co. v. United States, 475 F.2d 1377, 1381 (Ct. Cl. 1973).
180 George J. Bachrach & Cynthia E. Rodgers-Waire, *The Surety's Rights to the Contract Funds in the Principal's Chapter 11 Bankruptcy Case*, 35 TORT & INS. L. J. 1 (1999). *See also* Chapter 14, *infra*.
181 11 U.S.C. § 101., *et seq.*
182 371 U.S. 132 (1962).
183 371 U.S. at 141-42.
184 Am. States Ins. Co. v. United States, 324 B.R. 600 (N.D. Tex. 2005); *In re* Cone Constructors, Inc., 265 B.R. 302 (Bankr. M.D. Fla. 2001); *In re* Glover Constr. Co., 30 B.R. 873 (Bankr. W.D. Ky. 1983).

under the Bankruptcy Act. Subsequently, section 541 of the Code was adopted which substantially expands the definition of property of the estate to include all legal and equitable interests of the debtor.[185] With respect to the contract funds, whether those contract funds consist of earned and unpaid progress payments,[186] retainage,[187] or the settlement of certain contract claims of the debtor,[188] the surety's equitable lien on the contract funds as a result of the surety's performance of the work and payment of claimants supplying labor and materials relates back to the date of the bond[189] and gives the surety priority over the debtor to the contract funds.[190]

Bankruptcy courts have used a number of theories in recognizing the surety's superior subrogation rights to the contract funds. In several cases, the bankruptcy court determined that the debtor's failure to pay subcontractors and suppliers was equivalent to the debtor's failure to actually perform the contract.[191] Therefore, the obligee did not owe the contract funds to the debtor. Because the debtor had no legal or equitable interests in the contract funds, the contract funds did not become property of the estate under section 541 of the Code.[192] Other cases recognize that the broad scope of section 541 of the Code would bring the contract funds into the estate, subject to the equitable lien rights of

---

185   *In re* Alliance Props., Inc., 104 B.R. 306, 312 (Bankr. S.D. Cal. 1989).
186   *In re* E.R. Fegert, Inc., 88 B.R. 258, 261 (B.A.P. 9th Cir. 1988); *In re* Massart Co., 105 B.R. 610, 613 (W.D. Wash. 1989).
187   *In re* QC Piping Installations, Inc., 225 B.R. 553 (Bankr. E.D.N.Y. 1998); *In re* Glover Constr. Co., 30 B.R. 873, 882 (Bankr. W.D. Ky. 1983).
188   *In re* Alliance Props., Inc., 104 B.R. 306, 310 (Bankr. S.D. Cal. 1989).
189   *In re* Ward Land Clearing & Drainage, Inc., 73 B.R. 313, 315 (Bankr. N.D. Fla. 1987).
190   *In re* Glover Constr. Co., 30 B.R. 873, 882 (Bankr. W.D. Ky. 1983). In fact, the surety is subrogated to the debtor's rights to the contract funds in the hands of the obligee, and may obtain the contract funds ahead of the debtor. *In re* Alcon Demolition, Inc., 204 B.R. 440 (Bankr. D. N.J. 1997); *In re* Four Star Constr. Co., 151 B.R. 817 (Bankr. N.D. Ohio 1993).
191   *In re* Modular Structures, Inc., 27 F.3d 72 (3d Cir. 1994); *In re* Pac. Marine Dredging & Constr., 79 B.R. 924, 929 (Bankr. D. Or. 1987).
192   *In re* Arnold, 908 F.2d 52 (6th Cir. 1990); *In re* Underground Storage Tank Technical Servs. Group, Inc., 212 B.R. 564 (Bankr. E.D. Mich. 1997); *In re* Massart Co., 105 B.R. 610, 613 (W.D. Wash. 1989).

the surety pursuant to the surety's subrogation rights and section 541(d) of the Code.[193]

When the debtor continues the performance of the contract and looks to the progress payments to finance the performance of the work, the progress payments earned by the debtor have been found to be property of the estate.[194] However, bankruptcy courts have held that the surety has an interest in the progress payments pursuant to its subrogation rights that must be adequately protected under the Code.[195] As adequate protection, bankruptcy courts have given the surety the ability to control the debtor's payments to assure that the progress payments are dedicated to pay bona fide claims against the projects for which the surety would become liable under its bonds.[196] Furthermore, in those states that have either enacted trust fund statutes or recognized trust fund theories, all contract funds received by the debtor must be held in trust by the debtor for the benefit of the laborers and materialmen protected by the trust fund statute or trust fund theory, *and* the surety to the extent that the surety pays the laborers and materialmen, and such contract funds may not be allocated or disbursed to general creditors or be used by the debtor in its efforts to reorganize.[197]

The surety's subrogation rights relate back to the date of the bonds.[198] Therefore, post-petition payments by the surety as a result of claims against its bonds executed pre-petition do not allow the debtor to

---

193 *In re* Alliance Props., Inc., 104 B.R. 306, 312 (Bankr. S.D. Cal. 1989); *In re* Glover Constr. Co., 30 B.R. 873, 881 (Bankr. W.D. Ky. 1983).
194 *In re* Glover Constr. Co., 30 B.R. 873, 876 (Bankr. W.D. Ky. 1983).
195 *In re* Glover Constr. Co., 30 B.R. 873, 882 (Bankr. W.D. Ky. 1983); *cf. In re* Universal Builders, Inc., 53 B.R. 183 (Bankr. M.D. Tenn. 1985). The authors believe that *Universal Builders* may have been incorrectly decided by the court's failure to refer to applicable Tennessee law, Third National Bank v. Highlands Insurance Co., 603 S.W.2d 730 (Tenn. 1980).
196 *In re* RAM Constr. Co., 32 B.R. 758, 759 (Bankr. W.D. Pa. 1983); *In re* Glover Constr. Co., 30 B.R. 873, 882 (Bankr. W.D. Ky. 1983).
197 *In re* Marrs-Winn Co., 103 F.3d 584 (7th Cir. 1996); Universal Bonding Ins. Co. v. Gittens & Sprinkle Enters., Inc., 960 F.2d 366, 371 (3d Cir. 1992).
198 *In re* Massart Co., 105 B.R. 610, 612 (W.D. Wash. 1989); *In re* Alliance Props., Inc., 104 B.R. 306, 311 (Bankr. S.D. Cal. 1989); *In re* Pac. Marine Dredging & Constr., 79 B.R. 924, 929 (Bankr. D. Or. 1987).

intervene and claim the contract funds as a hypothetical lien creditor under section 544 of the Code.[199] Furthermore, the surety's payment of those claims post-petition is neither a violation of the automatic stay of section 362(a)(4) of the Code,[200] nor is it a preference under section 547 of the Code.[201] The surety has defeated the trustee's claims of preference under section 547 of the Code because of its equitable lien on the contract funds pursuant to its subrogation rights.[202] Finally, a performance bond surety completing multiple projects for the same obligee at a loss is subrogated to the obligee's common-law setoff rights on those other projects completed at a "profit" because allowing setoff under section 553 of the Code serves as an incentive for sureties to complete their performance bond obligations.[203]

In summary, during an ongoing Chapter 11 proceeding when the debtor is performing the work and the obligee is paying progress payments, both the debtor and the surety have an interest in the contract funds. The debtor will normally be authorized to use the contract funds (progress payments) with the surety obtaining some measure of adequate protection.[204]

When the work has been performed and the surety's payments exceed the remaining contract funds, whether they are progress payments, retainage or the settlement of certain contract claims, the surety maintains an equitable lien in the contract funds pursuant to its subrogation rights to the extent of its losses.[205]

---

199 *In re* Pac. Marine Dredging Constr., 79 B.R. 924, 928 (Bankr. D. Or. 1987).
200 Section 362(a)(4) of the Code stays any act of a creditor of the debtor to create, perfect, or enforce any lien against property of the debtor's estate, i.e., the remaining contract funds.
201 *In re* Pacific Marine Dredging Constr., 79 B.R. 924, 928-29 (Bankr. D. Or. 1987).
202 *In re* E.R. Fegert, Inc., 88 B.R. 258, 260-61 (B.A.P. 9th Cir. 1988). *See also* Newbery Corp. v. Fireman's Fund Ins. Co., 106 B.R. 186 (D. Ariz. 1989).
203 *In re* Larbar Corp., 177 F.3d 439 (6th Cir. 1999).
204 *In re* Glover Constr. Co., 30 B.R. 873 (Bankr. W.D. Ky. 1983).
205 *In re* Alliance Props., Inc., 104 B.R. 306 (Bankr. S.D. Cal. 1989).

4. Taxing Authorities Other Than the Obligee[206]

In a prior section of this chapter, we discussed the conflicting priorities and claims to the contract funds between a surety performing under its performance bond and a government obligee attempting to setoff taxes owed to the obligee by the principal. A surety, pursuant to its subrogation rights, may also compete for the contract funds against a government tax lien from a taxing authority that is not the obligee, and against other governmental agencies making statutory claims against the contract funds such as the federal government and state labor departments. When the surety is a performance bond surety completing the contract of its principal,[207] the surety will prevail over the tax lien rights of the taxing authority to the contract funds because the taxing authority can only claim those contract funds that the principal is entitled to receive.[208] In addition, the surety's subrogation rights arise at the time that it provides the bond and the rights become available to the surety when it suffers a loss.[209] Therefore, the surety's subrogation rights are superior to a government tax lien for unpaid taxes that arises after the date of the bond, but occurs prior to the date that the surety actually makes payment.[210]

However, when the federal government attempts to collect the principal's tax obligations by serving a notice of levy on an obligee in

---

206 Matthew M. Horowitz, *Evaluating Priority Disputes Between a Surety and the Internal Revenue Service* (1995) (unpublished paper submitted at the ABA program on Aug. 8, 1995 at the 1995 ABA Annual Meeting).

207 Cent. Sur. & Ins. Corp. v. Martin Infante Co., 272 F.2d 231 (3d Cir. 1959) (performing surety financed the principal); Aetna Cas. & Sur. Co. v. Port of N.Y. Auth., 182 F. Supp. 671, 673 (S.D.N.Y. 1960) (surety had priority to retainage and unpaid portion of a bonus for early substantial completion).

208 Amwest Sur. Ins. Co. v. United States, 870 F. Supp. 432 (D. Conn. 1994). *See* Matthew M. Horowitz, *Evaluating Priority Disputes Between a Surety and the Internal Revenue Service* (1995) (unpublished paper submitted at the ABA program on Aug. 8, 1995 at the 1995 ABA Annual Meeting). *But cf.* Capitol Indem. Corp. v. United States, 41 F.3d 320 (7th Cir. 1994); *In re* Constr. Alternatives, Inc., 2 F.3d 670 (6th Cir. 1993).

209 United States Fid. & Guar. Co. v. Triborough Bridge Auth., 74 N.E.2d 226, 227 (N.Y. 1947).

210 United States Fid. & Guar. Co. v. United States, 201 F.2d 118, 121 (10th Cir. 1952).

possession of contract funds that the surety claims, the surety must argue that the levy is wrongful because the contract funds are not the principal's property or are otherwise protected from a state law judgment lien. In order to protect its rights, the surety must file a complaint to contest the notice of levy within the nine-month statute of limitations provided under the statute.[211]

The federal government under the Davis-Bacon Act[212] and various state governmental agencies, such as state labor departments, may also compete with the surety's subrogation rights to the contract funds,[213] and some have found success, depending upon the federal or state statutes.

One issue that may affect the priority between the surety and the taxing authority to the contract funds is whether the principal is in default. One court has held that the surety has priority over the taxing

---

211 The requirement that the surety file a complaint to contest the levy is found in 26 U.S.C. § 7426(a)(1) and the nine-month statute of limitation period is found in 26 U.S.C. § 6532(c). The surety's failure to file a wrongful levy complaint within the nine-month period will bar the surety's right to contest the levy and assert its rights to the contract funds. Fid. & Dep. Co. of Md. v. City of Adelanto, 87 F.3d 334 (9th Cir. 1996). See Adam Cizek & Michael A. Safris, *IRS Notice of Levy on Bonded Contract Funds: What Does the Surety Do Next?* (2007) (unpublished paper submitted at the Eighteenth Annual Northeast Sur. & Fid. Claims Conference on Sept. 27, 2007).

212 See Michael A. Stover & Susan Getz Kerbel, *"Look Who's Bringing Home the Bacon"–How Recent Decisions Interpreting the Davis-Bacon Act Can Negatively Affect the Surety* (2003) (unpublished paper submitted at the Fourteenth Annual Northeast Sur. & Fid. Claims Conference on Sept. 18, 2003).

213 Titan Indem. Co. v. Triborough Bridge & Tunnel Auth., 135 F.3d 831 (2d Cir. 1998); City of New York v. Cross Bay Contracting Corp., 709 N.E.2d 459 (N.Y. 1999); RLI Ins. Co. v. N.Y. State Dep't of Labor, 97 N.Y.2d 256 (2002). See Darryl Weissman & Scott D. Baron, *The Surety's Priority Battle With State Labor Departments Over Unpaid Contract Funds–Whatever Happened to Subrogation?* (1998) (unpublished paper submitted at the Ninth Annual Northeast Sur. & Fid. Claims Conference on Oct. 22, 1998); John W. Morris, *The Labor Department Versus the Subrogated Surety, Who Wins?* (1999) (unpublished paper submitted at the 1999 National Bond Claims Association annual meeting program on Sept. 30, 1999).

authority's tax liens that are filed after the principal is in default, but not as to any tax liens filed before the principal is in default.[214] However, all that is necessary for the surety's subrogation rights and equitable lien to attach to the contract funds is for the principal to be in default as a matter of fact, and the surety has become obligated to pay subcontractors, laborers and materialmen under its payment bond. In that instance, formal notice of default need not be given to the surety before its subrogation rights accrue against the contract funds.[215]

C. Legal Competitors, Including the Principal's General Creditors and Judgment Creditors (Hereinafter the "General Creditors")

A surety may compete for the contract funds on a contract bonded by the surety with general creditors of the principal that are not claimants under any contract bonded by the surety.[216] This situation is very similar to the surety competing for the contract funds with a taxing authority other than the obligee that has a filed tax lien against the principal. The general creditor may have a judgment against the principal and may have executed or garnished the contract funds, or it merely may be owed a general unsecured debt from the principal.

When the surety has performed under its performance bond, the surety's subrogation rights to the contract funds are superior to those of general creditors even when the contract funds have been attached by general creditors first.[217] When the surety completes the performance of the contract at a cost greater than the remaining contract funds, and has deposited the full amount of the payment bond with the court, the surety is subrogated to the rights of the government obligee to the contract funds even though the payment bond did not fully compensate all of the

---

214 Int'l Fid. Ins. Co. v. United States, 949 F.2d 1042 (8th Cir. 1991).
215 Kansas City, Mo. v. Tri-City Constr. Co., 666 F. Supp. 170, 172 (W.D. Mo. 1987).
216 A general creditor may also include a subcontractor claimant who has failed to file a timely claim against the surety's payment bond. Gen. Acrylics v. United States Fid. & Guar. Co., 623 P.2d 839, 844-45 (Ariz. Ct. App. 1980).
217 Segovia Dev. Corp. v. Constructora Maza, Inc., 628 F.2d 724 (1st Cir. 1980); Stehle v. United Sur. Co., 107 Md. 470 (Md. 1908); Int'l Fid. Ins. Co. v. Ashland Lumber Co., 463 S.E.2d 664 (Va. 1995).

payment bond claimants, who then become general creditors of the principal.[218]

At least one court has found, in determining the priority rights to the contract funds in a dispute involving a bank as the assignee of the principal, a surety who issued a contract surety bond, and general creditors, including a general creditor that had issued a writ of garnishment after the surety bond was executed, that the surety's subrogation rights, which relate back to the date of the execution of the surety bond, took priority over the claims of the principal's general, unsecured creditors.[219]

When the principal has received progress payments from the obligee and paid general creditors on obligations not arising from the principal's performance of the bonded contract, courts have generally held that the general creditor may retain the payment received. When the principal paid the general creditor prior to the principal's default on the bonded contract, the general creditor could retain the payment barring any allegation or proof by the surety that the payment was a fraudulent conveyance by the principal.[220] When the general creditor had no knowledge of the principal's default, the surety may not, on a subrogation theory, recover from the general creditor the amount paid in satisfaction of a just debt.[221]

In those states that have enacted trust fund statutes, all contract funds received by the principal must be held in trust for the benefit of the laborers and materialmen protected by the trust fund statute, *and* the surety to the extent that the surety pays the laborers and materialmen, and such contract funds may not be allocated or disbursed to general creditors of the principal.[222]

---

218 Covenant Mut. Ins. Co. v. Able Concrete Pump, 609 F. Supp. 27 (N.D. Cal. 1984).
219 Kimberly-Clark Corp. v. Alpha Bldg. Co., 591 F. Supp. 198 (N.D. Miss. 1984).
220 Am. Cas. Co. of Reading, Pa. v. Line Materials Indus., 332 F.2d 393 (10th Cir. 1964).
221 Cal. Bank v. United States Fid. & Guar. Co., 129 F.2d 751 (9th Cir. 1942).
222 Universal Bonding Ins. Co. v. Gittens & Sprinkle Enters., Inc., 960 F.2d 366, 371 (3d Cir. 1992).

D. Setoff Issues: The Surety's Subrogation Rights to the Obligee's Setoff Rights to Defeat the Claims of Other Claimants ("Common Obligee Theory")

The surety is subrogated to all of the rights and remedies of the obligee as a result of its performance of the work under the performance bond and payment of claimants under the payment bond.[223] The obligee may have one or more contracts with the principal, whether bonded by the surety or not, and the principal may owe the obligee money as a result of other obligations (debts for taxes due and owing, debts on other contracts). Under these circumstances, the obligee may attempt to exercise its setoff rights against the contract funds the obligee owes the principal under the contract or contracts (funds in which the obligee has an interest) to reimburse itself for debts owed by the principal to the obligee. The issue of whether a performance bond surety may use its subrogation rights to the setoff rights of the obligee to obtain the proceeds owed by the obligee to the principal on one contract to reimburse the surety for losses it has incurred on another contract[224] is limited to those instances when the obligee is a mere stakeholder of the contract funds and has no independent interest in them.

A surety that performs its obligations under its performance bond[225] is subrogated to all of the rights and remedies of the obligee. As a result, several courts have held that, when the only claimants to certain monies held by the obligee as a stakeholder are the surety and the principal, the surety who has performed under its performance bond to complete the bonded contract of its principal, upon full satisfaction of its obligations, is subrogated to all of the rights and remedies that the obligee may have had against the principal had the obligee been forced to complete the bonded contract itself. Among those remedies is the common-law right of the obligee to setoff monies owed to the principal on one contract against debts owed by the principal to the obligee on another.[226] Courts have routinely affirmed that a surety should not be punished for

---

223 Pearlman v. Reliance Ins. Co., 371 U.S. 132 (1962).
224 Edward G. Gallagher, *Surety's Subrogation to Obligee's Right of Setoff*, 18 FORUM 73 (1982).
225 Prairie State Nat'l Bank v. United States, 164 U.S. 227 (1896).
226 *In re* Larbar Corp., 177 F.3d 439 (6th Cir. 1999); Transamerica Ins. Co. v. United States, 989 F.2d 1188 (Fed. Cir. 1993); Dist. of Columbia v. Aetna Ins. Co., 462 A.2d 428 (D.C. 1983).

completing a bonded contract as opposed to forcing the obligee to complete it and make a claim under the surety's performance bond for any resulting loss.[227] However, the surety did not prevail when it sought to use its status as a performance bond surety on some contracts to obtain funds due to its principal on another contract in which the surety had only a payment bond loss. The competing claimants to the contract funds were the surety and the government obligee, which was not a stakeholder but rather had its own claims as a taxing authority against the excess contract funds. The court found that the surety, as a payment bond surety, was not entitled to use its performance bond surety subrogation rights to require the obligee to setoff the contract funds in favor of the surety and ahead of the obligee's own tax claims against the principal.[228] The surety incurring a loss on a bonded contract does have the subrogation right to compel an obligee to assert its setoff rights against an insolvent principal on a separate contract in order to reduce the surety's loss.[229]

In the bankruptcy area, a performance bond surety completing multiple projects for the same obligee at a loss is subrogated to the obligee's common-law setoff rights on those other projects completed at a "profit."[230]

In summary, while some cases state that the surety's subrogation rights to the contract funds are limited to the contract on which the surety's loss was incurred and do not give the surety rights in the excess contract funds from another contract,[231] other cases hold just the

---

227 United States v. Munsey Trust Co., 332 U.S. 234, 244 (1947) ("A surety would rarely undertake to complete a job if it incurred the risk that by completing it might lose more than if it had allowed the government to proceed.").

228 Dependable Ins. Co., Inc. v. United States, 846 F.2d 65, 67 (Fed. Cir. 1988).

229 Merritt Commercial Sav. & Loan, Inc. v. Guinee, 766 F.2d 850 (4th Cir. 1985); In re Yale Express Sys., Inc., 362 F.2d 111 (2d Cir. 1966); United States *ex rel.* Johnson v. Morley Constr. Co., 98 F.2d 781 (2d Cir. 1938), *cert. denied sub nom.*; Md. Cas. v. United States *ex rel.* Harrington, 305 U.S. 651 (1938).

230 *In re* Larbar Corp., 177 F.3d 439 (6th Cir. 1999).

231 *In re* Eastern Marine, Inc., 104 B.R. 421 (Bankr. N.D. Fla. 1989); Transamerica Ins. Co. v. Barnett Bank of Marion County, N.A., 540 So. 2d 113, 117 (Fla. 1989).

opposite.[232] The decision of the United States Court of Appeals for the Federal Circuit in *Transamerica*[233] has decided the issue as far as contracts with the federal government are concerned.

IV. Unique Issues Involving the Federal Government as Obligee

The Miller Act requires a principal entering into a construction contract with the federal government to provide a performance bond and a payment bond from a qualified surety.[234] The principal's construction contract with the federal government is governed by the Federal Acquisition Regulations (the "FARs"),[235] which also address surety bonds generally[236] and the performance bond surety's rights and obligations. The unique issues involving a principal's construction contract with the federal government and the principal's and the surety's performance bond issued to the federal government include the surety's performance bond options when the federal government defaults and/or terminates the principal's construction contract, the surety's rights to the contract funds held by the federal government, and the resolution of the surety's disputes with the federal government with respect to the surety's rights to the contract funds.[237]

---

232 *In re* Larbar Corp., 177 F.3d 439 (6th Cir. 1999); Transamerica Ins. Co. v. United States, 989 F.2d 1188 (Fed. Cir. 1993); Dist. of Columbia v. Aetna Ins. Co., 462 A.2d 428 (D.C. 1983).
233 Transamerica Ins. Co. v. United States, 989 F.2d 1188 (Fed. Cir. 1993).
234 40 U.S.C. §§ 3131-34.
235 48 C.F.R. Parts 1-53.
236 48 C.F.R. Part 28.
237 For additional secondary materials concerning the federal government as the obligee under the surety's performance bond, see Donald G. Gavin et al., *Ch. 8, Public Works Projects*, in BOND DEFAULT MANUAL 287-311 (Duncan L. Clore et al. eds., 3d ed. 2005); George J. Bachrach & Robert F. Carney, *The Surety and the United States Court of Federal Claims–Revisited* (1999) (unpublished paper submitted at the Tenth Annual Northeast Sur. & Fid. Claims Conference on Oct. 21, 1999); George J. Bachrach & Robert F. Carney, *The Surety and the United States Court of Federal Claims* (1995) (unpublished paper submitted at the Surety Claims Institute program on June 22, 1995 at the 1995 Annual Meeting); David D. Crane, *A Critical Examination of the Federal Acquisition Regulations Related to Sureties* (1991) (unpublished paper

A. Surety Bonding with the Federal Government

1. The Miller Act

The Miller Act requires a performance bond for all contracts of more than $100,000 for the "construction, alteration, or repair of any public building or public work" of the federal government.[238] Under the Miller Act performance bond, the surety's obligation for payment of the penal sum is void if the principal "performs and fulfills all the undertakings, covenants, terms, conditions, and agreements of the contract."[239] If the principal fails to perform, the surety is bound for payment of the penal sum of the Miller Act performance bond. Essentially, the Miller Act performance bond is an indemnity bond.[240]

2. The Federal Acquisition Regulations

The FARs set forth the regulations concerning the principal's construction contracting with the federal government, including the requirement for the surety's performance and payment bonds, the performance bond surety's obligations, and its rights to the contract funds.

---

submitted at the ABA program on Aug. 13, 1991 at the 1991 Annual Meeting).
238 40 U.S.C. § 3131(b) (2009).
239 Standard Form 25, Performance Bond, 48 C.F.R. § 53.301-25 (2009).
240 *See* Trinity Universal Ins. Co. v. United States, 382 F.2d 317, 321 (5th Cir. 1967), *cert. denied*, 390 U.S. 906 (1968).

B. The Surety's Performance Bond Options When the Federal Government Defaults the Principal

The Miller Act performance bond does not set forth the surety's performance bond options or describe how the surety must fulfill its performance obligations under the Miller Act performance bond if the principal fails to fulfill its obligations under the contract with the federal government.[241]

Unlike the AIA Document A311 Performance Bond, the AIA Document A312 Performance Bond and the ConsensusDOCS 260 Performance Bond, which provide that the surety has rights to the balance of the contract funds, the Miller Act performance bond does not contain any such provision and the FARs condition the surety's rights to the contract funds. However, whatever Miller Act performance bond option the surety may have or may exercise, the surety will contend that it has rights to the balance of the contract funds.

The surety performance bond options of takeover and completion, tender, financing the principal and completion by the obligee are more fully described in Chapter 3. The only surety performance bond option specifically mentioned in the FARs is the surety's option to enter into a takeover agreement with the federal government.[242] The FARs specifically require the federal government, under a takeover agreement with the surety, "to pay the surety's costs and expenses up to the balance of the contract price unpaid at the time of default," subject to a number of conditions.[243] Because there may be conflicting demands by various

---

241 Nowhere in the Miller Act performance bond or the FARs does it say that the surety is obligated to complete. In fact, the FARs contain a provision for the contracting officer to arrange for completion in the event the surety does not do so. 48 C.F.R. § 49.405 (2009). However, the FARs do acknowledge that the "contracting officer should permit surety offers to complete the contract," 48 C.F.R. § 49.404(c) (2009), that a "surety has certain rights and interest in the completion of the contract work and the application of any undisbursed funds" and that "the contracting officer must consider carefully the surety's proposals for completing the contract." 48 C.F.R. § 49.404(b) (2009).
242 48 C.F.R. § 49.404 (2009).
243 48 C.F.R. § 49.404(e) provides:
Any takeover agreement must require the surety to complete the contract and the Government to pay the surety's costs and

parties to the contract funds, "the surety may include a 'takeover' agreement in its proposal, fixing the surety's rights to payment from those funds."[244]

Notwithstanding the language of the FARs, sureties have exercised their other performance bond options with the federal government, including the surety's tendering of a completion contractor to the federal government,[245] the surety's financing of the principal,[246] and the federal government choosing to complete the performance of the principal's

> expenses up to the balance of the contract price unpaid at the time of default, subject to the following conditions:
> (1) Any unpaid earnings of the defaulting contractor, including retained percentages and progress estimates for work accomplished before termination, must be subject to debts due the Government by the contractor, except to the extent that the unpaid earnings may be used to pay the completing surety its actual costs and expenses incurred in the completion of the work, but not including its payments and obligations under the payment bond given in connection with the contract.
> (2) The surety is bound by contract terms governing liquidated damages for delays in completion of the work, unless the delays are excusable under the contract.
> (3) If the contract proceeds have been assigned to a financing institution, the surety must not be paid from unpaid earnings, unless the assignee provides written consent.
> (4) The contracting officer must not pay the surety more than the amount it expended completing the work and discharging its liabilities under the defaulting contractor's payment bond. Payments to the surety to reimburse it for discharging its liabilities under the payment bond of the defaulting contractor must be only on authority of—
> (i) Mutual agreement among the Government, the defaulting contractor, and the surety;
> (ii) Determination of the Comptroller General as to payee and amount; or
> (iii) Order of a court of competent jurisdiction.

244 48 C.F.R. § 49.404(d) (2009).
245 48 C.F.R. § 49.404(b) and (c) (2009). *See* Transamerica Ins. Co. v. United States, 31 Fed. Cl. 532 (1994).
246 Aetna Cas. & Sur. Co. v. United States, 845 F.2d 971 (Fed. Cir. 1988); Morrison Assur. Co. v. United States, 3 Cl. Ct. 626 (1983); Great Am. Ins. Co. v. United States, 481 F.2d 1298, 1300 n.8 (Ct. Cl. 1973).

work under the construction contract,[247] and then making a claim against the surety's performance bond for any excess costs of completion.[248] As discussed previously in this chapter and in Chapter 3, the surety exercising one of its performance bond options is entitled under various theories to the balance of the contract funds.

However, in the federal government context, the surety's rights to the contract funds are governed by the FARs, the cases decided under the Miller Act, and, perhaps, more importantly, the various statutory restraints on the surety's resolution of any disputes with the federal government with respect to the contract funds. Whether the surety is asserting its contractual rights, statutory rights or common-law and equitable rights to the contract funds held by the federal government, the performance bond surety's rights to the contract funds will be affected by the Tucker Act and the Contract Disputes Act procedures as more fully described below.

C. The Surety's Disputes With the Federal Government—Jurisdictional Issues

The surety's disputes with the federal government concerning the contract funds are litigated primarily in the United States Court of Federal Claims (the "Claims Court") under two jurisdictional statutes, the Tucker Act[249] and the Contract Disputes Act,[250] which are generally applicable to the surety's claims for the contract funds against the federal government.[251]

---

247 Completion by another contractor, 48 C.F.R. § 49.405 (2009).
248 Liquidation of liability, 48 C.F.R. § 49.406 (2009). The "contracting officer must take action on the basis of the Government's interest," which may necessitate the federal government completing the performance of the principal's work under the contract, even though the contracting officer must take into account "the possible effect upon the Government's rights against the surety." 48 C.F.R. § 49.404(b) (2009).
249 28 U.S.C. § 1491 (2008).
250 41 U.S.C. § 601 (2008).
251 For a detailed discussion of the surety's involvement in cases before the Claims Court, see Gerald N. Carozza, Jr. & Cynthia E. Rodgers-Waire, *A Primer on the Tucker Act* (2008) (unpublished paper submitted at the Surety Claims Institute program on June 26, 2008 at the 2008 Annual Meeting); George J. Bachrach & Robert F. Carney, *The Surety and the*

1. The Tucker Act—Generally

The Tucker Act is federal legislation that is a limited waiver of sovereign immunity granting subject matter jurisdiction to the United States District Courts and the Claims Court[252] for certain non-tort monetary damage claims against the federal government based on any express or implied contract with the federal government or based on a constitutional, statutory or regulatory provision that grants a plaintiff a right to monetary relief.[253]

The Tucker Act does not confer substantive rights against the federal government; it merely provides authority for certain courts to entertain claims for money arising under the Constitution, statutes, regulations or express or implied contracts with the federal government when the substantive rights already exist.[254] The Tucker Act does not have general jurisdiction to grant equitable relief,[255] nor does it provide jurisdiction for non-monetary relief such as mandamus or declaratory judgment.[256]

United States Court of Federal Claims–Revisited (1999) (unpublished paper submitted at the Tenth Annual Northeast Sur. & Fid. Claims Conference on Oct. 21, 1999); George J. Bachrach & Robert F. Carney, *The Surety and the United States Court of Federal Claims* (1995) (unpublished paper submitted at the Surety Claims Institute program on June 22, 1995 at the 1995 Annual Meeting).

252 28 U.S.C. § 1346(a)(2) (2008).
253 28 U.S.C. § 1491(a)(1) (2008). For a discussion of the historical background of the Tucker Act and the present constitution of the Tucker Act, *see* Gerald N. Carozza, Jr. & Cynthia E. Rodgers-Waire, *A Primer on the Tucker Act* (2008) (unpublished paper submitted at the Surety Claims Institute program on June 26, 2008 at the 2008 Annual Meeting) at pp. 2-5 and the authorities and references cited therein; United States v. Mitchell, 463 U.S. 206, 212 (1983).
254 United States v. Testan, 424 U.S. 392 (1976); Int'l Fid. Ins. Co. v. United States, 41 Fed. Cl. 706, 710 (1998); Transamerica Ins. Co. v. United States, 31 Fed. Cl. 602, 604 (1994).
255 The Tucker Act contemplates equitable relief in contract actions only in limited circumstances prior to the award of the contract. 28 U.S.C. § 1491(a)(2) (2008).
256 United States v. King, 395 U.S. 1 (1969); Austin v. United States, 206 Ct. Cl. 719, 723, *cert. denied*, 423 U.S. 911 (1975).

All claims for which the Claims Court has jurisdiction must be filed within six years after the claim first accrues.[257]

The Tucker Act is important to sureties because it has been the salvation for the surety seeking a right to the contract funds. While the *Blue Fox* case, discussed later in this chapter, created concern over the continued viability of a surety's subrogation rights in the face of federal government assertions of sovereign immunity, the Federal Circuit has reaffirmed the surety's right to maintain such actions by virtue of the waiver of sovereign immunity granted by the Tucker Act for performance bond sureties in *Insurance Co. of the West v. United States*.[258] Performance bond sureties that execute takeover agreements with the federal government establish privity of contract with the federal government and clearly fall within the Tucker Act's waiver of sovereign immunity for claims that fit within the scope of the takeover agreement.

2. Contracts Under the Tucker Act

a. *Tucker Act Jurisdiction Based upon an Express Contract.* One way a claimant may establish jurisdiction under the Tucker Act is to plead and prove that it has an express contract with the federal government. An express contract with the federal government requires mutuality of intent to contract, an unambiguous offer and acceptance, consideration, and actual authority on the part of a government official to bind the federal government.[259]

---

257 28 U.S.C. § 2501 (2008).
258 243 F.3d 1367 (Fed. Cir. 2001). The Federal Circuit has also reaffirmed the payment bond surety's right to maintain such actions by virtue of the waiver of sovereign immunity granted by the Tucker Act. Nat'l Am. Ins. Co. v. United States, 498 F.3d 1301 (Fed. Cir. 2007).
259 *See* City of El Centro v. United States, 922 F.2d 816, 820 (Fed. Cir. 1990); Yachts Am., Inc. v. United States, 779 F.2d 656, 661 (Fed. Cir. 1985), *cert. denied*, 479 U.S. 832 (1986); H.F. Allen Orchards v. United States, 749 F. 2d 1571, 1575 (Fed. Cir. 1984), *overruled in part on other grounds by* Orff v. United States, 545 U.S. 596 (2005); OAO Corp. v. United States, 17 Cl. Ct. 91 (1989); Nitol v. United States, 7 Cl. Ct. 405, 415 (1985); Prevado Vill. P'ship v. United States, 3 Cl. Ct. 219, 223 (1983); Russell Corp. v. United States, 537 F.2d 474, 482 (Ct. Cl. 1976), *cert. denied*, 429 U.S. 1073 (1977); Boyd & Huffman, *The Treatment of Implied-in-law and Implied-in-fact Contracts and Promissory Estoppel in*

In contrast with the private sector, there is no recognition of apparent authority when seeking to establish a contract claim against the federal government.[260] Generally, only a contracting officer whose authority is established by written warrant has authority to bind the federal government.[261] Therefore, a prudent surety should verify that all contracts that it secures with the federal government are actually approved and executed by the authorized contracting officer or run the risk of having an unenforceable contract.

An express agreement requires an express oral or written manifestation of assent by the parties to the contract.[262] Federal procurement law prefers written contracts and disfavors oral contracts.[263]

---

the United States Claims Court, 40 CATH. U. L. REV. 605, 606 (1991) (hereinafter referred to as "Boyd & Huffman").

260 See Fed. Crop Ins. Co. v. Merrill, 332 U.S. 380, 384 (1947):
[W]hatever the form in which the Government functions, anyone entering into an arrangement with the Government takes the risk of having accurately ascertained that he who purports to act for the Government stays within the bounds of his authority. The scope of this authority may be explicitly defined by Congress or through the rule-making power. And this is so even though, as here, the agent himself may have been unaware of the limitations upon his authority.

261 The FARs, issued jointly by the Department of Defense, NASA, and the General Services Administration, vest contracting authority in the head of the agency. 48 C.F.R. § 1.601(a) (2009). For example, within DOD, the heads of the agencies are the Secretaries of Defense, the Army, the Navy, and the Air Force. 48 C.F.R. § 202.101 (2009). Agency heads or their designees select and appoint contracting officers in writing using the Standard Form (SF) 1402, Certificate of Appointment. 48 C.F.R. § 1.603-3 (2009).

262 Chavez v. United States, 18 Cl. Ct. 540, 545 (1989); Boyd & Huffman, supra note 259, at 608.

263 The FARs define a contract as "a mutually binding legal relationship obligating the seller to furnish supplies and services (including construction) and the buyer to pay for them. It includes all types of commitments that obligate the Government to an expenditure of appropriated funds and that, except as otherwise authorized, are in writing. In addition to bilateral instruments, contracts include (but are not limited to) awards and notices of awards; job orders or task letters issued under basic ordering agreements; letter contracts; orders, such as purchase orders, under which the contract becomes effective by written

It is a statutory requirement that an obligation of the federal government be supported by documentary evidence of a written binding agreement between an agency and another party.[264]

Surety bonds executed in favor of the federal government have been held not to constitute an express contract between the surety and the federal government because they are not signed by the federal government and the federal government does not undertake any obligations to the surety under the bonds.[265] The rationale behind this position is that the federal government is a beneficiary of, but not a party to, the bonds and owes no obligations to the surety thereunder.[266]

One of the express agreements most often relied on by a surety for Tucker Act jurisdiction is the original contract between the principal and the federal government, which will be discussed later in the context of the surety's subrogation rights. The second is the takeover agreement between the surety and the federal government.[267]

For the reasons discussed above, it is incumbent upon the surety to make sure that a takeover agreement or any other form of agreement to be relied upon is executed by a contracting officer or higher official whose warrant or position empowers the official to bind the federal government. A less formal letter agreement between the surety and federal government may also suffice for Tucker Act jurisdiction; however, prudence dictates that the surety not proceed with performance until such a letter is countersigned by a contracting officer.

In addition to the normal protections that a surety generally obtains with the execution of a takeover agreement (such as penal sum

---

acceptance or performance; and bilateral contract modifications." 48 C.F.R. § 2.101 (2009).
264   31 U.S.C. § 1501(a)(1) (2008).
265   Ransom v. United States, 900 F.2d 242, 244 (Fed. Cir. 1990); Am. Ins. Co. v. United States, 62 Fed. Cl. 151, 154-55 (2004).
266   Fireman's Fund Ins. Co. v. United States, 909 F.2d 495, 500 (Fed. Cir. 1990); Am. Ins. Co. v. United States, 62 Fed. Cl. 151, 154 (2004).
267   Travelers Indem. Co. v. United States, 16 Cl. Ct. 142, 151 (1988) ("Said agreement is unquestionably a contract between defendant and Travelers..."). An express contract is a written document signed by the federal government wherein the federal government undertakes obligations to the surety. Fireman's Fund Ins. Co. v. United States, 909 F.2d 495, 499-500 (Fed. Cir. 1990); Ransom v. United States, 900 F.2d 242, 244 (Fed. Cir. 1990).

limitations, agreements as to the scope of work, time for completion, and payment of the contract funds), in the federal government context, the surety also obtains a waiver of sovereign immunity for the purposes of bringing monetary claims against the federal government in the Claims Court. "The effect of finding privity of contract between a party and the United States is to find a waiver of sovereign immunity."[268]

b. *Tucker Act Jurisdiction Based upon an Implied-in-Fact Contract.* Notwithstanding federal procurement law's stated preference for contracts to be evidenced in writing, there are circumstances when the courts will find a contract to be implied-in-fact. The Claims Court has held that failure to reduce a contract to writing under 31 U.S.C. 1501(a)(1) should not preclude recovery; rather, a party may prevail if it introduces additional facts from which a court can infer a meeting of the minds.[269] Courts have held that the FARs do not prevent a court from finding an implied-in-fact contract.[270]

An implied-in-fact contract is "founded upon a meeting of the minds, which, although not embodied in an express contract, is inferred, as a fact, from conduct of the parties showing, in the light of the surrounding circumstances, their tacit understanding."[271] The requirements for an

---

268   Wagner v. United States, 71 Fed. Cl. 355, 362 (2006) (citing Nat'l Leased Hous. Ass'n v. United States, 105 F.3d 1423, 1436 (Fed. Cir. 1997)).

269   Narva Harris Constr. Corp. v. United States, 574 F.2d 508 (1978); The Judge Advocate General's Legal Center and School, U.S. Army, 159th Contract Attorneys Course Deskbook, at page 3-3 (Mar. 2008) (hereinafter referred to as "JAG 159 CAC Deskbook").

270   48 C.F.R. § 2.101. PacOrd, Inc. v. United States, 139 F.3d 1320 (9th Cir. 1998). The Armed Services Board of Contract Appeals, which is a creature of the Contracts Dispute Act discussed later in this chapter, has followed the *Narva Harris* position. Various correspondence between parties can be sufficient "additional facts" and "totality of circumstances" to avoid the statutory prohibition in 31 U.S.C. § 1501(a)(1) against purely oral contracts. Essex Electro Eng'rs, Inc., ASBCA Nos. 30118 and 30119, 88-1 B.C.A. ¶ 20,440 (Dec. 14, 1987); Vec-Tor, Inc., ASBCA Nos. 25807 and 26128, 84-1 B.C.A. ¶ 17,145 (Jan. 31, 1984); JAG 159 CAC Deskbook, *supra* note 269, at 3-3.

271   Balt. & Ohio R.R. Co. v. United States, 261 U.S. 592, 597 (1923). *See also* Employers Ins. of Wausau v. United States, 23 Cl. Ct. 579, 581 (1981).

implied-in-fact contract are the same as for an express contract; only the nature of the evidence differs.[272]

The Claims Court has found sufficient evidence of an implied-in-fact contract between the surety and the federal government and denied the federal government's motion to dismiss the surety's counts that were based on an implied contract.[273] However, as discussed previously, the surety's providing of bonds to the federal government does not create a contractual relationship between the surety and the federal government.[274] Furthermore, the federal government's requirement that the principal obtain surety bonds does not imply a contract between the federal government and the surety.[275]

---

272 OAO Corp. v. United States, 17 Cl. Ct. 91 (1989) (finding implied-in-fact contract for start-up costs for an early warning system). *See generally, Willard L. Boyd III, Implied-in-Fact Contract: Contractual Recovery against the Government without an Express Agreement*, 21 PUB. CONT. L. J. 84-128 (Fall 1991); JAG 159 CAC Deskbook, *supra* note 269, at 3-4.

273 Travelers Indem. v. United States, 16 Cl. Ct. 142, 151 (1988). (The court stated that when the parties have substantially interacted with one another in executing bonds and a takeover agreement, there existed conduct by the parties from which the court might reasonably infer the existence of intent to enter into a contract.)

274 Ransom v. United States, 900 F.2d 242, 243-44 (Fed. Cir. 1990) (The Federal Circuit Court noted that no authorized federal government official ever said anything that could be construed as intending to obligate the federal government towards the surety, that no federal government official signed the bonds or was asked to, and that there was no language in the bonds that even purported to obligate the federal government to the surety.).

275 Ransom v. United States, 900 F.2d 242, 245 (Fed. Cir. 1990) (The Federal Circuit stated that, at most, the federal government's requirement that a principal obtain a bond evidences an implied contract between the federal government and the principal. Without an express or implied contract, the surety could not establish jurisdiction for its claim of breach of good faith and fair dealing.). *See also* Fireman's Fund Ins. Co. v. United States, 909 F.2d 495, 500 (Fed. Cir. 1990) (The performance and payment bonds, and the events leading up to their execution, including the fact that the contract requires bonds, do not create an implied-in-fact contract directly between the surety and the federal government.); Nova Cas. Co. v. United States, 69 Fed. Cl. 284, 290 (2006).

An implied-in-fact contract should not be confused with an implied-in-law contract. An implied-in-law contract has been described as a legal fiction where "a promise is imputed to perform a legal duty, as to repay money obtained by fraud or duress."[276] An implied-in-law contract is not sufficient for invoking the jurisdiction of the Claims Court.[277]

Finally, implied covenants of good faith and fair dealing are not implied-in-law contracts, but are obligations implicitly contained within an existing contract.[278] "All contracts, including government contracts, contain an implied covenant of good faith and fair dealing."[279] Therefore, if a surety can establish an express or implied-in-fact contract, that contract comes with obligations of good faith and fair dealing on the part of each party to that contract, including the federal government.

3. The Contract Disputes Act

Unlike the Tucker Act, which only confers jurisdiction in the Claims Court when a separate substantive right of action exists, the Contract Disputes Act ("CDA")[280] is a federal statute that provides a means for certain claims against the federal government to be heard in the Claims Court. The CDA confers subject matter jurisdiction upon the Claims Court for certain claims,[281] establishes jurisdictional prerequisites for pursuit of claims in the Claims Court,[282] and creates substantive rights of action available to a surety pursuant to the terms of a takeover agreement between the surety and the federal government.[283] Furthermore, like the Tucker Act, the CDA confers subject matter jurisdiction in the Claims Court for appeals arising out of a contracting officer's final decision on the claim, whether it is a principal's claim or the surety's claim, most likely under a surety takeover agreement.

---

276 Balt. & Ohio R.R. Co. v. United States, 261 U.S. 592, 597 (1923); JAG 159 CAC Deskbook, *supra* note 269, at 3-4.
277 *See* Hercules, Inc. v. United States, 516 U.S. 417 (1996); JAG 159 CAC Deskbook, *supra* note 269, at 3-5.
278 Travelers Indem. Co. v. United States, 16 Cl. Ct. 142 (1988).
279 Temple-Inland, Inc. v. United States, 59 Fed. Cl. 550, 559 (2004) (quoting Centex Corp. v. United States, 48 Fed. Cl. 625, 632 (2001)).
280 41 U.S.C. § 601 (2008).
281 41 U.S.C. § 609(a) (2008).
282 41 U.S.C. §§ 605(a) and 605(c)(1) (2008).
283 41 U.S.C. § 605(a) (2008).

A surety's opportunities to pursue a successful claim under the CDA are more limited than under the Tucker Act. First, the CDA confers subject matter jurisdiction upon the Claims Court only for appeals arising out of a contracting officer's final decision on a claim. A principal or surety must file its action against the federal government under the CDA within one year after the issuance of the contracting officer's final decision on the claim or the claim is time-barred.[284]

Second, the CDA applies only to claims from "contractors" under "government contracts."[285] In order for a surety to qualify as a "contractor," the surety must be "a party to a government contract other than the government."[286] A "government contract" is an express or implied contract for the procurement of services or construction, alteration, repair or maintenance of real property.[287] The most likely government contract between a surety and the federal government is a takeover agreement executed upon the default of the principal.[288] Absent the execution of a

---

284   41 U.S.C. § 609(a)(3) (2008). Claims under the CDA are not governed by the six-year limitations set forth in 28 U.S.C. § 2501 applicable to actions over which the Claims Court has jurisdiction. The CDA contains two relevant time limitations. All claims must be submitted to the contracting officer within six years after the accrual of the claim. 41 U.S.C. § 605(a) (2008). Appeals from the final decision of a contracting officer must be filed within one year after the date of the final decision. 41 U.S.C.§ 609(a)(3) (2008).
285   41 U.S.C. § 605(a) (2008).
286   41 U.S.C. § 601(4) (2008).
287   41 U.S.C. § 602 (2008).
288   *See, e.g.*, Reliance Ins. Co. v. United States, 27 Fed. Cl. 815 (1993); Employer Ins. of Wausau v. United States, 23 Cl. Ct. 579 (1991). In denying the federal government's motion to dismiss, the Claims Court in *Travelers Indemnity Co. v. United States*, 16 Cl. Ct. 142 (1988) held:
   As Travelers, here, has executed such a takeover agreement, it necessarily possesses greater rights to sue the government than might a non-completing surety. In fact, upon the execution of said Takeover Agreement, Travelers became the prime party in privity with the government. It is, therefore, the holding of this court that where a surety has executed a takeover agreement, as herein, upon the default of the prime contractor in order to complete the work under the construction contract, it becomes a "party to a Government contract'" and thus, logically, a "contractor" within the meaning of § 601(4) of the CDA. . . . As

takeover agreement, the surety does not qualify as a "contractor" and cannot rely upon the CDA to create a substantive right of action for the surety.[289] The Claims Court has held that the surety's Miller Act bonds alone do not qualify as "government contracts" for the purposes of the CDA.[290]

After a takeover agreement is signed, the surety qualifies as a "contractor" under the CDA and is entitled to assert claims arising out of its performance of the work,[291] arising out of representations made by the federal government and the actions of the federal government leading up to the execution of the takeover agreement,[292] for alleged breaches of the underlying construction contract and/or the bonds themselves,[293] or for the federal government's alleged abuse of discretion in its failure to terminate the contract and for making improper payments after notice of

---

Travelers can maintain an action under the CDA based upon the Takeover Agreement, we hold that it may also maintain an action based upon the construction contract terms to the extent that they are incorporated by reference into such agreement. Id. at 153, 154.

289 Universal Sur. Co. v. United States, 10 Cl. Ct. 794, 800 (1986).
290 Westech Corp. v. United States, 20 Cl. Ct. 745, 749 (1990). In *Admiralty Construction, Inc. v. Dalton*, 156 F.3d 1217, 1221-22 (Fed. Cir. 1998), the court found that the surety was not a "contractor" for purposes of CDA jurisdiction because the surety had not executed a takeover agreement with the federal government to complete the defaulted contract. The court noted that the principal itself had already brought its own suit against the federal government on the same claim in the Claims Court and that the CDA attempted to prevent just such a duplication by requiring a "single point of contact" for contract claims, namely the principal and not its surety when that surety had not executed a takeover agreement with the federal government. The court found that the surety was neither a "contractor" nor an entity in privity with the federal government, and therefore was not eligible to appeal the contracting officer's final decision under the CDA. Furthermore, the court found that the surety could not act for the principal as the principal's attorney-in-fact under the terms of the indemnity agreement between the principal and the surety.
291 Reliance Ins. Co. v. United States, 27 Fed. Cl. 815, 821-24 (1993).
292 Travelers Indem. Co. v. United States, 16 Cl. Ct. 142, 152-54 (1988).
293 Id.

default.²⁹⁴ However, the surety's failure to submit its claim to the contracting officer arising out of the surety's performance of the takeover agreement will deprive the Claims Court of jurisdiction to consider the claim on appeal.²⁹⁵

A third potential impediment to bringing a successful claim under the CDA is the statutory requirement that claims having an alleged value of over $100,000 must be properly certified.²⁹⁶ Case law established that substantial compliance with the certification requirements was insufficient and that strict compliance would be required or the claim would be dismissed.²⁹⁷ In numerous cases, the Claims Court rejected certifications submitted by performance bond sureties that had executed takeover agreements as insufficient under the statutory language.²⁹⁸

---

294 Employers Ins. of Wausau v. United States, 23 Cl. Ct. 579 (1991).
295 Reliance Ins. Co. v. United States, 931 F.2d 863, 866 (Fed. Cir. 1991).
296 41 U.S.C. § 605(c) (2008). Prior to amendments to the CDA that took effect in 1992, the CDA required that all claims in excess of $50,000 be certified in accordance with very strict requirements. Prior to the 1992 change, 41 U.S.C. § 605(c) provided:
> (c)(1) For claims of more than $50,000, the contractor shall certify that the claim is made in good faith, that the supporting data are accurate and complete to the best of his knowledge and belief, and that the amount requested accurately reflects the contract adjustment for which the contractor believes the government is liable.

Public Law No. 102-572, signed into law on October 29, 1992, altered these certification requirements. Prior to the 1992 CDA amendments, the certification requirements frequently became a jurisdictional obstacle for sureties seeking to pursue their principals' claims against the government under the CDA. Transamerica Ins. Co. v. United States, 6 Cl. Ct. 367, 370 (1984).

297 Reliance Ins. Co. v. United States, 23 Cl. Ct. 108, 115-16 (1991).
298 *See, e.g.*, Reliance Ins. Co. v. United States, 27 Cl. Ct. 815, 824-25 (1993); Indus. Indem. Co. v. United States, 26 Cl. Ct. 443, 445 (1992); Nat'l Sur. Corp. v. United States, 20 Cl. Ct. 407, 410-12 (1990). One of the primary difficulties encountered by sureties attempting to certify claims prior to the 1992 amendments was that they could not produce a "senior company official in charge at the contractor's plant or location involved." This provision was interpreted to require a physical presence at the location of the primary contract activity. United States v. Grumman Aerospace Corp., 927 F.2d 575, 580 (Fed. Cir. 1991). Generally, a surety

After the 1992 amendments, the certification requirement was changed to allow the certification to be executed by "any person duly authorized to bind the contractor with respect to the claim."[299] In addition, the CDA as amended now provides that a defect in the certification does not deprive a court of jurisdiction over the claim and defects can be cured.[300] Thus, certification of claims should no longer prove to be the trap that it once was for the performance bond surety that executes a takeover agreement.

4. Comparing and Contrasting the Surety's Claims In the Claims Court Under the Tucker Act and the Contract Disputes Act

"The Court of Federal Claims is a court of special jurisdiction. Absent congressional consent to adjudicate a claim against the United States, this court lacks authority to grant relief."[301] Because the Claims Court is a court of limited statutory jurisdiction, it is imperative that parties seeking recovery from the federal government be able to prove the existence of jurisdiction.[302]

---

does not have a senior company official with a physical presence on the job site. The surety was therefore required to have the certification executed by "an officer or general partner of the contractor having overall responsibility for the conduct of the contractor's affairs." *Id.* Generally, bond claim managers and regional vice-presidents have been held not to meet this test even though they are the persons primarily responsible for handling the claim. Reliance Ins. Co. v. United States, 27 Fed. Cl. 815, 824-25 (1993).

299 41 U.S.C. § 605(c)(7) (2008). With this amendment, a regional vice-president or a bond claim manager should be able to execute the certification.

300 41 U.S.C. § 605(c)(6) (2008).

301 Transamerica Ins. Co. v. United States, 31 Fed. Cl. 602, 604 (1994). *See generally* United States v. Testan, 424 U.S. 392, 399 (1976).

302 Reliance Ins. Co. v. United States, 27 Fed. Cl. 815, 820 (1993). Understandably, in many opinions from the Claims Court, the discussion of whether the Claims Court has subject matter jurisdiction becomes a discussion of the merits of the surety's claims against the federal government. It is often difficult to figure out if the Claims Court is discussing jurisdiction or the merits. *See, e.g.,* Transamerica Premier Ins. Co. v. United States, 32 Fed. Cl. 308, 311-13 (1994). However, the surety

Both the Tucker Act and the CDA provide, in specified circumstances, a statutory waiver of the federal government's sovereign immunity that a surety may use to pursue claims against the federal government as obligee. As a result, the federal government's frequent first line of attack against the surety's claims to the contract funds is a motion to dismiss or a motion for summary judgment predicated upon the Claims Court's alleged lack of subject matter jurisdiction.[303] The surety must be prepared to argue the subject matter jurisdiction issue before it files its complaint with the Claims Court.[304] However, even if

---

should fight against having to prove its entire case in the context of a motion to dismiss based on jurisdictional grounds. *See* Employers Ins. of Wausau v. United States, 23 Cl. Ct. 579 (1991) (factual issues relating to the existence and terms of the contract(s) between the parties, which may affect the Claims Court's ultimate determination of jurisdiction as well as the merits of the case, require that the motion to dismiss for lack of subject matter jurisdiction be denied); Ransom v. United States, 17 Cl. Ct. 263, 267 (1989) (preferred practice is to assume jurisdiction where decision would involve deciding merits), *aff'd*, 900 F.2d 242 (Fed. Cir. 1990). Nonetheless, the surety should not focus exclusively on the merits of its action and forget about proving the existence of jurisdiction. *See, e.g.*, Balboa Ins. Co. v. United States, 775 F. 2d 1158, 1163 n.3 (Fed. Cir. 1985) (federal government's focus on merits of claim improper for jurisdictional argument); Fid. & Dep. Co. of Md. v. United States, 14 Cl. Ct. 421 (1988) (surety's focus on litigating the default termination apparently resulted in oversight of the jurisdictional requisites).

303 Some recent cases describe the federal government's attack on the surety's claim as being beyond the subject matter jurisdiction of the Claims Court. Int'l Fid. Ins. Co. v. United States, 41 Fed. Cl. 706, 711-12 (1998); Intercargo Ins. Co. v. United States, 41 Fed. Cl. 449, 456-57 (1998).

304 The burden is on the surety to establish that it has met the jurisdictional requirements of the Claims Court. Reliance Ins. Co. v. United States, 23 Cl. Ct. 108, 115 (1991). On a motion to dismiss for lack of subject matter jurisdiction, the Claims Court will accept the surety's allegations as true and will draw all reasonable inferences in the surety's favor, *Westech Corp. v. United States*, 20 Cl. Ct. 745 (1990), and will construe the allegations of the complaint favorably to the surety, *Reliance Ins. Co. v. United States*, 27 Fed. Cl. 815, 820 (1993). If a motion to dismiss for lack of subject matter jurisdiction challenges the truth of jurisdictional facts alleged in the complaint, the Claims Court may also consider relevant evidence in order to decide disputed facts. George W. Kane, Inc. v.

not faced with such an initial motion, a surety must remain vigilant as a motion asserting a lack of subject matter jurisdiction may be raised at any time and must be considered by the Claims Court.[305] Further, even in the unlikely event that the federal government consents to subject matter jurisdiction, the surety's claim may still face scrutiny from the Claims Court because subject matter jurisdiction may not be waived or granted by the consent of the parties.[306] Therefore, a surety should expect a fight over subject matter jurisdiction in every case and be prepared for the argument before the case is even filed.

There are important distinctions between the Tucker Act and the CDA that will determine which theory of subject matter jurisdiction is more viable and ensures the greatest likelihood of ultimate success in a particular case. Whether the Tucker Act or the CDA is the best or perhaps the only avenue for a surety to assert subject matter jurisdiction and succeed on the merits depends upon the underlying "contract" at issue and the nature of the claims being asserted.

The Tucker Act is the principal source of the Claims Court's jurisdiction in general and for surety claims in particular. The Tucker Act does not create a substantive right of recovery against the federal government; it only vests jurisdiction in the Claims Court when a substantive right already exists.[307] The surety must still prove the existence of a contract or other legal authority creating a substantive right to recover the contract funds (money damages) from the federal government.[308]

For performance bond sureties, the basis for Tucker Act jurisdiction will be an express or implied contract with the federal government. There are a number of ways that a surety may attempt to satisfy the Tucker Act requirements of contractual privity with the federal government or its substantive equivalent. Some of these ways, such as a written takeover

---

United States, 26 Cl. Ct. 655, 657 (1992). But where the jurisdictional facts alleged are closely intertwined with the merits, the preferred practice is to assume subject matter jurisdiction exists and to address the merits of the claim. Ransom v. United States, 17 Cl. Ct. 263, 267 (1989), *aff'd*, 900 F.2d 244 (Fed. Cir. 1990).

305 U.S.C.S. Cl. Ct. R. 12(h)(3) (2008).
306 George W. Kane, Inc. v. United States, 26 Cl. Ct. 655, 661 (1992).
307 Int'l Fid. Ins. Co. v. United States, 41 Fed. Cl. 706, 710 (1998); Transamerica Ins. Co. v. United States, 31 Fed. Cl. 602, 604 (1994).
308 Westech Corp. v. United States, 20 Cl. Ct. 745, 748 (1990).

agreement with the federal government, are obvious, while others, such as a surety asserting its subrogation rights, are not.

As discussed in more detail below, in the absence of a takeover agreement, a surety may use its subrogation rights to "stand in the shoes" of the principal to pursue recovery of contract funds under the Tucker Act.[309] The same cannot be said for a claim under the CDA. The courts have decided that a surety does not become subrogated to the principal's claims for purposes of pursuing a claim under the CDA.[310] Thus, absent a takeover agreement or some other form of written agreement with the federal government, the surety cannot assert substantive claims, either of its own or of its principal, under the CDA.[311]

On the other hand, the existence of a takeover agreement does not prevent the surety from asserting its subrogation rights. In *Transamerica*

---

309   The surety's traditional method of asserting a substantive right to recover money damages from the federal government is through its subrogation rights. Transamerica Premier Ins. Co. v. United States, 32 Fed. Cl. 308, 311 (1994). "To bring itself within the ambit of the Tucker Act, 28 U.S.C. § 1491 (1988) (the court's basic jurisdictional statute), a government contract surety must demonstrate the existence of a contract-based right to sue here. That right may rest either on the equitable doctrine of subrogation, *Balboa Ins. Co. v. United States*, 775 F.2d 1158, 1161 (Fed. Cir. 1985) or, alternatively, on a contract right of its own, *Fireman's Fund Ins. Co. v. United States*, 909 F.2d 495, 499 (Fed. Cir. 1990)." Fid. & Dep. Co. of Md. v. United States, 31 Fed. Cl. 540, 542 (1994).

310   Admiralty Constr., Inc. v. Dalton, 156 F.3d 1217, 1222-23 (Fed. Cir. 1998); Intercargo Ins. Co. v. United States, 41 Fed. Cl. 449 (1998); Westech Corp. v. United States, 20 Cl. Ct. 745, 749-50 (1990); Universal Sur. Co. v. United States, 10 Cl. Ct. 794, 800-01 (1986).

311   Westech v. United States, 20 Cl. Ct. 745 (1990). "The recovery available under equitable subrogation, however, has been limited to funds held by the government, or funds improperly disbursed to a third-party, only to the amount of the contract balance. In the instant case, Fireman's Fund has not asked for relief allowable under subrogation, *i.e.*, the recovery of funds held by the government or the retrieval of improper disbursements. Instead, Fireman's Fund has sought standing to recover for delay and acceleration damages suffered by Westech. As noted above, a surety's recovery of such damages suffered by a contractor is simply beyond the scope of equitable subrogation." *Id.* at 749-50 (citations and footnotes omitted).

Insurance Co. v. United States,[312] the Federal Circuit reversed the Claims Court's dismissal of the surety's complaint and held that the surety stated a cause of action against the federal government under the Tucker Act for subrogation to the federal government's rights to set off contract funds payable to the principal on a second contract against the losses incurred by the surety on the first (defaulted) contract.

On remand to the Claims Court,[313] the federal government again moved to dismiss, arguing that the Claims Court lacked subject matter jurisdiction because the surety executed a takeover agreement on the first contract, but failed to submit a properly certified claim to the contracting officer for the contract funds payable on the second contract. The surety argued that its subrogation rights to the contract funds on the second contract were independent of any contractual relationship between the surety and the federal government on the first contract, and that the certification requirements of the CDA (which were admittedly not met) did not operate to bar the surety's Tucker Act claims to the contract funds on the second contract. The issue became whether the surety's subrogation right was a claim "arising under or relating to" the takeover agreement.[314] The Claims Court held that the surety's subrogation rights did not arise under or relate to the takeover agreement and were not subject to the certification requirements of the CDA.[315]

---

[312] 989 F.2d 1188 (Fed. Cir. 1993).
[313] Transamerica Ins. Co. v. United States, 31 Fed. Cl. 602 (1994).
[314] *Id.* at 606.
[315] The Claims Court stated:
> By its very nature, plaintiff's claim for equitable subrogation is not related to the school contract takeover agreement. Transamerica's claim is derived from its subrogative right to step into the shoes of the government and recover proceeds withheld on a contract unrelated to the school project, which may result in recovery from the government for breach of its equitable duty to safeguard contract retainage. Although defendant correctly notes that plaintiff's equitable subrogation rights matured when it completed performance of the school contract takeover agreement, see Fidelity and Dep. Co. v. United States, 183 Ct. Cl. 908, 912, 393 F.2d 834 (1968) ("surety's potential rights become an actuality when it pays the obligations of its principal"), plaintiff merely discharged its obligations *under the performance bond of the defaulted contract* by completing the school project.

One final limit on subrogation rights under the CDA bears mention. The Claims Court has held that a contractor completing a project for the surety after the surety executed a takeover agreement with the federal government was not in privity of contract with the federal government. The completion contractor was not entitled to assert claims under the CDA because it was not a party to a federal government contract.[316]

D. The Use of a Surety's Subrogation Rights to Establish Tucker Act Jurisdiction

The surety's traditional means to establish jurisdiction under the Tucker Act is through its subrogation rights to the contract funds held by the federal government or wrongfully disbursed by the federal government.[317]

---

* * *

The existence of potential subrogation rights and contract retainage at the time of the contractor's default, the subsequent maturing of those rights whether by takeover agreement or in some other fashion, and the fact that a surety's rights relate back to the date of execution of the bonds, preclude the court from finding that Transamerica's claim relates to the takeover agreement. The court finds that plaintiff's equitable subrogation claim relates to the circumstances and duties of the defaulted school contract and the performance bond, rather than the takeover agreement executed by Transamerica.

* * *

The court concludes that neither execution nor performance of the school contract takeover agreement transformed the equitable nature of Transamerica's subrogation rights into rights arising under or relating to that contract as contemplated by the CDA.

31 Fed. Cl. at 606-07 (emphasis in original).

316 George W. Kane, Inc. v. United States, 26 Cl. Ct. 655, 660-61 (1992). Careful drafting of a completion contract may prevent this result by allowing the completion contractor to prosecute CDA claims in the name of the surety, which does have a contract with the federal government.

317 Balboa Ins. Co. v. United States, 775 F.2d 1158, 1161 (Fed. Cir. 1985); Int'l Fid. Ins. Co. v. United States, 41 Fed. Cl. 706, 711-12 (1998); Transamerica Premier Ins. Co. v. United States, 32 Fed. Cl. 308, 312 (1994). The Claims Court has jurisdiction over the subrogation claims of a performance bond surety that executes a takeover agreement with the

Although recently subject to vigorous attack based on *Blue Fox*, as discussed in detail below, the surety that has satisfied its obligations under a performance bond (or a payment bond)³¹⁸ may still, through its

---

federal government, *Transamerica Insurance Co. v. United States*, 31 Fed. Cl. 602, 605-07 (1994), finances the principal to completion, *Universal Surety Co. v. United States*, 10 Cl. Ct. 794, 800 (1986), or tenders a completion contractor and makes payment to the completion contractor of the excess costs to complete, *Transamerica Insurance Co. v. United States*, 31 Fed. Cl. 532, 536 (1994). A surety does not have standing to assert a claim against the federal government on the basis of an indemnity agreement between the principal and the surety pursuant to which the surety issued the performance and payment bonds to the federal government. An indemnity agreement may contain assignment provisions that assign a principal's rights, claims and causes of action to the surety. Such an assignment of the principal's claim against the federal government to the surety would be invalid under the Assignment of Claims Act, 31 U.S.C. § 3727, 41 U.S.C. § 15 (1998). *Intercargo Ins. Co. v. United States*, 41 Fed. Cl. 449, 460 (1998). For an excellent summary of the history of the Claims Court's long-standing recognition of the surety's subrogation rights, see *Nova Casualty Co. v. United States*, 69 Fed. Cl. 284, 292-93 (2006).

318 The question of whether the surety is operating pursuant to its performance bond or payment bond obligations may determine whether it has subrogation rights and, hence, whether the Claims Court has jurisdiction over the surety's claim. For example, the federal government is entitled to set off tax debts against claims made by a payment bond surety, but not claims made by a performance bond surety. *Int'l Fid. Ins. Co. v. United States*, 27 Fed. Cl. 107, 109 (1992). Whether payments are made pursuant to performance bond or payment bond obligations may be a disputed question of fact preventing the entry of summary judgment. *Id.* at 109-11. The United States Court of Appeals for the Federal Circuit in *Aetna Casualty & Surety Co. v. United States*, 845 F.2d 971, 975 (Fed. Cir. 1988), has discussed the criteria to be reviewed in determining whether a surety is operating pursuant to its performance bond or payment bond obligations:

> We agree with Aetna's position that there is no requirement that a performing surety must assume "the primary responsibility for the completion of the work." A performance bond gives the surety the option of completing performance or of assuming liability for the Government's costs in completing the contract which are in excess of the contract price. *Security Ins. Co. v.*

subrogation rights, establish jurisdiction under the Tucker Act to bring an action for recovery of the contract funds against the federal government either in the United States District Court for claims under $10,000 or in the Claims Court for claims in excess of $10,000.

One condition to the surety's subrogation rights establishing the existence of Claims Court jurisdiction is that the surety must prove that it has discharged its performance bond obligations and has incurred a loss.[319] A second condition to a surety's successful assertion of its subrogation rights may be that notice must be given to the federal government of the fact that the surety is discharging or has discharged its obligations under its bonds and that the surety has become entitled to the remaining contract funds.[320] Although notice is not a prerequisite for establishing Tucker Act jurisdiction, it may be essential to a successful cause of action on the merits.[321] There is an exception to the notice requirement when the claim is that the federal government had failed to

---

United States, 428 F.2d at 841 n.6. Neither formal termination of the contract by the Government nor execution of a take-over agreement by the surety is necessary in order for a surety to qualify as a performing surety. *Id.* at 839, 843. Thus, a performing surety may satisfy its obligation in various ways. For example, the surety may formally take over the project and contract for its completion, or it may allow the project to be defaulted and let the government complete or contract for the completion of the project, in which case the surety is responsible for costs in excess of the contract price. A performing surety may also satisfy its obligation by providing funds to an insolvent contractor to complete performance. (Citations omitted).

319 *See, e.g.*, Fid. & Dep. Co. of Md. v. United States, 31 Fed. Cl. 540 (1994) (when a surety had not paid out any funds under its performance bond, it could not assert its subrogation rights and was unable to prove the existence of Tucker Act jurisdiction to contest the default termination). Generally, proof of payment supported by an affidavit of a person with personal knowledge, a copy of the check by which payment was made, and proof of receipt by the claimant is sufficient to establish the fact and amount of payment. Transamerica Premier Ins. Co. v. United States, 32 Fed. Cl. 308, 312-13 (1994).

320 *See generally* Fireman's Fund Ins. Co. v. United States, 909 F.2d 495 (Fed. Cir. 1990); United States Fire Ins. Co. v. United States, 78 Fed. Cl. 308, 310 (2007).

321 United States Fire Ins. Co. v. United States, 78 Fed. Cl. 308, 325 (2007).

comply with a bonded contract requirement not to disburse the contract funds that the federal government disbursed anyway.[322] Furthermore, the surety's subrogation right is a right held uniquely by a surety, and may not be asserted by an indemnitor to the surety attempting to assert the surety's and the principal's rights against the federal government.[323]

E. The Surety's Claim to the Contract Funds Under a Takeover Agreement

Under a takeover agreement, the surety not only has rights to the contract funds that have not been paid to the principal under the original contract with the federal government, but also may have rights to various claims, extras, the contesting of liquidated damages, and improper payments made by the federal government.

1. Contract Funds

When the surety executes a takeover agreement with the federal government, it has all of the rights of one with a direct contract with the federal government.[324] A takeover agreement typically provides that the

---

322 Nat'l Sur. Corp. v. United States, 118 F.3d 1542, 1543 (Fed. Cir. 1997).
323 In *Nelson Construction Co. v. United States*, 79 Fed. Cl. 81 (2007), the indemnitors to a Miller Act surety attempted to assert a claim for the contract funds depleted by the federal government's overpayment on a theory of equitable subrogation, arguing that as indemnitors to the surety, they were equitably subrogated to the surety's rights, which surety was subrogated to the principal's rights for purposes of establishing Tucker Act jurisdiction. *Id.* at 86. The Claims Court denied relief, finding that the indemnitors were not a surety for purposes of equitable subrogation because they were not one of the three parties that make up the three-party relationship upon which Tucker Act equitable subrogation precedent has been based; that is, the federal government, the principal and the surety. *Id.* at 91-93. The three-party arrangement relied upon by the *Nelson* indemnitors was between the Nelson indemnitors, the principal and the surety.
324 In *Travelers Indemnity Co. v. United States*, 16 Cl. Ct. 142 (1988), the court stated:
> In Carchia v. United States, 202 Ct. Cl. 723, 735, 485 F.2d 622, 628 (1973), the court held that a completing surety, *i.e.*, one that has executed a Takeover Agreement to complete performance

surety will receive the contract funds that have not been paid to the principal that has defaulted under its contract with the federal government. Those contract funds include both ongoing progress payments and the retainage held by the federal government.

2. Claims and Extras for Delay, Acceleration, Wrongful Termination, Etc.

A surety executing a takeover agreement also has rights to make contractual claims for changes, extras, delay and acceleration, whether those claims are those of the principal[325] or the surety under the takeover

---

under the original construction contract upon the original contractor's default, had standing to sue the government *on the takeover contract* for extra work that it had performed in excess of that contemplated in the original contract price. With the existence of a takeover agreement, therefore, "the surety, in effect, becomes the contractor, subject to the terms of the new agreement." Universal Surety, 10 Cl. Ct. at 800; *see also* Transamerica Ins. Co. v. United States, 6 Cl. Ct. 367, 371 (1984); Morrison Assurance Co. v. United States, 3 Cl. Ct. 626 (1983).

16 Cl. Ct. at 153 (emphasis in original). The court held that when a surety executed a takeover agreement upon the default of the principal, it became a party to a federal government contract and a contractor within the meaning of the Contract Disputes Act. 16 Cl. Ct. at 153.

[325] The surety may have rights to assert the principal's pre-termination construction claims. See Robert G. Watt et al., *The Surety's Procedures for Preserving and Defending its Rights Following a Default Termination*, 22 CONSTR. LAW. 10 (2002). The cases that disallow the surety's rights to prosecute a principal's pre-termination construction claim are normally grounded under the Anti-Assignment Act. *See* Fireman's Fund Ins. Co. v. England, 313 F.3d 1344, 1349-50 (Fed. Cir. 2002); Admiralty Constr., Inc. v. Dalton, 156 F.3d 1217 (Fed. Cir. 1998). *See also* this chapter, Section V.F.2., *infra*. A surety does not have standing to assert a claim against the federal government on the basis of an indemnity agreement between the principal and the surety pursuant to which the surety issued the performance and payment bonds to the federal government. An indemnity agreement may contain assignment provisions that assign a principal's rights, claims and causes of action to the surety. The courts have not recognized the indemnity agreement assignment provision as complying with the Anti-Assignment Act

agreement.[326] The surety may "maintain an action based upon the construction contract terms to the extent that they are incorporated by reference into [a takeover agreement]."[327]

The surety executing a takeover agreement also has the right to challenge the termination of the principal's right to proceed under the original contract.[328] A surety that is default terminated under the terms of its takeover agreement with the federal government because of the

---

because the federal government has not signed the indemnity agreement. *See, e.g.,* United Pac. Ins. Co. v. Roche, 380 F.3d 1352, 1357 (Fed. Cir. 2004). Such an assignment of the principal's claim against the federal government to the surety would be invalid under the Assignment of Claims Act, 31 U.S.C. § 3727, 41 U.S.C. § 15 (1998). Intercargo Ins. Co. v. United States, 41 Fed. Cl. 449, 460 (1998).

[326] Carchia v. United States, 202 Ct. Cl. 723, 485 F.2d, 622 (1973). The Claims Court allowed a completing surety to claim payment for extra work beyond that contemplated in the original contract price. In *Carchia*, there was a separate takeover agreement between the federal government and the surety after the default by the principal. "In that circumstance, the surety in effect becomes the contractor, subject to the terms of the new agreement." Universal Sur. Co. v. United States, 10 Cl. Ct. 794, 800 (1986). See *Appeal of Atherton Constr., Inc.*, Armed Services Board of Contract Appeals ("ASBCA") No. 56040, 2008 WL 4981621 (Nov. 5, 2008), which held that a completion contractor that was a party to a takeover agreement along with the federal government and the surety had standing to assert a constructive changes claim for furnishing equipment that was not required by the original contract between the principal and the federal government.

[327] Travelers Indem. Co. v. United States, 16 Cl. Ct. 142, 154 (1988). A surety asserting claims, including claims for additional delay overhead, is bound by the terms of the construction contract. Reliance Ins. Co. v. United States, 931 F.2d 863 (Fed. Cir. 1991).

[328] In *Westech Corp. v. United States*, 20 Cl. Ct. 745, 749 (1990), the court stated:

> Had Fireman's Fund executed a takeover contract with defendant to complete the contract, it would have standing to sue. In fact, under that circumstance Fireman's Fund could even challenge the propriety of defendant's prior actions including the decision to terminate for default. *See* Carchia v. United States, 485 F.2d 622, 628-30, 202 Ct. Cl. 723 (1973); Travelers Indem. Co. v. United States, 16 Cl. Ct. 142, 153 (1988); Universal Sur. Co. v. United States, 10 Cl. Ct. 794, 800 (1986).

surety's alleged lack of significant progress may also challenge the default termination by the federal government.[329]

3. Liquidated Damages

The surety is entitled to contest the assessment of liquidated damages, both against the principal[330] and under the takeover agreement,[331] that reduce the amount of the remaining contract funds.

4. Improper Payments

Normally, the performance and payment terms of the construction contract between the principal and the federal government are incorporated into the takeover agreement.[332]

a. *Progress Payments.* In *Transamerica Insurance Co. v. United States*,[333] the federal government entered into a takeover agreement with the surety. Subsequently, the federal government discovered that, in making previous progress payments to the principal, it had overpaid the principal in an amount of $79,810.74 beyond the amount properly due the principal for the work accomplished. That amount was subsequently withheld from a progress payment due to the takeover surety. The surety made a claim for the amount withheld.[334]

---

329 Indem. Ins. Co. of North Am. v. United States, 14 Cl. Ct. 219 (1988).
330 While in *Transamerica Insurance Co. v. United States*, 31 Fed. Cl. 532 (1994), the surety tendered a completion contractor to the federal government rather than entering into a takeover agreement with the federal government, the surety was allowed to contest the federal government's assessment of liquidated damages against the default terminated principal. *But see*, United States Sur. Co. v. United States, 83 Fed. Cl. 306 (2008). *See* this chapter, Section V.F.3., *infra*, for more discussion of this topic.
331 If the federal government assesses liquidated damages against the surety under the takeover agreement, the surety, under its express contract with the federal government, may contest that assessment of liquidated damages for the surety's alleged late performance under the takeover agreement.
332 Travelers Indem. Co. v. United States, 16 Cl. Ct. 142 (1988).
333 6 Cl. Ct. 367 (1984).
334 *Id.* at 369.

The Claims Court questioned why the surety should bear the financial burden resulting from the federal government's mistake. Upon executing the takeover agreement, the surety's reasonable intent was to obtain the balance of the contract price remaining at the time of default. The Claims Court stated:

> It seems reasonable to conclude that when the parties provided that Transamerica's reimbursement should be limited to "the balance of the contract price unpaid at the time of default," the parties intended to exclude from Transamerica's reimbursement only those previous payments made to [the contractor] *in accordance with the provisions of the contract.* It would be unreasonable to believe that Transamerica would have undertaken to complete the defaulted contract if it had known there was a prospect that reimbursement of its costs might be jeopardized by unknown payments mistakenly made to [the contractor] in excess of contract requirements.[335]

The court went on to state that:

> [A] performance bond surety which completes a defaulted contract has conferred a benefit on the Government by relieving the Government of the burden of completing the contract, and, accordingly, that the surety should be able to recover its costs without being subject to claims which the Government may have against the defaulting contractor, seems to be applicable to the present case. In other words, Transamerica's right to recover its costs in completing this contract should not be reduced because the Government mistakenly made an excessive payment to [the contractor] before the default.[336]

b. *Retainage.* In *National Surety Corp. v. United States*,[337] the federal government terminated the principal's contract for default. The surety entered into a takeover agreement with the federal government providing that the surety would complete performance for the remaining contract funds. The surety then arranged for completion by another contractor. The work was accepted and the federal government paid the remaining contract funds to the surety.

---

335   *Id.* at 371.
336   *Id.* at 372.
337   118 F.3d 1542 (Fed. Cir. 1997).

Subsequently, the surety made a claim against the federal government for certain retainage paid to the principal before its default. The surety contended that the funds should have been held as retainage by the federal government, thereby reducing the surety's loss. The court held that the surety was entitled to recover from the federal government the retainage paid to the principal[338] because the "retainage provision in a bonded construction contract serves to protect the surety as well as the government. . . ."[339] The court found that the "duty devolves upon the government to administer the contract, during the course of its performance, in a way that does not materially increase the risk that was assumed by the surety when the contract was bonded."[340] The court went on to say:

> The ten percent retainage provision was in the contract between Dugdale and the government when National Surety set the price for and executed its surety bonds. The retainage requirement served as security for performance of the bonded contract, and this requirement contributed to the surety's assessment of the risk involved. The surety was entitled to rely on the government's obligation to retain this percentage in accordance with the terms of the bonded contract, and on its right of subrogation to this security. National Surety's right was fixed upon execution of the surety bonds, and was not dissolved or altered when the government failed to implement the retainage required by the contract. *See Balboa Insurance*, 775 F.2d at 1161 (subrogation rights encompass funds wrongfully disbursed). The government, with

---

[338] The Court of Federal Claims in *National Surety Corp. v. United States*, 31 Fed. Cl. 565 (1994), allowed the surety to recover damages in the amount that should have been retained by the government. However, the court in *National Surety Corp. v. United States*, 118 F.3d 1542 (Fed. Cir. 1997), concluded that the surety's "recovery should not exceed any losses that ensued, directly or indirectly, from the impairment of the security (the retainage paid to the contractor). Thus, it is relevant to consider what the contractor did with the released funds." *Id.* at 1548. The court remanded the case to the Court of Federal Claims because it concluded that "damages are fairly measured not by the calculated amount of the required retention, but by the injury, loss, or prejudice to the surety due to the government's failure to implement the required retention." *Id.* at 1545.

[339] 118 F.3d at 1545.

[340] *Id.* at 1546.

knowledge that Dugdale had not met the contractual condition predicate to release of the retainage, did not defeat National Surety's subrogation right. *Home Indemnity*, 376 F.2d at 895 (government held liable to surety despite having disbursed the retainages).[341]

The surety prevailed notwithstanding the fact that it did not give notice to the federal government. [342]

F. The Traditional Surety Claims for the Contract Funds Under the Tucker Act That Are Not Recoverable Under the Contract Disputes Act

Once the surety establishes its subrogation rights for Tucker Act purposes, it can proceed with certain types of claims, including claims

---

341 *Id.*
342 The court in *National Surety Corp. v. United States*, 118 F.3d 1542 (Fed. Cir. 1997) distinguished the case of *Fireman's Fund Insurance Co. v. United States*, 909 F. 2d 495 (Fed. Cir. 1990). In *Fireman's Fund*, the contract provided for the federal government's discretion in releasing the retainage. Because of the contract provisions contained in the original construction contract in *National Surety*, the federal government was bound by the limitations on its discretion for the release of the retainage. The court stated:
> In contrast [to *Fireman's Fund*], Dugdale's bonded contract gave no discretion to the government to depart from the requirement of the ten percent retainage until after the complete project arrow diagram was submitted and approved. That condition was never met. When the contractor abandoned performance before completion, as did Dugdale, and the government had knowledge of the default, as here, *Fireman's Fund* does not impose a further requirement that the surety notify the government that "the principal has defaulted." The holding in *Fireman's Fund* did not change the rules of subrogation, but simply dealt with the rights and obligations of the parties on the conditions of that case.
> We conclude that National Surety's right of subrogation was not defeated by the government's release of the retainage in contravention of the terms of the bonded contract.

118 F.3d at 1547.

for the contract funds,[343] that may not be recoverable under the narrow parameters of the CDA. However, even when the surety is successful in establishing jurisdiction under the Tucker Act, it has not always been successful on the merits of its claims.

1. Overpayment/Impairment of Suretyship

In *Fireman's Fund Insurance Co. v. United States*,[344] the contract required the federal government to retain a portion of each progress payment (10 percent) unless the principal made satisfactory progress during a progress payment period.[345] Subsequently, the principal requested the retainage because of "cash flow problems" and the federal government agreed to release the contract funds.[346] The principal subsequently abandoned the contract and six days later (and almost five months after the federal government had released the retainage), the surety notified the federal government not to make any further payments to the principal without the surety's consent.[347] The surety declined to takeover the project and the federal government reprocured and assessed the excess reprocurement costs against the surety.[348] The surety challenged the assessment based on what it considered to be a premature release of the progress payments and retainage by the federal government to the principal.[349] Although the surety succeeded in establishing jurisdiction, the Federal Circuit found that the federal government owed no equitable duty to the surety because the surety did not notify the

---

343 Generally, a performance bond surety's remedy in the Claims Court under its subrogation rights is "limited to recovery from a fund held by the government/owner pursuant to the construction contract." Universal Sur. Co. v. United States, 10 Cl. Ct. 794, 797 (1986). "The recovery available under equitable subrogation, however, has been limited to funds held by the government, or funds improperly disbursed to a third-party, only to the amount of the contract balance." Westech Corp. v. United States, 20 Cl. Ct. 745, 749 (1990).
344 909 F.2d 495 (Fed. Cir. 1990).
345 *Id.* at 496.
346 *Id.*
347 *Id.* at 496, 499.
348 *Id.* at 497.
349 *Id.*

federal government that the principal had defaulted under the bonds until five months after the release of the retainage.[350]

The surety in the recent case of *United States Fire Insurance Co. v. United States*[351] fared no better. For over three and a half years, as spelled out in eleven pages of the court's opinion laying out its findings of fact, the federal government struggled with the principal, noting and complaining of numerous deficiencies it its performance of the contract. Thirty months after the original completion date, the federal government terminated the principal.

The surety took over the project and reserved its rights against the federal government. The surety's completion contractor completed the project, the surety paid the completion contractor, and the federal government complied with the terms of the takeover agreement by paying to the surety the contract funds net of the stated liquidated damages.

The surety filed suit in the Claims Court alleging that the federal government made improper payments to the principal of $394,911.79 for work not performed and $296,839.20 for work improperly performed, for a total claimed amount of $691,750.99. After overcoming the federal government's jurisdictional attacks, the surety lost on the merits. The Claims Court found that the federal government's payments to the principal were not in violation of the terms of the contract which gave the contracting officer discretion in making payments to the principal and that the payments made were reasonable under the facts and circumstances of the case.[352]

Not all sureties have fared as poorly in making arguments of overpayment or material deviation from the contract terms. In *National*

---

350 *Id.* at 498-99. *See also* Lumbermens Mut. Cas. Co. v. United States, 67 Fed. Cl. 253 (2005) (the surety, the completion contractor and the federal government entered into a takeover agreement, the work was completed, and the federal government withheld substantial liquidated damages).

351 78 Fed. Cl. 308 (2007). In a prior decision in *United States Fire Insurance Co. v. United States*, 61 Fed. Cl. 494 (2004), the court denied the federal government's motion to dismiss the surety's suit seeking to recover overpayments because the takeover agreement between the surety and the federal government reserved the surety's overpayment claim and all other rights and defenses of both the surety and the federal government.

352 *Id.* at 328.

Surety Corp. v. United States,[353] the contract explicitly required the federal government to retain 10 percent of all progress payments, conditioned upon the federal government's approval of the principal's performance schedule.[354] The principal's schedule was not approved, or even submitted, but the federal government did not withhold the 10 percent retainage as required by the contract.[355] The surety completed the project under the performance bond. The surety then filed a claim for the retainage which the contract required to be withheld by the federal government from the progress payments.[356]

The court held that, because the contract gave no discretion to the federal government to depart from the requirement of the 10 percent retainage until after the complete project arrow diagram was submitted and approved, and that such condition was never met, the surety could recover when the federal government deviated from that provision of the contract, even when the surety failed to give notice to the federal government to refrain from making payments to the principal. [357] However, in order "to recover under this theory, it must be shown that the government actually departed from the terms of its contract with the primary obligor."[358]

---

[353] 118 F.3d 1542 (Fed. Cir. 1997). See a full discussion of *National Surety* in this chapter, Section V.E.4.b., *supra*.

[354] *Id.* at 1543.

[355] *Id.* at 1543-44.

[356] *Id.* at 1544.

[357] *Id.* at 1547; United States Fire Ins. Co. v. United States, 78 Fed. Cl. 308, 327 (2007); *see also* Hartford Fire Ins. Co. v. United States, 40 Fed. Cl. 520, 524 n.2 (1998) ("[T]he court [in *National Surety*] concluded that notice to the government regarding the need to retain payments was unnecessary where the contract required the government to retain a percentage of the progress payments."), *aff'd*, 185 F.3d 885 (Fed. Cir. 1999).

[358] United States Fire Ins. Co. v. United States, 78 Fed. Cl. 308, 327 (2007) (quoting Am. Ins. Co. v. United States, 62 Fed. Cl. 151, 157 (2004) (citing Nat'l Sur. Corp. v. United States, 118 F.3d 1542, 1546 (Fed. Cir. 1997)). A review of the *United States Fire* case above demonstrates that, when the contract affords some discretion to the contracting officer, including payments beyond those justified by the principal's performance of the work, the court is likely to find that the federal government action was reasonable and allowable under the contract.

2. Wrongful Termination and Pre-termination Claims– Takeover Agreement Required

On occasion, a principal may have a legitimate basis for asserting that the federal government's termination of the contract was wrongful or that the principal has legitimate and substantial claims against the federal government that arose pre-termination that would increase the amount of the contract funds. The difficulty becomes how, or if, the surety can preserve such claims in order to reduce or eliminate its own bond losses. The surety's problem is that the principal's pre-termination contract claims are not typically among those claims to which a surety may assert its subrogation rights.[359] Accordingly, the surety must establish Tucker Act jurisdiction for such a claim under an express or implied-in-fact contract.

A surety executing a takeover agreement *may* have rights to challenge the termination of the principal's right to proceed under the original contract. In *Westech Corp. v. United States*,[360] the Claims Court stated:

> Had Fireman's Fund executed a takeover contract with defendant to complete the contract, it would have standing to sue. In fact, under that circumstance Fireman's Fund could even challenge the propriety of defendant's prior actions including the decision to terminate for default. *See Carchia v. United States*, 485 F.2d 622, 628-30, 202 Ct. Cl. 723 (1973); *Travelers Indem. Co. v. United States*, 16 Cl. Ct. 142, 153 (1988); *Universal Sur. Co. v. United States*, 10 Cl. Ct. 794, 800 (1986).[361]

This statement from *Westech* is clearly dicta as it is speculating about outcomes if the facts of the case were different. In *Carchia*, cited in *Westech*, the Claims Court did hold that the surety who signed a takeover agreement could assert the claim of wrongful termination and, if

---

359 Fireman's Fund Ins. Co. v. England, 313 F.3d 1344, 1351 (Fed. Cir. 2002); *see also* Universal Sur. Co. v. United States, 10 Cl. Ct. 794, 798 (1986) ("[P]laintiff's right as subrogee amounts to a *security interest in the fund* generated pursuant to the construction contract. It does not give rise to an assignment of the contractor's legal status under that underlying contract.") (emphasis in original) (citing Pearlman v. Reliance Ins. Co., 371 U.S. 132 (1962)).

360 Westech Corp. v. United States, 20 Cl. Ct. 745 (1990).

361 *Id.* at 749.

successful, would be entitled to its costs of completion.[362] The emphasized *"may"* in the introductory sentence of this paragraph is cautionary because the contents of the takeover agreement may be critical to the surety's success in making pre-termination or wrongful termination claims.

A surety making a pre-termination claim or a claim for its completion costs based on a wrongful termination must be aware of the federal Anti-Assignment Act,[363] which prohibits an assignment of contract and claim rights to another party without the consent of the federal government.[364] The federal government will likely argue that the right to contest the termination of the contract or pursue the principal's pre-termination claims lies with the party to the contract, which cannot be assigned without the federal government's consent. However, if such an assignment were contained in a takeover agreement to which the federal government was a party, then the surety would stand a much better chance of being able to assert such claims for itself. If the principal is available and cooperative, the surety might convince the principal to sign the takeover agreement, which, when signed by the surety and federal government, would seem to satisfy the hurdles of the Anti-Assignment Act.[365] This logic would apply to claims for extras for delay and other pre-termination claims.

Several cases have been brought by sureties under the Tucker Act or the CDA asserting the principal's pre-termination construction claims. Their success or failure has been very fact-specific and dependant upon whether the court or board was convinced that the federal government had consented to the assignment of the claims from the principal to the surety. In *Security Insurance Co. of Hartford*,[366] the Armed

---

362 Carchia v. United States, 485 F.2d 622, 628-629 (Ct. Cl. 1973).
363 41 U.S.C. § 15 (2008) and 31 U.S.C. § 3727 (2008).
364 Gerard P. Sunderland, *The Surety and the Federal Government: Negotiating a Minefield* (2005) (unpublished paper submitted at the Surety Claims Institute program on June 23, 2005 at the 2005 Annual Meeting.)
365 *See* Rochester Gas & Elec. Corp. v. United States, 65 Fed. Cl. 431, 437 (2005) ("assigned contracts are valid when the assignment takes place by operation of law or when the government consents to and recognizes the assignment").
366 ASBCA No. 51813, 2001-2 B.C.A. ¶ 31,588, 2001 ASBCA LEXIS 151 (Aug. 24, 2001).

Services Board of Contract Appeals ("ASBCA") held that the surety's takeover agreement with the Air Force constituted the governmental consent necessary to take the claim outside the bar of the Anti-Assignment Act. Although the ASBCA found the actual language of the takeover agreement somewhat ambiguous as to whether the federal government had consented to the assignment of the principal's pre-termination claims for delays and changes to the work, the board found that the "totality of the circumstances" after the takeover agreement was signed evidenced that the federal government itself interpreted the takeover agreement as a valid assignment of claims.[367] The surety met with similar success in another ASBCA case, *Safeco Insurance Co. of America*,[368] but another surety with similar language in a takeover agreement was not as fortunate because it was unable to establish other extrinsic evidence that the federal government actually recognized it as the principal's assignee.[369]

3. Contesting the Assessment of Liquidated Damages

If a surety is unable to negotiate a sufficient time extension in the takeover agreement that eliminates liquidated damages, the surety, in an action for the recovery of the contract funds, may contest the assessment of liquidated damages.

In *Transamerica Insurance Co. v. United States*,[370] the performance bond surety sought to recover funds withheld by the federal government as liquidated damages when the original principal defaulted. The surety did not take over the contract. Rather, the surety tendered a completion contractor to the federal government. The surety paid funds both to the completion contractor for the completion of the performance of the work and to fulfill its obligations under the payment bond. The surety

---

367   2001 ASBCA LEXIS 151, at *18-20.
368   ASBCA No. 52107, 2003-2 B.C.A. ¶ 32,341, 2003 ASBCA LEXIS 83 (July 30, 2003).
369   Appeal of United Pac. Ins. Co., ASBCA No. 53051, 2001-2 B.C.A. ¶ 31,527, 2001 ASBCA LEXIS 125 (July 20, 2001), *further hearing* at United Pac. Ins. Co., ASBCA No. 53051, 2003-2 B.C.A. ¶ 32,267, 2003 ASBCA LEXIS 57 (June 4, 2003), *aff'd*, United Pac. Ins. Co. v. Roche, 380 F.3d 1352 (Fed. Cir. 2004).
370   31 Fed. Cl. 532 (1994).

contested the federal government's assessment of liquidated damages against the original principal.

The Claims Court stated that the surety did not have either an express or implied-in-fact contract with the federal government because it did not enter into a takeover agreement. However, the Claims Court found that the surety's subrogation rights as a performance bond surety (for funding the completion of the work[371]) allowed the surety to sue the federal government because, "[u]nder the doctrine of equitable subrogation, 'contract retainage' is determined as soon as the contractor defaults."[372] As a result, the surety could assert a claim to the contract funds as they existed at the time of the principal's default and could challenge the federal government's management of the remaining contract funds, including the federal government's decision to reduce them pursuant to a liquidated damages assessment.[373]

G. The Performance Bond's Surety's Competitors for the Contract Funds Held by the Federal Government

As discussed earlier in this chapter,[374] the surety may compete with other parties for the contract funds held by an obligee, including the federal government. The most common parties the surety competes against in the Claims Court are the federal government itself, which may assert its setoff and/or statutory or regulatory rights against the remaining contract funds as a result of other contracts, obligations or claims against the principal by the federal government; assignee/lenders, including assignees under the Assignment of Claims Act; trustees in bankruptcy and/or debtors-in-possession; and subcontractors and/or suppliers on the bonded projects. There appear to be no cases where the principal (other than the principal that has been wrongfully paid by the federal government as described below), other taxing authorities, or general creditors, including judgment creditors, have competed with the surety for the remaining contract funds held by the federal government.

---

371 *See* Aetna Cas. & Sur. Co. v. United States, 845 F.2d 971 (Fed. Cir. 1988).
372 Transamerica Ins. Co. v. United States, 31 Fed. Cl. 532, 536 (1994).
373 *Id.*
374 *See* this chapter, Section IV., *supra*.

1. Surety v. Government Exercising Its Setoff Rights

When the federal government has already "paid" itself by exercising its rights of setoff against the contract funds because the principal "owes" the federal government a debt on another obligation (a separate contract claim, an Internal Revenue Service claim for taxes due from the principal, etc.), the federal government will have to "repay" those funds to a performance bond surety.[375]

The same holds true if the federal government is holding the remaining contract funds as a stakeholder and intends to exercise its setoff rights against those contract funds. A performance bond surety will prevail against the setoff claims of the federal government.[376]

Notwithstanding the above cases, under the Davis-Bacon Act,[377] which provides that contractors on federal government construction projects must pay a prevailing wage rate decided from time to time in various labor markets, the surety's rights to the contract funds have not faired as well. An employee of a principal who does not receive the appropriate wages has an administrative remedy under the Davis-Bacon Act,[378] and that employee also has the right to file a payment bond claim

---

375 Aetna Cas. & Sur. Co. v. United States, 845 F.2d 971 (Fed. Cir. 1988); Morrison Assurance Co. v. United States, 3 Cl. Ct. 626 (1983).

376 Int'l Fid. Ins. Co. v. United States, 27 Fed. Cl. 107 (1992) (a question of fact whether the surety's payments were pursuant to its performance bond obligations or its payment bond obligations); Sec. Ins. Co. of Hartford v. United States, 428 F.2d 838 (Ct. Cl. 1970). However, the federal government's setoff rights will prevail over the claims of a payment bond surety. United States v. Munsey Trust Co., 332 U.S. 234 (1947); Sentry Ins. v. United States, 12 Cl. Ct. 320 (1987) (amounts owed by principal to the Small Business Administration); Am. Fid. Fire Ins. Co. v. United States, 513 F.2d 1375 (Ct. Cl. 1975) (even though the federal government wrongfully paid contract proceeds to the principal and was therefore liable to reimburse the payment bond surety for payments made to a subcontractor, the federal government was not further liable to pay contract retainages to the surety because the federal government was entitled to offset such retainages against the amount wrongfully paid to the principal); Great Am. Ins. Co. v. United States, 492 F.2d 821 (Ct. Cl. 1974); Royal Indem. Co. v. United States, 371 F.2d 462 (Ct. Cl. 1967); Barrett v. United States, 367 F.2d 834 (Ct. Cl. 1966).

377 40 U.S.C. §§ 3141, *et seq.*

378 *See* 29 C.F.R. §§ 1.8, 1.9 (2009).

against the surety for the amount of the underpayment of that person's wages.[379] While prior cases had held that a performance bond surety's rights to the contract funds came ahead of the Department of Labor, which enforces the Davis-Bacon Act, recent decisions have decided that the Department of Labor's demand to withhold the contract funds under the Davis-Bacon Act are superior to the performance bond surety's rights to the contract funds.[380]

2. Surety v. Assignee/Lenders

Assuming that there is a valid default[381] (actual or threatened), the performance bond surety[382] will prevail against the federal government if it has already paid the remaining contract funds to the assignee/lenders. If the federal government is holding the remaining contract funds as a stakeholder, the performance bond surety will prevail against the assignee/lender.[383] The surety's failure to "perfect" its rights under the

---

[379] *See generally* United States *ex rel.* Sherman v. Carter, 353 U.S. 210 (1957) (employees providing labor to project are within the class of claimants protected by Miller Act payment bond).

[380] *See* Westchester Fire Ins. Co. v. United States, 52 Fed. Cl. 567 (2002); *In re* Disputes Concerning the Payment of Prevailing Wage Rates and Proper Classifications, A.R.B. No. 00-018, A.L.J. No. 99-DBA-11, 2003 WL 21499861 (Dep't of Labor Adm. Rev. Bd. June 30, 2003). *See* Michael A. Stover & Susan Getz Kerbel, *"Look Who's Bringing Home the Bacon"–How Recent Decisions Interpreting the Davis-Bacon Act Can Negatively Affect the Surety* (2003) (unpublished paper submitted at the Fourteenth Annual Northeast Sur. & Fid. Claims Conference on Sept. 18, 2003).

[381] Nat'l Union Fire Ins. Co. of Pittsburgh, Pa. v. United States, 304 F.2d 465 (Ct. Cl. 1962) (no default by principal or notice to federal government by surety prior to payment to principal's assignee).

[382] Great Am. Ins. Co. v. United States, 481 F.2d 1298 (Ct. Cl. 1973); *see also* United States Fid. & Guar. Co. v. United States, 16 Cl. Ct. 541 (1989). The payment bond surety will also prevail against the federal government. *See* Great Am. Ins. Co. v. United States, 492 F.2d 821 (Ct. Cl. 1974); Newark Ins. Co. v. United States, 169 F. Supp. 955 (Ct. Cl. 1959).

[383] Prairie State Nat'l Bank v. United States, 164 U.S. 227 (1896); Reliance Ins. Co. v. United States, 15 Cl. Ct. 62 (1988). The payment bond surety will also prevail against the assignee/lender. *See* Henningsen v. United

Uniform Commercial Code does not prevent the surety from prevailing over an assignee/lender with a perfected security interest in the remaining contract funds. The Uniform Commercial Code does not alter the surety's subrogation rights.[384]

3. Surety v. Trustees in Bankruptcy/Debtors-In-Possession

The starting point is *Pearlman v. Reliance Insurance Co.*[385] In *Pearlman*, the federal government had turned over the remaining contract funds to the bankrupt's trustee. The Supreme Court held that a surety had a superior right to the remaining contract funds held by the federal government over the rights of the bankruptcy trustee.

When the federal government is holding the remaining contract funds as a stakeholder, the performance bond surety will prevail against the trustee in bankruptcy or the debtor-in-possession.[386]

4. Surety v. Subcontractors and Suppliers on the Bonded Projects

A subcontractor lacks standing to bring suit against the federal government for compensation due to the subcontractor under a subcontract with the federal government principal when both the principal and the surety have failed or refused to make payment, and the federal government has retained funds owing on the contract.[387] While the subcontractors lack standing to sue the federal government directly for any amounts retained by the federal government under a contract, the

---

States Fid. & Guar. Co., 208 U.S. 404 (1908); Reliance Ins. Co. v. United States, 15 Cl. Ct. 62 (1988); Argonaut Ins. Co. v. United States, 434 F.2d 1362 (Ct. Cl. 1970); Nat'l Sur. Corp. v. United States, 133 F. Supp. 381 (Ct. Cl. 1955) (Assignment of Claims Act does not affect the surety's equitable rights of subrogation).

384   Home Indem. Co. v. United States, 433 F.2d 764 (Ct. Cl. 1970).
385   371 U.S. 132 (1962).
386   United Pac. Ins. Co. v. United States, 319 F.2d 893 (Ct. Cl. 1963). The payment bond surety will also prevail against the trustee in bankruptcy or the debtor-in-possession. *See* Cont'l Cas. Co. v. United States, 164 Ct. Cl. 160 (1964); Cont'l Cas. Co. v. United States, 169 F. Supp. 945 (Ct. Cl. 1959).
387   United Elec. Corp. v. United States, 647 F.2d 1082 (Ct. Cl. 1981).

federal government owes the subcontractors an equitable obligation to see that they get paid. To the extent that the surety pays the subcontractors, the federal government is released from that equitable obligation.[388]

5. Common Obligee Theory

When the federal government is a stakeholder holding contract funds on one contract for the principal when the performance bond surety has incurred losses on a second contract between the federal government and the principal, the surety may assert its subrogation rights to the contract funds from the first contract.[389]

H. The Impact of the Blue Fox Case on the Surety's Use of the Tucker Act in Pursuit of Its Claims Against the Federal Government

1. What Is The Blue Fox Case?

In *Department of the Army v. Blue Fox, Inc.*,[390] Blue Fox, a subcontractor, sued the Department of the Army (the "Army") for monies owed to Blue Fox by the prime contractor under a construction contract with the Army.[391] Despite receiving notice from Blue Fox of the unpaid funds, the Army made a payment to the prime contractor. After the prime contractor defaulted, the Army paid the remaining contract funds to its completion contractor.[392]

Blue Fox was left with little choice but to attempt to pursue recovery from the Army directly because the prime contractor had become insolvent and there were no Miller Act bonds, the Army having removed

---

388 United States Fid. & Guar. Co. v. United States, 475 F.2d 1377 (Ct. Cl. 1973).
389 Transamerica Ins. Co. v. United States, 989 F.2d 1188 (Fed. Cir. 1993). See this chapter, Section IV.D., *supra*, for an in-depth discussion of the common obligee theory.
390 525 U.S. 255 (1999).
391 *Id.* at 256-57.
392 *Id.* at 258.

the bonding requirements from the prime contract by re-characterizing it as a "services contract."[393]

Blue Fox sought an "equitable lien" against any contract funds remaining in the Army's hands or any other funds owed to the prime contractor to the extent of its losses. Blue Fox argued that the Administrative Procedure Act ("APA") waived the government's sovereign immunity for equitable claims.[394] After losing at the trial court level, Blue Fox convinced the Ninth Circuit of the merits of its sovereign immunity argument. In agreeing with Blue Fox, the Ninth Circuit mentioned numerous surety equitable subrogation cases in support of its argument.[395]

The Supreme Court reversed, holding that there was no jurisdiction for Blue Fox's claim against the Army because the "equitable lien" sought by Blue Fox equated to a claim for money damages that fell outside of the APA's sovereign immunity waiver.[396] In so holding, the Supreme Court recognized long existing precedent that a subcontractor or materialman does not have standing to sue the federal government either in contract or for an equitable lien on the contract funds because those entities are not in privity with the federal government.[397]

2. Why Does the Blue Fox Case Matter to Sureties?

The *Blue Fox* case only exists because of the federal government's unwise decision to forego Miller Act surety bonds from the prime contractor. Ironically, the federal government and its counsel now attempt to use the *Blue Fox* decision against sureties. This is because the Supreme Court noted, in dicta, that the seminal surety cases of *Prairie State*, *Henningsen*, and *Pearlman* did not consider the question of sovereign immunity.[398]

Ever since the *Blue Fox* ruling, federal government counsel have argued that *Blue Fox*, in effect, although not expressly, overruled *Balboa*

---

393   *Id.* at 257-58.
394   *Id.*
395   *Id.* at 259.
396   *Id.* at 263.
397   *Id.* at 264.
398   *Id.*

Insurance Co. v. United States[399] and all prior case authority standing for the proposition that a surety's subrogation claims establish a basis for jurisdiction under the Tucker Act and that the Supreme Court has now established that the federal government has sovereign immunity from all surety claims founded upon the surety's subrogation rights.

3. Tucker Act Decisions Involving Sureties Since Blue Fox

Less than two months after the Supreme Court handed down the *Blue Fox* decision, the Insurance Company of the West ("ICW") brought suit against the federal government under the Tucker Act to recover $174,000 in contract funds that the federal government had improperly paid to ICW's principal, the prime contractor, P.C.E., Limited ("PCE"). Prior to the payment at issue, PCE sent a notice to the federal government advising the federal government that PCE was financially unable to complete the contract and the project, that ICW would take responsibility for completing the performance of the remaining work, and directing the federal government to pay all remaining contract funds to ICW. ICW sent a follow-up letter to the contracting officer confirming that it was to receive all further payments. After the above-described notices were given to the federal government, ICW financed the completion of the performance of the work under the contract at issue and incurred a loss of $354,744.34.

After receiving the notices, the federal government issued a contract modification directing that future payments be made payable to PCE but sent to ICW. Nevertheless, the federal government ignored both the notices and its own contract modification and made three payments directly to PCE. In its lawsuit, ICW alleged that the federal government breached its duties to ICW as a performing surety by making payments totaling $174,000 to PCE. The federal government moved to dismiss ICW's lawsuit, arguing that, in light of the *Blue Fox* decision, the federal government had not waived its right of sovereign immunity as to the surety's subrogation claims.

---

399   775 F.2d 1158 (Fed. Cir. 1985). The federal government is not the only governmental entity which alleges that sovereign immunity bars the surety's claims. *See* XL Specialty Ins. Co. v. Commonwealth of Va., 624 S.E.2d 658 (Va. Ct. App. 2006).

The Claims Court denied the federal government's motion to dismiss, but allowed, with ICW's consent, the issue to be brought before the Federal Circuit Court of Appeals through an interlocutory appeal. The Federal Circuit affirmed in *Insurance Co. of the West v. United States*,[400] stating:

> We conclude that the Tucker Act must be read to waive sovereign immunity for assignees as well as those holding the original claim, except as barred by a statutory provision such as the Anti-Assignment Act. No act here limits the right of subrogees to bring suit against the government, and thus sovereign immunity presents no barrier to such an action.[401]

On remand, the federal government tried again to dismiss ICW's claim, based upon two sentences uttered by the Federal Court in dicta:

> It is well-established that a surety who discharges a contractor's obligation to pay subcontractors is subrogated only to the rights of the subcontractor. Such a surety does not step into the shoes of the contractor and has no enforceable rights against the government.[402]

The Claims Court again agreed with ICW that the dicta contradicted long-established precedent that a surety is also subrogated to the rights of the defaulting principal:

> [T]he dicta in *West II* do not define the scope of a surety's rights under the doctrine of equitable subrogation. When a surety, after financing or completing the performance of a defaulted contractor, discharges the outstanding claims of the subcontractors, it may subrogate to the rights of both the defaulted contractor and the subcontractors. *Balboa*, 775 F.2d at 1161; *USFG*, 201 Ct. Cl. at 10, 475 F.2d at 1382. Because the subcontractors have no standing to sue the Government directly, the surety must invoke the contractor's right to sue in order to sustain its claim against the Government. *Id.* If a surety were limited to exercising the rights of only the subcontractors under the doctrine of equitable subrogation, the surety never would be able to recover directly from the

---

400   243 F.3d 1367 (Fed. Cir. 2001).
401   *Id.* at 1378.
402   *Id.* at 1371 (citing United States v. Munsey Trust Co., 332 U.S. 234, 240-41 (1947)).

contracting agency. Such a result would contradict a century of jurisprudence on equitable subrogation.[403]

Undaunted by the *ICW* decisions, the federal government has continued to assert that it has not waived its sovereign immunity for various different types of surety subrogation claims. In *United States Fire Insurance Co. v. United States*,[404] a performing surety under a takeover agreement sued the federal government for overpayment of its principal, thereby causing a depletion in the amount of contract funds available to complete the work after the principal was default terminated. Following the *ICW* decision, the Claims Court denied the federal government's motion to dismiss and held that the doctrine of equitable subrogation gave the Claims Court jurisdiction under the Tucker Act to hear the case. However, the surety ultimately lost on the merits of its claim based upon the fact, among others, that the surety had failed to give notice to the federal government to withhold payments from the principal.[405]

Although rejected at every turn to date, it is likely that the federal government will continue to persist in its efforts to establish that *Blue Fox* has eliminated Tucker Act jurisdiction arising from a surety's assertion of its subrogation rights.[406] One factual scenario that has not

---

403 Ins. Co. of the West v. United States, 55 Fed. Cl. 529, 538 (2003).
404 61 Fed. Cl. 494 (2004).
405 United States Fire Ins. Co. v. United States, 78 Fed. Cl. 308 (2007).
406 The federal government has also contended in numerous cases that *Blue Fox* has eliminated Tucker Act jurisdiction arising from a payment bond surety's assertion of its subrogation rights. While the payment bond surety's subrogation rights are beyond the scope of this chapter, those payment bond surety cases include: *Liberty Mutual Insurance Co. v. United States*, 70 Fed. Cl. 37 (2006). In *Liberty Mutual*, the Claims Court rejected the federal government's argument that a payment bond surety, as opposed to a performance bond surety, was only subrogated to the rights of the subcontractors that it paid, and that, therefore, the Claims Court lacked jurisdiction because it cannot hear claims of subcontractors against the federal government. 70 Fed. Cl. at 42-43. "Therefore, the rule remains unchanged that a payment bond surety is subrogated to the rights of the insured prime contractor." *Id*. at 43. The same argument was raised before two other judges of the Claims Court and received the same result. *See* Nova Cas. Co. v. United States, 69 Fed. Cl. 284 (2006) (court had jurisdiction to hear claim of payment bond surety for recovery of monies

yet arisen in the Claims Court since *Blue Fox* is the surety's assertion that it is subrogated to the rights of the federal government to set off the remaining contract funds owed to the principal on other (presumably more successful) projects. There is little doubt that the federal government will try to argue that such a scenario is factually distinguishable from *ICW* (and, for payment bond sureties, *National American)*, and will seek the dismissal of the surety's subrogation claims.

---

still held by the federal government and payment improperly paid by the federal government, but such claim was subject to the federal government's set off claim for excess completion costs) and Commercial Cas. Ins. Co. of Ga. v. United States, 71 Fed. Cl. 104 (2006) (court had jurisdiction to hear claim of payment bond surety for recovery of monies still held by the federal government after the federal government refused to pay the principal's final invoice); *see also* Cincinnati Ins. Co. v. United States, 71 Fed. Cl. 544 (2006) (denied the federal government's motion to dismiss a payment bond surety's suit for lack of jurisdiction); Capitol Indem. Corp. v. United States, 71 Fed. Cl. 98 (2006) (held that sovereign immunity does not bar a payment bond surety's suit against the federal government); Travelers Indem. Co. v. United States, 72 Fed. Cl. 56 (2006) (denying the federal government's motion to dismiss for lack of subject matter jurisdiction and granting summary judgment for the payment bond surety arising from the federal government's wrongful disbursement of contract funds to the principal after the surety's notice). In *National American Insurance Co. v. United States*, 72 Fed. Cl. 451 (2006), the Claims Court granted summary judgment in favor of a payment bond surety who had asserted that the federal government improperly paid the principal following notice by the surety of payment bond claims. In so doing, the Claims Court also held that the surety was equitably subrogated to the rights of its principal and that the Tucker Act's waiver of sovereign immunity extended to the surety as a subrogee. On appeal, the Federal Circuit, in *National American Insurance Co. v. United States*, 498 F.3d 1301 (Fed. Cir. 2007), following a lengthy review of long-standing Supreme Court and federal circuit case authority on the issue, affirmed the Claims Court and re-affirmed "that *Munsey Trust, Blue Fox*, and *ICW* did not change the established precedent that a payment bond surety that discharges a contractor's obligations to pay a subcontractor may be equitably subrogated to the rights of the contractor." 498 F.3d at 1304-07, 1307.

V. The Surety's Rights to the Contract Funds In the Principal's Bankruptcy Case

The United States Bankruptcy Code[407] provides a procedural and substantive overlay on top of the surety's rights to the contract funds.[408] The surety's rights to the contract funds are affected immediately by the principal's filing of its bankruptcy petition and becoming a debtor, including but not limited to the operation of the automatic stay,[409] the debtor's property rights,[410] the debtor's right to use property of the debtor's estate,[411] and the surety's rights to adequate protection in the event that the principal, now the debtor, uses the contract funds from the bonded contracts after the filing of the bankruptcy petition.[412]

The surety has both substantive rights and procedural issues when asserting its rights to the contract funds in the principal's bankruptcy case. The surety's substantive rights, including its contractual rights, statutory rights and common-law and equitable rights, have been discussed previously in this chapter, and many cases have been cited from bankruptcy court decisions. Procedurally, the surety must follow the Bankruptcy Code and the Federal Rules of Bankruptcy Procedure in order to effectively assert its rights to the contract funds. The performance bond surety has been successful under numerous theories in prevailing over the claims of the trustee in bankruptcy and/or the debtor-in-possession to the contract funds.[413]

---

407 11 U.S.C. §§ 101 *et seq.*
408 *See* Chapter 14, *infra*, and this chapter, Section IV.B.3, *supra. See also* George J. Bachrach & Cynthia E. Rodgers-Waire, *The Surety's Rights to the Contract Funds in the Principal's Chapter 11 Bankruptcy Case*, 35 TORT & INS. L.J. 1 (1999); T. Scott Leo, *The Financing Surety and the Chapter 11 Principal*, 26 TORT & INS. L.J. 45 (1990).
409 11 U.S.C. § 362 (2008).
410 11 U.S.C. § 541 (2008).
411 11 U.S.C. § 363 (2008).
412 11 U.S.C. §§ 361, 363 (2008).
413 *See* note 408, *supra.*

Conclusion

The performance bond surety may assert many rights to the contract funds. Whether it is making a claim for the contract funds held by the obligee under the performance bond or some performance agreement or it is competing with the claims of other creditors for the contract funds, the performance bond surety must sort out its many rights to the contract funds, assert those rights that may prevail, and obtain the contract funds to reduce its loss.

5

SURETY'S RIGHTS OF RECOVERY AGAINST PRINCIPALS AND INDEMNITORS UNDER THE GENERAL INDEMNITY AGREEMENT AND COMMON LAW

Brett D. Divers
Kenneth M. Givens, Jr.
P. Keith Lichtman

Introduction

General suretyship principles provide that a bond principal owes a duty to the surety to perform all of its obligations to the obligee. When a principal defaults or fails to perform its obligations and causes loss to the surety, the surety has various rights and remedies to recover its losses. These rights exist at common law, in equity, and by contract when the surety has required the principal to sign a general agreement of indemnity. Rights and remedies available to sureties in the event of loss include: equitable rights such as reimbursement, contribution, exoneration, and subrogation, and contractual rights under the indemnity agreement. All protect the surety against ultimate loss but each operates differently.

I. General Indemnity Agreement

The typical surety in today's marketplace requires its principal (and indemnitors) to sign a written indemnity agreement before issuing any bonds. The indemnity agreement often restates the surety's common law rights of contribution, exoneration, and subrogation. The intent of the written indemnity agreement is not to alter those fundamental rights, but to describe how, when, and where the surety can enforce them in the event of default. Thus, the indemnity agreement is the starting point to evaluate indemnitors' obligations to the surety and the surety's rights and remedies against the indemnitors.

Most importantly, the indemnity agreement addresses how the surety will handle the relationship with the indemnitors when the surety receives a claim against the bond. For example, it addresses the right of indemnity against liability, the right of exoneration, the right of the surety to demand collateral security from the indemnitors, the surety's right to access the principal's books and records, the right to financial information from third parties, and the right to refuse to execute further bonds.

Most indemnity agreements also address what happens when the surety actually pays a claim or when it must perform under a performance bond. In such cases, the indemnity agreement addresses the surety's right to indemnity against loss, indemnity for expenses and attorney's fees incurred in the defense of claims, and the right to recover fees and expenses incurred to enforce the indemnity obligation.

Not only does the indemnity agreement restate the surety's common law rights, but it also specifically describes how the surety can enforce these and other rights. For example, most indemnity agreements address subject matters permitting the surety to mitigate an impending loss. Some indemnity agreements give the surety the right to finance the principal to complete a project, or alternatively, the right to take over and complete the job itself. In addition, to give meaning to these rights, the indemnity agreement often provides a right to secure receivables on bonded and unbonded jobs. Likewise, it may contain an assignment of the principal's rights under other contracts, including the rights to payment under those contracts. Significantly, the indemnity agreement typically gives the surety the right to compromise and settle all claims made against the surety. The assignment and power of attorney provisions of the agreement give the surety the ability to settle the principal's own affirmative claims.[1]

To enhance these rights, the agreement may include a *"prima facie"* provision allowing the surety to submit vouchers and other evidence of payment to establish the right to indemnity. Moreover, it may give the surety the right to record the indemnity agreement under the Uniform Commercial Code to secure the right of assignment. Other miscellaneous rights such as the waiver of notices, defenses, jury trials, confessions of judgment, exemptions, and the right to enforce the agreement jointly or

---

1   Hutton Constr. Co. v. County of Rockland, 52 F.3d 1191 (2d Cir. 1995); Liberty Mut. Ins. Co. v. Aventura Eng'g & Constr. Corp. 534 F. Supp. 2d 1290, 1308-09 (S.D. Fla. 2008); Bell BCI Co. v. Old Dominion Demolition Corp., 294 F. Supp. 2d 807 (E.D. Va. 2003); James McKinney & Son, Inc. v. Lake Placid 1980 Olympic Games, Inc., 462 N.E.2d 137 (N.Y. 1984); Harlandale Indep. Sch. Dist. v. C2M Constr., Inc., No. 04-07-00304-CV, 2007 WL 2253510 (Tex. App. 2007).

severally against multiple indemnitors, may also exist in the agreement. Each indemnity agreement requires careful study to determine the precise rights and remedies available as these agreements vary among companies. One company may even use different forms of agreement depending on the type of bond issued.

Note: This chapter is specific to recovery rights. Other rights afforded under agreements of indemnity to minimize losses are addressed in Chapter 6.

A. Surety's Rights Prior to Payment

1. The Right to Indemnity Against Liability

a. *Generally.* A typical indemnity provision in an indemnity agreement provides as follows:

> The undersigned shall indemnify and keep indemnified the company against any and all liability, loss and expense of whatsoever kind or nature, including, but not limited to, court costs, attorney's fees, and interest, which the company may sustain or incur (i) by reason of having executed or procured execution of any bond or bonds as surety for any of the undersigned, (ii) by reason of the failure of the undersigned to perform or comply with this agreement, or (iii) to enforce any of the covenants and conditions of this agreement.

This clause requires indemnitors to indemnity the surety for all losses sustained in good faith.[2] If a court determines, or if the surety determines after investigating a claim, that the surety is liable to pay the principal's debt, the surety may pay the debt and require the indemnitors to reimburse it. If the surety has obtained collateral security from the indemnitors, it may immediately draw upon those funds to satisfy its indemnity right. Generally, however, the surety will have no remedy at law or equity until the loss actually occurs.[3] The indemnity clause broadens the surety's common law rights and requires the named indemnitors to indemnify the surety for all losses and expenses,

---

2 *See* Commercial Ins. Co. of Newark, N.J. v. Pacific-Peru Constr. Corp., 558 F.2d 948 (9th Cir. 1977).
3 74 AM. JUR. 2D SURETYSHIP § 178 (1974).

regardless of the surety's actual liability under the bond.[4] The validity of an indemnity clause, such as the one above, is ordinarily beyond legitimate attack.[5]

b. *Good Faith.* The right to indemnity under the indemnity agreement is not without limitation, however. Case law has established that every contract imposes on the parties a duty of good faith and fair dealing.[6] Thus, where a surety fails to act in good faith it may lose its indemnity rights.

Courts evaluate numerous factors based on the facts of each case to determine whether a surety acted in good faith. A few of these factors are whether: (1) the surety investigated the claim properly;[7] (2) the principal demanded that the surety deny the claim; (3) the principal cooperated with the surety in the defense of the claim; (4) the surety demanded that the principal and indemnitors post collateral security; (5) the principal (or indemnitors) complied with that demand; and, (6) the surety acted improperly with respect to any collateral it received.[8] Therefore, before the surety is entitled to pursue its rights under the indemnity agreement it must proceed in good faith with respect to the obligee's demands and those of the principal and all other indemnitors.

---

4   *See generally,* U.S. Fid. & Guar. Co. v. Feibus, 15 F. Supp. 2d 579, 583 (M.D. Pa. 1998).

5   *See, e.g.,* Fid. & Deposit Co. of Md. v. Bristol Steel & Iron Works, Inc., 722 F.2d 1160, 1163 (4th Cir. 1983); Commercial Ins. Co. of Newark, N.J. v. Pacific-Peru Constr. Corp., 558 F.2d 948, 953 (9th Cir. 1977); Ins. Co. of N. Am. v. Bath, 726 F. Supp. 1247, 1252 (D. Wyo. 1989); *see also* Borey v. Nat'l Union Fire Ins. Co., 934 F.2d 30 (2d Cir. 1991); Am. Motorist Ins. Co. v. United Furnace Co., 876 F.2d 293 (2d Cir. 1989); Fireman's Fund Ins. Co. v. Nizdil, 709 F. Supp. 975 (D. Or. 1989); Int'l Fid. Ins. Co. v. Spadafina, 596 N.Y.S.2d 453 (N.Y. App. Div. 1993).

6   RESTATEMENT (SECOND) OF CONTRACTS § 205 (1981); *see also* Cates Constr., Inc. v. Talbot Partners, 980 P.2d 407 (1999) (performance bond surety cannot be held liable for tort damages arising out of a breach of the common law implied covenant of good faith and fair dealing).

7   PSE Consulting, Inc. v. Frank Mercede & Sons, Inc., 838 A.2d 135 (Conn. 2004).

8   *See* Bernard Balkin & Keith Witten, *Current Developments in Bad Faith Litigation Involving the Performance in Payment Bond Surety,* 28 TORT & INS. L. J. 611 (1993).

2. The Collateral Deposit Clause

a. *Generally.* Claims against bonds are inevitable. Sureties incur fees and expenses to investigate and defend against claims and often have to pay valid claims. Even though the indemnity agreement is designed to allow the surety to avoid costly litigation and protect its rights against the principal and indemnitors, litigation often results when the surety attempts to enforce its contractual rights. Principals and indemnitors often seek to avoid fulfilling their obligations under the agreement.

Many indemnity agreements contain a provision allowing the surety to request and receive collateral security from the principal and indemnitors before the surety suffers a loss.[9] The contractual right to collateral security gives the surety the ability to pursue claims directly against the signatories to the indemnity agreement. In many instances, these signatories are the individuals who control the principal. Consequently, the surety obtains rights directly against individuals it would otherwise not have. Moreover, the surety obtains the right to pursue the assets of these individuals when it would otherwise be difficult to do so.

In general, the collateral security clause requires a principal and/or indemnitors to deposit funds with the surety when the surety faces potential liability under a bond. In practice, sureties prefer to receive cash or cash equivalents, such as letters of credit or certificates of deposit. The surety can easily hold such security and it is readily liquid and available to pay any loss.[10] Other types of collateral, such as real estate, may be subject to external factors that affect their value, such as fluctuating market value or other encumbrances making it potentially difficult and costly to liquidate. The typical collateral security provision allows the surety to determine in its sole discretion whether the collateral is satisfactory.[11] The amount of collateral must generally be sufficient to

---

[9] *See* Fid. & Deposit Co. of Maryland v. D.M. Ward Constr. Co., Inc., No. 06-2483-CM, 2008 WL 2761314 (D. Kan. July 14, 2008).

[10] Joseph T. Getz, *Collateral: What to Take, How to Take It, and What to Do with It Once You Have It*, 28 THE BRIEF 25, 47 (1999).

[11] *Id.*; Liberty Mut. Ins. Co. v. Aventura Eng'g & Constr. Corp., 534 F. Supp. 2d 1290, 1308-09 (S.D. Fla. 2008); BIB Constr. Co. v. Fireman's Ins. Co. of Newark, N.J., 625 N.Y.S.2d 550 (N.Y. App. Div. 1995) (indemnitor dealing at arm's length with surety must abide by amount of collateral requested by surety).

pay any judgment with interest plus any costs and attorneys' fees that the surety estimates would be incurred in litigating the claim.[12]

Since the collateral security clause is contained in the indemnity agreement, it is worth emphasizing that contract principles govern its enforcement. Thus, the usual claims and defenses applicable in the typical contractual setting also apply to the enforcement of the collateral security clause.

The collateral security clause gives the surety a contractual right to choose the triggering event that compels the principal and/or indemnitors to deposit the funds. Many clauses require the principal and indemnitors to deposit collateral upon the surety's establishment of a reserve. Others require the deposit of collateral only after liability is established. The terms of the specific clause at issue will govern the triggering event.

For example, the collateral security clause in the Model Agreement of Indemnity provides:

> The Undersigned will deposit with the Company as collateral security, immediately upon demand, a sum of money, at the option of the Company, equal to: (1) the liability of the Company, if established; (2) the liability asserted against the Company; or (3) the reserve established by the Company, or any increase thereof, to cover any liability, loss, expense, or possible liability for any loss or expense for which the Undersigned may be obligated to indemnify the Company under the terms of this agreement.[13]

This clause plainly gives the surety the right to collateralization from the principal and indemnitors "immediately upon demand." Before the surety can make an enforceable demand, one of three prerequisites must occur. Subsection (1) gives the surety the option to wait until liability is actually established. Subsections (2) and (3) do not require a determination of liability or the validity of a claim before the surety is entitled to the deposit of collateral. They merely require the assertion of liability against the

---

[12] Am. Home Assurance Co. v. Peter Gun, Inc., No. 98 Civ. 6970 (TPG), 1999 WL 672569 at *3 (S.D.N.Y. Aug. 26, 1999) ($100,000.00 was sufficient to secure $83,701.40 claim); Am. Motorists Ins. Co. v. Pa. Beads Corp., 983 F.Supp. 437, 440 (S.D.N.Y. 1997) ("sufficient" means enough collateral to cover surety's potential liability); BIB Constr. Co. v. Fireman's Ins. Co., 625 N.Y.S.2d 550, 552 (N.Y. App. Div. 1995).

[13] Model Agreement of Indemnity Project Update (1995).

Surety's Rights of Recovery Against Principals and Indemnitors   273

surety and the surety's establishment of a reserve. This clause can, thus, be extremely useful to protect the surety from losses when the surety has received several payment bond claims and is in the process of investigating them.

Another illustrative collateral security clause more clearly makes the surety's establishment of a reserve the triggering mechanism to require the principal and indemnitors to deposit collateral. This clause provides:

> If for any reason the surety shall be required to or shall deem it necessary to set up a reserve in any amount to cover any (a) judgment, actual or contingent, with interest and costs, in any action instituted against the principal and/or the surety of (b) unadjusted claims or (c) losses, costs, attorneys' fees, and disbursements and/or expenses in connection with said bond or (d) default(s) of the principal or (e) abandonment of the contract or (f) liens filed or (g) dispute with the owner or obligee or (h) for any reason whatever regardless of any proceedings contemplated or taken by the principal or the pendency of any appeal, the undersigned shall immediately upon demand, deposit with the surety funds in the amount of such reserve and any increase thereof, to be held by the surety as collateral with the right to use such fund or any part thereof, at any time, in payment or compromise of any judgment, claim, liability, loss, damages, attorneys' fees, and disbursements and/or other expenses.

This clause has the added benefit of entitling the surety to receive enough collateral to pay the surety's attorneys' fees and disbursements as well as the principal amount of the claim(s). A surety drafting a collateral security clause should be sure the clause entitles it to all loss, costs, and expenses including attorneys' fees, consulting fees, and other administrative costs or fees. If the clause itself does not entitle the surety to recover such fees and costs, the indemnity agreement should contain a separate clause entitling the surety to such recovery.[14]

---

14 For example, many indemnity agreements contain the following clause:
> The undersigned shall indemnify and keep indemnified the surety against any and all liability for losses and expenses of whatsoever kind or nature, including fees or disbursements of counsel, and against any and all said losses and expenses, which the surety may sustain or endure (i) by reason of having executed or procured execution of the bond or bonds hereinbefore applied for; (ii) by reason of the failure of the

Courts scrutinize the specific terms of the clause at issue to determine when the surety is entitled to the deposit of collateral. In *Safeco Insurance Co. of America v. Schwab*, the clause required the indemnitors to post collateral once a demand had been made upon the surety.[15] When Safeco sought specific performance of the collateral security clause, the court held that the creditor's demand against the bond immediately vested the surety with the right to collateralization.

Conversely, the collateral security clause at issue in *Fidelity & Deposit Co. of Maryland v. Rosenmutter* contained the following language:

> Indemnitors agree to pay any such amounts to Fidelity ... as soon as Fidelity shall be liable therefor, whether or not it shall have paid out any portion thereof.[16]

The surety tried to enforce the collateral security clause upon receiving a demand against the bond. The court rejected the surety's attempt finding that a determination of liability, not simply the receipt of a demand, was the triggering event specified in the clause that gave the surety the right to enforce the clause.

Regardless of the clause used, once the surety decides collateral security is necessary to shield it from a potential loss, it should demand that its principal and indemnitor(s) deposit sufficient collateral with the surety to cover the anticipated liability. If liability on the claim is established, the surety can pay the liability from this fund. If it is determined that there is no liability, the surety must return the remaining balance of the fund to the principal and indemnitors.[17]

b. *Enforcement.* As with all disputes, the facts of each particular situation will govern the desired method of enforcing the collateral security clause. The answers to the following questions, among others, may help the surety decide how quickly it needs to enforce the collateral security clause:

---

undersigned to perform or comply with the covenants and conditions of this Agreement; or (iii) enforcing any of the covenants and conditions of this Agreement.

15   739 F.2d 431 (9th Cir. 1984).
16   614 F. Supp. 348, 351 (N.D. Ill. 1985).
17   *Safeco*, 739 F.2d at 433.

- Is the principal solvent? (The surety should have a general understanding of the principal's financial well-being as a result of the underwriting process and any monitoring of the project.)
- Are the principal and indemnitors dissipating or hiding assets in an effort to exempt them from levy?
- Is the principal still in business?
- If the principal is still in business, what is the status of its other projects?
- What is the status of payment between the principal and obligee?
- How many claims against the bond have been received?
- Is the principal cooperating with the surety in response to the claims?

The greater the risk that the principal will be insolvent after months of litigation and/or that the principal and indemnitors will be judgment-proof, the greater the need to obtain prompt judicial enforcement of the collateral security clause. Regardless of the selected means to enforce the clause, it is important for the surety to argue that, through the agreement of indemnity, it bargained for the right to be collateralized. This right is separate and distinct from the surety's ultimate common law right of indemnity.[18] This argument should be a central theme any time the surety seeks to enforce the collateral security clause.

Perhaps the most common enforcement mechanism of the collateral security clause is an action of specific performance.[19] The court in *Employers Insurance of Wausau v. Bond* stated, "It is well settled that a surety may sue for specific performance for deposit of security to cover the surety's reserve if such a provision is in the indemnity agreement."[20]

---

18 *See* Northwestern Nat'l Ins. Co. of Milwaukee, Wis. v. Alberts, 741 F. Supp. 424 (S.D.N.Y. 1990) (where the court recognized the difference between the surety's right of indemnification and collateralization), *vacated in part on other grounds*, 937 F.2d 77 (2d Cir. 1991).

19 *See* Milwaukie Constr. Co. v. Glens Falls Ins. Co., 367 F.2d 964 (9th Cir. 1966); United Bonding Ins. Co. v. Stein, 273 F. Supp. 929 (E.D. Pa. 1967).

20 No. HAR-90-1139, 1991 U.S. Dist. LEXIS 951 (D. Md. 1991). *See also* Am. Ins. Co. v. Egerton, 59 F.3d 165, 1995 U.S. App. LEXIS 23230 (4th

Courts generally grant specific performance if the surety proves: (1) it has no adequate remedy at law; (2) the indemnity agreement is just and reasonable and supported by adequate consideration; (3) the terms of the indemnity agreement are sufficiently definite to allow enforcement by the court; and (4) the performance sought is substantially identical to that promised in the indemnity agreement.[21] Typically, the court will focus on whether the surety can prove that it lacks an adequate remedy at law. As noted in *BIB Construction Co. v. Fireman's Insurance Co. of Newark, New Jersey*, the surety can prove the lack of adequate remedy at law even if the amount of damages is in doubt.[22] There, the court held that the surety's legal remedies were inadequate because the future damages were not ascertainable.

Courts also recognize that the surety lacks an adequate remedy at law when the amount of the claim is indefinite because an action for indemnification is not yet ripe.[23] In addition, when an indemnitor fails to deposit collateral promptly after the surety's demand, courts generally hold that the surety has no adequate remedy at law.[24] In short, courts

---

Cir. June 21, 1995); U.S. Fid. & Guar. Co. v. Feibus, 15 F. Supp. 2d 579 (M.D. Pa. 1998); Standard Sur. & Cas. Co. of N.Y. v. Caravel Indus. Corp., 15 A.2d 258 (N.J. Ch. 1940).

21 Employers Ins. of Wausau v. Bond, No. HAR-90-1139, 1991 U.S. Dist. LEXIS 951 (D. Md. 1991).

22 625 N.Y.S.2d 550 (N.Y. App. Div. 1995); Milwaukie Constr. Co. v. Glens Falls Ins. Co., 367 F.2d 964 (9th Cir. 1966).

23 Safeco Ins. Co. of Am. v. Criterion Inv. Corp., 732 F. Supp. 834, 843 (E.D. Tenn. 1989) (court granted specific performance of the collateral security provision upon the surety's showing that it had obtained a judgment against the principal after the principal had defaulted on its bond).

24 Nat'l Sur. Corp. v. Titan Constr. Co., 26 N.Y.S.2d 227, 231 (N.Y. Sup. Ct. 1940) (where the court stated that the very purpose of the collateral security clause is to entitle surety, as soon as possible future liability appears, to security against any loss it may later sustain if the liability matures, and to save plaintiff from being in a position of a general creditor of the principal), *aff'd*, 24 N.Y.S.2d 141 (N.Y. App. Div. 1940). *See also* Safeco Ins. Co. of Am. v. Schwab, 739 F.2d 431 (9th Cir. 1984); BIB Constr. Co. v. Fireman's Fund Ins. Co. of Newark, N.J., 625 N.Y.S.2d 550 (N.Y. App. Div. 1995); Nat'l Sur. Corp. v. Titan Constr. Corp., 26 N.Y.S.2d 227 (N.Y. Sup. Ct. 1940), *aff'd*, 24 N.Y.S.2d 141 (1940).

hold that for the creditor to receive the benefit of the collateral security provision for which it bargained, the clause must be enforced so the surety can avoid suffering losses and then being placed in the position of a general creditor of the principal and indemnitors.[25] There are some courts that will not deem the indemnitor's failure to post collateral as satisfying the necessary requisites for injunctive relief. In *Abish v. Northwestern National Insurance Co. of Milwaukee, Wisconsin*,[26] *Borey v. National Union Fire Insurance Co. of Pittsburgh, Pennsylvania*,[27] and *Northwestern National Insurance Co. of Milwaukee, Wisconsin v. Alberts*,[28] the surety was denied preliminary injunctive relief to enforce collateral deposit obligations of the indemnitors, owing to an allegedly inadequate showing by the surety of irreparable injury.[29] As noted, these cases are contrary to other decisions that hold that irreparable injury is presumed from an indemnitor's failure to deposit collateral.[30]

The surety's right for specific performance of the collateral security clause is extinguished once the principal's debt becomes certain. At that point, courts hold that the surety has an adequate remedy at law since it is entitled to damages for indemnification under other provisions of the indemnity agreement.[31]

---

25 *See* Titan Constr., 26 N.Y.S.2d at 231; *see also* Safeco v. Schwab, 739 F.2d 431; BIB Constr., 625 N.Y.S.2d 550; Titan Constr., 26 N.Y.S.2d 227.
26 924 F.2d 448 (2d Cir. 1991).
27 934 F.2d 30 (2d Cir. 1991).
28 937 F.2d 77 (2d Cir. 1991).
29 *See also* Fireman's Ins. Co. of Newark, N.J. v. Keating, 753 F. Supp. 1146 (S.D.N.Y. 1990) (insufficient showing of irreparable injury); Transamerica Premium Ins. Co. v. Cavalry Constr., Inc., 552 So. 2d 225 (Fla. Dist. Ct. App. 1989) (insufficient showing of apprehension of loss).
30 *See* Safeco Ins. Co. of Am. v. Schwab, 739 F.2d 431 (9th Cir. 1984); Doster v. Cont'l Cas. Co., 105 So. 2d 83 (Ala. 1958). *See also* Am. Motorists Ins. Co. v. United Furnace Co., Inc., 876 F.2d 293 (2d Cir. 1989); Safeco Ins. Co. of Am. v. Criterion Inv. Corp., 732 F. Supp. 834 (E.D. Tenn. 1989) (court granted surety's request for enforcement of collateral security provision but would not enjoin indemnitor's transfer of assets to other persons).
31 Am. Motorists Ins. Co. v. United Furnace Co., 876 F.2d 293, 300 (2d Cir. 1989); Commercial Ins. Co. of Newark, N.J. v. Pacific-Peru Constr. Corp., 558 F.2d 948, 955 (9th Cir. 1977).

Specific performance can be useful regardless of the solvency of the principal. If the principal is solvent, the surety will receive cash or other unencumbered assets to secure its bond obligations. If the principal is insolvent, the surety can enforce the collateral security clause against the assets of the principal and indemnitors. With the help of a precise decree of specific performance, specifying the nature and classification of assets to be deposited with the surety, the surety can prevent indemnitors from hiding assets that should be applied to offset bond losses.

When the surety believes the principal and/or indemnitors are in the process of dissipating or hiding assets to avoid fulfilling their contractual obligation to deposit collateral, the surety should seek temporary injunctive relief in the action for specific performance. A decree of specific performance and an injunction ordering the principal and indemnitors to deposit collateral have a similar effect. The benefit of the motion for temporary injunction is that the court will consider a motion for temporary injunction relatively early in the case and before an adjudication on the merits of the claim for specific performance.

To obtain a temporary injunction, the surety must show: (1) likelihood of irreparable injury; (2) lack of adequate remedy at law; (3) substantial likelihood of the surety's success on the merits; and (4) the granting of the injunctive relief will not disserve the public interest.[32] In pursuing an injunction, the surety must be able to substantiate its assertion that it is exposed to a loss under the bond and substantiate the magnitude of damages to which it claims to be exposed. If the surety cannot make these showings, its effort to obtain an injunction will likely fail.[33]

If the principal and indemnitors are dissipating or hiding assets, the surety may only have a limited amount of time to enforce its rights and protect itself from exposure to liability that it specifically contracted to avoid. Without pursuing some type of injunctive relief in such circumstances, the surety will not be adequately secured and could forever and irreparably lose its rights to the collateral. As a result, courts recognize that the requirement of irreparable harm overlaps with the lack

---

32   *See, e.g.*, Bradley v. Health Coalition, Inc., 687 So. 2d 329 (Fla. 1997); Capraro v. Lanier Bus. Prods., Inc., 466 So. 2d 212 (Fla. 1985).
33   Transamerica Premium Ins. Co. v. Cavalry Constr., Inc., 552 So. 2d 225 (Fla. Dist. Ct. App. 1989).

of adequate remedy at law necessary to establish the right to injunctive relief.[34]

In determining whether the surety is likely to succeed on the merits, courts generally focus on whether the surety can show that it can likely succeed in its right to compel a deposit of collateral. Therefore, the surety stands a good chance of success if the claim is valid and the surety will, in fact, be exposed to liability.

The surety may have the option to file suit in state or federal court. A determination of which court in which to seek enforcement of the collateral deposit clause will depend on the facts of each case. Of course, the first inquiry is whether jurisdictional grounds exist to support the pursuit of claims in federal court. Assuming such grounds exist, the surety should next consider, among other things, the relative speed with which it might receive a ruling on its enforcement efforts, and the court in which the surety is likely to receive a favorable ruling. The surety should discuss with its counsel the numerous inter-related issues regarding the most appropriate forum in which to seek relief. Such discussions are particularly important given the Supreme Court's stated discomfort with injunctions based on purely equitable principles.[35] In *Grupo Mexicano de Desarrollo, S.A. v. Alliance Bond Fund, Inc.*, the Court held that a district court lacked the authority to issue a preliminary injunction preventing the dissipation of their assets before adjudication of the claimant's contract claim for monetary damages because such a remedy was historically not available from courts of equity.[36]

One way to mitigate the potential hurdles to obtaining injunctive relief is by relying on statutory authority that permits prejudgment relief. Statutes in some states allow for prejudgment attachment remedies that may help the surety prevent the dissipation of assets so long as the statutory prerequisites exist.[37] Also worth consulting is the Uniform

---

34 Northwestern Nat'l Ins. Co. of Milwaukee, Wis. v. Alberts, 741 F. Supp. 424 (S.D.N.Y. 1990), *vacated in part on other grounds*, 937 F.2d 77 (2d Cir. 1991).
35 Grupo Mexicano de Desarrollo, S.A. v. Alliance Bond Fund, Inc., 527 U.S. 308 (1999).
36 *Id.* at 319-21.
37 *See, e.g.*, Conn. Gen. Stat. § 52-278a (2008), *et. seq.*; Mass. R. Civ. P. 4.1 (2008).

Fraudulent Conveyance Act, as it may provide for equitable relief in appropriate circumstances.[38]

c. *Amount of Collateral.* The typical collateral security provision provides that the indemnitors are to post a sum with the surety sufficient to cover the liability established against the surety, the liability asserted, or the amount of the surety's reserve. Since the typical clause does not specify a precise monetary amount of security to demand, the question of how much collateral is sufficient can arise. In *American Motorists Insurance Co. v. Pennsylvania Beads Corp.*,[39] the court construed a provision requiring the posting of "sufficient collateral." It found that "sufficient collateral" meant enough collateral to cover the surety's potential liability and exposure.

However, in *BIB Construction Co. v. Fireman's Fund Insurance Co.*,[40] the court construed a provision providing that the amount of collateral to be posted was within the sole discretion of the surety. It held that the surety could demand that amount of collateral that is reasonable under the circumstances.

d. *The Demand.* The surety's demand for collateral to the indemnitors should, of course, be in writing. It should state at least the following:

(1) If the clause provides that the setting of a reserve is a condition precedent to demanding collateral security, it should state that the surety has posted a reserve and state the amount of the reserve;

(2) That the surety has received claims against bonds it posted and the dollar amount of those claims;

(3) The deadline by which the surety expects to receive the collateral security; and

---

38 Hartford Acc. & Indem. Co. v. Jirasek, 235 N.W. 836 (Mich. 1931); Cahill-Mooney Constr. Co. v. Ayres, 373 P.2d 703, 708 (Mont. 1962) (wherein the court stated that under the record facts "to hold that these plaintiffs do not have a right to equitable relief in this case is to say that the Uniform Fraudulent Conveyance Act affords a defrauded victim no remedy which he did not have prior to the enactment of this statute. For all practical purposes it would nullify the act.").

39 983 F. Supp. 437 (S.D.N.Y. 1997).

40 625 N.Y.S.2d 550, 552 (N.Y. App. Div. 1995).

(4) A reservation of the right to adjust the amount of collateral upward or downward based on new information, additional demands, or changes in the surety's analysis.

The agreement of indemnity may specify how the parties are to deliver notice to each other. If it does, the surety needs to comply with those provisions. Otherwise, it is a good practice to deliver the demand by a means providing proof of delivery (i.e., by certified mail, return receipt requested, or overnight mail).

The surety may acquire additional rights if the principal and indemnitors fail to post the requested collateral. For example, some courts have found that the surety may settle claims over the principal's objection and seek indemnification if the principal and indemnitors fail to deposit collateral as demanded.[41] Thus, proof of delivery may be important.

3. Right to Have Indemnitors Obtain Release of Surety

Many indemnity agreements provide that the principal and indemnitors will, at the request of the surety, procure the discharge of the surety from any bonds and all liability by reason of the surety having issued the bonds. There is little published authority construing this clause to illustrate the relative rights and liabilities of the parties. However, in *Continental Casualty Co. v. Funderburg*,[42] the court mentioned the provision indirectly and found it to be enforceable.

---

41 Liberty Mut. Ins. Co. v. Aventura Eng'g & Constr. Corp. 534 F. Supp. 2d 1290 (S.D. Fla. 2008); Feibus, 15 F. Supp. 2d 579, 585 (M.D. Pa. 1998); Banque Nationale de Paris S.A. Dublin Branch v. Ins. Co. of N. Am., 896 F. Supp. 163 (S.D.N.Y. 1995); Employers Ins. of Wausau v. Able Green, Inc., 749 F. Supp. 1100, 1103 (S.D. Fla. 1990); Fireman's Fund Ins. Co. v. Nizdil, 709 F. Supp. 975, 977 (D. Or. 1989); Fid. & Deposit Co. of Md. v. Fleischer, 772 S.W.2d 809, 816 (Mo. Ct. App. 1989); Hess v. Am. States Ins. Co., 589 S.W.2d 548, 552 (Tex. Civ. App. 1979).

42 140 S.E.2d 750 (N.C. 1965).

4. Right to Review Books and Records of the Principal and Indemnitors and to Obtain Other Financial Information

Most indemnity agreements give the surety the right to review and copy the principal's books and records. While reported authority construing such clauses is not plentiful, the existing case law holds that the clauses are enforceable.[43] While the provisions of the clause can vary among sureties, a typical clause might provide:

> Until such time as the potential liability of the company under any bond or bonds is terminated, the undersigned will promptly furnish to the company such information as the company may request from time to time, and the company shall have the right to examine and copy the books, records and accounts of the undersigned.

Access to the principal's books and records is especially important for performance and payment bond sureties. The review can provide useful information the surety can use to determine the principal's solvency. The review may also help the surety to understand and verify the legitimacy of bond claims and a principal's defenses to such claims. These defenses have included matters such as the failure of the obligee to make timely payments, the failure of the obligee to pay the principal in full, or the obligee's delay to the project schedule.[44] Likewise, the review may reveal and help document the obligee's overpayment of the principal. The obligee's overpayment can result in the surety's complete or partial discharge.[45] The books and records may disclose other potential defenses, such as the obligee's failure to perform according to the contract.

On the other hand, the review may identify weaknesses in the principal's stated defenses. Identification of these weaknesses may allow the surety to expeditiously resolve a claim without incurring considerable attorneys' fees and/or consulting expenses.

---

[43] *See generally* State v. Laconco, Inc., 430 So. 2d 1376 (La. Ct. App. 1983).

[44] *See, e.g.*, Granite Computer Leasing Corp. v. Travelers Indem. Co., 894 F.2d 547 (2d Cir. 1990).

[45] *See, e.g.*, Cont'l Ins. Co. v. City of Virginia Beach, 908 F. Supp. 341 (E.D. Va. 1995).

Sureties have also used the right to review the principal's books and records to enforce their rights to collateral security.[46]

5. Right to Financial Information From Third-Parties

It can be important for the surety to obtain financial information from the performance bond obligee before the surety determines how it will comply with its performance obligations. For example, a surety may want to know if the obligee has sufficient funds to complete performance of the contract. If the obligee fails to cooperate with the surety's request for information, the surety may seek a discharge of its bonded obligations.[47]

Many indemnity agreements give the surety the right to obtain financial or other information or documentation in the hands of third parties (e.g., banks, obligees, subcontractors, etc.). A typical clause provides:

> Any bank, depository, creditor, obligee of a bond, subcontractor, material supplier, or other person, firm, or corporation possessing records or having information concerning the financial affairs of the Undersigned is hereby authorized to furnish the Surety and its representatives or consultants any such records or information requested by the Surety.

The provision arguably constitutes consent from the principal or indemnitors for third parties to release information. In practice, some third-parties, particularly banks, are reluctant to release information without a valid subpoena or without additional express written authorization from the principal–usually its customer. Accordingly, if provided in the indemnity agreement, the surety can consider executing

---

46   Fed. Ins. Co. v. Project Control Sys., Inc., No. 5:06-cv-11328, 2006 U.S. Dist. LEXIS 23638 (E.D. Mich. Apr. 27, 2006) (Surety sued indemnitors for collateral security and indemnification, and sought a preliminary injunction, including an order requiring the indemnitors to provide access to books and records. The court granted a preliminary injunction, stating that indemnitors must allow surety "full and complete access to all of their financial books, records and accounts, and other asset documentation . . . that could be used to fulfill Defendants' collateralization obligation under the General Indemnity Agreement.").

47   *See generally*, Sumitomo Bank of Cal. v. Iwasaki, 447 P.2d 956 (Cal. 1968); First Nat'l Bank & Trust Co. of Racine v. Notte, 293 N.W.2d 530 (Wis. 1980).

consent forms on behalf of the principal and/or indemnitors according to the "attorney-in-fact" provision found in most indemnity agreements. One significant purpose for this provision is to allow the surety to receive financial information about the principal or indemnitors without having to rely on the principal and indemnitors to do so. A provision expressly consenting to a third-party's provision of the requested information can sometimes eliminate the reluctance of third-parties to provide the information.[48] The provision may also shield third parties from claims of the principal and indemnitor that the release of the information was not authorized.[49]

B. Surety's Rights After Payment

1. Indemnity After Loss

The rights of the surety to indemnity after loss are predicated upon provisions similar to the one set forth above in the section regarding rights of the surety to indemnity prior to loss. The comments above apply equally here with respect to the enforceability of such a provision, the need for the surety to act in good faith, the procedures available for the surety to enforce the provision, the relief available, and the method and manner for making demand. The right to compel the indemnitors to reimburse the surety under this provision continues to be reaffirmed on a regular basis.[50] Generally, in those cases where relief in the nature of

---

48 *See* Peterson v. Idaho First Nat'l Bank, 367 P.2d 284 (Idaho 1961) (confirming a bank's ability to protect its customers' records from the public except with the consent of the customer).

49 *See* Banaitis v. Mitsubishi Bank, Ltd., 879 P.2d 1288, 1294 (Or. Ct. App. 1994) (noting that "[A]t common law, the courts in a number of jurisdictions have recognized a bank's duty not to divulge to a third-party, without the customer's consent, any information relating to the customer acquired through the keeping of the customer's account").

50 Northwestern Nat'l Ins. Co. of Milwaukee, Wis. v. Alberts, 822 F. Supp. 1079 (S.D.N.Y. 1993); United States *ex rel.* Electrical Workers Local Pension Fund v. D Bar D Enters., Inc., 772 F. Supp. 1167 (D. Nev. 1991); Employers Ins. of Wausau v. Able Green, Inc., 749 F. Supp. 1100 (S.D. Fla. 1990); U.S. Fid. & Guar. Co. v. Lipsmeyer Constr. Co., 754 F. Supp. 81 (M.D. La. 1990); Cont'l Cas. Co. v. Guterman, 708 F. Supp. 953 (N.D. Ill. 1989); Safeco Ins. Co. of Am. v. Criterion Inv. Corp., 732 F. Supp. 834 (E.D. Tenn. 1989); Ins. Co. of N. Am. v. Bath, 726 F. Supp. 1247 (D. Wyo. 1989);

indemnity to the surety has been denied, it has been on the basis that the indemnitors asserted issues of fact relative to their underlying liability, which, in turn, caused the denial of summary judgment.[51]

2. Prima Facie/Conclusive Evidence Clauses

A clause that can help the surety recover from the indemnitors is the proof of payment clause. A typical clause might read:

> Vouchers, affidavits, or other evidence of payment by the company of any loss, cost, or expense incurred by reason of the execution of the bonds shall be prima facie evidence of the propriety thereof and of the liability of the undersigned therefor.

Courts have upheld such clauses to establish the surety's right of reimbursement and the indemnitor's liability.[52] As a result, where the surety seeks in court to enforce its indemnity rights against the indemnitors and provides affidavits and supporting documentation of payment, the courts will often consider this documentation prima facie proof of the indemnitor's liability to the surety and will likely grant summary judgment.[53]

In *Fallon Electric Co. v. Cincinnati Insurance Co.*,[54] the court held that where the indemnity agreement specifies that a voucher is prima facie evidence of payment, the surety is entitled to reimbursement of

---

Acstar Ins. Co. v. Am. Mech. Contractors, Inc., 621 So. 2d 1227 (Ala. 1993); Horton v. U.S. Fid. & Guar. Co., 392 S.E.2d 25 (Ga. Ct. App. 1990).

51 *See, e.g.*, Nat'l Union Fire Ins. Co. v. Turtur, 892 F.2d 199 (2d Cir. 1989); Northwestern Nat'l Ins. Co. v. Alberts, 769 F.Supp. 498 (S.D.N.Y. 1991). *See generally*, Palevac v. Mid Century Non Auto, 710 P.2d 1389 (Nev. 1985); Am. Bonding Co. v. Nelson, 763 P.2d 814 (Utah Ct. App. 1988).

52 *See, e.g.*, Transamerica Ins. Co. v. Bloomfield, 401 F.2d 357, 362 (6th Cir. 1968); Engbrock v. Fed. Ins. Co., 370 F.2d 784 (5th Cir. 1967); Wash. Int'l Ins. Co. v. Bucko Constr. Co., Inc., No. 2:06 CV 320, 2007 WL 2384273 (N.D. Ind. Aug. 17, 2007); Fid. & Deposit Co. of Md. v. Tri-Lam Co., No. SA-06-CA-207-XR, 2007 WL 1452632 (W.D. Tex. May 15, 2007); Hanover Ins. Co. v. Clark, No. 05 C 2162, 2006 WL 2375428 (N.D. Ill. Aug. 15, 2006); Cont'l Cas. Co. v. Am. Sec. Corp., 443 F.2d 649 (D.C. Cir. 1970).

53 Buckeye Union Ins. Co. v. Boggs, 109 F.R.D. 420 (S.D. W.Va. 1986); Ford v. Aetna Ins. Co., 394 S.W.2d 693 (Tex. Civ. App. 1965).

54 121 F.3d 125 (3d Cir. 1997).

monies it reasonably believed were owed. The burden is upon the principal/indemnitor to prove that indemnification is not warranted. The court found this burden requires the principal/indemnitor to show either that the surety did not believe its payment was reasonable or that its payment, in fact, was unreasonable. In such a circumstance, the principal/indemnitor would establish fraud or bad faith and thus defeat the surety's rights.[55]

Although many indemnity agreements contain a clause providing that a surety's documentation is prima facie proof of the indemnitor's liability, there are other clauses that purport to provide that the documentation operates as conclusive proof.[56] When reviewing such clauses, courts are less apt to enforce them because of their tendency to circumscribe the indemnitor's opportunity to rebut the surety's evidence.[57] Where the clause may deprive the indemnitor's right of rebuttal to the surety's evidence, courts may hold the clause to be against public policy.[58]

Before proceeding under this clause, the surety and its counsel should review it carefully to determine whether the evidentiary phrase creates a rebuttable or nonrebuttable presumption of liability and enforceability under local law.

3. Indemnity Against Expenses, Including Attorneys' Fees

Under the "American Rule," a plaintiff generally must have a statutory or contractual basis in order to recover its attorneys' fees, costs, and expenses against a defendant.[59] An exception exists in certain jurisdictions where the defendant breaches a contract with the plaintiff (or otherwise acts wrongfully), resulting in the plaintiff having to maintain or defend a suit with a third-party. In this instance, the plaintiff

---

55 *See e.g.*, Fid. & Deposit Co. of Md. v. Wu, 552 A.2d 1196 (Vt. 1988). *See also* Hartford v. Tanner, 910 P. 2d 872 (Kan. Ct. App. 1996); Gen. Ins. Co. of Am. v. K. Capolino Constr. Corp., 903 F. Supp. 623 (S.D.N.Y. 1995).

56 *See* Home Indem. Co. v. Wachter, 115 A.D.2d 590 (N.Y. App. Div. 1985).

57 *See generally* Fid. & Deposit Co. of Md. v. Davis, 284 P. 430 (Kan. 1930); Fid. & Cas. Co. of N.Y. v. Eickhoff, 65 N.W. 351 (Minn. 1895).

58 *See, e.g.*, Sork v. United Benefit Fire Ins. Co., 161 So.2d 54 (Fla. Dist. Ct. App. 1964). *But see* Engbrock v. Fed. Ins. Co., 370 F.2d 784 (5th Cir. 1967); Wachter, 115 A.D.2d 590 (where a conclusive evidence clause was enforced with the proviso that the surety act in good faith).

59 *See* Baja Energy, Inc. v. Ball, 669 S.W. 2d 836 (Tex. App. 1984).

may be able to recover from the defendant the plaintiff's reasonable attorneys' fees incurred in the suit with the third-party.[60] In the jurisdictions recognizing the exception, the attorneys' fees the plaintiff incurred as a result of defending the case the third-party brought are treated as "consequential damages," and thus, are different from the attorneys' fees the plaintiff incurs against the defendant in the case at issue.

Most indemnity agreements today provide in the indemnity provision for the reimbursement of attorneys' fees incurred as a consequence of having issued the bond. This includes attorneys' fees for the surety's defense of claims as well as fees incurred in enforcing the indemnity agreement. While the attorneys' fees clause generally is held to be enforceable by the courts,[61] securing the actual award of fees in an individual case is somewhat more problematic. One of the earliest cases confirming the surety's right to indemnification for attorneys' fees is *United States Fidelity & Guaranty Co. v. Hittle*[62] where the surety was permitted to recover attorneys' fees incurred in good faith and the court placed the burden of proof on the indemnitor to prove that the surety had acted in bad faith before denying the attorneys' fees application. Subsequent cases, however, seem to muddle the good faith/bad faith standard. For example, in *Fidelity & Casualty Co. of New York v. Mauney*,[63] the court adopted a standard that permitted the surety to recover attorneys' fees and costs against the indemnitors only if the surety acted reasonably, in good faith, and with due diligence. Reasonableness, in that case, was measured by the surety's reasonable cause to believe that expenditure for separate counsel was necessary.

In *Central Towers Apartments, Inc. v. Martin*,[64] and other cases following *Martin*, the court placed the burden squarely on the surety to establish good faith and show that the expenditure of attorneys' fees was reasonably necessary. In the *Central Towers* case, the court set out

---

60   *See* Ranger Constr. Co. v. Prince William County Sch. Bd., 605 F.2d 1298 (4th Cir. 1979); Baja Energy, Inc., 669 S.W. 2d 836.
61   *See, e.g.*, Abbott v. Equity Group, Inc., 2 F.3d 613 (5th Cir. 1993); Citizens State Bank of Big Lake v. Transamerica Ins. Co., 815 F. Supp. 309 (D. Minn. 1993); Agnew v. Alicanto, S.A., 125 F.R.D. 355 (E.D.N.Y. 1989).
62   96 N.W. 782 (Iowa 1903).
63   116 S.W.2d 960, 962 (Ky. 1938).
64   453 S.W.2d 789 (Tenn. Ct. App. 1969).

typical criteria to be examined on the question of reasonableness, including the following factors:

1. The amount of risk to which the surety was exposed;
2. Whether the principal was solvent;
3. Whether the surety called on the principal to deposit collateral;
4. Whether the principal refused to deposit collateral;
5. Whether the principal was notified of the action and given an opportunity to defend it;
6. Whether the principal hired the attorney for both itself and the surety;
7. Whether the principal notified the surety of the hiring of the attorney;
8. The competency of the attorney the principal hired;
9. The diligence of the principal and his attorney in the defense;
10. Whether there was a conflict of interest between the parties;
11. The attitude and cooperativeness of the surety; and
12. The amount charged and diligence of the attorney the surety hired.

Since the terms good faith and reasonableness have varying meanings to different courts, the question of a surety's right to indemnification for attorneys' fees, if reasonable and incurred in good faith, is less than crystal clear.[65] Under this clause it is important for the

---

65 *See, e.g.*, United Riggers & Erectors, Inc. v. Marathon Steel Co., 725 F.2d 87 (10th Cir. 1984) (Tenth Circuit reversed district court's ruling denying the surety indemnification of attorney's fees holding that the surety was entitled to reimbursement because of the refusal of the indemnitor, who was also the principal, to post collateral upon demand and because of the existence of separate surety defenses; the surety also had reason to doubt the indemnitor's ability to satisfy any judgment and to remain solvent until the completion of litigation); Perkins v. Tompson, 551 So. 2d 204 (Miss. 1989) (vacating attorney's fees award for the surety and remanding case to the trial court for a determination of the factual issue of whether it was reasonably necessary for the surety to employ separate counsel to protect its interests, whether the surety acted in good faith in

surety to make an unequivocal written demand that the indemnitor post sufficient collateral to cover any reserve that is set up on the underlying bond claim and to review the facts surrounding the underlying claims for the specific purpose of determining the existence of potential separate surety defenses.

In summary, courts will usually award attorney's fees under this clause if found to be reasonably incurred.[66] They also will typically award fees incurred in good faith.[67] Courts may not award fees if they were incurred to defend against a negligence action, unless the indemnity agreement specifically provides for indemnity against losses resulting from the surety's own negligence.[68] With respect to the recovery of fees incurred to enforce the indemnity agreement itself, courts have ruled this portion of the provision enforceable as well.[69] However, without a specific provision in the indemnity agreement for recovery of attorneys' fees in litigating the right to indemnity, or some other contractual or statutory right to recover them, recovery generally will be denied.[70]

II. Quia Timet and Exoneration

In addition to contractual-based remedies, quia timet relief and exoneration are equitable vehicles that may help shield the surety from loss or recover for losses after they are suffered. Since these remedies arise from the common law, they are available against the principal but not other indemnitors signing the indemnity agreement.

---

incurring those expenses with its principal, and whether the fees and expenses claimed were reasonable).

66 Citizens State Bank v. Transamerica Ins. Co., 815 F. Supp. 309 (D. Minn. 1993); Lamp, Inc. v. Int'l Fid. Ins. Co., 493 N.E.2d 146 (Ill. App. Ct. 1986); Int'l Fid. Ins. Co. v. Jones, 682 A.2d 263 (N.J. Super. Ct. App. Div. 1996) (attorney's fees equaled three times the amount paid by the surety on the bond held not unreasonable).
67 See Transamerica Premier Ins. Co. v. Nelson, 878 P.2d 314 (Nev. 1994).
68 See Cooper v. Am. Auto. Ins. Co., 978 F.2d 602 (10th Cir. 1992).
69 See, e.g., Mo. Pac. R.R. Co. v. Kan. Gas & Electric Co., 862 F.2d 796 (10th Cir. 1988); City of Boston v. S.S. Texaco Texas, 773 F.2d 1396 (1st Cir. 1985); Kan. Tpk. Auth. v. Morgan Guar. Trust Co., 751 F. Supp. 936 (D. Kan. 1990).
70 See, e.g., Goodridge v. Harvey Group, Inc., 778 F. Supp. 137 (S.D.N.Y. 1991); David v. Glemby Co., Inc., 717 F. Supp. 162 (S.D.N.Y. 1989).

A. Quia Timet

Often, a surety anticipates suffering a loss well before its principal defaults. Quia timet relief is an equitable vehicle through which a surety may try to require the principal to collateralize it before the surety actually incurs a loss. Quia timet literally means "because he [or she] fears or apprehends."[71] The fear of injury and the danger of irreparable harm, as opposed to actual injury, form the basis for quia timet relief.

While quia timet relief is still available to a surety in certain circumstances, some courts have been reluctant to grant it, particularly when a written indemnity agreement is in place. For example, in *Safeco Insurance Company of America v. Chiang*,[72] the surety filed a summary judgment motion seeking, among other things, quia timet relief, and $500,000 in collateral. The court dismissed the surety's claim for quia timet relief, suggesting (erroneously) that it is not available when an indemnity agreement is in place. While quia timet relief and indemnity rights springing from a written agreement are not mutually exclusive, sureties should recognize that some courts have limited experience in analyzing surety claims.

In that regard, a surety should carefully plead the key element of quia timet relief, namely, reasonable grounds for fearing irreparable harm resulting from the principal's actions or inactions. For example, in *United States Fidelity & Guaranty Co. v. Diaz Matos*,[73] the surety sued the principal and indemnitors on an indemnity agreement at issue and for quia timet relief. While the court granted specific performance of the collateral deposit provision of the indemnity agreement, it found that the surety had not adequately demonstrated the potential for irreparable harm; accordingly, the court denied the surety's request for quia timet relief.

B. Exoneration

Exoneration is another important equitable right available to the surety. It refers to the surety's right, upon the principal's default, to force the principal to honor its obligations or to furnish collateral security before

---

71 BLACK'S LAW DICTIONARY 1122 (5th ed. 1979).
72 No. C-04-1977 SC, 2006 WL 1867718 (N.D. Cal. July 6, 2006).
73 No. 05-1851 (PG), 2007 WL 878571 (D. P.R. Mar. 21, 2007).

the time that the surety is required to discharge the principal's obligations. Exoneration places the loss where it belongs, squarely on the principal, who is primarily responsible for it.[74] Exoneration is appropriate given the following circumstances: (a) the principal is primarily responsible for an obligation; and (b) the surety's obligation is "fixed."[75] An obligation can be "fixed" before a surety pays claims. Thus, it is not necessary for the surety to have suffered a loss and paid or discharged the principal's primary obligation. It is only necessary that the obligation has become fixed.

In *Morley Construction Co. v. Maryland Casualty Co.*,[76] a surety on a public job wanted to use installment payments due on the bonded contract to resolve claims. The outstanding bills on the bonded contract were $100,000. The surety argued that there was a danger the principal would convert or conceal funds (resulting in irreparable loss to the surety), unless principal exonerated the surety. The court held that the surety was entitled to exoneration.[77]

A principal's ability to pay a loss does not affect a surety's ability to seek exoneration, nor does a surety's right to indemnity (either at common law or *vis-à-vis* a written indemnity agreement) or reimbursement preclude an exoneration claim. This is important because recently, some courts have been reluctant to fashion equitable remedies where remedies at law may exist.

C. Distinction Between Quia Timet and Exoneration

While quia timet and exoneration have much in common, they are different.[78] The fear of injury, rather than an injury itself, forms the basis for quia timet relief. Alternatively, exoneration is not available to the surety unless, and until, its obligation to pay is "fixed." "Fixed" does not

---

74 Admiral Oriental Line v. United States, 86 F.2d 201, 204 (2d Cir. 1936).
75 *See* Admiral Oriental, 86 F.2d at 204; Borey v. Nat'l Union Fire Ins. Co. of Pittsburgh, Pa., 934 F.2d 30, 33 (2d Cir. 1991).
76 90 F.2d 976 (8th Cir. 1937).
77 *See also* United States v. King, 349 F.3d 964 (7th Cir. 2003), for a helpful description of exoneration and the surety (albeit not in the performance bond context).
78 Great Am. Ins. Co. v. General Contractors & Constr. Mgmt., Inc., No. 07-21489-CIV, 2008 WL 2245986, *5, 6 (S.D. Fla. May 29, 2008) (discusses the differences between quia timet and exoneration).

mean the surety must have actually paid the claim. Despite their differences, both remedies may result in similar ends, such as receiver's injunctions, orders directing funds to be paid into court, among other things.

In equity, and under some statutes, after maturity of the debt or accrual of liability, a surety may have the right to compel the principal to exonerate the surety from liability, or to secure the surety against loss, even where the surety has yet to pay the claim.[79] The Restatement (Third) of Suretyship and Guaranty (1995), provides in §21(1) that a principal has a primary duty to perform underlying obligations for which the surety is secondarily liable, and to refrain from conduct that impairs the surety's expectation that the principal will perform the underlying obligation. If the principal breaches one or both duties, the surety is entitled to relief.

Quia timet and exoneration complement the rights and remedies typically available to a surety under written agreements of indemnity. Sureties should carefully consider one or both remedies as part of any salvage/mitigation analysis.

D. Enforcement

Because quia timet and exoneration are equitable remedies, courts have considerable latitude in fashioning remedies. *Fidelity & Deposit Co. of Maryland v. McClintic-Marshall Corp.* highlights some or all of the following options potentially available:[80]

1. A decree directing either the appointment of a receiver to execute documents and to receive funds, such as contract funds, or to pay funds into court or directing that funds be placed in a joint control account for payment to the proper parties;[81]

---

79 72 C.J.S. *Principal and Surety* § 227 (1987); 11A John A. Appleman & Gene Appleman, INSURANCE LAW & PRACTICE § 6661 (1981).
80 171 A. 382 (N.J. 1934), *aff'd by* Plunkett v. Bd. of Pension Comm'rs, 176 A. 341 (N.J. 1935).
81 Martin v. Nat'l Sur. Co., 300 U.S. 588 (1937) (right of surety to control contract funds first confirmed by the United States Supreme Court in the form of quia timet relief due to failure of contractor to pay bills and default in obligations); Glades County, Fla. v. Detroit Fid. & Sur. Co., 57 F.2d 449 (5th Cir. 1932).

2. An injunction restraining an owner from disbursing the unpaid contract price to the contractor;[82] and/or
3. A decree directing the posting of collateral.[83]

III. Reimbursement and Contribution

A. *Reimbursement*

When a surety performs its principal's primary obligations, the principal is obligated to reimburse the surety.[84] In fact, there is an implied promise on the part of the principal to reimburse the surety for any amount the surety pays in good faith; however, a surety is not entitled to

---

82   *Martin*, 300 U.S. 588 (1937). The following cases set forth standards for injunctive relief in a quia timet actions; i.e., that the surety must suffer irreparable injury or harm in the absence of an adequate remedy at law: Milwaukie Constr. Co. v. Glens Falls Ins. Co., 367 F.2d 964 (9th Cir. 1966) (failure to post collateral on request presumes inadequacy of remedy and irreparable injury), and United Bonding Ins. Co. v. Stein, 273 F. Supp. 929 (E.D. Pa. 1967) (defendant's assertion of existence of a legal remedy for damages did not suffice to defeat injunctive relief where the indemnitor refused to voluntarily comply with surety's demand for collateral under the General Agreement of Indemnity). *But see* Northwestern Nat'l Ins. Co. of Milwaukee, Wis. v. Alberts, 937 F.2d 77 (2d Cir. 1991); Borey v. Nat'l Union Fire Ins. Co. of Pittsburgh, Pa., 934 F.2d 30 (2d Cir. 1991); Abish v. Northwestern Nat'l Ins. Co. of Milwaukee, Wis., 924 F.2d 448 (2d Cir. 1991) (surety must demonstrate inadequacy of legal remedy to specifically enforce collateral security clause and show irreparable injury to obtain an injunction); Commercial Ins. Co. of Newark, N.J. v. Pacific-Peru Constr. Corp., 558 F.2d 948 (9th Cir. 1977) (court believed surety had adequate remedy at law to collect an existing money judgment and, therefore, specific performance of indemnity agreement to post collateral denied). As to other requirements for injunctive relief, *see* Northwestern Nat'l Ins. Co. of Milwaukee, Wis. v. Barney, 886 F.2d 1316 (6th Cir. 1989), and Wingsco Energy One v. Vanguard Group Resources 1984 Inc., No. H-86-452, 1989 WL 223756 (S.D. Tex. Nov. 15, 1989).
83   Northwestern Nat'l Ins. Co. of Milwaukee, Wis. v. Alberts, 741 F. Supp. 424, 430 (S.D.N.Y. 1990), *rev'd. on other grounds*, 937 F.2d 77 (2d Cir. 1991); Doster v. Cont'l Cas. Co., 105 So. 2d 83 (Ala. 1958) (where essential elements were set forth for requiring the contractor transfer assets as collateral).
84   74 AM. JUR. 2D SURETYSHIP § 221 (1974).

reimbursement from the principal until the surety has suffered a loss or paid the debt for which it is secondarily liable.[85]

Moreover, absent an agreement of indemnity, or some other contract or statute providing otherwise, a principal's implied obligation of reimbursement is limited to the amounts it actually paid others to resolve claims. Thus, a surety is typically unable to recover attorneys' fees, costs, or expenses under an equitable reimbursement theory.

The Restatement (Third) of Suretyship and Guaranty (1995) discusses the right to reimbursement. Section 22 provides as follows:

> (1) Except as provided in section 24, when the principal obligor is charged with notice of the secondary obligation, it is the duty of the principal obligor to reimburse the secondary obligor to the extent that the secondary obligor:
> (a) performs the secondary obligation; or
> (b) makes a settlement with the obligee that discharges the principal obligor, in whole or in part, with respect to the underlying obligation.

Section 23 of the Restatement (Third) of Suretyship and Guaranty (1995) provides as follows:

> (1) When the principal obligor has a duty to reimburse the secondary obligor, that duty is to reimburse the secondary obligor for the reasonable cost of performing the secondary obligation, including incidental expenses.
> (2) If satisfaction of the principal obligor's duty to the obligee pursuant to the underlying obligation is limited to a particular fund or property, satisfaction of the duty of reimbursement is limited to the same fund or property.

The surety cannot profit from completing a principal's contract.[86] In other words, it can only recover in reimbursement that which it paid. Further, the surety is entitled to reimbursement if it pays an obligation

---

85   72 C.J.S. PRINCIPAL & SURETY §§ 224-25 (1987).

86   *See, e.g.*, Howell Constr., Inc. v. United Pac. Ins. Co., 824 F. Supp. 105 (W.D. Ky. 1993) (contract funds held in trust for payment obligations; surety's right to funds is qualified by payment obligations, and surety holds funds as a fiduciary).

for which the principal is liable, even if the surety has a defense to the obligee's claim. But, where the principal has a defense and the surety knows it but pays a claim anyway, the principal has no equitable duty to reimburse the surety.

Often when an obligee defaults a principal, the principal disputes the obligee's position, yet the surety decides it is best to complete the principal's work before the principal can litigate its potential defenses with the obligee. In such cases, the surety should be sure to preserve its rights in writing (to reimbursement, among other things) in case its principal later proves the default was improper.[87]

B. Contribution

Contribution is an equitable right of the surety for which it is critical that the loss have actually occurred. For example, in *RLI Insurance Co. v. John H. Hampshire, Inc.*,[88] the surety for a subcontractor sued the project architect for negligence and contribution. The court dismissed the contribution claim since the surety had not yet been found liable to the owner. Contribution often applies when a surety shares liability in bonding a principal with one or more other sureties.[89]

Absent a written contract addressing liabilities of co-sureties, they will typically be responsible for a proportionate share of the payment made under the bonds at issue.[90] The Restatement (Third) of Suretyship and Guaranty (1995) provides that each co-surety is entitled to contribution or reimbursement from the other for its losses.[91] A co-surety should have an expressed written agreement firmly establishing the specific reimbursement rights, rather than simply deferring to equitable rights.

---

87 Travelers Cas. & Sur. Co. of Am. v. Long Bay Mgmt. Co., No. 01-5490 BLS, 2004 WL 2341339 (Mass. Super. Ct. Sept. 7, 2004).
88 RLI Ins. Co. v. John H. Hampshire, Inc., 461 F. Supp. 2d 364 (D. Md. 2006).
89 Swiss Reinsurance Am. Co. v. Airport Indus. Park, Inc., No. 2:05-cv-01127, 2007 WL 2464504 (W.D. Pa. Aug. 27, 2007).
90 *See, e.g.*, Atalla v. Abdul-Baki, 976 F.2d 189 (4th Cir. 1992); Alberding v. Brunzell, 601 F.2d 474 (9th Cir. 1979); Phelps v. Scott, 30 S.W.2d 71, 76 (Mo. 1930).
91 *See generally In re* Wetzler, 192 B.R. 109 (Bankr. D. Md. 1996), *aff'd*, Wetzler v. Cantor, 202 B.R. 573 (D. Md. 1996).

Conclusion

The indemnity agreement remains an important tool for the surety to enforce its rights against the principal and indemnitors when faced with losses. While it provides the surety with many weapons, the surety must act in good faith to make the most of those weapons. The collateral deposit clause has withstood a great deal of litigation. In the absence of an indemnity agreement, or where the agreement fails to adequately protect the surety, common law rights such as exoneration and quia timet may shield the surety from losses.

6

SURETY'S RIGHTS UNDER THE GENERAL INDEMNITY AGREEMENT TO MINIMIZE LOSS

Richard E. Towle
Sam H. Poteet, Jr.
*Jeffrey S. Price**

Introduction[1]

The greatest multi-tool on the surety's belt, the General Indemnity Agreement (the "indemnity agreement") serves as the surety's primary basis of contractual recovery for its losses. Born out of the surety's common law rights of exoneration, indemnification, and subrogation, and serving as a powerful supplement to and enhancement of these common law rights, an indemnity agreement is given, generally, by the principal, the individual owners of the principal (and their spouses), and any other third-party willing to assume the obligations of the principal, such as subsidiary or parent companies of the principal. These parties are generally willing to execute the indemnity agreement because while a

---

*   Rebecca B. Howald, an associate at the firm of Manier & Herod, contributed to the research and drafting of this chapter.

1   This chapter is an expansion and bifurcation of Chapter 5 of the first edition of THE LAW OF PERFORMANCE BONDS. The authors respectfully acknowledge the original work of G. Steven Ruprecht, author of the first edition of this material. *See* G. Steven Ruprecht, *Surety's Rights and Remedies Against Principals and Against Indemnitors under the General Indemnity Agreement, in* THE LAW OF PERFORMANCE BONDS 77, 104-21 (Lawrence R. Moelmann & John T. Harris eds., 1999). In addition to updates on case law since the first edition was published, this chapter also addresses the additional concepts of the surety's right to have its indemnitors obtain a release of the surety, the surety's trust fund rights, and the right to financial information from third parties. For an excellent and in-depth analysis of many of the topics overviewed in this chapter, *see generally* THE SURETY'S INDEMNITY AGREEMENT: LAW & PRACTICE (Marilyn Klinger, George J. Bachrach & Tracey L. Haley eds., 2d ed. 2008).

contractor may be able to exist without a bank, it cannot exist without surety credit. Each indemnity agreement is worded differently, and it is generally held that "[t]he contract of indemnity forms the law between the parties and must be interpreted according to its own terms and conditions."[2]

Under many indemnity agreements, enforcement of the surety's rights is frequently triggered by an "event of default," which event is defined under the indemnity agreement.[3] Other indemnity agreements do not require any conditions precedent or triggering events at all.[4] Significantly, the event of default under an indemnity agreement does not necessarily depend upon the principal being in default by the terms of the bonded contract.[5] In fact, a default under the terms of the indemnity agreement can occur long before a principal is defaulted or terminated under a bonded contract. The broad triggering events for the exercise of rights under the indemnity agreement are an example of the tremendous value of an indemnity agreement over the rights available via subrogation and/or under the common law.

The indemnity agreement also vests in the surety rights based upon potential liability of the surety, not only actual liability. In fact, courts across the country have recognized that the difference between the right to indemnity under the common law and the right to indemnity under an indemnity agreement is that, "[a]bsent a written indemnity agreement, the surety's common law indemnity rights exist only when there is actual liability...however, there will usually exist a written indemnity agreement between the parties, which will typically provide, among other things, that the surety need only show potential liability or that it believed in good faith that it was necessary or expedient to satisfy a claim to invoke its rights."[6] Sureties should be aware, however, that despite the clear

---

2   *See e.g.*, Abbott v. Equity Group, 2 F.3d 613, 627 (5th Cir. 1993).
3   *See* Shannon J. Briglia, Mike F. Pipkin & David C. Olson, *The Surety's Enforcement of its Rights to Collateral from the Principal and the Indemnitors in* THE SURETY'S INDEMNITY AGREEMENT: LAW & PRACTICE 277, 320-21 (Marilyn Klinger, George J. Bachrach & Tracey L. Haley eds., 2d ed. 2008).
4   *See id.* at 309.
5   *See id.*
6   Liberty Mut. Ins. Co. v. Aventura Eng'g & Constr. Corp., 534 F. Supp. 2d 1290, 1309-10 (S.D. Fla. 2008) (quoting Armen Shahinian, Marc Brown & Joseph Monaghan, *Deciding to Litigate: The Surety's Recourse*

language of the indemnity agreement, and despite the correct interpretation that potential liability is sufficient to trigger indemnity obligations, some courts struggle with enforcing the concept that absent an actual loss or the setting of a reserve, the surety may enforce its rights against its indemnitors.

I. Provisions to Minimize Surety's Loss

Most indemnity agreements contain assignment provisions which assign to the surety property such as the principal's receivables on bonded and unbonded contracts, the principal's subcontracts, the principal's materials, inventory and equipment on bonded jobs, the principal's claims against others, and the right to prosecute those claims. Along with the assignment, the indemnity agreement will generally also include the right to make a collateral deposit demand (without regard to the settlement of claims); the right to serve as the principal's attorney-in-fact; and the right to record the indemnity agreement as a financing statement under the Uniform Commercial Code ("UCC") in order to perfect the surety's rights against other creditors of the principal. Working together, these provisions are the cornerstones for preserving the surety's rights, protecting the surety's interests, and recovering the surety's loss. Because they are so important to the surety's over-arching rights under the indemnity agreement, a brief discussion of the surety's right to demand collateral, the UCC provision and the attorney-in-fact provision is warranted.

A. *Collateral Deposit Demand (Without Regard to Settlement of Claims)*

One of the surety's strongest options to minimize its losses by virtue of the rights purveyed in the indemnity agreement is the right to demand and obtain collateral from the principal/indemnitors. This remedy, properly couched as a demand for specific performance, may, depending on the language of the indemnity agreement, be sought before making

---

Against its Principal and Indemnitors, in MANAGING AND LITIGATING THE COMPLEX SURETY CASE 115, 120 (Philip L. Bruner & Tracey L. Haley eds., 2d ed. 2007).

any payment under a bond.[7] The clause is a logistical adaptation of the common law rights of exoneration, the right of a surety to compel its principal to pay for a debt for which the surety's liability already has matured,[8] and quia timet, a right used to protect a party against an anticipated future injury when it cannot be avoided by a present action at law.[9] This provision is typically referred to as a "place-in-collateral" provision. There is a developing body of case law specifically addressing the collateral deposit obligation in the context of a commercial surety bond. Commercial bond indemnity agreements often provide that a surety may demand collateral, typically in the form of cash, at any time and for any reason.[10]

Collateral may be demanded upon an "event of default" as defined under the indemnity agreement, representing an extension of the common law right to exoneration or protection from loss. The surety determines the triggering event when negotiating the execution of the indemnity agreement.[11] Typical triggering events for surety to make collateral deposit demand include (but are not limited to): the setting of reserves; the receipt of a claim/demand; the actual incurring of liability; and request by principal to litigate a claim.

For example, in *Safeco Insurance Company of America v. Tarragon Corp.*,[12] a developer bonded off the prime contractor's mechanics lien. The prime contractor sued the developer and surety, and that case was pending. The developer encountered financial difficulties and liquidated certain assets. The surety demanded collateral and, when it was not provided, sued the developer on the indemnity agreement and for quia timet relief. The developer moved to dismiss the suit for failure to state a claim and the surety moved for an order directing the developer to deposit collateral equal to the amount of the bond. The court found that

---

7   *See generally* Briglia, Pipkin & Olson, *supra* note 3, at 284-290; Shahinian, Brown & Monaghan, *supra* note 6, at 138-45.
8   *See* BLACK'S LAW DICTIONARY 597 (7th ed. 1999).
9   *See* BLACK'S LAW DICTIONARY 1260 (7th ed. 1999).
10 *See* Bruce C. King, Julia Blackwell Gelinas, & James S. Kreamer, *Commercial Surety Indemnity Agreement Issues*, in THE SURETY'S INDEMNITY AGREEMENT: LAW & PRACTICE 447, 469-70 (Marilyn Klinger, George J. Bachrach & Tracey L. Haley eds., 2d ed. 2008).
11 *See* Briglia, Pipkin & Olson, *supra* note 3, at 285-86.
12 No. 2:07-cv-760-FtM-29DNF, 2008 WL 4279691 (M.D. Fla. Sept. 16, 2008).

the allegations of the complaint supported the surety's claims for breach of contract, quia timet, exoneration and specific performance of the collateral deposit provision of the indemnity agreement.[13] The court denied the developer's motion to dismiss. Although the court acknowledged that deposit of collateral security provisions are enforceable, it denied the surety's motion for immediate deposit of collateral because the evidence did not clearly establish a basis for the relief requested.[14]

The obligation to post collateral typically arises at the time a reserve is set by the surety, or even in some cases, "the indemnity agreement provides [the surety] with the right to be collateralized when, in it its sole judgment, it determines that potential liability exists."[15] The courts have consistently held the collateral deposit obligation to be valid and have upheld the surety's right to recovery from indemnitors who failed to post collateral.

Depending on the language of the indemnity agreement, the demand for collateral may occur only in regard to actual or threatened loss, or more generally, at the sole determination of the surety that the deposit is necessary to secure surety's guaranty.[16] However, if the surety makes demand that collateral be deposited, it will likely have to demonstrate a rational basis for the nature and approximate amount of collateral demanded.[17] For example, in *Great American Insurance Co. v. General Contractors & Construction Management, Inc.*,[18] where the indemnity agreement provided that the indemnitors were obligated to exonerate the surety against liability as soon as liability existed or was asserted against the surety (whether or not surety has made any payment related to such liability), the court held that the surety had the right to demand and receive collateral from the principal because the surety had a rational basis for its fear that it would suffer a loss based on the claim that had been made against the surety.[19] The other key issue that a court may struggle with is what amount of collateral is appropriate. Even where a

---

13 *See id.*
14 *Id.* at *4.
15 Liberty Mut. Ins. Co. v. Aventura Eng'g & Constr. Corp., 534 F. Supp. 2d 1290, 1322 (S.D. Fla. 2008).
16 *See* Briglia, Pipkin & Olson, *supra* note 3, at 287.
17 *See, e.g.*, Transamerica Premium Ins. Co. v. Cavalry Constr., Inc., 552 So. 2d 225 (Fla. Dist. Ct. App. 1989).
18 No. 07-21489-CIV, 2008 WL 2245986 (S.D. Fla. May 29, 2008).
19 *Id.* at *5.

court is willing to enforce the collateral deposit obligation, it may have difficulty determining what amount of collateral is appropriate. While the surety will typically take the position that the collateral should cover the penal sum of the bond, a court may limit the collateral required to the amount of the surety's imminent exposure to loss.

In any event, the ability to demand collateral to exonerate any actual or potential losses provides the surety with a very strong basis to mitigate its losses. Aside from the literal minimization of loss that the posting of collateral can provide to a surety, having a court order the specific performance of a deposit of collateral also signals to the indemnitors that the indemnity agreement will be enforced,[20] and can therefore encourage the cooperation of the third-party indemnitors.

B. The UCC Provision

The UCC provision is frequently read in tandem with the assignment and right-to-settle provisions. The following is a commonly found UCC recording provision:

> This Agreement shall constitute a Security Agreement to Surety and also a Financing Statement, both in accordance with the provisions of the Uniform Commercial Code of every jurisdiction wherein such Code is in effect, but the filing or recording of this Agreement shall be solely at the option of the Surety, and the failure to do so shall not release or impair any of the obligations of the Indemnitor under this Agreement or otherwise arising, nor shall such failure be in any manner in derogation of the rights of the Surety under this Agreement or otherwise.

This indemnity agreement provision constitutes not only a Security Agreement, but also a Financing Statement under the UCC. It provides the surety with the option to either file the indemnity agreement as a UCC Financing Statement ("UCC-1") or to rely on the express terms of the indemnity agreement and the surety's rights of equitable subrogation. This provision is typically utilized in conjunction with the power-of-attorney clause, giving the surety the right to execute all necessary documents to effect assignments made in the indemnity agreement.

---

20   *See* Shahinian, Brown & Monaghan, *supra* note 6, at 140 (citing multiple cases upholding the collateral deposit demand provision in favor of the surety).

There does not appear to be any case law challenging or interpreting this provision and its use is more of a practical question than a legal one, largely because the rights provided to the surety in the indemnity agreement attach at the time the agreement is executed,[21] and thus become immediately enforceable against the indemnitors. However, the establishment of a priority over another creditor to whom the indemnitors may have granted a security interest can only be achieved through perfection of the indemnity agreement.

In other words, if another creditor has been granted an interest in property of the principal or indemnitor, and the surety exercises its rights under this provision by filing the indemnity agreement as a UCC-1, the surety will obtain priority rights to materials, equipment and other property owned by the principal and described in the indemnity agreement against any subsequent filer. Filing also puts other creditors on notice of the surety's position. Best practices would dictate that a surety should always file the indemnity agreement in order to protect its priority secured interest. From a practical sense, however, the perfection of the indemnity agreement through the filing of a UCC-1 is often delayed until it is too late to be effective.

For a variety of reasons, sureties have historically avoided filing a UCC-1 until the principal is in financial difficulty or in default under the terms of the indemnity agreement.[22] For example, sureties may not want to incur the time and expense of filing the indemnity agreement. Additionally, there is a perception that the filing of a UCC-1 will have a negative market effect on the principal. A lender may be hesitant to provide capital to a principal if the lender's security interest in inventory and receivables is not the first-priority interest. However, these concerns can be (and often are) dealt with through negotiated inter-creditor agreements.

If provided for in the language of the agreement, the indemnity agreement should be filed as a UCC-1. But as stated above, an issue only

---

21 More precisely, attachment occurs once the secured party (surety) gives value, the debtor (principal) executes the security agreement (Indemnity Agreement), and the debtor (principal) has rights in the collateral or the power to transfer those rights. *See* U.C.C. § 9-203 (1998). Generally all three conditions are present at the time the Indemnity Agreement is executed. *See* Briglia, Pipkin & Olson, *supra* note 3, at 316.

22 *See* Briglia, Pipkin & Olson, *supra* note 3, at 318.

arises if there are other secured creditors with a superior perfected interest. Otherwise, the indemnity agreement is a security instrument under the terms of the UCC and standing alone, it provides the surety with the ability to enforce the rights granted under the indemnity agreement against the principal, the indemnitors and third parties as of the date of execution of the indemnity agreement.[23]

C. *Power-of-Attorney or Attorney-in-Fact*

An enormously important clause included in the indemnity agreement is the power-of-attorney or "attorney-in-fact" clause. The clause will generally spell out what specific authority is being granted to the surety.[24] The clause typically grants the surety, or its designated representative, the power to execute and deliver all necessary agreements and documents to vest title in the surety with regard to monies, properties and other rights assigned under the agreement.[25] It also allows the surety to assert claims in its own name or in the name of its principal against owners and subcontractors for the collection of accounts receivable and amounts due on bonded or unbonded contracts. Finally, it can also permit the surety to execute lien documents against the assets of the principal and the indemnitors, including mortgages and deeds of trust.[26]

This clause will be read in conjunction with, and frequently as giving effect to, the other substantive rights created in the indemnity agreement.[27] If the rights granted under the indemnity agreement are thought of as being held in a vault, the attorney-in-fact provision operates as the key that opens the vault door, especially if the indemnitors refuse

---

23 *See id.* at 316, 318.
24 Some clauses are carefully worded to state that the surety has the right, power and authority, *but not the obligation*, to serve as attorney-in-fact for the principal. *See* James P. Diwik, Denise C. Puente & Carol Z. Smith, *The Surety's Enforcement of its Rights of Reimbursement (Indemnity), in* THE SURETY'S INDEMNITY AGREEMENT: LAW & PRACTICE 225, 234-35 (Marilyn Klinger, George J. Bachrach & Tracey L Haley eds., 2d ed. 2008).
25 *See also generally* THE SURETY'S INDEMNITY AGREEMENT: LAW & PRACTICE (Marilyn Klinger, George J. Bachrach & Tracey L Haley eds., 2d ed. 2008).
26 *See* Diwik, Puente & Smith, *supra* note 24, at 235.
27 *See* Shahinian, Brown & Monaghan, *supra* note 6, at 160.

to cooperate.[28] For example, an assignment clause will often be coupled with the attorney-in-fact provision so that the surety can undertake the logistical steps necessary to enforce its right to take absolute and immediate title to supplies, materials, and property assigned to it.[29] Another example includes the importance of the attorney-in-fact provision as it relates to the right-to-settle provision. In *Liberty Mutual Insurance Co. v. Aventura Engineering & Construction Corp.*,[30] the court unambiguously found that the right-to-settle provision, read with the assignment and attorney-in-fact provisions, gave the surety the right, "at its option and sole discretion," to settle or compromise any claim or demand upon any bond.[31] The provision is also important when filing the indemnity agreement as a UCC-1 financing statement.[32] Essentially, the attorney-in-fact provision provides the surety with the tools needed to exercise the rights granted under the indemnity agreement.

D. Assignment of Contract Rights and Subcontracts, Including Receivables on Bonded and Unbonded Contracts

An important preliminary discussion is whether the indemnity agreement assignments of contract rights, subcontracts, property rights, affirmative claims and others, are to be read as "absolute" assignments or assignments for security. An absolute assignment divests the assignor of all rights and interest in the assigned property; whereas, an assignment as security restricts the recovery of an assignment up to the secured amount. Typically, the indemnity agreement is drafted in such way to imply that the

---

28   *See generally* Diwik, Puente & Smith, *supra* note 24, at 234.
29   For example, in *Hutton Construction Co. v. County of Rockland*, 52 F.3d 1191 (2d Cir. 1995), the court found that the right-to-settle provision in the Indemnity Agreement standing alone did not give the surety the power to settle the contractor's affirmative claims. However, the right-to-settle clause, when applied in conjunction with the assignment of claims provision *and the attorney-in-fact provision*, did give such a right. *See also* Shahinian, Brown & Monaghan, *supra* note 6, at 149.
30   534 F. Supp. 2d 1290 (S.D. Fla. 2008).
31   *Id.* at 1308.
32   *See* Diwik, Puente & Smith, *supra* note 24, at 232.

assignments contained therein were made as security and not intended to be absolute assignments.[33]

A typical assignment of contract rights provision may read in pertinent part:

> Effective in the event of a default,[34] the Indemnitor(s) do assign, transfer, and convey to the surety, as of the date of execution of any bond (a) all the rights of the Indemnitor(s) in, and growing in any manner out of the Bonds or any contracts referred to in the Bonds as well as (b) all the rights, title and interest of the Indemnitor(s) in and to all subcontracts let or to be let in connection with any and all contracts referred to in the Bonds, and in and to all surety bonds supporting such subcontracts.

Historically, this assignment of rights has not been a frequent topic of litigation. On the one hand, it could be argued that the provision is superfluous because of a surety's right of equitable subrogation with regards to the contract balances.[35] However, with the indemnity agreement in hand, a surety can easily and without litigation demonstrate to an owner/obligee that it has the right, title and interest in the contract balances. Having a fully executed contractual assignment provides the surety with unambiguous, written evidence of this right. The contractual assignment also gives the surety the right to recover bonded contract balances from all projects to offset all losses. In contrast, if a surety relies solely on its common law rights, it may be restricted to application of bonded contract proceeds to losses on the project from which the funds were received.

Demonstrating the significance of the assignment clause, the United States District Court for the District of Maryland relied on the

---

33   *See* J. Michael Franks, Matthew M. Horowitz & Cynthia E. Rodgers-Waire, *Documents and Agreements Related to the Indemnity Agreement*, *in* THE SURETY'S INDEMNITY AGREEMENT: LAW & PRACTICE 103, 142 (Marilyn Klinger, George J. Bachrach & Tracey L Haley eds., 2d ed. 2008).

34   Note that the "event of default" referenced in the Indemnity Agreement provision refers to an event of default *as defined under the Indemnity Agreement.*

35   *See* Nat'l Sur. Corp. v. Allen-Codell Co., 70 F. Supp. 189, 191 (E.D. Ky. 1947).

assignment of contract rights provision of an indemnity agreement in holding that an anti-assignment clause in the contract between the general contractor on project at a municipal waste disposal site and the site owner did not bar assignment of general contractor's claims to its surety, where, in light of routine practice and tradition in the construction industry, a reasonable person in the position of the parties to this three-way relationship would understand the anti-assignment clause to be inapplicable to surety.[36] The court in *Handex* found that the subrogation rights of the surety did not need to be addressed because the surety's rights under the indemnity agreement had resolved the question.[37] This case emphasizes that the surety's rights under the indemnity agreement not only complement its common law rights, but serve to supplant the common law rights in certain cases.

In *Harlandale Independent School District v. C2M Construction, Inc.*,[38] the principal sued the owner of a project for breach of contract. The owner sought dismissal for lack of standing on the grounds that the principal had assigned its right to bring the cause of action against the owner in its indemnity agreement with its surety. The principal, in turn, argued that the indemnity agreement in question did not specifically assign causes of action against the owner and therefore, it had standing to file suit.[39] The Texas Court of Appeals reversed the trial court and found in favor of the owner, specifically holding that the principal lacked standing because the indemnity agreement assigned "all rights 'in, and growing in any manner out of' the construction contract." Therefore, the assignment to the surety included the cause of action against the owner.[40]

Although the assignment of contract balances has not frequently been the subject of either use or dispute between sureties and indemnitors, these two examples demonstrate that the assignment of contract balances and subcontract rights can be critically important to a surety's success in mitigating its losses.

---

36 Handex of Md., Inc. v. Waste Mgmt. Disposal Servs. of Md., Inc., 458 F. Supp. 2d 266 (D. Md. 2006).
37 *Id.* at 274. While the court did discuss subrogation, it first stated, "[b]ecause the issues raised by Great American's motion can be disposed of without reaching the question of subrogation, the Court will discuss the issue only briefly here." *Id.*
38 No. 04-07-00304-CV, 2007 WL 2253510 (Tex. App. Aug. 8, 2007).
39 *Id.* at *2.
40 *Id.* at *3.

The indemnity agreement may also provide that effective upon default,[41] but retroactive to the date of the first bond written, the principal (and the indemnitors) assign to the surety payments due under all contracts, both bonded and unbonded. This will include not only contract balances due under those contracts but also claims for extras and other additional monies. The provision also will assign to the surety the right to prosecute the claims to their conclusion.

1. Contract Proceeds

The surety generally will proceed to collect contract proceeds under the surety's right of equitable subrogation, rather than relying upon the standard indemnity agreement assignment clause. However, there are circumstances where the indemnity agreement will provide the surety with a greater opportunity to recover contract proceeds and mitigate its losses than the equitable right. In the case of *United States v. MidPac Lumber Co.*,[42] the surety was denied a right of setoff against an IRS levy because the bonds did not provide for profits from one job to be setoff against unrelated debts. However, the court reviewed the assignment language of the indemnity agreement and said that it might defeat the IRS levy if the evidence at trial established that a true assignment was intended rather than a security agreement under Hawaii's version of the UCC.[43]

There are a number of cases which discuss the surety's contractual rights as assignee of the principal to obtain contract balances, earned but unpaid requisition payments, retainages and extra work claims, but most are decided pursuant to equitable principles of subrogation.[44] For

---

41 Note that the "event of default" referenced in the Indemnity Agreement provision refers to an event of default as defined under the Indemnity Agreement.
42 976 F. Supp. 1310 (D. Haw. 1997).
43 *Id.* at 1317.
44 *See* Balboa Ins. Co. v. Bank of Boston Connecticut, 702 F. Supp. 34 (D. Conn. 1988); *In re* V. Pangori & Sons, Inc., 53 B.R. 711 (Bankr. E.D. Mich. 1985); Transamerica Ins. Co. v. Barnett Bank of Marion County, N.A., 540 So.2d 113 (Fla. 1989); Old Kent Bank-Southeast v. City of Detroit, 444 N.W.2d 162 (Mich. Ct. App. 1989); Earl Dubey & Sons, Inc. v. Macomb Contracting Corp., 296 N.W.2d 582 (Mich. Ct. App. 1980);

example, the Sixth Circuit in *Kentucky Central Insurance Co. v. Brown (In re Larbar Corp.)*,[45] found that the surety was entitled to rely on its equitable subrogation rights to recover contract proceeds after its lien rights derived from the indemnity agreement failed due to belated perfection of the agreement.[46] Many cases have held that performing sureties are entitled to funds from other contracts for the same obligee.[47] With respect to collection by the surety of contract funds on contracts or projects on which it has not suffered a loss, the same is true.[48] Referring again to *Larbar*, the surety was able to set off contract balances from one project of the principal against balances from another project because its equitable subrogation rights (to step into its principal's shoes) caused the surety to meet the mutuality requirement for setoff under Section 553 of the Bankruptcy Code.[49] Absent the rights of equitable subrogation (or a similar right in an indemnity agreement), the surety would not be able to make such a claim to contract balances due to the principal on another bonded contract where no surety losses had been incurred.

Despite the court's general reliance on the principle of equitable subrogation when awarding contract proceeds to a surety, the indemnity agreement contractual arrangement serves an important purpose. Although equitable subrogation will provide the surety with a strong basis for recovery of contract proceeds, the doctrine creates no right to recover expenses in investigating and defending claims, nor does it allow the surety to lay claim to its principal's tools, equipment or inventory.[50] The indemnity agreement casts a wider net of recovery, demonstrating yet another example of the great advantages and additional rights that are available under the indemnity agreement. These additional rights and

---

Interfirst Bank Dallas, N.A. v. United States Fid. & Guar. Co., 774 S.W.2d 391 (Tex. App. 1989).
45   177 F.3d 439 (6th Cir. 1999).
46   *Id.* at 443.
47   Transamerica Ins. Co. v. United States, 989 F.2d 1188 (Fed. Cir. 1993); U.S. Fid. & Guar. Co. v. Hous. Auth. of Berwick, 557 F.2d 482 (5th Cir. 1977); Dist. of Columbia v. Aetna Ins. Co., 462 A.2d 428 (D.C. 1983). *But see* Ram Constr. Co., Inc. v. Am. States Ins. Co., 749 F.2d 1049 (3d Cir. 1984); W. Cas. & Sur. Co. v. Brooks, 362 F.2d 486 (4th Cir. 1966).
48   *See* Gray v. Travelers Indem. Co., 280 F.2d 549, 553 (9th Cir. 1960).
49   *In re* Larbar, 177 F.3d at 446-47.
50   Shahinian, Brown & Monaghan, *supra* note 6, at 148-49.

recovery options can be of great importance to a surety attempting to complete a job while mitigating its losses.

2. Claims

The assignment-of-receivables provision also assigns to the surety the principal's claims against others and proceeds obtained therefrom. This portion of the clause is generally enforceable.[51] In the case of *In re Alcon Demolition, Inc.*,[52] the principal's claim against the obligee for extra funds was enforced and the surety granted entitlement to the proceeds of an arbitration award. In *Amwest Surety Insurance Co. v. United States National Bank of Oregon (In re Comcraft, Inc.)*,[53] funds paid by the obligee to the principal were found to be held by the principal in constructive trust for laborers and materialmen and the surety's equitable lien followed the funds into the hands of the principal with a corresponding right of the surety to defeat the claim of a secured creditor.

In another case, *Handex of Maryland, Inc. v. Waste Management Disposal Services of Maryland, Inc.*,[54] the court held that the assignment of a principal's claims against the owner/obligee under its indemnity agreement was enforceable, notwithstanding an anti-assignment clause in the general contract. Specifically, the court found that the anti-assignment clause in the bonded contract (where the owner did not explicitly bar assignment of the principal's claims to its surety), in light of routine practice and tradition in the construction industry, a reasonable person in the position of the parties to this three-way relationship would understand the anti-assignment clause to be inapplicable to surety.[55]

E. Assignment of Material and Equipment on Bonded Projects

indemnity agreements frequently include language assigning to the surety rights to materials and equipment needed for completion of the bonded projects. Without the indemnity agreement, the surety would

---

51 *See generally id.* at 149; Briglia, Pipkin & Olson, *supra* note 3, at 312.
52 204 B.R. 440 (Bankr. D.N.J. 1997).
53 206 B.R. 551 (Bankr. D. Or. 1997).
54 458 F. Supp. 2d 266 (D. Md. 2006).
55 *Id.* at 273.

have a much more difficult argument claiming a right to the equipment. A common assignment provision reads as follows:

> Effective in the event of default, the indemnitors(s) assign, transfer and convey to the surety: all of the right, title and interest in and to supplies, tools, plant, equipment and materials (whether completely manufactured or not) of every nature and description that are or hereafter may be ordered or purchased for use in performing any contract or may be in, or about the site upon which such a contract is being performed.

In the past, conflicts regarding this provision have arisen in the context of disputes between the surety and the principal's secured creditor. If the indemnity agreement is perfected by filing under the UCC, the question, generally, is one of priority rather than of the terms, validity and enforceability of the assignment provision. However, even if another creditor has a prior-perfected interest in the material and equipment of a principal, the surety has not completely lost the ability to mitigate its losses. Frequently, the surety and the secured lender will enter into a separate equipment utilization agreement whereby the surety rents or leases the materials and equipment needed for completion of a project from the secured lender.[56] Thus, in the case where no other creditor has a prior interest, the indemnity agreement provides the surety with the unambiguous, written assignment of the property, which it can use to either utilize the materials and equipment to complete the job, or sell the materials and equipment to recover losses. In the case where a prior creditor does exist, and assuming the surety does not have the prior-perfected UCC filing, there still remain viable options for reducing the surety's loss.

In *United States Fidelity & Guaranty Company v. United Penn Bank*,[57] a Pennsylvania court addressed the respective priorities of a surety and secured lender as to the inventory purchased for a bonded project, but not paid for by the principal. When the principal defaulted on its loan, the secured creditor took a confessed judgment against the principal and then levied on the materials. The property was sold at a sheriff's auction and the proceeds, placed in escrow, were claimed by both the surety and the lender.

---

56 *See* Franks, Horowitz & Rodgers-Waire, *supra* note 33, at 163-64.
57 524 A.2d 958 (Pa. Super. Ct. 1987).

The lender asserted priority by virtue of its prior perfected security agreement under the UCC. The surety asserted priority under the theory of equitable subrogation (not under the indemnity agreement), stating that because the suppliers demanded payment, it "would be" obligated to pay these claims, and therefore it was equitably subrogated to the rights of the suppliers to recover the sale proceeds.[58] Adopting the line of thought that the surety would have priority to the proceeds to reimburse it for claims paid under the bond, the court concluded that the doctrine of equitable subrogation did not apply unless and until the surety had paid the outstanding debts of its principal or sustained a loss by reason of the suretyship. However, even if the surety had paid the supplier, the Pennsylvania court held that the surety would nonetheless have obtained no priority to the proceeds from the sale of the inventory because the surety would assume only the position of the supplier that sold the materials on credit and thus became a general unsecured creditor subject to the bank's UCC filing.[59]

Similarly, in *State Bank & Trust Co. v. Insurance Co. of the West*,[60] the Fifth Circuit agreed that equitable subrogation did not create priority rights in material and equipment of the principal over the interests of a secured lender. Specifically, the court held that

> when tangible personal property—distinct from contract proceeds—is at issue, the rationale for elevating the surety over the secured creditor has no application. Unlike the contractor's inchoate or potential rights in the contract proceeds, the contractor comes into the construction contract with present and effective ownership and the right to possess and use its own tools, equipment, and inventory. If the contractor has previously given a creditor a security interest in these materials—even those subsequently acquired—the creditor's right to realize on its collateral is not contingent on the contractor's full performance of its obligations.[61]

In other words, the surety may not be able to rely upon its equitable subrogation rights to take a priority interest in materials and equipment over that of a secured lender with a perfected interest in the property.

---

58   *Id.* at 963.
59   *Id.* at 965.
60   132 F.3d 203 (5th Cir. 1997).
61   *Id.* at 207.

One exception could be based upon the decision rendered in *Havens Steel Co. v. Commerce Bank (In re Havens Steel Co.)*,[62] in which the bankruptcy court held that an owner which had purchased project materials, but which materials had not yet been delivered to the project site, had a priority interest in the materials over the secured lender to the manufacturer of the materials.[63] The interest was ascribed to the owner based on a theory of constructive possession, which entitled the owner to "buyer-in-the-ordinary-course" status. The *Havens Steel* case was based on a thorough analysis of the UCC. A careful analysis of state law on secured transactions and equitable liens is necessary to evaluate the surety's rights to materials absent the surety's first priority, perfected security interest. A situation could arise where a surety performs under its performance bond, thus subrogating to the rights of its principal and the owner of a project, such that the surety could then assert a superior claim (under *Havens Steel*) to project materials that have been paid for by the owner. Note that an indemnity agreement in a junior priority position has little value with regard to materials, equipment and/or inventory. In such a case, the surety's fate will be determined through traditional equitable subrogation rights.

On the other hand, where the indemnity agreement assigns such rights, there is no question that the surety is entitled to recover the given equipment and materials, including materials that are on-site as well as materials that have been purchased and are in transit, in production, or in storage off-site.[64] Furthermore, if the indemnity agreement is perfected prior to a secured lender with an interest in the same materials, then the surety's rights will prevail.[65] This is another instance where the indemnity agreement can provide greater rights than what may be available under equitable subrogation.

---

62   317 B.R. 75 (Bankr. W.D. Mo. 2004), *rev'd on other grounds*, No. 04-41574-(JWV), 2005 U.S. Dist. LEXIS 16859 (W.D. Mo. Jan. 12, 2005).
63   *Id.* at 88.
64   *See* Shahinian, Brown & Monaghan, *supra* note 6, at 149.
65   *See generally*, Aetna Cas. & Sur. Co. v. J.F. Bunken & Son, Inc., 357 F. Supp. 290, 293 (D. S.D. 1973) (failure to file and perfect Article 9 security interests in compliance with U.C.C. § 9-102 provisions is fatal to a surety's claim on personal property).

F. Right of Surety to Takeover or Complete Performance of Bonded Contracts

A common takeover provision found in an indemnity agreement may read:

> In the event of default, the surety, in its sole discretion, is hereby authorized, but not required, to take possession of the work under any contract and, at the expense of the indemnitor, to complete the contract, or cause same to be completed, or to consent to the completion thereof, and to take any other action which the surety may deem appropriate to obtain the discharge of the surety's obligations as surety for the indemnitor including, but not limited to, a monetary settlement with the obligee at the indemnitor's expense.

This provision provides the surety with at least three distinct performance options in the event of default as defined under the indemnity agreement:[66] (1) complete the contract, (2) cause the contract to be completed, or (3) consent to the completion.[67] There is very little litigation on the takeover provision under the indemnity agreement, with one likely reason being that the performance bond typically governs this issue, and the myriad cases on takeover issues center around performance bond claims. Additionally, takeover issues generally occur with respect to the obligee as opposed to the principal and indemnitors.

In addition to the three common completion options found in many indemnity agreements, the provision above also grants to the surety blanket, "catch all" discretion to take any other action which the surety deems appropriate in order to obtain its discharge. This blanket discretion can be especially important when faced with a principal defending an indemnity action on the grounds that the surety "should not have paid." The phrase also

---

66 Note that the rights under the Indemnity Agreement should not be confused with the surety's rights and obligations under the Performance Bond itself.

67 Additional takeover options provided in an Indemnity Agreement include buying back the bond through a cash payment to the obligee and denying liability to the obligee. *See* M. Michael Egan, Jr., Omar J. Harb, & Brett D. Divers, *The Indemnity Agreement and the Handling of Surety Claims, in* THE SURETY'S INDEMNITY AGREEMENT: LAW & PRACTICE 323, 363 (Marilyn Klinger, George J. Bachrach & Tracey L. Haley eds., 2d ed. 2008).

bolsters the surety's position when urging courts to broadly interpret the overall clause.

Even absent a "catch-all" phrase, however, at least one court has held that while parties may expressly limit remedies by agreement, if a remedy is to be exclusive, "the contract must clearly indicate that the parties intend that the stipulated remedy be the sole or exclusive remedy."[68] In *Windowmaster Corp. v. Morse/Diesel, Inc.*,[69] the surety arranged completion of a defaulted contract with the owner by letter agreement. It utilized the defaulted principal to complete the work as well as his equipment and materials and advanced funds to pay subcontractors and suppliers.[70] The indemnitors claimed that the surety was limited exclusively to the three specific performance options contained in the indemnity agreement and argued that since the surety's actions did not conform strictly to one of the three remedies set forth in the clause, the surety could not recover against the indemnitors to recoup the loss.[71] The trial court found that the surety's options were "nonexclusive" and while no formal takeover agreement or financing documents existed, the facts demonstrated elements of both takeover and completion and financing by the surety. Therefore, the surety was granted summary judgment against the indemnitors. Thus, despite the absence of the "catch-all" language, the indemnity agreement terms prevailed, with the court finding that the letter agreement was an additional remedy available to the surety.

In *Fidelity & Deposit Co. of Maryland. v. A-Mac Sales & Builders Co.*,[72] the United States District Court for the Eastern District of Michigan held, as a matter of law, that surety had the right to undertake and complete the project in the manner of its choosing, pursuant to the terms of the respective indemnity agreement, which provided:

---

68 Windowmaster Corp. v. Morse/Diesel, Inc., 722 F. Supp. 1530, 1531 (N.D. Ill. 1988) (citations omitted), *vacated on other grounds*, Windowmaster Corp. v. Morse/Diesel, Inc., 722 F. Supp. 1532 (N.D. Ill. 1988).
69 722 F. Supp. 1530 (N.D. Ill. 1988).
70 *Id.* at 1530-31.
71 *Id.* at 1531.
72 No. 04-72643, 2006 WL 1555985 (E.D. Mich. June 5, 2006) (holding that indemnity takeover provision was sufficient for the court to grant summary judgment in favor of the surety regarding its right to takeover and complete the contract).

> SIXTH: In the event of any breach or default asserted by the obligee in any said Bonds, or the Contractor has abandoned the work on or forfeited any contracts covered by any said Bonds, or has failed to pay obligations incurred in connection therewith...the Surety shall have the right, at its option and in its sole discretion and is hereby authorized, with or without exercising any other right or option conferred upon it by law or in the terms of this Agreement, to take possession of any part or all of the work under any contract or contracts covered by any said Bonds, and at the expense of the Contractor and Indemnitors to complete or arrange for the completion of the same, and the Contractor and Indemnitors shall promptly upon demand pay to the Surety all losses, and expenses so incurred.[73]

Because the indemnity agreement in the *A-Mac Sales* case was void of ambiguity, the district court of Michigan determined that the surety could only be at fault (at best) if it exercised its sole discretion on completion of the contract in bad faith. On this point, the court held that the indemnitors "offered no basis for concluding that Plaintiff did not act in good faith in taking over the Project (assuming that there was such an implied covenant of good faith)."[74]

Notwithstanding the cases finding that the surety may freely exercise its "sole discretion" with respect to taking "other action deemed appropriate to discharge its obligations," the case of *Howell Construction, Inc. v. United Pacific Insurance Co.*,[75] circumscribed, at least in part, the extent of a surety's recovery options. The court in *Howell Construction* held that a surety which took over and completed construction of the project, thus discharging the obligations of the principal, was required to pay over to the principal all contract funds paid by the owner which were in excess of the surety's cost to complete (including the surety's costs and reasonable expenses).[76] Interpreting the indemnity agreement assignment as an assignment of security, as opposed to an absolute assignment, the court held that a surety who discharges obligation of its principal, even under an assignment from principal's creditor or obligee, may not thereafter realize a profit from its assignment.[77] This scenario is the

---

73 *Id.* at *4 (emphasis added).
74 *Id.* at *7 (parenthetical in original).
75 824 F. Supp. 105 (W.D. Ky. 1993).
76 *Id.* at 108.
77 *Id.* at 107.

exception and a surety which has been fully compensated rarely seeks to further profit from the principal's default. This case merely prevents a windfall to the surety and does not curtail its broad rights of recovery while it continues to suffer a loss.

G. Surety's Right to Finance Principal and Recover Financing Under Indemnity Agreement

If the principal is unable to perform solely because of the lack of financial resources, a surety may finance the principal to completion by paying the principal's bills as they become due. This option is most attractive when a shutdown of the project may result in substantial liquidated damages or the project is substantially complete. Without the indemnity agreement, the surety, as a financier, would not be able to recover its extension of funds or credit through the common law rights available to a performing surety for a defaulted principal (including equitable subrogation). However, by including the "right to finance" provision, the surety can mitigate its losses not only by funding a principal in an appropriate situation, but also by retaining the right to recover that funding under the indemnity agreement.

An illustrative financing provision is as follows:

> The surety at its sole election and discretion, is authorized and empowered but not obligated, to advance or loan to the principal any money which the surety may see fit to advance to said principal, and all monies so loaned or advanced, as well as all costs, counsel fees and expenses incurred by the surety in connection with such advances or loans, unless repaid with legal interest by the principal shall be a loss by the surety for which the indemnitor shall be responsible.

The key elements of this provision include the surety's ability to loan funds to its principal and have those loans be "loss payments" under the bond, and thus reimbursable to the surety. It may be disputed whether this type of provision is broad enough in scope to include indirect credit supplied by the surety including bank loans guaranteed by the surety, or whether it addresses loans made to the surety. A provision stating that the indemnitors are obligated to reimburse the surety for any type of "financial accommodation" made by the surety should remove any question about the surety's right of reimbursement from the indemnitors.

Although decided on other grounds, the outcome of *City of Kansas City, Missouri v. Tri-City Construction Co.*[78] supports the proposition that financing constitutes a loss to the surety as stated in the provision illustrated above. The United States District Court for the Western District of Missouri found that where a principal failed to pay its bills on time, it was in default under the indemnity agreement, even though it had not been declared to be in default by the owner. It was held that the surety's subsequent financing of the principal through its payment of subcontractors was just as much a loss entitling the surety to priority to contract balances over the IRS, as if payment bond claims had been paid directly by the surety.[79]

Also, the case of *Windowmaster Corp. v. Morse/Diesel, Inc.*[80] confirms that financing is a viable performance alternative for the surety under the indemnity agreement and that indemnitors will be responsible to repay such losses.[81]

Although not addressing recovery where a surety has opted to provide its principal with funding, the court in *Granite Computer Leasing Corp. v. Travelers Indemnity Co.*,[82] held that there is no legal support for the proposition that a surety is obligated to finance its principal. This case supports the provision of the indemnity agreement stating that the surety is empowered "but not obligated . . . to advance or loan to the contractor any money . . . ."

Before financing any principal (aside from indirect financing through the payment of payment bond claims), the surety should obtain a well-drafted financing agreement, promissory note, and security interest (if applicable) to make it clear exactly what obligations the surety is assuming.[83] The financing agreement should make it clear that the surety

---

78 666 F. Supp. 170 (W.D. Mo. 1987).
79 *Id.* at 172.
80 722 F. Supp. 1530 (N.D. Ill. 1988), *vacated on other grounds*, 722 F. Supp. 1532 (N.D. Ill. 1988).
81 *Id.* at 1531.
82 582 F. Supp. 1279 (S.D.N.Y. 1984), *rev'd on other grounds*, 751 F.2d 543 (2d Cir. 1984).
83 James E. McFadden, Inc. v. Baltimore Contractors, Inc., 609 F. Supp. 1102 (E.D. Pa. 1985) (determining that the surety did not take absolute and total control of contractor, but merely took steps to minimize its risks as a major creditor of it, and thus contractor did not become instrumentality of the bonding company by virtue of the financing

may terminate funding at any time and at the surety's sole and absolute discretion. Absent a clear written agreement to this effect, a principal/indemnitor may assert a "failure to fund" as an affirmative defense, i.e. that the failure to continue funding caused the loss to occur.

H. Designation of Contract Funds as Trust Funds

The inclusion of a trust fund provision in the indemnity agreement springs from the equitable trust or equitable lien theory espoused in *Pearlman v. Reliance Insurance Co.*[84] The provision is designed to establish trust fund rights in contract funds, with the indemnitors serving as the trustee(s) and the surety as the beneficiary. The intended funds to be held in trust include funds that the principal has already received, future payments owed to the principal (i.e. progress payments and/or retainage), as well as payments in the hands of others.[85] There are limitations and restrictions in the application of a trust fund theory. However, in general, the requirements to form a trust are: (1) a manifestation of an intent to create a trust, (2) a properly designated trust property, and (3) designated trust beneficiaries.[86]

One illustrative provision states:

> The indemnitor will hold all payments received pursuant to any contract as a trust fund for the payment of obligations incurred for labor, materials and services furnished for use in the prosecution of work required by the contracts.[87]

---

provided by the surety). In *McFadden*, although the court did not address the indemnity agreement, the court discussed numerous provisions of the financing agreement between the principal and surety, including those regarding repayment of funds advanced or loaned by the surety. *Id.*

84 371 U.S. 132 (1962).
85 *See* Briglia, Pipkin & Olson, *supra* note 3; Shahinian, Brown & Monaghan, *supra* note 6, at 166-67; George J. Bachrach, *The Surety's Right to Obtain Salvage–Exoneration, Reimbursement, Subrogation and Contribution, in* SALVAGE BY THE SURETY 1 (George J. Bachrach ed., 1998).
86 RESTATEMENT (SECOND) OF TRUSTS ch. 2 (1957) (Introductory Note).
87 For a collection of sample trust fund provisions, *see* Briglia, Pipkin & Olson, *supra* note 3, at 291-93.

1. Observe Local Law

The intent to establish a trust and the actual establishment under the law are two distinct occurrences. State law dictates whether a trust has been created,[88] and each jurisdiction may be inclined to interpret a trust fund provision in an indemnity agreement in its own way. Every state has its own peculiar law relative to the creation and enforcement of an express trust.[89] The wording of a particular state statute can vary the general discussions regarding trust fund rights under indemnity agreements, whereas other interpretations may be derived from the general common law of trusts. These features will tend to be the same from state to state, unless a state legislature has enacted a specific law to the contrary. It is imperative to consult local law when considering application of this indemnity agreement provision as an express trust.[90]

2. Courts Finding That a Trust was Formed

Due to the question of dischargeability of debts associated with fraud and/or defalcation as it applies to the debtor's handling of "trust funds," the bankruptcy courts most often address the issue of whether an indemnity agreement has created a trust. For example, after reviewing Pennsylvania and Kentucky law on the establishment of trusts, the Bankruptcy Court for the Western District of Kentucky determined that two separate indemnity agreements each created an express trust imposing fiduciary duties upon the debtor/indemnitors in the case.[91] Similarly, in *International Fidelity Insurance Co. v. Marques (In re*

---

88 Briglia, Pipkin & Olson, *supra* note 3, at 294 (citing *inter alia*, *In re* Johnson, 691 F.2d 249 (6th Cir. 1982); *In re* Pedrazzini, 644 F.2d 756 (9th Cir. 1981); *In re* W. Urethanes, Inc., 61 B.R. 243 (Bankr D. Colo. 1986)).

89 For a complete overview of states' trust fund statutes or other similar laws, *see Survey of Payment Provisions and Trust Fund Statutes*, in CONSTRUCTION LAW SURVIVAL MANUAL (Fullerton & Knowles ed., 2008), available at: http://www.fullertonlaw.com/ 14TrustFundLawsandAgreements.php (last visited July 14, 2008).

90 For an in-depth discussion of specific state laws on the formation of a trust, *see* Briglia, Pipkin & Olson, *supra* note 3, at 294-303.

91 Cumberland Sur. Ins. Co. v. Smith (*In re* Smith), 238 B.R. 664 (Bankr. W.D. Ky. 1999).

Marques),[92] the court held that the indemnity agreement clearly created a trust to the extent the specific conditions precedent were met. Explicitly setting out how the state law trust requirements were met, the court stated that:

> the [Indemnity Agreement] evidences an agreement . . . that all payments received on account of the contract (an ascertainable res) be held in trust (express intent to create a trust) by them (the trustees) for the payment of obligations under the contract and for labor, materials and services furnished in the prosecution of the work provided for in the contract (a sufficiently certain beneficiary). This language or some slight variant thereof has repeatedly been found to constitute an express trust . . . .[93]

Several other cases adopt similar lines of reasoning in finding that a trust was created by the indemnity agreement.[94]

Federal Insurance Co. v. Fifth Third Bank[95] is a demonstrative and frequently cited case finding that a trust was formed by agreement of the parties. Although the case involved a trust provision contained in the general contract, rather than the indemnity agreement, it nevertheless is instructive, and in fact has been interpreted as an indemnity agreement case.[96] The general contract provision in *Federal* read:

> All monies paid on account to any contractor . . . shall be regarded as fund [sic] in his trust for payment of any and all obligations relating to the contract . . . .

---

92 358 B.R. 188 (Bankr. E.D. Pa. 2006).
93 *Id.* at 194.
94 *See* Int'l Fid. Ins. Co. v. Fox (*In re* Fox), 357 B.R. 770, 772 (Bankr. E.D. Ark. 2006); Wright v. Gulf Ins. Co. (*In re* Wright), 266 B.R. 848, 851 (Bankr. E.D. Ark. 2001); *In re* Alcon Demolition, Inc., 204 B.R. 440 (Bankr. D.N.J. 1997).
95 867 F.2d 330 (6th Cir. 1989).
96 *See In re* Smith, 238 B.R. 664. Interestingly, the court in *Smith* specifically referred to the construction contract in the *Federal* case as a "general agreement of indemnity." *Id.* at 672 (stating that the *Federal* case "involved the question of whether a substantively identical provision in a general indemnity agreement created an express trust").

The principal's bank offset monies in the principal's account, including bonded job progress payments, due to a loan default. The surety alleged wrongful offset by the bank as to the progress payments which, in the surety's opinion, were trust funds under the contract. The surety also alleged it was subrogated to the rights of the subcontractors, suppliers, and vendors (and thus the protection of the trust fund provision) by reason of having performed and paid contract obligations.

The issue was whether a trust fund was created for the benefit of the subcontractors and suppliers and which of the two competing parties would prevail. There was no issue as to the legitimate subrogation rights of the surety after paying the claims.[97] Instead, the bank argued that the trust provision created a debt to the job creditors, not a trust fund, because the intention of the owner and the principal was that the principal would have unrestricted use of the job funds. The court, on the other hand, held that the provision did not give the principal unrestricted use of the money, but instead required the principal to pay all obligations relating to the contract out of the progress payments prior to allowing any amounts to accrue to the principal.[98] The bank also argued that there was no requirement for the principal to hold the money in a separate account. The court found this was not a determinative factor of whether a trust was formed.[99] To hold the money in a separate account was a fiduciary obligation of the principal as the trustee, regardless of the trust agreement wording. Since the bank could not offset funds held by a depositor in a fiduciary capacity, the bank could not accede to the funds, particularly since Ohio law followed the equitable rule that a bank cannot offset whether or not it has knowledge of the interest of a third-party.[100]

---

97   *Fifth Third Bank*, 867 F.2d at 332-33.
98   *Id.* at 334.
99   *Id.*
100 *See also* Ins. Co. of N. Am. v. Northampton Nat'l Bank, 708 F.2d 13 (1st Cir. 1983) (holding surety was entitled to funds in contractor's account at time of bank setoff where bank had knowledge of contractor's default prior to exercising its right of setoff); Cotton States Mut. Ins. Co. v. Citizens & S. Nat'l Bank, 308 S.E.2d 199 (Ga. Ct. App. 1983) (addressing the question of when the surety's obligation arose and whether or not the bank was aware that the depositor's general account was one for job funds upon which an apparent constructive trust would be imposed for the benefit of the surety).

3. Courts Finding that a Trust was not Formed

Four years after the *Fifth Third Bank* case, another Ohio case reached the Sixth Circuit, and came to a very different result. In the case of *Indiana Lumbermens Mutual Insurance Co. v. Construction Alternatives, Inc. (In re Construction Alternatives, Inc.)*,[101] the IRS was given a priority lien over the surety as to proceeds of a construction contract paid to the debtor principal (and into a cash collateral account) from a project on which the surety had paid claims under its bonds. The surety argued that the debtor/principal held the funds as the surety's trustee under the indemnity agreement, which contained the following trust provision:

> It is expressly understood and declared that all monies due and to become due under any contract or contracts covered by the Bonds are trust funds, whether in the possession of the Indemnitor or Indemnitors or otherwise, for the benefit of and for payment of all such obligations in connection with any such contract or contracts for which the Surety would be liable under any of said Bonds, which said trust also inures to the benefit of the Surety for any liability or loss it may have to sustain under any said Bonds, and this Agreement and declaration shall also constitute notice of such trust.[102]

The surety argued that it had a superior equitable interest in the funds while the debtor/principal had a mere legal interest, to which the IRS lien attached. However, Ohio common law did not provide for the creation of a constructive trust in favor of the subcontractors and suppliers to which the surety would be subrogated upon payment, nor was there a constructive trust statute to aid the surety.[103] The court held, therefore, that the provision contained in the indemnity agreement did not create an express trust under Ohio law, which required (a) manifest intent to create a trust; (b) a trust corpus; and (c) a fiduciary relationship between the trustee and the beneficiary.[104] Following the rule with respect to the creation of a trust, as set forth in *Fifth Third Bank*, the *Construction Alternatives* court stated that:

---

101   2 F.3d 670 (6th Cir. 1993).
102   *Id.* at 676, n.4.
103   *Id.* at 677.
104   *Id.*

no provision of the General Agreement of Indemnity required [Principal] to keep any portion of the progress payments as a separate trust fund, and the record does not indicate that [Principal] kept the progress payments in a separate account. Thus, since there was no trust corpus, no trust was created. Accordingly, we conclude that [Principal] was vested with both the legal and equitable interests in the Fund to which the tax liens could attach, and that [Surety] was not vested with an equitable interest by the General Agreement of Indemnity.[105]

It is difficult to speculate whether a change in the indemnity agreement provision requiring the establishment of a separate account would have altered the result in the *Construction Alternatives* case.

Several other cases have also distinguished themselves from the outcome of the *Fifth Third Bank* case and held that a trust was not created by virtue of an indemnity agreement trust fund provision.[106] One held that the surety had failed to establish that the four requirements of a constructive trust had been met by the language of the indemnity agreement provision.[107] Another held that no trust was created because the settler of the trust (the project owner) was not a party to the agreement creating the trust (the indemnity agreement).[108] Finally, a bankruptcy court has determined that allowing a surety to recover funds held "in trust" would disrupt the provisions of the Bankruptcy Code setting forth the priority of creditors' interests in estate distributions, and this would effectively allow an unsecured creditor priority over a secured

---

105 *Id.*
106 *See* Ohio Farmers Ins. Co. v. Hughes-Bechtol, Inc. (*In re* Hughes-Bechtol, Inc.), 225 F.3d 659 (6th Cir. 2000), *reported in full* at Nos. 98-4257, 98-4306, 2000 U.S. App. LEXIS 18741 (July 27, 2000); Acuity v. Planters Bank, Inc., 362 F. Supp. 2d 885 (W.D. Ky. 2005); Shapiro v. Jacob's Elec. Constr., Inc. (*In re* E. Concrete Paving Co.), 293 B.R. 704 (Bankr. E.D. Mich. 2003); *In re* William Cargile Contractor, Inc., 151 B.R. 854 (Bankr. S.D. Ohio 1993).
107 *See* Acuity, 362 F. Supp. 2d 885 (finding that although the Indemnity Agreement evidenced an original intent to create a trust, and although the beneficiaries seem sufficiently certain, these limited findings were a long way from establishing that specific contract funds were held in trust).
108 *In re* E. Concrete Paving Co., 293 B.R. 704 (declining to follow *Fifth Third Bank* on the grounds that the trust in *Fifth Third Bank* was created within the language of the contract, to which the obligee was a party).

creditor.[109] This decision was followed by another bankruptcy court agreeing that the priorities established in section 541 of the Bankruptcy Code should prevail over the terms of an indemnity agreement.[110]

In another case, *Insurance Company of the West v. Simon (In re Foam Systems Co.)*,[111] the surety lost a proceeding to recover funds held in a debtor's special bank account. The debtor entered into a contract where the obligee paid the entire contract in advance and required a surety bond for protection.[112] The contract price was placed in an account in the name of the debtor and the funds never were commingled into the general account of the debtor until after disbursement from the special depository account, clearly a segregated account.[113] The obligee declared the debtor in default and called upon the surety to make payment pursuant to its bond. The surety complied and was assigned the obligee's rights of the contract. The surety requested release of the funds in the special depository account but the trustee for the principal-debtor refused.[114] The surety asserted that the funds were held in trust pursuant to either an express or resulting trust, or both.[115]

The Ninth Circuit bankruptcy appellate panel rejected the arguments of the surety and denied access to the funds even though they were placed in a segregated account. The panel concluded that no express trust was created nor should be created under the facts.[116] It examined the relationship between the debtor and the surety as evidenced by the indemnity agreement and determined that the intent of the debtor was to create a security interest in the account as opposed to creating a trust fund. The indemnity agreement, according to the court, merely assigned collateral as security for the obligations under the bond and the indemnity agreement and did not provide specifically for an express trust.[117]

The court also rejected the surety's argument that a resulting trust was created noting that such a trust does not arise from the transfer of

---

109   *In re* William Cargile Contractor, Inc., 151 B.R. at 859-60.
110   *In re* Hughes-Bechtol, Inc., 225 F.3d 659.
111   92 B.R. 406 (B.A.P. 9th Cir. 1988).
112   *Id.* at 407.
113   *Id.*
114   *Id.*
115   *Id.* at 408.
116   *Id.*
117   *Id.* at 409.

property or funds under the circumstances whereby the transferee is not intended to have a beneficial interest. The express intent between the parties was to create a lien on the account as security, and because the surety did not perfect its secured interest, the funds belonged to the bankruptcy estate.[118]

One possible explanation for these differing results might be the tendency of the bankruptcy courts to preserve the funds of the principal for the benefit of the creditors rather than to give the surety any priority interest in such funds. Nevertheless, these cases do illustrate the peculiar problems a surety might have when attempting to enforce the trust fund provision.

In order to avoid the potential pitfalls of a trust fund dispute, a surety that intends to provide financing to its principal or to control the release of contract balances should set up a separate trust account that is controlled by the surety.

I. *Right to Compromise or Settle Claims*

The "right-to-compromise" or "right-to-settle" provision of an indemnity agreement can be crucial because it permits the surety to discharge its principal's obligations before suit, without endangering its indemnification rights. It also protects the surety from several of the most common defenses asserted to an indemnity claim: that the surety settled a claim voluntarily, unreasonably, and/or in bad faith, thereby forfeiting its right to indemnification.[119] Alternatively, if a surety does not settle a claim, it may find itself defending a bad faith action instigated by an obligee or claimant. In the spirit of avoiding a Morton's Fork dilemma (a choice between two equally unpleasant alternatives), the "right-to-settle" provision allows the surety to use its reasonable and prudent judgment when handling and resolving claims.

An illustrative provision would read:

> The Surety shall have the exclusive right for itself and for the Indemnitor to decide and determine whether any claim, demand, suit, or judgment shall, on the basis of liability, expediency or otherwise, be paid, settled, defended or appealed, and the Surety's determination shall be final, conclusive and binding upon the Indemnitor.

---

118 *Id.* at 410.
119 *See generally*, Egan, Harb & Divers, *supra* note 67, at 334-39.

If the Indemnitor desire that the Surety litigate such claim or demand, or defend such suit, or appeal from such judgment, they shall deposit with the Surety, at the time of such request, cash or collateral satisfactory to the Surety in kind and amount to be used in paying any judgment or judgments rendered, or which might be rendered, against Surety together with interest, costs and attorney's fees.

Right-to-settle clauses are generally enforced according to their terms. In other words, in the face of such a provision, a surety typically has wide discretion in settling claims made upon a bond, even if the principal is not liable for the underlying claim.[120] Under the common law, equity generally implies a right to indemnification in favor of a surety only when the surety pays a debt for which its principal is legally obligated to pay. However, "resort to implied indemnity principles is improper when an express indemnification contract exists; when there is such an express contract, a surety is entitled to stand upon the letter of the contract."[121] The surety's discretion to make settlement payments, however, does have to comport with general standards of good faith.[122]

1. Absence of Right-to-Settle Clause

Courts have held on common law grounds (as opposed to relying on a written provision in an indemnity agreement) that where a surety can prove it paid an obligation of a principal for which the principal was legally bound, the surety is entitled to indemnity.[123] If an indemnity agreement does not include a provision stating that the surety may settle a claim at its discretion, a court may hold the surety to the burden of

---

120 *See* PSE Consulting, Inc. v. Frank Mercede & Sons, Inc., 838 A.2d 135, 146 (Conn. 2004) (citing U.S. Fid. & Guar. Co. v. Napier Elec. & Constr. Co., 571 S.W.2d 644, 646 (Ky. Ct. App. 1978)); Fid. & Deposit Co. of Md. v. Fleischer, 772 S.W.2d 809 (Mo. Ct. App. 1989); Hess v. Am. States Ins. Co., 589 S.W.2d 548 (Tex. Civ. App. 1979); John W. Hinchey, *Surety's Performance Over Protest of Principal: Considerations and Risks*, 22 TORT & INS. L.J. 133, 146-47 (1986) (discussing enforceability of right-to-settle and *prima facie* evidence clauses).
121 U.S. Fid. & Guar. Co. v. Feibus, 15 F. Supp. 2d 579, 583 (M.D. Pa. 1998) (citing Fid. & Deposit Co. of Md. v. Bristol Steel & Iron Works, Inc., 722 F.2d 1160, 1163 (4th Cir. 1983) (applying Pennsylvania law)).
122 *PSE Consulting, Inc.*, 838 A.2d at 146.
123 *See* Egan, Harb & Divers, *supra* note 67, at 335.

proving actual liability as opposed to potential liability.[124] If the surety cannot prove that its principal had a legal obligation, or actual liability, to a claimant, a court may be inclined to consider the payment voluntary, and thus non-recoverable from the principal.[125] Where the surety holds an indemnity agreement with a right-to-settle clause (and especially if it also contains a prima facie clause), this burden can be eliminated.

2. Exercise of Discretion

A right-to-settle clause provides a surety with wide discretion in settling claims, "even where the principal is not liable for the underlying claim."[126] In *Liberty Mutual Insurance Co. v. Aventura Engineering & Construction Co.*,[127] the court unambiguously found that the right-to-settle provision, read with the assignment and attorney-in-fact provisions, gave the surety the right, "at its option and sole discretion," to settle or compromise any claim or demand upon any bond.[128]

The *Aventura Engineering* court also held that "it is a well settled principle that a surety may settle claims regardless of whether liability for the claim actually existed,"[129] and for the sole purposes of avoiding

---

124 *See* James v. Hyatt Corp. of Del., 981 F.2d 810 (5th Cir. 1993) (finding that an indemnity provision in a service contract agreement did not require indemnity in the case of a settled claim and therefore the indemnitee could only be indemnified by a showing of actual, not potential liability); United States *ex rel.* Trustees of the Elec. Workers Local Pension Fund v. D Bar D Enters., Inc., 772 F. Supp. 1167 (D. Nev. 1991) (finding that in absence of express agreement, the indemnitee must prove actual liability to be entitled to indemnification, but if written indemnification agreement exists, indemnitee need only show potential liability in order to be entitled to indemnification).
125 *See* Egan, Harb & Divers, *supra* note 67, at 336.
126 Liberty Mut. Ins. Co. v. Aventura Eng'g & Constr. Corp., 534 F. Supp. 2d 1290, 1306 (S.D. Fla. 2008) (citing Auto-Owners Ins. Co. v. Southeast Floating Docks, Inc., No. 6:05-cv-334-Orl-31JGG, 2007 WL 676217, at *5 (M.D. Fla. March 1, 2007)).
127 534 F. Supp. 2d 1290 (S.D. Fla. 2008).
128 *Id.* at 1308.
129 *Id.* at 1306 (citing Thurston v. Int'l Fid. Ins. Co., 528 So.2d 128, 129 (Fla. Dist. Ct. App. 1988)).

the cost of litigation.[130] In the same spirit as the *Aventura Engineering* holding, the United States District Court for the District of Pennsylvania stated that "[s]ureties enjoy such discretion to settle claims because of the important function they serve in the construction industry. The purpose of good faith clauses is to facilitate the handling of settlements by sureties and protect them from unnecessary and costly litigation."[131]

3. Burden of Proving Reasonableness of Settlement of Claim

Courts interpreting right-to-settle provisions found in an indemnity agreement routinely have concluded that, upon a finding that a surety has made a payment to a claimant upon a bond, the burden of proof shifts to the indemnitor to prove that the surety had not made the payment in good faith.[132] However, notwithstanding this sentiment and the *Aventura Engineering* court's deference to the indemnity agreement, some courts will impose a limitation on the exercise of the surety's discretion and fold the analysis into a "good faith" discussion.[133] For example, when reviewing the provision granting the surety the "exclusive right" or "sole discretion" to settle claims, the court in *City of Portland v. George D. Ward & Associates, Inc.*[134] held that the surety was bound to exercise its discretionary rights so that the reasonable expectations of all parties

---

130 *Id.* (citing generally Employers Ins. of Wausau v. Able Green, Inc., 749 F. Supp. 1100, 1103-1104 (S.D. Fla.1990) (surety's decision to forgo litigation and settle claims is not evidence of bad faith where litigation would far exceed the expense of settling the claims)); Gen. Accident Ins. Co. of Am. v. Merritt-Meridian Constr. Corp, 975 F. Supp. 511, 516 (S.D.N.Y. 1997)). *See also* Fid. & Deposit Co. of Md. v. Fleischer, 772 S.W.2d 809, 815 (Mo. Ct. App. 1989).
131 U.S. Fid. & Guar. Co. v. Feibus, 15 F. Supp. 2d 579, 584 (M.D. Pa. 1998). *See also* Egan, Harb & Divers, *supra* note 67, at 338.
132 Engbrock v. Federal Ins. Co., 370 F.2d 784, 786 (5th Cir. 1967) (where indemnity agreement has prima facie evidence provision, indemnitor may avoid liability "only by pleading and proving fraud or lack of good faith by [s]urety"); PSE Consulting, Inc. v. Frank Mercede & Sons, Inc., 838 A.2d 135, 146 (Conn. 2004) (citing Transamerica Ins. Co. v. Bloomfield, 401 F.2d 357, 362 (6th Cir. 1968); U.S. Fid. & Guar. Co. v. Napier Elec. & Constr. Co., 571 S.W.2d 644, 646 (Ky. Ct. App. 1978) (same)).
133 *See* Egan, Harb & Divers, *supra* note 67, at 337.
134 750 P.2d 171 (Or. Ct. App. 1988), *review denied*, 757 P.2d 422 (Or. 1988).

would be effected. It rejected the surety's argument that "sole discretion" to settle is limited only by the surety's duty not to act for dishonest purposes or improper motives and held that parties to an indemnity agreement "reasonably expect that compromise and payment will be made only after reasonable investigation of the claims, counterclaims and defenses asserted in the underlying action."[135] Similarly, in *Hartford v. Tanner*,[136] the court found a right-to-settle provision providing that the surety's decision was "final, conclusive and binding" was against public policy and that an implied covenant of reasonableness existed with respect to settlement by the surety. One conclusion that can be drawn, however, is that good faith is synonymous with good investigation. For example, in *Horton v. United States Fidelity & Guaranty Co.*,[137] the Georgia Court of Appeals held that the surety paid claims in good faith after proper investigation.

Other cases have also found that a surety's good faith may be generally required and that a showing of bad faith will be required to overcome an indemnity obligation of a principal. For example, in *Associated Indemnity Corp. v. CAT Contracting, Inc.*,[138] the court found no common law duty of good faith to the principal by virtue of the bond, but found there was a contractual duty of good faith under the indemnity agreement. *Employers Insurance of Wausau v. Able Green, Inc.*[139] acknowledged that the surety had an obligation to act in good faith, but concluded that for there to be any lack of good faith the surety must be deliberately malfeasant. In *Reliance Insurance Co. v. Romine*,[140] the court held that the only material issue in the case was whether the surety exhibited bad faith or abuse of discretion in paying claimants. Whether the payments were erroneous or excessive was immaterial with regard to the question of good or bad faith. In *United States Fidelity & Guaranty*

---

135 *Id.* at 175.
136 910 P.2d 872 (Kan. Ct. App. 1996).
137 392 S.E.2d 25 (Ga. Ct. App. 1990).
138 964 S.W.2d 276 (Tex. 1998).
139 749 F. Supp. 1100 (S.D. Fla. 1990) (noting that if made in good faith, the surety's decision whether to settle a claim would be subject only to the principal's posting of collateral as provided for in the indemnity agreement). *See also* Gen. Ins. Co. of Am. v. K. Capolino Constr. Corp., 903 F. Supp. 623 (S.D.N.Y. 1995) (noting no indemnity without good faith).
140 707 F. Supp. 550 (S.D. Ga. 1989).

Co. v. Feibus,[141] the court found that an alleged overpayment or negligent investigation of claims does not constitute bad faith in the suretyship context. The court emphasized that gross negligence, bad judgment and alleged excessive payments by the surety does not rise to the level of bad faith.[142] Additionally, in *Safeco Insurance Co. of America v. Criterion Investment Corp.*,[143] the court held that where bond claims are paid in good faith the surety is entitled to recover from the indemnitors. Good faith implies "honesty in fact," which is a lesser standard under the law than "reasonable under the circumstances" which is a negligence test.[144]

Finally, in *Travelers Indemnity Co. v. Harrison Construction Group Corp.*,[145] the court held that under the indemnity agreement, settlement of claims was within the surety's discretion, and the surety was entitled to indemnity as long as the settlement was in good faith and the amount paid was reasonable.[146] The court thought that good faith meant there was no fraud or collusion or, at most, that there was no conscious sinister motive.[147]

---

141   15 F. Supp. 2d 579 (M.D. Pa. 1998) (noting that failure to deposit collateral security, in violation of a surety agreement, weighs against a finding that the surety acted in bad faith in settling claims).
142   *Id.* at 586. *See also* Engbrock v. Federal Ins. Co., 370 F.2d 784, 785-87 (5th Cir. 1967) (allegations that surety made excessive payments at most alleges negligence); Frontier Ins. Co. v. Int'l, Inc., 124 F. Supp. 2d 1211 (N.D. Ala. 2000); Fireman's Fund Ins. Co. v. Nizdil, 709 F. Supp. 975, 976-77 (D. Or. 1989) (allegation that surety overpaid claim did not raise issue of material fact necessary to defeat summary judgment).
143   732 F. Supp. 834 (E.D. Tenn. 1989). *See also* U.S. Fid. & Guar. Co. v. Feibus, 15 F. Supp. 2d 579, 585 (M.D. Pa. 1998); Gen. Accident Ins. Co. of Am. v. Merritt-Meridian Constr. Co., 975 F. Supp. 511 (S.D.N.Y. 1997); PSE Consulting, Inc. v. Frank Mercede & Sons, Inc., 838 A.2d 135 (Conn. 2004); BIB Constr. Co. v. Fireman's Ins. Co., 214 A.D. 2d 521 (N.Y. App. Div. 1995) (settlement provision applies even if principal claims it had not defaulted).
144   *See also* Park v. Universal Sur. of Am., 25 S.W.3d 738 (Tex. App. 2000) (requiring a duty of reasonableness where indemnity agreement did not contain express language requiring good faith).
145   No. CV 06-4011(FB)(RML), 2008 WL 4725970 (E.D.N.Y. Oct. 22, 2008).
146   *Id.* at *3.
147   *Id.* at *5.

Because the indemnity agreement generally will not set forth a standard for good faith, courts may apply the common law standard of bad faith, finding that "bad faith or fraudulent payment is the sole limiting factor of a surety's enforcement of an indemnity agreement."[148] Under this standard, bad faith "is not simply bad judgment or negligence, but rather it implies the conscious doing of a wrong because of dishonest purpose or moral obliquity . . . [b]ad faith requires a showing of recklessness or improper motive such as self-interest or ill will."[149]

To minimize, if not avoid entirely, the burden of establishing "reasonableness" in the settlement of claims, upon receipt of a claim, the surety should immediately demand the deposit of collateral by the principal. If the principal refuses/fails to deposit collateral, it may thereby waive any objection to the surety's decision to settle a claim.

4. *Prima Facie or Conclusive Evidence Provision*

A "prima facie" clause in an indemnity agreement will generally provide that payment vouchers or other evidence of payment of claims shall be prima facie evidence of the propriety of the payment of such claims. Often read in conjunction with the right-to-settle provision, and sometimes included therein, the prima facie provision serves largely to shift the surety's burden of proving that a given payment was made in good faith back to the indemnitors to show that a payment was made in bad faith.[150]

Courts have generally upheld the concept that "[t]he purpose of [prima facie evidence] clauses . . . is to facilitate the handling of settlements by sureties and obviate unnecessary and costly litigation."[151] Consequently, in a case where the surety included a right-to-settle provision in its indemnity agreement, but did not provide that the payment of monies by the surety was prima facie evidence of a good faith payment, the court placed the burden upon the surety to prove the

---

148 Great Am. Ins. Co. v. Stephens, No. Civ.A. 04-3642, 2005 WL 2373866 (E.D. Pa. Sept. 27, 2005) (quoting U.S. Fid. & Guar. Co. v. Bilt-Rite Contractors, Inc., No. Civ.A. 04-1505, 2005 WL 1168374, at *4 n.9 (E.D. Pa. May 16, 2005)).

149 *Id.* (citations omitted). *See also* Travelers Indem. Co. v. Harrison Constr. Group Corp., 2008 WL 4725970 at *4-5.

150 *See generally* Shahinian, Brown & Monaghan, *supra* note 6, at 133-37.

151 Transamerica Ins. Co. v. Bloomfield, 401 F.2d 357, 363 (6th Cir. 1968).

reasonableness of its disbursements under the bond, rather than requiring the indemnitors to plead and prove unreasonableness or lack of good faith.[152]

5. Failure to Mitigate Damages

Along with the advantages of having full discretionary authority when settling claims comes the responsibility of the consequences of mishandling the settlement of a claim (if the increased damages can be traced to the surety's actions, not the principal's). At least one case has found that where the surety's action (or inaction) unreasonably increases the overall loss, only the original loss may be recovered under the indemnity agreement.[153] In other words, the surety's recovery from its principal will be limited to the amount owed before the increased loss accrued. Notably, it has not been found that an obligee can bring a bad faith action against a surety for "failure to settle," but instead held that the principal/indemnitor's liability to the surety may be limited as a result of a surety's bad faith.[154]

6. The Bond v. the Indemnity Agreement

Some cases have discussed the interrelationship of the bond and indemnity agreement when addressing the settlement of claims. In the case of *Insurance Co. of North America v. Bath*,[155] the court held that a

---

152 Hawaiian Ins. & Guar. Co. v. Higashi, 675 P.2d 767 (Haw. 1984). *See also* Great Am. Ins. Co. v. N. Austin Municipal Utility Dist. No. 1, 908 S.W. 2d 415, 418 (Tex. 1995) (compensated surety owes no duty of good faith to obligee).
153 Republic Ins. Co. v. Prince George's County, 608 A.2d 1301 (Md. Ct. Spec. App. 1992) (holding where surety allowed three years to pass before settling a claim despite repeated requests for payment by the claimant and by the time the claim was paid, the cost to complete had increased significantly from the original claim amount, surety was only allowed to recover the original claim amount from the principal).
154 Generally, a "failure to settle" claim will come in the form of a bad faith tort action, the validity of which will be determined on state law. *See* Bell BCI Co. v. HRGM Corp., 276 F. Supp. 2d 462 (D. Md. 2003) (finding that a tort action for "bad faith" was not available under Maryland law as a remedy for the surety's alleged breach of contract).
155 726 F. Supp. 1247 (D. Wyo. 1989).

surety was entitled to pay a claim and recover against the indemnitors where the express language of the bond waived all defenses of any kind that the principal might have to the claim (even though the principal alleged a fraud defense).[156] Without a showing of bad faith or fraud committed by the surety, the surety was entitled to judgment. However, the court in *National Union Fire Insurance Co. v. Alexander*[157] found that an unconditional obligation to pay contained in the bond (i.e., all defenses of principal waived as to the surety) was somewhat inconsistent with the terms and conditions of the indemnity agreement, and that a question of fact existed as to whether the surety's payment under the bond (without asserting the principal's defenses) breached the indemnity agreement obligation of the surety.[158]

Although the bond and the indemnity agreement are to be read together, the rights and liabilities in one (the indemnity agreement) may be broader than those contained in the other (the bond),[159] and in most jurisdictions, the indemnity agreement will trump.[160] For example, in *Liberty Mutual Insurance Co. v. Aventura Engineering & Construction Corp.*, the court held that under Florida law, "the indemnity agreement, and not the performance bond, delineates the rights and obligations of a principal and surety."[161]

---

156   *Id.* at 1252.
157   728 F. Supp. 192 (S.D.N.Y. 1989).
158   *Id.* at 199.
159   *See* Liberty Mut. Ins. Co. v. Aventura Eng'g & Constr. Corp., 534 F. Supp. 2d 1290, 1322 (S.D. Fla. 2008) (holding that the indemnity agreement, and not the performance bond, delineates the rights and obligations of a principal and surety); Fireman's Fund Ins. Co. v. Nizdil, 709 F. Supp. 975 (D. Or. 1989) (holding that indemnification depends upon interpretation of the indemnity contract and not on the validity or enforceability of the bond).
160   *Aventura Eng'g*, 534 F. Supp. 2d at 1309.
161   *Id.* (citing Aetna Ins. Co. v. Buchanan, 369 So.2d 351, 354 (Fla. Dist. Ct. App. 1979) ("The status of an indemnitor of a surety on a bond is to be determined by the indemnity agreement and not by the provisions of the bond."); Harrison v. Am. Fire & Cas. Co., 226 So.2d 28, 29 (Fla. Dist. Ct. App. 1969) (rejecting the argument that an indemnitor's liability shall be fixed by the terms of the bond since the status of an indemnitor is governed by the indemnity agreement, not the bond); Gen. Accident Ins. Co. of Am. v. Merritt-Meridian Constr. Corp, 975 F. Supp. 511, 517 (S.D.N.Y. 1997) ("[A] contractor, whose relationship with the surety is

7. Notice to Indemnitors

The question of whether a surety must notify indemnitors prior to settling a claim is often litigated. In *American Bonding Co. v. Nelson*,[162] the court examined the conflict between the indemnity agreement settlement provision and the provision in the indemnity agreement providing for waiver of notice to indemnitors of default, claims and the like. The court held that the reading of the two paragraphs together created an ambiguity in the indemnity agreement because one paragraph waived all notices to indemnitors by the surety while the other implied that the indemnitors would be notified so they could exercise their right to request the surety to litigate a claim upon deposit of collateral.[163] In strictly construing the indemnity agreement against the surety, the court found the settlement provision required that indemnitors be adequately notified of claims. Because notice to one indemnitor was deemed defective, that indemnitor was excused.[164] Another case, *Palevac v. Mid Century Non Auto*,[165] held that the lack of notice to an indemnitor rendered the surety's payment a non-obligatory or voluntary payment for which there was no recovery against the indemnitor.[166]

On the other hand, absent an explicit provision requiring notice to the indemnitors, the surety does not have any obligation to give notice to the indemnitors. In *Citizens State Bank of Big Lake v. Transamerica Insurance Co.*,[167] the court found that the surety's settlement was not suspect simply because the indemnitor was unaware of either settlement discussions or an agreement between the parties. Also, in *Safeco*

---

governed by an express indemnity agreement contract containing provisions that permit the surety to settle in good faith, may [not] avoid its obligation to indemnify by pointing to inconsistent provisions in a separate contract between itself and the subcontractor.")).
162 763 P.2d 814 (Utah Ct. App. 1988).
163 *Id.* at 816.
164 *Id.* at 816-17.
165 710 P.2d 1389 (Nev. 1985).
166 *Id.* at 1391.
167 815 F. Supp. 309 (D. Minn. 1993). *See also* Transamerica Ins. Co. v. Avenell, 66 F.3d 715 (5th Cir. 1995) (holding settlement of claims by surety while principal appealing not breach of Indemnity Agreement so long as surety acted in good faith).

Insurance Co. of America v. Gaubert,[168] the indemnitors argued that the surety had a duty to notify them of an action on the bond so they could participate in the trial. The court held there was no duty to contact or notify the indemnitors of the action on the bond. The surety need only act in good faith.[169] In *North American Specialty Insurance Co. v. Schuler*,[170] a New York appellate court rejected the contention of an indemnitor that the surety had breached the indemnity agreement by failing to notify the indemnitor before settling the claim. The *Schuler* court stated, "[A]bsent a specific provision in the indemnity agreement, an indemnitee is not required to give notice of claims on the underlying surety bond to the indemnitors . . . . The indemnification agreement herein not only contained no such provision for notice, but in fact contained a waiver of such notice requirement to the indemnitors."[171]

Both lines of cases demonstrate that the surety has wide latitude in settling claims under the right-to-settle provisions of the indemnity agreement. Notice to a principal of the intended settlement of a claim will be required only where the indemnity agreement specifically calls for such notice to be given.

To avoid arguments (however unfounded they may be), a surety should give separate notice to and make a collateral deposit demand upon all indemnitors early in the process of settling claims. In many cases, the individual indemnitors will pressure the principal to resolve matters and reduce the surety's loss. Although notice may not be required under the indemnity agreement, as a practical matter, giving notice to all indemnitors can help the surety limit the impediments toward summary resolution of the surety's indemnity rights.

8. *Deposit of Collateral*

In the context of settlement of claims, a surety may require a deposit of collateral from a principal/indemnitor seeking to have the surety litigate

---

168 829 S.W.2d 274 (Tex. App. 1992).
169 U.S. Fid. & Guar. Co. v. Lipsmeyer Constr. Co., 754 F. Supp. 81 (M.D. La. 1990) (finding that the surety paid monies in good faith and in compliance with the terms of the contract).
170 291 A.D.2d 924 (N.Y. App. Div. 2002).
171 *Id.* at 925 (quoting Republic Ins. Co. v. Real Dev. Co., 161 A.D.2d 189, 189-190 (N.Y. App. Div. 1990)).

or deny a given claim.[172] When a right-to-settle provision includes the requirement of the deposit of collateral before a surety is obligated to litigate a claim, the majority of courts will uphold the provision and give no relief whatsoever to a principal/indemnitor who fails to deposit collateral upon demand.[173] This is another example of the tremendous advantages an indemnity agreement provides to a surety in mitigating its losses. Without the clean, straightforward terms of the indemnity agreement, the surety would have to rely on its common law right of exoneration, which is only available to a surety after the principal's debt has become due.[174]

One case, *North American Specialty Insurance Co. v. Montco Construction Co.*, found that a principal's breach of indemnity agreement by failing to post collateral or otherwise exonerate the surety activated the attorney-in-fact and assignment clauses of the indemnity agreement and gave the surety the right to settle the principal's pending lawsuit against the owner/obligee.[175] In another case, *United States ex rel. Trustees of the Electrical Workers Local Pension Fund v. D Bar D Enterprises, Inc.*,[176] a surety was granted judgment on an indemnity agreement notwithstanding the fact that there may have been possible defenses against the claimant that the surety paid. The surety notified the indemnitors of the claim and settlement negotiations; however, the indemnitors failed to post collateral and instruct the surety to litigate, thus failing to preserve any objection to settlement.[177] Similarly, in *Transamerica Insurance Co. v. Avenell*,[178] the Fifth Circuit held that indemnitors wishing to prevent a surety from settling a claim must deposit collateral and request litigation. The court specifically stated that

---

172 *See* Shahinian, Brown & Monaghan, *supra* note 6, at 129.
173 *Id.* at 130.
174 *See, e.g.*, Great Am. Ins. Co. v. Gen. Contractors & Const. Mgmt., Inc., No. 07-21489-CIV, 2008 WL 2245986 (S.D. Fla. May 29, 2008) (citing Filner v. Shapiro, 633 F.2d 139, 142 (2d Cir. 1980); Borey v. Nat'l Union Fire Ins. Co. of Pittsburgh, Pa., 934 F.2d 30, 32 (2d Cir. 1991)).
175 N. Am. Specialty Ins. Co. v. Montco Constr. Co., No. 01-CV-0246E(SR), 2003 WL 21383231, at *7 (W.D.N.Y. May 9, 2003).
176 772 F. Supp. 1167 (D. Nev. 1991).
177 *Id.* at 1173.
178 66 F.3d 715 (5th Cir. 1995).

a failure to deposit collateral left the surety with no obligation "to hear, much less honor" the indemnitor's protest of the claim.[179]

In *Fidelity & Deposit Co. of Maryland v. Greenlee*,[180] the surety prevailed even though the indemnitor offered to defend the claim and/or pay defense costs because the indemnitor failed to post collateral.[181] The offer to defend was not considered the equivalent of a deposit of collateral. In *Continental Casualty Co. v. Gutterman*,[182] the surety's failure to assert the principal's defenses was held not to preclude the surety from seeking reimbursement, even if the surety paid off debts for which the principal was not liable. In another case, *Fidelity & Deposit Co. of Maryland v. Fleischer*,[183] the indemnitors made demand for defense but posted no collateral. The court found that absent the indemnitors posting collateral, as required by the indemnity agreement, the surety had the right to settle the claims.[184]

In *Liberty Mutual Insurance Co. v. Aventura Engineering & Construction Corp.*, the court specifically held that the indemnity agreement right-to-settle provision, which included collateral deposit demand language, gave the surety the right, at its option and sole discretion, to settle or compromise any claim or demand upon any bond. If the principal wanted to protect its claims against the owner of the bonds, the indemnity agreement set forth a mechanism to do so, specifically that the principal must "first ask [the surety] to deny the claim, and, at the same time, it must provide [the surety] with collateral that exonerates and indemnifies it against any potential loss."[185] Therefore, cases requiring the surety to demonstrate good faith or liability to recover under its indemnity agreement should be foreclosed where the surety had the ability to demand collateral and the indemnitors failed to place the surety in collateral.

---

179   *Id.* at 720. *See also* Am. Ins. Co. v. Egerton, 59 F.3d 165 (4th Cir. 1995), *reported in full at* No. 94-1911, 1995 WL 371452 (4th Cir. June 21, 1995); Employers Ins. of Wausau v. Able Green, Inc., 749 F. Supp. 1100 (S.D. Fla.1990).
180   660 P.2d 172 (Or. Ct. App. 1983).
181   *Id. See also* Fireman's Fund Ins. Co. v. Nizdil, 709 F. Supp. 975 (D. Or. 1989) (where no collateral was posted).
182   708 F. Supp. 953 (N.D. Ill. 1989).
183   772 S.W.2d 809 (Mo. Ct. App. 1989).
184   *Id.* at 818.
185   *Aventura Eng'g*, 534 F. Supp. 2d. at 1308 (emphasis in original).

In *Fidelity & Deposit Co. of Maryland v. D.M. Ward Construction Co.*,[186] the surety set aside a reserve and paid losses. Additional claims were pending, and the surety sued the principal and indemnitors and moved for summary judgment on the count seeking an order that the indemnitors deposit collateral equal to the reserve. The indemnitors argued that the surety had "unclean hands" because it had not handled the claims as they desired.[187] The court noted that the indemnitors had "bargained away the right to contest how plaintiff handled claims upon the bonds unless they were willing to post collateral satisfactory to plaintiff."[188] The court rejected the indemnitors' contentions and granted the surety summary judgment ordering deposit of collateral equal to the reserve.

9. Affirmative Claims of Principal

The indemnity agreement provides a surety with the ability to utilize the affirmative claims of its principal as a source of recovery to mitigate its losses. Although the right-to-compromise or right-to-settle claims provisions may not be sufficient alone to permit the surety to compromise affirmative claims of the principal against others, in those instances where a surety desires to pursue such a claim, it should look also to the indemnity agreement provisions regarding assignment-of-claims and the attorney-in-fact clause giving the surety the power to exercise all of its assignment rights. When taken as a whole, courts "have expressly recognized a surety's right to settle the principal's claims, by virtue of the assignment and power-of-attorney provisions of an indemnity agreement."[189] In *Hutton Construction Co. v. County of Rockland*,[190] a principal objected to the surety settling its affirmative claims arising out of the construction contract. The court found that the right-to-settle provision in the indemnity agreement standing alone did not give the surety the power to settle the principal's affirmative claims.[191] However, the right-to-settle clause, when applied in

---

186 No. 06-2483-CM, 2008 WL 2761314 (D. Kan. July 14, 2008).
187 *Id.* at *2.
188 *Id.* at *3.
189 *Aventura Eng'g*, 534 F. Supp. 2d at 1306 (citing Hutton Constr. Co. v. County of Rockland, 52 F.3d 1191 (2d Cir. 1995)).
190 52 F.3d 1191 (2d Cir. 1995).
191 *Id.* at 1192-93.

conjunction with the assignment-of-claims provision and the attorney-in-fact provision did give such a right. The court was compelled to this conclusion because the surety had demanded collateral of the principal and the principal had failed to post it.[192]

Many cases have followed the *Hutton Construction* decision regarding the surety's right to settle the affirmative claims of its principal. In *Liberty Mutual Insurance Co. v. Aventura Engineering & Construction Corp.*, the court found that when read together with the assignment provision, the settlement clause gave the surety the right to settle or compromise any claim or demand.[193] In *Bell BCI Co. v. Old Dominion Demolition Corp.*, the court held that the indemnity agreement's unambiguous provisions gave the surety the authority to settle and resolve the principal's claims against the owner.[194] Not persuaded by the principal's argument that allowing the surety to settle its affirmative claims would result in a bad faith settlement,[195] the *Bell* court found that the principal's failure to make certain indemnity payments constituted a breach of its obligations to the surety, thus activating an assignment clause assigning all of the principal's rights growing out of the bonded construction projects to the surety. This, combined with the fact that there was also an attorney-in-fact clause that unambiguously appointed the surety as the principal's attorney-in-fact with the power to exercise all rights assigned to it under the indemnity agreement, supported the court's holding that the assignment clause and the attorney-in-fact provision gave the surety the authority to settle all claims on behalf of the principal, including the affirmative claims growing out of the principal's insured contracts.[196]

In a case addressing the question of standing, *Harlandale Independent School District v. C2M Construction, Inc.*,[197] the court held that the surety had the right to settle principal's claims against the project owner based upon indemnity, assignment, settlement, and attorney-in-

---

192   *Id.* at 1192 (agreeing with the district court's findings).
193   *Aventura Eng'g*, 534 F. Supp. 2d 1290.
194   Bell BCI Co. v. Old Dominion Demolition Corp., 294 F. Supp. 2d 807 (E.D. Va. 2003).
195   *Id.* at 814.
196   *Id.*
197   No. 04-07-00304-CV, 2007 WL 2253510 (Tex. App. Aug. 8, 2007).

fact provisions that are "standard in the industry."[198] In *Harlandale*, because the surety paid claims and completed the construction in accordance with its payment and performance bonds, and because the principal had the option to, but did not deposit cash or collateral satisfactory to the surety to be used in paying any judgment or judgments rendered, with interest, costs, expenses and attorneys' fees, all of the principal's rights "growing in any manner out of" the construction contract were assigned to the surety.[199]

Finally, the court in *North American Specialty Insurance Co. v. Montco Construction Co.*,[200] held that the principal's breach of the indemnity agreement activated the attorney-in-fact and assignment clauses of the indemnity agreement and gave the surety the right to settle the principal's pending lawsuit against the owner/obligee.[201] In *Montco*, the principal was alleged to have breached the unambiguous terms of the indemnity agreement by failing to "post collateral security, make payment or otherwise exonerate or indemnify the surety pursuant to the terms of the agreement."[202] The court found that the terms of the indemnity agreement were unambiguous and therefore it was obligated to give effect to the express rights and obligations of the parties contained therein as a matter of law.[203] Further finding that the principal breached the indemnity agreement, the court held that such a breach activated the assignment and attorney-in-fact clauses of the indemnity agreement, thereby assigning to the surety all of the principal's rights arising from the bonded construction contract, including the surety's right to settle the principal's pending action against the owner of the project.[204]

---

198   *Id.* at *2.
199   *Id.*
200   No. 01-CV-0246E(SR), 2003 WL 21383231 (W.D.N.Y. May 9, 2003).
201   *Id.*
202   *Id.* at *4.
203   *Id.* at *5.
204   *Id.* at *7.

J. Principal's Obligation to Cooperate in Defense of Claims

Although courts have found that an indemnitor has an implicit duty to cooperate with the surety,[205] the indemnity agreement generally includes a provision expressly creating this obligation as well. An illustrative provision would state:

> The Indemnitor shall give the Surety prompt notice of any claim, demand, suit, arbitration proceeding or other action which purports to be instituted on any Bond and shall fully cooperate with the Surety in defense thereof.

The indemnitors' obligation to cooperate may be implied, however, a cooperation clause can be very useful in an indemnity agreement. In the case of *Harvey v. United Pacific Insurance Co.*,[206] the surety sued its principal for indemnification after the surety lost a lawsuit against it for failure to pay a claim. The surety had denied payment of the claim at the request of its principal. The principal failed to pay the claim as well and also refused to cooperate in the defense or settlement of it. In the surety's suit for indemnity, the principal counter-claimed for bad faith, breach of fiduciary duty, breach of implied covenant of good faith and fair dealing, unfair insurance practices, abuse of process, unfair trade practices, intentional infliction of emotional harm and conspiracy. These claims were unsuccessful and the trial court awarded the surety its bond loss ($25,000), plus attorneys' fees and expenses (over $100,000).[207] The appeal involved an issue regarding the amount of attorney's fees awarded to the surety. The attorney's fees for pursuing the indemnity against the principal were six times the fees incurred in defending the original action. The court carefully reviewed the principal's tactics employed in the indemnity action and concluded that its counterclaims were "frivolous and interposed solely for the purpose of obstructing the indemnity claim," and therefore chargeable to the indemnitors.[208]

---

205 *See* Egan, Harb & Divers, *supra* note 67, at 352.
206 856 P.2d 240 (Nev. 1993).
207 *Id.* at 240.
208 *Id.* at 241.

In *Premier Electrical Construction Co. v. American National Bank & Trust Co. of Chicago*,[209] a subcontractor sued the surety for recovery under a payment bond. The surety tendered the defense to its principal pursuant to its indemnity agreement, and its principal defended.[210] After partial summary judgment was entered for the claimant, the claimant amended its petition to allege bad faith against the surety. The principal refused to indemnify the surety on this cause of action, and the surety sued its principal seeking indemnification. After the surety successfully defeated the claimant's bad faith action, the trial court entered judgment in favor of the surety against the principal for substantial defense costs.[211] The principal appealed, arguing that the claim was based on the surety's negligence and bad faith and that the indemnity agreement should not be extended to cover that type of claim.[212] The Illinois Appellate Court acknowledged the general principle that an indemnitor was not liable to the surety for its own negligence, but concluded that in this case the principal took over the defense of the original claim and was responsible for the long delay in payment of the claim. Therefore, the principal was required to indemnify the surety for its attorneys' fees and costs in defense of the bad faith claim which also included litigation costs in defending the unsuccessful appeal.[213]

K. Right to Have Indemnitors Obtain Release of Surety

Another provision that reinforces common law suretyship rights is the provision directing the indemnitors to discharge the surety from any bond and all liability thereof.[214] An illustrative provision would read:

---

209 603 N.E.2d 733 (Ill. App. Ct. 1992).
210 *Id.* at 734.
211 *Id.* at 734-35.
212 *Id.*
213 *Id.* at 735.
214 *See generally* Randall I. Marmor & Jay M. Mann, *Complementary Provisions of the Indemnity Agreement, in* THE SURETY'S INDEMNITY AGREEMENT: LAW & PRACTICE 369, 370-75 (Marilyn Klinger, George J. Bachrach & Tracey L. Haley eds., 2d ed. 2008).

The Principal and Indemnitor will, at the request of the Surety, procure the discharge of the Surety from any bond and all liability by reason thereof.

Consistent with the surety's common law rights, this provision is comparable to the equitable remedy of exoneration.[215] There are very few cases, if any, specifically addressing this provision in the context of traditional performance bonds. However, some jurisdictions have created statutory provisions and procedures whereby a surety may obtain a discharge of its bond.[216] Generally, these provisions address the release of a surety that has paid obligations on the bond. A different situation arises, however, when despite no claims having been made, a surety has knowledge that a principal is in financial distress, that there is talk of a default under the construction contract, that no reserves are currently in place, and that the market conditions have changed significantly since the provision of the bond. The surety may seek exoneration and/or a mitigation of its anticipated losses by attempting to call into effect the right-to-discharge provision. However, a court may not be inclined to enforce an indemnity agreement provision that will force the principal into financial ruin because it has to either obtain new surety credit or post a large amount of working capital as a collateral deposit to secure the continuation of the present bonds.[217]

Similar to the analysis of a collateral deposit demand (in the absence of claims), the enforceability of the right-to-obtain release provision in the indemnity agreement may depend upon the surety's ability to provide

---

215   *See id.* at 371.
216   *See id.* at 370 (citing ALASKA STAT. § 45.70.010 (West 2007); ARIZ. REV. STAT. ANN. § 12-1641; CAL. CIV. PROC. CODE § 996.110 (West 2007); KAN. STAT. ANN. § 59-1107 (West 2006); ME. REV. STAT. ANN. tit. 18, § 8-306 (West 2007); MO. REV. STAT. § 433.130 (West 2007); N.J. STAT. ANN. § 3B:15-18 (West 2007); N.M. STAT. ANN. § 46-6-3 (West 2007); N.Y. C.P.L.R. LAW § 2510 (McKinney 2007)).
217   This scenario is more troublesome (and more likely to be found) in the context of commercial bonds. Commercial bonds, such as permit bonds, license bonds, improvements bonds, and subdivision bonds are performance bonds by nature, however they do not typically relate to an underlying bonded contract as would a construction performance bond. These types of commercial bonds carry a higher risk to the surety because of the duration of the surety's risk and its continuing exposure. *See generally*, King, Gelinas, & Kreamer, *supra* note 10, at 447.

a court with a rational and reasonable basis for seeking a discharge. Where claims have been paid and the surety's liability under the bonds has been fully vetted, the obligation of the principal/ indemnitors to obtain a release/discharge of the surety will likely be fully enforceable.

II. Other Provisions of the Indemnity Agreement

A. *Rights of Co-Sureties and Reinsurers*

Often an indemnity agreement will contain a provision which states that the indemnitors agree that all terms and conditions of the indemnity agreement will apply and operate for the benefit not only of the principal's surety but any co-sureties and reinsurance companies.[218] The purpose of this provision in the indemnity agreement is to provide other sureties or reinsurers, not in privity of contract with the indemnitors, third-party beneficiary status under the agreement and afford them the same rights as the original surety. In *Commercial Insurance Co. of Newark, New Jersey v. Pacific-Peru Construction Corp.*,[219] the Ninth Circuit directly addressed the issue and held that the reinsurer of the original surety was entitled to recover from the principal because the reinsurer was a third-party beneficiary of the indemnity agreement between the principal and the original surety pursuant to this indemnity agreement clause.[220] This premise was upheld in *Lyndon Property Insurance Co. v. Houston Barnes, Inc.*,[221] in which the court found that the terms of the indemnity agreement as well as the circumstances surrounding it indicate that the indemnitors in the indemnity agreement, intended to give the surety/reinsurer, as "beneficiary," the benefit of the promised performance.[222]

---

218   *See* Diwik, Puente & Smith, *supra* note 24, at 244-45.
219   558 F.2d 948 (9th Cir. 1977).
220   *See also* King v. Employers Nat'l. Ins. Co., 928 F.2d 1438 (5th Cir. 1991); Trans-Orient Marine Corp. v. Star Trading & Marine, Inc., 925 F.2d 566 (2d Cir. 1991); Sepulveda v. Pac. Marine Ass'n, 878 F.2d 1137 (9th Cir. 1989), *cert. denied*, 493 U.S. 1002 (1989).
221   No. 3:04 CV 174, 2005 WL 1840254 (E.D. Tenn. July 26, 2005).
222   *Id.* at *5.

B. Severability

Another important provision allows that if any provision in the indemnity agreement is void or unenforceable under any law governing the agreement, that the entire agreement will not be voided, but shall be construed with those void provisions severed. Courts uniformly find that if a contract contains provisions which are illegal or unenforceable, the invalid provisions may be severed, leaving the remainder of the contract enforceable, provided that the illegal provision is not an essential feature of the agreement.[223] The issue was addressed in *Transamerica Insurance Co. v. Avenell*[224] regarding a homestead exemption waiver. The indemnitors in that case sought to release themselves from their obligations under the indemnity agreement and argued that the indemnity agreement itself was against public policy because it required the waiver of their homestead exemptions in violation of the Texas Constitution.[225] The court reviewed the "invalidates clause" and found that clause severs the homestead waiver provision from the indemnity agreement and, therefore, the balance of the indemnity agreement was enforceable.[226]

C. Surety's Right to Bring Separate Suit

Many indemnity agreements also include a separate suit provision which allows suits to be brought as they accrue and that the pendency or termination of any such suit will not bar subsequent actions. This clause also has been held enforceable.[227] Suits may be brought against separate indemnitors and will be influenced by factors such as the cost of a suit versus the likelihood of recovery.[228]

---

223 *See* Samuel J. Arena, Jr., Adam P. Friedman, Dennis J. Bartlett & Dawn C. Stewart, *Creation of the Relationship Among the Surety, the Principal, and the Indemnitors—Who and How, in* THE SURETY'S INDEMNITY AGREEMENT: LAW & PRACTICE 29, 77-81 (Marilyn Klinger, George J. Bachrach & Tracey L. Haley eds., 2d ed. 2008).

224 66 F.3d 715 (5th Cir. 1995).

225 *Id.* at 721.

226 *Id.* at 722.

227 Republic Ins. Co. v. Culbertson, 717 F. Supp. 415 (E.D. Va. 1989).

228 Diwik, Puente & Smith, *supra* note 24, at 236-44.

D. Waiver of Notice

Another common clause is a provision allowing the surety, without notice to the indemnitors (which notice is waived), to accept any changes or modifications in bonds, contracts and all manner of agreements relating to them. This section is typically read in conjunction with the settlement-of-claims provisions and with the power-of-attorney provision. Some courts have required notice by the surety of intent to settle claims made.[229] However, others enforce the terms of the indemnity agreement as written. In *Developers Surety & Indemnity Co. v. Martin*, the court agreed that pursuant to the indemnity agreement, the indemnitors had waived any right to notice of claims and held that "[i]t is well settled that a party to a contract is presumed to know its contents and is bound by its terms."[230]

E. Waiver of Homestead and Other Exemptions

Another commonly found clause in the indemnity agreement provides that the indemnitors waive all right to claim property, including homestead, as exempt from levy, execution or sale. With respect to this clause, local law must be consulted. In one case, *Transamerica Insurance Co. v. Avenell*,[231] the indemnitors sought release from their indemnity agreement obligations based on the attempt of the surety to waive homestead exemptions in the indemnity agreement, which the indemnitors argued was against public policy. Fortunately for the surety, the court severed that clause from the balance of the indemnity agreement and enforced it as written. In general, the enforceability of a waiver of the homestead exemption will be determined on a state-by-state basis. States have a range of homestead exemption provisions, from

---

229 *See* Reliance Ins. Co. v. Penn Paving, Inc., 734 A.2d 833 (Pa. 1999) (declining to uphold the waiver of notice clause); Am. Bonding Co. v. Nelson, 763 P.2d 814 (Utah Ct. App. 1988) (finding notice inadequate despite waiver of notice provision); New Amsterdam Cas. Co. v. Lundquist, 198 N.W.2d 543 (Minn. 1972). For a more in depth analysis of waiver of notice provisions, *see* Marmor & Mann, *supra* note 214, at 383-84.
230 No. 3:05-CV-447, 2006 WL 1984425, at *6 (E.D. Tenn. July 14, 2006).
231 66 F.3d 715 (5th Cir. 1995).

a full and complete exemption,[232] to a partial exemption with a monetary limit. In some, the exemption may be waived by contract,[233] but in others, the waiver will be held invalid.[234]

F. Right to Financial Information from Third-Parties

An indemnity agreement may include a provision granting the surety access to financial information of the principal/indemnitor(s) that is held by a third-party, such as a bank, depository institution, creditor, subcontractor or any other party possessing relevant information. Driven by the need for efficiency and promptness when addressing claims, the provision can eliminate the hesitancy or reluctance that a third-party may express when facing a demand for its customer's information. Additionally, the indemnity agreement can serve as a shield not only for the surety, but also for the third-party, against claims of the principal/indemnitor that the release of records was unauthorized.

The provision may also serve to protect the surety by imposing a duty on creditors of the principal/indemnitors to disclose to the surety material information unknown to the surety.[235] This duty would apply, for example, where the creditor knows information that materially affects the surety's risk beyond the amount of risk the creditor believes the surety intended to assume.[236]

---

232 *See, e.g.*, Fla. Const. art. X, §4(a); Tex. Const. art. XVI, § 50.

233 *See* Marmor & Mann, *supra* note 214, at 389-91 (listing Alabama, Alaska, Arizona, Arkansas, Delaware, Georgia, Illinois, Kentucky, Louisiana, Massachusetts, Minnesota, Missouri, Nevada, New Mexico, North Carolina, North Dakota, Oklahoma, South Dakota, Tennessee, Utah, Virginia, Washington, and Wyoming as the states allowing the enforcement of contractual waivers of the homestead exemption).

234 *See id.* at 389-91 (citing California, Colorado, Connecticut, District of Columbia, Florida, Idaho, Iowa, Kansas, Maryland, Montana, Ohio, Pennsylvania, Texas as states where at least one court has struck down a waiver of homestead provision on various grounds).

235 *See* Arena, Friedman, Bartlett & Stewart, *supra* note 223, at 69 (citing Logan Bank & Trust Co. v. Letter Shop, Inc., 437 S.E.2d 271 (W. Va. 1993); First Nat'l Bank & Trust Co. of Racine v. Notte, 293 N.W.2d 530 (Wis. 1980); Peoples Nat'l Bank of Wash. v. Taylor, 711 P.2d 1021 (Wash. Ct. App. 1985)).

236 *See id.* at 69 and notes thereto.

Conclusion

Supplementing the rights a surety has by operation of law, including its rights of equitable subrogation, the indemnity agreement is the surety's primary tool through which it can minimize its losses: the assignment provisions enhance the surety's right to stand in the shoes of its principal, and depending on the language of a given indemnity agreement, attach those rights upon execution of the Agreement, as opposed to upon issuance of the bonds; the collateral deposit provision protects the surety before it has paid any loss; the trust fund provisions protect the surety by sequestering contract funds and holding the principal accountable in the event the funds are misused; the "right-to-settle" provisions allow the surety broad discretion in handling and resolving claims; and the various complementary provisions accentuate and bolster these contractual rights.

While the indemnity agreement is an undeniably powerful tool for the surety, especially with regard to the ability to pursue individual indemnitors, it may be over-relied upon by sureties making claim decisions. Without downplaying the value of a finely crafted indemnity agreement, sureties are well-advised to have a thorough understanding of the rights available under the indemnity agreement from the onset of its relationship with its principal and indemnitors. Too often and to their detriment, sureties base decisions strictly upon the indemnity agreement, waiting until an indemnity/collection action is necessary, when in truth, the indemnity agreement, when applied as a leveraging tool can carry far more value than the actual ability to obtain reimbursement of surety loss.

Specifically, a surety can often obtain the cooperation of its principal and the individual indemnitors before losses are incurred, based upon the reminder of indemnity obligations. When indemnitors find themselves facing the loss of personal property such as their private homes, they can often put more effective pressure on the principal to cooperate with the surety before the indemnity obligations become the only alternative for the surety to recover its losses. In other words, the surety should not wait until a collection action is necessary to review and enforce its indemnity agreement rights. Both prior to and after losses have occurred, the ability of the surety to minimize its losses is greatly augmented by a well-crafted indemnity agreement.

7

RIGHT OF THE SURETY TO PURSUE CLAIMS AGAINST THIRD-PARTIES

Christopher R. Ward
Nicholas Hyslop

Introduction

Sureties typically focus their salvage efforts on available claims against their principals and individual indemnitors, against whom they have formidable and well established common law rights and contractual rights per the general indemnity agreement signed as a condition to issuance of the bonds.[1] Available bonded project contract funds also provide a potential way to mitigate surety loss.[2] Unfortunately, usually a surety's principal and the individual indemnitors no longer have the financial wherewithal to indemnify the surety after a large default. Furthermore, contract funds, if any, remaining in the hands of owners seldom make the surety whole. Consequently, after suffering a loss, sureties must consider looking to other entities or individuals for recovery. This chapter will explore potential claims against third parties and their insurers.[3]

---

1 *See infra* at V.
2 *See infra* at IV.
3 For more discussion of claims against third parties, see Ronald F. Goetsch & Christopher R. Ward, *Deciding to Litigate: The Surety's Recourse Against Third Parties, in* MANAGING AND LITIGATING THE COMPLEX SURETY CASE 173-258 (Philip L. Burner & Tracey L. Haley eds., 2d ed. 2007); James D. Ferrucci & Scott D. Baron, *The Surety's Claims Against Third Parties, in* SALVAGE BY THE SURETY 209-262 (George J. Bachrach ed., 1998). For further discussion of claims against insurance policies, see Patrick J. O'Connor, Jr., *Deciding to Litigate: The Surety's Rights Against Property and Liability Insurers of the Obligee, Principal, and Subcontractors, in* MANAGING AND LITIGATING THE COMPLEX SURETY CASE 259-429 (Philip L. Burner & Tracey L. Haley eds., 2d ed. 2007); Christopher R. Ward & Mary Jean Pethick, *Considerations With Respect to Insurance Coverage, in* BOND DEFAULT MANUAL 393-430 (Duncan L. Clore et al. eds., 3d ed. 2005).

I. Source of a Surety's Rights Against Third Parties

In some situations, a third-party may directly aggrieve a surety, giving rise to a direct right of action against that third-party. In many instances, however, the surety becomes involved in a construction project after the third-party's wrongful act or inaction, and is forced to remedy the resulting damages. Due to the surety's unique role, it may lack the relationship, contractual or otherwise, with the third-party necessary to support a direct third-party claim. Thus, a surety's subrogation and assignment rights often play a crucial role in evaluating and pursuing third-party claims.[4] In addition, a surety's exoneration and indemnity rights in certain limited cases, give rise to a third-party claim. These concepts are discussed generally below.

A. *Subrogation*

Subrogation is defined as the "substitution of one party for another whose debt the party pays, entitling the paying party to rights, remedies, or securities that would otherwise belong to the debtor."[5] It is well established that a surety who discharges or performs the principal's obligations can assert the rights of any party whose claim the surety satisfies, by virtue of its equitable subrogation rights.[6] Accordingly, when a surety satisfies an obligee's performance claim, the surety will be entitled to pursue claims available to the obligee against third parties, such as claims against design professionals who are in privity with the obligee. Likewise, when a surety satisfies a subcontractor's payment bond claim, the surety steps into the shoes of that subcontractor with respect to claims it may have for losses suffered on the project, such as mechanic's lien claims or trust fund claims. The surety's equitable subrogation rights extend not only to the rights of the obligee or claimant whose claim it satisfies, but also to the rights of the defaulting principal.

---

4   For further and more detailed discussion of a surety's rights of subrogation and assignment, *see* George J. Bachrach & John V. Burch, *The Surety's Subrogation Rights, in* THE LAW OF SURETYSHIP 419-454 (Edward G. Gallagher ed., 2d ed. 2000).

5   BLACK'S LAW DICTIONARY 1467 (8th ed. 2004).

6   Pearlman v. Reliance Ins. Co., 371 U.S. 132, 139 (1962); Prairie State Bank v. United States, 164 U.S. 227, 231 (1896); *see also* 73 AM. JUR. 2d § 53 (2008).

As stated by one court, "[t]he general rule is that, upon answering for the default of its principal, a surety may be subrogated to any claims which the defaulting principal might have against third parties whose wrongful conduct allegedly were the cause of the default."[7] The principal's rights may be essential, for instance, when pursuing a claim against a subcontractor for defective work[8] or when pursuing the principal's insurer for project losses.[9]

As a general rule, subrogation rights arise only after the surety has satisfied an obligee's or claimant's claim.[10] Some courts have held that a surety may not pursue its subrogation rights until the obligee or claimant are paid in full.[11] In the event that a surety is exposed to, but has not yet suffered, a loss, the surety's assignment rights (discussed below), may be the only vehicle available to seek recovery from a third-party. Other courts, however, recognize a surety's right to pursue subrogation rights even though it has not yet suffered a loss or fully satisfied a claim.[12] The court's decision in *Menorah Nursing Home, Inc. v. Zukov*,[13] illustrates a court's recognition of a surety's contingent subrogation rights with a

---

[7] Menorah Nursing Home, Inc. v. Zukov, 548 N.Y.S.2d 702, 705 (App. Div. 1989).

[8] *See, e.g., id.*

[9] Auto Owners Ins. Co. v. Reliance Ins. Co., 227 F. Supp. 2d 1248, 1260 (M.D. Fla. 2002); W. World Ins. Co. v. Travelers Indem. Co., 358 So. 2d 602, 604 (Fla. Dist. Ct. App. 1978); Am. Ins. Co. v. Ohio Bur. of Workers' Comp., 577 N.E.2d 756, 758-59 (Ohio Ct. App. 1991); Travelers Indem. Co. v. Aetna Ins. Co., No. 89AP-816, 1989 Ohio App. LEXIS 4673, at *3 (Ohio Ct. App. Dec. 14, 1989); *see also* Robert F. Carney, *Subrogation Rights of the Surety Against its Principal's Insurer: Could The Principal Possibly Have a Deep Pocket?* (unpublished paper presented at the 6th Annual Northeast Surety & Fidelity Claims Conference, November 16-17, 1995).

[10] *See, e.g.*, Equilease Corp. v. United States Fid. & Guar. Co., 565 S.W.2d 125, 126 (Ark. 1978); Gen. Ins. Co. of Am. v. State Highway Comm'n, 414 P.2d 526, 530 (Mont. 1966).

[11] *See, e.g.*, Fid. & Deposit Co. of Md. v. Hay, 9 F.2d 749, 750 (3d. Cir. 1926), *cert denied*, 271 U.S. 663 (1926); Martin v. Nat'l Sur. Corp., 262 A.2d 672, 675 (Pa. 1970).

[12] *See, e.g.*, United States Fid. & Guar. Co. v. Sweeney, 80 F.2d 235, 237 (8th Cir. 1935); Corn Constr. Co. v. Aetna Cas. & Sur. Co., 295 F.2d 685, 689 (10th Cir. 1961); United Pac. Ins. Co. v. U.S., 319 F.2d 893, 895-96 (Ct. Cl. 1963).

[13] 548 N.Y.S.2d 702 (App. Div. 1989).

third-party claim. In *Menorah*, the obligee sued the surety to recover damages resulting from the principal's default.[14] In turn, the surety asserted third-party claims against four of its principal's subcontractors and one of the subcontractor's surety, alleging the wrongful conduct of such subcontractors caused the default and, hence, that they should be held responsible.[15] The appellate court reversed a dismissal of the surety's claims against the subcontractors and surety, holding that the principal's surety was entitled to recover from them "all or part of what [the surety] may ultimately be found to owe the [obligee] on account of deficiencies in the completion of the general contract."[16] Significantly, the court rejected the argument that the surety could not yet assert its claim simply because it had not yet paid the claim or been found liable.[17] Although recognizing that subrogation typically only arises after the claim of the obligee has been paid, the court nonetheless allowed the surety to proceed on a "contingent third-party claim based on subrogation."[18]

Subrogation rights rise only as high as the party to whose rights the surety is subrogated, and the surety is subject to all defenses available against the subrogor.[19] Some third-party particular defenses are discussed later in this chapter. In many cases, the surety has little ability to influence these defenses before they arise. However, with respect to claims against a principal's insurer, the surety may be able to stave off particular defenses. For instance, the insurer may raise defenses based on the insured's lack of timely notice, the insured's failure to cooperate in a claim investigation, or the insured's settlement of a claim without obtaining the requisite insurer consent.[20] By encouraging its principal, or other parties to whose rights the surety may be subrogated, to comply with all of the conditions in potentially applicable policies, the surety may help avoid such defenses. The surety might also consider providing

---

14   *Id.* at 704-05.
15   *Id.*
16   *Id.* at 710.
17   *Id.* at 706.
18   *Id.*
19   *See, e.g.,* Hartford Accident & Indem. Co. v. First Nat'l Bank & Trust Co., 287 F.2d 69, 72 (10th Cir. 1961).
20   *See* Ferrucci & Baron, *supra* note 3, at 248.

its own notices to insurers as a potential subrogee to the insureds' rights under potentially applicable policies.[21]

B. Assignment

In addition to its rights of subrogation, a surety typically has been assigned the rights of its principal by way of a general indemnity agreement. As such, with respect to potential claims against third parties asserted *vis-à-vis* its principal, a surety may not need to resort to the equitable remedy of subrogation. Likewise, when a surety satisfies the claims of an obligee or claimant, it often takes a direct assignment of that party's potential claims against third parties and need not assert subrogation rights when pursuing those claims. In many instances, the surety's assignment rights do not place it in any better position than with subrogation rights.[22] Like subrogation, the rights obtained by the surety through assignment can rise no higher than that of its principal, and the surety is subject to any defenses a subcontractor or supplier may have against the principal.[23] In certain situations, however, asserting a claim by way of assignment may present advantages over asserting a claim via subrogation.

Unlike the surety's subrogation rights, the surety's assignment rights typically arise upon a principal's default, as defined by the general indemnity agreement, rather than after the surety has expended funds to satisfy the obligations of its principal.[24] Although some courts have allowed sureties to assert a third-party "contingent subrogation claim" in order to sidestep the general rule that subrogation rights arise only upon

---

21 Joanne S. Brooks et al., *Importance of Insurance Coverage for Sureties* (unpublished paper presented at meeting of ABA Forum on the Construction Industry, January 27, 2005); Ferruci & Baron, *supra* note 3, at 249.
22 *See, e.g.*, Nat'l Sur. Corp. v. Allen-Codell Co., 70 F. Supp. 189, 191 (E.D. Ky. 1947) (surety's assignment right "seems to add nothing" to surety's subrogation claim); *see also* Ferrucci & Baron, *supra* note 3.
23 Ferrucci & Baron, *supra* note 3.
24 Fid. & Deposit Co. of Md. v. United States, 31 Fed. Cl. 540, 542-43 (1994) (where surety had not paid out any funds under performance bond, it could not assert equitable rights of subrogation); *see also* Armen Shahinian, *The General Agreement of Indemnity*, in THE LAW OF SURETYSHIP 517-25 (Edward G. Gallagher ed., 2d ed. 2000).

fund expenditure,[25] other courts may refuse to recognize "contingent" subrogation rights. In such situations, assignment may be the only available avenue for a surety to pursue claims against a subcontractor or supplier.

In addition, most general agreements of indemnity provide that they can be filed as financing statements under the UCC. If the surety has properly filed the general indemnity agreement as a UCC financing statement, thereby perfecting its security interest, the surety's assignment rights may prove extremely important against competing creditors. Having a perfected security interest in such claims will be particularly important if the principal is in bankruptcy, as it will place the surety in a better position to control the claim. Furthermore, some indemnity agreements provide the surety with a security interest in claims arising on any project, even if not bonded by the surety. Sureties seldom pursue assigned claims on projects they did not bond, simply due to the time and expense necessary to pursue such claims and because, in many cases, the surety's interest in such claims is inferior to prior perfected security interests. However, in certain situations, those rights may prove to be a viable salvage source, especially where the actions or inactions of a subcontractor or supplier on an unbonded project was the genesis of the principal's ultimate undoing.

In other situations, however, subrogation may present an advantage over assignment. For instance, a principal's contract with the third-party against whom a claim is being considered may contain an anti-assignment provision, barring the assignment of the principal's rights to the surety. Such anti-assignment provisions may be relied upon in an attempt to overcome assigned contract claims.[26] However, anti-

---

25 Menorah Nursing Home, Inc. v. Zukov, 548 N.Y.S.2d 702, 705 (App. Div. 1989). *But see* RESTATEMENT (THIRD) OF SURETYSHIP AND GUARANTY § 27(1) (1995).

26 Although some courts will invalidate an attempted assignment altogether when the contract contains an anti-assignment provision, the modern trend is to hold that such provisions only limit a parties' right to assign a contract, not its power to do so, unless the clause specifically declares any assignment to be void. *See e.g.*, Bank of America, N.A. v. Moglia, 330 F.3d 942, 947-48 (7th Cir. 2003); Bel-Ray Co. v. Chemrite Ltd., 181 F.3d 435, 441-43 (3d Cir. 1999); Pravin Banker Assocs. v. Banco Popular Del Peru, 109 F.3d 850, 856 (2d Cir. 1997); Cedar Point Apartments, Ltd. v. Cedar Point Inv. Corp., 693 F.2d 748, 753-54 (8th Cir. 1982); Wonsey v.

assignment provisions have been held not to have been implicated by the surety's subrogation rights, which arose upon the surety's payment of its principal's obligations.[27] Since subrogation rights do not arise under the contract, "anti-" or "no assignment" provisions in the contract do not affect the surety's rights as a subrogee.[28]

C. *Exoneration and Indemnification*

The surety's exoneration and indemnification rights may give rise to a claim against a principal's general liability insurer for defense and indemnity in certain cases. For instance, where the surety has been sued by the obligee, the principal's general liability insurer may have a duty to defend the surety due to the principal's contractual and common law obligations to exonerate and indemnify the surety.[29] Although most

---

Life Ins. Co. of N. Am., 32 F.Supp.2d 939, 943-44 (E.D. Mich. 1998); Int'l Telecomm. Exch. Corp. v. MCI Telecomm. Corp., 892 F. Supp. 1520, 1533-34 (N.D. Ga. 1995); Pro Cardiaco Pronto Socorro Cardiologica, S.A. v. Trussell, 863 F. Supp. 135, 137-38 (S.D.N.Y. 1994); Lomas Mortgage U.S.A., Inc. v. W.E. O'Neil Constr. Co., 812 F. Supp. 841, 843-44 (N.D. Ill. 1993); *In re* Freeman, 232 B.R. 497, 501-02 (Fla. Bankr. 1999); Rumbin v. Utica Mut. Ins. Co., 757 A.2d 526, 532-34 (Conn. 2000); Travertine Corp. v. Lexington-Silverwood, Ltd. P'ship, 683 N.W.2d 267, 272-74 (Minn. 2004); *In re* Kaufman, 37 P.3d 845, 851-52 (Okla. 2001). Under this reasoning, unless an anti-assignment clause specifically voids an assignment, the assignment is valid and the party contesting the assignment is relegated to a remedy in damages due to a breach of the clause. Typically, monetary damages do not flow from an assignment in derogation of an anti-assignment clause.

27 Reliance Ins. Co. v. City of Boston, 884 N.E.2d 524, 530 (Mass. App. Ct. 2008) ("Rights of subrogation, although growing out of a contractual setting and ofttimes articulated by the contract, do not depend for their existence on a grant in the contract, but are created by law to avoid injustice."(quoting Canter v. Schlager, 267 N.E.2d 492, 494 (Mass. 1971)).

28 Am. Mfrs. Mut. Ins. Co. v. Payton Lane Nursing Home, Inc., CV-05-5155, 2007 U.S. Dist. LEXIS 15160, at *24 (E.D.N.Y. Feb. 28, 2007) ("Subrogation is not a transfer of a cause of action." (quoting Liberty Mut. Fire Ins. Co. v. Perricone, 54 A.D.2d 975 (N.Y. 1976)).

29 Merrick Constr. Co. v. Hartford Fire Ins. Co., 449 So. 2d 85, 88 (La. Ct. App. 1984); Natchitoches Parish Sch. Bd. v. Shaw, 620 So. 2d 412, 414-

commercial general liability policies specifically exclude coverage for damages assumed by contract, the principal's common law duties to exonerate and/or indemnify the surety may prevent the application of such exclusion.

II. Claims Against Subcontractors and Material Suppliers

When a principal has encountered problems on a project stemming from a failure to comply with plans or specifications, defective materials, or delays in performing the work, responsibility for such problems often rests, at least in part, with the subcontractors and/or suppliers who contracted with the principal to perform the work and/or supply the material. In addition, when a surety has satisfied payment bond claims by a subcontractor's or supplier's downstream subcontractors or suppliers, the surety may have claims against the principal's subcontractor or supplier for such nonpayment, either by virtue of rights obtained via subrogation or assignment from those downstream subcontractors or suppliers the surety has paid or pursuant to an applicable construction trust fund statute.[30]

Courts have uniformly recognized a surety's right to recover via its subrogation rights from its principal's subcontractors and suppliers for breach of their underlying subcontract and/or warranties issued in connection therewith.[31] The principal's rights against its subcontractors and suppliers are also typically assigned to the surety by way of a general indemnity agreement. Of course, when a completing surety has entered into a formal ratification agreement with a subcontractor or supplier, it

---

15 (La. Ct. App. 1993); *see also* Carney, *supra* note 7, at 21-22; Ferrucci & Baron, *supra* note 3, at 247-48.

30 Construction trust fund statutes are discussed further *infra* at VII.A.

31 Kelley Island Lime & Transp. Co. v. City of Cleveland, 47 F. Supp. 533, 545 (E.D. Ohio 1942); Storm & Butts v. Lipscomb, 3 P.2d 567, 572 (Cal. Ct. App. 1931); Bewley Furniture Co. v. Md. Cas. Co., 285 So. 2d 216, 220 (La. 1973); Sentry Ins. v. Lardner Elevator Co., 395 N.W.2d 31, 32 (Mich. App. 1986); Menorah Nursing Home, Inc. v. Zukov, 548 N.Y.S.2d 702, 705 (App. Div. 1989); Md. Cas. Co. v. King, 381 P.2d 153, 157-58 (Okla. 1963); *see also* United States v. Am. Employers Ins. Co., 141 F. Supp. 281, 290-91 (E.D. Pa. 1956).

should be able to assert claims directly under that agreement without looking to its subrogation rights.[32]

A surety might also consider whether it can pursue a claim against a subcontractor or supplier by virtue of its subrogation rights vis-à-vis the obligee. Although obligees typically are not in privity with the subcontractors and suppliers on a project, the obligee may have potential tort claims against them based on negligent work performed, which may also give rise to a viable insurance claim.[33] In addition, the owner may have express or implied warranty claims against a subcontractor or supplier. The possibility of asserting such rights is especially prevalent when a performance claim is asserted after substantial completion of the project. Many of the warranties provided by subcontractors and suppliers, and turned over to the owner upon completion, may prove invaluable tools in a surety's salvage efforts.

Recoverable damages include the costs to cure the subcontractor's or supplier's breach, damages for delay, and even attorney's fees incurred by the surety in enforcing the underlying subcontract.[34] A surety may also be able to recover tort damages recovered from the general contractor's surety by a third-party which resulted from the negligent acts performed by the subcontractor on a project.[35] The surety's available rights against a subcontractor for damages resulting from performance defects, or failures to perform, the work called for by the subcontract, as well as claims arising from a subcontractor's failure to pay downstream subcontractors and suppliers, may also be asserted against the subcontractor's surety.[36]

---

32   *See* Ferrucci & Baron, *supra* note 3.
33   Insurance claims are discussed further *infra* at VIII.
34   Am. Employers Ins. Co., 141 F. Supp. at 290-91 (allowing partial recovery for delay damages); Sentry Ins., 395 N.W.2d at 35-36 (allowing recovery of cost to cure, delay damages, and attorney's fees).
35   United States Fid. & Guar. Co. v. Tomlinson-Arkwright Co., 141 P.2d 817, 826-827 (Or. 1943) (holding surety for general contractor entitled to recover from subcontractor and surety for damages recovered by individuals injured on highway as a result of defective work performed by subcontractor on the highway).
36   *Id.*, *see also* Mai Steel Service Inc. v. Blake Constr. Co., 981 F.2d 414, 421 (9th Cir. 1992) (holding that general contractor's surety is entitled to be indemnified by subcontractor's surety for any liability arising out of the subcontractor's breach, including failure to pay downstream

As addressed generally above, a surety's claim against a principal's subcontractors and suppliers asserted via subrogation or assignment is subject to any defenses that may be available to the subcontractor or supplier. As stated by the Eastern District of Kentucky in *National Surety Corp. v. Allen-Codell Co.*:

> [T]he surety stands in no better position that the principal contractor through whom his right is derived. The rights and remedies to which the surety succeeds are taken subject to all defenses, limitations and disqualifications incident to them in the hands of the party to whom he is subrogated. As against the subcontractor, the surety is not subrogated to rights which may have originally existed in favor of the principal contractor but is limited to such rights as the principal contractor had against the subcontractor as of the time the contract was completed. In other words, the surety stands in the shoes of the principal contractor, with no better right or remedy.[37]

One of the most common subcontractor defenses in response to surety claims asserted pursuant to its subrogation rights is that the principal committed a prior material breach by failing to pay the subcontractor per the subcontract, thereby relieving the subcontractor of its obligations. When a subcontractor or supplier asserts prior material breach as a defense, however, the subcontractor's actions after the alleged material breach may significantly influence a court's conclusion as to whether such a breach occurred. For instance, in *Sentry Ins. v. Lardner Elevator Co.*, the court considered the subcontractor's conduct after the alleged breach. After the default, the subcontractor continued to work on the project, dealing directly with the surety and obligee.[38] The court reasoned that if the subcontractor "insisted on a forfeiture when [the

---

subcontractors); Houston Fire & Cas. Ins. Co. v. E.E. Cloer Gen. Contactor, Inc., 217 F.2d 906, 911-12 (5th Cir. 1954); Cont'l Cas. Co. v. Hartford Accident & Indem. Co., 52 Cal. Rptr. 533, 537 (Cal. Ct. App. 1966); Argonaut Ins. Co. v. Commercial Standard Ins. Co., 380 So. 2d 1066, 1068 (Fla. Dist. Ct. App. 1980).

37 Nat'l Sur. Corp. v. Allen-Codell Co., 70 F. Supp. 189, 191 (E.D. Ky. 1947); *see also Sentry Ins.*, 395 N.W.2d at 34 ("Had [the principal] breached the subcontract...[the subcontractor] could assert that breach against [the surety] to excuse its performance.").

38 *Sentry Ins.*, 395 N.W.2d at 34.

principal] withdrew, it should have done so at once."[39] Accordingly, the court refused to find a prior material breach and allowed the surety to recover from the subcontractor.[40]

III. Claims Against Design Professionals

Design professionals, i.e., architects and engineers, are often involved in every aspect of a construction project. When a design professional's failure to perform his or her contractual and/or common law duties has contributed to or increased the surety's loss, the surety may be able to seek recourse against the design professional.[41]

A. *Potential Causes of Action Against Design Professionals*

Claims for professional negligence, whether against design or other professionals, are typically limited to claims by those who share privity with the professional. Obviously, a surety called upon to complete a project is not in contractual privity with the design professional. Accordingly, to pursue a claim against a design professional, the surety must overcome the traditional privity bar. The potential theories of recovery against a design professional, and the hurdles created by contractual limitations and the economic loss rule, are examined below.

1. *Breach of Contract Claims Asserted by Subrogation or Assignment*

One way around the traditional privity bar is for a surety to assert a breach of contract claim directly against the design professional by stepping into the shoes of the obligee. A performing surety is equitably

---

39 *Id.*
40 *Id.*; *see also Am. Employers Ins. Co.*, 141 F. Supp. at 290-91.
41 For further analysis of a surety's potential claims against design professionals, *see* Goetsch & Ward, *supra* note 3; Martha Crandall Coleman, *Design Professionals' Liability for Negligent Design and Project Management* (unpublished paper submitted at the ABA/TIPS Fid. & Sur. Law Committee annual meeting, January 24, 1997); Michael L. Chapman, *Liability of Design Professionals to the Surety*, 20 FORUM 591 (1985).

subrogated to the obligee's rights, including the obligee's claims of negligence and breach of the design contract against the design professional.[42] The surety may obtain a direct assignment of the owner's claims against the design professional.[43] In addition to avoiding problems of privity, a surety's breach of contract claim asserted through subrogation or assignment has the advantage of bypassing application of the economic loss rule in those jurisdictions that apply it to suits against design professionals.[44]

When asserting a breach of contract claim against a design professional, a surety may confront contractual provisions between the owner and design professional whereby the design professional attempts to limit his or her liability, either by limiting the scope of the undertaking or specifically disclaiming responsibility for delay, lost profits, lost use of equipment, increased expense of operation, or cost of purchased or replacement equipment.[45] A design professional may also attempt to limit his or her liability under the contract to the total amount of fees he or she charges for services.[46] Whether such disclaimers are effective may depend in large part on whether the surety's cause of action sounds in tort or in contract. A design professional's duty of due care and competence is a common law duty not subject to contract limitations and, thus, a negligence suit brought by a surety should not be affected by contractual limitations of liability. However, when the surety asserts a breach of contract claim against a design professional as the owner's subrogee or assignee, then the surety likely will be subject to contractual limitations that were fairly bargained for and lawful. As long as the

---

42   *See* Lyndon Property Ins. Co. v. Duke Levy & Assocs., 475 F.3d 268, 270-71 (5th Cir. 2007); Am. Mfrs. Mut. Ins. Co. v. Payton Lane Nursing Home, Inc., CV-05-5155, 2007 U.S. Dist. LEXIS 15160, at *24-25 (E.D.N.Y. Feb. 28, 2007); Hanover Ins. Co. v. Corrpro Cos., Inc., 312 F. Supp. 2d 816, 824 (E.D. Va. 2004).

43   *See* Berschauer/Phillips Constr. Co. v. Seattle Sch. Dist. No. 1, 881 P.2d 986, 993 (Wash. 1994) (recognizing right of owner to assign claims against design professional).

44   *See* discussion of economic loss rule *infra* at Section IV.A.3.

45   *See, e.g.*, Wausau Paper Mills Co. v. Chas. T. Main, Inc., 789 F. Supp. 968, 970 (W.D. Wis. 1992); J & J Elec., Inc. v. Gilbert H. Moen Co., 516 P.2d 217, 221 (Wash. 1973).

46   *See, e.g.*, Marbro, Inc. v. Borough of Tinton Falls, 688 A.2d 159, 161-62 (N.J. Sup. Ct. Law Div. 1996).

contractual limitations are not unconscionable, they will most likely be enforced, despite that the surety may be left without recourse to recover its losses.[47]

However, not all disclaimers will totally absolve the design professional of responsibility for its breach of contract. For instance, in *Lyndon Property Ins. Co. v. Duke Levy and Associates*, the Fifth Circuit held that the exculpatory clause at issue did not save the engineer from liability from anyone except the owner: "[T]he District cannot bargain away the engineer's potential duty to a surety that would step into the District's shoes under the doctrine of equitable subrogation."[48] It has also been held that when the design professional observes a known defect, he or she has a duty to notify the owner: "[A]n architect cannot close his eyes on the construction site and refuse to engage in any inspection procedure whatsoever and then disclaim liability for construction defects that even the most perfunctory monitoring would have prevented."[49] Likewise, when an architect certified payment in the face of direct notification of construction problems, the Mississippi Supreme Court held that the architect's duty to exercise ordinary professional skills and competence was non-delegable.[50] Accordingly, the court held that the architect breached the contract by failing to stop defective construction of which the architect had actual knowledge.[51]

2. Negligence

In most jurisdictions, a design professional owes a duty to the owner to perform with due care and competence, as defined by professional associations and common law, separate and apart from his or her contractual obligations.[52] Although separate from contract, privity has traditionally acted as a bar to third-party claims of professional

---

47 See *Wausau Paper*, 789 F. Supp. at 975.
48 Lyndon Property Ins. Co. v. Duke Levy and Associates, 475 F.3d 268, 270 (5th Cir. 2007).
49 Watson, Watson, Rutland/Architects, Inc. v. Montgomery County Bd. of Educ., 559 So. 2d 168, 174 (Ala. 1990).
50 U.R.S. Co. v. Gulfport-Biloxi Reg. Airport Auth., 544 So. 2d 824, 827 (Miss. 1989).
51 *Id.*
52 For a discussion of the duties owed by design professionals, *see* Goetsch & Ward, *supra* note 3, at 187-88.

negligence. However, many jurisdictions have created exceptions to the privity bar that may allow a surety to pursue a negligence claim against a design professional.

a. *Strict Privity Approach.* Jurisdictions that require strict privity for liability to attach in professional negligence generally treat the professional's duty as one arising solely by contract.[53] That is, no common law duty of care toward third parties is recognized, or the common law duty is overridden by policy reasons.[54] Policy reasons most frequently cited in favor of applying a strict privity approach are: (1) allocation of risk is best left to the contracting parties, and that allowing a negligence suit by one not in privity will open the design professional to potentially unlimited liability to a potentially unlimited class of persons or entities; and (2) allowing tort suits by parties not in privity will wrest control over contracts from those who make them.[55] In those jurisdictions adhering to a strict privity approach, a surety's only chance of prevailing against a design professional on a direct breach of contract claim will be by way of subrogation and/or assignment as discussed above.

b. *Quasi-Privity Approach.* Other courts have allowed sureties recourse against design professionals despite the lack of privity by finding that the relationship between a surety and a design professional is the functional equivalent of privity, or that the relationship between the parties is so close as to be tantamount to privity.[56] Cases employing such a quasi-privity approach have recognized the necessity of privity, but

---

53 The following jurisdictions have applied a strict privity bar to claims against design professionals: Nebraska: John Day Co. v. Alune & Assocs., Inc., 510 N.W.2d 462, 466-467 (Neb. Ct. App. 1993); New York: Widett v. United States Fid. & Guar. Co., 815 F.2d 885, 887 (2nd Cir. 1987) (applying New York law); Oklahoma: Am. Cas. Co. v. Bd. of Educ., 228 F. Supp. 843, 852 (W.D. Okla. 1964); Pennsylvania: Linde Enters., Inc. v. Hazelton City Auth., 602 A.2d 897, 900 (Pa. Super. Ct. 1992); Texas: Bernard Johnson, Inc. v. Cont'l Constructors, Inc., 630 S.W.2d 365, 370 (Tex. Ct. App. 1982).
54 *See John Day*, 510 N.W.2d at 466.
55 *See* Essex v. Ryan, 446 N.E.2d 368, 373 (Ind. Ct. App. 1983).
56 *See, e.g.*, Peerless Ins. Co. v. Cerny & Assocs., 199 F. Supp. 951, 955 (D. Minn. 1961); State *ex rel.* Nat'l Sur. Corp. v. Malvaney, 72 So. 2d 424, 430-31 (Miss. 1954); Westerhold v. Carroll, 419 S.W.2d 73, 78 (Mo. 1967).

have looked to all of the contract documents on a project as a whole to find the required privity.[57] That is, by looking at the prime contract, the design contract, and the bond, courts have found intertwining obligations running from the design professional to the owner and the surety.

This approach was discussed in *State ex rel. National Surety Corp. v. Malvaney*.[58] In that case, the contract between the architect and the owner obligated the architect to certify project completion and acceptance and that the balance of construction funds was due and payable to the contractor. The architect made such certifications without ascertaining if the contractor had paid its subcontractors, which the contractor had not done. Relying on such architect certifications, the owner released the funds to the contractor, who paid obligations unrelated to the project. The surety, called upon to complete the project, was left without sufficient project funds after the balances due to the subcontractors were paid, and sued the architect for negligent certification.[59]

The trial court found that the architect failed to exercise due diligence in ascertaining if the subcontractors had been paid and allowed the surety to recover the funds improperly released due to the architect's negligent certification.[60] On appeal, the Mississippi Supreme Court recognized that no privity of contract existed between the surety and the architect.[61] Nevertheless, the court upheld the judgment against the architect. In so doing, the court discussed the intertwined nature of the contract documents: "The contractual arrangement here consisted of the building contract, including the plans and specifications, and the bond which incorporated the contract as part thereof, with the mutually

---

57 *Peerless Ins.*, 199 F. Supp. at 955 (holding "architect's duty to protect the [o]wner and the subrogated surety arose out of the general and mutual contractual arrangements . . . "); Nat'l Sur. Corp., 72 So. 2d at 431 (finding architect under duty to protect surety's interest in retainage as part of contractual obligations arising under contract documents taken as whole); *Westerhold*, 419 S.W.2d at 80-81. *But see* Am. Mfrs. Mut. Ins. Co. v. Payton Lane Nursing Home, Inc., CV-05-5155, 2007 U.S. Dist. LEXIS 15160, at *17 (E.D.N.Y. Feb. 28, 2007) (applying quasi-privity approach, but found surety failed to have requisite link).
58 72 So. 2d 424 (Miss. 1954).
59 *Id.* at 425.
60 *Id.* at 429.
61 *Id.* at 431.

interdependent obligations and rights therein contained."[62] The contracts thus construed created a duty inuring to the benefit of both the owner and the surety, even though no direct contract existed between the surety and the architect.[63] Thus, the court found that the architect was under a duty to protect the surety's interest in the retainage as part of its contractual obligations arising under the contract documents taken as a whole.

Another case that recognized the quasi-privity nature of the relationship between surety and design professional was *Peerless Ins. Co. v. Cerny & Associates, Inc.*[64] Like *National Surety Corp.*, this case dealt with the architect's failure to properly supervise and approve the release of project funds to a defaulting contractor.[65] After being notified of the contractor's default, the surety completed the project and later sued the architect. The architect's inspector admitted that he did not question the contractor as to the accuracy of the project costs.[66] The owner paid the entire project fund to the contractor based on the inspector's certifications when the project was only two-thirds complete.[67]

At the end of a bench trial, the district court concluded that the architect's liability need not be predicated on privity: "Privity of contract between plaintiff and defendant was not a prerequisite to the existence of the defendant-architect's duty in the foregoing respect, for the reason that said architect's duty to protect the [o]wner and the subrogated surety arose out of the general and mutual contractual arrangements which included resulting independent rights and obligations."[68] The court found that the architect owed the surety an independent duty to ensure that retainage was not prematurely released.[69] The court also found that the architect had actual or constructive notice, knowledge of the surety bond, and the purpose of retainage.[70] Thus, the court found that the architect

---

62 *Id.*
63 *Id.*
64 199 F. Supp. 951 (D. Minn. 1961).
65 *Id.* at 953.
66 *Id.*
67 *Id.*
68 *Id.* at 955.
69 *Id.*
70 *Id.* at 954-55.

breached its duty to the surety by negligently certifying project completion and releasing retainage.[71]

c. *Restatement Approach.* Other courts have adopted the approach found in Restatement (Second) of Torts Section 552 to determine if a third-party, lacking privity, may pursue a claim against a design professional.[72] Section 552 provides as follows:

> (1) One who, in the course of his business, profession or employment, or in any other transaction in which he has a pecuniary interest, supplies false information for the guidance of others in their business transactions, is subject to liability for pecuniary loss caused to them by their justifiable reliance upon the information, if he fails to exercise reasonable care or competence in obtaining or communicating the information.
>
> (2) Except as stated in Subsection (3), the liability stated in Subsection (1) is limited to loss suffered
>
> > (i) by the person or one of a limited group of persons for whose benefit and guidance he intends to supply the information or knows that the recipient intends to supply it; and
> >
> > (ii) through reliance upon it in a transaction that he intends the information to influence or knows that the recipient so intends or in a substantially similar transaction.
>
> (3) The liability of one who is under a public duty to give the information extends to loss suffered by any of the class of persons

---

71   *Id.* at 955.

72   The following jurisdictions have applied the Restatement approach to claims against design professionals: Arizona: Donnelly Constr. Co. v. Oberg/Hunt/Gilleland, 677 P.2d 1292, 1297-98 (Ariz. 1984); Colorado: Wolther v. Schaarschmidt, 738 P.2d 25, 27-28 (Colo. Ct. App. 1986); Delaware: Guardian Constr. Co. v. Tetra Tech Richardson, Inc., 583 A.2d 1378, 1385 (Del. Super. Ct. 1990); Georgia: Robert & Co. Assocs. v. Rhodes-Harverty Partnership, 300 S.E.2d 503, 504 (Ga. 1983); Montana: Jim's Excavating Serv., Inc. v. HKM Assocs., 878 P.2d 248, 254-55 (Mont. 1994); North Carolina: Howell v. Fisher, 272 S.E.2d 19, 25-26 (N.C. Ct. App. 1980); Pennsylvania: Bilt-Rite Contractors, Inc. v. Architectural Studio, 866 A.2d 270, 287 (Pa. 2005); Tennessee: John Martin Co. v. Morse/Diesel, Inc., 819 S.W.2d 428, 432 (Tenn. 1991).

for whose benefit the duty is created, in any of the transactions in which it is intended to protect them.[73]

Like quasi-privity, the Restatement approach is a middle ground between privity and foreseeability, discussed below, in that it limits the class of potential claimants to those whom the professional knows will rely on the information, without the requirement that the parties be in privity. The Restatement approach has been successfully used in suits brought by contractors who, relying on an engineer's report, provide a low bid on a construction project that turns out to be too low due to report inaccuracies.[74] A contractor claim against an engineering firm for damages associated with delayed shop drawings was also successful.[75] However, even if the Restatement approach applies, the economic loss rule, discussed further below may prevent the claim.[76]

d. *Foreseeability.* A fourth approach to design professional liability in the absence of privity is the foreseeability approach.[77] In jurisdictions

---

73 RESTATEMENT (SECOND) OF TORTS § 552 (1977).
74 *See, e.g.,* Donnelly Constr. Co., 677 P.2d at 1293-94.
75 Malta Constr. Co. v. Henningson, Durham & Richardson, Inc., 694 F. Supp. 902, 907 (N.D. Ga. 1988).
76 *See* Berschauer/Phillips Constr. Co. v. Seattle Sch. Dist. No. 1, 881 P.2d 986, 993 (Wash. 1994) ("We hold that when parties have contracted to protect against economic liability, as is the case in the construction industry, contract principles override the tort principles in § 552 and, thus, purely economic damages are not recoverable.").
77 The foreseeability exception to privity has been applied in third-party claims against design professionals in several jurisdictions: Alabama: Berkel & Co. Contractors, Inc. v. Providence Hosp., 454 So. 2d 496, 503 (Ala. 1984); Arkansas: Carroll-Boone Water Dist. v. M & P Equip. Co., 661 S.W.2d 345, 349 (Ark. 1983); California: Huber, Hunt & Nichols, Inc. v. Moore, 136 Cal. Rptr. 603, 617 (Cal. Ct. App. 1977); Connecticut: Ins. Co. of N. Am. v. Town of Manchester, 17 F. Supp. 2d 81, 84-85 (D. Conn. 1998); Massachusetts: Parent v. Stone & Webster Eng'g Corp., 556 N.E.2d 1009, 1012, 1013 (Mass. 1990); Minnesota: Waldor Pump & Equip. Co. v. Orr-Schelen-Mayerson & Assocs., 386 N.W.2d 375, 377 (Minn. Ct. App. 1986); New Jersey: Conforti & Eisele, Inc. v. John C. Morris Assocs., 418 A.2d 1290, 1292 (N.J. Super Ct. Law Div. 1980), *aff'd* 489 A.2d 1233 (N.J. Super Ct. Law Div. 1985); North Carolina: Browing v. Maurice B. Levien & Co., 262 S.E.2d 355, 358 (N.C. Ct. App. 1980); Oklahoma: Keel v. Titan Constr. Corp., 639 P.2d 1228, 1232

applying this approach, a surety seeking liability against a design professional will need to establish that damages caused by the design professional's negligence were foreseeable. "The test is, would the ordinary man in the defendant's position, knowing what he knew or should have known, anticipate that harm of the general nature of that suffered was likely to result?"[78]

A foreseeability approach was discussed in *State ex rel. National Surety Corp v. Mulvaney*, mentioned above in the quasi-privity approach.[79] Although the court appeared to hold the contract documents created a quasi-privity relationship between the architect and surety, the court also suggested that the surety should recover against the architect for foreseeable harm resulting from the architect's negligent contract certification:

> There is still another basis for holding that the architect owed a duty to the surety not to approve the release of the retainage funds prior to the completion of the contract . . . [I]t was apparent that his failure to exercise due care and diligence to ascertain if there were outstanding bills for labor and material before approving the release of the retainage funds might result in loss to the surety by depriving it of its rights under the doctrine of subrogation to resort to such funds upon the default of the contractor. The architect, therefore, undertook the performance of an act which, it was apparent, if negligently done would result in loss to the surety, and the law imposed upon him the duty to exercise due care to avoid such loss.[80]

(Okla. 1981); South Carolina: Tommy L. Griffin Plumbing & Heating Co. v. Jordan, Jones & Goulding, Inc., 463 S.E.2d 85, 88-89 (S.C. 1995); South Dakota: Mid-Western Elec. Inc. v. DeWild Grant Reckert & Assocs. Co., 500 N.W.2d 250, 254 (S.D. 1993); Texas: Assoc. Architects & Eng'rs, Inc. v. Lubbock Glass & Mirror Co., 422 S.W.2d 942, 945 (Tex. Civ. App. 1967); Wisconsin: A.E. Inv. Corp. v. Link Builders, Inc., 214 N.W.2d 764, 768 (Wis. 1974).

78   Town of Manchester, 17 F. Supp. 2d at 85 (quoting Neal v. Shiels, Inc., 166 Conn. 3, 12-13, 347 A.2d 102 (1974)).
79   State *ex rel.* Nat'l Sur. Corp. v. Malvaney, 72 So. 2d 424, 431 (Miss. 1954).
80   *Id.*

In *Calandro Development, Inc. v. R. M. Butler Contractors, Inc.*,[81] the court held that a design professional is deemed to know that the services for which the engineer is engaged will be relied upon by both the owner and the surety:

> An engineer or architect must be deemed and held to know that his service are for the protection, not only of the interests of the owner, but also the surety on the contractor's bond who has no supervisory power whatsoever, and who must perforce rely on the architect or engineer to produce a completed project conformable with the contract plans and specifications.[82]

Thus, because it was foreseeable to the engineer that the surety's injury would result from its negligence, the surety's cause of action for negligence was proper.[83] Nevertheless, the court upheld the judgment against the surety on its claim against the engineer by ruling that the preponderance of evidence did not establish the degree of professional care and skill demanded of the engineer.[84]

A surety was also allowed to recover from an architect for negligent supervision based on a foreseeability approach in *Aetna Ins. Co. v. Hellmuth, Obata & Kassabaum, Inc.*[85] The Eighth Circuit reversed the ruling that the surety could not recover from an architect due to lack of privity, holding privity was not required as the two rationales for enforcing a privity requirement are absent when a surety sues a design professional for negligence.[86] That is, under a foreseeability analysis, an architect's lack of due care in its supervisory obligations does not create unlimited liability to an unlimited number of persons, because only foreseeable parties may assert a claim against the design professional.[87] Likewise, allowing a suit by a third-party surety does not deprive the contracting parties of control over their contracts, for the reason that the

---

81   249 So. 2d 254 (La. Ct. App. 1975).
82   *Id.* at 265.
83   *Id.*
84   *Id.* at 266. In particular, the court found that the testimony of the dueling experts was "in hopeless conflict" concerning the engineer's duty and, because of this, no breach of the engineer's duty was shown. *Id.*
85   392 F.2d 472 (8th Cir. 1968).
86   *Id.* at 475.
87   *Id.*

parties can freely change their obligations–a surety may be released from its obligations under the bond if its risks are enlarged, but the parties are under no obligation to the surety to keep their contract terms static.[88] Hence, the court held that because the surety could foreseeably be injured by the architect's negligence, the architect owed a duty to the surety:

> An architect is not a guarantor or an insurer but as a member of a learned and skilled profession he is under the duty to exercise the ordinary, reasonable technical skill, ability and competence that is required of an architect in a similar situation; and if by reason of a failure to use due care under the circumstances, a foreseeable injury results, liability accrues.[89]

e. *Other Approaches.* Some courts have adopted approaches to third-party claims against design professionals that do not readily fit into the categories discussed above. For instance in *Travelers Casualty & Surety Co. v. Dormitory Authority of New York*,[90] the court employed a three-part test developed in *Ossining Union Free School District v. Anderson LaRocca Anderson*,[91] requiring the plaintiff surety to show the following: (1) awareness on the part of the architect that its reports would be used for a particular purpose; (2) reliance by a known party or parties in furtherance of that purpose; and (3) some conduct by the architect linking it to the party and evidencing the architect's understanding of that reliance.[92] Like the quasi-privity approach discussed above, the *Dormitory Authority* court recognized that the relationship between the surety, the owner, and the architect is the functional equivalent of privity.[93] Unlike the other quasi-privity cases discussed above, however,

---

88　*Id.*
89　*Id.* at 476-77; *see also* Westerhold v. Carroll, 419 S.W.2d 73, 79 (Mo. 1967).
90　No. 04 Civ. 5101, 2005 U.S. Dist. LEXIS 9415 (S.D.N.Y. May 19, 2005).
91　539 N.E.2d 91, 95 (N.Y. Super. Ct. 1989).
92　*Dormitory Auth.*, 2005 U.S. Dist. LEXIS 9415, at *15; *see also* Reliance Ins. Co. v. Morris Assocs., 607 N.Y.S.2d 106, 107 (N.Y. App. Div. 1994).
93　*Dormitory Auth.*, 2005 U.S. Dist. LEXIS 9415, at *27.

the court did not rely on the intertwining obligations arising from the contract documents.

In addition, a few courts have recognized even more limited approaches to tort liability against a design professional for third-party claims. For instance, one court has held that a third-party can recover against a design professional only if the design professional's negligence presented "a clear danger of death or personal injury."[94] Another court found that third-party claims could be allowed only if the design professional had actual knowledge that the specific third-party at issue would rely on the design professional's representations.[95]

3. Impact of Economic Loss Rule on Negligence Claims

The economic loss rule bars negligence actions against design professionals for purely economic losses.[96] "Economic loss" is the loss associated with a party's expectancy interest derived from contract, and includes loss of value, loss due to the cost of repair or replacement, lost profits, loss due to increased cost of performance, and loss caused by delay or disruption.[97] These are the types of losses that often accrue when a design professional negligently undertakes its obligations or fails to perform.

The policy rationale behind the economic loss rule is the idea that economic interests are protected, if at all, in contract negotiations, and, by allowing tort recoveries for these losses, a party can realize benefits that it could not obtain in negotiation.[98] If a party is liable in tort for economic risks that it did not agree to assume in contract, the theory

---

94 Council of Co-Owners Atlantis Condominiums, Inc. v. Whiting-Turner Contracting Co., 517 A.2d 336, 345 n.5 (Md. 1986).
95 Essex v. Ryan, 446 N.E.2d 368, 372 (Ind. Ct. App. 1983).
96 *See Coleman, supra* note 41 at 934; *see also* Malcolm Cunningham & Amy Fisher, *The Economic Loss Rule: Deconstructing the Mixed Metaphor in Construction Cases*, 33 TORT & INS. L.J. 147 (1997).
97 *See Coleman, supra* note 41, at 934.
98 *See id.*; *see also* Casa Clara Condominium Ass'n v. Charley Toppino & Sons, Inc., 620 So. 2d 1244, 1246 (Fla. 1993) (recognizing "fundamental boundary between contract law, which is designed to enforce the expectancy interests of the parties, and tort law, which imposes a duty of reasonable care and thereby encourages citizens to avoid causing physical harm to others").

goes, then construction contracts will lose their utility as vehicles to allocate risks associated with commercial activities and those activities will become more expensive.[99] While the economic loss rule has been adopted in a majority of jurisdictions to prevent product liability claims or negligent manufacture claims against manufacturers and suppliers, its application to design professionals is not universal. Thus, a third-party negligence claim may be available to a surety against a design professional in certain jurisdictions.[100]

The economic loss rule was applied to a surety's claim against a quality assurance inspector in *Hanover Ins. Co. v. Corrpro Companies, Inc.*[101] In that case, a painting contractor working for the U.S. Department of the Navy hired a quality assurance inspector, as required under the prime contract. After the contractor defaulted, the surety completed the project at significant additional cost. The surety sought to recover against the quality assurance inspector for negligent inspection.

The district court granted the inspector's motion to dismiss for failure to state a claim, finding that the surety's failure to allege that the inspector owed a duty "imposed by law to protect the broad interests of social policy" precluded tort recovery for economic losses.[102] Although the court applied the economic loss rule in this case, it acknowledged that under proper circumstances, the same conduct that constitutes a breach of contract can also give rise to tort claims: "Such circumstances exist, however, only where the duty owed to the plaintiff by the defendant is a common law duty, not one that exists solely by virtue of the contract."[103] Because the surety did not allege that the inspector

---

99 Berschauer/Phillips Constr. Co. v. Seattle Sch. Dist. No. 1, 881 P.2d 986, 992 (Wash. 1994) ("The fees charged by architects, engineers, contractors, developers, vendors, and so on are founded on their expected liability exposure as bargained and provided for in the contract.").

100 *See* Ins. Co. of N. Am. v. Town of Manchester, 17 F. Supp. 2d 81, 86 (D. Conn. 1998) ("[T]he majority of jurisdictions have held that the absence of privity is no bar to recovery of economic losses by construction professionals against one another, when reliance by the plaintiff is reasonably foreseeable.").

101 312 F. Supp. 2d 816 (E.D. Va. 2004).

102 *Id.* at 820.

103 *Id.*; *see also* Int'l Fid. Ins. Co. v. T C Architects, Inc., C. A. No. 23112, 2006 Ohio App. LEXIS 4784, at **7 (Ohio Ct. App., Sept. 20, 2006)

breached a common law duty, however, no negligence claim was available.[104]

The *Corrpro* case highlights the importance of the independent common law duty of due care and competence owed by a design professional. The economic loss rule only applies when the breaching party's obligations arise strictly under contract. No reported cases exist in which a surety's negligence claim against a design professional has been dismissed or barred by applying the economic loss rule when the design professional's common law duty of due care and competence was recognized.

IV. Claims Against the Principal's Accountant

Unlike insurance, bonds are not issued based on an actuarial or spreading of the risk basis. Rather, bonds are, at least in theory, issued based on the assumption that no loss will occur.[105] As such, the surety's underwriting process is, or should be, aimed at obtaining sufficient information to satisfy itself that the surety will not, in fact, suffer a loss. Key parts of this analysis are whether the contractor has enough capital to complete its projects and whether he survives unanticipated losses and/or slow receivables. In short, good financial information is the backbone of a surety's underwriting process.[106]

Typically, the financial information provided by a principal to a surety will include information prepared by the principal's accountant, often including reviewed, compiled or audited financial statements. Sureties often request at least the principal's past three fiscal year-end

---

(holding that in the absence of an exception to privity, no cause of action for negligence against an architectural firm existed for economic losses).

104 *Corrpro*, 312 F. Supp. 2d at 820.

105 See Michael R. Seidl et al., *A Surety's Guide for Claims Against Providers of Inaccurate Underwriting Information* (unpublished paper presented at the ABA/TIPS Fid. & Sur. Law Committee Annual Meeting, January 28, 1994). For a detailed discussion of surety underwriting, *see* Stewart R. Duke & Mary Jeanne Anderson, *How Contract Surety Bonds are Underwritten, in* THE LAW OF SURETYSHIP (Edward G. Gallagher, ed., 2d. ed. 2000).

106 *Seidl, supra* note 105; *see also* Ferrucci & Baron, *supra* note 3, at 210-11.

financial statements,[107] which provides information to evaluate whether to bond the contractor, including, but not limited to, working capital trends and fluctuations, net worth, debt ratios, and other key financial information.[108] In addition, these financial statements may also raise important additional questions that need to be addressed before issuing bonds.[109] When a financial statement provided to a surety fails to accurately reflect the financial condition of the contractor and/or omits important information, the surety's risk of loss is significantly increased. When that financial statement has been prepared by the principal's accountant, the surety may have a claim against that accountant. The section below discusses potential causes of action against an accountant who has misrepresented the principal's financial condition, followed by a brief discussion of defenses that may be available to the accountant.

A. The Type of Financial Statement's Effect on the Accountant's Liability

The accountant's work product relied upon by sureties in the underwriting process may take various forms. In some circumstances, an accountant may interact directly with a surety to provide financial information regarding the contractor. Such direct interaction may significantly increase the possibility that a viable cause of action will be available to a surety against the accountant. In most situations, a surety is provided with an accountant's work product and opinions in the form of audited, reviewed, or compiled financial statements.[110]

The majority of cases considering an accountant's liability to third parties have centered on misstatements or omissions in audited financial statements, as opposed to compilations or reviews. This is because of the affirmative representation made by an accountant performing an audit. The scope of reviews and compilations is not only more limited, but also

---

107 Duke & Anderson, *supra* note 105, at 56; *see also* Marilyn Klinger, *A Toast–To the Underwriters: The Underwriters Process and Salvage by the Surety, in* SALVAGE BY THE SURETY 66-68 (George J. Bachrach ed., 1998).
108 Duke & Anderson, *supra* note 105, at 56.
109 *Id.* at 56-57.
110 For a discussion of the difference between these types of financial statements, *see* Goetsch & Ward, *supra* note 3; *see also* Ferrucci & Baron, *supra* note 3.

reviews and compilations often include express disclaimers or limitations in the accountant's opinion letters. Many courts have relied on the accountant's limited scope of reviews and compilations and/or express disclaimers or qualifications in denying recovery to third parties against accountants for negligently performing reviews and compilations. For instance, in *First Indemnity of America Ins. Co. v. Letters, Meyler & Co., P.C.*, the court held that given the unaudited report's express limitations, it was "not reasonably foreseeable at the time it was produced that a third-party would give it the unwarranted status and use of an audited financial statement."[111] Therefore, the surety was denied recovery.[112]

However, a number of courts have imposed third-party liability on accountants in connection with unaudited financial statement engagements.[113] These decisions have, in effect, created two exceptions

---

111 741 A.2d 176, 179 (N.J. Super. Ct. Law Div. 1998).
112 *Id.*
113 *See, e.g., In re ZZZZ Best Sec. Litig.*, 864 F. Supp. 960, 971 (C.D. Cal. 1994) (accountant held liable for negligence in "limited review"); Ryan v. Kanne, 170 N.W.2d 395, 401 (Iowa 1969) (accountant held liable for misstatement in unaudited financial statement); *see also* United States v. Natelli, 527 F.2d 311, 320 (2d Cir. 1975), *cert. denied*, 425 United States 934 (1976) (affirming criminal conviction of accountants in connection with unaudited financial statement; even if unaudited, accountant cannot "shut his eyes in reckless disregard of his knowledge of highly suspicious figures"); Cogan v. Triad Am. Energy, 944 F. Supp. 1325, 1333 (S.D. Tex. 1996); Zupnick v. Thompson Parking Partners, L.P. III., No. 89-Civ. 6607, 1990 U.S. Dist. LEXIS 9881, at *12 (S.D.N.Y. July 31, 1990); Seedkem, Inc. v. Safranak, 466 F. Supp. 340, 344 (D. Neb. 1979) ("The fact that the financial statements were marked 'unaudited' and contained an express disclaimer of opinion is not necessarily dispositive at this time"); Spherex, Inc. v. Alexander Grant & Co., 451 A.2d 1308, 1313 (N.H. 1982) (third-party can have cause of action for unaudited financial statement); 1136 Tenants' Corp. v. Max Rothenberg & Co., 319 N.Y.S.2d 1007, 1008 (N.Y. App. Div. 1971), *aff'd*, 281 N.E.2d 846 (N.Y. 1972) (accountant held liable for misrepresentations in unaudited "write-up" reports); Bonhiver v. Graff, 248 N.W.2d 291, 299 (Minn. 1976) (accountants liable to third-party who relied on erroneous work papers where accountant knew third-party was relying on such work papers); Blakely v. Lisac, 357 F. Supp. 255, 265-66 (D. Or. 1972) (accountants held liable for errors in financial statement contained in prospectus even though performing an unaudited write up); Robert Wooler Co. v. Fid.

to the general rule that limitations and disclaimers in unaudited financial statements are effective.[114]

First, notwithstanding attempts by an accountant to limit liability, courts should look to the nature of the accounting work contracted.[115] As was stated in the often cited case of *Ryan v. Kanne*:

> Although in this profession a distinction is made between certified audits where greater time and effort are expended to verify book items, and uncertified audits where greater reliance is placed on book items, it is clear to us that accountants, or any other professional persons, must perform those acts that they have agreed to do under the contract and which they claim have been done in order to make the determination set forth and presented in their report. Their liability must be dependent upon their undertaking, not their rejection of dependability. They cannot escape liability for negligence by a general statement that they disclaim its reliability. . . . He must perform as agreed whether the work is certified or not. This being so, we have here fact questions as to the substance of the agreement between the parties, as to the care exercised in its performance, and as to the representation made, rather than whether the report was certified or uncertified.[116]

Second, regardless of the type of engagement undertaken by the accountant, if the accountant discovers a materially false matter in the entity's books and fails to disclose it, he may be subject to liability.[117] This requirement, often referred to as the "suspicious inquiry" standard,

---

Bank, 479 A.2d 1027, 1032 (Pa. Super. Ct. 1984), *appeal denied*, 528 A.2d 957 (Pa. 1987) ("agreement to perform unaudited services was not a shield from liability . . . for ignoring suspicious circumstances which would have raised a 'red flag'"); First Nat'l Bank of Bluefield v. Crawford, 386 S.E.2d 310, 314-15 (W. Va. 1989) (claim available by third-party who relied on review report).

114   *First Nat'l Bank of Bluefield*, 386 S.E.2d at 314-15.
115   *Id.* at 314.
116   *Ryan*, 170 N.W.2d at 404 (citing C.I.T. Financial Corp. v. Glover, 2d Cir. 224 F.2d 44 (1955)). *See also* Ashland Oil, Inc. v. Arnett, 875 F.2d 1271, 1284 (7th Cir. 1989); Badische Corp. v. Caylor, 356 S.E.2d 198, 200 (Ga. 1987); Coleco Indus., Inc. v. Berman, 423 F. Supp. 275, 310 (E.D. Pa. 1976); *Spherex, Inc.*, 451 A.2d at 1313; *Bonhiver*, 248 N.W.2d at 299; *Seedkem, Inc.*, 466 F. Supp. at 345.
117   *First Nat'l Bank of Bluefield*, 386 S.E.2d at 315; *see also* Natelli, 527 F.2d at 320; *Bonhiver*, 248 N.W.2d at 299.

was enunciated in *1136 Tenants' Corp. v. Max Rothenberg & Co.*, in which the court found an accountant liable to a third-party based on an unaudited "write up."[118] In *1136 Tenants' Corp.*, the court stated that the "[d]efendant was not free to . . . consider suspicious circumstances as being of no significance and prepare its financial reports as if same did not exist."[119] The "suspicious inquiry" standard requires that an accountant perform additional investigative procedures whenever suspicious circumstances are or should have been discovered, even where such procedures are not contemplated by the original engagement.[120] If the accountant fails to investigate further when such investigation would have revealed substantial irregularities, the accountant may be held liable for such failure notwithstanding the limited scope engagement.[121]

B. Potential Causes of Action Against the Principal's Accountant

As with claims for professional negligence against design professionals, claims against accountants have traditionally been limited to claims by those with whom the accountant is in contractual privity, unless the accountant himself is guilty of fraud. Obviously, a surety is not in contractual privity with its principal's accountant. As a result, claims against accountants for negligence by third parties, including sureties, who relied on accountants' negligently prepared work product to their detriment initially met with little success because of the lack of contractual privity. By 1990, however, significant inroads had been made into the privity bar, allowing third parties, including sureties, to recover against accountants.[122] There are now a number of potential causes of action that may be available to a surety who has relied on the work product of its principal's accountant to its detriment. Potential causes of

---

118 *1136 Tenants' Corp.*, 319 N.Y.S.2d at 1008; *see also* John S. Dzienkowski, Note, *Accountants' Liability for Compilation and Review Engagement*, 60 TEX. L. REV. 759, 783 (April 1982).
119 *1136 Tenants' Corp.*, 319 N.Y.S.2d at 1008.
120 Dzienkowski, *supra* note 118, at 783.
121 *Id.*
122 Jerome M. Joseph, *Sureties' Claims for Negligence Against Accountants, Design Professionals, and Lenders*, 20 THE BRIEF 17 (Winter 1991); Jack I. Samet, et al., *The Attack on the Citadel of Privity*, 20 THE BRIEF 9 (Winter 1991).

action by sureties against their principals' accountants for negligent misrepresentation, breach of contract (as a third-party beneficiary), and fraud/intentional misrepresentation are discussed below.[123]

1. Negligent Misrepresentation

The primary focus of the case law concerning claims against accountants by third parties has been on the tort of negligent misrepresentation. Similar to negligence actions against design professionals, there are currently at least four approaches utilized by courts to determine whether an accountant owes a duty to a third-party which may give rise to a negligent misrepresentation claim: (1) the strict privity approach; (2) the near-privity approach; (3) the Restatement approach; and (4) the foreseeability approach.[124]

a. *Strict Privity Approach.* The most restrictive approach to an accountant's liability for negligent misrepresentation, and the harshest

---

123 For further discussion of accountant liability, *see, generally*, Goetsch & Ward, *supra* note 3; Christopher R. Ward, *Liability of the Principal's Accountant to the Surety*, (unpublished paper presented at the Surety Claims Institute Annual Meeting, June 22-23, 2005); Richard P. Swanson, *Theories of Liability*, in ALI-ABA, COURSE OF STUDY MATERIALS, ACCOUNTANTS' LIABILITY 27 (February 10-11, 2005); Jay M. Feinman, *Liability of Accountants for Negligent Auditing: Doctrine, Policy, And Ideology*, 31 F.S.U. L. REV. 17 (2003); Carl Pacini et al., *At the Interface of Law and Accounting: An Examination of a Trend Toward a Reduction in The Scope of Auditor Liability to Third Parties in the Common Law Countries*, 37 AM. BUS. L.J. 171 (2000). Because of the divergent approaches which have been utilized in the various jurisdictions it should be kept in mind that choice of law issues may arise that could significantly affect the viability of a claim by a surety against its principal's accountant. *See, e.g.*, KPMG Peat Marwick v. Asher, 689 N.E.2d 1283, 1287 (Ind. Ct. App. 1997), *transfer denied*, 706 N.E.2d 166 (Ind. 1998); Allied Inv. Corp. v. KPMG Peat Marwick, 872 F. Supp. 1076, 1083 (D. Me. 1995); Performance Motorcars of Westchester, Inc. v. KPMG Peat Marwick, 643 A.2d 39, 41 (N.J. Super. Ct. App. Div. 1994), *cert. denied*, 652 A.2d 172 (N.J. 1994); Banco Totta & Acores v. Stockton Bates & Co., No. 84 Civ. 7041, 1986 U.S. Dist. LEXIS 27845, at *2 (S.D.N.Y. March 21, 1986).
124 For a chart setting forth the approaches utilized in all fifty states and various other countries, *see* Pacini et al., *supra* note 123, at 226.

rule for a surety who relied to its detriment on its principal's accountant's work product, is the strict privity approach. Under the strict privity approach, a cause of action against an accountant for negligent misrepresentation is not available to a party not in contractual privity with the accountant.[125] As stated by one commentator, the privity approach is "arguably inconsistent with the two primary policy goals of tort law–compensating persons injured by the negligence of others and deterring future negligent conduct."[126] The strict privity approach is currently the minority position, but continues to be utilized in certain jurisdictions.[127]

In *Dworman v. Lee*,[128] the court addressed claims by individual sureties against their principal's accountant who had prepared consolidated financial statements upon which the sureties relied in deciding to issue bonds on behalf of their principal. Applying the strict privity approach adopted in *Ultramares Corp. v. Touche*, the court predictably upheld the dismissal of the sureties' complaint because of the lack of privity between the sureties and accountant.[129] Likewise, in *Seaboard Surety Co. v. Garrison, Webb & Stanaland, P.A.*, the Eleventh Circuit, relying on Florida law, refused to allow a surety to recover against its principal's accountant under a tort theory because of the lack of privity.[130] However, in *Seaboard Surety*, the court suggested that, under different facts, such as a contrary agreement or special circumstances, a surety may be able to recover as a third-party beneficiary to the contract between the principal and the accountant.[131]

---

125 *See* Ultramares Corp. v. Touche, 174 N.E. 441, 448 (N.Y. 1931) ("[I]f there has been neither reckless misstatement nor insincere profession of an opinion, but only honest blunder, the ensuing liability for negligence is one that is bounded by the contract, and is to be enforced between the parties by whom the contract has been made."); *see also* Landell v. Lybrand, 107 A. 783 (Pa. 1919).
126 *Swanson, supra* note 123, at 34.
127 *See, e.g., In re* Phar-Mor Sec. Litig., 892 F. Supp. 676, 694 (W.D. Pa. 1995); PNC Bank, Kentucky, Inc. v. Housing Mortgage Corp., 899 F. Supp. 1399, 1407 (W.D. Pa. 1994); Ward v. Ernst & Young, 435 S.E.2d 628, 631 (Va. 1993).
128 441 N.Y.S.2d 90 (N.Y. App. Div. 1981).
129 *Id.* at 91.
130 823 F.2d 434, 437 (11th Cir. 1987).
131 *Id.* at 437-38; *see also* discussion *infra* at Section V.C.

b. *Near-Privity Approach.* The same New York court which decided *Ultramares Corp.*, the case most often cited for the strict privity approach, had the opportunity to revisit the privity requirement in the 1985 decision of *Credit Alliance Corp. v. Arthur Andersen & Co.*[132] Although the court refused to expressly overrule the holding in *Ultramares*, the court effectively shied away from the strict privity approach, holding that the lack of strict privity should not preclude all claims by third parties against accountants.[133] The court enunciated what is now known as the near-privity approach as follows:

> Before accountants may be held liable in negligence to noncontractual parties who rely to their detriment on inaccurate financial reports, certain prerequisites must be satisfied: (1) the accountants must have been aware that the financial reports were to be used for a particular purpose or purposes; (2) in the furtherance of which a known party or parties was intended to rely; and (3) there must have been some conduct on the part of the accountants linking them to that party or parties, which evinces the accountants' understanding of that party or parties' reliance.[134]

Various courts outside of New York have applied a near-privity approach similar to that enunciated in *Credit Alliance*.[135]

The key question to be answered in jurisdictions applying the near-privity approach is whether the conduct of the accountant was such that it links the surety to the principal's accountant in such a way as to establish "an affirmative assumption of a duty of care to [the surety], for a specific purpose, regardless of whether there was a contractual relationship."[136] The surety must bring forward sufficient evidence to show that although

---

132 483 N.E.2d 110, 119 (N.Y. 1985).
133 *Id.*, 483 N.E.2d at 119.
134 *Id.* at 118.
135 *See, e.g.*, Toro Co. v. Krouse, Kern & Co., 827 F.2d 155, 161 (7th Cir. 1987); Colonial Bank of Alabama v. Ridley & Schweigert, 551 So. 2d 390, 395 (Ala. 1989), *overruled by implication*, Boykin v. Arthur Anderson & Co., 639 So. 2d 504, 510 (Ala. 1994); Twin Mfg. Co. v. Blum, Shapiro & Co., 602 A.2d 1079 (Conn. Super. Ct. 1991); Idaho Bank & Trust Co. v. First Bancorp, 772 P.2d 720, 722 (Idaho 1989); Walpert, Smullian & Blumenthal, P.A. v. Katz, 762 A.2d 582, 607-08 (Md. 2000).
136 *Credit Alliance*, 483 N.E.2d at 116; *see also* Toro, 827 F.2d at 163.

there was no formal contract between the surety and the principal's accountant, a duty was still owed due to the nature of the relationship.[137] Courts have reached various results, which often appear at odds, regarding what is required to create the requisite link between the accountant and a third-party who relied on the accountant's work product.[138] As the near-privity approach is typically applied, it may be difficult for a surety to establish the requisite link with the accountant to maintain a negligent misrepresentation action.[139] Even direct communications between the surety and the accountant may not establish the requisite relationship.[140]

However, at least one court considering a claim by a surety against its principal's accountant has found the requisite link. In *St. Paul Fire & Marine Ins. Co. v. Touche Ross & Co.*, the Nebraska Supreme Court considered whether the interaction between a surety and its principal's

---

137   *Idaho Bank & Trust*, 772 P.2d at 722.
138   *Compare, e.g.*, First Fed. Sav. & Loan of Pittsburgh v. Oppenheim, Appel, Dixon & Co., 629 F. Supp. 427, 433-35 (S.D.N.Y. 1986) *with* William Iselin & Co. v. Mann Judd Landau, 522 N.E.2d 21, 24 (N.Y. 1988). *See also* Westpac Banking Corp. v. Deschamps, 484 N.E.2d 1351, 1353 (N.Y. 1985).
139   *See, e.g., Twin Mfg.*, 602 A.2d at 1080 (no allegations that defendant prepared any financial statements for the plaintiff, that there was any direct contact between defendant and plaintiff, or that the defendant prepared financial statements for the purpose of the sale of assets to the plaintiff); Hamond v. Marks Shron & Co., 671 N.Y.S.2d 106, 107 (N.Y. App. Div. 1998) (summary judgment properly granted where limited partner failed to produce admissible evidence of relationship approaching privity with accounting firm); Common Fund for Non-Profit Orgs. v. KPMG Peat Marwick, LLP, 951 F. Supp. 498, 501-02 (S.D.N.Y. 1997) (no allegation that accountants promised to provide audit services to plaintiff, provided plaintiff with any written document or made any oral representation to plaintiff); CMNY Capital, L.P. v. Deloitte & Touche, 821 F. Supp. 152, 160-61 (S.D.N.Y. 1993) (fact that client's president contacted accountants and notified them that plaintiffs would be relying on financial report was insufficient; plaintiffs' use of the report was collateral and incidental).
140   *See, e.g.*, Sec. Pac. Bus. Credit, Inc. v. Peat Marwick Main & Co., 597 N.E.2d 1080, 1085 (N.Y. 1992) (single contact by plaintiff not enough); *Colonial Bank*, 551 So. 2d at 395 (contact as part of audit inquiry insufficient).

accountant was sufficient to support a cause of action for negligent misrepresentation.[141] In finding that the surety had stated a cause of action for negligent misrepresentations against its principal's accountant, the court stated:

> It is sufficient to note that the allegations at hand state a negligence cause of action in favor of St. Paul against Touche under the theories that Touche negligently performed its services and made negligent misrepresentations. Particularly significant are the allegations that despite its representation to the contrary, Touche did not perform in accordance with generally accepted accounting standards, that Touche met and communicated directly with St. Paul and made Touche's products available to the former for its use in dealing with Commonwealth, and that Touche intended that St. Paul rely on the documents Touche prepared for Commonwealth.
>
> As held by the Florida Supreme Court in *First Fla. Bank v. Max Mitchell & Co.*, 558 So. 2d 9 (Fla. 1990), when an accountant fails to exercise reasonable and ordinary care in preparing financial statements for its client and personally delivers and presents those statements to a third-party to induce the third-party to loan to or invest in the client, the accountant is liable to the third-party in negligence. That is to say, a duty arises by virtue of a contract implied from the conduct of the parties.[142]

Although the court did not specifically indicate that it was applying the near-privity approach, the above language suggests it was. However, regardless of whether the court intended to utilize the near-privity approach, the reasoning in *Touche Ross* strongly suggests that a surety can, at least under the circumstance described in *Touche Ross*, assert a viable cause of action for negligent misrepresentation against its principal's accountant under the near-privity approach.

c. *Restatement Approach.* The majority of courts have adopted the more moderate approach to accountant liability set forth in the Restatement (Second) of Torts, Section 552.[143] The Restatement

---

141 507 N.W.2d 275, 280-81 (Neb. 1993).
142 *Id.* at 280-81 (citing McVaney v. Baird, Holm, McEachen, 466 N.W.2d 499 (Neb. 1991).
143 *See, e.g.*, Scottish Heritable Trust v. Peat Marwick Main & Co., 81 F.3d 606, 612 (5th Cir. 1996) (applying Texas law), *cert. denied*, 519 U.S. 869

approach holds accountants responsible when they have intended to influence third persons, but avoids the unlimited and uncertain liability in cases of professional mistake.[144] As one court has noted, the Restatement approach is "most consistent with the elements and policy foundations of the tort of negligent misrepresentation."[145] As stated by the First Circuit in *North American Specialty Ins. Co. v. Lapalme*, discussed further

---

(1996); First Nat'l Bank of Commerce v. Monco Agency Inc., 911 F.2d 1053, 1061 (5th Cir. 1990) (applying Louisiana law); Reisman v. KPMG Peat Marwick LLP, 965 F. Supp. 165, 173 (D. Mass. 1997); Forcier v. Cardello, 173 B.R. 973, 982-83 (D.R.I. 1994) (applying Rhode Island law); Boykin v. Arthur Andersen & Co., 639 So. 2d 504, 509 (Ala. 1994); Standard Chartered PLC v. Price Waterhouse, 945 P.2d 317, 342 (Ariz. Ct. App. 1996); Bily v. Arthur Young & Co., 834 P.2d 745, 747 (Cal. 1992); First Fla. Bank, N.A. v. Max Mitchell & Co., 558 So. 2d 9, 14 (Fla. 1990); Badische Corp. v. Caylor, 356 S.E.2d 198, 199-200 (Ga. 1987); Kohala Agric. v. Deloitte & Touche, 949 P.2d 141, 162 (Haw. Ct. App. 1997); Ryan v. Kanne, 170 N.W.2d 395, 401 (Iowa 1969); Nycal Corp. v. KPMG Peat Marwick LLP, 688 N.E.2d 1368, 1371 (Mass. 1998); Aluma Kraft Mfg. Co. v. Elmer Fox & Co., 493 S.W.2d 378, 382-83 (Mo. Ct. App. 1973); Bonhiver v. Graff, 248 N.W.2d. 291, 301-02 (Minn. 1976); Noram Inv. Servs., Inc., f/k/a Equity Sec. Trading Co. v. Stirtz Bernards Boyden Surdel & Larter PA, 611 N.W.2d 372, 374-75 (Minn. Ct. App. 2000); Spherex, Inc. v. Alexander Grant & Co., 451 A.2d 1308, 1312 (N.H. 1982); Marcus Bros. Textiles, Inc. v. Price Waterhouse, LLP, 513 S.E.2d 320, 326 (N.C. 1999); Raritan River Steel Co. v. Cherry, Bekaert & Holland, 367 S.E.2d 609, 617 (N.C. 1988); Haddon View Inv. Co. v. Coopers & Lybrand, 436 N.E.2d 212, 215 (Ohio 1982); ML-Lee Acquisition Fund, L.P. v. Deloitte & Touche, 489 S.E.2d 470, 471 n.3 (S.C. 1997); Bethlehem Steel Corp. v. Ernst & Whinney, 822 S.W.2d 592, 595 (Tenn. 1991); Milliner v. Elmer Fox & Co., 529 P.2d 806, 808 (Utah 1974); First Nat'l Bank of Bluefield, 386 S.E. 2d at 313 (W. Va. 1989); *see also* Armen Shahinian & Scott D. Baron, *The Surety and Fidelity Insurer's Reliance Upon Accounting Professionals in Underwriting: Augmenting Salvage Prospects* (unpublished paper submitted at the 7th Annual Northeast Surety & Fidelity Claims Conference, October 24-25, 1996).

144 *Bily*, 834 P.2d at 769.
145 *Id.*; *see also* Kohala Agric., 949 P.2d at 162; Pahre v. Auditor of State, 422 N.W.2d 178, 180 (Iowa 1988); Nycal Corp., 688 N.E.2d at 1371; Spherex, 451 A.2d at 1312; Bethlehem Steel Corp., 822 S.W.2d at 594; *see also* RESTATEMENT (SECOND) OF TORTS § 552 (quoted *supra* at 73).

below, the Restatement approach has six elements: (1) inaccurate information; (2) negligently supplied; (3) in the course of an accountant's professional endeavors; (4) to a third person or limited group or third person whom the accountant actually intends or knows will receive the information; (5) for a transaction that the accountant actually intends to influence (or for a substantially similar transaction); (6) with the result that the third-party justifiably relies on such misinformation to his detriment.[146]

As compared to the near-privity approach, the Restatement approach significantly increases the class of potential third parties who may have a claim against an accountant upon whose work product such third parties have relied. More specifically, unlike the near-privity approach, the accountant need not have known the precise identity of the third-party claimant in order for a cause of action to be available to that third-party for negligent misrepresentation. Rather, under the Restatement approach, a claim for negligent misrepresentation is available not only to those who the accountant intends to supply information, but also to those who the accountant knows his client intends to supply information.[147] Whether the accountant knew that his client intended to supply the information to a particular class of third parties, such as sureties, may be established by direct or circumstantial evidence.[148] In short, the Restatement approach "creates an objective standard that looks to the specific circumstances . . . to ascertain whether [an accountant] has undertaken to inform and guide

---

146 258 F.3d 35, 41-42 (1st Cir. 2001) (applying Massachusetts law).
147 For cases considering the types of third parties who fall within class of potential claimants under the Restatement approach, *see* First Nat'l Bank of Commerce, 911 F.2d at 1062; Harbor Ins. Co. v. Essman, 918 F.2d 734, 737 (8th Cir. 1990); Indus. Indem. Co. v. Touche Ross & Co., 17 Cal. Rptr. 2d 29, 33 (Cal. Ct. App. 1993); Amwest Sur. Ins. Co. v. Ernst & Young, 677 So. 2d 409, 411 (Fla. Dist. Ct. App. 1996); First Fla. Bank, N.A., 558 So. 2d at 15; Badische Corp., 356 S.E.2d at 200; Ryan, 170 N.W.2d at 398-99; Raritan River Steel Co., 367 S.E.2d at 615; Haddon View Inv. Co., 436 N.E.2d at 215; Bethlehem Steel Corp., 822 S.W.2d at 592; Haberman v. Wash. Pub. Power Supply Sys., 744 P.2d 1032, 1066 (Wash. 1987); First Nat'l Bank of Bluefield, 386 S.E.2d at 312.
148 *See* First Nat'l Bank of Commerce, 911 F.2d at 1063; NCNB Nat'l Bank v. Deloitte & Touche, 458 S.E.2d 4, 9 (N.C. Ct. App. 1995), *cert. denied*, 462 S.E.2d 514 (1995).

a third-party with respect to an identified transaction or type of transaction."[149]

As applied to a surety's claim against its principal's accountant, the Restatement approach has met with mixed results. In *Amwest Surety Ins. Co. v. Ernst & Young*, a Florida appellate court applied the Restatement approach to a surety's claim against its principal's accountants for losses sustained on performance bonds issued by the surety in reliance on audited financial statements prepared by the accountants.[150] Applying Section 552 to the facts at issue, the court held that the surety was one for whose benefit the accountant had supplied the financial statements and, hence, was entitled to seek recovery.[151]

A surety seeking to recover from its principal's accountant met with less success under the Restatement approach in *Industrial Indemnity Co. v. Touche Ross & Co.*[152] The court concluded that there was no evidence that the accountant knew at the time it issued its opinion that the principal intended to provide the audit opinion to the surety.[153] Therefore, the court held that the surety, under those facts, was not in the "class of persons" the accountant intended to influence and, consequently, the surety was not entitled to recover from the principal's accountant as a matter of law. Although the surety was denied recovery, the court's application of the Restatement approach suggests that the principal's accountant could have been subject to liability to the surety had it known of the principal's transactions with the surety.[154]

A surety's claim against its principal's accountant under the Restatement approach was also unsuccessful in *Lapalme*,[155] where the surety brought a negligent misrepresentation claim against its principal's accountant. The claim was based on a review-level financial statement prepared by the principal's accountants that failed to disclose information regarding the recent transfer of ownership of the principal

---

149 *Bily*, 834 P.2d at 769.
150 677 So. 2d at 409.
151 *Id.* at 412 ("Ernst & Young were notified that a bonding company would utilize its audit in determining whether to issue bonds. That was enough. It was error to enter summary judgment for Ernst & Young in this case").
152 17 Cal. Rptr. 2d at 29.
153 *Id.* at 35.
154 *Id.*; *see also* Ferrucci & Baron, *supra* note 3, at 220.
155 258 F.3d at 35.

and contained arguably misleading comments.[156] After the district court granted summary judgment in favor of the principal's accountants, the surety appealed, challenging the district court's "interpretation and application of the legal regime governing an accountant's liability to third persons . . . ."[157] The surety argued that the principal's accountants sought to influence the transaction at issue (i.e., the issuance of the bonds upon which the surety suffered a loss), or, alternatively, that the accountants sought to influence a substantially similar transaction and, hence, that the surety was in the class of entities protected under the Restatement.[158] The surety made the following three arguments in support of its position.

First, the surety argued that the bonds at issue were issued as a part of a regular bonding program and that the principal had the subject financial statement prepared with that in mind. The surety explained that sureties typically "prequalify" contractors for future bonding by relying on data such as the financial statement at issue.[159] The First Circuit rejected that argument, pointing out that it is not the typical use of the financial statement by the surety that is controlling, but rather what the accountants actually knew at the time the accountants issued the financial statement about the surety's intent to use the financial statement in deciding whether to issue bonds on behalf of the principal.[160] The evidence suggested that the accountants were only aware that the financial statement would be used by the principal for "ongoing" bonds, rather than for "future" bonds.[161] Based on this evidence, the First Circuit concluded, as a matter of law, that the accountants did not subject themselves to the liability on future bonds.

Next, the surety argued that the defaulted bonds were transactions "substantially similar" to those that the accountants intended to influence, i.e., transactions involving "ongoing" bonds. The First Circuit concluded that the principal's use of the financial statement for "ongoing bonds," of which the accountants were aware, was not substantially

---

156   *Id.* at 36-37.
157   *Id.* at 37.
158   *Id.* at 42.
159   *Id.*
160   *Id.*
161   *Id.* at 42-43.

similar to use of the financial statement for "future bonds."[162] However, the First Circuit provided a useful analysis of other bonding situations in which it suggested a finding of substantial similarity might by found:

> To be sure, determinations of this type involve matters of degree. If, for example, D&L had agreed to release the 1995 financial statement in anticipation of allowing NASI to review it before issuing a $500,000 bond for a specific future project, and NASI thereafter issued a bond for that project in an amount that varied by, say, $50,000, D&L would be liable to NASI for any loss occasioned by a negligent misrepresentation. [Footnote omitted.] *See* Restatement (Second) Torts § 552 cmt. j. Similarly, if D&L had agreed to provide the 1995 financial statement in anticipation of allowing NASI to review it before bonding a project that was slated to start on May 1, but the project did not get underway until June 15, D&L would still be liable. *Id.* In each instance, the key is the accounting firm's actual knowledge of the surety's intention to rely on the financial statement for a specific purpose–deciding whether to issue a bond in a known amount for a known project. The firm thus could anticipate its likely exposure from attempting to influence the surety's decision, and the imposition of liability for negligence should not be defeated by modest variances that the firm, given the way in which business transactions typically develop, reasonably could have anticipated. *See id.*
>
> In this context, there is no scientific formula for ascertaining substantial similarity. Even if the change involves a new transaction, rather than merely a modification of the earlier (known) transaction, the accounting firm might still be held liable if the identity of the third-party is unchanged, the type of transaction pretty much the same, and the firm's exposure relatively constant. Imagine, for example, that D&L agreed to provide the financial statement in anticipation that NASI would review it in deciding whether to write a $500,000 bond referable to a specific roofing contract that CRS hoped to secure. Imagine, too, that the project fell through, but CRS instead obtained a different, roughly comparable roofing contract, likewise requiring a $500,000 bond, and NASI, relying on the financial statement, provided the bond. In that hypothetical situation, D&L likely would be liable to the surety for misinformation. *See id.* cmt. j, illus. 15.[163]

---

162 *Id.*
163 *Id.* at 43-44.

According to the First Circuit, the above examples "presume that the accountants knew the general nature of the risk they were taking and the approximate dollar amount of their potential liability."[164] Under the facts before the court, the First Circuit held that the accountants "accepted potential liability only for ongoing work—known projects in various stages of completion."[165] Therefore, the court concluded that "[w]ithout some evidence that the [accountants] knew that they were undertaking additional, open-ended liability with respect to future bonds by releasing the financial statements, [the surety's] second argument founders."[166]

Finally, the surety argued that the accountants were willfully blind and, hence, subject to liability.[167] The First Circuit disagreed, holding that the surety "failed to identify any plausible evidence of willful blindness or otherwise to demonstrate the existence of a genuine issue of material fact as to the defendants' actual knowledge of a substantially similar, loss inducing transaction."[168] Therefore, the court affirmed the district court's decision, dismissing the surety's action as a matter of law.[169]

A surety's claim against its principal's accountant under the Restatement approach was also rejected by the Eleventh Circuit in *Travelers Casualty and Surety Co. of America v. Reznick Group, P.C.*[170] In *Reznick*, the Eleventh Circuit affirmed the district court's dismissal of the surety's claim against the accountant for failure to state a claim for

---

164 *Id.* at 43.
165 *Id.*
166 *Id.* at 44.
167 *Id.* at 45.
168 *Id.*
169 The First Circuit's interpretation of the Restatement in *Lapalme* is arguably too restrictive. That the accountant knew that the financial statement would be provided by the principal to the surety for purposes of its bonding relationship with the surety arguably should have been enough under the Restatement approach. In any event, it is important to note that *Lapalme* does suggest that if an accountant knows that a principal is providing the financial statement prepared by the accountant to a surety for purposes of obtaining future bonding, which is the more common scenario, then the accountant very well may be subject to liability to a surety who relied on such financial statement to its detriment under the Restatement approach.
170 No. 07-12557, 2008 U.S. App. LEXIS 6425 (11th Cir. March 25, 2008).

which relief could be granted, reasoning that to state a viable claim under the Restatement approach, the accountant must know more than simply the broad purposes for which the financial statement will be used. Rather, the accountant must know that the financial statement will be used in the particular transaction with the surety or substantially similar transactions.[171]

   d. *Foreseeability Approach.* Some courts have applied a foreseeability approach in evaluating the liability of accountants to third parties for negligent misrepresentation.[172] Under the foreseeability approach, an accountant can be held liable to those whom the accountant should reasonably foresee will receive financial statements or other information prepared by the accountant. The foreseeability approach, the most liberal approach to accountant liability, has been adopted by very few jurisdictions.[173] In fact, what is, or at least was, the leading decision concerning the foreseeability approach, *H. Roseblum, Inc. v. Adler,* was statutorily overruled by the New Jersey legislature in 1996 in favor of a near-privity approach.[174]

In addition to the general principle that accountants "should be responsible for their careless misrepresentations to parties who justifiably relied upon their expert opinions,"[175] there are a number of possible rationales for adopting the foreseeability approach that have been

---

171 *Id.* at *2.
172 *See, e.g.,* Int'l Mortgage Co. v. John P. Butler Accountancy Corp., 223 Cal. Rptr. 218 (1986), *overruled by* Bily, 834 P.2d at 773-74; Touche Ross & Co. v. Commercial Union Ins. Co., 514 So. 2d 315, 322 (Miss. 1987); H. Rosenblum, Inc. v. Adler, 461 A.2d 138, 153 (N.J. 1983), *statutorily overruled by* N.J. STAT. ANN. § 2A:53A-25 (West Supp. 1996); Citizens State Bank v. Timm, Schmidt & Co., 335 N.W.2d 361, 366 (Wis. 1983); *see also* Bradford Secs. Processing Servs., Inc. v. Plaza Bank & Trust, 653 P.2d 188, 191 (Okla. 1982) (applying foreseeability approach to claim against attorney).
173 *See* cases cited *id.*; *see also* Bily, 834 P.2d at 755-757 (discussing the cases and commentators which have weighed in on the foreseeability approach).
174 *H. Rosenblum, Inc.,* 461 A.2d at 138; N.J. STAT. ANN. § 2A:53A-25 (West Supp. 1996) (adopting rule similar to near-privity approach); *see also* Ferrucci & Baron, *supra* note 3, at 215; Shahinian & Baron, *supra* note 143, at 10-11.
175 *H. Rosenblum, Inc.,* 461 A.2d at 155.

espoused by courts. First, with respect to the counter-argument made by accountants that imposing such sweeping liability on accountants would cripple the accounting profession, some courts adopting the foreseeability approach have suggested that accountants can address such increased risk by obtaining appropriate insurance or by increasing the price of their services.[176] Courts adopting the foreseeability approach have also stressed the importance of financial statements to third parties and the frequent reliance on financial statements by "investors, creditors, vendors, and insurers."[177] Finally, courts adopting the foreseeability approach have argued that by utilizing such an approach, accountants will be encouraged to exercise greater care.[178]

Because of the broad liability which may result under the foreseeability approach, some courts that have adopted the approach have recognized that it must be subject to some limitations. For instance, one court that adopted the approach indicated that public policy might prevent its application in certain circumstances.[179] Other courts adopting the foreseeability approach have limited the accountant's liability to those foreseeable users who have received financial statements directly from the accountant or the accountant's client.[180] Finally, one court that adopted the approach stated that the accountant "remains free to limit the

---

176   *Id.*; *Citizens State Bank*, 335 N.W.2d at 365.
177   *Touche Ross & Co.*, 514 So. 2d at 322. *See also H. Rosenblum, Inc.*, 461 A.2d at 149.
178   *H. Rosenblum, Inc.*, 461 A.2d at 152; *Citizens State Bank*, 335 N.W.2d at 365.
179   *Citizens State Bank*, 335 N.W.2d at 366. Public policy may dictate that accountants not be held liable in the following circumstances: "(1) The injury is too remote from the negligence; or (2) the injury is too wholly out of proportion to the culpability of the negligent tort-feasor; or (3) in retrospect it appears too highly extraordinary that the negligence should have brought about the harm; or (4) because allowance of recovery would place too unreasonable a burden on the negligent tort-feasor; or (5) because allowance of recovery would be too likely to open the way for fraudulent claims; or (6) allowance of recovery would enter a field that has no sensible or just stopping point." *Id.* at 366. *See also* Imark Indus., Inc. v. Arthur Young & Co., 414 N.W.2d 57, 65-66 (Wis. Ct. App. 1987).
180   *Touche Ross & Co.*, 514 So. 2d at 322-23; *H. Rosenblum, Inc.*, 461 A.2d at 153.

dissemination of his opinion through a separate agreement with the audited entity."[181]

The foreseeability approach is obviously the most favorable approach for sureties seeking to impose liability on their principals' accountants. The most obvious foreseeable users of an accountant's work product relating to a construction contractor are that contractor's surety, banker, and outside investors.[182]

2. Breach of Contract–The Surety as a Third-Party Beneficiary

Another possible theory of recovery against a principal's accountant is a claim for breach of contract asserted as a third-party beneficiary to the contract between the principal and accountant. There are numerous decisions in which courts have refused to find that third parties who relied upon accountants' work product are third-party beneficiaries of the contract between the accountants and their clients.[183] However, the Eleventh Circuit's decision in *Seaboard Surety Co. v. Garrison, Webb & Stanaland* suggests that a surety may qualify as a third-party beneficiary of a contract between its principal and its principal's accountant.[184]

Although the surety did not prevail in *Seaboard Surety Co.*, the decision demonstrates that a cause of action for breach of contract as a third-party beneficiary may be available to a surety against its principal's

---

181 *Touche Ross & Co.*, 514 So. 2d at 323.
182 Ferrucci & Baron, *supra* note 3, at 215.
183 *See, e.g.*, Blu-J, Inc. v. Kemper C.P.A. Group, 916 F.2d 637, 639-40 (11th Cir. 1990) (investor in corporation not third-party beneficiary); Software Design & Application Ltd. v. Price Waterhouse, LLP, 57 Cal. Rptr. 2d 36, 40 (Cal. Ct. App. 1996) (investor not an intended beneficiary); *In re* Sahlen & Assoc., Inc. Sec. Litig., 773 F. Supp. 342, 373 n.43 (S.D. Fla. 1991) (shareholders not third-party beneficiaries); Mulligan v. Wallace, 349 So. 2d 745, 746-47 (Fla. Dist. Ct. App. 1977) (*per curiam*) (officers, directors, and shareholders of corporation not third-party beneficiaries), *cert. denied*, 354 So. 2d 983 (Fla. 1977); Dubbin v. Touche Ross & Co., 324 So. 2d 128, 129 (Fla. Dist. Ct. App. 1975) (shareholders not third-party beneficiaries), *cert. denied*, 336 So. 2d 1181 (Fla. 1976); Pell v. Weinstein, 759 F. Supp. 1107, 1119 (M.D. Pa. 1991) (shareholders not third-party beneficiaries), *aff'd*, 961 F.2d 1568 (3d Cir. 1992).
184 823 F.2d 434, 437 (11th Cir.) (holding surety's cause of action sounded in contract, not tort).

accountant, even though it is unlikely to be the focus of a surety's claim against its principal's accountant. As later recognized by the Eleventh Circuit, "[i]n order for one to qualify as a third-party beneficiary under a contract, it must be shown that the intent and purpose of the contracting parties was to confer a direct and substantial benefit upon the third-party."[185] As such, a third-party beneficiary theory effectively limits the class of potential claimants in much the same way as the near-privity approach applied in a tort action.[186] Hence, in most cases, there will be little, if any, benefit to the surety in pursuing a contractual claim, as opposed to a tort claim.[187] In light of the adoption of the Restatement approach by the majority of courts, the burden on the surety to establish a right of recovery against an accountant will, in most cases, be easier to carry under a tort theory.

3. Fraud/Intentional Misrepresentation

A cause of action may be available to the surety for fraud and/or intentional misrepresentation if an accountant has engaged in fraudulent conduct in connection with the information relied upon by a surety.[188] Evidence of gross negligence by the accountant may give rise to an inference of fraud.[189] Even in jurisdictions adhering to a strict privity approach, it has long been held that lack of privity is not a defense to fraud.[190] As was astutely pointed out by one commentator, however, it

---

185 *Blu-J, Inc.*, 916 F.2d at 639 (citing Am. Sur. Co. of N.Y. v. Smith, 130 So. 440 (1930)).

186 *See* Goestch & Ward, *supra* note 3, at 237; Ferrucci & Baron, *supra* note 3, at 216; *see also* Joseph, *supra* note 122, at 19-20.

187 A breach of contract action against the principal's accountant may be useful in situations where the statute of limitations on a cause of action has expired. In many jurisdictions, the statute of limitations for a breach of contract cause of action is longer than for a tort cause of action. *See* discussion *infra* at V.B.

188 *See* Goestch & Ward, *supra* note 3, at 238; Ferrucci & Baron, *supra* note 3, at 216-17.

189 Ferrucci & Baron, *supra* note 3, at 217 (citing Roberston v. White, 633 F. Supp. 954 (W.D. Ark. 1986)).

190 Ultramares Corp. v. Touche, 174 N.E. 441, 448 (N.Y. 1931) ("Our holding does not emancipate accountants from the consequences of fraud. It does not relieve them if their audit has been so negligent so as to justify

should be kept in mind that the accountant's professional liability insurance likely excludes coverage for fraud.[191] That fact may weigh in favor of focusing the claim on negligence in order to heighten the chance of a meaningful recovery.

C. Potential Defenses that May be Asserted by the Accountant

1. Limitations By Statute

A number of states have enacted statutes which limit the liability of accountants.[192] Although these statutes recognize a cause of action for negligence against an accountant, they limit the situations under which an accountant may be held liable to a third-party or provide methods by which an accountant can effectively limit his or her liability.[193]

2. Lack of Causation

Causation defenses are common in accountant liability cases.[194] Losses suffered by third parties who rely on the work product of an accountant often involve numerous complex factors. The accountant's role in the loss is sometimes unclear.[195] This is no less the case with respect to a surety who has suffered a loss as a result of its reliance on information provided by its principal's accountant.[196] Courts have taken various approaches to the causation issue.[197]

---

a finding that they had no genuine belief in its adequacy, for this again is fraud.").

[191] Ferrucci & Baron, *supra* note 3, at 217-18.
[192] *See* ARK. CODE. ANN. §16-114-302 (Michie Supp. 1993); ILL. COMP. STAT. ANN. CHAP. 225 §450/30.1 (Smith-Hurd 1993); KAN. STAT. ANN. §1-402 (1991); MICH. COMP. LAWS ANN. §600.2962 (West. Supp. 1997); N.J. STAT. ANN. §2A:53A-25 (West Pocket Par 1998); UTAH CODE ANN. §56-26-12 (1994); WYO. STAT. §33-3-201 (Supp. 1995).
[193] *See* statutes cited *id.*
[194] *See* Swanson, *supra* note 123, at 61.
[195] *Id.*
[196] *See* Seidl et al., *supra* note 105.
[197] *See, e.g.*, AUSA Life Ins. Co. v. Ernst & Young, 206 F.3d 202 (2d Cir. 2000) (each judge on the panel taking a different approach to causation).

The accountant may argue that the surety simply did not make its underwriting decision based on the representations in the accountant's work product.[198] This type of defense will likely involve a fact intensive inquiry into what the underwriter did and did not rely on. However, even if it can be established that the surety would not have issued bonds on behalf of its principal "but for" its reliance on the accountant's work product (sometimes referred to as "transactional causation"), the accountant may still argue that the surety is not entitled to recover because the loss itself was not caused by any facts misrepresented by the accountant (sometimes referred to as "loss causation").[199] For instance, in *Standard Surety & Casualty Co. of N.Y. v. Plantsville National Bank*, a case involving claims by a surety against a bank as a result of misrepresentations by the bank regarding the principal's deposits and line of credit, the Second Circuit stated:

> Even if [the contractor] had had cash and credit . . . it does not follow, and neither the Bank nor its agent ever represented, that the cash and credit would be available some seven months later for the plaintiff's indemnification. The Bank's misrepresentation, made gratuitously, may not be stretched into a sweeping agreement to relieve the [surety] of the entire risk it assumed for a consideration.[200]

A strong argument can be made that this decision is too restrictive.[201] However, a surety can be expected to confront this very type of defense in connection with a claim against its principal's accountant.

3. *Contributory/Comparative Negligence*

A surety asserting a claim against its principal's accountant may confront a defense that the surety's negligence contributed to or caused the loss.[202] The accountant's argument will likely be that had the surety acted with reasonable care in performing its underwriting, the

---

198   *See* Standard Sur. & Cas. Co. v. Plantsville Nat'l Bank, 158 F.2d 422, 426 (2d Cir. 1946), *cert. denied*, 331 U.S. 812 (1947).
199   *See* Seidl et al., *supra* note 105, at 17; *see also* AUSA Life Ins. Co., 206 F.3d at 202.
200   *Standard Sur. & Cas. Co.*, 158 F.2d at 425.
201   *Seidl, et al., supra* note 105, at 19.
202   *Id.*, at 16.

circumstances not disclosed, or improperly disclosed, by the accountant would have been discovered. In making such an argument, the accountant may also contend that the surety underwriter had the undisclosed or improperly disclosed information in his or her hands from another source, which should have alerted the surety to the risk.[203]

Dispute exists as to whether a contributory or comparative negligence defense should be available to an accountant.[204] Where a contributory or comparative negligence defense is available, the surety should be prepared to defend and explain in detail its steps during the underwriting process.[205]

4. Failure to Mitigate

Sureties often confront mitigation defenses raised by principals and indemnitors in indemnification suits. Such defenses are often effectively addressed by applicable indemnity agreement terms that provide the surety with the right to settle claims it deems appropriate and/or by presenting evidence of the numerous surety letters to the principal and indemnitors asking them to address outstanding claims without the need for the surety's involvement. However, when a surety focuses its salvage efforts on a third-party such as an accountant, these typical surety responses will not be available. Therefore, if the surety is confronted with a mitigation defense asserted by an accountant, the surety should be ready to document and explain in detail its handling of the subject claims.[206]

5. Statute of Limitations

As a general rule, a cause of action accrues against an accountant when a wrongful act causes some legal injury, even if the injury is not discovered until later and even if all resulting damages have not yet

---

203 *Id.*
204 *See* Swanson et al., *supra* note 123, at 62; Eric R. Dinallo, Note, *The Peculiar Treatment of Contributory Negligence in* ACCOUNTANTS' LIABILITY CASES, 65 N.Y.U. L. REV. 329 (1990).
205 *Seidl, et al., supra* note 105, at 16.
206 *See id.*, at 19-21.

occurred.[207] Under that general rule, the statute of limitations for accounting malpractice may begin to run when the accountant's negligently prepared work product is provided to the accountant's client.[208] Under the discovery rule, the accrual of the cause of action may be postponed until the plaintiff knew or in the exercise of reasonable diligence should have known of the wrongful act and resulting injury.[209] However, in some jurisdictions, the statute of limitations applicable to professional negligence may not apply to a negligent misrepresentation claim by a surety against its principal's accountant, with whom the surety is not in privity.[210] Rather, the cause of action may be governed by the statute of limitations applicable to torts in general.[211]

V. Claims Against Lenders

Banks and other lenders play a vital role in most construction projects, often providing underwriting information concerning a contractor's financial well-being to the surety and owner, as well as disbursing project funds. Notwithstanding a lack of privity, a surety that relies on representations by the bank in bonding a project may be able to seek recovery of losses caused by those representations, typically either in negligence or as an intentional tort. In addition, when the bank has

---

207 *See* Consolidated Mgmt. Serv., Inc. v. Halligan, 368 S.E.2d 148, 150 (Ga. Ct. App. 1988), *aff'd*, 369 S.E.2d 745 (1988); Fronczak v. Arthur Andersen, LLP, 705 N.E.2d 1283, 1285 (Ohio Ct. App. 1997); Murphy v. Campbell, 964 S.W.2d 265, 270 (Tex. 1997); *see also* Sch. Dist. of the Borough of Aliquippa v. Md. Cas. Co., 587 A.2d 765, 770 (Pa. Super. Ct. 1991) (applying statute of limitations to claim by surety as subrogee of claims against accountant).
208 *See* World Radio Labs., Inc. v. Coopers & Lybrand, 557 N.W. 2d 1, 10 (Neb. 1996).
209 *Murphy*, 964 S.W.2d at 270.
210 *See* Barger v. McCoy Hillard & Parks, 488 S.E.2d 215, 223-24 (N.C. 1997) (holding that a claim for negligent misrepresentation by a third-party not in privity with accountant "does not accrue until two events occur: first, the claimant suffers harm because of the misrepresentation, and second, the claimant discovers the misrepresentation"). *But see* Ventura County Nat'l Bank v. Macker, 57 Cal. Rprt. 2d 418, 420 (Cal. Ct. App. 1996) (applying statute of limitations applicable to professional malpractice claim).
211 *Barger*, 488 S.E.2d at 223-24.

obligated itself to supervise the project and make progress disbursements, a surety may also be able to look to the bank to recover losses stemming from the bank's negligent disbursement of those funds.[212]

A. *Misrepresentation*

During the underwriting process, a surety may request bank statements in order to judge the current financial health of the principal. When those statements contain misrepresentations that lead the surety to believe the principal is in better financial shape than it actually is, the surety may bond a project that, but for those misrepresentations, it would not have. In the case of negligent misrepresentations, it may be proper, depending on the jurisdiction's stance toward privity, for the surety to look to the bank for recovery of losses associated with the contractor's poor financial health.[213]

A bank's intentional misrepresentations, on the other hand, may give the surety a direct intentional tort cause of action against the bank. For example, in the important case of *Associated Indemnity Corp. v. Del*

---

212 As one commentator has noted, there are three ways in which contract funds are disbursed to the contractor. Under a "draw system," the bank advances a portion of the project funds directly to the contractor upon completion of specified stages of the project. Under a "voucher system," the bank will pay subcontractors and materialmen directly based on vouchers submitted to the bank through the contractor. Finally, under an "escrow system," the bank pays the project funds to a third-party that assumes the obligation of disbursing the project funds. *See* Ferrucci & Baron, *supra* note 3, at 231. In addition, a lender may be liable to make periodic disbursement of project funds on an "obligatory" or "optional" basis. *See* Craig D. Tindall, *The Obligatory Advance Rule in the Construction Lending Context*, 12 CONSTR. LAW 13 (Jan. 1992). Under the obligatory structure, the bank must disburse project funds at predetermined stages of completion, whereas under the optional structure, the bank retains discretion to disburse funds when the bank is satisfied that progress warrants such disbursement. *See* Harold E. Leidner, *An Overview of Mechanics Lien & Future Advance Mortgages*, 3 PRAC. REAL EST. LAW., 39, 42-44 (May 1987).

213 *See generally* Robert J. Heyne and Scott O. Reed, *Third Party Liability to the Surety* (unpublished paper submitted at the ABA/TIPS Fid. & Sur. Law Committee annual meeting, August 8, 1988).

Guzzo,[214] the Supreme Court of Washington held that a cause of action was available to a surety against a bank that made fraudulent statements to the surety knowing that the surety was relying on those statements in bonding the contractor. The bank defended on the ground that it owed no duty toward the surety to provide complete or accurate financial information. The court disagreed, holding that the bank owed the surety a duty of good faith and a duty to speak:

> A duty to speak may arise from partial disclosure, the speaker being under a duty to say nothing or to tell the whole truth. One conveying a false impression by the disclosure of some facts and the concealment of others is guilty of fraud, even though his statement is true so far as it goes, since such concealment is in effect a false representation that what is disclosed is the whole truth.[215]

In response to the surety's inquiries, the bank's representatives made incomplete statements concerning the financial health of the principal and did not disclose debts the contractor owed to the bank. The court said the bank's intention was to aid the contractor in winning the project, which would allow the contractor to repay the bank its debt.[216] Because the bank owed the surety a duty of good faith, the breach of that duty made the bond voidable by the surety.[217]

Not every jurisdiction recognizes a bank's duty of good faith toward a surety.[218] And, even in those jurisdictions that do recognize such a duty, policy reasons may limit the surety's right to void the bond to those instances where the surety can show the bank's fraud and bad faith by a standard higher than the preponderance of evidence standard employed in most civil litigation. This was the holding in *Marine Midland Bank v. Smith*,[219] where the court said: "Before a bond can be voided, the fraud and bad faith should be brought home to the obligee by quite clear and decisive evidence, otherwise bonds of this character will furnish a very

---

214 81 P.2d 516, 521-22 (Wash. 1938).
215 *Id.* at 526.
216 *Id.* at 527.
217 *Id.*
218 *See* Greene v. Gulf Coast Bank, 593 So. 2d 630, 632 (La. 1992); Popp v. Dyslin, 500 N.E.2d 1039, 1043 (Ill. App. Ct. 1986).
219 482 F. Supp. 1279, 1286 (S.D.N.Y. 1979).

precarious security to the parties who take them."[220] The court found that it was the surety's duty to make proper inquiries, and that the bank did not have an obligation to make disclosures to the surety in the absence of such inquiry.[221]

B. Negligent Disbursement of Project Funds

A bank may undertake responsibility for supervising a construction project and making progress payments. When a bank performs such obligations negligently, the surety may incur losses associated with a lack of project funds to complete the project. Whether a surety will have a cause of action against the bank for negligent disbursement of project funds will depend on the jurisdiction's approach toward the necessity of privity and the concomitant duty owed, if any, to the surety.

The seminal case allowing a surety to sue a bank directly for negligent disbursement of project funds is *Commercial Standard Ins. Co. v. Bank of America*.[222] In that case, the surety brought a third-party claim against the bank after being sued by the project owner. The surety alleged that the bank, which had obligated itself to inspect the project and make progress payments to the contractor, carried out this obligation negligently by disbursing more project funds than were warranted based on the project's state of completion. Insufficient funds to complete the project remained after the contractor's default. The surety completed the project and sought recovery against the bank for the shortfall in project funds. The trial court dismissed the surety's negligence claim, finding that the bank did not owe it a duty.[223]

The California Court of Appeals reversed, employing a foreseeability analysis similar to that discussed above for claims by sureties against design professionals.[224] The court held that because the bank was aware of the performance and payment bonds (in fact, the bank had requested them), and because it was foreseeable that its negligence could cause

---

220 *Id.* at 1286 (citation omitted).
221 *Id.* at 1288.
222 129 Cal. Rptr. 91, 93 (Cal. Ct. App. 1976).
223 *Id.* at 93.
224 *Id.* at 95. The court considered, but rejected, as a basis for denying the surety's claim the fact that the surety, through the premiums charged for the bonds, was in a position to spread the risk of loss on a construction project throughout the construction industry. *Id.*

damages to the surety, the bank was under a duty to perform its disbursement obligations with reasonable care.[225] Thus, privity was not a bar to the surety's claim.

C. Improper Set-Off of Construction Funds

Construction funds held at a bank or other lending institution often are designated as trust funds, either by statute or through the express intention of the parties. Such funds must be applied to construction project debts and, although deposited in the contractor's accounts, belong to the project subcontractors and materialmen.[226] If the bank improperly sets-off the debts owed by the contractor with project funds that are trust funds, the surety may have a claim for those funds against the bank.

This principle was discussed in *Acuity v. Planters Bank, Inc.*[227] Although the court found that the construction funds were not held in trust, it recognized that the bank cannot circumvent a party's superior right to trust funds through set-off. "A bank may not apply a deposit, consisting of trust funds or funds belonging to one other than the depositor, to the individual indebtedness of the depositor if it knows, or can properly be charged with knowledge of, the trust character or true ownership of the funds."[228] Because the surety holds an equitable right to contract funds held in trust, it can properly assert a claim for those funds improperly set-off by the bank.[229]

---

225 *Id.*; *see also* Cmty. Nat'l Bank v. Fid. & Deposit Co. of Md., 563 F.2d 1319 (9th Cir. 1977) (the tort policy of preventing future harm is even more clearly served when the conduct at issue is intentional, rather than merely negligent); Garnter v. Atl. Nat'l Bank of Jacksonville, 350 So. 2d 495 (Fla. Dist. Ct. App. 1977); Cook v. Citizens Sav. & Loan Ass'n, 346 So. 2d 370 (Miss. 1977).
226 Acuity v. Planters Bank, Inc., 362 F. Supp. 2d 855, 890 (W.D. Ky.).
227 *Id.*
228 *Id.* at 889-890 (internal quotations omitted). The court denied the surety's claim, finding that the construction funds were not held in trust because neither state law nor the express intent of the parties created a trust. *Id.* at 893.
229 *Id.* at 890.

VI. Claims Against Third Parties for Violations of Trust Fund Statutes and Fraudulent Transfers

The misuse of project funds and/or fraudulent transfer of the principal's and/or indemnitor's assets may give rise to liability of third parties who were complicit in such actions. This section will touch on possible avenues that may be available to the surety to recover against third parties involved in the misuse of contract funds and/or fraudulent transfer of assets. With respect to the misuse of contract funds, a number of states have enacted statutes which require that contract funds be held in trust until all subcontractors and suppliers have been paid. Some of these statutes extend liability to certain employees, agents, officers, and directors of the contractor who were involved in or had knowledge of the misuse of the contract funds, and may provide an avenue for the surety to recover from such individuals who may not already be indemnitors. Furthermore, many states have enacted fraudulent transfer statutes that may provide the surety an avenue to recover assets of the principal and indemnitors wrongfully transferred to insiders to avoid the reach of creditors such as the surety.

The statutes and common laws that have arisen around trust fund and fraudulent transfer statutes vary significantly between jurisdictions. A comprehensive discussion of the various intricacies and differences between the laws in such jurisdictions is beyond the scope of this chapter.[230] Rather, the following discussion is intended to identify

---

230   For a more comprehensive discussion of potential trust fund statutes and theories of recovery, *see* Kim McNaughten *et al.*, *Surety's Rights to Contract Funds Under Trust Fund Provisions in Indemnity Agreements and Trust Fund Statutes* (unpublished paper presented at Surety Claims Institute, June 24-26, 1999); *see also* Robert F. Carney & Adam Cizek, *Payment Provisions in Construction Contracts and Construction Trust Fund Statutes: A Fifty State Survey*, 24 CONSTR. LAWYER 5, 7 (2004). For a comprehensive discussion of fraudulent transfer laws and processes as they relate to the surety, *see* Robert C. Niesley, *Dismantling an Asset Protection Plan Using Fraudulent Transfer Laws* (unpublished paper presented to ABA/TIPS Fid. & Sur. Law Committee annual meeting, August 2-6, 1996); Chad L. Schexnayder, *"Can't Touch That..." How Asset Protection Planning Affects Underwriting and Recovery* (unpublished paper presented to ABA/TIPS Fid. & Sur. Law Committee

possible theories of recovery that may be available to the surety after discovering a misuse of contract funds or a questionable dissipation of assets.

A. Claims Based on Violations of Trust Fund Statutes

Many states have enacted statutes providing that funds received by a contractor on a construction project are trust funds for the benefit of the subcontractors and suppliers who performed the work.[231] Some of these statutes expressly extend the duty to appropriately utilize construction draws to the employees, officers, and directors of the contractor or subcontractor who received the construction funds.[232] Even where the applicable statute does not expressly provide that it extends to individuals responsible for such misuse, some courts have nonetheless found that the statute will extend to responsible individuals.[233] By

---

annual meeting, August 2-6, 1996); *see also* Ferrucci & Baron, *supra* note 3, at 249-54.

231 *See, e.g.*, ARIZ. REV. STAT. § 33-1005 (2006); COLO. REV. STAT. ANN. § 38-22-127 (2005); DEL. CODE ANN. tit. 6, § 3502 (2006); 770 ILL. COMP. STAT. 60/21.02 (2005); MD. CODE ANN., REAL PROP. § 9-201 (2006); MICH. COMP. LAWS § 570.151 (2006); N.J. STAT. ANN. § 2A:44-148 (2004); N.Y. LIEN LAW § 70-79-a (2006); OKLA. STAT. ANN. tit. 42, § 152-53 (2004); S.D. CODIFIED LAWS § 44-9-13 (2004); TEX. PROP. CODE ANN. § 162.001 *et seq.* (Vernon 2004); WASH. REV. CODE § 60.28.010 (2004); WIS. STAT. § 779.02(5) (2003). Some states have enacted statutes that do not refer to funds received on a construction project as trust funds, but otherwise require that they be used first to pay subcontractors and suppliers. *See, e.g.*, GA. CODE ANN. § 16-8-15 (2006); KY. REV. STAT. ANN. § 376.070 (2004).

232 *See, e.g.*, MD. REAL PROPERTY CODE ANN. § 9-202 (duty extends to officer, director, or employee); OKLA. STAT. ANN. tit. 42, § 153 (duty extends to "natural persons having the legally enforceable duty for the management of the entity"); TEX. PROP. CODE ANN. § 162.002 (duty extends to "officer, director, or agent of a contractor, subcontractor, or owner, who receives trust funds or who has control or direction of trust funds"); WIS. STAT. § 779.02(5) (duty extends to "officers, directors, members, partners, or agents responsible for the misappropriation").

233 *See, e.g., In re* Baird, 114 B.R. 198, 204 (9th Cir. 1990) (holding that a corporate officer who knowingly causes the misappropriation of the trust property is personally liable for a breach of trust committed by the

extending the duty to individual officers, directors, employees, and/or agents of the contractor to appropriately use construction draws to pay the claims of subcontractors and suppliers before utilizing the funds for another purpose, the possibility arises that the surety may pursue such individuals for such misuse. As stated by the Fifth Circuit construing the Texas construction trust fund statute, one of the principal rights created by the act "is allowing materialmen or similar project creditors to impose personal liability on individuals whose corporations held and diverted construction trust funds even in the absence of a personal guaranty agreement from those individuals."[234]

In deciding whether to pursue such a claim, there are a number of factors the surety should consider in light of the law in the pertinent jurisdiction. First, the surety must determine whether there is a statute that provides for a civil right of recovery against the individual at issue. Although some of the trust funds statutes are criminal in nature, some courts have recognized a civil right of recovery.[235] If there is an applicable statute under which a party can pursue a civil right of recovery against an individual who has handled construction trust funds, the surety must next determine whether it has standing to pursue the claim. Most of the trust funds statutes specifically identify the subcontractors and suppliers as the beneficiaries of the statutory trust.[236] As such, the surety will have to establish its right to pursue the claim by and through the subcontractors and suppliers to whom it has paid payment bond claims. Typically, these claims can be pursued by virtue of the surety's rights of subrogation and/or express assignment received upon satisfaction of the claims of the payment bond claimants. It should be kept in mind, however, that to the extent the surety is forced to present its trust fund claim by and through the subcontractors, it is necessarily limited by the total amount of the payment bond claims it has paid. Furthermore, it will be subject to any defense the principal may have as to the particular subcontractors paid by the surety. Finally, it is possible that the particular

---

corporation even if the officer did not personally profit from the transaction).
234 *In re* Boyle, 819 F.2d 583, 589 (5th Cir. 1987).
235 *See, e.g.*, Lively v. Carpet Services, Inc., 904 S.W.2d 868, 871 (Tex. App. 1995) (establishing common law civil right of recovery under TEX. PROP. CODE ANN. § 162.001 et seq.); *see also In re* Boyle, 819 F.2d at 589.
236 *See, e.g.*, MD. CODE ANN., REAL PROP. § 9-201(b)(1); TEX. PROP. CODE § 162.003.

individuals involved in the misuse of the trust funds may be different depending on when payment was owed to each subcontractor or supplier through which the surety asserts the claim.

It is also important that the surety carefully consider what it will be required to establish in order to pursue a statutory trust claim. For instance, the surety should consider whether, and to what extent, it must establish that the individual at issue had the requisite intent to defraud the beneficiary of the trust. Even those statutes expressly providing for potential liability of individuals directing the use of construction funds may differ as to whether the individuals identified are considered to have fiduciary obligations and whether specific intent to defraud must be shown. For example, under the Maryland trust fund statute, in order to hold an officer liable for violations of the trust fund statute, the claimant is required to establish that the individual had the actual "intent to defraud."[237] On the other hand, under the Texas and Oklahoma trust funds statutes, the identified individuals may be held liable without a showing of specific intent to defraud.[238] Where intent must be shown, the expense and effort to establish a viable claim may be considerably higher, as it will undoubtedly require discovery as to the intent of the individual and a more exacting tracing of the funds. Where no intent is required, however, proof of a violation arguably can be established simply by showing that the amounts received by the principal were in excess of the amounts paid for legitimate project expenses.

Finally, when considering pursuing such a claim, the surety should take into account whether, and to what extent, it will be required to trace the construction funds in order to prevail. When a showing of specific intent of the individual is required, such as under the Maryland statute, it will be difficult to prevail without a detailed tracing of how the funds

---

[237] Ferguson Trenching Co., v. Kiehne, 618 A.2d 735, 739-40 (Md. 1993) (contrasting Maryland trust fund statute with Oklahoma and Texas trust fund statutes).

[238] *Id.*; *Lively*, 904 S.W.2d at 875 ("[I]ntent to defraud is only relevant in a criminal prosecution. Requiring a showing of intent to defraud would be inconsistent with the fiduciary relationship imposed by the Act."); *see also In re* Boyle, 819 F.2d at 586 ("The message of the statute . . . is not necessarily that the individuals do anything wrong in 'diverting' the funds, but is rather that if they do so 'divert' they had better be sure that the project debts to such creditors will be paid, as the risk of nonpayment then falls on them personally.").

were utilized. On the other hand, where a showing of intent is not required, the burden to trace the funds may effectively be shifted back to the defendant. For instance, the Texas trust fund statute, under which no showing of intent is required for civil recovery, provides:

> It is an affirmative defense to prosecution or other action brought under Subsection (a) that the trust funds not paid to the beneficiaries of the trust were used by the trustee to pay the trustee's actual expenses directly related to the construction or repair of the improvement or have been retained by the trustee, after notice to the beneficiary who has made a request for payment, as a result of the trustee's reasonable belief that the beneficiary is not entitled to such funds or have been retained as authorized or required by Chapter 53.[239]

By making a showing of proper use of the trust funds an affirmative defense, the Texas trust fund statute effectively puts the burden on the defendant to trace and explain the use of the contract funds received on a given project. In jurisdictions that shift the burden to the trustee to account for the trust funds, the expense of prosecuting such an action will obviously be significantly reduced.

B. *Claims Based on Fraudulent Transfer Laws*

Most states have enacted statutes that specifically provide a remedy to a creditor who has been the victim of a fraudulent transfer. The vast majority of the states have adopted the Uniform Fraudulent Transfer Act.[240] If a surety discovers that its principal or indemnitors have transferred their assets with the intent to defraud creditors, these statutes

---

239 TEX. PROP. CODE § 162.031(b).
240 UNIF. FRAUDULENT TRANSFER ACT, §§ 1-13, 7A U.L.A. 13 (2006) [hereinafter UFTA]. UFTA has been adopted in forty-four states. For a listing of the states that have that adopted UFTA and statutory citation for each, *see* UFTA, 7A U.L.A. at 2-3. For a discussion of the particular deviations from the statute in each state which has adopted UFTA, *see* UFTA, 7A U.L.A. at 7-12. For a more in depth discussion of these statutes and their application to the surety, *see* Robert C. Niesley, *Dismantling an Asset Protection Plan Using Fraudulent Transfer Laws* (unpublished paper presented to ABA/TIPS Fid. & Sur. Law Committee annual meeting, August 2-6, 1996); *see also* Ferrucci & Baron, *supra* note 3, at 249-54.

may allow the surety to recover such assets from the third-party transferee and/or obtain orders preventing further transfers. More specifically, such statutes may allow the surety to obtain the following relief: (1) an avoidance of the transfer to extent necessary to satisfy the surety's claim; (2) an attachment or other provisional remedy against the asset transferred pursuant to the procedures prescribed in the jurisdiction at issue; (3) an injunction against further disposition of assets by the principal and/or indemnitors and/or the transferee; (4) appointment of a receiver to take charge of the asset transferred or of other property of the transferee; (5) other relief the circumstances may require; and/or (6) if a judgment has been entered in favor or the surety, execution on the asset transferred or its proceeds.[241] If a principal or indemnitor who has fraudulently transferred assets is in bankruptcy, these remedies may also be pursued by the trustee in the bankruptcy court pursuant to the United States Bankruptcy Code.[242] Additionally, if it is determined that a third-party, such as an attorney or financial planning professional willfully participated in a conspiracy to hide the assets, that third-party may also be liable for damages caused to the surety by the transfer, even if that party did not receive the fraudulently transferred assets.[243]

In many cases, the potential fraudulent transfer being considered by the surety occurred prior to the surety incurring a loss. At that time the

---

241   UFTA § 7.
242   11 U.S.C.A. § 548 (2005); *see also* Ferrucci & Baron, *supra* note 3, at 251-52. Although the fraudulent transfer standards found in the Bankruptcy Code Section 548 are very similar to those in UFTA, a notable difference is that Section 548 only reaches to transfers made within two years prior to the bankruptcy filing whereas UFTA provides for a four year statute of limitation from the date of the transfer. *Compare* 11 U.S.C.A. § 548 with UFTA § 9. However, Section 544(b) of the Bankruptcy Code provides that the trustee can avoid any transfer "that is voidable under applicable law." 11 U.S.C.A § 544(b). Hence, a trustee should be able to reach back further than the two year limitation in Section 548 if the fraudulent transfer statute in the particular jurisdiction at issue has adopted UFTA's four year statute of limitation. Ferrucci & Baron, *supra* note 3, at 252.
243   Ferrucci & Baron, *supra* note 3, at 253-54 (citing McElhanon v. Hing, 728 P.2d 256 (Ariz. Ct. App. 1985), *aff'd in part and vacated in part*, 728 P.2d 273 (Ariz. 1986), *cert. denied*, 481 U.S. 1030 (1987); Dalton v. Meister, 239 N.W.2d 9 (Wis. 1976)).

surety is only a "contingent creditor." Accordingly, one of the most basic issues to address is whether the surety is the type of creditor entitled to pursue a fraudulent transfer action. It is well established that a contingent creditor is entitled to the protection of the fraudulent transfer statutes.[244]

Another very basic issue is whether there has been a "transfer" as defined in the pertinent statute. Significantly, UFTA defines "transfer" very broadly to include "every mode, direct or indirect, absolute or conditional, voluntary or involuntary, of disposing of or parting with an asset or an interest in an asset, and includes payment of money, release, lease, and creation of a lien or other encumbrance."[245] Based on this definition, there are very few, if any, modes of disposing of assets that will not at least qualify as a "transfer."

Having determined that a transfer has taken place, one must next consider whether the transfer was a "fraudulent transfer." Section 4(a) of UFTA defines "fraudulent transfer" as follows:

(a) A transfer made or obligation incurred by a debtor is fraudulent as to a creditor, whether the creditor's claim arose before or after the transfer was made or the obligation was incurred, if the debtor made the transfer or incurred the obligation:

   (1) with actual intent to hinder, delay, or defraud any creditor of the debtor; or

   (2) without receiving a reasonably equivalent value in exchange for the transfer or obligation, and the debtor:

   (i) was engaged or was about to engage in a business or a transaction for which the remaining assets of the debtor were unreasonably small in relation to the business or transaction; or

---

244 See Am. Sur. Co. of N.Y. v. Marotta, 287 U.S. 513, 517 (1933); United States v. Brickman, 906 F. Supp. 1164, 1172 (N.D. Ill. 1995); Smith v. Young, 55 So. 425, 427 (Ala. 1911); Reel v. Livingston, 16 So. 284, 286 (Fla. 1894); Peterson v. Wahlquist, 249 N.W. 678, 681 (Neb. 1933); Graeber v. Sides, 66 S.E. 600, 601 (N.C. 1909); Squire v. Cramer, 28 N8.E.2d 516, 520 (Ohio 1940); McDonald v. Baldwin, 148 S.W.2d 385, 388 (Tenn. Ct. App. 1940).

245 UFTA § 1(12).

(ii) intended to incur, or believed or reasonably should have believed that he [or she] would incur, debts beyond his [or her] ability to pay as they became due.[246]

Whether a principal or an indemnitor received an equivalent value in return for a transfer based on objective criteria is relatively easy to determine in most cases. On the other hand, determining whether the principal or indemnitor made the transfer with the requisite intent to qualify as a fraudulent transfer is much more difficult. To assist in such determination, UFTA provides the following nonexclusive list of factors that may be considered in determining whether the transfer at issue was made with the requisite intent:[247]

(1) the transfer or obligation was to an insider;
(2) the debtor retained possession or control of the property transferred after the transfer;
(3) the transfer or obligation was disclosed or concealed;
(4) before the transfer was made or obligation was incurred, the debtor had been sued or threatened with suit;
(5) the transfer was of substantially all the debtor's assets;
(6) the debtor absconded;
(7) the debtor removed or concealed assets;
(8) the value of the consideration received by the debtor was reasonably equivalent to the value of the asset transferred or the amount of the obligation incurred;
(9) the debtor was insolvent or became insolvent shortly after the transfer was made or the obligation was incurred;
(10) the transfer occurred shortly before or shortly after a substantial debt was incurred; and
(11) the debtor transferred the essential assets of the business to a lienor who transferred the assets to an insider of the debtor.[248]

If the surety determines that a fraudulent transfer has been made, the fraudulent transfer statutes in the jurisdiction at issue, in combination with applicable rules in the jurisdiction pertinent to such equitable relief, should be consulted to determine the steps that will need to be taken to

---

246 UFTA § 4(a).
247 These factors have been referred to by one commentator as "badges of fraud." Niesley, *supra* note 230, at 7.
248 UFTA, § 4(b) (2006).

recover from the third-party transferee.[249] In most cases, a fraudulent transfer action, if successful, will result in legal title to the asset being returned to the status it had before the transfer, subject to the lien of other creditors.[250]

VII. Insurance Claims

There are various types of insurance policies which may provide coverage for losses on a construction project. This section will focus on potential claims on commercial general liability and builder's risk policies.[251] A surety's principal and the obligee are typically named insureds in commercial general liability and builder's risk policies. Accordingly, a surety may be able to assert a direct claim on those policies by virtue of its subrogation and/or assignment rights.

A. *Commercial General Liability Coverage*

Most parties to a construction contract are insured by a commercial general liability policy ("CGL"). As its name implies, a CGL policy insures against certain "general liability" risks of the named insureds. The importance to the surety of the potential coverages provided by CGL policies can not be understated. A surety's subrogation, assignment, exoneration, and/or indemnity rights may allow the surety to seek recovery of all or a portion of its actual or anticipated loss in connection with a default from a CGL carrier. The "general liability" risks that are covered by CGL policies, the definitions, exclusions, conditions, and endorsements that effect such coverages, and the difference in the varying interpretations of CGL coverages across jurisdictions are expansive topics which cannot possibly be covered in full in this chapter. The following discussion is intended to identify many of the most

---

249   For a discussion of the recovery process, *see* Niesley, *supra* note 230, at 2; Ferrucci & Baron, *supra* note 3, at 252.
250   Ferrucci & Baron, *supra* note 3, at 253.
251   However, the practitioner should not lose sight of other potentially applicable policies. For instance, it is not uncommon in default situations that there will be questions regarding whether errors and omissions by design professionals on the project precipitated the default, caused significant delay on the project, or resulted in certain portions of the project not performing as intended.

prevalent issues that arise in connection with claims by sureties against CGL policies.

1. Coverage

CGL policies typically have three insuring agreements, which define the scope of the coverage.[252] Insuring Agreement A of the CGL policy covers "bodily injury" or "property damage" caused by an "occurrence" in the "coverage territory" and occurring during the policy period.[253] Insuring Agreement B of the CGL policy covers "personal injury" or "advertising injury."[254] Insuring Agreement C of the CGL policy covers certain medical expenses for "bodily injury" caused by an accident.[255]

Insuring Agreement A of the CGL policy is the insuring agreement most likely to be implicated in a surety default situation. Accordingly, the following analysis will focus on Insuring Agreement A of the CGL policy.

    a. *Bodily injury.* The CGL policy defines "bodily injury" as "bodily injury, sickness or disease sustained by a person, including death resulting from any of these at anytime."[256] Although coverage for "bodily injury" is very important, "property damage" is typically the type of damage pertinent to a surety in a default situation.

    b. *Property damage.* The CGL policy defines "property damage" to include two different forms of property damage:

> a. Physical injury to tangible property, including all resulting loss of use of that property. All such loss of use shall be deemed to occur at the time of the physical injury that caused it; or

---

[252] Insurance Service Office, Inc., Form CG 00 01 01 96 (1996 ISO Occurrence Policy) (hereinafter, the "CGL Policy"); Insurance Service Office, Inc., Form CG 00 02 01 96 (1996 ISO Claims Made Policy); *see also* Mathew Horowitz et al., CGL/BUILDER'S RISK MONOGRAPH (2004).
[253] CGL Policy, Section 1, Coverage A, ¶ 1.
[254] CGL Policy, Section 1, Coverage B, ¶ 1.
[255] CGL Policy, Section 1, Coverage C, ¶ 1.
[256] CGL Policy, Section V, ¶ 3.

b. Loss of use of tangible property that is not physically injured. All such loss of use shall be deemed to occur at the time of the "occurrence" that caused it.[257]

The definition of "property damage" in the CGL policy has occupied the attention of numerous courts and commentators over the years.[258] Whether damages sought to be recovered under a CGL policy constitute covered "property damage" will require careful consideration. Following is a brief discussion of how courts have addressed the issue of what constitutes "property damage" with respect to various types of damages often at issue in a default.

(i) *Poor workmanship.* While the analysis of whether poor workmanship is covered by a CGL policy is often focused on the definition of "occurrence" or the application of various so-called "business risk" exclusions found in the policy, whether poor workmanship qualifies as "property damage" must also be considered. Many courts have held that poor workmanship may qualify as "property damage."[259] However, some courts have held that poor workmanship, and the costs to repair the poor workmanship itself, are not covered "property damage."[260] Other courts have held that where the poor workmanship itself does not qualify as "property damage," the damages resulting from the poor workmanship may qualify as covered "property damage."[261]

---

257 CGL Policy, Section V, ¶ 12.
258 For a detailed discussion of these issues, *see* Patrick J. O'Connor, Jr., *supra* note 3, at 259; Scott C. Turner, INSURANCE COVERAGE OF CONSTRUCTION DISPUTES (2d ed. 2004), § 6:24-34.
259 *See, e.g.,* Southwest Metalsmiths, Inc. v. Lumbermen's Mut. Cas. Co., 85 Fed. Appx 552 (9th Cir. 2004); Summit Custom Homes, Inc. v. Great Am. Lloyd's Ins. Co., 202 S.W.3d 823 (Tex. Ct. App. 2006); Horowitz, et al., *supra* note 252, at 31.
260 *See, e.g.,* Dreis & Krump Mfg. Co. v. Phoenix Ins. Co., 548 F.2d 681, 686 (7th Cir. 1977); Hamilton Die Cast, Inc. v. United States Fid. & Guar. Co., 508 F.2d 417, 419 (7th Cir. 1975); F & H Const. v. ITT Hartford Ins. Co. of the Midwest, 12 Cal. Rptr. 3d 896 (Cal. Ct. App. 2004); St. Paul Fire & Marine Ins. Co. v. Coss, 145 Cal. Rptr. 836, 838-39 (Cal. Ct. App. 1978); West Orange Lumber Co., Inc. v. Ind. Lumbermens Mut. Ins. Co., 898 So. 2d 1147 (Fla. Dist. Ct. App. 2005).
261 *See, e.g.,* Maryland Cas. Co. v. Reeder, 270 Cal. Rptr. 719, 722 (Cal. Ct. App. 1990); LaMarche v. Shelby Mut. Ins. Co., 390 So. 2d 325, 326-27

(ii) *Failure to complete a contractual obligation.* An insured's failure to complete its contractual obligation does not generally constitute "property damage."[262] However, inadequate performance of a contractual obligation may give rise to covered "property damage" where contiguous property is damaged.[263]

(iii) *Consequential damages.* Consequential damages (e.g. loss of profits, good will, etc.) alone have been held not to constitute covered "property damage."[264] However, if consequential damages[265] result from damage otherwise qualifying as "property damage" under part a. of the definition of "property damage" quoted above, then such consequential damages may be covered.[266] Likewise, if such consequential damages result from the "loss of use of tangible property that is not physically injured," as set forth in part b. of the definition of "property damage" quoted above, then such consequential damages may be covered.[267]

(iv) *Diminution in value.* There is a split of authority as to whether diminution in value alone constitutes "property damage." Some courts have held that diminution in value, by itself, constitutes property

---

(Fla. 1980); W.E. O'Neil Constr. Co. v. Nat'l Union Fire Ins. Co., 721 F. Supp 984, 991 (N.D. Ill. 1989); *see also* Horowitz et al., *supra* note 252, at 30-31; Cunningham & Fischer, *supra* note 96, at 1071.

262 Cunningham & Fischer, *supra* note 96, at 1071-72 (citing Gulf Ins. Co. v. L.A. Effects Group, Inc., 827 F.2d 574 (9th Cir. 1987)); Coss, 145 Cal. Rptr. at 841.

263 *See, e.g.,* St. Paul Fire & Marine Ins. Co. v. Sears, Roebuck & Co., 603 F.2d 780, 784 (9th Cir. 1979) (insured's installation of defective urethane on roof caused insured physical damage to other property because entire roof had to be replaced to correct insured's defective performance).

264 Lazzara Oil Co. v. Columbia Cas. Co., 683 F. Supp. 777, 779 (M.D. Fla. 1988), *aff'd* 868 F.2d 1274 (11th Cir. 1989); Diamond State Ins. Co. v. Chester-Jenson Co., 611 N.E.2d 1083, 1088 (Ill. Ct. App. 1993); *see also* Turner, *supra* note 258, at § 6:75.

265 For a discussion of the types of consequential damages potentially covered, *see* Turner, *supra* note 258, § 6:49-53.

266 *See, e.g.,* Am. Home Assurance Co. v. Libbey-Owens-Ford Co., 786 F.2d 22, 27 (1st Cir. 1986). *But see* Liberty Mut. Ins. Co. v. Consol. Milk Producers Ass'n, 354 F. Supp. 879, 884 (D.N.H. 1973).

267 Woodfin Equities Corp. v. Hartford Mut. Ins. Co., 678 A.2d 116, 131 (Md. Ct. App. 1996) *aff'd in part, rev'd in part,* 687 A.2d 652 (Md. 1997); *see also* Turner, *supra* note 258, § 6:19.

damage.[268] Other courts have held that "property damage" does not result unless it occurs with physical injury to tangible property or loss of use.[269]

(v) *Delay damages.* Exclusion (m) of the CGL policy, the "impaired property" exclusion, excludes losses arising out of "a delay or failure by you or anyone acting on your behalf to perform a contract or agreement in accordance with its terms."[270] As a result of the impaired property exclusion, many pure delay claims will be excluded from coverage.[271] However, if the delay results from otherwise covered "property damage" to tangible property, there may be coverage for the resulting delay damages.[272]

c. *Occurrence.* The 1996 ISO form defines "occurrence" as "an accident, including continuous or repeated exposure to substantially the same general harmful condition."[273] The proper application of the term "occurrence" in connection with construction defect claims is a hotly debated topic. Although there are various exclusions in the CGL policy which exclude damages arising out of certain "business risks," insurers frequently argue that these exclusions need not be reached because faulty construction does not constitute an "occurrence." Courts have reached various conclusions with respect to whether the faulty workmanship can qualify as an "occurrence."[274]

---

268   *See, e.g.*, McDowell-Wellman Eng'g v. Hartford Accident & Indem. Co., 711 F.2d 521, 525 (3rd Cir. 1983); Western Cas. & Sur. Co. v. Polar Panel Co., 457 F.2d 957, 960 (8th Cir. 1972); Aetna Cas. & Sur. Co. v. PPG Indus., Inc., 554 F. Supp. 290, 294 (D. Ariz. 1983).

269   *See, e.g.*, N.H. Ins. Co. v. Vieira, 930 F.2d 696 (9th Cir. 1991); Travelers Ins. Co. v. Eljer Mfg., Inc., 757 N.E.2d 481, 493 (Ill. 2001); Federated Mut. Ins. v. Concrete Units, Inc., 363 N.W.2d 751, 756 (Minn. 1985).

270   CGL Policy, Section 1, ¶ 2(m). For a more detailed analysis of the impaired property exclusion, *see* Horowitz et al., *supra* note 252, at 52-54; Turner, *supra* note 258, § 26.

271   *See* Horowitz et al., *supra* note 252, at 55.

272   For a detailed discussion of the cases which have considered whether coverage exists for delay damages, *see* Turner, *supra* note 258, § 6:31.

273   CGL Policy, Section V, ¶ 12.

274   *See* O'Connor, Jr., *supra* note 3, at 269; Clifford J. Shapiro, *The Good, the Bad and the Ugly* (unpublished paper presented at the meeting of the ABA Forum on the Construction Industry, January 29, 2005).

Some courts have concluded that faulty workmanship qualifies as an "occurrence."[275] Other courts have concluded that while faulty workmanship by itself does not constitute a covered occurrence, if faulty workmanship results in damage to "other property" a covered occurrence may exist.[276] Finally, other courts have concluded that faulty workmanship simply does not constitute an "occurrence."[277] However, it should be noted that even if faulty work is determined to constitute an "occurrence," the loss may be excluded by specific policy exclusions.[278]

A related argument often made by CGL insurers against coverage for faulty workmanship under a CGL policy is that if a CGL policy were held to cover for faulty workmanship, the CGL policy would, in effect, be converted into a performance bond. Such an argument has met with some success.[279] However, such an argument is misplaced. A performance bond does not "insure" the contractor, but rather protects the owner from the contractor's failure to perform its contractual obligation. A claim under a CGL policy should be governed by the terms of the policy itself without reference to the obligations which arise under a performance bond. Where there is overlap, the surety should be able to

---

275 *See, e.g.*, Rando v. Top Notch Properties, L.L.C., 879 So. 2d 821 (La. Ct. App. 2004); Pine Oak Builders, Inc. v. Great Am. Lloyds Ins. Co., No. 14-05-00487-CV, 2006 Tex. App. LEXIS 5950 (Tex. Civ. App. July 6, 2006), *aff'd in part, rev'd in part*, 52 Tex. Sup. J. 30 (2009); Glendenning's Limestone & Ready-Mix Co. v. Reimer, 721 N.W.2d 704 (Wis. Ct. App. 2006); Am. Family Mut. Ins. Co. v. Am. Girl, Inc., 673 N.W.2d 65 (Wis. 2004).
276 *See, e.g.*, Auto-Owners Ins. Co. v. Home Pride Companies, Inc., 684 N.W.2d 571 (Neb. 2004); Acuity v. Burd & Smith Constr., Inc., 721 N.W.2d 33, 39-40 (N.D. 2006).
277 *See, e.g.*, Travelers Indem. Co. of Am. v. Miller Bldg. Corp., 142 Fed. Appx. 147 (4th Cir. 2005); Kvaerner Metals Div. of Kvaerner United States, Inc. v. Commercial Union Ins. Co., 908 A.2d 888 (Pa. 2006); L-J, Inc. v. Bituminous Fire & Marine Ins. Co., 621 S.E.2d 33 (S.C. 2005).
278 *See* discussion of exclusions *infra* Section VIII.A.2.
279 *See, e.g.*, Hartford Accident & Indem. Co. v. Pac. Mut. Life Ins. Co., 861 F.2d 250, 253 (10th Cir. 1988); William C. Vick Constr. Co. v. Pennsylvania Nat'l Mut. Cas. Ins. Co., 52 F. Supp. 2d 569, 591 (E.D.N.C. 1999); Reliance Ins. Co. v. Mogavero, 640 F. Supp. 84, 85 (D. Md. 1986).

look to the policy for covered losses suffered by the surety by virtue of its rights of subrogation, assignment, exoneration, and/or indemnity.[280]

2. Exclusions

Even if there is "property damage" resulting from an "occurrence," a loss may nonetheless may be excluded by one of the many exclusions in the CGL policy. The exclusions most likely to come into play in a construction default situation are discussed below.

1. Exclusion (a)—Expected or Intended

Exclusion (a) states:

> This insurance does not apply to:
>
> "Bodily injury" or "property damage" expected or intended from the standpoint of the insured. This exclusion does not apply to "bodily injury" resulting from the use of reasonable force to protect persons or property.[281]

It is important to recognize that it is the "bodily injury" or "property damage" that cannot be expected or intended for there to be coverage. In other words, exclusion (a) does not exclude unintended and unexpected damage that results from intentional acts.[282] As most acts on a construction project are intentional, this is an important distinction to make. However, if the insured intended or expected some damage to result, although different than what actually resulted, the exclusion may still apply.[283]

---

280 *See* Turner, *supra* note 258, § 3:10.
281 CGL Policy, Section I, ¶ 2(a).
282 *See* Koch Eng'g Co. v. Gibraltar Cas. Co., 78 F.3d 1291, 1294 (8th Cir. 1996); Allstate Ins. Co. v. Steinmeier, 723 F.2d 873, 875 (11th Cir. 1984); City of Johnstown, N.Y. v. Bankers Standard Ins. Co., 877 F.2d 1146, 1150 (2d Cir. 1989); *see also* Turner, *supra* note 258, § 9:2; O'Connor, Jr., *supra* note 3, at 232.
283 *See e.g.*, Chem. Leaman Tank Lines, Inc. v. Aetna Cas. & Sur. Co., 89 F.3d 976, 988 (3d Cir. 1996); Kuckenberg v. Hartford Accident & Indem. Co., 226 F.2d 225, 227 (9th Cir. 1955).

Considerable attention has been devoted by courts to the standard to be applied when determining whether the damage or injury was expected or intended by the insured. Some courts have applied an objective standard to the insured's conduct, questioning whether a reasonable person in the position of the insured would have expected or intended the damage to occur.[284] Some courts and commentators, however, have noted that the standard for determining whether injury or damage was intended or expected should not be "foreseeability." Because foreseeability is an element of a negligence action, if foreseeability was the standard utilized, coverage would effectively be eviscerated by this exclusion.[285] As such, some courts applying an objective standard have used a "substantial certainty" or "substantial probability" test.[286]

---

[284] Bituminous Cas. Corp. v. Tonka Corp., 9 F.3d 51, 53 (8th Cir. 1993), cert. denied, 511 U.S. 1083, (1994); Alert Centre, Inc. v. Alarm Prot. Services, Inc., 967 F.2d 161, 164 (5th Cir. 1992) (holding that exclusion (a) excludes an injury "which the insured intended, not one which the insured caused, however intentional the injury-producing act"); Auto-Owners Ins. Co. v. Jensen, 667 F.2d 714, 720 (8th Cir. 1981); Am. Cas. Co. v. Timmons, 352 F.2d 563, 566 (6th Cir. 1965); United States Fid. & Guar. Co. v Morrison Grain Co., 734 F. Supp. 437, 445 (D. Kan. 1990), aff'd, 999 F.2d 489 (10th Cir. 1993) (distinguishing an intentional injury and an unintended injury resulting from an intentional act to hold insured "had the desire to cause the consequences of his acts or he believed the consequences were substantially certain to result"); United States Fire Ins. Co. v. CNA Ins. Co., 572 N.E.2d 1124, 1128-29 (Ill. Ct. App. 1991) ("An insured need not know to a virtual certainty that a result will follow its acts or omissions for the result to be expected . . . the word 'expected' denotes that the actor knew or should have known that there was a substantial probability that certain consequences will result from his actions.") (quoting City of Carter Lake v. Aetna Cas. & Sur. Co. (8th Cir. 1979), 604 F.2d 1052, 1058-59; Green Constr. Co. v. Nat'l Union Fire Ins. Co., 771 F. Supp. 1000, 1002-1003 (W.D. Mo. 1991); Ohio Cas. Ins. Co. v. Terrace Enterprises, 260 N.W.2d 450, 452 (Minn. 1977); Am. Mut. Liab. Ins. Co. v. Neville Chem. Co., 650 F. Supp. 929 (W.D. Pa. 1987).

[285] See City of Johnstown, N.Y., 877 F.2d at 1150; Albuquerque Gravel Prods. Co. v. Am. Employers Ins. Co., 282 F.2d. 218 (10th Cir. 1960); Hutchinson Water Co. v. United States Fid. & Guar. Co., 250 F.2d 892, 894 (10th Cir. 1957); see also Turner, supra note 258, § 9:5.

[286] See, e.g., Bituminous Cas. Corp., 9 F.3d at 54; City of Carter Lake v. Aetna Cas. & Sur. Co., 604 F.2d 1052, 1059 n.4 (8th Cir. 1979).

Other courts have applied a subjective standard, excluding only those losses subjectively intended by the insured.[287] It is important to note that courts applying the subjective standard have concluded that gross negligence and recklessness do not fall within the exclusion.[288]

2. Exclusion (b)—Contractual Liability

Exclusion (b) states:

This insurance does not apply to:

"Bodily injury" or "property damage" for which the insured is obligated to pay damages by reason of the assumption of liability in a contract or agreement. This exclusion does not apply to liability for damages:

That the insured would have in the absence of the contract or agreement; or

Assumed in a contract or agreement that is an "insured contract", provided the "bodily injury" or "property damage" occurs subsequent to the execution of the contract or agreement. Solely for the purposes of liability assumed in an "insured contract", reasonable attorney fees and necessary litigation expenses incurred by or for a party other than an insured are deemed to be damages because of "bodily injury" or "property damage," provided:

a. Liability to such party for, or for the cost of, that party's defense has also been assumed in the same "insured contract"; and

b. Such attorney fees and litigation expenses are for defense of that party against a civil or alternative dispute resolution

---

[287] *See, e.g.*, Koch Eng'g Co., 78 F.3d at 1294; Stonewall Ins. Co. v. Asbestos Claims Mgmt. Corp., 73 F.3d 1178, 1205 (2d Cir. 1995); City of Johnstown, N.Y., 877 F.2d at 1150.

[288] Koch Eng'g Co., 78 F.3d at 1294; Andover Newton Theological Sch., Inc. v. Cont'l Cas. Co., 930 F.2d 89, 92 (1st Cir. 1991).

proceeding in which damages to which this insurance applies are alleged.[289]

Significantly, exclusion (b) is not intended to exclude all damages simply because they result from a breach of contract. Rather, the "contractual liability" at issue is liability arising from an insured's contractual "assumption" of another's liability, e.g., through an indemnity or hold harmless provision in a contract.[290] Damages resulting from an insured's failure to properly construct a structure pursuant to a construction contract are not the type of "contractual liability" intended to be excluded by exclusion (b).[291]

As will be noted, exclusion (b) has two explicit exceptions. First, exclusion (b) does not exclude damages for which the insured would be liable "in the absence of the contract or agreement."[292] For instance, where the insured would be liable for damages in tort, or by virtue of principles of equitable indemnity, contribution, or similar principles, separate and apart from its contractual assumption of liability, exclusion (b) will not apply.[293] This exception to the contractual liability exclusion is potentially very important to the surety. Although the principal has likely "assumed" liability to the surety by virtue of an indemnity agreement, the principal is also liable to the surety under common law principles of indemnification and exoneration. Therefore, pursuant to the first explicit exception, the principal's liability to the surety should not be excluded from coverage by exclusion (b).

Relying on an exception to exclusion (b) found in earlier policy forms, similar to that above, two Louisiana courts have concluded that exclusion (b) does not exclude coverage for an insured's liability to its

---

289 CGL Policy, Section I, ¶ 2.b.
290 *See* Federated Mut. Ins. Co. v. Grapevine Excavation, Inc., 197 F.3d 720, 726 (5th Cir. 1999); Dreis & Krump Mfg. Co. v. Phoenix Ins. Co., 548 F.2d 681, 683 (7th Cir. 1977); Am. Family Mut. Ins. Co. v. Am. Girl, Inc., 673 N.W.2d 65, 80-81 (Wis. 2004).
291 *See* Turner, *supra* note 258, § 10:3.
292 CGL Policy, Section 1, ¶ 2.b.
293 *See, e.g.*, Roger H. Proulx & Co. v. Crest-Liners, Inc., 119 Cal. Rptr. 2d 442, 451-52 (Cal. Ct. App. 2002); Reliance Ins. Co. v. Armstrong World Indus., Inc., 614 A.2d 642, 658 (N.J. Super. Ct. Law Div. 1992), *op. modified*, 625 A.2d 601 (N.J. Super 1993).

surety for the surety's investigative and defense costs.[294] Similarly, a Florida court held that exclusion (b) does not exclude coverage of the insured's liability to the surety for amounts paid by the surety on a personal injury judgment.[295] In that case, the court held that because the insured's liability to the surety for indemnification arose as a matter of law, and not solely under the provisions of an agreement of indemnity, exclusion (b) did not apply, and the insurer was liable to the surety for the amount paid to satisfy the judgment.[296]

The second exception to exclusion (b) is for obligations assumed in an "insured contract."[297] The definition of "insured contract" is a lengthy definition that will not be repeated in full here. However, of particular note is part f. of the definition of "insured contract" providing in relevant part that "insured contract" includes "that part of any other contract or agreement pertaining to your business . . . under which you assume the tort liability of another party to pay for 'bodily injury' or 'property damage' to a third person or organization."[298] Arguably, the agreement of indemnity executed by an insured in favor of its surety would fall under this part of the definition of "insured contract." Therefore, when confronted with litigation by the obligee, the claim may implicate coverage under the principal's CGL policy. If coverage is implicated, the surety may be able to demand a defense from the principal's insurer.[299]

3. Exclusion (j)—Damage to Property

The portions of exclusion (j) relevant to construction projects state:

---

294 Natchitoches Parish Sch. Bd. v. Shaw, 620 So. 2d 412, 414-15 (La. Ct. App. 1993); Merrick Constr. Co. v. Hartford Fire Ins. Co., 449 So. 2d 85, 88 (La. Ct. App. 1984).
295 Western World Ins. Co. v. Travelers Indem. Co., 358 So. 2d 602, 604 (Fla. Dist. Ct. App. 1978).
296 Id.
297 CGL Policy, Section I, ¶ 2.b.2.
298 Id.
299 Ferrucci & Baron, *supra* note 3, at 248. If the indemnity agreement is determined to be an "insured contract" and the surety seeks a defense from the insurer to a suit by the obligee, the Supplementary Payments provision of the 1996 ISO policy form, unlike prior forms, expressly addresses the conditions under which the insurer will undertake the defense of an indemnitee.

This insurance does not apply to:

(j) "Property damage" to:

. . .

(5) That particular part of real property on which you or any contractors or subcontractors working directly or indirectly on your behalf are performing operations, if the "property damage" arises out of those operations; or

(6) That particular part of any property that must be restored, repaired or replaced because "your work" was incorrectly performed on it.

. . .

Paragraph 6 of this exclusion does not apply to "property damage" included in the "products-completed operations hazard."[300]

Generally speaking, exclusions (j)(5) and (6) are so-called "business risk" exclusions.

a. Exclusion (j)(5)

Exclusion (j)(5) is intended to exclude coverage for damage to property on which construction "operations" are underway resulting from such "operations."[301] Exclusion (j)(5) is limited to property damage to the "particular part" of real property upon which operations are being performed. "Particular part" is not defined in the policy. Commentators and courts have concluded that "particular part" should apply only to the "smallest unit of division available to the work in question."[302] For instance, where an insured started a fire while cleaning equipment used to paint cabinets, which destroyed a large portion of the structure, it was held that the "particular part" excluded from coverage was the cost to

---

300 CGL Policy, Section I, ¶ 2(j).
301 OWEN SHEAN & DOUGLAS PATIN, CONSTRUCTION INSURANCE: COVERAGE AND DISPUTES (1994 & Supp. 2003); O'Connor, Jr., *supra* note 3, at 345.
302 Turner, *supra* note 258, § 29:5, *but see* Vandivort Const. Co. v. Seattle Tennis Club, 522 P.2d 198, 201 (Wash. Ct. App. 1974).

repair the cabinets being painted; the remainder of the damages were not subject to the exclusion.[303]

Exclusion (j)(5) further limits the exclusion to damages that occur while "performing operations." As such, the exclusion should not apply to damages which occur after the operations that caused the damage are complete.[304]

Exclusion (j)(5) is also limited to damages that "arise out of" the operations. As such, if the damages result from something other than the immediate operations (including the insured's previous operations), the exclusion should not apply. Further, if the damage resulted from defective materials rather than installation, the exclusion should not apply.[305]

b. Exclusion (j)(6)

Exclusion (j)(6), often referred to as the "faulty workmanship" exclusion, is intended to preclude coverage for the cost to repair the insured's faulty work.

---

[303] Columbia Mut. Ins. Co. v. Schauf, 967 S.W.2d 74, 81 (Mo. 1998) (case includes excellent discussion of "particular part" language); *see also* Travelers Ins. Co. v. Volentine, 578 S.W.2d 501 (Tex. Civ. App. 1979) (holding that when a contractor was hired to replace valves on an engine, ultimately causing the entire engine to explode, the damage to the engine itself was not excluded since the contractor had been hired only to perform operations on the valves not the entire engine); Blackfield v. Underwriters at Lloyd's, London, 53 Cal. Rptr. 838 (Cal. Ct. App. 1966) (The builders of a tract of homes were sued by buyers who discovered the homes had faulty foundations. The court interpreted an exclusion similar to (j)(5) to exclude only the damages to those parts of the house which were defective. The insurer argued that the whole house was "that particular part," since the insureds were responsible for overseeing all of the construction. The court held the insurer's interpretation of the policy exclusion to be unreasonable, requiring the insurer to cover all damages, except the damaged foundation itself.). *But see* Util. Maint. Contractors v. Western Am. Ins. Co., 866 P.2d 1093 (Kan. Ct. App. 1994); Jet Line Serv., Inc. v. Am. Employers Ins. Co., 537 N.E.2d 107 (Mass. 1989).

[304] Turner, *supra* note 258, § 29:3.

[305] Nat'l Union Fire Ins. Co. v. Structural Sys. Tech, Inc., 756 F. Supp. 1232, 1241 (E.D. Mo. 1991), *aff'd*, 964 F.2d 759 (8th Cir. 1992); *see also* Turner, *supra* note 258, § 29:7.

Exclusion (j)(6) is limited to "that particular part" of "any property" requiring repair due to "your work." First, it will be noted that as with exclusion (j)(5), exclusion (j)(6) is limited by the words "that particular part." As such, while the costs to repair the defective work performed may be excluded, the costs to repair other resulting damages to other portions of the project should not.

"Your work" is defined as:

a. Work or operations performed by you or on your behalf; or

b. Materials, parts or equipment furnished in connection with such work or operations.

"Your work" includes:

a. Warranties or representations made at any time with respect to the fitness, quality, durability, performance or use of "your work"; and

b. The providing of or failure to provide warnings or instructions.[306]

It should be noted that the definition of "your work" includes work performed by subcontractors. However, significantly, exclusion (j)(6) does not apply to property damage included in the "products-completed operations hazard." In short, exclusion (j)(6) does not apply when the project has been "completed."[307] The exception of damages falling within the "products-completed operations hazard" and the potential of expanded coverage for work performed by subcontractors is discussed below.[308]

Finally, it should also be noted that exclusion (j)(6) excludes property damage to property that must be restored, repaired or replaced because the insured work was incorrectly performed "on it." Although there is little case law addressing the significance of the inclusion of the

---

306 CGL Policy, Section V. ¶ 19.
307 *See* J.Z.G. Resources, Inc. v. King, 987 F.2d 98, 100 (2d Cir. 1993); Nat'l Union Fire Ins. Co., 756 F. Supp. at 1241.
308 *See infra* Section VIII.5.

words "on it," some commentators have suggested such language limits the application of exclusion (j)(6) to property damage to preexisting property "on" which the insured subsequently performed work.[309]

4. Exclusion (k)—Property Damage to "Your Product"

Exclusion (k) excludes from coverage "'property damage' to 'your product' arising out of it or any part of it."[310] Although exclusion (k) was always intended by insurers to apply to the manufacturing of products, rather than to contractors who perform services, the language of the 1973 ISO form did not make this clear.[311] Courts reached varying conclusions as to whether work performed by a contractor qualified as a "product" under the 1973 ISO form.[312] However, by excluding "real property" from the definition of "your product," the 1986 and later ISO policy forms strongly suggests that a contractor's work is not to be included as "your product."[313]

It should also be noted that the CGL policy includes material supplied in the definition of "your work."[314] This is further evidence that "your product" is not intended to include the work of, or materials provided by, contractors. However, some courts have reached a different conclusion.[315]

Whether or not the work of a contractor is determined to fall in the definition of "your product," it is important to recognize that exclusion (k) only excludes damage to the insured's product. Property damages to

---

309 Turner, *supra* note 258, § 32:6; Horowitz et al., *supra* note 252, at 32.
310 CGL Policy, Section I, ¶ 2.k. The definition of "your product" is found at Section V, paragraph 18, of the 1996 ISO form.
311 Turner, *supra* note 258, § 27:7.
312 For a citation to numerous cases construing the 1973 ISO form, *see id.* § 27:12 n.2.
313 *See* Underwriters at Interest v. SCI Steelcon, 905 F. Supp. 441 (W.D. Mich. 1995); *see also* Turner, *supra* note 258, § 27:7.
314 CGL Policy, Section V, ¶ 19.
315 *See, e.g.*, Thorn v. Caskey, 745 So. 2d 653, 666 (La. Ct. App. 1999); Commerce Ins. Co. v. Betty Caplette Builders, Inc., 647 N.E.2d 1211, 1214 (Mass. 1995); Fisher v. Am. Family Mut. Ins. Co., 579 N.W.2d 599, 606 (N.D. 1998).

other parts of a project resulting from the insured's product would not be excluded by exclusion (k).[316]

5. Exclusion (l)—Property Damage to "Your Work" and the "Products-Completed Operations Hazard"

Exclusion (l) states:

This insurance does not apply to:

> (1) "Property damage" to "your work" arising out of it or any part of it and included in the "products-completed operations hazard."

This exclusion does not apply if the damaged work or the work out of which the damage arises was performed on your behalf by a subcontractor.[317]

While exclusions (j)(5) and (j)(6), discussed above, exclude certain property damage resulting from a contractor's defective work which occurs while construction is ongoing, exclusion (l) excludes certain property damage which occurs after a project is completed.

Because the definition of "your work" includes the work of subcontractors, the first part of the exclusion, without more, would exclude coverage for property damage occurring after the project was complete caused by the work of the general contractor or its subcontractors. However, exclusion (l) specifically provides that the exclusion does not apply if "the damaged work or the work out of which the damage arises was performed on your behalf by a subcontractor." This exception is significant given the high percentage of work often subcontracted on construction projects. By excepting from the exclusion the work of subcontractors, the policy in essence expands coverage for general contractors after the project is complete, at least as compared to the coverage available during the progress of construction as limited by

---

316 *See* Stonewall Ins. Co. v. Asbestos Claims Mgmt. Corp., 73 F.3d 1178, 1205 (2d Cir. 1995); Lafarge Corp. v. Hartford Cas. Ins. Co., 61 F.3d 389, 394 (5th Cir. 1995); Imperial Cas. & Indem. Co. v. High Concrete Structures, Inc., 858 F.2d 128, 134-37 (3d Cir. 1988).
317 CGL Policy, Section I, ¶ 2(1).

exclusions (j)(5) and (j)(6). For this reason, the subcontractor exception to exclusion (l) is often referred to as "completed operations coverage," although it really is merely an exception to the exclusion.

Most courts recognize the broader coverage for property damage caused by or to the work of subcontractors after the project is complete.[318] However, notwithstanding what appears to be the clear intention of the drafters, some courts have refused to extend coverage for subcontractor's work in a completed operations context any further than in ongoing operations.[319]

B. Builder's Risk Coverage

1. Risks Covered

Damage to the structure being constructed is the primary property insured by a builder's risk policy.[320] However, builder's risk insurance also typically provides coverage for damage to other important property interests on a project. For instance, construction equipment, tools, materials and fixtures to be incorporated into the improvements may be on site. For a renovation project, existing property will also be on site. Whether items such as these are covered by a builder's risk policy depends in large part on the definitions, conditions, and exclusions contained in the coverage form utilized.[321]

---

318 *See, e.g.*, Fireguard Sprinkler Sys., Inc. v. Scottsdale Ins. Co., 864 F.2d 648 (9th Cir. 1988); United Capital Ins. Co. v. Special Trucks, Inc., 918 F. Supp. 1250 (N.D. Ind. 1996); Iberia Parish Sch. Bd. v. Sandifer & Sons Constr. Co., 721 So. 2d 1021 (La. Ct. App. 1998); O'Shaughnessy v. Smuckler Corp., 543 N.W.2d 99 (Minn. Ct. App. 1996).

319 *See, e.g.*, Lassiter Const. Co., Inc. v. Am. States Ins. Co., 699 So. 2d 768 (Fla. Dist. Ct. App. 1997); R.N. Thompson & Assoc., Inc. v. Monroe Guar. Ins. Co., 686 N.W.2d 160 (Ind. Ct. App. 1997); Knutsen Constr. Co. v. St. Paul Fire & Marine Ins. Co., 396 N.W.2d 229 (Minn. 1986); Blaylock & Brown Constr. Co. v. AIU Ins. Co., 796 S.W.2d 146, 153-54 (Tenn. Ct. App. 1990).

320 Ajax Bldg. Corp. v. Hartford Fire Ins. Co., 358 F.3d 795, 799 (11th Cir. 2004) (*citing* DEUTSCH, KERRIGAN & STILES, CONSTRUCTION INDUSTRY INSURANCE HANDBOOK (1991 & Supp. 1998)).

321 *See, e.g.*, Ajax Bldg. Corp., 358 F.3d at 799 (policy specifically excluding machinery, tools, equipment and other property not to become part of structure).

Builder's risk policies typically fall into one of two categories—"named peril" or "all risk" (or "open peril"). In a "named peril" policy, the covered causes of loss are specifically enumerated, and typically include property damages caused by fire, lightning, explosion, and vandalism, among others. Endorsements are available for named peril policies to expand the types of covered losses.

"All risk" policies, on the other hand, insure against risks of direct physical loss, except those specifically excluded, including losses resulting from events such as violations of building ordinances, earth movement, and governmental action. Other significant exclusions may include property damage resulting from faulty workmanship,[322] building collapse,[323] design defects,[324] improper excavation activities,[325] or freezing.[326]

Notwithstanding the often used description of an "all risk" policy as a policy that covers all losses except those specifically excluded, courts have recognized certain underwriting limitations in coverage. For instance, intentional misconduct and fraud are not covered.[327] Further, as with other insurance policies, in order to be covered, the loss must be fortuitous.[328] Probably of most significance is the recognition by most

---

322 Roy Anderson Corp. v. Westchester Fire Ins. Co., No. W2000-01489-COA-R3-CV, 2001 Tenn. App. LEXIS 545, at *1 (Tenn. Ct. App. July 26, 2001).
323 Loewenthal v. Sec. Ins. Co., 436 A.2d 493 (Md. Ct. App. 1981); Nat'l Fire Ins. Co. v. Valero Energy Corp., 777 S.W.2d 501, 506 (Tex. App. 1989).
324 Gen. Am. Transp. Corp. v. Sun Ins. Office, Ltd., 369 F.2d 906, 908 (6th Cir. 1966); Swire Pac. Holdings, Inc. v. Zurich Ins. Co., 139 F. Supp. 2d 1374, 1377 (S.D. Fla. 2001).
325 Gen. Constr. Co. v. Aetna Cas. & Sur. Co., 202 A.2d 146 (Conn. 1964); D'Agostino Excavators, Inc. v. Globe Indem. Co., 184 N.Y.S.2d 378, 379 (N.Y. App. Div. 1959).
326 Album Realty Corp. v. Am. Home Assurance Co., 607 N.E.2d 804 (1992).
327 Standard Structural Steel Co. v. Bethlehem Steel Corp., 597 F. Supp. 164, 191 (D. Conn. 1984); Avis v. Hartford Fire Ins. Co., 195 S.E.2d 545, 549 (N.C. 1973).
328 Intermetal Mexicana v. Ins. Co. of N. Am., 866 F.2d 71, 75 (3d Cir. 1989); Compaigne Des Bauxites De Guinee v. Ins. Co. of N. Am., 724 F.2d 369, 372 (3d Cir. 1983); *see also* Jane Massey Draper, *Annotation, Coverage Under "All-Risk" Insurance*, 30 A.L.R. 5th 170 (1995).

courts that a builder's risk policy is not intended to cover non-performance of contractual obligations that result in defective or deficient work.[329] Although most "all risk" policies contain an express exclusion for the costs to correct faulty workmanship, even in the absence of such an express exclusion, courts have held that the costs to correct faulty construction is not covered.[330] If, however, the defective work causes a covered loss, the loss may very well still be covered.[331] In short, when a surety is called upon to correct defective work as well as the property damages resulting therefrom, the surety should consider whether a claim can be made on a builder's risk policy.

2. Insureds

If an entity is not properly named in the builder's risk policy, that entity may not be able to make a claim on the policy.[332] Identifying the insureds under a builder's risk policy typically involves a straightforward analysis of a policy's named insureds. However, it is possible that the property interests of certain entities, although not specifically named, are described specifically enough in the policy to qualify such entities as insureds.[333]

Even if a party is a named insured, such named insured must have an "insurable interest" in the damaged property in order for there to be

---

329   Trinity Indus., Inc. v. Ins. Co. of N. Am., 916 F.2d 267, 270-71 (5th Cir. 1990).
330   Id.
331   See Tzung v. State Farm Fire & Cas. Co., 873 F.2d 1338, 1341 (9th Cir. 1989); S. Cal. Edison Co. v. Harbor Ins. Co., 148 Cal. Rptr. 106, 110 (Cal. Ct. App. 1978).
332   Bd. of Trustees of the Univ. of Ill. v. United States Fid. & Guar. Co., No. 90 C 1281, 1992 U.S. Dist. LEXIS 10191, at *16 (N.D. Ill. July 2, 1992); United States Fid. & Guar. Co. v. Royal Ins. Co., 1992 U.S. Dist. LEXIS 2911, at *8 (N.D. Ill. Mar 13, 1992); LeMaster Steel Erectors, Inc. v. Reliance Ins. Co., 546 N.E.2d 313, 319 (Ind. Ct. App. 1989); Metric Constructors, Inc. v. Indus. Risk Insurers, 401 S.E.2d 126, 128 (N.C. Ct. App. 1991), aff'd, 410 S.E.2d 392 (N.C. 1991); McBroome-Bennett Plumbing, Inc. v. Villa France, Inc., 515 S.W.2d 32, 37-38 (Tex. App. 1974). But see W. Am. Ins. Co. v. J.R. Const. Co., 777 N.E.2d 610, 616 (Ill. App. Ct. 2002).
333   See J. F. Shea Co. v. Hynds Plumbing & Heating Co., 619 P.2d 1207, 1209 (Nev. 1980).

coverage for such property damage under a builder's risk policy.[334] In order for a party to have an "insurable interest," the party must "either derive a pecuniary benefit from the continued existence of the property or suffer pecuniary loss from its destruction."[335] Because the interests of those involved in a project may change during the course of the project, whether a named insured has an "insurable interest" in damaged property may be a central issue in an analysis of whether coverage is available under a builder's risk policy.

Conclusion

When a surety's principal and indemnitors no longer have the financial ability to protect the surety from loss, potential claims against third parties and insurers may prove to be an invaluable source of recovery to the surety. Accordingly, sureties should carefully consider the law in the applicable jurisdiction early on in a project to ensure that such rights are protected.

---

334 St. Paul Fire & Marine Ins. Co. v. Daughtry, 699 S.W.2d 321, 322 (Tex. App. 1985).
335 *Id.*

8

LIABILITY OF THE PERFORMANCE BOND SURETY FOR DAMAGES (UNDER CONTRACT OF SURETYSHIP)

Keith A. Langley*
Marchelle M. Houston

Introduction

By undertaking a surety bond, a surety agrees to be a guarantor, and, as under a guaranty agreement, the liability of a surety is primarily defined by the language of the bond itself. Determining the liability of a performance bond surety is a fact intensive process and is determined on a case by case basis. While liability may be affected by statutes or common law, the first step in determining the liability of a surety is to read the bond. The promises and requirements of the bond are critical issues to be found in the language used.

I. General Principles of Construction and Interpretation

A. *Contract Principles of Interpretation*

A performance bond is a contract, and thus is governed by the normal rules of contract formation.[1] In most cases, by issuing a performance bond, a surety is making a promise to the obligee that the surety will guaranty the performance of the principal/primary obligor. In return, the surety receives a fee from the principal/primary obligor for the use of the surety's financial guaranty.[2]

---

*   Brandon Bains, Ryan Dry, and Rob Sayles of Langley Weinstein Hamel LLP rendered substantial assistance with respect to the research and preparation of this chapter.
1   RESTATEMENT (THIRD) OF SURETYSHIP AND GUARANTY § 7 (1996).
2   4 PHILIP L. BRUNER & PATRICK J. O'CONNOR, JR., BRUNER & O'CONNOR ON CONSTRUCTION LAW § 12:9 (West 2002 & Supp. 2008).

The liability of the performance bond surety–and recourse by an obligee–is tied to the bond itself.[3] To determine the liability of a performance bond surety, one must begin by reading the full language of the performance bond. Reading the bond–fully and carefully–should be the first step of the parties, counsel, and the court or arbitrators when analyzing liability. The nuances of each performance bond can vary a surety's liability dramatically. This analysis should continue with any other documents that are incorporated by reference into the bond,[4] most importantly the bonded contract. The terms of the bond and the underlying contract are to be construed together to determine the performance required of the surety and the ensuing liability.[5]

At its core, a performance bond is a contract to be construed as written.[6] When interpreting performance bonds, the courts will attempt to ascertain the true intentions of the parties.[7] Reading each bond is the only way to fully analyze a surety's liability, even when using standard forms. Differences, even in the standard forms, can be substantial. For instance, under the A311 bond, the surety is provided with three options upon the default of the principal, while the A312 bond provides the surety with five options. Each change and update serves as a reminder to read the full bond. The importance of reading both the bond and all contract documents is further evidenced by looking to the AIA A201 General Conditions. The "A201 General Conditions" was amended in 2007, and accordingly, it is best to be aware of differences between the old and new General Conditions incorporated into the bond. The 2007 A201 is a culmination of ten years of feedback and case law commenting on the 1997 A201 General Conditions.[8] Examples of the new changes include

---

3   RESTATEMENT (THIRD) OF SURETYSHIP AND GUARANTY § 17(2) (1996); *see, e.g.*, Geters v. Eagle Ins. Co., 834 S.W.2d 49, 50 (Tex. 1992) (citing Howze v. Surety Corp. of Am., 584 S.W.2d 263, 266 (Tex. 1979)).
4   *See* American Institute of Architects, AIA Document A-312, Performance Bond and Payment Bond, § 12.2 (1984).
5   Arthur A. Stearns, THE LAW OF SURETYSHIP § 2.4 (James L. Elder ed., 5th ed. 1951).
6   RESTATEMENT (THIRD) OF SURETYSHIP AND GUARANTY § 14 (1996) (stating that "[t]he standards that apply to interpretation of contracts in general apply to interpretation of contracts creating secondary obligations").
7   RESTATEMENT (SECOND) OF CONTRACTS § 202 (1981).
8   *See* Elizabeth M. Debaillon and Denis G. Ducran, *A201 2007: Exploring the Changes* (unpublished paper submitted at the 21st

identifying a neutral decision maker, mandatory arbitration, time limits for claims, consolidation and joinder, consequential damages, and insurance. It is also important to recognize that the new A201 form includes a "Statute of Repose" to bar any claims ten years after substantial completion.[9]

Each bond, and its underlying contract(s), differ. Some may be updated forms, some may be older forms, some may have handwritten cross-outs, and others may have amendments, addenda, or additions. Accordingly, an assumption that liability is standardized should be avoided, and a thorough review of the bond itself is required to ascertain with any certainty the liability that will flow from the terms of the bond. Total command of any project or case begins with reading the bond.

B. Suretyship Distinguished From Insurance

1. Liability of the Surety is Secondary

The liability of the surety on a surety performance bond is secondary and only triggered if the principal (the primary obligor) fails to perform.[10] This trait underlies the surety's assumption that it will not suffer a loss on a bond because of the presence of the principal (primary obligor). It is this assumption that drastically separates suretyship from insurance. Where the nature of the surety relationship is based on a "no loss" frame of mind, insurance expects losses and therefore distributes losses over a group or classification of risks.[11]

2. No Actuarial Based Expected Loss

This is not the only difference, however, between suretyship and insurance; there are several other important distinctions. For example, after the surety conducts a review of a principal and its perceived ability to perform, it then underwrites the principal on the basis of the capacity, character, and capital of the principal and indemnitors. An insurance

---

Annual Construction Law Conference on Feb. 28, 2008), *available at* http://www.cbylaw.com/publications/dgd-A201%20changes.pdf (last visited Jan. 15, 2009).

9   *Id.*
10 RESTATEMENT (THIRD) OF SURETYSHIP AND GUARANTY § 1(2) (1996).
11 WARREN FREEDMAN, RICHARDS ON THE LAW OF INSURANCE 98-99 (6th ed. 1990).

policy, on the other hand, is underwritten and premiums are set on the basis of anticipated losses. Additionally, where the surety can use the common law theory of indemnity and contractual indemnity agreements to pursue the principal for claims paid, an insurer cannot pursue its insured to recover the amount paid for a valid and covered claim. These distinctions are even more important, but often times blurred when surety bonds are issued by insurance companies. At times, some courts have held that suretyship constitutes the "business of insurance" for regulatory purposes.[12] A few courts have even imposed extra-contractual liability on the basis that the surety bond is akin to an insurance product for such purposes.[13] Imposition of extra-contractual liability is outside the mainstream, and such issues are beyond the scope of this chapter.[14]

II. Performance Bond Forms

A surety can find the definition of its liability under a performance bond in the language of the bond itself. It is essential to know the terms of the performance bond, to know the meaning behind those terms, and to understand how those terms will be construed to fully appreciate the extent and limits of the liability.

Since liability is tied to the terms of the bond, it is imperative to investigate and be comfortable with how the terms should be read and how strictly those terms are construed. To apply this reasoning to bond

---

[12] *See, e.g.*, Colorado Structures, Inc. v. Insurance Co. of the West, 167 P.3d 1125, 1140 (Wash. 2007)("There is little to distinguish construction performance bonds from other forms of insurance."); Mass. Bonding & Ins. Co. v. Feutz, 182 F.2d 752, 756 (8th Cir. 1950); Transamerica Premier Ins. Co. v. Brighton Sch. Dist. 27J, 940 P.2d 348, 352-53 (Colo. 1997); Am. Sur. Co. v. Plank & Whitsett, 165 S.E. 660, 663 (Va. 1932); *but see* Great Am. Ins. Co. v. N. Austin Mun. Util. Dist. No. 1, 908 S.W.2d 415, 424 (Tex. 1995) ("Absent a clear legislative directive, we conclude that suretyship, as historically understood in the insurance and suretyship fields, does not constitute the business of insurance" under the Texas insurance statutes.).

[13] Dadeland Depot, Inc. v. St. Paul Fire & Marine Ins. Co., 945 So. 2d 1216, 1236 (Fla. 2006) ("[O]bligee of a surety contract qualifies as an "insured" and is therefore entitled to sue its surety for bad faith refusal to settle claims pursuant to" Florida insurance statutes.).

[14] *See infra* Chapter 9 discussing extra-contractual liability.

interpretation, it is important to recognize the distinction between "statutory" performance bonds and "common law" performance bonds.[15]

A. Statutory Bonds

Statutory bonds, including bonds under the Miller Act and the "Little Miller" Acts, are dictated by statutory requirements, which include guidance for interpreting the terms through legislative intent and well developed bodies of case law.[16] As statutes (and court interpretations) vary, it is imperative to consult the applicable state or federal statute. Further highlighting the importance of consulting each statute and bond, some municipalities and government agencies have created their own unique bond forms.

B. Common Law Bonds

In contrast, "common law" bonds are created by contract. Therefore questions of construction and interpretation are governed by contract law.[17] Rather than adhering to legislative intent, the intent of the parties is taken into consideration to determine what the contract "means."[18] It is important to note that courts following contract law have usually construed "common law" bonds in favor of the surety, namely because the performance bonds are typically drafted and/or selected by the obligee.[19]

Some practitioners mistakenly construe the distinction between "statutory" and "common law" performance bonds as synonymous with

---

15 This chapter broadly discusses the varying bond forms as they may affect the liability of the performance bond surety. *See infra* Chapter 1 for a more detailed discussion of each bond, including A-311, A-312, indemnity bonds, Miller Act bonds, Little Miller Act bonds, and subcontractor bonds.
16 BRUNER & O'CONNOR, *supra* note 2, § 12:10.
17 RESTATEMENT (THIRD) OF SURETYSHIP AND GUARANTY § 14 (1996).
18 RESTATEMENT (SECOND) OF CONTRACTS § 202 (1981); *see also* Hightower & Co., Inc. v. U.S. Fid. & Guar. Co., 527 So. 2d 698, 703 (Ala. 1988); Hendricks v. Blake & Pendleton, Inc., 472 S.E.2d 482, 483 (Ga. Ct. App. 1996); Republic Ins. Co. v. Bd. of County Comm'rs, 511 A.2d 1136, 1138 (Md. 1986).
19 Marchelle M. Houston et al., *Ch. 1, Bond, Contractual, and Statutory Provisions and the General Agreement of Indemnity, in* BOND DEFAULT MANUAL 1, 5 (Duncan L. Clore et al. eds., 3d ed., Am. Bar Ass'n 2005).

the difference between public works projects and privately owned projects. This, however, is too general an understanding. Not all performance bonds issued on public works project are "statutory." For example, when a surety issues a bond that alters the notice requirements on a public works project, some courts have ruled that the surety has bound itself to the language of the altered bond, despite the statutory requirements.[20] Moreover, subcontract performance bonds on public works projects are typically common law bonds since they are not mandated by statute. Likewise, sureties do not always issue "common law" bonds in favor of private owners, because some states may utilize statutes which control the bond if certain conditions are met.[21]

Whether the bond is a "common law" or "statutory" bond, most, if not all, bonds contain terms that may operate as a complete defense to liability if certain conditions are not met. For instance, the AIA A-312 Performance Bond includes several conditions that must be satisfied before the surety's obligations are triggered, including notice of default to the surety and a waiting period before the contract is officially terminated by the obligee.[22] Courts have viewed these requirements as

---

20   *Id.*
21   *See, e.g.,* TEX. PROP. CODE ANN. §§ 53.001-.260 (Vernon 2005) (including statutory provisions governing bonds issued on private works projects).
22   American Institute of Architects, *supra* note 4, § 3. In particular, this provision states:
    3. If there is no Owner Default, the Surety's obligation under this Bond shall arise after:
       3.1 The Owner has notified the Contractor and the Surety at its address described in Paragraph 10 below that the Owner is considering declaring a Contractor Default and has requested and attempted to arrange a conference with the Contractor and the Surety to be held not later than fifteen days after receipt of such notice to discuss methods of performing the Construction Contract. If the Owner, the Contractor and the Surety agree, the Contractor shall be allowed a reasonable time to perform the Construction Contract, but such an agreement shall not waive the Owner's right, if any, subsequently to declare a Contractor Default; and
       3.2 The Owner has declared a Contractor Default and formally terminated the Contractor's right to complete the contract. Such Contractor Default shall not be declared earlier than

conditions precedent and have refused to impose liability on a surety when an owner has failed to comply with the terms of the bond.[23] In *City of Green River*, after an obligee terminated its contractor following significant delays, the obligee was not pleased with the surety's proposed completion timeline.[24] On this basis, it refused to allow the surety to complete the project.[25] The court determined that the "obligee's action that deprive[d the] surety of its ability to protect itself pursuant to performance options granted under a performance bond constitute[d] a material breach" and rendered the "bond null and void."[26] As illustrated, these conditions precedent are not to be taken lightly.

In addition, it is important to note that differing remedies may be available depending on the specific circumstances of the claim by the obligee. For instance, paragraph 6 of the AIA A-312 Performance Bond provides for three distinct remedies in the event the owner terminates the contractor's right to complete the construction contract.[27] If, however,

---

> twenty days after the Contractor and the Surety have received notice as provided in Subparagraph 3.1; and
>
> 3.3 The Owner has agreed to pay the Balance of the Contract Price to the Surety in accordance with the terms of the Construction Contract or to a contractor selected to perform the Construction Contract in accordance with the terms of the contract with the Owner.
>
> *See also* Chapter 2 discussing conditions precedent of the AIA A-312 Performance Bond.

23   *Houston, et al., supra* note 19, at 5; St. Paul Fire & Marine Ins. Co. v. City of Green River, 93 F. Supp. 2d 1170, 1178 (D. Wyo. 2000); Seaboard Sur. Co. v. Town of Greenfield, 370 F.3d 215, 220 (1st Cir. 2004) ("[N]otice requirements exist precisely to provide the surety an opportunity to protect itself against loss by participating in the selection of the successor contractor to ensure that the lowest bidder is hired and damages mitigated."); Hunt Constr. Group, Inc. v. Nat'l Wrecking Corp., 542 F. Supp. 2d 87, 96 (D.D.C. 2008)("Where the obligee fails to notify a surety of an obligor's default in a timely fashion, so that the surety can exercise its options under the controlling performance bond, the obligee renders the bond null and void.").

24   *Green River*, 93 F. Supp. 2d at 1178.

25   *Id.*

26   *Id.*

27   American Institute of Architects, *supra* note 4, § 6. This provision states as follows:

the surety is found not to have complied with the provisions of the performance bond, paragraph 5 of the AIA A-312 Performance Bond provides for expanded remedies.[28]

III. Design-Build

A. *Nature of the Design-Build Delivery Method*

Subject to some variation, "design-builders" have been described as "entities[29] willing to assume the single source responsibility to design

---

> 6. After the Owner has terminated the Contractor's right to complete the Construction Contract, and if the Surety elects to act under Subparagraph 4.1, 4.2, or 4.3 above . . . . the Surety is obligated without duplication for:
>   6.1 The responsibilities of the Contractor for correction of defective work and completion of the Construction Contact;
>   6.2 Additional legal, design professional and delay costs resulting from the Contractor's Default, and resulting from the actions or failure to act of the Surety under Paragraph 4; and
>   6.3 Liquidated damages, or if no liquidated damages are specified in the Construction Contract, actual damages caused by delay performance or non-performance of the Contractor.

28 American Institute of Architects, *supra* note 4, § 5. This provision states as follows:
> 6. If the Surety does not proceed as provided in Paragraph 4 [the paragraph listing the Surety's options upon default] with reasonable promptness, the surety shall be deemed to be in default on this Bond fifteen days after receipt of an additional written notice from the Owner to the Surety demanding that the Surety perform its obligations under this Bond, and the Owner shall be entitled to enforce any remedy available to the Owner.

29 The design-build "entity" usually falls into one of four categories:
  1. Joint venture between a general contractor and another construction and/or design firm;
  2. Sole venture general contractor who subcontracts the design services;
  3. Sole venture design firm who subcontracts the construction services; or

and construct–in conformance with applicable design professional and contractor licensing laws, building codes and the requisite 'standard of care'–work defined generally by owner performance requirements."[30] The nature of a design-build project can vary depending upon the involvement of the owner, and as a delivery method, can apply to projects covered by statutory or common law bonds. In some instances, the owner gives little to no input about the intricacies of the project's design (for example, in the construction of a generic, pre-fabricated warehouse). In other cases, the owner will require a specific product and the contractor must adapt its design to the end goal (for example, construction of a complex water station for a municipal utility district).

Sureties have historically been hesitant to bond design-build contracts due to the design risks associated with this type of contract. Some of this hesitation comes from the fact that the dual role of the design-build contractor expands the possible liability of the surety.[31] In a non-design-build project, the owner provides the design documents and therefore impliedly warrants that the plan and specifications for the project are adequate and sufficient.[32] In a design-build project, however, the contractor takes on the design, as well as the construction, and therefore provides the design warranty. This added liability–stemming from the extra warranty–can run to the surety.

---

    4.   Sole venture company that performs both the construction and the design services.

The first two categories are the most common design-build "entities."

[30] BRUNER & O'CONNOR, *supra* note 2, § 12.83, n.2.
[31] *Houston, et al.*, *supra* note 19, at 11.
[32] United States v. Spearin, 248 U.S. 132, 136 (U.S. 1918) ("[I]f the contractor is bound to build according to plans and specifications prepared by the owner, the contractor will not be responsible for the consequences of defects in the plans and specifications."); *see also* Rick's Mushroom Serv., Inc. v. United States, 521 F.3d 1338, 1344 (Fed. Cir. 2008); Stuyvesant Dredging Co. v. United States, 834 F.2d 1576, 1582 (Fed. Cir. 1987) ("Detailed design specifications contain an implied warranty that if they are followed, an acceptable result will be produced."); *but see* Lonergan v. San Antonio Loan & Trust Co., 104 S.W. 1061 (Tex. 1907); *compare to* Shintech, Inc. v. Group Constructors, Inc., 688 S.W.2d 144, 151 (Tex. Civ. App. 1985); Turner, Collie & Braden v. Brookhollow, Inc., 624 S.W.2d 203, 208 (Tex. Civ. App. 1981) *aff'd in part and rev'd in part on other grounds*, 642 S.W.2d 160 (Tex. 1982); Newell v. Mosley, 469 S.W.2d 481 (Tex. Civ. App. 1971).

B. Managing and Allocating the Risk of the Design-Build Contract

The most common ways to manage the design risk is either through indemnification or hold harmless clauses or through an insurance transfer. Indemnification or hold harmless clauses contained within a contract are typical ways to distribute the risk of loss to the more culpable party or the party who has the ability to insure for such a risk. When the design-build contractor subcontracts the design services to a professional firm (or is part of a joint venture), the surety can be better protected by the use of proper indemnification language in the services contract. Yet, even an indemnity clause that clearly establishes primary responsibility on the design firm may not be a foolproof solution. Indemnity or hold harmless clauses are only effective if the party providing the indemnification has the necessary financial resources to address the liability. If these resources prove inadequate, the design-build contractor's primary responsibility to the obligee will not change.[33] As a result, combining indemnification and hold harmless clauses with professional liability insurance has become a popular combination for dealing with design-build projects' long liability tail and effectively managing the projects' risks.

The professional Errors & Omissions insurance policies of design-build contractors generally protect the insured against liability arising from negligence, errors, and omissions in rendering professional services (including design services). Extreme care should be used, however, when evaluating this coverage since these policies tend to vary from carrier to carrier, and from insured to insured. Many of these policies have limitations that may impact such things as claims periods, design coverage, and potential claimants. In addition, many design-build entities seek project specific Errors & Omissions policies. In large, complex projects[34] a performance bond surety may want to verify the financial

---

33 Due to the increased risks, sureties often conduct more extensive prequalification checks for principals involved on design-build projects. Jeff C. Carey, *Design-Build Expands Surety Prequalification Process*, available at http://www. aia.org/nwsltr_print.cfm?pagename=db_a_200609_prequalify (last visited January 15, 2009).

34 Large projects typically contain Owner Controlled Insurance Programs and Contractor Controlled Insurance Programs that require the purchase of an Errors & Omissions policy to protect the entire project. In such cases, the performance bond surety should investigate the adequacy of the

stability of the providing insurance company to ensure that a substantial claim would be adequately backed. It is critical that the insurance policy's limits be adequate and that the policy's extended reporting period, or "tail," be long enough to cover any future exposures. Often, however, there will be a gap between the tail coverage, which is able to be secured in the E&O market, and the time-frame under which a claim might be made under the performance bond. In those cases, the primary responsibility shifts back to the design-build entity and any indemnity provisions in the contract between the principal and the designer.

Another approach performance bond sureties have used to address the added risks involved in design-build projects is to tailor the bonds to cover only the construction portion of the contract, leaving the principal solely liable for any design errors. This approach has been criticized, however, by the Design-Build Institute of America, which prefers that a single bond be issued for all aspects of the contract.[35] Owners may prefer, and expect, a "single bond" method.[36] Interestingly, the Associated General Contractors of America ("AGC") has taken a different approach and has promulgated various forms that remove design from under the umbrella of the performance bond.[37] The AGC's

---

    policy limits and whether the tail period is sufficient to cover any delayed exposures. If there is a gap between the tail coverage available and the state statutory time period in which a design errors and omissions claim can be perfected, the primary responsibility will shift back to the design-build contractor and the indemnification language of the contract.

[35] Michael C. Loulakis & Owen J. Shean, *Risk Transference in Design-Build Contracting*, in CONSTRUCTION BRIEFINGS No. 96-5, at 13 (Federal Publications Inc. April 1996).

[36] Carey, *supra* note 33.

[37] *See* Associated General Contractors of America, AGC Documents Nos. 470, 471 (1999). Document 470 (although including design costs) greatly limits the liability of the surety by removing any costs covered by the liability insurance of the principal. Specifically, Document 470 notes:

    This bond shall cover the costs to complete the Work, but shall not cover any damages of the type specified to be covered by the Design-Builder's Liability insurance or by the Professional Liability Insurance required pursuant to the Contract, whether or not such insurance is provided or in such an amount sufficient to cover such damages.

Where Document 470 limits the liability of a surety related to design errors, Document 471 completely removes design from the coverage of the performance bond, noting as follows:

reasoning for this divergence is based on the theory of indemnity: any loss suffered by a surety–whether for design or construction–will ultimately be sought from the principal in accordance with the surety's indemnity rights.[38] The AGC's approach anticipates this and, in essence, never allows the liability to pass through the surety.

Under circumstances where changing the terms and scope of the bond are not feasible, the scope of the surety's liability can be affected by changes made to the underlying contract. In an effort to cap the unknowns of future design-build liability, a surety will often attempt to contractually limit the consequential damages to a set amount or have them waived altogether. This method has garnered support from the AGC.[39] The standard design-build contract published by the AGC waives claims by the owner for "loss of use of the Property, all rental expenses incurred, loss of services of employees, or loss of reputation."[40] Other standard form contracts contain even broader waiver language.[41]

Another consideration that should be taken into account involves the increase in communications and analysis in the underwriting process between a principal and a surety when dealing with design-build. In the non-design-build construction contract, the underwriter generally considers whether the principal has the necessary construction expertise, as well as financial stability, to perform the scope of work in a contract. In a design-build contract, however, the underwriter is forced to make additional judgments about the principal's, or its chosen designer's, design expertise – a realm that is normally reserved for the owners and their architects. This challenge is magnified when considered with the expanded liability that design-build contracts already encompass. In light of this, added care in the review of any principal is necessary by any party who is considering executing a design-build contract, including underwriting the design-build entity, evaluating the design, and undertaking an examination of the project risk.

      [A] Surety shall be liable for all construction costs of the Work, up to the Bond Sum, but shall not be liable for any costs or damages arising from any design services provided pursuant to the Contract.

38   *See supra* Chapter 6 for a detailed review of a surety's indemnity rights.
39   ROBERT FRANK CUSHMAN & MICHAEL C. LOULAKIS, DESIGN-BUILD CONTRACTING HANDBOOK 234 (Aspen Law & Business, 2d ed. 2001).
40   *Id.*
41   *Id.*

IV. Claims by the Obligee

The most likely claimant on a construction contract performance bond will be an obligee following the default and/or termination of a bonded principal. The extent to which an obligee may have a valid claim depends chiefly on the language of the performance bond. Issues which should also be considered are provisions in an underlying contract (if it is incorporated into the performance bond), as well as statutes governing performance bond claims. Damages sought by obligees fall into two generic categories: direct damages and consequential damages. In the case of a performance bond claim, direct damages are typically the costs necessary to complete the project, including completion of unfinished work and repair of defective work. Consequential damages are those arising from "special circumstances" and normally include liquidated damages, expenses for increased overhead, and lost profits. In addition to both direct and consequential damages, obligees often seek to recover attorneys' fees.

A. *Costs to Complete*

An obligee is often entitled to recover the costs to complete the project over and above the remaining contract balances.[42] The costs to complete typically include costs associated with the completion of unfinished work and repair of defective work.[43] What constitutes "costs to complete" has been subject to debate, yet in one instance, the Second Circuit utilized a bright-line rule in calculating the costs of completion. In particular, the court held that "costs of completion" are all amounts paid after default and not only the costs that are incurred following default (the latter typically being a lower number since actual amounts paid usually includes pre-default obligations).[44]

---

42   Granite Computer Leasing Corp. v. Travelers Indem. Co., 894 F.2d 547, 552 (2nd Cir. 1990); Am. Sur. Co. of New York v. United States, 317 F.2d 652 (8th Cir. 1963); Miracle Mile Shopping Ctr. v. Nat'l Union Indem. Co., 299 F.2d 780 (7th Cir. 1962); McGovney & McKee, Inc. v. City of Berea, Ky., 448 F. Supp. 1049 (E.D. Ky. 1978), *aff'd*, 627 F.2d 1091 (6th Cir. 1980).
43   BRUNER & O'CONNOR, *supra* note 2, § 12.34.
44   U.S. Fid. & Guar. Co. v. Braspetro Oil Servs. Co., 369 F.3d 34, 67-70 (2nd Cir. 2004).

This principle that an obligee recovers the costs of completion, however, is not without several important restraints, chief of which is that the exposure of a surety is limited by the penal sum of the bond.[45] Almost as significant is the requirement of the obligee to mitigate its damages.[46] Courts also have held that the doctrine of economic waste will limit liability when demands by an obligee are not economically feasible.[47] Courts applying the economic waste doctrine have held a surety liable only for the difference between the value of the project as intended and the value of the project as constructed.[48]

B. Consequential Damages

In addition to direct damages, an obligee may seek consequential damages. The performance bond is a contract between the obligee and the surety, and as such, damages are subject to normal contract principles, including the long standing rule that consequential damages must be foreseeable.[49] Where the underlying contract is incorporated into

---

45   *See infra* Section VI for a more in depth discussion of the penal limit.
46   BRUNER & O'CONNOR, *supra* note 2, § 12.34; International Fidelity Ins. Co. v. United States, 25 Cl. Ct. 469, 479 (1992); Ketchikan Pulp Co. v. United States, 25 Cl. Ct. 164, 166 (1990) ("Under the doctrine of mitigation, the contractor in breach should not be charged with damages which the government could have avoided with reasonable effort and without undue risk or expense.").
47   *See* RESTATEMENT (SECOND) OF CONTRACTS § 348, cmt. c (1981) ("Sometimes, however, such a large part of the cost to remedy the defects consists of the cost to undo what has been improperly done that the cost to remedy the defects will be clearly disproportionate to the probable loss in value to the injured party. Damages based on the cost to remedy the defects would then give the injured party a recovery greatly in excess of the loss in value to him and result in a substantial windfall. Such an award will not be made."); BRUNER & O'CONNOR, *supra* note 2, § 12.63; Austin-Westshore Constr. Co. v. Federated Dep't Stores, Inc., 934 F.2d 1217, 1224 (11th Cir. 1991) ("The economic waste measure of damages clearly contemplates that one of the contracting parties did not receive what was contracted for and to insist on such compliance under the circumstances would be unreasonable and economically wasteful.").
48   5-6 BRUNER & O'CONNOR, *supra* note 2, §§ 18:13, 19:30.
49   Hadley v. Baxendale, 9 Exch. 341, 354 (1854); *see also* RESTATEMENT (SECOND) OF CONTRACTS § 351 (1981); EBWS, LLC v. Britly Corp., 928 A.2d 497 (Vt. 2007); Applied Equip. Corp. v. Litton Saudi Arabia Ltd.,

the performance bond, an obligee may argue that damages that were foreseeable when the underlying contract was executed are also recoverable.

1. Liquidated Damages

Parties will often include an express liquidated damages provision in the contract. Such provisions set the amount of damages available to an owner for each day that the principal delays the date of completion. Again, if the performance bond incorporates the underlying contract, the surety may potentially be held liable for the liquidated damages charged against the principal.[50]

Freedom of contract was an early consideration in determining the validity of a liquidated damages provision. As noted by the Supreme Court nearly a century ago:

> The parties to the contract, with full understanding of the results of delay and before differences or interested views had arisen between them, were much more competent to justly determine what the amount of damage would be, an amount necessarily largely conjectural and resting in estimate, than a court or jury would be . . . .[51]

In instances where a surety has challenged recovery of liquidated damages, it has done so on the following primary bases:[52]

1. The imposition of liquidated damages is an unenforceable penalty.[53]

---

    869 P.2d 454 (Cal. 1994); Wade & Sons, Inc. v. Am. Standard, Inc., 127 S.W.3d 814 (Tex. App. 2003).

50   Marilyn Klinger et al., *Ch. 6, Contract Performance Bonds, in* THE LAW OF SURETYSHIP 81, 109 (Edward G. Gallagher ed., 2d ed., Am. Bar Ass'n 2000).

51   Wise v. United States, 249 U.S. 361, 366 (U.S. 1919).

52   Additional items to consider include: (1) beneficial use of the project by the obligee, i.e. substantial completion; and (2) waiver by an obligee based on an extension of time to complete the project (assuming that this argument is not precluded by a provision in the bond).

53   *See* RESTATEMENT (SECOND) OF CONTRACTS § 356(1) (1981) ("Damages for breach by either party may be liquidated in the agreement but only at an amount that is reasonable in the light of the anticipated or actual loss caused by the breach and the difficulties of proof of loss. A term fixing

2. The obligee has failed to mitigate its damages, *e.g.*, waiting too long to terminate the contract of the principal.[54]
3. There were delays on the project outside of the control of the principal, include inclement weather[55] and *force majeure*,[56] as well as acts of concurrent delay by the owner.[57]
4. Liquidated or delay damages are not awardable under the terms of the bond.[58]

Even when liquidated damages have been contracted to by the parties, courts will render these damages unenforceable if there is no evidence that the damages were a reasonable estimate of the possible harm to the owner.[59] For example, the Second Circuit found that liquidated damages were not a reasonable estimate of possible harm (and

---

unreasonably large liquidated damages is unenforceable on grounds of public policy as a penalty."); U.S. Fid. & Guar. Co. v. Braspetro Oil Servs. Co., 369 F.3d 34, 73 (2nd Cir. 2004).

54 *See* BRUNER & O'CONNOR, *supra* note 2, § 12.34; International Fid. Ins. Co. v. United States, 25 Cl. Ct. 469, 479 (1992); Ketchikan Pulp Co. v. United States, 25 Cl. Ct. 164, 166 (1990).

55 *See* BARRY B. BRAMBLE & MICHAEL T. CALLAHAN, CONSTRUCTION DELAY CLAIMS § 3.06[A] (Aspen Law & Business, 3d ed. 2000).

56 *Id.* § 3.06[B] (quoting Akwa-Dowey Constr. Co., ASBCA No. 14823, 75-1 B.C.A (CCH) ¶ 11,254 (1975), which defined acts of God as a "singular unexpected and irregular visitation of a force of nature").

57 *See* Klingensmith, Inc. v. United States, 731 F.2d 805 (Fed. Cir. 1984) ("The general rule is that '[w]here both parties contribute to the delay neither can recover damage[s], unless there is in the proof a clear apportionment of the delay and the expense attributable to each party. Courts will deny recovery where the delays are concurrent and the contractor has not established its delay apart from that attributable to the government.'") (internal citations omitted); *see also id.* § 11.09.

58 Certain courts have held that liquidated or delay damages are not recoverable under AIA A-311 bonds. *See* Am. Home Assur. Co. v. Larkin Gen. Hosp., Ltd., 593 So.2d 195, 197 (Fla. 1999); Downington Area Sch. Dist. v. Int'l Fid. Ins. Co., 759 A.2d 560, 566 (Pa. Commw. 2001); Marshall Contractors, Inc. v. Peerless Ins. Co., 827 F. Supp. 91, 95 (D. R. I. 1993). Other courts have held that delay or liquidated damages are recoverable under an A-311 bond. *See* Cates Construction Co. v. Talbot Partners, 21 Cal. 4th 28, 41-42 (1999).

59 *See* U.S. Fid. & Guar. Co. v. Braspetro Oil Servs. Co., 369 F.3d 34, 73 (2nd Cir. 2004).

thereby, the liquidated damages provision was unenforceable) because (1) the underlying contracts provided for several forms of penalties, and (2) pursuant to the contracts, the obligees were permitted to recover delay-related damages as part of the actual damages.[60]

One court has held that liquidated damages will be allowed only if it can be shown that:

1. The damages are incapable of being estimated or were difficult to estimate at the time the contract was executed; and
2. The amount of the liquidated damages is a reasonable forecast of just compensation.[61]

In that same vein, the determination of whether a liquidated damages provision is enforceable sometimes includes a consideration of the actual damages incurred in contrast with the total claimed amount of liquidated damages.[62] An alternative approach in determining the validity of a liquidated damages provision is whether the provision is unconscionable.[63]

There is a split of authority (in part based on express contract provisions) as to whether liquidated damages can be recovered when, instead of a delay, there is no actual performance at all.[64] Additionally, in

---

60   *Id.*
61   Phillips v. Phillips, 820 S.W.2d 785, 788 (Tex. 1991); *see also* Stewart v. Basey, 245 S.W.2d 484 (Tex. 1952); Joe F. Canterbury & Robert J. Shapiro, TEXAS CONSTRUCTION LAW MANUAL § 8:16 (3d ed. 2005).
62   *See* Ridgley v. Topa Thrift & Loan Ass'n, 17 Cal. 4th 970, 977 (Cal. 1998) ("A liquidated damages clause will generally be considered unreasonable . . . if it bears no reasonable relationship to the range of actual damages that the parties could have anticipated would flow from a breach."); Loggins Constr. Co. v. Stephen F. Austin State Univ. Bd. of Regents, 543 S.W.2d 682 (Tex. Civ. App. 1976) (holding a liquidated damage clause unenforceable when actual damages totaled less than $6,500 and liquidated damages totaled $39,500); *see also* Muller v. Light, 538 S.W.2d 487 (Tex. Civ. App. 1976) (viewing liquidated damages as an unenforceable penalty when actual damages were $400 per month and the liquidated damages totaled $3,000 per month).
63   5 BRUNER & O'CONNOR, *supra* note 2, § 15:82 (citing Goetz & Scott, *Liquidated Damages, Penalties, and the Just Compensation Principle: Some Notes on an Enforcement Model and a Theory of Efficient Breach*, 77 COLUM. L. REV. 554 (1977)).
64   Klinger et al., *supra* note 50.

cases of abandonment by the contractor, an obligee generally has been permitted either to (1) enforce the liquidated damages provision, or (2) attempt to recover actual damages on the basis that the liquidated damages provision does not contemplate total abandonment of the project.[65] Finally, some jurisdictions preclude recovery of both liquidated damages and actual damages, as such awards would allow for double recovery.[66]

2. Actual Damages From Delay

In instances where delay damages are not expressly defined by a liquidated damages provision, obligees often are entitled to actual damages from delay. Unless the bond restricts such claims, delay damages may be sought for the following:

1. Extra labor costs related to lost productivity and wage escalation;
2. Extra material and equipment costs;
3. Extra overhead and supervision costs resulting from the lengthening of the project, which may be referred to as field office overhead;
4. Extended or unabsorbed home office overhead; and
5. Lost business opportunities and profits.[67]

Even though the availability of these damages will vary from case to case, recovery remains tempered by the rule of foreseeability.[68] In

---

65 5 BRUNER & O'CONNOR, *supra* note 2, § 15:82.
66 *See* Wechsler v. Hunt Health Sys., Ltd., 330 F. Supp. 2d 383, 426 (S.D.N.Y. 2004) ("Ordinarily plaintiffs are awarded either actual damages or liquidated damages, but not both when the predicate for the awards is the same.") Blood v. Gibbons, 418 A.2d 213, 217 (Md. 1980) ("[I]f a plaintiff receives liquidated damages, then a claim may not be made for actual damages.").
67 R. Daniel Douglass et. al., *Delay Claims Against the Surety*, 17 CONSTR. LAWYER 4 (July 1997).
68 RESTATEMENT (SECOND) OF CONTRACTS § 351, cmt. a (1981) ("A contracting party is generally expected to take account of those risks that are foreseeable at the time he makes the contract. He is not, however, liable in the event of breach for loss that he did not at the time of contracting have reason to foresee as a probable result of such a breach."); *see, e.g.*, Cates Constr., Inc. v. Talbot Partners, 980 P.2d 407,

addition, delay damages have not been awarded when the damages were inherently speculative.[69] It is important to note that some courts have declined to award *any* consequential/delay damages unless the terms of the performance bond expressly allow for recovery.[70] In that same vein, other courts have noted that the damages available under the performance bond are limited to the damages expressly enumerated in the bond, regardless of whether the underlying contract (providing a greater array of damages) is incorporated into the bond.[71]

---

414 (Cal. 1999) (holding delay damages recoverable based on the knowledge of the surety that contract completion was time sensitive); *cf. Texas Pattern Jury Charges–Business, Consumer, Insurance & Employment*, PJC 110.4 (2006 ed.) ("Consequential damages may be recovered only if proved to be the 'natural, probable, and foreseeable consequence' of the defendant's breach.") (internal citation omitted).

[69] Gurney Indus. v. St. Paul Fire & Marine Ins. Co., 467 F.2d 588, 598 (4th Cir. 1972) (declining to award lost profits because of the speculative nature the damages that were sought); *see also* Mai Steel Service, Inc. v. Blake Const. Co., 981 F.2d 414 (9th Cir. 1992) (holding that the surety for a general contractor could be liable under the Miller Act to a sub-subcontractor for increased labor and material costs, but not for lost profits caused by delay).

[70] *See* Am. Home Assur. Co. v. Larkin Gen. Hosp., Ltd., 593 So. 2d 195, 197 (Fla. 1999) ("[L]anguage of the performance bond, construed together with the purpose of the bond, clearly explains that the performance bond merely guaranteed the completion of the construction contract and nothing more."); Downington Area Sch. Dist. v. Int'l Fid. Ins. Co., 769 A.2d 560, 566 (Pa. Commw. 2001) ("[U]nderlying obligation is to pay the cost of completion. . . . The [Performance Bond] does not make [the surety] liable for delay damages caused by [the principal] . . . [The surety's] obligation is to provide 'sufficient funds to pay the cost of completion less the balance of the contract.' [There is no] other way of interpreting the term 'cost of completion' other than as the cost of obtaining a substitute contractor who will actually complete the job."); Marshall Contractors, Inc. v. Peerless Ins. Co., 827 F. Supp. 91, 95 (D. R. I. 1993) ("The bond makes no provision for consequential damages. On the contrary, it makes the measure of [] liability the amount by which the *cost of completion* exceeds the unpaid balance of the contract price . . . . Unlike an insurance policy, a performance bond is not intended to compensate for indirect losses or to indemnity against liability to others.") (emphasis in original).

[71] *See* N. Am. Specialty Ins. Co. v. Chichester Sch. Dist., 158 F. Supp. 2d 468, 471-72 (E.D. Pa. 2001).

An obligee who is working on the project, i.e., the general contractor, may seek to recover damages related to office overhead. Courts that have addressed home office overhead have segregated it into two categories: extended home office overhead (or field office overhead) and unabsorbed home office overhead. Extended home office overhead is "a concept unique to construction contracting" and is defined as the "additional costs incurred when a job's performance period is prolonged."[72] This usually includes costs associated with maintaining and supervising the job site.[73] Unabsorbed home office overhead "includes those expenses . . . that must be absorbed by fewer jobs because a job designated for that given period has been delayed."[74] These damages typically include the costs associated with continuing to operate an office (salary of employees, administrative costs, etc.).[75]

Due to difficulty in estimating office overhead damages, a calculation was utilized–and where the formula gets its shorthand reference–in the Army Services Board case of *Eichleay Corp.*[76] *Eichleay* damages, as they have come to be known, are calculated using the following formula: "overhead-per-day rate is multiplied by the number of days the job was extended to determine total overhead damages attributable to the delay."[77] Prior to utilizing the *Eichleay* formula, parties should look to the jurisdiction of the dispute to determine whether the formula has been accepted or rejected.[78] Regardless of whether the *Eichleay* formula is employed, recovery of office overhead damages is

---

[72] Southwestern Eng'g Co. v. Cajun Elec. Power Co-op., 915 F.2d 972, 978 (5th Cir. 1990) (citing Capital Elec. Co. v. United States, 729 F.2d 743, 745 n.3 (Fed. Cir. 1984)).

[73] *See, e.g.*, General Ins. Co. v. Hercules Constr. Co., 385 F.2d 13, 22 (8th Cir. 1967).

[74] Southwestern Eng'g Co. v. Cajun Elec. Power Co-op., 915 F.2d 972, 978 (5th Cir. 1990).

[75] *See, e.g.*, Fred R. Comb Co. v. United States, 103 Ct. Cl. 174, 183-84 (1945).

[76] *Eichleay Corp.*, ASBCA No. 5183, 60-2 B.C.A. (C.C.H.) ¶ 2688 (1960), *on reconsideration*, 61-1 B.C.A. (C.C.H.) ¶ 2894 (1961).

[77] Chilton Ins. Co. v. Pate & Pate Enters., Inc., 930 S.W.2d 877, 892 n.10 (Tex. App. 1996).

[78] *See, e.g.*, Canterbury & Shapiro, *supra* note 61 § 8:16 (noting that "no Texas cases expressly authorize [the *Eichleay* formula] to calculate damages").

subject to a heightened standard and courts have declined to award these damages in the absence of specific evidence supporting the claim.[79]

Lost profits have also been sought by obligees, which raises a host of issues, including foreseeability of this class of damages,[80] the extent to which these damages are calculable and not speculative,[81] and the diligence of the obligee in its mitigation efforts.[82] In addition, financing costs may be sought when an obligee has financed the project and a delay by the principal resulted in increased financing costs, which can be in the form of increased interest payments or an increase in the interest rate during the term of the loan.[83]

---

[79] *See* Guy James Constr. Co. v. Trinity Indus., Inc., 644 F.2d 525, 533 (5th Cir. 1981); Chilton Ins. Co. v. Pate & Pate Enters., Inc., 930 S.W.2d 877, 884 (Tex. App. 1996).

[80] *See* AgGrow Oils, L.L.C. v. National Union Fire Insur. Co. of Pittsburgh, Pa., 276 F. Supp. 2d 999 (D.N.D. 2003) (awarding lost profits when processing plant was not built to specifications, which included production guarantees).

[81] *See* Gurney Indus. v. St. Paul Fire & Marine Ins. Co., 467 F.2d 588, 598 (4th Cir. 1972) (declining to award lost profits because of the speculative nature of the damages that were sought); *see also* Mai Steel Service, Inc. v. Blake Const. Co., 981 F.2d 414 (9th Cir. 1992) (holding that the surety for a general contractor could be liable under the Miller Act to a sub-subcontractor for increased labor and material costs, but not for lost profits caused by delay).

[82] BRUNER & O'CONNOR, *supra* note 2, § 12.34; International Fid. Ins. Co. v. United States, 25 Cl. Ct. 469, 479 (1992); Ketchikan Pulp Co. v. United States, 25 Cl. Ct. 164, 166 (1990) ("Under the doctrine of mitigation, the contractor in breach should not be charged with damages which the government could have avoided with reasonable effort and without undue risk or expense.").

[83] *See, e.g.*, New Amsterdam Casualty Co. v. Mitchell, 325 F.2d 474 (5th Cir. 1964).

C. Attorneys' Fees and Interest

Attorneys' fees likely will be sought from the surety if provided by the language of the performance bond or by statute.[84] Where the bond or underlying contract addresses an award of attorneys' fees, the surety is in most instances responsible for these fees.[85] The American Rule against awarding fees is, however, tough to overcome and parties should be aware of the precise language used in the bond prior to seeking recovery of fees. The language of the performance bond proved critical in the case of *United States Fidelity & Guaranty Co. v. Braspetro Oil Services Co.*[86]

In *Braspetro*, one of the issues before the Second Circuit was whether attorneys' fees incurred by an obligee in litigation with the surety constituted "legal costs," which was the term used in the AIA A312 performance bonds at issue in the case.[87] In wrestling with this issue, the court turned to a series of opinions from the Eastern District of Pennsylvania in *North American Specialty Insurance Co. v. Chichester*

---

84 For a comprehensive review of jurisdictional distinctions in awarding attorney's fees, *see* Klinger et. al, *supra* note 50, at 112-114.
85 *See, e.g.*, Commonwealth v. Manor Mines, Inc., 544 A.2d 538, 543 (Pa. Commw. Ct. 1988) (granting attorneys' fees where "the parties executed a performance bond, wherein [the surety] agreed to be liable for the amount of the bond plus five per cent attorney[s'] fees added for collection"); Whitten v. Alling & Cory Co., 526 S.W.2d 245, 249 (Tex. Civ. App. 1975) (awarding attorneys' fees where the bond form dictated such); City of Sacramento v. Trans Pac. Indus., Inc., 159 Cal. Rptr. 514, 522 (Cal Ct. App. 1979) (awarding attorneys' fees to obligee in suit against surety "on the basis of [surety's] contractual obligation to pay, 'in case suit is brought upon this bond, such reasonable attorney[s'] fees as shall be fixed by the court'"); Klein v. Collins, 106 So. 120, 123 (La. 1925) (awarding attorneys' fees where bond "provided that 'any attorney[s'] fees connected with the enforcement of this contract shall be a charge against the builders and their surety.'").
86 369 F.3d 34 (2nd Cir. 2004).
87 U.S. Fid. & Guar. Co. v. Braspetro Oil Servs. Co., 369 F.3d 34, 74-78 (2nd Cir. 2004). *Id.* at 75. Paragraph 6 of the bond provided that "the Sureties [are] obligated without duplication for . . . additional legal, design professional, and delay costs resulting from the Contractor's Default, and resulting from the actions or failure to act of the Sureties under Paragraph 4 . . . ."

School District.[88] In analyzing what constitutes "legal costs," the *Chichester* court focused on the fact that the surety would have been liable for legal fees even if litigation was never commenced.[89]

Expanding on this observation, the Second Circuit opined "the 'legal costs' contemplated by the drafters of the AIA A312 bond form were purely administrative in nature . . . ."[90] Ultimately, the Second Circuit concluded (based in part on the above rationale) that the obligee did not meet its burden in overcoming the American Rule and was unable to establish that it was entitled to attorneys' fees incurred in the litigation with the surety.[91]

If the bond and contract are silent as to fees, a statute may overcome the American Rule against awarding fees. While some state statutes provide for the recovery of attorneys' fees,[92] other states hold the surety liable only if it has acted in bad faith.[93]

An award of pre-judgment interest likely will be sought by an obligee. As a general matter, pre-judgment interest "is an element of complete compensation,"[94] and "serves to compensate for the loss of use of money due as damages from the time the claim accrues until judgment is entered . . . ."[95] Sureties have been held liable for pre-judgment interest when an obligee asserted a valid claim against the performance bond.[96] In awarding pre-judgment interest, the Federal Circuit employed the following rationale:

---

[88] *Id.* at 76. The *Braspetro* court noted that *Chichester* was the "one case that has been identified as having endeavored to interpret the relevant language [of the AIA 312 performance bond]."
[89] *Id.* (citing N. Am. Specialty Ins. Co. v. Chichester Sch. Dist., 2002 U.S. Dist. LEXIS 11730, at *18 (E.D. Pa. 2002)).
[90] *Id.* at 76-77.
[91] *Id.* at 78. The holding by the court resulted in the overturn of an award in excess of $36 million.
[92] *See, e.g.*, ARIZ. REV. STAT. § 34-222 (2008); KAN. STAT. ANN. §40-256 (2007); NEB. REV. STAT. 44-359 (2007).
[93] *See, e.g.*, GA. CODE ANN. § 10-7-30 (2007); MO. ANN. STAT. § 375.420 (2007).
[94] West Virginia v. United States, 479 U.S. 305, 310 (1987).
[95] *Id.* at 310, n.2.
[96] Insurance Co. of North America v. United States, 951 F.2d 1244 (Fed. Cir. 1991); United States *ex rel.* Maris Equip. Co. v. Morganti, Inc., 175 F. Supp. 2d 458 (E.D.N.Y. 2001); Appley Bros. v. United States, 924 F. Supp. 935 (D.S.D. 1996).

The surety's obligation to pay does not wait for completion of legal contests between the principal and the creditor. If a surety's obligation to pay only arose upon conclusion of lawsuits, the creditor would lose a significant part of the protection it bargained to obtain.[97]

An award of pre-judgment interest is, however, restrained by the rule that a surety must be given proper notice of a claim against the performance bond.[98]

A final consideration is that courts, in some instances, will even award attorneys' fees[99] and interest[100] in excess of the penal sum of the performance bond.

D. *Warranty Claims and Latent Defects*

Many construction contracts require warranty periods. When an obligee has a valid warranty claim and the principal declines to honor its warranty obligations, a surety may be liable under its performance bond. The liability of a surety, however, generally does not extend past the liability of its principal. Thus, where an obligee is unable to prove that a defect is covered by a warranty, it may not be able to enforce any warranty obligations against the surety.[101]

In contrast to defects identified by an owner within a warranty period, latent defects are generally understood "as defective work that was not apparent at the time the contractor's work was accepted."[102] Such an understanding is, however, too simplistic, as undiscovered defects can be either latent or patent. With respect to the former, the defect is one that could not be discovered by a reasonable investigation, whereas a patent defect could have been discovered. In cases of latent defects, courts are split as to whether substantial completion will vitiate

---

97   Insurance Co. of North America v. United States, 951 F.2d 1244, 1246 (Fed. Cir. 1991).
98   United States v. Reul, 959 F.2d 1572, 1581 (Fed. Cir. 1992).
99   *See infra* Section VI.
100   *See* Fid. N.Y., FSB v. Aetna Ins. Co., 651 N.Y.S. 2d 58, 59 (App. Div. 1996); United States v. U.S. Fid. & Guar. Co., 236 U.S. 512, 530 (1915).
101   William J. Schwartzkopf, PRACTICAL GUIDE TO CONSTRUCTION CONTRACT SURETY CLAIMS § 15.02 (2d ed. 2006). The author goes on to note that "[i]t is for this reason that some owners require separate 'warranty' or 'maintenance' bonds."
102   *Id.* § 15.03.

the surety from liability; in cases where the defects were patent and could have been discovered, an argument by a surety that the defect claims have been waived upon occupancy by the owner may be available.

E. Dual Obligees

Although not as typical, there is a possibility of a dual obligee on a performance bond. Dual obligees are typically construction lenders or the FDIC (succeeding a failed financial institution) who were issued a dual obligee rider along with the performance bond. The dual obligee rider does not provide that the surety is guaranteeing the financial obligations of the owner to the lender. Instead, the rider only gives the dual obligee a direct right of action against the surety in the event of a breach by the principal. Without one, a construction lender has no claim against the performance bond.

In cases where there is a dual obligee rider, sureties often require language in the rider that requires that payments be made the principal "in strict accordance with the Contract." With this language, payments to the principal may be argued to be a condition precedent to the dual obligee's ability to make a claim against the bond. Nevertheless, unless the performance bond provides otherwise, the liability of the surety to the dual obligee should be no greater than the surety's liability to the primary obligee.

The above categories of damages are of course not exhaustive of every damage that may be sought by an obligee, but regardless of what damages are asserted, the primary focus should be on the language of the performance bond to determine if recovery of the damages is expressly provided for.

V. Claims by a Non-Obligee

Although claims against the performance bond by an obligee are the most common claims that are asserted, non-obligees may assert claims against the performance bond. By its express language, performance bonds are in favor of a specific obligee. Thus, by definition, non-obligees are not a party protected by the performance bonds, and as such, non-obligees typically face a heightened challenge in asserting a valid claim.

A. Subcontractors and Suppliers

Of the class of non-obligee claims, the most prevalent are third-party beneficiary claims made by unpaid subcontractors and suppliers who argue that they are "intended beneficiaries" of the performance bond. These claims are sometimes lodged because the subcontractor cannot assert a valid payment bond claim, either due to non-compliance with required payment notices or due to the lack of available monies in the bond's penal sum.[103] Attempts to turn a performance bond into a payment bond have not received wide support and should be viewed with skepticism.[104]

B. Assignees, Successors and Purchasers

In instances where a claim is asserted by either an assignee of the performance bond or a successor to the performance bond, the language of the bond should be closely examined. One court has denied recovery to an owner who received a full assignment of the bond, not because the assigned performance bond claim was *per se* invalid, but because the language of the bond limited claims solely to the named obligee or a successor to the bond.[105] With respect to successor owners, these claims

---

103 *See* THE MOST IMPORTANT QUESTIONS A SURETY CAN ASK ABOUT PERFORMANCE BONDS 15-18 (Steven J. Strawbridge & Lawrence Lerner eds., Am. Bar Ass'n 1997).

104 BRUNER & O'CONNOR, *supra* note 2, § 12:28 ("Such third-party arguments, however, overlook the fundamental proposition that the performance bond is intended specifically to protect the named obligee against the risk of contract nonperformance, and is not intended to offer financial balm to the hurts of everyone involved with the construction project."); see also RESTATEMENT (THIRD) OF SURETYSHIP AND GUARANTY § 69, illus. 1 (1996) ("P contracts to build a house for O. Pursuant to the contract, P and S both execute a payment bond to O whereby they promise O that all of P's debts for labor and materials on the house will be paid. P later employs C as a carpenter and buys lumber from L. C and L are intended beneficiaries of S's promise to O. In contrast, under a typical 'performance bond,' where the secondary obligor's promise is only to fulfill the principal obligor's duty to the obligee, laborers and suppliers would not be intended beneficiaries of the secondary obligor's promise.").

105 Southern Patrician Assoc. v. International Fid. Ins. Co., 381 S.E.2d 98 (Ga. Ct. App. 1989).

have had mixed success, based chiefly on the language of the performance at issue in the case.[106] Applying the same principle, the success of an assignee in asserting a claim against the performance bond depends on whether assignments are prohibited by the language of the bond.[107]

Recently, some state legislatures have enacted statutes mandating that warranties shall run to the purchasers of condominiums, effectively creating a new class of potential non-obligee claimants. These statutes typically impose a warranty on the developer for a specified amount of time and tend to cover structural defects, although the definition of what constitutes a "structural defect" varies from statute to statute.[108] While the statutory warranties are usually imposed on the developer, those warranties can be passed on to the contractor or subcontractors by virtue of contractual provisions, and consequently, may run to their sureties as well. Exposure may be limited by including language in the performance bond that strictly states that the surety's obligations shall not apply to any statutory warranties imposed upon its principal, any subcontractors, or the obligee.

C. Miscellaneous Claims

Although less common, some large projects are constructed by co-prime contractors. Attempts by a co-prime contractor to recover against the performance bond of another co-prime contractor have met with little

---

106 See Balboa Ins. Co. v. Snyder Consol. Indep. School Dist., 574 S.W.2d 879, 880-81 (Tex. Civ. App. 1978) (allowing claim by a successor because underlying contract incorporated into the bond bound the parties to "partners, successors, [and] assigns . . . ."); *but see* Board of Educ. v. Ockerlund & Assocs., Inc., 519 N.E.2d 95 (Ill. App. Ct. 1988) (affirming lower court decision that successor lacked standing to assert a claim against the performance bond because the bond was solely in favor of the named obligee).

107 *See* Chris Nelson & Son, Inc. v. Atlas Concrete Pipe, Inc., 269 N.W.2d 295, 296 (Mich. Ct. App. 1978).

108 *See e.g.*, FLA. STAT. ANN. § 718.203 (West 2004); VA. CODE ANN. § 55-79.79 (Michie 2006).

success, primarily on the basis that the performance bond is in favor of the owner of the project and not other co-prime contractors.[109]

Non-obligee claims for personal injury and/or wrongful death as a result of the negligence of the bonded principal also have begun to arise. As a general rule, "a performance bond is not a substitute for liability insurance and accords no third-party rights to those with claims for personal injury or wrongful death."[110] Likewise, attempts by the obligee or adjacent property owners seeking redress from the performance bond surety for property damage caused by the principal are typically rejected. As the Eighth Circuit explained, the performance bond coverage does not "operate as an all risks policy of public liability insurance for the benefit of tort claimants...."[111]

In sum, regardless of whether a claim is asserted by an obligee or a non-obligee, the extent to which damages may be recovered (in most instances) hinges on the language of the performance bond, and it is this document that should receive primary attention when evaluating the validity of a claim against the performance bond.

VI. Limitations to Liability

Liability under a performance bond may be limited or impacted by the penal limit of the bond and the performance option selected by the surety.

A. The Penal Limit

A bedrock principle of suretyship is that the liability of the surety is limited to the penal limit of its bond.[112] The penal limit, also known as

---

109 Moore Constr. Co. v. Clarksville Dep't of Elec., 707 S.W.2d 1, 12 (Tenn. Ct. App. 1985); Van Cor, Inc. v. American Casualty Co., 208 A.2d 267 (Pa. 1965).

110 BRUNER & O'CONNOR, *supra* note 2, § 12:31; *cf.* Itri Brick & Concrete Corp. v. Aetna Cas. & Sur. Co., 680 N.E.2d 1200, 1204 (N.Y. 1997) (rejecting broad indemnity language in several agreements "since their full enforcement would result in the contractors being indemnified for their negligence").

111 Tri-State Ins. Co. v. United States, 340 F.2d 542, 545 (8th Cir. 1965) (basing the decision on the specific language of the bond).

112 RESTATEMENT (THIRD) OF SURETYSHIP AND GUARANTY § 73, cmt. b (1996); Trainor v. Aetna Cas. & Sur. Co., 290 U.S. 47, 52 (1933); United

the penal sum or the bond penalty, is the sum stated on the face of the bond and is dictated by the bond statute or contract terms pursuant to which the bond is furnished. The purpose of the penal sum is to fix the limit of the surety's financial exposure under the bond.[113]

The principles of equity have put further limitations on the surety's liability. Historically, when the principal defaulted, the surety was required to surrender the entire penal sum, regardless of what damages the obligee sustained.[114] Now, courts will analyze the facts and circumstances in order to assess the obligee's damages. The surety may be liable for those assessed damages, but the rule still stands that the surety's liability does not extend beyond the penal limit.[115] According to

---

States v. Seaboard Sur. Co., 817 F.2d 956, 963 (2d Cir. 1987), *cert. denied*, 484 U.S. 855 (1987); Great Am. Ins. Co. v. N. Austin Mun. Util. Dist. No. 1, 908 S.W.2d 415, 426 (Tex. 1995); Houston Fire & Cas. Ins. Co. v. E.E. Cloer Gen. Contractor, Inc., 217 F.2d 906, 912 (5th Cir. 1954); Bill Curphy Co. v. Elliott, 207 F.2d 103, 106 (5th Cir. 1953); Mass. Bonding & Ins. Co. v. United States, 97 F.2d 879, 881 (9th Cir. 1938).

113 *See* Bill Curphy Co. v. Elliott, 207 F.2d 103, 106 (5th Cir. 1953) ("If appellant's contention that the surety's liability may exceed the sum stated on the face of the bond is correct, and it is not, it would be futile to state any amount of liability in the bond. This contention completely overlooks the well-established rule in Texas and elsewhere that the sole object of stating the penalty in a bond is to fix the limit of the liability of the signers, and no recovery can be had on such bond against the principal or surety beyond the penalty named on the bond.").

114 BRUNER & O'CONNOR, *supra* note 2, § 12:21. At one point in time, a surety bond was a forfeiture bond for a stipulated amount. In the event of a principal's default, the surety had to pay a penalty–a bond penalty–and surrender whatever it had promised. The fundamental premise was limitation of exposure. Without this limitation, the concept of surety would never have gained traction. A surety bond is no longer considered a forfeiture bond, and the term bond penalty has come to be known as the penal limit or penal sum. *See also* Bill Curphy v. Elliott, 207 F.2d 103, 106 (5th Cir. 1953) (holding that liquidated damages are generally not recoverable in excess of the penal sum).

115 RESTATEMENT (THIRD) OF SURETYSHIP AND GUARANTEE § 73, cmt. b (1996); Trainor v. Aetna Cas. & Sur. Co., 290 U.S. 47, 52 (1933); United States v. Seaboard Sur. Co., 817 F.2d 956, 963 (2d Cir. 1987), *cert. denied*, 484 U.S. 855 (1987); Great Am. Ins. Co. v. N. Austin Mun. Util. Dist. No. 1, 908 S.W.2d 415, 426 (Tex. 1995); Houston Fire & Cas. Ins. Co. v. E.E. Cloer Gen. Contractor, Inc., 217 F.2d 906, 912 (5th Cir.

the Texas Supreme Court: "[i]t is well settled that a performance bond is enforceable only to the extent of the obligee's actual damages. Likewise, when an obligee's actual damages exceed the penal amount of a bond, a surety's liability generally is limited to the penal sum of the bond."[116]

Although the penal sum is intended to limit the surety's liability to the obligee, the surety's exposure may extend beyond the penal sum in certain instances. A surety has been held to be liable beyond the penal sum for pre-judgment interest.[117] Such interest may begin to run either from the time the principal defaults, or when payment is demanded.[118] A surety will generally not be liable, however, for interest unless it has received a demand for payment.[119]

Attorney fees may also cause the surety's liability to exceed the penal limit of the bond, particularly when the bond or statute provides for payment of attorney fees. Sureties are not liable for attorneys' fee awards against its principal in excess of the penal sum of the bond, but have been required to pay attorneys' fees in excess of the penal sum where the surety unsuccessfully litigates a claim against the obligee when the bond

---

1954); Bill Curphy Co. v. Elliott, 207 F.2d 103, 106 (5th Cir. 1953); Mass. Bonding & Ins. Co. v. United States, 97 F.2d 879, 881 (9th Cir. 1938).

116 Great Am. Ins. Co. v. N. Austin Mun. Util. Dist. No. 1, 908 S.W.2d 415, 426 (Tex. 1995); Bill Curphy Co. v. Elliott, 207 F.2d 103, 106 (5th Cir. 1953).

117 *See* Fidelity N.Y., FSB v. Aetna Ins. Co., 651 N.Y.S. 2d 58, 59 (App. Div. 1996); Insurance Co. of North America v. United States, 951 F.2d 1244 (Fed. Cir. 1991); United States v. U.S. Fidelity & Guaranty Co., 236 U.S. 512, 528-29 (1915).

118 *See* U.S. Fid. & Guar. Co. v. Braspetro Oil Services Co., 369 F.3d 34, 78 (2d Cir. 2004) ("interest . . . shall be awarded from the time of default by the surety); Howze v. Surety Corp. of Am., 584 S.W.2d 263, 268 (Tex. 1979) (holding that if a surety is held liable on its bond, it is also liable for prejudgment interest commencing on the date demand was made); *see also* Seattle-First Nat'l Bank v. Aetna Life & Cas. Co., 642 P.2d 1259, 1261 (Wash. Ct. App. 1982); Ins. Co. of N. Am. v. United States, 951 F.2d 1244, 1246 (Fed. Cir. 1991); Fid. N.Y., FSB v. Aetna Ins. Co., 651 N.Y.S.2d 58, 59 (N.Y. App. Div. 1996).

119 U.S. Fid. & Guar. Co. v. Braspetro Oil Services Co., 369 F.3d 34, 79-80 (2d Cir. 2004); Aetna Ins. Co. v. Junction Warehouse Co., 389 F.2d 464, 467 (5th Cir. 1968); Golden West Constr. Co. v. United States *ex rel.* Bernadot, 304 F.2d 753, 757-58 (10th Cir. 1962).

provides for the payment of fees.[120] Liability for attorney fees in excess of the penal limit may be provided by statute even if the terms of the bond do not provide for liability for fees in excess of the bond amount.[121]

There may be circumstances, although rare, where the language of the surety bond allows for increases in the penal limit. Depending on the language of the bond, the penal amount may increase automatically upon certain changes, i.e. a unilateral change order issued under the principal's contract or a bilateral modification to the contract.[122] Bond language allowing these automatic increases amounts to an express waiver and authorization by the surety to increase the penal limit.[123] Regardless of such language, fundamental changes that materially alter the penal limit typically cannot be expressly waived – the surety must give actual waiver or authorization before any increase in the price of the bond contract will change the penal sum.[124]

---

120 Great Am. Ins. Co. v. N. Austin Mun. Util. Dist. No. 1, 908 S.W.2d 415, 426 (Tex. 1995); Trustees of Plumbers and Pipefitters Union Local 525 Health and Welfare Trust Plan v. Developers Sur. and Indem. Co., 84 P.3d 59 (Nev. 2004) (Under Nevada's attorney's fees statute, a surety may be assessed attorney's fees in excess of its bond limitation where the surety is directly involved in litigation over its liability under its bond or where the surety rejects a favorable offer of judgment or litigates without reasonable grounds.).
121 For a comprehensive review of jurisdictional distinctions in awarding attorney's fees, *see Klinger et al., supra* note 50, at 112-114.
122 BRUNER & O'CONNOR, *supra* note 2, § 12:21.
123 *See* Centex Constr. v. Acstar Ins. Co., 448 F. Supp. 2d 697 (E.D. Va. 2006) ("It is also well settled that the surety may waive its rights, or consent to the underlying agreement being altered or modified, and the general rule calling for the discharge of the surety does not apply where the suretyship or guaranty agreement itself permits the modification of the underlying obligation."); *In re* Technology For Energy Corp., 140 B.R. 214, 228-29 (Bankr. E.D. Tenn. 1992).
124 BRUNER & O'CONNOR, *supra* note 2, § 12:21; *see Centex Constr.*, 448 F.Supp. 2d at 697 ("Under Virginia law, a surety's bond obligation may be discharged by a modification to a construction contract if the alteration materially alteration increases the surety's risk without the surety's knowledge or consent. The surety need not demonstrate prejudice resulting from the material alteration because the material alteration, in itself, establishes sufficient prejudice."); *In re* Technology, 140 B.R. at 228-29.

B. The Surety's Performance Options

The surety's obligations upon receiving a performance bond claim include investigating the claim, establishing whether the principal is in default of its contractual obligations, and determining whether the surety has liability under the performance bond. After completing its investigation, the surety must decide the most appropriate means of responding to the obligee's performance bond claim.[125] The extent of the surety's liability will largely depend on the performance option selected by the surety. In certain circumstances, the surety's decision may result in a waiver of the general rule, and as a result of the waiver, its exposure may exceed the penal sum. Generally, a surety has six options available under a performance bond:

1. *Buy Back the Bond.* When the surety buys back the performance bond, it tenders payment to the obligee, not to exceed the penal sum of the bond, in full and final settlement of the claim.[126] This option provides certainty to all parties involved and can avoid additional disputes regarding the claim.

2. *Finance the Principal.* When the surety chooses to finance the principal, its liability may not be limited by the penal sum of the bond.[127] In some circumstances, a surety

---

125 See *supra* Chapter 3 for a detailed review of a surety's investigation and available performance options.

126 Philip L. Bruner et al., Ch. 3, *The Surety's Analysis of Investigative Results: "To Perform or Not to Perform—That is the Question,"* in BOND DEFAULT MANUAL 77, 152 (Duncan L. Clore et al. eds., 3d. ed., Am. Bar Ass'n 2005).

127 BRUNER & O'CONNOR, *supra* note 2, § 12:78. ("Unless the obligee is notified of and consents to the surety's financing as made pursuant to the surety's performance bond obligation, sums advanced by the surety may not be credited against the limit of the bond amount"); George J. Bachrach & Mathew L. Silverstein, *Financing the Principal, in* BOND DEFAULT MANUAL 155, 178 (Duncan L. Clore et. al. eds., 3d. ed. 2005) ("Unless agreed to by the obligee, money advanced by the surety to its principal under a financing agreement does not decrease the penal sum of the surety's performance bond"); Philip L. Bruner et. al., *Ch. 4, The Surety's Analysis of Investigative Results: "To Perform or Not to Perform–That is the Question"*, *in* BOND DEFAULT MANUAL 77, 149-50 (Duncan L. Clore et. al. eds., 3d. ed., Am. Bar Ass'n 2005).

advancing money to the principal may be recognized as a lender with no penal limit.[128] It is often the case that parties will enter into written agreements that will address this issue so that any advanced financing constitutes a reduction of the penal limit of the performance bond.

3. *Tender a Completion Contractor to the Obligee.* The surety may also arrange for the obligee to enter into a contract with a completion contractor who, in addition to the new contract, may also tender a new performance bond. Under this option, the costs to be paid by the original surety will not exceed the penal sum of the bond.[129]

4. *Execute a Takeover Agreement.* By executing a takeover agreement, the surety agrees to takeover and complete the project. Once this occurs, the takeover agreement controls the surety's obligation, and the surety often includes a clause in the new agreement limiting its liability to the original penal amount.[130] The takeover agreement may also provide that sums spent by the surety will be reduced from the penal amount. Absent these clauses, courts appear to apply an objective standard to determine whether the surety "stepped into the contractor's shoes," making it responsible for completion costs even in excess of the bond limit.[131]

---

128 *Schwartzkopf, supra* note 101, § 11.04.
129 BRUNER & O'CONNOR, *supra* note 2, § 12:80; E.A. "Seth" Mills, Jr. & Susan M. Moore, *Ch. 6, Tender, in* BOND DEFAULT MANUAL 243, 243-45 (Duncan L. Clore et. al. eds., 3d. ed., Am. Bar Ass'n 2005); *Bruner, supra* note 126, at 151; *see also* Scott v. Red River Waterway Comm'n, 926 So. 2d 830 (La. Ct. App. 2d Cir. 2006), *writ denied*, 936 So. 2d 1269 (La. 2006) (holding that a surety which tendered a completing contractor after default of the principal, and which was not otherwise involved in completion of the bonded contract, was not liable for alleged defects in the completed work).
130 *Bruner, supra* note 126, at 150.
131 Gregory L. Daily & Todd C. Kazlow, Ch. 5, *Takeover and Completion, in* BOND DEFAULT MANUAL 223, 228 (Duncan L. Clore et. al. eds., 3d. ed., Am. Bar Ass'n 2005); *see, e.g.*, Employers Mut. Cas. Co. v. United Fire & Cas. Co., 682 N.W.2d 452, 457 (Iowa Ct. App. 2004) ("When a surety takes over performance of a contract, the surety's liability is no longer limited by the amount of the bond."); U.S. Fid. & Guar. Co. v. Braspetro Oil Services Co., 369 F.3d 34 (2d Cir. 2004) (reducing a judgment for reasons other than exceeding the aggregate penal sum limit of bonds);

5. *Allow the obligee to mitigate.* There may be a number of circumstances where the easiest and most effective way to solve the problem is to allow the obligee to mitigate. The surety may select this option for any number of legal or factual reasons, including the following: (1) the surety is uncertain whether the obligee has formally declared the principal in default; (2) the surety is not in a position to effectively mitigate; (3) the surety disagrees with the scope of the undertaking; (4) the obligee needs to mitigate immediately; (5) there is disagreement on the amount of the demand; or (6) the obligee is in better position to mitigate the damages. Under this option, the surety's liability is generally limited to the penal amount of the bond.
6. *Deny the claim.* When the surety denies the claim made against the performance bond, the surety's liability is generally limited to the penal sum of the bond.[132]

VII. Defenses

A. *Substantial Completion*

The liability of a surety under a performance bond is not triggered unless there is a default by the principal.[133] Therefore, the possibility of liability can effectively end when a project reaches the point where a default can no longer be declared. As a leading treatise has noted:

> [T]he bond duration traditionally has been deemed to extend only to the point of 'substantial completion' . . . at which point the owner is determined to have received performance substantially as bargained for

---

Caron v. Andrews, 284 P.2d 544 (Cal. Ct. App. 1955); McWaters & Bartlett v. United States, 272 F.2d 291 (10th Cir. 1959).

132   *See* Great Am. Ins. Co. v. N. Austin Mun. Util. Dist. No. 1, 908 S.W.2d 415, 426 (Tex. 1995); Bill Curphy Co. v. Elliott, 207 F.2d 103, 106 (5th Cir. 1953); *see also* AIA 312 bond form.

133   *Klinger et al., supra* note 50, at 82 ("If the principal on the project defaults on the underlying contract, the surety has a contractual obligation to the obligee with regard to completion of the project.").

and thus is not legally justified in terminating the bonded contract for default.[134]

Arguably, when substantial completion has occurred, the owner should look to retainage funds to cover any additional "punch list" items that remain.

The definition of "substantial completion" can be difficult to define. For example, the definition expressed in the standard AIA General Conditions somewhat loosely states that substantial completion is achieved when the project "is sufficiently complete in accordance with the contract documents so that the owner can occupy or utilize the work for its intended purpose."[135] In the absence of specific language defining substantial completion, some courts have imposed strict guidelines, including that the contractor act in good faith. As one court opined:

> To constitute substantial compliance the contractor must have in good faith intended to comply with the contract, and shall have substantially done so in the sense that the defects are not pervasive, do not constitute a deviation from the general plan contemplated for the work, and are not so essential that the object of the parties in making the contract and its purpose cannot, without difficulty, be accomplished by remedying them. Such performance permits only such omissions or deviation from the contract as are inadvertent and unintentional, are not due to bad faith, do not impair the structure as a whole, and are remediable without doing material damage to other parts of the building in tearing down and reconstructing.[136]

Without an express definition of substantial completion, the term will be subject to the common law. Keeping this in mind, one must examine the language of the contract documents to determine whether substantial completion has been defined.

---

134 BRUNER & O'CONNOR, *supra* note 2, § 12:22.
135 *American Institute of Architects, supra* note 4, § 9.8.
136 Turner, Collie & Braden, Inc. v. Brookhollow, Inc., 642 S.W.2d 160, 164-65 (Tex. 1982).

B. Material Alteration

Discharge of liability under the performance bond is the result of some affirmative act of the obligee. The reasoning for the discharge is that the obligee has done something, without the consent of the surety, which rises to such a level of prejudice to the surety that the law dictates that the bond liability be terminated.[137] Over time courts have expanded the situations that warrant a discharge of the performance bond.[138]

A material alteration is a "nonconsensual increase of the surety's risk by some act of the obligee that changes the bonded contract."[139] Yet not every nonconsensual act qualifies as a material alteration. The change must represent a "material, substantial departure from the original risk,

---

137 M. Michael Egan & Marla Eastwood, Ch. 7, *Discharge of the Performance Bond Surety, in* THE LAW OF SURETYSHIP 119, 119 (Edward G. Gallagher ed., 2d ed., Am. Bar Ass'n 2000); United States v. Reliance Ins. Co., 799 F.2d 1382, 1385-86 (9th Cir. 1986); Old Colony Ins. Co. v. Quitman, 163 Tex. 144, 148 (Tex. 1961) (quoting Bullard v. Norton, 182 S.W. 668, 580 (Tex. 1916) ("It is well settled that sureties are only bound by the precise terms of the contract whose performance they secure, and that any material alterations in the terms of the contract without their consent will release them from liability.")).

138 BRUNER & O'CONNOR, *supra* note 2, § 12:68 (noting discharge warranted in the following situations:
   1. Material alteration of the bonded contract by fundamental change or by abandonment and substitution of a new contract;
   2. Changes in the obligee or principal;
   3. Impairment of contract funds by wrongful overpayment;
   4. Untimely or insufficient notice;
   5. Failure to follow statutory requirements;
   6. Time limitations on commencement of suit on the bond;
   7. Misrepresentation or fraud;
   8. Release of the principal; and
   9. Impairment of collateral available to the surety).

   See also Chapter 11 *infra* for a complete analysis of all defenses to liability available to a surety.

139 RESTATEMENT (THIRD) OF SURETYSHIP & GUARANTY § 41(b)(i) (1996) ("[T]he secondary obligor is discharged from any unperformed duties pursuant to the secondary obligation . . . if the modification creates a substituted contract or imposes risks on the secondary obligor fundamentally different from those imposed pursuant to the transaction prior to modification . . . .").

so that a reasonable person would either have not undertaken the risk at all, or would have charged a greater premium."[140]

Given the subjective standard of determining if a material alteration exists, this is a fact dependent inquiry often to be decided by a jury.[141] Certain trends have emerged, however, that can provide some guidance. For example, material alterations were found when the change significantly increased the surety's exposure without the surety's knowledge.[142] Relatively minor changes, however, do not amount to material alterations. Such minor changes, as noted by a respected treatise, include:

1. Slight increase in building height, change in window size, and omission of one window;
2. Change of location of building from one lot to another;
3. Small changes to the plans and specifications; and
4. Construction of an additional story to a building when cost of extra story was less than ten percent of the penal sum.[143]

---

140 Egan & Eastwood, *supra* note 137, at 132 (citing Varlotta Constr. Corp. v. Sette-Juliano Constr. Corp., 651 N.Y.S.2d 484, 484 (N.Y. App. Div. 1996); *In re* Liquidation of Union Ins. Co. of New York, 632 N.Y.S.2d 788, 788 (N.Y. App. Div. 1995)); *see also* Nat'l Surety Corp. v. United States, 118 F.3d 1542, 1544-45 (Fed. Cir. 1997); Leila Hosp. & Health Center v. Xonics Med. Sys., 948 F.2d 271, 275 (6th Cir. 1991); United States v. Reliance Ins. Co., 799 F.2d 1382, 1385 (9th Cir. 1986); Reliance Ins. Co. of Phila., Pa. v. Colbert, 365 F.2d 530, 534-35 (D.C. Cir. 1966); Carriage Town, Inc. v. Landco, Inc., 998 F. Supp. 646, 648 (D.S.C. 1998).

141 Egan & Eastwood, *supra* note 137, at 135 (citing Fireman's Fund Ins. Co. v. United States, 15 Cl. Ct. 225, 230 (Cl. Ct. 1988), *judgment rev'd on other grounds*, 909 F.2d 495 (Fed. Cir. 1990); Reliance Ins. Co. v. Colbert, 365 F.2d 530, 534-35 (D.C. Cir. 1966)).

142 *See In re* Liquidation of Union Ins. Co. of New York, 632 N.Y.S.2d 788, 788 (N.Y. App. Div. 1995) (finding material alteration when contract price increased from $195,000 to $545,000); Employer's Ins. of Wausau v. Constr. Mgmt. Eng'rs of Fla., Inc., 377 S.E.2d 119, 121-22 (S.C. Ct. App. 1989) (finding material alteration when contract price increased from $2.3 million to $6.2 million).

143 *Egan & Eastwood, supra* note 137, at 133-34.

C. Overpayment or Improper Payment

Obligees typically retain 10 percent of the progress payments as retainage until the contractor completes the work. This money serves as protection for the obligee and for use on outstanding "punch-list" items. The retainage also serves as protection for the surety, and the surety's consent is required prior to a reduction in retainage or the release of the final payment.[144] When an obligee improperly pays a principal without the consent of the surety, this act can result in a discharge of the performance bond.[145] Improper payments include:

1. Making progress payments for work not completed;
2. Paying for work which the obligee knew or should have known was defective;
3. Prematurely releasing the contract retainage; or
4. Making final payment without the required consent of the surety.[146]

As is the case with a material alteration, a surety must prove that it has been harmed as a result of the improper payment. For instance, the Third Restatement of Suretyship and Guaranty recognizes harm to the surety where payments are prematurely released, namely because the surety has lost a portion of contract balances that it otherwise would have been entitled to under its subrogation rights.[147] In contrast, a premature

---

144 BRUNER & O'CONNOR, *supra* note 2, § 12:71; *see, e.g.*, Fort Worth Indep. Sch. Dist. v. Aetna Cas. & Sur. Co., 48 F.2d 1 (5th Cir. 1931).
145 *Houston et al.*, *supra* note 19, at 16.
146 BRUNER & O'CONNOR, *supra* note 2, § 12:71 (citing Fireman's Fund Ins. Co. v. United States, 15 Ct. Cl. 225, 231 (1988), *judgment rev'd on other grounds*, 909 F.2d 495 (Fed. Cir. 1990); Ohio Cas. Ins. Co. v. United States, 12 Cl. Ct. 590, 594-96 (Cl. Ct. 1987); Merchant's Bonding Co. (Mutual) v. Pima County, 860 P.2d 510, 512-13 (Ariz. Ct. App. 1993); Cent. Towers Apartments, Inc. v. Martin, 453 S.W.2d 789, 796-97 (Tenn. Ct. App. 1969)).
147 RESTATEMENT (THIRD) OF SURETYSHIP AND GUARANTY § 31, cmt. c. (1996) ("If the obligee pays the return performance to the principal obligor before such payment is owed under the contract between the principal obligor and the obligee, the ability of the secondary obligor to be made whole through subrogation may be impaired if the secondary obligor is called upon to perform. Accordingly, such a payment may constitute impairment of collateral.").

release of payments by joint check to both the principal and its subcontractors has not been seen to constitute any harm, because the joint check relieves the surety of any obligation it would have had to the subcontractors under the payment bond.[148]

An additional component in this issue is the architect's role in approving progress payments. By and large, progress payments are processed monthly and involve three steps: (1) the contractor submits a payment application; (2) the architect certifies the payment application; and (3) the obligee accepts the payment application.[149] In this process, the obligee relies on the architect's proper certification of the payment application, as an assurance that the actual amount of money due has been verified and the proper amount of work has been performed. Courts have been reluctant to discharge the bond when an obligee has relied in good faith on the architect's certification, even if the obligee overpaid the contractor as a result of an improperly certified payment application.[150] A surety may assert affirmative defenses of negligent inspection and overpayment in this situation.

D. Termination for Convenience and Release of the Principal

Construction contracts normally include provisions for termination of the contract and may include clauses for termination for cause and/or termination for convenience. A termination for cause provision establishes what constitutes sufficient cause for the owner to terminate the contract and enumerates the rights the contractor has under the contract to cure such a default. A termination for convenience clause allows the owner to terminate the contract without cause and without having to justify the termination decision. Where termination of the contract is for convenience, the obligee (the owner) cannot call upon the surety to perform because no default has occurred that triggers any obligation on the part of the surety. Similar to a termination for

---

148 Egan & Eastwood, *supra* note 137, at 125 (citing United Bonding Ins. Co. v. W.S. Newell, Inc., 232 So. 2d 616, 627 (Ala. 1969); St. John's College v. Aetna Indem. Co., 94 N.E. 994, 995-98 (N.Y. 1911); Am. Sur. Co. v. Noe, 53 S.W.2d 178, 181 (Ky. Ct. App. 1932)).
149 BRUNER & O'CONNOR, *supra* note 2, § 12:71 (footnote omitted).
150 *See, e.g.*, Argonaut Ins. Co. v. Town of Cloverdale, Ind., 699 F.2d 417, 419 (7th Cir. 1983); *see also* U.S. Fidelity and Guaranty Co. v. Braspetro Oil Services Co., 369 F.3d 34, 64-65 (2d Cir. 2004).

convenience, an obligee cannot pursue any remedies against the surety after the obligee has released the principal in a settlement agreement.[151] In both of these situations, the obligee has selected its remedy and has discharged the surety from any potential liability.

Conclusion

A performance bond is a guaranty, and as such it is a creature of contract. As a contract, the liability of the surety is properly found within the four corners of the bond, and as appropriate, the intentions of the parties. While determining the liability of a performance bond surety requires fact intensive analysis, such analysis must have a common starting point: the bond itself. While this chapter serves as an overview of the liability of the performance bond surety, applicable state statutes and laws must also be given consideration.

---

151   BRUNER & O'CONNOR, *supra* note 2, § 12:65.

9

EXTRA-CONTRACTUAL LIABILITY OF PERFORMANCE BOND SURETIES

David C. Olsen
Peter E. Karney*

Introduction

Other chapters in this book will cover issues regarding the creation of the performance bond relationship, how to assert performance bond claims and the rights and responsibilities of the parties to the performance bond. This chapter addresses situations in which the surety is asked to respond to claims that go beyond the "four corners" of the bond. Since a surety bond is properly viewed as a contract, this potential exposure is considered "extra-contractual liability" and includes claims for "bad faith" asserted by the bond obligee or others.

On construction projects, sureties typically provide two types of bonds: a performance bond and a payment bond. The potential beneficiaries of a payment bond are usually not specified in the instrument itself and are unknown at the time the bond is issued. A performance bond, on the other hand, has a specified obligee (or group of obligees) that is known and identified in the bond.

When the surety provides a performance bond on a construction project, it assumes the risk that the contractor will not be able to complete its contractual obligations. For performance bonds, the surety can identify the potential claimant, namely the obligee, which could potentially assert extra-contractual liability claims. Upon a proper and valid declaration of default as specified in the bond, the surety becomes exposed to the expenses and losses that may arise as a result of the obligation to complete the work. The maximum extent of this potential liability is reflected in the bond itself by reference to the penal sum of the bond. But at times, tort claims may be presented which go beyond the penal sum of the bond or beyond the stated terms of the bond. It is these risks which are the focus of this chapter.

---

*   The author wishes to acknowledge the valuable assistance of Lisa Weekley Coulter of Frost Brown Todd LLC for her writing and editing.

The risk of "extra-contractual liability" for the surety may extend beyond the costs associated with the completion of the work. Further, these potential claims may arise from risks and obligations which are not set forth in either the bonded contract or the bond. Accordingly, the risk of extra-contractual liability may be created by the terms of the bond, the contract that is bonded, or claims by the obligee which attempt to expand the reach of the bond. These claims expose the surety to potential losses which go beyond the "four corners" of the bond and are often beyond the costs directly associated with the work.

I. Bad Faith

A term that often arises in the context of extra-contractual liability is "bad faith." This concept arises more frequently in the handling of insurance claims rather than surety claims. In the early twentieth century, courts began to discuss the implied duty to act in good faith and to engage in fair dealing for contracts. This concept was expanded in 1930 when the principles of bad faith were applied to situations where insurance carriers failed to settle claims which were within the scope of the insurance policy limits.[1] Black's Law Dictionary defines "bad faith" as follows:

> Insurance company's unreasonable and unfounded (though not necessarily fraudulent) refusal to provide coverage in violation of the duties of good faith and fair dealing owed to insured.[2]

Claims for "bad faith" are often defined by reference to what constitutes "good faith" in the handling of claims. A performance bond by definition is a contract, and the Restatement of Contracts provides one source to identify the basic elements of "good faith." The lack of some or all of those elements may lead to the conclusion that there is some basis for a claim of bad faith in the surety context. Section 205 of the Restatement (Second) of Contracts (1979) is entitled "Duty of Good Faith and Fair Dealing" and states as follows: "Every contract imposes upon each party a duty of good faith and fair dealing in its performance and its enforcement."

---

1   Hilker v. Western Automotive Ins. Co., 231 N.W. 257 (Wis. 1930).
2   BLACK'S LAW DICTIONARY, 149 (8th ed. 2004).

Comment D is entitled "Good Faith Performance" and states:

> Subterfuges and evasions violate the obligation of good faith in performance even though the actor believes his conduct to be justified. But the obligation goes further: bad faith may be overt or may consist of inaction, and fair dealing may require more than honesty. A complete catalog of types of bad faith is impossible, but the following types are among those which have been recognized in judicial decisions: evasion of the spirit of the bargain, lack of diligence and slacking off, willful rendering of imperfect performance, abuse of a power to specify terms, interference with or failure to cooperate in the party's performance.

As noted in the Restatement, a large number of jurisdictions recognize a common law duty of good faith and fair dealing in the performance of contracts, especially insurance contracts.[3] For sureties, a comprehensive review of the various elements and contexts within which a breach of "good faith" can arise may be found in *PSE Consulting, Inc. v. Frank Mercede & Sons, Inc.*[4] That case examined the use of "bad

---

[3] *See* Lockwood Int'l, B.V. v. Volm Bag Co., 273 F.3d 741, 745 (3rd Cir. 2001) ("The duty of good faith is read into every insurance contract, as it is into contracts generally."); Alevy v. Alliance Gen. Ins. Co., 1996 U.S. App. LEXIS 27826, at *8 (9th Cir., Oct. 24, 1996) ("Every insurance contract contains an implied contract of good faith and fair dealing."); Kansas Bankers Sur. Co. v. Lynass, 920 F.2d 546, 548 (8th Cir. 1990) ("A duty to act in good faith is part of every insurance contract."); A & E Supply Co. v. Nationwide Mut. Fire Ins. Co., 798 F.2d 669, 676 (4th Cir. 1986) ("All contracting parties owe to each other a duty of good faith in the performance of the agreement."); Egan v. Mutual of Omaha Ins. Co., 24 Cal. 3d 809, 818 (Cal. 1979) ("[T]he law implies in every contract a covenant of good faith and fair dealing."); Dairyland Ins. Co. v. Herman, 954 P.2d 56, 60 (N.M. 1997) ("[W]ith insurance contracts, as with every contract, there is an implied covenant of good faith and fair dealing that the insurer will not injure its policyholder's right to receive the full benefits of the contract."); Helmbolt v. Le Mars Mut. Ins. Co., 404 N.W.2d 55, 57 (S.D. 1987) ("[A] duty to act or deal in good faith is found in all insurance contracts."); McCullough v. Golden Rule Ins. Co., 789 P.2d 855, 858 (Wyo. 1990) ("The insurance contract is one of these special classes of contracts so that this duty of good faith and fair dealing imposed by law arises from the contractual relationship.").

[4] 267 Conn. 279, 838 A. 2d 135 (2004).

faith" as a defense to a claim of indemnity by the surety. After reviewing the various precedents, the *PSE Consulting* court stated the following:

> After full consideration of the issues before us, we join those jurisdictions that define bad faith as requiring an "improper motive" or "dishonest purpose" on the part of the surety. This standard is in substantial accord with our definition of bad faith in other contexts.[5]

The exposure of a surety to a claim of "bad faith" may arise in a variety of circumstances. Many of those circumstances are beyond the scope of this chapter. For example, many indemnity agreements provide that the surety may seek reimbursement for claims "paid in good faith." This chapter focuses on the potential for claims by the obligee for "bad faith." Claims by the principal for "bad faith" are the focus of the next chapter.

A. Recovery from Surety by Obligee for Surety's Alleged Bad Faith

1. Recovery Against Surety Allowed

Some states allow a cause of action by the obligee for bad faith against a surety.[6] The basis for such claims usually begins with a policy argument, noting that the parties entered into the surety bond with certain expectations which were not met. In these cases, the courts discuss how suretyship is a three-party relationship which identifies the obligee as the beneficiary of the bond. The courts that recognize a claim for bad faith seek to protect the obligees from the allegedly improper actions taken or

---

5 *Id.* at 304-05.
6 U.S. Fid. & Guar. Co. v. Braspetro Oil Servs. Co., 369 F.3d 34 (2nd Cir. 2004); States *ex. rel.* Don Siegel Constr. Co., Inc. v. Atul Constr. Co., 85 F. Supp. 2d 414 (D.N.J. 2000); Loyal Order of Moose, Lodge 1392 v. Int'l Fid. Ins. Co., 797 P.2d 622 (Alaska 1990); Dodge v. Fid. & Deposit Co. of Maryland, 778 P.2d 1240 (Ariz. 1989); Transamerica Premier Ins. Co. v. Brighton Sch. Dist., 940 P.2d 348 (Col. 1997); Dadeland Depot, Inc. v. St. Paul Fire & Marine Ins. Co., 945 So. 2d 1216 (Fla. 2006); Atlantic Contracting & Material Co., Inc. v. Ulico Cas. Co., 380 Md. 285 (Md. App. 2004) (applying a "reasonable manner" rather than "good faith" standard); Worldlogics Corp. v. Chatham Reinsurance Corp., 108 P.3d 5 (Okla. Civ. App. 2004).

wrongful failure to act by the surety to deny them the benefits of the bond. These courts also must address and resolve the fundamental differences between suretyship and insurance. The courts that recognize the validity of bad faith claims treat suretyship as insurance.[7] Since the concept of bad faith is recognized in the insurance context, such a finding is crucial to the analysis. Once a court finds that insurance and suretyship are in this context identical, the tort claim of bad faith that is available in the insurance setting becomes recognized under the suretyship relationship.[8]

One of the first cases to acknowledge the liability of a surety for bad faith was *Suver v. Personal Service Ins. Co.*[9] In that case, the surety provided a financial responsibility bond to the principal, an individual who was not able to secure standard insurance for the operation of an automobile. When the driver was involved in an accident and the carrier did not promptly respond to the claim, the injured party brought a bad faith claim against the surety under the bond. The trial court dismissed the claim, but the Ohio Supreme Court reversed, writing a headnote[10] that provided:

> The issuer of a financial responsibility bond has a duty to act in good faith in the handling and payment of claims by one who may be injured by the principal. Bad faith actions are a breach of this duty and will give rise to a cause of action in tort against the issuer of the bond.

The headnote did not state that the surety bond was in many respects a substitute for an insurance product. The *Suver* court held, however, that

---

[7] See Dodge v. Fid. & Deposit Co. of Maryland, 778 P.2d at 346 ("As insurers, sureties have the same duty to act in good faith...").

[8] See, e.g., Loyal Order of Moose, Lodge 1392 v. Int'l Fid. Ins. Co., 797 P.2d at 627 ("[S]ureties are insurers; insurers are subject to bad faith tort liability; therefore, sureties are subject to bad faith tort liability... Although simple, this proposition is supported by our statutes, case law and sound policy reasons.").

[9] 11 Ohio St. 3d 6 (1984).

[10] The Supreme Court of Ohio writes its own headnotes which, under Ohio law, become the holding court of the case and define the legal principles decided by the case.

the claimant was entitled to pursue a claim against the surety for the tort of bad faith when the claim was not paid.[11]

Five years later, Arizona recognized a claim for bad faith against a surety in the context of a construction bond. In *Dodge v. Fidelity & Deposit Co. of Maryland*,[12] the court acknowledged that the question before the court was one of first impression in Arizona.[13] In 1978, the Dodges signed a contract with a contractor to build a single family residence.[14] The contract for the residence required a performance bond.[15] The terms of the bond required that, upon declaration of default, the surety had the obligation to: (1) remedy the default; (2) complete the contract in accordance with its terms and conditions; or (3) obtain a bid or bids for completing the contract.[16] After a default was declared, the Dodges asserted that the surety refused to investigate the claim or remedy the default.[17]

The Dodges filed suit against the contractor and the surety alleging breach of contract. In accordance with the terms of the contract, the claim was submitted to arbitration, and the arbitrator awarded the Dodges less than $10,000. The Dodges filed suit to confirm the arbitration award and also sought damages for bad faith.[18] The contractor

---

11   In subsequent cases, the Supreme Court of Ohio has narrowed the focus of *Suver*. In Dean v. Seco Elec. Co., 35 Ohio St. 3d 203 (1988), the supreme court confronted the issue of whether a surety is obligated to pay a statutory penalty under the terms of the labor and material payment bond. The surety had paid the unpaid wages due the employees but refused to pay a statutory penalty over and above the unpaid wages. The court reasoned that the statutory requirement for an employer to pay a penalty over and above the actual wages due was, indeed, penal in nature. The court reasoned that "punitive damages are not recoverable against a surety unless the act of the principal was authorized, participated in, or ratified by the surety." Since there was no evidence submitted that showed that the surety was guilty of "actual malice, fraud, or oppression" the plaintiff could not recover the penalty. The court discussed but did not apply the principles espoused in *Suver*.
12   161 Ariz. 344; 778 P. 2d 1240 (Arizona 1989).
13   *Id.* at 345.
14   *Id.*
15   *Id.*
16   *Id.*
17   *Id.*
18   *Id.*

paid the amount of the judgment into the court and was dismissed as a party. The trial court also dismissed the claim against the surety for bad faith. The court of appeals confirmed that decision, citing the differences between casualty insurance and suretyship. The Supreme Court of Arizona, however, reversed.

In its analysis, the *Dodge* court recognized a tort based on an insurer's bad faith refusal to pay a claim submitted by the insured.[19] The court then accepted the plaintiffs' contention that sureties are insurers and are, therefore, subject to tort claims for bad faith. In reaching this conclusion, the *Dodge* court acknowledged that Arizona's statutes defined suretyship arrangements as akin to insurance.[20] The court went on to hold that "sureties have the same duty to act in good faith" as recognized in the insurance context.[21] The court stated that the purpose of "insurance" is to have the carrier pay valid claims, and this purpose is defeated when the company refuses to pay a proper claim without valid justification.[22] Citing *Suver*, the *Dodge* court reached the following conclusion:

> We hold that a surety has a duty to act in good faith in responding to its obligee's claims that the principal has defaulted. Breach of this duty entitles the obligee to maintain a tort action and recover tort damages.[23]

In *Loyal Order of Moose, Lodge 1392 v. International Fidelity Ins. Co.*, the Supreme Court of Alaska also held that a surety could be liable for the tort of bad faith.[24] The Moose Lodge had accepted a proposal for the construction of a new facility and obtained performance and payment bonds with Moose Lodge identified as the obligee.[25] The contractor had substantially completed the project and had been paid 97% of the

---

19 *Id.*
20 *Id.* at 345-46.
21 *Id.* at 346.
22 *Id.* at 347, *citing* Noble v. Nat'l Am. Life Ins. Co., 128 Ariz. 188, 190, 624 P.2d 866 (Ariz. 1981).
23 *Id.* at 348.
24 797 P. 2d 622, 626 (Alaska 1990) ("We conclude that an implied covenant of good faith and fair dealing exists between a surety and its obligee on payment and performance bonds.").
25 *Id.* at 623.

contract price.[26] The contractor refused to perform the punch list until he had been paid for additional items of work beyond the scope of the original contract.[27] The obligee refused to honor the change order, and the contractor did not finish the work.[28] The contractor and the obligee exchanged correspondence identifying, and refuting, claims of poor workmanship and incomplete performance.[29] Ultimately, the obligee filed suit against the surety asserting a claim of bad faith. The trial court dismissed the claim, holding that there was a legitimate dispute as to whether a default had occurred, leading to the conclusion that the surety had no obligation to investigate the claim.[30]

The question presented to the Alaska Supreme Court was whether state law recognized the tort of bad faith in the context of a surety bond for a commercial construction project.[31] The court began with an analysis of the policy considerations that form the basis for a tort claim for bad faith in the context of insurance policies.[32] The court then cited *Dodge*, holding that a similar analysis would apply in the context of suretyship. The court held that the relationship between the surety and obligee is analogous to that of an insurer/insured such that the tort claim of bad faith was viable.[33]

In *Brighton School District 27 J. v. Trans America Premiere Ins. Co.*, the school district sought to remodel a facility and signed a contract to retrofit its HVAC and plumbing.[34] In accordance with state law, the contract required a performance bond.[35] Soon after the work began, questions arose regarding the performance by the contractor.[36] The school district notified the contractor and the surety of its claims and

---

26 *Id.* at 624.
27 *Id.*
28 *Id.*
29 *Id.* at 624-25.
30 *Id.* at 626.
31 *Id.*
32 *Id.*
33 *Id.* at 628 ("In our view the relationship of a surety to its obligee–an intended creditor third-party beneficiary–is more analogous to that of an insurer to its insured than to the relationship between an insurer and an incidental third-party beneficiary.").
34 923 P. 2d 328, 330 (Colo. 1996).
35 *Id.*
36 *Id.*

executed an agreement setting forth amended completion dates.[37] After the contractor missed these amended deadlines and new defects were discovered, the contractor was ordered to leave the project.[38] Thereafter, the school district terminated the contractor and demanded that the surety complete the work.[39] After negotiations between the surety and the school district, a contract was awarded for the completion of the work, but the surety refused to make payments for the completion costs.[40] The surety claimed that the school district had not complied with its obligations under the bond.[41] Ultimately, the school district prevailed in its claim for the payment of the cost to compete the work, and the jury awarded the school district damages on its claim of bad faith. On appeal, the surety contended that the trial court erred in allowing the jury to consider the bad faith claim.

The *Brighton School* court first looked at the state statutes governing practices of the insurance industry, similar to the analysis conducted in *Dodge*.[42] While the court held that the state statutes did not allow for a private action for their breach, the court held that these statutes formed the basis of a common law action in tort for breach of the duty of good faith and fair dealing.[43] The court further reasoned that, similar to the policy underlying a tort of bad faith in the insurance context, the availability of a tort remedy in this surety relationship would deter a breach by the surety of its obligations to the obligee.[44] The court cited with approval the *Dodge* holding and held that the trial court acted properly in submitting the claim to the jury.[45]

---

37 *Id.*
38 *Id.*
39 *Id.*
40 *Id.* at 331.
41 *Id.*
42 *Id.*
43 *Id.*
44 *Id.* at 332 ("If the only damages a surety has to pay upon a judgment of breach are the amounts that it would have owed under the surety contract plus interest, it is motivated to retain the money, earning perhaps higher rates of interest on the outside market and hoping eventually to force the bond obligee into a settlement for less than the policy amount. Permitting the obligee a tort remedy...provides the same deterrence against breach by a surety that it provides against breach by any other insurer.").
45 *Id.*

In the case of *Bd. of Directors of the Assoc. of Apartment Owners of the Discovery Bay Condominium v. United Pacific Ins. Co.*,[46] the association sought repairs of a condominium project. The association engaged G.W. Murphy to perform the painting. G. W. Murphy provided a performance bond and maintenance bond for the work. A year after completion of the work, problems with the paint became apparent and the association filed a claim with the surety. After conducting an inspection, the surety denied the claim. The association pursued various claims under the bonds including claims for punitive damages based on the allegation that the surety failed to properly investigate the claims. The case proceeded to arbitration on the issue of liability under the two bonds.

The arbitrator found no breach of the contract and thus no claim under the performance bond. Further, the panel found no breach of the maintenance bond. The trial court affirmed the award and dismissed the claims based on the alleged failure to investigate. The association appealed. Citing *Dodge*, the Hawaii Supreme Court acknowledged that "the surety owes a duty of good faith to *both* the principle [sic] and the obligee on the bond." (emphasis in original)[47] The court found that the association was bound by the award of the arbitration and thus there was no liability under either bond. Accordingly, dismissal of the claims was appropriate. The court also said that there was no need to address the issue of whether Hawaii recognized "a tort action against a surety for its bad faith failure to investigate a claim." However, the citation to *Dodge*, and the court's statement shows the court's view that a surety does owe a duty of good faith to an obligee.

In *Dadelend Depot, Inc. v. St. Paul Fire & Marine Ins. Co.*, the United States Court of Appeals for the Eleventh Circuit certified certain questions of law to the Florida Supreme Court.[48] One question was whether an obligee could pursue a claim against a surety for a bad faith refusal to settle. The court analyzed the Florida insurance code and found that a surety was included within the definition of an insurer under the applicable Florida statutes. The court cited with approval *Dodge, Loyal Order of Moose, Lodge 1392* and *United Pacific*. It also noted the cases which had rejected similar claims but observed that those cases included

---

46   77 Haw. 398 (1994).
47   *Id.*
48   945 So. 2d 1216; 2006 Fla. LEXIS 2953 (Dec. 21, 2006).

an analysis of the statutory provisions of the applicable state's insurance code. The majority of the court concluded that a surety may be liable for its refusal to settle a claim in good faith.

In the dissent, the minority noted that the Florida statutes upon which the majority relied had been modified to now hold that the surety issuing the performance and payment bonds is not an insurer for purposes of the act.

2. *Recovery Against Surety Not Allowed*

In the cases cited in the previous section, the courts imposed liability on the surety for punitive damages or "bad faith" after an analysis based on perceived similarities between insurance and suretyship. Cases in other states, however, have rejected this analysis and specifically hold that a surety does not owe a duty of good faith and fair dealing to the obligee. *The Cincinnati Ins. Co. v. Centec Building Corp.*[49] is such a case. A number of disputes and legal squabbles arose on a large-scale construction project. At the center of the claims were allegedly fraudulently created surety bonds issued by a former agent of the surety. The surety had previously appointed an agent in North Carolina and provided the appropriate materials to document the authority granted to the agent. The surety terminated the agency and directed the agent to destroy all powers-of-attorney and other documents used to execute bonds. The agent wrote the surety saying that the documents had been destroyed, but the surety had a lingering doubt as to whether that had occurred. Several years later, a project was let for the construction of a motel. The agency working with the contractor forged a bond in the name of the surety and fabricated a power-of-attorney. Shortly after the project began, the general contractor fell behind schedule and a number of claims were submitted under the forged bonds. Litigation ensued raising a number of claims, including a claim of bad faith by the obligee against the surety. The court rejected this theory with the following language:

> As for DEG's common law counterclaim of bad faith, the court finds that summary judgment is appropriate against this counterclaim as well. Here again the distinction between suretyship and insurance is fatal to the claim. The duty of good faith and fair dealing required to sustain a

---

49   286 F. Supp. 2d 669 (N.D.N.C. 2003).

common law bad faith claim is a concept of insurance law and attaches because of the special relationship between insureds and insurers.[50]

In reaching this conclusion, the court cited with approval *Great American Ins. Co. v. North Austin Municipal Utility District No. 1*.[51]

The *Great American* case acknowledged that other jurisdictions had imposed the duty of good faith and fair dealing upon commercial sureties in favor of their bond obligees.[52] The *Great American* court held, however, that the essential predicate for these holdings, namely a finding of similarity between insurance and suretyship, was not appropriate. The court identified a number of the factors that are usually found in the insurer/insured relationship which are lacking in the suretyship relationship. The court stressed the lack of unequal bargaining power and the ability of the obligee to select the bond form as features that would prevent the application of insurance principles in the surety bond context.

A similar conclusion was reached in *Schwerdt v. International Fidelity Ins. Co.*[53] in the context of surety bonds outside of the construction industry. Schwerdt, the owner of a computer hardware and software company, entered into a contract to sell its technology. A bond was provided to guarantee compliance with the terms of the contract for sale. The bond provided that the penal sum would be paid in the event that the buyers failed to pay the amount due or failed to return the technology. After the buyer failed to perform, Schwerdt sought payment under the bond. The surety responded saying that it would not pay unless a court determined that the buyer had breached the contract. After the court had entered judgment in favor of the principal, Schwerdt sought payment under the bond. Again the surety refused to make the payment claiming that its liability had been discharged pursuant to an order from a state court in another jurisdiction. The obligee persisted with its claims and filed an action for bad faith.

While the court acknowledged that California law imposed a covenant of good faith and fair dealing in every contract, the court noted that the damages flowing from the breach of this covenant were recoverable as contract damages and not through tort remedies. The court

---

50   *Id.* at 690.
51   908 S.W. 2d 415 (Tex. 1995).
52   The court cited to *Dodge* and *United Pacific*.
53   2002 U.S. App. LEXIS 1486 (9th Cir. Jan. 25, 2002).

noted that one limited exception to this rule allowed the imposition of tort damages arising in the insured/insurer context. The court based its holding upon a prior state court ruling in *Cates Construction, Inc. v. Talbot Partners*, which had denied a claim for tort remedies in the breach of a construction performance bond.[54] The court found no elements of adhesion or disparate bargaining power in that the obligee had selected the bond form that he was willing to accept. On this basis, the court rejected the claim of bad faith.[55]

B. Recovery from Surety by Principal for Surety's Alleged Bad Faith

In some cases the principal asserts tort claims on the basis of "bad faith" against the surety. As tort claims those theories are typically not successful. A more viable approach is for a principal to use allegations of "bad faith" as a defense to the surety's claims for indemnity.

In the case of *Masterclean, Inc. v. Star Insurance Co.*[56] the federal district court had certified certain questions to the Supreme Court of South Carolina. The essential question was:

> Does South Carolina recognize a cause of action in tort by a principal against its surety for the surety's bad faith refusal to pay first party benefits to an obligee pursuant to a construction performance bond?[57]

The court answered both questions in the negative.

The University of South Carolina had contracted with Masterclean, Inc. to remove asbestos from a school building. A performance bond was obtained from Star Insurance Company pursuant to state law. The obligee notified the surety of a default on the contract and made a claim on the bond. As the surety was conducting its investigation, the obligee formally terminated the contract. The surety concluded that its principal had defaulted on the contract but refrained from paying the claim pending negotiations with the obligee. As those negotiations continued, the school hired a replacement contractor. Thereafter, the school's procurement officer issued a ruling finding a default and allocating

---

54   21 Cal. 4th 28; 980 P. 2d 407 (1999).
55   *Id.*
56   347 S.C. 405; 556 S.E. 2d 371 (S.C. 2001).
57   *Id.* at 407.

damages between the surety and the principal. Masterclean contended that the surety should have mitigated its damages by performing its bond obligation and therefore was liable to Masterclean as the principal for its bad faith refusal to honor the claim under the performance bond. The question, therefore, was whether the principal stated a viable claim in bad faith against the surety.

In an approach similar to the analysis of the bad faith claims brought by an obligee, the court began with an examination of the differences between suretyship and insurance. The court reviewed the split of authority citing to *Trans America, Dodge, Loyal Order of Moose, United Pacific* as well as cases from New Jersey[58] and discussed *Cates Construction, Great American Insurance Company* and *Institute of Mission Helpers of Baltimore City* as cases that reject bad faith claims by obligees against their sureties.

The *Masterclean* court then analyzed the South Carolina insurance code and observed that, even though sureties are regulated, that regulatory scheme does not automatically result in an application of all insurance principles to sureties.[59] The court then discussed the differences between suretyship and insurance. The court further noted that public policy did not support claims for bad faith. The most important difference was that the surety bond itself does not define the underlying relationship between the principal and the obligee; rather, the construction contract defines the duties and obligations of the parties to the transaction. The court drew a "claim/defense" distinction between how bad faith could be a factor in the relationship between a surety and its principal:

> In holding that a principal cannot sue a surety in tort for bad faith refusal to pay a first party claim, it is important to note we do not preclude a principal from using a surety's bad faith in all instances. Several courts, including those not recognizing a principal's right to sue on bad faith and tort, allow the principal to assert a surety's bad faith as a defense to indemnification. [Citations omitted] . . . While a principal may not use bad faith as a sword to extract damages from the surety in

---

58   United States for the use of Don Siegel Constr. Co., Inc. v. Atul Constr. Co., 85 F. Supp. 2d 414 (2002), (court applied New Jersey law to allow an obligee to sue for bad faith damages against surety).

59   *Id.*

tort, a principal is not precluded from using bad faith as a shield in contract against a surety seeking indemnification.[60]

The court in *International Fidelity Ins. Co. v. Vimas Painting Co., Inc.*[61] engaged in a similar analysis. In that case, the surety provided a performance bond and a maintenance bond for *Vimas* in favor of the Ohio Department of Transportation for the painting of certain bridges. In consideration for the issuance of the bonds, an indemnity agreement was required. ODOT contended that the work was not performed in a proper fashion and brought a claim under the maintenance bond. The surety established a reserve and then demanded the deposit of collateral equal to the reserve. The principal refused. The surety filed suit against the individual indemnitors seeking specific performance of the contractual obligation to deposit collateral. In response, the indemnitors filed counterclaims against the surety contending, *inter alia*, that the surety had engaged in bad faith in handling the claims and refusing to accept a tender of a defense from the indemnitors and principal.[62] The surety moved to dismiss the counterclaims for bad faith.

The court observed that Ohio law does not recognize a tort claim for breach of a contract, and the exception allowing a bad faith claim in the insurance context arises from the fiduciary relationship existing in that context.[63] The court distinguished *Suver*, noting that the underlying document that established the relationship between the parties in *Suver* was an insurance product that was called a financial responsibility bond and was, therefore, more analogous to an insurance product. The court said that those courts which found a duty of good faith owing by the surety to the obligee found no such corresponding duty owing by the surety to the principal. On this basis, the court held:

> The obligee requests a bond to protect itself from loss in case the principal defaults. The bond is issued for the benefit of the obligee, not the principal. The principal, who remains primarily liable, does not look to the surety for protection as the insured does to the insurer.

---

60   *Id.* at 414.
61   2008 U.S. Dist. LEXIS 27018 (S.D. Ohio, Apr. 3, 2008).
62   *Id.* at 3.
63   *Id.* at 12-13.

Therefore, while an obligee may bring a bad faith against a surety, a principal may not.[64]

The court observed that the indemnity agreement may impose a duty of good faith since it may provide that the surety may recover indemnity only for payments made "in good faith." As noted in *Masterclean*, however, this argument is a defense to an indemnity claim as opposed to the foundation for an affirmative tort claim for damages. On this basis, the court dismissed the claim for bad faith.

The court in *PSE Consulting, Inc. v. Frank Mercede & Sons, Inc.* performed a similar analysis.[65] While the context was complicated, the basic claim was brought by the surety against the principal for indemnity. The surety contended that it had the right to settle claims under the terms of the written indemnity agreement, and Mercede claimed that this discretion was limited by the requirement to act "in good faith." The court cited the many jurisdictions which held that a surety was entitled to indemnification only for payments made in good faith regardless of whether this was an implied duty or one based on common law. The court held that the majority of jurisdictions required some finding of good faith in the actions of the surety to justify indemnity.[66]

C. Statutory Causes of Action–Model Unfair Claims Settlement Practices Act

In the area of insurance law, claimants sometimes try to use statutes imposing obligations on carriers to handle and process claims in a proper manner as a basis for direct causes of action. A number of states have

---

64 *Id.* at 16.
65 267 Conn. 279; 838 A. 2d 135 (Conn. 2004).
66 The *Mercede* court cited a long list of cases to support its contention that there is a basic need to show good faith in payments by the surety to recover indemnity. Grundle Lining Constr. Corp. v. Adams County Asphalt, Inc., 85 F. 3d 201 (5th Cir. 1996); Fidelity & Deposit Co. of Maryland v. Bristol Steel & Iron, 722, F. 2d 1160 (4th Cir. 1983); Trans America Ins. Co. v. Bloomfield, 401 F. 2d 362; Engbrock v. Federal Ins. Co., 370 F. 2d 786; Carroll v. National Surety Co., 58 U.S. App. D.C. 3 (D.C. Cir. 1928); United States Fidelity & Guarantee Co. v. Feibus, 15 F. Supp. 2d 583; National Surety Corp. v. People's Milling Co., 57 F. Supp. 281 (W.D. Ky. 1944).

adopted individual Unfair Claims Settlement Practices Acts ("UCSPA") that are frequently based on a model act formulated by the National Association of Insurance Commissioners.[67] The state statutes seek to regulate the insurance companies, and list a number of practices which are specifically prohibited to an insurance carrier. The statutes outline practices that are deemed "unfair" in the settlement and handling of claims. Accordingly, a state's UCSPA provides a guideline for carriers as to actions they should take in processing claims. More than 35 years ago, states began to enact most, if not all, of the model legislation.[68] The thrust of these laws is to protect the insureds which are presumably in a position of unequal bargaining position and less informed as to the intricacies of insurance claims handling. The issues are whether the statutes allow a private cause of action for a violation of the statutory guidelines and whether these claims handling practices apply to sureties.

Some states, such as Montana, recognize claims for violation of the unfair claims settlement practice.[69] In *K-W Industries v. National Surety Corp.*[70] the Montana Supreme Court held that a surety could be held liable for violations of the statutory scheme. As with states that find sureties liable for claims of bad faith, the *K-W Industries* court reviewed the insurance/surety distinction but found that the surety was subject to the same requirements for claims handling as insurance companies. Once this was determined, the court imposed liability for bad faith tort damages.

Other courts have found that there is no private right of action under comparable state statutes.[71] Many states which have enacted their own

---

67 A good discussion of the origin of the act can be found in Casamassima, Aronson & Marchetti, *Extra Contractual Damage,* THE LAW OF SURETYSHIP (2d ed. 2000) and Egan, *"Dispute Resolution,"* TIPS Fidelity and Surety Law Committee, Mid-Winter Meeting, 1995.

68 Earth Scientists, Ltd. v. United States Fidelity & Guaranty Co., 619 F. Supp. 1465 (D. Kan. 1985) lists a number of states which have enacted some legislation. The case also cited to Houser, *The Unfair Claims Settlement Practices Act*, 15 FORUM 336 (1979).

69 Holmgren v. State Farm Mutual Auto Ins. Co., 976 F. 2d 573 (9th Cir. 1992); Maher v. Continental Cas. Co., 76 F. 3d 535 (4th Cir. 1996) (applying West Virginia law).

70 231 Mont. 461, 754 P.2d 502 (Mont. 1988).

71 Hipsky v. Allstate Ins. Co., 304 F. Supp. 2d 284 (D. Conn. 2004); Anderson v. Lancaster Aviation, Inc., 220 F. Supp. 2d 524 (N.D. N.C.

versions of the model UCSPA fail to mention surety claims. However, a surety should be mindful of these claims handling procedures. In general, compliance with the state regulatory process governing settlement practices requires a state-by-state analysis. Accordingly, the insurance code for the applicable states should be reviewed to determine whether a UCSPA enacted in a particular state would apply to sureties and whether there is a private right of action for breach of the statutory prohibitions.

II. Fraudulent Or Illegal Activities Of The Principal

A. *Fraud Committed on the Surety*

A question that may arise under the terms of performance bond is whether the commission of fraud upon the surety renders the performance bond void or voidable. The Restatement provides that, if the obligee secures the surety bond through a material or fraudulent misrepresentation, the surety bond is voidable.[72] However, if the principal engages in fraud or misrepresentation leading to the execution of the surety bond, the bond is voidable *unless* the obligee gives value or materially relies on the bond in good faith and without knowledge of the misrepresentation.[73] The court in *American Manufacturing Mutual Insurance Co. v. Tison Hog Market, Inc.* applied these concepts.[74] Two livestock dealers obtained a surety bond under the Packers and Stockyards Act of 1921.[75] Prior to issuing the bonds, the surety sought indemnification agreements which allegedly were signed by various individuals. With the bonds in hand, the dealers bought livestock from a variety of suppliers but failed to pay as agreed. The suppliers then filed claims against the surety bonds.

When presented with the claims, the surety conducted an investigation and learned that the indemnity agreements had been forged. The surety thereafter filed an action seeking a declaratory judgment that

---

2002); Crawford v. Guide One Mut. Ins. Co., 420 F. Supp. 2d 584 (N.D. Tex. 2006); Julian v. New Hampshire Ins. Co., 694 F. Supp. 1530 (D. Wyo. 1988); Strack v. Westfield Co., 515 N.E.2d 1005 (Ohio 1986).
72 RESTATEMENT THIRD, SURETYSHIP AND GUARANTY § 12(1).
73 RESTATEMENT THIRD, SURETYSHIP AND GUARANTY § 12(2).
74 182 F. 3d 1284 (11th Cir. 1999).
75 7 U.S.C. § 181 *et seq.*

it was not liable under the bonds. After addressing the issue of jurisdiction, the court ruled:

> It is well established under common law of suretyship that fraud or misrepresentation practiced by the principal alone on the surety, without any knowledge or participation on the part of the creditor or obligee, in inducing the surety to enter into a suretyship contract will not affect the liability of the surety.

On this basis, the court held that the surety could not avoid liability under the surety bonds.

In *Commercial Money Center, Inc. v. Illinois Union Insurance Co.*,[76] an equipment leasing business had been structured in the form of a Ponzi-type scheme since several leases were nonexistent. Various banks had advanced significant sums secured by the alleged lease payments and insurance companies provided assurances of payment on the leases. Sureties had issued "lease bonds" naming the leasing business as the obligee. One of the primary legal issues was whether the business arrangements amounted to a surety relationship. The court found that, even though the papers identified the relationship as one of insurance, a review of the overall transaction showed that a surety relationship had been established as a matter of law.[77] The court held:

> The finding of a suretyship is significant in this case because "[t]he rule is well established and generally followed that fraud of the principal debtor will not relieve the guarantor or surety who acted at the request of the debtor from liability, if the creditor did not have notice of the fraud and did not participate therein." [Citations omitted][78]

The court in *National Union Fire Insurance Co. v. Robuck* reached a similar conclusion.[79] A contract was written to sell certain property for the construction of a shopping center in Florida. The agreement provided for a down payment and future periodic payments secured by a note and mortgage. The buyer was required to provide the sellers with a surety bond for completion of the shopping center. The buyer had used the

---

76 508 F. 3d 327 (6th Cir. 2007).
77 *Id*. at 341-42.
78 *Id*. at 342.
79 203 So. 2d 204 (Ct. App. Fla. 1967).

same surety for prior bonds. In order to secure this new bond, the contractor presented the surety with a forged construction contract. The surety conducted no investigation to determine the validity of the contract and issued the bond. Using the bond, the buyer bought the property and secured a loan for the cost of construction. The contractor began the work but soon ran into financial difficulties. Ultimately, the contractor abandoned the project. The obligee and various claimants filed suit against the surety under both the performance and payment bonds. As a defense, the surety contended that the bonds were void due to the fraud committed against it. The court rejected this defense and entered summary judgment in favor of the claimants. The surety appealed. The appellate court affirmed:

> This holding is often explained on the ground that where one of two innocent parties must suffer from the fraud of another, the loss must be born by the one who through his negligence or misplaced confidence has enabled the third-party to consummate the fraud.[80]

The court found that its holding was consistent with prior rulings in which the bond obligation was deemed unenforceable when the obligee had participated in the wrongdoing.[81] Both of these holdings were consistent with the Restatement Third of Suretyship and Guaranty, Section 12.

B. Penalties/Punitive Damages

Another means of imposing liability on a surety beyond specific terms of the bond is through the imposition of liability for penalties or exemplary damages. The Restatement discusses this issue:

> When the secondary obligation is a legally mandated bond, that obligation does not include any penalties imposed on the principal obligor for failure to fulfill the underlying obligation unless the secondary obligation so provides.[82]

---

80 *Id.* at 206.
81 Lambert v. Heaton, 134 So. 2d 536 (App. Fla. 1961).
82 RESTATEMENT THIRD OF SURETYSHIP AND GUARANTY, § 73.

A number of courts have adopted this provision in a variety of contexts. In *C & I Steel LLC v. Travelers Casualty & Surety Co. of America*,[83] the public owner had awarded a contract to construct a middle school. As required by state law, the contractor provided a surety bond in the penal sum of the contract.[84] The terms of the bond required the surety to pay for labor, materials and equipment furnished in performance of the construction contract. The subcontractor provided structural steel for the project, and numerous disputes arose on the project concerning extra work, back charges and delays. The subcontractor filed suit against the contractor, the architect and the surety. Under the terms of an arbitration clause, the contractor stayed the judicial proceeding and compelled arbitration. Pursuant to the stay, the subcontractor demanded arbitration but named only the contractor to that proceeding. While the surety knew of the arbitration, it did not participate. In the arbitration, the panel awarded contract damages and imposed exemplary or punitive damages pursuant to a Massachusetts statute.[85] The award was confirmed against both the contractor and the surety. The surety opposed the motion to confirm the amount claiming that it was not liable for punitive damages assessed against its principal and that punitive damages were not covered by the bond.[86]

Observing that the Restatement reflected the well-established law in Massachusetts, the court stated:

> By its terms, then, the bond did not cover punitive damages, a payment of which is payment for punishment, not for "labor, materials, and equipment." [Citations omitted] To conclude that the bond encompassed punitive damages would be to rewrite the agreement Travelers made with Peabody and to risk diluting through punitive awards to a few subcontractors and material men the "security to [all] subcontractors and material men on public works." [Citations omitted]

The court noted, however, that the surety was neither immune to punitive damages nor immune to claims arising from its own misdeeds.[87]

---

83 70 Mass. App. Ct. 653; 2007 Mass. App. LEXIS 1188 (Nov. 6, 2007).
84 *Id.*
85 MASS. GEN. L., § 93 A.
86 *Id.*
87 *Id.*

The court in *North Marion School District v. Acstar Insurance Co.* reached a similar result.[88] The school district hired a general contractor for a public improvement and the general contractor obtained a surety bond pursuant to the state law. The general contractor engaged a subcontractor which provided surety bonds to the general contractor for its work. The subcontractor became financially insolvent and could not pay its employees. The surety paid the wages to the employees but not on a timely basis. The employees presented claims against the surety pursuant to a state law that required the timely payment of wages. If the wages were not paid in a timely fashion, liability under the statute could be imposed for "penalty wages," liquidated damages and attorneys fees.[89]

The surety paid all of the actual wages but refused to pay the statutory penalties. The trial court upheld that course of action, and the plaintiff/employees appealed. In its analysis, the appellate court stated that the determination was one of statutory construction.[90] The court noted that penalty wages under the statute are not the same as wages that are earned for work performed by the employee. Accordingly, the court observed that "penalty wages, as a matter of law, cannot be payment for labor supplied for the prosecution of the work in a public contract and cannot be recovered against a surety under ORS 279.526 under such a theory."[91] The court used a similar analysis to reject claims for payments of prevailing wages and liquidated damages.

Courts have followed this same approach to assess claims under surety bonds issued in areas outside of construction projects. For example, in *Pennsylvania Turnpike Comm'n v. United States Fidelity & Guarantee Co.*,[92] a member of the Pennsylvania Turnpike Commission was indicted, tried and convicted for conspiracy as a result of actions while in office. Pursuant to Pennsylvania law, surety bonds had been provided for the commission member as a result of the various offices that he held. After his conviction, the commission filed suit against the former commissioner as well as his surety to recover the penal sum of

---

88   205 Ore. App. 484; 136 P. 3d 42; 2006 Ore. App. LEXIS 557 (May 3, 2006).
89   *Id.*
90   *Id.*
91   *Id.*
92   412 Pa. 222; 194 A. 2d 423 (1963).

the various bonds. The trial court denied the claim, and the appellate court upheld this denial. The appellate court stated that "the majority of decisions on this question uniformly hold that the liability of a surety on an official bond is limited to the actual damages sustained."[93]

In *Butler v. United Pacific Insur. Co.*[94] the Oregon Supreme Court upheld a similar ruling denying liability to a surety under an automobile dealer's bond. The court said that the general rule is that "a surety is liable only for the payment of actual damages caused by the principal, and may not be held for exemplary or punitive damages, in the absence of any statutory provision imposing such liability."[95] Similar rulings have been issued in Alabama,[96] Arizona,[97] Connecticut,[98] Florida,[99] Kansas,[100] Kentucky,[101] Mississippi,[102] Missouri,[103] Nevada,[104] North Dakota,[105] Ohio,[106] Oklahoma,[107] and Texas.[108]

III. Tort Claims Against The Principal

Another way to extend the potential claims against a surety beyond the "four corners" of the bond is to assert liability for *all* damages caused by

---

93 *Id.*
94 265 Ore. 473; 509 P. 2d 1184 (1973).
95 *Id.*
96 Bull v. Albright, 254 Ala. 29; 37 So. 2d 266 (1950).
97 Rogers v. Speros Constr. Co., Inc., 119 Ariz. 289; 580 P.2d 750 (1978).
98 Ames v. Comm'r of Motor Vehicles, 267 Conn. 524; 839 A.2d 1250 (2004).
99 Amer. Home Assur. Co. v. Larkin Gen. Hosp., Ltd., 593 So. 2d 195 (Fla. 1992).
100 Smith v. Merchants Mut. Bonding Co., 211 Kan. 397; 507 P.2d 1989 (1973).
101 Growbarger v. U.S. Fid. & Guar. Co., 126 Ky. 118; 102 S.W. 873 (1907).
102 U.S. Fid. & Guar. Co. v. State for Use and Benefit of Stringfellow, 254 Miss. 812, 182 So.2d 919 (Miss. 1966).
103 Coates v. U.S. Fid. & Guar. Co., 525 S.W. 2d 654 (Mo. App. 1975).
104 The New Hampshire Ins. Co. v. Gruhn, 99 Nev. 771; 670 P.2d 941 (1983).
105 Yesel v. Watson, 58 N.D. 524; 226 N.W. 624 (1929).
106 Troyer v. Horvath, 13 Ohio App. 3d 155; 468 N.E. 2d 351 (Ct. App. Ohio 1983).
107 Stumpf v. Pederson, 180 Okla. 408; 70 P. 2d 101 (1937).
108 Dawson v. Reliance Ins. Co., 482 S.W. 2d 882 (Tex. App. 1972).

the contractor performing work on the project. Such damages could include tort claims against the principal performing work on the project. Case law, however, does not extend the liability of a surety bond to cover such tort claims. The policy supporting this determination is that, while surety bonds are read broadly to provide relief to the designated or intended beneficiaries, there is a limit beyond which the bond coverage should not run.

An example of this holding is found in *Long v. City of Midway*.[109] The city issued a contract for the construction of a water distribution system. As required by state law, a surety bond was provided guaranteeing completion of the work and payment of the various claimants providing labor or materials for the project. The principal defaulted on the contract, and the surety undertook completion of the work. While the work was being performed, the contractor caused damages to the adjacent property owner by causing a flood and interrupting the business for an excessive period of time.[110] The liability of the surety was premised solely upon the issuance of the bond, and the claimant admitted that the contractor's negligence was the cause of the damage to the property. The court held that the purpose of the bond was to protect the obligee through the performance bond and to satisfy legitimate claims of third-parties which had provided labor or materials to complete the project. The claimant fell into neither category.

The court noted that the purpose of the statutory bond was to provide protection for those who did not have a right to file lien claims against public projects. While the coverage afforded by this bond through the statute was extensive, it had its limits. In dismissing the claim, the court explained:

> If this court were to extend the coverage of such bonds to cover claims by third-party tort claimants for damage either to person or property, it would have the affect of allowing personal injury or property damages claimants to compete with or exhaust funds designated to guarantee the payments for labor for material arising out of public contract. They conclude that unless the surety contracts expressly provide for a third-party liability coverage, third-party claimants such as Long should look

---

109   169 Ga. App. 72; 311 S.E. 2d 508 (Ct. App. Ga. 1983).
110   *Id.*

to coverage under liability insurance to be provided by the contractor, a contractual requirement imposed on Van's in this case.[111]

The court reached a similar conclusion in *Tri-State Ins. Co. v. United States*, where a property owner sued for damages sustained when lateral support was removed in the course of an excavation for a public structure.[112] A contract was issued to build a church, and a surety bond was provided for the project. The scope of the work included certain excavation which removed the lateral support for adjoining land. While the parties agreed that the damage occurred, the issue before the court was the scope of the protection afforded by the surety bond. In dismissing the claims, the court gave the following analysis:

> A bond given by appellant ensured to Baptist and the mortgage lender the performance of Building's contract and all cost and damage suffered by these obligees from a breach thereof. It also gave a direct right of action on the bond to any laborer or material men for claims arising under the contract. The bond does not specify that its coverage is to operate as an all risks policy of public liability insurance for the benefit of tort claimants such as appellee.[113]

In these cases, the courts examined the scope of the bond and the intended beneficiaries of the instrument. Absent language that would expand the definition of claims to include unidentified third-parties who have suffered tort losses, surety bonds are not read to provide such extended coverage.

IV. Tax Obligations of the Principal

A. *Miller Act Bonds*

The liability of a Miller Act performance bond surety for the principal's unpaid federal withholding tax obligations is codified in 40 U.S.C. § 3131(c).[114] Prior to 1966 and the passage of the Federal Tax Lien Act,

---

111 *Id.*
112 340 F. 2d 542 (8th Cir. 1965).
113 *Id.*
114 The citation to the Miller Act changed from 30 U.S.C. § 279 to 40 U.S.C.§ 3131 in August 2002.

the surety generally prevailed in cases where the government argued that Miller Act performance bonds covered withholding taxes. *See, e.g. United States Fidelity & Guaranty Co. v. United States*,[115] where the Court of Appeals for the Tenth Circuit held that the employer alone was liable for withholding taxes. In its analysis, the court explained:

> ... no case to which our attention has been called goes so far as to hold that an employer's tax liability is within the provision of the bond merely because wages were used in paying the employee's tax liability and creating that of the employer.[116]

The Federal Tax Lien Act, which applies to all contracts entered into pursuant to invitations for bids issued after June 30, 1967, amended the Miller Act by adding the following provision:

> Every performance bond required under this section specifically shall provide coverage for taxes the Government imposes which are collected, deducted, or withheld from wages the contractor pays in carrying out the contract with respect to which the bond is furnished.[117]

With this modification of the Miller Act, the performance bond surety became statutorily liable for the principal's unpaid federal withholding taxes.[118] At least one court has held that a Miller Act *payment* bond surety may also be held liable for interest and penalties on the unpaid federal withholding taxes.[119] As for the remaining contract proceeds, a Miller Act performance bond surety that takes over a project from a defaulting principal *and* pays for the completion of the project, is entitled to those proceeds free from setoff for the principal's unpaid taxes, including withholding taxes.[120]

---

115 201 F.2d 118 (10th Cir. 1952).
116 *Id.* at 120-21.
117 40 U.S.C. § 3131(c)(1).
118 United States v. Fid. & Deposit Co. of Md., 690 F. Supp. 905 (D. Haw. 1988); 17 AM. JUR. 2d CONTRACTORS' BONDS § 158 (1990); Katzman, *Type of Claims Covered,* in THE LAW OF PAYMENT BONDS 47 (Lybeck & Shreves, eds., 1998).
119 United States v. Am. Mfr. Mut. Cas. Co., 901 F.2d 370, 373 (4th Cir. 1990).
120 Morrison Assur. Co. v. United States, 3 Cl. Ct. 626 (Cl. Ct. 1983); *but see*, Dependable Ins. Co. v. United States, 846 F.2d 65 (Fed. Cir. 1988)

In the analysis of the surety's potential liability, a distinction is drawn between an action to *collect unpaid taxes* from the surety, and efforts to *set off the unpaid taxes* against the contract proceeds. In attempting to collect from the performance bond surety, the Miller Act has several requirements. The government must give notice to the surety of the unpaid taxes within 90 days after the principal files a return, or, in any event, no later than 180 days from the date the principal should have filed the return.[121] Suit to collect these amounts must be filed within one year of the notice.[122] Given the fact that with proper notice to the surety, unpaid withholding taxes are statutorily recoverable under the performance bond, attempts to set off the principal's unpaid taxes against the contract proceeds could be the result of the government's failure to comply with the notice requirements.[123]

B. Little Miller Act Bonds

The provisions of Little Miller Act bonds, in contrast, vary among the states as to whether the completing performance bond surety takes the remaining contract balance free from setoff for the principal's unpaid state taxes. Alabama, New Jersey and Texas, for example, have chosen to follow the federal Miller Act and hold that the completing performance bond surety takes the remaining contract balance free from setoff.[124] Other jurisdictions have reached the opposite result.

(holding that a surety's status as a Miller Act performance bond surety on one project did not give the surety the right to take the contract balance of a separate project free from setoff for taxes).

121 40 U.S.C. § 3131(c)(2).
122 40 U.S.C. § 3131(c)(3).
123 In *Morrison Assurance Co.*, 3 Cl. Ct. at 626, although not specifically discussed, it appears that the IRS did not give timely notice to the surety of the principal's delinquent taxes. If the IRS had given timely notice of the tax delinquency, it may have been able to recover the tax delinquency from the surety for the reasons set forth in *Fidelity & Deposit Co. of Md.*, 690 F.Supp. at 905. Instead, the IRS attempted to set off the principal's past due taxes against the contract retainage, but because the surety had taken over the project and completed construction, the IRS was not entitled to the retainage.
124 *See* Alabama v. Bessemer Materials, Inc., 224 F.Supp. 182 (N.D. Ala. 1963); New Amsterdam Cas. Co. v. Bd. of Educ., 193 F.Supp. 305 (D.

In *Hartford Accident & Indemnity Co. v. Arizona Dept. of Transportation*,[125] a case decided pursuant to Arizona's Little Miller Act, the court held that a performance bond surety on a road construction contract that completed a contract for its defaulting principal was liable for the principal's unpaid unemployment insurance taxes and that the state was permitted to set off the unpaid taxes against unpaid contract funds. The surety argued that the court should follow the cases decided under the federal Miller Act and allow the completing performance surety to take contract funds free of setoff for the principal's unpaid taxes.[126] The court rejected this argument, holding that the Arizona Little Miller Act requires that the bond be conditioned on the full performance of the contract, which contract required the principal to pay all taxes.[127]

In *Safeco Insurance Co. v. State of New York*,[128] the court created a hybrid approach. The court of claims held that the state could not set off the principal's unpaid sales and use tax against contract funds payable to the performance bond surety that completed the project for a defaulting principal where those funds represented work completed subsequent to the contractor's default. The state could, however, set off the unpaid taxes against retainage being held on work that was completed by the principal prior to default.[129]

N.J. 1961); Liberty Mut. Ins. Co. v. Sharp, 874 S.W.2d 736, 738, n.2 (Tex. Ct. App. 1994).

125   838 P.2d 1325 (Ariz. Ct. App. 1992).
126   *Id.* at 1328. *See also In re* CQ Piping Installations, Inc., 225 B.R. 553 (Bankr. E.D.N.Y. 1998) (holding that the Dormitory Authority of the State of New York is not entitled to setoff debts owed to the state, as the Dormitory Authority is a public benefit corporation and not the state itself).
127   *Hartford Accident*, 838 P.2d at 1329 (the court relied heavily on Employment Security Comm'n v. C. R. Davis Contracting Co., 462 P. 2d 608 (N.M. 1969)).
128   392 N.Y.S.2d 976 (N.Y. Ct. Cl. 1977).
129   *Id. See also* Reliance Ins. Co. v. Kentucky, 576 S.W.2d 231 (Ky. Ct. App. 1978) (holding that the state could set off detailing contractors' unpaid taxes and unemployment insurance against contract funds earned prior to the default but which had not yet been disbursed).

V. Interest and Attorney Fees

A. *Interest*

Judicial or post-judgment interest on *judgments* against sureties is payable at the applicable rate, based on the specific statutes governing the jurisdiction. Courts addressing the liability of a surety for *prejudgment interest* under the terms of the performance bond have reached different conclusions.[130] Historically, courts have recognized the government's common law right to recover prejudgment interest on contract claims.[131] The award of prejudgment interest is an issue decided as a matter of law and is usually committed to the sound discretion of the trial court.[132] In a number of instances, courts have been willing to assess prejudgment interest against a performance bond surety.[133] The date the interest begins to run is also an issue where the courts differ.

In *United States v. Seaboard Surety Co.*,[134] the District Court for the Eastern District of New York awarded prejudgment interest on a defaulted contract against two performance bond sureties from the date the sureties denied liability under their bond. In reversing, the Second Circuit concluded that the lower court's calculation of prejudgment interest was an abuse of discretion, noting, "From the government's perspective, it was harmed only insofar as it was forced to pay for completion that should have been financed by proceeds from the bond. Interest, therefore, cannot be assessed prior to the date the government began paying to complete the . . . project."[135] In Arizona, the supreme

---

130 Contracts and bonds that are silent on the interest issue require an examination of the respective state's case law and statutes governing awards of interest on contract claims to determine whether a particular court may assess prejudgment interest against a performance bond surety.
131 Royal Indemnity Co. v. United States, 313 U.S. 289 (1941); Billings v. United States, 232 U.S. 261 (1914).
132 United States *ex rel.* Maris Equip. Co. v. Morganti, Inc., 175 F. Supp. 2d 458, 460 (E.D.N.Y. 2001); *Royal Indemnity Co.*, 313 U.S. at 296.
133 *See, e.g., Maris*, 175 F. Supp. 2d 458; Ins. Co. of N. Am. v. United States, 951 F.2d 1244 (1991); Summit Contractors v. United States, 21 Cl. Ct. 767 (1990); United States v. Am. Mfr. Mut. Cas. Co., 901 F.2d 370 (4th Cir. 1990).
134 817 F. 2d 956 (2d Cir. 1987).
135 *Id.* at 965.

court ruled that the performance bond surety is liable for interest from the date the sums become due,[136] not the date the complaint is filed. In Illinois, the interest runs from the date of the filing.[137] In Colorado, interest is recoverable from the surety only from the time of notice and demand.[138] If demand is not made prior to the filing of the claim, the date of filing becomes the date of demand.[139]

Another issue is whether an award of prejudgment interest will increase the surety's potential liability beyond the penal sum of the bond. The surety views the penal sum of the bond as the limit of its exposure. Some courts agree,[140] but others do not. Further, in an early decision the United States Supreme Court upheld the assessment of interest beyond the penal sum of a surety bond under certain circumstances.[141]

Courts have found that a surety may be held liable for prejudgment interest beyond the penal sum of the bond for various reasons. Interest may be awarded if the surety refuses to promptly pay the claims of the obligee, as the interest begins to run from the time the principal defaults, or demand has been made for payment.[142] Prejudgment interest above the penal sum of the bond has also been allowed where the surety delays payment after proper notification of its liability.[143] The court in *Insurance Co. of North America v. United States* explained the rationale for this rule: "[i]f a surety's obligation to pay only arose upon conclusion of lawsuits, the creditor would lose a significant part of the protection it bargains to obtain."[144] As observed by another court, the assessment of

---

136   Webb v. Crane Co., 80 P.2d 698 (Ariz. 1938).
137   Fisher v. Fid. & Deposit Co., 466 N.E.2d 332 (Ill. Ct. App. 1984).
138   Autocon Indus., Inc. v. Western States Constr. Co., 782 P.2d 372 (Colo. Ct. App. 1986).
139   *Id.* at 376.
140   *See, e.g.,* Polk v. Amer. Cas. Co., 816 S.W.2d 178 (Ky. 1991).
141   United States v. U.S. Fid. & Guar. Co., 236 U.S. 512 (1915).
142   Seattle-First Nat'l Bank v. Aetna Life & Cas. Co., 642 P.2d 1259 (Wash. Ct. App. 1982).
143   *See* Ins. Co. of N. Am. v. United States, 951 F.2d 1244 (Fed. Cir. 1991); Clarkstown v. N. River Ins. Co., 803 F. Supp. 827 (S.D.N.Y. 1992); *cf.* Morse/Diesel, Inc. v. Trinity Industries, Inc., 875 F.Supp. 165 (when it is not clear that the principal has been defaulted, and it cannot be shown that there was a clear date on which the surety was aware of and wrongfully ignored a mature obligation to pay, no prejudgment interest is available).
144   *Ins. Co. of N. Am.*, 951 F.2d at 1246.

prejudgment interest "merely compensates the creditor for the surety's use of the money already due."[145] Prejudgment interest beyond the penal sum may also be awarded by statute. Such is the case in Missouri "if the principal is found liable and/or the surety litigates the issue of liability."[146]

Unliquidated claims for damages ordinarily do not result in the assessment of prejudgment interest,[147] but in *Tonkin v. Bob Eldridge Constr. Co.*[148] such interest was awarded because the surety's failure to pay was "unreasonable and vexatious."[149] A few jurisdictions hold that an award of prejudgment interest in a contract action involving *liquidated* sums is mandatory, not discretionary.[150]

B. Attorney Fees

Generally, attorney fees cannot be recovered from the performance bond surety if they exceed the penal sum of the bond.[151] However, if the surety is found to have acted in bad faith or to have violated some specific statutory provision, courts may allow claims for attorney fees against the surety.[152] In *Tonkin v. Bob Eldridge Constr. Co.*,[153] the court held that a performance bond surety was liable for attorney fees under a Kansas statute penalizing an insurer for failure to pay a claim without just cause.

---

145 *Id.*
146 MO. ANN. STAT. 408.020.
147 *See, e.g.,* City of Milwaukee v. Cement Div., Nat'l Gypsum Co., 515 U.S. 189, 197 (1995); Continental Bk. & Tr. Co. v. Amer. Bonding Co., 630 F.2d 606 (8th Cir. 1980).
148 808 S.W.2d 849 (Mo. Ct. App. 1991) (applying Kansas statutory law).
149 *Id.* at 855.
150 *See, e.g.,* Amtote Int'l, Inc. v. PNGI Charles Town Gaming, Inc., 66 F. Supp. 2d 782 (N.D. W.Va 1999) (applying West Virginia law); Turner Constr. Co. v. First Indem. of Am. Ins. Co., 829 F.Supp. 752 (E.D. Pa. 1993) (applying Pennsylvania law).
151 *See, e.g.,* Nat'l Technical Sys. v. Superior Court, 97 Cal. App. 4th 415 (2002); Guardianship of Davison v. Aetna Life and Cas. Co., 642 P.2d 1259 (Wash. Ct. App. 1982); *contra* Iowa Concrete Breaking Corp. v. Jewat Trucking Inc., 444 N.W.2d 865 (Minn. Ct. App. 1989).
152 *Davison*, 642 P.2d at 1259. For a complete discussion of bad faith and recoverable damages, see Section I on bad faith, *supra.*
153 808 S.W.2d at 849.

"Without just cause" was held to be determinable by the finder of fact according to the particular circumstances of a given case.

The leading case denying the recovery of attorney fees against a surety (specifically, a Miller Act surety) is *F. D. Rich Co. v. United States ex rel. Industrial Lumber Co.*[154] In *F. D. Rich*, the Supreme Court held that attorney fees were not recoverable because the Miller Act did not expressly provide for the recovery of attorney fees. Although the case involved a payment bond, the same legal principles and analysis should apply to claims against performance bonds. For bonds not governed by the Miller Act,[155] courts look to applicable state law on the issue of the recovery of attorney fees against the surety, and have at times awarded fees where the state law provides for such recovery.[156]

Some states have implemented statutes providing for the recovery of attorney fees against a performance bond surety.[157] Other state statutes only provide for the recovery of attorney fees when the surety has acted in bad faith or vexatiously in refusing to pay the claim.[158] A few state statutes provide for the recovery of attorney fees as a percentage of the claim.[159] To analyze the exposure of a surety to attorney fees, consideration should be given to the applicable statutes, including public work statutes, building construction statutes, insurance statutes, and general litigation fee shifting statutes. Some courts will award attorney fees where the underlying contract provides for the recovery of attorney fees and the bond is conditioned upon the contractor performing all terms

---

154 417 U.S. 116 (1974).
155 *See, e.g.,* United States *ex rel.* Vulcan Materials v. Volpe Constr., 622 F.2d 880 (5th Cir. 1980).
156 *Id.*
157 *See, e.g.,* ARK. CODE ANN. §23-79-208; ARIZ. REV. STAT. §34-222-B; FLA. STAT. §§255.05, 627.428, 627.756; IDAHO CODE §§54-1929, 41-1839; KAN. STAT. ANN. §40-256; LA. REV. STAT. 22:658; MINN. STAT. §574.26; MO. ANN. STAT. §375.420; MONT. CODE ANN. §18-2-207, 33-1-616; NEB. REV. STAT. § 44-359; N.C. GEN. STAT. §44A-35; OR. REV. STAT. §742.061.
158 GA. CODE ANN. §10-7-30; 215 ILL. COMP. STAT. 5/155; MO. ANN. STAT. §375.420; MONT. CODE ANN. §33-1-616; VA. CODE ANN. §38.2-209.
159 ARK. CODE ANN. §23-79-208; ALA. RULES OF CIV. P. 82.

under the contract,[160] while some will only award attorney fees if the bond expressly obligates the surety to pay such fees.[161]

The Texas Supreme Court held in *Great American Insurance Co. v. North Austin Municipal Utility District No. 1* that the performance bond surety cannot be held liable for attorney fees resulting from the principal's breach of the contract where the fees would exceed the penal sum of the bond, unless the contract specifically provides otherwise.[162] The court did, however, find the surety liable for attorney fees resulting from its own breach of the performance bond.[163] Nearly a century ago, the United States Supreme Court reached the same conclusion in *United States v. United States Fidelity & Guaranty Co.*,[164] holding the surety "liable for its own default in unjustly withholding payment after being notified of the default of the principal."[165]

Relying on the Florida statute on attorney fees, the Supreme Court of Florida took the opposite approach in *Trans Coastal Roofing Co. v. David Boland, Inc.*[166] After a jury found the surety and the principal jointly and severally liable to the plaintiff for $31,654.42 in compensatory damages, the district court awarded the plaintiff an additional $357,121.52 in attorney fees. Since the performance bond's penal sum was only $167,800, the district court limited the plaintiff's recovery to that amount. The plaintiff appealed to the Eleventh Circuit, claiming that the applicable Florida statute[167] providing for attorney fees to a prevailing plaintiff did not limit recovery to the penal sum of the bond.[168] The surety responded by arguing that its liability could only exceed the penal sum if the plaintiff could show misconduct by the

---

160 *See* Austin v. Parker, 672 F.2d 508 (5th Cir. 1982); Mason v. City of Albertville, 158 So. 2d 924 (Ala. 1963).
161 *See, e.g.,* J.K. Tomlinson v. Century Eng'g & Constr., Inc., 777 F.2d 918 (4th Cir. 1985).
162 908 S.W.2d 415 (Tex. 1995).
163 *Id.* at 427.
164 236 U.S. 512 (1915).
165 *Id.* at 530-31.
166 851 So. 2d 724 (Fla. 2003) (answering certified question from the 11th Circuit case *Trans Coastal Roofing Co. v. David Boland Inc.*, 309 F.3d 758 (11th Cir. 2002)).
167 FLA. STAT. § 627.428 (2002).
168 309 F.3d at 760-61.

surety.[169] The Eleventh Circuit certified the question to the Supreme Court of Florida. The Florida Supreme Court found that while it had previously found that pursuant to statute attorney fees were limited to the penal sum for a guardianship bond surety absent misconduct by the surety, no such limitation existed with respect to performance bonds. The court found that the surety's liability for compensatory damages was limited to the performance bond's penal sum, but held that Florida's statute allowed recovery of attorney fees beyond the penal limit even in the absence of misconduct by the surety.[170]

In *Boliver v. Surety Co. of the Pacific*,[171] the defendant performance bond surety appealed an award of $2,395 in damages and $1,000 in attorney fees. The surety had issued two separate performance bonds to the plaintiff each in the amount of $2,500. Taken together, the award of $3,395 in damages and fees exceeded the $2,500 penal sum of each performance bond. The surety argued that the plaintiff's total award of attorney fees should be limited to $105–the difference between the $2,395 in damages and the $2,500 penal limit.[172] The court rejected the surety's position, holding the penal sum of the bonds were to be considered together. Since the $3,395 award did not exceed the $5,000 *combined* penal sum, the court refused to reduce the judgment against the surety.[173]

---

169 *Id.* at 761.
170 *Boland*, 851 So. 2d at 727.
171 72 Cal. App. 3d Supp. 22 (1977).
172 *Id.* at 34.
173 *Id.*

VI. Liability for Environmental Claims[174]

A. Federal Statutes Governing Hazardous Materials and Environmental Degradation

The three federal statutes that may expose a surety to liability for environmental claims are the Comprehensive Environmental Response, Compensation and Liability Act of 1980 ("CERCLA") (as amended by Superfund Amendments and Reauthorization Act of 1986 ("SARA")[175]), the Resource Conservation and Recovery Act ("RCRA")[176] and the Surface Mining Control and Reclamation Act ("SMCRA").[177]

CERCLA was enacted to prevent the spread of hazardous materials from abandoned waste sites by imposing liability for the cleanup costs on the party or parties responsible for the contamination. CERCLA, as amended by SARA, enumerates potentially responsible parties ("PRPs") as: (1) the owner and operator of any facility used for the disposal of hazardous substances; (2) any person who at the time of disposal of any hazardous substance owned or operated any facility at which the substance was disposed of; (3) any person who arranged for disposal or treatment, or arranged for transport for disposal or treatment, of hazardous substances; and (4) any person who accepts or accepted any hazardous substances for transport to disposal or treatment facilities, incineration vessels or sites from which there is a release or a threatened

---

[174] For a detailed discussion of potential surety liabilities for environmental issues, see THE SURETY'S ENVIRONMENTAL RISK (Donald G. Gavin & Robert M. Wright eds., Tort & Ins. Practice Section, Am. Bar Ass'n 1997); Welge et al., *Good News for Sureties? Sharing the Risk: A Discussion of Joint and Several Liability, and Contribution Under CERCLA*, (National Bond Claims Association 1996); *Environmental Construction: Market or Minefield?*, unpublished paper (TIPS Fidelity and Surety Law Committee, Mid-Winter Meeting 1994); Shreves et al., *Liability of Sureties Under CERCLA and RCRA*, (Defense Research Institute Fidelity & Surety Committee, Chicago, May 10, 1991); and Manko, *Surety's Exposure to Environmental Claims Against Construction Contractors*, (Surety Claims Institute 1989).
[175] 42 U.S.C. § 9601 *et seq.*
[176] 42 U.S.C. § 6901 *et seq.*
[177] 30 U.S.C. § 1202 *et seq.*

release of a hazardous substance.[178] Courts have liberally construed CERCLA in order to achieve its objectives. [179]

Congress enacted RCRA to promote the protection of health and the environment and to conserve valuable material and energy resources.[180] RCRA differs from CERCLA in that it covers (1) "hazardous waste" (a subset of hazardous substances, which are regulated by CERCLA); (2) regulation of solid and hazardous waste activities including the generation and disposal of hazardous waste from "the cradle to the grave"; (3) the permitting scheme for facilities that treat, store and dispose of hazardous waste ("TSD" facilities); and (4) the regulation of underground storage tanks ("USTs") containing hazardous waste.[181] Under RCRA, any past or present generator or transporter of waste, or any past or present owner or operator of the facility at which waste is disposed, may be liable.

The intent of SMCRA is to provide protection against environmental degradation from coal mining while ensuring an adequate supply of coal to meet the nation's energy requirements.[182] SMRCA requires strip-mined land be reclaimed for post-mining use as soon as is practicable.[183] Under SMCRA, before surface mining operations can begin, the contractor must submit and have approved a permit for the work.[184] After the permit is approved but before it will be issued, the applicant must provide a performance bond.[185]

---

178 42 U.S.C. § 9607(a); *see also Shreves et al., supra* note 174.
179 Kaiser Aluminum & Chemical Corp. v. Vetalis Development Corp., 976 F.2d 1338 (9th Cir. 1992); Brookfield-North Riverside Water Comm'n v. Martin Oil Marketing, Inc., 1992 U.S. Dist. LEXIS 2920, 1992 WL 63274 (N.D. Ill., March 10, 1992).
180 *See* 42 U.S.C. § 6902.
181 42 U.S.C. § 6901 *et seq.*
182 30 U.S.C. § 1202(a),(f).
183 30 U.S.C. § 1202.
184 30 C.F.R. § 773.11.
185 30 C.F.R. § 800.11; *see also* Pennsylvania Fed'n of Sportsmen's Clubs, Inc. v. Kempthorne, 497 F.3d 337, 340-41 (3d Cir. 2007); West Virginia Highlands Conservancy v. Norton, 238 F.Supp. 2d 761, 763 (4th Cir. 2003).

1. Liability Under CERCLA

If a surety bonds a contractor for work at a conventional non-hazardous waste construction site at which the contractor discovers hazardous waste and ultimately defaults, the terms of the bond may require the surety to (1) complete the work, (2) finance the principal to complete the work, or (3) hire a third-party completion contractor to conclude the work.[186] Sureties which bond a "response action contractor" (RAC)[187] procured by the federal government under the Miller Act, however, are immune from suit accruing on the bond, and are not obligated to indemnify or compensate the obligee for loss or liability arising from personal injury or property damage.[188] If the RAC defaults, the surety's liability is limited to the cost to complete the work in accordance with the plans and specifications, minus the balance of funds remaining to be paid under the contract, up to the penal sum of the bond.[189]

2. Liability Under RCRA

A surety that bonds a contractor involved in cleaning up a hazardous waste site can, under certain circumstances, be deemed an "operator" of a hazardous waste facility and subject to permitting requirements or RCRA.[190] If the original contractor discovered hazardous waste on the project after the project has been commenced, upon default the completing surety may be liable for punitive damages, consequential damages, and even liability to third-parties for personal injury or property damage claims.[191] A surety may even face "bad faith" claims if the surety refuses to issue a performance or payment bond (especially in the instance where a bid bond has already been issued) and the construction contract does not protect the contractor from potential liability if hazardous waste or substances are eventually discovered at the project site.[192]

---

186 *See Shreves et al., supra* note 174 at 9-30.
187 A response action contractor is one that contracts to clean up a hazardous waste site.
188 42 U.S.C. § 9619(g)(2)-(3).
189 42 U.S.C. § 9619(g)(3).
190 42 U.S.C. § 6901, *et seq.*
191 *Id.*
192 *Id.; see also Shreves et al., supra* note 174 at 31-37.

Despite the potential liability for sureties under CERCLA and RCRA, an insurance market has evolved for environmental contractors. The availability of contractors' pollution liability ("CPL") and commercial general liability ("CGL") insurance for environmental remediation projects, coupled with increased limits of CPL insurance from $1 million per occurrence to as high as $50 million per occurrence, has benefited the surety industry.[193] However, regardless of the availability of insurance, claims may be made on performance bonds resulting in costly and time-consuming litigation.

3. Liability Under SMCRA

Under the applicable federal regulations, a surety may be unable to obtain a discharge of its bond until such time as the responsible contractor has satisfactorily sealed the mine and all state environmental laws and regulations are fully met.[194] As such, in the event of the contractor's default, the performance surety may be liable for both "satisfactorily" sealing the mine and complying with all state environmental laws and regulations. Even in the absence of default, the bond might not be released for an extended period of time due to the inherent complications in complying with these requirements. Thus, in addition to evaluating the contractor receiving the bond, the surety may also investigate the project, its scope, inherent problems in the work, and applicable statutes. Securing indemnity for such exposure may also be desirable.

B. Practical Application of Federal Statutes to Sureties

Consideration may also be given to the liberal construction of these environmental statutes in light of their stated objectives. For instance, in a West Virginia mining case, the regulatory authority sought the passage of an amendment to the West Virginia act which would expand liability for reclamation costs beyond the intended parties, operators, and

---

193 *See Environmental Construction: Market or Minefield?, supra* note 174 at pp. 2-17.
194 *See* 30 C.F.R. § 784.13 (requiring underground mines to adopt a reclamation plan); 30 C.F.R. § 806 (requiring posting of a performance bond on reclamation); 30 C.F.R. § 800.40 (stipulating requirements for release of the performance bond).

permitees to include landowners and "other responsible parties."[195] The "other responsible parties" could have included a performance surety.[196] The court did not reach that issue since it held that notice of the proposed regulation was inadequate and that the amendment was arguably inconsistent with the Surface Mining Control and Reclamation Act ("SMCRA"). The amendment failed to clearly define this, thus, the court found the amendment was invalidly approved.[197] The *Cat Run Coal* case is illustrative of the potential extracontractual liability of a surety with reference to mining operations and related projects.

The surety is more likely to increase its potential liability for these claims by taking over the project (thereby becoming an "operator"), than by merely bonding the project. In cases where the contractors are required to handle materials of environmental concern, the surety should endeavor to assess its exposure at an early stage or, in the event that the risk is added during the work, to review the change order submitted by the contractor in order to assess the new risk at that time.

With the emergence of environmental activism in the past twenty-five years, sureties should give greater attention to the risks of potential claims before bonding projects for sites and projects where environmental difficulties may be or have been encountered. The extent or likelihood of this risk has yet to be fully realized.[198]

Under reported cases, the surety's liability has been limited to damages that were reasonably foreseeable or within the realm of a normal recovery under surety or contract law. Moreover, none of the cases involved the award of punitive damages against the surety that arose from a contractor's default. When faced with such claims, there are several defenses available to the surety. First, the surety may assert any defense the principal can assert so long as it is not personal to the principal.[199] Additionally, the surety may also raise defenses such as

---

195   Cat Run Coal Co. v. Babbitt, 932 F.Supp. 772 (S.D. W.Va. 1996).
196   *Id.* at 779.
197   *Id.*
198   See *Environmental Construction: Market Or Minefield?, supra* note 174.
199   U.S. Fid. & Guar. Co. v. Town of Dothan, 56 So. 953, 174 Ala. 480 (1911).

lack of jurisdiction of the regulatory agency;[200] expiration of the statute of limitations;[201] and material change in obligation,[202] among others.

C. Mold–The Performance Bond Surety's New Generation of Environmental Claims

Beginning in the early 1990s, mold and fungi claims have emerged as the latest environmental concern. According to statistics released by the insurance industry, the amount paid on mold-related claims more than doubled between the years 2000 and 2001.[203] As the number of mold claims increased, insurers reacted.[204] They redrafted coverage provisions and vigorously litigated claims to enforce applicable policy exclusions. As a result, some claimants were forced to look beyond their commercial general liability policies to find coverage for mold claims. One potential alternative in the construction industry for claimants to pursue is the project's performance bond.

1. Basis for the Mold-Related Bond Claim

Under standard building contracts, the contractor is required by the contract documents to procure insurance for personal injury and property damage claims. In order to "fit" a mold exposure claim into one of the general liability coverage clauses, creative claimants' attorneys came up with various theories of recovery, including claims that mold exposure causes bodily injury; the presence of mold constitutes property damage;

---

200 Commercial Standard Ins. Co. v. Ala. Surface Mining Reclamation Comm'n, 570 A.2d 122 (Pa. Commw. Ct. 1990).
201 Natural Resources and Environmental Protection Cabinet v. Whitley, 940 S.W.2d 904 (Ky. App. 1997).
202 Am. Druggists Ins. Co. v. Commw. of Kentucky Dept. for Natural Resources and Environmental Protection, 670 S.W.2d 485 (Ky. App. 1983).
203 Insurance Information Institute, *see* www.iii.org/medical/hottopics/hot/house.
204 An excellent discussion of the insurance industry's reaction to the rising number of mold claims can be found in *Construction Dilemmas: Caught Between "The Rock" and A Hard Place*, Moelmann and Strobel (ABA Forum on The Construction Industry/TIPS Fidelity & Surety Law Committee 2004).

or, the migration of mold constitutes a personal injury due to the "wrongful invasion of the right of privacy occupancy." Despite these efforts, insurers steadfastly rejected the claims.

As the number of denials under the commercial general liability policies increased, some building owners elected to forgo litigation with the insurer in favor of declaring a default under the construction contract.[205] These owners blamed mold-related problems on poor building design or faulty construction, looking to the contractor and, ultimately, the surety for relief. In essence, the aggrieved owners claim that the mold is a result of a breach of contract and the surety is responsible to cure the defect by remediating the mold damage and repairing the construction defect. Thus, while it was never the intent of the performance bond surety to assume the risk of mold claims, the potential exposure has, in some cases, become a reality.[206]

2. *The Surety's Response to Mold-Related Bond Claims*

Given the increasing number of mold claims, performance bond underwriters, like insurers, reacted to the threat. Bond underwriters are now more carefully examining the insurance and indemnity obligations imposed by contract on the principal to ensure that the policy the contractor procures will cover all of its contractual obligations. If the policy does not, the surety can require the contractor to purchase a special insurance policy specifically designed to cover mold claims before the surety will agree to bond the project. These specialty policies are, however, expensive. Thus, requiring them is likely to result in higher, and ultimately less competitive, bids for the contractor who is trying to pass along the added cost.

---

205 *See, e.g.*, Centex-Rooney Constr. Co. v. Martin Cty., 70 So. 2d 20 (Fla. Dist. Ct. App. 1998); Polk Cty. v. Reliance Ins. Co., No. 94-7135 (Fla. Cir. Ct. 1995).

206 Three states, Louisiana, New Jersey and Washington have eliminated this concern for the surety by passing statutes that prohibit obligees from asserting against the surety personal injury or property damages claims arising from the negligence of the principal. The rationale for this prohibition lies in the very purpose underlying the performance bond–the completion of the construction project. If personal injury or property damage claims are permitted, the bond may not have sufficient funds to complete the project.

Another way for the surety to reduce its risk is by revising bond forms to exclude mold-related claims. This solution has limited application, however, since such revisions are not usually possible when contracting with public entities. Sureties can also require indemnification agreements or simply refuse to write bonds for those contractors that are financially unable to handle a mold-related loss. In the alternative, some sureties are trying to work with the contractor by looking closely at construction modifications to minimize the risk of mold growth.

Once a claim is asserted, there are arguments that can be made based on the language setting forth the insurance requirements of the General Conditions.[207] These arguments may be sufficient for a court to conclude that an ambiguity exists in the policy, which, under the rules of contract construction, must be construed against the drafter. The surety may also rely on, as defenses, the proof and causation issues inherent in mold-related litigation.

Even if the surety prevails in litigation, the cost of defending mold-related claims is extremely high. Thus, the proactive measures suggested above, while seemingly difficult to implement, may be the best defense available to the performance bond surety for this new generation of claims.

Conclusion

In a handful of states sureties have some exposure to extra-contractual liability for claims asserted by the obligee that may extend the exposure beyond the stated terms of the bond. In those cases which have sustained claims for such liability, the courts have found that suretyship coverage parallels the coverage available through an insurance product. In those cases which have rejected these claims, the courts have recognized the differences in the coverage provided by surety bonds and the financial nature of the suretyship underwriting process.

---

207 *See, Construction Dilemmas: Caught Between "The Rock" and a Hard Place, supra* note 204, at pgs. 36-37.

10

CLAIMS AND DEFENSES ASSERTED BY PRINCIPALS OR INDEMNITORS AGAINST THE SURETY

Lee McGraw Brewer
Bogda M.B. Clarke
Phillip G. Alber

Introduction

With increasing frequency, principals and/or indemnitors[1] file claims against the surety in tort. Many such claims are aimed at thwarting the surety's efforts to recover its losses, costs, expenses and attorney's fees, while others are asserted for the purpose of recovering tort damages from the surety. More often, in response to a surety's indemnity claim, indemnitors assert surety misconduct as an affirmative defense, including allegations that the surety breached a contractual duty to issue payments or make expenditures in "good faith" or that it breached the implied common law covenant of good faith and fair dealing.

This chapter will examine both the principal's or indemnitors' affirmative bad faith claims (contractual or common law) and the defenses raised by indemnitors seeking to be relieved of their indemnity obligations to the surety.

---

[1] For ease of reference in this chapter, principals and indemnitors will collectively be referred to as "indemnitors" unless otherwise noted.

I. The Surety's Duty to Act in Good Faith Stems Either From the Indemnity Agreement or Common Law

The indemnity agreement executed by the indemnitors in favor of the surety establishes both the surety's rights and the indemnitors' obligations and is the document upon which the surety, indemnitors and courts should rely in examining a surety's rights. These rights include exoneration, indemnity, collateral and assignment, among others. The predominant duty courts have imposed upon the surety under most indemnity agreements is the contractual, or in some jurisdictions, the implied common law duty to make payments or incur expenses in good faith.

Because of the limited availability of other defenses to indemnity suits, indemnitors frequently allege, either in the form of an affirmative claim or as a defense to a surety's indemnity action, that the surety acted in bad faith by its a) failure to perform an adequate investigation, b) overpayment of claims, c) interference with the principal's contract while exercising assignment rights, d) unreasonable collateral demands despite the principal's belief that neither it nor the surety are obligated to the obligee, e) unreasonable refusal to finance or issue further bonds to the principal, or f) unreasonable refusal to allow the principal to complete the project. While these are the typical claims or defenses raised by indemnitors, such list is not exhaustive.

Since the last publication of *The Law of Performance Bonds* in 1999, there have been many decisions wherein courts in various jurisdictions have addressed claims and/or defenses raised by indemnitors seeking to avoid a surety's express rights under an indemnity agreement. This chapter will address decisions that provide insight into the recent trends in case law.

The cases decided in recent years consistently hold that if the facts demonstrate that the surety exercised express rights conferred upon it by the indemnity agreement, conducted a reasonable investigation, consulted or attempted to consult with its principal and retained an expert, where necessary, to assist the surety in evaluating its principal's defenses to the owner's claim, the surety will likely be deemed to have acted reasonably and in good faith, thus defeating the indemnitors' defenses to their indemnity obligations.[2] However, it should be noted that the indemnity agreement does not typically impose an obligation on the surety to conduct a reasonable investigation, consult with its principal or retain an expert.[3]

Whether a court in a given jurisdiction will limit its analysis to the rights granted the surety under the indemnity agreement and not impose common law obligations such as the implied covenant of good faith and fair dealing, will depend upon the case law in that jurisdiction. The majority of jurisdictions hold that the implied covenant of good faith and fair dealing is implicit in all contracts, including indemnity agreements. Accordingly, courts often examine the conduct of the surety to determine whether it breached this implied covenant, or failed to act in "good faith."

---

[2] U.S. Fid. & Guar. v. Diggs, No. A.03-1023, 2004 U.S. Dist. LEXIS 43, 2004 WL 32917 (E.D.La., Jan. 5, 2004); PSE Consulting, Inc. v. Frank Mercede and Sons, Inc., 267 Conn. 279; 838 A.2d 135 (Conn. 2004); U.S. Fid. & Guar. Co. v. Stanley Contracting, Inc., 303 F. Supp. 2d 1169 (D.C.Or. 2004); First Nat'l Ins. Co. of America v. Joseph Wunderlich, Inc., 358 F. Supp. 2d 44 (N.D.N.Y. 2004).

[3] See, e.g., Travelers Ins. Co. v. Harrison Constr. Group, Corp., No. CV 06-4011, 2008 WL 4725970 (E.D.N.Y., Oct. 22, 2008) (Indemnitors alleged surety did not contact them concerning obligee's performance bond claim. The indemnity agreement expressly stated that the indemnitors waived any such notice. The court noted that even if the indemnitors did not waive notice, absent express provisions obligating the surety to provide notice to indemnitors, no such notice is required) (citing Republic Ins. Co. v. Real Dev. Co., 554 N.Y.S.2d 574, 575 (1st Dep't 1990)).

II. Affirmative Claims Asserted by Indemnitors Against the Surety

A. Claims That Surety Breached Duty of Good Faith

Courts have applied differing standards in determining whether a surety acted in bad faith. However, courts have generally agreed that indemnitors may use bad faith of the surety as a defense to their indemnity obligations, but, with very few exceptions,[4] not to prosecute affirmative claims against the surety. Below are some of the issues that have been significant in the courts' decisions.

1. Lambert (Surety Asserts Rights to Contract Balances and Refuses Further Financial Assistance)

Courts traditionally examine bad faith claims against a surety by examining whether the surety's conduct was authorized by the indemnity agreement. *Lambert v. Maryland Casualty Co.*[5] is a landmark case on the issue of an indemnitors' affirmative claims against the surety, wherein the court upheld a surety's right to enforce the express provisions of its indemnity agreement. When the surety first learned that its principal–the largest road contractor in Louisiana–was experiencing cash flow problems, the surety had $30,000,000 in outstanding bonds. The surety, in an effort to mitigate its damages and provide support to its principal, agreed to guarantee specific loans in exchange for the indemnitors' agreement formally to provide the surety with collateral and to formally

---

[4] PSE Consulting, Inc. v. Frank Mercede and Sons, Inc., 838 A.2d 135, 150, 267 Conn. 279, 300 (Conn. 2004) (court upheld a lower court judgment against the surety for its breach of the implied covenant of good faith and fair dealing); Western Sur. Co. v. WGG, Inc., No. 1:07-CV-1551, 2009 WL 130187 (M.D. Pa., Jan. 29, 2009) (court denied surety's motion to dismiss indemnitors' affirmative claim for the surety's alleged breach of the implied covenant of good faith and fair dealing).

[5] 403 So.2d 739, 748 (La. App. 1981), *aff'd*, 418 So.2d 553 (La. 1982).

acknowledge that the assignment clause in the indemnity agreement was "executory."

Despite the surety's efforts to assist the principal, the principal's financial condition further declined. The principals' labor and/or material suppliers filed liens and asserted claims against the surety. The surety ceased writing bonds for the principal and issued notices to the obligees on its bonded projects advising them of the surety's right to contract balances by way of assignment, subrogation or otherwise. The surety's notices caused an immediate reduction of cash flow to the principal and the principal was no longer able to function.

The principal filed for Chapter 11 bankruptcy protection, which was later converted to Chapter 7. Thereafter, the owners of the construction company filed a lawsuit against the surety seeking $33,000,000 in damages and alleging that the surety wrongfully attempted to take over and destroy their corporation, and that the surety conspired with the principal's lenders. The trial court entered judgment in favor of the owners and against the surety for $9,866,739.50, which judgment the surety appealed.

The appellate court conducted a three-part analysis. The court first reviewed the record to determine whether the principal assigned its contract rights to the surety.[6] It concluded the documents executed by the principal resulted in an assignment to the surety of the principal's contract proceeds.[7]

Second, the court analyzed whether the surety had the legal right to send the stop payment letters. The owners argued that the surety's assignment was not perfected and could not be perfected absent the principal's default upon its obligations under the bonded contracts, which they alleged had not occurred as of the date upon which the surety sent the stop payment letters. The appellate court, looking to the express provisions of the indemnity agreement and the letter declaring that the surety's assignment rights were rendered "executory," concluded that the surety had the legal right to issue the

---

6   *Id.*
7   *Id.*

stop payment letters and cease issuing bonds or providing financial assistance to the principal.[8]

In addition, the appellate court determined that, even in the absence of the assignment clause, the surety had, by legal subrogation, the right to claim funds due to the principal on the outstanding contracts it bonded, citing to *Prairie State Bank v. United States*.[9]

The appellate court next considered whether the surety was liable to the indemnitors for a "bad faith breach of a fiduciary relationship on an 'abuse of rights' theory."[10] The court found that the surety assumed additional obligations by providing assistance to the principal over and above those owed by a surety. Therefore, the surety became a guarantor and direct creditor of the principal. While the trial court had determined that the surety owed the principal a duty of good faith and that the surety was a fiduciary, the appellate court characterized the trial court's conclusion as "an oversimplification."[11] The appellate court held that the surety neither breached its good faith duty nor any fiduciary obligation owed to the principal.

> The conclusion of the trial judge that Maryland was a fiduciary with regard to the corporation and owed it a duty of acting in good faith is an oversimplification. That corporation, as principal of the public works bonds, made certain indemnity agreements which were unilaterally enforceable both prospectively and retrospectively by written agreement. We also note Maryland has a duty to its shareholders, and perhaps to its creditors, to manage its business in a prudent manner in order to avoid jeopardizing the corporate entity, the equity interests of its shareholders, and the right of its creditors to be paid amounts owed by it.
>
> We cannot construe the action of Maryland as being in bad faith or in violation of any fiduciary relationship to the corporation.

---

8   *Id.* at 748-52.
9   *Id.* at 752 (citing Prairie State Bank v. United States, 164 U.S. 227, 17 S. Ct. 142, 41 L. Ed. 412 (1896)).
10 *Id.* at 755.
11 *Id.* at 754.

Maryland was under no legal obligation to furnish additional public works bonds; it was under no legal obligation to furnish additional release of lien bonds; and it had no obligation to make further direct cash advances to or for the benefit of the corporation. Maryland did not lull the corporation into a "false sense of security" by the agreement of August 20, 1975. . . .

We agree with the trial court's conclusion that Maryland intended to cut off its financial support to the corporation with the full knowledge that such action would effectively place the corporation in bankruptcy. However, we do not see in this a breach of good faith or of a fiduciary violation since we know of no law requiring even a surety company much less a guarantor and creditor to continue to put additional money into a corporation which it reasonably believes is in a financially hopeless condition, once it has legally obtained the right to take whatever actions are necessary to cease operations in connection with such a corporation.[12]

The Supreme Court of Louisiana affirmed the decision rendered by the appellate court.[13] The supreme court focused its review upon the contractual relationship between the parties, stating that "[c]ontracts must be construed in such a way as to lead to logical conclusions and to give effect to the obvious intentions of the parties."[14] The supreme court held that the principal contractually agreed to indemnify and hold harmless the surety; assigned to the surety all payments due or to become due under contracts covered by the bonds; and, in the subsequent letter agreement, confirmed the effectiveness of the assignments and agreed to execute upon the surety's demand whatever documents might be required to evidence to third-parties the effectiveness of the assignment. The supreme court rejected the owners' argument that the principal must first

---

12   *Id.*
13   Sharon W. Lambert and Donald C. Lambert v. Maryland Cas. Co., 418 So. 2d 553 (La. 1982).
14   *Id.* at 559 (citing to St. Ann v. American Ins. Cos., 182 So.2d 710 (La. App. 1966)).

default upon its obligations under the bonded contract before the assignment rights were triggered, stating that the subsequent letter agreement "altered and modified the indemnifying agreements to the extent that it made the assignments of contract proceeds executory and effective as of that date."[15]

The supreme court stated that the surety was obligated under the Louisiana State Constitution to act in good faith[16] towards its principal and indemnitors, but found that the facts amply demonstrated that the principal was financially incapable of completing its performance, and that the surety had the right to exercise its rights for its own protection.[17]

Accordingly, the appellate court and the supreme court focused on the surety's rights under the indemnity agreement. While they found that the surety did owe certain duties to the indemnitors, the courts recognized that the surety was entitled to protect its own interest in exercising its indemnity agreement rights.

2. Standards for the Surety's Good Faith

The Supreme Court of Connecticut in *PSE Consulting, Inc. v. Frank Mercede and Sons, Inc.*,[18] observed that the standards for imposing the duty of good faith are not uniform. While the majority of jurisdictions recognize that a surety has a duty to act in good faith, even if such requirement is not contained in the indemnity agreement, there is no consensus as to what that duty requires. However, courts in most states hold that mere negligence by the surety is insufficient to prove bad faith.[19]

---

15   *Id.* at 561.
16   *Id.* (citing to LSA-C.C. Art. 1934). Note that common law doctrines are not applicable in this jurisdiction as its laws are based upon the Napoleonic Code.
17   *Id.*
18   267 Conn. 279, 838 A.2d 135 (Conn. 2004).
19   *Id.* at 303 (citing Engbrock v. Federal Ins. Co., 370 F.2d 787 (C.A. Tex. 1967) ("neither lack of diligence nor negligence is the equivalent of bad faith"); Frontier Ins. Co. v. Int'l, Inc., 124 F. Supp. 2d 1211, 1214 (N.D. Ala. 2000); U.S. Fid. & Guar. Co. v. Feibus, 15

A minority of jurisdictions impose a less forgiving standard by defining bad faith as conduct that was unreasonable or negligent.[20] A

F. Supp. 2d 587 (M.D. Pa. 1988) ("gross negligence or bad judgment is insufficient to amount to bad faith"); Employers Ins. of Wausau v. Able Green, Inc., 749 F. Supp. 1100, 1103 (S.D. Fla. 1990) (surety's actions may have been negligent but did not rise to level of deliberate malfeasance required to establish bad faith); Am. Employers' Ins. Co. v. Horton, 35 Mass. App. 921, 924, 622 N.E. 2d 283 (Mass. App. 1993) ("bad judgment, negligence or insufficient zeal" not evidence of bad faith); Fid. & Deposit Co. of Maryland v. Wu, 150 Vt. 231 (Vt. 1988) ("at best, the jury could draw the conclusion that [the] plaintiff was negligent. . . there was no evidence of lack of good faith for the jury")).

20   *Id.* at 304. *PSE Consulting* cited the minority jurisdictions imposing a less forgiving standard, i.e., conduct that was unreasonable or negligent: Rush Presbyterian St. Luke's Medical Center v. Safeco Ins. Co. of Am., 712 F. Supp. 1344, 1346 (N.D. Ill. 1989) ("negligence and bad faith are synonymous" in context of determining good faith); Arntz Contracting Co. v. St. Paul Fire & Marine Ins. Co., 47 Cal. App. 4th 483, 54 Cal. Rptr. 2d 888 (Cal. App. 1996) (surety's bad faith can be demonstrated by proof of "objectively unreasonable conduct, regardless of the actor's motive"); Hawaiian Ins. & Guar. Co., Ltd. v. Higashi, 67 Haw. 12, 675 P. 767 at 14 (Ha. 1985) ("Burden of establishing that the amount paid in settlement . . . was reasonable and in good faith [is] upon the indemnitee"); Hartford v. Tanner, 22 Kan. App. 2d 76 (Kan. App. 1986) ("good faith requires a surety seeking indemnification to show that its conduct was reasonable"); Portland v. George D. Ward & Associates, Inc., 89 Or. App. 458, 750 P.2d 171 (Or. App. 1988) (to prove bad faith in settling claim, indemnitors "needed only to prove that [the surety] failed to make a reasonable investigation of the validity of the claims against them or to consider reasonably the viability of their counterclaims and defenses, not that [the surety] acted for dishonest purposes or improper motives"). *See also* E. Gallagher, *The Law Of Suretyship* (2d ed. 2000) pp. 492-95, and, courts requiring actual fraud by the surety for its conduct to rise to the level of bad faith: Firemen's Ins. Co. of Newark, New Jersey v. Todesca Equip. Co., 310 F.3d 37 (R.I. 2002) (bad faith requires fraud or collusion under Rhode Island law); Gen. Accident Ins. Co. of Am.

few jurisdictions have demonstrated a reluctance to find bad faith on the part of the surety if it exercised express rights granted to it under the indemnity agreement.[21]

---

v. Merritt-Meridian Constr. Corp., 975 F. Supp. 511, 516 (S.D.N.Y. 1997) (Indemnity agreement's right-to-settle clause is invoked "in the absence of an indication of fraud or collusion"); Banque Nationale de Paris S.A. v. Ins. Co. of N. Am., 896 F. Supp. 163, 165 (S.D.N.Y. 1995) (analogizing to business judgment rule and ruling that absent self-interest or fraud, surety's decision should be regarded as presumptively correct); Reliance Ins. Co. v. Romine, 707 F. Supp. 550, 552 (S.D. Ga. 1989) (bad faith equated with arbitrary or capricious standard for proving abuse of discretion), *aff'd*, 888 F.2d 1344 (11th Cir. 1989); Hess v. Am. States Ins. Co., 589 S.W.2d 548 at 551 (Tex. App. 1979) (Indemnity agreement "lodged in the indemnitee a discretion limited only by the bounds of fraud.").

21 *See, e.g.*, Gundle Lining Constr. Corp. v. Adams County Asphalt, Inc., 85 F.3d 201, 210-11 (5th Cir. 1996); Fid. & Deposit Co. of Maryland v. Bristol Steel & Iron Works, Inc., 722 F.2d 1160, 1162-63 (4th Cir. 1983); Transamerica Ins. Co. v. Bloomfield, 401 F.2d 357, 362 (6th Cir. 1968); Engbrock v. Fed. Ins. Co., 370 F.2d 786; Carroll v. Nat'l Sur. Co., 58 U.S. App. D.C. 3, 58 App. D.C. 3, 24 F.2d 268, 270-71 (D.C. Cir. 1928); U.S. Fid. & Guar. Co. v. Feibus, 15 F. Supp. 2d 579, 582-83 (M.D. Pa. 1998); Nat'l Sur. Corp. v. Peoples Milling Co., 57 F. Supp. 281, 282-83 (W.D. Ky. 1944); Martin v. Lyons, 98 Idaho 102, 105-106, 588 P.2d 1063 (Idaho 1977); U.S. Fid. & Guar. Co. v. Klein Corp., 190 Ill. App. 3d 250, 255, 558 N.E.2d 1047, 137 Ill. Dec. 736 (1989); Hartford v. Tanner, 22 Kan. App. 2d 64, 70, 910 P.2d 872 (Kan. App. 1996), *review denied*, 259 Kan. 927 (1996); U.S. Fid. & Guar. Co. v. Napier Elec. & Constr. Co., 571 S.W.2d 644 at 646 (Ky. App. 1978); Int'l Fid. Ins. Co. v. Spadafina, 192 App. Div. 2d 637, 639, 596 N.Y. S.2d 453 (N.Y. A.D. Dept. 1993); Portland v. George D. Ward & Assoc., Inc., 89 Or. App. 452, 456-57, 750 P.2d 171 (Or. App. 1988), *review denied*, 305 Or. 672, 757 P.2d 422 (1988); Hess v. Am. States Ins. Co., 589 S.W. 2d 548, 550 (Tex. App. 1979); Fid. & Deposit Co. of Maryland v. Wu, 150 Vt. 230, 552 A.2d 1196 (1988); *but see* Firemen's Ins. Co. of Newark, New Jersey v. Todesca Equip. Co., 310 F.3d 32, 37 (1st Cir. 2002); Associated Indem. Corp. v. CAT Contracting, Inc., 964 S.W.2d 276, 278 (Tex. 1998). *See also*, Am.

The *Mercede* court held that under Connecticut law the covenant of good faith and fair dealing applied to sureties[22] and joined with those courts that define a surety's bad faith as requiring an "improper motive" or "dishonest purpose."[23]

As noted by the *Mercede* court, the weight of authority in the majority of jurisdictions is to recognize a duty of good faith, though there is no consensus about what that duty requires.[24] Chapter 9 of this publication discusses, in depth, how the various jurisdictions define bad faith. The decision in *Mercede* was officially released on January 13, 2004, and has since been cited in the Second, Third, Sixth and Eleventh Circuits in cases where the surety's indemnity rights were at issue.[25]

Motorist Ins. Co., et. al v. Southcrest Constr., Inc., et. al, 2006 U.S. Dist. LEXIS 19933 2006 WL 995202 at *5 (N.D.Tex. 2006) (by granting exclusive discretion to surety in indemnity agreement, without tempering discretion with good faith provision, principal "bargained away any protections provided under Illinois common law duty of good faith and fair dealing."); Amwest Sur. Ins. Co. v. Szabo, 2003 WL 21789033 (N.D.Ill. 2003) at *4 ("In any event, the implied duty of good faith does not modify contractual provisions which plainly define the duties of the parties. LaSalle Nat'l Bank v. Metro Life Ins. Co., 1993 WL 191803, at *3 (N.D.Ill. June 4, 1993), *aff'd* 18 F.3d 1371 (7th Cir. 1994).")

22 *PSE Consulting*, 267 Conn. at 304.
23 *Id.*
24 *Id.* at 302 (citing T. Harris, *Good Faith, Suretyship, and the IUS Commune*, 53 MERCER L. REV. 5811, 587 (2002)).
25 *See* Acoustics, Inc. v. Travelers Ins. Co., 2004 WL 1559214, *4, 37 Conn. L. Rptr. 301, 301 (Conn. Super. 2004); Mountbatten Sur. Co., Inc. v. Jenkins, No. 02-CV-8421, 2004 WL 2297405, *6 (E.D.Pa., Oct. 13, 2004); In re Oakwood Homes Corp., 342 B.R. 59, 69, 46 Bankr. Ct. Dec. 140 (Bankr. D. Del., 2006); Atl. Contracting & Material Co., Inc. v. Ulico Cas. Co., 844 A.2d 460, 380 Md. 285, 320 (Md. App. 2004) (dissent); Int'l Fid. Ins. Co. v. Vimas Painting Co., Inc., No. 2107-CV-291 2008 WL 926577, *6 (S.D. Ohio, Apr. 3, 2008); *cf.* Auto-Owners Ins. Co. v. S.E. Floating Docks, Inc., 2007 WL 1559214, at *3, 20 Fla. L. Weekly Fed. D 599, 599 (M.D.Fla. 2007).

It is necessary to understand the facts in *Mercede* that led to the court's determination that the surety breached the implied covenant of good faith and fair dealing. A sub-subcontractor on the bonded contract filed a payment bond claim with the surety seeking reimbursement for labor and/or material it provided to the project under an oral agreement with the principal's subcontractor.[26]

The surety responded to the notice of claim and stated that there were "a number of bona fide or otherwise unresolved disputes" between the principal and the claimant and that much of the claim against the principal and surety was "likely to be subject to reasonable defenses."[27] In its response, the surety sought further documentation, which the claimant provided.

Approximately two months after the surety received notice of the claim, the claimant's attorney advised the surety that it breached its obligations under the payment bond by failing to explain the basis for any disputed amounts within forty-five days of the surety's receipt of the claim. The surety responded by stating that it was conducting a detailed investigation and that the principal fully disputed the claim.[28]

The claimant then filed a formal complaint with the state insurance commissioner. Thereafter, per the decision, the surety "shifted its position on the PSE claim." The surety met with the principal and suggested that the surety or the principal issue a partial payment to the claimant. The principal agreed to pay the remaining contract balance but refused to pay retainage, essentially asserting a pay when paid defense.[29]

The claimant filed suit against both the principal and surety for breach of contract and brought a separate claim against the surety alleging bad faith. Nearly two years after the surety received notice of the claim, and almost a year after the lawsuit was filed, the surety enlisted its in-house engineer to evaluate the fair market value of the

---

26 PSE Consulting, Inc. v. Frank Mercede and Sons, Inc., 838 A.2d 135, 267 Conn. 279, 285 (Conn. 2004).
27 *Id.*
28 *Id.*
29 *Id.* at 286.

claimant's work on the project. The surety's engineer concluded that the plaintiff was due a significant portion of its claim based solely on work the plaintiff performed on the base contract, which did not include its extra work claims.[30]

The surety then met with the plaintiff and agreed to issue a partial payment of the claim. The principal was unaware of this meeting. The surety issued partial payment and made demand upon the indemnitors for reimbursement and to either resolve the balance of the claim or provide the surety with collateral under the indemnity agreement. The principal refused to comply with either demand. Thereafter, the surety settled plaintiff's claims against the surety, leaving the principal as the sole defendant.[31] The principal settled with the plaintiff on the first day of trial.

In the action, the surety filed a cross-claim seeking indemnification from the principal and the principal filed a cross-claim against the surety alleging that the surety breached the implied covenant of good faith and fair dealing. The case proceeded to trial on the cross claims of the principal and surety.

The surety pursued indemnification from the principal and the principal claimed damages arising from a breach of contract and breach of the implied covenant of good faith and fair dealing. The principal argued that the surety's sole motivation for settling the claim was to secure a dismissal of the bad faith claim and avoid any potential adverse decision by the state insurance department.[32] The jury returned a verdict for the principal and against the surety on both the surety's cross-claim and the principal's cross-claim. In response to jury interrogatories, the jury stated its finding that the surety failed to prove its claim for indemnification; that the principal proved its special defense that the surety breached the implied covenant of good faith and fair dealing; and, that the principal proved its special defenses of estoppel and waiver. The principal was

---

30   *Id.* at 287.
31   *Id.* at 288.
32   *Id.* at 296-97.

awarded nominal damages.[33] The jury also found that the surety did not breach the indemnity agreement.

On appeal, the surety claimed that the trial court improperly disregarded the terms of the indemnity agreement by instructing the jury that the surety had the burden to prove, as an element of its indemnification claim, that its payments to the claimant were proper. In addition, the surety pointed to the jury's inconsistent findings that the surety did not breach the indemnity agreement but did breach the covenant of good faith and fair dealing.[34]

The indemnity agreement required that the principal indemnify and save the surety harmless from every claim inclusive of all losses, costs and expenses and further contained a provision that the surety's voucher or other evidence of such payments constituted *prima facie* evidence to establish the principal's liability.[35] Further, the indemnity agreement included a right to settle clause, which "typically provide the surety with wide discretion in settling claims made upon a bond, even where the principal is not liable for the underlying claim."[36]

The *Mercede* court agreed that the indemnity agreement expressly granted the surety the right to settle a payment bond claim on behalf of both the surety and principal and that evidence, in the form of vouchers and other evidence of payment by the surety, constituted *prima facie* evidence of the propriety of that payment,

---

[33] The supreme court mentioned the judgment in favor of the principal against the surety, in dicta, but undertook no analysis of the propriety of the award, presumably because only nominal damages were awarded.

[34] *Id.* at 288.

[35] *Id.* at 291.

[36] *Id.* at 291-92 (citing U.S. Fid. & Guar. Co. v. Napier Elec. & Constr. Co., 571 S.W.2d 644 (Ky. Ct. App. 1978); Fid. & Deposit Co. of Maryland v. Fleischer, 772 S.W.2d 809, 816 (Mo. App. 1989); Hess v. Am. States Ins. Co., 589 S.W.2d 548, 551 (Tex. App. 1979); J. Hinchey, *Surety's Performance Over Protest of Principal: Considerations and Risks*, 22 TORT & INS. L.J. 133, 1446-47 (1986) (discussing enforceability of right-to-settle and prima facie evidence clauses).

thus shifting to the indemnitors the burden to rebut.[37] However, the court concluded that a surety's right to settle is "not unfettered"[38]

The indemnity agreement did not expressly require that the surety act in good faith. However, the parties recognized "that the implied covenant of good faith is an overlay that applies to sureties."[39] The *Mercede* court defined bad faith as "requiring an 'improper motive' or 'dishonest purpose' on the part of the surety."[40]

The *Mercede* court found that the jury could reasonably have concluded that the surety acted in bad faith. Facts indicated that the surety failed to conduct a sufficient investigation and respond to the claimant within the prescribed forty-five days, as required by the bond. Though the surety argued it settled a valid payment bond claim and that the principal failed to produce any evidence at trial that the claim was not due and owing, the *Mercede* court deferred to the jury which determined that the surety issued payment solely in its self-interest.[41] Accordingly, the *Mercede* court upheld the jury finding that the surety breached its implied covenant of good faith and fair

---

37   *Id.* at 293.
38   *Id.*
39   *Id.* at 301-02 (citing Arntz Contracting Co. v. St. Paul Fire & Marine Ins. Co., 47 Cal. App. 4th 464, 482, 54 Cal. Rptr. 2d 888 (Cal. App. 1996) (standard of good faith implied in every contract to surety conduct; doctrine has "particular application in situations where one party is invested with discretionary power affecting the right of another"); *see also* Portland v. George D. Ward & Assocs., Inc., 89 Or. App. at 457-58, 780 P.2d 171 (Or. App. 1996) (applying reasonableness standard to bad faith where indemnity agreements subjects right to compromise claim to surety's sole discretion).
40   *PSE Consulting, Inc.,* 267 Conn. at 304. The *Mercede* court held that "the failure to investigate standing alone and not accompanied by other evidence of an improper motive, is not enough to constitute bad faith." The court distinguished circumstances "where a party fails to make an inquiry for the purpose of remaining ignorant of the facts which he believes or fears would disclose a defect in the transaction," and reasoned that this type of intentional or reckless conduct could lead to a finding of bad faith on behalf of the surety.
41   *Id.* at 318.

dealing. The court further found that ". . . subsumed in this finding is the jury's implicit finding that National's payments to PSE were not the result of PSE's claims under the payment bond."[42]

3. Cases Finding No Tort Claim For Surety's Alleged Failure to Act in Good Faith

Texas and Nevada courts have rejected a principal's claim in tort for a surety's alleged bad faith conduct.[43] In *Associated Indemnity Corp. v. CAT Contracting, Inc.*[44] the Texas Supreme Court concluded that the surety had a contractual obligation to make payments under the bond in good faith.[45] However, the court held that a principal does not have a common law tort claim against a surety for bad faith. The court further rejected the argument that statutory causes of action for unfair insurance practices apply to commercial sureties.[46] The court also defined good faith in the indemnity agreement as follows:

> . . . conduct which is honest in fact, free of improper motive or wilful ignorance of the facts at hand. It does not require proof of a "reasonable" investigation by the surety. Stating the proposition conversely for purposes of our evidentiary review for this particular case, "bad faith" means more than merely negligent or unreasonable conduct; it requires proof of an improper motive or wilful ignorance of the facts."[47]

The trial court in *CAT* found that the surety breached a common law duty of good faith and fair dealing, breached the indemnity agreement by failing to act in good faith, breached a fiduciary duty owed to the principal, violated the Insurance Code, and committed fraud, tortious

---

42   *Id.* at 321.
43   Associated Indem. Corp. v. CAT Contracting, Inc., 964 S.W.2d 276 (Tex. 1998); Great Am. Ins. Co. v. Gen. Builders, Inc., 934 P.2d at 257.
44   964 S.W. 2d 276 (Tex. 1998).
45   *Id.* at 283.
46   *Id.* at 278.
47   *Id.* at 285.

interference with contract, and negligent misrepresentation. The trial court rendered judgment denying indemnity for the surety and awarding the principal $4,163,305 in lost profits, $425,579 for contract damages, and awarded the indemnitors and their spouses $700,000 in mental anguish damages.

The Texas Supreme Court, reversed and vacated the judgment in favor of the principals and indemnitors. The court found that, under Texas law, the surety owes no common law duty of good faith to the bond principal.[48] The court went on to find that there was some evidence in the record of bad faith by the surety and affirmed the judgment of the court of appeals insofar as it denied the surety relief under the indemnity agreement.[49]

In *Great American Insurance Co. v. General Builders, Inc.*[50] the Supreme Court of Nevada similarly rejected the principal's affirmative bad faith claim against the surety. In *General Builders*, the principal alleged that the surety breached the implied covenant of good faith and fair dealing because the surety canceled bonds that its agent issued without consent. At trial, the jury found that the surety acted in bad faith and awarded the indemnitors compensatory and punitive damages.

On appeal, the supreme court vacated the jury award for damages. The court found that no special relationship existed to create such a cause of action by the principal against a surety in tort for the breach of the implied covenant of good faith and fair dealing. The court noted that such claims are limited to "special relationships characterized by elements of public interest, adhesion and fiduciary responsibility."[51] It further found that all parties to the indemnity agreement were experienced commercial entities and were never inherently in unequal bargaining positions.[52]

---

48   *Id.* at 282.
49   *Id.* at 286.
50   113 Nev. 346, 934 P.2d 257 (Nev. 1997).
51   *Id.* at 263.
52   *Id.*

Relying on *General Builders,* the Supreme Court of Nevada in *Insurance Company of the West v. Gibson Tile Company*[53] dismissed the principal's claim for compensatory and punitive damages and reversed a judgment rendered by the lower court for tortious breach of the covenant of good faith and fair dealing.[54] The principal claimed that the surety refused to issue further bonds. The *Gibson* court found that there was no oral agreement by the surety to continue bonding the principal and distinguished the role of a surety and its indemnitors from insurer/insured relationships:

> For ICW to be liable to Gibson for a tortious breach of the covenant of good faith and fair dealing, the parties had to be in a special relationship. We conclude, as a matter of law that no such special relationship existed between ICW and Gibson.
>
> Although every contract contains an implied covenant of good faith and fair dealing, an action in tort for breach of the covenant arises only "in rare and exceptional cases" when there is a special relationship between the victim and tortfeasor. A special relationship is "characterized by elements of public interest, adhesion, and fiduciary responsibility." [Citations omitted] Examples of special relationships include those between insurers and insureds, partners of partnerships, and franchisees and franchisers. Each of these relationships shares a special element of reliance common to partnership, insurance, and franchise agreements. We have recognized that in these situations involving an element of reliance, there is a need to "protect the weak from the insults of the stronger" [Citations omitted] that is not adequately met by ordinary contract damages. In addition, we have extended the tort remedy to certain situations in which one party holds "vastly superior bargaining power."[55]

---

53   134 P.3d 698, 122 Nev. Adv. Rep. 40 (Nev. 2006).
54   *Id.* The court specifically opined that the lower court erred when it denied the surety its right to pursue its indemnity claim for attorneys' fees and expenses on the basis that the surety did not pay any claims.
55   *Id.* at 702.

The *Gibson* court declined to extend tort liability for breach of the good faith covenant to a surety.[56]

In *International Fidelity Insurance Company v. Vimas Painting Co.*,[57] the principal and indemnitors filed a counterclaim for the tort of bad faith in response to the surety's claim for indemnity. The *Vimas* court held that under Ohio law, a principal does not have such a cause of action against a surety. The indemnitors alleged, among other things, that the surety acted in bad faith by refusing to tender its defense to the principal and failing to counsel the principal that the penal sum of the bond exceeded the amount required under the principal's contract with the obligee. The surety argued that Ohio does not recognize a tort claim of bad faith filed by a principal against a surety. The *Vimas* court agreed, stating that "a tort claim of bad faith filed by a principal against its surety is not cognizable."[58]

The *Vimas* court observed that other courts addressing the issue of whether a principal has a cause of action in tort against a surety have held that the surety owes no such duty to its principal.[59] Thereafter, the *Vimas* court dismissed the indemnitors' counterclaim against the surety for "bad faith." However, it held that the surety's

---

56 *Id.*
57 No. 2007-CV-298, 2008 U.S. Dist. LEXIS 27018, 2008 WL 926577 (S.D. Ohio Apr. 3, 2008).
58 *Id.* at 12.
59 *Id.* at 16 (citing Associated Indem. Corp. v. CAT Contracting, Inc., 964 S.W.2d 276, 278 (Tex. 1998) ("a surety does not owe a common law duty of good faith to its principal"); Ins. Co. of the West v. Gibson Tile Co., 134 P.3d 698 (Nev. 2006) (since no fiduciary relationship exists between the performance bond surety and its principal, the principal cannot sue the surety in tort for bad faith or breach of the covenant of good faith and fair dealing); Masterclean, Inc. v. Star Ins. Co., 347 S.C. 405, 556 S.E.2d 371, 276-77 (S.C. 2001) (because the surety bond is designed to protect the obligee and not the principal, a principal cannot maintain a bad faith claim against the surety); Cates Constr., Inc. v. Talbot Partners, 21 Cal. 4th 28, 86 Cal. Rptr. 2d 855, 980 P.2d 407 (Cal. 1999) (no tort recovery is available for breach of implied covenant of good faith and fair dealing in the context of a construction performance bond).

alleged bad faith conduct may constitute a defense to the surety's indemnity claim."[60]

The Supreme Court of South Carolina likewise distinguished the relationship among a surety, principal and indemnitors from the relationship between an insurer and insured and concluded that no special relationship exists in the surety context to justify the imposition of a cause of action for the tort of bad faith. The court in *Masterclean, Inc. v. Star Insurance Company*[61] examined whether a surety was subject to the same common law obligations as an insurer. The indemnitors argued that they had a cause of action in tort against the surety because, under South Carolina law, sureties are subject to regulation by the South Carolina Insurance Department. The court held that the mere fact that the surety is part of the regulatory scheme does not mean that common law duties of an insurer apply to a surety.[62] The court reasoned that the surety bond "does not exist to protect the principal against an unknown calamity but to protect the obligee against the principal's potential default. It cannot be said a principal is the true intended beneficiary of the bond."[63] The court then clarified its holding and stated that a principal may be able to use a surety's bad faith as a defense to indemnification, "While a principal may not use bad faith as a sword to extract damages from a surety in tort, a principal is not precluded from using bad faith as a shield in contract against a surety seeking indemnification."[64]

In *Travelers Casualty & Surety Co. of America v. Dennis J. Amoroso, et al.*,[65] the principal asserted causes of action against the surety for breach of written contract, bad faith, breach of the covenant of good faith and fair dealing, fraud, negligent misrepresentation and tortious interference with contract. The surety filed a motion to dismiss the principal's claims. The court held that because the surety

---

60   *Id.* at 17.
61   347 S.C. 405, 556 S.E.2d 371 (S.C. 2001).
62   *Id.* at 410.
63   *Id.* at 414.
64   *Id.*
65   No. C-03-5746 PJH, 2004 U.S. Dist. LEXIS, 2004 WL 1918890 (N.D. Cal. Aug. 24, 2004).

exercised express rights granted to it under the indemnity agreement, the implied covenant of good faith and fair dealing did not apply.[66]

Accordingly, the majority of courts that have reviewed the issue have concluded that principals and indemnitors may be entitled to defend a surety's indemnity claim by alleging bad faith, but cannot use such allegations to prosecute an affirmative claim against the surety.

B. Claims Based Upon Breach of Fiduciary Duties

Courts that have considered whether a surety has a fiduciary duty to the principal have declined to impose such a duty. In *Travelers Property & Casualty Insurance Co. v. Triton Marine Construction Corp.*,[67] the principal argued that the completing surety was its fiduciary and that the surety's refusal to pass through the principal's appeal of a re-work claim breached duties owed to the principal. The court noted that "in general a surety does not owe a fiduciary duty to its principal."[68] Under Connecticut law, a fiduciary relationship may exist in "situations in which there is a justifiable trust confided on one side and a resulting superiority and influence on the other."[69] The court held that there are no circumstances that would justify classifying Travelers' relationship with Triton as a fiduciary one. Under the indemnity agreement, the surety had the exclusive right to determine whether bond claims should be paid, settled, defended, or appealed. In the court's opinion the surety was not "under a duty to represent the interest" of its principal. A reasonable jury could not find that Triton confided a "justifiable trust" in Travelers, resulting in the latter's "superiority and influence" over Triton.[70] Accordingly, no fiduciary relationship existed.

---

66   *Id.* at *9.
67   473 F. Supp. 2d 321 (D. Conn. 2007).
68   *Id.* (citing Nat'l Union Fire Ins. Co. of Pittsburgh, Pa. v. Woodhead, 917 F.2d 752, 757 (2d Cir. 1990)).
69   *Id.* at 322 (citing Dunham v. Dunham, 204 Conn. 303, 320, 528 A.2d 1123 (1987)).
70   *Id.*

In *Far West Insurance Company v. J. Metro Excavating, Inc.*,[71] the court found that "[s]ome states have held that, in contrast with an insurer in a bilateral insurance relationship, a fiduciary duty or a special implied duty of good faith and fair dealing does not apply to the tripartite relationship of a surety, its principal, and the obligee under a bond."[72] The court concluded that the surety owed no common law fiduciary duty to the principal under the bond.[73]

In *Insurance Company of the West v. Gibson Tile Company, Inc.*,[74] the court held that the trial court erred in submitting an instruction on fiduciary duty to the jury, stating that "because a surety's role in providing bonds on behalf of a principal is distinct from that of an insurance company providing a policy to protect its insured, a surety is not held to owe the same fiduciary duty to its principal."[75]

Accordingly, courts have declined to impose on a surety the type of fiduciary relationship with the principal that exists between an insurer and its insured.

---

71 No. 2:07-CV-11 PRC, 2008 WL 859182 (N.D. Ind. Mar. 28, 2008).
72 *Id.* at 29 (citing to 4 BRUNER §12:7 SURETYSHIP AND "BAD FAITH"; Bruce v. Martin, Nos. 87 Civ. 7737, 90 Civ. 0870, 90 Civ. 4561, 1993 U.S. Dist. LEXIS 21382, 1993 WL 148904, at *6 (S.D. N.Y. May 5, 1993); Nat'l Union Fire Ins. Co. of Pittsburgh, Pa. v. Turtur, 892 F.2d 199, 207 (2d Cir. 1989); Cates Constr., Inc. v. Talbot Partners, 21 Cal. 4th 28, 86 Cal. Rptr. 2d 855, 980 P.2d 407 (Cal. 1999); Associated Indem. Corp. v. CAT Contracting, Inc., 964 S.W.2d 276, 282 (Tex. 1988); Great Am. Ins. Co. v. Gen. Builders, Inc., 113 Nev. 346, 934 P.2d 257, 263 (Nev. 1997)).
73 *Id.* at 30.
74 134 P.3d 698, 122 Nev. 455 (Nov. 2006).
75 *Id.* at 703; *see also* Associated Indem. Corp. v. CAT Contracting, Inc. 964 S.W.2d 276, 278 (Tex. 1998); Kmart Corp. v. Ponsock, 732 P.2d 1364, 1370 (Nev. 1987) (an action in tort for breach of the covenant arises only "in rare and exceptional cases" when there is a special relationship between the victim and the tortfeasor).

C. Claims Based Upon Abuse of Rights

Principals may argue that a surety, in exercising its indemnity rights, assumed control of the principal's business to such an extent that any loss the surety incurred should be borne by the surety and not the indemnitors. Indemnitors have advanced the abuse of rights doctrine as an affirmative defense to the surety's indemnity demand and an affirmative claim against the surety for damages suffered by the principal due to the surety's exercise of its indemnity rights.

In *Lambert v. Maryland Casualty Co.*,[76] the Louisiana Court of Appeals rejected the principal's claim that the surety "abused its rights." The court found that the abuse of rights doctrine requires that "for one to be held in damages for exercising a right legally conferred upon him there must exist (1) no benefit to the person exercising the legal right, and (2) damage or injury to the person against whom the legal right is asserted."[77] The court found that the surety's desire to dominate and control its principal was entirely reasonable under the circumstances, and that the surety simply acted to protect its serious and legitimate interests.[78] The court concluded that the first prong of the test had not been met, and therefore held that the "abuse of rights" doctrine did not apply.

The Louisiana Supreme Court reviewed the decision by the court of appeals.[79] In addressing the principal's claims against the surety for its alleged breach of the abuse of rights doctrine, the supreme court held that "[t]hese contentions of plaintiffs were analyzed, discussed in detail and correctly decided by the court of appeal."[80]

As with affirmative tort claims for a breach of fiduciary duty, indemnitors have been unsuccessful in persuading courts that a surety's conduct should give rise to an "abuse of rights" cause of action.

---

76 403 So.2d 739 (La. App. 4th Cir. 1981), *aff'd,* 418 So. 2d 553, 561 (La. 1982).
77 *Id.* at 756.
78 *Id.* at 757.
79 Lambert v. Maryland Cas. Co., 418 So. 2d 553 (La. 1982).
80 *Id.* (citing 403 So.2d at 754-57).

III. Defenses Raised By Indemnitors to Surety's Indemnity Claims

A. Breach of Covenant of Good Faith and Fair Dealing

Indemnitors frequently use the surety's alleged bad faith conduct as a shield to liability rather than as a sword to seek damages from the surety for the tort of bad faith. They typically argue that the surety breached a contractual duty to issue payments or make expenditures in good faith, or that the surety breached the implied covenant of good faith and fair dealing.

In a recent Florida decision, *Liberty Mutual Insurance Co. v. Aventura Engineering & Construction Corp.*,[81] the court observed, "Courts have consistently upheld contractual rights of a surety as long as the surety acted in the good faith belief that it was required to act or pay, regardless of whether any liability actually existed."[82] In analyzing whether the surety acted in good faith, the court determined that the principal had to show that the surety acted with deliberate malfeasance, defined as, "an intentional wrongful act which the actor has no legal right to do, or any wrongful conduct which affects, interrupts, or interferes with the performance of an official legal duty." The court ruled that a "lack of diligence or negligence is not the equivalent of bad faith, and even gross negligence is not the same as bad faith."[83]

The *Aventura* decision sets forth how a surety may undertake its investigation and protect its rights under the indemnity agreement. From the inception of the claim, the surety advised the indemnitors of each right it intended to exercise; made a demand for collateral; and frequently reiterated and reserved all of its rights and defenses. In granting summary judgment for the surety, the *Aventura* decision recognized the surety's right to recover its losses and expenses; its

---

81   534 F. Supp. 2d 1290 (S.D. Fla. 2008).
82   *Id.* at 1316 (citing Employers Ins. of Wausau v. W. Able Green, Inc., 749 F. Supp. at 1103 (S.D. Fla. 1990)).
83   *Id.*

right to settle the principal's claim against the obligee; its right to settle the obligee's claim against the surety; its right to be placed in collateral for outstanding claims; and its right to compel specific performance of the indemnitor's obligation to pledge collateral.

After securing an indemnity agreement, the surety in *Aventura* executed multiple performance and payment bonds. In response to a notice from one obligee of its intent to declare the principal in default, the surety undertook an investigation of the principal's books and records. The surety discovered through the principal's admission that the cost to complete the project exceeded the remaining contract balances by $900,000. The principal acknowledged to the obligee that it under-bid the project by $1,700,000.

The surety made demand upon the principal to post $900,000 in collateral.[84] The principal responded that it had not been terminated or declared in default, therefore there was no justification for the surety's involvement in the matter. Although the principal agreed to provide collateral, it did not agree to the amount the surety requested, but rather said that the amount would be determined from further analysis. The surety in multiple communications persisted in its demand and reiterated its reservation of rights.

The obligee eventually terminated the principal's contract. The principal maintained that the obligee breached the bonded contract by its refusal to issue payments, and demanded that the surety not honor the obligee's claim against the bond. Rather, the principal requested that it be allowed to litigate its claim against the obligee. The surety sought the principal's cooperation in securing ratification agreements with the principal's major subcontractors and material suppliers and then negotiated a takeover agreement with the obligee, to which the principal was a party. The surety proposed to complete the project under a reservation of rights.

Despite the surety's multiple demands that the principal post collateral, the principal refused. The surety then issued a letter formally invoking its assignment rights and its right to settle as the principal's "attorney-in-fact." The surety proceeded to settle with the obligee and utilized its power of attorney to release all claims that

---

84 *Id.* at 1297.

the principal had against the obligee growing out of the bonded contract.

Subsequently, the surety received claim notices on three other projects. Similarly, the surety conducted its investigation, made a demand for collateral and reserved all of its rights.

The surety filed an indemnity action alleging that the principal breached the indemnity agreement by failing to provide collateral upon demand, by demanding that the surety deny the obligee's claim without providing collateral security to the surety, and by failing to provide any indemnification to the surety. The surety argued the principal's breaches invoked all of the surety's rights under the indemnity agreement.

The principal defended by alleging a) that the obligee did not have a proper claim against the bond due to its default in issuing progress payments; b) that the right-to-settle clause is limited to claims against the bond and the attorney-in-fact provision is limited to rights assigned elsewhere in the indemnity agreement; c) that if the surety was authorized to settle the principal's claim, the surety waived such rights; and d) that the surety's bad faith vitiates any right, otherwise not waived, to release the principal's claim against the obligee.[85]

The *Aventura* court rejected the principal's argument that the surety had no rights under the indemnity agreement because the owner was in default. The court held that the indemnity agreement, and not the bond, delineates the rights and obligations of the principal and surety.[86] The court further held that the principal's

---

85   *Id.* at 1306.
86   *Id.* at 1309 (citing Aetna Ins. Co. v. Buchanan, 369 So.2d 351, 354 (Fla. App. 1979) ("The status of an indemnitor of a surety on a bond is to be determined by the indemnity agreement and not by the provisions of the bond."); Harrison v. Am. Fire & Cas. Co., 226 So.2d 28, 29 (Fla. App. 1969) (rejecting the argument that an indemnitor's liability shall be fixed by the terms of the bond since the status of an indemnitor is governed by the indemnity agreement, not the bond)); *see also,* Gen. Accident Ins. Co. of Am., 975 F. Supp. at 517 (S.D.N.Y. 1997) ("[A] contractor, whose relationship with the

failure to post the demanded collateral defeated the principal's claim of bad faith.[87]

The court found that the indemnitors granted to the surety in the indemnity agreement the right to settle. Therefore, the validity of the claims against the surety and principal was immaterial.[88] The principal's argument that the surety had no obligation under the performance bond and thus no valid bond claims lacked merit.

In *Atlantic Contracting & Material Company Inc. v. Ulico Casualty Co.*, the Maryland Court of Special Appeals applied a "reasonableness" standard in evaluating the surety's good faith in settling a claim.[89] The court concluded that the indemnity agreement grants a surety the discretion to pay a claim and the surety's discretion is limited by the bounds of reasonableness and not the bounds of fraud. In defining Maryland's good faith standard, the court rejected the lower court's holding that the surety's "good faith" required only that the surety subjectively believed that it was or would be liable to the claimant. The court instead considered the following factors: a) the surety's obligation to the claimant under the bond; b) whether the principal generally demanded that the surety deny payment or cooperated in the surety's claim investigation; and c) the thoroughness of the surety's claim investigation.

In determining the surety's obligation, the *Atlantic Contracting* court looked to both the bond and the indemnity agreement. The court found that the surety acted reasonably and in good faith when it paid the underlying claims. The *Atlantic Contracting* court was not persuaded by the principal's argument that it had viable defenses to

---

surety is governed by an express indemnity agreement contract containing provisions that permit the surety to settle in good faith, may [not] avoid its obligation to indemnify by pointing to inconsistent provisions in a separate contract between itself and the subcontractor.").

87   *Id.* at 1316.
88   *Id.* at 1310.
89   380 Md. 285, 309, 844 A.2d 460 (Md. 2004).

the claims, noting that the principal failed to respond when the surety requested that the principal submit available defenses.[90]

Some jurisdictions require that the principal must demonstrate that the surety acted with a dishonest purpose or some moral obliquity in order to avoid indemnity obligations.[91]

Courts in other jurisdictions have held that the surety is entitled to indemnity for its losses and expenses absent a showing of "fraud or extravagance;"[92] improper motive or dishonest purpose;[93] or "more than merely negligent or unreasonable conduct [requiring] proof of an improper motive or willful ignorance of the facts.[94] One court held that, ". . . payments made in good faith shall be deemed to include any and all payments made by the surety except those made with deliberate and willful malfeasance."[95] Other courts have stated, ". . . generally when an indemnity agreement gives a surety broad discretion to pay claims triggering the indemnity agreement, the only defense an indemnitor may raise against a claim by the surety for

---

90 *Id.* at 311.
91 Nguyen v. Lumbermans Mutual Ins. Co., 261 Ga. App. 553, 583 S.E.2d 220 (Ga. App. 2003).
92 First Nat'l Ins. of Am. v. Joseph Wunderlich, Inc., 358 F. Supp. 2d 44 (N.D.N.Y. 2004), *aff'd*, 144 Fed. Appx. 125, 2005 U.S. App. LEXIS 6580 (2d Cir. N.Y. 2005).
93 The Mountbatten Sur. Co. v. William H. Jenkins, No. 02-CV-8421, 2004 U.S. Dist. LEXIS 20653, 2004 WL 2297405 (E.D. Pa. Oct. 13, 2004).
94 Bituminous Cas., et. al v. Texas Window Specialties, Inc., No. C.V.A. SA-03-CA-98, 2006 U.S. Dist. LEXIS 9272, 2006 WL 864277 (D.C. Tx. Mar. 7, 2006).
95 U.S. Fid. & Guar. Co. v. Bilt-Rite Contractors, Inc., No. Civ. A. 04-1505, 2005 U.S. Dist. LEXIS 9299, 2005 WL 1168374 (E.D. Pa. May 16, 2005).

indemnification is that the surety committed fraud or collusion, or otherwise acted in bad faith in paying a claim."[96]

B. Wrongful Settlement and Release of the Principal's Affirmative Claims

When a surety releases the principal's affirmative claims against the obligee as part of a broader settlement of the obligee's claims, such claims are often settled over the principal's objections. In addressing such objections,[97] the *Aventura* court reviewed the provisions in the indemnity agreement pertaining to settlements, assignments and attorney-in-fact designations. The court found that the principal agreed to indemnify the surety against any potential liability and granted the surety, in its sole discretion, the right to settle not only

---

96 Constructora Andrade Guiterrez, S.A. v. Am. Int'l Ins. Co., 467 F.3d 38 (1st Cir. 2006) (citing Fireman's Ins. Co. of Newark, New Jersey v. Todesca, 310 F.3d 32 (1st Cir. 2002)). For further discussion of the standards of "good faith" employed by various courts, see Section II(A)(2) of this chapter.
97 See Section III (A) of this chapter.

the claims against the surety but also the claims held by the principal against the obligee,[98] especially if the indemnitors refused the

---

[98] Liberty Mutual Ins. Co. v. Aventura Eng. & Const. Corp., 534 F. Supp.2d 1290, 1306-07. The *Aventura* court explained the wide-ranging acceptance in other jurisdictions of a surety's right to settle claims:

> While neither the Florida Supreme Court, Florida intermediate courts of appeals, nor the Eleventh Circuit have addressed the specific question of whether the surety may, in addition to settling a claim on the bond, also settle the principal's claims against the owner of the bond, other courts that have done so have expressly recognized a surety's right to settle the principal's claims, by virtue of the assignment and power-of-attorney provisions of an indemnity agreement. *See, e.g.*, Hutton Constr. Co. v. County of Rockland, 52 F.3d 1191 (2d Cir.1995) (affirming trial court's decision to enforce a settlement which included the surety's dismissal of its principal's affirmative claims, over the principal's objections). The Hutton Court reasoned that the principal breached the indemnity agreement by failing to make the demanded indemnity payments. *Id.* at 1192. This breach triggered the assignment clause and caused assignment to the surety of all of the principal's rights growing out of the construction contracts. *Id.* The assignment clause, and the attorney-in-fact clause, which unambiguously appointed the surety as the principal's attorney-in-fact with the power to exercise all rights assigned to them, gave the surety the right to settle the principal's claims against the owner. *Id.* 1192-93.

Similarly, in Mezzacappa Brothers, Inc. v. City of New York, No. 03-0223, 2003 WL 22801429, *6-7 (S.D.N.Y. Nov. 24, 2003), the Court found that the assignment provision in the indemnity agreement, which stated that "[Principal] assigns to [Surety] ... [a]ny actions, causes of action, claims or demands whatsoever which [Principal] may have or acquire against any party to the Contract, or arising out of or in connection with any Contract . . . and [Surety] shall have the full and exclusive right, in its name or in the name of

surety's demand for collateral.[99] If the principal wanted to preserve its claims against the owner, the indemnity agreement required that the indemnitors deliver to the surety sufficient collateral that would exonerate and indemnify the surety against any potential loss.[100]

> The Settlements provision gives the surety "the right, *at its option and sole discretion,* to adjust, settle or compromise *any* claim [or] demand . . ." (*Id.* at § 13) (emphasis added). The Assignment provision assigns "all of the right, title and interest of the Indemnitors and/or Principals in, and growing in any manner out of, all contracts referred to in the Bonds, or . . . out of the Bonds." In turn, the Attorney-in-Fact provision appoints the Surety as Defendants' "attorney-in-fact ... to exercise all the rights . . . assigned . . . over to the Surety . . . in this Agreement, with full

---

> [Principal] . . . to prosecute, compromise, release or otherwise resolve such actions, causes of action, claims or demands," gave the surety the authority to release and settle the principal's affirmative claims. *Id.*; see also, Bell BCI Co. v. Old Dominion Demolition Corp., 294 F. Supp.2d 807, 812 (E.D. Va. 2003) (applying Virginia Law and finding that the Indemnity Agreement's unambiguous assignment and attorney-in-fact provisions conferred on the Surety the authority to settle and resolve the principal's claims against the owner); Harlandale Independent Sch. Dist. v. C2M Constr., Inc., No. 04-07-00304, 2007 WL 2253510, at *2 (Tex. App. Aug. 8, 2007) (finding that the industry standard indemnity, assignment, settlement, and attorney-in-fact provisions give the surety the right to settle principal's claims against the project owner); N. Am. Specialty Ins. Co. v. Montco Constr. Co., Inc., No. 01-0246E, 2003 WL 2138321, at *7 (W.D.N.Y. Apr. 25, 2003) (finding that a principal's breach of indemnity agreement by failing to post collateral or otherwise exonerate the indemnity surety activated the attorney-in-fact and assignment clauses of the Indemnity Agreement and gave the surety the right to settle the principal's pending lawsuit against the owner/obligee). Courts that have addressed this question answer it by construing the language of the Indemnity Agreement to ascertain the surety's rights and obligations. *See id.*

99 *Id.* at 1308.
100 *Id.*

power and authority to execute on behalf of and sign any Indemnitor or Principal to any ... release ...."

Nowhere in these provisions does the indemnity agreement require that the owner's claim on the bond be "valid" before Liberty may exercise its contractual rights to indemnity, exoneration, assignment and settlements of claims. Rather, these provisions unequivocally state that Liberty's rights arise once Liberty determines that it may incur potential liability and that actual liability need not be shown. *Cf. Thurston,* 528 So.2d at 129 ("A surety is entitled to reimbursement pursuant to an indemnity contract for any payments made by it in a good faith belief that it was required to pay, regardless of whether any liability actually existed."). Therefore, whether Goodwill's claim is ultimately found to have been "proper" or "valid" is immaterial. The Indemnity Agreement simply does not provide that Liberty must receive a valid claim before it can exercise its rights.[101]

While indemnitors will often disagree with a surety's decision to settle the principal's affirmative claims against the obligee, courts generally find, as in *Aventura*, that the indemnity agreement assignment, settlement and attorney-in-fact provisions give the surety the right to release the principal's claims.[102]

C. Obligee's Breach of Its Duties to the Principal

Indemnitors frequently maintain, as they did in the *Atlantic Contracting* and *Aventura* cases,[103] that the obligee breached the

---

101 *Id.* at 1310.
102 For a detailed analysis of a surety's right to settle the principal's affirmative claims, *see* M. Michael Egan, Brett D. Divers and Omar J. Harb, The Indemnity Agreement and the Handling of Surety Claims, in *The Surety's Indemnity Agreement–Law & Practice*, 2d ed. 323 (Marilyn Klinger, George J. Bachrach, & Tracey L. Haley, eds., 2008).
103 Atl. Contracting & Material Co., Inc. v. Ulico Cas. Co., 844 A.2d 460 at 470 (Md. 2004); Liberty Mutual Ins. Co. v. Aventura Eng'g & Constr. Corp, 534 F. Supp. 2d 1290 at 1305 (S.D. Fla. 2008).

provisions of the bonded contract. Accordingly, they deny indemnity liability to a surety that issues payment to an obligee that is in default. In *United States Fidelity and Guaranty Company v. Stanley Contracting, Inc.*,[104] the surety sought to enforce its indemnity rights after having settled claims against its bond. The indemnitors argued that the obligee wrongfully terminated the principal. They further argued that if the principal had been allowed to perform the contract, there would have been no claims under the bond.[105] The indemnitors further maintained that the surety failed to conduct a reasonable investigation into the obligee's claims and the principal's defenses.

The surety argued that the indemnity agreement provided the right to settle claims which the surety thought were valid. Thus, whether the obligee wrongfully terminated the principal was irrelevant. The reasonable investigation standard was not applicable because the parties agreed in the indemnity agreement that the surety's discretion was limited only by the standard of good faith. The *Stanley* court held that the parties agreed that the surety's "good faith term is fulfilled if there is no bad faith or wrongful motive on the part of the [surety]."[106] Thereafter, the court concluded that the indemnitors failed to establish that the surety acted with bad faith or a wrongful motive when it paid the claims and completed the project.[107]

In *Mercede*,[108] the court imposed a good faith standard of whether the surety had an improper motive or dishonest purpose in making the payments to the claimant in evaluating the principal's obligation to indemnify. Unlike the *Stanley* court, the *Mercede* court considered the surety's alleged lack of a reasonable investigation as evidence of bad faith and found sufficient evidence from which the jury could conclude that the surety acted in bad faith and acted with an improper motive in satisfying the claim.

---

104   303 F. Supp. 2d 1169 (D. Or. 2004).
105   *Id.* at 1171.
106   *Id.* at 1174.
107   *Id.*
108   *Mercede* is discussed extensively in Section II(A)(2) of this chapter.

In *Liberty Mutual Insurance Co. v. Aventura Engineering & Construction Corp.*,[109] the court rejected the principal's argument that the surety had no obligation under the bond due to "owner default." Like the court in *Stanley,* the *Aventura* court reasoned that the indemnity agreement, not the bond, delineates the rights and obligations of the principal and surety.[110] The *Aventura* court concluded that the indemnitors breached the indemnity agreement by failing to post collateral. Thus, their arguments that the surety engaged in bad faith had no merit.[111] The court further concluded that the indemnitors expressly granted the surety the right to settle and that the indemnity agreement provided to the indemnitors the mechanism whereby they could compel the surety to litigate the obligees' claims by providing sufficient collateral to the surety.[112]

D. Demand for Collateral by Surety is Excessive

Indemnity agreements typically require that the indemnitors deposit collateral with the surety upon demand or upon the establishment of a reserve by the surety. The surety's right to collateral in the indemnity agreements is not expressly conditioned upon the surety being obligated to pay the claim. Rather, the typical indemnity agreement requires only that the indemnitors deposit collateral upon receiving the surety's demand.

The indemnity agreement grants the surety the discretion to demand collateral if it has a good faith belief that it might be liable under the bond.[113] In *United States Fidelity & Guaranty Co. v. Stanley Contracting, Inc.*,[114] the surety sought to enforce the collateral security provision after receiving claims on the bonds. The *Stanley* court looked to the express language of the indemnity

---

109 534 F. Supp. 2d 1290 (S.D. Fla. 2008).
110 *Id.* at 1309.
111 *Id.* at 1316.
112 *Id.* at 1308.
113 *Id.*
114 303 F. Supp. 2d 1169 (D. Or. 2004).

Claims and Defenses Asserted by Principals or Indemnitors 547

agreement and ordered the principal to post collateral equal to the amount of the surety's reserve.[115]

The indemnitors' failure to provide collateral to the surety constitutes a breach of the indemnity agreement, invoking the surety's rights under the indemnity agreement for specific performance or a judgment in the amount of the collateral demanded plus costs and attorney fees.[116] If the surety demands collateral, the surety needs only prove that the indemnitors breached the indemnity agreement by failing to comply.[117]

Failure of the indemnitors to deposit collateral in accordance with the indemnity agreement and to pay costs associated with litigation constitutes a breach by the indemnitors.[118] A surety is entitled to demand collateral security from its indemnitors to protect the surety from any possible liability flowing from pending claims.[119]

An issue might arise if the surety seeks collateral to cover a bond claim that the indemnitors believe has no merit. The *Aventura* court resolved this issue in favor of the surety:

> Contrary to Defendant's assertions, the indemnity agreement does not condition Liberty's rights on a "proper" or "valid" claim upon the Bond. Instead, Liberty and Aventura executed an indemnity agreement giving Liberty the right to seek collateral in order to be exonerated and to be indemnified for all costs associated with the issued bonds. The Indemnity provision states that if the "Surety determines, *in its sole judgment,* that *potential liability* exists" the principals must deposit a sum of money satisfactory to the Surety, regardless of whether the Surety has made any payments or even

---

115 *Id.* at 1174.
116 Mountbatten Sur. Co., Inc. v. Szabo Contracting, Inc., 349 Ill. App. 3d 857, 812 N.E.2d 90 (2004), *appeal denied*, 211 Ill. 2d 582, 812 N.E.2d 90; Fid. and Dep. Co. of Maryland v. A-MAC Sales & Builders, No. 04-72643, 2006 U.S. Dist. LEXIS 35308, 2006 WL 1555985 (E.D. Mich. June 5, 2006).
117 *Id.*
118 Safeco Ins. Co. of Am. v. Lori Chiang, No. C-04-1977, 2006 U.S. Dist. LEXIS 86695, 2007 WL 460842 (N.D. Cal. Feb. 7, 2007).
119 *Id.* at *8.

received a notice of a claim on the bond. . . . [T]he Settlements provision gives the surety "the right, *at its option and sole discretion,* to adjust, settle or compromise *any* claim [or] demand . . .

[N]owhere in these provisions does the indemnity agreement require that the owner's claim on the bond be "valid" before Liberty may exercise its contractual rights to indemnity, exoneration, assignment and settlements of claim. Rather, these provisions unequivocally state that Liberty's rights arise once Liberty determines that it may incur potential liability and that actual liability need not be shown. *Cf. Thurston,* 528 So. 2d at 129 ("A surety is entitled to reimbursement pursuant to an indemnity contract for any payments made by it in a good faith belief that it was required to pay, regardless of whether any liability actually existed."). Therefore, whether Goodwill's claim is ultimately found to have been "proper" or "valid" is immaterial. The Indemnity Agreement simply does not provide that Liberty must receive a valid claim before it can exercise its rights.[120]

Once the surety is placed in collateral, the indemnitors might argue that the surety did not properly disburse such funds. In *Travelers Casualty & Surety Co. of America v. Dennis J. Amoroso,*[121] the principal deposited collateral with the surety. The principal claimed that the surety orally agreed that the principal could direct the surety's disbursement of the collateral. The principal asserted that the surety breached the covenant of good faith and fair dealing by failing to follow directions from the principal. The court concluded that there can be no claim for breach of the implied covenant based upon alleged verbal contracts because the indemnity agreements required that any modifications must be in writing and signed by an officer of the surety.

---

120   Liberty Mutual Ins. Co. v. Aventura Eng. & Constr. Corp., 534 F. Supp. 2d 1290, 1310 (S.D. Fla. 2008) (emphasis in original).
121   Travelers Cas. & Sur. Co. of Am. v. Dennis J. Amoroso, No. C03-746 PJH, 2004 U.S. Dist. LEXIS 17604, 2004 WL 1918890 (N.D. Cal. Aug. 24, 2004).

The *Amoroso* court found that the indemnity agreement required that the indemnitors deposit collateral upon demand and granted the surety the express right to use those funds in its discretion:

> Therefore, because Travelers had the express right to demand the $3 million collateral paid by Amoroso and the express right to use those funds in its discretion, Amoroso cannot state a claim for the breach of the covenant of good faith based on the indemnity agreement.[122]

In response to a surety's collateral demand, indemnitors might challenge the amount of the surety's demand as excessive. In *Hanover Insurance Company v. Clark*,[123] the surety argued that Illinois courts and other jurisdictions have routinely granted motions for summary judgment in favor of a surety for specific performance of the collateral security obligation under an indemnity agreement.[124] The court recognized the surety's right to determine the amount of its collateral demand in denying the indemnitors' assertion that the amount demanded was excessive.

> As the Second Circuit noted in *American Motorists*, in the event that the claims against Plaintiff are reduced in value, Defendant

---

122 *Id.* at 9.
123 No. 05-C-2162, 2006 U.S. Dist. LEXIS 62418; 2006 WL 2375428 (N.D. Ill. Aug. 15, 2006).
124 *Id.* at 17 (citing U.S. Fid. & Guar. Ins. Co. v. Cler Constr. Servs., Inc., 2003 U.S. Dist. LEXIS 19810, No. 03 C 1405, 2003 WL 22508169 at *2 (N.D. Ill. Nov. 3, 2003); Am. Motorists Ins. Co. v. United Furnace Co., Inc., 876 F.2d 293, 299-300 (2d Cir. 1989) ("Courts have traditionally analyzed the plain language of the indemnity agreement to determine a surety's right to obtain specific performance of collateral security"); Safeco Ins. Co. v. Schwab, 739 F.2d 431, 433-34 (9th Cir. 1984) (an indemnity agreement with a surety should be construed as requiring the indemnitor to provide collateral security upon demand by the surety and prior to actual bond loss)).

would be entitled to the return of any of the excess collateral funds.[125]

In *American Motorists Insurance Co. v. Pennsylvania Beads Corp.*,[126] the surety demanded collateral after receiving a claim from the obligee on a customs bond. The indemnitors refused to post the collateral and argued that the indemnity agreement was ambiguous and that enforcement of the collateral security provision was contrary to public policy. The court held that the collateral provision was both "clear and precise." The court further found that the parties agreed the principal would be obligated to provide sufficient collateral which would protect the surety against liability.[127]

The principal in *Pennsylvania Beads* also argued that the collateral provision of the indemnity agreement was unconscionable and void as against public policy because it forces the indemnitor to post collateral before there has been a judicial determination as to the surety's liability.[128] The *Pennsylvania Beads* court agreed with the indemnitors' "characterization of the practical effect of the indemnity agreement," but held that the purpose of the collateral provision was to protect the surety against its indemnitors' insolvency and provide security before the surety is required to make bond payments:

> Defendant's characterization of the practical effect of the indemnity agreement is entirely accurate. Indeed, the very purpose of the Agreement is to provide plaintiff with collateral security before it is required to discharge any potential Customs liability. That purpose is neither unconscionable, nor void as against public policy, and has been enforced consistently by our courts. *See e.g. American Motorists Ins. Co., 876 F.2d at 302* (holding that under an identical provision, AMICO was entitled to receive the collateral security it had bargained for); *Northwestern National*

---

125   *Id.* at 19 (citing Am. Motorists v. United Furnace Co., Inc., 876 F.2d at 293, 300 (CA 2 N.Y. 1989)).
126   983 F. Supp. 437 (S.D.N.Y. 1997).
127   *Id.* at 440.
128   *Id.*

> *Insurance Co. of Milwaukee, Wisconsin v. Alberts, 741 F. Supp. 424, 429 (S.D.N.Y. 1990)* (enforcing surety's rights to collateral security for an anticipated liability as provided for by an indemnity agreement); *Safeco Ins. Co. of America v. Schwab, 739 F.2d 432, 433 (9th Cir. 1984)* ("Sureties are ordinarily entitled to specific performance of collateral security clauses. 'If a creditor is to have the security position for which he bargained, the promise to maintain the security must be specifically enforced.'" *(quoting Marine Midland Trust Co. of New York v. Alleghany Corp., 28 F. Supp. 680, 683-84 (S.D.N.Y. 1939)).*
>
> The only remaining support for defendant's public policy argument is its unsubstantiated claim that the financial hardship which would result from enforcement of the indemnity agreement would bankrupt PB Co. "needlessly." *Id.* While that possible outcome would indeed be unfortunate, it does not, standing alone, provide a valid justification for denying plaintiff access to the security it specifically bargained for. In fact, absent enforcement of the indemnity agreement's collateral security clause, plaintiff could–in the bankruptcy situation contemplated by defendant–be relegated to an unsecured claim and therefore be forced to share its debtor's property with other creditors. If anything, public policy considerations dictate against such a result, since it is that precise situation which AMICO sought to avoid in bargaining for the collateral security clause.[129]

Therefore, the *Pennsylvania Beads* court enforced the surety's collateral security rights. Courts have consistently held that the ultimate validity of the claims for which the surety demands collateral is immaterial, and indemnitors have been unsuccessful in avoiding their obligations on that ground.

E. Failure to Litigate Claims Asserted by Obligee

Sureties are typically granted the right, under the indemnity agreement, to settle claims against its bonds. Despite this express right, indemnitors, as a defense to their indemnity obligations, argue

---

129   *Id.* at 441.

that the surety essentially failed to mitigate its damages by paying an excessive amount to the claimant(s) or by failing to commence litigation against the allegedly responsible party, such as the obligee.

In *Reliance Insurance Co. v. Dipietro Plumbing Corp.*,[130] the court rejected the indemnitors' arguments that the surety's payment was excessive and that the surety had an obligation to litigate the obligee's claims against the performance bond. The *Dipietro* court concluded that the surety's conduct was expressly authorized by the indemnity agreement, wherein the indemnitors granted the surety the right to settle claims in its sole discretion.

The court addressed multiple defenses raised by individual indemnitors, including that the surety a) had a duty to commence litigation against the bond obligee; b) acted in bad faith by paying excessive amounts to secure its release of its bond obligations; c) failed to offer the principal the opportunity to complete the bonded contract after the principal's contractual rights were terminated by the obligee; and d) breached its fiduciary obligations to the individual indemnitors by acts of its agent. In rejecting these defenses, the court noted that "written contracts are to be enforced according to their terms."[131] The indemnity agreement expressly granted the surety the right to settle claims.

> [T]he right, at its option and sole discretion . . . (c) [t]o adjust, settle or compromise any claim, suit or judgment upon said bond or bonds or any of them, unless the undersigned shall request in writing the surety to litigate such claim or demand, or defend such a suit, or appeal from such judgment, and shall deposit with the surety, at the time of such request, cash or collateral satisfactory to the surety in kind and amount to be used in paying any judgment or judgments rendered with interest, costs and attorney's fees.[132]

---

130 No. 85-C-6985, 1989 U.S. Dist. LEXIS 3545, 1989 WL 32935 (N.D. Ill. Apr. 3, 1989).
131 *Dipietro*, 1989 WL 32935, at *4.
132 *Id.* at *2.

Claims and Defenses Asserted by Principals or Indemnitors 553

The *Dipietro* court observed that these provisions, though strict, are common in indemnity agreements and have been "uniformly sustained and upheld subject to a single exception." The exception is when the payment(s) was made "through fraud or lack of good faith."[133]

The court stated that the surety has broad discretion to settle claims unless the indemnitors exercised their right to require the surety to litigate the claims. The court observed that at no time did the indemnitors make such a request in writing.[134] Further, the indemnitors did not deposit collateral with the surety. In rejecting all of the indemnitors' defenses, the court stated that none of the alleged conduct "even raises the issue of bad faith."[135]

Despite possessing the exclusive right for itself and for its principal to settle claims against its bond, the surety in *Hartford v. Tanner*[136] was denied its indemnity rights.[137] In *Tanner*, the indemnitors argued that the surety had an obligation to administratively challenge the obligees' claims.

The *Tanner* court held that a "conclusive evidence" clause is contrary to public policy.[138] The court also held that the implied covenant of good faith and fair dealing and the "reasonableness

---

133 *Id.* at *3 (citing Fid. & Deposit Co. of Maryland v. Bristol Steel, 722 F.2d 1160, 1163 (4th Cir. 1983); U.S. For Use & Benefit of St. Paul A.M.E., 541 F.2d 463, 464 (4th Cir. 1976) ("Buckeye remains free to adjust, settle, or compromise any claim, limited only by whatever legally-imposed duty of good faith may exist")).
134 *Id.* at *2.
135 *Id.* at *4.
136 22 Kan. App. 2d 64, 910 P.2d 872 (Kan. App. 1996).
137 Note that the court in Associated Indem. Corp. v. CAT Contracting, Inc., 41 Tex. Sup. Ct. J. 389, 389, 964 S.W.2d 276, 281 (Tex. 1998) disagreed with the *Tanner* decision and the court in PSE Consulting, Inc. v. Frank Mercede and Sons, Inc., 267 Conn. 279, 300, 838 A.2d 135, 150 (Conn. 2004). The *Tanner* decision was examined in Atl. Contracting & Material Co., Inc. v. Ulico Cas. Co., 844 A.2d 460, 472, 380 Md. 285, 307 (Md. 2004).
138 *Tanner*, 22 Kan. App. 2d at 74.

standard" apply to suretyship agreements.[139] The trial court ruled that the surety's payment on the bond was not reasonable and denied the surety's indemnity claims.[140] The indemnity agreement at issue did not include a *prima facie* evidence clause. The court concluded that the fact that the surety's actions, pursuant to the indemnity agreement, were "final, conclusive and binding" on the indemnitors resulted in a "conclusive evidence clause." Such a clause would have required the court to simply grant judgment in favor of the surety without regard to whether the surety's conduct was reasonable, which the court deemed to be a violation of public policy.[141]

In *Tanner*, the surety secured an application containing indemnity obligations prior to issuing customs bonds. The obligee asserted claims against three bonds. The principal disputed two of the claims and the surety disputed the third claim. In response to the surety's letter disputing the obligee's claim on the third bond, the obligee withdrew its claim. The surety then paid the obligee's other two claims and sought recovery against the indemnitors.[142]

The *Tanner* court defined general principles of suretyship;[143] to support its finding that a good faith requirement is implied in indemnity contracts.[144] The court applied a reasonableness standard as adopted in cases involving insurance.[145] The appeals court

---

139 *Id.*

140 *Id.* at 68.

141 *Id.* at 73 (citing Fid. and Deposit Co. v. Davis, 129 Kan. 790, 801, 284 P. 430 (1930) ("The court held that a 'conclusive evidence' clause in an indemnification contract given by a principal to a surety was invalid because it violated public policy by making the court ministerial.")).

142 *Id.* at 66-67.

143 *Id.* at 70 (citing Hinchey, *Surety's Performance Over Protest of Principal: Considerations and Risks*, 22 TORT & INS. L.J. 133, 134 (1986)).

144 *Id.* (citing Hinchey, *supra*, at 143; Commercial Union Ins. Co. v. Melikyan, 430 So.2d. 1217, 1221 (La. App. 1983)).

145 *Id.* at 74-76 (citing Hinchey, *supra*, at 133, 149; First Hays Bancshares, Inc. v. Kansas Bankers Sur. Co., 244 Kan. 576, 580, 769 P.2d 1184 (1989)); *see* Docking v. Nat'l Sur. Co., 122 Kan. 235, 240,

affirmed the trial court's holding that the surety's actions were unreasonable.

F. Settlement Motivated by Bad Faith Claims Asserted By Obligee

Some indemnitors have argued that the surety had an improper motive to settle the claim(s), which improper motive is tantamount to bad faith or a self-interested settlement. Courts addressing this defense have reached differing conclusions. In *PSE Consulting, Inc. v. Frank Mercede and Sons, Inc.*,[146] the court held that the surety had an improper motive for settling a payment bond claim, thereby releasing the indemnitors from their obligations to the surety. In *Mercede*, the payment bond claimant alleged that the surety acted in bad faith and in violation of Connecticut law by failing to promptly investigate and pay the claim. In response to the bad faith allegation, the surety settled the claim and within the same action sought recovery from the indemnitors. Upholding the trial court verdict against the surety for bad faith, the Supreme Court of Connecticut determined that the jury could have reasonably concluded that the surety acted out of its own self-interest.[147]

The *Mercede* court then considered whether a surety acting in its own self-interest in paying a claim could support a finding of bad faith.[148] The court considered *Fidelity & Deposit Co. of Maryland v. Bristol Steel & Iron Works, Inc.*,[149] wherein the surety settled a performance bond claim after the Pennsylvania Department of Transportation threatened that it would no longer accept bonds issued by the surety. In *Bristol Steel,* the court held that the surety had the right to reimbursement for payments that it believed were necessary or expedient, whether or not such liability, necessity, or

---

252 P. 201 (1927); Rush Presbyterian St. Luke's Medical Center v. Safeco Ins. Co., 712 F. Supp. 1344, 1345-46 (N.D. Ill. 1989).
146 267 Conn. 279, 838 A.2d 135 (Conn. 2004).
147 *Mercede*, 267 Conn. at 316.
148 *Id.* at 315.
149 722 F.2d 1160 (4th Cir. 1983).

expediency existed.[150] The *Mercede* court distinguished the *Bristol Steel* ruling:

> Those facts are distinguishable from the present case wherein the jury reasonably could have found that the principal, Mercede, at various times, either was unaware of the fact that National was making payments to PSE, or had objected to those payments once it was made aware of them. In fact, Mercede presented evidence showing that, initially, National actually had supported Mercede's defenses against PSE's claims against the payment bond. Mercede also presented evidence that, only after PSE had filed a complaint with the insurance commissioner and had threatened litigation against National based upon bad faith and CUTPA claims, did National abandon this approach. Moreover, we observe that Pennsylvania law required the principal in *Fidelity & Deposit Co. of Maryland* "'not simply to indemnify the surety but to keep it unmolested'"; id.; a standard not at play in the present case. Therefore, unlike in *Fidelity & Deposit Co. of Maryland,* the self-interested settlement in the present case was not cloaked in good faith garb, but, rather, was tainted by a confluence of circumstances from which a jury could properly have inferred improper motive.[151]

The *Mercede* court determined that just self-interest is not sufficient to support a finding of bad faith. However a self-interested settlement, when accompanied by other evidence of improper motive, can constitute bad faith.[152]

---

150 *Id.* at 1163.
151 *Mercede*, 267 Conn. at 316 (citing Fid. & Deposit Co. of Maryland v. Bristol Steel & Iron Works, Inc., 722 F.2d at 1165).
152 *Id.* at 318 (citing Arntz Contracting Co. v. St. Paul Fire & Marine Ins. Co., 47 Cal. App. 4th 464, 485-86 (Ca. App. 1996) (holding indemnification of settlement costs properly denied where costs were attributable to obligee's action against surety for bad faith claims and claims involving willful malfeasance in managing project); *see also*, U.S. Fid. & Guar. Co. v. Feibus, 15 F. Supp. 2d 586-87 (no evidence submitted that surety made payments because of "improper motive or purpose")).

In *Auto-Owners Insurance Co. v. Southeast Floating Docks, Inc.*,[153] the court reversed a jury's finding that the surety acted in bad faith when it settled the obligee's claim against the performance bond. In response to the surety claim, the indemnitors argued that the surety failed to conduct an adequate investigation. The indemnitors also asserted that the claim payment, as in *Mercede*, was motivated by a "self-interested settlement" that was "tainted by a confluence of circumstances from which a jury could properly have inferred improper motive."[154] The court rejected the indemnitors' argument that the *Mercede* ruling should apply.

> Although these facts parallel some of the facts present in [*Mercede*], the Court finds that they are not sufficient to permit a reasonable jury to conclude that Auto-Owners acted in bad faith. A mere expression of concern over a bad faith claim cannot support a finding that the bad faith claim was the primary basis for Auto-Owner's settlement with Rivermar. And the fact that the bad faith claim was included in the release is also not significant; no reasonable surety would leave even minor claims hanging over its head when it could obtain a release as to all potential liability. Finally, Auto-Owners was under no obligation, contractually or otherwise, to include Southeast and Simpson in the settlement negotiations or to reach a settlement that benefitted them. . . . A right to settle clause, such as Section 4(g) of the Indemnity Agreement, typically provides a surety with 'wide discretion' in settling claims, 'even where the principal is not liable for the underlying claim' . . . The Defendants have not challenged Auto-Owner's *prima facie* case and have failed to produce any evidence from which a reasonable jury could conclude that Auto-Owners acted in bad faith in settling Rivermar's claim."[155]

Accordingly, outcomes have varied in cases in which the surety settles claims which are accompanied by actual or potential bad faith

---

153 No. 6:05-cv-334-orl-31-JGG, 2007 U.S. Dist. LEXIS 14252, 2007 WL 676217, 20 Fla. L. Weekly Fed. D 599 (M.D. Fla., March 1, 2007).
154 *Southeast Floating Docks*, 2007 WL 676217, at *4.
155 *Id.* at *4-5.

claims asserted by the claimant. Courts will consider the surrounding circumstances in determining whether a purported "improper" motive was the primary motive for the settlement.

G. Attorney's Fees Incurred by the Surety Are Excessive or Incurred in Bad Faith

Indemnitors frequently argue they have no obligation to reimburse the surety for its legal fees, alleging the surety breached the covenant of good faith and fair dealing or failed to act in good faith. Further, indemnitors often argue that the surety's attorney fees were not reasonable or were duplicative.

Indemnity agreements often require that the indemnitors reimburse the surety for all expenses, including attorney's fees, which the surety incurs by reason of having issued any bonds. Most indemnity agreements provide that the surety's sworn statement as to fees incurred or evidence in the form of vouchers constitute *prima facie* evidence of the surety's loss. Indemnity provisions may also include a requirement that the surety incur the legal expenses in good faith or require that the surety incur the attorney's fees under the reasonable belief that the legal fees were necessary or expedient. These distinctions in the indemnity agreement have led courts to reach differing results.

1. Burden of Proof Issues

The indemnity agreement provides guidance as to whether the surety is required to show that its legal fees were proper, or whether the indemnitors must prove they are not recoverable. In *Central Towers Apartments, Inc. v. Martin*,[156] the indemnity agreement did not include a *prima facie* provision expressly shifting the burden to the indemnitors to prove that the surety failed to act in good faith or that the fees incurred were not reasonably necessary. The indemnity agreement provided:

---

156   61 Tenn. App. 244; 453 S.W. 2d 789 (Tenn. App. 1969).

> The undersigned will indemnify the Surety and hold it harmless from and against any and all claim, liability, cost, charge, counsel fee (including fees of special counsel), expense, suit, order, judgment and adjudication, whatsoever. Liability hereunder shall extend to any and all disbursements made by the Surety in good faith under the belief that it was liable for the amount so disbursed or that it was necessary or expedient to make such disbursements, whether such liability, necessity or expediency existed or not.[157]

In *Central Towers*, the surety initially tendered its defense to the principal. Thereafter, the surety learned that the owner prematurely paid the principal a portion of the retainage and that the principal accepted a note from the owner as partial payment for its work. The surety determined that these events created a conflict of interest between the surety and principal and elected to retain its own counsel.

The *Central Towers* court concluded that there was no conflict of interest between the surety and principal. It then considered whether the surety, in retaining its own counsel, acted reasonably and in good faith. This court identified "those facts which will have a bearing on the reasonable necessity of action and good faith under the circumstances," which included:

> [S]uch matters as the amount of risk to which the surety was exposed, whether the principal was solvent; whether the surety has called on the principal to deposit with it funds to cover the potential liability; whether the principal on demand by the surety to deposit with it the amount of the claim has refused to do so; whether the principal was notified of the action and given an opportunity to defend for itself and the surety; whether the principal hired the attorney for both himself and the surety; whether the principal notified the surety of the hiring of the attorney; the competency of the attorney hired by the principal; the diligence displayed by the principal and his attorney in the defense; whether there is a conflict of interest between the parties; the

---

157 *Id.* at 253-54.

attitude and cooperativeness of the surety; and the amount charged and diligence of the attorney hired by the surety.[158]

The principal settled the obligee's claim for $28,000, and the court concluded that a surety, given its "broad experience and daily encounter with claims of owners against contractors charged the surety with knowledge, if it acted in good faith, of at least an approximate amount of the potential liability."[159] The court further determined, on the issues of good faith and reasonable necessity, that the principal was solvent, engaged competent attorneys to represent the surety's interests and notified the surety to this effect.[160] Although the court held that the indemnity agreement rendered the contractor liable for attorney fees properly incurred by the surety, it denied the surety's indemnity claim on the basis that the surety did not act in good faith in incurring the attorney fees claimed.[161]

If the indemnity agreement specifies that the indemnitors must indemnify the surety for attorney fees incurred in good faith or with reasonable necessity and also includes a *prima facie* evidence provision, the surety's proffer of evidence in the form of an affidavit or other specified proof that it incurred the fees will, in the majority of jurisdictions, shift the burden of proof to the indemnitors to show that the surety failed to act in good faith.

The court in *Fallon Electric Co., Inc. v. Cincinnati Insurance Company*[162] distinguished *Central Towers*, noting that the indemnity agreement before it contained a *prima facie* evidence clause, thereby shifting the burden of proof to the indemnitors to show that the surety failed to act in good faith or demonstrate reasonable necessity.

In *Fallon*, the indemnity clause provided that the indemnitors must:

---

158   *Id.* at 268.
159   *Id.*
160   *Id.*
161   *Id.* at 269.
162   121 F.3d 125 (3rd Cir. 1997).

Claims and Defenses Asserted by Principals or Indemnitors 561

Exonerate, indemnify and keep indemnified [Surety] from and against any and all liability for losses and expenses of whatsoever kind or nature, including the fees and disbursements of counsel, and against any and all said losses and expense which [Surety] may sustain or incur: (i) by reason of having executed or procured the execution of any Bond or Bond; (ii) by reason of the failure of [Indemnitor] to perform or comply with the covenants and conditions of this Agreement; or (iii) in enforcing any of the covenants and conditions of this Agreement. [Surety] may pay or compromise any claim, demand, suit, judgment or expense arising out of such Bond or Bonds and any such payment or compromise shall be binding upon [Indemnitor] and included as a liability, loss or expense covered by this Indemnity Agreement, provided the same was made by [S]urety in the reasonable belief that it was liable for the amount disbursed, or that such payment or compromise was reasonable under all circumstances. In the event of any such payment or compromises by [Surety], an itemized statement thereof sworn to by any representative of [Surety] familiar with the facts, or the voucher or vouchers of other evidence of such payment or compromise shall be prima facia [sic] evidence of the facts and the amount of the liability of [Indemnitor] under this Agreement.[163]

On appeal, the surety argued that the trial court erred by imposing a reasonableness requirement on the amount of the surety's attorney fees in light of the "prima faci[e] evidence" language in the indemnity agreement.[164] The appellate court rejected the trial court's finding that "a surety may recover fees and expenses under an indemnity agreement only if it was 'reasonably necessary' for the surety to incur them . . . even where the contract of indemnity contains no explicit provision mandating reasonableness on the part of the surety."[165]

---

163   *Id.* at 126.
164   *Id.* at 127.
165   *Id.* at 128 (rejecting the holdings in U.S. Fid. & Guar. Co. v. Love, 260 Ark. 374, 538 S.W.2d 558, 559 (Ark. 1976); Redfern v. R.E. Dailey & Co., 146 Mich. App. 8, 379 N.W.2d 451, 456-57 (Mich. App. 1985); Perkins v. Thompson, 551 S. 2d 204, 209 (Miss. 1989);

The *Fallon* court was persuaded by the decision in *Transamerica Premier Insurance Co. v. Nelson*,[166] which ruled, "When the parties contractually agree that good faith is the standard, undertaking a determination of anything other than good faith is inappropriate."[167] The court also considered the following ruling in *United States Fidelity & Guaranty Co. v. Napier Electric & Construction Co.*:[168]

> The agreement further provided that vouchers or other evidence of payments or an itemized statement of payments sworn to by an officer of the surety shall be prima facie evidence of the fact and extent of the liability of the indemnitor to the surety.[169]

The *Fallon* court held that under such an agreement, "the indemnitor may successfully attack payments made by the surety only by pleading and proving fraud or lack of good faith by the surety."[170] The court also held that a *prima facie* evidence clause in an indemnity agreement shifts to the indemnitor the burden of proving that the costs incurred were not recoverable. Finally, the court concluded that "what an indemnitor must demonstrate to escape liability for attorney's fees depends upon the precise language used in the agreement."[171] Since the indemnitor failed to present any

---

Sentry Ins. Co. v. Davison Fuel & Dock Co., 60 Ohio App. 2d 248, 396 N.E.2d 1074, 1074 & n.2 (Ohio App. 1978); Cent. Towers Apts., Inc. v. Martin, 61 Tenn. App. 244, 453 S.W.2d 789, 799 (Tenn. App. 1969); James Constructors, Inc. v. Salt Lake City Corp., 888 P.2d 665, 667-69 (Utah App. 1994)).

166 110 Nev. 951, 878 P.2d 314, 318 (Nev. 1994).
167 *Id.*
168 571 S.W.2d 644, 645 (Ky. App. 1978).
169 *Id.*
170 *Fallon*, 121 F.3d at 129 (3rd Cir. 1997) (quoting Hawaiian Ins. & Guar. Co. v. Higashi, 67 Haw. 12, 675 P.2d 767, 769 (Haw. 1984) ("Obviously, where such a provision is in the agreement, the burden of proof on the issue [of reasonableness and good faith] shifts")).
171 *Fallon*, 121 F.3d at 129 (citing U.S. Fid. & Guar. Co. v. Napier Elec. & Constr. Co., 571 S.W.2d 644, 646 (Ky. App. 1978); Transamerica

evidence that the expenses sought by the surety were incurred in bad faith and without reasonable necessity, the court ruled in favor of the surety and directed the district court to enter judgment in the full amount of the attorney's fees and expenses claimed by the surety.[172]

In *Capitol Indemnity Corp. v. Weatherseal Roofing & Renovations, Inc.*,[173] the indemnity agreement imposed upon the indemnitor the obligation to undertake the surety's defense. The surety initially tendered its defense to the principal's counsel. Due to its concern that the principal's counsel was not adequately representing its interests, the surety retained its own counsel.

The indemnity agreement imposed upon the indemnitors the obligation to indemnify and hold harmless the surety from and against all loss and expense, including fees and disbursements of counsel and imposed a duty that the indemnitors defend any action against the surety arising out of its execution of any bonds. The trial court held that the indemnitors discharged their indemnity obligation when it undertook the surety's defense and denied the surety's indemnification claim.[174]

On appeal, the court determined that the indemnitors' obligation to the surety was two-pronged: (1) The principal and indemnitors have an obligation to defend the surety and (2) to provide the surety a "full and proper defense."[175] The court acknowledged that the surety met its *prima facie* burden to show its legal fees and expenses under the indemnity agreement and that the burden of proof that the fees were unreasonable shifted to the indemnitors. Citing to case law in other jurisdictions, the appellate court concluded that the *prima facie* evidence clause did not conclusively prove that the fees and

---

Premier Ins. Co. v. Nelson, 110 Nev. 951, 878 P.2d 314, 317-18 (Nev. 1994)).

172 *Fallon*, 121 F.3d at 129-30.
173 No. L-02-1174, 2003 Ohio App. LEXIS 3565, 2003 WL 21716002 (Ohio App. July 25, 2003).
174 *Capitol Indem. Corp.*, 2003 WL 21716002, at *1.
175 *Id.* at *5-6.

expenses were reasonable.[176] The indemnity agreement did not contain a provision that the surety's expenses must be incurred in good faith or under a reasonable belief that the expenses were necessary. The appellate court remanded the case to the trial court to determine whether the indemnitor provided the surety a "full and proper defense."[177]

The Supreme Court of New Hampshire agreed that by reason of the *prima facie* evidence clause, the burden of proof that the surety was not entitled to indemnity shifted to the indemnitors. In *Gulf Insurance Company v. AMSCO, Inc.*,[178] the surety sought indemnity for attorney fees and loss adjustment expenses. The indemnity agreement provided as follows:

> [F]or any payment or compromise of "any claim demand, suit, judgment or expense arising out of any [bond]" so long as "the same was made by [Gulf] in the reasonable belief that it was liable for the amount disbursed, or that such payment or compromise was reasonable under all circumstances.[179]

The *AMSCO* court disagreed with the surety's argument that the principal is required to prove subjective "bad faith" through dishonest purpose, conscious wrongdoing, or breach of duty motivated by self-interest or ill will.[180] Instead, the court held that the appropriate standard is whether the indemnitors proved that the surety's claimed expenses were unreasonable.

Although the surety had tendered its defense to the principal in two prior lawsuits, it refused to tender its defense in a third lawsuit. The surety sought to recover its loss adjustment expense and attorney fees incurred in monitoring the second case, plus collateral on the third claim, as a condition to tendering its defense to the principal in

---

176   *Id.* at *3 (citing Ideal Elec. Sec. Co., Inc. v. Int'l Fid. Ins. Co., 129 F.3d 143 (D.C. Cir. 1997)).
177   *Id.* at *6.
178   153 N.H. 28, 889 A.2d 1040 (N.H. 2005).
179   *Id.* at 35.
180   *Id.* at 36.

the third lawsuit. The principal failed to post the requested collateral or reimburse the surety for its fees and expenses.

The court found that it was not reasonable for the principal to have to reimburse the surety for independent adjusting expenses, which constituted an "ordinary cost of doing business" and that they constituted "administrative and housekeeping expenses," which were "an ordinary cost of doing business and not recoverable under the [indemnity agreement]."[181] The court further found that the surety's legal fees were unreasonable because the principal agreed to undertake the surety's defense and granted only reasonable fees for the surety's monitoring of the lawsuits.[182]

The court was not persuaded that the principal's failure to provide the requested collateral served as a basis for the surety's retaining separate counsel.[183] Further, the court did not believe the surety had unique defenses.[184] The surety argued that it was not obligated to tender to its principal and that its principal's failure to indemnify the surety for costs it incurred on the first two cases constituted a default under the indemnity agreement. The court rejected the surety's arguments, finding that the surety failed to sufficiently develop its appeal and failed to raise certain issues at the trial court level.[185] With the exception of legal fees incurred to monitor the various lawsuits, the surety was denied its indemnity claims.

Accordingly, the cases examining the surety's entitlement to attorney fees in the face of an objection by the indemnitors often turn on whether the specific language of the indemnity agreement shifts the burden to the indemnitors through a *"prima facie* evidence" clause. The courts then typically look to the indemnity agreement to determine whether the party with the burden of proof must prove either good or bad faith, or whether a reasonableness standard should

---

181 *Id.* at 37.
182 *Id.* at 38.
183 *Id.* at 39.
184 *Id.*
185 *Id.* at 40.

2. Surety Not Limited to "Reasonable and Necessary" Expenses

In a case where the indemnity agreement did not require that the surety incur expenses in good faith or under a reasonable belief that they were necessary, the surety was not limited to recovering only "reasonable and necessary" expenses. In *American Contractors Indemnity Co. v. Nicole Gas Production, Ltd.*,[186] the court held that the surety is not limited to recovery of "reasonable and necessary" attorney fees, but is entitled to recover, pursuant to the indemnity agreement, any and all attorney fees incurred. The court explained the basis for its ruling:

> In response, appellees point out that the indemnity agreement does not limit recovery to only "reasonable and necessary" attorney fees. Its plain language provides for payment of "any and all" of ACIC's and Goldleaf's attorney fees. We agree. Review of the indemnity agreement reveals no language limiting an award of attorney fees to only those fees proven to be "reasonable and necessary." It is axiomatic that "[t]he intent of the parties to a contract is presumed to reside in the language they chose to employ in the agreement." *Kelly v. Med. Life Ins. Co.* (1987), 31 Ohio St.3d 130, 31 OBR 289, 509 N.E.2d 411, paragraph one of the syllabus. "When enforcing an indemnity agreement, the court must determine the intent of the parties from the language of the indemnity contract." *Capitol Indemn. Corp. v. Weatherseal Roofing & Renovations, Inc.*, Lucas App. No. L-02-1174, 2003 Ohio 3982, citing *Worth v. Aetna Cas. & Sur. Co. (1987)*, 32 Ohio St.3d 238, 240, 513 N.E.2d 253, reversed in part on other grounds in *Worth v. Huntington Bancshares, Inc.* (1989), 43 Ohio St.3d 192, 540 N.E.2d 249. "[T]he language of the indemnity Agreement controls the issue of whether the surety may charge the principal for the surety's defense fees and expenses." *Id.*

---

186 No. 07AP-1039, 2008 WL 4416671 (Ohio App. Sept. 30, 2008).

Appellants cite no case law for support of their third assignment of error, and we note that the cases requiring that attorney fees be proven to be "reasonable and necessary" involve statutes or contracts whose plain language limits a prevailing party to recovery of "reasonable and necessary" fees. See, e.g. *Bittner v. Tri-Cty. Toyota, Inc.* (1991), 58 Ohio St.3d 143, 569 N.E.2d 464 ("reasonable attorney's fee" available to prevailing party for knowing violation of Consumer Sales Practices Act); *Don Keyser Co. v. Niles Mfg. & Finishing, Inc.,* Trumbull App. No. 2003-T-0089, 2004 Ohio 7228, discretionary appeal not allowed, 105 Ohio St. 3d 1519, 2005 Ohio 1880, 826 N.E.2d 316 (contract provided for indemnification of "reasonable attorney fees").[187]

In holding that the surety was entitled to its attorney fees without regard to whether they were "reasonable and necessary," the court in *Nicole Gas* further found that the magistrate's decision affirmed by the trial court applied the correct standard to determine whether the surety acted in good faith. The court rejected the indemnitors' argument that the surety must conduct a reasonable investigation and held that the "general duty, implied in all contracts, to exercise good faith and fair dealing" is "[a] compact reference to an implied undertaking not to take opportunistic advantage in a way that could not have been contemplated at the time of drafting, and which therefore was not resolved explicitly by the parties."[188] The court upheld the trial court decision.

In *Fallon Electric*,[189] the court specifically overturned the trial court's judgment that awarded less than the amount sought by the surety in its indemnity action and rejected the trial court's imposition of a "reasonably necessary" attorney fees standard that was not set forth in the indemnity agreement. Rather, the indemnity agreement included a *"prima facie evidence"* clause.[190] Accordingly, the court

---

187 *Id.* at *6, n. 1.
188 *Id.* at *3.
189 121 F.3d 125 (3rd Cir. 1997).
190 *Id.* at 127-28 (citing U.S. Fid. & Guar. Co. v. Love, 260 Ark. 374, 538 S.W.2d 558, 559 (Ark. 1976); Redfern v. R.E. Dailey & Co., 146 Mich. App. 8, 379 N.W.2d 451, 456-57 (Mich. Ct. App. 1985);

found that the indemnitor had the burden of showing that the expenses were incurred in bad faith.

3. Case Law or Statute Might Override the Express Language of the Indemnity Agreement

The surety's contractual right to recover attorney fees might be overridden by statute. For example, in a North Carolina case, the surety sought to recover the loss payments and attorney fees it incurred. Though the surety was deemed entitled to recover attorney fees, its recovery was limited to a percentage of the unreimbursed loss, pursuant to statute.[191]

Case law in a given jurisdiction may also determine the surety's contractual right to indemnity for legal fees. In *Ideal Electronic Security Co., Inc. v. International Fidelity Insurance Company*,[192] the court held that the surety reasonably elected to retain its own counsel, despite the principal's offer to undertake the surety's defense due to the principal's failure to post collateral upon the surety's demand.[193] The court further held that pursuant to the indemnity agreement the surety was entitled to be indemnified for attorney fees and costs it incurred.[194] However, this did not conclude the court's discussion. The court further inquired into the reasonableness of the fee amount claimed.[195] Citing to precedent in the very same court, the court stated that "the determination of a reasonable fee

---

Perkins v. Thompson, 551 So. 2d 204, 209 (Miss. 1989); Sentry Ins. Co. v. Davison Fuel & Dock Co., 60 Ohio App. 2d 248, 396 N.E.2d 1071, 1074 & n. 2 (Ohio App. 1978); Cent. Towers Apartments, Inc. v. Martin, 61 Tenn. App. 244, 453 S.W.2d 789, 799 (Tenn. App. 1969); James Constructors, Inc. v. Salt Lake City Corp., 888 P.2d 665, 667, 668-69 (Utah App. 1994)).

191 New York Marine and Gen. Ins. Co. v. Beck Elec. Co., Inc., No. 3:05 CV 373-H, 2007 U.S. Dist. LEXIS 3499, 2007 WL 160689 (W.D. N.C., Jan. 16, 2007), *aff'd*, 254 Fed. Appx. 235 (4th Cir. N.C.).
192 129 F.3d 143 (D.C. Cir. 1997).
193 *Id.* at 149.
194 *Id.* at 150.
195 *Id.*

award is for the trial court in light of the relevant circumstances,"[196] and held that the trial court, as opposed to a jury, determines whether the requested fees are reasonable.[197]

H. Surety Failed to Mitigate its Damages

The indemnity agreement language that gives the surety the right to settle claims has tended to discourage indemnitor defenses based upon the surety's failure to mitigate damages.[198] In *American Motorists Insurance Co. v. Southcrest Construction. Inc.*,[199] the indemnitors attempted to defeat the surety's indemnity claims for performance and payment bond payments by claiming in its affidavit that the surety appropriated its contract for the benefit of others and that pursuant to the express terms of the indemnity agreement, the principal was not in default. The obligee declared the principal in default and the surety, through its consultant, retained a completion contractor. The indemnitors further alleged that the surety allowed the completion contractor to include a 30 to 40 percent profit margin in its price when the principal had included only a 10 percent profit margin in its bid.

The surety filed its indemnity complaint in the U.S. District Court for the Northern District of Texas. The indemnitors argued that the indemnity agreement contained a choice of law provision requiring that the court apply Illinois law. The surety argued that the "duty of good faith and fair dealing, which Illinois courts apply to sureties in dealing with their principals, violates Texas policy."[200] Applying Texas' choice of law rules, the court examined the applicable contract provisions:

---

196 *Id.*
197 *Id.*
198 Patrick J. O'Connor, Jr., et al., *Defenses in The Surety's Indemnity Agreement: Law & Practice*, 2d (Marilyn Klinger, George J. Bachrach, & Tracey L. Haley, eds., 2008) at 405, 429.
199 No. 3:04-cv-2575 M, 2006 U.S. Dist. LEXIS 19933 (N.D. Tex. Apr. 17, 2006); 2006 WL 995202 (N.D. Tex. 2006).
200 *Southcrest*, 2006 WL 995202, at *3.

> This contractual language vests the Plaintiffs with discretion, untempered by any requirement of bad faith, unlike the language found in the contract at issue in *Mountbatten* or *USF&G*. Arguably, Southcrest bargained away any protections provided by the Illinois common law duty of good faith and fair dealing.[201]

The *Southcrest* court found that, per the *prima facie* evidence clause, the surety met its burden of proof and that the indemnitors failed to meet their burden to prove that the surety acted in bad faith.

> Illinois case law demonstrates the very limited circumstances when a principal can successfully prove a duty of good faith and fair dealing under an indemnity agreement that vests a surety with "sole discretion" to settle or compromise any claim.[202]

The *Southcrest* court held that, because the principal failed to provide any evidence of bad faith under Illinois law, there was no genuine issue of material fact as to whether the surety breached its duty of good faith and fair dealing. Therefore, the court granted summary judgment for the surety in the amount of losses and expenses incurred.[203]

I. Burden of Proof

Where the indemnity agreement or common law imposes an obligation of good faith upon the surety, an issue that arises is whether the burden of proof as to the surety's good faith rests with the surety or is imposed upon the indemnitors. In *Fidelity & Deposit*

---

201 *Id.* at *5 (citing U.S. Fid. & Guar. Co. v. Klein Corp, 190 Ill. App. 3d 250, 558 N.E.2d, 1047, 1050 (Ill. App. 1989); Mountbatten Sur. Co. v. Szabo Contracting, Inc., 349 Ill. App. 3d 857, 812 N.E.2d 90, 94 (Ill. App. 2004)).

202 *Southcrest*, 2006 WL 995202 *4 (citing Reliance Ins. Co. v. Dipietro Plumbing Corp., No. 85 C 6985, 1989 U.S. Dist. LEXIS 3545; 1989 WL 32935 (N.D. Ill. Apr. 3, 1989)).

203 *Southcrest*, 2006 WL 995202, at *6.

Company of Maryland v. Marian Professional Construction, Inc.,[204] the court held the surety's good faith shall be presumed absent an affirmative showing of fraud or bad faith by the indemnitors, thereby shifting the burden of proof to the indemnitors. In *Marian*, the indemnitors argued that they had no obligation to indemnify the surety because the surety acted in bad faith by paying claims for which the principal was not liable, by paying a claim without conducting an adequate investigation into the circumstances of the principal's alleged default and by overpaying on a completion contract. The court rejected the indemnitors' affidavit alleging the affirmative bad faith claims on procedural and substantive grounds.

> While the arguments regarding F&D's duties to investigate and to mitigate damages *might* have some legal footing, the argument that F&D acted in bad faith by allegedly paying on claims on which MPC was not liable is untenable. Again, briefly, the Indemnity Agreement provides: "The Surety shall be entitled to charge for any and all disbursements made by it in good faith in and about the matters herein contemplated by this Agreement under the belief that it is or was liable for the sums and amounts so disbursed, or that it was necessary or expedient to make such disbursements, whether or not such liability, necessity or expediency existed." Illinois courts have held that such language vests the surety with discretion to make payments and demand indemnity if it "believed in good faith that it *might* be liable for the payments" see *Klein Corp.*, 190 Ill.App.3d at 255; *Lamp, Inc. v. Int'l Fidelity Insurance Co.*, 142 Ill.App.3d 692, 695, 493 N.E.2d 146, 97 Ill. Dec. 664 (2d Dist. 1986), and such discretion is "limited only by a showing of fraud or bad faith." *Klein Corp.* 190 Ill.App.3d at 255. Taking it a step further, under such indemnity agreements, 'absent an affirmative showing of fraud or bad faith, the good faith of the plaintiff-surety [is] presumed.' *Mountbatten Surety Co., Inc. v. Szabo Contracting, Inc.*, 349 Ill.App.3d 857, 812 N.E.2d 90, 204 Ill. App. LEXIS 720, Mountbatten Surety Co., No. 2-03-0171, 2004 Ill. App. LEXIS 720, 2004 WL 1380189 at *12. Therefore, even if F&D *did* pay off debts for which MPC was not liable, the

---

204 No. 99 C 6787, 2004 U.S. Dist. LEXIS 14558, 2004 WL 1718655 (N.D. Ill. July 29, 2004).

Agreement entitles F&D to full reimbursement, that is, absent an affirmative showing of bad faith. And of course, conduct expressly allowed by the contract cannot *itself* support that bad faith showing.[205]

The *Marian* court recognized the clear and unambiguous provisions of the indemnity agreement that granted the surety the right to settle claims if the surety believed it was obligated to do so. The *Marian* court observed that an affirmative showing that the surety's acts rise to the level of fraud or bad faith is a defense to indemnity which the indemnitors must establish.

In *Mercede*,[206] the Supreme Court of Connecticut addressed the issue of whether the trial court committed error by failing to instruct the jury that the burden of proof on the issue of good faith had shifted to the indemnitors. The court agreed that there should have been an instruction that shifted the burden of proof to the indemnitors but, under the circumstances, concluded that it was harmless error.[207]

In *State Farm Automobile Mutual Insurance Co. v. Horst Reschke*,[208] the court agreed that the surety does not bear the burden to prove the good faith of its payments once it has met its *prima facie* burden of proof. The surety settled multiple payment and performance claims against its bond and thereafter filed an indemnity action. The indemnity agreement contained the *prima facie* evidence provision specifying that upon the surety's providing an itemized statement of payments, sworn to by an officer of the surety, or the voucher(s) of such payments, the surety shall have met its *prima*

---

205 *Marian*, 2004 WL 1718655, at *5, n. 8.
206 PSE Consulting, Inc. v. Frank Mercede and Sons, Inc., 267 Conn. 279, 838 A.2d 135 (Conn. 2003). The *Mercede* case is discussed in detail in Section II(A)(2) of this chapter.
207 *Mercede*, 267 Conn. at 289.
208 No. 2:06-cv-15410, 2008 WL 4937971 (E.D. Mich., Nov. 14, 2008).

facie burden of proof of its damages and the burden thereafter shifts to the indemnitors to prove the existence of a material fact for trial.[209] The surety provided its itemized statement of payments, sworn to by an officer, and therefore the burden of proof rebutting the surety's evidence shifted to the indemnitors.[210]

In another recent decision the court held that a duty of good faith is implied in indemnity agreements, and that duty requires the surety to show that its conduct with regard to a bond claim was reasonable.[211] The court suggested factors for a court to consider in evaluating whether the surety's conduct in paying the bond claims was reasonable, such as the thoroughness of the investigation performed by the surety, the cooperation or lack thereof by the principal, and whether the surety made attempts to mitigate the claims. The court concluded that the surety met its burden of proof and that the surety acted reasonably after observing that the surety attempted to mitigate its damages; the indemnitors did not cooperate with the surety by responding to its requests for information; and, that none of the indemnitors informed the surety that they disputed the claim settlement.[212]

---

[209] *Reschke*, 2008 WL 4937971, at *6 (citing Transamerica Ins. Co. v. Bloomfield, 401 F.2d 357, 362 (6th Cir. 1968); U.S. Fid. & Guar. Co. v. Feibus, 15 F. Supp.2d 579, 585 (M.D. Pa., 1998)).

[210] *Id.* at *6-7; *see also* Am. Motorists Ins. Co. v. Southcrest Constr., Inc., No. 3:04-cv-2575 M, 2006 U.S. Dist. LEXIS 19933, 2006 WL 995202, at *4 (N.D. Tex., Apr. 17, 2006) ("To survive a motion for summary judgment, Defendants must provide evidence of Plaintiff's bad faith").

[211] Hartford Fire Ins. Co. v. P & H Cattle Co., Inc., 451 F. Supp.2d 1262 (D. Kan. 2006), *aff'd*, 248 Fed. Appx. 942.

[212] *Id.* at 1279.

Conclusion

The terms of the indemnity agreement, as with any other contract, should be enforced as written. As is evident in this chapter, some jurisdictions strictly enforce the express provisions of the indemnity agreement while others apply stricter standards upon the surety. The majority of courts, however, apply the implied covenant of good faith and fair dealing to evaluate whether the surety failed to act in good faith. The provisions of the indemnity agreement must be viewed in conjunction with the case law in the jurisdiction where the indemnitors' default will be determined through litigation.

11

DEFENSES AVAILABLE TO THE SURETY

Julia Blackwell Gelinas
Genise W. Teich*

Introduction

The surety has many defenses available to it which are not available to insurers because of the unique tripartite relationship which exists among the surety, the obligee, and the principal. Although compensated sureties have fewer defenses available than uncompensated sureties, the numerous defenses that are still available serve to limit the surety's liability to that which was intended by the parties to the relationship. Sureties may waive any and all of these defenses,[1] which makes a good working knowledge of the primary defenses important.

The following is a discussion of several of the more common defenses available to a performance bond surety.

The terms of the performance bond may affect the availability of these defenses. Therefore, when the possibility of a claim first arises it may be important to evaluate the conduct of the principal and the obligee as well as the myriad of other factors related to the claim, to determine the parameters of the surety's obligations. Prompt and properly focused information gathering can be critical to determine whether the surety has any defenses available which could serve to limit or otherwise reduce its liability.

---

*   Eric D. Foerg of Frost Brown Todd LLC rendered substantial assistance with respect to the research and preparation of this chapter.
1   Citibank, N.A. v. Plapinger, 485 N.E.2d 974, 975 (N.Y. 1985). In a more recent Sixth Circuit case, the court concluded that there was "sufficient evidence for the jury to have concluded that by waiting to raise its affirmative defense," NAS waived its right to the defense. N. Am. Specialty Ins. Co. v. J.A. Jones Envtl. Servs., Co., 64 Fed. Appx. 426, 428-29 (6th Cir. 2003).

I. The Surety Succeeds to All of the Defenses of Its Principal

Of primary importance to the surety, in terms of its liability to an obligee, is determining whether its principal is liable to the obligee. A surety's liability under a performance bond is generally derived from that of its principal. If the principal is not liable to the obligee, in most instances, neither will the surety be liable to the obligee. If the principal has a defense available to the obligee's claim,[2] more often than not, the surety will also be able to successfully assert that same defense.[3] There are exceptions to this general rule.[4]

Defenses which are available to both the principal and the surety include an obligee's failure to provide plans and specifications which are free from defects,[5] an obligee's failure to timely issue change orders or extensions of time,[6] impossibility of performance,[7] an obligee's failure to disclose information material to the principal's performance of the work,[8] the wrongful termination of the principal's contract by the obligee,[9] failure to provide an opportunity to cure,[10] and failure of the owner to make timely payment.[11]

---

2   "A variety of such defenses may be available." Millgard Corp. v. Goldberg-Zoino Assocs. of New York, 99 Civ. 2952 (LBS), 2002 U.S. Dist. LEXIS 23921, at *49 (S.D.N.Y. Dec. 12, 2002).

3   *See* Housing Authority of the City of Huntsville v. Hartford Accident and Indemn. Co., 954 So.2d 577, 580 (Ala. 2006) (holding surety could assert principal's statute of limitation defense even though statute was limited to builders and design professionals).

4   In United States v. Gov't Tech. Servs., LLC, 531 F. Supp. 2d 1375, 1378 (N.D. Ga. 2008), the court denied the surety's pay-when-paid defenses, fearing that doing "otherwise would turn a pay-when-paid contract provision into an implicit waiver of the subcontractor's Miller Act rights." *Id.* "A surety's liability is governed by the obligations imposed by the Miller Act." *Id.* "A contract provision that would deny the subcontractor its federal remedy under the [Miller] Act cannot be used as a defense by a surety." *Id.*

5   *See* Section I, A.
6   *See* Section I, B.
7   *See* Section I, C.
8   *See* Section VI.
9   *See* Section I, D.
10 *See* Section I, E.
11 *See* Section I, F.

A. The Obligee's Failure to Provide Plans and Specifications Which are Free From Defects

Frequently a conflict can arise between an owner and a contractor as to who bears the responsibility for defects in the plans and specifications. Although the contractor typically warrants that its work will be free from faults and defects, this warranty does not limit the owner's responsibility to provide adequate plans and specifications. As a general rule, if the contractor is required to build according to plans and specifications prepared by or on behalf of the owner, the contractor will not thereafter be held responsible for the consequences of any defects contained in the plans.[12] This rule is known as the "*Spearin* Doctrine," named after a 1918 United States Supreme Court decision.[13]

In *United States v. Spearin*, the government had supplied a contractor with very detailed plans for the construction of a sewer and dry-dock.[14] These detailed specifications were held by the Court to have "imported a warranty that, if the specifications were complied with, the sewer would be adequate."[15]

This doctrine has been extended to situations where the "defect" in question was the designation of materials which themselves proved to be defective.[16] In *Trustees of Indiana University v. Aetna Casualty and Surety Co.*, Indiana University sued Aetna on its performance bond to

---

[12] United States v. Spearin, 248 U.S. 132, 136 (1918); Trs. of Indiana Univ. v. Aetna Cas. & Sur. Co., 920 F.2d 429, 436 (7th Cir. 1990) (where owner directs the contractor to perform in a particular way, and contractor follows the plans and specifications and disaster ensues, the contractor is not liable) (*abrogated on other grounds*, Watson v. Amedco Steel, Inc., 29 F.3d 274, 278 (7th Cir. 1994)); Lake Union Drydock Co., Inc. v. United States, No. C05-2146RSL, 2007 U.S. Dist. LEXIS 78282, at *29-30 (W.D. Wa. Oct. 10, 2007); CEMS, Inc. v. United States, 59 Fed. Cl. 168, 213 (Fed. Cl. 2003) (holding that design specifications created by government contain implied warranty that, if contractor adheres to the specifications, the result will be acceptable to the government).

[13] United States v. Spearin, 248 U.S. 132, 136-37 (1918).

[14] *Spearin*, 248 U.S. at 133-34.

[15] *Id.* at 137.

[16] *Trs. of Indiana*, 920 F.2d 429, 436 (7th Cir. 1990); Wood-Hopkins Contracting Co. v. Masonry Contractors, Inc., 235 So. 2d 548, 551-52 (Fla. Ct. App. 1970).

recover damages for defective work which it alleged was performed by Aetna's principal, Mid Republic.[17] Mid Republic had installed brick on several buildings which showed some signs of deterioration over time. Indiana University had chosen and specified the use of brick by brand name and type. Tests performed on the bricks showed that the bricks did not meet quality standards with respect to initial rate of absorption, that the bricks were excessively porous and that a very real possibility of spalling existed. Indiana University argued that Mid Republic had breached its warranty by using bricks with a latent defect. Aetna countered that the deterioration was a design and maintenance problem, in that the bricks were not suited for the "severe" weather they encountered. The court determined that Indiana University, having chosen and specified the use of the brick, warranted that they would be suitable for the use to which they were put.[18] Indiana University's breach of this warranty served to discharge Aetna.[19]

An owner may also be responsible for delays caused by the inadequacy of its plans. In *Beard Family Partnership v. Commercial Indemnity Insurance Co.*,[20] a court upheld a jury verdict in favor of a performance bond surety who had taken over and completed a project after the default of its principal.[21] The owner, Beard Family Partnership (Beard), contracted with Round Rock Construction for the construction of the infrastructure of a residential subdivision.[22] Beard's engineer miscalculated the topography of the site, causing the plan elevations to be off by six to eight vertical feet.[23] Correction of the plans caused a delay, and the elevation changes led to further changes and problems in downstream aspects of the job.[24] Adhering to the *Spearin* doctrine, the court upheld a jury's verdict finding that Beard breached the contract because the inadequacies of its plans, which it impliedly warranted, caused delay in the completion of the work.[25]

---

17   *Trs. of Indiana*, 920 F.2d at 430.
18   *Id.* at 436-37.
19   *Id.* at 435-36.
20   116 S.W.3d 839 (Tex. Ct. App. 2003).
21   *Beard*, 116 S.W.3d at 842-43.
22   *Id.* at 842-43.
23   *Id.* at 843.
24   *Id.* at 843, 847-48.
25   *Id.* at 847.

B. Obligee's Failure to Act

Unreasonable delays by the obligee, as well as the obligee's failure to act, may also constitute a breach that will relieve the principal, and ultimately the surety, from liability.

In *Granite Computer Leasing Corp. v. Travelers Indemnity Co.*,[26] a subcontractor had provided a bond to a federal government contractor, the obligee on the bond.[27] The government contractors allegedly caused delays by deficient specifications and failure to give timely approvals for alternate material sources.[28] The principal argued that these delays caused serious financial problems and ultimately caused it to shut down its production operations.[29] The contract had a disputes clause that required the subcontractor to proceed diligently pending resolution of any disputes.[30] The court held, however, that the subcontractor was not obligated to proceed under any and all circumstances, and remanded for determination of two questions: whether the government contractors had breached the contract in respect to design or construction aspects of the subcontract; and, if so, whether the delay in responding to the subcontractor's claim for funds was reasonable.[31] If both were true, the court concluded, the obligee had committed a material breach that discharged the principal's duty to perform as well as the surety's liability under its bond.[32]

In *Mayfair Construction Co. v. Waveland Associates*,[33] the issue was the owner/obligee's failure to take certain actions which ultimately proved prejudicial to the contractor.[34] The contract between the parties provided that the parties were to take their disputes to the architect for

---

26 894 F.2d 547 (2d Cir. 1990).
27 *Granite*, 894 F.2d at 553.
28 *Id.* at 548.
29 *Id.*
30 *Granite*, 894 F.2d at 550.
31 *Id.* at 552.
32 *Id.* at 553. *But see* William Ziegler & Son v. Chicago Northwestern Development Co., 389 N.E.2d at 199 (failure to make reasonably prompt payment of extras may not provide a basis for repudiating the entire contract).
33 619 N.E.2d 144 (Ill. Ct. App. 1993), *appeal denied*, 624 N.E.2d 809 (Ill. 1993).
34 *Mayfair*, 619 N.E.2d at 146.

resolution, so as to allow quick, binding decisions which would keep the project moving.[35] The owner refused to submit the disputes to the architect and refused to allow the architect to review disputes submitted by the contractor regarding extensions of time and change orders which had a financial impact on the contractor.[36] The court found that submission of disputes to the architect constituted a condition precedent to litigating them.[37] The court concluded that the remedy for the owner's refusal to fulfill the condition was to preclude the owner from either asserting defenses to the contractor's claims or from asserting its own counterclaims for any issue that should have been submitted to the architect.[38]

In *Fru-Con Construction Corp. v. Sacramento Utility Engineering Corp.*,[39] the court denied motions for summary judgment against the contractor and its surety, which argued that the owner/obligee may have acted improperly in failing to grant a time extension to the principal where the evidence showed that the obligee directed the principal to omit any mentions of weather delays in its scheduling reports.[40] Under the contract, the principal may have been entitled to time extensions for flooding and other abnormal and unforeseeable causes, and the obligee may have confounded the principal's ability to request time extensions for heavy rain and standing water.[41]

C. Impossibility of Performance

A determination that work which the principal was to have performed has become impossible to perform, can constitute a defense available to

---

35   *Id.*, 619 N.E.2d at 154.
36   *Id.*, 619 N.E.2d at 146.
37   *Id.*, 619 N.E.2d at 156.
38   *Id.*, 619 N.E.2d at 158-159.
39   No. CIV. S-05-583 LKK/GGH, 2008 U.S. Dist LEXIS 25592 (E.D. Cal. March 28, 2008).
40   *Fru-Con*, 2008 U.S. Dist. LEXIS 25592, at *60-62.
41   *Id.* at *52-56.

the surety.[42] Like other defenses, however, impossibility of performance is subject to waiver.[43]

In *Caron v. Andrew*,[44] the obligee was the owner of low-lying lands in the San Joaquin River Valley.[45] The principal had contracted to level off the entire ranch of the obligee. During the fall, when the principal began its work, the San Joaquin Valley experienced heavy rain.[46] The principal abandoned its work later the same fall and the surety took over the principal's leveling work. Five days after the surety began working, an unusually heavy storm caused several breaks in the master levees surrounding the obligee's land, partially flooding the land. A second flooding occurred approximately three weeks later due to further levee breaks and "almost completely inundated the property."

The *Caron* court stated the general rule that "'[w]here a party has agreed, without qualification, to perform an act which is not in its nature impossible of performance, he is not excused by the difficulty of performance, or by the fact that he himself became unable to perform.'"[47] "The impossibility which will excuse the performance of a contract must consist in the nature of the thing to be done and not in the inability of the obligor to do it."[48] The court in *Caron* explained that "if the thing to be done is not naturally or necessarily impossible under all circumstances, a positive contract to do it is binding, though the performance is rendered impracticable, or even impossible, by some unforeseen cause over which the promisor has no control but against which he might have provided in his contract."[49]

In *Caron,* the court ultimately found that it was common knowledge that lands, such as those of the obligee, lying behind protective levees of

---

42   *But see* City of Montpelier v. Nat'l Sur. Co., 122 A. 484, 487 (Vt. 1923) (appointment of receiver for principal did not render principal's obligations impossible).

43   Excell Constr., Inc. v. Michigan State Univ. Bd. of Trs., No. 228310, 2003 Mich. App. LEXIS 59, at *10 (Mich. Ct. App. 2003) ("because NASIC failed to raise lack of notice or impossibility of performance as affirmative defenses, these defenses were waived").

44   133 Cal. App. 2d 402 (Cal. Ct. App. 1955).

45   *Caron*, 133 Cal. App. 2d at 403-04.

46   *Id.* at 405.

47   *Id.* at 408 (*quoting* 12 Cal. Jur. 2d 'Contracts,' p. 461, sec. 238).

48   *Id.*

49   *Id..*

the San Joaquin River are "subject to inundation by flood waters which over-top or break through the levees."[50] The *Caron* court found that because no protective provision was included in the contract, the principal and its surety "accepted the hazard that such floods might occur."[51] The *Caron* court recognized the fact that neither the principal nor the surety made any request for an extension of time to complete the work.[52] Further, evidence existed that the principal had slowed down the work and moved equipment away from the job site before the first flooding even occurred.[53]

In *Peerless Casualty Co. v. Weymouth Gardens, Inc.*,[54] the obligee advanced a claim against a surety related to construction of houses on the obligee's land.[55] The surety asserted that the work of its principal in completing construction had become impossible.[56] The court found that "dislocations in this country's economy caused by the Korean conflict made it impossible for the contractor to finish the houses on time, and thus excused it from that feature of the contract . . . ."[57] However, the court found that "it was the [principal's] financial inability to cope with those economic dislocations which made it unable to complete the houses at all."[58] The court reasoned that "unexpected increases in costs is a risk every contractor takes in entering into a fixed price contract" and "an increase in costs caused by the unexpected outbreak of a war does not constitute the intervention of a superior force which ends the obligation of a valid contract by preventing its performance."[59] The principal in *Weymouth Gardens* "undertook the contractual duty to build the houses regardless of cost and at least one purpose of the bond was to secure performance of that duty regardless of the principal's financial capacity to carry out its obligation."[60]

---

50 *Id.* at 407.
51 *Id.*
52 *Id.* at 411-12.
53 *Id.* at 407.
54 215 F.2d 362 (1st Cir. 1954).
55 *Peerless*, 215 F.2d. at 363.
56 *Id.* at 364.
57 *Id.*
58 *Id.*
59 *Id.*
60 *Id.*

D. Obligee's Wrongful Termination of the Principal's Contract

The wrongful termination by the obligee of its contract with the principal may constitute a material or substantial breach of contract. A surety can assert such wrongful termination of the principal as a basis for relieving the surety of liability to the obligee.[61] As a general rule, an obligee may only terminate its contract with the principal based upon inadequate or incomplete performance if the principal commits a material breach or legal default.[62] As observed by one court, termination of a principal "is believed to require a material breach or series of breaches which are sufficient to justify termination of the contract by the owner/obligee."[63]

In *Village of Fox Lake v. Aetna Casualty and Surety Co.*,[64] a surety disputed whether termination of its principal/contractor by the village-obligee was proper.[65] The village claimed that the principal had failed to pay various subcontractors and suppliers, which had purportedly demanded payment of amounts due.[66] The surety countered that its principal had not committed a material breach.[67] The court explained that the test of whether a breach is substantial or material "is whether the breach is so substantial and fundamental as to defeat the objects of the parties in making the agreement, or whether the failure to perform renders performance of the rest of the contract different in substance from the original agreement."[68] "The breach must be so material and important as to justify the injured party in regarding the whole

---

61 *See* William Green Constr. Co. v. United States, 477 F.2d 930, 937-38 (Ct. Cl. 1973), *cert. denied*, 417 U.S. 909 (1974); Gulf Ins. Co. v. Fid. & Deposit Co. of Maryland, 16 Misc. 3d 1116(A), 2007 WL 2162885 at *5 (N.Y. Sup. Ct. July 20, 2007) (subcontractor's breach of the contract, including the wrongful termination of its subcontractor, relieved the latter subcontractor's surety from any liability under the bond).
62 L&A Contracting Co. v. Southern Concrete Servs., Inc., 17 F.3d 106, 110 (5th Cir. 1994).
63 *Id.* at 110 n.11.
64 534 N.E.2d 133 (Ill. App. Ct. 1989), *appeal denied*, 541 N.E.2d 1116 (Ill. 1989).
65 *Village of Fox Lake*, 534 N.E.2d at 139.
66 *Id.* at 138.
67 *Id.* at 140-41.
68 *Id.* at 141.

transaction as at an end."[69] The court in *Village of Fox Lake* found that where the principal failed to pay the subcontractors and suppliers "some $59,000 plus" and the total contract price was nearly $2.5 million, the principal's breach could not be deemed a material breach of the contract.[70]

In *Carchia v. United States*,[71] the Post Office wrongfully terminated the principal-contractor and looked to the surety to complete the remainder of the work.[72] The surety entered into a written agreement to complete the work.[73] The surety expended approximately $280,000 in completion costs and received only $212,000, leaving a difference of approximately $68,000 unpaid by the Post Office.[74] The court awarded the $68,000 as damages to the surety, reasoning that, if the surety had refused to complete the project, the Post Office would have had to pay a completing contractor these excess costs ($68,000).[75] The court explained that in such a case the Post Office would not have been able to recoup the $68,000 either from the principal or the surety since "the termination of [the principal's] contract being wrongful, neither the contractor nor the surety would be liable for the excess costs of reprocurement."[76] The court held that "the Post Office's agreement with [the surety] should be read to contain the implicit term that, if the [principal's] termination was admitted or found to be wrongful and if [the surety] reasonably incurred excess costs in completing, the Government would be liable to [the surety] under the completion agreement for those additional expenses–just as it would be responsible to the outside completing contractor."[77] The court explained that "[w]ith respect to such costs, the agreement will not be construed to leave the [Post Office] scot-free and the surety remediless."[78]

---

69   *Id.*
70   *Id.*
71   485 F.2d 622 (Ct. Cl. 1973).
72   *Carchia*, 485 F.2d at 624-25.
73   *Id.* at 628-29.
74   *Id.* at 629.
75   *Id.*
76   *Id.*
77   *Id.* at 630.
78   *Id.*

E. Failure to Provide Notice and An Opportunity to Cure

The obligee's failure to provide the principal and the surety with notice and an opportunity to cure incomplete or inadequate performance by the principal may constitute a breach of contract which can relieve the principal and surety of liability to the obligee.[79] If the parties agree to a notice requirement, courts are usually willing to uphold it.[80]

In *Dragon Construction, Inc. v. Parkway Bank & Trust*,[81] Dragon was hired to build a hardware store for the obligees.[82] The contract entitled the obligees to terminate the contract under certain specified conditions.[83] Seven days written notice was required prior to termination. The performance bond incorporated the construction contract by reference. When the project ran behind schedule, the obligees terminated Dragon for failing to provide enough labor. Four days after hiring a replacement contractor, the obligees sent notice to the surety, stating that their architect was taking competitive bids. In actuality, no bids were ever taken. The surety did not contact the architect until nearly three months later, by which time the store was fully constructed.

The court found the surety bond null and void because of the obligees' material breach of contract in failing to provide the required notice of contract termination.[84] The obligees argued that the surety had waived its right to assert lack of notice by failing to respond to the late notice until the store was built.[85] The court found that the obligees waived this potential defense by not raising it in a timely manner, with the result that the lack of timely notice by the obligees was dispositive.[86]

While courts will strictly construe a requirement for notice of default, they generally will not enforce requirements that are not clearly

---

79 *See* Carriage Town, Inc. v. Landco, Inc., 998 F. Supp. 646, 649 (D.S.C. 1998).
80 Elkins Manor Assoc. v. Eleanor Concrete Works, Inc., 396 S.E.2d 463, 470 (W.Va. 1990). *See also* Continental Bank & Trust Co. v. A. M. Bonding Co., 605 F.2d 1049, 1057 n.17 (8th Cir. 1979).
81 *Dragon*, 678 N.E.2d 55 (Ill. App. Ct. 1997).
82 *Id.* at 56.
83 *Id.*
84 *Id.* at 59.
85 *Id.* at 58.
86 *Id.*

specified.[87] For example, a notice-of-default requirement will not be read to require notice of missed interim completion dates, especially where the obligee acted in accordance with its own procedures and industry practice in allowing a struggling contractor to try to perform under revised working schedules before declaring a default.[88] The parties may agree, however, to notice requirements that are triggered earlier than an actual declaration of default if such requirements are clearly specified.[89]

In *School Board of Escambia County v. TIG Premier Insurance Co.*, the court noted that "[c]ourts have consistently held that an obligee's action that deprives a surety of its ability to protect itself pursuant to performance options granted under a performance bond constitutes a material breach, which renders the bond null and void."[90] The school board argued that TIG was required to "show it was prejudiced or damaged" by the failure to provide notice.[91] The court declined "to place a burden on the non-defaulting surety to come forth with affirmative evidence that it was 'prejudiced.'"[92] The court was motivated in part by the fact that the school board's action blocked the surety's "opportunity to gather the data necessary to demonstrate prejudice."[93]

In *Solai & Cameron, Inc. v. Plainfield Community Consolidated School District*, the court initially distinguished *Dragon* by noting that the bond at issue did "not require any notice to the surety" as to the decision to declare a default and then make the termination.[94] Other

---

87   *See, e.g.*, Millgard Corp. v. Goldberg-Zoino Assocs. of New York, 99 Civ. 2952 (LBS), 2002 U.S. Dist. LEXIS 23921, at *33 (S.D.N.Y. Dec. 12, 2002) ("Under New York law, notice of a principal's default is not a condition precedent to asserting a claim against a surety in the absence of an express contractual provision requiring such notice").

88   Turner Constr. Co. v. First Indem. of Am. Ins. Co., 829 F. Supp. 752, 762 (E.D. Pa. 1993), *aff'd*, 22 F.3d 303 (3rd Cir. 1994).

89   Section 3.1 of Document A312, published by the American Institute of Architects, requires that notice be given when declaration of default is being considered, whereupon a meeting of all three affected parties (principal, surety and obligee) is to be held within 15 days to discuss methods of performing.

90   110 F. Supp. 2d 1351, 1354 (N.D. Fla. 2000).

91   *Sch. Bd. of Escambia County*, 110 F. Supp. 2d at 1354.

92   *Id.*

93   *Id.*

94   871 N.E.2d 944, 956 (Ill. App. Ct. 2007).

factors made *Dragon* persuasive, however, such as the school's actions in hiring a replacement contractor before terminating the principal, which prevented the surety from exercising its options.[95] Specifically, the surety was left to only "investigate and then agree to pay or deny payment."[96]

As with the cases which address wrongful termination as a defense to the surety, there is a spirited debate surrounding *Dragon*. Courts have held that a self-declared default by the principal does not necessarily trigger the surety's contractual obligations.[97] And, as is typically the case, the general rule that a decision to terminate before the end of a cure is improper, is not without exception. Courts have found that termination prior to the expiration of a cure period "may be 'appropriate and provide no basis for setting aside the termination for default' if there is 'no evidence that the contractor had taken any action which would have permitted it to perform the contract satisfactorily, or that it had taken any actions which were in any way affected by the termination prior to the expiration of the . . . cure period.'"[98] Further, a surety may be deprived of the defense upon an owner's showing that it acted generally to mitigate its damages and selected a reasonable replacement contractor.[99]

F. Setoffs or Counterclaims

As a general rule, a surety is entitled to assert any setoffs available to its principal against the obligee much in the same way that it may assert those defenses available to its principal.[100] In *Kalfountzos v. Hartford Fire Insurance Co.*, the principal brought suit against a subcontractor for completion costs after the subcontractor was removed from the project

---

95 *Solai*, 871 N.E.2d at 956.
96 *Id.*
97 Liberty Mut. Co. v. Constr. Mgmt. Servs., Inc., Case No. 99 C 6906, 2004 U.S. Dist. LEXIS 23635, at *8-10, 12 (N.D. Ill. Oct. 6, 2004).
98 Bell BCI Co. v. HGRM Corp., Civil No. JFM-03-1357, 2004 U.S. Dist. LEXIS 15305, at *15 (D. Md. Aug. 6, 2004) (*quoting* Appeals of Soledad Enters., Inc., 77-2 BCA P 12, 552, 1977 WL 2287 (ASBCA 1977)).
99 *Bell*, 2004 U.S. Dist. LEXIS 15305, at *26.
100 Kalfountzos v. Hartford Fire Ins. Co., 44 Cal. Rptr. 2d 714, 715 (Ct. App. 1995) *overruled on other grounds*, Wm. R. Clarke Corp. v. Safeco Ins. Co., 938 P.2d 372 (Cal. 1997).

for failing to pay prevailing wages.[101] The subcontractor filed a counterclaim against the principal for unpaid progress payments. The principal subsequently went out of business and a default judgment was entered against it. The subcontractor sought to prevent the surety from asserting any of the defenses and setoffs available to the principal on the grounds that the principal could no longer assert such defenses. The court, however, found:

> [t]he surety may raise any defenses or set-offs, with respect to the obligation, to reduce or eliminate the amount due on the bond, even though the principal, as here, is precluded from raising those defenses and set-offs because of a legal disability having nothing to do with the validity of the defenses and set-offs.[102]

In *Kentucky Central Insurance Co. v. Brown (In re Larbar Corp.)*,[103] the surety entered into an indemnity agreement with its principal/contractor whereby its principal agreed to indemnify the surety against losses on the bonds and assigned its rights to the surety under any contract under which the principal abandoned its obligations. The principal entered into several construction contracts to build guardrails on highways. The principal, as subcontractor, surety, and a general contractor entered into side agreements that stated the bond was unaffected by the terms of the side agreement. The principal filed for bankruptcy protection and the trustee attempted to avoid the surety's interest under the Bankruptcy Code.

The court held that the surety could setoff its losses against the profits earned on some of the subcontracts under Section 553 of the Bankruptcy Code.[104] "[A] surety who pays the debts of its principal (here the bankruptcy debtor Larbar) is entitled to step into the shoes of the creditor and assert the creditor's rights of setoff against the debtor in order to recover the payments that the surety has made."[105] The court found that the surety could establish mutuality between the contracts, even though one of the contracts had two general contractors, because the mutuality requirement is met when partners are jointly and severally

---

101   *Kalfountzos*, 44 Cal. Rptr. 2d at 715.
102   *Id.* at 716.
103   177 F.3d 439 (6th Cir. 1999).
104   *Kentucky Central*, 177 F.3d at 446.
105   *Id.*

liable for joint obligations.[106] Likewise, "the surety's rights of equitable subrogation relate back to the date of the bond under which it incurred surety obligations," thus meeting the requirement that the obligations were established prior to commencement of the bankruptcy proceeding.[107] Finally, while § 553 is discretionary, allowing the surety the right of setoff did not prejudice other third-party creditors because general creditors of the estate, such as the Internal Revenue Service, were the only outstanding creditors.[108] The court argued that not allowing the surety the right to setoff may tempt the surety to "cut corners" on its losing contracts, rather than complete them promptly and properly.[109]

G. Prior Material Breach by Obligee

A prior material breach of the contract by the obligee may also relieve the surety of liability under the performance bond. In *Bank of Brewton, Inc. v. International Fidelity Insurance Co.*,[110] the bank made threats to terminate the contractor, withheld payment from the contractor, and inquired with the surety how the bank could declare the contractor in default. In the meantime, the contractor substantially completed the work, under the bank's direction, before the bank actually declared the principal in default.[111] The court found that the bank failed to follow the proper procedures, according to the contract, in declaring the subcontractor in default and, because the bank allowed the contractor to complete the job, the surety was no longer liable.[112]

II. Acts of the Obligee Prejudicial to the Surety

In addition to defenses which are available to its principal, and, therefore, available to the surety, other defenses exist by reason of certain actions taken by the obligee which serve to prejudice the surety. These actions, although prejudicial to the surety, many times can be seen as having provided a benefit to the principal. When considering such defenses, it

---

106 *Id.*
107 *Id.* at 446-47.
108 *Id.* at 447.
109 *Id.*
110 827 So. 2d 747 (Ala. 2002).
111 *Bank of Brewton*, 827 So. 2d at 754.
112 *Id.*

may be important to note whether the obligee's actions have changed the underlying contractual obligations between the parties and whether the actions have placed the surety at a disadvantage or resulted in actual harm to the surety.

A. Surety Must Be Given Notice of Default and Opportunity to Perform

1. Declaration of Default Must be Clear

Surety contractual documents often require the owner to formally declare default and to formally terminate the principal.[113] When notice is required, it should state in clear, direct and unequivocal terms the basis for the obligee's claim that the principal is in default.[114] Because of the significant consequences of a default, the notice should inform the surety (1) that the principal has materially defaulted on its obligations, (2) that the obligee regards the contract as terminated, and (3) that the surety must begin to perform under the terms of its bond immediately.[115]

In *L&A Contracting Co. v. Southern Concrete Services, Inc.*, a judgment against the surety for a subcontractor that was supplying concrete for a bridge construction project was reversed on appeal.[116] The general contractor had experienced problems with slow deliveries and the poor quality of the concrete, prompting it to notify the subcontractor and its surety that the subcontractor had breached the agreement and would have five days to cure the breach. More than two months later, the surety sent a routine inquiry as to the subcontractor's performance, and was told in reply that performance was satisfactory. A few months later

---

113 Mid-State Surety Corp. v. Thrasher Eng'g, Inc., 575 F. Supp. 2d 731, 742 (S.D. W. Va. 2008) (noting that the purpose of such clauses is to avoid common-law rules holding that secondary obligors need no notice).

114 "As the Court has previously held, any declaration of default sufficient to trigger a surety's obligation on a performance bond should be direct and unambiguous." CC-Aventura, Inc. v. Weitz Co., Case No. 06-21598-Civ., 2008 U.S. Dist. LEXIS 49988, at *14 (S.D. Fla. June 20, 2008). *See also* Elm Haven Constr. Ltd. P'ship v. Neri Constr. LLC, 376 F.3d 96, 100 (2d Cir. 2004); L&A Contracting Co. v. Southern Concrete Svcs., Inc., 17 F.3d 106, 111 (5th Cir. 1994).

115 *L&A*, 17 F.2d at 111.

116 *Id.*

another letter of complaint was sent, requesting that the surety "take the necessary steps to fulfill this contract to prevent further delays and costs . . . ." The subcontractor completed its contractual obligations several months later, and the general contractor accepted the performance. Within a couple of months the general contractor sued the surety for breach of contract.[117]

The court found that there were two prerequisites to bond liability under the bond's terms: a default by the subcontractor and a declaration of default by the general contractor.[118] The court found the terminology "declared . . . to be in default" unambiguous, and held that a declaration of breach did not constitute a declaration of default, because not every breach rises to such a magnitude that it triggers a surety's obligations.[119] For legal default, the breach must be material enough to justify the obligee's terminating the contract.[120] None of the correspondence offered as evidence by the general contractor contained the term "default."[121] Thus, the obligee's evidence was insufficient as a matter of law to support liability by the surety on the bond.[122]

A consistent result was reached in *Balfour Beatty Construction v. Colonial Ornamental Iron Works*,[123] with the court holding that notice of delay does not satisfy a requirement of notice of default.[124] There, the performance bond language itself required notice of default.[125] When delays in the work occurred, two letters were sent. The first stated that the contractual obligation of complete delivery by a specified date had not been met, and that the obligee was being delayed and intended to pursue any and all damages arising from the principal's late performance. The second letter, sent four months later, again stated that the delivery deadline had not been met, that the principal "continues to fail to perform in accordance with its contractual obligations," and that

---

117 *L&A*, 17 F.2d at 108.
118 *Id.* at 109.
119 *Id.* at 109-110.
120 *Id.* at 110.
121 *Id.* at 111.
122 *Id.*
123 986 F. Supp. 82 (D. Conn. 1997).
124 *Balfour*, 986 F. Supp. at 86.
125 *Id.* at 85.

the obligee intended to pursue any and all damages "including all remedies against the surety."[126]

The court concluded that the two letters did not provide the surety with actual notice of default.[127] The letters only discussed delays and, as a result, did not provide sufficient notification to allow the surety to step in and take over the principal's contractual obligations.[128] Although courts will not find an implied duty to notify where none is stated in the written agreements, they may be willing to require strict adherence to notice requirements to which the parties have agreed.

A further example is found in *Seaboard Surety Company v. Town of Greenfield*.[129] The town was required to give the surety 15 days written notice to cure any defects before the town could deem the surety in default.[130] While the town and surety exchanged many letters over the course of several months with regard to the completion of the new school building, the court found that none of the letters reasonably put the surety on notice that the town considered the surety in breach of its duties.[131] The town failed to include language in those letters that was "clear, direct, and unequivocal," which would have been sufficient to place the surety on notice.[132] Ultimately, the town hired another construction manager and notified the surety that the town would proceed without the surety's involvement.[133] The court found that because the town failed to give the surety proper notice of its alleged breach and proceeded to complete without the surety, it had materially breached the surety agreement and the surety was absolved from liability with regard to the project.[134]

---

126 *Id.* at 84.
127 *Id.* at 85.
128 *Id.* at 86.
129 370 F.3d 215 (1st Cir. 2004).
130 *Greenfield*, 370 F.3d. at 216-17.
131 *Id.* at 225-26.
132 *Id.* at 223.
133 *Id.* at 217-18.
134 *Id.* at 223-24. *See also* Elm Haven Construction Limited Partnership v. Neri Construction LLC, 376 F.3d 96, 100 (2d Cir. 2004) (surety was absolved from liability where the principal's letters regarding the subcontractor's default did not "even contain the word 'default' or an 'unequivocal declaration of default'" and "the letters clearly evidenced [the principal's] desire to continue its arrangements with [the

In a more recent case, the owner sent the surety a letter which stated that the contractor was in "default," but requested a meeting and indicated a willingness to consider a resolution.[135] Such a letter did "not directly, unequivocally inform" the surety that the author "now looks to it . . . to fulfill the requirements of the Subcontract."[136]

The above line of cases is not without its detractors. For instance, in *Colorado Structures, Inc. v. Insurance Co. of the West*,[137] the court found that the surety's liability on the bond was not conditioned on a declaration of default, and the obligee's failure to declare a default did not relieve the surety of its liability under the bond.[138]

Similarly, in an unpublished Michigan case involving an obligee who retained a completion contractor prior to declaration of default and termination, the court stated that it declined "to follow cases from other jurisdictions that allow a surety's responsibilities to be discharged for technical violations of the bond."[139] Examining Restatement (Third) of Suretyship and Guaranty § 37, the court determined that, because the surety could not demonstrate "serious impairment or any resulting harm, excusing it from its obligations under the bond would bestow upon it an unwarranted windfall–at taxpayers' expense."[140]

In another recent case, a surety pushed for a broader definition of default than that presented in *L&A*, to support its argument that the principal had been in default earlier than contended by the obligee.[141] The court, in dismissing the proposed alternative as amorphous and

---

    subcontractor] and to keep the subcontract agreement in force") (quoting United States Fid. & Guar. Co. v. Braspetro Oil Servs. Co., 369 F.3d 34, 51 (2d Cir. 2004)).

135 CC-Aventura, Inc. v. Weitz Co., LLC, Case No. 06-21598-Civ., 2008 U.S. Dist. LEXIS 49988, at *16-17 (S.D. Fla. June 20, 2008).

136 *Id.* at *17.

137 167 P.3d 1125 (Wash. 2007).

138 *Colorado Structures*, 167 P.3d at 1133. *But see* Hunt Constr. Group, Inc. v. Nat'l Wrecking Corp., 542 F. Supp. 2d 87, 94 (D.D.C. 2008) (court declined to adopt reasoning of *Colorado Structures*, "as it would turn a performance surety into a commercial guarantor").

139 Kilpatrick Bros. Painting v. Chippewa Hills Sch. Dist., No. 262396, 2006 Mich. App. LEXIS 736, slip op. at *13 (Mich. Ct. App. March 16, 2006).

140 *Id.*

141 John A. Russell Corp. v. Fine Line Drywall, Inc., No. 2:05-cv-321, 2008 U.S. Dist. LEXIS 13098, at *6 (D. Vt. Feb. 21, 2008).

unworkable, noted that "[t]he *L&A* approach offers a clear benchmark for determining whether a default has occurred by requiring a material breach."[142]

Such instances of disagreement are indicative of a spirited debate on this issue within the case law. The particular facts of each case, along with the body of law within the jurisdiction, will control the outcome of each case.

2. Surety Must Be Given An Opportunity To Perform

Hand in hand with the requirement that a surety must be given a clear declaration of default by the obligee is the requirement that a surety be given an opportunity to perform. Thus, notice must be timely to be effective. A failure by the obligee to provide the principal and the surety an opportunity to cure incomplete or inadequate performance by the principal can also constitute a breach which can relieve the principal and the surety of liability to the obligee.[143]

In *Insurance Co. of North America v. Metropolitan Dade County*,[144] the county sued a "common law" performance surety to recover for latent defects in construction work done nearly a decade earlier at Opa Locka Airport, which defects were discovered when Hurricane Andrew blew off part of the roofs of two airport buildings. Notice of the defects was not given to the surety until five months after the necessary repairs had been made, thereby depriving the surety of its contractual right to complete the contract or, at least, to participate in selection of a contractor to properly complete the work. The court found the lack of timely notice to be a material breach which relieved the surety of all liability.[145]

In *St. Paul Fire and Marine Insurance Co. v. City of Green River*,[146] the owner terminated the principal and refused to allow St. Paul, the surety, to complete the project.[147] The owner attempted to justify its

---

142 *Id.* at *8.
143 *See* Carriage Town, Inc. v. Landco, Inc., 998 F. Supp. 646, 649 (D.S.C. 1998).
144 705 So. 2d 33 (Fla. Ct. App. 1997).
145 *Ins. Co. of N. Am.*, 705 So. 2d at 35.
146 93 F. Supp. 2d 1170 (D. Wyo. 2000), *aff'd* 6 Fed. Appx. 828 (10th Cir. 2001).
147 *Green River*, 93 F. Supp. 2d at 1172.

refusal by arguing that the surety committed an anticipatory breach by announcing it was unable to complete the behind-schedule project before the original project completion date and that it planned to use the principal's personnel to complete the project. Under the performance bond, the surety had four options for performance in the event of the contractor's default: "(1) arrange for [the principal] to complete the Project; (2) complete the Project itself; (3) arrange for a new contractor to complete the Project; or (4) determine the amount of its liability under the performance bond and tender that amount to the [owner]." The bond also provided that the surety would proceed "with reasonable promptness." The court rejected the owner's arguments that the surety had committed an anticipatory breach of the contract, finding the surety within its rights under the bond.[148]

The court found that the owner materially breached the performance bond, by refusing to allow the surety to complete the project. By refusing to allow completion, the owner divested the surety of its ability to minimize its liability by selecting the lowest cost provider and by directing the construction or participating in the contractor selection process. The court held that "an obligee's action that deprives a surety of its ability to protect itself pursuant to performance options granted under a performance bond constitutes a material breach, which renders the bond null and void."[149] The court concluded that, since the surety would not have entered into the performance bond without the four performance options in the event of a contractor's default, the owner's action depriving the surety of those options was a material breach, and the surety was discharged from the bond's obligations.[150]

B. Material Alteration in the Underlying Contract

The rule of strict construction–*strictissimi juris*–which says that any deviation in the original contract discharges the surety, was traditionally available as a suretyship defense, under the presumption that the suretyship was gratuitous and the surety therefore deserved maximum

---

[148] *Id.* at 1175-78.
[149] *Id.* at 1178.
[150] *Id.* at 1179.

protection under the law.[151] Courts, however, have long abandoned this favorable treatment toward compensated sureties, reasoning that "'[s]ureties for hire are not wards of court to be shielded from heedlessness or folly.'"[152] Bond sureties may not insist upon an absolute proscription of change.[153] Nevertheless, a material alteration of the terms of the original contract, without the knowledge or consent of the surety, may serve to discharge the surety from liability under the performance bond.[154] As with other defenses, a surety may waive the defense by action (or inaction) or via contract.[155] Similarly, the surety is required to exercise due diligence.[156]

---

151 Southwood Builders, Inc. v. Peerless Ins. Co., 366 S.E.2d 104, 106 (Va. 1988).

152 *Id.* at 106-07 (*quoting* C.S. Luck & Sons v. Boatwright, 162 S.E. 53, 54 (Va. 1932)).

153 U.S. Fid. & Guar. Co. v. Braspetro Oil Servs., 369 F.3d 34, 61 (2d Cir. 2004).

154 XL Specialty Ins. Co. v. Virginia Dep't of Transp., 611 S.E.2d 356, 370 (Va. 2005) ("if the owner and contractor engage in practices that constitute a material change in the construction contract provisions, and the contractor subsequently defaults on the contract, the surety is entitled to a discharge of its obligation to pay the contractor's debt"). *See also* Success Constr. Corp. v. Superintendent of Ins. (In re Liquidation of Union Indem. Ins. Co. of New York), 220 A.D.2d 339, 340 (N.Y. App. Div. 1995) (by amending the contract to include previously excluded work and substantially increasing the contract price, claimant materially altered the underlying obligation, thus discharging the surety). *But see* Town of Southington v. Commercial Union Ins. Co., 805 A.2d 76, 84 (Conn. App. Ct. 2002) (holding that surety was still liable under performance bond, as there was not a material alteration of the underlying obligation, even though the municipality purchased the land at a foreclosure sale after the developer filed bankruptcy, thus becoming the successor developer).

155 *See, e.g.*, Travelers Indem. Co. v. Ballantine, 436 F. Supp. 2d 707, 712 (M.D. Pa. 2006) ("However, a surety may consent to material modifications that will affect his obligations in the suretyship contract. Further, a surety may waive notice of material modifications with specific language in the surety agreement.").

156 *See* Augusta Fuel Co. v. Bond Safeguard Ins. Co., 502 F. Supp. 2d 124, 133-34 (D. Me. 2007) (even where the change was found to be material, court found surety's failure to investigate did not relieve the surety of its obligations under the bond). *See also* Spencer v. Frontier Ins. Co., No. 05-2391, No. 06-1551, 2008 U.S. App. LEXIS 18572, at *14 (4th Cir.

1. Prejudice to the Surety

In many instances, discharge for even a material modification will only be allowed if actual prejudice results to the surety.[157] In *Mergentime v. Washington Metropolitan Area Transit Authority*, the court looked to various jurisdictions to determine the standard for discharge of a compensated surety.[158] The court ultimately looked to the Restatement of Security, section 128(b), comment (f), which states:

> The modifications of contract between creditor and principal may be such as are contemplated by the contract in which case no surety would be discharged. They may be slight variations which by the technical rules which have prevailed in respect to non-compensated sureties would discharge them, although not in fact disadvantageous to the surety. In such a case the compensated surety would not be discharged. They may cause slight and easily measured damage to the compensated surety, so that the penalty of a total discharge of the surety would be disproportionate to the blame attaching to the creditor for the modification. In such a case the surety is discharged only to the extent of the loss. The compensated surety, however, should not be held to his obligation if the creditor and principal have so modified the contract as to impose a risk of a loss substantially different from the one covered by his obligation. If the change imposes a danger of loss upon the surety which cannot fairly be measured, the surety is discharged entirely.[159]

Aug. 26, 2008) ("Frontier, a sophisticated party, chose to execute its surety bond three days prior to closing without specifically examining the terms of the promissory note it knew would be delivered at closing...[c]onsequently, Frontier cannot escape its obligation as surety by failing to examine a promissory note it knew was being delivered").

157   Mergentime Corp. v. Washington Metro. Area Transit Auth., 775 F. Supp. 14, 17 (D.D.C. 1991). *But see* Centex Constr. v. Acustar Ins. Co., 448 F. Supp. 2d 697, 713 (E.D. Va. 2006) ("The surety need not demonstrate prejudice resulting from the material alteration because the material alteration, in itself, establishes sufficient prejudice").
158   *Mergentime*, 775 F. Supp. at 16-18.
159   *Mergentime*, 775 F. Supp. at 20-21 (*quoting* RESTATEMENT OF SECURITY § 128(b), cmt. (f)(1941)). *See also* RESTATEMENT (THIRD) OF SURETYSHIP AND GUARANTY § 41, cmt. (e)(1996) (fundamental modifications).

In *Mergentime*, the focus of analysis shifted from the nature and magnitude of the modification itself to the effect of the modification on the surety's risk. The court found that the obligee bore the burden of persuasion on the issue of prejudice, relying on *Reliance Insurance Co. v. Colbert*.[160]

In *Colbert*,[161] the court held that, if the prejudice to the surety proves impossible of rational measure, the surety must receive a total discharge.[162] If the prejudice is subject to measurement, the surety may receive only a partial discharge, measured by the extent of the prejudice.[163]

The court, in *Board of Supervisors of Fairfax County v. Southern Cross Coal Corp.*,[164] took a similar view, holding that discharge of the surety may be contingent on a showing of harm (by the surety) even when the obligee undertakes without the surety's consent to complete the work after the principal has defaulted.[165]

In *Southern Cross*, the contractor was obligated to complete road improvements in a subdivision.[166] After its default, it became apparent that the contractor had paved over deficient substructures. The county explored alternatives for correcting the problem within state transportation standards and adopted the least costly option. The surety claimed that the departure from original plans was a material variation that should relieve it from liability. The court disagreed, holding that the surety had failed to meet its burden of proof on the issue of material variation, since it had failed to rebut the county's evidence that it had

---

160 *Mergentime*, 775 F. Supp. at 13-14, 17-18, 21-22, 29 (*citing* Reliance Ins. Co. v. Colbert, 365 F.2d 530 (D.C. Cir. 1966)).
161 365 F.2d 530 (D.C. Cir. 1966).
162 *Colbert*, 365 F.2d at 535.
163 *Id.*
164 380 S.E.2d 636, 638-39 (Va. 1989).
165 *Southern Cross*, 380 S.E.2d at 638-39. Similarly, the Third Circuit, in a non-precedential opinion, has stated that compensated sureties "are discharged only when there has been a material modification without the surety's consent *and* that modification substantially increases the surety's risk." WRS Inc. v. Plaza Entm't, Inc., 285 Fed. Appx. 872, 876 slip op. (3d Cir. 2008) (emphasis in original).
166 *Id.* at 637.

taken the least expensive route to complete its goal of completing the streets to state standards.[167]

Despite the general rule that a surety's liability is discharged if its undertaking is altered so that the bond covers a different obligation, courts are unlikely to entertain an argument that a modification permitted by the bonded subcontract is a material alteration that should relieve the surety of liability.[168] In *In re Liquidation of Union Indemnity*, the obligee entered into an assumption agreement with a new subcontractor after the bonded subcontractor defaulted.[169] The subcontract was incorporated into the bond and specifically allowed the obligee to retain a completion contractor upon the subcontractor's default.[170] The court held that the actions taken by the obligee to complete the work were therefore within the contemplation of the surety.[171]

2. *Cardinal Change*

A change which is not fairly within the contemplation of the parties when the contract was executed may constitute a material departure that will release the surety. Courts have referred to such changes as fundamental or "cardinal changes," where the parties could not have reasonably anticipated the change in question as being within the scope of the work at the time the contract was signed.[172] A cardinal change is more than a mere alteration in the underlying contract. In many instances it amounts to a completely new contract. Additionally, courts have viewed such changes as constituting a breach of contract, relieving the contractor of its obligations.[173] It is worth noting, however, that the cardinal change doctrine has not been universally adopted.[174]

---

167 *Id.* at 639.
168 *In re* Liquidation of Union Indem. Ins. Co. of New York, 234 A.D.2d 120, 122-23 (N.Y. App. Div. 1996).
169 *Id.* at 122-23.
170 *Id.* at 122.
171 *Id.* at 122-23.
172 Allied Materials & Equip. Co. v. United States, 569 F.2d 562, 563 (Ct. Cl. 1978) (cardinal change defined as "an alteration in the work so drastic that it effectively requires the contractor to perform duties materially different from those originally bargained for").
173 In a Georgia federal district court case, the court found well-supported one party's argument that a cardinal change "is not a 'change' or

In the case of *Success Construction Corp. v. Superintendent of Insurance (In re Liquidation of Union Indem. Ins. Co. of New York)*, change orders were issued that substantially expanded the scope of work by adding stonework that was explicitly excluded in the original contract and that added $350,000 to the contract price.[175] The court found sufficient prejudice to justify release of the surety from its $195,000 bond obligation.[176]

Similarly, in *Employers Insurance of Wausau v. Construction Management Engineers of Florida*,[177] the surety was discharged from liability on its bond where the principal's contract was increased from a $2.3 million subcontract to a $6.2 million general contract.[178]

In *Wagner v. Frazier*,[179] however, the court found that a $77,000 extra for rock removal on a $250,000 contract did not increase the risk to the surety so as to constitute a discharge.[180]

The surety may also be released from its obligations if the contractor and subcontractor settle their dispute without the surety's consent. In *R.P. Richards v. Chartered Construction Corp.*,[181] the subcontractor sued the general contractor under a stop notice and stop notice release bond for payment on work that the subcontractor had completed. The general and subcontractor agreed on a settlement, but when the general

---

'modification' in the typical sense of these terms, but is instead a 'material breach' of the contract." Global Eng'g & Constr., LLC v. Merchants Bonding Co., Case No. CV 404-1, 2007 U.S. Dist. LEXIS 43588, at *4-6 (S.D. Ga. June 15, 2007). The court observed that, "it is well-established that a cardinal change is a material breach of contract that relieves a contractor from its obligations under a disputes clause." *Global Eng'g*, 2007 U.S. Dist. LEXIS 43588, at *6.

174 *See* Metro. Transp. Comm'n v. Motorola, Inc., No. C-06-2302 MMC, 2007 U.S. Dist. LEXIS 11286, at *30-31 (N.D. Cal. Jan. 31, 2007) ("California courts have not addressed the question of whether California should adopt the cardinal change doctrine").

175 Success Constr. Corp. v. Superintendent of Ins. (In re Liquidation of Union Indem. Ins. Co. of New York), 220 A.D.2d 339, 340 (N.Y. App. Div. 1995).

176 *Success Constr.*, 220 A.D.2d at 340.

177 377 S.E.2d 119 (S.C. Ct. App. 1989).

178 *Wausau*, 377 S.E.2d at 121.

179 712 S.W.2d 109 (Tenn. Ct. App. 1986).

180 *Wagner*, 712 S.W.2d at 116.

181 83 Cal. App. 4th 146 (Cal. Ct. App. 2000).

contractor missed a payment to the subcontractor, the subcontractor brought a claim against the general contractor and the surety. The court held that the general contractor's settlement of the subcontractor's claim, without the surety's consent, amounted to a release of the surety's liability, because it operated as a material alteration of the principal obligation in a manner that was not originally contemplated by the surety.[182]

In *Carriage Town, Inc. v. Landco, Inc.*, the underlying agreement between the obligee and the principal afforded the principal a ninety-day window to cure any default.[183] After litigation was initiated relating to another aspect of the obligee-principal agreement, the principal obtained a bond from the surety in order to guard against the effect of a wrongfully issued preliminary injunction. The principal and the obligee ultimately entered into a settlement agreement, without the consent or knowledge of the surety. The settlement agreement provided, among other things, that the cure period for late payments made by the principal would be reduced from ninety days to ten days.

The court in *Carriage Town* explained that "an alteration of the underlying risk assumed by the surety will discharge the surety from its obligations under the bond where the surety does not receive notice or consent to the additional risk."[184] The surety had "issued its bond in view of the generous 90-day cure period contained in the original lease-purchase agreement" between the obligee and the principal.[185] The court explained that "[t]he amended terms, however, cut the cure period to a more onerous ten days, clearly altering the conditions that served as part of the foundation for [the surety's] initial risk analysis," in addition to adding a liquidated damages provision automatically triggered in the event of a default by the principal under the significantly shorter ten-day cure period.[186] The court in *Carriage Town* found that the reduction in the opportunity to cure afforded to the principal and the surety was material and "significantly impacted the risk undertaken" by the

---

182 *R.P. Richards*, 83 Cal. App. 4th at 155.
183 Carriage Town, Inc. v. Landco, Inc., 998 F. Supp. 646, 647 (D.S.C. 1998).
184 *Id.* at 648.
185 *Id.* at 649.
186 *Id.*

surety.[187] Because the surety "was provided no notice of these changes, it is discharged from its obligation to pay the proceeds of the bond.[188]

3. Changes in the Parties to the Contract

A change in the parties to the transaction may give rise to a material modification defense by the surety. Although a "mere formalistic" change in the principal's identity will not discharge the surety, a substantial alteration can result in discharge if made without the surety's knowledge or consent.[189] It can be assumed that the surety based its decision to provide the bond in large part upon the principal's specific financial situation and ability to perform. Thus, a change in the principal can materially increase the risk to the surety.[190]

In *Aetna Casualty and Surety Co. v. New York City School Construction Authority*, work on the contract was suspended when federal arrest warrants were issued for the president and the founder of the bonded contractor.[191] A separate corporation was created to remove the two individuals from further involvement and the obligee entered into an agreement with the new corporation to complete the project. No notice was given to the surety. The new corporation ultimately was terminated. When a bond claim was later filed, the surety argued that the restructuring discharged its liability.

In its analysis, the court in *New York City School Construction Authority* cited three factors that determine whether a change in the bonded entity is significant enough to change the risk undertaken:

> [w]hether ownership or management control of the principal has been changed, whether there has been any change in the principal's business activities which would relate to the guarantee, and whether the changes

---

187   *Id.*
188   *Id.*
189   Aetna Casualty & Sur. Co. v. New York City Sch. Constr. Auth., No. 95 Civ. 9412, 1997 U.S. Dist. LEXIS 7145, at *8 (S.D.N.Y. May 21, 1997).
190   *But see* Leila Hosp. & Health Center v. Xonics Medical Sys., Inc., 948 F.2d 271, 275-76 (6th Cir. 1991) (sale by the principal of its sales and service functions did not relieve the surety from its bonded obligations with regard to the manufacture of equipment).
191   *New York City Sch. Constr. Auth.*, 1997 U.S. Dist. LEXIS 7145, at *2-3.

in form or structure of the principal would have reasonably been within the contemplation of the surety when it issued the guarantee.[192]

The court found that the application of these factors was unnecessary because the performance bond explicitly provided that any transfer or assignment of work to be performed by the principal would be treated as performed or not performed by the principal.[193] The surety was therefore bound to fulfill its obligations.[194]

As with other types of modifications, contractual provisions allowing transfers or assignments without notice and/or consent will be generally enforced.[195] But in the absence of such a provision, an assignee of an obligee may not be allowed to assert a claim against a surety where the bond language provides no right of action except by the owner and its successors, with no reference to its assignees.[196]

C. Prepayments and Overpayments by the Obligee

Early payments and overpayments, which frequently come in the form of premature release of retained funds, can harm the surety in two ways. First, the surety's access to remaining contract funds to cover its completion costs is reduced.[197] Second, early payments may reduce the principal's incentive to complete the project.[198]

---

192 *Id.* at *8.
193 *Id.* at *9-10.
194 *Id.* at *9-11.
195 *Id.*
196 TRST Atlanta, Inc. v. 1815 the Exch., Inc., 469 S.E.2d 238, 240 (Ga. Ct. App. 1996).
197 The surety has an equitable interest in the collateral held by the obligee as security for the principal's obligation. The obligee's overpayment of the contract funds constitutes a release of that security which impairs the surety's rights of subrogation to those funds. Prairie State Nat'l Bank v. United States, 164 U.S. 227, 232-33 (1896). *But see* United States Sur. Co. v. United States, 83 Fed. Cl. 306, 310-11 (Ct. Cl. 2008) (While a surety has "a right to withheld contract funds free from claims of set-off," this "right extends only to the unexpended contract balance," which "does not include liquidated damages").
198 *Southwood Builders*, 366 S.E.2d at 108.

As noted by one court, older jurisprudence "granted sureties a total discharge from their obligations in the event of overpayment."[199] Modern cases recognize that a surety is not helpless and can undertake measures to protect itself.[200] The basic principle that a surety may pursue an affirmative defense or claim against an obligee who impairs its suretyship status by a material overpayment to the principal, knowing the principal has failed to meet contractual requirements, continues to apply. However, this defense has been somewhat limited in recent years.[201] Where the defense does apply, however, the basic principle forms the starting point for analysis by any surety seeking to assert this defense.[202]

The more controversial questions involve the relief to which the surety is entitled, if any, should an overpayment occur and the method of calculating the amount to which the surety is entitled. Some courts take the approach that a material prepayment is enough to justify discharge of the surety's obligation without any showing of prejudice to the surety.[203]

In *Southwood Builders, Inc. v. Peerless Insurance Co.*, the bonded contractor was behind schedule and the obligee made advances on progress payments to allow the contractor to add more labor.[204] The surety successfully argued that prepayments of $31,000 on an original contract price of $79,500 constituted material variations and that no

---

199 N. Am. Specialty Ins. Co. v. Chichester Sch. Dist., Civil Action No. 99-2394, 2000 U.S. Dist. LEXIS 10745, at *36 (E.D. Pa. July 20, 2000) (Court noted that the "modern rule...holds that 'when there has been a material departure from contractual provisions relating to payments and the security of retained funds, a compensated surety is discharged from its obligations on the performance bond to the extent that such unauthorized payments result in prejudice or injury'–*i.e.* the pro tanto rule." (*quoting* United States v. Continental Cas. Co., 512 F.2d 475, 477 (5th Cir. 1975)).

200 *See, e.g.*, Great Am. Ins. Co. v. Norwin Sch. Dist., 544 F.3d 229, 246 n.15 (3d Cir. 2008) ("We note that a surety is not necessarily without protection when a construction contract makes retainage permissive rather than obligatory." Sureties have other means to protect themselves.).

201 *See* Argonaut Ins. Co. v. Town of Cloverdale, 699 F.2d 417, 419 (7th Cir. 1983). *See also* Mergentime Corp. v. Washington Metro. Area Transit Auth., 775 F. Supp. 14, 16-17 (Fed. Cir. 1991).

202 Nat'l Sur. Corp. v. United States, 118 F.3d 1542, 1545 (Fed. Cir. 1997).

203 *Southwood Builders*, 366 S.E.2d at 108.

204 *Id.* at 105-06.

separate showing of prejudice was necessary.[205] The court said that proof that the subcontractor was paid money before it was due and without the required approvals established a material deviation.[206]

It may be more common for courts to hold that a surety is discharged in such instances only to the extent that it can establish prejudice. In *Continental Insurance Co. v. City of Virginia Beach*,[207] the bonded contract implicitly provided that work would be paid for only after satisfactory completion of testing and inspection.[208] When a default occurred, it was discovered that the city had paid over $1 million to the contractor but had done very little testing and inspection of the contractor's work.[209] The court held that the surety was discharged, but only to the extent that the city's actions prejudiced the surety's interest.[210]

Other courts have similarly held that discharge is limited to the extent of prejudice suffered by the surety. In *National Surety Corp. v. United States*,[211] the court recognized that contract terms which provide security for the bonded performance cannot be "ignored, waived or modified without consideration of the surety's interests."[212] The extent to which a surety can recover based on an owner's failure to consider the surety's interests in prematurely releasing retainage to the principal, however, should be measured not by the amount released, but by the actual damage attributable to the release.[213]

---

205   *Id.* at 108.
206   *Id.*
207   *Virginia Beach*, 908 F. Supp. 341, 345 (E.D. Va. 1995).
208   *Id.* at 343.
209   *Id.*
210   *Id.*
211   *Nat'l Surety Corp.*, 118 F.3d at 1547.
212   *Id.* at 1547.
213   *Id.* at 1548. *See also* Ramada Dev. Co. v. U.S. Fid. & Guar. Co., 626 F.2d 517, 522 (6th Cir. 1980) (Discharge in any amount is inappropriate, if overpayments are made in good faith to allow the contractor to complete the job and if the contractor actually uses the overpaid funds to pay amounts due and to further completion of the contract); *Town of Cloverdale*, 699 F.2d at 419 ("[W]hether the advances increase the surety's risk depends on what the principal did with them; if he used them on the project the amount at risk to the surety may be unaffected").

This reasoning was followed by the court in *Freeman & Associates, Inc. v. Travelers Casualty & Surety Co. of America*.[214] The *Freeman* court allowed a partial discharge of the surety's obligations for the portion of payments that had been applied by the principal to pay other loans and not loans on the bonded project.[215]

Two factors that can come into play in determining whether the surety is entitled to relief based on overpayments are the reasonableness of the obligee's actions and its good faith.[216] In *Transamerica Insurance Co. v. City of Kennewick*, the court held that a prepayment would excuse a surety only if it caused the surety pecuniary disadvantage or otherwise deprived the surety of some privilege or protection reserved in the bond.[217] The court found that the surety had not been prejudiced by a premature payment made in good faith for materials that were actually delivered to the site and for which the contractor had paid.[218] However, the city's overpayment in reliance on negligent certifications by its own employee, for pipe which was never installed, deprived the city of the good faith defense and resulted in a recovery by the surety.[219]

---

214 5:05-CV-34-(WDO), 2006 U.S. Dist. LEXIS 59687, at *23 (August 23, 2006 M.D. Ga.).
215 *Freeman*, 2006 U.S. Dist. LEXIS 59687, at *23.
216 Transamerica Ins. Co. v. City of Kennewick, 785 F.2d 660, 662 (9th Cir. 1986). "[C]ourts have held that this defense does not apply when the owner has in good faith relied upon the certifications of its architects or engineers." RLI Ins. Co. v. Indian River Sch. Dist., 536 F. Supp. 2d 356, 364 (D. Del. 2008). *But see Chichester*, 2000 U.S. Dist. LEXIS 10745, at *40 ("Even if the prepayment or overpayment resulted from mere negligence, such negligence exonerates the surety's duty to the extent of the prejudice caused by the payment").
217 *Kennewick*, 785 F.2d at 662-63.
218 *Id.* at 661.
219 *Id.* at 662. *But see* Fid. & Deposit Co. of Maryland v. County of Lake, No. 97 C 6276, 2000 U.S. Dist. LEXIS 5497, at *16 (N.D. Ill. 2000) (holding that surety was not discharged from liability where the city paid the contractor prior to receiving waivers because distributing funds prior to receiving waivers was standard practice in the construction industry, was the procedure outlined by the performance bond, and the payments did not amount to unauthorized advances under the two-prong test).

D. Extensions of Time

Extensions of the time allowed for the performance of a construction contract often provide a clear benefit to the principal, and in many instances do not cause significant prejudice to the interests of the surety. This defense, like other material alterations, is also frequently waived by contractual provisions (either in the bond or the underlying contract) that permit reasonable extensions of time without prior notice to the surety.[220] Because of the surety's inability in most instances to establish prejudice as a result of such extensions, this defense has become less viable over time.

The defense may have a place, however, in those cases where an obligee has granted extension after extension with no notice to the surety, and then upon the default of the principal, seeks to recover for delay damages. One author recently observed, the Restatement (Third) of Suretyship and Guaranty may breathe new life into this defense.[221] Section 40 of the Restatement addresses extensions of time and reaffirms that, to the extent the extension of time causes a loss to the surety, the surety will be discharged.[222] A showing of prejudice, as with most cases involving an alteration to the underlying contract, is the key to the surety's ability to argue for discharge.

E. Failure to Mitigate

The scenario most commonly giving rise to a "failure to mitigate" defense is one in which the obligee takes over arrangements for project completion without affording the surety an opportunity to complete.[223] In

---

220 *See, e.g.*, McWane, Inc. v. Fid. & Deposit Co. of Maryland, 372 F.3d 798, 804 (6th Cir. 2004) (surety's payment bond contract expressly waived notice of any extension of time).

221 J. Knox, *The Surety's Extension of Time Defense*, 33 TORT & INS. L. J., 891 (1998).

222 RESTATEMENT (THIRD) OF SURETYSHIP AND GUARANTY § 40(b)(1996).

223 *See, e.g.*, Enter. Capital, Inc. v. San-Gra Corp., 284 F. Supp. 2d 166, 177 (D. Mass. 2003) ("the seven-day notice requirement in the Construction Contract exists precisely to provide the surety an opportunity to protect itself against loss by participating in the selection of the successor contractor to ensure that the lowest bidder is hired and damages mitigated").

Dragon Construction, Inc. v. Parkway Bank & Trust,[224] the obligee failed to provide the required notice on a timely basis, and hired a successor contractor before eventually giving notice.[225] This action stripped [the surety] of its contractual right to minimize its liability under the performance bond by ensuring that the lowest responsible bidder was selected to do the job."[226] The result was a material breach that rendered the surety bonds null and void.[227] A similar result was reached in *Balfour Beatty Construction Co. v. Colonial Ornamental Iron Works, Inc.*,[228] where the court held that failure to declare the principal in default and allowing the principal to complete the project, released the surety from liability because it denied the surety the opportunity to exercise its options under the performance bond.[229]

F. Other Actions of the Obligee

Other actions by obligees have served to discharge the surety from partial or full liability. In *United States Fidelity and Guaranty Co. v. Orlando Utilities Commission*,[230] a deliberate delay in the commercial operation date of a plant by the obligee for economic reasons relieved the surety of damages for the period of the delay.[231] In *St. Paul Fire and Marine Insurance Co. v. Commodity Credit Corp.*,[232] a government agency/obligee that condoned kiting of obligations by the principal was precluded from recovering on the suretyship agreement that secured performance of those obligations.[233]

Simple negligence by the obligee, however, may not be enough to discharge a surety. In *City of Houma v. Municipal and Industrial Pipe Service, Inc.*,[234] the negligence of engineers hired by the city to certify

---

224 678 N.E.2d 55 (Ill. Ct. App. 1997), *appeal denied*, 684 N.E.2d 1335 (Ill. 1997).
225 *Dragon*, 678 N.E.2d at 57.
226 *Id.* at 58.
227 *Id.*
228 *Balfour*, 986 F. Supp. 82 (D. Conn. 1997).
229 *Id.* at 86.
230 *Orlando Utilities*, 564 F. Supp. 962 (M.D. Fla. 1983).
231 *Id.* at 967.
232 *Commodity Credit*, 646 F.2d 1064 (5th Cir. 1981).
233 *Id.* at 1073.
234 *Houma*, 884 F.2d 886 (5th Cir. 1989).

progress, who failed to make site visits, was not imputed to the city.[235] The surety, however, was entitled to indemnification from the engineering firm.[236]

Despite the existence of an enforceable bond, the obligee may be estopped from seeking recovery against the surety. In *Cornell & Co. v. First Indemnity of America Insurance Co. (In re Muratone Co.)*,[237] the general contractor/obligee specifically required satisfactory performance and payment bonds.[238] Bonds issued by First Indemnity for a premium of $56,000 were forwarded for review and approval to the obligee, but the obligee rejected these as unacceptable based on the surety's substandard financial strength.[239] Meanwhile, the subcontractor/ principal was permitted to proceed with work on the project.[240] The subcontractor sought replacement bonds and a refund of its premium from First Indemnity.[241] First Indemnity asserted that the bonds were non-cancelable and that the premium had been earned.[242] When the subcontractor defaulted, the general contractor/obligee sought recovery under the First Indemnity performance bond.[243] The court held that, although a suretyship contract had been formed at the time the surety's offer was accepted by the subcontractor/principal, the obligee could not enforce the bond because it had not accepted the bond within a reasonable time.[244]

---

235 *Id.* at 891.
236 *Id.* at 887, 891 (noting that the bonded contractor in the case had committed fraud by falsifying work logs in order to obtain payment for work that was not done).
237 *Cornell*, 198 B.R. 871 (Bankr. E.D. Pa. 1996).
238 *Id.* at 873.
239 *Id.*
240 *Id.*
241 *Cornell*, 198 B.R. at 874.
242 *Id.*
243 *Cornell*, 198 B.R. at 875.
244 *Id.* at 875-76.

III. Impairment to Security or Collateral

The security held by the obligee in a performance bond setting is generally the remaining unremitted balance of contract funds.[245] Premature release of these funds may result in the partial release of a surety, as discussed above. Other situations, however, may arise where the obligee takes certain actions which jeopardize the surety's rights to look to collateral which would otherwise be available to the surety to offset any loss incurred by reason of claims made on the performance bond. In these situations, the obligee may be estopped from asserting a claim on the bond.[246]

A. Impairment of Collateral

In *United States v. Continental Casualty Co.*,[247] Continental Casualty issued a performance bond for a general contractor that had failed to pay its subcontractor for partially fabricated equipment.[248] The general contractor had received payment from the government owner, but had not paid its subcontractor.[249] The subcontractor subsequently declared a lien on the partially completed equipment.[250] The government eventually terminated the general contract, notifying the surety that the subcontractor was still obligated to deliver the completed equipment and that all of the equipment covered by the progress payments made to the general contractor was the property of the government.[251]

The government eventually granted a reprocurement contract for the equipment and paid the subcontractor the original purchase price for the

---

245 *See, e.g.*, Nat'l Fire Ins. Co. of Hartford v. Fortune Constr. Co., 320 F.3d 1260, 1271 (11th Cir. 2003) ("the surety has a right to all retained funds and any remaining progress sums, and the obligee does not possess a right to set-off").
246 *See* RESTATEMENT (THIRD) OF SURETYSHIP AND GUARANTY § 42 (1996).
247 *Continental Casualty,* 512 F.2d 475 (5th Cir. 1975).
248 *Id.* at 476.
249 *Id.*
250 *Id.*
251 *Id.*

equipment.[252] The reprocurement contract ignored the original payments which had already been made to the general contractor.[253]

The surety successfully argued that its obligation was discharged because the government had unreasonably prejudiced the surety's right of subrogation by paying for the equipment under the reprocurement contract.[254] The court observed:

> [A] surety is entitled to be subrogated to the benefit of all securities and means of payment under the creditor's control, and any act by the creditor depriving the surety of this right discharged it pro tanto; thus, the creditor must, for the surety's benefit, apply to the debt all money or security within his control and which he has a right to apply. If he voluntarily surrenders or releases such security, the surety is discharged pro tanto.[255]

The court further found that the government could have protected the surety's rights without impairing its own interests by simply initiating litigation against the subcontractor to determine title to that percentage of the equipment for which the government had already paid, while at the same time paying the full amount of the contract into court.[256] While the suit was in progress, the government could have entered into the reprocurement contract with the subcontractor, and demanded payment of the amount from the surety.[257] The surety would then have been subrogated to any rights that the government was eventually determined to have had in the partially completed equipment.[258]

Recent cases confirm that the government, like other obligees, may be liable to a surety for improper release of retainage. In *National Surety Corp. v. United States*,[259] the court held that "the retainage provision in a bonded construction contract serves to protect the surety as well as the

---

252 *Id.*
253 *Id.*
254 *Continental Casualty Co.*, 512 F.2d at 478-79.
255 *Id.* at 478.
256 *Id.*
257 *Id.*
258 *Id.*
259 *National Surety Corp.*, 118 F.3d 1542 (Fed. Cir. 1997).

government, and is an interest of the surety that can not be disregarded or diminished by a party to the contract."[260]

A few courts, however, have held that different performance standards apply to governmental obligees. In *United Pacific Insurance Co. v. United States*,[261] the court held that the premature issuance of progress payments related to construction contracts awarded by the government should be reviewed under an "abuse of discretion" standard.[262]

B. Release of Collateral

An obligee's intentional release of contract funds to a principal in total disregard of the surety's interest in the funds, as distinguished from a negligent premature payment, will serve to release the surety to the extent of release. In *Pennsylvania National Mutual Casualty Insurance Co. v. City of Pine Bluff*,[263] the city entered into a contract with a general contractor to remove debris caused by an ice storm.[264] The city ultimately terminated the contractor but later settled with the contractor and released the remaining contract funds despite conflicting claims from the contractor, its subcontractors, and the surety.[265] Prior to the city disbursing funds to the contractor, the surety had given the city notice that the city was not to distribute any funds without the surety's written consent given that numerous claims had been asserted against the payment bond.[266] The court held that the city was liable to the surety for the amounts paid out by the surety on payment bond claims because the city's decision to pay funds to the principal increased the surety's risk and impaired its right to reimbursement from the remaining security.[267]

---

260 *Id.* at 1545.
261 *United Pacific*, 16 Ct. Cl. 555 (Ct. Cl. 1989).
262 *Id.* at 559 (also holding that, although public policy supports granting the government great flexibility in contract administration, an "unbelievable disregard of prominent warning signals" and knowing use of taxpayer money to pay for nonexistent items did, in fact, constitute abuse of discretion).
263 *Pine Bluff*, 354 F.3d 945 (8th Cir. 2004).
264 *Id.* at 949.
265 *Id.*
266 *Pine Bluff*, 354 F.3d at 948.
267 *Id.* at 953-54.

In *Continental Insurance Co. v. City of Virginia Beach*,[268] the obligee's failure to make reasonable and prompt inspections before paying the full contract price to the principal for materials installed discharged the surety from its obligations to the extent that the surety was prejudiced by the failure.[269] In *City of Virginia Beach*, a city employee admitted that the city was unconcerned about its lax payment and inspection procedures because it had a surety to hold responsible.[270] The court expressed concern that these procedures provided no inducement for construction contractors to complete projects on schedule or indeed at all.[271] For reasons of public policy, the court held that the city had materially deviated from the contract, thereby discharging the surety to the extent of prejudice suffered.[272]

Similar principles apply to federal government contracts. In *National Surety Corp. v. United States*,[273] a 10 percent retainage, releasable only upon submission of a "project arrow diagram," was provided for in the contract, and served as security for performance of the contract.[274] The court held that, because this provision had contributed to the surety's assessment of risk, the surety was entitled to rely on it.[275] In reaching its conclusion, the court stated that, "[c]ontract terms that provide security for the bonded performance can not be ignored, waived, or modified without consideration of the surety's interests."[276]

IV. Release or Discharge of Principal

Generally speaking, a surety's liability is limited by that of its bonded principal. Thus, if the principal receives a discharge from its bonded obligation, the surety's liability terminates as well.[277] Whether such a

---

268 *Virginia Beach*, 908 F. Supp. 341 (E.D. Va. 1995).
269 *Id.* at 348.
270 *Id.*
271 *Id.*
272 *Id.*
273 *National Surety Corp.*, 118 F.3d 1542 (Fed. Cir. 1997).
274 *Id.* at 1546.
275 *Id.*
276 *National Surety Corp.*, 118 F.3d at 1547. See also RESTATEMENT (THIRD) OF SURETYSHIP AND GUARANTY § 39 (1996).
277 Continental Bank & Trust Co. v. American Bonding Co., 605 F.2d 1049, 1054 (8th Cir. 1979).

discharge has occurred can be a fact-specific question. In *Safeco Insurance Co. v. City of White House*,[278] the principal submitted a winning bid to construct a sanitary system for the city and was awarded the contract for the project.[279] The principal agreed to perform the work according to bid specifications, which included compliance with the Environmental Protection Agency's equal employment opportunity policy.[280] The principal failed to comply with the policy because of its inability to secure a subcontract with a minority business enterprise.[281] When the city insisted on compliance with the policy, the principal withdrew its bid.[282] The city then awarded the job to the second lowest bidder and made a demand upon the surety, based upon what it characterized as an anticipatory breach by the principal, for the difference of approximately $350,000 between the lowest and second lowest bid amounts.[283]

The surety argued that no binding contract existed between the principal and obligee because Environmental Protection Agency approval was a condition precedent to formation of the contract.[284] The court held otherwise, concluding that the city had unconditionally accepted the principal's conditional promise, which resulted in formation of a valid contract.[285] The court went further, however, to find that the issue of breach centered on whether the principal's efforts to fulfill the condition were made in good faith.[286] If a good faith effort was made, but the condition could not be met, the principal had no further duty to perform under the contract.[287] The case was remanded for further proceedings.[288]

A problematic issue, related to release of the principal as a defense of the surety, arises where the obligee releases the principal, but expressly reserves recourse against the surety. The Eleventh Circuit Court of

---

278 *White House,* 36 F.3d 540 (6th Cir. 1994).
279 *Id.* at 542.
280 *Id.*
281 *White House,* 36 F.3d at 543.
282 *Id.*
283 *Id.* at 542-43.
284 *Id. at* 546.
285 *Id.* at 547.
286 *Id.* at 548.
287 *Id.*
288 *Id.*

Appeals addressed this question in *Hardaway Co. v. Amwest Surety Insurance Co.*.[289] *Hardaway* involved a bonded subcontractor that experienced financial difficulties, which led to the surety's completion of the project.[290] The subcontractor then sued the obligee/general contractor for cost overruns.[291] The claim between the general contractor and subcontractor was settled by release of the claim of default by the general contractor against the subcontractor (but not the surety) in exchange for the release of the cost overrun claim by the subcontractor.[292]

The Eleventh Circuit certified the following question to the Georgia Supreme Court: Does release of a principal, with express reservation of rights against the surety and without the surety's consent, release the surety from liability, or merely serve as a covenant not to sue the principal?[293] The Georgia Supreme Court held that although such a release did not discharge the surety, the surety would be entitled to assert any claims against the obligee which were waived by the principal in consideration of the release.[294] Thus, the surety was allowed to assert the claim for cost overruns that the principal had released as part of the settlement agreement against the general contractor.[295]

An arbitration award that settles an obligee's claim against a principal may, under certain circumstances, operate as res judicata in discharging the surety from liability.[296] In *Westcott Construction Corp. v. Firemen's Fund of New Jersey*, the court assessed costs against a general contractor based on its continued efforts to seek indemnification of additional costs from the surety, after an arbitration award had already established the extent of the general contractor's damages against the subcontractor/principal.[297]

---

[289] *Hardaway Co.*, 15 F.3d 172 (11th Cir. 1994) (*rev'g* Hardaway Co. v. Amwest Sur. Ins. Co., 986 F. 2d 1395 (11th Cir. 1993)).
[290] *Id.* at 173.
[291] *Id.*
[292] *Id.*
[293] *Id.* at 172-73.
[294] Hardaway Co. v. Amwest Sur. Ins. Co., 436 S.E.2d 642 (Ga. 1993).
[295] *Hardaway Co.*, 15 F.3d at 174.
[296] Westcott Constr. Corp. v. Firemen's Fund of New Jersey, 996 F.2d 14, 16 (1st Cir. 1993).
[297] *Id.* at 17.

V. Obligee's Lack of Good Faith

Courts are not in total agreement as to what is required of both the obligee and the surety in terms of the disclosure of information. The failure to disclose material facts to a surety may result in discharge of the surety's liability on the bond if the surety can establish a duty on the part of the obligee to disclose such information. Courts, however, are much more uniform in their treatment of actual misrepresentations made by an obligee.

A. *Concealment*

An obligee has no general duty to disclose information not requested by the surety.[298] A surety who fails to seek reasonably available and important information cannot assert ignorance of such facts as a defense in the absence of fraud.[299] The surety may have a defense to liability if, before the obligation is undertaken, (1) the obligee knows of facts unknown to the surety, which the obligee has reason to believe are not known to the surety; (2) the facts materially increase the surety's risk; and (3) the obligee has adequate time to disclose these facts but fails to do so.[300]

Not all courts, however, are amenable to such a defense. The court in *Rachman Bag Co. v. Liberty Mutual Insurance Co.*,[301] added two requirements to the test for fraudulent concealment.[302] First, the obligee must have had reason to believe that the surety would not be willing to assume the higher risk indicated by the undisclosed information.[303] The second, and more significant, additional requirement was that the obligee "must have the duty to disclose the information based upon its relationship to the surety, its responsibility for the surety's misimpression, or other circumstances."[304]

---

298   St. Paul Fire & Marine Ins. Co. v. Commodity Credit Corp., 646 F.2d 1064, 1072 (5th Cir. 1981).
299   *Id.* at 1072.
300   *Id.* at 1073 (citing RESTATEMENT OF SECURITY § 124 (1941)). *See also* SURETYSHIP AND GUARANTY § 47 (1996).
301   *Rachman*, 46 F.3d 230 (2nd Cir. 1995).
302   *Id.* at 237.
303   *Id.*
304   *Id.*

The court in *Rachman Bag* began its analysis by stating that policy does not support protecting sureties from their own "laziness or poorly considered decision[s]."[305] Therefore, under New York law, sureties are responsible for taking the initiative to obtain information that is important to their bonding decisions.[306] If a surety makes appropriate inquiries of an obligee, the obligee's silence can constitute fraudulent concealment.[307] However, where the surety fails to make such inquiries, the obligee's silence amounts to fraud only if some basis is established for an affirmative duty of disclosure by the obligee.[308]

There are certain circumstances under which such a duty might arise, such as where the obligee dealt directly with the surety in securing the bond.[309] In addition, an obligee who affirmatively creates an erroneous impression, such as by signing a contract that contains a statement known by the obligee to be false, may have a duty to correct it.[310] An obligee that colludes in a deception with the principal may have a disclosure duty, even if the misrepresentation is by the principal.[311] Finally, if the obligee has unique access to material information within its control, it may have a duty to disclose. However, mere difficulty by the surety in obtaining information will not suffice.[312]

B. *Non-Disclosure*

Closely related to the issue of concealment is the issue of non-disclosure. A surety asserting nondisclosure by the obligee has the burden of proving nondisclosure of facts unknown to the surety and material to the surety's risk, and reliance by the surety in issuing the bond.[313] However, as with concealment, the obligee generally has no duty to disclose

---

305 *Id.* at 235 (*quoting* Cam-Ful Indus. v. Fid. & Deposit Co., 922 F.2d 156, 162 (2d Cir. 1991)).
306 *Id.*
307 *Id.*
308 *Id.* at 235-36.
309 *Id.* at 236.
310 *Id.* at 236-37.
311 *Id.* at 236.
312 *Id.* at 237.
313 Rocky Mountain Tool & Mach. Co. v. Tecon Corp., 371 F.2d 589, 597 (10th Cir. 1966).

information which allegedly increases the risk to the surety, absent an inquiry by the surety or fraud by the obligee.[314]

C. Misrepresentation

A surety may be discharged from all liability under its bond if it can prove an affirmative misrepresentation by the obligee, even if it could have discovered the misrepresentation through additional investigation.[315] In *Pinkerton & Laws, Inc. v. Macro Construction, Inc.*, the surety issued bonds after talking with the obligee's project manager, who misrepresented the terms of the subcontract, but without reviewing a copy of the bonded contract.[316] The surety offered testimony that this practice was common in the industry.[317] The court held that the surety had exercised due diligence, and therefore could assert a defense of fraudulent misrepresentation by the obligee.[318]

In *Ground Improvement Techniques, Inc. v. Merchants Bonding Co.*,[319] the surety issued a performance bond after speaking with the contractor, who stated that he was comfortable with the subcontractor/principal to the bond, but failed to disclose that the owner, contractor, and subcontractor were engaged in an on-going dispute regarding the excavation.[320] The court applied Section 12 of the Restatement (Third) of Suretyship and Guaranty's three-part, "intensely fact-based inquiry"

---

314 Iowa Concrete Breaking Corp. v. Jewat Trucking, Inc., 444 N.W.2d 865, 868 (Minn. Ct. App. 1989) (holding that the surety knew or should have known that the principal had already begun work when the bond was issued). *See also* Plant Process Equipment, Inc. v. Continental Carbonic Products, Inc., No. 87 C 193, 1994 WL 201218, *3 (N.D. Ill. May 17, 1994) (court recognized application of RESTATEMENT OF SECURITY § 124 (1)(1941) to issue of nondisclosure).
315 Pinkerton & Laws, Inc. v. Macro Constr., Inc., 485 S.E.2d 797, 798-99 (Ga. Ct. App. 1997).
316 *Pinkerton*, 485 S.E.2d at 799.
317 *Id.*
318 *Id.* at 798-99. *See also* Employers Ins. of Wausau v. Construction Mgmt. Engrs. of Florida, Inc., 377 S.E.2d 119, 122 (S.C. Ct. App. 1989) (replacement of a $2.3 million bonded contract with a $6.2 million contract discharged the surety from its obligation, because the first contract appeared valid and gave surety no reason to investigate).
319 *Ground Improvement,* 63 F. Supp. 2d 1272 (D. Colo. 1999).
320 *Id.* at 1274.

VI. Matters Affecting the Bonded Obligation

In a variety of circumstances, the surety may be able to successfully assert that the bond itself was not valid. For example, in *American Insurance Co. v. Donatelli Construction Co., Inc.*,[323] the performance and payments bonds submitted by the principal to the obligee had been forged.[324] The obligee argued that the would-be surety should be held accountable for having negligently allowed critical power-of-attorney forms to fall into the wrong hands.[325] However, the obligee was unable to prove that the form attached to the forged bond had been negligently handled, nor was it able to identify the forger.[326] Furthermore, no basis for strict liability was offered to, or perceived by, the court.[327] Therefore, the obligee was unable to obtain any recovery against the surety listed on the bonds.[328]

Courts have held that precontractual obligations are not covered by performance bonds.[329] In *JCM Construction Co., Inc. v. Orleans Parish School Board*, the principal was responsible for obtaining builder's risk coverage, but failed to do so.[330] The obligee's insurance consultant failed to detect the oversight when reviewing the certificate of insurance.[331] After work commenced on the project, vandals started a fire that burned two portable buildings.[332] The obligee sought recovery from the surety on the basis that the surety had guaranteed performance of all of the

---

321 *Id.* at 1276.
322 *Id.* at 1277.
323 *Donatelli*, 713 A.2d 237 (R.I. 1998).
324 *Id.*
325 *Id.* at 238.
326 *Id.*
327 *Id.* at 239.
328 *Id.*
329 JCM Constr. Co., Inc. v. Orleans Parish Sch. Bd., 663 So. 2d 429, 433 (La. Ct. App. 1995).
330 *Id.* at 430.
331 *Id.* at 431.
332 *Id.* at 430.

principal's contractual obligations.[333] The court disagreed, holding that although the surety's obligation was to guarantee performance of the contract, the principal's obligation to obtain builder's risk insurance was a precontractual obligation.[334]

Courts will not imply a duty to issue a performance bond solely from the issuance of a bid bond.[335] In *Charles H. Tompkins Co. v. Lumbermens Mutual Casualty Co.*, the principal breached its bid bond obligation by failing to obtain a performance bond.[336] Nonetheless, the obligee allowed the principal to proceed with performance until the principal declared bankruptcy and ceased work thirteen months later.[337] The obligee on the bid bond unsuccessfully argued that the bid bond surety was expressly or impliedly responsible for issuance of a performance bond.[338] The court noted that the two risks are substantially different, with a bid bond breach typically limited to 5 to 10 percent of the bid amount, and the performance bond generally covering the entire bid amount.[339]

Where a later contract, substantially broader in scope, supersedes the contract on which the surety is liable, a surety who returns the premium on the first contract after learning of the second is released from liability.[340] On the other hand, billing and collection of a premium may serve to ratify a surety's bond obligation.[341] In *Wagner v. Frazier*, the

---

333 *Id.* at 431.
334 *Id.* at 432. *But see* Carroll-Boone Water Dist. v. M&P Equip. Co., 661 S.W.2d 345, 354 (Ark. 1983) (surety liable for damages as a result of the contractor's failure to provide builder's risk policy).
335 Charles H. Tompkins Co. v. Lumbermens Mut. Cas. Co., 732 F. Supp. 1368, 1372-73 (E.D. Va. 1990).
336 *Id.* at 1370.
337 *Id.*
338 *Id.* at 1370-71.
339 *Id.* at 1373. *See also* Avallone Architectural Specialties v. DBCS Corp., 839 So. 2d 1045, 1050 (La. Ct. App. 2003) (holding that school board's failure to obtain performance and payment bonds, although it did acquire a bid bond, absolved bid bond insurer of liability when the contractor completed the work and was paid by the school board, but failed to pay a subcontractor).
340 Employers Ins. of Wausau v. Construction Mgmt. Engrs. of Florida, Inc., 377 S.E.2d 119, 121-22 (S.C. Ct. App. 1989).
341 Wagner v. Frazier, 712 S.W.2d 109, 115 (Tenn. Ct. App. 1986).

obligee learned, upon asserting a claim, that the surety had never received payment from the agents and, therefore, had not issued a bond.[342] The agents who had improperly retained the premium persuaded the obligee to tell the surety that the bond had been placed with another company.[343] The obligee later sought reinstatement of the bond on the basis that she had acted under a mistake of fact.[344] The surety billed the agency and collected the bond premium.[345] Although the surety thereafter asserted that the bond was invalid, the court found, in the act of collection, there was a ratification of the bond by the surety.[346]

Conclusion

A strong working knowledge of the above defenses available to the surety can greatly assist a surety in its efforts to limit its liability under performance bonds to that upon which the parties originally agreed. Because sureties may waive any and all of these defenses, it is important that a surety become familiar with the primary defenses so as to be able to better address its options from the moment it first receives notice of a potential claim. Such action can greatly aid the surety in formulating a successful defense against a claim.

---

342 *Id.* at 112.
343 *Id.*
344 *Id.*
345 *Id.*
346 *Id.* at 115.

12

LITIGATION ISSUES

Denise C. Puente*
Steven D. Nelson

Introduction

This chapter shall address procedural issues which arise regardless of the type of performance bond involved in the litigation. Although the primary focus of this chapter will deal with Miller Act claims, procedural issues relating to claims filed against payment and performance bonds issued in connection with private or Little Miller Act claims will also be discussed. Regardless of what type of bond is involved, certain common issues arise. Who are proper parties? Where should suit be filed? When should suit be filed? What happens if one of the parties is in bankruptcy? This chapter shall address issues frequently encountered by practitioners in litigation involving performance bond claims. This chapter will also discuss what limitations may apply to any such action including but not limited to issues such as when or if notice must be given and what statute of limitations is to be applied.

I. Federal Court Jurisdiction

Jurisdiction in federal courts may be based upon diversity jurisdiction or on matters of federal questions, such as Miller Act claims. The issue of federal court jurisdiction is relevant not only in determining whether a suit should be filed in federal district court, but also in whether it may be removed to federal court.

---

* The authors would like to express their appreciation for the assistance of Betty F. Mullin and law clerks, Chris Otten and Jason Wixom in researching and writing this chapter.

A. Diversity Jurisdiction

Federal courts have original jurisdiction over all civil actions arising between citizens of different states or foreign nations where the amount in controversy exceeds $75,000.[1] Therefore, under diversity jurisdiction there are two requirements: diversity between the parties and minimum amount in controversy. For purposes of diversity among the parties, a business has two citizenships: the state of incorporation and the state where it has its principal place of business.[2] Furthermore, in order for the diversity requirement to be met, every defendant's citizenship must be diverse from the plaintiff's.

Because federal courts have original jurisdiction over diversity suits, if both the diversity and amount in controversy requirements are met, the action may be removed from state court upon motion by the defendant to the federal district court in which the state court sits.[3] The cardinal rule for removal is that only defendants may remove.[4] Thus, if a plaintiff mistakenly files a properly diverse suit in state court, there is no procedural device available for him to remove the action to federal court.

The requirement of diversity among the parties for removal turns on who should be named a party to an action centered on a performance bond.[5] The court is vested with substantial discretion in determining whether joinder is required.[6] In determining questions concerning removal, only indispensable and necessary parties are considered.[7] Indispensable parties are those who have such an interest in the subject matter that a final decree cannot be made without either affecting their interests or leaving the controversy in such condition that a final determination may be wholly inconsistent with equity and good conscience.[8] Necessary parties "are those whose presence is necessary to

---

1   28 U.S.C. § 1332(a).
2   *Id.* at (c)(1).
3   28 U.S.C. § 1441(a).
4   Croy v. Buckeye Int'l, Inc., 483 F. Supp. 402 (D.C. Md. 1979).
5   FED. R. CIV. P. 19(a).
6   Liberty Mut. Ins. Co. v. Aventura Engineering & Constr. Corp., 534 F. Supp. 1290 (S.D. Fla. 2008) (citing Swerhun v. General Motors Corp., 141 F.R.D. 342 (M.D. Fla. 1992)).
7   Leadman v. Fid. & Cas. Co. of New York, 92 F. Supp.782, (D.C. W.Va. 1950).
8   *Id.*

adjudicate the entire controversy, but whose interests are so far separable that the court can proceed to final judgment without adversely affecting them."[9]

Who is a necessary party to an action based on a performance bond is entirely dependent on the nature of the claim and the nature of the parties. Thus, the insolvent principals on surety bonds who were citizens of the same state as the plaintiff, were neither "indispensable" nor "necessary" parties.[10] Neither architect nor owner were considered indispensable parties in an action between a surety and its indemnitor in *Liberty Mutual Insurance Co. v. Aventura Engineering & Construction Corp.*[11]

B. Federal Question Jurisdiction

Federal courts have original jurisdiction over cases "arising under the constitution, laws or treaties of the United States." 28 U.S.C. §1331. Although Section 1331 is considered the general federal question statute, Congress has enacted other more specific statutes conferring jurisdiction in matters involving specific causes of action.

For example, since the Miller Act provides a federal cause of action, the scope of its remedy as well as the substance of the rights created thereby is a matter of federal and not state law.[12] Federal district courts have exclusive jurisdiction of suits brought under 40 U.S.C. § 3133(b)(3)(b).[13] Therefore, state courts may not entertain suits against

---

9 Sechrist v. Palshook, 95 F. Supp. 746 (M.D. Pa. 1951). *See, also*, Dunham v. Robertson, 198 F.2d 316 (C.A. Wyo. 1952); Edwards v. Rogers, 120 F. Supp. 499 (D.C. S.C. 1954); Gregory v. West Virginia Pulp & Paper Co., 112 F. Supp. 8 (D.C. N.C. 1953); Horwich v. Price, 25 F.R.D. 500 (D.C. Mich. 1960); Savoia Film S.A.I. v. Vanguard Films, 10 F.R.D. 64, (D.C. N.Y. 1950).
10 Leadman v. Fid. & Cas. Co. of New York, 92 F. Supp. 782 (D.C. W.Va. 1950).
11 534 F. Supp. 1290 (S.D. Fla. 2008).
12 F.D. Rich Co., Inc. v. U.S., Indus. Labor Co., Inc., 417 U.S. 116, 94 S.Ct. 2157 (1974).
13 United States *ex rel.* Gigliello v. Sovereign Const. Co., 311 F. Supp. 371 (D. Mass 1970); Blanchard v. Terry and Wright, Inc., 331 F.2d 467 (6th Cir 1964), *cert. denied* 379 U.S. 831, 85 S.Ct 62 (1964); United States *ex rel.*, Central Rigging & Contracting Corp. v. Paul Tishman Co., 32

a Miller Act surety.[14] Moreover, the Miller Act surety cannot be named as a party in a state court suit or permitted to intervene and the surety is not bound by a judgment rendered in state court.[15] Because jurisdiction is based on a federal question, there are no diversity of citizenship or jurisdictional amount requirements. The parties may not contractually waive jurisdiction.

The exclusivity of federal court jurisdiction does not apply if the claim does not fall within the purview of the Miller Act. For example, performance bonds issued by a subcontractor are not governed by the Miller Act because the obligee is not the United States. Therefore, the Miller Act's jurisdictional requirements are inapplicable.[16] The provisions of the Miller Act relating to performance bonds do apply to contracts let by the United States Postal Service.[17] Similarly, state law claims for attorneys' fees are not precluded under the Miller Act.[18]

In *George W. Kane, Inc. v. United States*,[19] the issue was whether the court had subject matter jurisdiction pursuant to the Contract Disputes Act over a completion contractor's complaint seeking recovery of home office overhead under a contract performed pursuant to a surety takeover agreement. The United States filed a motion to dismiss alleging that because the plaintiff lacked privity with the government, it was not the

---

F.R.D. 223 (E.D. N.Y. 1963); Koppers Co. v. Cont'l Cas. Co., 337 F.2d 499 (8th Cir. 1964).

14   American Ins. Co. v. Kinder, 640 S.W.2d 537 (Mo. W.D. App. 1982).

15   U.S. Fid. & Guar. Co. v. Hendry, 391 F.2d 13 (5th Cir. 1968), *cert. denied*, Hendry Corp. v. U.S. Fid. & Guar. Co. 393 U.S. 978, 89 S.Ct. 446 (1968); American Ins. Co. v. Kinder, 640 S.W.2d. 537, (Mo. App. W.D. 1982); Pierce Contractors, Inc. v. Peerless Cas. Co., 81 So.2d 747 (Fla. 1955). *But see*, United States *ex rel.* Frank M. Sheesley Co. v. St. Paul Fire and Marine Ins. Co., 239 F.R.D. 404, *cert. denied* (W.D. Pa. 2006) (calls holding of *Hendry* into question).

16   Dominion v. L&M Concrete Forms, Inc., 1997 WL 839887 (R.I. Super. 1997).

17   39 U.S.C. § 410 (b)(4)(a); Fid. & Deposit Co. of Maryland v. Stromberg Sheet Metal Works, Inc., 532 A.2d 676 (D.C. 1985).

18   United States *ex rel.* Cal's A/C and Elec. v. Famous Const. Corp., 220 F.3d 326, 27-28 (5th Cir. 2008). *But see*, United States *ex rel.* Metric Elec., Inc. v. Enviroserve, Inc., 301 F. Supp. 2d 56, 73 (D. Mass. 2003) (disagreeing with narrow interpretation of *F.D. Rich* in *United States ex rel Cal's A/C and Elec.*).

19   26 Cl. Ct. 655 (Cl. Ct. 1992).

real party in interest. The court granted the motion. The mere fact that plaintiff is a completion contractor does not automatically subrogate it to all of the rights and responsibilities of the original contractor. Moreover, the fact that the surety hired the plaintiff to complete the original scope of work did not confer upon it any right to bring suit against the government. Thus, there was no subject matter jurisdiction under either the Tucker Act[20] or under the Contract Disputes Act.[21]

Similarly, in *Dorey Electric Co. v. Pittman Mechanical Contractors, Inc.*,[22] a general contractor on a federal project filed suit against its subcontractor and the subcontractor's performance bond surety. The plaintiff alleged that the subcontractor failed to comply with the Davis-Bacon Act[23] and the Contract Work Hours and Safety Standards Act.[24] The government assessed back charges against the general contractor for these violations. The plaintiff sought a declaratory judgment as to the surety's liability on the performance bond. The court reasoned that the claim did not fall under the Miller Act because the performance bond was provided by the subcontractor for the benefit of the general contractor, and not the government. Since federal law addresses only a claim by employees of the prime contractor or any subcontractor against a prime contractor under the Davis-Bacon Act, and against the surety under the Miller Act, the court concluded that Congress intended to relegate prime contractors to state law claims against its subcontractor.[25]

In *Wagner v. United States*,[26] the issue was whether the surety could sue the United States. The court granted the defendant's motion to dismiss. The court noted that although there is necessarily a three party relationship in any surety arrangement, there is no privity of contract between the United States and the surety to a government contract, and therefore the court lacks jurisdiction.

The Louisiana First Circuit Court of Appeals recognized and affirmed the exclusive jurisdiction under the Miller Act in *Cajun*

---

20 28 U.S.C. § 1491.
21 41 U.S.C. §§ 601-613 (1982).
22 789 F. Supp. 734 (E.D.Va. 1992).
23 40 U.S.C. § 3141 *et seq.; formerly* 40 U.S.C. § 276(a) *et seq.*
24 40 U.S.C. § 327 *et seq.*
25 789 F. Supp. 734, 738 (E.D. Va. 1992).
26 71 Fed. Cl. 355, 362 (Fed. Cl. 2006).

Constructors, Inc. v. Fleming Construction Co., Inc.[27] While the court recognized that the Miller Act may not be the exclusive remedy, remedies under the Miller Act are exclusively federal. The court reversed the trial court's state law surety judgment on that basis.

C. *Counterclaims and Cross-Claims*

In the case that an obligee brings a suit against a surety, the surety must assert compulsory counterclaims against the obligee. Compulsory counterclaims are those arising out of the same transaction or occurrence that is the subject matter of the obligee's claim.[28] However, the surety need not state such a claim if it was the subject of another pending action when the primary action against the surety was commenced.[29]

The usual issues that exist between a surety and an obligee revolve around improper contract balances, change orders, delay damages, and wrongful termination.[30] Additionally, if the surety claims fraud on the part of the obligee, then this must be asserted as a counterclaim.[31]

Pursuant to the Federal Rules of Civil Procedure, a surety may file a cross-claim against its indemnitors named as defendants in the suit.[32] Individual indemnitors may need to be brought in as third-party defendants, if not already in the suit.[33] In some instances, courts have required sureties to wait until a loss is actually incurred before suit may

---

27 951 So.2d 208, 219-220 (La. App. 1st Cir. 2006), *writ denied*, 954 So.2d 146 (La. 2006) (citing Bernard Lumber Co., Inc. v. Lanier-Gervais Corp., 560 So.2d 465, 466 (La. App. 1st Cir. 1990)).
28 FED. R. CIV. P. 13(a)(1). Potential subrogation claims against third-parties, such as design professional, may not be compulsory counterclaims that must be asserted against the obligee. *See* Acuity v. McGhee Engineering, Inc., 2008 WL 5234743 (Tenn. Ct. App. 2008).
29 FED R. CIV. P. 13(a)(2).
30 Potential subrogation claims against third-parties, such as design professional may not be compulsory counterclaims that must be asserted against the obligee. *See* Acuity v. McGhee Engineering, Inc., 2008 WL 5234743 (Tenn. Ct. App. 2008).
31 Adam v. Jacobs, 950 F.2d 89 (N.Y. 1991).
32 FED R. CIV. P. 13(g).
33 FED R. CIV. P. 14(a). *See also*, KLINGER, BACHRACH, HALEY, THE SURETY'S INDEMNITY AGREEMENT: LAW AND PRACTICE, 2nd ed.

be filed.[34] If the general indemnity agreement allows the surety to seek indemnity for any liability, such as investigation or defense costs, a cross-claim or third-party demand may be filed prior to any payments being made under the bond.

The doctrine of *res judicata* encompasses "two distinct barriers to repeat litigation: claim preclusion and issue preclusion."[35] Claim preclusion bars a party from relitigating a claim or cause of action on which final judgment has been rendered. Issue preclusion bars a party from relitigating an issue once it has suffered an adverse determination on the issue, even if the issue arises when the party is pursuing or defending against a different claim.[36]

A recent case regarding counterclaims questions whether claims primarily involving architects and engineers must be brought against the owner as a counterclaim or may be brought after the bond claims are resolved pursuant to the surety's subrogation rights. Such claims may involve alleged over-certification of payments or approval of defects. A Tennessee appeals court held that such claims are not compulsory counterclaims under Rule 13, and thus were not barred by *res judicata* because of an earlier suit filed by the surety against the owner.[37]

D. Ancillary Jurisdiction

Generally, a federal court has ancillary jurisdiction over a third-party claim notwithstanding a lack of independent grounds for jurisdiction, so long as it has jurisdiction of the main action.[38] Fed. R. Civ. P. 14(a) provides the basis for bringing third-parties into actions:

---

34 *See* Lawyers Sur. Co. v. Cagle, 898 S.W. 2d 476 (Ark. Ct. App. 1995).
35 Park Lake Resources, Ltd. v. U.S. Dept. of Agriculture, 378 F.3d 1132 (10th Cir. 2004).
36 *Id.* at 1136; *See also* Dodge v. Cotter Corp., 203 F. 3d 1190, 1198 (10th Cir. 2000); New Hampshire v. Maine, 532 U.S. 742, 121 S.Ct. 1808 (2001).
37 Acuity v. McGhee Engineering, Inc., 2008 WL 5234743 (Tenn. Ct. App. 2008).
38 King Fisher Marine Serv. v. 21st Phoenix Corp., 893 F.2d 1155 (10th Cir. 1990); Dery v. Wyer, 265 F.2d 804 (2d Cir. 1959); 6 WRIGHT, MILLER & KANE, *FEDERAL PRACTICE AND PROCEDURE: CIVIL 2D* § 1444, (West 2008).

(a) When Defendant May Bring in Third-Party.

(1) Timing of the Summons and Complaint. A defending party may, as third-party plaintiff, serve a summons and complaint on a nonparty who is or may be liable to it for all or part of the claim against it. But the third-party plaintiff must, by motion, obtain the court's leave if it files the third-party complaint more than 10 days after serving its original answer.

Rule 14(a) should be read in light of Fed. R. Civ. P. 18 (a) which allows a party asserting a claim (whether original, counterclaim, cross-claim or third-party claim) to join as many claims as it has against a party.[39] However, since the federal rules do not confer jurisdiction, independent jurisdiction must be established to allow a federal court to decide those additional claims.[40]

Even though some parties may not be expressly named as the obligee of a performance bond, they may still have claims as "third-party beneficiaries." The general rule in the context of suretyship is stated in Restatement (Third), Suretyship and Guaranty § 69 as follows:

> When (i) pursuant to the underlying obligation, a duty of the principal obligor to a third person is created and (ii) the secondary obligor promises the obligee to fulfill the principal obligor's duty to the third person, the third person is an intended beneficiary of the secondary obligor's promise unless the agreement creating the secondary obligation expressly disclaims such liability.

The most obvious interested third-parties would be subcontractors and suppliers to whom the contractor owes numerous duties. However, because the modern performance bond contract is drafted specifically to prevent these parties from claiming protection as third-party "intended" beneficiaries, subcontractors and suppliers must rely on the ancillary jurisdiction of the district court in addressing their claims. The test of whether an additional claim may be asserted against a third-party

---

39 FED R. CIV. P. 18 (a) provides:
   A party asserting a claim, counterclaim, cross-claim or third-party claim, may join, as independent or alternate claims, as many claims as the party has against an opposing party.
40 King Fisher Marine Serv. v. 21st Phoenix Corp., 893 F.2d 1155 (10th Cir. 1990).

defendant under ancillary jurisdiction is whether the claim involves the same core of facts as the third-party claim and whether both arise out of the same transaction.[41]

Though third-parties may have claims that should be joined in the primary action, the nature of suretyship presents a unique question of when such claims can be asserted because the surety's rights are subrogated to the obligee's until the obligee is "made whole." As a matter of federal procedure a complaint may state a claim against the defendant before the defendant's contingent liability has become absolute.[42]

A surety which is sued by the government as a result of a default by the principal may file a third-party claim against the personal indemnitors under the indemnity agreement in order to have all claims relative to the completion cost decided in one forum.[43] Even if the principal claim is settled, the federal court may retain jurisdiction over the third-party claims under the ancillary jurisdiction doctrine.[44]

E. Abstention

The doctrine of abstention permits a federal court, in the exercise of its jurisdiction, to relinquish jurisdiction when necessary to avoid needless conflict with the administration by a state of its own affairs.[45]

Abstention is appropriate when the case concerns (1) a federal constitutional issue which might be mooted or presented in a different posture by a state court determination of pertinent state law, or (2) difficult questions of state law bearing on policy problems of substantial import whose importance transcends the result in the case at bar.[46]

---

41 Executive Fin. Services, Inc. v. Heart Check, Inc., D.C. Colo. 1982, 95 F.R.D. 383.
42 United States v. Cisco Aircraft, Inc., 54 F.R.D. 181 (D.C. Mont. 1972).
43 United States *ex rel.* Payne v. United Pacific Ins. Co., 472 F.2d 792 (9th Cir.) *cert. denied*, 411 U.S. 982, 93 S.Ct. 2273 (1973).
44 United States v. City of Twin Falls, Idaho, 806 F.2d 862 (9th Cir. 1986); United States *ex rel.* Payne v. United Pacific Ins. Co., *supra*.
45 Railroad Comm'n of Texas v. Pullman Co., U.S. 496, 61 St. Ct. 643 (1941).
46 Colorado River Water Conservation Dist. v. U.S., 424 United States 800, 96 S.Ct. 1236 (1976); Burford v. Sun Oil Co., 320 U.S. 214, 63 S.Ct. 1442 (1943).

Abstention is also appropriate if federal review would disrupt state efforts to establish a coherent policy in a matter of substantial public concern.[47]

The mere fact that there is a concurrent state court proceeding does not constitute grounds for abstention unless the federal case duplicates the state court proceeding.[48] If a case does not present difficult questions of state law or does not upset the state's interest in uniform regulation, then abstention under the United States Supreme Court decision in *Burford v. Sun Oil Co.*[49] is not warranted. The mere fact that a surety may be in receivership is not sufficient to warrant abstention under *Burford*.[50]

In *Aetna Casualty & Surety Co. v. Manshul Construction Corp.*,[51] Genetech, a subcontractor and third-party defendant, filed a motion to dismiss the third-party complaint of Aetna or alternatively to stay the suit pending resolution of a state court action. The suit was procedurally complex: Manshul entered into a contract with Nassau County to build a project. Aetna was Manshul's surety and issued both payment and performance bonds. Manshul was defaulted and Aetna became the completion surety. However, Aetna was subsequently defaulted by the county. Aetna filed suit against Manshul under the indemnity agreement. Manshul, in turn, filed a third-party demand against the county. Aetna amended and named the county as a direct defendant. The county, in turn, asserted a counterclaim against Aetna which precipitated the third-party demand against Genetech, Manshul's subcontractor.

Prior to the commencement of Aetna's third-party action, Genetech had sued Aetna in state court for damages under Aetna's payment bond. Genetech sought to dismiss the federal court action based on abstention. Citing *Colorado River*,[52] the court noted that in cases of concurrent state and federal jurisdiction, federal courts have a "virtually unflagging

---

47 New Orleans Pub. Serv., Inc. v. New Orleans, 491 U.S. 350, 109 S.Ct. 2506 (1989).
48 TransDulles Center, Inc. v. USX Corp., 976 F.2d 219 (4th Cir. 1992); McLaughlin v. United Virginia Bank, 955 F.2d 930 (4th Cir. 1992).
49 319 U.S. 315, 63 S.Ct. 1098 (1943).
50 *See* Spencer v. Frontier Ins. Co., 290 Fed. Appx. 571, 2008 WL 3914622 (C.A.S.C. 2008).
51 1998 WL 401558 (S.D. N.Y. 1998).
52 424 U.S. 800 (1976).

obligation to exercise the jurisdiction given them."[53] The court noted that abstention can only be justified by the existence of "exceptional circumstances," and thereafter undertook an analysis of the factors a court should consider when making a determination of when exceptional circumstances exist: (1) the assumption of jurisdiction over res; (2) the inconvenience of the forum; (3) the avoidance of piecemeal litigation; (4) the order in which the actions were filed; (5) whether state or federal laws supply the rule of decision; and (6) whether the state court proceeding will adequately protect the rights of the parties seeking to invoke federal jurisdiction. Each factor is considered with the balance heavily weighted in favor of exercising jurisdiction.

The court was not convinced that the state and federal actions were identical. Specifically, the court found that although the question of whether Genetech adequately performed under its subcontract with Manshul was at issue in both lawsuits, each court would address that issue in a different context. The state suit only involved determining whether Aetna breached its payment bond by refusing to pay Genetech, while the federal action involved the issue of Aetna's responsibility under the performance bond.

In *Hospital Service District No. 3 of Parish of Lafourche, State of Louisiana v. Fidelity and Deposit Co. of Maryland*,[54] the owner, a public entity, filed suit against F&D in state court. The surety removed the case to federal court. The owner sought a remand on the basis of lack of subject matter jurisdiction, or in the alternative abstention pursuant to 28 U.S.C. § 1334(C). The general contractor on the project, Keeper Co., Inc., filed bankruptcy. Suit by the owner against the surety was filed subsequent to the bankruptcy proceeding. The claims against the surety were under the performance bond for the costs to complete the project after the general contractor's default and liquidated damages for late completion. A non-diverse subcontractor of Keeper was also named as a defendant. The bankruptcy debtor asserted a claim against the owner in the bankruptcy alleging that the owner's failure to pay the balance prevented Keeper from fulfilling its obligations. F&D argued that bankruptcy jurisdiction also constituted a basis to allow the case to remain in federal court.

---

53 1998 WL 401558, at *2 (S.D. N.Y. 1998).
54 1999 WL 294795 (E.D. La. 1999).

The surety argued that the subcontractor was fraudulently joined to defeat diversity since the owner has no direct claim against the subcontractor; however, the court found that surety failed to establish that there was absolutely no possibility that the owner would be able to establish the third-party beneficiary cause of action against the subcontractor and therefore joinder of the subcontractor was not "fraudulent" (in the technical federal jurisdictional sense of the term). With respect to the argument that the court had jurisdiction over plaintiff's claims under bankruptcy jurisdiction,[55] the court undertook an extensive analysis to determine whether the claims were subject to either mandatory or discretionary abstention. Mandatory abstention applies only to proceedings related to a case under Title 11 or arising in a case under Title 11.[56] The court found that the facts of the case did not justify mandatory abstention. The plaintiff's state contract law claims did not involve rights created by federal bankruptcy law, and these claims can clearly exist outside of bankruptcy. Alternatively, the court also reviewed discretionary abstention under § 1334(c)(1). This section provides that a district court "in the interest of justice or in the interest of comity with State court or respect for state law" may abstain from hearing a particular proceeding from arising under Title 11 or arising in a case related to Title 11.[57] In deciding whether to abstain, the court looked at the following factors: (1) *forum non conveniens*; (2) bifurcation of the civil action; (3) centralization of the entire action; (4) expertise of the particular court; (5) duplicative or wasteful use of judicial resources; (6) prejudice to involuntarily removed parties; (7) comity issues; and (8) a diminished likelihood of inconsistent results.

The court held that the owner's claims against the defendants were state law contract claims and claims for violation of a state law obligation of good faith. The state court being familiar with the legal issues raised in the case, believed trial in state court of plaintiff's claims would diminish the likelihood of inconsistent state law decisions. Another factor weighing in favor of abstention was the presence of non debtor parties. The fact that the owner demanded a jury which would be unavailable in bankruptcy court without the consent of all parties also

---

55   28 U.S.C. § 1334.
56   *Matles of Gober*, 100 F.3d 1195 (5th Cir. 1996) (citing 28 U.S.C. § 157(b)(1) 1334(c)(2)).
57   1998 WL 294795, at *8 (E.D. La. 1999).

weighed in favor of abstention. Moreover, because the proceeding is not considered a core proceeding, further delay would result if the dispute is resolved by bankruptcy court in that the district court would have to review the decision de novo. The court further noted that the same abstention factors weighed in favor of equitably remanding the case pursuant to 28 U.S.C. § 1452(b). Therefore, the federal court permissibly abstained and equitably remanded the case to state court.

In a somewhat unusual case, a Georgia district court denied a party's request for abstention. In *United States ex rel. ACCA Construction Services, LLC v. F.A.S. Development Co., Inc.*,[58] the North Carolina insurance commissioner took control of Commercial Casualty pursuant to a statutory rehabilitation process. This statute prohibited the further prosecution of claims against the company, and the state court issued a preliminary injunction barring any and all pending claims against Commercial Casualty. On the basis of that order, Commercial Casualty filed a motion to stay any proceedings in federal court, or in the alternative on the basis of abstention. The court denied Commercial Casualty's motion, noting that abstention is permissible only when the district court has discretion to grant or deny relief. Since Miller Act claims can exclusively be brought in federal court, the state court's stay of proceedings does not apply to the federal court or give it the ability to abstain.

Abstention may also arise in the context of a case in which arbitration is mandated by the underlying contract. The federal court may, a minimum, stay a proceeding pending arbitration.[59] A stay of a proceeding is distinct from abstention. For a full discussion of the effect of arbitration provisions on a pending matter, see Chapter 13, Arbitration.

Conversely, pursuant to the All Writs Act, a federal court may issue an injunction to enjoin an arbitration when the claim which is the subject of an arbitration has been resolved. In *Liberty Mutual Insurance Co. v. Aventura*,[60] the court granted summary judgment in favor of the surety holding that it had authority to settle its principal's claims against the

---

58 304 F. Supp.2d 1359 (N.D. Ga. 2004).
59 United States *ex rel.* Wrecking Corp. of Am. v. Marden Corp., 407 F.2d 525 (1st Cir. 1969).
60 534 F. Supp. 1290 (S.D. Fla. 2008).

obligee and therefore, enjoined the principal from proceeding in arbitration with its suit against the obligee.[61]

II. Venue

The Federal Rules of Civil Procedure contain various venue provisions, both general and specific in nature. The primary focus of a venue inquiry generally is the "convenience of litigants and witnesses."[62] The general venue statute is 28 U.S.C. § 1391. Suit may be filed in the judicial district where any defendant resides, if all defendants reside in the same state,[63] or in a district in which a substantial part of the events or omissions giving rise to the claim occurred or a substantial part of property that is subject of the action is situated.[64] If there is no district in which the action may otherwise be brought, a suit may be filed in a judicial district in which any defendant is subject to personal jurisdiction at the time the action is commenced.[65] A defendant that is a corporation is deemed to reside in any judicial district in which it is subject to personal jurisdiction at the time the action is commenced.[66]

There are numerous statutes dealing with venue for particular kinds of actions. These special venue provisions take precedence over the general venue statutes.[67]

For example, the Federal Arbitration Act ("FAA") contains venue provisions. 9 U.S.C. §§ 9, 10, 11. The Supreme Court in *Cortez Byrd Chips, Inc. v. Harbert Construction Co.*,[68] held that the provisions contained in the FAA are permissive rather than mandatory; accordingly, an action to confirm, vacate or modify an arbitration award can be

---

61 *Id.* at 1324.
62 WRIGHT, MILLER & COOPER, FEDERAL PRACTICE AND PROCEDURE: JURISDICTION 3d § 3801.
63 28 U.S.C. 1391(a)(1).
64 *Id.* at (a)(2).
65 *Id.* at (a)(3).
66 *Id.* at (c).
67 Fourco Glass Co. v. Transmirra Prods. Corp., 353 U.S. 222, 77 S.Ct. 787 (1957).
68 529 U.S. 193, 120 S.Ct. 1331 (2000).

brought in the district where the award was made or in any district that would be proper under the general venue statute.[69]

The law does not appear to be settled as to proper venue for filing of suits to compel arbitration. Section 4 of the FAA provides that an action to compel arbitration may be brought in "any United States District Court which, save for such agreement, would have jurisdiction under Title 28." This would seem to imply that the general venue provisions may govern. However, the statute further provides:

> The court shall hear the parties, and upon being satisfied that the making of the agreement for arbitration or the failure to comply therewith is not an issue, the court shall make an order directing the parties to proceed to arbitration in accordance with the terms of the agreement. The hearing and proceedings, under such agreement, shall be within the district in which the Petition for an Order directing such arbitration is filed.

The latter part of the statute would indicate that the venue for the arbitration must be in the district where the court order was issued. This appears to be somewhat contradictory to the earlier part of the statute which appears to allow for application of general venue provisions.[70] At least one court has held that § 4 of the FAA does not require that the proper venue be the location specified in the arbitration agreement, but rather only limits the arbitration to the district in which the petition to compel is filed. *Textile Unlimited, Inc. v. A.BMH & Co.*[71] Other courts have construed the FAA to mean that a petition to compel arbitration can be granted only by a court in the district in which the arbitration is mandated to take place, as provided in the arbitration agreement between the parties.[72]

Venue in Miller Act cases is set forth in 40 U.S.C. § 3133 (b)(3)(b) which provides:

---

69   *See also* Azammi, L.P. v. Mitchell Gold Co., 2007 WL 1556833 (D.C. Tex. 2007); Prof. Transp., Inc. v. American Cas. Co. of Reading, P.A. 2007 WL 30554 (D.C. Ind. 2007).
70   WRIGHT, MILLER AND COOPER, FEDERAL PRACTICE AND PROCEDURE: JURISDICTION 3d § 3825.
71   240 F.3d 781, 783 (9th Cir. 2001).
72   Ansari v. Quest Communications Corp., 414 F.3d 1214 (10th Cir. 2005).

a civil action brought under this section must be brought in . . . the United States District Court for any district in which the contract was to be performed and executed. . .

The law is well settled that the Miller Act provision requiring plaintiff to sue in federal district court for the district in which contract was to be performed is considered a venue provision benefitting the surety and not the plaintiff, and that it was not jurisdictional.[73] Venue may be waived by a failure to object timely.[74] Since this section is merely a venue requirement, there is no jurisdictional bar to transferring the case.[75] The distinction between jurisdictional requirements and venue requirements was addressed by Justice Frankfurter in *Nierbo Co. v. Bethlehem Shipbuilding Corp.*,[76] a non-Miller Act case:

> The jurisdiction of the federal courts–their power to adjudicate is a grant of authority to them by congress and thus beyond the scope of litigants to confer. But the locality of a lawsuit–the place where judicial

---

73   F.D. Rich Co., Inc. v. United States *ex rel.* Industrial Labor Co., Inc., 417 U.S. at 118.
74   United States *ex rel.* Bryant Elec. Co. v. Aetna Cas. & Sur. Co., 297 F.2d 665 (2nd Cir 1962); Commercial Cas. Ins. Co. v. Consol. Stone Co., 278 U.S. 177, 49 S.Ct. 98 (1929).
75   United States *ex rel.* Capolino Sons, Inc. v. Elect. & Missile Facilities, Inc., 364 F.2d 705 (2nd Cir. 1966); United States *ex rel.* Bryant Elec. Co. v. Aetna Cas. & Sur., Co., 297 F.2d 665, 100 ALR 2d 451 (2nd Cir. 1962); Elec. & Missile Facilities, Inc. v. United States *ex rel.* Moseley, 306 F.2d 554 (5th Cir. 1962), *rev'd on other grounds*, 374 U.S. 167, 83 S.Ct. 1815, (1963); Texas Const. Co. v. United States for the Use of Caldwell Foundry & Mach. Co., Inc., 236 F.2d 138 (5th Cir. 1956); United States *ex rel.* Mitchell Bros. Truck Lines v. Jen-Mar Const. Co., 223 F. Supp. 646 (D. Or. 1963); United States *ex rel.* Industrial Eng'r & Metal Fabricators, Inc. v. Eric Elevator Corp., 214 F. Supp. 947 (D. Mass. 1963); United States *ex rel.* Bailey-Lewis-Williams, Inc. v. Peter Kiewit Sons Co., Ltd., 195 F. Supp. 752 (D.C. Cir. 1962), Indemnity Ins. Co. of N. Am. v. United States *ex rel.* Bailey-Lewis-Frank A. Trucco & Sons Co. v. Bergman Const. Co., 256 F.2d 851 (7th Cir. 1958); United States *ex rel.* Fairbanks Morse & Co. v. Bero Const. Corp., 148 F. Supp. 295 (S.D.N.Y. 1957); United States *ex rel.* Expedia v. Altex Enterprises, 734 F. Supp. 972 (M.D. Fla. 1990); United States v. Alaskan Insulations, Inc., 1990 WL 67257 (E.D. Pa. 1990).
76   308 U.S. 165, 60 S.Ct. 153 (1939).

authority may be exercised–though defined by legislation relates to the convenience of litigants and is subject to their disposition.[77]

Thus, it is important to distinguish between the exclusive federal court jurisdiction of a Miller Act claim, and the locale of the particular federal district where suit is to be filed, which may be agreed to by the parties or determined by the court based upon the doctrine of *forum non conveniens*.

It is also important to note courts generally have ruled that the venue requirement's language "performed" limits the proper Miller Act venue to the location in which the government project is located. In *United States ex rel. Straightline Corp. v. CNA Surety*,[78] the court rejected Straightline's argument that the court follow the minority position that any district in which a substantial aspect of contract performance takes place is a proper venue for Miller Act claims.[79] Although fabrication, which constituted roughly 70 percent of the total work, occurred in Pennsylvania, the court held that venue was only proper in West Virginia, the site of the actual government project.

Any objection to venue must be raised timely, otherwise it is waived.[80] An indemnitor may waive an objection to venue by signing an indemnity agreement that includes a forum selection provision.[81] A waiver of an objection to improper venue does not constitute a waiver to seek a transfer of venue.[82]

A. *Forum Non Conveniens*

A federal district court has the authority to transfer a case to another more convenient venue if such transfer is in the interest of justice.[83] This

---

77   *Id.* at 167-168.
78   411 F. Supp.2d 584, 85-86 (W.D. Pa. 2006).
79   *See* United States *ex rel.* Expedia, Inc. v. Altex Enter., Inc., 734 F. Supp. 972 (M.D. Fla. 1990) (minority position).
80   Stjernholm v. Peterson, 83 F. 3d 347 (10th Cir. 1996), *cert. denied*, 519 U.S. 930, 117 S. Ct. 301 (Oct. 1996); Tri-State Employment Serv., Inc. v. Mountbatten Sur. Co., 295 F.3d 256 (2nd Cir. 2002).
81   *See* Bell BCI Co. v. Developers Serv. & Indem. Co, No. 06-CV-6211 – CJS(F), 2006 WL 4070760, at *2 (W.D. N.Y., Nov. 21, 2006).
82   *See*, WRIGHT, MILLER & COOPER, § 3829.
83   28 U.S.C. § 1404(a).

can be done in lieu of dismissing a case improperly filed in the wrong district. The court can transfer the case *sua sponte* or on motion of the defendant.[84] *Forum non conveniens* applies to Miller Act claims just like any other type of suit.[85] Likewise, a valid contractual forum selection clause may also mandate a venue different than that specified by the Miller Act. There are several factors which courts consider in determining whether a transfer is appropriate, including the convenience of parties and witnesses, relative ease of access to sources of proof, access to premises (project), location of relevant documents and other tangible evidence, calendars of respective courts, desirability of having the case tried by forum familiar with the substantive law and how best to serve the interest of justice based on assessment of the totality of circumstances.[86]

The right to transfer venue for convenience lies within the sound discretion of the trial judge.[87] It does not matter which case is filed first.[88]

In *LaCorte Electrical Construction v Centron Security Systems, Inc.*,[89] a general contractor filed suit against its subcontractor in state court in New York for breach of the subcontract. The project involved implementation of a card access security system for an airport in Kentucky. The subcontractor removed the case to federal court on diversity grounds. It also filed its own suit in federal court in Kentucky against the general contractor's performance bond for amounts allegedly

---

84 United States *ex rel.* Coffey v. William R. Austin Const.. Co., 436 F. Supp. 626 (W.D. Okla. 1977).
85 *In re* Fireman's Fund Ins. Cos., Inc., 588 F.2d 93 (5th Cir. 1979).
86 Gulf Oil Corp. v. Gilbert, 330 U.S. 501, 57 S.Ct. 839 (1974); Alfadda v. Fenn, 159 F.3d 41 (2d Cir. 1998).
87 Ervin and Assoc. Inc. v. Cisneros, 939 F. Supp. 793 (D. Colo. 1996); Ashmore v. Northeast Petroleum Div. of Cargill, Inc., 925 F. Supp. 36 (D. Me. 1966); Linzer v. EMI Blackwood Music, Inc., 904 F. Supp. 207 (S.D. N.Y. 1995); State Street Capital Corp. v. Dente, 855 F. Supp. 192 (S.D. Tex 1994); K&F Mfg. Co. Inc. v. Western Litho Plate & Supply Co., 831 F. Supp. 661 (N.D. Ind. 1993).
88 Riviera Trading Corp. v. Oakley, Inc., 944 F. Supp. 1150 (S.D.N.Y. 1996).
89 894 F. Supp. 80 (N.D. N.Y. 1995).

due for extra work.[90] The subcontractor filed a motion to transfer the New York action to Kentucky based on *forum non conveniens*. The court held that jurisdiction existed in both New York and Kentucky. In denying the motion to transfer the case to Kentucky, the court reasoned that movant had failed to establish that witnesses would be inconvenienced by having to travel to New York, or that evidence located in Kentucky was really necessary for trial. It also noted that the action against the surety pending in Kentucky although arising from the same factual scenario had little or no bearing upon the venue of the action pending in New York.[91]

The case of *United States ex rel. Bailey–Lewis–Williams of Florida, Inc. v. Peter Kiewit Sons Co. of Canada, Ltd*,[92] involved a construction project in Canada owned by the United States. The subcontractor-plaintiff filed suit in the District of Columbia. The surety moved to dismiss relying on Section 270(b)[93] of the Miller Act. The surety argued that suit should be instituted in Canada since that was where the project was located. The court denied the motion and undertook a *forum non conveniens* analysis. The court noted that the project was situated in a different locale in Canada than the general contractor's Canadian office. Moreover, the principal office of the governmental agency concerned with the contract and the surety were located in the District of Columbia. Therefore, transferring the case to Canada would not be any more convenient. The ruling denying the motion was affirmed by the appellate court, which also noted that venue was proper in the District of Columbia since the surety company was licensed to do business there and no other

---

90 Although referred to as a "performance bond," because of the nature of claims asserted against the bond and the party by whom it is asserted–a subcontractor, in all likelihood the bond is a payment bond. *Compare*, Glens Falls Indem. Co. v. United States, 229 F.2d 370 (9th Cir. 1955), wherein the court ruled that the performance bond covered claims for materials furnished to project because failure to pay also constitutes breach of duty to perform construction contract obligations.
91 *Id.* at 85.
92 195 F. Supp. 753 (D.C. 1961), *aff'd sub nom.*, Indemnity Ins. Co. of N. Am. v. United States *ex rel.* Bailey-Lewis-Williams of Fla., Inc. 299 F.2d 930; New Hampshire v. Maine (D.C. Cir. 1962).
93 *Currently* 40 U.S.C. § 3133 (b)(3).

judicial district in the United States was suggested as an alternative forum.[94]

A motion by an indemnitor to transfer to a different forum on the basis of *forum non conveniens* was granted in *National Surety Corp. v. Robert M. Barton Corp.*[95] In *Barton*, a claim was made against the performance bond issued by National Surety Corp. The surety filed suit in Oklahoma against the indemnitor. The obligee on the bond was the City of Waco. The court stated that the absence of any significant contact with the forum state (Texas) reduced the weight that is generally given to plaintiff's right to select the forum. The defendants were all citizens of Oklahoma. The plaintiff, a surety company, was a New York corporation. The court further reasoned that suit could have been filed in the transferee district. Moreover, because all the books, documents, research and exhibits were located in Texas, it would have been unduly burdensome and expensive to produce them in Oklahoma. The issue of whether the contractor defaulted on the project would require witnesses who were located in Texas. The court noted that the facts which plaintiff would be required to prove, such as execution of the indemnity agreement, would not require any of plaintiff's employees. Furthermore, the issues relating to breach of the indemnity agreement and losses under the bond would be determined more conveniently in the district where the project was located. The defendants would be extremely inconvenienced if the case were to remain in Oklahoma. Therefore, since a transfer would permit a greater access to the source of proof, greater availability of compulsory process for unwilling witnesses, less expense in obtaining willing witnesses and the events given rise to the action all took place in Texas, the motion was granted and the case transferred.

In *U.S. Fidelity & Guaranty Co. and Home Association Co. v. Petroleo Brasilero S.A. Petrobras*,[96] two plaintiff surety companies filed a declaratory judgment action regarding their obligations, if any, on two performance bonds guaranteeing construction of two oil field production facilities in Brazil. The defendants filed a motion to dismiss for lack of subject matter jurisdiction and *forum non conveniens*. The complaint also

---

[94] 299 F.2d 931, 932 (D.C. Cir. 1962).
[95] 484 F. Supp. 222 (W.D. Okla. 1979).
[96] 1999 WL 307642 (S.D. N.Y. 1999), *aff'd*, U.S. Fidelity and Guaranty Co. v. Braspetro Oil Services, Co., 199 F.3d 94 (2nd Cir. 1999).

sought specific performance of the defendant's obligations under the indemnity agreements.

With respect to the motion to dismiss based on *forum non conveniens*, the court went through each of the factors to be considered. First, it found that generally the plaintiff's choice of forum should be honored, especially where the plaintiff is a United States citizen and the alternative forum is foreign. Second, weighing the private and public interests "tips strongly in favor of the plaintiff's choice of a New York forum."[97] The interest of the litigants in the forum also weighs in favor of New York as the indemnity agreement expressly accepts the Southern District of New York as an appropriate forum and New York law as the governing law. The defendant, although a Brazilian company, maintains an office in New York and the documents relating to the bond are all located in New York. The sureties' rights arise under bonds that were negotiated, executed and issued in New York and under indemnity agreements that incorporate New York law. For these reasons, the defendants' motion to dismiss under the doctrine of *forum non conveniens* was denied.

Similarly, in *United States ex rel. Essex Machine Works, Inc. v. Roundout Marine, Inc.*,[98] the plaintiff subcontractor manufactured all of its boat components in Connecticut. New York was the state where the general contractor was located and where the contract for manufacturing of utility boats for the U.S. government was supposed to be performed originally. Subsequently, the government decided it wanted the boats to be built in Florida. Thus, the court held that the Miller Act venue mandated that the claims between the general contractor and its subcontractor be litigated in Florida.

The case of *United States ex rel. Harvey Gulf International Marine, Inc. v. Maryland Casualty Co.*[99] involves a payment bond. The case contains a helpful discussion of the factors considered by the court in reviewing a motion to dismiss based upon improper venue. The case involved three different government contracts all governed by the Miller Act. Two of the contracts were performed in the Eastern District of Louisiana and the third in the Western District of Louisiana. Suit was filed in the Eastern District on all three contracts. The surety moved to

---

97 *Id.* at 10.
98 312 F. Supp. 846 (S.D. N.Y. 1970).
99 573 F.2d 245 (5th Cir. 1978).

dismiss for improper venue on the claim involving the project in the Western District of Louisiana. The court denied the motion without reason. On appeal, the Fifth Circuit reversed, holding that the district court erred in not dismissing the claim or in the alternative not transferring it to the proper venue pursuant to 28 U.S.C. §1406(a).[100]

Since Section 270b(b) is considered merely a venue requirement, it may be contractually waived by a valid forum selection clause.[101]

The Fifth Circuit in *In re Fireman's Fund*[102] reasoned that forum selection clauses in Miller Act cases should especially be given effect where the defendants for whose special protection the venue clause exists move to transfer in accordance with the forum selection clauses.[103] Alternatively, if a forum selection clause is found to be invalid, then venue will be governed by the Miller Act.[104] In the St. Paul case, the court found that the forum selection clause which designated a state court forum was invalid because it contravened the Miller Act's exclusive jurisdictional requirement. If, however, the forum selection clause is sufficiently broad to allow the federal court to maintain its exclusive jurisdiction under the Miller Act, the clause will be upheld.[105] The issue of forum selection clauses is discussed in greater detail below.

---

100 *Id.* at 247.
101 National Equip. Rental, Ltd. v. Szukhent, 375 U.S. 311, 84 S.Ct. 411 (U.S. N.Y. 1964); FGS Constructors, Inc. v. Carlow, 64 F.3d 1230, 1233 (8th Cir. 1995) *cert. denied*, 517 U.S. 1134, 116 S.Ct. 1417 (1996); United States *ex rel.* Pittsburgh Tank & Tower, Inc. v. G&C Enterprises, 62 F.3d 35 (1st Cir. 1995); *In re* Fireman's Fund Ins. Cos., 588 F.2d 93 (5th Cir. 1979).
102 588 F.2d 93 (5th Cir. 1979).
103 *Id.* at 95 (citing Elec. & Missile Facilities, Inc. v. United States, 306 F.2d 534 (5th Cir. 1962), *rev'd on other grounds, sub nom.*, Moseley v. Elec. & Missile Facilities, Inc., 374 U.S. 167, 83 S.Ct. 1815 (1963).
104 United States v. *ex rel.* B&D Mechanical Contractors, Inc. v. St. Paul Mercury Ins. Co., 70 F.3d 1115 (10th Cir. 1995), *cert. denied*, 517 U.S. 1167, 116 S.Ct. 1568 (1996).
105 United States v. Ross Group Constr. Corp., 2007 WL 3119691 (W.D. Tex. 2007).

B. Forum Selection Clauses

Generally, forum selection clauses are accorded *prima facie* validity.[106] The enforceability of a forum selection clause is governed by the standard as stated by the Supreme Court in *The Bremen v. Zapata Offshore Co.*[107]

The Bremen is an admiralty case which involved a U.S. owner of an oil drilling rig, Zapata, who sued a German company which had contracted to tow Zapata's rig from the U.S. to Italy. The rig was damaged during a storm in the Gulf of Mexico and put into port in Tampa, Florida. The contract between the parties contained a provision requiring litigation in England. The Supreme Court gave effect to the forum selection clause, holding that such a clause is *"prima facie* valid and should be enforced unless enforcement is shown by the resisting party to be 'unreasonable' under the circumstances."[108] A party resisting enforcement of a forum selection clause carries a heavy burden of showing that the provision itself is invalid due to broad or overreaching or that enforcement would be unreasonable or unjust under the circumstances.[109]

---

106 United States v. Miller-Stauch Const. Co. Inc., 904 F. Supp. 1209 (D. Kan. 1995); Public Water Supply Dist. No. 1 of Mercer County, Missouri v. Am. Ins. Co., 471 F. Supp. 1071 (W.D. Mo. 1979).

107 407 U.S. 1, 92 S.Ct. 1907, (1972). *See also* the following U.S. Court of Appeal decisions that have examined and adopted *The Bremen* holding of the Supreme Court: Royal Bed and Spring Co., Inc. v. Famossul Industria e Comercio de Moveis Ltda., 906 F.2d 45, 48 (1st Cir. 1990); Evolution Online Systems, Inc. v. Koninklijke PTT Nederland N.V., 145 F.3d 505, 509, (2nd Cir. 1998); Foster v. Chesapeake Ins. Co., Ltd., 933 F.2d 1207, 1212 (3rd Cir. 1991); Sterling Forest Associates, Ltd. v. Barnett-Range Corp., 840 F.2d 249, 250 (4th Cir. 1988); Int'l Software Systems, Inc. v. Amplicon, Inc., 77 F.3d 112, 113 (5th Cir. 1996); Shell v. W. Sturge, Ltd., 55 F.3d 1227, 1229 (6th Cir. 1995); Sun World Lines, Ltd. v. March Shipping Corp., 801 F.2d 1066, (8th Cir. 1986); Richards v. Lloyd's of London, 135 F.3d 1289, 1292 (9th Cir. 1998); Riley v. Kingsley Underwriting Agencies, Ltd., 969 F.2d 953, 957 (10th Cir. 1992); Lipcon v. Underwriters at Lloyd's, London, 148 F.3d 1285, 1291 (11th Cir. 1998).

108 407 U.S. at 10.

109 Riley v. Kingsley Underwriting Agencies, Ltd., 969 F.2d 953, 957 (10th Cir. (Colo.) 1992), *cert. denied*, 506 U.S. 1021, 113 S.Ct. 658 (1992);

To establish that a particular choice of forum clause is unreasonable, a resisting party must present evidence of fraud, undue influence, overweening bargaining power or such serious inconvenience in litigating in the selected forum that is effectively deprived of its day in court.[110] The forum selection clause is also unenforceable if enforcement would contravene a strong public policy of the forum in which the suit is brought.[111]

It is important to look at the actual language of the forum selection clause to determine its applicability. For example, the use of the word "shall" in a forum selection clause generally indicates a mandatory intent unless a convincing argument to the contrary is made.[112] The prevailing rule is that where venue is specified with mandatory language, the clause will be enforced.[113]

The Bremen, 407 U.S. at 10; Seward v. Devine, 888 F.2d 957, 962 (2nd Cir. 1989).

110 Fireman's Fund American Ins. Co. v. Puerto Rican Forwarding Co., 492 F.2d 1294, 1297 (1st Cir. 1974); *The Bremen*, 407 U.S. at 12.

111 *The Bremen*, 407 U.S. at 15. *See also* the following decisions which declined to extend and/or distinguish the holding of the Supreme Court in *The Bremen*: Perkins v. CCH Computax, Inc., 415 S.E. 2d 755 (N.C. App. 1992); Thompson v. Founders Group Int'l, Inc., 886 P.2d 904 (Kan. App. 1994); First Nat'l City Bank v. Nanz, Inc., 437 F. Supp. 184 (S.D.N.Y. 1975); Int'l Ass'n of Bridge, Structural and Ornamental Iron Workers, Local Union 348, AFL-CIO v. Koski Const. Co., 474 F. Supp. 370, (W.D. Pa. 1979); City of New York v. Pullman, Inc., 477 F. Supp. 438 (S.D.N.Y. 1979); Union Ins. Co. of Canton, Ltd. v. S.S. Elikon, 642 F.2d 721, (4th Cir. 1981); McDonnell Douglas Corp. v. Islamic Republic of Iran, 591 F. Supp. 293, (E.D. Mo. 1984); Appalachian Ins. Co. v. Superior Court, 208 Cal. Rptr. 627 (Cal. App. Ct. 1984); McDonnell Douglas Corp. v. Islamic Republic of Iran, 758 F.2d 341 (8th Cir. 1985); Weidner Communications, Inc. v. H.R.H. Prince Bandar Al Faisal, 859 F.2d 1302 (7th Cir. 1988); Carnival Cruise Lines, Inc. v. Shute, 499 U.S. 585, 111 S.Ct. 39 (1991); Underwriters at Lloyd's of London v. M/V Steir, 773 F. Supp. 523 (D. P.R. 1991); Cannelton Industries, Inc. v. Aetna Cas. & Sur. Co. of America, 460 S.E.2d 1 (W.Va. 1994); Mayeux's A/C & Heating, Inc. v. Famous Const. Corp. 1997 WL 567955 (E.D. La. 1997); Lambert v. Kysar, 983 F.2d 1110 (1st Cir. 1993).

112 Milk 'N' Moore, Inc. v. Beavert, 963 F.2d 1342, 1346 (10th Cir. 1992).

113 Zimmerman Metals, Inc. v. United Engineers & Constructors, Inc., Stearns-Roger Div., 720 F. Supp. 859, 861 (D. Colo. 1989).

In *Rice Contracting Corp. v. Callas Contractors, Inc.*,[114] the court granted defendant's motion to dismiss under Fed. R. Civ. P. 12(b)(3) ruling that the forum selection clauses in subcontracts requiring the parties submit to jurisdiction of state court in particular counties, did not allow for suit in federal court even if the court was located in the county referenced in the contract.

There has been substantial litigation in Miller Act cases as to whether forum selection clauses are enforceable. The confusion initially arose under former 40 U.S.C. § 270b (b), which provides:

The statute as now codified in 40 U.S.C. § 3133(3)(b) now provides:

A civil action brought under this subsection must be brought . . .

(B) in the United States District Court for any district in which the contract was to be performed and executed, regardless of the amount in controversy.

Every suit instituted under this action shall be brought in the name of the U.S. for the use of the person suing in the U.S. District Court for any district in which the contract was to be performed and executed and not elsewhere . . .

In the past, lower federal courts were split as to whether § 270b(b) was jurisdictional and hence mandatory, or a venue provision that could be modified by contract. However, the Supreme Court seems to have settled the question in *F.D. Rich Co. v. United States, ex rel. Industrial Lumber Co.*,[115] which held that the statutory language of § 270b (b) was "merely a venue requirement" and not jurisdictional.[116] Most of the subsequent cases have followed *Rich* and held that the disputed provision is simply a venue statute.[117]

Under conventional venue statutes, venue provisions have long been subject to contractual waiver through a valid form selection

---

114 2009 WL 21597 (E.D. Va. 2009).
115 417 U.S. 116, 94 S.Ct. 2157 (1974).
116 417 U.S. at 124-126.
117 United States *ex rel.* Pittsburgh Tank & Towing, Inc. v. G&C Enterprises, Inc., 62 F.3d 35, 36 (1st Cir. 1995); *In re* Fireman's Fund Ins. Cos., Ins., 588 F.2d 93, 95 (5th Cir. 1979); Arrow Plumbing & Heating, Inc. v. N. Am. Mechanical Servs. Corp., 810 F. Supp. 369, 370 (D.R.I. 1993).

agreement.[118] Consequently, the venue requirement under the Miller Act, 40 U.S.C. § 270b (b),[119] is like any other conventional provision; it can be contractually waived by a valid forum selection clause.[120]

The reasoning of the Supreme Court in *Rich* is consistent with the intent behind the enactment of the venue provision of the Miller Act. For example, it has been held that the Miller Act venue provision was intended to benefit defendants, not plaintiffs.[121] The Miller Act venue provision was intended to protect the surety from liability beyond the amount of the bond that might result from multiple suits in several different jurisdictions.[122] Since the legislative history of the venue provision of the Miller Act was to benefit defendants, the courts have held that valid forum selection clauses accomplish the same thing and should be enforced.

The U.S. Fifth Circuit has specifically held that a valid forum selection clause can override a Miller Act venue provision.[123] The Fifth Circuit Court in *In re Fireman's Fund* stated:

> The Miller Act venue provision exists for the convenience of the parties. Such a provision is subject to variation by their agreement which should especially be given effect in a case such as this, where the defendants, for whose special protection the venue clause exists,

---

118 *See, e.g.*, Nat'l Equip. Rental, Ltd. v. Szukhent, 375 U.S. 311 (1964).
119 *Currently* 40 U.S.C. §3133(3)(B).
120 United States on Behalf of Pittsburgh Tank & Towing, Inc. v. G&C Enterprises, Inc., 62 F.3d 35, 36 (1st Cir. 1995); *In re* Fireman's Fund Ins. Co., Inc., 588 F.2d 93, 95 (5th Cir.1979); Arrow Plumbing & Heating, Inc. v. N. Am. Mechanical Servs. Corp., 810 F. Supp. 369, 370 (D.R.I. 1993).
121 United States *ex rel.* Aurora Painting, Inc. v. Fireman's Fund Ins. Co., 832 F.2d 1150, 1152 (9th Cir. 1987).
122 *Aurora Painting*, 832 F.2d at 1152 (citing United States *ex rel.* Capolino Sons, Inc. v. Electronic & Missile Facilities, Inc., 364 F.2d 705, 707 (2d Cir.1966)), *cert. denied* 385 U.S. 924 (1966); Electronic & Missile Facilities, Inc. v. United States *ex rel.* Moseley, 306 F.2d 554, 556 (5th Cir. 1962), *rev'd on other grounds*, Moseley v. Electronic & Missile Facilities, Inc., 374 U.S. 167 (1963)).
123 *In re* Fireman's Fund Insurance Co., 588 F.2d 93 (5th Cir. 1979).

themselves have moved for transfer in accord with the forum selection clause.[124]

In re Fireman's Fund involved a construction project located in Louisiana. Suit was filed under the Miller Act in the Eastern District of Louisiana by Fireman's Fund, the subcontractor's assignee, against the general contractor and its surety. The defendants moved to transfer the case to New Jersey based on a provision in the subcontract stating that "venue of such suit or action shall be laid in the County of Essex and the State of New Jersey." The Fifth Circuit ruled that the venue provision of the Miller Act was and the transfer order was affirmed. Other courts have followed the Fifth Circuit's reasoning in upholding the enforceability of arbitration clauses in subcontract agreements.[125]

There has been a shift in some states regarding the enforceability of forum selection clauses if deemed to be against public policy. For example, the law has changed in Louisiana with respect to forum selection clauses since the *In re Fireman's Fund* decision. It is now considered against public policy to have forum selection provisions that require disputes to be resolved in a forum outside of Louisiana or require the application of another state's laws, if one of the parties to the contract is domiciled in Louisiana and the work to be done or equipment or materials to be supplied involved construction projects in Louisiana.[126] With respect to public construction projects in Louisiana, any provision in a public contract which requires that disputes be settled in a different forum or that law of a different state be applied is null and void.[127] This applies to contracts involving the State of Louisiana, or any of its political subdivisions, where the work is done in the state or the services are to be provided or materials to be supplied in the state. This same prohibition applies to provisions requiring that arbitration be conducted in a forum outside of Louisiana. Other states have enacted similar statutes declaring forum selection clauses in construction contracts invalid.[128]

---

124 *Id.* at 95.
125 United States *ex rel.* Capolino Sons, Inc. v. Electronic & Missile Facilities, Inc., 364 F.2d 705 (2d Cir.1966).
126 LA. REV. STAT. 9:2779.
127 LA. REV. STAT. 38:2196.
128 For specific requirements regarding place of construction and citizenship of the parties, *see*: ARIZ. REV. STAT. § 32-1129.05; CALIF. CIV. PROC.

The Georgia Court of Appeals, in *Harry S. Peterson v. National Union Fire Insurance Co.*,[129] has upheld a forum selection clause in a contract executed in Maryland for a project in Virginia. The bond contained a clause providing in pertinent part:

> [n]o claim or action shall be commenced hereunder by any claimant . . . other than in a state court of competent jurisdiction in and for the country [sic] or other political subdivision of the state in which the Project, or any part thereof, is situated, or in the U.S. District Court for the district in which the project, or any part thereof, is situated and not elsewhere.

The plaintiff filed suit in state court in Georgia. The court reasoned that the contract sued upon (the bond) was entered into by two parties, the principal and the surety, to provide a benefit to specified claimants under certain conditions, including one limiting suit to the project's situs, i.e. Virginia. Since this provision was not contrary to Georgia public policy, it was held to be enforceable and thus suit was improperly filed in Georgia.

In *United States ex rel B&D Mechanical Contractors, Inc. v. St. Paul Mercury Insurance Co.*,[130] the court held that because the forum selection clause was invalid, the Miller Act's venue provision prevailed and the case must be brought in the district where the contract was to be performed.[131]

Even entities not party to the contract which contains the forum selection clause can invoke the forum selection provisions. For example, in *Arrow Plumbing v. North American Mechanical Services*,[132] the court held that even though the surety was not a party to the subcontract, it could invoke the forum selection clause contained in the subcontract

---

CODE § 410.42; 815 ILCS 665/10; IND. CODE § 32-28-3-17; FLA. STAT. § 47.025; MINN. STAT. § 337.10; MONT. CODE § 28-2-2116; N.Y. GEN. BUS. LAW 35-E § 757; N.C. GEN. STAT. § 22B-2; OHIO REV. CODE § 4113.62; OR. REV. STAT. § 701.640; 73 P.S. 514; R.I. GEN. LAWS § 6-34.1-1; TENN. CODE § 66-11-208; TEX. BUS. & COM. CODE § 35.52; UTAH CODE 13-8-3; VA. CODE § 8.01-262.1; WIS. STAT. § 779.135.

129   434 S.E.2d 778 (Ga. App. 1993).
130   70 F.3d 1115 (10th Cir. 1995), *cert. denied*, 517 U.S. 1167 (1966).
131   *Id.* at 1118.
132   810 F. Supp. 369 (D.R.I. 1993).

agreement. The court reasoned that since the surety generally stands in the shoes of its principal, it may avail itself of any defense which is available to the principal, except those that are purely personal, such as bankruptcy or infancy.[133] The court stated:

> Although a surety is not a party to a subcontract agreement, its liability under a payment bond is determined by the agreements between its principal and the subcontractor. The surety therefore should have all of the benefits and suffer all of the disadvantages that would accrue to the general contractor under these agreements.[134]

Courts often disregard a forum selection clause if it considered permissive rather than mandatory.[135]

Forum selection clauses in contracts on both federal and state projects will be generally enforced unless found to be unreasonable. But, nuances do exist, and one should check the law of the particular state to determine whether a forum selection clause is voidable for certain projects between certain parties.

C. Bankruptcy Venue

The venue for bankruptcy proceedings is governed by 28 U.S.C. §§ 1408-1409.[136] The basic venue provision, 28 U.S.C. § 1408, gives two venue choices for an entity planning to file a case under Title 11. One is based upon the domicile, residence, location of the debtor's principal place of business in the U.S. or principal assets in the U.S.,

---

133 *Arrow Plumbing*, 810 F. Supp. at 372.
134 *Id.* (citing United States *ex rel.* Fireman's Fund Ins. Co. v. Frank Brisco Co., Inc., 462 F. Supp. 114, 117 E.D. La. 1978)). *See also In re* Fireman's Fund Ins. Co., 588 F.2d 93 (5th Cir. 1979) (holding that forum selection clauses in subcontracts overrides Miller Act venue provisions and warrants transfer of action against contractor and surety).
135 GMAC Commercial Mortgage Corp. v. LaSalle Bank Nat'l Ass'n, 242 F. Supp. 23d 279 (D.C. N.Y. 2002); Nat'l Council on Compensation Ins., Inc. v. Caro & Graifman, P.C., 259 F. Supp. 172 (D.C. Conn. 2003); Von Graffenreid v. Craig, 246 F. Supp. 2d 553 (D.C. Tex. 2003) (forum selection clause considered permissive where nothing in the agreement precluded parties from litigating elsewhere).
136 For an excellent detailed discussion on bankruptcy related issues, see Chapter 14 "Bankruptcy Issues."

during the greatest portion of the one hundred eighty days before the actual filing. The other choice is a district in which an affiliate of the filing entity has a pending Title 11 case. The statute provides:

> Except as provided in section 1410 of this title, a case under title 11 may be commenced in the district court for the district–
>
> (1) in which the domicile, residence, principal place of business in the U.S., or principal assets in the U.S., of the person or entity that is the subject of such case have been located for the one hundred and eighty days immediately preceding such commencement, or for a longer portion of such one-hundred-and-eighty-day period than the domicile, residence, or principal place of business, in the U.S., or principal assets in the U.S., of such person were located in any other district; or
>
> (2) in which there is pending a case under title 11, concerning such person's affiliate, general partner, or partnership.

The wording of § 1408(1), which does not make a distinction between the venue options of natural persons and other entities such as corporations, has led to what many perceive to be forum shopping, with the Delaware Bankruptcy Court appearing to be the venue of choice for corporate debtors. In many of these cases, the debtor's only connection to Delaware is the fact that it is incorporated under the laws of Delaware. Venue is found to be proper in Delaware (or any other state of incorporation) by reference to the general federal venue statute, 28 U.S.C. § 1391(c) which states:

> A corporation may be sued in any judicial district in which it is incorporated or licensed to do business or is doing business, and such judicial district shall be regarded as the residence of such corporation for venue purposes.

28 U.S.C. § 1408(2) provides a venue alternative for affiliates of a person or entity already involved in a case filed under Title 11. Thus, an affiliate has the option of filing a proceeding in the district in which it has its domicile, residence, principal place of business or principal assets, or in the district where its affiliate, general partner or partnership already has a case pending. The apparent reason for this alternative venue provision for affiliates is the assumption that a court which has

jurisdiction over the affiliate, general partner or partnership's proceeding should also have jurisdiction over the affiliate's proceeding.[137]

Venue for civil proceedings that arise during a Chapter 11 proceeding, such as various forms of adversary proceedings are governed by 28 U.S.C.§ 1409. The general venue rule for these proceedings is that they are to be filed in the court where the Chapter 11 case is pending.

Section 1409 provides:

(a) Except as otherwise provided in subsections (b) and (d), a proceeding arising under title 11 or arising in or related to a case under title 11 may be commenced in the district court in which such case is pending.
(b) Except as provided in subsection (d) of this section, a trustee in a case under title 11 may commence a proceeding arising in or related to such a case to recover a money judgment of or property worth less than $1,000 or a consumer debt of less than $5,000 only in the district court for the district in which the defendant resides.
(b) Except as provided in subsection (d) of this section, a trustee in a case under title 11 may commence a proceeding arising in or related to such a case to recover a money judgment of or property worth less than $1,100 or a consumer debt of less than $16,425, or a debt (excluding a consumer debt) against a non-insider of less than $10,950, only in the district court for the district in which the defendant resides.
(c) Except as provided in subsection (b) of this section, a trustee in a case under title 11 may commence a proceeding arising in or related to such a case as statutory successor to the debtor or creditors under section 541 or 544(B) of title 11 in the district court for the district where the state or federal court sits in which, under applicable non-bankruptcy venue provisions, the debtor or creditors, as the case may be, may have commenced an action on which such proceeding is based if the case under title 11 had not been commenced.
(d) A trustee may commence a proceeding arising under title 11 or arising in or related to a case under title 11 based on a claim arising after the commencement of such case from the operation of the business of the debtor only in the district court for the district where a state or federal court sits in which, under applicable non-bankruptcy venue provisions, an action on such claim may have been brought.

---

137 *See*, 1 COLLIER ON BANKRUPTCY, ¶ 4.01[3].

(e) A proceeding arising under title 11 or arising in or related to a case under title 11, based on a claim arising after the commencement of such case from the operation of the business of the debtor, may be commenced against the representative of the estate in such case in the district court for the district where the state or federal court sits in which the party commencing such proceeding may, under applicable non-bankruptcy venue provisions, have brought an action on such claim, or in the district court in which such case is pending.

28 U.S.C.§ 1409(c) provides an alternative venue for suits brought by a trustee as the statutory successor to the debtor or creditors under § 541 or 544(b) of the bankruptcy court (the strong-arm clause). This alternative venue is the district court which would have been a suitable venue under applicable non-bankruptcy venue provisions. It should be noted that this provision is rarely invoked since trustees, for obvious reasons, prefer to litigate these cases in the bankruptcy court where the overall proceeding is pending.

III. Change of Venue in Bankruptcy Cases[138]

Change of venue of a bankruptcy case is governed by 28 U.S.C. § 1412, which provides:

> A district court may transfer a case or proceeding under title 11 to a district court for another district, in the interest of justice or for the convenience of the parties.

This statute applies both to changes of venue of cases filed under Title 11 and related civil proceedings arising under Title 11 or during Title 11 cases. Changes of venue are also dealt with by Bankruptcy Rule 1014(a)(1), which states:

> If a petition is filed in a proper district, on timely motion of a party in interest, and after hearing on notice to the petitioners, the U.S. trustee, and other entities as directed by the court, the case may be transferred

---

138 This section addresses changes of venue in connection with bankruptcy cases. Change of venue under 28 U.S.C. § 1404 is addressed elsewhere in the chapter.

to any other district if the court determines that the transfer is in the interest of justice or for the convenience of the parties.

The courts have developed the following primary criteria to determine whether to transfer a Title 11 case: (1) proximity of the creditors to the court; (2) location of the debtor's assets; (3) the proximity of the debtor to the court; (4) the proximity of witnesses necessary to the administration of the estate; and (5) the economic administration of the estate.[139]

It should be noted that the burden of proof relating to the transfer is borne by the moving party.[140] As one commentator has noted, there is a presumption that civil proceedings should be tried in the "home" court.[141]

Normally, venue issues are not important to sureties. However, situations may arise where a principal or an indemnitor has filed in a presumably friendly forum far removed from its assets, its creditors, including the surety, and witnesses relevant to existing or potential disputes. In these instances, the surety should consider moving for a change of venue, keeping in mind the criteria employed by the courts and the need to "timely" move for change of venue.

IV. Removal of State Proceedings to Federal Court

A. Actions Removable Generally Under 28 U.S.C. § 1441

Any case filed in state court in which a federal court would have original jurisdiction may be removed to federal court.[142] Therefore, if there is diversity of citizenship and the amount in controversy exceeds

---

139 *See* Commw. of Puerto Rico v. Commonwealth Oil Ref. Co., 596 F.2d 1239 (5th Cir. 1979), *cert. denied*, 444 U.S. 1045, 100 S.Ct. 732 (1980) (interpreting former Bankruptcy Rule 116, the predecessor of Federal Rule of Bankruptcy Procedure 1014).

140 *See In re*: Peachtree Lane Assocs. Ltd., 150 F. 3d 788 (7th Cir. 1999); *In re* Commw. Oil Ref. Co., 596 F.2d 1239 (5th Cir. 1979); *cert. denied*, 444 U.S. 1045, 100 S. Ct. 732, (1980).

141 *See* 1 COLLIER ON BANKRUPTCY, ¶4.04[1].

142 28 U.S.C. §1441(a).

$75,000[143] or the cause of action is based upon a federal question,[144] then the case is removable. The procedure for removal is governed by federal statute and not the Federal Rules of Civil Procedure.[145]

In order to effectuate the removal, a notice of removal is filed in the federal district court to which the case is being removed. The notice should include the grounds for the removal. A copy of the notice must also be filed in the state court in which the original petition was filed and should also be sent to the plaintiff. The removal must occur within thirty days from when the defendant is served with a copy of the complaint[146] or from when a suit becomes removable, if still within one year of the filing of the original suit.

Only a defendant may remove a case to federal court and only on the basis of claims filed against them and not on basis of third-party claims or counter-claims.[147] All defendants who have been served at the time the removal is sought must concur in the removal.

In *Lloyd v. Cabell Huntington Hospital, Inc.*,[148] the court granted the plaintiff's motion to remand the case because all co-defendants failed to consent to removal of the case. Moreover, the court held that it lacked the jurisdiction to stay an action over which it lacked any jurisdiction. In the case, the plaintiff claimed that without the consent of all defendants, removal was defective.[149] The defendant manufacturer then moved for a stay of the proceedings.[150] The court, however, held that that it could not "stay proceedings in an action over which it lacks jurisdiction."[151] The court also held that the removal was defective, reasoning that "[b]ecause the right of removal is jointly held by all the defendants, the failure of one defendant to join in the notice precludes removal."[152] While the defendants do not all have to join in a single notice of removal, all

---

143 28 U.S.C. § 1332.
144 28 U.S.C. § 1331.
145 WRIGHT, MILLER AND COOPER, FEDERAL PRACTICE AND PROCEDURE: JURISDICTION 3d § 3730.
146 28 U.S.C. § 1441(e)(1).
147 Dixie Elec. Co-op v. Citizens of State of Alabama, 789 F.2d 852 (11th Cir. 1986), *reh'g denied*, 794 F.2d 687 (11th Cir. 1986).
148 58 F. Supp. 694 (S.D. W.Va. 1999).
149 *Id.* at 696.
150 *Id.*
151 *Id.*
152 *Id.* (citing MOORE'S FEDERAL PRACTICE, § 107.11[1][c]).

defendants are required to join within thirty days of receiving service of the complaint.[153]

The only limitation to removal based upon diversity is that none of the defendants may be a citizen of the state in which the district court is located and diversity must have existed at the time original suit was filed and at the time the notice of removal is filed.[154]

In *Town of Gordon v. Great American Insurance Co., Inc.*,[155] the Middle District Court of Alabama found when a defendant brings a new party into a case through a third-party complaint asserted against the new party, a plaintiff may assert any claim against that third-party defendant which arises out of the same transaction or occurrence that is the subject matter of the plaintiff's claim against the third-party plaintiff.[156] Moreover, when such an amendment of a plaintiff's complaint is allowed against a third-party defendant, and the inclusion of that claim destroys diversity, remand of the case is appropriate.[157]

The issue of whether a forum selection clause could preclude removal of an action to federal court was discussed by the court in *Karl Koch Erecting Co., Inc. v. New York Convention Center Development Corp.*[158] In *Koch*, the plaintiff, a public benefit corporation organized to develop a New York City convention center brought suit against the contractor and its surety in state court over contractual disputes.[159] Following the state court claim, the contractor brought a separate diversity action against the corporation, which served to remove the corporation's state court action to federal court.[160] However, the contract over which suit was brought contained a forum selection clause, which provided that in the event of a dispute, the contractor could only bring an action against the corporation in state court.[161]

---

153 *Id.*
154 Houston & T.C. Ry. Co. v. Shirley, 4 S.Ct. 472, 111 U.S. 358 (U.S. 1984); Kaneshire v. N. Am. Co. for Life and Health Ins., 496 F. Supp. 452 (D.C. Haw. 1980).
155 331 F. Supp. 1357 (M.D. Ala. 2004).
156 *Id.* (citing FED. R. CIV. P. 14).
157 *Id.* at 1359-60.
158 56 F. Supp. 464 (S.D.N.Y. 1987).
159 *Id.* at 465.
160 *Id.* at 466.
161 *Id.*

The court was thus confronted with the issue of whether the forum selection clause would render the contractor's removal of the action improper.[162] The court found that in interpreting the applicability of the forum selection clause, it "must construe it in light of its actual purpose, as manifested by an objective consideration of the language in the contract."[163] The court then found that the clause was applicable and to allow the contractor to remove the action brought by the corporation in state court would allow the contractor to choose the forum, thus contravening the forum selection clause.[164] The court concluded that the clause was enforceable because the contractor had not shown that the clause resulted from fraud or was overreaching, or that it was unreasonable or unfair, or that it would contravene some strong public policy of the forum.[165]

If removal is based upon federal question jurisdiction, then it must appear on the face of the complaint that resolution of the case depends upon a federal question.[166]

Removal of a case does not waive a party's contractual right to arbitrate.[167]

B. Removal to Bankruptcy Court Under § 28 U.S.C. § 1452

Removal of civil proceedings to bankruptcy court may be based on the general removal statute (28 U.S.C. § 1441), as well as the bankruptcy removal statute (28 U.S.C. § 1452).[168] Removal under either statute is to the federal district court where the litigation is pending.[169] After

---

162 *Id.*
163 *Id.* (citing *In re* Robertson Class Plaintiffs, 479 F. Supp. 657, 668-69 (S.D.N.Y. 1979)), *aff'd in part, rev'd in part*, 625 F.2d 407 (2d Cir. 1980).
164 *Id.*
165 *Id.* at 467.
166 Chronologic Simulation, Inc. v. Sanguinetti, 892 F. Supp. 318 (D. Mass. 1995).
167 Baker v. Securitas Sec. Servs. USA, Inc., 432 F. Supp. 2d 120.
168 Things Remembered, Inc. v. Petrarca, 516 U.S. 124, 116 S.Ct. 494, (1995).
169 Removal of cases to an improper district is a recurring problem which some courts view as a jurisdictional flaw. *In re* Trafficwatch, 138 B.R.

removal, the district court automatically refers the claim or causes of action to the bankruptcy court in accordance with local standing orders promulgated under 28 U.S.C. § 157(a).

In practical terms, use of Section 1441 will be limited in as much as there is a much narrower window for filing the notice of removal–i.e., thirty days after the receipt of service of process.[170] Other tactical issues to consider include the following: (1) removal under Section 1441 can be done only by a defendant, whereas any party can remove under Section 1452;[171] and (2) Section 1441 removal transfers the entire case, whereas Section 1452 only removes a claim or cause of action over which the federal district court has jurisdiction under 28 U.S.C. § 1334 pertaining to bankruptcy jurisdiction.

1. Jurisdictional Requirements of 28 U.S.C. § 1452

Section 1452 provides that "any claim or cause of action" may be removed "to the district court . . . if such district court has jurisdiction of such claim or cause of action under Section 1334 of this title." Section 1334 is the jurisdictional font for bankruptcy cases and related proceedings. Under 28 U.S.C. § 157 proceedings under the Bankruptcy Code are classified as either core or non-core proceedings.[172] Generally speaking, core proceedings are the specialized function of the bankruptcy case–e.g., administration of the bankruptcy estate, allowance or disallowance of claims against the estate, orders concerning the use,

---

841 (Bankr. E.D. Tex. 1992). As noted in *Trafficwatch*, if the strategy is to move the litigation to the district where the bankruptcy case is pending and the removal is to another district, a motion to transfer venue can be filed.

170 28 U.S.C. § 1446(b).

171 Typically, the debtor as plaintiff or defendant utilizes Section 1452 to remove a previously pending state court suit to bankruptcy court after initiation of bankruptcy. In the event the debtor is a defendant in the litigation which another party seeks to remove, it would be advisable to seek relief from the automatic stay before attempting the removal, as courts have held that removing a state court case in which the debtor is a defendant violates the automatic stay. *In re* Hoskins, 266 B.R. 872, 877 (Bankr. W.D. Mo. 2001); *In re* Brateman Bros., Ins., 135 B.R. 853, 855 (Bankr. N.D. Ind. 1991).

172 *See* Section 157 for a list of examples of core proceedings.

lease or sale of property, and confirmation of bankruptcy plans. Non-core matters are ". . . otherwise related to a case under (the Bankruptcy Code)."[173]

Removal under Section 1452 will ordinarily involve a claim or cause of action which is a non-core matter. Under the test used by most circuit courts, a civil proceeding is related to a bankruptcy case only when "the outcome of that proceeding could conceivably have any effect on the estate being administered in bankruptcy."[174]

2. Exceptions of Removal Under 28 U.S.C. § 1452

Section 1452 provides that certain proceedings are not removable–i.e., non-civil actions, tax court proceedings and certain civil actions by governmental units enforcing the unit's police or regulatory power. Non-civil actions which would not be removable would be criminal, administrative or arbitration proceedings.[175]

3. Procedure for Removal Under 28 U.S.C. § 1452

Federal Bankruptcy Rule 9027 sets out the specifics detailing the procedure and timing for removal under Section 1452. Notices must be

---

173 28 U.S.C. § 157(c)(1).
174 Pacor, Inc. v. Higgins, 743 F.2d 984, 994 (3d Cir. 1984); *In re* A. H. Robins Co., Inc., 86 F.3d 364, 372 (4th Cir. 1996), *cert. denied, sub nom*, Bergstrom v. Dalkon Shield Claimants Trust, 519 U.S. 993, 117 S.Ct. 483, 136 L.Ed.2d 377 (1996); Specialty Mills, Inc. v. Citizens St. Bank, 51 F.3d 770 (8th Cir. 1995); *In re* G.S.F. Corp., 938 F.2d 1467, 1476 (1st Cir. 1991); Robinson v. Michigan Consol. Gas Co., 918 F.2d 579 (6th Cir. 1990); *In re* Feitz, 852 F.2d 455 (9th Cir. 1988). However, the Seventh and Fifth Circuits have used different tests. *Matles of Xonics, Inc.*, 813 F.2d 127, 131 (7th Cir. 1987) (the proceeding is "'related to' the bankruptcy when it affects the amount of property available for distribution or the allocation of property among creditors."); Bass v. Denney, 171 F.3d 1016 (5th Cir. 1999) (a proceeding is related "if the outcome could alter the debtor's rights, liabilities, options, or freedom of action (either positively or negatively) and . . . in any way impacts upon the handling and administration of the estate."). This Fifth Circuit test was approved as an alternative test by the First Circuit in *In re* Middlesex Power Equip. & Marine, Inc., 292 F.3d 61, 68 (1st Cir. 2002).
175 *In re* Adams Delivery Serv., Inc., 24 B.R. 589 (9th Cir. BAP 1982).

filed with the respective courts which are more detailed and contain bankruptcy related provisions, not required under the general removal statute. The time for removal is computed on the basis of whether the claim or cause of action was or was not pending at the time of the commencement of the bankruptcy case. If the claim or cause of action in a civil action was pending when the bankruptcy case was filed, a notice of removal may be filed only within the longest of (A) ninety days after the order for relief in the case under the Bankruptcy Code, (B) thirty days after entry of an order terminating a stay, if the claim or cause of action in a civil action has been stayed under Section 362 of the Bankruptcy Code, or (C) thirty days after a bankruptcy trustee qualifies in a Chapter 11 reorganization case but not later than 180 days after the order for relief.[176] If a claim or cause of action was asserted in another court after the commencement of the bankruptcy case, a notice of removal may be filed with the clerk only within the shorter of (A) thirty days after receipt, through service or otherwise, of a copy of the initial pleading setting forth the claim or cause of action sought to be removed or (B) thirty days after receipt of the summons if the initial pleading has been filed with the court but not served with the summons.

4. Remand

Section 1452(b) permits the court to remand a claim or cause of action on any equitable grounds. Examples of remand grounds include: *forum non conveniens*; if the civil action has been bifurcated by removal then the entire action should remain with the trial court; a state court is better prepared to interpret state law; and the trial court had a specific expertise (e.g. court of federal claims).

V. Issues Relating To Limitations

The limitation period in which suit must be brought on a claim may be established by contract, (i.e., those contained in the bond or construction contract) or by statute. (i.e., those specified by particular state statutes). This section will address issues arising from limitation periods.

---

[176] The time for removal may be reduced or enlarged. Federal Bankruptcy Rule 9006(b), (c).

A. Contractual Limitations

1. Limitation Periods Stated in the Bond

Many performance bonds contain an express limitations period. For example, the standard form AIA Performance Bond provides:

> Any proceeding, legal or equitable, under this Bond may be instituted in any court of competent jurisdiction in the location in which the work or part of the work is located and shall be instituted within two years after Contractor Default or within two years after the Contractor ceased working or within two years after the Surety refuses or fails to perform its obligations under this Bond, whichever occurs first. If the provisions of this Paragraph are void or prohibited by law, the minimum period of limitation available to sureties as a defense and the jurisdiction of the suit shall be applicable.[177]

Performance bonds are governed by the usual rules of construction of adhesion contracts, and contracts, and contractual time limitations contained therein are to be strictly construed against the surety.[178] Provisions which shorten the statutory time limitation are generally enforceable so long as the limitations period provided is reasonable.[179] For example, the two-year limitation period provided in standard form AIA Performance Bond was upheld as valid by the court in *Yeshiva*

---

177 *AIA Document A312, Performance Bond*, § 9, (1984 ed.).
178 Menorah Nursing Home, Inc. v. Zukov, 153 A.D.2d. 13, 20 (N.Y. A.D. 2 Dept. 1989).
179 V. Petrillo & Sons, Inc. v. Am. Constr. Co., 371 A.2d 799, 801 (N.D.J. Super A.D. 1977); Yeshiva Univ. v. Fid. & Deposit Co. of Md., 116 A.D.2d 49 (N.Y. A.D. 1 Dept. 1986); Raymond Int'l, Inc. v. City of New York, 511 F.Supp 773, 776 (S.D.N.Y. 1981); Order of United Commercial Travelers of Am. v. Wolfe, 331 U.S. 586, 67 S.Ct. 1355 608 (1947); Moreno v. Sanchez, 131 Cal. Rptr. 2d 684, 695 (Cal. Ct. App. 2003) (in which the court recognized the validity of freedom for contractual parties to limit the length of a statute of limitations, provided; however, in order for such an action to be valid, a party must be aware that the event triggering the shortened period occurred, and cannot be a latent event, undetectable to a party); Techcon Contracting, Inc. v. Village of Lynbrook, 2007 WL 702801 (N.Y. Sup. 2007).

University v. Fidelity & Deposit Co. of Maryland.[180] At least one court has held that reasonableness is not relevant. In *Rory v. Continental Insurance Co.*,[181] the court held that "an unambiguous contractual provision providing for a shortened period of limitations is to be enforced as written regardless of reasonableness"; see also *Clark v. DaimlerChrysler Corp.*,[182] (in which the court, by virtue of *Rory*, was compelled to enforce a contract as written, regardless of reasonableness, provided that the contract was not contrary to law or public policy, or was otherwise unenforceable under recognized traditional contract defenses). *Yeshiva* involved suit by an owner against a surety on a subcontractor's performance bond. The performance bond was the standard form AIA Performance Bond containing a two-year limitation. The owner brought his action after two years has passed in contravention of the bond's provisions. The court upheld the two-year limitation provision in a AIA Performance Bond. The court found that such a limitation was not void as against public policy as it is construed as a shortening rather than a waiver or extension of the statute of limitations.[183] Had the bond limitation provision not been applicable, the action by the owner would have been timely under New York's six-year statutory limitation for contractual suits.

Similarly, Illinois allows private parties to negotiate a limitations period shorter than that provided by statute, if the agreed period is reasonable and not contrary to public policy.[184] Reasonableness was the issue before the court in *Continental Illinois National Bank & Trust Co. of Chicago v. Indemnity Insurance Co. of North America*.[185] The case involved suit by trustees of property against a surety under a performance bond in favor of a contractor. The performance bond provided that any suit to compel performance "must be instituted within ninety (90) days from the date on which final payment under the contract falls due."[186] The surety moved for summary judgment contending that

---

180 116 A.D.2d 49 (App. Div. 1986).
181 703 N.W.2d 23, 31 (Mich. 2005).
182 706 N.W.2d. 471, 473-74 (Mich. App. 2005).
183 116 A.D.2d at 51-52.
184 Bd. of Educ. of Community High Sch. Dist. No. 99, DuPage County v. Hartford Acc. & Indem. Co., 504 N.E.2d 1000 (2nd Dist. 1987).
185 1989 WL 27127 (N.D. Ill. 1989).
186 *Continental Illinois*, 1989 WL 27127 at 3.

the trustee to the property failed to institute the action within the ninety-day period as provided in the bond. Absent the performance bond limitation provision, Illinois has a ten-year statute of limitation period that would have been applicable to the performance bond for private works.[187] In analyzing the ninety-day period, the court noted that the supreme court has upheld a two-year limitation period and indicated that a six-month period would not be unreasonable.[188] Nonetheless, the court in *Continental Illinois* denied the surety's motion for summary judgment finding that under the circumstances of the case the ninety-day limitation period was unreasonable.[189]

However, reasonableness is not always an issue courts consider when examining contractual limitation periods which are shorter than what would otherwise be an applicable statute of limitations. This was true for the court in the matter of *Rory v. Continental Insurance Co.*[190] In a decision that expressly overruled *Camelot Excavating Co. v. St. Paul Fire & Marine Insurance Co.*,[191] the court held that "a mere judicial assessment of 'reasonableness' is an invalid basis upon which to refuse to enforce contractual provisions," and that unambiguous contractual provisions providing for a shortened period of limitations should be enforced unless the provision would violate law or public policy.[192]

Some states have enacted statutes that void a private party's efforts at contractually shortening the time period afforded by statute for commencement of a suit.[193] Miss. Code Ann. § 15-1-5 states:

> The limitations prescribed in this chapter shall not be changed in any way whatsoever by contract between parties, and any change in such limitations made by any contract's stipulation whatsoever shall be absolutely null and void, the object of this section being to make the

---

187 *Id.* (citing ILL. REV. STAT. Ch. 110, ¶13-206 (1983)).
188 Bd. of Educ. of Community High Sch. Dist. No. 99, DuPage County v. Hartford Acc. & Indem. Co., 504 N.E.2d 1000 (2nd Dist. 1987).
189 *Continental Illinois*, 1989 WL 27127 at *3.
190 703 N.W.2d 23 (Mich. 2005).
191 280 N.W. 2d 491, 494 (Mich. App. 1979), *aff'd*, 301 N.W. 2d 275 (Mich. 1981).
192 *Id.* at 31.
193 4 PHILIP BRUNER & PATRICK J. O'CONNOR, JR., BRUNER & O'CONNOR ON CONSTRUCTION LAW § 12:74.

period of limitations for the various causes of action the same for all litigants.

The question of whether a limitation of liability clause in a home inspection agreement was valid came before the court in the matter of *Pitts v. Watkins*.[194] The liability clause required that any legal action arising from the home inspection agreement must occur within one (1) year from the date of inspection.[195] After reviewing the liability clause, the Mississippi Supreme Court declared that the limitation of liability clause was "substantively unconscionable" and "oppressive and in violation of statutory law."[196]

Florida has adopted similar legislation which nullifies any attempt to shorten statutory guidelines for commencement of a suit through contractual language. Fla. Stat. Ann. § 95.03 states:

> Any provision in a contract fixing the period of time within which an action arising out of the contract may be begun at a time less than that provided by the applicable statute of limitations is void.

Many bonds also contain mandatory notice provisions. If the notice requirement is not met, a subsequent suit may be barred.[197] In addition to the timing of the notice, the bond may also specify the form the notice must take. Generally, the notice should identify the bond, the underlying contract, the date of the alleged default and specifics regarding the default. Failure to provide correct notice may affect the claimant's right to bring suit.[198] Full compliance does not always result in dismissal.[199]

In *Balfour Beatty Construction Co. v. Colonial Ornamental Iron Works Inc.*,[200] the surety issued a performance bond for Colonial

---

194 905 So.2d 553 (Miss. 2005).
195 *Id.* at 558.
196 *Id.*
197 Coleman Capital Corp. v. Travelers Indem. Co., 443 F.2d 47 (2d Cir. 1971).
198 Ulster Elec. Supply Co. v. Md. Cas. Co., 35 A.D. 2d 309 (N.Y.A.D. 1970).
199 Fleischer Eng'g & Const. Co. v. United States, 311 U.S. 15, 61 S.Ct. 886 (1940); Village of Warwick v. Republic Ins. Co., 104 Misc. 2d 514 (N.Y. Sup. 1980).
200 986 F.Supp. 82 (D. Conn 1997).

Ornamental Iron Works, Inc. ("Colonial"). Colonial had a contract with Balfour Beatty Construction Co. ("Balfour") to supply materials for a bridge project. The parties utilized the standard AIA 312 bond. Balfour sent two notice letters to surety advising of the delay in delivery of the materials. The court held that the claimant failed to comply with the notice requirements of the bond because it failed to actually declare the principal in default. Therefore, as the obligee failed to meet a condition precedent for the surety's liability, summary judgment in favor of the surety was granted dismissing the claims against it.

However, Washington courts have held that violation of a notice requirement exonerates a surety only to the extent of resulting prejudice even when notice is an express condition precedent to liability under the surety bond.[201]

Under the A-312 bond form, the period is measured from the date upon which the principal "ceased work" on the contract. This includes the work performed by subcontractors on the project.[202] However, in *Eagle Fire Corp. v. First American Insurance. Co.*,[203] a case involving a payment bond, the New Jersey Supreme Court held that the term "cease work" did not extend to work performed by subcontractors performing work directly for owner due to general contractor's bankruptcy. The court distinguished this from the situation in which the subcontractor is still working on this project pursuant to its contract with the general contractor.

---

201 Colorado Structures, Inc. v. Insurance Co. of the West, 167 P.3d. 1125, 1150 (Wash. 2007); *see also* Lazelle v. Empire State Sur. Co., 109 P. 195, 196 (Wash. 1910) ("the surety cannot complain when it can show no loss or substantial damage by reason of the failure to receive notice, in the exact and technical language of the contract, or make it appear that its failure to receive notice has prevented it from taking proper steps for its protection."); Heffernan v. U.S. Fid. & Guar. Co., 79 P. 1095, 1097 (Wash. 1905) ("yet when the notice serves its purpose as well when given after the prescribed time as it does before–that is, when it is equally effective in protecting the surety from loss–it is inequitable, and a manifest abuse of the purposes of this provision of the bond, to hold that the mere technical variance shall relieve the obligor entirely").

202 Petrillo & Son, Inc. v. Am. Constr. Co., 371 A.2d 799 (N.J. Sup. Ct. App. Div.) *cert. denied*, 379 A.2d 235 (N.J. 1977) (General contractor does not "cease work" if subcontractors are still working on the project.)

203 678 A.2d 699 (N.J. 1996).

2. Limitation Periods Stated in the Underlying Contract

In addition to finding a contractual limitation clause in the performance bond, the construction contract itself may include an express limitations period, as was the case in *Raymond International, Inc. v. City of New York*.[204]

Raymond involved a suit by a contractor to recover additional monies claimed to be due under a public contract. The limitation period contained in the contract provided that the period for filing suit must be within six months of the filing of the certificate of completion. The contractor in the action did not file his suit until two years after the certificate of completion. The court held that the contractor's action was barred by the six-month limitation period contained in the contract. In reaching its holding, the court noted that to uphold a shortened contractual limitation period, the period must be reasonable and its terms will be strictly construed.[205] However, after review of other New York decisions, the court in *Raymond* found that contractual six-month limitation clauses had consistently been upheld in previous decisions as valid and is enforceable.[206]

Although clauses that shorten the time to bring an action are generally enforceable, clauses that lengthen or extend the statutory limitation period have been held null and void. For example, in *John Jay Kassner & Co. v. City of New York*,[207] the court nullified the identical clause that was at issue in *Raymond* where its practical effect was to

---

204 Raymond Int'l, Inc. v. City of New York, 511 F. Supp. 773 (S.D.N.Y. 1981).
205 *Id.* at 776, (citing Redington v. Hartford Acc. & Indem. Co., 463 F. Supp. 83, 86 (S.D.N.Y. 1978); Hurlbut v. Christiano, 63 A.D.2d 1116, 1118 (N.Y.A.D. 4 Dept. 1978); Stanley R. Benjamin, Inc. v. Fid. & Cas. Co. of New York, 72 Misc.2d 742, 744 (N.Y. Sup. 1972); *but see Rory, supra* note 190.
206 *Raymond*, 511 F. Supp. at 776 (citing Sando Parisi & Sons, Inc. v. Bd. of Educ., 32 A.D.2d 909 (N.Y.A.D. 1 Dept. 1969); City of New York v. Alpha Contracting Corp. 182 Misc. 115 (N.Y.Sup. App. 1944) (*per curiam*)).
207 John Jay Kassner & Co., Inc. v. City of New York, 389 N.E.2d 99 (N.Y. 1979).

extend the statutory limitation period beyond six years, the statutory maximum period.[208]

Kassner involved a plaintiff who had performed some engineering work for the City of New York. The plaintiff did not institute suit until five months after payment by the city and almost seven years after notification by the city of the amount to be paid. The court determined that the breach accrued, for statute of limitations purposes, when the plaintiff received notification of the amount to be paid by the city.[209] The court refused to apply the six-month limitation clause, because it was predicated upon filing of the certificate of completion, which was not done until six and one-half years after the breach and thus would have extended the period of limitations beyond the statutory maximum under New York's six-year statute of limitations for contractual suits.[210]

Yet another example of the court's unwillingness to extend a period of limitations beyond what is statutorily dictated can be found in the matter of *West Gate Village Association v. Dubois*.[211] *West Gate Village* involved a non-profit, homeowners association that filed suit against homeowners in an effort to collect home assessments.[212] The homeowners association eventually placed liens on the homeowners' property, which prompted the homeowners to move for the district court to find the homeowners association in contempt for, among other things, placing liens on their property for unpaid assessments.[213] The district court denied the motion, and the homeowners filed a superior court action in equity against the homeowners association, seeking a declaratory judgment and injunctive relief from the liens that the homeowners association had placed against the homeowners' property.[214] The homeowners association counter-claimed and brought a separate civil action to recover annual assessments for a period of six years.[215]

The homeowners association moved for summary judgment on its counterclaim and civil complaint, which was granted by the superior

---

208 *Raymond*, 511 F. Supp. at 776 (citing *Kassner*, 389 N.E.2d 99).
209 *Kassner*, 389 N.E.2d at 102-03.
210 *Id.* at 103-04.
211 761 A.2d 1066 (N.H. 2000).
212 *Id.* at 1068.
213 *Id.*
214 *Id.* at 1069.
215 *Id.*

court.[216] The homeowners appealed to the New Hampshire Supreme Court and argued, in part, that they were not granted the opportunity to argue that an amendment to the covenant between the homeowners association and the homeowners which contractually extended the timeframe for the homeowners association to bring suit on a lien from the statutorily mandated three years to six years was inapplicable.[217] The court agreed with the homeowners and, citing to *Kassner*, held that a party cannot, in advance, make a valid promise that a statute founded in public policy shall be inoperative.[218]

A contrary holding is found in *Milwaukee Metropolitan Sewerage District v. Fidelity & Deposit Co. of Maryland*.[219] *Milwaukee Sewerage* involves suit by a public entity, the sewerage district, against a surety under a performance bond with a contractor. The performance bond contained a one-year limitation provision for actions for defective workmanship or material against the bond. The district court granted summary judgment in favor of the surety due to the sewerage district's failure to institute its action within the one-year period as provided in the performance bond. The sewerage district contended that Wisconsin's six-year statute of limitation for contractual actions was applicable.[220] The Seventh Circuit affirmed the summary judgment, but for different reasons. It found that Wisconsin's one-year statute of limitations for public works was applicable since there was no conflict with the performance bond.[221] Either under the bond's provisions or under the one-year statute, the sewerage district's action was untimely, but the court noted that had the performance bond provided a longer period than Wisconsin's statute, then the longer period of the bond would have been applicable.[222] In other words Wisconsin would allow expansion of a statutory limitation period unlike New York and New Hampshire.

---

216   *Id.*
217   *Id.*
218   *Id* at 1071, citing to Kasnner, *supra* note 207.
219   56 F.3d 821 (7th Cir. 1995).
220   WIS. STAT. ANN. § 893.43.
221   *Id.* at § 779.14.
222   *Milwaukee Sewerage*, 56 F.3d at 824, n. 2.

B. Statutory Limitations

In addition to contractual provisions concerning the time to institute an action against a performance bond, specific statutes may control the period of limitation with respect to performance bonds.

1. Statutes

Some states provide express statute of limitations.

a. Illinois. Illinois has a six-month limitation statute for suits on payment or performance bonds for public works.[223] All bonds issued for public works in Illinois are deemed statutory bonds subject to the six-month limitation period and any provisions in the bond or the contract to the contrary are disregarded.[224]

b. Louisiana. Louisiana has a specific statute applicable to public works. It provides:

> Any action against the contractor on the contract on the bond, or against the contractor or the surety or both on the bond furnished by the contractor, all in connection with the construction, alteration, or repair of any public works let by the State or any of its agencies, boards or subdivisions shall prescribe five years from the substantial completion . . . [225]

c. Minnesota. Minnesota requires that suits against sureties on performance bonds for defective and unsafe conditions on real property are subject to a two-year statute of limitations.[226]

---

223 ILL. COMP. STAT. 550/1, 2; *formerly* Ill. S.H.A. ch. 29, ¶¶ 15, 16.
224 Concrete Structures of the Midwest, Inc. v. Fireman's Ins. Co. of Newark, New Jersey, 790 F.2d 41 (7th Cir. 1986); *see also* Shaw Ind. Inc. v. Cmty. Coll. Dist. No. 515, 741 N.E.2d 642 (Ill. App. 1 Dist. 2000) (in which the court held that an unpaid subcontractor that asserted third-party beneficiary contract claim against state college under Public Construction Bond Act was required to comply with the act's six-month limitations period, even though college failed to procure payment bond from general contractor as required by the act).
225 LA. REV. STAT. ANN. 38:2188.
226 Travelers Indem. Co. v. Hennepin Cty., Minn., 918 F.2d 66 (8th Cir. 1990) (citing MINN. STAT. § 541.051 (the portion of MINN. STAT. § 541.051 pertaining to the statute of repose has been rendered

d. Nevada. In *Trustees of Bricklayers & Allied Craftsman Local 3 Health and Welfare Trust v. Reynolds Elec. & Engineering Co., Inc.*,[227] a Miller Act case, where neither the contract nor the bond contained any specific limitation clause, the court applied Nevada's six-year statute of limitation applicable to contracts.

e. Pennsylvania. Pennsylvania has a specific statute that provides for a limitation period with regard to performance bonds. The Pennsylvania statute provides in pertinent part:

§5523 One year limitation
The following actions and proceedings must be commenced within one year:

* * *

(3) An action upon any payment or performance bond.[228]

f. Wisconsin. Wisconsin has a one-year limitation period for actions on performance bonds for public works.[229]

In addition to specific statutes governing limitation on actions against performance bonds, many states have adopted special statutes of limitations applicable to suits brought against architects, contractors, and others for latent defects in construction work.[230] Some courts have held these special statutes of limitations apply to bar an action against the surety where an action against the principal would have been barred.[231] Other courts have held that special statutes do not provide protection for

---

unconstitutional by Brink v. Smith Co. Constr., Inc. v. D.A. Distribution, Inc., 703 N.W.2d 871 (Minn. App. 2005), however, the section referred to above is still good law)).

[227] 747 F. Supp. 606 (D. Nev. 1990), *aff'd*, Trustees of Brick Layers and Allied Craftsman Local No. 3 Health and Welfare Trust v. Structures Midwest Corp., 958 F.2d 378 (9th Cir. 1992).
[228] 42 PA. CONS. STAT. ANN. § 5523(3).
[229] WIS. STAT. ANN. § 779.14.
[230] CAL. CIV. PROC. CODE §337.15; FLA. STAT. ANN. § 95.11; ILL. ANN. STAT. Ch. 83, § 24f; MICH. COMP. LAWS § 600.5839; N.J. STAT. ANN. § 2A:14-1.1.
[231] Hudson County v. Terminal Const. Corp., 381 A.2d 355 (N.J. Super A.D. 1977); President and Directors of Georgetown College v. Madden, 660 F.2d 91 (4th Cir. 1981).

the sureties. The terms of the construction contract may also expressly limit the period in which an action may be brought.[232]

In addition to statutory limitations, equitable remedies, such as laches, may apply to estop a party's action against a performance bond.[233] However, a party raising estoppel by laches bears the burden of establishing undue prejudice or injustice by the passage of time and that the other party's conduct was responsible for said damage.[234]

Generally, contractual limitation provisions in performance bonds or building contracts are enforceable, unless they are determined to be unreasonable. Where the bond or contract is silent, the limitation period applicable to contracts is generally employed, barring a specific statute addressing performance bonds. In cases involving public works, some states have specific statutes that may supersede contractual limitation periods.

2. Miller Act Claims

The Miller Act does not have an express limitation period with regard to performance bond claims. It does however provide for a one-year period relative to payment bond claims. The action must be brought no later than one year after the day on which the last of the labor or material was supplied for the project.[235] Moreover, filing of an arbitration demand against a principal does not interrupt the period for suit against the surety.[236]

Another issue which arises is when does the limitation begin to run? With respect to Miller Act bonds, generally warranty work or repair of

---

232   Indep. Consol. Sch. Dist. No. 24, Blue Earth County v. Carlstrom, 151 N.W.2d 784 (Minn. 1967).
233   *In re* ADL Contracting Corp., 184 B.R. 436 (Bankr. S.D.N.Y. 1995) (where lessor of equipment raised doctrine of laches in an attempt to prevent surety's claim to bankruptcy proceed to prime its own.).
234   *In re* ADL Contracting Corp., 184 B.R. at 443 (citing *In re* Hooker Investments, 162 B.R. 426 (Bankr. S.D.N.Y. 1993)).
235   40 U.S.C. § 3133(4), *formerly* 40 U.S.C.§ 270b(b).
236   United States *ex rel.* Wrecking Corp. v. Edward M. Marden Corp., 406 F.2d 525 (1st Cir. 1969).

defective work does not re-start the time period. The period begins to run upon completion of the original work required by the contract.[237]

3. Tax Claims

A surety of a Miller Act performance bond may also be liable for federal withholding taxes. There are, however, certain notice requirements which must be met. 40 U.S.C. Section 270a(d) provides that the U.S. shall give the surety written notice with respect to any unpaid taxes attributable to any period within ninety (90) days after the date when such contractor files a return for the period, except that no such notice shall be given more than 180 days from the date when a return for the period was required to be filed under Title 26.

The notice requirement is simply to alert the surety of its principal's default on payment of its withholding taxes and that payment of the debt is expected. It is not necessary for the government to detail with any specificity the contract, bonds and amount of delinquent taxes; only that timely notice of the contractor's default be given so that the surety is aware that payment from such contractor is not forthcoming. *United States v. American Manufacturers Mutual Casualty Co.*[238]

C. Impact of Bankruptcy

The filing of a bankruptcy petition results in the automatic stay of the commencement or continuation of most litigation against the debtor.[239] The Bankruptcy Code contains a specific statute governing the effect of

---

237 United States *ex rel.* General Elec. Co. v. Gunnar I. Johnson & Son, Inc., 310 2d 899 (8th Cir. 1962); United States *ex rel.* Mod-Form v. Bartan & Barton, 769 F. Supp. 235 (E.D. Mich. 1991); United States *ex rel.* T. Square Equip. Corp. v. Gregor J. Schaefer Sons, Inc., 272 F. Supp. 962 (E.D. N.Y. 1967); United States *ex rel.* T.L. Wallace Constr. Inc. v. Fireman's Fund Ins. Co., 790 F. Supp. 680 (S.D. Miss. 1992).

238 901 F.2d 370 (4th Cir. 1990); United States *ex rel.* Jinks Lumber Co. v. Fed. Ins. Co., 452 F.2d 485 (5th Cir. 1971); United States v. Fid. & Deposit Co. of Md., 690 F. Supp. (D. Hawaii 1988); CTI/DC, Inc. v. Selective Ins. Co. of Am., 392 F.3d 114 (4th Cir. 2004).

239 11 U.S.C. § 362. Exceptions to the automatic stay are contained in § 362(b).

the automatic stay on non-bankruptcy statutes of limitation. 11 U.S.C. § 108(c) provides:

> Except as provided in section 524 of this title, if applicable nonbankruptcy law, an order entered in a nonbankruptcy proceeding, or an agreement fixes a period for commencing or continuing a civil action in a court other than a bankruptcy court on a claim against the debtor, or against an individual with respect to which such individual is protected under section 1201 or 1301 of this title, and such period has not expired before the date of the filing of the petition, then such period does not expire until the later of–
> (1) the end of such period, including any suspension of such period occurring on or after the commencement of the case; or
> (2) 30 days after notice of the termination or expiration of the stay under section 362, 922, 1201, or 1301 of this title, as the case may be, with respect to such claim.

Section 108(c) extends the time a creditor has to commence or continue a civil suit against the debtor that is stayed by § 362.[240] It states that any applicable nonbankruptcy deadline for commencing and continuing an action against a debtor is extended to thirty days after notice of termination of the automatic stay, if the deadline would have occurred earlier.

Under § 362(c) of the Bankruptcy Code, the stay continues until the earlier of the time a case is closed, dismissed, or at the time a discharge is granted or denied. Further, under § 362(c)(1) the stay terminates as to property of the estate at a time when the property is no longer property of the estate. The stay also terminates in those cases where a creditor successfully obtains relief from the stay.

Although the automatic stay can terminate at the close of Chapter 11 reorganization proceedings, ordinarily the bankruptcy court thereafter imposes an injunction to prohibit any collection activities directed against the reorganized debtor to the extent the activities are inconsistent with the confirmed plan of reorganization.

---

240 By contrast, §108(a) allows the trustee or debtor-in-possession to commence an action in a nonbankruptcy proceeding within the applicable statute of limitations or within two years after the order for relief, whichever is later. *See* United States *ex rel.* American Bank v. C.I.T. Const., Inc. of Texas, 944 F.2d 253 (5th Cir. 1991).

Sureties should be particularly aware of the fact that the extension contained in § 108(c) does not apply to claims against co-debtors who are not protected by a co-debtor stay. This simply means that no extension is available for claims against nonbankrupt principals or indemnitors. Thus, the bankruptcy of a single indemnitor or of a principal, does not toll or suspend any limitations period with respect to claims against these parties.

Conclusion

As with any type of litigation, basic issues relating to jurisdiction and limitation periods are very important to practitioners. For example, when defending a claim, verify that the suit has been filed in the proper forum. If not, then grounds may exist to have the case dismissed and in some instances it may be too late for the obligee to re-file the claim. Timing is also an important issue. The practitioner should determine what the appropriate time periods are, whether they are statutory or contractual, and whether the claimant has properly complied with these limitations. These issues are not limited only to individuals defending such claims, but should also be considered by plaintiffs. It is helpful in deciding where to file suit to know what one's options are as to where suit can be filed. It is also important to know how long is remaining before suit can be filed and to determine what other claims can or must be joined in the litigation.

13

EFFECT OF AN ARBITRATION PROVISION IN THE PRINCIPAL'S CONTRACT WITH THE OBLIGEE

James D. Ferrucci
R. Scott Cochrane[*]

Introduction

The presence of an arbitration clause in the principal's contract with the obligee confronts the surety with unique issues which result from the convergence of suretyship law, arbitration law and preclusion law. When a performance bond claim arises, the obligee may invoke the arbitration provision and demand that the surety arbitrate the claim. The surety will want to consider whether submitting the dispute to arbitration is to its advantage.[1] That choice, however, may not rest with the surety.

The principal has an enforceable contractual obligation to arbitrate disputes with the obligee, but does the surety? Many courts have held that, even though the performance bond does not contain an agreement to arbitrate, typical performance bond language incorporates by reference the construction contract between the obligee and the principal and thereby imports the arbitration provision of the construction contract into the bond. Such incorporation operates to make the arbitration provision binding on

---

[*] Scott Lichtenstein of Wolff & Samson PC rendered substantial assistance with respect to the research and the preparation of this chapter.

[1] For a discussion of the critical advantages of litigation over arbitration, *see* United States *ex rel.* Pensacola Construction Co. v. St. Paul Fire and Marine Insurance Co., 705 F. Supp. 306, 313 (W.D. La. 1989), which held that, on the basis of such advantages, a payment bond surety under the Miller Act, 40 U.S.C.A. §§ 3131-34 (West 2005 & Supp. 2008), should not be bound by the results of an arbitration between the claimant and the principal when the surety had not agreed to arbitrate because binding the surety would be inconsistent with the surety's right under the Miller Act to a federal court adjudication of claims against it. *But see* U.S. *ex rel.* Skip Kirchdorfer, Inc. v. AEGIS/Zublin Joint Venture, 869 F. Supp. 387, 394-96 (E.D. Va. 1994) (assuming that arbitrators based their award in a Miller Act case on proper grounds).

the surety. Courts are divided on the question whether such incorporation warrants compelling the surety to submit its disputes with the obligee to arbitration for determination. The majority holds that it does. For the minority, the effect of an incorporated arbitration provision is limited to binding the surety to the result of the arbitration between the obligee and the principal as to disputes under the construction contract. On the other hand, it may be the surety which wishes to arbitrate and the obligee which seeks to avoid that forum. In general, the surety will be able to compel a reluctant obligee to arbitrate in a given jurisdiction to the same extent that the obligee could force the surety to arbitrate.

If a court orders the surety to arbitrate, the issue is decided, absent a desire to contest contempt sanctions. If, however, a court refuses to issue such an order or the obligee simply serves a demand for arbitration without seeking one, the surety may have the option of declining the obligee's invitation to arbitrate. The risk in choosing not to participate in the arbitration is that the obligee will prevail and seek to hold the surety liable on the basis of an award adverse to the principal. The preclusive effect against the surety which is accorded to an arbitration award against the principal varies widely from jurisdiction to jurisdiction. Some apply the traditional doctrines of res judicata and collateral estoppel, others fashion preclusion principles based on substantive suretyship law, and still others view the incorporation of the arbitration provision into the performance bond as the determining factor. Despite the variation, it is unlikely that the surety will be permitted to litigate anew the issue of the principal's liability, at least if the principal contested the arbitration or the surety had the opportunity to do so. If, however, the surety has personal defenses to a claim, its ability to litigate those defenses may well not be foreclosed by an arbitration award against the principal.

Any effort to navigate the complexities of such issues requires an understanding of the basic tenets of arbitration law, and a primer on that subject is presented in Part I of this chapter. Part II analyzes the bases upon which the surety may be compelled to arbitrate, while Part III does the same with respect to the obligee's obligation to arbitrate. Part IV discusses the consolidation of related arbitrations. Finally, Part V considers preclusion issues including the extent to which suretyship defenses may survive an arbitration award adverse to the principal.

I. Arbitration in General–A Brief Overview

A. *Statutory Framework*

At common law, a provision in a contract which required that future disputes arising therefrom be resolved by arbitration was generally unenforceable, and courts refused to compel an unwilling party to submit to arbitration in lieu of a court action.[2] Although some states adopted statutes to reverse those results, the effectiveness of such statutes was open to question.[3] As a result, the federal government enacted the Federal Arbitration Act[4] to make agreements to arbitrate enforceable,[5]

---

2   *See* Allied-Bruce Terminix Cos. v. Dobson, 513 U.S. 265, 270-71 (1995); Dean Witter Reynolds Inc. v. Byrd, 470 U.S. 213, 219-20 (1985).
3   Southland Corp. v. Keating, 465 U.S. 1, 14 (1984) ("The problems Congress faced [when enacting the Federal Arbitration Act] were twofold: the old common-law hostility toward arbitration, and the failure of state arbitration statutes to mandate enforcement of arbitration agreements.").
4   9 U.S.C.A. §§ 1-16 (West 1999 & Supp. 2008).
5   "[W]hen Congress passed the [Federal] Arbitration Act in 1925, it was 'motivated, first and foremost, by a desire' to change this antiarbitration rule." *Allied-Bruce Terminix Cos.*, 513 U.S. at 270-71 (quoting *Dean Witter Reynolds*, 470 U.S. at 220); *see also* Buckeye Check Cashing, Inc. v. Cardegna, 546 U.S. 440, 443 (2006) ("To overcome judicial resistance to arbitration, Congress enacted the Federal Arbitration Act"). As of 1995, "[o]nly Alabama, Mississippi, and Nebraska still hold all executory arbitration agreements to be unenforceable, though some other States refuse to enforce particular classes of such agreements," *Allied-Bruce Terminix Cos.*, 513 U.S. at 295 (Thomas, J., dissenting). For a discussion of arbitration in the suretyship context, *see* Jacqueline T. Lewis and James D. Ferrucci, *Bond Claimant vs. Surety's Principal in Arbitration– the Surety's Rights and Strategies* (unpublished paper submitted at the 18th Annual Northeast Surety & Fidelity Claims Conference on September 27-28, 2007); James D. Ferrucci, *Sureties and Arbitration– Some Issues and Strategies* (unpublished paper submitted at the 6th Annual Northeast Surety & Fidelity Claims Conference on November 16-17, 1995); Gregory R. Veal, *Arbitration and the Surety: When You Should, How Far You Should, and What If You Don't?* (unpublished paper submitted at the 6th Annual Southern Surety & Fidelity Claims Conference on Apr. 20-21, 1995).

and the states have adopted similar statutes.[6] In general, the federal statute and similar state statutes typically provide, among other things, that written agreements to arbitrate are "valid, irrevocable, and enforceable, save upon such grounds as exist at law or in equity for the revocation of any contract,"[7] that a court action brought upon any issue referable to arbitration under an arbitration agreement shall, "on the application of one of the parties," be stayed until arbitration has been had,[8] that upon the failure or refusal of a party to an arbitration agreement to arbitrate, the court "shall make an order directing the parties to proceed to arbitration in accordance with the terms of the agreement,"[9] and that a court shall enter judgment upon an arbitration award unless the award is vacated, modified or corrected in accordance with the statutes.[10]

The Federal Arbitration Act applies to, and makes enforceable, a written arbitration provision in "a contract evidencing a transaction

---

[6] Twenty-seven states and the District of Columbia adopted the 1956 version of the Uniform Arbitration Act, UNIF. ARBITRATION ACT §§ 1-25 (1956), 7 U.L.A. §§ 1-25 (West, Westlaw through 2006 Ann. Mtg. of Nat'l Conf.). *See id.* Gen. Notes, ULA ARB Refs. & Annos. (Table of Jurisdictions Wherein Act Has Been Adopted). In 2000, the National Conference of Commissioners on Uniform State Laws promulgated the Revised Uniform Arbitration Act, UNIF. ARBITRATION ACT §§ 1-33 (2000), 10 U.L.A. §§ 1-33 (West, Westlaw through 2007 Ann. Mtg. of Nat'l Conf.). The revised act has been adopted by Alaska which did not repeal the 1956 act when it adopted the revised act, by the District of Columbia which repealed the 1956 Act effective 2009, and by eleven additional states. *See id.* Gen. Notes, ULA ARB Refs. and Annos. (Table of Jurisdictions Wherein Act Has Been Adopted). For a discussion and compilation of state statutes generally, *see* Veal, *supra* note 5, at 2-4, app. A. The impact of the revised act in draft form is discussed at length in James L. Knoll, *Revised Uniform Arbitration Act–Draft 4, Key Elements of the Revision, in* ARBITRATION AND THE CONTRACT SURETY: WHEN BOUND TO THE PROCESS, ARE THE COURTS BEYOND REACH? (unpublished paper submitted at the ABA/TIPS Fidelity & Surety Law Committee and Alternative Dispute Resolution Committee program on August 9, 1999 at the 1999 ABA Annual Meeting).

[7] 9 U.S.C.A. § 2; *see also* 7 U.L.A. § 1; 10 U.L.A. § 6(a).
[8] 9 U.S.C.A. § 3; *see also* 7 U.L.A. § 2(d); 10 U.L.A. § 7(g).
[9] 9 U.S.C.A. § 4; *see also* 7 U.L.A. § 2(a); 10 U.L.A. § 7(a).
[10] 9 U.S.C.A. § 9; *see also* 7 U.L.A. §§ 11, 14; 10 U.L.A. §§ 22, 25.

involving commerce"[11] which is defined as both interstate and international commerce.[12] The Supreme Court has held that the words "involving commerce" are the functional equivalent of the term "affecting commerce" and therefore "signal the broadest permissible exercise of Congress' Commerce Clause power."[13] In the context of arbitration provisions in construction contracts, parties opposing arbitration have argued that because the actual construction activities took place in a single state, the interstate commerce requirement was not satisfied and that even if a project involved some interstate activity, the federal statute required substantial interstate contacts. Those arguments were rejected in *Del E. Webb Construction v. Richardson Hospital Authority*.[14] There, the court found that even though the general contractor maintained a substantial in-state presence, it was from another state, some of its employees traveled interstate, and mail and materials used for the project moved interstate. Those facts were sufficient to meet

---

11   9 U.S.C.A. § 2.
12   *Id.* § 1.
13   Citizens Bank v. Alafabco, Inc., 539 U.S. 52, 56 (2003); Allied-Bruce Terminix Cos. v. Dobson, 513 U.S. 265, 277 (1995); *see also* Perry v. Thomas, 482 U.S. 483, 490 (1987) (the Federal Arbitration Act provides for "the enforcement of arbitration agreements within the full reach of the Commerce Clause."); Foster v. Turley, 808 F.2d 38, 40 (10th Cir. 1986) (the commerce requirement "is to be broadly construed so as to be coextensive with congressional power to regulate under the Commerce Clause."); Snyder v. Smith, 736 F.2d 409, 418 (7th Cir. 1984) ("Congress intended the [Federal Arbitration Act] to apply to all contracts that it could constitutionally regulate."), *overruled on other grounds* by Felzen v. Andreas, 134 F.3d 873 (7th Cir. 1998).
14   823 F.2d 145 (5th Cir. 1987). The United States Supreme Court's decision in *Green Tree Financial Corp. v. Bazzle*, 539 U.S. 444 (2003), is regarded has having effectively overruled *Del E. Webb*'s holding that the court, rather than the arbitrator, should decide whether an arbitration agreement permits consolidation, Pedcor Mgmt. Co., Inc. Welfare Benefit Plan v. Nations Personnel of Tex., Inc., 343 F.3d 355, 363 (5th Cir. 2003); *see* discussion *infra* Parts IV.A.1-B.1. The Fifth Circuit's rulings as to the interstate commerce requirement of section 2, however, remain intact.

the commerce requirement.[15] The commerce requirement has been found to have been satisfied as to a construction project when the only interstate connections were that paint used by the painting contractor was manufactured out of state and that the contractor's surety was headquartered in another state.[16]

Because of its reach, the Federal Arbitration Act is likely to apply to all but the smallest and most local construction projects.[17] Moreover, the Act "creates a body of federal substantive law"[18] which embodies "a congressional declaration of a liberal federal policy favoring arbitration agreements, notwithstanding any state substantive or procedural policies to the contrary."[19] When applicable, the Federal Arbitration Act governs the construction and enforceability of agreements to arbitrate, and state courts as well as federal courts are bound to apply the substantive federal law.[20] Accordingly, the Act preempts any state laws which "undercut the enforceability of arbitration agreements"[21] because "Congress [has] declared a national policy favoring arbitration and withdrew the power of the states to require a judicial forum for the resolution of claims which

---

15 *Del E. Webb*, 823 F.2d at 147-48.
16 Lost Creek Mun. Util. Dist. v. Travis Indus. Painters, Inc., 827 S.W.2d 103, 105 (Tex. App. 1992).
17 For a discussion of the scope of the Federal Arbitration Act in general and its applicability to construction disputes, *see* Ferrucci, *supra* note 5, at 10-13.
18 Moses H. Cone Mem'l Hosp. v. Mercury Constr. Corp., 460 U.S. 1, 25 n.32 (1983) (applying the Act to a dispute arising under a construction contract).
19 *Id.* at 24.
20 *Id.* at 25; *accord* Alfano v. BDO Seidman, LLP, 925 A.2d 22, 30 (N.J. Super. Ct. App. Div. 2007) ("The arbitration agreement between the parties unquestionably is governed by the [Federal Arbitration Act], notwithstanding the filing of the action in state court."); Industra/Matrix Joint Venture v. Pope & Talbot, Inc., 142 P.3d 1044, 1050-51 (Or. 2006) (holding that federal substantive law governs issue of arbitrability even though the arbitration provision mandated that the state arbitration statute apply to any arbitration hearings).
21 Southland Corp. v. Keating, 465 U.S. 1, 16 (1984) (holding that a California franchise investment statute, construed by California courts to nullify an agreement to arbitrate disputes arising under that statute, was preempted by the Federal Arbitration Act).

the contracting parties agreed to resolve by arbitration."[22] Nevertheless, because the purpose of the federal statute is to "place arbitration agreements on equal footing with all other contracts,"[23] state law may invalidate arbitration agreements on the basis of defenses which apply to all contracts, such as fraud, duress, or unconscionablity.[24] State "[c]ourts may not, however, invalidate arbitration agreements under state laws applicable *only* to arbitration provisions."[25]

B. Limited Judicial Review of Arbitration Awards

As a general proposition, an arbitrator's ruling is, for all practical purposes, virtually unreviewable on the merits. The Federal Arbitration Act and typical state statutes permit judicial vacatur of an arbitration

---

22   *Id.* at 10.
23   Buckeye Check Cashing, Inc. v. Cardegna, 546 U.S. 440, 443-44 (2006) (noting that the Federal Arbitration Act makes agreements to arbitrate enforceable "save upon such grounds as exist at law or in equity for the revocation of any contract."); 9 U.S.C.A. § 2 (West 1999).
24   Doctor's Assocs., Inc. v. Casarotto, 517 U.S. 681, 687 (1996).
25   *Id.* In *Doctor's Associates*, the Supreme Court held that a Montana statute which required that a contract with an arbitration clause must contain on the first page a notice, in underlined capital letters, that the contract is subject to arbitration is incompatible with, and therefore preempted by, the Federal Arbitration Act because the special notice requirement was imposed on only contracts providing for arbitration and was not applicable to contracts generally. *Id.* The proponent of the Montana statute argued that the notice requirement was permissible under Volt Information Sciences, Inc. v. Board of Trustees of Leland Stanford Junior University, 489 U.S. 468 (1989) which upheld a California statute authorizing a court to stay an arbitration pending resolution of a related litigation when there was a possibility of inconsistent rulings. The Court rejected the argument because *Volt* involved only a state procedural rule which "did not affect the enforceability of the arbitration agreement itself." *Doctor's Assocs.*, 517 U.S. at 688. By contrast, the Montana statute would invalidate the agreement to arbitrate absent the first-page notice requirement and that such "threshold limitations placed specifically and solely on arbitration provisions" are "antithetical" to the goals and policies of the Federal Arbitration Act. *Id.*

award only on specified and very narrow grounds which pertain generally to the fairness of the arbitration process itself. The federal statute, for example, permits a court to vacate an award where the award was procured by corruption, fraud, or undue means; where there was evident partiality or corruption of the arbitrators; where a reasonable postponement of hearings was not granted, material evidence was not heard, or the arbitrator engaged in prejudicial misbehavior; or where the arbitrators exceeded their powers or failed to render a mutual, final and definite award upon the subject matter submitted.[26] Resolving a split among the courts of appeal, the Supreme Court recently held that the grounds stated in the Federal Arbitration Act for vacating or modifying an arbitration award are exclusive when the "expedited" procedures of the Act are invoked and the parties may not expand upon them by contract.[27]

---

26   9 U.S.C.A. § 10(a) (West 1999 & Supp. 2008). Both versions of the uniform act specify similar grounds. UNIF. ARBITRATION ACT § 12 (1956), 7 U.L.A. § 12 (West, Westlaw through 2006 Ann. Mtg. of Nat'l Conf.); UNIF. ARBITRATION ACT § 23 (2000), 10 U.L.A. § 23 (West, Westlaw through 2007 Ann. Mtg. of Nat'l Conf.). The grounds for vacating an arbitration award are discussed fully with an appended state-by-state analysis in Laird E. Lawrence & Christopher R. Ward, *The Availability and Scope of Appeal of Arbitration Awards Under the Federal, Uniform, and State Acts*, in ARBITRATION AND THE CONTRACT SURETY: WHEN BOUND TO THE PROCESS, ARE THE COURTS BEYOND REACH? (unpublished paper submitted at the ABA/TIPS Fidelity & Surety Law Committee and Alternative Dispute Resolution Committee program on August 9, 1999 at the 1999 ABA Annual Meeting).

27   Hall St. Assocs., L.L.C. v. Mattel, Inc., 128 S.Ct. 1396 (2008) (holding that an award may not be vacated under the Federal Arbitration Act for the arbitrator's erroneous conclusions of law even though the parties' agreement expressly provided for vacatur on that ground). The Court noted, however, that the Federal Arbitration Act "is not the only way into court for parties wanting review of arbitration awards: they may contemplate enforcement under state statutory or common law, for example, where judicial review of different scope is arguable." *Id.* at 1406. Under the Federal Arbitration Act, an application for an order confirming, vacating or modifying an arbitration award "will get streamlined treatment as a motion, obviating the separate contract action that would usually be necessary to enforce or tinker with an arbitral award in court." *Id.* at 1402. If litigants want to take advantage of this

Parties disappointed with the merits of an arbitration award have often sought a vacatur by trying to clothe their objections in the guise of one of the statutory grounds; they have usually failed. The following is a typical example of a court's response:

> Thus, in reviewing arbitral awards, a district or appellate court is limited to determining whether the arbitrators did the job they were told to do – not whether they did it well, or correctly, or reasonably, but simply whether they did it. Courts are not free to overturn an arbitral result because they would have reached a different conclusion if presented with the same facts. . . .
>
> . . . .
>
> . . . The statutory grounds for vacatur permit challenges on sufficiently improper conduct in the course of the proceedings; they do not permit rejection of an arbitral award based on disagreement with the particular result the arbitrators reached. Accordingly, parties may not seek a second bite at the apple simply because they desire a different outcome. To permit such attempts would transform a binding process into a purely advisory one.[28]

"FAA shortcut," *id.* at 1403, they are limited to the grounds for vacatur as provided in that statute and may not expand them by agreement. Speaking of *Hall St. Assocs.*, one district court recently said that "[t]he scope of review is so narrow that unless 'dishonesty is alleged, an arbitrator's improvident, even silly, fact finding does not provide a basis' to set aside an award." Andorra Servs., Inc. v. M/T Eos, Civil Action No. 06-373 (PGS), 2008 WL 4960449, at *2 (D.N.J. Nov. 20, 2008) (quoting Gateway Funding Diversified Mortgage Servs., L.P. v. Field, Civil Action No. 04-4428, 2008 WL 2758877, at *6 (E.D. Pa. July 10, 2008) (quoting United Paperworkers Int'l Union v. Misco, Inc., 484 U.S. 29, 39 (1987), (decided under the Labor Management Relations Act of 1974, 29 U.S.C.A. §§ 171-187 (West 1998 & Supp. 2008), because the Federal Arbitration Act does not "apply to contracts of employment of . . . workers engaged in foreign or interstate commerce," 9 U.S.C.A. § 1 (West 1999)).

28 Remmey v. PaineWebber, Inc., 32 F.3d 143, 146 (4th Cir. 1994) (internal quotation marks omitted) (citations omitted). *See also* Grundstad v. Ritt, 166 F.3d 867, 872 (7th Cir. 1999) ("[F]ederal courts do not sit in review of an arbitrator's interpretation of a contract absent extraordinary circumstances").

The most generous statement that one is likely to find as to a court's power to vacate an arbitrator's decision is that "a court may vacate an award if the conduct of the arbitrator constitutes 'manifest disregard' of applicable law."[29] Such statements, however, are usually accompanied by qualifications such as the following: "'that a court is convinced [the arbitrator] committed serious error does not suffice to overturn his decision.'"[30] That any difference between "manifest disregard of applicable law" and "serious error" would appear to be evanescent at best only emphasizes the unwillingness of courts to review an arbitrator's ruling on the merits. In its recent holding that the statutory grounds for vacatur are exclusive, the Supreme Court summed up as follows:

> [I]t makes more sense to see the three provisions, §§ 9-11, as substantiating a national policy favoring arbitration with just the limited review needed to maintain arbitration's essential virtue of resolving disputes straightaway. Any other reading opens the door to the full-bore legal and evidentiary appeals that can "rende[r] informal arbitration merely a prelude to a more cumbersome and time-consuming judicial review process," and bring arbitration theory to grief in post-arbitration process.[31]

---

29 NCR Corp. v. Sac-Co., Inc., 43 F.3d 1076, 1079 (6th Cir. 1995) (internal quotation marks omitted) (citations omitted). *See also* Wilko v. Swan, 346 U.S. 427, 436-37 (1953) (holding that parties bound by arbitrator's decision on the merits which is not in "manifest disregard" of the law), *overruled on other grounds* by Rodriguez de Quijas v. Shearson/American Express, Inc., 490 U.S. 477 (1989).

30 *Id.* (footnote omitted) (internal quotation marks omitted) (citations omitted). Some jurisdictions take an even more limited view by refusing to overturn an award even for "manifest disregard of the law," "gross errors of law," or errors of law as to principles which are not "reasonably debatable," Perini Corp. v. Greate Bay Hotel & Casino, Inc., 610 A.2d 364, 397-99 (N.J. 1992) (Wilentz, C.J., concurring), *concurring opinion adopted by* Tretina Printing, Inc. v. Fitzpatrick & Assocs., Inc., 640 A.2d 788, 792-93 (N.J. 1994).

31 *Hall St. Assocs*, 128 S.Ct. at 1405 (quoting Kyocera Corp. v. Prudential-Bache Trade Servs., Inc., 341 F.3d 987, 998 (9th Cir. 2003) and citing Ethyl Corp. v. United Steelworkers of Am., 768 F.2d 180, 184 (7th Cir. 1985)). In *Lewis v. Circuit City Stores, Inc.*, 500 F.3d 1140 (10th Cir. 2000), the losing party in an arbitration sued the same party on the same

Despite the desire to limit judicial review of arbitration awards, a payment bond surety has been permitted to maintain an action to vacate or modify an award even though it was not a party to the arbitration proceeding. In *Westra Construction, Inc. v. United States Fidelity & Guaranty Co.*,[32] the court observed that although sections 10 and 11 of the Federal Arbitration Act restricted the right to seek review of an award to parties to the arbitration,[33] nonparties who are adversely affected are sometimes allowed to challenge an award.[34] The court applied that exception to the surety because the surety knew of, but did not join, the arbitration and therefore might be bound by the award[35] and because the surety relied upon the principal to seek review of the award and the principal's unexpected bankruptcy filing deprived the surety of that opportunity.[36]

---

claim. In affirming dismissal on res judicata grounds, the Tenth Circuit observed that "[c]ourts cannot prevent parties from trying to convert arbitration losses into court victories, but it may be that we can and should insist that if a party on the short end of an arbitration award attacks that award in court without any real legal basis for doing so, that party should pay sanctions," *id.* at 1154. Nevertheless, the court denied sanctions, finding that although the claims were "meritless," they were not "completely frivolous," *id.*

32 Civil Action No. 1:03-CV-0833, 2006 WL 1149252, at *2 (M.D. Pa. Apr. 28, 2006).

33 9 U.S.C.A. § 10(a) (court may vacate an award "upon the application of any party to the arbitration"); *id.* § 11(a) (court may modify an award "upon the application of any party to the arbitration").

34 *Westra*, 2006 WL 1149252 at *2 (citing Ass'n of Contracting Plumbers of City of New York, Inc. v. Local Union No. 2 United Ass'n of Journeymen, 841 F.2d 461, 466-67 (2d Cir. 1988) and Bruscianelli v. Triemstra, No. 99-C-6446, 2000 WL 1100439, at *1 (N.D. Ill. Aug. 4, 2000)).

35 The preclusive effect of an award on a surety which had notice of, and the opportunity to defend in, the arbitration is discussed *infra* Part V.B.2.b.

36 *Westra*, 2006 WL 1149252 at *2.

C. The Consensual Nature of Arbitration

While establishing that the Federal Arbitration Act embodies a strong federal policy in favor of arbitration, the United States Supreme Court has also reaffirmed that any duty to submit to arbitration can arise only from a party's consent.[37] In *AT&T Technologies, Inc. v. Communications Workers of America*,[38] the court reviewed the basic precepts underlying arbitration and stated:

> The first principle . . . is that "arbitration is a matter of contract and a party cannot be required to submit to arbitration any dispute which he has not agreed so to submit." This axiom recognizes the fact that arbitrators derive their authority to resolve disputes only because the parties have agreed in advance to submit such grievances to arbitration.[39]

That requirement was invoked by the First Circuit to deny arbitration of claims arising out of a contract to purchase corporate stock in *McCarthy v. Azure*.[40] After reiterating that a "party seeking to substitute an arbitral forum for a judicial forum must show, at a bare minimum, that the protagonists have agreed to arbitrate *some* claims,"[41] the court also observed that "[t]his imperative is in no way inconsistent with the acknowledged 'federal policy favoring arbitration.'"[42] The court

---

37 Howsam v. Dean Witter Reynolds, Inc., 537 U.S. 79, 83 (2002).
38 475 U.S. 643 (1986).
39 *Id.* at 648-49 (quoting United Steel Workers of Am. v. Warrior & Gulf Navigation Co., 363 U.S. 574, 582 (1960)) (citation omitted). The Supreme Court has also held that "[w]hen deciding whether the parties agreed to arbitrate a certain matter ..., courts generally ... should apply ordinary state-law principles that govern the formation of contracts." First Options of Chicago, Inc. v. Kaplan, 514 U.S. 938, 944 (1995).
40 22 F.3d 351 (1st Cir. 1994).
41 *Id.* at 354-55; *accord* IDS Life Ins. Co. v. SunAmerica, Inc., 103 F.3d 524, 529 (7th Cir. 1996); Thomson-CSF, S.A. v. Am. Arbitration Ass'n, 64 F.3d 773, 776 (2d Cir. 1995).
42 *McCarthy*, 22 F.3d at 355 (quoting Moses H. Cone Mem'l Hosp. v. Mercury Constr. Corp., 460 U.S. 1, 24 (1983)); *accord* MPACT Constr. Group, LLC v. Superior Concrete Constructors, Inc., 802 N.E.2d 901, 906 (Ind. 2004).

explained that the federal policy applies once an agreement to arbitrate has been demonstrated and requires that doubts as to the scope of the agreement be resolved in favor of arbitration. The court further explained that requiring arbitration to rest on a consensual basis can also be viewed in terms of one's right to seek relief in the courts:

> Subject matter jurisdiction over an action or series of claims can be conceptualized as conferring a personal right on the parties to have that action, or those claims, adjudicated in a judicial forum. Though a person may, by contract, waive his or her right to adjudication, *see* 9 U.S.C. § 2, there can be no waiver in the absence of an agreement signifying an assent.[43]

Thus, under the Federal Arbitration Act, the authority of courts to order parties to proceed with arbitration[44] or to stay an action to permit

---

43 *McCarthy*, 22 F.3d at 355. "[A] party who has not agreed to arbitrate will normally have a right to a court's decision about the merits of its dispute...." *First Options*, 514 U.S. at 942. Because of the consensual basis of arbitration, the question of arbitrability is "an exception" to the pro-arbitration federal policy and "is 'an issue for judicial [as opposed to arbitral] determination [u]nless the parties clearly and unmistakably provide otherwise.'" Howsam v. Dean Witter Reynolds, Inc., 537 U.S. 79, 83 (2002) (quoting *AT&T Technologies*, 475 U.S. at 649); *see also First Options*, 514 U.S. at 944 ("Courts should not assume that the parties agreed to arbitrate arbitrability unless there is clea[r] and unmistakabl[e] evidence that they did so") (internal quotation marks omitted), *distinguished in* Green Tree Fin. Corp. v. Bazzle, 539 U.S. 444, 452 (2003) (holding that whether the arbitration agreement permitted class arbitration is a question which falls outside of the narrow class of "gateway" questions of arbitrability and therefore is to be decided by the arbitrator), discussed in detail *infra* Part IV.A.2. Questions of "procedural" arbitrability, such as whether contractual conditions precedent to arbitration have been met, are presumptively for the arbitrator, not the judge. *Howsam*, 537 U.S. at 84 (holding that whether a NASD limitations rule barred an arbitration demand was a procedural issue for the arbitrator to decide); *see also* UNIFORM ARBITRATION ACT § 6(c), 10 U.L.A. § 6(c) (2000) (West, Westlaw through 2007 Ann. Mtg. of Nat'l Conf.) ("An arbitrator shall decide whether a condition precedent to arbitrability has been fulfilled ....").

44 9 U.S.C.A. § 4 (West 1999).

arbitration[45] presupposes, and requires a showing, that the party sought to be compelled to arbitrate entered into an agreement to do so.[46]

II. The Surety's Obligation to Arbitrate

A surety is no different from any other party when it comes to arbitration: in the absence of a preexisting agreement to arbitrate, the surety may not be compelled to submit to arbitration against its wishes.[47] The contract between the obligee and the performance bond surety is the

---

45 *Id.* § 3.
46 *See IDS Life Ins. Co.*, 103 F.3d at 529 (holding that guarantors which were not parties to an arbitration agreement were not entitled to a stay of the action commenced by the plaintiffs which were parties to that agreement); *but cf.* Westra Constr., Inc. v. U.S. Fid. & Guar. Co., Civil Action No. 1:03-CV-0833, 2006 WL 1149252, at *2 (M.D. Pa. Apr. 28, 2006) (permitting a surety to seek to modify or vacate an arbitration award even though it was not a party to the arbitration). Guarantors and sureties so resemble one another that generally the same principles of law apply to both, *see* RESTATEMENT (THIRD) OF SURETYSHIP AND GUARANTY § 1 cmt. c (1996), including arbitration law, *see, e.g.*, Grundstad v. Ritt, 106 F.3d 201, 204 (7th Cir. 1997) ("'Guarantors and sureties for the performance of a contract are bound by the arbitration clause in that contract only when they expressly agree to the obligation to arbitrate,'" (quoting 1 DOMKE ON COMMERCIAL ARBITRATION § 10.07, at 133 (Supp. 1996))); Gingiss Int'l, Inc. v. Bormet, 58 F.3d 328, 331-32 (7th Cir. 1995) ("Under federal law, a subcontract with a guarantor or surety may incorporate a duty to arbitrate by reference to an arbitration clause in a general contract." (footnote omitted) (citation omitted)); Scinto v. Sosin, 721 A.2d 552, 559-60 (Conn. App. Ct. 1998) (citing *Grundstad* and holding that guarantors of a construction contract with an arbitration clause were not obligated to arbitrate with the owner because the guaranties did not expressly incorporate the contract).
47 *See, e.g., Grundstad*, 106 F.3d at 205 (holding that guarantors of the performance of a non-competition agreement had not agreed to arbitrate a claim of a breach of that agreement); *Scinto*, 721 A.2d at 559-60 (holding that guarantors of a construction contract had not agreed to arbitrate a claim of breach of the contract); *In re* Interactive Video Res., Inc., 170 B.R. 716, 722 (S.D. Fla. 1994) (holding that a surety on a contract for the production of video "courseware" had not agreed to arbitrate a claim of a breach of that agreement).

performance bond which has been referred to as "the surety contract,"[48] the "bond agreement"[49] or "the suretyship agreement"[50] and which typically does not contain an arbitration provision. Thus, even if the principal's contract with the obligee contained an arbitration provision, the surety did not sign that contract, and cannot be compelled to arbitrate as a party to that contract unless there is some basis for finding that the surety otherwise consented to arbitrate pursuant to that contract.

There is such a basis. A substantial body of law holds that the performance bond's incorporation of the construction contract binds the surety to an arbitration clause in that contract. Such arbitration clauses typically provide that the obligee and the principal will arbitrate disputes arising under the construction contact.[51] Nevertheless, most courts which have considered the issue have held, at least implicitly, that an incorporated arbitration provision has the effect of making the surety a party to the agreement to arbitrate and, on that basis, have concluded that the surety has an enforceable obligation to arbitrate its performance bond liability with the obligee.[52] A minority holds that the terms of such an arbitration clause, even though incorporated, do not call for arbitration by the surety and therefore can provide no basis for ordering the surety to arbitrate.[53] Because of the majority's expansive reading of the incorporated arbitration provision, that approach may appropriately be characterized as "super incorporation."[54] Conversely, the minority's literal view can accurately be called "limited incorporation." Under limited incorporation, only the obligee and the principal may be compelled to arbitrate, but the surety will be bound by the results of that proceeding. The performing surety which has taken over completion of

---

48 Choctaw Generation Ltd. P'ship v. Am. Home Assurance Co., 271 F.3d 403, 404, 406 (2d Cir. 2001).
49 Matson, Inc. v. Lamb & Assocs. Packaging, Inc., 947 S.W.2d 324, 325 (Ark. 1997).
50 Bolingbrook Park Dist. v. Nat'l–Ben Franklin Ins. Co. of Ill., 420 N.E.2d 741, 743 (Ill. App. Ct. 1981).
51 *See infra* discussion accompanying notes 69-70.
52 *See* discussion *infra* Part II.A.2.
53 *See* discussion *infra* Part II.A.3-4.
54 The majority position has been described as "an expansive view of incorporation by reference . . . ." C.I. Steel, LLC v. Travelers Cas. & Sur. Co. of Am., 876 N.E.2d 442, 451 (Mass. App. Ct. 2007) (Brown, J., dissenting).

the bonded project may be compelled to arbitrate with the obligee without the application of incorporation by reference. By undertaking completion in accordance with the principal's contract, the surety assumes the obligations of the principal's contract including the obligation to arbitrate disputes with the obligee if the contract contains an arbitration clause.[55] Moreover, there is at least one state statute which requires a surety to arbitrate and thereby provides a basis for an order compelling it to do so.[56] Even when the surety is not held to have an enforceable obligation to arbitrate, however, the prospect of being bound by an award rendered against the principal in an arbitration with the obligee may create an incentive to participate in that arbitration which effectively, though indirectly, compels the surety to arbitrate.[57]

A. Direct Compulsion–Incorporation by Reference

1. Incorporation–The Basic Principle

While a party cannot be forced to arbitrate unless it has consented to do so, the expression of that consent need not be limited to the party's signing an agreement which contains an arbitration provision. "[A]s a matter of contract law, incorporation by reference is generally effective to accomplish its intended purpose where . . . the provision to which reference is made has a reasonably clear and ascertainable meaning."[58]

---

55   *See* discussion *infra* Part II.B.
56   *See* discussion *infra* Part II.D.
57   *See* discussion *infra* Part II.C.
58   J. S. & H. Constr. Co. v. Richmond County Hosp. Auth., 473 F.2d 212, 215 (5th Cir. 1973) (holding that an arbitration provision in a prime contract which was incorporated by reference in a subcontract was binding on the subcontractor). *See also* Thomson-CSF, S.A. v. Am. Arbitration Ass'n, 64 F.3d 773, 776-77 (2d Cir. 1995) (recognizing incorporation by reference as one of five "common law principles of contract and agency law" under which a nonsignatory may be bound to the arbitration agreement of others); Choctaw Generation Ltd. P'ship v. Am. Home Assurance Co., 271 F.3d 403, 404 (2d Cir. 2001) (holding that an obligee was estopped by its execution of a construction contract with an arbitration provision from avoiding arbitration with a surety, even though the surety was not a party to that contract, when issues which the surety sought to resolve were intertwined with the construction contract); *see generally* Randy J. Sutton, Annotation, *Enforcement of Arbitration*

Agreement Contained in Construction Contract by or Against Nonsignatory, 100 A.L.R. 5th 481 §§ 3-6 (2002) (discussing enforcement against nonsignatory); 6 PHILIP L. BRUNER & PATRICK J. O'CONNOR, JR., BRUNER & O'CONNOR ON CONSTRUCTION LAW § 20:71 (2002) (discussing enforcement of arbitration provisions by or against sureties as nonsignatories). To be effective, however, the incorporating instrument must expressly, specifically and unambiguously refer to and incorporate the underlying agreement. *Compare* Grundstad v. Ritt, 106 F.3d 201, 203 (7th Cir. 1997) (holding that the guarantors' statement, which appeared on the underlying agreement, that "'[w]e hereby guarantee all of the provisions of the within Agreement'" was insufficient to bind the guarantors to the arbitration provision of the underlying agreement) *with* Gingiss Int'l, Inc. v. Bormet, 58 F.3d at 330, 332 (7th Cir. 1995) (holding that the guarantors' written agreement to be bound by all of the obligations of a franchisee under an identified franchise agreement constituted an express incorporation of the arbitration provision of the franchise agreement). In *Kvaerner ASA v. Bank of Tokyo-Mitsubishi, Ltd., N.Y. Branch*, 210 F.3d 262 (4th Cir. 2000), guarantors which guaranteed a joint venture's performance of a construction contract sought to compel the financing bank to arbitrate its claim under the guaranties that the joint venture failed to substantially complete the project. The court held that a guaranty provision which gave the guarantors "'the same rights and remedies'" as the joint venture "'operate[d] to incorporate into the Guaranties the rights and remedies available to the joint venture under the Construction Agreement,'" *id.* at 265 (quoting guaranty), and that as the bank's failure-to-complete claim related to the construction contract, the bank was required to arbitrate that claim, *id.* at 266. But *cf.* Dunn Indus. Group, Inc. v. City of Sugar Creek, 112 S.W.3d 421, 436 (Mo. 2003) (en banc) (holding that the guarantor was not required to arbitrate because "[m]ere reference to [as opposed to incorporation of] the construction contract in the guaranty is insufficient to establish that [the guarantor] bound itself to the arbitration provision of the construction contract." (citing *Grundstad*, 105 F.3d at 205)). Typically, the incorporating language of performance bonds is sufficiently explicit to meet this standard easily. *See* cases cited *infra* notes 69-70. In *AgGrow Oils, L.L.C. v. National Union Fire Insurance Co. of Pittsburgh, Pa.*, 242 F.3d 777, 781-82 (8th Cir. 2001) (applying North Dakota law), discussed in detail *infra* Part II.A.3-4, however, the court found that the incorporation clause of the performance bond was ambiguous in that it did not clearly reflect an agreement between the surety and the obligee to arbitrate disputes between them. As there was no agreement to arbitrate, the surety was not entitled to a stay of the obligee's performance bond lawsuit against it. In a

Accordingly, performance bond sureties have been held to have agreed to arbitrate the obligee's claim when the bond incorporated by reference the principal's contract with the obligee and that contract contained an arbitration provision. The opinion in *Cianbro Corp. v. Empresa Nacional de Ingeniera y Technologia, S.A.*[59] presents a typical scenario. The surety in that case issued a performance bond which secured the principal's subcontract with the general contractor. In familiar language, the bond declared that the "subcontract is by reference made a part hereof,"[60] and the subcontract included an arbitration clause. When the surety refused to arbitrate the obligee's claim, the obligee sought to compel the surety to arbitrate pursuant to section 4 of the Federal Arbitration Act.[61] The surety argued in opposition that because it was not a party to the subcontract and its bond did not contain any arbitration provision, it had never agreed to arbitrate and could not be compelled to do so against its will. Relying on the effectiveness of incorporation by reference, the court answered that by issuing a performance bond which incorporated a contract with an arbitration clause, the surety "ha[d] voluntarily agreed to

---

later case involving identical bond language, *Liberty Mutual Insurance Co. v. Mandaree Public School District # 36*, 503 F.3d 709 (5th Cir. 2007), *aff'g* 459 F. Supp. 2d 866 (D.N.D. 2006), the obligee sought to stay the surety's suit and to compel the surety to arbitrate. There, the Eighth Circuit abandoned any ambiguity argument and held simply that the incorporation provision of the performance bond did not reflect a mutual intent to arbitrate obligee-surety disputes. *Id.* at 711. The court in WindowMaster Corp. v. B. G. Danis Co., 511 F. Supp. 157 (S.D. Ohio 1981) (applying Ohio law), *disapproved of by* Exchange Mutual Insurance Co. v. Haskell Co., 742 F.2d 274, 276 (6th Cir. 1984), also found that the performance bond did not create an agreement to arbitrate between the surety and the obligee. Though the opinion is unclear, it appears that the subcontract performance bond may not have incorporated the subcontract because, although incorporation cases were discussed, there is no suggestion in the opinion that the obligee's contentions in support of its application to compel the surety to arbitrate included an incorporation argument.

59   697 F. Supp. 15 (D. Me. 1988).
60   *Id.* at 16 n.2.
61   9 U.S.C.A. § 4 (West 1999).

arbitrate disputes consistent with that clause."[62] Accordingly, the court entered an order compelling the surety to arbitrate. A number of other courts, both federal and state, have adopted that reasoning to compel a performance bond surety to arbitrate with the obligee.[63] Still other courts,

---

62   *Cianbro Corp.*, 697 F. Supp. at 20. The court also stated that the "strong federal policy favoring arbitration back[ed]" its decision to compel the surety to arbitrate, *id.* at 18. That argument, which is typically cited in such cases, *see* cases cited *infra* note 89, is unpersuasive. As the First Circuit pointed out in McCarthy v. Azure, 22 F.3d 351, 354-55 (1st Cir. 1994), the policy favoring arbitration does not come into play in deciding whether a party has made an agreement to arbitrate but only after such an agreement has been established and the issue is whether its scope encompasses the particular dispute in question.

63   *See, e.g.*, Jewish Fed'n of Greater New Orleans v. Fid. & Deposit Co. of Md., No. 01-30371, 273 F.3d 1094, 2001 WL 1085096, at *1 (5th Cir. Aug. 29, 2001) (unpublished table decision) (2-1 decision) (King, C.J., dissenting) (holding that because the performance bond incorporated a construction contract with a broad arbitration provision, the surety was required to arbitrate its limitation defense with the obligee); U.S. Fid. & Guar. Co. v. West Point Constr. Co., Inc., 837 F.2d 1507, 1508 (11th Cir. 1988) (stating that the performance bond "incorporated by reference" the bonded contract and therefore expressed the intention of the surety to arbitrate disputes concerning "the adequacy of [the principal's] performance"); Exch. Mut. Ins. Co. v. Haskell Co., 742 F.2d 274, 276 (6th Cir. 1984) (holding that the surety was required to arbitrate the obligee's claim because the performance bond incorporated the bonded subcontract and the subcontract incorporated the general contract which contained an arbitration provision); Compania Espanola de Petroleos, S.A. v. Nereus Shipping, S.A., 527 F.2d 966, 973-74 (2d Cir. 1975) (holding that a guaranty, which provided that the guarantor of the obligations of the charterer under a maritime shipping contract was "'to assume the rights and obligations of [the charterer] on the same terms and conditions as contained in [the shipping contract]' as well as [to] 'perform the balance of the contract,'" required the guarantor to arbitrate the claim of the vessel owner pursuant to the arbitration provision of the shipping contract); Shores of Pan. Inc. v. Safeco Ins. Co. of Am., Civil Action No. 07-00602-KD-B, 2008 WL 4417558, at *2 (S.D. Ala. Sept. 29, 2008) (staying the obligee's court action against the surety and, because the performance bond incorporated a construction contract with arbitration provision, ordering the surety to participate, and resolve the issue of its bond liability, in the pending arbitration between the obligee

and principal); U.S. Sur. Co. v. Hanover R.S. Ltd. P'ship, 543 F. Supp. 2d 492, 495-96 (W.D.N.C. 2008) (holding that the incorporation of a broad arbitration provision in subcontract performance bond required the surety to arbitrate the obligee's bond claim and suretyship defenses thereto); Spinks v. Krystal Co., C.A. No. 6:07-2619-HMH, 2007 WL 4568992, at *1 (D.S.C. Dec. 20, 2007) (holding that guaranty agreements, which provided that the guarantors agreed to be bound by every provision of the guaranteed franchise agreements, incorporated the arbitration provision of the franchise agreements and therefore required the guarantors to arbitrate the franchisor's claims); Capitol Indem. Corp. v. Dayton Bd. of Educ., 492 F. Supp. 2d 829, 836 (S.D. Ohio 2006), *reconsideration den.*, No. 3:03cv404, 2006 WL 2233429, at *1 (S.D. Ohio Aug. 3, 2006) (holding that the performance bonds incorporated construction contracts requiring arbitration and therefore the surety was required to arbitrate the issue of its liability under bonds with the obligee); Ohio Cas. Co. v. City of Moberly, Mo., No. 4:05 CV 5 JCH, 2005 WL 2491461, at *3 (E.D. Mo. Oct. 7, 2005) (holding that the surety was bound by the incorporated arbitration provision "the same as it would be if there were an arbitration agreement in the Bond itself and therefore surety is obligated to arbitrate its surety defenses to obligee's bond claim"); Fid. & Guar. Ins. Co. v. West Point Reality, Inc., No. 02 Civ. 1951 LMM, 2002 WL 1933780, at *5 n.3 (S.D.N.Y. Aug. 21, 2002) (in a confusing opinion, also discussed *infra* note 158, holding that the arbitration provision had been incorporated into both the performance bond and the takeover agreement and therefore ordering the surety to arbitrate the obligee's claims); Taylor Ridge Estates, Inc. v. Statewide Ins. Co., No. Civ. 4-01-CV-90058, 2001 WL 1678745, at *11 (S.D. Iowa Oct. 1, 2001) (purporting to follow the limited incorporation approach of AgGrow Oils, L.L.C. v. Nat'l Union Fire Ins. Co. of Pittsburgh, Pa., 242 F.3d 777 (8th Cir. 2001), discussed in detail *supra* Part II.A.4, but holding that incorporation required the surety to arbitrate such of the obligee's claims and its own defenses as "are dependent upon defining [the obligee's] duties or the Surety's secondary obligations under the Construction Contract" such as, in that case, the surety's overpayment defense); Transamerica Premier Ins. Co. v. Collins & Co., Gen. Contractors, Inc., 735 F. Supp. 1050, 1051 (N.D. Ga. 1990) (holding that "[t]he [performance] bond references the subcontract as follows: 'Which subcontract is hereby referred to and made a part hereof'" and therefore that the surety was required to join the arbitration between the obligee and the principal); Hoffman v. Fid. & Deposit Co. of Md., 734 F. Supp. 192, 193 (D.N.J. 1990) (holding that the performance bond incorporated a construction contract with an arbitration provision and therefore required

while not being called upon to order the surety or guarantor to arbitrate, have adopted and applied incorporation by reference to a surety or guarantor where the underlying contract contained an arbitration

---

surety to arbitrate its performance bond liability including its suretyship defenses); Boy's Club of San Fernando Valley, Inc. v. Fid. & Deposit Co. of Md., 8 Cal. Rptr.2d 587, 589 (Cal. Ct. App. 1992) (holding that a performance bond which incorporated a contract with an arbitration provision required the surety to arbitrate disputes including the obligee's bond claim); St. Paul Fire & Marine Ins. Co. v. Woolley/Sweeney Hotel # 5, 545 So. 2d 958, 958-59 (Fla. Dist. Ct. App. 1989) (holding that "the performance bond incorporated the construction contract by reference" and that the surety thereby bound itself to arbitrate claims including the obligee's bond claim); City of Piqua v. Ohio Farmers Ins. Co., 617 N.E.2d 780, 781 (Ohio Ct. App. 1992) (holding that a performance bond which incorporated a contract with an arbitration clause required the surety to arbitrate with the obligee). Cases which have held that a performance bond surety is bound by the obligee's award against the principal, in an arbitration to which the surety was not a party, because the bond incorporated the principal's contract with the obligee which contained an arbitration clause, but which did not call upon the court to compel the surety to arbitrate, are discussed *infra* Part V.C.

provision.[64] Some of the courts applying incorporation, however, have not concluded that incorporation required the surety or guarantor to

---

[64] *See, e.g.*, AgGrow Oils, L.L.C. v. Nat'l Union Fire Ins. Co. of Pittsburgh, Pa., 242 F.3d 777 (8th Cir. 2001) (recognizing that the construction contract was incorporated into the performance bond but finding that the incorporation provision was ambiguous because it did not clearly express an intent by the obligee and the surety to arbitrate a performance bond claim); Kvaerner ASA v. Bank of Toyko-Mitsubishi, Ltd., N.Y. Branch, 210 F.3d 262 (4th Cir. 2000) (holding that guaranties of a joint venture's performance of a construction contract incorporated the arbitration clause of that contract and that therefore the bank, one of the beneficiaries of guaranties, was required to arbitrate its claim against guarantors); Thomson-CSF, S.A. v. Am. Arbitration Ass'n, 64 F.3d 773 (2d Cir. 1995) (recognizing in dicta that incorporation by reference is one of five ordinary principles of contract and agency law by which a nonsignatory may be bound to an arbitration agreement, but finding no such incorporation on the facts); Gingiss Int'l, Inc. v. Bormet, 58 F.3d 328 (7th Cir. 1995) (holding that guarantors were bound by an arbitration award because they were obligated to arbitrate with the creditor by a guaranty which incorporated an underlying agreement with an arbitration provision); Commercial Union Ins. Co. v. Gilbane Bldg. Co., 992 F.2d 386 (1st Cir. 1993) (staying the obligee's court action against the surety because the incorporation into the performance bond of a contract with an arbitration provision obligated the surety and obligee to arbitrate all disputes arising under performance bond); Sue Klau Enters., Inc. v. Am. Fid. Fire Ins. Co., 551 F.2d 882 (1st Cir. 1977) (applying Puerto Rico law and holding that the surety was bound by the architect's decision in favor of the obligee because the performance bond incorporated a contract providing for initial resolution of disputes by the architect); J & S Constr. Co. v. Travelers Indem. Co., 520 F.2d 809 (1st Cir. 1975) (in a confusing opinion, apparently finding that the principal's contract with the obligee, which contained an arbitration provision, was incorporated into the performance bond and, on that basis, staying the subcontractor's court action against the surety); St. Paul Fire & Marine Ins. Co. v. La Firenza, LLC, No. 8:06-CV-1855-JDW-TGW, 2007 WL 2010759, at *1 (M.D. Fla. July 6, 2007) (refusing to stay, under 9 U.S.C.A. § 3 (West 1999), the surety's declaratory judgment action against the obligee because the surety was bound by the arbitration provision in a construction contract that was incorporated into the performance bond); Firemen's Ins. Co. of Newark, N.J. v. Edgewater Beach Owner's Ass'n, Inc., No. 3:96CV256/RV, 1996 WL 509720, at *1 (N.D. Fla. June 25, 1996) (compelling the obligee to arbitrate its performance bond claim with the

surety because the surety was also a party to the arbitration provision in the construction contract as that contract was incorporated into the performance bond); Aetna Cas. & Sur. Co. v. L'Energia, Ltd. P'ship., No. Civ. A. 96-10098-GAO, 1996 WL 208497, at *4 (D. Mass. Mar. 4, 1996) (refusing to compel the surety to join "a massive, consolidated" arbitration but noting that the surety "presumably could be compelled to participate in some arbitration" as incorporation into the performance bond of a contract constituted the surety's assent to the arbitration provision of that contract); Rashid v. U.S. Fid. & Guar. Co., Civ.A.No. 2:91-0141, 1992 WL 565341, at *1 (S.D.W. Va. Sept. 28, 1992) (holding that the surety was bound under federal law by an arbitration award in favor of the obligee and against the principal because the performance bond incorporated a contract with arbitration provision), *approved in related case*, Rashid v. Schenck Constr. Co., 438 S.E.2d 543 (W. Va. 1993) (agreeing that, under West Virginia law, the surety had agreed to arbitrate all disputes as to the construction contract and the performance bond because the bond incorporated the construction contract which included an arbitration provision); Thomas O'Connor & Co. v. Ins. Co. of N. Am., 697 F. Supp. 563 (D. Mass. 1988) (staying the subcontractor's court action against the surety pending arbitration between the subcontractor and the principal because the subcontract incorporated a prime contract with an arbitration provision and the performance bond also incorporated the prime contract); Loyal Order of Moose, Lodge 1392 v. Int'l Fid. Ins. Co., 797 P.2d 622 (Alaska 1990) (staying the obligee's court action against the surety pending arbitration between the obligee and the principal pursuant to their contract because the performance bond incorporated that contract); Matson, Inc. v. Lamb & Assocs. Packaging, Inc., 947 S.W.2d 324 (Ark. 1997) (requiring that the obligee arbitrate with the principal pursuant to an arbitration provision in the bonded contract before suing surety because the obligee was party to the performance bond which incorporated the bonded contract); Cumberland Cas. & Sur. Co. v. Lamar School Dist., No. CA 03-961, 2004 WL 2294409, at *3 (Ark. Ct. App. Oct. 13, 2004) (not designated for publication) (holding that the surety may compel the obligee to arbitrate its performance bond claim because the arbitration provision incorporated by the performance bond is binding on the parties to the bond); Henderson Inv. Corp. v. Int'l Fid. Ins. Co., 575 So. 2d 770 (Fla. Dist. Ct. App. 1991) (holding that the surety may compel the obligee to arbitrate when the performance bond incorporated a construction contact with an arbitration provision); Bolingbrook Park Dist. v. Nat'l–Ben Franklin Ins. Co. of Ill., 420 N.E.2d 741 (Ill. App. Ct. 1981) (dismissing the obligee's court action against the surety because the performance bond incorporated a contract with an arbitration provision and therefore required the obligee to arbitrate its claim against the surety); Buck Run Baptist Church, Inc. v. Cumberland Sur. Ins. Co., 983 S.W.2d 501 (Ky. 1998) (requiring the obligee to arbitrate with the performing surety because, *inter alia*, the performance bond incorporated a contract with arbitration provision); Hartford Accident & Indem. Co. v. Scarlett Harbor Assocs. Ltd. P'Ship, 695 A.2d 153 (Md. 1997) (refusing to compel the obligee to arbitrate with the surety because the terms of the arbitration provision of the construction contract that was incorporated into the performance bond required only that the obligee and the principal arbitrate with each other); Kearsarge Metallurgical Corp. v. Peerless Ins. Co., 418 N.E.2d. 580 (Mass. 1981) (applying New Hampshire law and holding that the surety was bound by an arbitration award in favor of the obligee and against the principal because the performance bond incorporated a contract with an arbitration provision and therefore the surety had agreed to arbitrate with the obligee); Travelers Cas. & Sur. Co. of Am. v. Long Bay Mgmt. Co., 792 N.E.2d 1013 (Mass. Ct. App. 2003) (compelling the obligee to arbitrate its performance claim against the surety because bond incorporated a construction contract containing an arbitration provision); Powers Regulator Co. v. U.S. Fid. & Guar. Co., 388 N.E.2d. 1205 (Mass. Ct. App. 1979) (binding the surety by an arbitration award in favor of the subcontractor-claimant and against the principal because the payment bond incorporated a contract with an arbitration provision and the surety therefore had agreed to arbitration as the method for determining the principal's liability to claimants); Dunn Indus. Group, Inc. v. City of Sugar Creek, 112 S.W.3d 421, 435 (Mo. 2003) (en banc) (recognizing in dicta that "due to the strong federal policy in favor of arbitration, arbitration agreements are enforced against guarantors or sureties where the arbitration agreement is incorporated by reference into the guaranty or performance bond" but holding that the guaranty before the court referred to, but did not incorporate, the guaranteed contract and therefore did not obligate guarantor to arbitrate); Sheffield Assembly of God Church, Inc. v. Am. Ins. Co., 870 S.W.2d 926 (Mo. Ct. App. 1994) (binding the surety by arbitration award in favor of the obligee and against the principal because the performance bond incorporated a contract with an arbitration provision); Gloucester City Bd. of Educ. v. Am. Arbitration Ass'n, 755 A.2d 1256, 1262-63 (N.J. Super. Ct. App. Div. 2000) (refusing to compel the surety to arbitrate the obligee's performance bond claim because incorporation into the performance bond of a contract with an arbitration provision required the surety to arbitrate only those disputes which the principal would have been required to arbitrate); Fid. & Deposit Co. of Md. v. Parsons &

participate in an arbitration, finding instead that incorporation has a more limited effect.[65]

Finally, the supreme courts of at least two states, although holding that the performance bond surety could be bound by the results of the principal's arbitration with the obligee, have expressly declined to decide whether the surety can be compelled to participate in an arbitration with the obligee when the performance bond incorporates by reference an underlying contract with an arbitration provision.[66]

Whittemore Contractors Corp., 397 N.E.2d 380 (N.Y. 1979) (holding that the surety was bound by an arbitration award as to the principal's contract liability to the obligee because the performance bond incorporated the contract between the obligee and the principal which contained an arbitration provision); Walter Concrete Constr. Corp. v. Lederle Labs., 734 N.Y.S.2d 80 (N.Y. App. Div. 2001), aff'd, 788 N.E.2d 609 (N.Y. 2003), (holding that the surety for a subcontractor was bound by an award in an arbitration between the general contractor and the subcontractor because the performance bond incorporated the subcontract which contained an arbitration provision); Robert J. Denley Co., Inc. v. Neal Smith Constr. Co., No. W2006-00629-COA-R3-CV, 2007 WL 1153121, at *10 (Tenn. Ct. App. Apr. 19, 2007) (compelling the developer to arbitrate its performance bond claim with the surety because the bond incorporated the contract between the developer and the principal which contained an arbitration provision); Tipton County Dep't of Pub. Instruction v. Delashmit Elec. Co., No. 02A01-9704-CH-00084, 1998 WL 158774, at *3 (Tenn. Ct. App. Apr. 7, 1998) (compelling the school board to arbitrate its performance bond claim against the surety because the bond incorporated the construction contract between the school board and the principal which contained an arbitration provision).

65   *See* discussion *infra* Part II.A.3-4.
66   Loyal Order of Moose, Lodge 1392 v. Int'l Fid. Ins. Co., 797 P.2d 622, 629 n.18 (Alaska 1990); Raymond Int'l Builders, Inc. v. First Indem. of Am. Ins. Co., 516 A.2d 620, 623 (N.J. 1986); *but see* Gloucester City Bd. of Educ. v. Am. Arbitration Ass'n, 775 A.2d 1256, 1263 (N.J. Super. Ct. App. Div. 2000) (limiting surety's obligation to arbitrate, and therefore by implication the extent to which it may be bound by an award adverse to the principal, to disputes as to the principal's performance of the bonded contract).

2. Super Incorporation

On the basis of the incorporation doctrine, the court in *Hoffman v. Fidelity and Deposit Co. of Maryland*,[67] ordered, pursuant to section 4 of the Federal Arbitration Act, that the surety arbitrate with the obligee the issue of the surety's liability including its personal defenses.[68] The arbitration provision of the construction contract which was incorporated into the performance bond was quoted by the court as follows:

> "8.1.14. Dispute Resolution. All claims, disputes and other matters in question between the parties to this Agreement, arising out of or related to this Agreement or the breach thereof, shall be decided by arbitration or litigation at the election of the owner . . . ."[69]

Provisions calling for the arbitration of disputes between the parties to the construction contract arising from that contract or the performance thereof appear to be common in the construction setting. So far as the opinions disclose, the incorporated arbitration clauses in the other cases which compelled the surety to arbitrate with the obligee were, in

---

[67] 734 F. Supp. 192 (D.N.J. 1990). A New Jersey state intermediate level appellate court, however, held ten years later in *Gloucester City Bd. of Educ.*, 775 A.2d at 1263, that the surety could be compelled to arbitrate only disputes which the principal could have been required to arbitrate. The *Gloucester City Bd. of Educ.* court did not refer to either the Federal Arbitration Act, 9 U.S.C.A §§ 1-16 (West 1999 & Supp. 2008), or the New Jersey analogue, N.J. STAT. ANN. §§ 2A:24-1 to -11 (West 2000), *superceded* by N.J. STAT. ANN. §§ 2A:23B-1 to -32 (West Supp. 2008) (effective Jan. 1, 2003), and did not otherwise indicate whether its ruling was limited to the state statute or was intended to overrule *Hoffman's* interpretation of the federal statute. *See also* discussion *infra* notes 141-50.

[68] *Hoffman*, 734 F. Supp. at 194-95.

[69] *Id.* at 193 (quoting construction contract between owner and principal). There, the owner exercised his option by serving a demand for arbitration on both the principal and the surety. *Id.*

Effect of an Arbitration Provision in the Principal's Contract 703

substance, the same as that in the *Hoffman* case.[70] Such provisions, it

---

70   *See, e.g.* Jewish Fed'n of Greater New Orleans v. Fid. & Deposit Co. of Md., No. 01-30371, 273 F.3d 1094, 2001 WL 1085096, at *1 (5th Cir Aug. 29, 2001) (unpublished table decision) (2-1 decision) (King, C.J., dissenting) ("'Any controversy or Claim arising out of or related to the Contract, or the breach thereof, shall be settled by arbitration,'" (quoting construction contract)); U.S. Fid. & Guar. Co. v. West Point Constr. Co, Inc., 837 F.2d 1507, 1508 (11th Cir. 1988) (describing the contract as providing that "[d]isputes arising under the contract, including disputes concerning the adequacy of [the principal's] performance, were subject to arbitration"); Exch. Mut. Ins. Co. v. Haskell Co., 742 F.2d 274, 275 (6th Cir. 1984) (arbitration of all claims and disputes "'arising out of, or relating to this contract or the breach thereof ... which cannot be resolved by negotiation between the Contractor and the Owner,'" (quoting construction contract)); Shores of Pan., Inc. v. Safeco Ins. Co. of Am., Civil Action No. 07-00602-KD-B, 2008 WL 4417558, at *1 (S.D. Ala. Sept. 29, 2008) ("The Contract states that any controversy or claim 'arising out or related to' the Contract or the breach thereof shall be settled by arbitration," (quoting bonded contract)); U.S. Sur. Co. v. Hanover R.S. Ltd. P'ship, 543 F. Supp. 2d 492, 493 (W.D.N.C. 2008) ("'Any dispute arising out of or relating to this Agreement shall ... be settled by ... binding arbitration,'" (quoting bonded subcontract)); Capitol Indem. Corp. v. Dayton Bd. of Educ., 492 F. Supp. 2d 829, 832 (S.D. Ohio 2006), *reconsideration den.*, No. 3:03cv404, 2006 WL 2233429, at *1 (S.D. Ohio Aug. 3, 2006) (describing bonded contracts as containing "a provision, providing that any claim arising out of or related to the contract is subject to resolution through arbitration"); Ohio Cas. Co. v. City of Moberly, Mo., No. 4:05 CV 5 JCH, 2005 WL 2491461, at *2 (E.D. Mo. Oct. 7, 2005) ("Contract provides for arbitration of all 'claims, disputes, and other matters in question arising out of, or relating to, the CONTRACT DOCUMENTS,'" (quoting bonded contract)); Taylor Ridge Estates, Inc. v. Statewide Ins. Co., No. Civ. 4-01-CV-90058, 2001 WL 1678745, at *11 (S.D. Iowa Oct. 1, 2001) ("the Construction Contract requires that '[a]ny controversy or Claim arising out of or related to the Contract, or the breach thereof' shall be settled by arbitration," (quoting bonded contract)); Transamerica Premier Ins. Co. v. Collins & Co., Gen. Contractors, Inc., 735 F. Supp. 1050, 1050 (N.D. Ga. 1990) (arbitration of all claims and disputes "'arising out of, or relating to this agreement or the breach thereof ..., unless the parties mutually agree otherwise,'" (quoting construction contract)); Cianbro Corp. v. Empresa Nacional de Ingeniera y Technologia, S.A., 697 F. Supp. 15, 16 (D. Mass. 1988) (arbitration of all claims and disputes "'arising out of or relating to

will be noted, say nothing about the surety's being required to arbitrate with either of the parties to the construction contract, both of whom have expressly consented to do so; nor do those provisions include within the scope of issues to be submitted to arbitration claims or disputes as to the rights, liabilities and defenses arising under the performance bond. The surety in *Hoffman* argued that the arbitration clause applied only to the parties to the construction contract and that, therefore, even if the arbitration clause was incorporated into the bond, it did not require the surety to arbitrate "its defenses to liability on the Bond."[71] Citing *Cianbro Corp. v. Empresa Nacional de Ingeniera y Technologia, S.A.*[72] and *Exchange Mutual Insurance Co. v. Haskell Co.*,[73] the court responded that "courts have not construed such references to the parties as limiting the applicability of the arbitration clause to the parties to the main contract."[74] Because"[f]ederal policy favors arbitration and dictates liberal construction of arbitration clauses[,]"[75] the court compelled the surety to arbitrate with the obligee all issues regarding its liability under the performance bond.

In addition to the Sixth Circuit, with its decision in *Exchange Mutual*, the *Hoffman* court said that the First, Second, Fifth, and Eleventh Circuits agreed that incorporation requires the surety to arbitrate its performance bond liability with the obligee.[76] The *Hoffman*

---

this Agreement or the breach thereof, if not settled between the parties by agreement,'" (quoting construction contract)); Boy's Club of San Fernando Valley, Inc. v. Fid. & Deposit Co. of Md., 8 Cal. Rptr. 2d 587, 588 (Cal. Ct. App. 1992) (arbitration of all claims and disputes "'between the Contractor and the Owner arising out of, or relating to, the Contract Documents or the breach thereof,'" (quoting construction contract)); City of Piqua v. Ohio Farmers Ins. Co., 617 N.E.2d 780, 781 (Ohio Ct. App. 1992) (arbitration of all claims and disputes "'that cannot be resolved ... between the owner ... and the contractor arising from the provisions and performance of this contract,'" (quoting construction contract)).

71   *Hoffman*, 734 F. Supp. at 194.
72   697 F. Supp. 15 (D. Me. 1988), discussed in detail *supra* text accompanying notes 59-62.
73   742 F.2d 274 (6th Cir. 1984).
74   *Hoffman*, 734 F. Supp. at 194-95.
75   *Id.* at 195.
76   *Id.* at 194 (citing U.S. Fid. & Guar. Co. v. West Point Constr. Co., 837 F.2d 1507 (11th Cir. 1988), Compania Espanola de Petroleos v. Nereus

court was quite correct that most of the courts which had considered the incorporation of arbitration provisions in connection with sureties or guarantors adopted the super incorporation approach.[77] Such was the

---

Shipping, 527 F.2d 966 (2d Cir. 1975), and J & S Constr. Co. v. Travelers Indem. Co., 520 F.2d 809 (1st Cir. 1975)).

[77] In addition to the seventeen cases cited *supra* notes 59 and 63, which directly compelled the surety to arbitrate with the obligee, the following twenty of the thirty cases cited *supra* note 64 stated in dicta that an incorporated arbitration provision would obligate the surety or guarantor to arbitrate with the obligee or creditor, or vice versa; relied expressly on such a conclusion as a basis for their ruling; or employed reasoning from which such a conclusion is clearly inferable: Kvaerner ASA v. Bank of Tokyo-Mitsubishi, Ltd., New York Branch, 210 F.3d 262 (4th Cir. 2000); Thomson-CSF, S.A. v. American Arbitration Ass'n, 64 F.3d 773 (2d Cir. 1995); Gingiss International, Inc. v. Bormet, 58 F.3d 328 (7th Cir. 1995); Commercial Union Insurance Co. v. Gilbane Building Co., 992 F.2d 386 (1st Cir. 1993); Sue Klau Enterprises, Inc. v. American Fidelity Fire Insurance Co., 551 F.2d 882 (1st Cir. 1977); St. Paul Fire & Marine Insurance Co. v. La Firenza, LLC, No. 8:06-CV-1855-JDW-TGW, 2007 WL 2010759, at *1 (M.D. Fla. July 6, 2007); Firemen's Insurance Co. of Newark, New Jersey v. Edgewater Beach Owner's Ass'n, Inc., No. 3:96CV256/RV, 1996 WL 509720, at *1 (N.D. Fla. June 25, 1996); Aetna Casualty & Surety Co. v. L'Energia, Ltd. Partnership, No. CIV. A. 96-10098-GAO, 1996 WL 208497, at *1 (D. Mass. Mar. 4, 1996); Rashid v. United States Fidelity & Guaranty Co., Civ.A.No. 2:91-0141, 1992 WL 565341, at *1 (S.D.W. Va. Sept. 28, 1992), *approved in a related case*, Rashid v. Schenck Construction Co., 438 S.E.2d 543 (W. Va. 1993); Cumberland Casualty & Surety Co. v. Lamar School District, No. CA 03-961, 2004 WL 2294409, at *1 (Ark. Ct. App. Oct. 13, 2004) (not designated for publication); Henderson Investment Corp. v. International Fidelity Insurance Co., 575 So. 2d 770 (Fla. Dist. Ct. App. 1991); Bolingbrook Park District v. National–Ben Franklin Insurance Co. of Illinois, 420 N.E.2d 741 (Ill. App. Ct. 1981); Buck Run Baptist Church, Inc. v. Cumberland Surety Insurance Co., 983 S.W.2d 501 (Ky. 1998); Kearsarge Metallurgical Corp. v. Peerless Insurance Co., 418 N.E.2d 580 (Mass. 1981) (applying New Hampshire law); Travelers Casualty and Surety Co. of America v. Long Bay Management Co., 792 N.E.2d 1013 (Mass. Ct. App. 2003); Dunn Industrial Group, Inc. v. City of Sugar Creek, 112 S.W.3d 421, 435 (Mo. 2003); Sheffield Assembly of God Church, Inc. v. American Insurance Co., 870 S.W.2d 926 (Mo. Ct. App. 1994); Robert J. Denley Co., Inc. v. Neal Smith Construction Co., No.

W2006-00629-COA-R3-CV, 2007 WL 1153121, at *1 (Tenn. Ct. App. Apr. 19, 2007); Tipton County Dep't of Public Instruction v. Delashmit Electric Co., No. 02A01-9704-CH-00084, 1998 WL 158774, at *1 (Tenn. Ct. App. Apr. 7, 1998). Of the remaining ten cases, the following three invoked incorporation as grounds for either granting the surety a stay of a payment bond claimant's court action pending arbitration of the claim with the principal, thus necessarily finding that the surety and the claimant were parties to an arbitration agreement, or holding that the surety was bound by the award in such an arbitration and hence not involving the question of the surety's obligation to arbitrate with the obligee at all. Those three payment bond incorporation cases are: J & S Construction Co. v. Travelers Indemnity Co., 520 F.2d 809 (1st Cir. 1975); Thomas O'Connor & Co. v. Insurance Co. of North America, 697 F. Supp. 563 (D. Mass. 1988); Powers Regulator Co. v. United States Fidelity & Guaranty Co., 388 N.E.2d 1205 (Mass. Ct. App. 1979). Because a payment bond incorporates the principal's contract with the obligee and not its agreements with subcontractors, arbitration provisions in the latter instruments cannot be imported into the payment bond under any recognizable version of the incorporation doctrine, however expansive; and thus those three cases must be regarded as aberrational. *See* Gen. Accident Ins. Co. of Am. v. Merritt-Meridian Constr. Corp., 975 F. Supp. 511, 517 (S.D.N.Y. 1997) (stating that "while the payment bonds expressly incorporate the prime contract with the owner by reference, there is no similar language incorporating subcontracts" and therefore holding that conditions precedent to payment in the subcontracts were not incorporated into the payment bonds); C I Steel, LLC v. Travelers Cas. & Sur. Co. of Am., 876 N.E.2d 442, 449 (Mass. App. Ct. 2007) (payment bond surety not bound by arbitration award in favor of subcontractor and against the principal because the subcontract, which contained the arbitration agreement, was not incorporated in the bond and therefore the surety had no obligation to arbitrate with the subcontractor); *see also* James D. Ferrucci, *Ch. 8, Effect Of An Arbitration Provision In The Principal's Contract With A Claimant*, in THE LAW OF PAYMENT BONDS 159, 166-72 (Kevin L. Lybeck & H. Bruce Shreves, eds. Am. Bar Ass'n 1998 & Supp. 2001). Six of the last seven cases adopt a limited incorporation approach, *see* discussion *infra* Part II.A.3-4, and the seventh, Loyal Order of Moose, Lodge 1392 v. International Fidelity Insurance Co., 797 P.2d 622 (Alaska 1990), declined to decide whether the surety could be compelled to arbitrate with the obligee on the basis of an incorporated arbitration provision.

case when *Hoffman* was decided in 1990 and, despite a revival of limited incorporation reasoning beginning in the late 1990s,[78] it remains the case.

In *Firemen's Insurance Co. of Newark, New Jersey v. Edgewater Beach Owner's Ass'n, Inc.*,[79] it was the surety which sought an order under the Federal Arbitration Act to compel the obligee to arbitrate. Section 4 of that statute authorizes the court to issue such an order upon the application of a "party aggrieved" by the failure or refusal of the other party to arbitrate.[80] Accordingly, only a person who is a party to an arbitration agreement may obtain such an order,[81] which requires a showing that the parties entered into a written agreement to arbitrate.[82] Thus, in *Edgewater Beach*, although the surety and the obligee had reversed positions, the issue remained precisely the same; that is, whether the surety was a party to an agreement to arbitrate with the obligee.

The incorporated arbitration clause in *Edgewater Beach* required arbitration of "'[a]ll claims, disputes and other matters in question between OWNER and CONTRACTOR arising out of or relating to the Contract Documents or the breach thereof.'"[83] The court had little trouble with the fact that the scope of the arbitration provision was limited to claims or disputes arising out of the construction contract. The court stated that it was "well settled that where a performance bond incorporates the provisions of a contract, the arbitration provisions of the contract are made a part of the bond *and are applicable to disputes involving the surety*."[84] The court also directly addressed the obvious fact that under the terms of the arbitration clause, only the obligee and the principal had agreed to arbitrate.[85] As with the court in *Hoffman*, the

---

78   *See* discussion *infra* Part II.A.4.
79   No. 3:96CV256/RV, 1996 WL 509720, at *1 (N.D. Fla. June 25, 1996).
80   9 U.S.C.A. § 4 (West 1999).
81   Lorber Indus. of Cal. v. L.A. Printworks Corp., 803 F.2d 523, 525 (9th Cir. 1986). *See also* discussion *supra* Part I.C.
82   *See* discussion *supra* Part I.C.
83   *Edgewater Beach*, 1996 WL 509720, at *1 (quoting construction contract).
84   *Id*. at *2 (emphasis added).
85   In opposing arbitration, the obligee also invoked a provision of the construction contract prohibiting joinder in the arbitration of non-parties to contract. *Id*.

court in *Edgewater Beach* was unfazed by the omission of the surety: "[c]ourts have consistently applied this principle [that incorporated arbitration provisions apply to disputes involving the surety] even where the arbitration provision in the contract limits its application to the parties of the agreement."[86] Therefore, the court concluded, the consequence of incorporating into the performance bond a construction contract with an arbitration provision is that "the surety becomes a real party in interest and a joint and several obligor"[87] in and under the construction contract. Accordingly, the court denied the obligee's motion to dismiss the surety's application for an order compelling arbitration. A few months later, the court, having already held that the surety was a party to the arbitration agreement, issued a second opinion which included an agreed-upon final order directing that the obligee arbitrate with the surety "[a]ll claims, disputes and other matters in question between [the obligee] and [the surety] arising out of *the performance bond*."[88]

---

86   *Id.* The Second Circuit neatly side stepped this issue in Choctaw Generation Ltd. Partnership v. American Home Assurance Co., 271 F.3d 403 (2d Cir. 2001). There, the obligee sued the surety on the performance bond, and the surety moved to compel the obligee to arbitrate pursuant to an arbitration provision of the construction contract with the principal which was incorporated in the performance bond. The district court denied the surety's motion because the arbitration provision was limited to disputes between the parties to the construction contract and therefore the obligee's dispute with the surety was excluded. Expressly refusing to review that ruling, the Second Circuit reversed and found that the obligee was estopped by its execution of a contract containing an arbitration provision from avoiding arbitration with the surety because the issues involved in the obligee's dispute with the surety were closely related to those involved in its dispute with the principal. *Id.* at 406-07. Estoppel, however, does not provide a basis for compelling the surety to arbitrate because although the obligee executed a contract containing the arbitration provision, the surety did not.

87   *Edgewater Beach*, 1996 WL 509720, at *2 (citing Henderson Inv. Corp. v. Int'l Fid. Ins. Co., 575 So. 2d 770, 772 n.1 (Fla. Dist. Ct. App. 1991) and concluding that the surety could enforce an incorporated arbitration clause against the obligee because of "the surety's status as the real party in interest/joint and several obligor").

88   *Id.* at *1 (emphasis added).

It is clear that for those courts which compel the surety to participate in an arbitration proceeding with the obligee, incorporation by reference has an effect which goes far beyond simply making the construction contract part of the performance bond. Through the alchemy of incorporation, the surety becomes a full-fledged party to the construction contract and, moreover, the scope of the arbitration provision itself is transformed to include disputes arising under the performance bond as well as those arising under the construction contract. This expansive conception of the incorporation doctrine might as well be called "reverse incorporation." In practical effect, such super incorporation does not import the arbitration provision, as it appears in the construction contract, into the performance bond; rather, it incorporates the surety and the performance bond into the construction contract. Such an extreme treatment of incorporation is ultimately justified on the basis of federal or state policies which are regarded as strongly favoring arbitration.[89] At this point, it is well to recall the admonition of the First Circuit in *McCarthy v. Azure*[90] that the policy favoring arbitration comes into play only *after* it has been demonstrated, on the basis of ordinary contract principles,[91] by the party proposing the existence of an obligation to arbitrate, that the parties have, in fact, made an agreement to arbitrate. Once that agreement is shown, *then*, if there are doubts as to whether a particular dispute falls within the agreement, those doubts should be resolved in favor of arbitration.[92] "The federal policy, however, does not extend to situations in which the identity of the parties who have agreed

---

89 *See, e.g.*, Jewish Fed'n of Greater New Orleans v. Fid. & Deposit Co. of Md., No. 01-30371, 273 F.3d 1094, 2001 WL 1085096, at *2 (5th Cir Aug. 29, 2001) (unpublished table decision) (2-1 decision) (King, C.J., dissenting); Commercial Union Ins. Co. v. Gilbane Bldg. Co., 992 F.2d 386, 388 (1st Cir. 1993); U.S. Fid. & Guar. Co. v. West Point Constr. Co., Inc., 837 F.2d 1507, 1507 (11th Cir. 1988); Exch. Mutual Ins. Co. v. Haskell Co., 742 F.2d 274, 275 (6th Cir. 1984); U.S. Sur. Co. v. Hanover R.S. Ltd. P'ship, 543 F. Supp. 2d 492, 495-96 (W.D.N.C. 2008); Hoffman v. Fid. & Deposit Co. of Md., 734 F. Supp. 192, 195 (D.N.J. 1990); Boy's Club of San Fernando Valley, Inc. v. Fid. & Deposit Co. of Md., 8 Cal. Rptr. 2d 587, 590 (Cal. Ct. App. 1992).
90 22 F.3d 351 (1st Cir. 1994), also discussed *supra* Part I.C.
91 *See* First Options of Chicago, Inc. v. Kaplan, 514 U.S. 938, 944 (1995).
92 *McCarthy*, 22 F.3d at 354-55

to arbitrate is unclear."[93] Under the literal terms of construction contract arbitration provisions which seem most often to be involved in incorporation cases, it is clear that the surety is *not* one of the parties which is identified as having agreed to arbitrate. The mechanism of incorporation does not amend those terms, and policies favoring arbitration, if applied as intended, cannot do so either.

3. Limited Incorporation

Although most courts have embraced the super incorporation approach, there are courts which have resisted that trend and adopted more limited incorporation reasoning.[94] Under limited incorporation, the agreement to arbitrate is enforced according to its terms. When, as appears generally to be the case,[95] the incorporated arbitration provision identifies the principal and the obligee as the parties which agreed to arbitrate and/or limits the disputes subject to arbitration to those arising under their contract, neither the surety nor the obligee will be compelled to arbitrate with each other the latter's performance bond claim against the former. The obligee's agreement to arbitrate with the principal will be enforced, and the resulting award will determine whether the principal has breached its contract. While the surety will likely be bound by an award adverse to the principal on that issue, it will not be precluded from asserting its personal defenses when the obligee sues on its bond claim.[96]

Limited incorporation reasoning is well illustrated in *Hartford Accident & Indemnity Co. v. Scarlett Harbor Associates Ltd. Partnership*.[97] In that case, the Maryland Court of Appeals confronted the same issue as the Northern District of Florida Court in *Edgewater Beach*;[98] namely,

---

93   *Id.* at 355; *cf.* AgGrow Oils, L.L.C. v. Nat'l Union Fire Ins. Co. of Pittsburgh, Pa., 242 F.3d 777, 781 (8th Cir. 2001) (finding that the performance bond's incorporation clause was ambiguous as to an intent by the obligee and the surety to arbitrate a performance bond claim and holding therefore that the surety was not entitled to a stay of the obligee's suit).
94   *See also* cases discussed *infra* Part II.A.4.
95   *See supra* notes 69-70, 83 and accompanying text.
96   The preclusive effect of an arbitration award against the principal is discussed *infra* Part V.
97   695 A.2d 153 (Md. 1997).
98   No. 3:96CV256/RV, 1996 WL 509720, at *1 (N.D. Fla. June 25, 1996).

whether a surety may, on the basis of an arbitration provision of a construction contract which was incorporated into a performance bond, compel an obligee to arbitrate the obligee's claim against the surety. The *Edgewater Beach* court, which granted the surety's application for arbitration, began its analysis by invoking the "broad deference [which should be given] to the enforcement of arbitration clauses."[99] On the other hand, the *Scarlett Harbor* court, which refused to order arbitration, started by asserting that "[t]he question presented is answered by a return to the fundamentals"[100] of arbitration law: that arbitration is consensual; that a party may be compelled to arbitrate only if it has agreed to do so and that such a party may be required to submit to that process only those disputes which it has agreed to submit.[101] The surety argued that the obligee had agreed to arbitrate because the performance bond incorporated the obligee's contract with the principal which contained an arbitration provision and to which the obligee was a party.[102] Applying the principle that a party can be compelled to arbitrate only to the extent of its agreement to do so, the court found that incorporation was beside the point:

> By incorporating into the [performance] bond in the instant matter the contract that contains SHALP's [the obligee's] promise to arbitrate with Kraus [the principal], The Hartford [the surety] literally has incorporated as to SHALP only SHALP's promise to arbitrate with Kraus. The bond does not, by its terms, express any enlargement of the obligations of the obligee, and, even if The Hartford, acting unilaterally, or The Hartford and Kraus, acting by agreement, undertook to enlarge the obligations of SHALP under its contract with Kraus, that attempted enlargement ordinarily would be ineffective.[103]

Incorporation did not transform the terms of the obligee's agreement to arbitrate. Although acknowledging Maryland's strong policy favoring arbitration, the court of appeals ruled that "the judicial power to enforce an agreement to arbitrate cannot properly be exercised [in this case] because there is no agreement by SHALP to arbitrate with The

---

99 *Id.*
100 *Scarlett Harbor*, 695 A.2d at 155.
101 *Id.*
102 *Id.* at 156.
103 *Id.*

Hartford."[104] The court politely chided those cases which employed incorporation to compel the surety to arbitrate with the obligee[105] because "[t]he analysis" in those cases "does not go beyond the fact that the contract containing an arbitration provision has been incorporated into the bond."[106]

---

104   *Id.* at 157. The court also ruled that the obligee cannot be considered to have agreed to arbitration simply because it accepted the performance bond as conforming to the requirements of the construction contract, *id.*
105   *See* cases cited *supra* notes 59, 63.
106   *Scarlett Harbor*, 695 A.2d at 156 n.7. It should be noted that there is a well-developed body of case law in the Second Circuit, which, in an approach somewhat similar to that in *Scarlett Harbor*, limited the effect of an incorporated arbitration provision to its terms. Those are cases involving bills of lading or guaranties, which incorporated the provisions of "charter parties" (contracts by which merchants lease ships for the conveyance of goods) containing an arbitration provision. Where the arbitration clause was limited to disputes between the "Owners" and the "Charterers," the courts in those "charter party" cases have held that the guarantor or holder of a bill of lading was not a party to the incorporated arbitration clause and thus could not be compelled to arbitrate. Import Export Steel Corp. v. Miss. Valley Barge Line Co., 351 F.2d 503 (2d Cir. 1965); Cont'l U.K., Ltd. v. Anagel Confidence Compania Navieras, S.A., 658 F. Supp. 809 (S.D.N.Y. 1987); Gen. Auth. for Supply Commodities v. S.S. Capetan Costis I, 631 F. Supp. 1488 (S.D.N.Y. 1986); Prod. Steel Co. of Ill. v. SS Francois L.D., 294 F. Supp. 200 (S.D.N.Y. 1968). Where, however, the arbitration clause in the charter party contract was not limited to "Owners" and "Charterers," but was more broadly-worded to apply to all "disputes ... arising out of [the] charter [party]," the courts have held that the arbitration clause "binds not only original parties, but also those who have subsequently agreed to be bound by its terms." Lowry & Co., Inc. v. S.S. Le Moyne D'Iberville, 253 F. Supp. 396, 398 (S.D.N.Y. 1966); *accord*, Compania Espanola de Petroleos, S.A. v. Nereus Shipping, S.A., 527 F.2d 966 (2d Cir. 1975); Southwind Shipping Co., S.A. v. S/T Stoic, 709 F. Supp. 79 (S.D.N.Y. 1989); Amstar Corp. v. SS Union Australia, 445 F. Supp. 940 (S.D.N.Y. 1978). Outside of the shipping context, it presently appears that only one case has cited any of the "charter party" cases as authoritative on the issue of the effect of an incorporated arbitration clause: Progressive Cas. Ins. Co. v. C.A. Reaseguradora Nacional De Venezuela, 991 F.2d 42 (2d Cir. 1993) (involving reinsurance agreements and finding that the incorporated arbitration clause bound the "contracting parties" to arbitrate); *see, also,*

While the court in *Scarlett Harbor* refused to compel the obligee to arbitrate with the surety, it noted that the lower court had the power to stay further court proceedings by the obligee against the surety pending the outcome of the arbitration between the obligee and the principal which had already been ordered.[107] That court had no need to consider the impact on the surety of the results of the arbitration between the obligee and the principal. The New York Court of Appeals, however, had to address that issue in *Fidelity and Deposit Co. of Maryland v. Parsons & Whittemore Contractors Corp.*[108] There, the obligee, a general contractor, appealed from a stay, granted upon the surety's application, of the arbitration which the obligee had commenced against the principal, a subcontractor, and the subcontractor's surety. The performance bond incorporated the subcontract which contained a provision requiring the arbitration of "'[a]ll disputes arising out of this Contract, its interpretation, performance or breach.'"[109] Invoking that incorporation language, the obligee argued that the issue of the surety's liability under the bond, as well as the principal's liability under the construction contract, was subject to compulsory arbitration.

The New York court found that "a critical distinction must be drawn"[110] between disputes arising under the construction contract and "possible unrelated differences which may arise between Fidelity [the surety] and Parsons [the obligee] as to the liability of the surety company

---

Cont'l Group, Inc. v. NPS Commc'ns, Inc., 873 F.2d 613, 619, n.3 (2d Cir. 1989) (noting that the arbitration clause in the underlying agreement was limited to the specific, identified "parties," which did not include the guarantor, and that finding an "agreement by [the guarantor] to arbitrate its obligations under the guarantee cannot be fashioned out of such stuff as this.").

107 *Scarlett Harbor*, 695 A.2d at 157 n.8. Even though Maryland also had "a strong policy to avoid repetitious hearings," that policy could not overcome the fact that the obligee had not agreed to arbitrate with the surety, *id*. at 157. *Cf*. Dean Witter Reynolds Inc. v. Byrd, 470 U.S. 213 (1985) (holding that when arbitrable and non-arbitral claims are pending, a motion to compel arbitration of the arbitrable claims must be granted, even though the claims are related and despite the federal policy favoring arbitration, because a court must enforce the parties' arbitration agreement as written).
108 397 N.E.2d 380 (N.Y. 1979).
109 *Id*. at 381.
110 *Id*. at 382.

under the terms of its performance bond."[111] Clearly, the principal and the obligee had expressly agreed to arbitrate disputes in the first category. Therefore, the obligee's claim against the principal should proceed to arbitration, and the surety was not entitled to a stay of that proceeding. Noting that "the agreement made by the surety company must be precisely defined,"[112] the court found as follows:

> By contrast, there was no agreement on the part of *any* party that controversies arising as to rights and obligations under the terms of the performance bond would be submitted to arbitration.
>
> In defining the agreement made by the surety company it is accurate to say that it cannot be held to have agreed to participate in arbitration proceedings with respect to *any* dispute whatsoever. Certainly there is no language in the performance bond on which to base any argument that it was obligated to submit disputes arising under its performance bond (as distinguished from disputes arising under the subcontract) to resolution by arbitration. The arbitration clause in the subcontract provided *only* for arbitration of disputes arising under that contract.[113]

Accordingly, the surety could not be compelled to arbitrate with the obligee the latter's performance bond claim. Yet, the performance bond had incorporated the principal's contract with the obligee which contained an arbitration provision, and that fact was not without significance:

> Although it [the surety] did not agree to participate in any arbitration, it did accept the agreement of the general contractor [the obligee] and the subcontractor [the principal] that disputes between them would be settled by arbitration. An implicit corollary of that acceptance was agreement by the surety company that for purposes of later determining its liability under its performance bond, it would accept and be bound by the resolution reached in the arbitration forum of any dispute between the general contractor and the subcontractor.[114]

---

111 *Id.*
112 *Id.*
113 *Id.* (emphasis added).
114 *Id.*; *see* Walter Concrete Constr. Corp. v. Lederle Labs, 734 N.Y.S.2d 80 (N.Y. App. Div. 2001), *aff'd*, 788 N.E.2d 609 (N.Y. 2003) (citing

Unlike those courts applying the super incorporation approach, for the *Parsons & Whittemore* court, the mechanism of incorporation by reference did not operate to alter the incorporated arbitration provision. In conformity with the contractual basis of arbitration, an incorporated arbitration provision is to be enforced, as any other arbitration agreement, according to its terms. The principal and the obligee are to arbitrate the obligee's claim that the principal is in default of its obligations under their construction contract. As neither the incorporated arbitration clause nor the performance bond provides for arbitration by the surety as to any issue, there is no basis for inferring that the surety consented to its liability being decided by arbitration, and therefore the surety cannot be compelled to arbitrate that issue.[115]

Parsons & Whittemore and holding that the performance bond surety was bound by an award against the principal in an arbitration between the principal and the obligee), discussed *infra* text accompanying note 442.

115 The *Parsons & Whittemore* opinion was seriously misread in S & R Co. of Kingston v. Latona Trucking, Inc. (*In re* S & R Co. of Kingston, Application to Compel Arbitration), 984 F. Supp. 95 (N.D.N.Y. 1997). In that case, a surety, which issued a bond securing a developer's contractual obligation to pay a contractor, and the developer petitioned under section 4 of the Federal Arbitration Act, 9 U.S.C.A. § 4 (West 1999), for an order compelling the contractor to arbitrate the claims which the contractor had asserted in its lawsuit against them. Although the court ultimately held that the petitioners had waived any right to arbitration as a result of their extensive participation in the lawsuit, it nevertheless considered whether, under New York law, the contractor was obligated to arbitrate with the surety on the basis of the incorporation into the bond of the contractor's contract with the developer which contained an arbitration provision. The court tried to side-step *Parsons & Whittemore* by declaring that the court of appeals in that case "did not reach the issue of whether the parties could compel the surety to arbitrate *its* disputes arising under the subcontract, or vice-versa," *id.* at 99 (emphasis added). Thus, the district court in *Latona Trucking* felt free to follow the super incorporation cases and conclude that the contractor did have an obligation to arbitrate with the surety, calling that ruling "a logical extension" of *Parsons & Whittemore, id.* at 100. The issues which the court did not reach in *Parsons & Whittemore*, however, were whether the surety could be compelled to participate in the arbitration between the obligee and the principal as to the principal's default under the construction contract or whether the surety could force its way into that arbitration over the objection of either or both of those parties. *Parsons &*

By incorporating the construction contract, however, the surety can reasonably be taken to have accepted the choice by the principal and obligee of arbitration as the method for resolving disputes between them. Accordingly, if the arbitration award is adverse to the principal, the surety will not be permitted to relitigate the issue of the principal's default. The successful obligee will have established that element of the surety's liability under the bond. To the extent that the surety has defenses which are independent of the issue of the principal's default, it will not be precluded from litigating those defenses because, by definition, they do not arise under the construction contract and hence could not have been submitted to or adjudicated in the arbitration.[116]

4. Rediscovery of Limited Incorporation

The 1979 ruling in *Parsons & Whittemore*, with its limited incorporation reasoning, was one of the first cases to consider whether incorporation of an arbitration provision in a performance bond constituted an agreement by the surety and obligee to arbitrate disputes between them.[117]

Whittemore, 397 N.E.2d at 382-83. While the court in *Parsons & Whittemore* recognized that the surety had an interest in the outcome of the arbitration between the principal and the obligee, it is clear that the court conceived of the surety's liability as arising solely from the performance bond (only one of the conditions of liability under which was the principal's default under the construction contact), and therefore the surety could not be compelled to submit the issue of its liability to arbitration. For the *Parsons & Whittemore* court, the only issue which could be decided by a compelled arbitration was the principal's liability, and that reasoning is entirely inconsistent with district court's conclusion in *Latona Trucking* that the bond obligee could be compelled by the surety to arbitrate the issue of the surety's liability. On appeal, the Second Circuit affirmed the denial of the petition to compel arbitration but did so only on the waiver grounds, *Latona Trucking*, 159 F.3d 80 (2d Cir. 1998); there was no reference to the incorporation issue.

116   *See infra* Part V for a full discussion of the preclusive effect on the surety of an arbitration award against the principal.

117   There was at least one earlier New York lower court opinion holding that the surety was not bound by an arbitration provision in the bonded contract even though that contract was incorporated into the performance bond. *In re* Transamerica Insurance Company v. Yonkers Contracting Co., 267 N.Y.S.2d 669, 671 (N.Y. Sup. Ct. 1966). In that case, however,

Nevertheless, that case became and remains the minority view. The Sixth Circuit decision in *Exchange Mutual Insurance Co. v. Haskell Co.*,[118] decided five years later in 1984, and its super incorporation approach attracted a substantial following[119] while *Parsons & Whittemore* stood as virtually the only limited incorporation opinion for nearly twenty years.[120] Beginning in 1997, however, some courts began to rediscover

---

      the court held that incorporation could have no effect whatever on the surety. The surety did not sign the bonded contract and did not "evidence any intention thereafter to be included as a party . . . , or to be bound thereby, merely by executing. . . the performance bond . . . ," and incorporation of the bonded contract "cannot serve to alter the relationships of the original parties to the arbitration agreement or to add a party thereto . . . ." *Id.* Such reasoning, the court of appeals said in *Parsons & Whittemore*, 397 N.E.2d at 871, "withstands analysis only in part" because incorporation establishes that the surety accepted the agreement of the obligee and principal to arbitrate their disputes and therefore is bound by the outcome. *Id.* at 871-72.

118   742 F.2d 274 (6th Cir. 1984).

119   *See supra* notes 59, 63, and 77 and accompanying text. *Exchange Mutual* was preceded by cases binding nonsignatories who invoked the benefit of a contract which contained an arbitration provision. *See, e.g.*, Wells Fargo Bank Int'l Corp. v. London Steam-Ship Owners' Mut. Ins. Ass'n, 408 F. Supp. 626 (S.D.N.Y. 1976) (ship mortgagee seeking to recover as loss payee on an insurance contract was bound by arbitration provision in the contract); Psaty & Fuhrman, Inc. v. Cont'l Cas. Co., 103 N.Y.S.2d 849 (N.Y. App. Div. 1951) (dictum) (surety asserting principal's contract claims against obligee as an off-set to the obligee's bond claim would be bound by the arbitration provision in the contract if obligee demanded arbitration). Such cases, however, did not involve consideration of incorporation as a basis for imposing the arbitration obligation on the nonsignatory).

120   In 1981, the court in *WindowMaster Corp. v. B.G. Danis Co.*, 511 F. Supp. 157 (S.D. Ohio 1984) (applying Ohio law), held that because the surety was not a party to the bonded contract, it could not be compelled to arbitrate the obligee's performance bond claim. Although the court quoted *Yonkers Contracting*, 267 N.Y.S.2d at 671, at some length, it did not quote the bond or state that the bond incorporated the underlying contract. In fact, the court did not mention incorporation at all or otherwise suggest that either the obligee's argument or its ruling was based on that doctrine. In any event, *WindowMaster* was effectively overruled three years later by the Sixth Circuit in *Exchange Mutual*, 742

Parsons & Whittemore and found limited incorporation appealing. In that year, the Maryland Court of Appeals applied limited incorporation reasoning to reject the surety's attempt to compel the obligee to arbitrate a performance bond claim in the *Scarlett Harbor* case.[121] Also in 1997, the Supreme Court of Arkansas held in *Matson, Inc. v. Lamb & Associates Packaging, Inc.*[122] that an obligee may not sue the surety on the performance bond until the obligee had arbitrated with the principal the issue of the principal's liability under the construction contract.[123]

F.2d at 276. Likewise, there is no indication that incorporation was considered in *Episcopal Housing Corp. v. Federal Insurance Co.*, 239 S.E.2d 647, 652 (S.C. 1977), in which the court tangentially ruled that the surety, not having signed the bonded contract, could not be compelled to arbitrate the obligee's performance bond claim. In that case, the obligee did not seek to compel the surety to arbitrate; instead it opposed the principal's petition to require the obligee to arbitrate on the ground that an arbitration agreement which ousts the court of jurisdiction is unenforceable under South Carolina law. The court held that the case involved interstate commerce and therefore the arbitration provision was valid under the Federal Arbitration Act, 9 U.S.C.A. §§ 1-16 (West 1999 & Supp. 2008), *id.* The surety's obligation to arbitrate became an issue only because the obligee argued that the arbitration provision was invalid even under the federal statute because the surety was not a party to the contract which contained that provision. In an apparent effort to blunt that argument, the lower court conditioned its referral of the matter to arbitration upon the surety's also joining that proceeding. It was in the course of excising that condition that the South Carolina Supreme Court ruled that the surety could not be compelled to arbitrate.

121 *See supra* Part II.A.3 for a detailed discussion of *Scarlett Harbor*.
122 947 S.W.2d 324 (Ark. 1997).
123 An incorporation analysis which limits the obligee's obligation (or right) to arbitration to the issue of the *principal's* liability on the underlying contract is a key component of limited incorporation because such a limitation is inescapably inconsistent with requiring the surety to arbitrate its liability under the performance bond with the obligee. Nevertheless, in *Cumberland Casualty & Surety Co. v. Lamar School District*, No. CA 03-961, 2004 WL 2294409, at *3 (Ark. Ct. App. Oct. 13, 2004), an Arkansas intermediate level appellate court cited Matson for the proposition that "incorporation by reference [of an arbitration provision] in a performance bond is binding upon the parties to the bond" and held that the surety was entitled to compel the obligee to arbitrate its performance bond claim. There are opinions which, while otherwise inconclusive as to whether the

Effect of an Arbitration Provision in the Principal's Contract 719

The construction contract contained an arbitration provision and was incorporated by reference in the performance bond. Therefore, even though the performance bond was a separate agreement, the obligee could not be permitted to circumvent its agreement to arbitrate the issue of the principal's liability under the construction contract simply by suing the surety. To the argument that its ruling nullified the performance bond, the court noted "the possibility that a remedy may remain against USF&G [the surety] if it is determined through arbitration that Matson [the principal] has not performed or has not properly performed the contract."[124] The court's further statement that "there remains the possibility that effect may be given to both the arbitration clause and the performance bond"[125] expresses its objective of enforcing agreements according to their terms and may reasonably be taken as a strong signal that the court would bind the surety to the results of the arbitration as to the principal's liability but would not preclude the surety from asserting any personal defenses. Such a resolution, of course, would mirror precisely the *Parsons & Whittemore* approach to incorporation.[126]

---

    surety can be compelled to arbitrate with the obligee, suggest, with varying degrees of apparent deliberation, that arbitration under incorporation is limited to the issue of the principal's liability. For example, in *Loyal Order of Moose, Lodge 1392 v. International Fidelity Insurance Co.*, 797 P.2d 622, 629, 629 n.18 (Alaska 1990), the court expressly ruled that the surety may compel the obligee to arbitrate the question of the principal's default under the construction contract, although it declined to decide whether the surety could be compelled to participate in that arbitration on the basis of an incorporated arbitration clause.

124 *Matson*, 947 S.W.2d at 328.
125 *Id.*
126 Citing *Parsons & Whittemore*, the court in *Walter Concrete Construction Corp. v. Lederle Laboratories*, 734 N.Y.S.2d 80, 81 (N.Y. App. Div. 2001), *aff'd*, 788 N.E.2d 609 (N.Y. 2003), held that the surety was bound by an arbitration award against the principal in an arbitration between the principal and the obligee. One case that provoked two Seventh Circuit opinions yielded a result which was analogous to that reached in Parsons & Whittemore. In the first appeal, *Grunstad v. Ritt*, 106 F.3d 201 (7th Cir. 1997), the court held that the fact that guarantors signed a guaranty, which appeared at the end of the underlying agreement and stated that "[w]e hereby guarantee all of the provisions of the within Agreement, and especially the performance of Atlantic [the primary obligor] hereunder,"

In 2001, with its decision in *AgGrow Oils, L.L.C. v. National Union Fire Insurance Co. of Pittsburgh, Pa.*,[127] the Eighth Circuit became the first, and so far the only, federal appellate court to refuse to find that an arbitration provision of a construction contract which was incorporated into a performance bond constituted an agreement by the surety and the obligee to arbitrate the latter's bond claim. The court therefore held that the surety was not entitled to a stay under section 3 of the Federal Arbitration Act[128] of the obligee's lawsuit. The incorporated construction contact required arbitration of "'[a]ny controversy or Claim arising out of or related to the Contract or the breach thereof.'"[129] The construction contract also provided that it was not to be construed to create a contractual relationship between any parties other than the obligee and the principal,[130] and the performance bond stated that "'[a]ny proceeding, legal or equitable, under this Bond may be instituted in any court of competent jurisdiction in the location in which the work or part of the work is located.'"[131] The court found that the language of the incorporation clause of the performance bond was ambiguous because it did not clearly express "an intent by AgGrow [the obligee] and National

---

did not result in the incorporation of the arbitration provision of the agreement into the guaranty because the guaranty lacked sufficiently express incorporation language. Thus, the court held, the guarantor could not be compelled to arbitrate. In the second appeal, *Grunstad v. Ritt*, 166 F.3d 867 (7th Cir. 1999), one of the guarantors sought review of the judgment which had been entered against him on the basis of an arbitration award against the principal debtor. The court held that the guarantor was bound by the arbitration award as to the interpretation of the underlying agreement because, in assenting to guarantee an agreement with an arbitration clause, the guarantor took the risk that an arbitrator would interpret that agreement adverse to his interests, *id.* at 872. The court did, however, consider on the merits the guarantor's argument that the assignment of the agreement by one of the parties materially changed his risk and therefore discharged him from liability, although the court ultimately found the argument to be without merit.

127 242 F.3d 777 (8th Cir. 2001) (applying North Dakota law).
128 9 U.S.C.A. § 3 (West 1999).
129 *AgGrow Oils*, 242 F.3d at 780 n.1 (quoting construction contract).
130 *Id.* at 781.
131 *Id.* at 780 (quoting performance bond).

[the surety] to arbitrate *their* disputes under the bond,"[132] especially as the contract created a contractual relationship between only the parties to it and the bond referred to judicial resolution of disputes.[133] The court also found that there was no extrinsic evidence which shed any light on the question. An ambiguous provision was an insufficient basis for finding an agreement to arbitrate:

> Mindful of the fundamental principle that "[a]rbitration under the [Federal Arbitration] Act is a matter of consent, not coercion," *Mastrobuono v. Shearson Lehman Hutton, Inc.*, 514 U.S. 52, 57, 115 S. Ct. 1212, 131 L.Ed.2d 76 (1995), we are unwilling to construe an incorporation clause whose obvious purpose was to clarify the extent of the surety's secondary obligation as also reflecting a mutual intent to compel arbitration of all disputes between the surety and the obligee under the bond.... [W]e conclude there was no such agreement to arbitrate. Therefore, National [the surety] is not entitled to a mandatory stay under section 3 of the Act.[134]

---

[132] *Id.* at 781. On the basis of *AgGrow Oils*, the Eighth Circuit in *Liberty Mutual Insurance Co. v. Mandaree Public School District # 36*, 503 F.3d 709 (8th Cir. 2007) (applying North Dakota law), *aff'g* 459 F. Supp. 2d 866, 871-72 (D.N.D 2006), held that the incorporation into a performance bond of a construction contract with an arbitration clause did not require that the surety arbitrate its dispute with the obligee and that therefore the obligee was not entitled to a stay of the surety's court action for a declaratory judgment that the obligee had discharged the surety of any bond obligation.

[133] Courts applying the super incorporation approach typically find that the bond's express reference to a court action is not inconsistent with an agreement between the surety and obligee to arbitrate the surety's performance bond liability. *See, e.g.*, Transamerica Premier Ins. Co. v. Collins & Co., Gen. Contractors, 735 F. Supp. 1050, 1052 (N.D. Ga. 1990) ("'[S]uit' is a generic term that does not necessarily exclude arbitration. *See* BLACK'S LAW DICTIONARY 1286 (5th ed. 1979) ....").

[134] *AgGrow Oils*, 242 F.3d at 782. In *Ohio Casualty Insurance Company v. City of Moberly, Mo.*, No. 4:05 CV 5 JCH, 2005 WL 2491461, at *1 (E.D. Mo. Oct. 7, 2005), the court held that the surety was obligated, on the basis of an incorporated arbitration provision, to arbitrate its personal defenses to the obligee's performance bond claim and, in the process, distinguished *AgGrow Oils* because the bond in the case before it did not contain language referring to a judicial resolution of disputes, *id.* at *3

In support of that conclusion, the court cited the *Parsons & Whittemore* and *Scarlett Harbor* cases.[135] It acknowledged the super incorporation cases[136] but found them unpersuasive because those cases did not consider "the significance of construing the incorporation clause [of a performance bond] as an express agreement to arbitrate between the obligee and the bonding company."[137] Such a construction, the court observed, would permit the surety to compel the obligee to arbitrate even when the principal was in bankruptcy and no party to the underlying contract desired to arbitrate and would also permit the obligee to compel an unwilling surety to arbitrate "its unique defenses."[138] The court's invocation of the consensual nature of arbitration is typical of the cases

---

n.2, and noted that the definition of "Contract Documents" in the construction contract included the performance bond, *id.* at *2. In *Mandaree Public School District*, 503 F.3d at 711, however, the performance bond specified that legal or equitable proceedings may be brought in any court located where the work or part thereof was performed, and therefore the court found *AgGrow Oils* controlling and denied the obligee's motion to compel the surety to arbitrate its claim for a declaratory judgment that the obligee had discharged the surety's obligations under the performance bond. In *Taylor Ridge Estates, Inc. v. Statewide Insurance Co.*, No. Civ. 4-01-CV-90058, 2001 WL 1678745, at *11 (S.D. Iowa Oct. 1, 2001), the court distinguished *AgGrow Oils* on another ground: while ostensibly agreeing that the surety could not be compelled to arbitrate "claims solely based upon interpretation of the Performance Bond," the court found that the obligee's claims and the surety's defenses, particularly its overpayment defense, were not collateral to the construction contract but required interpretation of the parties' duties thereunder and therefore held that the surety was obligated to arbitrate the performance bond claim. That reading of *AgGrow Oils* is disingenuous at best in light of the Eighth Circuit's reference to the surety's "unique defenses" in connection with its discussion of the consequences of construing a performance bond incorporation provision as an agreement to arbitrate between the obligee and the surety. *AgGrow Oils*, 242 F.3d at 782.

135   *AgGrow Oils*, 242 F.3d at 782.
136   *Id.* at 782 n.4.
137   *Id.* at 782.
138   *Id.*

following limited incorporation reasoning.[139] By contrast, courts applying the super incorporation approach rely heavily on the legislative policy favoring arbitration.[140]

In 2000, a New Jersey intermediate appellate court decided *Gloucester City Board of Education v. American Arbitration Ass'n*,[141] and created confusion as to whether, in New Jersey, super incorporation or limited incorporation applies to the surety's obligation to arbitrate. The case was commenced by the obligee to compel the surety to arbitrate the obligee's performance bond claim. The court expressly adopted the limited incorporation reasoning of *Parsons & Whittemore* and held that because the arbitration provision, which was incorporated in the performance bond, required arbitration of only disputes arising under the construction contract, the surety had not agreed, and therefore could not be compelled, to arbitrate the obligee's performance bond claim.[142] The court's only reference to the *Hoffman* case,[143] in which the federal court for the District of New Jersey had ten years earlier applied super incorporation to compel the surety, pursuant to section 4 of the Federal Arbitration Act,[144] to arbitrate the obligee's performance bond claim, was a single citation to that case as "*contra*" without any further consideration.[145] Moreover, the court did not discuss, or even cite, either the Federal Arbitration Act or the New Jersey arbitration statute,[146] thereby giving no indication whether the obligee based its application, or the court its ruling, on the federal or state statute. The court was bound to

---

139 *See, e.g.*, Hartford Accident & Indem. Co. v. Scarlett Harbor Assocs. Ltd. P'Ship, 695 A.2d 153, 155 (Md. 1997), discussed in detail *supra* Part II.A.3.
140 *See, e.g.*, U.S. Fid. & Guar. Co. v. West Point Constr. Co., 837 F.2d 1507, 1508 (11th Cir. 1988); Hoffman v. Fid. & Deposit Co. of Md., 734 F. Supp. 192, 195 (D.N.J. 1990); Boy's Club of San Fernando Valley, Inc. v. Fid. & Deposit Co. of Md., 8 Cal. Rptr. 2d 857, 590 (Cal. Ct. App. 1992).
141 755 A.2d 1256 (N.J. Super. Ct. App. Div. 2000).
142 *Id.* at 1263.
143 Hoffman v. Fid. and Deposit Co. of Md., 734 F. Supp. 192 (D.N.J. 1990), discussed *supra* Part II.A.2.
144 9 U.S.C. § 4 (West 1999).
145 *Gloucester City*, 755 A.2d at 1263.
146 N.J. STAT. ANN. §§ 2A:24-1 to -11 (West 2000), *superceded* by N.J. STAT. ANN. §§ 2A:23B-1 to -32 (West 2008) (effective Jan. 1, 2003).

apply the Federal Arbitration Act if the interstate requirement was met.[147] Because the surety was not a corporation of or located in New Jersey,[148] it is likely that the requirement was satisfied; however, the court ignored the issue entirely. For all that can be gleaned from the opinion, the court decided the arbitration issue as a matter of common law as if no statute at all applied.

Thus, in New Jersey, whether or not the surety is obligated to arbitrate the obligee's performance bond claim may well depend on whether the obligee applies for an order compelling the surety to do so in the federal or state court and/or on whether the issue is decided under the federal or state statute. The *Hoffman* case is a classic application of the super incorporation approach and would clearly require issuance of an order compelling arbitration under section 4 of the Federal Arbitration Act.[149] Although the court in *Gloucester City* expressly adopted limited incorporation, it did not purport to overrule the *Hoffman* court's interpretation of the federal statute. It is certainly possible that both federal and state courts will limit *Gloucester City* to the New Jersey arbitration statute with the result that limited incorporation will apply only to the most local of construction projects. There is, however, no *a priori* reason why New Jersey state courts could not adopt a reading of the Federal Arbitration Act which is contrary to that of the federal district court.[150] In that case, resolution of the issue would depend entirely on which court makes the decision. So far, neither the federal nor state courts in New Jersey have issued a reported decision which clarifies the confusion.

Despite the revival of limited incorporation reasoning over the last dozen years, super incorporation cases have remained in the majority.

---

147   *See supra* Part I.
148   The surety was Amwest Surety Insurance Company, *Gloucester City*, 755 A.2d at 1258, which was a Nebraska corporation with its principal office in Calabasas, Cal., Notice, Nebraska Dep't of Ins., Notice of Liquidation–Amwest Surety Insurance Company (June 8, 2001).
149   Hoffman v. Fid. & Deposit Co. of Md., 734 F. Supp. 192, 195 (D.N.J. 1990) (ordering, pursuant to 9 U.S.C.A. § 4 (West 1999), the surety to arbitrate the obligee's performance bond claim).
150   Unlike the situation in which a federal court applying state law must follow the interpretations of state courts, there is no requirement that state courts must defer to the construction of the Federal Arbitration Act of a federal court except for the United States Supreme Court.

Effect of an Arbitration Provision in the Principal's Contract 725

For example, in 2001, when the Eighth Circuit became the first federal court of appeals to endorse limited incorporation in the *AgGrow Oils* case,[151] the Fifth Circuit, joining the First, Second, Fourth, Sixth, and Eleventh Circuits,[152] embraced super incorporation and upheld an order compelling the surety to arbitrate the obligee's performance bond claim in *Jewish Federation of Greater New Orleans v. Fidelity & Deposit Co. of Maryland*.[153] Even so, that ruling provoked a polite but firm dissent which evaluated the two contrary lines of authority on the issue and found the limited incorporation cases to be better reasoned.[154] Because the arbitration provision of the construction contract limited the obligation to arbitrate to claims asserted by one of the parties to that contract, the dissent concluded by pointing out that "the plain language of the contract would not have put Fidelity [the surety] on notice that, in incorporating the contract into the performance bond, it was agreeing to arbitrate disputes grounded in the language of the bond itself."[155]

---

151 242 F.3d 777 (8th Cir. 2001).
152 Commercial Union Ins. Co. v. Gilbane Bldg. Co., 992 F.2d 386 (1st Cir. 1993); Campania Espanola de Petroleos, S.A. v. Nereus Shipping, S.A., 527 F.2d 966 (2d Cir. 1975); Kvaener ASA v. Bank of Tokyo-Mitsubishi, Ltd., N.Y. Branch, 210 F.3d 262 (4th Cir. 2000); Exch. Mut. Ins. Co. v. Haskell Co., 742 F.2d 274 (6th Cir. 1984); U.S. Fid. & Guar. Co. v. West Point Constr. Co., 837 F.2d 1507 (11th Cir. 1988).
153 No. 01-30371, 273 F.3d 1094, 2001 WL 1085096, at *2 (5th Cir. Aug. 29, 2001) (unpublished table decision) (2-1 decision) (King, J. dissenting); *see also* post-1996 cases cited *supra* notes 59, 63, and 77.
154 *Id.* at *3 (citing Gloucester City Bd. of Educ. v. Am. Arbitration Ass'n, 755 A.2d 1256 (N.J. Super. Ct. App. Div. 2000); Fid. & Deposit Co. of Md., 397 N.E.2d 380 (N.Y. 1979)).
155 *Id.* The surety was asserting a limitations defense which was apparently based on a provision in the performance bond, *id.* at *2. Super incorporation cases, of course, take the opposite view, relying on the federal policy favoring arbitration. *See, e.g.*, Hoffman v. Fid. & Deposit Co. of Md., 734 F. Supp. 192, 194-95 (D.N.J. 1990) (surety "reads the arbitration clause too narrowly" in arguing that the limitation to claims of the parties to the construction contract excluded the surety).

B. Direct Compulsion–As Performing Surety

After a default termination of the principal, the performance bond surety may decide to exercise its option to arrange for the completion of the project. Often it will do so under a negotiated takeover agreement with the obligee, though sureties have undertaken to complete without such an agreement. In either situation, if the bonded contract contained an arbitration provision, the obligee will be entitled to compel the surety to arbitrate completion disputes unless the surety has arranged a takeover agreement which expressly negates the arbitration provision in the principal's contract.

For example, in *International Fidelity Insurance Co. v. Saratoga Springs Public Library*,[156] the obligee sought to compel the performing surety to arbitrate delay claims arising after the surety took over completion. The obligee relied on its original contract with the principal which contained an arbitration provision. The surety had arranged completion under a takeover agreement which expressly provided that it was acting solely in its capacity as performance bond surety. The surety argued that because the obligee's claims arose from post-default events, those claims related to the adequacy of the surety's performance under the performance bond and/or the takeover agreement, neither of which included an arbitration clause. Although the surety persuaded one member of the appellate panel,[157] the majority held that the takeover agreement incorporated by reference the original contract and that therefore the surety had agreed to arbitrate with the obligee.[158]

---

156 653 N.Y.S.2d 729 (N.Y. App. Div. 1997).
157 *Id.* at 730-31 (Mikoll, J., dissenting).
158 *See also* Fid. & Guar. Ins. Co. v. West Point Realty, Inc., No. Civ.1951 LMM, 2002 WL 1933780, at *4 (S.D.N.Y. Aug. 21, 2002) (directing that the performing surety arbitrate the obligee's claim because the construction contract, which contained an arbitration provision, had been incorporated in both the performance bond and the takeover agreement between the surety and the obligee); Town of Berlin v. Nobel Ins. Co., 758 A.2d 436, 440 (Conn. App. Ct. 2000) (holding that incorporation in a takeover agreement of a construction contract with an arbitration provision satisfied a state statute requiring that arbitration agreements be in writing and that therefore the obligee was required to arbitrate the surety's claims).

The majority in *Saratoga Springs* attempted to employ an incorporation analysis and relied on *Parsons & Whittemore*[159] to support its conclusion.[160] That reasoning is unpersuasive because *Parsons & Whittemore* held that incorporation of an arbitration provision did *not* obligate the surety to arbitrate the obligee's claims.[161] There is, however, another basis for binding a nonsignatory to an arbitration provision which applies to the performing surety: "[i]n the absence of a signature, a party may be bound by an arbitration clause if its subsequent conduct indicates that it is assuming the obligation to arbitrate."[162] Takeover agreements typically provide that the surety will complete or procure the completion of the project in accordance with the terms and conditions of the bonded contract. When the surety signs such a takeover agreement and the bonded contract includes an arbitration provision, the surety has assumed the principal's contract and, with it, the arbitration provision.

The performing surety can be bound by assumption even without entering into a takeover agreement. In *Buck Run Baptist Church, Inc. v. Cumberland Surety Insurance Co., Inc.*,[163] the performing surety sought to compel the obligee to arbitrate disputes arising from the work of the relet contractor in accordance with an arbitration provision in the bonded contract. The court concluded that the obligee was obligated to arbitrate because the performance bond incorporated the principal's contract and because the surety, "in effect, stood in the shoes of Z & J [the principal] and became the contractor on the project."[164] As the opinion refers to the performance bond and the construction contract and analyzes the incorporation of the latter into the former, but makes no mention of a takeover agreement, the surety presumably undertook completion without one. Nevertheless, the court ruled that the surety was entitled to enforce the arbitration provision of the bonded contract, which means

---

159 Fid. & Deposit Co. of Md. v. Parsons & Whittemore Contractors Corp., 397 N.E. 380 (N.Y. 1979), discussed in detail *supra* Part II.A.3.
160 *Saratoga Springs*, 653 N.Y.S.2d at 730.
161 *See supra* text accompanying notes 112-14.
162 Thomson-CSF, S.A. v. Am. Arbitration Ass'n., 64 F.3d 773, 777 (2d Cir. 1995) (recognizing assumption, as well as incorporation, as one of the five principles of contract or agency law by which a nonsignatory may be bound to an arbitration agreement).
163 983 S.W.2d 501 (Ky. 1998).
164 *Id*. at 503.

that the surety would likewise be bound by it.[165] Although the court invoked incorporation, that analysis was completely unnecessary. Even if the performance bond had not incorporated the arbitration provision, the surety, by arranging for completion, would still have occupied the principal's shoes and become the contractor and would thereby have assumed the principal's obligations which included the agreement to arbitrate.[166]

The completing surety might also find itself compelled to arbitrate with the defaulted principal's subcontractors.[167] In *Travelers Indemnity Co. v. Hayes Contractors, Inc.*,[168] all of the principal's rights in and to subcontracts were assigned to the surety upon the principal's default by operation of the general indemnity agreement. One subcontractor sought to compel the surety to arbitrate in the surety's capacity as assignee of the subcontract which incorporated the prime contract which, in turn, contained an arbitration provision. That arbitration provision, however, conditioned the owner's obligation to arbitrate upon its consent. As assignee, the surety was bound only to the extent of the terms of the arbitration provision and therefore could not be compelled to arbitrate against its wishes. For that reason, the court declined to decide whether the assignment effected an assumption by the surety of the principal's subcontract obligation to arbitrate with the subcontractor. Nevertheless, there is a possibility that an indemnity agreement assignment of the principal's subcontracts could result in the surety's being bound to an arbitration provision in the subcontract once the surety has taken over for the defaulted principal.

In *Employers Insurance of Wausau v. Bright Metal Specialties, Inc.*,[169] an Eleventh Circuit panel majority compelled the performing surety to arbitrate a subcontractor's claim pursuant to an arbitration provision in a subcontractor's agreement with the defaulted principal

---

165 *See* discussion *supra* text accompanying notes 79-82.
166 *See* U.S. Fid. & Guar. Co. v. Bangor Area Joint School Auth., 355 F. Supp. 913 (E.D. Pa. 1973) (performing surety, to which the defaulted principal had assigned a bonded contract with an arbitration provision, could compel the obligee to arbitrate the surety's claim for the contract balance).
167 The issue of the surety's obligation to arbitrate with a payment bond claimant generally is discussed fully in *Ferrucci, supra* note 77.
168 389 N.W.2d 257 (Minn. Ct. App. 1986).
169 251 F.3d 1316 (11th Cir. 2001).

because the surety had executed a takeover agreement with the obligee, a completion agreement with the relet contractor and a ratification agreement with the subcontractor. Reading those agreements together, the panel majority "conclude[d] that Wausau [the surety] gained the benefits and obligations of the Subcontract between A-1 [the principal] and Bright [the subcontractor] [and that] [t]hus, Wausau became bound by the arbitration provision in the Subcontract."[170] The surety did not contest that it acquired the principal's rights under the subcontract including the right to assign the acquired rights to a relet contractor which it exercised. Under those circumstances, the majority saw the surety's refusal to accept an obligation to arbitrate as "tantamount to Wausau asking the court to recognize its rights under the Subcontract without the correlative duties therein."[171]

That reasoning was too much for Judge Garwood who filed a dissenting opinion.[172] As to the three agreements relied upon by the majority, he said:

> The net result was in essence that Wausau paid Bright for unpaid work performed to date and Rogers [the relet contractor] was substituted for A-1 in the Subcontract as to the uncompleted work thereunder, and the subcontract's arbitration clause binds Rogers and Bright, but not Wausau, just as it had [prior to termination] bound Bright and A-1, but not Wausau. There is nothing unusual or unfair about this.[173]

Judge Garwood pointed out that the takeover agreement simply allowed the surety to fulfill its performance bond obligation and neither contained nor incorporated an arbitration provision. The completion contract obligated the surety to assign uncompleted subcontracts to the relet contractor but did not purport to recognize any obligations of the surety under those subcontracts to which it had never been a party. Moreover, the subcontractor was a party to neither the takeover agreement nor the completion agreement. The only agreement to which both the surety and the subcontractor were parties was the ratification agreement. In that agreement, however, the subcontractor expressly disclaimed any obligation of the surety. Judge Garwood concluded that:

---

170   *Id.* at 1323.
171   *Id.*
172   *Id.* at 1326-28.
173   *Id.* at 1327.

It is illogical to say that in these circumstances Wausau is somehow *implicitly* bound by the Subcontract, when Bright has *expressly* agreed to look only to the new prime completion contractor–Rogers–for "all further payments" and has agreed that Wausau's payment of the $7,730.45 retainage for work done for A-1 "will constitute complete fulfillment of the obligations of Surety to Subcontractor.[174]

The performing surety may also find itself bound to an arbitration agreement in a contract which it did not sign when relying on its subrogation rights. In *Liberty Mutual Insurance Co. v. N. Picco & Sons Contracting Co.*,[175] the surety sued the owner's construction manager and others to recover the cost of remedial work which the surety contended was outside the scope of the bonded contract and hence its takeover agreement. As it had completed the project, the surety asserted that it was subrogated to the rights of the owner under its contract with the construction manager and that therefore the surety was entitled to recover for the alleged breach of that contract by the construction manager. The court held that while a subrogee acquires the rights and remedies of the subrogor, it does so subject to any defenses or claims which may be raised against the subrogor. "Therefore, a surety who is a nonsignatory to a contract containing an arbitration clause can be required to arbitrate if the subrogor would have been required to arbitrate."[176] Because the owner's contract with the construction manager contained an arbitration provision, the court ordered that the surety submit its claims to arbitration.[177]

The cases discussed in this section are a warning, and the performing surety should take heed. Before establishing its arrangements for completion, the surety should determine whether the bonded contract

---

174 *Id.* at 1328.
175 No. 05 Civ. 217(SCR), 2008 WL 190310, at *1 (S.D.N.Y. Jan. 16, 2008).
176 *Id.* at 11.
177 *Id.* at 13. The surety also asserted a negligence claim against the construction manager. The court directed the surety to arbitrate that claim as well because the underlying factual allegations of negligence were closely related to the allegations of breach of a contract with an arbitration provision. *Id.* In addition, the surety, as subrogee, had asserted contract and negligence claims against the owner's architect whose contract also contained an arbitration provision. The architect, however, did not seek to enforce that provision, and the court therefore did not order the surety to arbitrate those claims. *Id.* at 9, 13.

contains an arbitration provision. If it does and if the surety does not wish to arbitrate disputes arising from completion, the surety must negotiate a takeover agreement which either expressly eliminates the arbitration provision or gives the surety the option whether or not to arbitrate. For the same reason, the surety must be alert to arbitration provisions in the principal's agreements with subcontractors which the surety may wish to retain and assign to the relet contractor. Unless the surety is prepared to arbitrate post-default disputes with such subcontractors, the surety must insist that the subcontractors enter into ratification agreements which expressly negate the obligation to arbitrate or conditions it upon the surety's consent.

The worst of all worlds for a performing surety is the situation in which the bonded contract contains an arbitration agreement but the ratified subcontract does not, or vice versa. If the surety finds itself facing disputes with both the obligee and the subcontractor with overlapping components, it could well be forced to arbitrate with one but litigate with the other. In addition to the cost inefficiency, that scenario raises the prospect of inconsistent results with possible drastic consequences for the surety. Courts are highly unlikely to bail out the surety by, for example, staying the arbitration with one party until the litigation with the other has concluded or forcing either to give up its chosen forum and consolidate its dispute with the other in one forum. As arbitration is a matter of consent, the court's function is to enforce arbitration agreements as written "even where the result would be the possibly inefficient maintenance of separate proceedings in different forums."[178] If a party agreed to an arbitration provision which might result in inefficiency or inconsistent results, it must live with that agreement.

C. *Indirect Compulsion–Preclusion*[179]

There are several bases upon which a performance bond surety will be subject to a court order which requires it to arbitrate with the obligee. Courts which take the super incorporation approach will, upon an

---

178 Dean Witter Reynolds, Inc. v. Byrd, 470 U.S. 213, 217 (1985). The consolidation of related arbitration proceedings is discussed in detail *infra* Part IV.

179 The preclusive effect upon the surety of an arbitration award against the principal is discussed fully *infra* Part V.

application by the obligee, issue an order under section 4 of the Federal Arbitration Act[180] compelling the surety to arbitrate with the obligee and will stay pursuant to section 3 of that statute,[181] or more likely dismiss outright, any court proceeding commenced by the surety so that arbitration may be had.[182] Similarly, the completing surety will almost certainly be required to arbitrate with the obligee under the assumption doctrine,[183] and there is at least one state statute which specifically requires a construction contract surety to arbitrate and one which exempts sureties from any arbitration agreement.[184]

On the other hand, courts which apply limited incorporation will not compel the surety to arbitrate nor stay or dismiss any court action brought by or against it.[185] Those courts, however, will enforce the agreement of the obligee and the principal to arbitrate with each other as to the performance of the underlying contract and will very likely preclude the surety from relitigating the results of that arbitration.[186] Even jurisdictions which have expressly not yet decided whether the surety can be compelled to arbitrate on the basis of an incorporated arbitration provision will bind the surety to the outcome of the arbitration

---

180 9 U.S.C.A. § 4 (West 1999). State statutes usually have a similar provision, *see supra* note 9 and accompanying text.
181 *Id.* § 3. See *supra* note 8 and accompanying text for equivalent state provision.
182 *See, e.g.*, Hoffman v. Fid. & Deposit Co. of Md., 734 F. Supp. 192 (D.N.J. 1990), discussed in detail *supra* text accompanying notes 67-76. *See also* cases discussed *supra* Part II.A.2.
183 *See* discussion *supra* Part II.B.
184 *See* discussion *infra* Part II.D.
185 *See, e.g.*, Liberty Mut. Ins. Co. v. Mandaree Public School Dist. # 36, 503 F.3d 709, 711 (8th Cir. 2007) (affirming denial of the obligee's motion to stay the surety's declaratory judgment action to permit arbitration), also discussed *supra* note 122; AgGrow Oils, L.L.C. v. Nat'l Union Fire Ins. Co. of Pittsburgh, Pa., 242 F.3d 777, 782 (8th Cir. 2001) (holding that the surety was not entitled to a mandatory stay under section 3 of the Federal Arbitration Act, 9 U.S.C.A. § 3 (West 1999)), discussed in detail *supra* Part II.A.4. Courts may, however, exercise discretionary authority to stay actions sufficiently related to disputes subject to arbitration. *See* discussion *infra* text accompanying notes 209-10.
186 *See* cases discussed *supra* Part II.A.3,4.

Effect of an Arbitration Provision in the Principal's Contract 733

between the obligee and the principal.[187] There is a wide variation among the cases as to the conditions upon which the surety will be foreclosed and as to the extent of the preclusion imposed.[188] Nevertheless, the surety will probably be bound to some degree by the outcome of the arbitration between the principal and the obligee—at least as to the issue of the existence and amount of the principal's liability to the claimant — if the principal contested the arbitration on the merits or the surety had the opportunity to do so. Accordingly, even if the surety has the option of declining to participate in an arbitration, it may wish to join that proceeding voluntarily.[189] Before exercising that choice, the surety should carefully consider the principal's willingness and ability to defend the claim effectively; for by choosing not to participate, the surety may well be putting its fate into the principal's hands.

D. *Statutory Compulsion*

The Federal Arbitration Act and most state statutes[190] apply to only the parties to the contract containing the arbitration provision, and thus, under the terms of those statutes, only parties to that contract may be compelled to arbitrate.[191] Two states, however, have adopted provisions

---

187 *See, e.g.*, Loyal Order of Moose, Lodge 1392 v. Int'l Fid. Ins. Co., 797 P.2d 622, 629 (Alaska 1990) (declining to decide whether the surety may be compelled to participate in an arbitration between the obligee and the principal but stating that the surety would be bound by the results of such an arbitration if the surety, with adequate notice of the arbitration and opportunity to participate, decided to forego arbitration).

188 For a detailed discussion of the preclusive effect of an arbitration award against the principal, *see infra* Part V.

189 *See* Aetna Cas. & Sur. Co. v. L'Energia Ltd. P'ship, No. Civ. A. 96-10098-GAO, 1996 WL 208497 at *4 n.4 (D. Mass. Mar. 4, 1996) (observing that "since [the surety] can be bound by the consequences of an unfavorable arbitral decision against [the principal], it potentially disregards the arbitration at its own peril."); WindowMaster Corp. v. B.G. Danis Co., 511 F. Supp. 157, 160 (S.D. Ohio 1981) (noting that "[s]ince it [the surety] may well be bound by an award between the other two [the obligee and the principal], it would certainly seem the better course for it voluntarily to participate in the arbitration."), *disapproved of by* Exch. Mut. Ins. Co. v. Haskell Co., 742 F.2d 274, 276 (6th Cir. 1984).

190 *See* discussion *supra* Part I.A.

191 *See* discussion *supra* Part I.C.

which appear to bear directly on the surety's obligation to participate in an arbitration. A Rhode Island statute[192] specifically makes an arbitration provision to which a construction contractor is a party binding on, and enforceable by, the claimant, the contractor or the contractor's surety with respect to the surety's bond liability. The statute provides in pertinent part:

> (a) If a contractor principal on a bond furnished to guarantee performance or payment on a construction contract and the claimant are parties to a written contract with a provision to submit to arbitration any controversy thereafter arising under the contract, the arbitration provisions shall apply to the surety for all disputes involving questions of the claimant's right of recovery against the surety. Either the claimant, the contractor principal, or surety may demand arbitration in accordance with the written contract in one arbitration proceeding. The arbitration award shall decide all controversies subject to arbitration . . . including all questions involving liability of the contractor principal and surety on the construction bond, ...[193]

In Georgia, by contrast, a surety on either a performance bond or a payment bond may be statutorily exempted from a duty to arbitrate. The Georgia arbitration statute provides that the enforceability of arbitration agreements shall not apply to "[a]ny contract of insurance, as defined in . . . Code Section 33-1-2."[194] That provision defines "Insurer" to include "any person engaged as . . . surety,"[195] and another provision of the same title defines "[s]urety insurance" to include "guaranteeing and executing bonds, undertakings, and contracts of suretyship."[196] On the basis of those statutes and a case stating that a contractor's surety bond is "a form of insurance contract,"[197] it has been argued that "the Georgia Arbitration Code and the provisions of the Insurance Code together exclude sureties from the scope of the only basis for compelling

---

192 R.I. GEN. LAWS § 10-3-21 (West, Westlaw through end of 2007 legislation.).
193 Id.
194 GA. CODE ANN. § 9-9-2(c)(3) (West, Westlaw through 2008 Reg. Sess.).
195 Id. § 33-1-2(4).
196 Id. § 33-7-7(2).
197 Houston Gen. Ins. Co. v. Brock Constr. Co., 246 S.E.2d 316, 318 (Ga. 1978).

arbitration under Georgia law."[198] If, however, arbitration is demanded in connection with a project to which the Federal Arbitration Act applies and the Georgia statute is deemed to undercut the enforceability of the obligee's arbitration agreement with the principal by excluding the surety from its purview, the Georgia statute would be nullified by preemption, and the federal statute would govern.[199] Preemption would not necessarily result in the surety's being compelled to arbitrate because the federal act does not, by its terms, require a surety to arbitrate. The net result of preemption would leave open the possibility of compelling the

---

[198] Veal *supra* note 5 at 3. That author cautions, however, that "[n]o appellate decisions have addressed this question directly; as a caveat to the above, at least one trial judge has rejected this conclusion without explanation." *id.* Arbitration statutes also exclude insurance contracts or policies in Kansas, KAN. STAT. ANN. § 5-401(a) (West, Westlaw through 2008 Reg. Sess.) (excluding "[c]ontracts of insurance, except for those contracts between insurance companies, including reinsurance contracts"); Missouri, MO. ANN. STAT. § 435.350 (West, Westlaw through end of 2008 2nd Reg. Sess. of 94th Gen. Assemb.) (excluding "contracts of insurance"); and South Dakota, S.D. CODIFIED LAWS § 21-25A-3 (West, Westlaw through 2008 Reg. Sess., 2008 Gen. Election, and Sup. Ct. Rule 08-09) (excluding "insurance policies"). It is not clear from other statutory provisions or available case law, however, whether or not surety bonds in general, or performance bonds in particular, are included within those statutory exclusions.

[199] *See* discussion *supra* text accompanying notes 18-25. In *Northwestern Corp. v. National Union Fire Insurance Co. of Pittsburgh, Pa. (In re Northwestern Corp.)*, 321 B.R. 120, 127 (Bankr. D. Del. 2005), the court held that the Federal Arbitration Act preempted a Montana statute which provided that its arbitration statute did not apply to "any agreement concerning or relating to insurance policies," MONT. CODE ANN. § 27-5-114(2)(c) (West, Westlaw through end of 2007 Reg. Sess. and May 2007 Spec. Sess). The court rejected the argument that the McCarran-Ferguson Act, 15 U.S.C.A. §§ 1011-12 (West 1997), which prohibits enactment of federal statutes impairing state laws regulating the business of insurance, "reverse preempted" the Federal Arbitration Act, finding that the dispute to be arbitrated involved a coverage issue under a single, private policy and had nothing to do with Montana's regulation of the business of insurance, *id.* at 124-27 (collecting cases). *See also,* Doctor's Assocs., Inc. v. Casarotto, 517 U.S. 681, 687 (1996) (holding that the Federal Arbitration Act preempted a provision of the Montana arbitration statute imposing special notice requirements on agreements to arbitrate).

surety to arbitrate upon a demonstration, under Georgia law,[200] that the surety was a party to the arbitration agreement by reason, for example, of the incorporation into the performance bond of a construction contract with an arbitration provision.

III. The Obligee's Obligation to Arbitrate

In the super incorporation cases at least, the obligee has been able to compel the surety to submit to arbitration on the basis of the incorporation by reference in the performance bond of a construction contract which contains an arbitration provision. Such incorporation has also provided the basis for courts to require the obligee to arbitrate, although the surety has not always been the party entitled to compel that arbitration and the issue referred to arbitration has not always been the surety's liability under the performance bond.

The surety which seeks to compel the obligee to arbitrate has the same problem as the obligee who wishes to require the surety to arbitrate. The surety and the obligee have not signed an arbitration agreement. Only a person who is a party to an arbitration agreement may enforce it by obtaining an order directing the other party to arbitrate.[201] Just as application of the super incorporation approach permits the obligee to compel the surety to arbitrate, it will also allow the surety to force the obligee to arbitrate. The super incorporation cases, either expressly or in practical effect, hold that the surety becomes a party to an arbitration provision in a construction contract when the performance bond incorporates that contract by reference. Concluding that the surety is a party to the arbitration agreement resolves the standing issue *ipso facto*. Thus, under the super incorporation approach, when the surety is sued by the obligee, the surety may compel the obligee to submit its performance bond claim for resolution to arbitration with the surety.[202]

---

200 First Options of Chicago, Inc. v. Kaplan, 514 U.S. 938, 944 (1995).
201 *See* discussion *supra* text accompanying notes 80-82.
202 *See, e.g.*, Kvaerner ASA v. Bank of Tokyo-Mitsubishi, Ltd., N.Y. Branch, 210 F.3d 262 (4th Cir. 2000); Commercial Union Ins. Co. v. Gilbane Bldg. Co., 992 F.2d 386 (1st Cir. 1993); Shorcs of Pan., Inc. v. Safeco Ins. Co. of Am., Civil Action No. 07-00602-KD-B, 2008 WL 4417558, at *1 (S.D. Ala. Sept. 29, 2008); Firemen's Ins. Co. of Newark, N.J. v. Edgewater Beach Owner's Ass'n, Inc., No. 3:96CV256/RV, 1996 WL 509720, at *1 (N.D. Fla. June 25, 1996), discussed in detail *supra*

Part II.A.4; Cumberland Cas. & Sur. Co. v. Lamar School Dist., No. CA 03-961, 2004 WL 2294409 (Ark. Ct. App. Oct. 13, 2004); Town of Berlin v. Nobel Ins. Co., 758 A.2d 436 (Conn. App. Ct. 2000); Bolingbrook Park Dist. v. Nat'l–Ben Franklin Ins. Co. of Ill., 420 N.E.2d 741 (Ill. App. Ct. 1981); Travelers Cas. & Sur. Co. of Am. v. Long Bay Mgmt. Co., 792 N.E.2d 1013 (Mass. App. Ct. 2003) (compelling arbitration over the objection of the principal, not the obligee); Robert J. Denley Co. v. Neal Smith Constr. Co., No. W2006-00629-COA-R3-CV, 2007 WL 1153121, at *1 (Tenn. Ct. App. Apr. 19, 2007); Tipton County Dep't of Public Instruction v. Delashmit Elec. Co., No. 02A01-9704-CH-00084, 1998 WL 158774, at *4 (Tenn. Ct. App. Apr. 7, 1998). In *Henderson Investment Corp. v. International Fidelity Insurance Co.*, 575 So. 2d 770 (Fla. Dist. Ct. App. 1991), the court affirmed the granting of the surety's motion to compel the obligee to arbitrate with the surety its claim under the performance bond on the grounds that the performance bond incorporated the construction contract with an arbitration provision. The opinion is not quite clear because it refers to incorporation as binding the surety and obligee to arbitrate "disputes under the construction contract," *id.* at 772, but also notes that the surety's right to invoke the incorporated arbitration provision rests on its "status as the real party in interest/joint and several obligor" under the construction contract, *id.* at 772 n.1. The court, however, emphasized that the "obligations of a surety under its bond agreement are coextensive with that of a contractor (principal). Thus, if the contractor owes the debt, so does the surety," *id.* at 771. For the *Henderson* court, there simply may have been no distinction between the surety and the obligee arbitrating disputes under the construction contract and arbitrating disputes under the performance bond. In *Choctaw Generation Ltd. Partnership v. American Home Assurance Co.*, 271 F.3d 403 (2d Cir. 2001), the Second Circuit ordered the obligee to arbitrate its performance bond claim against the surety, not because of incorporation, but on the grounds of estoppel. Although the performance bond incorporated a construction contract with an arbitration provision, the court expressly declined to rule on that basis. *Id.* at 406. Instead, it held that the obligee was estopped from avoiding arbitration with the surety because the obligee had agreed by signing the construction contract to resolve disputes arising thereunder by arbitration and because the obligee's bond claim was so closely related to the construction contract dispute which was the subject of a pending arbitration proceeding between the obligee and the principal. *Id.* at 406-408.

Moreover, the surety is entitled to at least a stay, if not a dismissal, of the obligee's action as a necessary component of enforcing the arbitration agreement between those parties.[203]

On the other hand, courts applying the limited incorporation approach have denied applications by the surety to compel the obligee to arbitrate, rather than litigate, its claims against the surety.[204] Those courts emphasize that arbitration is consensual and that therefore arbitration agreements must be enforced as written. By signing a construction contract with an arbitration provision, the obligee has agreed to arbitrate disputes thereunder with the other contracting party, the principal. The incorporation of that contract into the performance bond does not operate to transform the arbitration clause into an agreement by the obligee to arbitrate disputes with the surety.[205] Thus, despite incorporation, the surety is not a party to the obligee's arbitration agreement with the principal and therefore is not entitled to enforce that agreement by an order requiring the obligee to arbitrate its performance bond claim which would deprive the obligee of its right to a judicial determination of the surety's liability.

While the surety may not be a party to the obligee's arbitration agreement, the principal is. Therefore, if the obligee sues the surety on

---

203   See e.g., *Gilbane Bldg. Co.*, 992 F.2d at 386 (the surety was entitled to a stay of the obligee's counterclaim for arbitration of that count seeking recovery on the performance bond which incorporated a construction contract with arbitration provision); *Shores of Pan.*, 2008 WL 4417558, at *1 (the surety was entitled to a stay of the obligee's action and to an order compelling the obligee to arbitrate claims against the surety pursuant to the performance bond which incorporated a construction contract with an arbitration provision); *Bolingbrook Park Dist.*, 420 N.E.2d at 743 (surety entitled to dismissal of the obligee's action and to an order compelling the obligee to arbitrate claims against the surety under the performance bond which incorporated a construction contract with an arbitration provision); *Robert J. Denley Co.*, 2007 WL 1153121 at *10 (surety has standing to compel developer to arbitrate its performance bond claim because bond incorporated contract between developer and principal which contained an arbitration provision).

204   *E.g.*, AgGrow Oils, L.L.C. v. Nat'l Union Fire Ins. Co. of Pittsburgh, Pa., 242 F.3d 777 (8th Cir. 2001), discussed in detail *supra* text Part II.A.4; Hartford Accident & Indem. Co. v. Scarlett Harbor Assocs. Ltd. P'ship, 695 A.2d 153 (Md. 1997), discussed in detail *supra* Part II.A.3.

205   *E.g., Scarlett Harbor*, 695 A.2d at 156-57.

the performance bond, the principal may intervene and compel the obligee to arbitrate with the principal the issue of the principal's liability under the construction contract.[206] The obligee's agreement to arbitrate with the principal has been incorporated into the performance bond, however; and though the obligee may not be forced to relinquish its right to a judicial resolution of the surety's liability, the obligee's court action against the surety may be stayed in order to enforce the obligee's obligation to arbitrate with the principal.[207] Moreover, such a stay might be ordered upon the surety's motion, alone,[208] even though it is the principal, not the surety, which is regarded as the party to the arbitration agreement.[209] Nevertheless, a nonparty to an arbitration agreement

---

206   *See, e.g.*, Matson, Inc. v. Lamb & Assocs. Packaging, Inc., 947 S.W.2d 324 (Ark. 1997) (so holding), discussed *supra* Part II.A.4. *See also* Loyal Order of Moose, Lodge 1392 v. Int'l Fid. Ins. Co., 797 P.2d 622 (Alaska 1990) (holding that the surety was entitled to require the obligee to arbitrate the principal's liability under the construction contract); Sheffield Assembly of God Church, Inc. v. Am. Ins. Co., 870 S.W.2d 926 (Mo. Ct. App. 1994) (holding that surety was bound by the arbitration award in favor of the obligee rendered after the principal had successfully moved to stay the obligee's action against the surety and principal to permit arbitration of the principal's liability).

207   *See Matson*, 947 S.W.2d at 328.

208   *Loyal Order of Moose*, 797 P.2d at 629. In that case, the court affirmed an order requiring the obligee to arbitrate the principal's liability. While it is unclear whether the order below was entered on the surety's motion or the lower court's own motion, the Alaska Supreme Court stated that the surety "may require" the obligee to arbitrate the underlying dispute. *Id.* at 629. As that court expressly declined to decide whether the surety could be compelled to participate in such an arbitration, *id.* at 629 n.18, the court left open the possibility that the surety might ultimately be determined to be a party to the arbitration agreement.

209   In *AgGrow Oils*, 242 F.3d at 782, the Eighth Circuit denied the surety's motion for a mandatory stay under section 3 of the Federal Arbitration Act, 9 U.S.C.A. § 3 (West 1999), because it did not regard the bond's incorporation clause as constituting an agreement to arbitrate disputes between the obligee and the surety under the performance bond. Nevertheless, the court remanded the case and instructed the district court to consider whether it should exercise its discretionary authority to stay a third-party litigation which is sufficiently related to an issue within the scope of an arbitration agreement. *Id.* at 782-83. In *Scarlett Harbor*, 695 A.2d 153 at 157 n.8, even though the principal had already obtained an

generally does not have a statutory right to stay a related court proceeding.[210] Thus, if the obligee sues the surety in a jurisdiction which is expected to apply the limited incorporation approach and the surety wishes to stay the court action and to compel the obligee to arbitrate the principal's liability, the surety should enlist the principal, if it is cooperative, as a co-movant for a stay, either as a party to the action or as an intervenor. The principal's participation will likely ensure that the stay is granted.

IV. Consolidation of Related Arbitrations

A surety may find itself subject to an arbitration demand in an overall context in which there are related claims and disputes among other parties involved with the project. Such a situation is particularly likely to arise with multi-prime contracts in which several co-primes commence separate arbitrations under their individual contracts against the owner, and the owner asserts counterclaims seeking indemnification against each co-prime for the claims asserted by the others and perhaps commences an arbitration or action against the architect. Depending on the circumstances of the particular case, the surety may benefit from

---

order requiring the obligee to arbitrate the principal's liability and was no longer a party to the case, the Maryland Court of Appeals noted that the lower court had the power to stay the obligee's action against the surety pending the outcome of the arbitration between the obligee and the principal. Given that the court of appeals had already held that the surety was not entitled to compel the obligee to arbitrate its claim against the surety, the surety's entitlement to such a stay could not arise from its status as a party to the arbitration agreement. The statutory requirement for a stay pending arbitration is that the movant be a party to the arbitration agreement. IDS Life Ins. Co. v. SunAmerica, Inc., 103 F.3d 524, 529 (7th Cir. 1996) (so holding with respect to section 3 of the Federal Arbitration Act, 9 U.S.C.A. § 3 (West 1999)). Nevertheless, when an action and an arbitration involve the same issues and related parties, courts have discretionary authority to stay the litigation, even on the motion of a nonparty to the arbitration agreement, under the "parallel-proceeding abstention" doctrine, *IDS Life Ins. Co.*, 103 F.3d at 530, or a "[c]ourt's inherent power to conserve judicial resources by controlling its own docket," Cost Bros., Inc. v. Travelers Indem. Co., 760 F.2d 58, 60 (3d Cir. 1985), at least when a party is trying to evade a duty to arbitrate.

210   *See* IDS Life Ins. Co., 103 F.3d at 529.

resolving its dispute in a proceeding into which all of the arbitrations have been consolidated or in its own separate arbitration. Parties seeking to consolidate proceedings that involve common questions of fact or law typically emphasize the inefficiencies and possible inconsistent determinations that may result from separate proceedings.[211] The problem generally arises when the arbitration agreement is silent on the issue and a party to one of the separate arbitrations opposes consolidation.

The Federal Arbitration Act[212] does not address consolidation and neither does the original 1956 Uniform Arbitration Act[213] or most of the traditional state arbitration statutes.[214] Thus, in cases arising under those statutes, applications for compulsory consolidation have been resolved as a matter of common law, and the rule applied under the federal statute has differed from that used under many state statutes. The Revised Uniform Arbitration Act,[215] however, contains a new provision which gives courts the discretion to order consolidation and specifies the factors to be considered in deciding whether to do so.[216]

A. Under the Federal Arbitration Act

1. Before Green Tree

Before the United States Supreme Court decided *Green Tree Financial Corp. v. Bazzle*[217] in June, 2003, it was fairly clear that under the Federal Arbitration Act, a court did not have the authority to order an unwilling party to participate in a consolidated arbitration when that party had not agreed to do so and that the question whether or not a party had agreed

---

211 *See e.g.*, Gov't of the U.K. of Gt. Brit. & N. Ir. v. Boeing Co., 998 F.2d 68, 74 (2d Cir. 1993).
212 9 U.S.C.A. §§ 1-16 (West 1999 & Supp. 2008).
213 UNIF. ARBITRATION ACT, §§ 1-25 (1956), 7 U.L.A. §§ 1-25 (West, Westlaw through 2006 Ann. Mtg. of Nat'l Conf.).
214 Timothy J. Heinsz, *The Revised Uniform Arbitration Act: Modernizing, Revising, and Clarifying Arbitration Law*, 2001 J. DISP. RESOL. 1, 12 (2001).
215 REVISED UNIF. ARBITRATION ACT §§ 1-33 (2000), 10 U.L.A. §§ 1-33 (West, Westlaw through 2007 Ann. Mtg. of Nat'l Conf.).
216 *Id.* § 10; *see* discussion *infra* Part IV.B.2.
217 539 U.S. 444 (2003); *see* discussion *infra* Part IV.A.2.

was to be decided by the court, not the arbitrator, as a matter of federal common law[218] under the Act. That view emanated from Supreme Court opinions emphasizing that despite the liberal federal policy favoring arbitration, the fundamental purpose of the Act was to put private arbitration agreements on the same footing as contracts generally and that therefore courts were required to enforce those agreements as written.

In *Moses H. Cone Memorial Hospital v. Mercury Construction Corp.*[219] for example, a contractor brought a federal court action under section 4 of the Federal Arbitration Act to compel the owner to arbitrate delay and impact claims pursuant to the arbitration provision in their contract. The owner opposed arbitration on the ground that it was required to bring its related indemnification claims against the architect in state court because its contract with the architect did not contain an arbitration clause. The owner argued that it should not be forced to litigate common issues before two tribunals with the possibility of inconsistent results. For the court, those considerations did not abrogate the command of section 4; it said that "[u]nder the [Federal] Arbitration Act, an arbitration agreement must be enforced notwithstanding the presence of other persons who are parties to the underlying dispute but not to the arbitration agreement."[220]

Two years later, in *Dean Witter Reynolds, Inc. v. Byrd*,[221] the court reinforced that point in a dispute between a securities broker-dealer and its customer involving state law claims that were subject to the arbitration provision of the agreement between them and claims under federal securities statutes which were not arbitrable. The court held that the broker-dealer's application to compel arbitration of the state law claims should have been granted "even where the result would be the possibly inefficient maintenance of separate proceedings in different forums."[222] It explained that "[b]y its terms, the Act leaves no place for

---

218 *See* Moses H. Cone Mem'l Hosp. v. Mercury Constr. Corp., 460 U.S. 1, 24 (1983) ("The effect of the section [section 2 of the Federal Arbitration Act, 9 U.S.C.A. § 2 (West 1999)] is to create a body of federal substantive law of arbitrability, applicable to any arbitration agreement within the coverage of the Act.").

219 460 U.S. 1.

220 *Id.* at 20.

221 470 U.S. 213 (1985).

222 *Id.* at 217.

the exercise of discretion ... but instead mandates that the district court *shall* direct the parties to proceed to arbitration on issues as to which an arbitration agreement has been signed."[223] In short, the Act "requires that the courts compel arbitration of arbitrable claims, when asked to do so ... and 'not substitute [its] own views of economy and efficiency' for those of Congress."[224]

Courts of appeal invoked *Moses H. Cone* and *Byrd* to deny consolidation when not agreed to. For example, in *Government of the United Kingdom of Great Britain and Northern Ireland v. Boeing Co.*,[225] the Second Circuit held that the Federal Arbitration Act did not authorize a court to consolidate related arbitration proceedings which were being conducted pursuant to separate contracts. Although both contracts contained arbitration clauses, neither referred to consolidation and therefore the court held that "[w]e simply have no grounds to conclude that the parties consented to consolidated arbitration"[226] and arbitration contracts must be enforced as written "*despite* possible inefficiencies created by such enforcement."[227] Citing cases from the Fifth, Sixth, Eighth, Ninth, and Eleventh Circuits, the Second Circuit said that each of the other circuits which had considered the issue since *Moses H. Cone*, *Byrd*, and *Volt Information Sciences, Inc. v. Board of Trustees of the Leland Stanford Junior University*,[228] had also concluded that consolidation could not be ordered absent the consent of all parties.[229]

One of the cases cited by *United Kingdom*, *Del E. Webb Construction v. Richardson Hospital Authority*,[230] denied consolidation in a case involving the provision limiting consolidation or joinder in "the American Institute of Architects document A201, entitled General Conditions of the Contract for Construction"[231] which appeared in both

---

223 *Id* at 218.
224 *Id*. at 217 (quoting Dickinson v. Heinold Secs., Inc., 661 F.2d 638, 646 (7th Cir. 1981)).
225 998 F.2d 68 (2d Cir. 1993).
226 *Id*. at 70.
227 *Id*. at 72.
228 489 U.S. 468 (1989).
229 *United Kingdom*, 998 F.2d at 72-73 (footnote omitted).
230 823 F.2d 145 (5th Cir. 1987).
231 *Id*. at 147 (internal quotation marks omitted). As the relevant contracts were entered into in 1981, *id*. at 146, the court had before it a pre-1987 edition of the AIA Document A201.

the owner's contract with the contractor and the owner's contract with the architect.[232] The court quoted that provision as follows:

> No arbitration arising out of or relating to the Contract Documents shall include, by consolidation, joinder or in any other manner, the Architect, his employees or consultants except by written consent containing a specific reference to the Owner-Contractor Agreement and signed by the Architect, the Owner, the Contractor and any other person sought to be joined. No arbitration shall include, by consolidation, joinder or in any other manner, parties other than the Owner, Contractor, and any other persons substantially involved in a common question of fact or law, whose presence is required if complete relief is to be accorded in the arbitration. No person other than the Owner or Contractor shall be included as an original third-party or additional third-party to an arbitration whose interest or responsibility is insubstantial. Any consent to arbitration involving an additional person or persons shall not constitute consent to arbitration of any dispute not described therein or with any person not named or described therein.[233]

Relying on that provision in the owner-contractor contract, the district court ordered, under § 4 of the Act, that all of the claims among the owner, contractor and architect be arbitrated in a single, consolidated proceeding. Reversing, the Fifth Circuit said:

> We are not persuaded by the district court's reading because it ignores the first sentence, excluding the architect from arbitration absent consent, and treats the second sentence as an affirmative grant of authority, though the sentence is phrased as a limitation on arbitration. To give both sentences meaning, the architect must be excluded from arbitration absent consent. In short, since under the grant of authority in § 4 the district court was limited to enforcing arbitration agreements according to their terms, and since the parties agree that the architect has not consented in writing, the district court should not have ordered consolidation.[234]

Some courts have agreed with *Del E. Webb* that the second sentence of the quoted provision is a limitation on arbitration rather than an

---

232   *Id.*
233   *Id.* at 150.
234   *Id.*

affirmative grant of authority to consolidate.[235] Other courts have disagreed, holding that that sentence does authorize consolidation of related arbitrations.[236] In the 2007 edition of AIA Document A201, the American Institute of Architects revised the consolidation and joinder provision to the following:

§ 15.4.4 CONSOLIDATION OR JOINDER

§ 15.4.4.1 Either party, at its sole discretion, may consolidate an arbitration conducted under this Agreement with any other arbitration to which it is a party provided that (1) the arbitration agreement governing the other arbitration permits consolidation, (2) the arbitrations to be consolidated substantially involve common questions of law or fact, and (3) the arbitrations employ materially similar procedural rules and methods for selecting arbitrator(s).

§ 15.4.4.2 Either party, at its sole discretion, may include by joinder persons or entities substantially involved in a common question of law or fact whose presence is required if complete relief is to be accorded in arbitration, provided that the party sought to be joined consents in writing to such joinder. Consent to arbitration involving an additional person or entity shall not constitute consent to arbitration of any claim, dispute or other matter in question not described in the written consent.

§ 15.4.4.3 The Owner and Contractor grant to any person or entity made a party to an arbitration conducted under this Section 15.4, whether by joinder or consolidation, the same rights of joinder and consolidation as the Owner and Contractor under this Agreement.[237]

---

235 Hilton Constr. Co. v. Martin Mech. Contractors, Inc., 308 S.E.2d 830, 832 (Ga. 1983) (applying the Federal Arbitration Act); and Baldwin Co. v. Weyland Mach. Shop, Inc., 685 S.W.2d 537, 538-39 (Ark. Ct. App. 1985) (applying Arkansas' version of the original Uniform Arbitration Act).
236 *E.g.*, Maxum Founds., Inc. v. Salus Corp., 817 F.2d 1086, 1087-88 (4th Cir. 1987) (holding, under the Federal Arbitration Act, that the language required consolidation of an arbitration between general contractor and subcontractor with a related arbitration).
237 Am. Inst. of Architects, AIA Document A201 – 2007, General Conditions of the Contract for Construction § 15.4.4 (2007), *available for purchase at* http://www.aia.org/contractdocs/purchase/licensing/AIAS076585.

The 2007 revision brings much needed clarity to the provision which should eliminate the confusion evident in the *Del E. Webb* case. Among other things, the new provision affirmatively authorizes both the consolidation of separate arbitrations and the joinder of additional parties, whereas its predecessors spoke of only adding parties. Section 15.4.4.1 authorizes consolidation of a related arbitration by either party to the contract—even over the objection of the other party to the contract or parties to the separate proceeding—so long as the agreement governing the other arbitration also permits arbitration and the other criteria are met. A significant limitation, however, is the requirement that the party invoking consolidation must be a party to both proceedings. Thus, if, for example, the AIA owner-architect contract documents contain a similar provision, the owner could force the consolidation of its separate arbitrations with the contractor and the architect because it is in contract with both, while the contractor or the architect, who are not parties to each other's contract with the owner, could not. Although that limitation is not imposed on the joinder of parties, the consent of the party to be joined is required. Overall, the new provision permits the joinder of an unwilling nonparty but under limited circumstances.

2. After Green Tree

In 2003, a sharply divided United States Supreme Court ruled in *Green Tree Financial Corp. v. Bazzle*[238] that the question whether the arbitration provision in a contract between a commercial lender and its customers permits a class action arbitration is a question that must be decided by the arbitrator under state law, not by a court applying federal common law under the Federal Arbitration Act. Two groups of customers sued the lender separately in a South Carolina state court on state law claims arising from the lender's claimed failure to provide disclosure forms required under state statutes. The contract pertaining to each group provided broadly in substantially identical language that all disputes arising under or related to the contract or the relationships resulting from the contract would be resolved by arbitration by one arbitrator selected by the lender with the consent of the customer. In each case, the customers sought class certification and the lender moved to stay the court proceeding and to compel arbitration; the court certified a

---

238   539 U.S. 444 (2003).

class action and ordered a class arbitration by an arbitrator selected by the lender and consented to by the named plaintiffs in that case; and the arbitrator ruled in favor of the class and awarded $10 million in damages. On a consolidated appeal, the South Carolina Supreme Court upheld the awards, ruling that under South Carolina law, class arbitrations are permitted unless prohibited by the arbitration agreement.

On appeal to the Supreme Court, the principal question was whether the contractually specified method for selecting the arbitrator had the effect of prohibiting class arbitrations because that method guaranteed the lender the right to choose a separate, and perhaps different, arbitrator for its dispute with each of the class members separately and the imposition of the class procedure abrogated that right except as to the dispute with the named plaintiffs.[239] A four-Justice plurality[240] held that the question could not be resolved by the court, "not simply because it is a matter of state law, but also because it is a matter for the arbitrator to decide."[241] The plurality reasoned that because the ultimate purpose of the Federal Arbitration Act is to ensure that arbitration agreements are enforced according to their terms and because the arbitration provision in that case was so broad, it must be concluded that, except for a very narrow exception, the parties intended that all issues be decided by the arbitrator, not the courts. Because the Act charges the courts to determine only whether a valid agreement to arbitrate exists, the narrow exception includes only issues as to "the validity of the arbitration clause ... [or] its applicability to the underlying dispute between the parties."[242] Whether the arbitration provision permitted class arbitrations did not pose the question "*whether [the parties] agreed to arbitrate*" but instead the question "*what kind of arbitration proceeding* the parties agreed to."[243]

---

[239] In a dissenting opinion, Chief Justice Rehnquist, joined by Justices O'Connor and Kennedy, suggested that it would be reasonable to select different arbitrators "in order to avoid concentrating all of the risk of substantial damages awards in the hands of a single arbitrator," *id.* at 459 (Rehnquist, C.J., dissenting). Justice Thomas dissented separately on the basis of his belief that the Federal Arbitration Act does not apply at all to proceedings in a state court, *id.* at 460 (Thomas, J., dissenting).

[240] Justice Breyer announced the judgment of the Court and delivered an opinion in which Justices Scalia, Souter, and Ginsburg joined, *id.* at 447.

[241] *Id.* at 447.

[242] *Id.* at 452.

[243] *Id.*

The plurality relied on *Howsam v. Dean Witter Reynolds, Inc.*,[244] in which the Court held without dissent[245] that the arbitrator, not the court, should decide whether the arbitration was barred by a six-year limitation period contained in the National Association of Securities Dealers' Code of Arbitration Procedure to which the parties had agreed in the arbitration provision of their contract. The court found that the applicability of the limitations provision was a matter of "procedural" arbitrability, which the parties would have expected the arbitrator to decide, rather than of "substantive" arbitrability—a "gateway" issue which the contracting parties would likely have expected a court to decide.[246] For the *Green Tree* plurality, consolidation was an issue of the former, rather than of the latter, variety; and therefore the judgment of the court was to reverse and remand the case so that the arbitrator could decide the issue.[247]

The dissenters disagreed entirely. For them, "the choice of arbitrator is as important a component of the agreement to arbitrate as is the choice of what is to be submitted to him."[248] Moreover, the dissenters found that the class action format was so completely inconsistent with the contractually specified method of selecting the arbitrator that imposition of the former violated the latter. Therefore, the state court ruling ran afoul of the Federal Arbitration Act, which required that the parties' agreement be enforced as written, and should be reversed.[249] Both the plurality and the dissenters started with the same conception of the ultimate intent of the Act but came to completely different conclusions as to the result produced when that intent is applied to the facts of the case.

---

244   537 U.S. 79 (2002).
245   Only Justice O'Connor, who took no part in the consideration or decision in the case, *id.* at 86, and Justice Thomas, who concurred in the judgment, *id.* at 87, did not join in Justice Breyer's opinion of the Court.
246   *Id.* at 83-85.
247   Justice Stevens concurred in the judgment and dissented in part. He concluded that as the state court decision to conduct class arbitration was correct, he saw no need for a remand but would simply affirm the judgment below. He added that because the plurality opinion "expresses a view of the case close to my own, I concur in the judgment." *Green Tree*, 539 U.S. at 455 (Stevens, J., concurring in the judgment and dissenting in part).
248   *Id.* at 456-57 (Rehnquist, C.J., dissenting).
249   *Id.* at 459-60.

The *Green Tree* decision raised the question whether consolidation would be treated like class arbitrations. If so, then in cases under the Federal Arbitration Act, the arbitrator will decide the issue presumably by construing the parties' contract under state law as he would to resolve any other issue. The result would be the abrogation of cases such as *United Kingdom* and *Byrd* which held, as a matter of federal common law, that unless the arbitration agreement provides for consolidation, the court may not order it. As most arbitration provisions do not address consolidation,[250] the pre-*Green Tree* view would usually result in the denial of consolidation. If *Green Tree* does apply to consolidation, then the outcome will depend on how that issue is resolved under applicable state law. If, for example, state law provides that consolidation is permitted unless expressly prohibited in the arbitration agreement,[251] consolidation will likely be ordered in most cases as agreements generally do not consider the issue.

The courts of appeals appear to be lining up in favor of the view that consolidation is analogous to class arbitration and therefore should be decided by the arbitrator rather than the court. Even before *Green Tree* itself was decided, the First Circuit held that consolidation of related arbitrations under collective bargaining agreements was procedural under *Howsam* and therefore should be decided by the arbitrator.[252] After *Green Tree*, the Fifth Circuit in an ERISA case said in dicta that "*Green Tree* has effectively overruled our holding in *Del E. Webb Construction v. Richardson Hospital Authority*"[253] which held that consolidation should be decided by the court. In two reinsurance cases, the Third and Seventh Circuits ruled that the decision whether to consolidate related

---

250 *See* UNIF. ARBITRATION ACT (2000) § 10 cmt. 1, 10 U.L.A. § 10 (West, Westlaw through 2007 Ann. Mtg. of Nat'l Conf.); Heinsz, *supra* note 214.

251 The Revised Uniform Arbitration Act takes that position, UNIF. ARBITRATION ACT (2000) § 10, 10 U.L.A. § 10; *see* discussion *infra* Part IV.B.2.

252 Shaw's Supermarkets, Inc. v. United Food and Commercial Workers Union, Local 791, 321 F.3d 251, 254 (1st Cir. 2003).

253 Pedcor Mgmt. Co., Inc. Welfare Benefit Plan v. Nations Personnel of Tex., Inc., 343 F.3d 355, 363 (5th Cir. 2003).

arbitration proceedings was for the arbitrator not the court.[254] Although discussing *Howsam*, the Third Circuit ultimately invoked *Green Tree* in holding that consolidation, like class arbitration, does not involve whether the parties made a valid agreement to arbitrate but instead goes to the kind of arbitration to which they agreed and therefore falls outside of the narrow exception of issues that are for the court to decide.[255] The Seventh Circuit, however, chose to rely on *Howsam*, but not *Green Tree*, because that court did not believe that Justice Stevens had agreed with the reasoning of the *Green Tree* plurality and therefore could not "identify a single rationale endorsed by a majority of the court."[256] At least one state court has also held that *Green Tree* requires that the issue of consolidation be decided by the arbitrator.[257] No contrary reported

---

254 Certain Underwriters at Lloyd's London v. Westchester Fire Ins. Co., 489 F.3d 580, 582 (3d Cir. 2007); Employers Ins. Co. of Wausau v. Century Indem. Co., 443 F.3d 573, 574 (7th Cir. 2006).
255 *Certain Underwriters*, 489 F.3d at 587.
256 *Employers Ins. Co.*, 443 F.3d at 580.
257 Yuen v. Superior Court, 18 Cal. Rptr. 3d 127, 130 (Cal. Ct. App. 2004). The *Yuen* decision and its holding that *Green Tree* required that consolidation be decided by the arbitrator was acknowledged in *Parker v. McCaw*, 24 Cal. Rptr. 3d 55, 62 (Cal. Ct. App. 2005) wherein the court nevertheless applied a California statute empowering a court, not an arbitrator, to consolidate arbitration proceedings in certain circumstances, CAL. CIV. PROC. § 1281.3 (West, Westlaw through Ch. 765 of 2008 Reg. Sess., Ch. 1 of 2007-08 1st Exec. Sess., Ch. 1 of 2007-08 2nd Exec. Sess., Ch. 7 of 2007-08 3rd Exec. Sess., and all propositions on 2008 ballots), and state court decisions interpreting its provisions without stating that the Federal Arbitration Act did not apply, *id.* at 63-64, although it appears from the opinion that the transactions involved may have been sufficiently intrastate. The lower court had consolidated two arbitrations involving separate agreements, one of which provided for arbitration by a three-arbitrator panel and the other by a single arbitrator. Among other things, the *Parker* court held that the right to a three-judge panel is a substantial contractual right and that therefore the lower court, when consolidating arbitrations, erred by resolving the conflict between the agreements in favor of one arbitrator, *id. See also* Szuts v. Dean Witter Reynolds, Inc., 931 F.2d 830 (11th Cir. 1991) (holding under the Federal Arbitration Act that the arbitrators exceeded their authority when two arbitrators rendered an award after the disqualification of the third when the agreement called for an arbitration before at least three arbitrators).

decisions have been found. It appears, therefore, that for cases within the purview of the Federal Arbitration Act, which must be applied by both federal and state courts in such cases,[258] the question whether to consolidate related arbitrations is for the arbitrator, not the court, to decide, at least when there is a broad arbitration clause, and cases such as *United Kingdom* and *Del E. Webb*, which until recently held sway, have been abrogated.

B. Under State Statutes

Because the Federal Arbitration Act applies to the full extent of Congress's power under the Commerce Clause,[259] that statute has dominated arbitration litigation. *Green Tree*, however, has apparently turned the tables as to the consolidation issue. State law on consolidation has now become paramount in cases governed by the federal statute. Some commentators see a trend toward consolidation,[260] and to the extent that proves true, *Green Tree* will have reversed the result under earlier federal cases such as *United Kingdom* and *Del E. Webb*. Perhaps the most significant evidence of such a trend was the decision of the National Conference of Commissioners on Uniform State Laws to adopt a provision empowering courts to order consolidation when it issued the Revised Uniform Arbitration Act in 2000.[261] The American Institute of Architect's 2007 edition of the A201 General Conditions revised and clarified its provision on arbitration by affirmatively authorizing consolidation in certain circumstances.[262] The American Arbitration Association has added to its Construction Industry Arbitration Rules a section permitting the association to compel consolidation "[i]f the

---

258   But cf. Muhammad v. County Bank of Rehoboth Beach, Del., 912 A.2d 88, 95 (N.J. 2006) (distinguishing *Green Tree* because the arbitration agreement there was ambiguous while that before the court unambiguously prohibited class arbitrations and therefore holding that the validity of waivers of class treatment in the arbitration agreement was to be decided by the court as a question of whether the agreement to arbitrate was valid).
259   U.S. CONST. art. 1, § 8, cl. 3.
260   See UNIF. ARBITRATION ACT (2000) § 10 cmt. 2, 10 U.L.A. § 10 (West, Westlaw through 2007 Ann. Mtg. of Nat'l Conf.).
261   Id. § 10; see discussion *infra* Part IV.B.2.
262   See discussion *supra* text accompanying note 237.

parties' agreement or the law provides for consolidation or joinder of related arbitrations," even if the parties cannot agree on how to accomplish it.[263]

1. Statutes Which Do Not Address Consolidation

The arbitration statutes of many states are similar to the Federal Arbitration Act. Indeed, the New York arbitration statute[264] was the model for the federal statute itself.[265] Most state statutes, like the federal statute, do not contain a provision addressing consolidation,[266] and neither does the original Uniform Arbitration Act[267] promulgated in

---

263   CONSTR. INDUS. ARBITRATION R. R-7, Am. Arbitration Ass'n (effective Sept. 1, 2007), http://www.adr.org/sp.asp?id=22004&printable=true.

264   N.Y.C.P.L.R. §§ 7501-14 (McKinney 1998 & Supp. 2009).

265   Hall St. Assocs., L.L.C. v. Mattel, Inc., 128 S. Ct. 1396, 1406 n.7. (2008).

266   A few states have included in their arbitration statutes a provision authorizing a court to order consolidation and/or joinder in certain circumstances. *See e.g.*, CAL. CIV. PROC. § 1281.3 (West, Westlaw through Ch. 765 of 2008 Reg. Sess., Ch. 1 of 2007-08 1st Exec. Sess., Ch. 1 of 2007-08 2nd Exec. Sess., Ch. 7 of 2007-08 3rd Exec. Sess., and all propositions on 2008 ballots); MASS. GEN. LAWS ANN. ch. 251, § 2A (West, Westlaw through Ch. 461, except for Ch. 451, of 2008 2nd Ann. Sess.); S.C. CODE ANN. § 15-48-60 (West, Westlaw through end of 2008 Reg. Sess.). *See also* Travelers Cas. & Sur. Co. of Am. v. Long Bay Mgmt. Co., 792 N.E.2d 1013, 1018 (Mass. App. Ct. 2003) (compelling arbitration of the obligee's performance bond claim against the surety and ordering, over the principal's objection, the consolidation of the obligee-surety arbitration with the pending obligee-principal arbitration under chapter 251, section 2A of the Massachusetts General Laws because the two arbitrations arose from the same contract, involved common issues of fact and law, and the principal could show no prejudice resulting from consolidation); Aetna Cas. & Sur. Co. v. L'Energia, Ltd. P'ship, No. Civ. A. 96-10098-GAO, 1996 WL 208497, at *3 (D. Mass. Mar. 4, 1996) (citing chapter 251, section 2A and noting in dicta that "[t]he fact that arbitration agreements do not expressly provide for consolidation certainly does not preclude consolidation.").

267   UNIF. ARBITRATION ACT, §§ 1-25 (1956), 7 U.L.A. §§ 1-25 (West, Westlaw through 2006 Ann. Mtg. of Nat'l Conf.).

1956.²⁶⁸ Courts in some of those states, taking the approach of pre-*Green Tree* federal cases such as *United Kingdom* and *Del E. Webb*, have held that courts have no authority to order consolidation absent affirmative consent thereto by all parties. For example, the Connecticut Supreme Court in *W.J. Megin, Inc. v. Connecticut*²⁶⁹ held that there is no judicial authority to consolidate a general contractor's arbitration with the owner and its arbitration with a subcontractor on the same project, both of which concerned the effect of the same change order, because "the duty to arbitrate and the scope of that duty depend on the terms of the agreement between the parties ... [and] [a] party that has agreed to arbitrate certain matters cannot, for that reason alone, be compelled to arbitrate other matters that it has not agreed to submit to arbitration."²⁷⁰

Courts in other states, however, though beginning their reasoning at the same point, have come to the opposite conclusion.²⁷¹ In *County of Sullivan v. Edward L. Nezelek, Inc.*,²⁷² for example, a county college commenced an arbitration against the architect pursuant to a contract between them, and the general contractor on the same project commenced a related arbitration against the county, as "local sponsor" of

---

268   See Heinsz, *supra* note 214, at 12 ("The UAA, the FAA, and most state arbitration statutes do not specifically address consolidation of arbitration proceedings.").
269   434 A.2d 306 (Conn. 1980).
270   *Id.* at 308-09; Seretta Constr., Inc. v. Great Am. Ins. Co., 869 So. 2d 676, 679-80 (Fla. Dist. Ct. App. 2004) (holding that a court did not have authority to compel consolidation of an arbitration between a general contractor and a subcontractor with an arbitration between the same general contractor and another subcontractor on the same project which involved related work). *See also* Patricia C. Kussmann, Annotation, *Consolidation by State Court of Arbitration Proceedings Brought Under State Law*, 31 A.L.R.6th 433 §§ 4-6 (2008) (collecting cases); Daniel E. Feld, Annotation, *State Court's Power To Consolidate Arbitration Proceedings*, 64 A.L.R.3d 528 § 4 (1975 & Supp. 2007) (collecting cases); UNIF. ARBITRATION ACT (2000) § 10 cmt. 1, 10 U.L.A. § 10 (West, Westlaw through 2007 Ann. Mtg. of Nat'l Conf.) (collecting cases); *Heinsz, supra* note 214, at 12 n.76 (collecting cases).
271   *See, e.g.*, Kussmann, *supra* note 270, §§ 7-8 (collecting cases); Feld, *supra* note 270, § 3 (collecting cases); UNIF. ARBITRATION ACT (2000) § 10 cmt. 1 (collecting cases); *Heinsz, supra* note 214, at 12 n.75 (collecting cases).
272   366 N.E.2d 72 (N.Y. 1977).

the college, in accordance with the contract between them. The New York Court of Appeals held that a court had the power to consolidate the two arbitrations even though the architect objected.[273] While recognizing that arbitration must be based on the agreement of the parties, the court reasoned that "[i]n recent times, given the decisions of our court and others, parties signing an agreement to arbitrate must be held to do so in contemplation of the announced authority of the courts in proper cases to direct consolidation" and noted that parties wishing to avoid consolidation were free to prohibit it expressly in their arbitration agreements.[274] Thus, under that approach, compulsory consolidation is permitted unless forbidden in the arbitration agreement; for courts reaching the opposite conclusion, compulsory arbitration is forbidden unless expressly permitted in the agreement.[275]

2. *The Revised Uniform Arbitration Act*

In August, 2000, the National Conference of Commissioners on Uniform State Laws promulgated the Revised Uniform Arbitration Act.[276] One of the major changes from the original 1956 Uniform Arbitration Act was the addition of a new section 10 which authorizes a court to compel consolidation of arbitration proceedings in certain circumstances.[277] Section 10 provides as follows.

> § 10. Consolidation of Separate Arbitration Proceedings
>
> (a) Except as otherwise provided in subsection (c), upon [motion] of a party to an agreement to arbitrate or to an arbitration proceeding, the court may order consolidation of separate arbitration proceedings as to all or some of the claims if:

---

273 *Id.* at 73.
274 *Id.* at 75.
275 *See, e.g.*, Gov't of the U.K. of Gr. Brit. & N. Ir. v. Boeing Co., 998 F.2d 68, 71 (2d Cir. 1993) ("[T]he FAA does not authorize consolidation of arbitration proceedings unless doing so would be 'in accordance with the terms of the agreement.' 9 U.S.C. § 4.").
276 UNIF. ARBITRATION ACT (2000) §§ 1-33, 10 U.L.A. §§ 1-33 (West, Westlaw through 2007 Ann. Mtg. of Nat'l Conf.), which has so far been adopted by twelve states and the District of Columbia, *see supra* note 6.
277 *Heinsz, supra* note 214, at 11.

(1) there are separate agreements to arbitrate or separate arbitration proceedings between the same persons or one of them is a party to a separate agreement to arbitrate or a separate arbitration proceeding with a third person;
(2) the claims subject to the agreements to arbitrate arise in substantial part from the same transaction or series of related transactions;
(3) the existence of a common issue of law or fact creates the possibility of conflicting decisions in the separate arbitration proceedings; and
(4) prejudice resulting from a failure to consolidate is not outweighed by the risk of undue delay or prejudice to the rights of or hardship to parties opposing consolidation.

(b) The court may order consolidation of separate arbitration proceedings as to some claims and allow other claims to be resolved in separate arbitration proceedings.
(c) The court may not order consolidation of the claims of a party to an agreement to arbitrate if the agreement prohibits consolidation.[278]

The commentary to section 10 states that consolidation is desirable in order to avoid inefficiency and the possibility of conflicting results.[279] Moreover, by establishing "a default provision" providing for consolidation, the commissioners hoped to encourage drafters of agreements to consider the issue expressly and enhance the possibility that parties will be on notice regarding the issue.[280]

The limiting conditions of section 10 were considered in *Biber Partnership, P.C. v. Diamond Hill Joint Venture, LLC*,[281] in which an architectural firm was a party to two separate arbitration proceedings involving the same construction project, one with a structural engineering firm and the other with the project owner which asserted claims for design defects implicating the engineering firm's work. The

---

278 UNIF. ARBITRATION ACT (2000) § 10. Section 10 is an adaptation of the consolidation provisions of the California and Georgia arbitration statutes, UNIF. ARBITRATION ACT (2000) § 10 cmt. 3; *see supra* note 266. Section 10, however, "is not intended to address the issue as to the validity of arbitration clauses in the context of class-wide disputes," UNIF. ARBITRATION ACT (2000) § 10 cmt. 3.
279 UNIF. ARBITRATION ACT (2000) § 10 cmt. 3.
280 *Id.*
281 960 A.2d 774 (N.J. Super. Ct. App. Div. 2008).

architectural firm moved for consolidation of the two proceedings which both the engineering firm and the owner opposed and the trial court denied. On appeal, a New Jersey intermediate appellate court affirmed the denial in a case of first impression under New Jersey's version of the Revised Uniform Arbitration Act.[282] As the engineering firm and owner did not dispute that subsections (a)(1), (2) and (3) of section 10[283] had been met, the court decided the case under subsection (4) by considering whether "the risk of undue delay or prejudice to the rights of or hardship to parties opposing consolidation" outweighed any "prejudice resulting from a failure to consolidate."[284] The court found two kinds of prejudice to the opposing parties each of which was separately sufficient to justify denial of consolidation. First, the agreement between the architectural firm and the engineering firm provided that the arbitration would be conducted by a single arbitrator who was specified by name, and consolidation would have required that the arbitration be conducted before a panel of three arbitrators as provided in the agreement between the architectural firm and the owner. The court agreed with the commentary to the Revised Uniform Arbitration Act that the contractually specified arbitrator or method of selecting the arbitrator was a right the deprivation of which ordinarily precludes consolidation.[285] Second, the architectural firm had allowed both arbitrations to proceed separately for twenty months before commencing the action for consolidation on the day scheduled for the beginning of hearings in one of the arbitrations even though it had known for a year that the owner alleged defects in the engineering firm's work. Again, the court agreed with the commentary that waiting until one of the arbitrations has reached the hearings stage before seeking consolidation would ordinarily constitute delay and hardship sufficient to bar consolidation.[286] The court also noted that section 10 gives the trial court the discretion to determine whether or not to order consolidation and that therefore an appellate

---

282 N.J. STAT. ANN. §§ 2A:23B-1 to -32 (West Supp. 2008).
283 *Id.* § 2A:23B-10.
284 *Id.* § 2A:23B-10(a)(4).
285 *Biber*, 960 A.2d at 778 (citing UNIF. ARBITRATION ACT (2000) § 10 cmt. 3, 10 U.L.A. § 10 (West, Westlaw through 2007 Ann. Mtg. of Nat'l Conf.); Szuts v. Dean Witter Reynolds, Inc. 931 F.2d 830, 831 (11th Cir. 1991); Parker v. McCaw, 24 Cal. Rptr. 3d 55, 63 (Cal. Ct. App. 2005)).
286 *Id.* at 778-79 (citing UNIF. ARBITRATION ACT (2000) § 10 cmt. 3).

court reviews the trial court's ruling under the abuse of discretion standard.[287]

V. Preclusion

A. *Basic Principles of Preclusion*[288]

---

287 *Id.* at 777.
288 For a comprehensive analysis of preclusion as it applies to suretyship, *see* James D. Ferrucci, *Ch. 9, Preclusive Effect Upon The Surety Of Prior Judgment Or Arbitration Award Against The Principal*, in THE LAW OF PAYMENT BONDS 159 (Kevin L. Lybeck & H. Bruce Shreves, eds. Am. Bar Ass'n 1998 & Supp. 2001). Although that chapter emphasizes preclusion issues arising in the payment bond context, there appears to be no difference as to preclusive effect between judgments against the principal which were rendered in favor of a performance bond obligee and those which were rendered in favor of a payment bond claimant. *Compare* Monmouth Lumber Co. v. Indem. Ins. Co. of N. Am., 122 A.2d 604 (N.J. 1956) (holding that a surety was not bound by a prior default judgment against the principal and in favor of payment bond claimants when the surety did not have notice of and the opportunity to defend the prior action), *with* Raymond Int'l Builders, Inc. v. First Indem. of Am. Ins. Co., 516 A.2d 620 (N.J. 1986) (applying the same principles to hold that a performance bond surety was not bound by a confirmed arbitration award rendered by default against the principal and in favor of the obligee). Accordingly, that chapter discusses and cites performance bond and guarantor cases as well as payment bond cases. Guarantors and sureties are generally governed by the same law with respect to preclusion issues, *see* Motion Picture Indus. Pension Plan v. Hawaiian Kona Coast Assocs., 823 P.2d 752, 757 (Haw. Ct. App. 1991) ("Sureties may or may not be guarantors, but guarantors are sureties. With respect to a privity issue in the res judicata and collateral estoppel context, we conclude that the law applicable to a guarantor should be the same as the law applicable to a surety."); R.I. Hosp. Trust Nat'l Bank v. Ohio Cas. Ins. Co., 789 F.2d 74, 77-78 (1st Cir. 1986); Escambia Chem. Corp. v. Rocker, 184 S.E.2d 31, 34 (Ga. Ct. App. 1971); Ind. Univ. v. Ind. Bonding & Sur. Co., 416 N.E.2d 1275, 1278 (Ind. Ct. App. 1981); Trinity Universal Ins. Co. v. Briarcrest Country Club Corp., 831 S.W.2d 453, 455 (Tex. App. 1992); *see also* RESTATEMENT (THIRD) OF SURETYSHIP AND GUARANTY § 1 cmt. c, § 15 cmts. c & d (1996); *see also* discussion *supra* note 46. Arbitration awards which are binding on the performance

The surety's liability under either the performance bond or the payment bond arises from the breach by the principal of the bonded obligation. This has often led courts to conclude that the surety's liability is coextensive with that of the principal.[289] As a result, when the principal's liability to the obligee has been adjudicated—even in a proceeding to which the surety was not a party—a court may see no reason to permit the surety to litigate the issue of the principal's liability a second time when the obligee subsequently seeks to recover from the surety. Relitigating issues which have already been decided burdens courts and litigants alike, and the preclusion of unnecessary adjudication is the basic purpose of the related doctrines of res judicata and collateral estoppel.[290] Sureties and principals, however, are not simply alter egos of each other. The surety may have defenses which are unique to it and hence unavailable to the principal.[291] Even in the absence of such defenses, the

---

bond surety under the incorporation doctrine are an exception to the proposition that a judgment or arbitration award against the principal is given the same preclusive effect whether the surety is the obligor under a performance bond or payment bond, *see* discussion *infra* Part V.C. Though there are other exceptions, they should have little, if any, affect on the performance bond surety, *see* discussion *infra* note 437. *See also* J. Michael Franks & John W. Heacock, *Arbitration and the Contract Surety: Inclusion and Preclusion*, 32 TORTS & INS. L.J. 977 (1977).

289 *See, e.g.*, Henderson Inv. Corp. v. Int'l Fid. Ins. Co., 575 So. 2d 770, 771-72 (Fla. Dist. Ct. App. 1991) (performance bond incorporation issues), discussed *supra* note 202.

290 *See* Ufheil Constr. Co. v. Town of New Windsor, 478 F. Supp. 766, 767-68 (S.D.N.Y. 1979), *aff'd*, 636 F.2d 1204 (2d Cir. 1980) ("The doctrine of collateral estoppel, . . . 'like the related doctrine of res judicata, has the dual purpose of protecting litigants from the burden of relitigating an identical issue with the same party or his privy and of promoting judicial economy by preventing needless litigation.'" (quoting Parklane Hosiery Co. v. Shore, 439 U.S. 322, 326 (1979)). Selected federal and state cases deciding preclusion questions in the suretyship or guaranty context are listed on a state-by-state basis in *id.* at 218-21, app.

291 Such defenses are personal to the surety and are generally referred to as the surety's "suretyship defenses." In the performance bond context, such suretyship defenses would include the obligee's failure to adhere to notice requirements, overpayment of the principal, release of security, discharge of the principal, and misrepresentation or failure to disclose material facts. *See* RESTATEMENT (THIRD) OF SURETYSHIP AND GUARANTY, Title

principal may lack the resources, interest or expertise to present an effective defense to a claim. The potential incongruence between the interests of the surety and the principal has led some courts to reject the proposition that an adjudication of the principal's liability results in the surety's having had its day in court—at least not in all cases or for all purposes. Because of differing perceptions by courts as to the identity of the interests of the surety and the principal, the cases are in conflict over the preclusive effect to be given to a judgment or arbitration award against the principal.

1. Res Judicata, Collateral Estoppel and Privity

The common law has developed the doctrines of res judicata and collateral estoppel to attempt to reconcile the competing policies of avoiding the relitigation of decided matters and preserving everyone's right to be heard. At the most basic level, res judicata prohibits contesting parties, or those in privity with them, from relitigating the *claims* which those same parties previously litigated to a final judgment[292] and is therefore often referred to as "claims preclusion."[293] Collateral estoppel prohibits the relitigation of *issues* which have already been adjudicated in a previous case between the same parties and is called "issue preclusion."[294] The elements of collateral estoppel have been defined variously. A typical formulation requires that the issue in the first case was adjudicated on the merits, was essential to the judgment therein and is identical to the issue in the second case; that the party sought to be estopped was a party or in privity with a party to the first case; and that such party or its privy had a full and fair opportunity to litigate the issue in the first case.[295]

B, Suretyship Defenses, Introductory Note, §§ 37-49 (1996); Julia Blackwell Gelinas, *Ch. 9, Defenses Available to Surety, in* THE LAW OF PERFORMANCE BONDS 201, 210-19 (Lawrence R. Moelmann & John T. Harris, eds. Am. Bar Ass'n 1999). The extent to which suretyship defenses survive a judgment or arbitration award against the principal is discussed *infra* Part V.D.

292 *See Ferrucci, supra* note 288, at 187.
293 *See* Taylor v. Sturgell, 128 S. Ct. 2161, 2171, 2171 n.5 (2008).
294 *Id.*
295 Mellon Bank, East Nat'l Ass'n v. Rafsky, 535 A.2d 1090, 1093 (Pa. Super. Ct. 1987) (holding that a guarantor was bound by a prior judgment

Thus, it is fairly clear that while a party is entitled to its day in court, it should, generally speaking, be limited to only that one day. For the purposes of abstract analysis, the term "party" has a straightforward meaning. In practical application, however, the concept is ambiguous. Parties which may be separate legal entities for some purposes may otherwise have such a close relationship that the policies underlying preclusion require that they be treated as the same "party" for the purposes of barring the relitigation of previously settled claims or issues. The question whether such a relationship exists has traditionally been addressed by asking whether there exists "privity" between the party against which preclusion is asserted and the entity which was a party to the prior proceeding. Imposing preclusion on a related party is most often justified, either explicitly or implicitly, on the ground that the interests of the party against which preclusion is sought were adequately represented by or through the related party in the prior action.[296]

Whether the nature of the relationship between the surety and the principal is such that a judgment against the latter should be binding on the former is almost always the central issue with which courts struggle,

---

obtained by the creditor against the debtor); *see also* QDR Consultants & Dev. Corp. v. Colonia Ins. Co., 675 N.Y.S.2d 117, 118-19 (N.Y. App. Div. 1998) (reducing the elements of collateral estoppel to two: that the issue in the second case be identical to that decided in the first and that the party opposing collateral estoppel must have had a full and fair opportunity to contest that issue in the earlier proceeding); *Ferrucci, supra* note 288, at 187-88. The 'full and fair opportunity to contest' element of collateral estoppel should not be confused with the surety's 'notice and opportunity to defend' which, for many courts, is the critical factor in binding the nonparty surety. The former refers to the fairness of the first proceeding, the latter to the surety's opportunity to intervene in it. The nature and significance of the difference is discussed *infra* note 385.

296 A sufficient identity of interest between a party and non-party, and the resulting adequacy of the representation by the former of the latter, may be an exception to the general rule that a person cannot be deprived of his legal rights in a proceeding to which he is not a party and therefore may permit preclusion of nonparties. There are, however, important due process limitations on nonparty preclusion, *see* discussion *infra* Part V.A.2.

either expressly or tacitly, in deciding preclusion issues.[297] The formal

---

[297] Conversely, when the prior adjudication has been in *favor* of the principal, that judgment conclusively bars a subsequent action against the surety by the losing obligee or claimant, unless the principal prevailed on defenses personal to it or those arising from the operation of law. That result is based on the substantive principle of suretyship law that the surety is not liable to a bond beneficiary unless the principal is liable. *See, e.g.*, R.I. Hosp. Trust Nat'l Bank v. Ohio Cas. Ins. Co., 789 F.2d 74, 79 (1st Cir. 1986) (applying Rhode Island law and holding that the obligee's assignor was barred from suing the surety by prior judgment against the obligee and in favor of the principal). The same result has been based on both res judicata, Westcott Constr. Corp. v. Firemen's Fund of N.J., 996 F.2d 14 (1st Cir. 1993) (finding *sub silentio* that the surety was privy of the principal and holding therefore that prior confirmed arbitration award in favor of the principal and against the obligee barred the obligee's action against surety under res judicata), Tucker v. United Fire & Cas. Co., No. Civ. A. 3:98CV20-DA, 1998 WL 433954, at *4 (N.D. Miss. May 29, 1998) (stating that "a surety-principal relationship does not by itself establish privity" but nevertheless holding that res judicata applied because the "narrow exception" to the mutuality requirement *"makes the benefits of preclusion available to anyone who, if defeated in the second action, would be entitled to demand indemnification from the party who won the first action"* and that therefore the surety on a public official's bond was entitled to dismissal of the suit against it); Pye v. Dep't of Transp., 513 F.2d 290, 292-93 (5th Cir. 1975) (same), and collateral estoppel, Burdick Assocs. Owners Corp. v. Indem. Ins. Co. of N. Am., 560 N.Y.S.2d 481, 482 (N.Y. App. Div. 1990) (stating that "[i]t is beyond dispute that collateral estoppel applies to arbitration awards" and holding that because the surety's liability is measured by that of the principal, an arbitration award in favor of the principal determined that issue and therefore collateral estoppel barred the obligee's subsequent action against the surety); *accord* Venus Mech., Inc. v. Ins. Co. of N. Am., 667 N.Y.S.2d 60, 61 (N.Y. App. Div. 1997). Courts have also reasoned that any other result would render the principal indirectly liable, through its indemnification obligation to the surety, after it had been exonerated in the direct action against it. *See, e.g.* Mestek, Inc. v. United Pac. Ins. Co., 667 N.E.2d 292, 294 (Mass. App. Ct. 1996). *But cf.* Cashman Equip. Corp. v. Acadian Shipyard, Inc., No. Civ. A.01-2411, 2001 WL 1387921, at *3 (E.D. La. Nov. 6, 2001) (holding, on the basis of federal preclusion law, that the obligee was not precluded under res judicata by a prior arbitration award in favor of the principal from seeking the rescission of the liquidated damages provision of the bonded contract on a claim of

definition of privity, "'mutual or successive relationships to the same rights of property,'"[298] is exceedingly general and provides virtually no effective guidance. As a result, courts often look to suretyship law for the substance of the relationship between the surety and the principal to which they apply preclusion principles.[299] Some courts, finding that the surety's liability is coextensive with that of the principal, conclude that the surety and the principal are in privity. Other courts, however, see the obligations and interests of the surety and principal as fundamentally independent and incongruent and hold that there is no privity.[300]

2. Due Process Limitations on Nonparty Preclusion

Binding a person to a judgment rendered in a litigation to which he was not a party raises serious federal constitutional issues as the United States Supreme Court reminded everyone as recently as 2008 in *Taylor v. Sturgell*.[301] There, Taylor, "an antique aircraft enthusiast,"[302] sued Sturgell, Acting Administrator of the Federal Aviation Administration (FAA), in the United States District Court for the District of Columbia to enforce his Freedom of Information Act (FOIA)[303] request for all technical documents about the F-45 airplane, a vintage aircraft manufactured in the 1930s. The district court ruled that Taylor's action was barred by claim preclusion because less then a month earlier, the

---

fraudulent inducement in a subsequent court action against the principal and the surety because the arbitrator declined to consider that claim for procedural reasons). Unless otherwise stated, the analysis and authorities set forth in this chapter assumes the prior judgment or arbitration award was adverse to the principal.

298 Shire Realty Corp. v. Schorr, 390 N.Y.S.2d 622, 625 (N.Y. App. Div. 1977) (quoting *In re* Shea, 132 N.E.2d 864, 868 (N.Y. 1956)).

299 *See* Ind. Univ. v. Ind. Bonding & Sur. Co., 416 N.E.2d 1275, 1283 (Ind. Ct. App. 1981) (citing Ager, *Problem: The Effect on the Surety of a Judgment Against the Principal, Solution: The Due Process Clause*, 36 INS. COUNS. J. 245 (1969) and holding that a guarantor was not bound by a judgment against the debtor because the issue of the debtor's liability had not been actually litigated in the prior proceeding).

300 *See generally, Ferrucci, supra* note 288, at 188-91 and cases cited and discussed therein.

301 128 S. Ct. 2161 (2008).

302 *Id.* at 2168.

303 5 U.S.C.A. § 552 (West 2007 & Supp. 2008).

Tenth Circuit affirmed the District of Wyoming's rejection of a FOIA request to the FAA for the same documents which had been made by Herrick, a friend of Taylor's who owned and was restoring an F-45. The FAA had denied Herrick's request under FOIA's exemption for trade secrets or other confidential information[304] when the aircraft manufacturer's corporate successor objected to the release and simply ignored Taylor's request. The District of Columbia court held that even though Taylor was not a party to the earlier suit, Taylor's interests had been "virtually represented" by Herrick.[305] At that time, a number of federal courts had adopted varying conceptions of virtual representation as grounds for applying claim preclusion to nonparties.[306]

Announcing its own test for virtual representation, the District of Columbia Circuit affirmed because there was an identity of interests between Taylor and Herrick as both sought the same documents; Herrick had adequately represented Taylor's interests even though Taylor had received no notice of Herrick's suit; and there was a close relationship between Herrick and Taylor as Herrick asked for Taylor's assistance in restoring his F-45 and provided to Taylor information Herrick had acquired through discovery in his action. In addition, Taylor was represented in the case by the same attorney who had represented Herrick in the earlier suit. The court of appeals raised but left open the question whether Taylor had engaged in "tactical maneuvering" to avoid preclusion.[307]

The Supreme Court reversed in an unanimous opinion by Justice Ginsburg which opened by quoting a 1940 opinion of the Court: "'It is a principle of general application in Anglo-American jurisprudence that one is not bound by a judgment *in personam* in a litigation in which he is not designated as a party or to which he has not been made a party by service of process.'"[308] Invoking other of its prior opinions, the Court reiterated that one who was not a party to an action generally has not had

---

304   *Id.* § 552(b)(4).
305   128 S. Ct. at 2169.
306   *Id.* at 2167, 2173. For example, the district court in *Taylor* employed the Eighth Circuit's seven-factor test, Tyus v. Schoemehl, 93 F.3d 449 (8th Cir. 1996), while the Fourth Circuit had fashioned a much narrower test, Klugh v. United States, 818 F.2d 294 (4th Cir. 1987). *Taylor*, 128 S. Ct. at 2169.
307   *Taylor*, 128 S. Ct. at 2170.
308   *Id.* at 2166-67 (quoting Hansberry v. Lee, 311 U.S. 32, 40 (1940)).

a "'full and fair opportunity to litigate'"[309] the matters settled in that action. Therefore, "[t]he application of claim and issue preclusion to nonparties . . . runs up against the 'deep-rooted historic tradition that everyone should have his own day in court,'"[310] and "[t]he federal common law of preclusion is, of course, subject to due process limitations."[311]

The Court acknowledged that there are exceptions to the general rule against nonparty preclusion. Because of "the fundamental nature of the general rule,"[312] however, those exceptions must be narrowly construed and limited to the following six categories of "recognized exceptions": (1) when the nonparty has agreed to be bound by an action to which he is not a party;[313] (2) when there is a certain type of pre-existing substantive legal relationship between the party and nonparty, such as those between succeeding owners of property, bailor and bailee, and assignor and assignee; (3) in limited circumstances, when the nonparty has been adequately represented by someone with the same interests who was a party to the suit, such as in properly conducted class actions or suits brought by trustees, guardians and other fiduciaries; (4) when the nonparty assumed control over the litigation in which the judgment was entered[314]; (5) when the party bound by the earlier adjudication attempts to avoid preclusion by relitigating through a proxy, such as when the nonparty brings the later suit as the agent for the party who is bound; and (6) if otherwise consistent with due process, when a special statutory scheme expressly forecloses successive litigation by nonparties, such as bankruptcy or probate statutes.[315] Because the virtual representation

---

309   *Id.* at 2171 (quoting Montana v. United States, 440 U.S. 147, 153-54 (1979)).
310   *Id.* at 2171 (quoting Richards v. Jefferson County, 517 U.S. 793, 798 (1996)).
311   *Id.* at 2171.
312   *Id.* at 2175.
313   In the suretyship context, this exception would include judgment bonds; see discussion *infra* note 356.
314   That exception has been applied to bind sureties, *see, e.g.*, Mass. Bonding & Ins. Co. v. Robert E. Denike, Inc., 92 F.2d 657 (3d Cir. 1937); E.B.R. Corp. v. PSL Air Lease Corp., 313 A.2d 893 (Del. 1973).
315   *Taylor*, 128 S. Ct. at 2172-73.

theory "permit[s] nonparty preclusion in cases that do not fit within any of the established exceptions,[316] the court rejected that doctrine."[317]

Emphasizing the limited nature of the exceptions, the Court held that in claiming that Taylor had been adequately represented by Herrick, the District of Columbia Circuit had employed too broad a definition of that exception. A party's representation of a nonparty can be "adequate" only if the interests of those two parties are aligned *and* either the party understood that he was acting in a representative capacity in the first suit or the court in that suit had in place and employed special procedures to protect the interests of the nonparty. In addition, notice of the first suit to the persons supposedly represented is sometimes required.[318] The Court presented notice as a factor which may be required in addition to, not in lieu of, the other requirements.[319] Even assuming that the interests of Taylor and Herrick were aligned, none of the other factors were present.

It had also been argued that Taylor's suit was a collusive attempt to relitigate Herrick's action. Again, the argument failed for overbreadth. The exception for relitigation by proxy requires that the nonparty was the agent of the party bound or the functional equivalent. "[P]reclusion is appropriate only if the putative agent's conduct of the [later] suit is subject to the control of the party who is bound by the prior adjudication."[320] Nothing in the record showed that Herrick controlled Taylor's suit.

The Court also rejected the argument that preclusion should not be limited to defined grounds but should be applied "whenever 'the relationship between a party and nonparty is "close enough" to bring the second litigant within the judgment.'"[321] This determination, it was urged, should be made through a heavily fact-driven and equitable inquiry. The fundamental nature of the rule against nonparty preclusion, however, required "the deliniat[ion] [of] discrete exceptions that apply in 'limited circumstances'" and "Respondents' amorphous balancing test is

---

316   *Id.* at 2173.
317   *Id.* at 2167.
318   *Id.* at 2174, 2176. Those limitations are implemented in class action cases by court rule, such as Federal Rule of Civil Procedure 23; *id.* at 2176.
319   128 S. Ct. at 2176.
320   *Id.* at 2179.
321   *Id.* at 2174-75 (quoting Brief for Respondent FAA).

at odds with the constrained approach to nonparty preclusion our decisions advance."[322]

Of the six categories of exceptions identified in *Taylor*, the one which would most likely be invoked against the surety is the second–the presence of certain kinds of pre-existing substantive legal relationships between the party to the adjudication and the person to be bound.[323] Is the relationship between the principal and surety one such relationship?[324] The Court cited as examples of qualifying relationships those between succeeding owners of property, between bailor and bailee, and between assignee and assignor but did not include that between principal and surety. Although the Court said that there were a "variety" of such relationships and that this category was not limited to those which were noted, it also commented that "[t]hese exceptions originated 'as much from the needs of property law as from the values of preclusion by judgment.'"[325] As the comment suggests, that which connects the persons in the cited relationships is property. In each relationship, the parties to it have an interest, either concurrent or successive, in the same property, either real or personal. The surety and principal, as such, however, do not have interests in the same property or, for that matter, any property at all. The essence of the surety-principal relationship is not found in any shared property interests but in the shared obligation that each assumes in executing a bond. Therefore, suretyship law has no "need" for preclusion which in any way resembles that arising from property interests. In the case of successive owners of property, for example, preclusion prevents the losing party from defeating an adverse judgment as to the property by the simple expedient of conveying the property. The property law need is for the continuity of settled rights in the property and that is accomplished by the rule that "the estoppel runs

---

322 *Id.* at 2175 (quoting Martin v. Wilks, 490 U.S. 755, 762 n.2 (1989)).

323 The Court noted that relationships within this exception "are sometimes collectively referred to as 'privity'" but eschewed use of that term because it has "come to be used more broadly, as a way to express the conclusion that nonparty preclusion is appropriate on any ground," *id.* at 2172 n.8.

324 *See* Pye v. Dep't of Transp., 513 F.2d 290, 292 (5th Cir. 1975) (stating that under federal preclusion law, "a surety-principal relationship does not by itself establish privity").

325 *Taylor*, 128 S. Ct. at 2172 (quoting 18A C. WRIGHT, A. MILLER & E. COOPER, FEDERAL PRACTICE AND PROCEDURE § 4448 (2d ed. 2002)).

with the property, that the grantor can transfer no better right or title than he himself has, and that the grantee take cum onere."[326] As the bailor-bailee and assignor-assignee relationships are also defined by the interests of the parties in the same property, the law governing those relationships has a similar need for settled rules governing those interests.

In *Taylor v. Sturgell*, the Supreme Court applied federal common law to determine the preclusive effect on nonparties of a federal district court judgment in a federal question case. Seven years earlier, in *Semtek International Inc. v. Lockheed Martin Corp.*,[327] the court applied federal common law to a preclusion issue arising from a federal district court judgment rendered in a diversity action. In that case, a Maryland state court dismissed Semtek's claims against Lockheed on the basis of a prior California federal court judgment against Semtek that the same claims against Lockheed were barred by California's two-year statute of limitations. Even though California law did not preclude Semtek from pursuing the claims in another jurisdiction with a longer limitations period, such as Maryland which had a three-year limitations period, the state court held that the federal court judgment was res judicata because it stated that the dismissal against Semtek was on the merits and with prejudice and the claims-preclusive effect of the federal court judgment was governed by federal law.

Unanimously reversing, the Supreme Court agreed that the preclusive effect of all federal court judgments, whether in federal question or diversity cases, was a matter of federal common law. In a diversity case, however, the federal rule was that the federal court judgment should be accorded the preclusive effect to which it would be entitled under the laws of the state where the federal court was located.[328] Therefore, Semtek was not precluded from attempting to show that the prior judgment would not be res judicata under California law.

---

326 WRIGHT et al., *supra* note 325, § 4462 (quoting Postal Tel. Cable Co. v. City of Newport, 247 U.S. 464, 475-75 (1918)).
327 531 U.S. 497 (2001).
328 *Id.* at 508-09. The Court did observe that the federal reference to state law would not obtain in situations in which state law is incompatible with federal interests. As an example, the Court posited a state law which did not give claims-preclusive effect to dismissals for willful violations of discovery orders. *Id.* at 509.

The Supreme Court's concern about nonparty preclusion has not been limited to the effect given to federal court judgments. In *Richards v. Jefferson County*,[329] another unanimous ruling, the court held that a state court's application of state preclusion law to bind a nonparty violated the Due Process Clause of the Fourteenth Amendment.[330] There, the Alabama Supreme Court held that a suit by two taxpayers to invalidate a county occupational tax was barred because the tax had been upheld in an earlier action brought by different taxpayers. Reversing, the Court held that the state court ruling deprived the *Richards* taxpayers of the due process of law to which they were entitled under the U.S. Constitution.[331] While acknowledging that "[s]tate courts are generally free to develop their own rules for protecting against relitigation of common issues or the piecemeal resolution of disputes," the Court emphasized that "[w]e have long held, however, that extreme applications of the doctrine of res judicata may be inconsistent with a federal right that is 'fundamental in character.'"[332] Employing reasoning later applied to the preclusive effect of federal judgments in *Taylor* and *Semtek*, the court declared that one such right is the "'deep-rooted historic tradition that everyone should have his own day in court'" and that therefore "'[a] judgment or decree among parties to a lawsuit resolves issues as among them, but does not conclude the rights of strangers to those proceedings.'"[333]

To be sure, there is an exception to the general rule against nonparty preclusion "when it can be said that there is 'privity' between a party to the second case and a party who is bound by an earlier judgment" as, for example, a judgment against a guardian or trustee binding the ward or the beneficiaries of a trust.[334] While recognizing that the term "privity" has expanded to include relationships between litigants that would not have come within its traditional definition, the court also warned that "there are clearly constitutional limits on the 'privity' exception."[335] In addition, exceptions may be warranted when the nonparty's interests were adequately represented by one who is a party as in class actions,

---

329   517 U.S. 793 (1996).
330   U.S. CONST. amend. XIV, § 1.
331   *Richards*, 517 U.S. at 797.
332   *Id.* (quoting Postal Tel. Cable Co. v. Newport, 247 U.S. 464, 476 (1918)).
333   *Id.* at 798 (quoting Martin v. Wilks, 490 U.S. 755, 761-62 (1989)).
334   *Id.*
335   *Id.*

when the nonparty controls the litigation, or where "a special remedial scheme" forecloses successive litigation such as in bankruptcy or probate proceedings.[336] The Court acknowledged the same exceptions in *Taylor*.[337]

None of the exceptions, however, justified imposing nonparty preclusion on the *Richards* plaintiffs. As to the claim of adequate representation, the court observed that the taxpayers in the earlier suit had not provided notice to other taxpayers including those who brought the second suit. The court found the failure "troubling" because "the right to be heard ensured by the guarantee of due process 'has little reality or worth unless one is informed that the matter is pending and can choose for himself whether to appear or default, acquiesce or contest.'"[338] Moreover, mere notice may not be enough to preserve one's right to be heard because "[t]he general rule is that '[t]he law does not impose upon any person absolutely entitled to a hearing the burden of voluntary intervention in a suit to which he is a stranger.'"[339] In addition, the plaintiffs in the first case could not have represented the *Richards* taxpayers "in a constitutionally adequate manner"[340] because in the earlier suit, unlike the situation in a class action, the plaintiffs had not understood that they were litigating as representatives of absent taxpayers and there were no special procedures by which the court could protect the interests of absent taxpayers.[341]

Three years after *Richards*, in *South Central Bell Telephone Co. v. Alabama*,[342] the Supreme Court held that another Alabama state court judgment precluding a nonparty violated the Due Process Clause of the Fourteenth Amendment.[343] That case involved a state franchise tax which had been upheld in an initial action brought by taxpayers but was subsequently attacked in a second action by other taxpayers. The court

---

336 *Id.* at 798-99.
337 *Taylor*, 128 S. Ct. at 2172-73.
338 *Richards*, 517 at 799 (quoting Mullane v. Cent. Hanover Bank & Trust Co., 339 U.S. 306, 314 (1950)).
339 *Id.* at 800 n.5 (quoting Chase Nat'l Bank v. Norwalk, 291 U.S. 431, 441 (1934) but citing as a comparison Penn-Cent. Merger and N&W Inclusion Cases, 389 U.S. 486, 505 n.4 (1968) (noting that absent parties were invited to intervene by the court)).
340 *Id.* at 802.
341 *Id.*
342 526 U.S. 160 (1999).
343 *Id.* at 168.

found that the case was indistinguishable from *Richards*,[344] even though the taxpayers in the second suit had been aware of the earlier case and one of the lawyers for the taxpayers in the first case also represented the taxpayers in the second. The Court made it clear that the existence of notice had no bearing on the constitutional issue:

> These circumstances, however, created no special representational relationship between the earlier and later plaintiffs. Nor could these facts have led the later plaintiffs to expect to be precluded, as a matter of res judicata, by the earlier judgment itself, even though they may well have expected that the rule of law announced in *Reynolds Metals* [the first suit] would bind them in the same way that a decided case binds every citizen.[345]

This quartet of unanimous Supreme Court rulings—*Taylor*, *Semtek*, *Richards*, and *South Central Bell*—recognize that principles of fundamental fairness circumscribe the constitutionally permissible application of preclusion doctrines to parties who did not participate in the original litigation. Together, those cases establish that whether the prior judgment was rendered by a federal court, in either a federal question or diversity case, or by a state court applying state law, the requirements of due process forbid the imposition of that judgment on a stranger to the litigation unless a recognized exception can be properly applied. Although a few of the cases involving preclusion of the surety

---

344   *Id.* at 167.
345   *Id.* at 168. In *National Technical Systems v. Superior Court*, 118 Cal. Rptr. 2d 465, 470 (Cal. Ct. App. 2002), a California intermediate level appellate court held that the surety on a stop notice release bond undertook to be held only for breach of its own obligations and therefore may not be bound by a prior judgment against the principal, because "'[i]t is a general principle that no party can be so held without an opportunity to be heard in defense. *This right is not divested by the fact that another party has defended on the cause of action and has been unsuccessful.* As the surety did not stipulate that [it] would be bound by the judgment against the principal ... the fact that the principal has unsuccessfully defended has no effect on their rights.'" *Id.* (quoting All Bay Mill & Lumber Co. v. Sur. Co. of the Pacific, 255 Cal. Rptr. 790, 793-94 (Cal. Ct. App. 1989)).

address due process issues,[346] sometimes without express recognition of the constitutional dimension,[347] most do not even consider the question. Often, courts and parties alike, unable to see the forest for the trees, debate whether suretyship can be fitted into the categories of res judicata and collateral estoppel without pausing to ask whether those doctrines may be constitutionally applied at all. The due process restrictions on nonparty preclusion, however, offer strong arguments to the surety opposing preclusion, particularly when sought on res judicata or collateral estoppel grounds pursuant to a finding of privity.

The Supreme Court cases teach that the general rule is that nonparty preclusion is forbidden and that exceptions are limited to defined categories and must be narrowly construed and applied only if they do not subvert the fundamental right to be heard. Nevertheless, courts will often intone the word "privity" as a justification for binding the surety with little or no analysis of its applicability to the relationship between the surety and principal. In light of the examples of the relationships that permit nonparty preclusion in *Taylor* and *Richards*, however, the surety-principal relationship should not qualify because its essential nature does not inhere in its members' interests in the same property. For the same reason, the concept of privity cannot be used to evaluate whether

---

346 *E.g.*, U.S. *ex rel.* Skip Kirchdorfer, Inc. v. M.J. Kelley Corp., 995, F.2d 656, 661-62 (6th Cir. 1993) (recognizing the general rule against preclusion of nonparties but holding that the Miller Act surety could be bound by an arbitration award against the principal because of the privity relationship between them); U.S. *ex rel.* Davis Contracting, L.P. v. B.E.N. Constr., Inc., Civil Action No. 05-1219-MLB, 2007 WL 293915, at *1 (D. Kan. Jan. 26, 2007) (finding that the Miller Act surety had sufficient notice of, and opportunity to defend, the arbitration against the principal and therefore rejecting the surety's argument that preclusion would violate its due process rights under the Fourteenth Amendment, U.S. Const. amend. XIV, § 1).

347 *E.g.*, U.S. *ex rel.* Frontier Constr., Inc. v. Tri-State Mgmt. Co., 262 F. Supp. 2d 893, 897 (N.D. Ill. 2003) (refusing to preclude the Miller Act surety by a default arbitration award against the principal because the principal's liability was never adjudicated on the merits and therefore precluding the surety from asserting either the principal's or its own defenses would "deny it its day in court"); *Nat'l Technical Sys.*, 118 Cal. Rptr. 2d at 470 (precluding the surety by a default judgment rendered against the principal in an action to which the surety was not a party would deprive the surety of its right to be heard in its own defense).

preclusion can be justified by the extent to which the surety's liability may overlap that of the principal. The significance of that overlap for preclusion purposes is better analyzed on its own terms rather than under traditional preclusion doctrine.[348]

Courts will often bind the surety simply because the surety had notice of the proceeding against the principal and the opportunity to assert defenses in that proceeding.[349] *Taylor* and *Richards*, however, state that notice may be relevant, if at all, only as an additional requirement for applying the adequate representation exception and suggest that notice standing alone will not support nonparty preclusion. The adequate representation exception itself does not apply unless the prior proceeding was characterized by protections of absent parties which approximate those of a formal class action. In *South Central Bell*, notice was not seen as an adequate substitute for those protections. Further, the court in *Richards* made a point of noting the rule that a person entitled to a hearing is not required voluntarily to intervene in a proceeding to which he is a stranger.[350] That rule is entirely inconsistent with the cases that bind the surety because the surety knew of the proceeding against the principal and could have defended by joining that proceeding.[351] Such arguments are based on Supreme Court opinions and should be considered by sureties faced with preclusion. At the least, the arguments should give pause to courts bent on conclusively precluding the surety for no reason other than the perception that the surety's liability is coextensive with that of the principal.

---

[348] *See* discussion *infra* Part V.B.1.c.
[349] *See* discussion *infra* Part V.B.2.b.
[350] In *C & I Steel, LLC v. Travelers Casualty and Surety Co. of America*, 876 N.E.2d 442, 449 (Mass. App. Ct. 2007), also discussed *infra* 441, the court rejected the argument that the surety should be bound by an arbitration award against the principal because the surety did not intervene in the arbitration, saying that the surety's "absence from an arbitration to which it was not a party and in which no claims had been asserted directly against it produces neither surprise nor the detrimental reliance that is the hallmark of estoppel."
[351] *See* cases discussed *infra* Part V.B.2.b.

B. Preclusion in the Suretyship Context

The difficulty with trying to apply a traditional preclusion analysis to the surety is that either res judicata or collateral estoppel requires an all or nothing result; it is a zero-sum game. Some courts and other authorities abjure that approach because its rigidity does not adequately accommodate the realities of the surety's relationship with the principal. They have searched for a "middle ground." Two basic approaches have evolved. One focuses on the extent of the preclusive effect to be given to a prior judgment or award as to the principal's liability.[352] Thus, a judgment or award against the principal, which was contested on the merits, will be binding on the surety but only as prima facie evidence of the surety's liability or as a rebuttable presumption of the principal's liability.[353] The other approach focuses on the conditions under which a prior adjudication against the principal will have any preclusive effect at all. The most common condition is the requirement that the surety have notice and an opportunity to defend in the prior proceeding before the resulting judgment against the principal will have some binding effect.[354] The former doctrine arises from suretyship law;[355] the latter from traditional preclusion doctrine.

---

352 That approach was adopted by the American Law Institute in 1941 in RESTATEMENT OF SECURITY § 139 (1941) and was continued in RESTATEMENT (THIRD) OF SURETYSHIP AND GUARANTY § 67 (1996). For a discussion of the extent to which section 139 of the old RESTATEMENT OF SECURITY has been followed in the courts, see Dolores A. Parr & E.A. "Seth" Mills, Jr., *Res Judicata, Collateral Estoppel and the Surety* (unpublished paper submitted at Surety Claims Institute on June 21, 1996). Technically, section 139 of the RESTATEMENT OF SECURITY addresses prior adjudication between a principal and a "creditor," which appears to be defined as the obligee, see RESTATEMENT OF SECURITY § 82 cmt. d. Section 67 of the new RESTATEMENT OF SURETYSHIP AND GUARANTY expressly uses the term "obligee."
353 *See* discussion *infra* Part V.B.1.c.
354 *See* discussion *infra* Part V.B.2.b.
355 *See* Motion Picture Indus. Pension Plan v. Hawaiian Kona Coast Assocs., 823 P.2d 752, 757-58 (Haw. Ct. App. 1991).

1. Extent of Preclusive Effects

Judgments against the principal have been given three basic preclusive effects as against the surety. First, the judgment may have no binding effect at all. Second, it may be conclusive as to the surety's liability. Third, an adjudication of the principal's liability may constitute prima facie evidence of the surety's liability or a rebuttable presumption as to the principal's liability.[356]

---

[356] There is one type of bond, however, under which courts appear generally to agree as to the binding effect of a judgment against the principal. If, by the express terms of its bond, the surety undertakes to pay a judgment rendered against the principal, then the surety will be conclusively bound by such a judgment, even if it was rendered by default, so long as it was not the product of fraud or collusion. Such bonds are sometimes called "judgment bonds." Judgment bonds are distinguished from bonds in which the surety contracts to be liable for general undertakings of the principal and which are sometimes referred to as "general undertaking bonds." Contract surety bonds, such as performance and payment bonds, are general undertaking bonds. *See* Axess Int'l Ltd. v. Intercargo Ins. Co., 183 F.3d 935, 940 (9th Cir. 1999) (distinguishing between judgment bonds as to which even a default judgment against the principal is conclusively binding on the surety and non-judgment bonds as to which a default judgment against the principal has no preclusive effect on the surety, citing RESTATEMENT (THIRD) OF SURETYSHIP AND GUARANTY § 67(3) (1996)); Nat'l Technical Sys. v. Superior Court, 118 Cal. Rptr. 2d 465, 470-71 (Cal. Ct. App. 2002) (distinguishing between bonds by which the surety agrees to be absolutely bound by a judgment against the principal and bonds under which the surety can be held only for breach of its own obligations, such as a stop notice release bond, and holding that as to the latter type, a judgment against the principal is not binding in a separate action against the surety); McIntyre Square Assocs. v. Evans, 827 A.2d 446, 456-59 (Pa. Super. Ct. 2003) (distinguishing between bonds by which the surety agrees to pay a judgment against the principal, such as attachment bonds, and those by which the surety agrees only to answer for the principal's default and holding that a landlord's default judgment against the tenant under a commercial lease was not evidence of the liability of guarantors of the tenant's obligations); Old Republic Sur. Co., v. Bonham State Bank, 172 S.W.3d 210, 214 (Tex. App. 2005) (distinguishing between a general undertaking bond as to which a default judgment against the principal is only *prima facie* evidence of the surety's liability, if the surety had not been given an opportunity to

a. *No Preclusive Effect.* Very few cases suggest that an adjudication on the merits of the principal's liability will have no binding effect at all upon the surety.357 By far, most of the courts which have given no binding effect to a judgment against the principal did so when the judgment against the principal was rendered by default, or without notice to, or opportunity to defend by, the surety, or both.358 Section 139(3) of

---

defend the underlying action, and a judgment bond as to which a default judgment against the principal is conclusive as to the surety whether or not the surety had an opportunity to defend); *see also* Ferrucci, *supra* note 288, at 191-92.

357 *Nat'l Technical Sys.*, 118 Cal. Rptr. 2d at 471, however, seems to be such a case. Stating that "[i]t is well established that a judgment against a principal is not binding in a separate action against a surety," the court held that the surety on a stop notice release bond undertook to be held only for breach of its own obligations and therefore may not be bound by a court judgment against the principal even though the judgment against the principal resulted from a contested trial on the merits had not been entered by default, *id.* at 470-71 (quoting All Bay Mill & Lumber Co. v. Sur. Co. of the Pacific, 255 Cal. Rptr. 790, 793 (Cal Ct. App. 1989)). Addressing the preclusive effect of an arbitration proceeding, as opposed to a court action, a California statute provides that "[a]n arbitration award rendered against a principal alone shall not be, be deemed to be, or be utilized as, an award against his surety." CAL. CIV. CODE § 2855 (West, Westlaw through Ch. 1 of 2009 Reg. Sess., Ch. 12 of 2009-10 2nd Exec. Sess., and Ch. 19 of the 2009-10 3rd Exec. Sess.). In West Virginia, it is provided by statute that a judgment against the principal in any action to which the surety was not a formal party will have no preclusive effect on the surety. W. VA. CODE § 45-1-3 (West, Westlaw through end of 2008 Extraordinary Sess.). *But see* Rashid v. U.S. Fid. & Guar. Co. Inc., Civ.A.No. 2:91-0141, 1992 WL 565341, at *1, *5, *12 (S.D.W. Va. Sept. 28, 1992) (noting that the statute had been construed as not applying to judgment bonds and holding that a performance bond which incorporated an arbitration provision was equivalent to a judgment bond and therefore an arbitration award against the principal was binding on the surety under collateral estoppel), *approved in a related case*, Rashid v. Schenck Constr. Co., Inc., 438 S.E.2d 543, 546-47 (W. Va. 1993).

358 *See, e.g.*, Raymond Int'l Builders, Inc. First Indem. of Am. Ins. Co., 516 A.2d 620 (N.J. 1986) (holding that the surety was not bound at all by the obligee's arbitration award against the principal, which did not appear at the proceedings, because the surety had insufficient notice of, and therefore an inadequate opportunity to defend, in the arbitration);

the Restatement of Security[359] took the position, which is continued in the new Restatement of Suretyship and Guaranty,[360] that if a "judgment is obtained by default or confession against the principal, and the creditor subsequently brings an action against the surety, proof of the judgment against the principal is evidence only of the fact of its rendition."[361]

b. *Conclusively Binding.* Aside from cases involving judgment bonds, decisions which hold that a contract bond surety, without more, is conclusively bound under all circumstances by a judgment or arbitration award against the principal, particularly if rendered by default, are exceedingly rare. Usually, a surety is not conclusively bound by an adjudication adverse to the principal, default or otherwise, in the absence of some other factor.[362] That factor can be the incorporation into the

---

Monmouth Lumber Co. v. Indem. Ins. Co. of N. Am., 122 A.2d 604 (N.J. 1956) (holding that a payment bond surety was not bound by default judgments against the principal which had little probative value). Since *Raymond Int'l* and *Monmouth Lumber*, a New Jersey intermediate level appellate court decided *Gloucester City Board of Education v. American Arbitration Ass'n*, 755 A.2d 1256, 1263 (N.J. Super. Ct. App. Div. 2000) which expressly adopted the limited incorporation approach and held therefore that the surety's liability to the obligee under the performance bond is not an arbitrable issue. Thus, under a limited incorporation approach, occasions for the application of the notice and opportunity doctrine should arise much less frequently in the performance bond context because the surety cannot be compelled to arbitrate the obligee's bond claim and the result of the obligee-principal arbitration will be binding on the surety even though it was not a party to that proceeding but only as to the principal's liability under the bonded contract. *See also* discussion *infra* Parts V.B.2.b, V.D.2.

359 RESTATEMENT OF SECURITY § 139(3) (1941).
360 RESTATEMENT (THIRD) OF SURETYSHIP AND GUARANTY § 67(3).
361 RESTATEMENT OF SECURITY § 139(3).
362 One case which appears conclusively to bind the surety by an uncontested judgment against the principal without any other factor is *International Fidelity Insurance Co. v. China Construction of America (SC) Inc.*, 650 S.E.2d 677, 679 (S.C. 2007), also discussed *infra* note 468. There, the South Carolina Supreme Court held that the performance bond surety was conclusively bound by a judgment in favor of the obligee and against the principal which was rendered upon a trial at which the principal failed to appear. The court declared that the general rule is that "'where the liability of a surety is dependent on the outcome of litigation in which his principal is or may be involved, a judgment against a principal is binding

performance bond of the principal's agreement to arbitrate with the obligee which courts applying limited incorporation regard as an agreement by the surety to be bound by the results of the arbitration between the obligee and the principal.[363] Another factor is that the surety was given notice of, and the opportunity to defend in, the proceeding against the principal and failed to do so.[364] In addition, under general preclusion doctrine, a nonparty to an action "who controls or substantially participates in the control of the presentation on behalf of a party is bound by the determination of issues decided as though he were a party."[365] That principle has been applied to bind sureties.[366]

c. *Rebuttable Presumption and Prima Facie Evidence.* Section 139(2) of the Restatement of Security[367] provides as follows:

> (2) Where, in an action by a creditor against a principal, judgment is given, other than by default or confession, in favor of the creditor, and the creditor subsequently brings an action against the surety, proof of the judgment in favor of the creditor creates a rebuttable presumption of the principal's liability to the creditor.[368]

---

and conclusive on the surety, ...'" and that "'[t]he rule is applicable even though the surety had no notice of the suit or opportunity to defend,'" *id.* at 680 (quoting Ward v. Fed. Ins. Co., 106 S.E.2d 169, 170 (1958)). The formulation of that proposition looks much like the description of a judgment bond, *see* discussion *supra* note 356; however, the performance bond in both *China Construction* and *Ward* appear to have been contract bonds.

363 *See, e.g.*, Fid. & Deposit Co. of Md. v. Parsons & Whittemore Contractors Corp., 397 N.E.2d 380, 382 (N.Y. 1979), discussed in detail *supra* Part II.A.3.
364 *See also* discussion *infra* Part V.B.2.b.
365 RESTATEMENT (SECOND) OF JUDGMENTS § 39 (1982).
366 *See, e.g.*, Mass. Bonding & Ins. Co. v. Robert E. Denike, Inc., 92 F.2d 657 (3d Cir. 1937); E.B.R. Corp. v. PSL Air Lease Corp., 313 A.2d 893 (Del. 1973).
367 RESTATEMENT OF SECURITY § 139(2) (1941).
368 *Id.; accord* RESTATEMENT (THIRD) OF SURETYSHIP AND GUARANTY § 67(2) (1996) which continues the basic section 139(2) rule. Because the new Restatement was published relatively recently, most court citations are to section 139(2), and therefore the Restatement position will be represented by reference to that section. As the two sections are

As stated in the commentary, "[t]he rule . . . expresses a middle ground between the possible rule that a judgment against the principal is conclusive of the principal's liability, even in an action against the surety, and that such a judgment is evidence only of the fact of its rendition."[369] Thus, section 139(2) represented a deliberate compromise which reflects substantive surety law; that is, the view that the nature of the relationship between the surety and the principal is not such that a judgment against the principal should conclusively bind the surety. Section 139(2) does not derive from principles of res judicata or collateral estoppel which establish the conditions which must be shown in order for a prior judgment to be held conclusively binding in a subsequent proceeding. Instead, section 139(2) reflects a willingness to concede that a judgment against the principal, so long as it was not taken by default, will *always* have *some* preclusive effect upon the surety; but it tempers that imposition by limiting the extent of the effect. Thus, although a judgment on the merits against the principal will always have some preclusive impact, the surety will also *always* have the opportunity of demonstrating that the principal had not breached the bonded obligation.

A common variant of section 139(2) of the Restatement of Security is the rule that a judgment against the principal is prima facie evidence of the surety's liability. In *P.R. Post Corp. v. Maryland Casualty Co.*,[370] the

---

        substantively identical, however, courts should treat section 67(2) as they have section 139(2). Cf. Broadmoor/Roy Anderson Corp. v. XL Reinsurance Am., Inc., No. Civ.A. 02-0703, 2006 WL 2873473, at *1 (W.D. La. Oct. 4, 2006) (arbitration award in favor of the claimant and against the principal "is presumptive of the accuracy of [the claimant's] claims against Sureties.").

369   RESTATEMENT OF SECURITY § 139(2) cmt. c. The commentary to section 67(2) of the new Restatement is substantially the same except that it explicitly states that even if the surety cannot rebut the presumption, it may still raise its suretyship defenses. RESTATEMENT (THIRD) OF SURETYSHIP AND GUARANTY § 67(2) cmt. b (1996). The issue of suretyship defenses is discussed *infra* Part V.D.

370   271 N.W.2d 521 (Mich. 1978). *See also Robert E. Denike*, 92 F.2d at 658 (holding that a prior judgment against the principal is prima facie evidence against the surety in a later action, unless the surety participated in the prior proceeding in which case "he is concluded as to the issues therein decided against his principal."); Westra Constr., Inc. v. U.S. Fid. & Guar. Co., Civil Action No. 1:03-CV-0833, 2006 WL 1149252, at *2

Michigan Supreme Court, invoking preclusion principles applicable to judgments, held that an obligee's arbitration award against the principal constituted prima facie evidence of the performance bond surety's liability.[371] Because the court so held despite the fact that the surety had not been given notice of the arbitration,[372] the court employed the section 139(2) theory in that the court applied the prima facie rule without requiring a precondition, such as adequate notice, for the imposition of a preclusive effect.[373] According to the court, the legal effect of admitting a prior judgment as prima facie evidence of the surety's liability "is to shift the burden of proof to the party calling the evidence into question" which "requires the defendant [the surety] to come forward with evidence to rebut or contradict its liability for the arbitration award against its principal."[374]

---

n.1 (M.D. Pa. Apr. 28, 2006) (citing *Robert E. Denike*, 92 F.2d at 658, for the proposition that a judgment against the principal is prima facie evidence against the surety and is conclusive if the surety participated in the action against the principal and therefore finding that the surety would be adversely affected by an arbitration award against the principal and could maintain motion to vacate or modify the award).

371 *P.R. Post*, 271 N.W.2d at 525 (citing 74 AM. JUR. 2D *Suretyship* § 152 (1974)). Although the performance bond incorporated the construction contract containing an arbitration provision, the court found that applying the prima facie approach, which permitted the surety to rebut the assertion of liability, made it unnecessary to address the surety's contention that it had never agreed to arbitrate with the obligee, *id.* at 523.

372 *Id.* at 523.

373 In fact, the court expressly adverted to section 139(2) as stating a "similar rule," *id.* at 523 n.1. *See also* MacDonald v. Standard Accident Ins. Co., 111 A.2d 347, 349-50 (Conn. Super. Ct. 1955) (holding that a prior judgment against the principal on a statutory public official's bond was *prima facie* evidence against the surety whether or not the surety had notice thereof).

374 *P.R. Post*, 271 N.W.2d at 525; cf. Ins. Co. of N. Am. v. Metro. Dade County, 705 So. 2d 33, 35 (Fla. Dist. Ct. App. 1998) (holding that a default judgment against the principal was prima facie evidence of the surety's liability).

2. Conditions Affecting the Imposition of Preclusive Effects[375]

a. *Default Judgments or Awards.* Judgments or arbitration awards entered by default are generally regarded as having little probative value as to whether or not the principal breached the bond condition and is therefore liable to the claimant, obligee or other creditor and do not implicate preclusion policies against relitigation.[376] Accordingly, the imposition or extent of the preclusive effect of a default adjudication against the principal is almost always limited. In some cases, such a judgment is given no effect at all;[377] in others, the effect is restricted to

---

375 The conditions affecting the preclusive effect of a judgment or arbitration award against the principal which will be imposed upon the surety are discussed in detail in Ferrucci, *supra* note 288, at 199-203.

376 *See* RESTATEMENT OF SECURITY § 139(3) cmt. e (1941) ("The probative significance of a judgment obtained by confession or default is much less than that of a judgment after trial on the merits. Moreover, the arguments of policy and convenience against duplication of trials have little weight where there has not been a determination after consideration of evidence introduced by both sides to a litigation."); RESTATEMENT (THIRD) OF SURETYSHIP AND GUARANTY § 67(3) cmt. c (1996) (same); Axess Int'l Ltd. v. Intercargo Ins. Co., 183 F.3d 935, 940 (9th Cir. 1999) (while holding that a surety on a judgment bond issued pursuant to a federal statute was bound by a prior default judgment, the court stated that "[g]enerally a default judgment obtained by an obligee against a principal obligor does not have preclusive effect in a subsequent action against a secondary obligor." (citing RESTATEMENT (THIRD) OF SURETYSHIP AND GUARANTY § 67(3))); Monmouth Lumber Co. v. Idem. Ins. Co. of N. Am., 122 A.2d 604, 608 (N.J. 1956) ("[T]he default judgments [against the principal]... are not only of little probative significance; in the circumstances of these cases and the rule of this State they are not conclusive against the surety." (citing RESTATEMENT OF SECURITY § 139(3))). For cases adopting the Restatement position, *see* Ferrucci, *supra* note 288, at 194 n.63.

377 *See, e.g.,* Axess Int'l, 183 F.3d at 935; U.S. *ex rel.* Frontier Constr., Inc. v. Tri-State Mgmt. Co., 262 F. Supp. 2d 893, 896 (N.D. Ill. 2003) ("[A] majority of federal courts . . . do not give preclusive effect to default judgments."); U.S. *ex rel.* PCC Constr., Inc. v. Star Ins. Co., 90 F. Supp. 2d 512 (D.N.J. 2000); authorities cited *supra* notes 352, 376; *but see* discussion *infra* text accompanying notes 396-424.

the prima facie or rebuttable presumption level,[378] and in still others, no effect is given unless the surety ignored an opportunity to join and defend itself or was unable to do so.[379] Even when the surety is regarded

---

[378] See, e.g., MacDonald v. Standard Accident Ins. Co., 111 A.2d 347 (Conn. Super. Ct. 1955); Ins. Co. of N. Am. v. Metro. Dade County, 705 So. 2d 33, (Fla. Dist. Ct. App. 1998); Heritage Ins. Co. of Am. v. Foster Elec. Co., 393 So. 2d 28 (Fla. Dist. Ct. App. 1981); Old Republic Sur. Co. v. Bonham State Bank, 172 S.W.3d 210 (Tex. App. 2005) (dicta).

[379] For example, in both *United States Fidelity & Guaranty Co. v. St. Mary's Hospital*, 458 P.2d 966 (Ariz. Ct. App. 1969), and *Kentucky Insurance Guaranty Ass'n v. Dooley Construction Co.*, 732 S.W.2d 887 (Ky. Ct. App. 1987), the court affirmed summary judgment against the surety on the basis of a default judgment against the principal. In *St. Mary's Hospital*, the judgment appears to have been rendered in the action in which the surety and the principal had been sued jointly, and in *Dooley*, the judgment was rendered in a prior suit. In both cases, however, it appears that the surety had been given the opportunity to contest the claim on the merits, notwithstanding the default judgment against the principal, but did not, or could not, present evidence sufficient to raise an issue of fact as to the principal's liability; see United Fire & Cas. Co. v. Eldridge, No. 2006-CA-002609-MR, 2008 WL 991641, at *1 (Ky. Ct. App. May 9, 2008) (holding that a payment bond surety was conclusively bound by a default judgment against the principal in a suit against the principal and the surety because the surety had an opportunity to contest the principal's liability but did not do so). See also Fewox v. McMerit Constr. Co., 556 So. 2d 419, 424-25 (Fla. Dist. Ct. App. 1989) (en banc) (holding that the principal's voluntary payment of an arbitration award in favor of the obligee was the "functional equivalent" of a confession of judgment and is conclusively binding on the surety which had actual knowledge of the arbitration and ample opportunity to appear and defend therein); McIntyre Square Assocs. v. Evans, 827 A.2d 446, 459 (Pa. Super. Ct. 2003) (holding that a confessed judgment against the debtors did not constitute evidence against the guarantors in a subsequent suit because the guarantors did not have an opportunity to defend in the first suit). Thus, despite rhetoric that the surety is bound by a judgment against the principal, default or otherwise, cases in which the surety offered to contest a claim on the merits but was precluded from doing so solely because a default judgment had been entered against the principal, without the presence of any other factor, are exceedingly rare. *See also* cases discussed *infra* note 404. There are, however, a very few cases which conclusively preclude the surety by a default judgment against the

as being in privity with the principal, conclusive preclusion may not be had under collateral estoppel because the issue of the principal's liability has not been litigated and decided on the merits.[380] Therefore, to bind conclusively the surety, a nonparty, by a default judgment against the principal should be regarded as a violation of the surety's right to due process of law because the surety would have been deprived of both its day in court and the benefit, if any, of the principal's defense and because the obligee or payment bond claimant will have recovered without ever having had to prove its right to recovery on the merits.[381]

---

principal on the basis of a misapplication of the notice and opportunity doctrine; see discussion *infra* text accompanying notes 396-424.

380 See S.D.I. Corp. v. Fireman's Fund Ins. Cos., 617 N.Y.S.2d 790, 792 (N.Y. App. Div. 1994); Firedoor Corp. of Am., Inc. v. Merlin Indus. Ltd., 446 N.Y.S.2d 325, 326 (N.Y. App. Div. 1982). In both cases, the court held that a default judgment obtained by a payment bond claimant against the principal constituted prima facie, but not conclusive, evidence as to the surety's liability because, under New York law, collateral estoppel bars relitigation of an issue only if there was a full and fair opportunity in the first case to contest an identical issue. *Accord* Corless v. Leonard, 748 N.Y.S.2d 620, 623 (N.Y. App. Div. 2002) (holding that a judgment by confession against the debtor constituted prima facie evidence of the liability of the guarantors); Sette-Juliano Contracting, Inc./Halcyon Constr. Corp. v. Aetna Cas. & Sur. Co., 674 N.Y.S.2d 654, 658 (N.Y. App. Div. 1998) ("Generally, a judgment entered against a principal upon default is only prima facie evidence against the surety. The latter remains at liberty to contest its own liability by establishing affirmatively that the principal was not liable."). Collateral estoppel as applied generally, however, would not give any preclusive effect to a default judgment because a prerequisite is that the issue, as to which preclusion is sought, was determined on the merits in the prior proceeding. *See* Bush v. Balfour Beatty Bahamas, Ltd. (*In re* Bush), 62 F.3d 1319, 1323 (11th Cir. 1995) (recognizing that "the general federal rule ... is ... [that] ... a default judgment will not support the application of collateral estoppel because '[i]n the case of a judgment entered by confession, consent, or default, none of the issues is actually litigated.'" (quoting RESTATEMENT (SECOND) OF JUDGMENTS § 27 cmt. e (1982))).

381 *See, e.g.*, U.S. *ex rel.* Frontier Constr., Inc. v. Tri-State Mgmt. Co., 262 F. Supp. 2d 893, 897 (N.D. Ill. 2003) (denying preclusive effect upon the surety of a default arbitration award against the principal in part because doing so would deprive the surety of its day in court). In addition, the surety-principal relationship should not be regarded as justifying an

b. *Notice and Opportunity To Defend.* For many of the courts which have considered the problem, whether and the extent to which a judgment or arbitration award against the principal will be given preclusive effect depends decisively on whether the surety had notice of the proceeding against the principal and an opportunity to assert in that proceeding all defenses including those of the principal.[382] For those courts, if the surety did have such notice and opportunity, it will be bound either conclusively or to the rebuttable presumption or prima facie level.[383]

Because the imposition of preclusion is justified by the surety's "standing idly by"[384] instead of litigating the principal's liability as well as its own defenses in the original proceeding, the surety must have had a realistic opportunity to defend its interests.[385] If the opportunity was

---

exception to the due process rule against nonparty preclusion, *see* discussion *supra* text accompanying notes 323-26.

382   *See Ferrucci, supra* note 288, at 193-95, 198-99 and cases cited therein. Decisions which bind the nonparty surety primarily because it had the opportunity to intervene in the proceeding against the principal appear to be inconsistent with the United States Supreme Court's due process analysis. *See* discussion *supra* text accompanying notes 349-51.

383   The extent to which such an award precludes the assertion of suretyship defenses is discussed *infra* text accompanying notes 473-77.

384   U.S. *ex rel.* Vigilanti v. Pfeiffer-Neumeyer Constr. Corp., 25 F. Supp. 403 (E.D.N.Y. 1938), discussed in detail *infra* text accompanying notes 401, 405-10.

385   That issue should not be confused with the collateral estoppel requirement that "the party opposing the use of collateral estoppel must have been afforded a full and fair opportunity in the prior proceeding to contest the issue," QDR Consultants & Dev. Corp. v. Colonia Ins. Co., 675 N.Y.S.2d 117, 118 (N.Y. App. Div. 1998), which refers to the fairness of the first proceeding, not to opportunity to intervene in it. Under general collateral estoppel analysis, the preclusive effect of the adjudication in the first proceeding on a nonparty is addressed by asking whether the nonparty's relationship with the party was such that the fairness of the first proceeding should be attributable to the nonparty; that is, by asking whether the nonparty was in "privity" with the party, *see supra* notes 295-300 and accompanying text. In New York, the answer is that the surety is in privity with the principal and hence will be collaterally estopped as to issues decided in the proceeding against the principal, *id.* at 119. By contrast, inquiring whether the nonparty had the

inadequate, the surety will not be bound. In *Raymond International Builders, Inc. v. First Indemnity of America Insurance Co.*,[386] a general contractor-obligee sought judgment against the surety on the basis of an award against the subcontractor-principal rendered in an arbitration in which the principal, although served with a demand, did not appear. The obligee did not serve an arbitration demand on the surety and did not notify the surety of the existence of the arbitration until three weeks before the hearings commenced on a claim worth $800,000. Under those circumstances, the court found that three weeks' notice was insufficient to allow the surety properly to prepare its defense to a claim of such magnitude and therefore held that the surety was not bound by the award.[387]

---

opportunity to intervene in the first proceeding has become a substitute for analyzing and evaluating the nature of the relationship of the nonparty (the surety) to party (the principal). The similarity of the phrases 'notice and opportunity to [intervene and] defend' and 'a full and fair opportunity to contest' may well have bred much of the confusion evident in many of the cases attempting to apply preclusion analysis to the surety, particularly when the issue of the overlap of the liability of the surety and the principal, which is relevant to the "privity" question, is combined with the inquiry as to whether the surety had the opportunity to intervene in the first proceeding.

386   516 A.2d 620 (N.J. 1986).
387   *Id.* at 621-22; cf. U.S. *ex rel.* Davis Contracting, L.P. v. B.E.N. Constr., Inc., Civil Action No. 05-1219-MLB, 2007 WL 293915, at *6 (D. Kan. Jan. 26, 2007) (ruling that 10-days' notice of the arbitration hearings against the principal was sufficient to permit the surety to prepare a defense to a claim of $34,000). Since *Raymond Int'l*, a New Jersey intermediate level appellate court decided Gloucester City Board of Education v. American Arbitration Ass'n, 755 A.2d 1256, 1263 (N.J. Super. Ct. App. Div. 2000) which expressly adopted the limited incorporation approach and held therefore that the surety's liability to the obligee under the performance bond is not an arbitrable issue. Thus, occasions for the application of the notice and opportunity doctrine should arise much less frequently in the performance bond context because the surety cannot be compelled to arbitrate the obligee's bond claim and the result of the obligee-principal arbitration will be binding on the surety even though it is not a party to that proceeding but only as to the principal's liability under the bonded contract.

In *United States ex rel. Aurora Painting, Inc. v. Fireman's Fund Insurance Co.*[388] and *United States ex rel. Skip Kirchdorfer, Inc. v. M.J. Kelley Corp.*,[389] the Ninth and Sixth Circuits, respectively, held that sureties on bonds issued under the Miller Act[390] were bound by an adverse award rendered against the principal in an arbitration to which the sureties were not parties but which the principal apparently contested.[391] Applying the same analysis, both courts concluded that

388   832 F.2d 1150 (9th Cir. 1987).
389   995 F.2d 656 (6th Cir. 1993).
390   40 U.S.C.A. §§ 3131-34 (West 2005 & Supp. 2008). There has been disagreement as to whether the Miller Act's provision of exclusive federal court jurisdiction prohibits binding the surety to a prior state court judgment that the principal was liable to the claimant, *compare* U.S. Fid. & Guar. Co. v. Hendry Corp., 391 F.2d 13 (5th Cir. 1968) (holding that the Miller Act overrode the Full Faith and Credit Statute, 28 U.S.C.A. § 1783 (West 2006) because giving preclusive effect to the state court judgment would undermine Congress' intent that only federal courts could determine the surety's liability under the Miller Act), *with Aurora Painting*, 832 F.2d at 1152-53 (agreeing with the dissent in Hendry and holding that as the Miller Act does not by its terms create an exception to the Full Faith and Credit Statute, there is no incompatibility and no reason not to accord preclusive effect as required by the latter statute). Since those cases, the United States Supreme Court decision in *Marrese v. American Academy of Orthopaedic Surgeons*, 470 U.S. 373, 380-83 (1985) has been applied to deny preclusive effect to a state court judgment in a Miller Act suit, U.S. *ex rel.* PCC Constr., Inc. v. Star Ins. Co., 90 F. Supp. 2d 512 (D.N.J. 2000). *See* discussion *infra* note 437. Courts continue to reach contrary conclusions as to the preclusive effect of a state court judgment or arbitration in Miller Act cases, *see*, e.g., U.S. *ex rel.* Davis Contracting, L.P. v. B.E.N. Constr., Inc., Civil Action No. 05-1219-MLB, 2007 WL 293915, at *1 (D. Kan. Jan. 26, 2007) (holding that prior arbitration award was binding on the surety); U.S. *ex rel.* Frontier Constr., Inc. v. Tri-State Mgmt. Co., 262 F. Supp. 2d 893 (N.D. Ill. 2003) (holding that a confirmed arbitration award was not binding on the surety); U.S. *ex rel.* Pensacola Constr. Co. v. St. Paul Fire & Marine Ins. Co., 705 F. Supp. 306 (W.D. La. 1989) (entering declaratory judgment that an award in an arbitration between the principal and the claimant would not be binding the surety).
391   The *Aurora Painting* opinion recites that the claimant commenced a state court action against the surety and obtained an order compelling arbitration, that an award was entered in the claimant's favor, and that the

preclusion could properly be imposed on the nonparty sureties because there existed privity between them and the principal and therefore the sureties' interests had been adequately represented by the principal in the prior arbitration. In reaching that conclusion, both courts relied solely on the fact that the sureties had adequate notice of the proceeding against, and the opportunity to defend, the principal and on an assumed, but unexamined, identity of interests between the sureties and the principal. As primary legal authority, both courts cited dicta in *Frederick v. United States*[392] for the proposition that a judgment against the principal is conclusively binding on the surety if the surety had notice of the proceeding against the principal. The Ninth Circuit accurately paraphrased *Frederick* as stating that a judgment against the principal established the fact and amount of the *principal's* liability but the Sixth mischaracterized the opinion as stating that such a judgment established the fact and amount of the *surety's* liability.[393]

Neither court, however, attempted to analyze, or even define, the concept of privity or to examine the nature of the surety-principal relationship other than to assume that the liability of those parties was coextensive. Certainly, neither court so much as suggested that the sureties and the principal had an interest in the same property which is the factor identified by the Supreme Court as significant for preclusion purposes.[394] As to the constitutional requirements for adequate representation, neither court claimed that the principal understood that it was acting as a representative for the absent sureties or that procedures to

---

      award was confirmed by the state court. *Aurora Painting*, 832 F.2d at 1151. There is no suggestion that the principal did not appear in and contest the arbitration, which the surety would likely have raised had that been the case. In *Skip Kirchdorfer*, the principal informed the arbitrator that it had valid defenses which it could not present for lack of funds and did not appear at the arbitration; after the hearing, however, the principal presented evidence to the arbitrator which the arbitrator considered, *Skip Kirchdorfer*, 995 F.2d at 658.

392   386 F.2d 481, 486 n.6 (5th Cir. 1967).
393   *Aurora Painting*, 832 F.2d at 1153; *Skip Kirchdorfer*, 995 F.2d at 661. The Sixth Circuit also represented that the paraphrased proposition from *Frederick* was a holding when it was dicta, and other courts have also misread *Frederick*. *See* discussion *infra* note 418.
394   *See* discussion *supra* text accompanying notes 323-26.

protect nonparties were in place in the arbitration proceedings.[395] Thus, on the analysis presented, neither the *Aurora Painting* nor the *Skip Kirchdorfer* opinion meets the due process requirements established by the Supreme Court. In effect, the Ninth and Sixth Circuits fashioned an exception to the rule against nonparty preclusion which applies to only sureties.

At least the preclusion imposed in *Aurora Painting* and *Skip Kirchdorfer* rested on an adjudication contested by the principal. An even more simplistic and rigid application of the notice and opportunity doctrine, however, has led a few courts to hold that the surety is conclusively bound as to its liability by a judgment or arbitration award entered against the principal *by default* in the *same proceeding* to which the surety was a party. Most prominently perhaps, the Eleventh Circuit, in *Drill South, Inc. v. International Fidelity Insurance Co.*,[396] affirmed a summary judgment against a Miller Act surety based solely on a default judgment against the principal entered in the same action in which the surety was actively defending against the claim. Asserting that "the general rule that has emerged is that the surety is bound by any judgment against its principal, default or otherwise, when the surety had full knowledge of the action against the principal and an opportunity to defend,"[397] the Eleventh Circuit declared that the surety should be bound

---

395 *See* discussion *supra* text accompanying notes 318-19. Interestingly, the Ninth Circuit stated that privity required such procedures but then dropped the subject without considering whether such procedures had been in place; *Aurora Painting*, 832 F.2d at 1153.

396 234 F.3d 1232 (11th Cir. 2001) (per curiam).

397 *Id.* at 1235. In support of that assertion, the court cited *Lake County ex rel. Baxley v. Massachusetts Bonding & Insurance Co.*, 75 F.2d 6 (5th Cir. 1935); however, there is no indication in that case that the judgment against the principal was rendered by default. Moreover, federal common law—even in the Eleventh Circuit—held that a default judgment will not be given preclusive effect, *see* Bush v. Balfour Beatty Bahamas, Ltd. (*In re* Bush), 62 F.3d 1319, 1323 (11th Cir. 1995) (recognizing that "the general federal rule ...is [that] ... a default judgment will not support the application of collateral estoppel" but finding an exception when the party did not simply fail to appear but substantially participated in and actively obstructed the proceeding and then abandoned the proceeding); Axess Int'l, Ltd. v. Intercargo Ins. Co., 183 F.3d 935, 940 (9th Cir. 1999) (noting that a default judgment against the principal has no preclusive effect on the surety unless the claim was on a judgment bond). In *United*

because it "had the right, and therefore the opportunity, to defend Enviro-Group [the principal] as its surety and attorney-in-fact."[398] The court rejected the surety's argument that even if it had the right to defend the principal, it did not have the obligation to do so: "We believe that the issue is not whether the Agreement of Indemnity imposed an obligation on International Fidelity [the surety] to defend Enviro-Group, but whether it conferred a right to defend. The law requires only that a surety have notice and an opportunity to defend before it is bound by a judgment against its principal."[399] The court repudiated[400] cases such as

> States ex rel. Frontier Construction, Inc. v. Tri-State Management Co., 262 F. Supp. 2d 893, 896 (N.D. Ill. 2003), the court refused to bind the Miller Act surety by a default arbitration award against the principal in part because "a majority of federal courts (including the Seventh Circuit) do not give preclusive effect to default judgments." In reaching the opposite conclusion in *Drill South*, the Eleventh Circuit ignored *United States v. Maryland Casualty Co.*, 204 F.2d 912 (5th Cir. 1953) and *Interstate Electric Co. v. Fidelity & Deposit Co. of Maryland*, 153 So. 427 (Ala. 1934) both of which held, under Alabama law, that a prior adjudication *on the merits* against the principal had no preclusive effect at all upon the surety because the surety was not in privity with the principal and therefore neither res judicata nor collateral estoppel could apply. Citing *Firemen's Insurance Co. v. McMillan*, 29 Ala. 147, 1856 WL 346 (1856), the Eleventh Circuit also claimed that its application of preclusion was consistent with Alabama law. *Drill South*, 234 F.3d at 1236 n.5. The assertion rests upon an inexplicable misreading of the *McMillan* case in which the Alabama Supreme Court stated flatly that "[t]he true rule is, that a recovery against the principal cannot be used as evidence to charge the surety, except in cases where the contract of the surety can be construed into an undertaking to be bound by the result of legal proceedings against the principal [that is, a judgment bond]." *McMillan*, 1856 WL 346, at *13. Perhaps a failure to recognize the difference between a judgment bond and a contract bond accounts for the misreading.

398 *Drill South*, 234 F.3d at 1236 (citing provisions of the Agreement of Indemnity between the principal and the surety).
399 *Id.; contra* Trinity Universal Ins. Co. v. Briarcrest Country Club Corp., 831 S.W.2d 453, 456-57 (Tex. App. 1992) ("There is nothing in the law relating to contracts of sureties that places a duty on the surety to defend a suit on behalf of or in the name of the principal. Under a typical performance bond, the surety is merely the guarantor of the performance of the principal. Such are different from contracts of indemnity which

Effect of an Arbitration Provision in the Principal's Contract 789

United States ex rel. Vigilanti v. Pfeiffer-Neumeyer Construction Corp.[401] and *Gearhart v. Pierce Enterprises, Inc.*[402] which held that the surety had no duty to provide a defense to the principal when they were codefendants.[403]

The *Drill South* court could discern no difference between a default judgment against the principal which was rendered in a prior, separate action and such a judgment which was rendered in an action in which the principal and the surety were sued together.[404] There is, however, a very

---

often create a duty to defend."); Gearhart v. Pierce Enters., Inc., 779 P.2d 93, 95 (Nev. 1989) ("[A]lthough [the surety] knew about the lawsuit and presumably knew about the prospect of a default judgment against [the principal] [as the principal and the surety were sued in the same action], because [the surety] was not responsible for [the principal's] derelictions [failure to answer interrogatories], it was not required to defend against such a contingency.").

400 *Drill South*, 234 F.3d at 1236-37.
401 25 F. Supp. 403, 405 (E.D.N.Y. 1938).
402 *Gearhart*, 779 P.2d at 93.
403 At the same time, the Eleventh Circuit also rejected *United States ex rel. Fidelity National Bank v. Rundle*, 107 F. 227, 229-230 (9th Cir. 1901), in which the Ninth Circuit refused to preclude the surety by a default judgment against the principal because the notice and opportunity doctrine did not apply to a judgment rendered in an action in which the principal and the surety were codefendants and noted that even if that doctrine did apply, the judgment could have no more than a prima facie effect, and *North Jersey Savings & Loan Ass'n v. Wright, Eagan & Associates*, Civ. A. No. 85-4211, 1987 WL 5259, at *1-*2 (E.D. Pa. Jan. 13, 1987), in which the court, applying New Jersey law, held that pursuant to RESTATEMENT OF SECURITY § 139(3) (1941), a consent judgment rendered against the principal in an action in which the principal and sureties were sued jointly is evidence of only its rendition and has no preclusive effect against the surety. *See also* Kalfountzos v. Hartford Fire Ins. Co., 44 Cal. Rptr. 2d 714, 716 (Cal. Ct. App. 1995) (holding that the surety was not precluded from asserting the principal's defenses by a default judgment rendered against the principal in the same action to which the surety was a party), *disapproved of on other grounds*, Wm. R. Clarke Corp. v. Safeco Ins. Co. of Am., 938 P.2d 372, 380-81 (Cal. 1997).
404 *Drill South*, 234 F.3d at 1237. The court cited four cases for the proposition that a judgment against the principal binds the surety which had notice and opportunity to defend whether the surety was sued in the

significant distinction between the two circumstances for preclusion analysis. Even while disapproving *Vigilanti*, the Eleventh Circuit relied upon that case to support its assertion that a surety which could have defended in the proceeding against the principal is conclusively precluded by the resulting judgment against the principal, default or otherwise.[405] The *Vigilanti* case was the first to coin the "stand idly by" rationale for the notice and opportunity rule as follows:

> same action or separately. While those cases bound the surety by a default judgment against the principal in the same action, they do not otherwise support the extreme result in *Drill South*; *see* First Mobile Home Corp. v. Little, 298 So. 2d 676, 682-83 (Miss. 1974) (agreeing with *Rundle*, 107 F. at 229, that an exception to the general rule that a default judgment against the principal binds the surety arises when the principal and surety are sued jointly because the surety "had the same right to defend the action as its principal" and holding that the surety had the opportunity to oppose the claim on the merits even though a default judgment had been entered against the principal); Mass. Bonding & Ins. Co. v. Cent. Fin. Corp., 237 P.2d 1079, 180-81 (Colo. 1951) (stating, in a confusing opinion, that the default judgment against the principal was conclusively binding on the surety but also reciting that at the trial below the surety had the opportunity to submit evidence in support of its defense notwithstanding the default judgment); Home Ins. Co. of N.Y. v. Savage, 103 S.W.2d 900, 902 (Mo. Ct. App.) (holding that a default judgment against the principal constituted only prima facie evidence of the fact and amount of the principal's liability and noting that the surety failed to contest those issues at the trial below); Charleston & W.C. Ry. Co. v. Robert G. Lassiter & Co., 179 S.E. 879, 882 (N.C. 1935) (holding that a default judgment against the principal constituted only prima facie evidence of the surety's liability and noting that the surety did not undertake to present opposing evidence at the trial below). The surety was also bound by a default judgment rendered against the principal in an action in which the surety and principal had been sued jointly in *United States Fidelity & Guaranty Co. v. St. Mary's Hospital*, 458 P.2d 966 (Ariz. Ct. App. 1969) and *United Fire & Casualty Co. v. Eldridge*, No. 2006-CA-002609-MR, 2008 WL 1991641, at *1 (Ky. Ct. App. May 9, 2008). In both of those cases, however, the surety seemed to have had the opportunity to contest the claim on the merits, notwithstanding the default judgment against the principal, but was unable to do so.

405   *Drill South*, 234 F.3d at 1235.

A surety cannot stand idly by with full knowledge of an action pending against its principal, permit a judgment to be taken against the principal, and later on, when an action is brought upon its bond, require the plaintiff to retry his case. This would result in two trials of the same issue. It would retard and not promote the administration of justice.[406]

In *Vigilanti*, however, the court distinguished the case before it from *Lake County ex rel. Baxley v. Massachusetts Bonding & Insurance Co.*,[407] the case upon which the *Drill South* court built its conclusion,[408] because the judgment against the principal in *Baxley* was rendered in an earlier action to which the surety had not been a party:

> This case is readily distinguishable from the cases which have been cited in this opinion [primarily, *Baxley*[409]]. Here a judgment of default was entered against the principal in this action which the surety defended. The surety was not responsible for the principal defaulting in this action. Upon the trial of this action it was entitled to offer its defenses. It was not in any wise bound by the default judgment obtained against the principal. *See United States, to Use of Fidelity National Bank v. Rundle et al.*, 9 Cir. 107 F. 227, 52 L.R.A. 505 in which the Court decided (page 229) . . . . "This is not the ordinary case in which a judgment has first been obtained against the principal, and a second action is brought against the sureties to compel its payment. In such a case the first judgment is held to be evidence against the sureties, for the reason that it is the result of a judicial investigation in which the sureties might have availed themselves of the opportunity to make a defense for their principal. Here the action is brought in the first instance against the principal and his two sureties. The principal, presumably for the reason that he owed the bank the full amount for which the action was brought, and had no defense, made no appearance in the action. Judgment by default was rendered against him. But at the same time that this was done the sureties were in court in the same

---

406   *Vigilanti*, 25 F. Supp. at 404.
407   75 F.2d 6 (5th Cir. 1935).
408   *Drill South*, 234 F.3d at 1235.
409   *Baxley* was cited in *Vigilanti*, 25 F. Supp. at 404, by the proponent of preclusion for the proposition that the surety was conclusively bound by a judgment against the principal when the surety knew of the proceeding against the principal and had the opportunity to defend therein. As stated *supra* note 397, there is no indication from the *Baxley* opinion that the judgment against the principal in that case had been rendered by default.

action with their answer to the complaint denying the assignment of the claims to the bank, and denying, so far as the unassigned claims were concerned, their own, and incidentally their principal's, liability upon the bond. Upon what principle can it be said that the silence of the contractor—his failure to make answer—can be shown in evidence against the sureties upon the very issues which they had raised both for him and themselves upon their denial that certain of these claims had been assigned to the bank?"[410]

Upon what principle, indeed? The purpose of the notice and opportunity rule is to compel the surety to join in an action which had been commenced against the principal alone and thereby avoid the relitigation that would occur if the claimant, after having obtained a judgment against the principal, must then bring a second action against the surety. That is to say, the notice and opportunity rule serves underlying preclusion principles. By mechanically applying that rule to bind the surety conclusively in *Drill South*, the Eleventh Circuit divorced the rule from its purpose and rationale and thereby produced a nonsensical result: the claimant recovered, and the surety suffered, a judgment without the claimant's being required to prove its case on the merits even once. What value is advanced by such a result?

Moreover, it is difficult to see how the result in *Drill South* can be squared with "the deep-rooted historic tradition that everyone should have his own day in court"[411] which the Supreme Court has acknowledged is a fundamental right protected by the federal guaranty of due process of law.[412] Even though the surety in *Drill South* was a party and therefore could theoretically have protected itself by providing a

---

410 *Vigilanti*, 25 F. Supp. at 405 (quoting U.S. *ex rel.* Fid. Nat'l Bank v. Rundle, 107 F. 227, 229 (9th Cir. 1901) (denying preclusive effect to a default judgment against the principal rendered in same action in which the surety was actively defending and stating that even if the notice and opportunity doctrine applied, the judgment would constitute, at most, prima facie evidence against the surety)).

411 Richards v. Jefferson County, 517 U.S. 793, 798 (1996) (internal quotation marks omitted). *See also* U.S. *ex rel.* Frontier Constr., Inc. v. Tri-State Mgmt. Co., 262 F. Supp. 2d 893, 897 (N.D. Ill. 2003) (denying preclusive effect upon the surety of a default arbitration award against the principal in part because doing so would deprive the surety of its day in court).

412 *See* discussion *supra* Part V.A.2.

defense to the principal in that case,[413] precluding the surety conclusively for not doing so is a dubious proposition. Aside from according the claimant the windfall of a judgment without its having had to prove its case on the merits,[414] there is absolutely no reason for, nor benefit to be gained from, such an outcome. The practical effect of the ruling is to impose upon the surety the burden of providing a defense to the principal. That burden becomes the cost to the surety of its day in court, and a fundamental right should not come with a price tag when there is no need for it and when courts have traditionally held that the surety has no duty to defend the principal.[415] Thus, application of the notice and opportunity doctrine makes the surety's defense of the principal, when it has the opportunity to do so, a condition precedent to its right to defend itself. That fact appears most dramatically when the principal and the surety have been sued jointly and the surety is, in fact, actively contesting the merits of the plaintiff's claim.

The approach and outcome of cases such as *Drill South* are ultimately justified by the belief that the surety's liability is coextensive

---

[413] *Drill South*, 234 F.3d at 1236. The court based its reasoning on the fact that the surety could have, but failed to, "step in and defend the merits of [the claimant's] claims against [the principal]," *id*. On the other hand, when the surety argued that service of process on the principal was defective and that therefore the district court did not have jurisdiction to enter the default judgment, the court said that, while not deciding the issue, "it is not entirely clear that [the surety] has the right to raise the argument" because "[l]ack of personal jurisdiction is arguably a personal defense that can only be raised by the party over whom jurisdiction is lacking," *id*. at 1238 n.9. As the court saw fit to raise the possibility that the argument would be unavailable to the surety, how could the court also conclude that the surety had a full and fair opportunity to defend the principal?

[414] *See* Kalfountzos v. Hartford Fire Ins. Co., 44 Cal. Rptr. 2d 714, 716 (Cal. Ct. App. 1995) ("[T]he surety may raise any defenses or set-offs, with respect to the obligation [of the principal], ... even though the principal, as here, is precluded from raising those defenses and set-offs because of a legal disability having nothing to do with the validity of the defenses and set-offs. Any other conclusion would provide the creditor with an unjustified windfall."), *disapproved of on other grounds*, Wm. R. Clarke Corp. v. Safeco Ins. Co. of Am., 938 P.2d 372, 380-81 (Cal. 1997).

[415] *See supra* notes 402-03 and accompanying text.

with that of the principal.[416] That notion, however, is fundamentally inaccurate. While the principal's liability is necessary to establishing that of the surety, it may not be sufficient as the surety may have personal defenses that are unavailable to the principal. The problem is that the relationship between the surety and the principal is not monolithic or immutable; it simply does not lend itself to the all-or-nothing preclusion analysis applied in *Drill South*. The difficulties embedded in such cases, particularly the often overlooked due process issues, would largely be eliminated by use of the Restatement's "middle ground" approach with little, if any, real damage being done to the interests underlying the preclusion doctrine. Even on its own terms, however, the *Drill South* reasoning should limit the preclusive effect of a default judgment against the principal to only the issue of the principal's liability because it was only the claim against the principal which the surety failed to defend. The surety was in fact defending the claim asserted against it, and there is no justification for making the default judgment against the principal *conclusively* binding on the surety, thereby precluding it from asserting suretyship defenses.

Two payment bond cases have invoked *Drill South* and its conception of the notice and opportunity approach as authority for precluding the surety on the basis of a default judgment against the principal in the same case in which the surety was presenting its own defense. In one case, *American Safety Casualty Insurance Co. v. C.G. Mitchell Construction, Inc.*,[417] the default judgment had been entered as a discovery sanction because the principal, a defunct corporation, failed to obey an order to name a designee to give deposition testimony on its behalf. The surety argued that judgment by preclusion should not be entered against it because it did not have the ability to make a corporate designee appear and because other than a conclusory affidavit, the

---

416 Although unspoken in *Drill South*, that belief was expressly espoused in the two cases which have cited *Drill South* as support for precluding the surety. U.S. *ex rel.* Davis Contracting, L.P. v. B.E.N. Constr., Inc., Civil Action No. 05-1219-MLB, 2007 WL 293915, at *5 (D. Kan. Jan. 26, 2007) ("[S]ureties have the same defenses as the principal; no more, no less."); McAlpine v. Zangara Dodge, Inc., 183 P.3d 975, 982 (N.M. Ct. App. 2008) ("'[T]he liability of the surety depends upon the liability of the principal.'" (quoting Holland v. Lawless, 623 P.2d 1004, 1011 (N.M. Ct. App. 1981))).

417 601 S.E.2d 633 (Va. 2004).

claimant had not proved the amount of its damages.[418] Those arguments were unavailing; for the Virginia Supreme Court, all that mattered was that the surety did not even attempt to name a corporate designee.[419] Under that analysis, not only must the surety defend the principal, it must in effect *become* the principal and, because a default judgment against the principal is given conclusive preclusive effect, suffer the sanctions resulting from the principal's unwillingness or inability to comply with discovery orders.

In the other case to follow *Drill South*, *McAlpine v. Zangara Dodge, Inc.*,[420] the default judgment against the principal was also entered as a sanction for an unspecified failure to provide discovery. The surety

---

418   Along with *Drill South*, the court cited *Frederick v. United States*, 386 F.2d 481, 486 n.6 (5th Cir. 1967) as holding that the surety is bound by any judgment against the principal, default or otherwise, when the surety had notice of the proceeding against the principal and the opportunity to defend. *C.G. Mitchell*, 601 S.E.2d at 638-39. In *Frederick*, however, the court refused to bind the surety by a default judgment which had been rendered against the principal in a prior action, not in the action which the surety was defending, because the plaintiff's affidavit as to the amount of its damages was insufficient. *Frederick*, 386 F.2d at 485-86. Thus, the statements in that case as to the preclusive effect on the surety of a judgment against the principal were dicta. See U.S. *ex rel.* Frontier Constr., Inc. v. Tri-State Mgmt. Co., 262 F. Supp. 2d 893, 895 (N.D. Ill. 2003) (referring to "the rule expressed in the *Frederick* dicta"). Other courts have misread *Frederick*. In *U.S. ex rel. Skip Kirchdorfer, Inc. v. M.J. Kelley Corp.*, 995 F.2d 656 (6th Cir. 1993), also discussed *supra* text accompanying notes 388-95, the Sixth Circuit, in holding that Miller Act sureties were bound by a prior arbitration award against the principal because they had been aware of the arbitration, stated that "[i]n *Frederick*, the court *held* that a judgment against a principal conclusively establishes the liability of a *surety*, as long as the surety had notice of the proceedings against the principal," *id.* at 661 (emphasis added) (citing *Frederick*, 386 F.2d at 486 n.6). The statement is wrong on two counts. First, *Frederick* footnote 6 was dicta. Second, the footnote stated that a judgment against the principal "establishes against a surety the fact of, and amount of, the *principal's* liability . . . . ," *id.* (emphasis added). The distinction between those two formulations can mean the difference between the surety's being permitted to assert its suretyship defenses or its being precluded from doing so.
419   *C.G. Mitchell*, 601 S.E.2d at 637.
420   183 P.3d 975 (N.M. Ct. App. 2008).

argued that it did not have "the access or ability to defend [the principal] from sanctions based on bad conduct."[421] The court was unmoved: "The purpose of the notice and opportunity inquiry is not to speculate about what the outcome of a certain action might have been. Instead, we consider whether the surety took advantage of an opportunity to defend the principal against a judgment as to [its] liability."[422] In other words, no matter how futile, the surety must make the effort or face preclusion; form, not substance, prevails. The preclusion imposed in *McAlpine*, however, was limited to the "defenses which were or could have been asserted by [the principal] to the claim of fraud made against [the principal],"[423] and presumably would not extend to the surety's personal defenses. The appellate court did, in fact, consider in detail, though it ultimately rejected, the surety's defense based on contentions as to the bond coverage mandated by the applicable statute.[424]

Other courts, however, have found the *Drill South* reasoning unpersuasive.[425] For example, in *Angelo Iafrate Construction, LLC v. Potashnick Construction, Inc.*,[426] the Eighth Circuit, the court which eschewed the then-unanimous federal court endorsement of super incorporation in favor of limited incorporation,[427] "decline[d] to extend the language in *Drill South* to cover a situation where, as here, the surety has obtained a judgment in its favor before the default judgment against its principal was entered."[428] In *United States ex rel. Frontier Construction, Inc. v. Tri-State Management Co.*,[429] a Miller Act claimant sought to enforce against the surety a prior default arbitration award[430]

---

421 *Id.* at 982.
422 *Id.*
423 *Id.* at 979 (quoting trial court's summary judgment order against the surety which was affirmed).
424 *Id.* at 977-79.
425 For pre-*Drill South* cases which declined to preclude the surety on the basis of a default judgment against the principal, *see* discussion *supra* Part V.B.2.a.
426 370 F.3d 715 (8th Cir. 2004).
427 AgGrow Oils, L.L.C. v. Nat'l Union Fire Ins. Co. of Pittsburgh, Pa., 242 F.3d 777 (8th Cir. 2001), discussed in detail *supra* Part II.A.4.
428 *Angelo Iafrate*, 370 F.3d at 722.
429 262 F. Supp. 2d 893 (N.D. Ill. 2003).
430 The court regarded an award entered in an arbitration at which the principal did not appear as "essentially a default judgment." *Id.* at 896.

against the principal. The court held that such enforcement was unwarranted under either federal or state law. The court found that "a majority of federal courts (including the Seventh Circuit) do not give preclusive effect to default judgments" under federal law[431] and that cases applying Illinois law reached the same conclusion.[432] In addition, the court noted that Illinois "stresses the importance of allowing a surety to present defenses to its own liability on a bond" as well as those of the principal and that imposing preclusion on the basis of a default judgment would "deny [the surety] its day in court."[433]

C. Preclusive Effect of an Arbitration Award Against the Principal

Neither the federal statute nor the great majority of the state arbitration statutes have any provision which addresses the preclusive effect of an award on a nonparty to the arbitration. As a result, that issue has been determined by decisional law.[434] Arbitration statutes do, however, provide that arbitration awards may be confirmed by a court proceeding and judgment entered on the award.[435] Accordingly, for preclusion purposes, courts generally treat confirmed arbitration awards as they would any other court judgment. The cases apply to arbitration awards the same preclusion analysis and authorities as are applied to court judgments and accord arbitration awards the same binding effect given to judgments.[436]

---

431 *Id.* at 896.
432 *Id.* at 897.
433 *Id.*
434 See discussion *supra* Part V.B.
435 See discussion *supra* Part I.A.
436 *See, e.g.*, Lewis v. Circuit City Stores, Inc., 500 F.3d 1140, 1147 (10th Cir. 2007) (noting that preclusion law has been applied to valid arbitration awards under federal, Kansas and Virginia law); Rouse Constr., Inc. v. Transamerica Ins. Co., 750 F.2d 1492 (11th Cir. 1985) (applying Georgia law); Cashman Equip. Corp. v. Acadian Shipyard, Inc., No. Civ. A. 01-2411, 2001 WL 1387921, at *1 (E.D. La. Nov. 6, 2001) (applying res judicata and collateral estoppel principles in determining the effect of an arbitration among the performance bond surety, the obligee and the principal); Moore Bros. Constr. Co. v. Brown & Root, Inc., 962 F. Supp. 838, 841 (E.D. Va. 1997) (applying Virginia

An exception is the category of cases in which the surety is held to have agreed to arbitration by incorporating by reference into its bond a contract of the principal which contains an arbitration provision.[437] The

---

law), *order aff'd in part and rev'd in part*; 207 F.3d 717 (4th Cir. 2000); Ufheil Constr. Co. v. Town of New Windsor, 478 F. Supp. 766, 768 (S.D.N.Y. 1979), *aff'd*, 636 F.2d 1204 (2d Cir. 1980) (applying New York law); Von Eng'g Co. v. R. W. Roberts Constr. Co., 457 So. 2d 1080 (Fla. Dist. Ct. App. 1984); P. R. Post Corp. v. Md. Cas. Co., 271 N.W.2d 521, 524 (Mich. 1978); Azevedo & Boyle Contracting, Inc. v. J. Greaney Constr. Corp., 728 N.Y.S.2d 743, 744 (N.Y. App. Div. 2001) ("It is well settled that the doctrine of collateral estoppel is applicable to issues resolved in an earlier arbitration proceeding."); QDR Consultants & Dev. Corp. v. Colonia Ins. Co., 675 N.Y.S.2d 117, 118 (N.Y. App. Div. 1998); Shire Realty Corp. v. Schorr, 390 N.Y.S.2d 622 (N.Y. App. Div. 1977); McIntyre Square Assocs. v. Evans, 827 A.2d 446, 459 (Pa. Super. Ct. 2003). Under RESTATEMENT (SECOND) OF JUDGMENTS § 84 (1982), arbitration awards are to be accorded the same preclusive effect as a court judgment unless the arbitration procedure is "so radically unfair as to justify nullifying the agreement to abide by it." *Id.* cmt. b. In *United States ex rel. Pensacola Constr. Co. v. St. Paul Fire and Marine Ins. Co.*, 705 F. Supp. 306 (W.D. La. 1989), the court found the differences between arbitration and litigation so significant as to justify refusing to accord any binding effect upon a Miller Act surety of an arbitration between a claimant and the principal. In *United States ex rel. Skip Kirchdorfer, Inc. v. AEGIS/Zublin Joint Venture*, 869 F. Supp. 387, 394-96 (E.D. Va. 1994), however, the court assumed that arbitrators based their award in a Miller Act case on proper grounds.

437 There are other exceptions which should have little, if any, effect in the performance bond context. For example, the Full Faith and Credit Statute, 28 U.S.C.A. § 1738 (West 2006), applies only to "judicial proceedings" and therefore does not require federal courts to give preclusive effect to an arbitration award as it does to state court judgments, Dean Witter Reynolds, Inc. v. Byrd, 470 U.S. 213, 222 (1985). Also, there is a line of United States Supreme Court cases which holds that an arbitration award on a contract claim will not necessarily preclude a later court case seeking to vindicate a federal statutory right, *see, e.g.*, McDonald v. West Branch, 466 U.S. 284 (1984) (an adverse award in a labor arbitration did not preclude a subsequent suit under 42 U.S.C.A. § 1983 (West 2003) for deprivation of First Amendment rights), and therefore suggests that an arbitration award might be treated differently than a court judgment. Later cases, however, state *McDonald* and similar cases arose only when

preclusive effect of an arbitration award against the principal arises, naturally, much more frequently under the limited incorporation approach than under super incorporation.[438] Limited incorporation presupposes an arbitration between the obligee and the principal, to which the surety is not a party, as to the issue of the principal's breach of the underlying contract. As set forth in the *Parsons & Whittemore* case,[439] incorporation in the performance bond of a construction contract with an arbitration provision manifests the surety's agreement to be bound by the results of the arbitration between those parties as to the

---

an arbitration of a contractual right is later invoked to bar assertion of a related, but distinct, federal statutory right, and involved the tension between a union which controlled the contract grievance procedure and the individual employee, and were not decided under the Federal Arbitration Act and its policy favoring arbitration, *see, e.g.*, Gilmer v. Interstate/Johnson Lane Corp., 500 U.S. 20, 35 (1991) (distinguishing *McDonald* and like cases on those grounds and holding that a securities dealer was required to arbitrate with his employer a claim under the Age Discrimination in Employment Act, 29 U.S.C.A. §§ 621-34 (West 2008)). The issue could conceivably arise in payment bond claims under the Miller Act, 40 U.S.C.A. §§ 3131-34 (West 2005 & Supp. 2008), because that statute provides for exclusive federal court jurisdiction; *see* discussion *supra* note 390. Thus far, however, such cases have treated confirmed arbitration awards as state court judgments governed by the Full Faith and Credit Statute, *see, e.g.*, U.S. *ex rel.* Aurora Painting, Inc. v. Fireman's Fund Ins. Co., 832 F.2d 1150, 1152-53 (9th Cir. 1987). Under *Marrese v. American Academy of Orthopaedic Surgeons*, 470 U.S. 373, 380-83 (1986), the Full Faith and Credit Statute requires that a federal court, when faced with a state court judgment on a claim involving exclusive federal jurisdiction, look first to the law of the rendering state and only if that state would accord preclusive effect to such a judgment, address whether or not the federal statute should be read as an exception to the Full Faith and Credit Statute, *see* U.S. *ex rel.* PCC Constr., Inc. v. Star Ins. Co., 90 F. Supp. 2d 512, 516-18 (D.N.J. 2000) (holding that a New Jersey state court judgment in favor of a Miller Act claimant had neither claim nor issue preclusion effect in the claimant's subsequent federal court suit against the sureties because New Jersey law would not accord preclusive effect to a state court judgment when jurisdiction was exclusively federal).

438   The incorporation cases are discussed *supra* Parts II.A-III.
439   Fid. & Deposit Co. of Md. v. Parsons & Whittemore Contractors Corp., 397 N.E.2d 380 (N.Y. 1979).

principal's liability.[440] Thus, the reasoning underlying limited incorporation virtually mandates that courts applying that approach will preclude the surety from relitigating the principal's liability and will bind the surety conclusively to an award adverse to the principal as to its liability.[441] Two recent New York intermediate appellate court decisions

---

440   *Id.* at 382.
441   *Id.* See also AgGrow Oils, L.L.C. v. Nat'l Union Fire Ins. Co. of Pittsburgh, Pa., 242 F.3d 777, 783 (8th Cir. 2001) (denying the surety's application for a mandatory stay of the obligee's performance bond claim litigation pending arbitration between the obligee and principal but remanding for consideration of a discretionary stay to permit the arbitration); Grundstad v. Ritt, 166 F.3d 867, 872 (7th Cir. 1999) (holding that the guarantor was bound by an arbitration award interpreting the guaranteed contract); WindowMaster Corp. v. B.G. Danis Co., 511 F. Supp. 157, 160 (S.D. Ohio 1981) (suggesting, though the issue was not before it, that the surety "may well be bound by an award between" the obligee and principal), *disapproved of by* Exch. Mut. Ins. Co. v. Haskell Co., 742 F.2d 274, 276 (6th Cir. 1984); Loyal Order of Moose, Lodge 1392 v. Int'l Fid. Ins. Co., 797 P.2d 622, 629 (Alaska 1990) ("Such arbitration, pursuant to and limited to the underlying contract, will bind the surety as well as the principal and beneficiary."); Matson, Inc. v. Lamb & Assocs. Packaging, Inc., 947 S.W.2d 324, 328 (Ark. 1997) (granting the principal's motion to intervene and compel the obligee to arbitrate and strongly suggesting that the surety will be bound by the results of the arbitration between the obligee and principal); Hartford Accident & Indem. Co. v. Scarlett Harbor Assocs. Ltd. P'ship, 695 A.2d 153, 157 n.8 (Md. 1997) (denying the surety's application to compel the obligee to arbitrate claims asserted in a court action but reminding lower court that it had the power to stay the obligee's action pending the outcome of the arbitration between the obligee and the principal); Gloucester City Bd. of Educ. v. Am. Arbitration Ass'n, 755 A.2d 1256, 1262-63 (N.J. Super. Ct. App. Div. 2000) (expressly adopting the reasoning of *Parsons & Whittemore* and stating that by incorporating an arbitration provision in performance bond, the surety agreed to arbitrate any dispute which the principal was required to arbitrate); *but cf.* C & I Steel, LLC v. Travelers Cas. & Sur. Co. of Am., 876 N.E.2d 442, 449 (Mass. App. Ct. 2007) (although the surety's payment bond did not incorporate the subcontract between the claimant and principal and therefore there was no basis for inferring that the surety had agreed to arbitrate with claimant, the surety might be bound as to any issue actually decided in the arbitration between the claimant and principal).

applied *Parsons & Whittemore* in reaching such a result. In *Walter Concrete Construction Corp. v. Lederle Laboratories*,[442] the court affirmed a summary judgment against the surety on a subcontract performance bond, holding that the surety was bound by an award against the principal in an arbitration between the principal and the obligee. In *Zacher v. Oakdale Islandia Limited Partnership*,[443] the court held that the performance bond surety was liable on the obligee's arbitration award against the principal. Although the surety was permitted to assert, but could adduce no evidence to support, bond defenses which were beyond the scope of the award, it was precluded from presenting "claims regarding its liability for the arbitration award" because "such claims relate to the scope and content of the award and cannot be relitigated."[444]

Cases such as *Parsons & Whittemore* and the other limited incorporation cases are outside of any preclusion analysis whether it be traditional doctrines of res judicata or collateral estoppel or approaches based on suretyship principles such as the Restatement's rebuttable presumption rule. For the limited incorporation courts, the resolution of the preclusion question is easy; it is answered by the surety's perceived consent to be bound. There is no need to navigate the complexities of privity, of the conditions which should give rise to preclusion in a given case, or of the extent of the preclusive effect which should be imposed in particular circumstances.

Not all courts faced with a performance bond which incorporated a construction contract with an arbitration provision have embraced such a solution. For the Michigan Supreme Court in *P.R. Post Corp. v. Maryland Casualty Co.*,[445] it seemed that the more difficult issue was not the preclusion question but the incorporation question. That court chose

---

[442] 734 N.Y.S.2d 80, 81 (N.Y. App. Div. 2001), *aff'd*, 788 N.E.2d 609 (N.Y. 2003).
[443] 775 N.Y.S.2d 155, 156 (N.Y. App. Div. 2004).
[444] *Id. See also* QDR Consultants & Dev. Corp. v. Colonia Ins. Co., 675 N.Y.S.2d 117, 118-19 (N.Y. App. Div. 1998) (holding in connection with a payment bond claim that collateral estoppel precluded the surety as to only the issues resolved in a prior arbitration between the claimant and the principal and that therefore the surety was free to assert defenses under the bond).
[445] 271 N.W.2d 521 (Mich. 1978), discussed in detail *supra* Part V.B.1.c.

to apply its usual preclusion rule for judgments[446] against the principal to an arbitration award and hold that the award was prima facie evidence of the surety's liability.[447] That approach was preferable to having to decide whether incorporation constituted an agreement by the surety to arbitrate with the obligee and, if so, whether such an agreement should or could have preclusive consequences when the surety had no notice of the arbitration between the obligee and the principal.[448] In effect, the *P.R. Post* court simply ignored the fact that the performance bond incorporated an arbitration provision. In doing so, that court adopted a rule which is, of course, more generous to the surety. Even if the arbitration award is adverse to the principal, the surety, though it now has the burden of proof, may present any defenses which were available to the principal as well as those personal to itself.[449]

Under the super incorporation approach, the surety is a party to the arbitration provision and therefore may be compelled pursuant to arbitration statutes to arbitrate with the obligee all disputes including the

---

446 Other courts have applied their ordinary preclusion principles in cases involving an incorporated arbitration provision and an arbitration award. *See, e.g.*, Moore Bros. Constr. Co. v. Brown & Root, Inc., 962 F. Supp. 838, 842 (E.D. Va. 1997) (applying Virginia collateral estoppel principles), *order aff'd in part and rev'd in part*; 207 F.3d 717 (4th Cir. 2000); Raymond Int'l Builders, Inc. v. First Indem. of Am. Ins. Co., 516 A.2d 620, 621-22 (N.J. 1986) (applying principles and precedent involving judgments). *Cf.* Rashid v. U.S. Fid. & Guar. Co., Inc., Civ.A.No.2:91-0141, 1992 WL 565341, at *1, *13 (S.D.W. Va. 1992), (binding the surety to an arbitration award against the principal on the basis of the federal super incorporation cases but finding that the same result would be reached under West Virginia collateral estoppel principles), *approved in related case*, Rashid v. Schenck Constr. Co., Inc., 438 S.E.2d 543, 546-47 (W. Va. 1993) (agreeing that "principles of collateral estoppel would preclude [the surety] from relitigating the issues decided in the arbitration" between the obligee and the principal). For decisions in which courts applied their usual preclusion principles to arbitration awards against the obligee, *see* cases discussed *supra* note 297.

447 *P.R. Post*, at 525.
448 *Id.* at 523.
449 *Id.* at 525.

surety's liability under the bond.[450] In jurisdictions which follow that doctrine, the obligee can obtain a court order requiring a reluctant surety to arbitrate, and the resulting award would be binding on the surety as a party to the arbitration under the applicable arbitration statute. Thus, there appear to be few reported cases, arising under super incorporation principles, which involved an arbitration between the obligee and the principal alone and which therefore called for consideration of the preclusive effect upon the absent surety of an award adverse to the principal. One court, speaking of the federal court incorporation cases,[451] has said that it was "implicit" in those decisions that the surety would be bound by the award to the extent that it would have been obligated to arbitrate.[452] If that analysis is correct, then the surety would automatically be liable for the amount of the arbitration award rendered against the principal. In effect, such an approach would transform a performance bond into a judgment bond.[453] Indeed, that same court explicitly stated that a performance bond incorporating a contract with an arbitration clause is "deemed to be the equivalent of an express agreement to pay a judgment based on an arbitration award rendered

---

450 See, e.g., Hoffman v. Fid. & Deposit Co. of Md., 734 F. Supp. 192 (D.N.J. 1990) (surety is required to arbitrate all issues including any personal defenses with the obligee under section 4 of the Federal Arbitration Act, 9 U.S.C.A. § 4 (West 1999)), discussed in detail *supra* Part II.A.2.
451 See federal cases cited *supra* notes 59, 63 and 77.
452 Rashid v. U.S. Fid. & Guar. Co., Inc., Civ.A.No.2:91-0141, 1992 WL 565341, at *9 n.9 (S.D.W. Va. Sept. 28, 1992); *see also* Aetna Cas. & Sur. Co. v. L'Energia, Ltd. P'ship, No. CIV. A. 96-10098-GAO, 1996 WL 208497, at *4, n.4 (D. Mass. Mar. 4, 1996) (presuming that surety could be required to participate in some arbitration, but refusing to compel surety to join a massive, consolidated arbitration that included the obligee and principal and noting that the surety would be bound by an arbitration award adverse to the principal); Dunn Indus. Group, Inc. v. City of Sugar Creek, 112 S.W.3d 421, 436 n.6 (Mo. 2003) (per curiam) (expressly not addressing whether the guarantor of a subsidiary's performance of a construction contract, who could not be compelled to arbitrate with the obligee, would be bound by the results of an arbitration between the subsidiary and the obligee).
453 See discussion *supra* note 356.

against [the principal]."[454] Consequently, the fact of an arbitration award against the principal would be sufficient basis, in and of itself, without any other factors, upon which to enter a judgment against the surety for the amount of the award against the principal.

It appears, however, that even the super incorporation approach will not always support such a harsh result. In *Kearsarge Metallurgical Corp. v. Peerless Insurance Co.*,[455] for example, the obligee obtained an arbitration award against the principal which was rendered in a proceeding in which neither the principal nor the surety participated but of which both had notice. The Massachusetts Supreme Judicial Court, undertaking to apply New Hampshire law, held that the award was conclusively binding on the surety because the performance bond incorporated a construction contract with an arbitration provision.[456] The performance bond and the incorporated arbitration clause, read together, "required Peerless [the surety] to arbitrate '(a)ll claims and disputes relating to this (construction) contract.'"[457] Because the surety was obligated to arbitrate all such claims and disputes, the court refused to entertain the surety's defense that the obligee had agreed to waive

---

454 *Rashid*, 1992 WL 565341, at *12. In that case, the court held that the surety was conclusively bound by an arbitration award in favor of the obligee and against the principal because the performance bond incorporated the construction contract and its arbitration provision. The court seemed driven to transform the performance bond into a judgment bond in order to fit within an exception to a West Virginia statute prohibiting any preclusive effect on a nonparty surety, W. VA. CODE § 45-1-3 (West, Westlaw through end of 2008 2nd Extraordinary Sess.), and thus enable itself to say that the same result would be reached under West Virginia law. Nevertheless, the court did not go as far as its rhetoric: "While federal law would doubtless have required [the surety] to arbitrate its defenses along with those of [the principal], that scenario did not occur and [the surety] should not be bound by the award to the extent that it is based in whole or in part on unbonded obligations.," *id.* at 14. Although the surety appears to have partly financed the principal's arbitration effort, it was never served with an arbitration demand or made a party to that proceeding, *id.* at *3.
455 418 N.E.2d 580 (Mass. 1981).
456 *Id.* at 582-83.
457 *Id.* at 584 (quoting the arbitration provision).

liquidated damages if the surety agreed to complete the project.[458] In making its ruling, the court was faced with a case in which the Supreme Court of New Hampshire held that an unopposed summary judgment obtained by the creditor against the debtor had no preclusive effect at all on the guarantor.[459] One of the bases upon which the Massachusetts court distinguished the New Hampshire case was that the guarantor was not afforded the opportunity to participate in the summary judgment proceedings, while in the case before it, "the surety repeatedly was given notice of the arbitration proceedings, and chose not to participate."[460] Thus, even for a court which holds that incorporation imposes a duty on the surety to arbitrate with the obligee and which wishes to find that the surety's liability is conclusively determined by an award adverse to the principal will not bind the surety unless it had notice of the arbitration and the opportunity to participate in it–at least where the principal did not appear and contest the obligee's claim.

A surety which, itself, invokes an arbitration provision of an incorporated bonded contract may find itself conclusively bound by the result of that arbitration with no ability to raise any defenses at all. In *Sheffield Assembly of God Church, Inc. v. American Insurance Co.*,[461] the surety, in joining the principal's motion to stay the court action to permit arbitration between the principal and the obligee, argued that the issue of the amount of the obligee's damages was exclusively for the

---

458 *Id.* at 585. The court attempted to side-step *Fidelity & Deposit Co. of Maryland v. Parsons & Whittemore Contractors Corp.*, 397 N.E.2d 380 (N.Y. 1979) by characterizing the defenses not precluded under *Parsons & Whittemore* as those which were "'separate and distinct' from the issue of its [the surety's] liability under the terms of the construction contract" while labeling the defenses asserted by the surety before it as arising "directly under that contract, and therefore were required to be settled in arbitration," *id.* at 585 n.12. Thus, although the court formulated the surety's obligation to arbitrate in terms of claims and disputes arising under the construction contract, its refusal to recognize that the surety's defenses arose from an asserted modification of the performance bond and the scope of its obligations thereunder requires this case to be included among those applying the super incorporation approach.

459 C-E Bldg. Prods., Inc. v. Seal-Rite Aluminum Prods. of N.H., Inc., 316 A.2d 198 (N.H. 1974).

460 *Kearsarge*, 418 N.E.2d at 583 n.9.

461 870 S.W.2d 926 (Mo. Ct. App. 1994).

arbitrator and that the obligee could seek to enforce any award against the principal and the surety. The court, taking the surety at its word, held that the surety's assertion of the arbitration provision was a "judicial admission" that the surety would be bound by the arbitration results and therefore affirmed the judgment entered against the surety in the amount of the award.[462]

When courts base their preclusion analysis on the fact of incorporation, rather than employing ordinary preclusion principles, an arbitration award can have a greater binding effect on the surety than an adverse court judgment against the principal. It should also be noted, however, that arbitration can also narrow the scope of preclusion in comparison to court judgments, at least in those jurisdictions which apply traditional collateral estoppel principles. As recognized in *Ufheil Construction Co. v. Town of New Windsor*,[463] arbitrators are not required to make findings of fact or to state conclusions of law and frequently refrain from doing so.[464] In that case, the plaintiff obtained an arbitration award against the defendant town on several claims and thereafter commenced an action against the town. Moving for summary judgment, the plaintiff argued that the prior arbitration award collaterally estopped the town as to the claims asserted in the lawsuit. It could not be determined whether the claims upon which the arbitrators rendered an award in favor of the plaintiff included the claims which the plaintiff asserted in the lawsuit. Because collateral estoppel requires that the issue in the second case be the same as that decided in the first, the court denied summary judgment. Although the mere fact that the award did not contain findings of fact does not preclude the application of collateral estoppel, the court held that when an award is ambiguous as to the issues decided in the arbitration, collateral estoppel may not be invoked.[465]

---

462 *Id.* at 931-32.
463 478 F. Supp. 766 (S.D.N.Y. 1979), *aff'd*, 636 F.2d 1204 (2d Cir. 1980) (applying New York law).
464 *Id.* at 768.
465 *Id.* 768-69. Arbitration awards are to be accorded the same preclusive effect as a court judgment unless the arbitration procedure is "so radically unfair as to justify nullifying the agreement to abide by it," RESTATEMENT (SECOND) OF JUDGMENTS § 84 cmt. b (1982). For cases considering the procedural acceptability of arbitration, *see* discussion *supra* note 436.

Effect of an Arbitration Provision in the Principal's Contract 807

D. Suretyship Defenses

Even if a ruling against the principal precludes the surety to some extent from relitigating the issue of the principal's liability, may the surety still assert defenses that were not available to the principal but are personal to the surety? In the performance bond context, such suretyship defenses might include overpayment, material modification of the bonded contract and notice requirements or limitations provisions. Outside of the cases involving the effect of an incorporated arbitration provision, very few decisions speak to that issue directly, either as to arbitration awards or judgments, but some inferences can be made from the particular approach to preclusion that is applied.

1. Under General Preclusion Principles

Under res judicata, a judgment or confirmed arbitration award bars relitigation of all claims that were raised, or could have been raised, in the prior proceeding. That bar also applies to defenses which could have been asserted in the first proceeding even if they were not then raised.[466] The prohibitions of res judicata apply to the parties in the original case

---

466 RESTATEMENT (SECOND) OF JUDGMENTS § 18(2) (1982). In *Cashman Equipment Corp. v. Acadian Shipyard, Inc.*, No. Civ.A. 01-2411, 2001 WL 1387921, at *1 (E.D. La. Nov. 6, 2001), the obligee commenced an arbitration against the principal and surety for liquidated damages for the principal's late delivery of a vessel. After the arbitrator's deadline for the submission of claims, the obligee sought to assert claims for rescission of the liquidated damages provision and reformation of the contract to permit a claim for actual damages. The arbitrator refused to hear the claims because doing so would remove from the contract the basis for the obligee's demand for arbitration. The obligee then brought suit seeking a court order for the rescission and reformation which had been denied in the arbitration. The court held that the rescission and reformation claims were not barred by res judicata because the obligee tried to raise the claims in the arbitration and the claims were barred as not being subject to adjudication in the arbitration. The court also made a point of noting that the principal and surety had opposed the obligee's application to assert the claims in the arbitration. While permitting the assertion of the claims, however, the court also held that collateral estoppel applied to preclude relitigation of specific fact issues which had been determined in the arbitration.

and to those in privity with those parties. Conceivably, therefore, a court which is persuaded that the surety and principal are in privity could apply res judicata to preclude the assertion of suretyship defenses on the ground that such defenses could have been asserted by the principal in the first action.[467] Even under res judicata, however, there is the question of whether the principal could have raised the surety's personal defenses; and if not, the surety should not be precluded from doing so.[468]

Despite loose usage of the term res judicata, courts employing that rubric usually apply the issue preclusion analysis of collateral estoppel. In *United States ex rel. Aurora Painting, Inc. v. Fireman's Fund Insurance Co.*,[469] for example, the court purported to ask whether a payment bond claimant's arbitration award against the principal bound

---

467   That possibility was raised in J. Michael Franks and John W. Heacock, *Arbitration and the Contract Surety: Inclusion and Preclusion*, 32 TORTS & INS. L. J. 977, 992-93 (1997).

468   In *International Fidelity Insurance Co. v. China Construction America (SC) Inc.*, 650 S.E.2d 677 (S.C. 2007), the obligee sued the surety for a declaration that the surety was obligated to discharge liens of the principal's creditors and sued the principal for breach of contract. The surety ultimately discharged the liens, leaving only the obligee's breach of contract claim against the principal for trial. On the day of trial, the principal failed to appear, and the obligee consented to the surety's motion for dismissal without prejudice and proceeded to try its breach of contract claim against the absent principal which resulted in the entry of judgment against the principal. When the surety later sued the obligee for the contract balance, the obligee counterclaimed on the basis of its judgment against the principal. The court held that the judgment was conclusively binding on the surety and that "Surety may not now argue defenses which should or might have been raised in the action in which the judgment was recovered, especially where Surety had notice and an opportunity to defend in that action," *id.* at 679. Presumably, the court thought that when the principal failed to appear for the trial, the surety should have gone forward to defend the claim against the principal, which the court apparently regarded as a consequence of the surety's liability being joint and several with that of the principal. If, however, the surety had personal defenses, one may reasonably ask how the surety could have raised its defenses when the obligee's claim against it had been mooted by the surety's discharge of the liens and the suretyship defenses would have been irrelevant to the obligee's claim against the principal.

469   832 F.2d 1150 (9th Cir. 1987), discussed in detail *supra* text accompanying notes 388-95.

the surety under res judicata. The court found privity between the surety and the principal and then concluded that "a judgment against a principal conclusively establishes against a surety the fact of and the amount of the principal's liability as long as the surety has notice of the proceeding against the principal."[470] That conclusion represents the classic issue preclusion analysis of collateral estoppel.

Under collateral estoppel, parties to an action and their privies are precluded from relitigating *issues* which were previously determined. The issue which is usually decided by an award against the principal in an arbitration between the principal and the obligee is the principal's liability to the obligee. Thus, courts which apply collateral estoppel principles often conclude that the surety and the principal are in privity and that, therefore, a judgment or award against the principal establishes the principal's liability and the surety is precluded from relitigating that particular issue.[471] Such courts should conclude, therefore, that collateral

---

470 *Id.* at 1153.
471 *See, e.g.,* Moore Bros. Constr. Co. v. Brown & Root, Inc., 962 F. Supp. 838, 842 (E.D. Va. 1997) (applying Virginia law), *order aff'd in part and rev'd in part*, 207 F.3d 717 (4th Cir. 2000); Rashid v. U.S. Fid. & Guar. Co., Inc., Civ.A.No.2:91-0141, 1992 WL 565341, at *1, *13 (S.D.W. Va. Sept. 28, 1992) (binding the surety to an arbitration award against the principal on the basis of the federal incorporation cases but finding that the same result would be reached under the application of West Virginia collateral estoppel principles), *approved in related case*, Rashid v. Schenck Constr. Co., Inc., 438 S.E.2d 543, 546-47 (W. Va. 1993) (agreeing that "principles of collateral estoppel would preclude [the surety] from relitigating the issues decided in the arbitration" between the obligee and the principal); Greenwell v. Am. Guar. Corp., 277 A.2d 70, 76 (Md. 1971); Mayfield v. Hicks, 575 S.W.2d 571, 574 (Tex. App. 1978). *Cf.* Venus Mech., Inc. v. Ins. Co. of N. Am., 667 N.Y.S.2d 60 (N.Y. App. Div. 1997). In *Venus Mechanical*, an arbitration between a payment bond claimant and the principal resulted in an award that the principal was to pay a sum certain owed to the claimant only when the principal received payment from the obligee. The court held that the surety "stands in its principal's shoes for collateral estoppel purposes" and that therefore the claimant was precluded from relitigating against the surety the conditional nature of the principal's obligation, *id.* at 61. Although the case arose after "pay-when-paid" provisions were held to be against public policy in New York in *West-Fair Electric Contractors. v. Aetna Cas. & Sur. Co.*, 661 N.E.2d 967 (N.Y. 1995), the court held that

estoppel does not preclude the surety from later asserting its personal defenses.[472]

In those cases holding that the surety will be bound by an arbitration award against the principal when the surety had adequate notice of and the opportunity to defend in the arbitration, it is frequently unclear from the reported opinion whether the court intended that, or even considered whether, the assertion of suretyship defenses would also be precluded. The language of such cases, however, seems to suggest that the surety will be bound only as to the issue of the principal's liability. For example, in *Raymond International Builders, Inc. v. First Indemnity of America Insurance Co.*,[473] the court said that "the surety's decision to forego joinder [in an arbitration between the obligee and the principal] in the face of adequate notice and a request or demand for joinder will result in its being bound by *the results of the arbitration proceedings*."[474]

---

the impact of that ruling could not be litigated because it had not been raised in the proceeding to confirm the award, *Venus Mechanical*, 667 N.Y.S.2d at 61.

[472] QDR Consultants & Dev. Corp. v. Colonia Ins. Co., 675 N.Y.S.2d 117, 119 (N.Y. App. Div. 1998) (holding that the recoverability of lost profits under a payment bond was not resolved in the prior arbitration between the claimant and the principal and therefore collateral estoppel did not preclude the surety from contesting that issue in a subsequent action by the claimant).

[473] 516 A.2d 620 (N.J. 1986).

[474] *Id.* at 622 (emphasis added). The court in *Seaboard Surety Co. v. Board of Chosen Freeholders*, 537 A.2d 310, 314 (N.J. Super. Ct. App. Div. 1988), said that it read *Raymond Int'l* as holding that the surety will be bound by the arbitration award "against the principal" if the surety had adequate notice of the arbitration and opportunity to participate in it. Since then, a New Jersey intermediate level appellate court decided *Gloucester City Board of Education v. American Arbitration Ass'n*, 755 A.2d 1256, 1263 (N.J. Super. Ct. App. Div. 2000) which expressly adopted the limited incorporation approach and held therefore that disputes between the surety and the obligee "concerning the enforceability of the terms of the performance bond ... [are] not arbitrable." Thus, as to disputes arbitrated thereafter, the surety's personal defenses should not be precluded. Note, however, that *Gloucester City* directly contradicts the super incorporation decision in *Hoffman v. Fidelity and Deposit Co. of Maryland*, 734 F. Supp. 192 (D.N.J. 1990). Thus, the preclusive effect of an arbitration in New Jersey may depend on

Effect of an Arbitration Provision in the Principal's Contract 811

If such language is applied as written, the surety should not be foreclosed from presenting any personal defenses.[475] In a case where the guarantor was bound by its partial participation in the action against the principal debtor, however, the court said that the guarantor was thereby "concluded as to issues therein decided against the principal, or issues which could have been raised."[476] Despite the use of the res judicata formulation, the holding was that the guarantor was collaterally estopped from relitigating the defense which had been asserted and determined in the prior suit.[477]

The rebuttable presumption established by section 139(2) of the Restatement of Security is as to the *principal's* liability.[478] Thus, courts

---

whether it was compelled pursuant to *Gloucester City* or *Hoffman* and/or whether the preclusion issue arises in state or federal court. *See* discussion *supra* text accompanying notes 141-50. In *Von Engineering Co. v. R.W. Roberts Construction Co., Inc.*, 457 So. 2d 1080, 1082 (Fla. Dist. Ct. App. 1984) in which the court bound the surety to an arbitration award in favor of a payment bond claimant and against the principal because "when a surety has notice of a suit against the principal and is afforded an opportunity to appear and defend, a judgment . . . is conclusive against the surety as to all material questions therein determined." The court also noted that if the surety did not have notice and an opportunity to defend, a judgment against the principal would constitute only prima facie evidence of the surety's liability.

475 *Cf.* Old Republic Sur. Co. v. Bonham State Bank, 172 S.W.3d 210, 214 (Tex. App. 2005) (stating in dicta that a default judgment against the principal would constitute only prima facie evidence against the surety on "[a] general undertaking bond" which had not been made a party to or given an opportunity to defend the prior suit and that therefore the surety "will be permitted to assert any valid defense which the principal could have asserted").

476 E.B.R. Corp. v. PSL Air Lease Corp., 313 A.2d 893, 895 (Del. 1973).

477 *Id.* at 896-97; *cf.* Mass. Bonding & Ins. Co. v. Robert E. Denike, Inc., 92 F.2d 657, 658 (3d Cir. 1937) (holding that the surety was conclusively bound as to issues decided against the principal in the prior proceeding because of the surety's participation therein but without referring to either res judicata or collateral estoppel analysis).

478 RESTATEMENT OF SECURITY § 139(2) (1941); accord RESTATEMENT (THIRD) OF SURETYSHIP AND GUARANTY § 67(2) (1996); *cf.* Broadmoor/Roy Anderson Corp. v. XL Reinsurance Am., Inc., No. Civ.A. 02-0703, 2006 WL 2873473, at *1 (W.D. La. Oct. 4, 2006) (holding that an arbitration award in favor of the claimant and against the

which adopt that rule should permit the assertion of suretyship defenses free of the burden of the presumption. The prima facie rule, however, is usually stated as follows: a judgment against the principal is "prima facie evidence against the surety"[479] or is admissible as "prima facie evidence against the surety in an action on the bond."[480] That formulation suggests that the rule applies to all issues, not just the question of the principal's liability. Indeed, one court has said that the prima facie rule requires the surety "to rebut or contradict its liability for the arbitration award against its principal."[481] Under either the rebuttable presumption or the prima facie approach, of course, the surety will be able to assert its personal defenses. The only question is whether in doing so, the surety must carry the burden of proof when otherwise it would have remained with the obligee.

2. Under the Incorporation Doctrine

The super incorporation cases rest on the proposition that an incorporated arbitration provision requires the surety to arbitrate with the obligee all issues including its performance bond liability.[482] Thus, it is likely that courts applying that approach will not permit the surety to assert personal defenses, at least when the surety had notice of the arbitration and the opportunity to participate in it.[483]

---

principal "is presumptive of the accuracy of [the claimant's] claims against [the payment bond sureties].").

479 S.D.I. Corp. v. Fireman's Fund Ins. Cos., 617 N.Y.S.2d 790, 792 (N.Y. App. Div. 1994).

480 P. R. Post Corp. v. Md. Cas. Co., 271 N.W.2d 521, 525 (Mich. 1978).

481 *Id.*

482 *See* discussion *supra* Part II.A.2. Super incorporation cases often expressly require the surety to arbitrate its suretyship defenses; *see, e.g.*, Shores of Pan., Inc. v. Safeco Ins. Co. of Am., Civil Action No. 07-00602-KD-B, 2008 WL 4417558, at *9 (S.D. Ala. Sept. 29, 2008); U.S. Sur. Co. v. Hanover R.S. Ltd. P'ship, 543 F. Supp. 2d 492, 496 (W.D.N.C. 2008); Ohio Cas. Ins. Co. v. City of Moberly, Mo., No. 4:05 CV 5 JCH, 2005 WL 2491461, at *3 (E.D. Mo. Oct. 7, 2005); Taylor Ridge Estates, Inc. v. Statewide Ins. Co., No. Civ. 4-01-CV-90058, 2001 WL 1678745, at *11 (S.D. Iowa Oct. 1, 2001); Hoffman v. Fid. & Deposit Co. of Md., 734 F. Supp. 192, 194-95 (D.N.J. 1990).

483 *See* discussion *supra* text accompanying notes 450-65.

The limited incorporation approach, on the other hand, contemplates a two-stage procedure for adjudicating the surety's liability under the performance bond.[484] Assuming that the surety does not decide that it wishes to arbitrate, the obligee and the principal will arbitrate the principal's liability under the construction contract. An award in favor of the obligee will establish that the principal breached the bond condition and the surety will be bound as to that issue. Armed with that ruling, the obligee may then seek a judgment against the surety. There would be no need for a second proceeding if the award in favor of the obligee conclusively bound the surety as to its liability. Clearly, courts applying the limited incorporation approach will allow the surety to present any personal defenses.[485] Some cases have said so explicitly.[486] With other

---

484 *See generally* discussion *supra* Part II.A.3-4.
485 Fid. & Deposit Co. of Md. v. Parsons & Whittemore Contractors Corp., 397 N.E.2d 380, 382 (N.Y. 1979); Gloucester City Bd. of Educ. v. Am. Arbitration Ass'n, 755 A.2d 1256, 1263 (N.J. Super. Ct. App. Div. 2000) (adopting limited incorporation and therefore holding that disputes as to the enforcement of the performance bond were not arbitrable); Zacher v. Oakdale Islandia Ltd. P'ship, 775 N.Y.S.2d 155, 156 (N.Y. App. Div. 2004) (surety was "permitted to raise defenses arising under the terms of its performance bonds which were outside of the scope and content of the arbitration award," but as surety failed to produce evidence in support of the defenses, it was bound by the award). *See also* QDR Consultants & Dev. Corp. v. Colonia Ins. Co., 675 N.Y.S.2d 117, 119 (N.Y. App. Div. 1998) (citing *Parsons & Whittemore* as authority for holding that collateral estoppel did not preclude the payment bond surety from contesting issues that were not resolved by the arbitration award previously obtained by the claimant against the principal). *But cf.* Taylor Ridge Estates, Inc. v. Statewide Ins. Co., No. Civ. 4-01-CV-90058, 2001 WL 168745, at *11 (S.D. Iowa Oct. 1, 2001) (purporting to follow the limited incorporation approach of AgGrow Oils, L.L.C. v. Nat'l Union Fire Ins. Co. of Pittsburgh, Pa., 242 F.3d 777 (8th Cir. 2001) but holding that incorporation required the surety to arbitrate its overpayment defense to the obligee's performance bond claim because that issue involved the surety's secondary obligations and therefore was dependent on, not independent of, interpretation of the construction contract)).
486 *E.g., Parsons & Whittemore*, 397 N.E.2d at 382; *see also* Town of Melville v. Safeco Ins. Co. of Am., 651 So. 2d 404, 406 (La. Ct. App. 1995).

cases, that conclusion is necessarily implied from the use of limited incorporation reasoning.[487]

Conclusion

The incorporation doctrine dominates the performance bond surety's obligation to arbitrate pursuant to an arbitration provision in the principal's contract with the obligee. Incorporation by reference is a well-established principle of contract law, and will almost certainly result in giving some effect to the incorporation language which typically appears in performance bonds. The only question will be whether the super incorporation or the limited incorporation approach governs. Under the former, the surety will be compelled by court order to arbitrate, and under the latter, the surety will be bound to some degree by the arbitrator's determination of at least the principal's liability. While the preclusive effect of an award against the principal will vary widely from jurisdiction to jurisdiction and even if an award conclusively forecloses the surety as to the principal's liability, the surety's personal defenses should survive in many circumstances.

---

487   *See* cases cited *supra* note 441.

14

BANKRUPTCY

Chad L. Schexnayder
J. Blake Wilcox

Introduction

It has been ten years since the first edition of The Law of Performance Bonds. In that time, the Bankruptcy Code has been the subject of a significant package of amendments,[1] but the key bankruptcy issues confronting the performance bond surety have remained largely the same. In the bonded principal's bankruptcy case, the primary focus of the performance bond surety will be the bonded project itself, and contract funds paid and to be earned for the bonded project work. The surety, either consensually or through litigation, will seek to preserve, and if necessary, to control both the project and the contract funds, as the primary means to fulfill its surety obligations and mitigate its potential loss.

The involvement of the claims department of a performance bond surety presupposes some extraordinary event in the business operations of the bond principal. Whether it be a declaration of default by the project owner, a request for financing from a struggling principal, or voluminous payment claims, the surety knows from experience that the possibility of a bankruptcy filing exists. Modern times have seen the perception of a bankruptcy filing evolve from an admission of moral and economic failure into a legitimate business reorganization tool. This shift in perception has increased the frequency of the performance bond surety's appearance before the bankruptcy courts.

Not so long ago, if only because of unfamiliarity, a surety might take extraordinary steps to avoid being dragged into the bankruptcy abyss by its faltering principal. Thus, a surety might agree to finance an undeserving

---

[1] The Bankruptcy Abuse Prevention and Consumer Protection Act of 2005, Pub. L. No. 109-8 ("BAPCPA"). Most of BAPCPA's amendments are effective in cases filed after October 17, 2005.

principal, a decision that would later be seen with hindsight to have increased the surety's loss. However, because of the aforementioned shift in perception, many sureties have become familiar, even comfortable, with the bankruptcy forum. Sureties have developed expertise in the bankruptcy field and may even prefer the bankruptcy court to local jurisdictions.

One challenge is that bankruptcy law is not a user-friendly body of law. It is based upon a "code," set out sections, paragraphs and sub-paragraphs, each likely containing exceptions, numerical cross- references, as well as exclusive and non-exclusive lists.[2] If this were not enough, an entire body of shorthand expressions are regularly used by practitioners and courts alike, most of which appear nowhere within the four corners of the Bankruptcy Code.[3] Thus, one humble purpose of this chapter is to attempt to extract and focus on some of the more significant bankruptcy principles, from the perspective of a performance bond surety.

This chapter begins with a quick presentation of several fundamental bankruptcy law concepts. The chapter then discusses the most immediate impacts of the principal's bankruptcy filing upon the surety, particularly as it relates to the surety's efforts to complete the bonded work. Then, the focus turns to the unique bankruptcy perspective on the ubiquitous battles over control and ownership of the bonded contract proceeds, followed by the impact of bankruptcy on the surety's ability to finance the completion of the bonded work by the principal. Finally, the chapter looks at the rights of the surety when the principal blindly pursues its own improbable agenda of reorganization, to the detriment of the surety's interests.

I. Fundamental Purposes and Principles of Bankruptcy Law

From a creditor's perspective, bankruptcy law might seem to serve a sole pernicious purpose, i.e. to permit the debtor to break his promise to pay a debt. However, the justification for bankruptcy law and the outcome in

---

[2] The Bankruptcy Code, with the Federal Rules of Bankruptcy Procedure, plus local rules that vary from district to district, will govern the progress of the modern bankruptcy case.

[3] Richard I. Aaron, *Hooray for Gibberish! A Glossary of Bankruptcy Slang for the Occasional Practitioner or Bewildered Judge*, 3 DEPAUL BUS. & COM. L.J. 141 (2005).

particular bankruptcy cases can best be understood in the context of several fundamental principles.

A. *Forgiveness of Indebtedness*

The first fundamental principle is "discharge." Bankruptcy law provides the debtor with the opportunity to discharge personal liability and thereby get a "fresh start."[4] The "fresh start" is intended to be a societal "relief valve," providing the honest debtor with a means whereby he or she may escape insurmountable liabilities. Absent such a relief valve, a debtor, irretrievably burdened, will arguably lose all incentive to achieve productivity and, hence, become a burden to society.[5]

B. *Sharing*

The second fundamental principle is the equal distribution of assets among the debtor's creditors, which concept is known as the principle of "ratable distribution to creditors." Certain Code provisions provide the mechanisms to collect and liquidate the debtor's assets. Other Code provisions distribute the proceeds to creditors in proportion to the amount of their debt. Still other provisions may "reach back" into the months just prior to the bankruptcy filing. These provisions may reclaim property from a greedy (or vigilant) creditor, who has seized the debtor's property or has received the debtor's preferential treatment, in the form of last minute payments or property conveyances, thereby gaining a larger share of the debtor's limited assets. Because these mechanisms return the seized or conveyed property to the bankruptcy estate for later equitable redistribution,[6] the "reach back" powers further the fundamental bankruptcy purpose of "ratable distribution" or "sharing."

---

4   "The overriding purpose of the Bankruptcy Code is to relieve debtors from the weight of oppressive indebtedness and provide them with a fresh start." *In re* Cohn, 54 F.3d 1108, 1113 (3d Cir.1995).

5   R.P. Williams v. U.S. Fid. & Guar. Co., 236 U.S. 549, 554-555, 35 S.Ct. 289, 290, 59 L.Ed. 713 (1915).

6   *Matter of Kennesaw Mint, Inc.*, 32 B.R. 799, 805 (Bankr.N.D.Ga. 1983). Another purpose of the preference doctrine is to eliminate any incentive for creditors to race one another in an attempt to dismember a weak debtor on the eve of bankruptcy–behavior which tends to hasten or even

C. Breathing Space

The third fundamental principle is that a bankruptcy filing immediately protects a debtor from further seizures of its property or creditor collection actions. Bankruptcy law imposes an "automatic stay" of all creditor action. In the context of a debtor who seeks to reorganize and continue its business operations, the stay is intended to create "breathing space" for the debtor to assess its financial condition and to propose a plan to pay its creditors and reorganize its business. 11 U.S.C. § 362(a) is the "automatic stay" provision of the Bankruptcy Code. Upon the filing of a petition under the Bankruptcy Code, this section imposes a stay, applicable to all entities, against virtually all collection activities or other acts that would improve a creditor's position against the debtor or the debtor's property. Section 362(a) lists acts which violate the automatic stay:

(1) commencement or continuation of any legal proceedings against the debtor to enforce the surety's indemnification rights under the indemnity agreement [§ 362(a)(1)];

(2) enforcement against the debtor or any property of the estate of a judgment for reimbursement and indemnification obtained before the commencement of the debtor's case [§ 362(a)(2)];

(3) any act to obtain possession of or to exercise control over property of the debtor's estate [§ 362(a)(3)];

(4) any act to create, perfect, or enforce any lien against property of the estate [§ 362(a)(4)];

(5) any act to create, perfect, or enforce any lien against property of the estate to the extent such lien secures a claim that arose before the commencement of debtor's case [§ 362(a)(5)];

---

cause the bankruptcy filing. *See, In re* Balducci Oil Co., Inc., 33 B.R. 843, 845 (Bankr.D. Colo. 1983).

(6) any act to collect, assess, or recover a claim against the debtor that arose before the commencement of the debtor's case [§ 362(a)(6)];

(7) any act to setoff any debt under § 553 [§ 362(a)(7)].[7]

The performance bond surety will find that most of the actions that it contemplates taking may be viewed as a violation of the stay. The automatic stay will prohibit the surety from filing or continuing to

---

[7] Except as provided in subsection (b) of this section, a petition filed under section 301, 302, or 303 of this title, or an application filed under section 5(a)(3) of the Securities Investor Protection Act of 1970 (15 U.S.C. 78(a)(3)), operates as a stay, applicable to all entities, of –
   (1) the commencement or continuation, including the issuance or employment of process, of a judicial, administrative, or other action or proceeding against the debtor that was or could have been commenced before the commencement of the case under this title, or to recover a claim against the debtor that arose before the commencement of the case under this title;
   (2) the enforcement, against the debtor or against property of the estate, of a judgment obtained before the commencement of a case under this title;
   (3) any act to obtain possession of property of the estate or of property from the estate, or to exercise control over property of the estate;
   (4) any act to create, perfect, or enforce any lien against property of the estate;
   (5) any act to create, perfect, or enforce against property of the debtor any lien to the extent that such lien secures a claim that arose before the commencement of the case under this title;
   (6) any act to collect, assess, or recover a claim against the debtor that arose before the commencement of the case under this title;
   (7) the setoff of any debt owing to the debtor that arose before the commencement of the case under this title against any claim against the debtor; and
   (8) the commencement or continuation of a proceeding before the United States Tax Court concerning the debtor.
11 U.S.C. § 362(a).

prosecute a lawsuit for indemnification. In addition, the automatic stay (1) impacts the surety's right to demand or seize information, including the books, records, and accounts of the principal/debtor, (2) affects the surety's collection of the contract funds, including progress payments and retainage, (3) limits the surety's rights to the debtor's property, including the surety's rights under the assignment or trust provisions of the indemnity agreement, (4) affects the surety's ability to enforce its rights against the principal/debtor with respect to equipment claims and subcontracts under the assignment provision of the indemnity agreement, (5) prohibits the surety's demands for exoneration, reserve deposits, or the posting of collateral to resist or litigate claims, and (6) limits the surety's ability to exercise its takeover rights and its rights to terminate the underlying bonded contracts. In short, the automatic stay is a factor in the exercise of virtually every right available to the performance bond surety.

D. An Important Definition–"Property of the Estate"

Upon the filing of a bankruptcy petition, an "estate" is created consisting of all property and property interests of the principal/debtor. All of the "property of the estate" becomes a part of the bankruptcy case, and subject to restrictions and protections imposed by bankruptcy law. 11 U.S.C. § 541 defines "property of the estate." Section 541[8] is so broad as to include within its scope almost every conceivable interest of the debtor in property.[9] The statute's legislative history supports a broad

---

8   Unless otherwise indicated, all citations to "section ___," "§ ___," or "Code § ___" are to Title 11 of the United States Code, as amended, popularly known as the "Bankruptcy Code."

9   (a) The commencement of a case under section 301, 302, or 303 of this title creates an estate. Such estate is comprised of all the following property, wherever located and by whomever held:
       (1) Except as provided in subsections (b) and (c)(2) of this section, all legal or equitable interests of the debtor in property as of the commencement of the case.
       (2) All interests of the debtor and the debtor's spouse in community property . . .
       (3) Any interest in property that the trustee recovers under section 329(b), 363(n), 543, 550, 553, or 723 of this title.

interpretation of its scope.[10] Thus, the "estate" will ordinarily include all of the principal/debtor's property of any interest to the surety, such as subcontracts, equipment, contract proceeds, and claims against the project owners.

II. The Impact of Bankruptcy on the Completing Surety

The bankruptcy filing of the bond principal will affect the surety's efforts to discharge its duties in a number of ways. The most pervasive effect on the surety is undoubtedly the delay associated with a bankruptcy. The challenges ordinarily facing a performance bond surety are significant, such as persistent owner demands for action in the face of incomplete or conflicting information, or securing the cooperation of the principal and third parties to complete the bonded work. The bankruptcy filing introduces the automatic stay and bankruptcy court approval requirements for certain kinds of actions, to greatly increase the effort and cost required to meet these challenges.

---

(4) Any interest in property preserved for the benefit of or order transferred to the estate under section 510(c) or 551 of this title.

(5) Any interest in property that would have been property of the estate if such interest had been an interest of the debtor on the date of the filing of the petition, and that the debtor acquires or becomes entitled to acquire within 180 days after such date
   (A) by bequest, devise, or inheritance;
   (B) as a result of a property settlement agreement with debtor's spouse, or of an interlocutory or final divorce decree; or
   (C) as a beneficiary of a life insurance policy or of a death benefit plan.

(6) Proceeds, product, offspring, rents, or profits of or from property of the estate, except such as are earnings from services performed by an individual debtor after the commencement of the case.

(7) Any interest in property that the estate acquires after the commencement of the case.

11 U.S.C.A. § 541(a) (1993 & Supp. 1998).

10 H.R. Rep. No. 95-595, 95th Cong., 1st Sess. 367-8 (1977); S. Rep. No. 95-989, 95th Cong. 2d Sess. 82-3 (1978).

A. The Need for Information–Bankruptcy Rule 2004 Examination

In the early days and weeks of any bond default, the need for information is critical to the surety. Decisions must be made, and delay is often costly to the surety. The initial information concerning the status of contract payments on the bonded job, the identity and amounts owed to suppliers and subcontractors, overall job progress, etc. is normally obtained from the principal. However, when a principal files bankruptcy, it becomes difficult to obtain that information, notwithstanding the surety's contractual right to the records.[11] A principal that has just filed bankruptcy is faced with a myriad of conflicting demands and administrative obligations.[12] Faced with these burdens and deadlines, it is not unusual for the debtor to view the surety's information demands as being of secondary importance. This is particularly true if the principal views the surety as an adversary who wishes to "steal" the bonded projects.

Yet, the surety simply cannot make proper strategic decisions, or forecast its losses, without this information. Because of the automatic stay, the surety cannot simply demand and seize information from the principal. Fortunately, the Federal Rules of Bankruptcy Procedure provide an avenue of relief to the surety under these circumstances. Federal Rule of Bankruptcy Procedure, Rule 2004 authorizes an examination, not unlike a deposition, where the principal or its agents may be compelled to appear, produce and explain documentation.[13]

---

11   "At any time and until such time as the liability of the Surety under any and all bonds or undertakings executed for or on the application of the undersigned is terminated, the Surety shall have the right to free access to the books, records and accounts of the undersigned. . . ." *Indemnity Agreement Update*, 52 INS. COUNSEL J. 118, 144.

12   These bankruptcy obligations may include the preparation and filing of extensive schedules of assets and liabilities, a statement of financial affairs, interim operating reports, assembling documentation required by the United States Trustee's office, and preparation for the first meeting of creditors, to name a few.

13   Federal Rule of Bankruptcy Procedure 2004 provides:
    (a) Examination on Motion. On motion of any party in interest, the court may order the examination of any entity.
    (b) Scope of Examination. The examination of an entity under this Rule . . . may relate to the acts, conduct, or property or

One advantage of this Rule is that it does not require the surety to commence litigation against the principal before it may be used. The Rule does not incorporate an extended waiting period before the inspection is allowed or the documents must be produced, unlike ordinary discovery procedures under the Federal Rules of Civil Procedure.

Rule 2004 requires only that a motion or application be filed by the surety with the bankruptcy court, requesting the issuance of an order for examination. Pursuant to the advisory committee note to the Rule, it is contemplated that the motion may be heard ex parte and granted as a matter of course. In most districts, this is the practice, though local district rules should be consulted and observed in the filing of such a motion.

The scope of the Rule 2004 examination is very broad, as the language of the Rule would suggest.[14] Thus, the surety can use this rule to examine the debtor with respect to many aspects of bonded job performance,

> to the liabilities and financial condition of the debtor, or to any manner which may affect the administration of the debtor's estate, or to the debtor's right to a discharge. In . . . a reorganization case under Chapter 11 of the Code, . . . the examination may also relate to the operation of any business and the desirability of its continuance, the source of any money or property acquired or to be acquired by the debtor for purposes of consummating a plan and the consideration given or offered therefore, and any other matter relevant to the case or to the formulation of a plan.
> (c) Compelling Attendance and Production of Documentary Evidence. The attendance of an entity for examination and the production of documentary evidence may be compelled in the manner provided in Rule 9016 for the attendance of witnesses at a hearing or trial.
> (d) Time and Place of Examination of Debtor. The court may for cause shown and on terms as it may impose order the debtor to be examined under this Rule at any time or place it designates, whether within or without the district wherein the case is pending.

[14] Courts have stated the scope of the Rule 2004 examination to be "so all encompassing as semantically to include and encourage harassment on every human subject." *In re* Georgetown of Kettering, 17 Bankr. 73, 75 (Bankr. S.D.Ohio 1981).

subrogation issues, and any other particular matters of interest to the surety.

Attention should be given to the identification of the individual to be examined. Where a specific key project manager or principal of the debtor is known to possess the knowledge needed by the surety, that individual can be designated. However, the Rule 2004 procedure may be combined with the provisions of Federal Rule of Civil Procedure 30(b)(6), allowing the surety to place upon the debtor/principal the duty to designate a spokesperson(s) with knowledge of the identified subject matters.[15] Thus, the surety need only identify the project or records on which testimony will be required, shifting to the principal the duty to produce knowledgeable individuals.

The order of the court under Rule 2004 is sufficient to compel the attendance of the debtor at the examination. No subpoena is required.[16] If the debtor does not appear in response to the court's order, Federal Rule of Bankruptcy Procedure, Rule 2005 provides an additional procedure whereby an order to apprehend the debtor and bring the debtor before the court can be obtained.

B. Notice of Default/Termination of Bonded Contracts

When the performance bond surety receives a notice from the obligee or is contacted for assistance by the principal, the principal is likely to be in default in the performance of the bonded contract work. However, many contracts require formal notice, followed by a cure period, before a default is said to exist. It is not uncommon that the notice and opportunity to cure period has not fully passed prior to the principal's bankruptcy petition. In fact, the date of filing of the bankruptcy petition may have chosen by the principal specifically to prevent the default of a perceived valuable contract.

The Bankruptcy Code recognizes the interest of a party in a pending contract to be property of the estate, and thus protected by the automatic stay. Upon the filing of bankruptcy by the principal, the section 362 automatic stay precludes any act or notice to terminate the contract by

---

15   *In re* Analytical Systems, Inc., 71 Bankr. 408 (Bankr. N.D.Ga. 1987).
16   *In re* Fulton, 52 Bankr. 627, 631 (Bankr. D.Utah 1985); Advisory Committee Note to Fed. R. Bankr. P. 2004.

the owner. Thus, the project owner is often under a duty to file for relief from the automatic stay to effectively declare a default of the principal and thereafter place demand upon the surety to complete. The Code would similarly require that a surety file for stay relief before attempting to take over or re-let any uncompleted project not yet formally rejected by the principal.[17] A court order granting stay relief is required, no matter how hopeless the debtor's financial condition may be and no matter how improbable the debtor's ability to assume and complete the contract may be.[18]

Stay relief must be obtained before terminating the debtor/principal or taking over the debtor/principal's work, even if the principal voluntarily concedes the default or abandons the project. Even if all the affected parties agree not to rely upon or invoke the provisions of the automatic stay, the court can insist that the Code requirements relative to relief from the stay be met.[19] Consensual agreements between parties concerning the application of the automatic stay are permitted under the Bankruptcy Code, but only pursuant to the applicable rules and procedures and only as specifically authorized by court order after appropriate notice and opportunity for hearing.[20] Actions taken without observance of the procedures can be held "invalid, void and of no force and effect."[21] Thus, even the obliging principal who abandons the job the day after the petition is filed and acquiesces in the re-letting of the contract work should be required to execute a stipulation for stay relief and that stipulation should be presented to the court for approval. Normal notice periods can be shortened under the rules in appropriate circumstances.

---

17   11 U.S.C.A. §§ 362, 541 (1979 & Supp. 1989). *In re* Computer Communications, Inc., 824 F.2d 725, 728 (9th Cir. 1987); *In re* Edwards Mobile Home Sales, Inc., 119 Bankr. 857, 860 (Bankr. M.D. Fla. 1990).
18   *In re* Edwards Mobile Home Sales, Inc., 119 Bankr. 857, 860 (Bankr. M.D. Fla. 1990) (although surety bond was not assumable by the debtor under the provisions of 11 U.S.C. § 365(c)(2), relief from the automatic stay must still be sought to terminate.)
19   *In re* Randall Enters., Inc., 115 Bankr. 292 (Bankr. D. Colo. 1990).
20   *Id.* at 295.
21   *Id. See also*, COLLIERS ON BANKRUPTCY, ¶ 362.11[1], p. 362-115 (15th ed. rev.)

C. Assumption or Rejection of Executory Contracts

Generally speaking, a contract of the debtor that is pending at the time of the bankruptcy filing may be "assumed" by the debtor or may be "rejected" by the debtor. Unfortunately, in a Chapter 11 case, the debtor can also delay its declaration whether to assume or reject. This delay is often prejudicial to the performance bond surety. The bankruptcy term for such a pending contract is an "executory contract."

The Bankruptcy Code does not define "executory contract" but the legislative history identifies it as a contract "on which performance remains due to some extent on both sides."[22] Under this definition, construction contracts in various stages of completion will generally be

---

22 The House and Senate Reports discuss section 365 as follows:
> Though there is no precise definition of what contracts are executory, it generally includes contracts on which performance remains due to some extent on both sides. A note is not usually an executory contract if the only performance that remains is repayment. Performance on one side of the contract would have been completed and the contract is no longer executory.

H.R. Rep. No. 595, *supra* note 47 at 347-48; S. Rep. No. 989, 95th Cong., 2d Sess. 58 (1978), *reprinted* in 1978 U.S. CODE CONG. & ADMIN. NEWS 5787, 5844.

Many courts rely on the following definition:
> [A] contract under which the obligation of both the bankrupt and the other party to the contract are so far unperformed that the failure of either to complete the performance would constitute a material breach excusing the performance of the other.

Countryman, *Executory Contracts in Bankruptcy, Part I*, 57 MINN. L. REV. 439, 460 (1973); *see also* Countryman, *Executory Contracts in Bankruptcy, Part II*, 58 MINN. L. REV. 479 (1974).

Some courts have questioned the *Countryman* definition of executory contracts and held contracts to be executory as long as substantial performance is left on the part of the debtor (or estate). *In re* Oxford Royal Mushroom Prods., Inc., 45 Bankr. 792 (Bankr. E.D. Pa. 1985) (unrecorded easement is executory contract); *In re* Narquist, 43 Bankr. 224 (Bankr. E.D. Wash. 1984) (covenant not to compete is executory contract).

considered executory contracts.[23] However, a contract is not considered executory if the debtor has defaulted and the contract has been terminated by the owner prior to the petition being filed.[24] The prepetition termination must be complete and not subject to cure or reversal under either the terms of the contract or under state law.[25] The principal's interest in an executory contract is property of the estate under the Bankruptcy Code, and is protected by the automatic stay.[26]

Under Section 365, the debtor has three options: (1) assume the contract under Section 365(b)(1(A)-(C); (2) assign the underlying contract under Section 365(f)(1)-(3); or (3) reject the contract. If the principal has filed under Chapter 7, the trustee has 60 days from the date of filing to accept or reject the contract or it is deemed rejected.[27] However, if the petition has been filed under Chapter 11, the debtor-in-possession can assume or reject executory contracts at any time before confirmation of a plan of reorganization.[28]

1. Standards for Assumption

To assume an executory contract, the debtor must show that the contract is executory in nature, i.e., that it has not been completely terminated prior to the date of the bankruptcy filing. If there has been any default, the debtor must promptly cure the defaults,[29] and must demonstrate the ability to provide adequate assurances of future performance under the executory contract.[30] Where there has been no default by the debtor, the debtor may assume an executory contract without satisfying the above

---

23 Surety bonds and surety indemnity agreements have even been held to be executory contracts. *In re* Padula, 118 Bankr. 143 (Bankr. S.D. Fla. 1990); *In re* Evans, 91 Bankr. 1003 (Bankr. S.D. Fla. 1988).
24 *See, e.g.*, Moody v. Amoco Oil Co., 734 F.2d 1200 (7th Cir. 1984); COLLIER ON BANKRUPTCY ¶ 365.02[2], p. 365-20 (15th ed. rev. 1997).
25 *Moody*, 734 F.2d at 1212; COLLIER ON BANKRUPTCY ¶ 365.02[2], p.365-20-21 (15th ed. rev. 1997); *cf. In re* Waterkist Corp., 775 F.2d 1089 (9th Cir. 1985) (bare possessory interest in leasehold premises may be enough to allow debtor to assume lease).
26 *In re* Computer Communications, Inc., 824 F.2d 725 (9th Cir. 1987).
27 11 U.S.C.A. § 365(d)(1).
28 11 U.S.C.A. § 365(d)(2).
29 11 U.S.C.A. § 365(b)(1)(A).
30 11 U.S.C.A. § 365(b)(1)(B), (C).

tests, so long as the assumption appears to be in the best interests of the estate.[31]

The courts have applied two different tests in ruling on a debtor's motion to assume or reject: the "burdensome property" test and the "business judgment" test.[32] The business judgment test is used by the majority of jurisdictions.[33] Under the business judgment test, the trustee or debtor-in-possession need only demonstrate that assumption or rejection of the executory contract will benefit the estate.[34] The court, in approving the application to assume or reject, must balance the benefits and burdens of assuming or rejecting a given contract.[35]

2. Opposing the Assumption

A debtor-in-possession who truly has the finances and personnel to complete a project, and who seeks to assume the executory bonded project is regrettably, quite rare. In some bankruptcies, the surety may encounter a debtor in possession who seeks to assume the executory bonded contract, but whom the surety concludes lacks the ability to successfully complete. Continued performance by a failing principal can, in some cases, exacerbate project problems, and increase the surety's ultimate loss. If the surety believes that the debtor in possession's continued presence on the project is a detriment, the surety can consider two options to oppose assumption of the bonded executory construction contract. First, the surety may seek relief from the automatic stay, under Section 362(d)(1),[36] to permit the surety to take control over the bonded contract work. The "cause" as required under Section 362(d)(1) for the

---

31 *See In re* Westview 74th Street Drug Corp., 59 Bankr. 747, 754 (Bankr. S.D.N.Y. 1986); *In re* Great Northwest Recreation Ctr., Inc., 74 Bankr. 846, 856 (Bankr. D. Mont. 1987) and cases cited therein.
32 *In re* Huff, 81 Bankr. 531 (Bankr. D. Minn. 1988).
33 *Id.* at 537.
34 *Id.*
35 *See, e.g., In re* Food City, Inc., 94 Bankr. 91 (Bankr. W.D. Tex. 1988) (court analyzed sixteen separate items in denying debtor-in-possession's request to assume executory labor contract).
36 The two subsections in Section 362(d) are in the disjunctive. Therefore, subsections 362(d)(1) and 362(d)(2) provide separate bases for relief from stay. *In re* Sedona San Carlos Development Co., 59 Bankr. 113 (Bankr. D. Ariz. 1986).

automatic stay to be lifted is that the construction contract is an executory contract that is not assumable by the principal. The construction contract is not assumable because the debtor-in-possession cannot cure the existing defaults and cannot provide adequate assurance of its future performance.[37] Typically, the debtor-in-possession has not paid numerous subcontractors, laborers, and materialmen. This failure will be a default under most construction contracts. If the debtor-in-possession has no ability to cure these defaults, the court may give the surety relief from stay to complete the bonded projects. It will be incumbent upon the surety to advise the court of the amount of bonded contract funds remaining, the amount of unpaid subcontractors, laborers and materialmen, and the estimated cost to complete the bonded project.

The second option of the surety is to file a motion requesting the court to set a date by which the debtor/principal must assume or reject the contract. Because the order that will result from this motion does not compel a rejection, but only imposes a future deadline for the decision, this procedure is ordinarily too slow and unwieldy to be an effective tool for the surety.[38] A motion to compel a deadline for assumption or rejection is specifically authorized by 11 U.S.C. § 365(d)(2).[39] The section speaks of a motion brought by a "party to such contract." The standing of a surety to bring such a motion may be challenged, but the close relationship of the surety to the bonded contract, and the broad equitable powers of the bankruptcy court to fashion necessary relief should permit such a filing. It may be useful to persuade the obligee to bring this motion or to join in a motion with the surety.[40] An alternative way to bring this issue before the court is found in Code section 105. The

---

37 11 U.S.C.A. § 365(b)(1) (1993 & Supp. 1997).

38 The courts construing this section have generally required that the debtor be given a reasonable time in which to assume or reject. *See* Matter of Dunes Casino Hotel, 63 Bankr. 939, 948 (D. N.J. 1986).

39 "This provision will prevent parties in contractual and lease relationships with the Debtor from being left in doubt concerning their status vis-à-vis the estate." S. Rep. No. 95-595, at 348-49 (1977), *reprinted* in 1978 U.S.C.C.A.N. 5787, 6304-05.

40 The bond obligee is often a public entity that may not be able to act as promptly or decisively as the circumstances require. The surety often accompanies the request to the obligee with an offer to bear the cost of preparing the necessary court filings.

section now speaks of a mandatory duty[41] to set a status conference, if requested, from which conference the court may issue an order that "sets the date by which the [debtor] must assume or reject an executory contract."[42] If the contract contains a clause requiring that the contractor pay all materialmen and subcontractors, the owner and surety will argue that to cure the default, the debtor-in-possession must bring current the unpaid subcontractors and materialmen. If a court orders that all unpaid materialmen and subcontractors must be brought current by the debtor who wants to assume the contract, the performance bond surety is obviously benefitted.

At the hearing on a motion to compel assumption or rejection, the surety's goal will be to prove that the debtor/principal cannot meet the requirements to assume an executory contract. The surety should request the court to set an immediate deadline. A good example of how this process should work can be found in the reported decision of *CM Systems, Inc.*[43] In that case, the debtor-in-possession had not been declared in default under the subject contract when the debtor filed its Chapter 11 petition. The Florida bankruptcy court analyzed the information about the project presented by the surety and the obligee and determined that the debtor-in-possession was behind schedule and that the project would lose money. Based upon these factors and this analysis, the court denied the debtor's motion to assume the contract, notwithstanding the fact it was not technically in default. The court noted that the rejection would benefit the estate by reducing claims. "Moreover, in the case of a large construction project where there is a payment and performance bond posted, an early takeover of the project by the bonding company may minimize, if not completely eliminate, damage claims."[44] In the *CM Systems* case, the surety had the good fortune to have the debtor promptly file a motion to assume the contract, thereby placing the issue in front of the court on a prompt basis. A more common scenario is that the debtor simply chooses to defer the assumption/rejection issue and to continue to perform. In that event, a

---

41   The sentence regarding the setting of status conferences upon the request of a party in interest, was changed from "may" to "shall" in the 2005 BAPCPA amendments.
42   11 U.S.C. § 105(d)(2)(A).
43   64 Bankr. 363 (Bankr. M.D. Fla. 1986).
44   *Id.* at 365.

request for a Section 105 status conference, or a Section 365(d)(2) motion, filed by the surety alone, or in cooperation with the obligee, may be necessary to place the performance issues in front of the court.

D. Right to Use Debtor's Subcontractors

Often the performance bond surety will require or desire the continued performance of the principal's subcontractors. These subcontractors may have already obtained or manufactured long lead time materials or have access to personnel and equipment uniquely necessary to timely completion of the bonded contract. In a default not involving bankruptcy, the surety will attempt to obtain agreements from these parties to deliver their performance to the completing surety or a replacement contractor. Some of these subcontractors will view this as an opportunity to obtain a new and higher price for their previously agreed upon performance.

If the debtor promptly rejects the bonded subcontracts, the subcontractors may contend that they are now freed of all duties under their subcontract. However, the surety may assert that the rejection, being only a surrender by the debtor of its interest in the contract,[45] did not terminate the subcontract, but only removed the subcontract from the debtor's estate, and therefore the surety's pre-petition assignment of the bonded subcontract from the debtor, set out in the surety's indemnity agreement, now becomes effective, and the subcontractor owes a duty of performance to the surety/assignee.

In this particular situation, the bankruptcy of the principal may assist the performance bond surety in mitigating its loss. If it is clear that the surety will complete the work, the Bankruptcy Code provides a mechanism whereby the subcontractors will be legally obligated to deliver their agreed future performance directly to the surety. The debtor/principal may move to assume the executory subcontract agreements, and to assign those subcontracts to the surety.[46] The same

---

[45] The exact meaning and significance of "rejection" has been, and remains, the subject of some debate. *See* M. Andrew, Executory Contracts in Bankruptcy: Understanding "Rejection," 59 COLO. L. REV. 845 (1988) and J. Westbrook, A Functional Analysis of Executory Contracts, 74 MINN. L. REV. 227 (1989).

[46] 11 U.S.C.A. § 365(f)(2). This motion to assume and assign the bonded executory subcontracts benefits the debtor and the creditors of the estate, because if the subcontractors are not bound to deliver their performance

standards for assumption of an executory contract discussed in the preceding section apply. However, it is a simple matter for the surety to establish to the court that it will cure existing defaults (pay the payment bond claims of the subcontractors) and provide adequate assurance of future performance (pay the subcontractors for the balance of their work). The assumption and assignment procedure permits the surety, working with the debtor, to obtain full performance of subcontractors, and grants a measure of immunity from opportunistic profiteering.

E. Right to Use Debtor's Equipment and Tools in Completion of Bonded Projects

Typically, the principal has executed an agreement of indemnity containing a provision that permits the surety to take possession of and to use the principal's equipment to complete the bonded work.[47] Such provisions have been enforced in favor of the surety.[48] It has been held that the surety's indemnity agreement passed title to all construction equipment on the project site upon the principal's default. The court referred to the passing of title as a "prior equitable assignment."[49] However, the surety's right to use the principal's equipment after the principal has filed its bankruptcy petition is problematic and is

---

for the previously agreed price, then the surety will pay the subcontractor, or someone else, more to complete the work. This additional amount will increase the surety's loss, thereby increasing the dollar total of creditor claims in the distribution pool, and thereby decreasing each other creditor's proportionate share.

47   A typical indemnity agreement provision is:
     Upon the happening of an Event of Default, the Surety shall have the right to take immediate possession of the supplies, tools, plant, equipment and materials and to use, and consume if necessary, the same in the performance of the contracts by itself or by others.

48   Travelers Indem. Co. v. West Georgia Nat'l Bank, 387 F.Supp. 1090 (N.D. Ga. 1974) (the court held that the surety's right to equipment and materials were greater than that of a general creditor claiming under an attachment or judgment).

49   Id. at 1096.

complicated by the interplay of the doctrines of executory contracts, the automatic stay, and setoff or recoupment defenses.[50]

1. The Surety as a Creditor With an Interest in the Equipment

If the surety's claim to the right to use the principal's equipment arises from the indemnity agreement, it must be determined "what is the nature of the surety's claim under that agreement?" If the agreement of indemnity has been filed as a financing statement under the Uniform Commercial Code, sufficiently in advance of the bankruptcy to avoid attack as a preferential transfer, the surety may be a secured creditor, pursuant to assignment clauses traditionally found in such agreements.[51] The surety should seek relief from the automatic stay to take possession and use the equipment.

Where the agreement of indemnity has not been filed as a financing statement under the Uniform Commercial Code, the surety will encounter difficulties competing against prior perfected security interests.[52] The surety's arguments will be based upon the "equitable assignment" of equipment that pre-dates the perfected security interest,[53] and by analogy to cases that have recognized the surety's rights in other collateral to be created, effective even in bankruptcy, under the assignment clause of the indemnity agreement.[54] The surety's simplest recourse will often be to make appropriate arrangements with the lienholder in order that the equipment can be utilized to complete the bonded project.

---

50 *See* 11 U.S.C.A. §§ 365, 362, 542 and 553 (1979 & Supp. 1989), respectively.
51 *See* Sentry Select Ins. Co. v. LBL Skysystems (U.S.A.), Inc., 2007 WL 1459308 (E.D. Pa. 2007); Travelers Cas. & Sur. Co. of Am. v. Target Mech. Sys. Inc., 2004 WL 3050798 (N.Y.App.Div. Dec. 30, 2004) (unpublished).
52 *See* Aetna Cas. & Sur. Co. v. J.F. Brunken & Son, Inc., 357 F. Supp. 290 (D.S.D. 1973).
53 Travelers Indem. Co. v. West Georgia Nat'l Bank, 387 F. Supp. 1090 (N.D. Ga. 1974)
54 THE SURETY'S INDEMNITY AGREEMENT–LAW & PRACTICE, 2d ed. p. 512, n.168, *citing In re* Jones Construction & Renovation, Inc., 337 B.R. 579, 585 (Bankr.E.D.Va.2006).

2. Surety's Right to Use Debtor's Equipment Obtained by Subrogation to Obligee's Position

An obligee may have contractual rights to use the debtor's equipment after the debtor defaults. Under the doctrine of equitable subrogation, the surety stands in the shoes of the obligee and is subrogated to the obligee's right to use the debtor's equipment once the surety becomes liable to the obligee under its performance bond.[55] Where the construction contract between the obligee and the principal is executory, arguments may be made for the enforcement of the obligee's right to use the equipment, particularly in conjunction with a motion to compel the debtor to either assume or reject the contract. However, most often the claim of the obligee is that of an unsecured creditor, and for the reasons discussed above, that position will not be of great assistance to the surety seeking use of the debtor's equipment.

F. Taking Control Over or Compromising Debtor's Affirmative Claims

The performance bond surety may be significantly impeded in its ability to discharge its duties by the presence of an affirmative claim asserted by the debtor/principal. For example, the debtor may have asserted a large extra work claim against the project owner, which the project owner demands be resolved before the project can be closed out, and final monies paid. Or, the debtor may have asserted delay claims against a subcontractor, who is otherwise owed money, and the surety lacks the ability to resolve the dispute, without the ability to control, and therefore compromise, the debtor's claims. Often surety indemnity agreements have a provision that authorizes the surety to take control over and/or to settle its principal's claims relating to the bonded contract. Such a clause may be worded as an assignment of rights or as a provision appointing the surety as the principal's attorney-in-fact. Outside of bankruptcy, these provisions are widely enforced by courts.[56] *In re Jones*

---

55   *See, e.g.,* United States v. Munsey, 332 U.S. 234 (1947); Pearlman v. Reliance Ins. Co., 371 U.S. 132 (1962).

56   *See, e.g.,* Hutton Constr. Co., Inc. v. County of Rockland, 52 F.3d 1191 (2nd Cir. 1995); Bell BCI Co. v. Old Dominion Demolition Corp., 294 F.Supp.2d 807 (E.D.Va. 2003); S. Briglia, *Surety's Right to Settle its*

Construction & Renovation, Inc.,[57] the bankruptcy court held that the surety's rights also were recognized in bankruptcy. The court found that the assignment provision provided for the transfer of all sums due under the bonded contract to the surety upon the principal's default, that the surety's subrogation rights related back to the date of the bond, and therefore, the trustee had no property interest in the contract proceeds and affirmative claims, which did not constitute property of the estate. *Jones Construction* expressly recognizes the surety's right to the pre-petition affirmative compensation and damages.[58] *James McKinney & Son, Inc. v. Lake Placid 1980 Olympic Games, Inc.*, reached a similar result. The New York Court of Appeals held that a principal was not the real party in interest and thus could not assert an affirmative claim that its surety had already compromised, notwithstanding that the principal had filed its bankruptcy petition prior to the date of the surety's settlement with the project owner and construction manager.[59]

G. *Non-Dischargeability of the Indemnity Obligation*

In Section I.A. of this chapter, we posited the concept of "forgiveness of indebtedness" or "discharge" as one of the fundamental bankruptcy principles. In addition to the bond principal, the surety may have obtained the indemnity promise of select individuals to secure the surety's repayment in the event of loss. These individuals are most frequently officers or owners of the entity that is the bond principal.

The individual indemnitors may also file for bankruptcy when the bond principal files. Believing that their debt owed to the surety will be wiped clean, the individual indemnitors may be unwilling to cooperate or even communicate with the performing surety. Because these individuals frequently occupied management and supervisory roles within the company before the bankruptcy, the loss of their institutional knowledge and assistance can delay and complicate the surety's efforts to complete the bonded work, ultimately increasing the surety's cost of performance and loss. Following bankruptcy, such individuals have been known to offer to sell their knowledge to the surety, notwithstanding their pre-

---

Principal's Claims, Under Construction (March 2004), ABA Forum on the Construction Industry.
57 337 B.R. 579 (Bankr.E.D.Va. 2006).
58 *Id.* at 587.
59 61 N.Y.2d 836, 462 N.E.2d 137 (1984).

existing promise to furnish such assistance. Some individuals, embittered by their own dim short term financial future, have even acted intentionally to thwart the surety's efforts, or cause the surety harm, either by destroying property or records, or encouraging subcontractors and suppliers not to work with the surety in the completion effort. Such acts may be motivated entirely by spite, but other times have been seen as a means to extort payment from the surety in exchange for cooperation.

In such unusual circumstances, the bankruptcy discharge ends up shielding a wrongdoer, or removing the incentive of a party to behave in a commercially responsible fashion. A performing surety may be well served therefore, by an investigation into facts that call into question an individual indemnitor or company officer's right to a bankruptcy discharge. The bankruptcy discharge is not absolute entitlement. There are specifically enumerated grounds for the denial of any discharge to a particular debtor,[60] or the denial of the discharge of a particular debt.[61]

Among the multiple exceptions to the "general rule" of discharge, several are of particular interest to the performance bond surety.[62] If the individual debtor used bonded contract funds for purposes other than payment of project bills, the individual may lose the ability to discharge the surety's indemnity claim. Under Section 523(a)(4), any theft or embezzlement of the bonded contract funds may give rise to a non-dischargeable debt.[63] The misdirection of bonded contract funds may

---

[60] 11 U.S.C § 727. Section 727 provides grounds for objecting to the discharge of the debtor. Those grounds include the failure to keep adequate records to document the debtor's financial condition, the making of a false account or the removal or transfer of property of the estate with intent to defraud creditors.

[61] 11 U.S.C § 523(a). Section 523 provides for objections to the discharge of specific obligations to a creditor. The debtor will not be entitled to discharge of a particular obligation if the creditor can show, among other things, fraud, breach of fiduciary duty or that it had no knowledge of the pendency of the proceeding and was not scheduled by the debtor as a creditor.

[62] See Mark S. Gamell, *Objections And Exemptions To Discharge: Surety And Fidelity Considerations*, (unpublished paper submitted at the ABA Annual Meeting on August 10, 1993).

[63] 11 U.S.C. § 523(a)(4). *In re Snellgrove*, 15 B.R. 149 (Bankr. Fla. 1981). (Surety's claim against the debtors, former officers of the principal, non-dischargeable by reason of embezzlement of bonded contract funds.)

also give rise to a non-dischargeable debt even without the specific intent to defraud. Section 523(a)(4) provides that any "defalcation" or fraud, committed while acting in a fiduciary capacity, may make the claim against the individual debtor non-dischargeable.

The surety's indemnity agreement will often contain a provision impressing a trust upon property in the hands of the principal, including the bonded contract funds. Bankruptcy courts have held that the trust fund provision creates a valid trust and, therefore, imposes fiduciary obligations upon the individual indemnitors. The diversion or misuse of bonded contract funds, even without an intent to defraud, can cause the surety's indemnity claim for the loss of those funds to be non-dischargeable.[64] A trust created by contract is not the sole source of fiduciary duties imposed upon the principal and indemnitors in their handling of bonded contract funds. Some states have statutes which impress a trust upon contract proceeds for the benefit of the employees, subcontractors, and suppliers who work to create the fund.[65] When contract funds are impressed with such a trust, and the individual debtor has used the contract funds for other purposes, the conduct may violate the fiduciary obligation and the losses created thereby may be declared a non-dischargeable debt.

---

64   The bankruptcy court *In re* Fox, 357 B.R. 770, 727 (Bankr. E.D. Ark. 2006) expressly found that the indemnity agreement provision created a trust, and that the surety's debt was, therefore, excepted from discharge. The court cited approvingly language from *In re* Matheson, 10 B.R. 652, 656 (Bankr. Ala. 1981) ("It is the mere act of using the trust fund for any purpose other than the purpose for which the trust was created that constitutes misuse or misappropriation of the trust fund which is a defalcation committed by the fiduciary.") *See also* Favre v. Lyndon Property Ins. Co., 2008 WL 3271100 (S.D.Miss. August 6, 2008); *In re* Smith, 238 B.R. 664 (Bankr. W.D.Ky. 1999); *In re* McCormick, 283 B.R. 680 (Bankr. W.D.Pa. 2002); *In re* Herndon, 277 B.R. 765 (Bankr. E.D. Ark. 2002); *In re* Wright, 266 B.R. 848 (Bankr. E.D. Ark. 2001) (Existence of an express trust and that the use of the contract funds for purposes other than the payment of the laborers and suppliers on the bonded project was a textbook example of a defalcation.); *In re* Jenkins, 110 B.R. 74 (Bankr. M.D.Fla. 1990); *In re* McIntosh, 2005WL213978, 320 B.R. 22 (Bankr. M.D.Fla. 2005).
65   Robert F. Carney, *Payment Provisions in Construction Contracts and Construction Trust Fund Statutes: A Fifty-State Survey*, THE CONSTRUCTION LAWYER, Vol. 24, No. 4, Fall 2004.

There are two additional grounds for non-dischargeability that may apply to the surety, both found in Section 523(a)(2)[66] concerning the furnishing of false information to the surety in order to obtain "money," "property," or "credit." The indemnity agreement may contain certain representations and warranties that the signatures placed on the agreement are valid and binding. Under Section 523(a)(2)(A), when the debtor has knowledge that this representation is false, he or she may be liable for a non-dischargeable debt to the surety from the harm resulting from this misrepresentation or fraud.[67]

The indemnity agreement may contain express representations and warranties that the financial information that the principal and indemnitors provided to the surety is accurate. Section 523(a)(2)(B)

---

[66] (a) A discharge...does not discharge an individual debtor from any debt–

. . . .

    (2) from money, property, services, or an extension, renewal, or refinancing of credit, to the extent obtained, by-
        (A) false pretenses, a false representation, or actual fraud, other than a statement respecting the debtor's or an insider's financial condition;
        (B) use of a statement in writing-
            (i) that is materially false;
            (ii) respecting the debtor's or an insider's financial condition;
            (iii) on which the creditor to whom the debtor is liable for such money, property, services, or credit reasonably relied; and
            (iv) that the debtor caused to be made or published with intent to deceive;

[67] In *In re* Liberati, 11 B.R. 54 (Bankr. Pa. 1981) the court held that the husband's forging of the wife's signature on the indemnity agreement caused the debt to the surety to be non-dischargeable pursuant to Section 523(a)(2)(A). *In re* Romano, 262 B.R. 429 (Bankr. N.D. Ohio 2001). (Although the deadline for non-dischargeability objections in the husband's bankruptcy had passed more than a year before the surety discovered that the wife's signature was forged, the court denied the debtor's motion to dismiss the surety's complaint and permitted the surety to proceed with its fraud claim against the debtor/husband.)

concerns the furnishing of false[68] *written* statements of the financial condition of the debtor or an insider. When the individual knows that the information provided to the surety is false, or the debtor's actions are so reckless in making the representation as to warrant a finding that it acted fraudulently,[69] the debt resulting from the false representation may not be discharged.[70]

Aside from preserving for the surety the ability to collect in the future for its losses, the discovery of facts to support a finding of non-dischargeability of the indemnity debt may provide the basis for the surety to request and receive the cooperation of the officers and shareholders of the bond principal, even after they have filed their own personal bankruptcy petitions.

III. The Surety's Rights in Bonded Contract Proceeds

The issue most likely to embroil the performance bond surety in bankruptcy court litigation is the ownership and control of the balance of contract funds from the bonded construction contracts. Based upon longstanding and legion authority, the surety assumes and believes that its priority to these funds is paramount.[71] However, just about every other constituency in the bankruptcy case will have some theory why, in this particular circumstance, the body of case law is distinguishable, and the bonded contract proceeds should belong to the bankruptcy estate, and not the surety, and be used to pay general creditors.

---

68 The misrepresentation of financial condition must be "materially" false. Not every error will give rise to a non-dischargeable debt. *In re Bartomeli*, 303 B.R. 254 (Bankr. D.Conn. 2004) (8 percent overstatement of assets not sufficiently material for debt to be non-dischargeable).

69 *In re Cohn*, 54 F. 3d 1108, 1119 (3rd Cir.1995).

70 *In re Adams*, 312 B.R. 576 (Bankr. M.D.N.C. 2004)(debt owed to surety was non-dischargeable by virtue of false financial information submitted to surety and material misrepresentations made; *In re Young*, 995 F.2d 547 (5th Cir. 1993)(affirming non-dischargeability ruling for surety).

71 See Bachrach and Rodgers-Waire, *The Surety's Rights to the Contract Funds in the Principal's Chapter 11 Bankruptcy Case*," 35 TORT & INS. L. J. 1 (1999).

A. Are Bonded Contract Proceeds Property of the Estate?

The performance bond surety acquires rights of "equitable subrogation" to the balance of funds payable from the owner on the contract for which the bond was written. A surety's priority to bonded contract proceeds was firmly developed through a line of United States Supreme Court cases.[72]

In *Pearlman v. Reliance Insurance Company*,[73] the Supreme Court held that as between a surety and a trustee in bankruptcy, the surety is entitled to receive the contract proceeds to the extent necessary to reimburse it for its losses.[74] In *Pearlman*, the trustee in bankruptcy sought to recover funds held for retention by the United States Government for its contract with the debtor, Dutcher Construction Company. The surety paid payment bond losses in excess of the amount of the retention as a result of Dutcher's failure to make those payments. The surety, therefore, sought to recover the retention funds to reimburse itself for the payments it made in discharging its payment bond obligations. The Supreme Court held that the surety possessed a prior and superior right to the retained funds to the extent of its loss. The Court also held that, to the extent of the surety's subrogation right to the contract retention, the contract funds were not property of the debtor's estate. The Court found the surety's right to the retained funds was superior to any right or interest held by the Chapter 7 trustee.[75]

Pearlman was decided in 1962, under the provisions of the 1898 Bankruptcy Act.[76] In 1978, Congress adopted the Bankruptcy Code.[77] A concern existed, following enactment of the Code, that given the

---

72 Prairie State Bank v. United States, 164 U.S. 227, 17 S.Ct. 142, 41 L.Ed. 412 (1896); Henningson v. United States Fid. & Guar. Co., 208 U.S. 404, 28 S.Ct. 389, 52 L.Ed. 547 (1908); United States v. Munsey Trust Co., 332 U.S. 234, 67 S.Ct. 1599, 91 L.Ed. 2022 (1947).
73 371 U.S. 132, 83 S.Ct. 232, 9 L.Ed.2d 190 (1962).
74 "The Bankruptcy Act simply does not authorize a trustee to distribute other people's property among a bankrupt's creditors." *Id.* at 135.
75 THE SURETY'S INDEMNITY AGREEMENT – LAW & PRACTICE, 2d ed. p. 497-498 (2008).
76 Act of July 1, 1898, Ch. 541, 30 Stat. 544 (amended 1938), *repealed* by Pub. L. No. 95-598, Title IV, §401(a), Nov. 6, 1978, 92 Stat. 2682.
77 11 U.S.C.A. §§ 101-1330.

changes, particularly the broadened definition of "property of the estate" contained in Section 541,[78] that some courts might question *Pearlman's* continued viability. However, this concern has been largely unfounded, and bankruptcy courts have repeatedly affirmed *Pearlman's* continued authority over this question.[79]

While the fundamental holding of *Pearlman* remains unimpaired, one portion of the *Pearlman* Court's holding, that the bonded contract proceeds are not part of the bankruptcy estate, continues to generate confusion in the bankruptcy courts. This confusion seems to stem from the belief that the fundamental question of control over the bonded contract funds is answered by the threshold determination whether bonded contract funds are, or are not, "property of the estate" under Section 541 of the Code. In fact, shortly after enactment of the Code, one commentator correctly identified this issue as inconsequential to the overall resolution of whether the surety's rights to the bonded contract proceeds are superior to the debtor, or general creditors.

> As can be seen from the cited cases, the courts have been struggling with the new concept of 'property of the estate' as defined in § 541 of the new Code. However, as I have pointed out, this new concept should not significantly affect the surety's rights in bonded contract proceeds. The courts are for the most part finding that the surety in a bankruptcy situation has the right to see that the contract proceeds are first paid to those who created the fund (laborers and materialmen) and to reimburse the surety before the debtor can use them to pay other expenses or the funds can be paid to general creditors. In this context it

---

78   *See* note 9 for the text of 11 U.S.C § 541(a).
79   Am. States Ins. Co. v. United States, 324 B.R. 600 (W.D. Tex. 2005) (Bankruptcy Code does not overrule *Pearlman*.); *In re* Cone Constructors, Inc., 265 B.R. 302, 307-08 (Bankr.M.D.Fla.2001). (Clearly, *Pearlman* was decided prior to the enactment of the Bankruptcy Code. Recent cases have established, however, that the holding set forth in *Pearlman* remains controlling law. *citing In re* QC Piping Installations, Inc., 225 B.R. 553 (Bankr. E.D.N.Y. 1998), *In re* Padula Construction Company, Inc., 118 B.R. 143 (Bankr. S.D. Fla. 1990), *In re* Caddie Construction Co., Inc., 125 B.R. 674 (Bankr. M.D. Fla. 1991); *Massart Company*, 105 B.R. 610 (W.D. Wash.1989); *In re* E.R. Fegert, Inc., 88 B.R. 258, 260 (9th Cir. BAP 1988)).

may make little difference to the surety whether the proceeds are deemed property of the estate or not.[80]

As the cases discussed below establish, if the bankruptcy courts recognize the surety's superior interest in the bonded contract funds, whether because the funds are not property of the bankruptcy estate at all, or because they are property of the estate, but are impressed with a trust or equitable lien in favor of the surety, then does the "property of the estate" issue have any substantive meaning? In bankruptcy practice, the distinction matters, because the automatic stay applies to prohibit actions to assert control over "property of the estate." In a jurisdiction where the courts have held bonded contract funds are not property of the estate, the surety may be able to act sooner to use the contract funds to discharge its bonded performance obligations. Where the answer is unclear, or where the courts have held the bonded contract proceeds are property of the estate, the surety will have to approach the bankruptcy court and seek relief from the automatic stay, or protection for its cash collateral, with the attendant delay and increased expense.

1. Contract Funds Are Not Property of the Estate

Some post Bankruptcy Code enactment decisions have simply adopted the *Pearlman* holding, finding that the equitable subrogation rights of the surety are superior to those of the debtor, and that the bonded contract proceeds are not property of the estate under Section 541.[81] Other courts have also held that bonded contract proceeds are not property of the estate, but have employed different rationales.

    a. *Unsatisfied Conditions Precedent to the Debtor's Right to Payment.* Some courts have concluded that the debtor has no interest in contract proceeds, where the debtor's failure to pay for labor and materials would excuse the owner's duty to make the payment under the construction contract. In *In re Pacific Marine Dredging and*

---

80   Haug and Haug, *Bankruptcy 1984 vs. The Surety's Right to Contract Proceeds*, 20 FORUM 725, 747 (1985).

81   *In re* Massart Co., 105 Bankr. 610, 613 (W.D. Wash. 1989). *See also, In re* QC Piping Installations, Inc., 225 Bankr. 553 (Bankr. E.D.N.Y. 1998); *In re* Four Star Construction Co., 151 Bankr. 817 (Bankr. N.D. Ohio 1993); *In re* Big Idea Productions, Inc., 372 B.R. 388 (N.D.Ill.2007).

Construction,[82] a surety was required to pay the debtor/contractor's laborers and materialmen as a result of having issued a payment bond on the debtor's behalf. The issue was whether the surety or the debtor-in-possession had the superior claim to the retained contract funds. The court held that the funds were not property of the estate, and stated:

> This court agrees with other courts that have found that the contractor's failure to pay for labor and materials is just as much a failure to perform and carry out the terms of the contract as an abandonment of work. [Citations omitted.] *In short, plaintiff is not contractually obligated to pay the fund to debtor.* Due to debtor's breach of contract, the debtor does not have any legal or equitable interest in the fund. *Accordingly, the fund is not property of the estate.*[83] [emphasis added]

Several subsequent decisions have focused on contractual clauses that make payment of subcontractors and suppliers a precondition to the principal's right to be paid by the owner. The Third Circuit Court of Appeals has held that such a clause prevented the balance of contract funds from being paid to the bankruptcy court.[84] The principal had not paid the project bills, and the general conditions of the contract (American Institute of Architects, Document A201, 1987 Edition) provided that payment did not become due until the condition precedent was satisfied.

An Arizona court confronted the same issue and held that the principal's failure to provide lien waivers required by the contract documents caused the contract payment not to be due. The funds were therefore never a part of the contractor's bankruptcy estate.[85]

---

82   79 Bankr. 924 (Bankr. D. Or. 1987).
83   *Id.* at 929.
84   *In re* Modular Structures, Inc., 27 F.3d 72 (3rd Cir. 1994). *But see, In re* Construction Alternatives, Inc., 2 F.3d 670 (6th Cir. 1993). (The surety argued that the principal had contractual duties to see that the subcontractors and materials suppliers were paid. However, the court focused on the absence of a right to withhold funds or an express condition precedent. The court refused to find that the fund was not due and payable to the debtor. While the decision held that the bonded contract proceeds were property of the estate, the court recognized the surety's interest in the funds.)
85   Merchants Bonding Co. v. Pima County, Arizona, 860 P.2d 510, 512 (App. 1993).

Where the law imposes the duty to see that the subcontractors and suppliers are paid, the owner's right to pay project bills, and the owner's concomitant right of recoupment against the contract proceeds for the amounts it has paid, furnish the basis for the surety to keep the funds away from the bankruptcy of the principal. Because the surety is subrogated to the rights of the owner, and because the owner could retain funds to recover payments it has made to subcontractors and suppliers, the surety can also reimburse itself.[86]

The applicability of these particular decisions will depend upon the presence of a contract clause or state law that establishes a precondition to the payment obligation. However, the holdings of these cases strongly support the surety's claim that the bonded contract proceeds never became a part of the principal's bankruptcy.

b. *The Bonded Contract Funds Are Held In "Trust" For The Benefit of Another.* Some courts have found bonded contract proceeds not to be property of the estate, relying not upon contractual conditions precedent, but upon trusts imposed upon the contract funds, under the provisions of state law or pursuant to contractual clauses. It is bankruptcy "black letter law" that property held in trust by the debtor does not become a part of the bankruptcy estate.[87] The existence of a valid trust is a question determined by reference to state law.[88]

---

86   *See* Transamerica Ins. Co. v. United States, 989 F.2d 1188 (Fed. Cir. 1993). In this case, the court acknowledges the surety's right of subrogation to set-offs the owner could have asserted. Interestingly, the court distinguished a case decided under Ohio law, noting that the applicable state law did not give the relevant rights of setoff to the state. Thus, the strength of this subrogation argument will vary from state to state.

87   "The United States Supreme Court has stated that Congress had plainly excluded from the estate the property of others held by the debtor in trust at the time of the filing of the petition. We stated in *In re* Gurs, 34 Bankr. 755, 757 (9th Cir. BAP 1983), that where the debtor possesses only a legal and not an equitable interest in property, the equitable interest does not become part of the bankrupt estate. Other sections of the Code, such as Sections 548 and 547, cannot be used to allow a bankrupt estate to benefit from property that the debtor did not own." *In re* Torez, 63 Bankr. 751, 753-54 (Bankr. 9th Cir. 1986), *aff'd*, 827 F.2d 1299 (9th Cir. 1987).

     See Begier v. Internal Revenue Service, 110 S.Ct. 2258 (1990) ("A 'debtor' does not own an equitable interest in property he holds in trust for another, that interest is not 'property of the estate,' nor is such an

Some state laws impose a trust on money owed to a contractor where subcontractors and materialmen remain unpaid. Courts have recognized these state trust fund statutes to find the funds belong to the unpaid suppliers and subcontractors, not the debtor.[89] *In re D&B Electric, Inc.*[90] materialmen claimed uncashed checks made jointly payable to the materialmen and the debtor. Since the materialmen's equitable lien rights had expired, they contended that the funds held by the general contractor were held in trust for their benefit. Relying in part upon on a Kentucky statute, the court concluded that the funds were held in trust and were therefore not property of the estate. The court awarded the funds to the materialmen.[91]

Even in the absence of an express statute creating a trust, the court may find a trust to exist in favor of unpaid subcontractors and suppliers in prior decisional law.[92] The *Universal Bonding Ins. Co. v. Gittens and Sprinkle Enterprises, Inc.* decision demonstrates the possible breadth of these holdings, finding a trust to exist both under New Jersey's state law trust fund statute, and on federal jobs under the authority of *Pearlman v.*

---

equitable interest 'property of the debtor' for purposes of § 547(b)."); United States v. Whiting Pools, Inc., 462 U.S. 198, 205 n. 10, 103 S.Ct. 2309, 2314 n. 10, 76 L.Ed.2d 515, 522 n. 10 (1983) ("Congress plainly excluded property of others held by the debtor in trust at the time of the filing of the petition."); *In re* California Trade Technical Schools, Inc., 923 F.2d 641 (9th Cir. 1991) (funds held "in trust" were not property of the debtor for preferential transfer purposes).

88 *In re* California Trade Technical Schools, Inc., 923 F.2d 641 (9th Cir. 1991).

89 Selby v. Ford Motor Co., et al., 590 F.2d 642 (6th Cir. 1979); Parker v. Klochko Equipment Rental Co. Inc., et al., 590 F.2d 649 (6th Cir. 1979), *cert. denied*, 444 U.S. 831, 100 S.Ct. 60, 62 L.Ed.2d 40 (1979); *See also, In re* Dunwell Heating & Air Conditioning Contr. Corp., 78 Bankr. 667 (Bankr. E.D.N.Y. 1987); *In re* Comcraft, 206 B.R. 551 (Bankr. D. Or. 1997) (Constructive trust found to result from Oregon statute).

90 4 Bankr. 263 (Bankr. W.D. Ky. 1980).

91 *Id.* at 270.

92 Universal Bonding Ins. Co. v. Gittens and Sprinkle Enterprises, Inc., 960 F.2d 366, 371 (3rd Cir. 1992). *See also* U. S. Fid. & Guar. v. United States, 475 F.2d 1377 (Ct. Cl. 1973) (*en banc*); United Elec. Corp. v. United States, 647 F.2d 1082 (Fed. Cir. 1981).

Reliance Ins. Co.[93] Interestingly, the *Universal Bonding* court found that the bonded contract proceeds were property of the estate under Section 541, but the rights of the unpaid subcontractors and suppliers were superior to the debtor's rights in that money (as would be the surety's rights by subrogation to those it paid).[94]

Valid trusts can be created by agreement, as well as by statute.[95] The bonded construction contract may contain provisions impressing a trust on contract proceeds. General Agreements of Indemnity commonly contain a pledge by the principal to hold bonded contract funds in trust for the surety and the benefit of subcontractors and suppliers. Less

---

93   Universal Bonding Ins. Co. v. Gittens and Sprinkle Enterprises, Inc., 960 F.2d 366, 375-376.

94   The *Universal Bonding* holding and the holdings cited in note 76 highlight the continued language confusion in court decisions between the label of "property of the estate" and ultimate beneficial ownership of property. Some courts hold that if the beneficial interest of property is with someone other than the debtor, then the property is not "property of the estate." Other courts recognize that the disputed asset may be "property of the estate" under Section 541, but the rights of another party are superior, and the debtor may not use the asset in its case. In the end, the cases reach the same result.

95   *In re* Alcon Demolition, Inc., 204 Bankr. 440, 448-49 (Bankr. D. N.J. 1997) (Court found elements of trust established by terms of indemnity agreement.); Federal Ins. Co. v. Fifth Third Bank, 867 F.2d 330 (6th Cir. 1989) (Court found funds held in trust from provision in bonded construction contract); *In re* Gonzales, 22 Bankr. 58 (Bankr. 9th Cir. 1982) (contractual provision validly created trust of contract funds). Other bankruptcy court decisions examining state law have found indemnity agreement trust provisions create an enforceable trust: *In re* Marques, 2006 WL 3850025, Case No. 05-31854-DWS (Bankr. E.D. Pa. Nov. 30, 2006); *In re* Suprema Specialties, Inc., 2006 WL 2583648, Case No. 02-10823 (Bankr. S.D.N.Y. June 8, 2006) (found language may establish trust but strictly construed the trust language against the drafter-surety); *In re* Maxon Eng'g Serv., Inc., 2005 W.L. 2896958, Case No. 04-04781 (Bankr. D. P.R. May 5, 2005) (indemnity language created trust under Puerto Rico law); *see also In re* Marrs-Winn Co., Inc., 103 F. 3d 584 (7th Cir. 1996) (a trust provision in a subcontract met the requirements of a trust under Missouri law); Matter of Jenkins, 110 B.R. 74 (Bankr. M.D. Fla. 1990).

frequently, sureties have special collateral agreements or "fund control" agreements which may create a trust.

Generally, more than a contractual recitation of intent is required to establish a valid trust.[96] Some courts require that the formalities of a trust must be present and observed.[97] The parties must have treated the contract proceeds like a trust fund before the bankruptcy. For example, courts may look to see if the fund has been segregated.[98] A failure to observe the trust formalities ordinarily required by state law may cause the surety's "trust fund" claim to the bonded contract proceeds to fail.

c. *The Bonded Contract Proceeds Were Assigned Pre-Petition.* Most indemnity agreements provide for the principal's assignment to the surety of the receivables, accounts and claims arising out of the bonded contracts. In some instances, the assignment to the surety of a claim or receivable under the indemnity agreement will be superior to the rights of any other creditor or secured party because the terms of the indemnity agreement will have fully assigned those rights to the surety prior to any subsequent perfection of an assignment or the creation of a lien in favor of any other creditor.[99]

In *Jones Constr. & Renovation*, the bankruptcy court held that the proceeds of bonded contracts were the property of the surety, and not the

---

96 *In re* H&A Construction Co., 65 Bankr. 213 (Bankr. D. Mass. 1986). Some courts have required a de facto trust exist, not mere contractual recitation. *In re* Construction Alternatives, Inc., 2 F.3d 670 (6th Cir. 1993); *In re* Foam Systems Co., 92 B.R. 406 (9th Cir. BAP 1988); *In re* Eastern Concrete Paving Co., 293 B.R. 704 (Bankr. E.D. Mich. 2003).

97 The general requirements for a trust include the following: (1) intent to create a trust, (2) an identifiable trust property or res, (3) defined and ascertainable trust beneficiaries, and (4) there must be a trustee. *See* Bachrach and Rodgers-Waire, *The Surety's Rights to the Contract Funds in the Principal's Chapter 11 Bankruptcy Case*, 35 TORT INS. L.J. 1, 17 (Fall 1999), *citing In re* Alcon Demolition, Inc., 204 B.R. 440 (Bankr. D.N.J. 1997) (the terms of a typical surety indemnity agreement met the four elements of a trust).

98 *In re* Construction Alternatives, Inc., 2 F.3d 670, 677 (6th Cir. 1993) (General indemnity agreement trust provision found insufficient to award fund to the surety, where principal had not segregated fund.)

99 *In re* Jones Constr. & Renovation, Inc., 337 B.R. 579 (Bankr. E.D. Va. 2006) (claim assigned to the surety under the indemnity agreement prior to the filing of the petition not property of the estate).

property of the estate[100] because of the operation of the assignment clause of the indemnity agreement.[101]

2. Bonded Contract Proceeds Held to be Property of the Estate

A number of bankruptcy courts have concluded that the bonded contract proceeds are "property of the estate" in the principal's bankruptcy.[102] However, these courts have also acknowledged the surety's "interest" in these funds, either under the doctrine of equitable subrogation, or because they were held in trust. Under some decisions, the debtor/principal has obtained limited use of contract progress payments earned prior to bankruptcy. However, the bankruptcy court has generally not allowed the debtor unrestricted use of the funds.

In *In re Alliance Properties, Inc.*,[103] the court concluded that the proceeds were property of the estate, noting the expansive definition of

---

100 *Id.* at 586-87.
101 Sureties are entitled to claim rights arising by operation of law and under the assignment clause of their indemnity agreements. Plant Process Equip., Inc. v. Continental Carbonic Prods., Inc., 1994 WL 201218 at *3, n.7 (N.D.Ill.1994) (*citing* Armen Shahinian, *The General Agreement of Indemnity in* THE LAW OF SURETYSHIP, 27-3 to 21-21 (ABA Tort & Ins. Prac. Sec., Gallagher, E., ed. 1993)). Moreover, when an express indemnification agreement exists, "'a surety is entitled to stand upon the letter of his contract.'" Fid. and Deposit Co. of Maryland v. Bristol Steel & Iron Works, Inc., 722 F.2d 1160 (C.A.Va.1983) (*quoting* Commercial Ins. Co. of Newark v. Pacific-Peru Const., 558 F.2d 948, 953 (9th Cir. 1977)). Therefore, although Western Surety enjoys the rights of equitable subrogation, it is also entitled to enhance and supplement those rights through the use of the assignment provisions of the indemnity agreement. *Id.* at 585.
102 *See e.g., In re* Maxon Engineering Services, Inc., 332 B.R. 495 (Bankr. D.P.R. 2005) (trust); *In re* Glover Const. Co., Inc., 30 Bankr. 873, 378 (Bankr. W.D. Ky. 1983) (Court concluded that progress payments were "property of the estate" noting the "remarkably broadened definition" of this phrase in 11 U.S.C. §541). *In re* Alliance Properties, Inc., 104 Bankr. 306 (Bankr. S.D. Cal. 1989); *In re* Universal Builders, Inc., 53 Bankr. 183 (Bankr. M.D. Tenn. 1985); *In re* Ram Constr. Co. Inc., 32 Bankr. 758 (Bankr. W.D. Pa. 1983); Universal Bonding Ins. Co. v. Gittens and Sprinkle Enterprises, Inc., 960 F.2d 366, 371 (3rd Cir. 1992).
103 104 B.R. 306 (Bankr. S.D. Cal. 1989).

this phrase in Section 541.[104] The court also concluded that once the surety paid various subcontractors' claims the surety obtained an equitable lien on the contract proceeds which was superior to any rights of the defaulting contractor and/or the estate. Thus, even though the *Alliance Properties* court concluded that the bonded contract funds were property of the estate, the court awarded the funds to the surety because the funds were subject to the surety's equitable lien, a lien that related back to the time the bonds were written.

In *Maxon Engineering Services*[105] the bankruptcy court expressly found that the bonded contract proceeds were property of the estate. The court also found that the surety had an equitable interest in the proceeds, and so therefore permitted the debtor to use the funds, but only with adequate protection of the surety's interest. This took the form of adequate protection requested by the surety, which was that the proceeds were segregated and used on a job by job basis, and not therefore used by the debtor as general funds.[106] This decision, like *Alliance Properties*, is a good example of a bankruptcy court holding that bonded contract proceeds are property of the estate, without losing sight of the ultimate question of the surety's right to the equitable or beneficial interest in those funds.[107]

---

104 "The parties devote major portions of their pleadings to the issue of whether this fund is property of the estate. I conclude that the fund is included within the property of this estate but find that, under the facts of this case, this conclusion does not change the ultimate outcome. . . . For these reasons, I hold that INA has established an equitable lien in the remaining fund in the amount of $273,390.65, and that this lien is superior . . . ." *Id*. at 312.

105 *In re* Maxon Engineering Services, Inc., 332 B.R. 495 (Bankr. D.P.R.2005).

106 *Id*. at 500.

107 *See also, In re* Glover Const. Co., Inc., 30 B.R. 873 (Bankr. W.D. Ky. 1983); *In re* Ram Constr. Co. Inc., 32 B.R. 758 (Bankr. W.D. Pa. 1983) where debtors were permitted to use contract funds, with limitation designed to protect the sureties' interests.

IV. Actions to Protect Surety's Rights in Bonded Contract Proceeds

The previous section discussed the rights of the performance bond surety to bonded contract proceeds in the context of the principal's bankruptcy filing. Virtually all cases recognized the surety's superior rights in the funds. However, there are multiple legal theories that support the surety's rights, and the variability of the facts and circumstances of each performance bond loss require the selection of the legal theory that best supports the surety's immediate need. The variables can be "In whose hands are the bonded contract funds currently held?" or, "Has the surety already paid a loss?" or, "What particular language is found in the bonded construction contract, the indemnity agreement, or state statutes that support the surety's rights?" The surety must select and prioritize the proper legal theories to support its rights in the bonded contract proceeds. The surety will also make choices how, when and where it will act to protect its interest in the bonded contract funds. Bankruptcy law factors into the surety's strategic decisions.

When its principal has filed for bankruptcy, a surety must ordinarily act promptly to protect its interests in bonded contract proceeds. The surety may consider communicating to the bond obligee the surety's priority claim to contract proceeds. The surety may need to file motions before the bankruptcy court seeking: (1) to lift the automatic stay, (2) sequestration of the surety's cash collateral (the contract proceeds), (3) "adequate protection," if the court will permit the principal some use of the surety's cash collateral, and less frequently, (4) to compel the principal to assume or reject executory contracts. The surety may take action to compel the bond obligee to exercise its setoff rights against contract proceeds in a manner that will protect and benefit the surety.

A. *Giving Notice to the Obligee*

When a bond default has occurred, and the principal has not filed bankruptcy, one of the first items on the surety's "things to do" list might be to send a letter to the bond obligees, typically the project owners. This letter to the obligee may have multiple purposes, but one important purpose will be to place demand upon the obligee to disburse no further contract funds to the defaulting principal.[108]

However, what if the principal has filed bankruptcy before the surety has sent such a notice to the bond obligee? Can the surety still write a letter to the obligee demanding that further contract proceeds be withheld from the principal? To answer this question requires consideration of Sections 362 and 541 of the Bankruptcy Code. As will be explained in more detail below, there is bankruptcy court authority permitting a less mandatory notice to be sent by the surety to the obligee without violating the bankruptcy stay. Such a carefully drafted communication from the surety, coupled with the obligee's self-interest, may be effective to prevent a transfer of bonded contract proceeds from happening before bankruptcy court relief can be sought.

11 U.S.C. § 362(a) imposes a stay, applicable to all entities, against virtually all collection activities or other acts that would improve a creditor's position against the debtor or the debtor's property, effective upon the filing of a petition under the Bankruptcy Code.[109] In this situation, the inquiry is whether the surety's communication with the obligee that results in the withholding of contract funds is an act to exercise control over "property of the estate," an act that is prohibited by 11 U.S.C. § 362(a)(3).

As discussed in the previous section, there is conflicting bankruptcy case law on the threshold question of whether bonded contract proceeds are "property of the estate." The surety can contend that because the bonded contract funds are not "property of the estate" under case authority, a letter from the surety to the obligee demanding that the funds be withheld from the debtor does not constitute a violation of the automatic stay (i.e., is not an act to exercise control over "property of the estate").

Although the surety can serve an emphatic demand upon the obligee to withhold all contract proceeds, supported by its argument that the

---

108 This letter is such a basic part of the surety's response to a bond default, that the letter appears in some published literature as a practice form. *See* Charles A. Meeker and John W. Dondanville, Construction Forms for Sureties, CONSTRUCTION INDUSTRY FORMS, p. 329, ll. 13-8; Robert F. Cushman and George L. Blick, Eds. (1988); BOND DEFAULT MANUAL, (2d ed.) Clore, Duncan L., ed., Fidelity & Surety Law Committee, Tort and Insurance Practice Section, American Bar Association, Exhibit 13.7.
109 *See supra* note 8 for text of 11 U.S.C. § 362(a).

contract funds are not property of the estate, proceeding in this manner creates a risk. First, if the bankruptcy court finds that the stay has been violated by the surety's demand, it may award damages to the debtors against the surety, if it finds the stay violation was willful.[110] Second, a direct demand to the obligee may simply be ineffective. If the bankruptcy court determines that the automatic stay was applicable, then the surety's notice to the bond obligee is said to have been "invalid, void and of no force and effect."[111] Outside of the bankruptcy context, a bond obligee that pays funds to the principal over the surety's objection risks liability to the surety for those funds paid and lost. However, if the notice to the bond obligee from the surety is held by the bankruptcy court to have been "void" because it violated the automatic stay of 11 U.S.C. § 362(a), it is as if the notice was never given, and there may be no consequence to the obligee for having ignored the demand.

Several reported decisions from the United States Bankruptcy Court for the Southern District of Ohio articulate a solution to the surety's "demand" dilemma. These decisions, issued by two different judges in that court, both hold that it is not a violation of the automatic stay to send a notice to a third party advising them of their rights to withhold funds from the debtor.[112] In the *Hughes-Bechtol* decision, the party who sent the notice was a construction surety, who wrote the bond obligees. The debtor complained that the surety had violated the automatic stay. The court found that the surety's correspondence was predominantly informational in character, represented an isolated contact, and would therefore not be a violation of the automatic stay.[113] In the *Hughes-Bechtol* case, the surety sent letters advising the obligees that the principal had failed to pay certain claims and that those claimants had asserted claims against the bond written by the surety. The surety advised that it had paid claims and that it believed it had a direct right to the contract proceeds held by the obligee. In non-demanding language, the surety went on to state that it believed its claim to the contract fund was

---

110   11 U.S.C. § 362(h).

111   *In re* Schwartz, 954 F.2d 569 (9th Cir. 1992); *In re* Randall Enterprises, Inc., 115 Bankr. 292, 295 (Bankr. D. Colo. 1990); *In re* Advent Corp., 24 Bankr. 612 (Bankr. 1st Cir. 1982); COLLIER ON BANKRUPTCY, ¶ 362.11 [1], p. 362-111 (15th ed. rev. 1997) and cases cited at note 1.

112   *In re* U.S. Electric, Inc., 123 Bankr. 262 (Bankr. S.D. Ohio 1990); Matter of Hughes-Bechtol, Inc., 117 Bankr. 890 (Bankr. S.D. Ohio 1990).

113   *Hughes-Bechtol*, 117 Bankr. 890, 906.

superior, and that the surety might continue to have a claim against the obligee if the contract funds were disbursed or any other action were taken by the bond obligee that prejudiced the surety's position.

What distinguishes the letters in *Hughes-Bechtol* from the normal surety form "notice to obligee" is that the *Hughes-Bechtol* letters contains no demand for the funds nor do they direct how the fund should be paid. Instead, the letters advise the bond obligee of certain facts and state the surety's position with respect to the bonded contract funds. The *Hughes-Bechtol* letters also avoid any statement that the letter constitutes a declaration of default by the surety against the principal under the indemnity agreement or otherwise. Such a declaration would be a violation of the stay.[114]

Thus, the surety may choose to send an informational letter to the bond obligee, closely tracking the language approved by the court in the *Hughes-Bechtol* decision.[115] Demands, payment directions and default language should be avoided. If the surety's carefully drafted communication is nonetheless attacked as a violation of the automatic stay, it can be persuasively argued that an "informational notice" is not the type of conduct the automatic stay was meant to prohibit, in reliance upon these case authorities. Even if a particular bankruptcy court chose to disagree with the Ohio decisions, the use of the language expressly approved by a reported bankruptcy court decision would strongly assist the surety in defending a claim that the alleged violation of the stay was "willful," a predicate finding before most courts would assess any sanction or penalties against the surety.

---

114 *In re* Computer Communications, Inc., 824 F.2d 725 (9th Cir. 1987); Matter of Edwards Mobile Home Sales, Inc., 119 Bankr. 857 (Bankr. M.D. Fla. 1990).

115 It appears the *Hughes-Bechtol* court knew the importance that would be placed upon its holding. The court attached copies of the letters as an appendix to the reported decision, removing any doubt as to the exact phraseology it found did not violate the automatic stay.

B. Motion For Relief From The Automatic Stay Regarding Bonded Contract Proceeds

When the principal files for bankruptcy, the automatic stay provisions of the Bankruptcy Code operate to prevent any actions that may have a detrimental effect on the debtor, its property, or any interest of the debtor in any property.[116] Given this exhaustive list of potential acts proscribed by Code Section 362(a), the surety must be exercise care to avoid running afoul of the automatic stay provisions. In many cases, the automatic stay significantly hampers the surety's ability to discharge its duties and protect its interests.

Knowledge of the bankruptcy filing is the legal equivalent of knowledge of the automatic stay.[117] Some bankruptcy courts hold that violations of the stay must be intentional and deliberate to be sanctionable.[118] However, some courts have held that monetary sanctions may be imposed for inadvertent violations of the automatic stay.[119] The sanctions available for a willful violation are the actual damages incurred by the debtor, court costs, attorneys' fees, and in appropriate circumstances, punitive damages.[120]

If the surety will need to take control of the bonded contract proceeds, then the surety may wish to promptly prepare and file a motion

---

116 11 U.S.C.A. § 362(a).
117 *See, e.g., In re* NWFX, Inc., 81 Bankr. 500 (Bankr. W.D. Ark. 1987).
118 *See, e.g., In re* Withrow, 93 Bankr. 436 (Bankr. W.D.N.C. 1988).
119 *See, e.g., In re* Inslaw, Inc., 76 Bankr. 224 (D.D.C. 1987).
120 11 U.S.C.A. §362(h) (1993 & Supp. 1997); *see also In re* Computer Communications, Inc., 824 F.2d 725 (9th Cir. 1987). The threat to the surety of paying sanctions or actual damages to the bankrupt principal will be greatly reduced where the principal is a corporation. Better reasoned decisions have held that corporate debtors may not recover sanctions under §362(h) because only an "individual" injured by a willful violation of the stay may recover damages under this section. *In re* Manlon, 168 Bankr. 594, 597 (Bankr. E. D. Ky. 1994); *In re* Goodman, 991 F.2d 613, 620 (9th Cir. 1993); *In re* Pace, 67 F.3d 187, 193 (9th Cir. 1995); *In re* Cascade Roads, Inc., 34 F.3d 756, 766 (9th Cir. 1994); *In re* Chateaugay Corp., 920 F.2d 183, 187 (2d Cir. 1990); *But see In re* Atlantic Bus. and Community Corp., 901 F.2d 325 (3rd Cir. 1990); Budget Service Co. v. Better Homes of Virginia, 804 F.2d 289 (4th Cir. 1986). A debtor may still seek sanctions under the bankruptcy court's contempt powers, but such an award is discretionary.

for relief from the automatic stay under Section 362(d).[121] This motion may contain the surety's request for relief from stay to take other necessary actions. For example, the surety may also seek to declare a default and thereby terminate the debtor-in-possession's control of the work on the bonded projects.

There is no need to file a motion to lift the automatic stay if the contract funds are not property of the estate. For example, if the debtor was declared to be in contractual default and terminated before the bankruptcy filing, the contract funds are likely not part of the bankruptcy estate. Also, the debtor loses all legal and equitable interests in the contract funds when it rejects an executory contract in its bankruptcy case.[122] However, in most circumstances, actions taken by the surety to obtain contract funds without first seeking relief from the automatic stay have an element of risk. It is always possible that a court may later find that the bonded contract funds were property of the estate, notwithstanding the surety's belief otherwise. In the interests of prudence and to avoid sanctions, a surety can file a precautionary motion for relief from the stay under Section 362(d)(2). Such a motion need not contain an admission that the automatic stay applies to the surety's contract proceeds. Instead, the surety is merely seeking a court determination that the debtor has no interest in the bonded contract proceeds, due to the surety's superior rights of equitable subrogation, trust fund rights, or pre-petition assignment.

In opposing the surety's stay relief motion, the principal can be expected to argue that the contract funds are essential to the debtor's effective reorganization. Especially in the early days of the bankruptcy case, such an argument may predispose the court to permit the debtor to

---

121   (d)   On request of a party in interest and after notice and a hearing, the court shall grant relief from the stay provided under subsection (a) of this section, such as by terminating, annulling, modifying, or conditioning such stay–
(1)   for cause, including the lack of adequate protection of an interest in property of such party in interest; or
(2)   with respect to a stay of an act against property under subsection (a) of this section, if–
(A)   the debtor does not have an equity in such property; and
(B)   such property is not necessary to an effective reorganization.
11 U.S.C.A. § 362(d) (1993 & Supp. 1997).

122   *In re* Pacific Marine Dredging, 79 B.R. 924 (Bankr. D. Or. 1987).

use progress payments.[123] It is often true that a debtor-in-possession will have little hope of successfully reorganizing without use of the bonded contract proceeds. However, that truth alone is not sufficient to permit the debtor to use the contract proceeds under the Bankruptcy Code. The grounds for stay relief under Section 362(d)(2) are that the debtor lacks equity in the property that is the subject of the motion and that the property in not necessary to an effective reorganization. The surety bears the burden of showing (1) that it is owed a debt, and (2) that the debtor lacks "equity" in the bonded contract proceeds. Importantly, the debtor has the burden of proof that the contract proceeds are necessary to an effective reorganization.[124]

Because of the broad scope of the automatic stay, there are a fairly large number of circumstances where the surety may need to file a stay relief motion. An overly cautious project owner may refuse to make further payments to the surety post-petition, absent a stay relief order. Another common situation is when an owner is holding retainage that is the subject of competing claims by the debtor, its financing bank, and the surety. The surety may promptly move for stay relief asking the court to determine that the debtor lacks "equity" in the bonded contract proceeds (by virtue of the surety's superior rights) and to lift the stay to permit the surety to collect the funds from the owner. In yet another scenario, the surety may have been financing its principal by utilizing a trust fund account in which the principal holds legal title but the surety holds the equitable interest to the funds in the account. The debtor-in-possession may claim the funds in the trust account to be property of the estate because the account bears the principal's name. The debtor may wish to use those funds to finance its reorganization or a bankruptcy trustee may claim the funds to be used for distribution to the unsecured creditors. The surety can move for stay relief to have the court determine its priority in the funds and to permit the surety to use those funds.

---

123 Less stringent standard applied on the "necessity" requirement in stay relief earlier in the case. *See* FGH Realty Credit Corp. v. Newark Airport/Hotel Ltd. Partnership, 155 B.R. 93 (D.N.J. 1993).

124 11 U.S.C. § 362(g).

C. Motion to Sequester Cash Collateral and, Alternatively, for Adequate Protection

If the bonded contract funds have been received by the debtor and are property of the bankrupt estate,[125] those funds are referred to as the surety's "cash collateral."[126] The trustee or debtor-in-possession is required to segregate and account for any cash collateral in its possession, custody or control.[127] The debtor is not permitted to use any cash collateral unless (a) the surety consents or (b) the court, after notice and a hearing, authorizes such use.[128]

Although the clear language of the Bankruptcy Code prohibits the debtor's use of cash collateral, it is not uncommon for the surety to learn that its cash collateral has been dissipated.[129] For this reason, the surety

---

125 Of course, numerous cases cited in the preceding section hold that the bonded contract funds are not property of the estate, but are the surety's property.
126 11 U.S.C. § 363(a) provides: "'[C]ash collateral' means cash, negotiable instruments, documents of title, securities, deposit accounts, or other cash equivalents whenever acquired in which the estate and an entity other than the estate have an interest and includes the proceeds, products, offspring, rents, or profits of property ... subject to a security interest as provided in section 552(b) of this title, whether existing before or after the commencement of a case under this title."
127 11 U.S.C. § 363(c)(4).
128 11 U.S.C. § 363(c)(2).
129 Although the Bankruptcy Code specifically prohibits the debtor's use of cash collateral without consent of all interested parties or court order upon notice and a hearing, the Code does not specify any sanctions for the unapproved use of cash collateral. Therefore, in practice, a debtor-in-possession will often use the surety's cash collateral, i.e., contract proceeds, until the surety moves the bankruptcy court for an order restricting such use. The surety is not without recourse, however, for the misuse by the debtor of contract proceeds. One bankruptcy court, while recognizing the absence of any express sanctions in the Bankruptcy Code, used Section 105 to impose sanctions on a debtor-in-possession for its use of cash collateral without consent or court order. The court granted the secured creditor a replacement lien on the debtor-in-possession's post-petition accounts receivable and, to the extent that was not sufficient, a priority administrative claim. *In re* Aerosmith Denton Corp., 36 Bankr. 116 (Bankr. N.D. Tex. 1983); *see also In re* Rankin, 49 Bankr. 565

should promptly put its principal and the court on notice, by a short court filing, that it does not consent to the use of bonded contract funds. The surety may also file a motion pursuant to Section 363(e) to prohibit or condition the principal's use of cash collateral. The motion should request that the principal be prohibited from using the surety's cash collateral. As a fall back position, the motion should alternately request that the cash collateral be segregated and the surety be provided "adequate protection" for any use of the funds by the principal.[130]

If the court will not prohibit the Chapter 11 debtor/principal's use of cash collateral, then the surety should be prepared to suggest the form of adequate protection.[131] A debtor-in-possession completing a bonded

---

(Bankr. W.D. Mo. 1985) (creditor allowed administrative priority claim to extent debtor-in-possession misused cash collateral where no other property available). In another case, where the debtor-in-possession and the secured party had stipulated to the use of cash collateral but the debtor-in-possession violated the terms of the stipulation, the court refused the debtor-in-possession's subsequent motion for court-approved use of cash collateral over the creditor's objections. *In re* Oxford Royal Mushroom Prods., Inc., 19 Bankr. 974 (Bankr. E.D. Pa. 1982).

130 Adequate Protection
When adequate protection is required under section 362, 363 or 364 of this title of an interest of an entity in property, such adequate protection may be provided by–
(1)   requiring the trustee to make a cash payment or periodic cash payments to such entity, to the extent that the stay under section 362 of this title, use, sale, or lease under section 363 of this title, or any grant of a lien under section 364 of this title results in a decrease in the value of such entity's interest in such property.
(2)   providing to such entity an additional or replacement lien to the extent that such stay, use, sale, lease, or grant results in a decrease in the value of such entity's interest in such property; or
(3)   granting such other relief, other than entitling such entity to compensation allowable under section 503(b)(1) of this title as an administrative expense, as will result in the realization by such entity of the indubitable equivalent of such entity's interest in such property.
11 U.S.C. § 361.

131 The courts have fashioned adequate protection in a variety of ways to meet the needs of individual cases. *In re* Anchorage Boat Sales, Inc., 4 Bankr. 635 (Bankr. E.D.N.Y. 1980) (debtor enjoined from taking any action to transfer, sell, or dispose of cash collateral subject to interest of creditor); *In re* Earth Lite, Inc., 9 Bankr. 440 (Bankr. M.D. Fla. 1981)

contract can be required to (1) limit its disbursement of funds to only those expenses required to keep the bonded contracts going, (2) permit the surety to control the debtor's payment of expenditures to assure the bonded monies are dedicated to the ongoing expenses of the bonded contracts, (3) provide an accounting for each project, so that income and expenses can be reviewed, (4) limit any salary payments to the debtor's stockholders, officers or their relatives, and (5) not pay for equipment or expenses not necessary on the ongoing projects.[132]

Even if the surety is willing to permit the debtor to continue to perform on bonded projects after the bankruptcy filing, the surety should obtain a stipulation from the debtor, and court approval thereof, providing adequate protection to the surety, in order to protect the surety's cash collateral interest in the bonded contract proceeds.

(equity cushion and personal guarantee of principals not sufficient; debtor allowed use of cash collateral if it cures default and make monthly contractual payments); *In re* Certified Corp., 51 Bankr. 154 (D. Hawaii 1985) (debtor authorized to use cash collateral where creditor granted replacement liens and authority to inspect inventory while debtor required to file detailed daily reports with creditor and court and place all amounts collected in special account).

[132] *In re* Maxon Engineering Services, Inc., 332 B.R. 495 (Bankr. D.P.R.2005) (proceeds required to be segregated on a job by job basis, as requested by surety for adequate protection); *See Ram Const.*, 32 B.R. at 759. The *Glover Construction* court required progress payments to be used first to pay all bona fide claims against the bonded projects that the surety may become liable, and any surpluses could be used for the debtor's job-related operating and overhead expenses "most stringently viewed." 30 B.R. at 882. But see *In re Kuhn Constr. Co.*, Inc., 11 Bankr. 746 (Bankr. S.D. W.Va. 1981) (Court concluded that surety's equitable right of subrogation was subject to requirements of Article 9 of the UCC; the court held that the surety was not entitled to adequate protection and allowed the debtor to use the cash without the surety's consent); *In re* Universal Builders, Inc., 53 Bankr. 183 (Bankr. M.D. Tenn. 1985) (Court denied surety's action for adequate protection as concerns unpaid progress payments finding that the surety had not perfected its interest in the funds.

D. Common Obligee–The Surety's Right to Contract Proceeds From Other Projects

The bonded principal will sometimes have multiple construction contracts with the same obligee, for example, a local municipality. While the principal/debtor's default on one project may result in a claim against the surety, another project may be completed, with retention funds payable to the debtor. When the principal files for bankruptcy protection, the principal will claim the retention money should be paid into its bankruptcy, expecting the surety to pay the debtor's full liability to the obligee on the other project. The surety can and should require the obligee to use the contract proceeds in its possession to reduce the performance bond claim.

Put differently, the surety may seek the contract or claim proceeds in the hands of an obligee, which contract proceeds are owed to the principal for work performed on an unbonded contract with that same obligee. Every circuit court that has considered the surety's rights in this context has affirmed the surety's position. The circuit court opinions, and the Restatement (Third) of Suretyship and Guaranty take slightly different paths, but reach the same result, i.e., that the surety is entitled to assert the principal's claim against the obligee on projects other than the single bonded project where the surety suffered its loss.

The circuit court opinions analyze the surety's right in terms of the surety's subrogation to the obligee's right to setoff losses and claims on one project against another. The surety, standing in the shoes of the obligee, may claim money owed to its principal on an unbonded project, to recover losses on the bonded project. By way of example, on the bonded project, assume that bills to the principal's subcontractors went unpaid. These subcontractors can assert claims against the project and the obligee's property in the form of mechanic's liens, stop notices or quantum meruit claims. The obligee would be entitled to withhold money owed to the principal on a different project to protect itself and pay the principal's subcontractors on the first project. The obligee's ability to assert this "setoff" is viewed by the courts as a form of security for the surety's loss, which security is held by the obligee. The decisions hold that the obligee is compelled to exercise these rights of setoff, in order to potentially reduce the loss to the surety.

The Restatement[133] takes a slightly different approach, describing the surety's right to the monies as one of subrogation to the rights of the principal who would otherwise be entitled to recover the money from the obligee on the second unrelated contract. Notwithstanding the different approach, the result reached is the same, the surety is entitled to the monies on a second unrelated contract, to reduce its loss on the first, bonded contract.

The Sixth, Fourth, Second, and Federal Circuit Courts of Appeal have all affirmed the surety's rights to benefits flowing from "unrelated contracts" with a common obligee.[134] The *Corbitt* case provides a good illustration of this equitable right. In the *Corbitt* case, the debtor, Corbitt Company, owed the county $68,433.30 on bonded contracts, for which judgment had already been entered against both the debtor and its surety. However, the county held $40,850.00 of the debtor's funds pursuant to unrelated unbonded contracts. After the debtor filed bankruptcy, the trustee of the estate sought to obtain turnover of the proceeds from the

---

133 *See* Section 35, Comment b.
134 *In re* Larbar Corporation, 177 F.3d 439 (6th Cir. 1999) (the court allowed the surety to setoff against losses incurred in completing bonded projects against the profits gained on other bonded contracts, inasmuch as all laborers and materialmen on the contracts had been paid and the debtor's only outstanding creditors were general estate creditors. *Id.* at 447. The court reasoned that the setoff under Section 553 of the Bankruptcy Code provides the surety with a practical incentive to fulfill its bond obligations. Further, the court rejected the trustee's "lack of mutuality" argument suggesting that setoff was improper because the general contractors were not identical on the contracts that the surety was attempting to setoff. *Id.* at 446. Rather, the court found that where the general contractors were joint venturers, the mutuality requirement is met because the joint venturers would be jointly and severally liable for both contract's obligations.); Transamerica Insurance Co. v. U.S., 989 F.2d 1188 (Fed. Cir. 1993)(The Federal Circuit followed the reasoning of the District of Columbia v. Aetna Ins. Co., 462 A.2d 428 (D.C. 1983), where the District contracted with CSH Contractors, Inc. on two construction projects. Aetna was surety for CSH on one contract and suffered a loss. Over Aetna's objection, the District paid CSH contract funds on the other project. The court rejected the District's argument that the surety's right of subrogation was limited to the bonded contract. *Id.* at 432.); Merritt Commercial Savings & Loan, Inc. v. Guinee (*In re* James R. Corbitt Co.), 766 F.2d 850 (4th Cir. 1985) (and cases cited therein).

unbonded contract. Thereafter, the trustee and the county sought to enter into a settlement agreement which would have resulted in $33,350.00 of the unbonded funds being returned to the debtor by the county. The surety, Merritt, sought to intervene and objected to the settlement. Both the bankruptcy court and district court overruled the objection and refused to allow the surety to intervene. The Fourth Circuit Court of Appeals concluded that the "surety Merritt has the right to compel the county to assert its setoff right against the insolvent debtor...to reduce its liability to the county by the amount of the county's setoff right against the estate...."[135]

In reaching its conclusion, the *Corbitt* court relied heavily on Judge Friendly's analysis in *In re Yale Express System, Inc.*[136] In the *Yale Express* case, an insolvent motor carrier held claims against various of its clientele for unpaid freight charges. The carrier's clients held claims against the carrier and its surety for loss or damages to cargo it had placed with the carrier. The carrier's surety was allowed to "reduce its liability to the creditors by the amount of the freight charges owed by the creditors to the debtor."[137]

Of equal importance is Judge Friendly's recognition that a surety has a right to assert counterclaims on behalf of the principal against a creditor of the estate upon the principal becoming insolvent.[138] Both Judge Friendly and Judge Learned Hand found that not only does the surety have the equitable right to compel setoff, but one way in which this can be done is by the surety having the right to pursue the principal's counterclaims against the creditor. Judge Learned Hand stated that

> ... the upshot of denying the surety a right to assert the counterclaim is to enhance the principal's estate at the expense of the surety, which is contrary to the fundamental relation between the two, the truth is that after insolvency, the counterclaim becomes a creditor's security for his own claim, a means by which it can be paid dollar for dollar through his right of setoff. However, it is only after the surety pays the creditor that he is subrogated to all the creditor's securities, and that would be a

---

135 *In re* James R. Corbitt, *id.* at 855.
136 362 F.2d 111 (2nd Cir. 1966).
137 *In re* James R. Corbitt, *id.* at 854.
138 *In re* Yale Express System, Inc., *supra* note 136, at 195 (*citing* United States *ex rel.* Johnson v. Morley Construction Company, 98 F.2d 781, 789-790 (2nd Cir. 1938)).

condition here, except that the surety cannot pay the debt without losing the security, for it consists only of the creditor's power to defeat the counterclaim by using his claim to cancel it. Therefore, to exact of the surety, the normal condition of paying the debt, would be to destroy the security, and that follows that he must be allowed to set it up himself.[139]

Thus, the surety has the right to require the obligee to setoff amounts owed by the obligee to the debtor against the amounts owed by the debtor in order to prevent "unjust enrichment" at the expense of the surety.[140] Similarly, the surety would have the right to pursue the debtor's counterclaims against the debtor in order to ensure that the obligee does "what his [obligee's] self interest would lead him to do but for the existence of the surety . . . ."[141]

V. Impact of Bankruptcy Upon the Surety's Ability to Finance the Principal's Completion of Bonded Work

One of the performance bond surety's options in a default is to finance the principal's completion of the bonded work. If the principal needs the surety's financing, the principal is necessarily facing financial challenges. A bankruptcy filing or the potential of a bankruptcy filing will be an important consideration in the decision to finance and the terms that must be incorporated into a financing agreement. Bankruptcy law has substantial effects on both financing arrangements entered into outside of bankruptcy, and upon financing arrangements that will be entered into with a principal who has already filed a petition. These are addressed in turn.

A. Pre-Petition Financing of the Principal

1. Introduction

A performance bond surety might elect to provide the contractor with the money needed to complete bonded projects. This chapter does not discuss the advisability or hazards of this particular surety option, but

---

139 U.S. *ex rel.* Johnson v. Morley, *supra* note 138, at 790.
140 *Corbitt, supra* note 136, at 855.
141 *Id.* at 855.

other authors have addressed this topic.[142] Assuming the decision to finance has been made, how may the surety and its financing arrangement be affected by the subsequent bankruptcy filing by the principal?

By far the most important bankruptcy principle affecting any agreement with a financially distressed principal is the law of "avoidable preferences." The law of bankruptcy preferences examines past transactions against standards not necessarily contemplated at that time. This examination is triggered by the filing of a petition under the Bankruptcy Code. By way of example, in an avoidance action the bankrupt principal may argue that the assignment of the bonded contract proceeds to the surety contained in a financing agreement were a preference and/or that any security interests given to the surety were a preference.

2. The Law of Preference Liability

Once the principal files for bankruptcy, all transfers of property by the principal to the surety or other creditors within ninety days of bankruptcy may be avoided or undone under the preference provision of the Bankruptcy Code.[143] The financing agreement between the surety and its principal may be the target of a preference attack. Whether the agreement and the surety's benefits thereunder survive the attack will be affected by certain provisions in the financing agreement and the surety's actions under the agreement.

a. *Elements of Preference.* The Bankruptcy Code allows a trustee or debtor in possession to avoid[144] a pre-bankruptcy transfer[145] of the

---

142 Joyce & Haug, *Financing the Contractor*, BOND DEFAULT MANUAL (R. Wisner. ed. 1987); Schroeder, *Providing Financial Support to the Contractor*, 17 FORUM 1190 (1982); Schroeder, *Procedures and Instruments Utilized to Protect the Surety who Finances the Contractors*, 14 FORUM 830 (1979); Leo, *The Financing Surety and the Chapter 11 Principal*, 26 TORT & INS. L.J. 45 (1990).

143 11 U.S.C. § 547(b).

144 11 U.S.C. § 547(b).

145 "Transfer" is a broadly defined term, including every mode, voluntary and involuntary of disposing of property, including the granting of security interests in property. 11 U.S.C. § 101(54).

debtor's property[146] if certain conditions are met. There are six necessary elements to a preference action. They are:

(1) a transfer of property of the debtor,
(2) the transfer must be to or for the benefit of a creditor,
(3) the transfer must be for or on account of an antecedent debt owed by the debtor before the transfer was made,
(4) the transfer must have been made when the debtor was insolvent,
(5) the transfer must have been made during the ninety days immediately preceding the commencement of the case. If the transfer was made to an insider,[147] the transfer may be

---

146 The Code does not define property as it is used in 11 U.S.C. § 547(b) but items constituting the debtor's estate are listed at 11 U.S.C. § 541: Section 541's definition of property of the estate is helpful in determining what constitutes property of the debtor under Section 547 because (1) property of the debtor is property of the estate (except for statutory exemptions); and (2) the goal of Section 547 is to avoid only those preferential transfers that result in depletion of the estate. *In re* General Office Furniture Wholesalers, Inc., 42 Bankr. 232 (Bankr. E.D. Va. 1984).

147 11 U.S.C. § 101(31) defines "insider" as follows:
"Insider" includes –
(A) if the debtor is an individual -
    (i) relative of the debtor or of a general partner of the debtor;
    (ii) partnership in which the debtor is a general partner;
    (iii) general partner of the debtor; or
    (iv) corporation of which the debtor is a director, officer, or person in control;
(B) if the debtor is a corporation -
    (i) director of the debtor;
    (ii) officer of the debtor;
    (iii) person in control of the debtor;
    (iv) partnership in which the debtor is a general partner;
    (v) general partner of the debtor; or
    (vi) relative of a general partner, director, officer, or person in control of the debtor;
(C) if the debtor is a partnership -
    (i) general partner of the debtor
    (ii) relative of a general partner in, general partner of, or person in control of the debtor;

avoided if it occurred during the period that begins one year before the filing of the petition and ends ninety days before the filing, if the insider to whom the transfer was made had reasonable cause to believe the debtor was insolvent at the time the transfer was made, and

(6) The transfer must enable the creditor, to or for whose benefit the transfer was made, to receive a greater percentage of his claim than he would receive under the distributive provisions of the Bankruptcy Code. Specifically, the creditor must receive more than he would have received if the case were a liquidation case and if the transfer had not been made.[148]

All six of the elements of preference must be present before the court will order the transfer avoided. A close examination of the elements of the preference action brought against the surety arising out of its financing agreement will often show that the allegedly preferential transfer to the surety simply does not satisfy all elements. For example, the debtor may attack as preferential, a payment made just days before the bankruptcy from a trust account established under the financing agreement with the surety. Financing agreements commonly provide for the establishment of joint control trust accounts. The joint control trust accounts will likely receive all of the deposits for project completion, including all the principal's accounts receivable, the principal's current funds and the surety's advances. The agreement will typically state that the funds are held in trust for the benefit of the surety.

(iii) partnership in which the debtor is a general partner;
(iv) general partner of the debtor; or
(v) person in control of the debtor;
(D) if the debtor is a municipality, elected official of the debtor or relative of an elected official of the debtor;
(E) affiliate or insider of an affiliate as if such affiliate were the debtor; and
(F) managing agent of the debtor;

11 U.S.C. § 101(31).

148 H.R. Rep. No. 95-595, 95th Cong., 1st Sess. 372 (1977); S. Rep. No. 95-989, 95th Cong., 2d Sess. 87 (1978); 11 U.S.C. § 547b.

Bankruptcy courts look to state law to determine whether a valid trust was created.[149] In most states, the essential elements of a trust are: competent settler and a trustee, an intent to create a trust, an ascertainable trust res (i.e. property), and identifiable beneficiaries. For a surety/ principal joint control trust account, the trust res is the funds in the joint control trust accounts, the settler is both the surety and the principal and the trustees are the various banks where the joint control trust accounts are located. The surety will be the beneficiary if the financing agreement has been properly worded.

The intent to create a trust may be further supported by explicit procedures for funding the completion of the bonded projects in the financing agreement. If the latitude granted to the principal to use the surety's funds is broad, it may indicate the funds are not "in trust," but were merely loaned to the principal. However, if specific procedures are observed during the financing period, the surety can effectively argue that it had no intention of giving the beneficial interest to the funds in the joint control trust account to its principal.[150] The ownership of the beneficial interest will be the owner of any monies left in accounts held in trust if the principal files for bankruptcy.[151] Thus, the principal's preference attack on a payment under the financing agreement might be

---

149 Matter of Torrez, 63 B.R. 751 (9th Cir. Bankr. 1986), *aff'd*, 827 F.2d 1299 (9th Cir. 1987).
150 *In* Askew v. Resource Funding Ltd., 94 Cal.App.3d 402, 156 Cal.Rptr. 208 (1979), an agreement created a project account and contemplated that the funds would be spent on a specific project. The court held that a trust relationship was created because the agreement, between the transferor and the transferee of funds, provided for various safeguards and restrictions on the use of those funds by creating a committee which oversaw and approved expenditures before permitted withdrawals from the project account. The Askew court stated:

> We thus conclude that the *language of the Agreement makes it clear that the transferor, NCPA, did not intend the transferee, RGL, to have the beneficial interest in the property transferred, i.e., The $837,500, much less the "ownership" thereof.* Seemingly, it would be difficult to draw a document with terminology more manifest as to the purpose of the funds in question than the Agreement before us.

94 Cal.App.3d at 409, 156 Cal.Rptr. at 211. (emphasis added). *See also* RESTATEMENT (SECOND) OF TRUSTS, §12 cmt. g (1959).
151 *See* 11 U.S.C. § 541(d).

defeated by demonstrating that the monies were not "property of the debtor,"[152] but were instead funds held in trust for the surety and/or completion creditors.

In another example, not every principal who needs surety financing is "insolvent" for preference purposes. The challenges facing the principal may be related to cash flow, and not balance sheet insolvency. A transfer is not a preference unless it is made while the principal is insolvent.[153] Increasingly, companies are advised by bankruptcy counsel to strategically time their bankruptcy filing, often before the financial situation becomes irreparable. As transfers subject to attack become increasingly distant in time from the day of bankruptcy filing, investigation may reveal that the principal was not in fact insolvent, thereby defeating the preference claim.

The surety's defense may be aided by a financing agreement that contains a recitation by the principal concerning its present balance sheet solvency. Such a representation may also offer some measure of protection against later fraudulent conveyance claims, whether brought by the principal in his bankruptcy or by third parties.

 b. *Exceptions To Preference.* There are seven statutory exceptions to the Code's preference avoiding power.[154] Even if a surety has received a transfer that satisfies the six elements of preference, if a surety can qualify under any one of the exceptions, then it is protected from avoidance of the preference. If it can qualify under several exceptions, it is protected by each to the extent it qualifies under each. Two sections provide exceptions of particular use in defending a financing agreement from preference attack, Sections 547(c)(1) and (4).[155] Both of these

---

152 *See* Begier v. Internal Revenue Service, 110 S.Ct. 2258 (1990) ("A 'debtor' does not own an equitable interest in property he holds in trust for another, that interest is not 'property of the estate,' nor is such an equitable interest 'property of the debtor' for purposes of § 547(b)."); United States v. Whiting Pools, Inc., 462 U.S. 198, 205 n. 10, 103 S.Ct. 2309, 2314 n. 10, 76 L.Ed.2d 515, 522 n. 10 (1983) ("Congress plainly excluded property of others held by the debtor in trust at the time of the filing of the petition."); *In re* California Trade Technical Schools, Inc., 923 F.2d 641 (9th Cir. 1991) (funds held "in trust" were not property of the debtor for preferential transfer purposes).

153 11 U.S.C. § 101(32).

154 11 U.S.C. § 547(c).

155 (C) The trustee may not avoid under this section a transfer–

exceptions to preference incorporate the concept of "value" received by the debtor from the creditor who it is claimed received a transfer considered preferential. Because the execution of a financing agreement and transfers occurring pursuant to a financing agreement involve benefit flowing to the debtor from the surety, these exceptions should offer defenses to preference attack in the principal's bankruptcy.

To use the Section 547(c)(1) exception, the surety must give "new value," as defined in Section 547(a)(2),[156] contemporaneously with the receipt of the debtor's transfer. The surety could defend the principal's preference action by showing that any transfers of assets or security by the principal to the surety were a contemporaneous exchange for the surety's new value (i.e. the surety's financing).

The financing agreement may be protected by the acknowledgement or modification of the surety's equitable lien on bonded contract funds. These valuable rights may aid the surety's defense of a preference action relating to the debtor's payment of bills that would be covered by the surety's bond obligations.[157]

---

    (1) to the extent that such transfer was–
(A) intended by the debtor and the creditor to or for whose benefit such transfer was made to be a contemporaneous exchange for new value given to the debtor; and
(B) in fact a substantially contemporaneous exchange;

. . . .

    (4) To or for the benefit of a creditor, to the extent that, after such transfer, such creditor gave new value to or for the benefit of the debtor–
(A) not secured by an otherwise unavoidable security interest; and
(B) on account of which new value the debtor did not make an otherwise unavoidable transfer to or for the benefit of such creditor.
11 U.S.C. § 547(c)(1) and (c)(4), respectively.

156 11 U.S.C. § 547(a)(2) provides: "'New Value' means money or money's worth in goods, services, or new credit, or release by a transferee of property previously transferred to such transferee in a transaction that is neither void nor voidable by the debtor or the trustee under any applicable law, including proceeds of such property, but does not include an obligation substituted for an existing obligation."

157 *See In re* E. R. Fegert, Inc., 88 Bankr. 258 (9th Cir. Bankr. 1988), *aff'd*, 887 F.2d 955 (9th Cir. 1989). The Chapter 7 trustee brought a preference claim seeking to recover from the surety for pre-petition payments made by a debtor/contractor to two subcontractors. The court held that the release of the subcontractors' rights against the surety, because the surety

If a court were to conclude that the principal's transfer of its property interests to the surety and the surety's commitment to finance were not a "substantially contemporaneous" exchange of new value, then the preference exception for a "subsequent advance" of new value in Section 547(c)(4) may apply. Illustrative of the exception is the decision of *In Re Amarex, Inc.*[158] The debtor entered into an agreement with a group of creditors, under which the debtor made payments within ninety days of filing bankruptcy. The *Amarex* court concluded that the creditors' payments to third party vendors, made on behalf of the debtor, were a "subsequent advance" of new value each time the creditors paid the debtor's vendors.[159] Therefore, the surety's commitment to finance and its cash advances can be "new value" under Section 547(a)(2). Whether the surety's new value is perceived as "contemporaneous" or "subsequent" to the debtor's transfer of property to the surety, the exceptions to preference in Sections 547(c)(1) or 547(c)(4) should apply to defeat the avoidance action.

The bankrupt principal may argue that the surety's finance money, used to pay expenses on the bonded projects, is not "new value" because the surety had a pre-existing duty under its bond to pay those expenses. The court must be made to understand that financing the principal goes significantly beyond the surety's bond obligations. A performing surety is not required to finance its principal to complete the bonded projects.[160] A surety is entitled to decide how to best complete bonded projects upon

---

could have exercised its lien rights under the doctrine of equitable subrogation against the contract proceeds if the subcontractors had not been paid, constituted "new value" given to the debtor in a substantially contemporaneous exchange.

158 88 Bankr. 362 (W.D.Okla. 1988).
159 *See also* Matter of Global Int'l Airways Corp., 80 Bankr. 983 (Bankr. W.D. Mo. 1987) (Debtor's payment of prior purchases was not a voidable preference because creditor's subsequent transfer of goods was "subsequent value" under 11 U.S.C. § 547(c)(4)); Matter of Marin Aviation, Inc., 53 Bankr. 497 (Bankr. D.N.J. 1984) (Debtor's transfer of security interest in helicopter was not a voidable preference because bank gave new value to debtor after transfer occurred).
160 Fischer Construction Co. v. Fireman's Fund Insurance Co., 420 F.2d 271 (10th Cir. 1969).

the principal's default.[161] Furthermore, the surety's financing may protect the principal's reputation, preserve favorable credit terms and relationships with suppliers and subcontractors, and provide other benefits to the principal. It will be helpful if the principal has considered and acknowledged these types of benefits in the written financing agreement. The financing agreement may also require the surety to cover a portion of the principal's overhead or other expenses not covered by the surety's bonds. These benefits also constitute new value.

3. Other Financing Clauses That May Assist the Surety in Bankruptcy

A clause attempting to prohibit the principal or indemnitors from filing a bankruptcy petition will be void as against public policy.[162] In rare cases, some courts have dismissed a bankruptcy petition, in order to enforce the provisions of a pre-bankruptcy workout agreement.[163] A comprehensive financing or default agreement between the surety and principal could be very similar to the "workout agreements" that the courts have favored in the reported decisions dismissing bankruptcies. Such an agreement would need to comprehensively drafted and used as an intended alternative to bankruptcy.

---

161 Aetna Cas. and Sur. Co. v. U.S., 845 F.2d 971, 975 (Fed. Cir. 1988); Thompson, *Completion Options Available to a Performance Bond Surety Other than Financing its Principal*, 17 FORUM 1215 (1982).

162 *In re* Joshua Slocum Ltd., 922 F.2d 1081 (3d Cir. 1990); *In re* Club Tower L.P., 138 Bankr. 307 (Bankr. N.D. Ga. 1991).

163 *In re* Colonial Ford, Inc., 24 Bankr. 1014, 1020 (Bankr. D. Utah 1982) (in order to encourage non-judicial workouts that are expeditious, economic, and sensible, "[w]here . . . the workout is comprehensive, and designed to end, not perpetuate, the creditor-company relations, dismissal under section 305 (a) (1) is appropriate."); *In re* Pengo Industr., 962 F.2d 543, 549 (5th Cir. 1992), *cert. denied*, 506 U.S. 1000 ("[w]e strongly disfavor a judicial interpretation of the Bankruptcy Code that contravenes the substantial congressional policy favoring out-of-court consensual workouts."); *see also, In re* Chateaugay Corp., 961 F.2d 378, 383 (2d Cir. 1992) (the court "will not attribute to Congress an intent to place a stumbling block in front of debtors seeking to avoid bankruptcy with the cooperation of their creditors [r]ather . . . Congress inten[ded] to encourage consensual workouts and . . . minimiz[e] bankruptcy filings . . .").

The financing agreement may also include clauses that entitle the surety to immediate relief from the automatic stay if the financing agreement is unsuccessful and the principal later files a bankruptcy petition. Again, in rare cases, some bankruptcy courts have upheld such clauses, interpreting the pre-petition agreement to be "cause" for relief from the automatic stay under 11 U.S.C. § 362 (d) (1).[164] Even where such a clause is found in the financing agreement, and bankruptcy counsel believes the court will likely enforce the stipulated stay relief, it would be advisable to first file a motion with the court and await the court ruling, rather than relying upon language stating that the stay is not applicable to the surety's actions at all.[165]

Financing or default agreements may provide a release to indemnitors or may reduce or "cap" the amount of the indemnity obligation owed to the surety. This concession may be given in exchange for cooperation, collateral or some other consideration. A "claw-back" clause is intended to take away the benefits granted by the agreement, if the principal later files bankruptcy. The claw-back provision may be triggered if there is any subsequent bankruptcy filing or only if the bankruptcy filing occurs within the preference period.

A claw-back clause has two positive effects. First, it prevents the principal or indemnitors from unfairly claiming the benefits of the

---

164 *In re* Powers, 170 Bankr. 480 (Bankr. D. Mass. 1994); *In re* Cheeks, 167 Bankr. 817 (Bankr. D. S.C. 1994); *In re* Wheaton Oaks Office Partners, 1992 WL 381047 (N.D. Ill.), (a provision regarding stay relief could constitute "cause" under 11 U.S.C. §362 (d) (1)); *In re* Club Tower L.P., 138 Bankr. 307 (Bankr. N.D. Ga. 1991) (stay relief clause enforceable); *Contra,* Farm Credit of Cent. Fla. v. Polk, 160 Bankr. 870 (D. M.D. Fla. 1993); *Sky Group Int'l, Inc.*, 108 Bankr. 86 (Bankr. W.D. Pa. 1989); *Best Finance Corp.*, 74 Bankr. 243 (Bankr. P.R. 1987); *In re* Jenkins Court Assoc. Ltd Partnership, 181 Bankr. 33 (Bankr. E.D. Pa. 1995) (Court declined to enforce waiver, but considered representations in pre-petition settlement agreement with hearing evidence to determine whether to grant stay relief.) *See, Why Courts Should Refuse to Enforce Pre-Petition Agreements That Waive Bankruptcy's Automatic Stay Provision*, 28 IND. L. REV. 1 (1994); *The Case for Limited Enforceability of a Pre-Petition Waiver of the Automatic Stay*, 32 SAN DIEGO L. REV. 1133, (1995); *Games Lawyers Play: Waivers of the Automatic Stay in Bankruptcy and the Single Asset Loan Workout*, 43 U.C.L.A. L. REV. 1117 (1996).

165 *In re* Powers, 170 Bankr. 480, 483 (Bankr. D. Mass. 1994).

agreement, when their bankruptcy filing has destroyed or delayed benefits that should have flowed to the surety. Second, it creates incentives for the indemnitors and principal to avoid bankruptcy, at least for the preference period. This incentive is particularly important where the surety has obtained generous new collateral under the terms of the agreement. The security interests may be avoidable if a bankruptcy is filed within the preference period, generally ninety (90) days.

A clause in the financing agreement that states that financial statements provided by the indemnitors and the principal have been requested, received and relied upon by the surety in entering into the agreement can later be helpful to the surety. The same clause might further state that the principal and indemnitors understand and intend for the surety to rely upon the statements, and that this reliance is reasonable. If the information in the financial statements turns out to be inaccurate, the amounts loaned or the losses incurred under the agreement may be a non-dischargeable debt in the later bankruptcy case of the principal or the indemnitors.[166] A non-dischargeable claim benefits the surety in two ways. First, the debt can be pursued for possible collection even after the bankruptcy. Second, the principal or indemnitors may resist or avoid a bankruptcy filing altogether, because of the inability to discharge the debt owed to the surety.

B. Post-Petition Financing of the Principal

1. Introduction

A surety's decision to finance its debtor/principal after bankruptcy begins with the same considerations that apply outside of bankruptcy. The obvious goals are to minimize the surety's losses by enabling the debtor/principal to complete the work and possibly obtain collateral to offset potential losses. In addition to the ordinary considerations surrounding a decision to finance, the surety contemplating Chapter 11 financing should weigh the code's inducements to provide financing to a debtor-in-possession.[167] The extension of credit may entitle the surety to collateral either in a first priority or junior position, may be combined

---

166   11 U.S.C. § 523(a)(2)(B).
167   For a superior treatment on this topic, see Leo, *The Financing Surety and the Chapter 11 Principal*, 26 TORT & INS. L.J. 45 (1990).

with cross-collateralization clauses, and may be conditioned upon a waiver of actions an antagonistic debtor/principal or indemnitors may threaten to bring against the surety.[168]

In addition to providing money to principal, the surety may, under certain circumstances, agree to write new bonds for the principal. The extension of additional surety credit is also viewed as a form of post-petition financing under the Bankruptcy Code. A post-petition extension of surety credit is far rarer than traditional financing, and therefore most of the discussion in this section refers to money financing, although the discussion of relevant legal principles is equally applicable to both types of post-petition credit.[169]

2. The Four Types of Post-Petition Credit

The four different types of borrowings permissible under the Bankruptcy Code are set forth in Section 364(a), (b), (c) and (d).[170] Section 364(a)

---

168 *In re* Ellingsen MacLean Oil Co., Inc., 834 F.2d 599 (6th Cir. 1987), *cert. denied*, 488 U.S. 817 (1987) (Sixth Circuit affirmed bankruptcy court's financing order that provided for a waiver by the debtor of any possible fraudulent transfer claims against a lender).

169 Because of the unique nature of an extension of post-petition surety credit, and the lack of an exact fit between bankruptcy financing nomenclature and surety credit, it is highly advisable to engage bankruptcy counsel with specific experience in this area to negotiate and document the agreement, motion and order.

170 Obtaining Credit.
  (a) If the trustee is authorized to operate the business of the debtor under section 721, 1108, 1304, 1203, or 1204 of this title, unless the court orders otherwise, the trustee may obtain unsecured credit and incur unsecured debt in the ordinary course of business allowable under section 503(b)(1) of this title as an administrative expense.
  (b) The court, after notice and a hearing, may authorize the trustee to obtain unsecured credit or to incur unsecured debt other than under subsection (a) of this section, allowable under section 503(b)(1) of this title as an administrative expense.
  (c) If the trustee is unable to obtain unsecured credit allowable under section 503(b)(1) of this title as an administrative expense, the court, after notice and a hearing, may authorize the obtaining of credit or the incurring of debt–

provides that if the "trustee" (which term also includes the debtor)[171] is authorized to operate the debtor's business, the trustee may obtain unsecured credit and incur unsecured debt in the ordinary course of business, unless the court orders otherwise. Any such debt, usually trade debt, which is not fully repaid will be given an administrative expense priority in distributions pursuant to Section 503(b)(1). This level of priority receives first distribution of unsecured funds under the plan or in liquidation. The risk of this type of financing is that a court may later determine it was incurred outside the ordinary course of business.[172] If prior court approval was not obtained, the creditor may lose its claim against the estate for the amount of the credit extended.[173] A surety who will finance post-petition or who may execute bonds post-petition, should avoid the risk of financing under Section 364(a) and obtain court approval.

---

(1) with priority over any or all administrative expenses of the kind specified in section 503(b) or 507(b) of this title;

(2) secured by a lien on property of the estate that is not otherwise subject to a lien; or

(3) secured by a junior lien on property of the estate that is subject to a lien.

(d) (1) The court, after notice and a hearing, may authorize the obtaining of credit or the incurring of debt secured by a senior or equal lien on property of the estate that is subject to a lien only if—

(A) the trustee is unable to obtain such credit otherwise; and

(B) there is adequate protection of the interest of the holder of the lien on the property of the estate on which such senior or equal lien is proposed to be granted.

. . . .

11 U.S.C. § 364.

171 11 U.S.C. § 1107 (Debtor-in-possession has the rights and duties of a trustee).

172 *In re* Media Cent., Inc., 115 Bankr. 119 (Bankr. E.D.Tenn. 1990); *In re* Lockwood Enterprises, Inc., 52 Bankr. 871 (Bankr. S.D.N.Y. 1985) (there was no proof that the debtor normally or customarily borrowed funds to meet payroll and operating expenses). Additionally, credit under Section 364(a) or (b) must be extended for "the actual, necessary costs and expenses of preserving the estate" to be given Section 503(b)(1) priority.

173 *In re* Photo Promotion Associates, Inc., 881 F.2d 6 (2d Cir. 1989); *In re* J.L. Graphics, Inc., 62 Bankr. 750 (Bankr. D.N.H. 1986).

Credit incurred outside the ordinary course of business may also be given an administrative expense priority under Section 364(b). A court order approving this credit is required.

While Sections 364(a) and (b) provide administrative expense priority, inducements available under Sections 364(c) can provide the surety with superior protections for its post-petition financing. Section 364(c) offers three possible protections to the financing surety: (1) super priority status over all administrative expenses, (2) lien(s) on unencumbered property of the debtor, and/or (3) junior lien(s) on already encumbered property.[174]

To obtain protections under Section 364(c), the debtor must demonstrate that credit is unavailable on more favorable terms.[175] The debtor's burden includes establishing that credit under Section 364(b) is unavailable, that the credit is necessary for preservation of the estate, and that the "terms of the transaction are fair, reasonable, and adequate, given the circumstances of the debtor-borrower and the proposed lender."[176] In *Crouse Group*, the debtor/principal sought a financing order that gave the surety a super priority claim under Section 364(c)(1). In return, the surety would provide financing for another payroll period, but not for the completion of the bonded projects. Evidence suggested that the surety desired to keep the debtors/principals on the project only until the surety could find replacements for its principals. Thus, the *Crouse Group* court denied the motion to approve the financing order.

Conversely, in *In Re Ames Dept. Stores, Inc.*,[177] the court granted a lending arrangement which gave Chemical Bank a super priority claim under Section 364(c)(1). The court found that the proposed financing would benefit the estate.

The differing results of these two cases highlights the requirement that the surety's financing must benefit the estate for a court to grant the protections of Section 364(c). This benefit is more likely to be proven where the financing order contains a commitment by the surety to fund

---

174 11 U.S.C. § 364(c)(1), (2) and (3), respectively.
175 *In re* Ames Dept. Stores, Inc., 115 Bankr. 34 (Bankr. S.D.N.Y. 1990) (Court concluded that the debtors met their burden of showing the unavailability of alternative unsecured financing by approaching four lending institutions with the capability of loaning the large sums necessary to sustain the debtors' operations).
176 *In re* The Crouse Group, Inc., 71 Bankr. 544, 549 (Bankr. E.D. Pa. 1987).
177 115 Bankr. 34 (Bankr. S.D.N.Y. 1990).

the projects to completion, subject to various default provisions. Lesser financing commitments may be approved by the court, but the risk of rejection is increased.

A surety may be granted extraordinary protections under Section 364(d), if the debtor has no other recourse for financing.[178] This section permits the post-petition financier to "prime" an existing secured creditor on encumbered property as a condition to granting new or continued financing to the debtor. Similar to Section 364(c) financing, Section 364(d) financing requires that other financing on more favorable terms be unavailable.[179] Existing lienholders who will be primed must be adequately protected.[180] The debtor/principal has the burden of proving that the requirements of Section 364(d) are met.[181] In *In Re Snowshoe Co., Inc.*,[182] the court affirmed the district court's holding that an equity cushion in the primed property and the trustee's financial projection of repayment of the super priority loan were adequate to approve Section 364(d) financing.[183]

---

178 *In re* Seth Co., Inc., 281 B.R. 150, 153 (Bankr. D. Conn. 2002) (extraordinary remedy).
179 11 U.S.C. § 364(d)(1)(A).
180 11 U.S.C. § 364(d)(1)(B).
181 *In re* 495 Cent. Park Ave. Corp., 136 Bankr. 626 (Bankr. S.D.N.Y. 1992) (Debtor presented evidence that demonstrated that both prongs of 11 U.S.C. § 364(d) were met).
182 789 F.2d 1085 (4th Cir. 1986).
183 *In re* Beker Industries Corp., 58 Bankr. 725 (Bankr. S.D.N.Y. 1986) (Court authorized Section 364(d) borrowing that primed existing liens; case contains good discussion of adequate protection, valuation and cross-collateralization). *Contra In re* Chevy Devco, 78 Bankr. 585 (Bankr. C.D.Cal. 1987) (Section 364(d) motion denied where existing lienor was not granted adequate protection). Most courts have recognized that an equity cushion may constitute adequate protection. *In re* Mellor, 734 F.2d 1396 (9th Cir. 1984); *In re* McCombs Properties VI, Ltd., 88 Bankr. 261 (Bankr. C.D.Cal. 1988). *But see In re* Alyucan Interstate Corp., 12 Bankr. 803 (Bankr. D.Utah 1981) (Court rejects equity cushion as means of providing adequate protection, but contains list of cases at note 14 supporting the contrary view).

3. Cross-Collateralization

One significant benefit that the surety may obtain for financing the debtor/principal is the opportunity to cross-collateralize. For example, the surety may seek collateral that will cover its pre-petition losses.

Some courts have held that cross-collateralization of a pre-petition debt with post-petition assets may never be approved.[184] Other courts examine cross-collateralization on a case-by-case basis to determine if the financing is in the best interests of the estate, rather than principally the pre-petition creditor.[185] For example, in *In Re Vanguard Diversified, Inc.*,[186] the court approved a financing agreement with a cross-collateralization clause because without the lender's continued financing, the debtor would probably cease business and be forced to liquidate.

Cross-collateralization should be sought by a surety providing financing for its principal to complete bonded projects. The court will rigorously scrutinize a cross-collateralization provision to determine the preferential treatment the surety's pre-petition claim will receive, as compared with the benefit the financing will bring to the estate. The debtor and the surety will be required to demonstrate how the financing benefits the estate.

4. The Safe-Harbor for the Post-Petition Financier

It is often necessary to put bankruptcy financing in place on an expedited basis. Even where the bankruptcy court approved financing, if a lender withheld funds until the appeal period passed, or until all appeals were concluded, the patient would die waiting for the medicine. Section 364(e) provides lenders with protection from the possibility that an appeal will unwind the transactions.[187] This section provides that if an appellate

---

184 Shapiro v. Saybrook Manuf. Co., 963 F.2d 1490 (11th Cir. 1992); *In re Monarch Circuit Indus., Inc.*, 41 Bankr. 859 (Bankr. E.D.Pa. 1984) (Cross-collateralization amounts to impermissible preference and is not authorized by 11 U.S.C. §364).

185 *In re* Keystone Camera Prods. Corp., 126 Bankr. 177 (Bankr. D.N.J. 1991); *In re* Baker Indus., Inc., 58 Bankr. 725 (Bankr. S.D.N.Y. 1986); *In re* Roblin Indus., Inc., 52 Bankr. 241 (Bankr. W.D.N.Y. 1985).

186 31 Bankr. 364 (Bankr. E.D.N.Y. 1983).

187 11 U.S.C. § 364(e) provides:

court reverses or modifies the financing order it will not affect the validity of the debt or any priority or loan granted to secure the debt, even though the lender knew of the pendency of the appeal, provided: (1) the appeal was not stayed under Federal Rule of Bankruptcy Procedure 8005,[188] and (2) the lender extended the credit in good faith. These two requirements for the safe harbor provided in Section 364(e) are addressed serially.

There is no automatic ten-day supercedeas or stay of a financing order under Federal Rule of Bankruptcy Procedure 7062. Thus, credit extended during the ten-day period after entry of the financing order should be protected.[189] Additionally, if no stay of the financing order is obtained, an appeal of the order may be dismissed because of mootness. A lender should be aware that if a financing order is affirmed on appeal by the district court or bankruptcy appellate panel, then an automatic ten-day stay of the financing order will be in place.[190]

Good faith is not defined in the Bankruptcy Code or Bankruptcy Rules. Therefore, courts have looked to standards employed in other areas of law for guidance (i.e. the Uniform Commercial Code).[191] As long as the loan serves the purpose of the Bankruptcy Code the lender will be deemed to have extended the credit in good faith and will be entitled to the protection of Section 364(e).[192]

> The reversal or modification on appeal of an authorization under this section to obtain credit or incur debt, or of a grant under this section of a priority or a lien, does not affect the validity of any debt so incurred, or any priority or lien so granted, to an entity that extended such credit in good faith, whether or not such entity knew of the pendency of the appeal, unless such authorization and the incurring of such debt, or the granting of such priority or lien, were stayed pending appeal.

188 *In re* Adams Apple, Inc., 829 F.2d 1484 (9th Cir. 1987) (An order granting a lender a secured lien is a final order for purposes of appeal under 28 U.S.C. § 158(d)).
189 *Id.*
190 Fed. R. Bankr. P. 8017.
191 *Adams Apple*, 829 F.2d at 1489 (court looked to good faith standard applied in foreclosure sales, i.e. misconduct defeating good faith includes fraud, collusion, or an attempt to take grossly unfair advantage of others).
192 *Adams Apple*, 829 F.2d at 1485 (knowledge of illegality of a transaction destroys good faith); *Ellingsen MacLean Oil*, 834 F.2d 599 (loan by existing secured lenders was not improper because it involved the

The finding that the lender extended credit in good faith must be an explicit finding.[193] To avail itself of this safe harbor provision, the surety should require that any financing order explicitly contain a court finding that the surety is providing credit in good faith.

5. Implementing the Post-Petition Financing Agreement and Order

Similar to a pre-petition financing agreement, identification of the parties, bonds, bonded projects, and indemnity agreements, and acknowledgments of the principal's default and that the surety has an equitable lien on bonded contract funds should be set forth in the post-petition financing agreement. A statement of the specific purposes for which the surety's financing is intended should be included in the agreement.

Most importantly, the post-petition financing agreement should enumerate the protections the surety will receive under the various provisions of Section 364 (i.e. super priority, lien on unencumbered property and/or a priming lien) and recite all the predicate elements for that level of financing protection. The extent and nature of cross-collateralization given to the surety should be detailed. If a surety will receive any security interests in property of the estate, the financing order should specifically provide that all such interests are automatically perfected by the entry of the financing order, and that the automatic stay is lifted for the surety to enforce the security interests in the event of a default.

The agreement may also provide that the debtor/principal has no objection to the surety's claim in the bankruptcy proceeding and no

---

settlement of a preexisting dispute as well as the extension of post-petition credit). *But see In re* EDC Holding Co., 676 F.2d 945 (7th Cir. 1982) (lender's priority was revoked where the loan proceeds were used to fund a settlement between the debtor and a labor union involving payment of the union's legal expenses as a wage priority where they were not entitled to payment from the estate at all–effect was improper under the Bankruptcy Code).

193   *In re* Revco D.S., Inc., 901 F.2d 1359 (6th Cir. 1990).

objection to the validity, extent and priority of the surety's equitable rights of subrogation to the bonded contract proceeds.[194]

The indemnitors to the surety should be required to reaffirm their guarantees to the surety. The financing agreement and order should provide that they are binding on the debtor's successors and assigns. Moreover, the terms of the agreement and order should explicitly state that they survive the confirmation of a plan of reorganization, the appointment of a trustee, a subsequent bankruptcy filing, or a dismissal of the bankruptcy case.

The surety's obligation to finance must be terminable upon a default. The events of default suggested for inclusion in a financing agreement are: (1) conversion of the case to Chapter 7, (2) appointment of a trustee (or examiner with wide discretion), (3) debtor's filing of a plan of reorganization unacceptable to the surety, (4) an attack by a creditor on the surety's claim or the post-petition financing order, (5) debtor's failure to assume executory bonded construction contracts, and (6) if applicable, debtor's noncompliance with a budget included as a part of the financing order.

Finally, the surety should require that affirmative evidence be put in the record regarding the surety's good faith at the hearing to approve the financing. The financing order must make explicit and specific findings of the surety's good faith so as to provide the surety with the safe harbor protection of Section 364(e).

A surety should confirm that proper notice of the motion to approve financing was given. Notice of post-petition lending must be given to the creditors' committee, if appointed, or else to the twenty largest unsecured creditors, to any creditors with security interests or liens on post-petition assets, and to the U.S. Trustee.[195] Lack of sufficient notice may invalidate any financing agreement between the surety and the debtor-in-possession.[196]

Federal Rule of Bankruptcy Procedure 4001(c) in addition to notice and timing requirements, now outlines some of the substantive contents

---

194 Such agreements are permissible in connection with financing. *In re* Stein & Day, Inc., 87 B.R. 290, 292 (Bankr. S.D.N.Y. 1988) (providing for validation of debt); *In re* Quigly Gen. Elect. Co., 43 B.R. 336, 338 (Bankr. W.D. Wash. 1984) (stipulation conceded validity of lien).
195 Fed. R. Bankr. P. 4001(c).
196 *In re* Monarch Circuit Indus., Inc., 41 Bankr. 859 (Bankr. E.D.Pa. 1984).

that must appear in the motion to approve financing. This rule, in conjunction with local rules in an increasing number of districts, mandates a heightened disclosure of material or oft-contested financing agreement provisions. These required disclosures may take the form of a specific table that must be attached to the motion to approve financing, or a separate description that must be included within the motion. These rules do not necessarily indicate that the court will not approve such provisions, but certainly point out that the court intends to focus scrutiny on such provisions. Accordingly, the local rules of the bankruptcy court district where the financing agreement will be negotiated should be consulted before the financing agreement is prepared.

VI. Opposing the Principal's Control of the Reorganization

A. *Motion to Convert Chapter 11 Reorganization to Chapter 7 Liquidation*

Under certain circumstances a surety can request that a Chapter 11 case be converted to a Chapter 7 proceeding under Section 1112(b). Often times a motion to convert will also request the appointment of a trustee as an alternative. If either of these requests is granted, then the debtor/principal's management will be displaced by an independent trustee. Mismanagement by the principal's officers and directors, the absence of any reorganization prospects, threats by management of groundless suits against the surety, or any number of other circumstances suggesting the bankruptcy process is not working may indicate that the surety should seek a conversion of the reorganization case to a liquidation.

On April 20, 2005, President Bush signed the Bankruptcy Abuse Prevention and Consumer Protection Act of 2005 (BAPCPA), which among its numerous provisions were statutory changes to Section 1112(b) that were intended to make it easier for parties in interest to obtain conversion or dismissal of a case. Prior law had provided that the court "may" order conversion or dismissal based on certain factors establishing "cause." After BAPCPA, the court is now directed that it "shall" order conversion or dismissal for "cause."[197]

---

197   11 U.S.C. § 1112(b) provides in relevant part:

Federal Rule of Bankruptcy Procedure 1017 provides the procedure for a voluntary conversion and the procedure for a creditor to seek conversion. Proceedings to convert a case are commenced by motion.[198] In general, in a Chapter 11 case, the court will take into consideration the best interests of both the creditors and the estate to determine whether conversion is appropriate. With the enactment of BAPCPA came an expanded list of the factors in Section 1112(b) that constitute "cause" to convert or dismiss a case.[199] The listed causes are not exclusive or

---

> [O]n request of a party in interest, and after notice and a hearing, absent unusual circumstances specifically identified by the court that establish that the requested conversion or dismissal is not in the best interests of creditors and the estate, the court shall convert a case under this chapter to a case under chapter 7 or dismiss a case under this chapter, whichever is in the best interests of creditors and the estate, if the movant establishes cause.

198 Fed. R. Bankr. P. 9013, 9014.
199 11 U.S.C. § 1112(b)(4) provides in relevant part:
For purposes of this subsection, the term 'cause' includes–
(A)   substantial or continuing loss to or diminution of the estate and the absence of a reasonable likelihood of rehabilitation;
(B)   gross mismanagement of the estate;
(C)   failure to maintain appropriate insurance that poses a risk to the estate or to the public;
(D)   unauthorized use of cash collateral substantially harmful to 1 or more creditors;
(E)   failure to comply with an order of the court;
(F)   unexcused failure to satisfy timely any filing or reporting requirement established by this title or by any rule applicable to a case under this chapter;
(G)   failure to attend the meeting of creditors convened under section 341(a) or an examination ordered under rule 2004 of the Federal Rules of Bankruptcy Procedure without good cause shown by the debtor;
(H)   failure timely to provide information or attend meetings reasonably requested by the United States trustee (or the bankruptcy administrator, if any);
(I)   failure timely to pay taxes owed after the date of the order for relief or to file tax returns due after the date of the order for relief;
(J)   failure to file a disclosure statement, or to file or confirm a plan, within the time fixed by this title or by order of the court;

exhaustive. Other "cause" may support conversion.[200] Whether "cause" for conversion has been proven lies in the sound discretion of the court.[201]

With BAPCPA's transition to a mandatory conversion or dismissal, came the addition of three specified exceptions.[202]

The surety should look first to Section 1112(B)(1) as a basis to convert a case to Chapter 7. The general deterioration of the debtor/principal's business since filing for bankruptcy may be the requisite "cause" to support conversion of the case.[203] Deterioration of the debtor/principal's business is not uncommon because the debtor

---

    (K)   failure to pay any fees or charges required under chapter 123 of title 28;
    (L)   revocation of an order of confirmation under section 1144;
    (M)   inability to effectuate substantial consummation of a confirmed plan;
    (N)   material default by the debtor with respect to a confirmed plan;
    (O)   termination of a confirmed plan by reason of the occurrence of a condition specified in the plan; and
    (P)   failure of the debtor to pay any domestic support obligation that first becomes payable after the date of the filing of the petition.

200   11 U.S.C. § 102(3); *In re* C.J. Corp., 78 Bankr. 273 (Bankr. D. Haw.1987).
201   *In re* Heatly, 51 Bankr. 518 (Bankr. E.D.Pa. 1985).
202   (2) The relief provided in paragraph (1) shall not be granted absent unusual circumstances specifically identified by the court that establish that such relief is not in the best interests of creditors and the estate. . .
    (A) there is a reasonable likelihood that a plan will be confirmed within the timeframes established in sections 1121(e) and 1129(e) of this title, or if such sections do not apply, within a reasonable period of time; and
    (B) the grounds for granting such relief include an act or omission of the debtor other than under paragraph (4)(A)–
    (i) for which there exists a reasonable justification for the act or omission; and
    (ii) that will be cured within a reasonable period of time fixed by the court.
    11 U.S.C. 1112(b)(2).
203   *In re* Photo Promotion Associates, Inc., 47 Bankr. 454 (Bankr. S.D.N.Y. 1985) (Court converted Chapter 11 case to Chapter 7 because the debtor's business generally deteriorated over five months after filing for bankruptcy).

generally loses his ability to obtain new bonds either prior to or after filing for bankruptcy. Without bonding, the debtor will probably be unable to bid and obtain new work necessary to generate cash flow. Absence of new work generally exacerbates the financial problems that were the original cause of the bankruptcy filing.

In addition to showing a "continuing loss or diminution of the estate," Section 1112(b)(1) requires a showing of an "absence of a reasonable likelihood of rehabilitation." Language in the U.S. Supreme Court Case of *United Savings v. Timbers of Inwood Forest, Ltd.*,[204] suggests that the debtor must have some "realistic" possibility of reorganizing, rather than a mere subjective belief that the debtor can reorganize. Although the *Timbers* case dealt with relief from the automatic stay under Section 362(d)(2), the court stated that for property to be necessary for an effective reorganization the debtor must demonstrate an effective reorganization is in "prospect" and that the debtor has "a reasonable probability of a successful reorganization within a reasonable time."[205] The surety can argue that the analogous standard in Section 1112(b)(1) and (4) also require that the debtor demonstrate more than a hope of reorganization. The continuing diminution of the estate, coupled with other negative financial factors, (i.e. lack of bonding support and inability to bid or obtain new work) makes Section 1112(b)(1) a viable basis for the surety to move to convert the case.

Sections 1112(b)(4)(A) and (b)(4)(J) may also be grounds for conversion after a case has been pending for a significant period of time.[206] In most cases, a motion would not be made under either of these sections at the beginning of the case because they would probably not be well received by the court. However, if the debtor has been unable to bid or obtain new work and the debtor has been consuming assets of the

---

204   484 U.S. 365, 108 S.Ct. 626, 98 L.Ed.2d 740 (1988).
205   484 U.S. at 376. *See also In re* Oklahoma P.A.C. First Ltd. Partnership, 122 Bankr. 394 (Bankr. D.Ariz. 1990) (court follows *Timbers* and states, "In essence, a mini-feasibility analysis of the Debtor's Plan is required."). *Id.* at 400.
206   These cases referred to analogous sections which were re-worded on the 2005 BAPCPA amendments, specifically, "cause" under Section 1112(b)(2) ("inability to effectuate a plan") and/or (b)(3) ("unreasonable delay by the debtor that is prejudicial to creditors"). *In re* Belcher, 65 Bankr. 47 (Bankr. S.D.Fla. 1986); *In re* Eden Associates, 13 Bankr. 578 (Bankr. S.D.N.Y. 1981); *Matter of Bock*, 58 Bankr. 374 (Bankr. M.D.Fla. 1986).

estate for officers' salary and overhead for some time, the surety should be able to demonstrate "cause" under Section 1112(b)(1)·that would justify conversion.

If the Chapter 11 case is converted to Chapter 7, then an independent trustee will be appointed to manage all the assets in the estate. The debtor/principal is required to turn over all assets and records of the estate to the Chapter 7 trustee.[207] Additionally, a new time period for filing proofs of claim and objections to discharge commences after the conversion of the case.[208]

B. Motion to Appoint Trustee or Examiner

In most cases the debtor/principal will remain in possession of the estate in a Chapter 11 case.[209] The surety may move to appoint a Chapter 11 trustee or an examiner under Section 1104.

1. Trustee

A motion to appoint a Chapter 11 trustee is brought under Section 1104(a).[210] When the circumstances of a case suggest something

---

207 Fed. R. Bankr. P. 1019(5).
208 Fed. R. Bankr. P. 1019(3).
209 See e.g., In re Colorado–Ute Elec. Ass'n, Inc., 120 Bankr. 164 (Bankr. D.Colo. 1990) (appointment of a Chapter 11 trustee is an extraordinary remedy because there is a strong presumption that the debtor should remain in possession of the estate); In re TS Industries, Inc., 125 Bankr. 638 (Bankr. D. Utah 1991).
210 11 U.S.C. § 1104(a) provides:
At any time after the commencement of the case but before confirmation of a plan, on request of a party in interest or the United States trustee, and after notice and a hearing, the court shall order the appointment of a trustee–
(1) for cause, including fraud, dishonesty, incompetence, or gross mismanagement of the affairs of the debtor by current management, either before or after the commencement of the case, or similar cause, but not including the number of holders of securities of the debtor or the amount of assets or liabilities of the debtor; or
(2) if such appointment is in the interests of creditors, any equity security holders, and other interests of the estate, without

seriously wrong with management of the debtor's affairs, or some form of fraud is suspected, the surety should not hesitate to move to have a trustee appointed. Essentially, Section 1104 mandates appointment of a trustee if "fraud, dishonesty, incompetence or gross mismanagement" by the debtor can be demonstrated, or if such appointment is in the best interests of creditors.[211] A new subsection was added in Section 1104 by BAPCPA, which mandates a motion to appoint a trustee be filed by the United States Trustee, where there are reasonable grounds to suspect the corporate debtor's current management participated in actual fraud.[212]

Evidence of embezzlement or intentional fraud will clearly support appointment of a trustee. Other behavior that will permit the appointment of a trustee include failure to pay post-petition taxes, failure to maintain insurance, commingling of personal and business assets, gross mismanagement or an inability to reorganize the debtor. The surety may also seek to appoint a trustee under the "best interests" test of Section 1104(a)(2). Under this alternative ground, the court will balance the equities to the creditors, the estate and the debtor. If possible, the surety should move under both grounds.

There are a large number of reported cases discussing the conduct and standards that will be considered in a motion to appoint a trustee.

---

regard to the number of holders of securities of the debtor or the amount of assets or liabilities of the debtor.

211 *In re* Sharon Steel Corp., 871 F.2d 1217 (3rd Cir. 1989). (standards for appointment of a trustee are flexible and subject to the discretion of the bankruptcy court). It should be noted that a trustee may be appointed by the court for reasons not explicitly enumerated in Section 1104(a). *See* 11 U.S.C. §102(3); *In re* Oklahoma Refining Corp., 838 F.2d 1133 (10th Cir. 1988); *In re* V. Savino Oil & Heating Co., Inc., 99 Bankr. 518 (Bankr. E.D.N.Y. 1989).

212 The United States trustee shall move for the appointment of a trustee under subsection (a) if there are reasonable grounds to suspect that current members of the governing body of the debtor, the debtor's chief executive or chief financial officer, or members of the governing body who selected the debtor's chief executive or chief financial officer, participated in actual fraud, dishonesty, or criminal conduct in the management of the debtor or the debtor's public financial reporting. 11 U.S.C. § 1104(e).

Secondary sources provide a thorough discussion of these cases and the many fact patterns justifying the appointment of a trustee.[213]

2. Examiner

The surety may also move to appoint an examiner. An examiner is essentially a trustee with limited powers. A lesser standard of "cause" is required to appoint an examiner, as opposed to having a trustee appointed, because an examiner may only displace the debtor from possessing specified assets of the estate or from performing certain functions. From a timing perspective, a motion to appoint an examiner will generally be better received at the beginning of a case than motions to appoint a trustee or to convert the case

The grounds for appointment of an examiner under Section 1104(c), are (1) that the appointment is in the best interests of the estate and creditors, or (2) that the debtor's fixed, liquidated, unsecured debts exceed $5,000,000.[214] The "best interest" test will generally be met where the surety demonstrates allegations of fraud, misconduct and/or mismanagement. The alternative provision to appoint an examiner, i.e. upon the request of any party in interest, when unsecured non-trade debt

---

213 Berdan and Arnold, *Displacing the Debtor in Possession: The Requests for and Advantages of the Appointment of a Trustee in Chapter 11 Proceedings*, 67 MARQ. L. REV. 457 (1984); Comment, *When the Bank Wants its Borrowers in Bankruptcy: Benefits of Bankruptcy for Lenders and Lender Liability Defendants*, 40 ME. L. REV. 375, 399 (1988).

214 11 U.S.C. § 1104(c) provides:

If the court does not order the appointment of a trustee under this section, then at any time before the confirmation of a plan, on request of a party in interest or the United States trustee, and after notice and a hearing, the court shall order the appointment of an examiner to conduct such an investigation of the debtor as is appropriate, including an investigation of any allegations of fraud, dishonesty, incompetence, misconduct, mismanagement, or irregularity in the management of the affairs of the debtor of or by current or former management of the debtor, if--

(1) such appointment is in the interests of creditors, any equity security holders, and other interests of the estate; or

(2) the debtor's fixed, liquidated, unsecured debts, other than debts for goods, services, or taxes, or owing to an insider, exceed $5,000,000.

of the debtor exceeds $5,000,000, is easily invoked and will necessarily be successful, because of the mandatory language in the Code section.

From the surety's perspective, an examiner can serve a number of useful functions. An examiner can review the debtor's financial condition and controls. Such actions can lead to conservation of assets of the estate, and possibly to additional discoveries that will support appointment of a trustee. Examiners may be appointed for the purpose of investigating and reviewing litigation the debtor has commenced or proposes to commence.[215] A debtor may be threatening preference, subordination and/or surety/lender liability suits. Having an examiner appointed will displace the debtor/principal with an impartial third party to review the alleged action(s) threatened against the surety to determine whether it is in the best interests of the estate to pursue the action(s) or not.[216] Other purposes and uses for an examiner may exist in a particular case, and the bankruptcy judge has broad discretion to establish the scope of duties and investigations of an examiner.[217]

C. *The Creditor Plan*

In a Chapter 11 case, the debtor is given a specified length of time during which only the debtor may propose a plan of reorganization to the creditors for vote and approval. (the "exclusivity" period) The initial

---

[215] 11 U.S.C. § 1106(b) requires an examiner to perform the duty of investigating causes of action available to the estate, as required under 11 U.S.C. § 1106(a)(4). *In re* Carnegie Intern. Corp., 51 Bankr. 252 (Bankr. S.D.Ind. 1984) (examiner appointed to investigate and, if warranted, pursue causes of action available to the estate); Williamson v. Roppollo, 114 Bankr. 127 (W.D.La. 1990).

[216] *See* Meyer v. Fleming, 327 U.S. 161, 165-167, 66 S.Ct. 382, 385-386, 90 L.Ed. 595 (1946) (The trustee should "make the choice which is most advantageous to the estate."); *In re* Independent Clearing House Co., 41 Bankr. 985, 992 (D. Utah 1984) ("A bankruptcy trustee is not bound to pursue every cause of action, and may properly decide that the speculative nature of the suit and the expense do not warrant prosecution."); *In re* Jefferson, 59 Bankr. 707, 711 (S.D.Miss. 1986) ("Furthermore, the trustee is not bound to bring every possible suit . . . it was prudent for him to refrain here when considering the interest of the estate as a whole.").

[217] *In re* Revco, 898 F.2d 498, 501 (6th Cir.1990).

exclusivity period is 120 days from the petition filing.[218] However, the debtor can ask the court to extend the exclusivity period.[219] The debtor frequently does so. However, pursuant to the Bankruptcy Abuse Prevention and Consumer Protection Act of 2005 (BAPCPA), the exclusivity period, which could previously be extended without limit, now may not be extended more than 18 months after the petition date.[220]

Chapter 11 bankruptcy cases are very expensive. The cost of debtor's counsel, counsel for any official appointed committees, financial advisors, management salaries and United States Trustee fees can quickly consume all the money available for distribution to creditors, if a case is allowed to remain pending too long. Accordingly, unsecured creditors may wish to cause a plan to be confirmed sooner than the debtor and its employed professionals. Creditors might understandably want to see a prompt transfer of the decision making authority from debtor's embittered former management to an independent liquidating trustee, whose fiduciary responsibilities are clear. A creditor's plan can cause this to happen.

The surety may wish to oppose the debtor's requests to extend the exclusive time during which only the debtor can propose a plan, where the debtor's continued existence in Chapter 11 serves no clear economic benefit. The end of exclusivity tends to present two options. It often causes the debtor and its professionals to knuckle down and get a plan on file before the period expires. This shortens the administration period and reduces the cost drain. If the debtor does not file a plan, then any creditor, or a committee of creditors, is free to file a simple plan that provides for prompt confirmation and distribution of assets.

The surety may file a motion to shorten or terminate the debtor's exclusivity period.[221] The burden of proof rests with the movant when a termination or reduction of exclusivity is sought.[222] The Bankruptcy Code does not define what constitutes "cause" for reducing exclusivity. Courts, however, have considered a listing of non-exclusive factors when

---

218   11 U.S.C. § 1121(b).
219   11 U.S.C. § 1121(d).
220   11 U.S.C. § 1121(d)(2)(A).
221   Section 1121(d) of the Bankruptcy Code provides that, "[o]n request of a party in interest made within the [exclusivity periods] and after notice and a hearing, the court may for cause reduce or increase the 120-day period or the 180-day [exclusivity periods]." 11 U.S.C. § 1121(d).
222   *In re* Dow Corning Corp., 208 B.R. 661, 665 (Bankr.E.D. Mich. 1997).

deciding whether sufficient "cause" exists either to terminate–or extend–exclusivity. For example, some courts have looked to the following factors:

   a. the size and complexity of the case;
   b. the necessity for sufficient time to permit the debtor to negotiate a plan of reorganization and prepare adequate information;
   c. the existence of good faith progress toward reorganization;
   d. whether the debtor is paying its bills as they come due;
   e. whether the debtor has demonstrated reasonable prospects for filing a viable plan;
   f. whether the debtor has made progress in negotiations with its creditors; and
   g. the amount of time which has elapsed in the case;[223]

Unlike the attempt to wrest control away from the debtor with Section 1104 motions, which may not be well received by the court, the creditors' request to end exclusivity, and thereby open up the Chapter 11 plan drafting process to any interested party, tends to be well received, as it furthers the interests of creditors.

VII. Surety's Use of Involuntary Bankruptcy Remedy

A. *The Involuntary Petition*

Sureties generally view with trepidation the bankruptcy filing of their principal. However, under rare circumstances it may be to the surety's advantage to see an involuntary bankruptcy petition filed against the principal. Generally, the benefit to be derived from an involuntary bankruptcy is the prevention or "recapture" of fraudulent conveyances and preferential transfers of the principal's (or indemnitor's) property.[224]

---

[223] *In re* Adelphia Communications Corp., 352 B.R. 578, 586-87 (Bankr. S.D.N.Y. 2006); *see also In re* Dow Corning Corp., 208 B.R. 661, 664 (Bankr. E.D. Mich. 1997); *see also* Official Comm. of Unsecured Creditors v. Henry Mayo Newhall Mem. Hosp. (*In re* Henry Mayo Newhall Mem. Hosp.), 282 B.R. 444, 452 (B.A.P. 9th Cir. 2002).

[224] To illustrate, when a principal will imminently default on its bonded projects, the principal may transfer assets without consideration, or may

An involuntary bankruptcy proceeding may be justified where the surety becomes aware that the proceeds from bonded projects are substantially funding the completion of unbonded work. It is not unusual for a cash-starved principal to "rob Peter to pay Paul." The surety may become aware of insiders "raiding" the company as its financial decline becomes irreversible. Or, the surety may learn that the bonded job proceeds are being diverted to pay bank debt that was personally guaranteed by the owners of the company. If the amounts diverted are significant, or if the practice is ongoing, the surety may wish to consider recourse to the bankruptcy court. Due to the drastic nature of the consequences that a petitioning creditor may visit upon the involuntary debtor, the Bankruptcy Code provides remedies in favor of the debtor against a petitioning creditor who has acted in bad faith in commencing an involuntary petition.

The filing of an involuntary petition is authorized by 11 U.S.C. § 303 against an entity that is generally not paying its debts as they become due.[225] A petitioning creditor must hold a claim that is not contingent as

---

repay loans to insiders (i.e. officers and directors, family) or other favored creditors. The surety will desire to stop this hemorrhaging of assets. The involuntary bankruptcy proceeding can quickly divest the debtor of control of its assets.

Pursuant to the avoiding powers of the Bankruptcy Code, it will also be possible to file actions against those who have received fraudulent conveyances or preferential transfers and to recover those funds for distribution to the principal's creditors pro rata. The surety's claim may be a substantial component of the total pool of unsecured claims, thereby making the pro rata distribution to the surety substantial enough to justify the expense of an involuntary proceeding.

225   Involuntary Cases.

. . . .

(b)   an involuntary case against a person is commenced by the filing with the bankruptcy court of a petition under Chapter 7 or 11 of this title–
(1)   by three or more entities, each of which is either a holder of a claim against such person that is not contingent as to liability or the subject of a bona fide dispute as to liability or amount, . . . if such noncontingent, undisputed claims aggregate at least $13,475 more than the value of any lien on property of the debtor securing such claims held by the holders of such claims;
(2)   if there are fewer than 12 such holders, excluding any employee or insider of such person and any transferee of a transfer that is voidable

to liability,[226] nor the subject of a bona fide dispute as to liability or amount. Generally, the involuntary petition must be commenced by three creditors, whose unsecured claims aggregate over $13,475.[227] A single petitioning creditor is permissible, if the debtor has less than 12 creditors.[228] A single petitioning creditor must be able to demonstrate that it made some reasonable inquiry to determine that the debtor had less than 12 creditors.[229] An involuntary petition should substantially follow official form No. 5.[230]

---

under section 544, 545, 547, 548, 549, or 724(a) of this title, by one or more of such holders that hold in the aggregate at least $13,475 of such claims;

. . . .

(h) . . . the court shall order relief against the debtor in an involuntary case under the chapter under which the petition was filed only if –
(1) the debtor is generally not paying such debtor's debts as such debts become due unless such debts are the subject of a bona fide dispute as to liability or amount; . . .
11 U.S.C. § 303(b) and (h)(1), respectively.

226 The Bankruptcy Code provides that creditors with contingent claims as to liability cannot be petitioning creditors. 11 U.S.C. § 303(b)(1) Contingency as to liability is generally determined based upon whether the debtor's obligation to pay has come to fruition or rests upon some future event. *In re* Taylor & Associates, L.P., 193 B.R. 465 (Bankr. E.D. Texas 1996) *rev. on other grounds*, 249 B.R. 431 (E.D. Tenn. 1996). A surety's claim under a general indemnity agreement may or may not be contingent. Where a debtor has agreed to indemnify a surety under a general indemnity agreement and all the requirements set forth in the GIA have occurred, then the obligation is no longer contingent for purposes of involuntary bankruptcy. *In re* McNeil, 13 BR 434 (E.D. Tenn. N.E. Div. 1981) (debtor was an indemnitor under the surety agreement supporting bonds issued by surety to cover losses for a corporation owned by the debtor. Corporation defaulted on its obligations on the construction projects and surety was required to pay under the terms of the bonds. There was not going to be sufficient salvage to satisfy the indebtedness to the surety. The court concluded that the surety's claim was not contingent as to liability.)

227 11 U.S.C. § 303(b). This amount is subject to periodic adjustment under 11 U.S.C. § 104(b).

228 11 U.S.C. § 303(b)(2).

229 *In re* Mollen Drilling Co., 68 Bankr. 840 (Bankr. D.Mont. 1987).

230 Official and Procedural Bankruptcy Forms (as amended, 1991).

If the petition is challenged, it will be the surety's burden to prove that the debtor is generally not paying its debts as they become due.[231] Among the factors that will be considered in making this determination are the number of debts, the amount of the delinquency, the materiality of non-payment, and the way the debtor conducts its financial affairs.[232]

The determination whether a creditor holds a claim that is not subject to a "bona fide dispute" requires the consideration of factors in a case-by-case analysis.[233] The court will generally look to the nature of the dispute, the extent of evidence supporting a creditor's claim and a debtor's objection, whether the creditor's claim and the debtor's objection appear to have been made in good faith and without fraud or deceit, and whether, on the balance, the interests of the creditor outweigh those of the debtor.[234]

---

231 *In re* Caucus Distributors, Inc., 83 Bankr. 921, 931 (Bankr.E.D.Va. 1988), 106 Bankr. 890, 918 (Bankr. E.D.Va. 1989).

232 *In re* Reed, 11 Bankr. 755, 759-60 (Bankr. S.D.W.Va. 1981). *See also In re* Galaxy Boat Mfg. Co., Inc., 72 Bankr. 200 (Bankr. D.S.C. 1986) (length of time debt remains unpaid); *In re* All Media Properties, Inc., 5 Bankr. 126 (Bankr. S.D.Tex. 1980) (missing significant number of payments). The Ninth Circuit has stated that "a finding that a debtor is not generally paying his debts requires a more general showing of the debtor's financial condition and debt structure than merely establishing the existence of a few unpaid debts." *In re* Dill, 731 F.2d 629, 632 (9th Cir.1984); *see also In re* 7H Land & Cattle Co., 6 B.R. 29, 31 (Bankr. D. Nev. 1980)("it is clear that a court must find more than a prospective inability by the debtor to pay only a few of his debts, and more than a past failure to pay a few of such liabilities."). Ordinarily, the failure to pay a single creditor will not satisfy the standard. *See In re* Smith, 123 Bankr. 423 (Bankr. MD. Fla. 1990); *but see* Matter of 7H Land & Cattle Co., 6 Bankr. 29 (Bankr. D. Nev. 1980); Paroline v. Doling, 116 Bankr. 583 (Bankr. S.D. Ohio 1990).

233 The petitioning creditor has the burden of establishing a prima facie case that a bona fide dispute does not exist. Rubin v. Belo Broadcasting Corporation (*In re* Rubin), 769 F.2d 611, 615 (9th Cir.1985); Subway Equipment Leasing Corp. v. Sims (*In re* Sims), 994 F.2d 210, 221 (5th Cir.1993); *Atlas Machine & Iron Works*, 986 F.2d at 715. Once this is done, the burden shifts to the debtor to present evidence demonstrating that a bona fide dispute does exist. *Subway Equipment Leasing Corp.*, 994 F.2d at 221.

234 *In re* Johnston Hawks, Ltd., 49 Bankr. 823 (Bankr. D. Haw. 1985).

Much of the existing case law on the issues of a "disputed claim," while helpful, may not be dispositive, as Section 303 relating to involuntary petitions was amended by BAPCPA in 2005, with the addition of the requirement that a claim not be disputed "as to liability or amount" and cases have not yet come down regarding the effect of such amendments.

B. Principal Advantages of an Involuntary Bankruptcy

A financially troubled contractor will very frequently "take care of its own." This behavior may take the form of fraudulent conveyances of funds, stipulated judgments to favored creditors, premature payments to personally guaranteed debts, or a myriad of other practices, limited only by the imagination of the debtor.

Pursuant to the avoidance powers under the Bankruptcy Code, most, if not all, of such transactions can be avoided and the funds returned to the bankruptcy estate. Transfers made without consideration or other fraudulent conveyances can be attacked outside the bankruptcy court under state law remedies. However, pursuant to 11 U.S.C. § 547, the Bankruptcy Code adds the doctrine of "preference" to the recapture tools that would be available outside of bankruptcy. The preference doctrine is unique because it permits the avoidance of transactions that would be legitimate if there were no subsequent bankruptcy filing. Bankruptcy Code preference provisions generally permit the court to recover amounts paid to a creditor within ninety days of the bankruptcy filing. The recovery power includes payments that were made to entities holding a legitimate claim against the debtor. The "reach back" period for preference recovery, where the transaction involved an insider, is a full year prior to the bankruptcy filing.

The goal may also be to avoid fraudulent transfers, including both transfers that are considered fraudulent under state laws or transfers that are fraudulent under Bankruptcy Code Section 548. This Code provision enables the trustee or debtor-in-possession to avoid transfers within two years prior to the bankruptcy filing if made with actual intent to hinder, delay or defraud creditors or if made without an exchange of "reasonably equivalent value."[235] Another goal may be to marshal assets of the

---

235 Avoidance under the "reasonably equivalent value" test also requires a showing that the debtor was insolvent on the date of the transfer or was

debtor[236] or to compel turnover of property from an entity not entitled to keep such property from the debtor.[237] The principal benefit of the involuntary bankruptcy is that all of the remedies available under the Bankruptcy Code may be employed for the benefit of the surety and other unsecured creditors. When the need to halt or undo preferential transfers outweighs the inconvenience of the automatic stay, the use of an involuntary filing can be justified.

C. Principal Disadvantages of Filing an Involuntary Petition

The principal disadvantage to the surety who files an involuntary petition is the risk that the court will find the petition was filed in bad faith.[238] A

---

rendered insolvent by the transfer, or that the debtor was engaged in a business funded with reasonably small capital, or that the debtor intended to incur debt beyond his ability to pay when the debts matured. 11 U.S.C. § 548(a).

236 *See* Meyer v. United States, 375 U.S. 233 (1963); *In re* Beacon Distribs., Inc., 441 F.2d 547 (1st Cir. 1971).

237 11 U.S.C.A. § 542 (1979 & Supp. 1989). Turnover is a broad concept, which may include property in which debtor has a partial undivided interest. *In re* Ford, 3 B.R. 559 (Bankr. D. Md), *aff'd*, 638 F.2d 14 (4th Cir. 1981).

238 *In re* John Richards Home Building Co., L.L.C., 439 F.3d 248 (6th Cir. 2006), *cert. denied,* Adell v. John Richards Home Bldg. Co., L.L.C., 549 U.S. 818, 127 S.Ct. 85, 166 L.Ed.2d 31, 74 USLW 3687, 75 USLW 3021, 75 USLW 3150, 75 USLW 3164 (U.S. Oct. 2, 2006) (compensatory damage award and multi-million dollar punitive damage award affirmed against petitioning creditor who held claim subject to bona fide dispute). In *In re* Wavelength, 61 B.R. 614 (9th Cir. BAP 1986), the BAP identified the standard to be applied in the context of an involuntary petition to find bad faith. As that court stated, "Whether a party acted in bad faith is essentially a question of fact. Bad faith should be measured by an objective test that asks what a reasonable person would have believed." *Id.* at 620; *see also In re* Johnston Hawks Ltd., 72 B.R. 361, 365-66 (Bankr. D. Hawaii 1987)(finding that involuntary petition was filed in bad faith and describing two tests for finding the existence of bad faith in the context of an involuntary petition: "One view finds 'bad faith' to exist where the petition is motivated by ill will, a sense of malice, or to embarrass or harass the debtor. . . . A second view finds 'bad faith' to exist when the creditor's actions were an improper use

debtor may recover costs and reasonable attorneys' fees against a petitioning creditor where the petition was filed in bad faith.[239]

When a contractor is in dire financial straits, and when the surety holds an executed indemnity agreement and has possibly already begun paying losses, and when fraudulent transfers or other property conveyances are occurring, the likelihood of a bad faith finding is relatively small. Nonetheless, the challenge to the involuntary petition must be answered by the petitioning creditors. This challenge may entail significant litigation expense.

As an illustration of how a surety's petition can result in bad faith finding, it is useful to review the facts of the *In re Vincent J. Fasano, Inc.*[240] case from the Bankruptcy Court of New York. In that case, the surety filed an involuntary bankruptcy petition. The court found the surety acted in bad faith, due to the manner in which it solicited other parties to be co-petitioners in the involuntary bankruptcy. The court's concern related to the surety's solicitation of an unpaid subcontractor to join in the involuntary petition. The surety made this solicitation, but withheld from the subcontractor the fact that there may be a possible Miller Act bond claim. The debtor argued that the surety purposely delayed payment of the subcontractor's bond claim until it was time-barred, so as to qualify the subcontractor to be a petitioning creditor. The

---

of the Bankruptcy Code as a substitute for customary collection procedures.") *accord In re* WLB-RSK Venture, 296 B.R. 509 (Bankr. C.D. Cal. 2003); *accord In re* Grecian Heights Owners' Ass'n, 27 B.R. 172, 173 (Bankr. D. Or. 1982)(good faith test is "what a reasonable person would have believed.").

239 If the court dismisses a petition under this section other than on consent of all petitioners and the debtor, and if the debtor does not waive the right to judgment under this subsection, the court may grant judgment–
 (1) against the petitioners and in favor of the debtor for–
  (A) costs; or
  (B) a reasonable attorney's fee; or
 (2) against any petitioner that filed the petition in bad faith, for–
  (A) any damages proximately caused by such filing; or
  (B) punitive damages.
 11 U.S.C. § 303(i).

240 55 Bankr. 409 (Bankr. N.D.N.Y. 1985), *rev'd*, 58 Bankr. 1008 (N.D.N.Y. 1986) (district court reversed because of bankruptcy court's failure to consider surety's subjective motivation for filing petition).

court adopted the debtor's version of the facts.[241] The court found bad faith on the part of the surety. The involuntary bankruptcy petition was dismissed.[242]

Without question, the involuntary bankruptcy remedy is one that would be used by the surety only in unique circumstances. However, the pre-bankruptcy dissipation of assets by a principal is not such a rare occurrence. Furthermore, the gross misuse of bonded contract funds from a project that is not yet technically in default may require quick and decisive action by the surety.

Conclusion

Knowledge of bankruptcy law is invaluable to the performance bond surety. There is a relatively high likelihood of a financially distressed principal paying a visit to the bankruptcy court at some point. However, it is not possible to accurately predict which principals will file such a petition. Accordingly, all performance bond losses must be assessed with the thought of how a bankruptcy filing may delay the project completion, imperil the contract proceeds, or subject the surety to vexatious litigation. This chapter could not cover all of the law of bankruptcy that might be invoked by or against the surety. Instead, this chapter's presence in this publication acknowledges the importance of this body of law generally, to the performance bond surety.

---

241   "Turning to the facts as presently before the Court, it is now clear that at the time USF&G contacted Schalk in early May, 1982, Schalk's claim was not time barred against USF&G. Utilizing an objective test for determining bad faith, the court finds USF&G's failure to notify Schalk of its possible Miller Act bond claim evidences bad faith on its part in soliciting Schalk as a petitioning creditor." *Id.*, at 421.

242   This decision should not be interpreted to suggest that a bonded claimant may not join the surety in a voluntary petition. A claimant who had a claim only partially covered by the bond would be an acceptable petitioning creditor for the unbonded balance. Often attorneys' fees, delay damages, or other contractual items will not be covered by the bond, but will be an obligation of the debtor.